40-66
270-97

620-26
616-20
582-616

supp. § 242, 242A & 242B

718-30
759-70
878-84

511-12

770-804
860-61

339-61
370-75

IMMIGRATION:

PROCESS AND POLICY

Third Edition

By

Thomas Alexander Aleinikoff
Professor of Law (on leave)
University of Michigan Law School

David A. Martin
Henry L. & Grace Doherty Professor of Law
F. Palmer Weber Research Professor of Civil Liberties
and Human Rights
University of Virginia

Hiroshi Motomura
Professor of Law
University of Colorado School of Law

AMERICAN CASEBOOK SERIES®

WEST PUBLISHING CO.
ST. PAUL, MINN., 1995

COPYRIGHT © 1985, 1990, 1991 WEST PUBLISHING CO.

COPYRIGHT © 1995 By WEST PUBLISHING CO.
            610 Opperman Drive
            P.O. Box 64526
            St. Paul, MN 55164–0526
            1–800–328–9352

Library of Congress Cataloging-in-Publication Data

Aleinikoff, Thomas Alexander, 1952–
    Immigration process and policy / by Thomas Alexander Aleinikoff,
David A. Martin, and Hiroshi Motomura. — 3rd ed.
        p.   cm. — (American casebook series)
    Includes index.
    ISBN 0–314–06104–5 (Bd. Vol)
    1. Emigration and immigration law—United States—Cases.
I. Motomura, Hiroshi, 1953–   . II. Title.   III. Series.
KR4818.A43   1995
342.73'082—dc20
   [347.30282]   95–12826
                                       CIP

ISBN 0–314–06104–5

 TEXT IS PRINTED ON 10% POST CONSUMER RECYCLED PAPER  PRINTED WITH SOY INK™

*To the Aleinikoffs, Marrows, Mays, and Wises
And for Rachel, Shoshana, Sam, and Eli*

*To the Martins, Meekers, Johnstons, and Bowmans
And for Cyndy, Amy, and Jeff*

*To the Motomuras, Sakumas, Kishis, and Katos
And for Linda and Amy*

*

Preface to the Third Edition

"Immigration is an issue you can hardly mention without having steam coming out of people's ears."[1] So wrote David Broder, one of America's foremost political commentators, in October 1994. Anyone who followed the news during the 1994 elections, particularly the news from California, knows what he is talking about. The political climate now could hardly be more different from early 1991, when we finished work on the second edition. Congress then had just enacted a major revision of the immigration laws, the Immigration Act of 1990. Among many other changes, that legislation increased the level of annual legal immigration by a few hundred thousand. The bill excited little public debate or focused commentary in the United States, even though the increase ran sharply against a global tide of restrictionism then gaining force. Our challenge in writing that edition was to provide a vehicle for understanding an unnecessarily complex new law and the policies it embodied, at a time when many of the implementing regulations were not in force.

By 1994 it seemed that political debaters were trying to make up for the lack of public discussion—or simple lack of volume—that surrounded the 1990 changes. California, suffering more than the rest of the country from recession, but also the home to more immigrants, both legal and illegal, than any other state, blazed the trail. Proposition 187 presented its voters with a direct opportunity to vote on measures that would crack down on illegal migration (or so it was argued), by denying to undocumented aliens most state services, including even elementary education, and by requiring state officials to check the immigration status of virtually all their clientele. Some politicians called for a constitutional amendment to deny birthright citizenship to children born in this country of undocumented alien mothers. Members of Congress joined in with proposals to impose a moratorium on immigration or to slash admission levels permanently. Opponents denounced these measures, from the left, as discriminatory scapegoating, and sometimes from the free-market right as unrealistic restrictions in a world of tighter interdependence where goods and capital already move with few hindrances across national borders. Proposition 187 nonetheless passed with nearly 60 percent of the California vote; implementation was immediately stayed by litigation challenging its constitutionality. The Constitution remains intact, as do the immigration levels established in 1990, but these issues will probably figure prominently in the 104th Congress and indeed in the 1996 elections. And Congress and the President have both supported steep increases in the budgets of the immigration agencies, in order to respond more directly to the challenge of controlling illegal migration.

Meantime, two of the country's most serious foreign policy crises centered on migration—the boat migrations from Haiti and Cuba. The former was largely resolved, at least for the time being, by a massive U.S. military

---

1. Broder, *Immigration: 'Time for Reason and Logic,'* Wash. Post, Oct. 4, 1994, at A17.

intervention in Haiti, under UN authority. The Cuban raft flow brought an end to the open-door policy for all Cubans who escaped the island, a policy that had lasted 35 years and had defied the Cold War's demise for a half-decade. It also launched the United States on a new and untested scheme for increased legal migration from Cuba, including a guaranteed minimum of 20,000 admissions per year. But both solutions left open new questions about the use of offshore "safe havens" of the kind still in operation at the U.S. naval base at Guantanamo.

In short, immigration is no longer a stepchild of policy analysis (indeed, migration is increasingly counted as a legitimate issue of high politics by national security scholars and analysts), and it commands increasing attention in the law schools. None of these developments have made the policy questions easier to resolve, of course, but they have produced an abundance of new practice and new analysis upon which we draw extensively here. For example, Section 3C, which examines the issue of undocumented migration, has been completely rewritten and significantly expanded, including analysis of Proposition 187. Chapter Eight takes account of the Cuban and Haitian cases and of new asylum regulations that went into effect in early 1995, as well as the increasingly salient issue of gender-based claims to refugee status. We have also tried throughout the book to incorporate expanded attention to the treatment of aliens after admission—both constitutional doctrine and ongoing legislative policy changes. Thus we discuss such cases as *Graham v. Richardson, Mathews v. Diaz, Cabell v. Chavez-Salido* and *Plyler v. Doe* in Chapter Three and often refer to these issues elsewhere. And of course we are now able to present the 1990 statutory changes in the full light cast by the implementing regulations and four years of operation. Comparable updating, covering both case law and policy, will be evident in each of the chapters.

For this edition of the casebook, the two veteran authors are also pleased to welcome a new collaborator, who has brought a fresh perspective and a remarkable level of energy to the task. This change proved quite timely, because just as we were considering that expansion of the team, Alex Aleinikoff joined the ranks of the Immigration and Naturalization Service as its General Counsel. As a result, he has played only a minimal role in the preparation of this volume, and is certainly not to be held accountable for the editorial comments, speculations, or argumentative questions included in these materials. A *fortiori* the traditional disclaimer applies with full force: opinions expressed or implied here are not to be taken as representing the views of the INS or the U.S. government.

Most of our work on the book was completed in December 1994. We have found it possible, however, to incorporate brief mention of a few later developments, through February 1995. The casebook is designed to be used with an accompanying supplement containing relevant statutes, treaties, regulations, and forms.[2]

---

2. Immigration and Nationality Laws of the United States: Selected Statutes, Regulations and Forms (T. Aleinikoff, D. Martin, & H. Motomura eds., West Publishing Co., 1995 ed.). Updated statutory supplements are expected as legislative changes warrant.

Acknowledgments. Again we express our gratitude to colleagues who have provided support and suggestions, either as users of the book or as inspired analysts of the immigration scene. At the risk of overlooking some we should cite, we would mention Deborah Anker, Lenni Benson, Carolyn Patty Blum, Linda Bosniak, Michael Churgin, David Cole, Joan Fitzpatrick, Maryellen Fullerton, Lucas Guttentag, Susan Gzesh, Michael Heyman, Stephen Legomsky, Gerald Neuman, Michael Olivas, Juan Osuna, Maurice Roberts, Paul Schmidt, Peter Schuck, Peter Spiro, Margaret Taylor, Ibrahim Wani, Leon Wildes, and Stephen Yale-Loehr. Much-appreciated research assistance was provided by Tracy Ashmore, Craig Barber, Jackson Boggs, Charles Brower, Melissa Decker John Griffin, Julie Murray, and Judith Smith. And we owe a continuing debt of gratitude to those who helped us in typing manuscripts and correcting drafts: Marjorie Brunner, Cynthia Carter, Anne Guthrie, Barbara McLean, Marian Ryerson, Vanessa Smith, and Kay Wilkie.

ALEX ALEINIKOFF
DAVID MARTIN
HIROSHI MOTOMURA

April 1995

*

Preface to the First Edition

For decades, immigration and nationality law has been something of a neglected stepchild in the law schools. Most schools offer no immigration course at all. Where courses exist, they typically focus on the practical business of learning a complex statute and preparing students for careers as immigration attorneys, often finding little time to devote to larger issues of policy and principle.

Immigration law has suffered from the lack of sustained academic attention. All too often, instead of measured policy debate, one encounters in this field merely the polarized confrontation of charge and counter-charge: government supporters reflexively advocating a hardline response; government opponents reflexively assuming that maximum advocacy for the particular aliens involved will bring about the best public policy. We don't deny that the issues are the kind that stir—and ought to stir—deep feelings. But we believe there is far more room for careful and balanced study of long-term policy options, even among those who care passionately about the ultimate values at stake. Law schools should serve as one important forum for such exploration.

As law students, we too enjoyed little exposure to the subject. Later, during stints in government service in Washington, each of us found himself dealing occasionally with immigration matters, but we discovered our mutual interest in the subject only when the Cuban boatlift of 1980 brought lawyers from the Departments of Justice and State together. There is nothing like a full-fledged crisis—especially one offering no satisfactory solutions—to cement an appreciation of the subject's fascinations and frustrations. We carried that interest with us when we moved into the academy, along with vague intentions to teach immigration law, but with little idea of just what was in store.

Now, after teaching and writing in the field for several years, we have come to wonder how the intrinsic attractions of the subject for classroom teaching have gone so widely unnoticed. Immigration law, we have learned, can be one of the richest and most rewarding subjects for both students and professors. It is redolent of our national history, reflecting both successes that are the legitimate source of national pride, and dispiriting failures. Major public policy issues appear repeatedly, posing deeper questions concerning national identity, membership, moral philosophy, constitutional interpretation, public law, public administration, international relations, and the limits of practical politics. Immigration law also furnishes a vital setting for studying the interaction of our three branches of government. Indeed, we have been struck by how many major Supreme Court decisions on larger questions of administrative and constitutional law have been decided in immigration cases—the legislative veto case, *INS v. Chadha,* 103 S.Ct. 2764 (1983), being only the latest example.

An immigration course, however, need not always keep the student at the heights occupied by great questions of philosophy, public policy, and constitutional interpretation. Immigration law also provides a worthy vehicle for refining basic lawyering skills, especially the capacity for close reading of an intricate statute and the discipline of mastering a specialized technical vocabulary. One judge who had just struggled through a complex interpretive task reflected on his experience:

> Whatever guidance the regulations furnish to those cognoscenti familiar with [immigration] procedures, this court, despite many years of legal experience, finds that they yield up meaning only grudgingly and that morsels of comprehension must be pried from mollusks of jargon.

Dong Sik Kwon v. INS, 646 F.2d 909, 919 (5th Cir.1981). Students ought to learn how to wield their *escargot* forks expertly, and then they should be inspired to ask whether the food could not be prepared in a more sensible way.

Beyond this, the student of immigration law must develop an awareness of how legislation evolves and an ability to make use of the materials of legislative history—for today's Immigration and Nationality Act (INA) is the product of over a hundred years of congressional efforts to fashion laws that regulate immigration. There are also thousands of administrative and judicial precedents, often in remarkable conflict with one another in both holding and spirit. These provide excellent raw materials for practice in the art of advocacy, hypothetically representing either a private client or a government agency.

There may be many reasons for immigration law's historical insularity. But we wrote this book with the conviction that a lack of good teaching materials has played a role--materials with which nonspecialists might feel comfortable but which specialists might also find challenging. (In this respect, we remember well our own problems when we first taught the course.) When we began our work on this book, there was no casebook at all on the subject of immigration law. Treatises existed, and various kinds of manuals that have been used as the basis for the course by practitioners of many years' experience. But it is a daunting prospect for nonspecialists to put together workable supplemental materials on their own, especially if they aspire to teaching more than just the technical details.

We hope this book will contribute toward ending the law schools' neglect and the subject's insularity. We have consciously sought to make the reader aware of the broader dimensions of the subject, but without ignoring the nuts-and-bolts foundation that a novice practitioner in the field would find necessary. We don't spend time, for example, exploring all 19 grounds for deportation appearing in INA § 241(a). We do devote enough attention to selected grounds, however, as well as the basic structure of those provisions, so that a student would know where to turn for answers to the detailed questions that might arise in practice. We have aimed, above all, at recapturing immigration law as a worthy and exciting area for academic study, without losing sight of the basic learning a student must master if he or she chooses to open an immigration practice the following year. Whether we have succeeded in these aims remains to be seen, but we invite users of this book—instructors and students—to write us with their reactions and suggestions for expanded or reduced coverage.

We have also consciously tried to avoid the polarities that often beset the field. It is easy to develop sympathy for the individual alien involved in a particular case, and to strive to mold the legal doctrine to bring about a warm-hearted result for that person. Too many law review notes, and often judges as well, succumb to this temptation, neglecting to take adequate account of the long-term implications for an immigration system that must cope with millions of applications each year. We try to keep the reader aware of that larger systemic perspective—without suggesting that systems should always prevail over warm-heartedness, of course.

* * *

ALEX ALEINIKOFF
DAVID MARTIN

November 30, 1984

*

Technical Matters

EDITING STYLE

In editing cases and other materials reprinted here, we have marked textual deletions with asterisks, but we have often omitted simple citations to cases or other authorities without any printed indication. Similarly, we have deleted footnotes from reprinted materials without signalling the omission. Where we chose to retain a footnote, however, we have maintained the original numbering. Our own footnotes appearing in the midst of reprinted materials are marked with alphabetical superscripts; they also end with the notation "—eds." When we drop footnotes to text that we wrote ourselves, we have used the ordinary numerical designations.

INA CITATIONS

How to cite the sections of the Immigration and Nationality Act (INA) posed a special problem. Most—but not all—court decisions refer to INA provisions by means of the numbers employed in Title 8 of the U.S. Code, where the Act is codified. This is understandable, even though the system used to translate Act numbers into U.S. Code numbers strikes us as eccentric and unpredictable. But specialists in the field almost religiously employ the INA section numbers and would be mystified at references to the U.S. Code enumeration.

We decided ultimately to use the section numbers of the Act consistently throughout this book, to the exclusion of the U.S. Code numbers—and not only because we expect our readers to count themselves as specialists before they are finished. The administrative framework for regulations and Operations Instructions is intimately linked to the numbering scheme of the original Act. For example, regulations implementing the exclusion provisions, § 212 of the INA, appear in Part 212 of 8 C.F.R. Operations Instructions are similarly coded. Anyone even minimally active in the field therefore will profit from acquaintance with this fundamental numbering scheme.

Consequently, to avoid confusion, we have excised references to the Act using the U.S. Code numbering system from all cases and materials, and substituted direct INA section references, without expressly indicating where such substitutions have occurred. Readers who must know the corresponding U.S. Code number will find a conversion chart below.

ABBREVIATED CITATION FORMS

Most citations in the book conform generally to *A Uniform System of Citation,* customarily used by law journals. For a few items that are cited frequently, however, we have abbreviated even further.

GM & Y C. Gordon, S. Mailman, and S. Yale-Loehr, Immigration Law and Procedure (rev. ed. 1995). (The leading treatise in the field, available now as a 12-volume looseleaf set, including five volumes containing primary materials [INA, regulations, Operations Instructions, etc.].)

IMFA   Immigration Marriage Fraud Amendments of 1986, Pub.L. No. 99–639, 100 Stat. 3537.

INA   The Immigration and Nationality Act. (Passed in 1952, Pub.L. No. 82–414, 66 Stat. 163, as a comprehensive codification replacing earlier immigration and nationality laws, and frequently amended since then. The Act itself is codified, according to an idiosyncratic numbering scheme, in Title 8 of the United States Code; a conversion chart, showing corresponding section numbers, appears below. We cite by INA section number, *not* U.S.C. section number, to the current amended statute.)

IRCA   Immigration Reform and Control Act of 1986, Pub.L. No. 99–603, 100 Stat. 3359.

INS Statistical Yearbook
              United States Department of Justice, Immigration and Naturalization Service, Statistical Yearbook of the Immigration and Naturalization Service.

Interp.Rel.   Interpreter Releases. (The leading reporting service on administrative, legislative and judicial developments in the immigration field. It is published weekly by Federal Publications, Inc.)

1990 Act Immigration Act of 1990, Pub.L. No. 101–649, 104 Stat. 4978

O.I.   Operations Instructions. (The manual of detailed guidelines and policy statements issued by the Immigration and Naturalization Service and used by immigration officers in implementing the statute and the regulations. Those Instructions which have been released to the public are reprinted in Volume 9 of the GM & Y treatise.)

SCIRP, Final Report; SCIRP, Staff Report; SCIRP, Appendix A, etc.
              Select Commission on Immigration and Refugee Policy (SCIRP), U.S. Immigration Policy and the National Interest, Final Report and Recommendations (1981); *id.*, Staff Report, Supplement to the Final Report and Recommendations of [SCIRP]; *id.*, Appendix A to the Staff Report, etc. (The Select Commission, composed of four public members, four Cabinet officers, four Senators, and four Representatives, was chartered by statute in 1978. Act of October 5, 1978, Pub.L. No.

95–412, 92 Stat. 907. Each lettered appendix to the staff report was published as a separate volume; the appendices represent important compilations of research materials on the specific subject to which the volume is dedicated.)

*

Conversion Chart

CORRESPONDENCE OF SECTIONS OF THE IMMIGRATION AND
NATIONALITY ACT AND SECTIONS OF TITLE 8,
UNITED STATES CODE

INA §	8 U.S.C. §	INA §	8 U.S.C. §	INA §	8 U.S.C. §
101	1101	242A	1252a	282	1352
102	1102	242B	1252b	283	1353
103	1103	243	1253	284	1354
104	1104	244	1254	285	1355
105	1105	244A	1254a	286	1356
106	1105a	245	1255	287	1357
201	1151	245A	1255a	288	1358
202	1152	246	1256	289	1359
203	1153	247	1257	290	1360
204	1154	248	1258	291	1361
205	1155	249	1259	292	1362
206	1156	250	1260	293	1363
207	1157	251	1281	301	1401
208	1158	252	1282	302	1402
209	1159	253	1283	303	1403
210	1160	254	1284	304	1404
211	1181	255	1285	305	1405
212	1182	256	1286	306	1406
213	1183	257	1287	307	1407
214	1184	258	1288	308	1408
215	1185	261	1301	309	1409
216	1186a	262	1302	310	1421
216A	1186b	263	1303	311	1422
217	1187	264	1304	312	1423
218	1188	265	1305	313	1424
221	1201	266	1306	314	1425
222	1202	271	1321	315	1426
223	1203	272	1322	316	1427
224	1204	273	1323	317	1428
231	1221	274	1324	318	1429
232	1222	274A	1324a	319	1430
234	1224	274B	1324b	320	1431
235	1225	274C	1324c	321	1432
236	1226	275	1325	322	1433
237	1227	276	1326	324	1435
238	1228	277	1327	325	1436
239	1229	278	1328	326	1437
240	1230	279	1329	327	1438
241	1251	280	1330	328	1439
242	1252	281	1351	329	1440

INA §	8 U.S.C. §	INA §	8 U.S.C. §	INA §	8 U.S.C. §
329A	1440–1	339	1450	356	1488
330	1441	340	1451	357	1489
331	1442	341	1452	358	1501
332	1443	342	1453	359	1502
333	1444	343	1454	360	1503
334	1445	344	1455	361	1504
335	1446	346	1457	411	1521
336	1447	347	1458	412	1522
337	1448	349	1481	413	1523
338	1449	351	1483	414	1524

Acknowledgments

The authors wish to express their thanks to copyright holders and authors for permission to reprint excerpts from the following materials.

Ackerman, Bruce, Social Justice in the Liberal State, pp. 89–95. Copyright © 1980 by the Yale University Press. Reprinted by permission of the publisher.

Aleinikoff, T. Alexander, Aliens, Due Process and "Community Ties": A Response to Martin, 44 University of Pittsburgh Law Review 237 (1983). Copyright © 1983. Reprinted by permission.

Aleinikoff, T. Alexander, The Meaning of "Persecution" in U.S. Asylum Law, 3 International Journal of Refugee Law 1 (1991). Copyright © 1991. Reprinted by permission of the Oxford University Press.

Barich, Bill, Reporter at Large: La Frontera, in The New Yorker, December 17, 1990. Copyright © 1984 by Bill Barich. Originally in The New Yorker. Reprinted by permission of International Creative Management.

Bickel, Alexander, The Morality of Consent, ch. 2. Copyright © 1975 by the Yale University Press. Reprinted by permission of the publisher.

Borjas, George, Friends or Strangers (1990). Copyright © 1990. Reprinted by permission of the author.

Bruck, Connie, Springing the Haitians, The American Lawyer, September 1982, pp. 36–39. Copyright © 1982. Reprinted by permission.

Calavita, Kitty, Employer Sanctions Violations: Toward a Dialectical Model of White Collar Crime, 24 Law and Society Review 1041 (1990). Copyright © 1990. Reprinted by permission of the Law and Society Association.

Calavita, Kitty, The Immigration Policy Debate: Critical Analysis and Future Options, in Mexican Migration to the United States: Origins, Consequences, and Policy Options 151 (W. Cornelius & J. Bustamante eds. 1989). Copyright © 1989 by the Center for U.S.-Mexican Studies, University of California, San Diego. Reprinted by permission.

Carens, Joseph H., Aliens and Citizens: The Case for Open Borders, 49 Review of Politics 251 (1987). Copyright © 1987. Reprinted by permission of the editors of The Review of Politics, University of Notre Dame.

Clark, Rebecca L., Passel, Jeffrey S., Zimmerman, Wendy N., and Fix, Michael, Fiscal Impacts of Undocumented Aliens: Selected Estimates for Seven States (1994). Copyright © 1994. Reprinted by permission.

Cornelius, Wayne A., Mexican Migration to the United States: Introduction, in Mexican Migration to the United States: Origins, Consequences, and Policy Options 1 (W. Cornelius & J. Bustamante eds., 1989). Copyright

Motomura, Hiroshi, Immigration Law After a Century of Plenary Power: Phantom Constitutional Norms and Statutory Interpretation, 100 Yale Law Journal (1990). Copyright © 1990. Reprinted by permission of The Yale Law Journal Company and Fred B. Rothman & Company.

Note, Consular Discretion in the Immigrant Visa-Issuing Process, 16 San Diego Law Review 87 (1978). Copyright © 1978 by the San Diego Law Review Association. Reprinted by permission.

Note, Developments in the Law: Immigration Policy and the Rights of Aliens, 96 Harvard Law Review 1286 (1983). Copyright © 1983 by the Harvard Law Review Association. Reprinted by permission.

Novotny, Ann, Strangers at the Door: Ellis Island, Castle Garden, and the Great Migration to America, pp. 10–23, 127–30. Copyright © 1971 by Devin-Adair Publishing Co. Reprinted by permission.

Portes, Alejandro, and Böröcz, József, Contemporary Immigration: Theoretical Perspectives on its Determinants and Modes of Incorporation, 23 International Migration Review 606 (1989). Copyright © 1989 by the Center for Migration Studies of New York, Inc. Reprinted by permission.

Refugees or Prisoners?, Newsweek, February 1, 1982. Copyright © 1982, Newsweek, Inc. All rights reserved. Reprinted by permission.

Roberts, Maurice, The Exercise of Administrative Discretion Under the Immigration Laws, 13 San Diego Law Review 144 (1975). Copyright © 1975 by the San Diego Law Review Association. Reprinted by permission.

Rosberg, Gerald M., Aliens and Equal Protection: Why Not the Right to Vote?, 75 Michigan Law Review 1092 (1977). Copyright © 1977. Reprinted by permission.

Rumbaut, Ruben G., and Portes, Alejandro, Immigrant America: A Portrait, pp. 6–27, 34–48 (1990). Copyright © 1990 The Regents of the University of California. Reprinted by permission.

Schuck, Peter H., The Transformation of Immigration Law, 84 Columbia Law Review 1 (1984). Copyright © 1984. Reprinted by permission.

Schuck, Peter H., Membership in the Liberal Polity: The Devaluation of American Citizenship, in Immigration and the Politics of Citizenship in Europe and North America 51 (W.R. Brubaker ed. 1989). Copyright © 1984. Reprinted by permission.

Simon, Julian, Auction the Right to Be an Immigrant, New York Times, Jan. 28, 1986, at A25. Copyright © 1986 by The New York Times Company. Reprinted by permission.

Simpson, Alan, Legal Immigration Reform, 25 San Diego L.Rev. 215 (1988). Copyright © 1988, by the San Diego Law Review Association. Reprinted by permission.

Suhrke, Astri, Global Refugee Movements and Strategies of Response, in U.S. Immigration and Refugee Policy: Global and Domestic Issues

(M.M. Kritz ed. 1983). Copyright © 1983 by D.C. Heath and Company). Reprinted by permission.

Trillin, Calvin, Making Adjustments, in The New Yorker, May 28, 1984. Copyright © 1984 Calvin Trillin. Originally in The New Yorker. Reprinted by permission.

Vobejda, Barbara, Births, Immigration Revise Census View of 21st Century U.S., The Washington Post, Dec. 4, 1992, at A10. Copyright © 1992 The Washington Post. Reprinted with permission.

Walzer, Michael, Spheres of Justice: A Defense of Pluralism and Equality (New York, N.Y.: Basic Books, Inc., 1983), pp. 31–34, 37–40, 47–50, 61–62. Revised from Michael Walzer, "The Distribution of Membership," in Peter G. Brown and Henry Shue, eds., Boundaries: National Autonomy and its Limits (Totowa, N.J.: Rowman and Littlefield © 1981). Reprinted by permission.

Watkins, Henry G., Streamlining Deportation Proceedings: Self-Incrimination, Immunity from Prosecution and the Duty to Testify in a Deportation Context, 22 San Diego L.Rev. 1075 (1985). Copyright © 1985, by the San Diego Law Review Association. Reprinted by permission.

Weiss, Elaine, A Day in the Life of an Immigration Practitioner, The Florida Bar Journal, May 1992, at 74–75. Copyright © 1992. Reprinted by permission.

Weissbrodt, David, Immigration Law and Procedure in a Nutshell (3d ed. 1992). Copyright © 1992. Reprinted by permission of the West Publishing Corporation.

Wildes, Leon, The Nonpriority Program of the Immigration and Naturalization Service Goes Public: The Litigative Uses of the Freedom of Information Act, 14 San Diego Law Review 42 (1976). Copyright © 1976, 1977 by the San Diego Law Review Association. Reprinted by permission.

Whelan, Frederick, Citizenship and Freedom of Movement: An Open Admission Policy?, in Open Borders? Closed Societies?: The Ethical and Political Issues 3 (M. Gibney ed. 1988).

The Year of the Refugee, in The Economist, December 23, 1989. Copyright © 1989 The Economist Newspaper Group, Inc. Reprinted with permission. Further reproduction is prohibited.

Zolberg, Aristide R., Suhrke, Astri, and Aguayo, Sergio, Escape From Violence: Conflict and the Refugee Crisis in the Developing World (1989). Copyright © 1989 by the Oxford University Press. Reprinted by permission.

*

Using WESTLAW
to help you understand
Immigration Law

Introduction: As a law student, you want to master your courses as completely as possible. Obtaining that mastery is the key to higher levels of performance in law school and better preparedness for the bar exam. Using **WESTLAW** with **West books** is an excellent way to acquire the knowledge and information necessary to understand the legal concepts that you will encounter during law school.

The following examples will show you how to use **WESTLAW** to quickly retrieve relevant information that will increase your understanding of the many topic areas in Aleinikoff, Martin and Motomura's **Immigration: Process and Policy**. All you need is your WESTLAW password and WESTMATE software (if you are going to use WESTLAW from your home computer). To begin, simply type your password, enter a research session identifier and continue with one of the sections below.

I. HOW TO RETRIEVE THE FULL TEXT OF A PRINCIPAL CASE OR NOTE CASE

The principal and note cases in this text are generally not included in full. Reading the entire case, however, may help you understand the court's reasoning and holding, and give you a better grasp of the theories involved. The authors may also provide citations to cases for additional reading to better highlight a particular point of law. For example, in Chapter 3, *Admission and Exclusion*, **at the top of page 352**, the authors cite a case that speaks to Congress' power to determine whether certain restrictions to individual liberties can be tolerated. To see that case, *United States v. Robel*, 389 U.S. 258 (1967), use the **find** command by typing

find 389 us 258 (then press ENTER)

*Use the format above to retrieve cases on WESTLAW, i.e., from anywhere in WESTLAW type the word **find** (or **fi**) followed by the **volume number, reporter abbreviation,** and **page number** of the case you wish to view.*

II. HOW TO RETRIEVE LAW REVIEW AND LAW JOURNAL ARTICLES

Often a cited law review or journal article will provide valuable insight into and analysis of a particular issue or topic. Your professor may even suggest or require that you read some of these articles. For example, **on page 622,** Chapter 6, *Deportation Procedures*, footnote 8, the authors cite an article titled, *Reexamining the Constitutionality of Workplace Raids After the Immigration Reform and Control Act of 1986*, 100 Harv. L. Rev.

1979 (1987). To view this article, first go to the WESTLAW FIND PUBLI-CATIONS INDEX (to obtain the appropriate citation format) by typing

find pubs (*then press* **ENTER)**

To view publication abbreviations for law reviews and law journals, locate LAW REVIEWS *(the last entry)* and type its corresponding page number *(and press* **ENTER**). To view publications that begin with the letter **H** (for **H**arvard University Law Review) locate the letter **H** and type its corresponding page number *(and press* **ENTER**). Page ahead (by using the **PAGE DOWN** key or typing **p** then pressing **ENTER**) until you locate the Harvard University Law Review entry and its WESTLAW citation format. Combine the abbreviation with the volume and page numbers of the article you wish to view, then use the **find** command by typing

find 100 harv. l. rev. 1979 (*then press* ENTER)

Use the format above to retrieve law review and law journal articles on WESTLAW, i.e., from anywhere in WESTLAW type the word **find** *(or* **fi**) *followed by the* **volume number, appropriate law journal or law review abbreviation,** *and* **page number** *of the article you wish to view.*

III. HOW TO USE WEST'S TOPIC AND KEY NUMBER SYSTEM TO OBTAIN MORE INFORMATION ABOUT IMMIGRATION LAW

Cases reported in West Publications are organized in its *topic* and *key number system* (see Note following). The cases you read on WESTLAW contain paragraphs of information called *headnotes*. The headnotes contain concise statements of law that are designated by *topic* and *key number*. The system is designed to allow you to efficiently retrieve other cases that contain the same topic and key number, meaning that the cases will have similar "on-point" law.

Page forward in any case you are viewing until you find a topic and key number discussing a point of law relevant to your research. Then enter that topic and key number in a case law database to retrieve other cases discussing the same point of law, for example, **Aliens** (topic number 24) and **Restriction of number permitted to enter within given time** (key number 511/2). This example will use the U.S. Courts of Appeals cases database. You can also determine how the courts in your state (or any other state or federal jurisdiction) have decided this and other issues by using your state case law database, e.g., **vt-cs** (Vermont), **ne-cs** (Nebraska), **ut-cs** (Utah), etc. Access the U.S. Courts of Appeals cases database by typing

db cta (*then press* **ENTER)***

* You may type **db cta** from anywhere in your WESTLAW research session except from a **find** result. Typing **gb** (go back) then pressing **ENTER** will return you from a found document to your previous research location. If you have used FIND more than once in succession, it will be necessary for you to type **gb** more than once.

At the U.S. Courts of Appeals cases database Enter Query Screen type
24k511/2 *(then press* **ENTER)**

This will retrieve all cases that contain a headnote classified under West topic **24 (Aliens)** under key number **511/2 (Restriction of number permitted to enter within given time)**. Pressing **ENTER** will take you to the first page of each retrieved case and then to the topic and key number page(s).

Note: West's **Key Number service** contains the entire, current West Publishing Company Digest System topic and key number outline on WESTLAW. When you don't know which topic you are searching for, type **key**. The topic list will be displayed. When you know the topic name or number, type key followed by the name or number, e.g., **key jury** or **key 230**. The Analysis, which is a list of major headings for the topic, will be displayed.

Follow up: Many, but not all of the law review and journal articles referenced in this book are contained in a WESTLAW database. If you have any questions about WESTLAW or the preceding sections, call West Customer Service at 1–800–WESTLAW (1–800–937–8529), or speak to your WESTLAW Academic or student representative.

*

Summary of Contents

	Page
PREFACE TO THE THIRD EDITION	v
PREFACE TO THE FIRST EDITION	ix
TECHNICAL MATTERS	xiii
CONVERSION CHART	xvii
ACKNOWLEDGMENTS	xix
USING WESTLAW TO HELP YOU UNDERSTAND IMMIGRATION LAW	xxv
TABLE OF CASES	xliii
TABLE OF AUTHORITIES	liii
TABLE OF STATUTES, RULES AND REGULATIONS	lxvii

Chapter One. Foundations of the Immigration Power **1**

Sec.

A.	The Sources of the Federal Immigration Power	1
B.	A Brief History of Immigration to the United States	40
C.	Theories of Migration	66
D.	The Exercise of the Immigration Power: The Moral Constraints	74

Chapter Two. Federal Agencies **100**

A.	The Department of Justice	100
B.	The Department of State	115
C.	Other Federal Agencies	118

Chapter Three. Admission and Exclusion: Substantive Provisions **122**

A.	Immigrants	122
B.	Nonimmigrants	229
C.	Undocumented Aliens in the United States	270
D.	Grounds for Exclusion	339
E.	Parole	379

Chapter Four. Admission and Exclusion: Procedures **385**

A.	Due Process in Exclusion Proceedings	385
B.	Admission Procedures: A Glance Backward	412
C.	Modern Procedures and Documents	421
D.	Due Process Revisited: Detention of Excludable Aliens	445

Chapter Five. Entry **474**

A.	The Definition of "Entry" and Its Relevance	474
B.	The Re–entry Doctrine	486
C.	A Concluding Conversation	505

Page

Chapter Six. Deportation -- **511**
Sec.
A.   The Deportation Power -- 512
B.   Deportation Procedures --- 582
C.   Due Process, Exclusion and Deportation: Towards a New Ap-
        proach -- 629

Chapter Seven. Relief From Deportation ---------------------- **640**
A.   Voluntary Departure -- 640
B.   Prosecutorial Discretion --- 647
C.   Regularization of Status --- 652
D.   A Concluding Question -- 716

Chapter Eight. Refugees and Political Asylum -------------- **718**
A.   Introduction -- 718
B.   Overseas Refugee Programs ------------------------------------ 735
C.   Political Asylum --- 759
D.   Safe Haven --- 884

Chapter Nine. Judicial Review ------------------------------------ **899**
A.   Background --- 901
B.   Petitions for Review of Orders of Deportation -------------- 908
C.   Review in the District Court ------------------------------------ 927
D.   Other Restrictions on Judicial Review ----------------------- 934
E.   Habeas Corpus in Deportation Cases ------------------------ 960

Chapter Ten. Citizenship --- **974**
A.   Is Citizenship Important? --------------------------------------- 975
B.   Acquisition of Nationality by Birth --------------------------- 990
C.   Naturalization and Denaturalization ------------------------- 996
D.   Expatriation --- 1045
E.   A Concluding Problem: Citizens, Aliens, and the Right to Vote 1084

INDEX -- 1091

Table of Contents

—————

Page

PREFACE TO THE THIRD EDITION -- v
PREFACE TO THE FIRST EDITION --- ix
TECHNICAL MATTERS -- xiii
CONVERSION CHART --- xvii
ACKNOWLEDGMENTS -- xix
USING WESTLAW TO HELP YOU UNDERSTAND IMMIGRATION LAW ---------- xxv
TABLE OF CASES -- xliii
TABLE OF AUTHORITIES --- liii
TABLE OF STATUTES, RULES AND REGULATIONS ------------------------------- lxvii

Chapter One. Foundations of the Immigration Power ---------- 1
Sec.
A. The Sources of the Federal Immigration Power ----------------- 1
    Chinese Immigration --- 2
    Federal Regulation of Chinese Immigration -------------------- 3
    Chinese Exclusion Case (Chae Chan Ping v. United States) ---- 5
    Sources of the Immigration Power ----------------------------- 7
    The Chinese Exclusion Laws and Equal Protection -------------- 17
    From Exclusion to Deportation -------------------------------- 20
    Fong Yue Ting v. United States ----------------------------- 21
    Notes -- 35
B. A Brief History of Immigration to the United States ---------- 40
    Select Commission on Immigration and Refugee Policy [SCIRP], U.S.
        Immigration Policy and the National Interest ------------- 41
    Later Developments --- 61
C. Theories of Migration --- 66
    George J. Borjas, Friends or Strangers: The Impact of Immigrants on
        the U.S. Economy --- 66
    Alejandro Portes & József Böröcz, Contemporary Immigration: Theoreti-
        cal Perspectives on Its Determinants and Modes of Incorporation 70
    Note --- 74
D. The Exercise of the Immigration Power: The Moral Constraints 74
    Timothy King, Immigration From Developing Countries: Some Philo-
        sophical Issues -- 75
    Bruce Ackerman, Social Justice in the Liberal State ---------- 80
    Michael Walzer, Spheres of Justice: A Defense of Pluralism and Equality 85
    Joseph H. Carens, Aliens and Citizens: The Case for Open Borders 91
    Notes -- 94

Chapter Two. Federal Agencies ------------------------------- 100
A. The Department of Justice ------------------------------------- 100
    1. The Immigration and Naturalization Service --------------- 101
        Calvin Trillin, Making Adjustments ---------------------- 105
    2. Special Inquiry Officers, a/k/a Immigration Judges ------- 107
    3. Appeals -- 112

Sec.   **Page**

A. The Department of Justice—Continued

4. Other Units 115

B. The Department of State 115

C. Other Federal Agencies 118

1. The Department of Labor 118

2. The Public Health Service 118

3. The United States Information Agency 118

Elaine Weiss, A Day in the Life of an Immigration Practitioner 119

Chapter Three. Admission and Exclusion: Substantive Provi-

sions **122**

A. Immigrants 122

1. Overview 122

a. Family–Sponsored Immigration 125

b. Employment-based Immigration 128

c. Diversity Immigration 129

d. Ceilings and Floors 131

Notes to Table 3.6 135

Problems 136

e. Changing Patterns of American Immigration 137

Alejandro Portes & Rubén G. Rumbaut, Immigrant America: A

Portrait 139

Census Bureau Releases Statistics on Foreign–Born Population

in the U.S. 146

Barbara Vobejda, Births, Immigration Revise Census View of

21st Century U.S. 148

Further Questions 149

2. Constitutional Standards for Evaluating Admission Catego-

ries 150

Fiallo v. Bell 150

Notes 159

Constitutional Protection of Aliens After Admission 161

3. Family Reunification Categories 166

a. Offspring 166

De Los Santos v. INS 166

Notes 170

b. Immigration Based on Marriage 175

Bark v. INS 176

Calvin Trillin, Making Adjustments 178

Sham Marriages and the Ethical Responsibilities of an Attorney 179

Dabaghian v. Civiletti 181

Notes 182

The Immigration Marriage Fraud Amendments of 1986 184

Problems 186

Notes and Questions 187

c. The Backlog Problem 189

4. Labor Certification and Employment–based Immigration 192

a. Labor Certification 192

(i) Background and Basic Procedures 192

Calvin Trillin, Making Adjustments 196

Notes 198

(ii) Job Requirements and Employer's "Personal Pref-

erences" 199

Sec.		Page
A.	Immigrants—Continued	
	Pesikoff v. Secretary of Labor	200
	Notes	203
	The Current Administrative Approach: Business Necessity	204
	(iii) The Prevailing Wage Requirement	206
	(iv) The Requirement of a Genuine Employment Relationship	208
	(v) Labor Certification and an Attorney's Professional Responsibility	209
	Ethical Considerations in Immigration Cases	210
	(vi) Easing the Task of Labor Certification—or Avoiding it Altogether	212
	Exercise	213
	(vii) Other Problems With Labor Certification	214
	Yui Sing Tse v. INS	214
	Notes	216
	(viii) The Future of Labor Certification	216
	b. The Employment–Based Preferences	220
	Exercise	223
	Investors as Immigrants	223
	5. Diversity Immigration	225
	Statement of Senator Alan K. Simpson, Commissioner, Select Commission on Immigration and Refugee Policy	225
	James Fallows, Immigration: How It's Affecting Us	227
	Notes	228
B.	Nonimmigrants	229
	1. Nonimmigrant Visas for Students and Scholars	233
	Austin T. Fragomen, Jr., Alfred J. Del Rey, Jr. & Sam Bernsen, Immigration Law and Business	233
	Notes	239
	2. Business and Entrepreneurial Nonimmigrants	240
	Exercise	242
	a. H, O, and P Nonimmigrant Visas	243
	b. L Nonimmigrant Visas	248
	c. E Nonimmigrant Visas	250
	Charles Gordon, Stanley Mailman & Stephen Yale–Loehr, Immigration Law and Procedure	250
	Matter of Walsh and Pollard	254
	Notes	258
	d. B Nonimmigrant Visas	260
	International Union of Bricklayers and Allied Craftsmen v. Meese	261
	Notes	268
	e. The North American Free Trade Agreement (NAFTA)	270
C.	Undocumented Aliens in the United States	270
	Bill Barich, A Reporter at Large: La Frontera	271
	Notes	273
	1. Why Do Undocumented Aliens Enter the United States?	275
	Kitty Calavita, The Immigration Policy Debate: Critical Analysis and Future Options	276
	Douglas S. Massey, Luin Goldring, and Jorge Durand, Continuities in Transnational Migration: An Analysis of Nineteen Mexican Communities	278

Sec.   **Page**

C.   Undocumented Aliens in the United States—Continued
     2. Impact of Illegal Migration in the United States 283
        a.   Impact on Social Services 283
        b.   Impact on the Labor Market 289
             Wayne A. Cornelius, Mexican Migration to the United States:
                Introduction 289
             Note 292
     3. Controlling Undocumented Migration: the IRCA Response   293
        a.   Legalization 294
        b.   Employer Sanctions 297
        c.   Antidiscrimination Provisions 298
             Questions on Employer Sanctions and Discrimination 299
             Collins Foods International, Inc. v. U.S. INS 300
             Notes 304
        d.   The Impact of IRCA 304
             (i)   Discrimination 304
                   Note 307
             (ii) Effects on Undocumented Immigration 307
                   Kitty Calavita, Employer Sanctions Violations: Toward a
                      Dialectical Model of White–Collar Crime 308
                   Wayne A. Cornelius, Mexican Migration to the United
                      States: Introduction 313
                   Note 315
     4. After IRCA: The Future of Immigration Control 315
        a.   Border Enforcement 315
             U.S. Commission on Immigration Reform, U.S. Immigration
                Policy: Restoring Credibility 315
             Notes 317
        b.   Employer Sanctions 318
             U.S. Commission on Immigration Reform, U.S. Immigration
                Policy: Restoring Credibility 318
             Notes 322
        c.   Public Benefits 323
             Plyler v. Doe 325
             Notes 336
D.   Grounds for Exclusion 339
     1. Overview 339
        Problems 341
     2. Exclusion Based on National Security and the Search for
        Substantive Constitutional Constraints on Exclusion
        Grounds 343
        Kleindienst v. Mandel 345
        Notes 352
        Later Developments 354
        Congressional Action 357
        Notes 359
        Implementation 361
     3. A Brief Digression: Judicial Review of Consular Visa Denials   362
        Pena v. Kissinger 363
        Notes 366
        Standing and Visa Denials 368
     4. The Public Charge Provision 370
        Matter of Kohama 372
        Note 374

Sec.   **Page**

D. Grounds for Exclusion—Continued

     5. Fraud and Willful Misrepresentation of Material Facts 375

        U.S. Department of State, Foreign Affairs Manual 376

        Problems 378

E. Parole 379

Chapter Four. Admission and Exclusion: Procedures 385

A. Due Process in Exclusion Proceedings 385

    United States ex rel. Knauff v. Shaughnessy 386

    Shaughnessy v. United States ex rel. Mezei 389

    Henry Hart, The Power of Congress to Limit the Jurisdiction of the Federal Courts: An Exercise in Dialectic 397

    T. Alexander Aleinikoff, Aliens, Due Process and "Community Ties": A Response to Martin 400

    Notes 401

    Landon v. Plasencia 405

    Notes 410

B. Admission Procedures: A Glance Backward 412

    Ann Novotny, Strangers at the Door: Ellis Island, Castle Garden, and the Great Migration to America 413

    The Evolution of the Visa Requirement 419

C. Modern Procedures and Documents 421

    1. Nonimmigrant Admissions 421

    2. Immigrant Visas and Visa Petitions 424

    3. At the Border 427

        Elizabeth J. Harper, Immigration Laws of the United States 427

        Notes 430

    4. Adjustment of Status 433

        Jain v. INS 434

        Notes on Adjustment of Status 439

        The Special Adjustment Provisions of INA § 245(i) 442

        Adjustment Based on Marriage 443

        Rescission of Adjustment of Status 444

D. Due Process Revisited: Detention of Excludable Aliens 445

    Notes 451

    Jean v. Nelson 452

    Notes 460

    Jean v. Nelson in the Supreme Court 461

    Notes 464

    The Cuban Detainees: Later Developments 465

    Questions 472

Chapter Five. Entry 474

A. The Definition of "Entry" and Its Relevance 474

    The Difference Between Exclusion and Deportation Proceedings 475

    Defining "Entry" 476

    Matter of G– 476

    In the Matter of the Application of Phelisna 481

    Notes 484

B. The Re–entry Doctrine 486

    United States ex rel. Volpe v. Smith 487

    Note 488

    Rosenberg v. Fleuti 490

    Notes 497

    Applying *Fleuti* 499

    The Ripples of *Fleuti* 500

Sec.   **Page**

B.   The Re–entry Doctrine—Continued

    Where Is the *Fleuti* Question Resolved? 501

    Proposals to Modify the Re–entry Doctrine 505

C.   A Concluding Conversation 505

Chapter Six.   Deportation **511**

A.   The Deportation Power 512

    1.   Constitutional Perspectives 512

        A Brief Note on the Deportation of "Subversives" 513

        Harisiades v. Shaughnessy 518

        Statutory Developments After *Harisiades* 526

        Constitutionally Protected Liberties and the Deportation Power 527

        Congress' Power to Discriminate 531

        Deportation Statutes and the *Ex Post Facto* Clause 531

        On the Construction of Immigration Statutes 535

    2.   Grounds of Deportation 535

        a.   Immigration Control Grounds 536

            (i)   Excludable at Time of Entry 536

            (ii)   Entry Without Inspection or Presence in the United States in Violation of Law 537

            (iii)   Failure to Maintain Nonimmigrant Status 539

            (iv)   Document Fraud 539

        b.   Crime-Related Grounds 540

            (i)   Crimes Involving Moral Turpitude: A Discussion of the Meaning of Statutes 542

                The Statutory History of "Moral Turpitude" 542

                Administrative and Judicial Interpretation of "Moral Turpitude" 544

                Goldeshtein v. INS 546

                Notes 549

                "Void for Vagueness" 552

                Jordan v. De George 552

                Notes 558

            (ii)   Drug Offenses, Aggravated Felonies, and Firearms Offenses 559

                Flores-Arellano v. INS 561

                Note 564

            (iii)   What Is a Conviction? 564

                Matter of Ozkok 565

                Notes 569

         c.   Participants in Nazi Persecution 572

            Linnas v. INS 572

            Notes 578

        d.   Deportation Statutes and "Statutes of Limitations" 580

            Time between Entry and the Commission of a Deportable Act 580

            Time between Commission of Act and Initiation of Proceedings 581

    3.   The Consequences of Deportation 582

B.   Deportation Procedures 582

    1.   The Constitutional Requirement of Due Process 582

        The Japanese Immigrant Case (Yamataya v. Fisher) 583

        Notes 586

    2.   Initiation of Proceedings 587

        a.   Arrest and the Order to Show Cause 587

        b.   Bond and Detention 588

Sec. **Page**

B. Deportation Procedures—Continued
   3. The Deportation Hearing ---- 591
      a. The Conduct of a Deportation Hearing ---- 591
         Charles Gordon, Stanley Mailman & Stephen Yale-Loehr, Immigration Law and Procedure ---- 592
         Notes ---- 595
      b. Constitutional and Statutory Rights in Deportation Hearings ---- 595
         (i) An Independent Decisionmaker ---- 595
         (ii) Counsel ---- 597
            Aguilera-Enriquez v. INS ---- 599
            Notes ---- 604
         (iii) Evidence: Quality ---- 606
         (iv) Evidence: Standard of Proof ---- 606
            Woodby v. INS ---- 606
            Notes ---- 612
            The *Woodby* Standard in Action ---- 613
            Silence and Adverse Inferences ---- 616
         (v) Evidence: Fifth and Fourth Amendment Exclusionary Rules ---- 617
            Fifth Amendment: "*Miranda* Warnings" ---- 617
            Fourth Amendment ---- 620
            Notes ---- 626
      c. Special Deportation Procedures ---- 627
C. Due Process, Exclusion and Deportation: Towards a New Approach ---- 629
   A Concluding Dialogue ---- 638
   Questions ---- 639

Chapter Seven. Relief From Deportation ---- 640
A. Voluntary Departure ---- 640
   1. Why Voluntary Departure? ---- 640
   2. The Standards for Voluntary Departure ---- 642
      Campos-Granillo v. INS ---- 643
      Notes ---- 646
B. Prosecutorial Discretion ---- 647
   1. Deferred Action Status ---- 647
      Leon Wildes, The Nonpriority Program of the Immigration and Naturalization Service Goes Public: The Litigative Use of the Freedom of Information Act ---- 648
   2. Stay of Deportation ---- 651
C. Regularization of Status ---- 652
   1. Suspension of Deportation: Ina § 244 ---- 653
      a. "Continuous" Physical Presence ---- 654
      b. "Extreme Hardship" under § 244(a)(1) ---- 655
         Section 244 in Action ---- 656
         Motions to Reopen in Suspension of Deportation Cases ---- 657
         INS v. Jong Ha Wang ---- 662
         Notes ---- 666
         Suspension of Deportation in the Post-*Wang* Era ---- 666
         Ravancho v. INS ---- 667
         Notes ---- 676
      c. The Discretionary Aspect of § 244 Relief ---- 678
         (i) Administrative Discretion ---- 678

Sec.   **Page**

C.   Regularization of Status—Continued
      (ii) Judicial Review of Administrative Discretion in
        § 244 Cases --- 681
          INS v. Rios–Pineda ------------------------------- 681
          Notes --- 684
          Wong Wing Hang v. INS --------------------------- 686
          Note -- 688
    2. Waiver of Exclusion Grounds in Deportation Hearings of
       Long–Term Permanent Resident Aliens: INA § 212(c) ----- 689
      Francis v. INS ----------------------------------- 691
      Notes -- 694
      Beyond *Francis?* --------------------------------- 697
      Matter of Hernandez–Casillas -------------------- 698
      Notes -- 703
      Bedoya-Valencia v. INS -------------------------- 704
      Notes -- 708
      Section 212(c) in Action -------------------------- 709
    3. Registry: INA § 249 ----------------------------- 712
    4. Private Bills ----------------------------------- 713
    5. Estoppel --------------------------------------- 714
    6. Additional Forms of Relief ----------------------- 716
    7. Relief in the Context of Judicial Deportation ------- 716
D.   A Concluding Question ----------------------------------- 716

Chapter Eight.   Refugees and Political Asylum ------------------ **718**
A.   Introduction -- 718
    1. The Controversy -------------------------------- 718
    2. Overview --------------------------------------- 721
    3. The Refugee Definition: An Introduction --------- 723
      Astri Suhrke, Global Refugee Movements and Strategies of Response   724
      Aristide R. Zolberg, Astri Suhrke, & Sergio Aguayo, Escape From
        Violence: Conflict and the Refugee Crisis in the Developing World   728
      David A. Martin, Reforming Asylum Adjudication: On Navigating
        the Coast of Bohemia ------------------------------- 730
      Notes -- 734
B.   Overseas Refugee Programs ------------------------------- 735
    1. The Legal Framework --------------------------- 735
      Presidential Determination No. 95–1 of October 1, 1994 ------ 739
      Notes -- 741
      David A. Martin, The Refugee Act of 1980: Its Past and Future   745
      Notes -- 748
    2. The Overseas Refugee Program in Operation -------- 750
      a. Indochina, 1981 -------------------------------- 750
      b. Soviet Refugees -------------------------------- 751
        Notes --- 754
      c. Indochinese Refugees -------------------------- 755
        Notes --- 757
C.   Political Asylum --- 759
    1. Introduction ----------------------------------- 759
      Asylum Procedures -------------------------------- 764
      Trends and Statistics ----------------------------- 767
    2. The Relationship Between § 208 and § 243(h): Standards for
      Analyzing the Threat an Applicant Faces in the Homeland   770

Sec.   **Page**

C. Political Asylum—Continued

      a. *Salim* 770

      b. *Stevic* and *Cardoza–Fonseca* 771

           INS v. Cardoza–Fonseca 773

           Notes 785

      c. The BIA's Response to *Cardoza–Fonseca* 787

           Exercise 789

           Questions 790

      d. Current Standards 790

           The 1990 Regulations 791

           Past Persecution 792

  3. Discretionary Denials of Asylum Under § 208 793

      a. Early Administrative Use of Discretion Under § 208 793

      b. Discretion, According to the Ninth Circuit 795

      c. The BIA's Approach to Discretion After *Cardoza–Fonseca* 797

           Matter of Pula 797

           Notes 802

      d. The Issue of Transit Through Third Countries 803

  4. Bootstrap Refugees 804

  5. What Is Persecution? 807

      a. Overview 807

           Matter of Chang 808

           Notes 814

           Later Developments Involving Chinese Family Planning Policy 816

      b. Coup Plotters 819

           Notes 821

      c. Conscientious Objectors 822

           Notes 827

  6. "Persecution on Account of ..." (Including Various Problems in Applying Refugee Standards in Civil War Situations) 828

      a. Neutrality and Imputed Political Opinion 829

           Notes 833

           INS v. Elias–Zacarias 835

           Notes 839

           Elias-Zacarias and Judicial Review 841

      b. Civil War Situations: The Effect on Political Asylum Determinations 842

           Fuentes and Risks From Nongovernmental Actors 842

           Matter of Fuentes 842

           Notes 845

           Maldonado–Cruz and "Military Discipline" 846

           A Middle Ground? 848

      c. Membership in a Particular Social Group 850

      d. Applying the Standards: Gender-based Asylum Claims 851

           Fatin v. INS 852

           Notes 859

  7. The Exception Clauses 860

      Exercise: The Asylum Standards Applied 862

  8. The Facts and the Procedures 863

      a. The Factfinding Challenge 863

      b. The Role of the State Department 869

      c. Later Controversies over Administrative Notice ... 872

Sec.		Page
C.	Political Asylum—Continued	
	9. Deterrence of Asylum Seekers	873
	Detention of Asylum Seekers	875
	Interdiction	878
	Denial of Work Authorization	882
	Summary Exclusion	884
D.	Safe Haven	884
	EVD: The Historical Pattern	886
	Special EVD Legislation	889
	The Salvadoran Controversy and "Temporary Protected Status"	889
	Later Legislative and Administrative Developments	894
	Cuba and the Use of Offshore Safe Havens	896
	Chapter Nine. Judicial Review	**899**
A.	Background	901
B.	Petitions for Review of Orders of Deportation	908
	Cheng Fan Kwok v. INS	909
	Notes	915
	Kavasji v. INS	916
	Notes	919
	Jurisdiction Under *Chadha*	919
	Mohammadi–Motlagh v. INS	921
	Notes	923
	Ongoing Problems with the Doctrine of *Cheng Fan Kwok*	925
C.	Review in the District Court	927
	A Pictorial Summary	931
D.	Other Restrictions on Judicial Review	934
	1. Exhaustion of Remedies and Ripeness Doctrine	934
	Bak v. INS	935
	Notes	937
	The *HRC* Exception	937
	Notes	940
	McNary v. Haitian Refugee Center, Inc.	942
	Notes	949
	Reno v. Catholic Social Services, Inc.	950
	2. Departure From the Country While Review Is Pending	953
	Notes	954
	3. The Effect of Motions to Reopen on Administrative and Judicial Review	957
	Ongoing Controversies	958
E.	Habeas Corpus in Deportation Cases	960
	United States ex rel. Marcello v. District Director	960
	Daneshvar v. Chauvin	967
	Notes	970
	Chapter Ten. Citizenship	**974**
A.	Is Citizenship Important?	975
	Alexander M. Bickel, Citizen or Person?: What Is Not Granted Cannot Be Taken Away	976
	Sugarman v. Dougall	984
	Peter H. Schuck, Membership in the Liberal Polity: The Devaluation of American Citizenship	985
	Notes	988
B.	Acquisition of Nationality by Birth	990
	Problems	995

Sec.		Page
C.	Naturalization and Denaturalization	996
	1. Acquiring U.S. Citizenship Through Naturalization	996
	Charles Gordon, Stanley Mailman, and Stephen Yale-Loehr, Immigration Law and Procedure	996
	Naturalization Procedures	1000
	The Basic Substantive Provisions	1002
	David Weissbrodt, Immigration Law and Procedure in a Nutshell	1002
	Problems	1007
	Petition for Naturalization of Kassas	1008
	Price v. INS	1010
	Notes	1014
	2. Denaturalization	1015
	Chaunt v. United States	1017
	Notes	1022
	In Re Petition of Haniatakis	1023
	United States v. Sheshtawy	1026
	Questions	1029
	Kungys v. United States	1029
	Notes	1044
D.	Expatriation	1045
	Donald K. Duvall, Expatriation Under United States Law, *Perez* to *Afroyim*: The Search for a Philosophy of American Citizenship	1046
	Perez v. Brownell	1050
	Questions	1054
	A Note on Dual Nationality	1055
	Afroyim v. Rusk	1062
	Notes	1067
	Vance v. Terrazas	1069
	Notes	1077
	Procedures in Expatriation Cases	1079
	The State Department's New Leaf	1081
	Expatriation and Denaturalization: Some Statistics	1083
E.	A Concluding Problem: Citizens, Aliens, and the Right to Vote	1084
	Gerald M. Rosberg, Aliens and Equal Protection: Why Not the Right to Vote?	1085
	Questions	1089
Index		1091

*

Table of Cases

The principal cases are in bold type. Cases cited or discussed in the text are roman type. References are to pages. Cases cited in principal cases and within other quoted materials are not included.

A–, Matter of, 485
Abbott Laboratories v. Gardner, 362, 900
Abdelhamid v. Ilchert, 685, 928
Abourezk v. Reagan, 356, 368, 404
Abreu–Semino, Matter of, 552
Acosta, Matter of, 773, 789, 829, 850, 859, 864
Acupuncture Center of Washington v. Brennan, 204
Adams v. Howerton, 171
Afroyim v. Rusk, 976, 994, **1062,** 1067, 1068, 1069, 1082
A–G–, Matter of, 822
Agosto v. Immigration and Naturalization Service, 908
Aguilera–Cota v. United States I.N.S., 865
Aguilera–Enriquez v. I.N.S., 599
Agunobi v. Thornburgh, 590
Alcantar, Matter of, 560
Aldecoaotalora, Matter of, 183
Alfaro–Orellana v. Ilchert, 883, 883
Ali v. Reno, 362
Allende v. Shultz, 845 F.2d 1111, p. 356
Allende v. Shultz, 605 F.Supp. 1220, pp. 355, 356
Alma Motor Co. v. Timken–Detroit Axle Co., 498
Almeida–Sanchez v. United States, 621
Alvarez–Mendez v. Stock, 467
Amanullah v. Cobb, 795
Amanullah v. Nelson, 384, 464, 877
Amarante v. Rosenberg, 424
Ambach v. Norwick, 164
American Arab Anti–Discrimination Committee v. Meese, 529
American–Arab Anti–Discrimination Committee v. Nelson, 530, 531
American Baptist Churches v. Meese, 885
American Baptist Churches v. Thornburgh, 767, 895
American Hosp. Ass'n v. N.L.R.B., 173
Ananeh–Firempong v. I.N.S., 791, 841
Anderson v. McElroy, 955, 960
Andrade v. Esperdy, 160, 175
Andreacchi v. Curran, 552

Anetekhai v. I.N.S., 443
Annang, Matter of, 175
Antoine–Dorcelli v. I.N.S., 171
Anwo, Matter of, 695
Application of (see name of party)
Ardestani v. I.N.S., 108, 597, 952
Arnett v. Kennedy, 412
Artee Corp., Matter of, 244
Artiga Turcios v. I.N.S., 790
Artukovic v. I.N.S., 534
Ashbrook–Simon–Hartley v. McLaughlin, 206
Asylum Case (Colombia / Peru), 762
Athehortua–Vanegas v. I.N.S., 937
Attoh v. I.N.S., 958
Augoustinakis v. I.N.S. at New York, N.Y., 934
Avila v. Rivkind, 402
Ayuda, Inc. v. Reno, 952
Ayuda, Inc. v. Thornburgh, 948 F.2d 742, p. 950
Ayuda, Inc. v. Thornburgh, 880 F.2d 1325, pp. 941, 942
Aziz v. Sullivan, 374
Azizi v. Thornburgh, 443
Azzouka v. Meese, 404
Azzouka v. Sava, 404

Bachelier v. I.N.S., 919
Baggett v. Bullitt, 558
Bak v. I. N. S., 935, 937, 957
Balzac v. People of Porto Rico, 975
Baltazar, Matter of, 618
Baria v. Leno, 444
Bark v. I.N.S., 176, 182, 183, 189
Barraza Rivera v. I.N.S., 827, 871
Barrera–Echavarria v. Rison, 44 F.3d 1441, p. 473
Barrera–Echavarria v. Rison, 21 F.3d 314, pp. 467, 472
Batoon v. I.N.S., 677
Baxter v. Palmigiano, 616
Bedoya–Valencia v. I.N.S., 704, 708
Belenzo, Matter of, 445
Belfield, United States v., 403
Beltran–Zavala v. I.N.S., 862
Berdo v. I.N.S., 805

Berlin Democratic Club v. Rumsfeld, 369
Bertrand v. Sava, 384, 448, 876
Bilokumsky, United States ex rel. v. Tod, 616
Bindczyck v. Finucane, 1015
Blackie's House of Beef, Inc. v. Castillo, 622
Blancada v. Turnage, 652, 955, 959
Blas, Matter of, 441
Board of Regents v. Roth, 411, 412
Boddie v. Connecticut, 605
Bodre, United States v., 534
Bolanos–Hernandez v. I.N.S., 830, 831, 838, 841, 848
Bolling v. Sharpe, 19
Bong Youn Choy v. Barber, 230
Bonilla v. I.N.S., 959
Bonnette, Matter of, 161
Boromand, Matter of, 183
Bothyo v. I.N.S., 940
Boutilier v. I.N.S., 340, 499
Brandenburg v. Ohio, 344, 361, 527
Bridges v. Wixon, 15, 528, 529
Brignoni–Ponce, United States v., 15, 621, 622
Brown v. Board of Ed. of Topeka, Shawnee County, Kan., 19
Brownell v. Shung, 904
Bruce v. Slattery, 464
Buckley v. Valeo, 19
Bueno–Carrillo v. Landon, 655, 677
Bugajewitz v. Adams, 512
Buletini v. I.N.S., 213
Bulk Farms, Inc. v. Martin, 209
Burbano, Matter of, 711
Burgess v. Meese, 175
Burr v. I.N.S., 564
Burrafato v. Department of State, 367
Bustos–Torres v. I.N.S., 606, 618
Butros v. I.N.S., 960
Butros v. I.N.S., 697

Cabell v. Chavez–Salido, 164, 165, 166, 1084
Cabral–Avila v. I.N.S., 616
Califano v. Sanders, 919, 928
Califano v. Yamasaki, 431
Callow, Ex parte, 539
Camacho–Bordes v. I.N.S., 955
Caminetti v. United States, 9
Camp v. Pitts, 926
Campos v. I.N.S., 16 F.3d 118, p. 534
Campos v. I.N.S., 961 F.2d 309, p. 704
Campos v. Smith, 500
Campos–Granillo v. I.N.S., 643, 646
Campos–Guardado v. I.N.S., 848, 859
Canas, Matter of, 828
Canas–Segovia v. I.N.S., 828
Canjura–Flores v. I.N.S., 864
Caporali v. Whelan, 589
Cardenas v. Smith, 369
Cardoza–Fonseca v. I.N.S., 807, 864
Carnejo Molina v. I.N.S., 646
Cartier v. Secretary of State, 432
Carvajal–Munoz v. I.N.S., 790, 841
Castillo–Felix v. I.N.S., 695
Castillo–Villagra v. I.N.S., 873

Castro–O'Ryan v. I.N.S., 598
Catholic Social Services, Inc. v. Thornburgh, 950, 952, 953
Cerna, Matter of, 696
Cerrillo–Perez v. I.N.S., 677
Chang, Matter of, 808, 814, 815, 817, 818, 850
Chaunt v. United States, 1017, 1022, 1023, 1029, 1044
Chavez–Calderon, Matter of, 500
Chavez–Ramirez v. I.N.S., 792 F.2d 932, p. 411
Chavez–Raya v. I.N.S., 519 F.2d 397, p. 619
Chen, Matter of, 792, 793
Chen v. Carroll, 484, 818
Chen v. Slattery, 818
Chen Chaun–Fa v. Kiley, 929, 931
Cheng Fan Kwok v. I.N.S., 909, 916, 919, 920, 926, 927, 934, 959, 973
Chevron, U.S.A., Inc. v. Natural Resources Defense Council, Inc., 173, 174, 551, 666
Chinese Am. Civic Council v. Attorney General, 369
Chinese Exclusion Case (Chae Chan Ping v. United States), 3, 5, 10, 11, 13, 15, 19, 20, 21, 36, 39, 74
Ching and Chen, Matter of, 485
Chin Yow v. United States, 902
Chiravacharadhikul v. I.N.S., 695
Choe v. I.N.S., 432
Chong v. Director, United States Information Agency, 240, 928
Chong v. I.N.S., 570
Chu Drua Cha v. Noot, 744
Chudshevid v. I.N.S., 958
Chukwura, United States v., 628
Chy Lung v. Freeman, 8, 12
Cisternas–Estay v. I.N.S., 806
Citizens to Preserve Overton Park, Inc. v. Volpe, 685, 901
City of (see name of city)
Clark v. Smith, 464
Collins Foods Intern., Inc. v. United States I.N.S., 300
Colyer v. Skeffington, 517
Commissioner of Immigration, United States ex rel. Vajtauer v., 517
Compagnie Generale Transatlantique, People v., 11
Conceiro, Matter of, 384
Connecticut Bd. of Pardons v. Dumschat, 412
Coriolan v. I.N.S., 805
Corona–Palomera v. I.N.S., 614, 615
Crespo v. United States, 175
Crespo–Gomez v. Richard, 861
Cruz v. Canada (Minister of Employment & Immigration), 827
Cruz–Lopez v. I.N.S., 790, 841
Cuban, In re, 467
Cunanan v. I.N.S., 606
Curtiss–Wright Export Co., United States v., 14, 15

Dabaghian v. Civiletti, 175, **181,** 183, 188, 189

Dally v. I.N.S., 864
Damaize–Job v. I.N.S., 865
Daneshvar v. Chauvin, 967, 971, 972, 973
Darby v. Cisneros, 934
Dass, Matter of, 867
Davis v. District Director, I.N.S., 1079
Dawood–Haio v. I.N.S., 864
De Brown v. Department of Justice, 1080
De Canas v. Bica, 337
De Figueroa v. I.N.S., 424
De la Cruz v. I.N.S., 571
de la Llana Castellon v. I.N.S., 873
Delgado v. I.N.S., 170, 175
De Los Santos v. I.N.S., 166, 170, 172, 174, 175
Del Rosario, United States v., 571
Demjanjuk, United States v., 1084
Dennis v. United States, 527, 530
Deris, Matter of, 570
Dhangu v. I.N.S., 940, 959, 973
Di v. Carroll, 818
Diaz v. I.N.S., 883
Diaz v. Pan Am. World Airways, Inc., 205
Diaz–Chambrot, Matter of, 697
Diaz–Escobar v. I.N.S., 865
Dill v. I.N.S., 955
Dina v. Attorney General, 240, 685, 928
District Director, United States ex rel. Marcello v., 906, **960,** 971
Dodig v. I.N.S., 425
Doe I v. Meese, 883
Doherty v. Meese, 685, 927
Douglas v. California, 605
Downer, People v., 3
Dunar, Matter of, 761, 771
Dunn v. I.N.S., 159
Dwomoh v. Sava, 819, 821, 822

E., Matter of, 994
Eain v. Wilkes, 860
Echeverria–Hernandez v. I.N.S., 885
Edmond v. Nelson, 869
Edwards v. California, 9
Elk v. Wilkins, 991
El Rescate Legal Services, Inc. v. E.O.I.R., 586
El–Werfalli v. Smith, 402, 403, 404
El–Youssef v. Meese, 971, 973
Enriquez, Matter of, 443
Escobar v. I.N.S., 444
Espinoza v. Farah Mfg. Co., Inc., 298
Estrada v. Ahrens, 369
Etugh v. I.N.S., 845
Exilus, Matter of, 869
Ex parte (see name of party)
Extradition of Demjanjuk, Matter of, 1083
Extradition of McMullen, Matter of, 861

Fatin v. I.N.S., 851, **852,** 859
Fedorenko, Matter of, 579, 764
Fedorenko v. United States, 1029, 1083

Fefe, Matter of, 864
Fernandez v. Wilkinson, 402
Fernandez–Roque v. Smith, 734 F.2d 576, pp. 450, 452, 460
Fernandez–Roque v. Smith, 567 F.Supp. 1115, p. 449
Feroz v. I.N.S., 862
Ferrer–Mazorra v. Meese, 466
Fiallo v. Bell, 150, 159, 161, 162, 171, 367, 443, 513, 531
Fisher v. I.N.S., 859
Fleary v. I.N.S., 958
Flemming v. Nestor, 531
Flores v. I.N.S., 971
Flores, Matter of, 548
Flores–Arellano v. I.N.S., 561
Florida Power & Light Co. v. Lorion, 926
Fok Young Yo v. United States, 902
Foley v. Connelie, 164
Fong Haw Tan v. Phelan, 497, 535
Fong Yue Ting v. United States, 21, 36, 37, 40, 61, 74, 513, 559, 581, 586, 628, 630
Fook Hong Mak v. I.N.S., 173
Fortman v. Aurora Civil Service Commission, 550
Foti v. I.N.S., 972
Francis v. I.N.S., 689, **691,** 694, 695, 697, 704, 708
Franklin, Matter of, 551
Fuentes, Matter of, 842, 846, 860

G., Matter of, 476, 484, 486, 509, 768, 818
G.A., Matter of, 690, 691, 692, 694, 695
Gaglioti, Matter of, 550
Gagnon v. Scarpelli, 604
Galaviz–Medina v. Wooten, 973
Gallanosa by Gallanosa v. United States, 940
Galvan v. Press, 532, 533
Gando–Coello v. I.N.S., 959
Garay v. Slattery, 960
Garberding v. I.N.S., 570
Garcia–Alzugaray, Matter of, 743
Garcia–Mir v. Meese, 466
Garcia–Mir v. Smith, 465, 940
Gebremichael v. I.N.S., 678
Gegiow v. Uhl, 370, 902
Gena v. I.N.S., 806
Ghadessi v. I.N.S., 806
Ghaelian v. I.N.S., 924
Ghebllawi v. I.N.S., 842
Giddens, In re, 550
Gillars v. United States, 1079
Giova v. Rosenberg, 959, 972
Gloria, United States v., 550
Goesaert v. Cleary, 995
Golabek v. Regional Manpower Admin., 206
Goldberg v. Kelly, 411
Goldeshtein v. I.N.S., 546, 549
Gomez v. I.N.S., 859
Gomez–Vigil v. I.N.S., 872, 873
Goncalves v. I.N.S., 696
Gonzales v. Barber, 550
Gonzales v. Williams, 975
Gonzalez v. I.N.S., 711

Gonzalez Batoon v. I.N.S., 654, 685
Gonzalez–Julio v. I.N.S., 908
Gonzalez–Rivera v. I.N.S., 627
Gottesman v. I.N.S., 919
Graham v. Richardson, 20, 162, 163, 164, 166, 337, 529, 976
Griffiths, In re, 164, 984
Guarneri v. Kessler, 545
Guevara, Matter of, 615, 616
Guevara Flores v. I.N.S., 787
Gunaydin v. United States I.N.S., 538
Gurbisz v. I.N.S., 890, 924, 930
Gutierrez, Matter of, 432
Guzman–Guzman v. I.N.S., 606

Hagans v. Lavine, 923
Haitian Centers Council, Inc. v. McNary, 880, 950
Haitian Centers Council, Inc. v. Sale, 880
Haitian Refugee Center v. Civiletti, 806
Haitian Refugee Center v. Meese, 940, 952
Haitian Refugee Center v. Smith, 767, 807, 937, 940
Haitian Refugee Center, Inc. v. Baker, 880
Haitian Refugee Center, Inc. v. Gracey, 879, 880
Hall v. McLaughlin, 208, 209, 223
Hamide and Shehadeh, Matter of, 530
Haniatakis, In re, 1023, 1029
Harisiades v. Shaughnessy, 513, **518,** 526, 527, 529, 530, 531, 532, 533, 534, 580, 581, 631
Hartooni v. I.N.S., 865
Harvard Law School Forum v. Shultz, 355
Hathaway Children's Services, Matter of, 207
Head Money Cases, 8
Heckler v. Chaney, 685
Heckler v. Community Health Services of Crawford County, Inc., 714
Hee Yung Ahn v. I.N.S., 678
Heikkila v. Barber, 901, 903
Henderson v. New York, 8
Henry v. I.N.S., 697
Hensley v. Municipal Court, San Jose Milpitas Judicial Dist., Santa Clara County, California, 970, 971, 972
Hermina Sague v. United States, 368
Hernandez–Casillas v. I.N.S., 704, 707, 708
Hernandez–Casillas, Matter of, 697, **698**
Hernandez–Cordero v. United States I.N.S., 677
Hernandez–Ortiz v. I.N.S., 795, 796, 808, 831, 833
Hernandez–Patino v. I.N.S., 677
Hernandez–Rivera v. I.N.S., 908
Hess v. Indiana, 527
Hibbert v. I.N.S., 647
Hill v. I.N.S., 340
Hines v. Davidowitz, 13, 427
Hintopoulos, United States ex rel. v. Shaughnessy, 678
Hira, Matter of, 268
Hirsch v. I.N.S., 586

Hitai v. I.N.S., 159
Ho Ah Kow v. Nunan, 3
Holland, United States v., 907
Holley v. Lavine, 886
Hong Kong T.V. Video Program, Inc. v. Ilchert, 246
Horta–Ruiz v. United States Dept. of Justice, 183
Hosseinpour, Matter of, 232
Huang, Matter of, 403
Hotel & Restaurant Employees Union, Local 25 v. Smith, 594 F.Supp. 502, p. 871
Hotel & Restaurant Employees Union, Local 25 v. Smith, 563 F.Supp. 157, p. 890

Ignacio v. I.N.S., 908, 957
Illinois Migrant Council v. Pilliod, 622
In Matter of Information Industries, Inc. on Behalf of Ravichandran (Mayuram), 205, 206
In re (see name of party)
I.N.S. v. Abudu, 659, 765
I.N.S. v. Cardoza–Fonseca, 770, **773,** 786, 787, 788, 789, 790, 791, 793, 796
I.N.S. v. Chadha, 653, 920, 924, 926
I.N.S. v. Delgado, 622
I.N.S. v. Doherty, 662, 861
I.N.S. v. Elias–Zacarias, 835, 839, 840, 842
I.N.S. v. Hector, 171, 655
I.N.S. v. Jong Ha Wang, 662, 666, 667, 677, 957
I.N.S. v. Legalization Assistance Project of Los Angeles County Federation of Labor, 947, 953
I.N.S. v. Lopez–Mendoza, 583, 623, 627
I. N. S. v. Miranda, 714
I.N.S. v. National Center for Immigrants' Rights, Inc., 589
I.N.S. v. Phinpathya, 501, 654
I.N.S. v. Rios–Pineda, 654, 657, **681,** 684, 685
I.N.S. v. Stevic, 770, 772, 773, 786
International Ladies' Garment Workers' Union, AFL–CIO v. Sureck, 622
International Molders' and Allied Workers' Local Union No. 164 v. Nelson, 622
International Union of Bricklayers and Allied Craftsmen v. Meese, 261, 268, 269
Iran v. I.N.S., 606
Ishtyaq v. Nelson, 464
Izatula, Matter of, 821, 848

Jaa v. I.N.S., 934
Jaimez–Revolla v. Bell, 369
Jain v. I.N.S., 434, 437, 439, 440, 441, 442, 443
Jang Man Cho v. I.N.S., 216
Janus and Janek, Matter of, 805
Jaramillo v. I.N.S., 696
Jara–Navarrette v. I.N.S., 677
Jay v. Boyd, 404
Jean v. Nelson, 472 U.S. 846, pp. 460, 461, 464, 465, 466

Jean v. Nelson, 727 F.2d 957, p. **452**
Jean v. Nelson, 711 F.2d 1455, p. 449
Jenkins v. I.N.S., 908, 957
Johannessen v. United States, 1015
Johnson v. Eisentrager, 1007, 1012
Jones v. Cunningham, 970, 972
Joo v. I.N.S., 953
Jordan v. De George, 552, 558, 559
Joseph v. I.N.S., 695
Joseph v. Landon, 196
Juan, Matter of, 834
Ju Toy, United States v., 1080

Kabongo v. I.N.S., 552
Kaczmarczyk v. I.N.S., 872
Kahane v. Secretary of State, 1079
Kahane v. Shultz, 1078
Kahn v. I.N.S., 171
Kaliski v. District Director, 175
Kane, Matter of, 403, 411
Kaplan v. Tod, 506
Karimian–Kaklaki v. I.N.S., 908
Karmali v. I.N.S., 930
Kashani v. Nelson, 766
Kashefi–Zihagh v. I.N.S., 678
Katsis v. I.N.S., 696
Kavasji v. I.N.S., 916, 919, 920, 927
Kawakita v. United States, 1055
Kellman v. District Director, 590
Kennedy v. Mendoza–Martinez, 976, 1061
Kessler v. Strecker, 517, 518
Keyishian v. Board of Regents, 529
Keyte, Matter of, 953
Khalik, Matter of, 549
Kim v. Meese, 444
Kleindienst v. Mandel, 162, 344, **345,** 352,
    353, 354, 356, 362, 365, 366, 367, 368,
    369, 384, 443, 528
**Knauff, United States ex rel. v. Shaugh-
    nessy,** 385, **386,** 389, 405, 412, 448, 461,
    507
Kohama, Matter of, 372
Kolender v. Lawson, 559
Kooritzky v. Reich, 218
Koreh, United States v., 1083
Kotasz v. I.N.S., 791, 792
Kovac v. I.N.S., 805, 814
Kras, United States v., 605
K.R.K. Irvine, Inc. v. Landon, 196
Kulle v. I.N.S., 579
Kulle, Matter of, 579
Kungys v. United States, 375, **1029,** 1044,
    1045
Kwock Jan Fat v. White, 903
Kwong Hai Chew v. Colding, 403, 461
Kwong Hai Chew v. Rogers, 403

L., Matter of, 689, 690, 695, 698
Laipenieks v. I.N.S., 579
Laipenieks, Matter of, 764
Lam, Matter of, 744, 772
Landgraf v. USI Film Products, 534

Landon v. Plasencia, 385, **405,** 410, 411,
    450, 460, 476, 498, 501, 504, 510, 529,
    582, 630, 635
Larson v. Valente, 369
Lassiter v. Department of Social Services,
    604, 605
Lau v. Kiley, 170, 174, 183
Lauvik v. I.N.S., 232
Lazo–Majano v. I.N.S., 846, 859
Leal–Rodriguez v. I.N.S., 704
Leblanc v. I.N.S., 677
LeBrun v. Thornburgh, 161
Lee, Matter of, 174, 175
Lee Wee, Petition of, 974
Lemhammad, Matter of, 185
Lem Moon Sing v. United States, 902
Lemons v. City and County of Denver, 207
Lemos–Garcia v. Weiss, 973
Leng May Ma v. Barber, 381, 474, 475
Lenning, Matter of, 183
Leon, United States v., 627
Leon–Leon, United States v., 586
Li v. Greene, 384, 464
Lignomat USA, Ltd., Matter of, 209
Li Hing of Hong Kong, Inc. v. Levin, 368
Lin, Matter of, 485, 506, 509
Lin v. Meissner, 817
Lincoln v. Vigil, 362, 900
Linnas v. I.N.S., 572, 576
Lin Sing v. Washburn, 3
Lok v. I. N. S., 681 F.2d 107, p. 695
Lok v. I.N.S., 548 F.2d 37, p. 695
Longstaff, Matter of, 340
Lopez v. INS, 619
Lopez–Alegria v. Ilchert, 959
Lopez–Amaro v. I.N.S., 534
Lopez–Amaro, Matter of, 560
Louis v. Nelson, 402, 448, 449, 876
Louis Padnos Iron & Metal Co., United
    States v., 300
L–R, Matter of, 569
Ludecke v. Watkins, 10
Lujan v. Defenders of Wildlife, 369
Luna v. I.N.S., 666, 677
Lynch v. Cannatella, 465

M., Matter of, 552, 698
M.A. v. I.N.S., 899 F.2d 304, p. 825, 833, 841
M.A. v. I.N.S., 858 F.2d 210, p. 824
MacKenzie v. Hare, 995, 1049, 1061
Madany v. Smith, 196
Mahini v. I.N.S., 861
Mahler v. Eby, 533
Maikovskis v. I.N.S., 846
Maldonado–Cruz v. I.N.S., 848
Maldonado–Cruz, Matter of, 846
Maniego, United States v., 180
Manwani v. United States Dept. of Justice,
    444
Manzella v. Zimmerman, 552
Marcello v. Bonds, 108, 533, 534, 592, 596,
    904
Marcello v. I.N.S., 906, 907
**Marcello, United States ex rel. v. Dis-
    trict Director,** 906, **960,** 971

Marciano v. I.N.S., 550
Marczak v. Greene, 384, 464
Marin, Matter of, 711
Maringolo, Application of, 589
Marrero v. I.N.S., 955
Marroquin–Manriquez v. I.N.S., 841
Martinez v. Bell, 368, 930
Martinez v. Bynum, 697
Martinez De Mendoza v. I.N.S., 924
Martinez–Fuerte, United States v., 621
Martinez–Montoya v. I.N.S., 570
Martinez–Romero, Matter of, 772
Martins v. I.N.S., 862
Marti–Xiques v. I.N.S., 696
Mason v. Brooks, 384
Masonry Masters, Inc. v. Thornburgh, 217
Mathews v. Diaz, 20, 163, 164, 337, 339, 633
Mathews v. Eldridge, 405, 431, 598, 604, 605, 636, 639
Matter of (see name of party)
Mayor of City of New York v. Miln, 370
McCarthy v. Madigan, 934
McGrath v. Kristensen, 903
McGuire v. I.N.S., 423
McKee, Matter of, 183
McLeod v. I.N.S., 870
McLeod v. Peterson, 937
McMillan, Matter of, 161, 764, 860, 861
McMullen v. I.N.S., 788 F.2d 591, pp. 860, 861
McMullen v. I.N.S., 658 F.2d 1312, pp. 807, 846
McNary v. Haitian Refugee Center, Inc., 273, 296, **942,** 952
McNaughton v. I.N.S., 549
M'Culloch v. Maryland, 8
Medellin v. Bustos, 218
Medina v. I.N.S., 432
Medina, Matter of, 885
Medina v. O'Neill, 465
Medrano–Villatoro v. I.N.S., 937
Medvid by Jeziersky v. New Orleans Police Dept., 761
Melian v. I.N.S., 695
Mendelsohn v. Meese, 369
Mendenhall, United States v., 622
Mendes, Matter of, 185, 188
Mendez v. I.N.S., 953, 954
Mendez v. Major, 239
Mendoza v. I.N.S., 500
Mendoza–Lopez, United States v., 907
Mendoza Perez v. I.N.S., 833, 865
Mesa v. I.N.S., 666
Meyer v. Nebraska, 412
Mezei, United States ex rel. v. Shaughnessy, 385, **389,** 402, 403, 404, 405, 410, 411, 445, 446, 447, 448, 450, 451, 461, 466, 498, 507, 582, 586, 629, 630, 631, 635, 638
Milosevic v. I.N.S., 791
Minor v. Happersett, 1085
Miranda v. Arizona, 618, 619, 620
Miranda v. I.N.S., 715
Mogharrabi, Matter of, 787, 790, 797, 864
Mohammadi–Motlagh v. I.N.S., 921, 924
Montes v. Thornburgh, 941
Montoya de Hernandez, United States v., 621
Moore v. East Cleveland, 190, 354
Moore v. I.N.S., 657

Moore, Matter of, 552
Morales–Alvarado v. I.N.S., 571
Moreira, Matter of, 160, 161
Moret v. Karn, 384
Morris, United States ex rel. Parco v., 971
Morrissey v. Brewer, 604
Morrobel v. Thornburgh, 590
Mundell, Matter of, 500
Munoz–Santana v. I.N.S., 689
Murillo v. Musegades, 622

Nagaro–Garbin, United States v., 571
Naji v. Nelson, 404
Naranjo–Aguilera v. I.N.S., 952
Narayan v. Ilchert, 960
Narenji v. Civiletti, 12, 160, 539
Nasan v. I.N.S., 442, 934
Nasseri v. Moschorak, 841
Navia–Duran v. I.N.S., 620
Nazareno v. Attorney General, 174
Neelly, United States ex rel. Rongetti v., 903
Ness, United States v., 1015
Newton v. I.N.S., 239
New York, City of v. Baker, 356
Ng Fung Ho v. White, 655, 902, 908, 1080
Nghiem, Matter of, 806
Nguyen v. United States Catholic Conference, 744
Nikoi v. Attorney General of United States, 993
Nishikawa v. Dulles, 1061
Nishimura Ekiu v. United States, 14, 902
Nocon v. I.N.S., 958
Noorani v. Smith, 384, 876
Norberto La Rosa, Matter of, 207
Nose v. Attorney General, 423
Novoa–Umania v. I.N.S., 848
Nwolise v. United States I.N.S., 696
Nyquist v. Mauclet, 164

Ogio v. I.N.S., 958
Okechukwu v. United States, 971
Okoh, Matter of, 953
Okoroha v. I.N.S., 552
Olaniyan v. District Director, 539, 926
Oloteo v. I.N.S., 444
Orantes–Hernandez v. Meese, 641, 876
Orantes–Hernandez v. Thornburgh, 767, 877
Orhorhaghe v. I.N.S., 627
Ortega v. Vermont Bread, 299
Ortiz, United States v., 621
Ortwein v. Schwab, 605
Osaghae v. I.N.S., 808
Ozkok, Matter of, 565, 569, 570, 571

Padilla, People v., 571
Palma v. Verdeyen, 448
Palmer v. Reddy, 161
Papachristou v. City of Jacksonville, 558
Parco, United States ex rel. v. Morris, 971
Parham v. J. R., 604
Parness v. Shultz, 1077
Parrino, United States v., 571

Passenger Cases, 8, 10, 370
Patel, Matter of, 189, 588
Paul v. Davis, 412
Pazandeh, Matter of, 189
Pearson v. Williams, 432, 537
Pei–Chi Tien v. I.N.S., 440
Pelupo de Toledo v. Kiley, 653
Pena v. Kissinger, 363, 368, 928
Pena–Urrutia v. I.N.S., 183
Pension Ben. Guar. Corp. v. R.A. Gray & Co.,
  533
People v. _____ (see opposing party)
Perales v. Casillas, 685, 928
Perez v. Brownell, 1050, 1060, 1061, 1067
Perez–Alvarez v. I.N.S., 767
Pergament United Sales, Inc. v. N.L.R.B.,
  865
Perkovic v. I.N.S., 841
Perlera–Escobar v. Executive Office for Im-
  migration, 833, 841
Pesikoff v. Secretary of Labor, 199, **200,**
  203, 204
Petition for Naturalization of Kassas,
  1008, 1014
Petition of (see name of party)
Petkiewytsch v. I.N.S., 580
Phelisna, Matter of Application of, 481,
  484, 486, 507, 509
Pierre v. I.N.S., 958
Pierre, Matter of, 486, 501, 504
Pineda, Matter of, 161
Plyler v. Doe, 164, **284, 325,** 336, 337
Portales, Matter of, 744
Posadas de Puerto Rico Associates, Inc. v.
  Secretary of Labor, 195
Pozo, People v., 571
Price v. I.N.S., 531, **1010,** 1014
Proa–Tovar, United States v., 907
Production Tool Corp. v. Employment and
  Training Admin., 195
Pula, Matter of, 771, **797,** 802, 829

Quezada v. I.N.S., 954
Quinn v. Robinson, 860

R., Matter of, Int. Dec. 3195, p. 840
R., Matter of, 6 I & N Dec. 444, pp. 549, 550
R., Matter of, 4 I & N Dec. 644, p. 550
Rabang v. Boyd, 993
Rabang v. I.N.S., 993
Rafeedie v. I.N.S., 880 F.2d 506, pp. 411, 934
Rafeedie v. I.N.S., 795 F.Supp. 13, pp. 356,
  531, 558
Raghunandan, United States v., 552
Rajaratnam v. Moyer, 841
Ramirez–Gonzalez v. I.N.S., 653
Ramirez–Osorio v. I.N.S., 877
Ramirez–Ramos v. I.N.S., 861
Ramsey, United States v., 621
Randall v. Meese, 934
Ratnayake v. Mack, 203, 204, 205
Ravancho v. I.N.S., 667, 678
Ray v. Turner, 403

Reddy, Inc. v. United States Dept. of Labor,
  196, 368
Reid v. Covert, 39, 975
Reid v. I.N.S., 537
Rejaie v. I.N.S., 772
Reno v. Catholic Social Services, Inc., 296,
  951
Reno v. Flores, 591
Requested Extradition of Smyth, Matter of,
  856, 860
Reyes v. I.N.S., 677
Reyes–Arias v. I.N.S., 719
Reyes–Palacios v. United States I.N.S., 598
R.G., Matter of, 538
Richards v. Secretary of State, 1077
Richardson v. Perales, 596
Rios–Carrillo, Matter of, 586
Rivera de Gomez v. Kissinger, 368
Rivers v. Roadway Exp., Inc., 534
Rodriguez v. I.N.S., 704
Rodriguez v. Thornburgh, 467
Rodriguez–Fernandez v. Wilkinson, 447, 448,
  450, 451, 473
Rodriguez–Majano, Matter of, 861
Rodriguez–Padron v. I.N.S., 704
Rogers v. Bellei, 994, 995, 1067, 1068, 1069
Roldan v. Racette, 954
Romero v. Consulate of United States, 368,
  370
Rongetti, United States ex rel. v. Neelly, 903
Rosario, Matter of, 551
Rosenberg v. Fleuti, 490, 497, 498, 499,
  500, 501, 504, 505, 510, 654
Rosenberg v. Yee Chien Woo, 744
Ross v. McIntyre, 39
Ruginski v. I.N.S., 924
Ruis, Matter of, 538
Runnett v. Shultz, 995
Runyon v. McCrary, 4
Rusk v. Cort, 1081
Russian Volunteer Fleet v. United States, 462

S, Matter of, 5 I & N Dec. 425, p. 552
S, Matter of, 6 I & N Dec. 392, p. 690
S, Matter of, 9 I & N Dec. 548, p. 445
S, Matter of, 9 I & N Dec. 688, pp. 550, 552
Saadi v. I.N.S., 954
Sacco, United States v., 189
Safaie v. I.N.S., 859
Sakhavat v. I.N.S., 806
Salas–Velazquez v. I.N.S., 185
Saldina v. Thornburgh, 467
Sale v. Haitian Centers Council, Inc., 486,
  880
Salehi v. District Director, I.N.S., 972
Salim, Matter of, 770, 785, 786, 793, 795,
  797, 802, 804
Samras v. United States, 974
Sanchez, Matter of, 113, 697
Sanchez–Linn, Matter of, 647
Sanchez–Trujillo v. I.N.S., 801 F.2d 1571, pp.
  806, 850
Sanchez–Trujillo v. I.N.S., 632 F.Supp. 1546,
  p. 424

Sandoval, Matter of, 626
Sang Ryup Park v. Barber, 760
Sannon v. United States, 402
Santiago v. I.N.S., 714
Santos, Matter of, 885, 916
Santosky v. Kramer, 612
Sarvia–Quintanilla v. United States I.N.S., 865
Saunders, Matter of, 445
Saxbe v. Bustos, 193
Schellong v. I.N.S., 808
Schellong, United States v., 1083
Schenck v. United States, 344
Schlesinger v. Councilman, 934
Schneider v. Rusk, 1061
Schneiderman v. United States, 1016, 1022
Segovia–Melgar, United States v., 618
Serna, Matter of, 552
Shaughnessy v. Pedreiro, 904
Shaughnessy, United States v., 688
Shaughnessy, United States ex rel. Hintopoulos v., 678
Shaughnessy, United States ex rel. Knauff v., 385, **386,** 389, 405, 412, 448, 461, 507
Shaughnessy v. United States ex rel. Mezei, 385, **389,** 402, 403, 404, 405, 410, 411, 445, 446, 447, 448, 450, 461, 466, 498, 507, 582, 586, 629, 630, 631, 635, 638
Shen v. United States Consulate General, 367
Sherbert v. Verner, 529
Sheshtawy, United States v., 1026, 1029
Shirazi–Parsa v. I.N.S., 841
Shoaee v. I.N.S., 539
Shung v. Brownell, 903
Sibrun, Matter of, 790, 864
Sida v. I.N.S., 685
Silva v. Bell, 369
Silva, Matter of, 694, 698
Singh v. I.N.S., 971
Singh v. Moyer, 240
Singh v. Nelson, 464, 795, 877
Sivaainkaran v. I.N.S., 791
Skalak v. I.N.S., 792
Slaughter–House Cases, 18
Slyper v. Attorney General, 928
Smith v. Goguen, 559
Smith, Matter of, 692
Smith, United States v., 545
Smith, United States ex rel. Volpe v., 487, 488, 489, 537
Soleimani, Matter of, 744, 803
Soriano, People v., 571
Sotelo–Aquije v. Slattery, 842, 845
Sotelo Mondragon v. Ilchert, 971
Sovich v. Esperdy, 805
Stevic v. Sava, 771
Stone v. I.N.S., 958
Subramaniam v. District Director, United States I.N.S., Denver, Colo., 849
Suciu v. I.N.S., 404
Sudomir v. McMahon, 882
Sugarman v. Dougall, 164, **984**
Sugay, Matter of, 588
Sussex Engineering, Ltd. v. Montgomery, 245, 259

Swain v. Pressley, 902
Sweet Life v. Dole, 934, 937

T., Matter of, 841
Tapia–Acuna v. I.N.S., 695
Tashnizi v. I.N.S., 616
Tejeda–Mata v. I.N.S., 586
Terry v. Ohio, 620
Thack v. Zurbrick, 486
Thunder Basin Coal Co. v. Reich, 362
Tiaco v. Forbes, 17
Tillinghast v. Edmead, 545
Tisi, United States ex rel. v. Tod, 517
Tiwari, Matter of, 552
Toboso–Alfonso, Matter of, 859
Tod, United States ex rel. Bilokumsky v., 616
Tod, United States ex rel. Tisi v., 517
Toma v. Turnage, 908
Toquero v. I.N.S., 937
Torres v. Puerto Rico, 975
Townsend v. United States Dept. of Justice I.N.S., 937, 940
Trias–Hernandez v. I.N.S., 618
Trop v. Dulles, 402, 976, 1060, 1061
Tseung Chu v. Cornell, 552
Turner, United States ex rel. v. Williams, 514
Tuskegee University, Matter of, 206, 207
Tutun v. United States, 1015

Umanzor v. Lambert, 954, 971, 973
United Mine Workers of America v. Gibbs, 923
United States v. _____ (see opposing party)
United States ex rel. v. _____ (see opposing party and relator)
Usery v. Turner Elkhorn Min. Co., 533

V., Matter of, 994
Vajtauer, United States ex rel. v. Commissioner of Immigration, 517
Valencia, Matter of, 937
Valeros v. I.N.S., 616
Vance v. Terrazas, 612, **1069,** 1077, 1078, 1079, 1082
Vaughn v. I.N.S., 678
Velez–Lozano v. I.N.S., 552, 559
Verdugo–Urquidez, United States v., 622, 975
Vieira–Candelario, United States v., 907
Vigil, Matter of, 806
Vlandis v. Kline, 697
Volpe, United States ex rel. v. Smith, 487, 488, 489, 537

Wadman v. I.N.S., 552
Wadud, Matter of, 703
Walai v. United States I.N.S., 795
Walsh and Pollard, Matter of, 254, 258, 259
Walters v. Reno, 540
Warmtex Enterprises v. Martin, 195

Warth v. Seldin, 369
Wauchope v. United States Dept. of State, 995
Weedin v. Chin Bow, 994
Williams v. I.N.S., 925, 972
Williams, Matter of, 806
Williams, United States ex rel. Turner v., 514
Winship, In re, 613
Wong Kim Ark, United States v., 41, 993
Wong Wing v. United States, 15, 37, 39, 162, 445, 447, 462, 513, 528, 628
Wong Wing Hang v. I.N.S., 686, 901
Wong Yang Sung v. McGrath, 15, 108, 402, 592, 596
Woodby v. I.N.S., 606, 612, 613, 615, 616, 628
Wright v. I.N.S., 424

Xin–Chang v. Slattery, 484, 818

Yacoubian, United States v., 534

Yamataya v. Fisher (The Japanese Immigrant Case), 402, 453, 528, **583,** 586, 591, 604, 628, 629, 634, 902
Yang v. Reno, 952
Yassini v. Crosland, 160, 887
Y–G–, Matter of, 375
Yick Wo v. Hopkins, 18, 19, 20, 36, 39, 162, 447
Yim Tong Chung v. Smith, 766, 930
Yiu Sing Chun v. Sava, 433
Yui Sing Tse v. I.N.S., 214, 216, 440
Yurick v. Commonwealth, 550

Zacarias v. I.N.S., 848
Zalman, United States v., 180
Zamora v. I.N.S., 869, 870, 872
Zaoutis v. Kiley, 444
Zavala–Bonilla v. I.N.S., 678, 772, 871
Zayas–Marini v. I.N.S., 846, 850
Zheng v. I.N.S., 818
Zucca, United States v., 1015

*

Table of Authorities

Abrams & Abrams, Immigration Policy--Who Gets In and Why?, 38 The Pub.Int. 3 (1975)--217

Accepting the Immigration Challenge: The President's Report on Immigration--150, 322

Ackerman, B., Social Justice in the Liberal State (1980)--80

Adelman, H., Canada and the Indochinese Refugees (1982)--735

Administration's Proposals on Immigration and Refugee Policy, Joint Hearing before the House Subcommittee on Immigration, Refugees, and International Law and the Senate Subcommittee on Immigration and Refugee Policy, 97th Cong., 1st Sess. 6 (1981)--875

Aguayo, S. & P. Weiss Fagen, Central Americans in Mexico and the United States (1988)--804

Alba, Mexico's International Migration as a Manifestation of Its Development Pattern, 12 Int'l Migration Rev. 502 (1978)--73

Aleinikoff, Aliens, Due Process and 'Community Ties': A Response to Martin, 44 U.Pitt.L.Rev. 237 (1983)--400, 507, 633-34, 637-38

Aleinikoff, Citizens, Aliens, Membership and the Constitution, 7 Const.Comm. 9 (1990)--17

Aleinikoff, Meaning of "Persecution" in United States Asylum Law, 3 Int'l J. Refugee L. 5 (1991)--815

Aleinikoff, Political Asylum in the Federal Republic of Germany and the Republic of France: Lessons for the United States, 17 U.Mich.J.L.Ref. 183 (1984)--719

Aleinikoff, Theories of Loss of Citizenship, 84 Mich.L.Rev. 1471 (1986)--1079

Alvarez, Haitians Get Longer Hearings at Sea, Miami Herald, March 16, 1991, at B1--879

American Civil Liberties Union, Immigrants' Rights Project, Justice Detained: Conditions at the Varick Street Immigration Detention Center (1993)--590

Amsterdam, The Void-For-Vagueness Doctrine in the Supreme Court, 109 U.Pa. L.Rev. 67 (1960)--558

Anker, Blum, & Johnson, The Supreme Court's Decision in INS v. Elias-Zacarias: Is There Any "There" There?, 69 Interp.Rel. 285 (1992)--840

Anker, Discretionary Asylum: A Protection Remedy for Refugees under the Refugee Act of 1980, 28 Va.J.Int'l L. 1 (1987)--797

Anker, Report of the Findings and Recommendations of An Empirical Study of Adjudication Before the Immigration Court, 2 Int'l J.Refugee L. 252 (1990)--865

Anker & Blum, New Trends in Asylum Jurisprudence: The Aftermath of the U.S. Supreme Court Decision in INS v. Cardoza-Fonseca, 1 Int'l J. Refugee L. 67 (1989)--797, 829

Annotation, 62 A.L.R.Fed. 402 (1983)--216

Arendt, H., The Origins of Totalitarianism (1951)--988

Ascencio, F., Bringing it Back Home: Remittances to Mexico from Migrant Workers in the United States (A. Yanez, trans. 1993)--283

Atkinson, Congressmen, Others Denounce Denial of Visas to U.S. Critics, Wash. Post, Dec. 3, 1983--355

Avery, Refugee Status Decision-Making: The Systems of Ten Countries, 19 Stan.Int'l L.J. 235 (1983)--719, 871

B-1 in Lieu of H-1 Visas: A Brouhaha Brews, 69 Interp.Rel. 1495 (1992)--269

Bach, R. & D. Meissner, America's Labor Market in the 1990s: What Role Should Immigration Play? (1990)--208

Bari, Refugee Status Determination under the Comprehensive Plan of Action (CPA): A Personal Assessment, 4 Int'l J. Refugee L. 487 (1992)--757

Barich, B., A Reporter at Large: La Frontera, The New Yorker, December 1990, at 72--271-73

Barry, B., The Liberal Theory of Justice (1973)--76

Bar-Yaacov, N., Dual Nationality (1961)--1057

Becker, An Open Door for Immigrants--The Auction, Wall St.J., Oct. 14, 1992, at A14--98

Beitz, C., Political Theory and International Relations (1979)--76, 96

Benefits for Spouses Under the Immigration and Nationality Act, 1 Imm.Law Rep. 121 (1982)--183, 187, 189

Benson, By Hook or by Crook: Exploring the Legality of an INS Sting Operation, 31 San Diego L.Rev. 813 (1994)--598

Berlowitz, Beattie, & O'Brien, Labor Certification: The Statutory and Regulatory

Evolution of the Business Necessity Requirement--Part I, 12 Imm.J. 1 (1989)--205

Berns, The Constitution and the Migration of Slaves, 78 Yale L.J. 198 (1968)--10

Bernsen, Withdrawl of Applications for Admission, 71 Interp.Rel. 441 (1994)--433

Beyer, Affirmative Asylum Adjudication in the United States, 6 Geo.Imm. L.J. 253 (1992)--765

Beyer, Establishing the United States Asylum Officer Corps: A First Report, 4 Int'l J. Refugee L. 455 (1992)--765

Beyer, Reforming Affirmative Asylum Processing in the United States: Challenges and Opportunities, 9 Am.U.J. Int'l L. & Pol'y 43 (Special Issue 1994--766

Bickel, A., The Least Dangerous Branch (1962)--666

Bickel, A., The Morality of Consent (1975)--976-84

Black, C., Structure and Relationship in Constitutional Law (1969)--16, 1067

Black's Law Dictionary--544-45

Blum, License to Kill: Asylum Law and the Principle of Legitimate Governmental Authority to "Investigate Its Enemies", 28 Willamette L.Rev. 719, 746-48 (1992)--821, 841

Blum, The Ninth Circuit, and the Protection of Asylum Seekers Since the Passage of the Refugee Act of 1980, 23 San Diego L.Rev. 327 (1986)--791, 814

Borchard, Diplomatic Protection of Citizens Abroad (1919)--520, 1057, 1059

Borjas, G., Friends or Strangers: The Impact of Immigrants on the U.S. Economy (1990)--66

Bosniak, Exclusion and Membership: The Dual Identity of the Undocumented Worker under United States Law, 1988 Wisc. L.Rev. 955--339

Bosniak, Membership, Equality, and the Difference that Alienage Makes, 69 N.Y.U.L.Rev:___(1994)--99, 166

Bouve, C., A Treatise on the Laws Governing the Exclusion and Expulsion of Aliens in the United States (1912)--592

Bracete, A Primer on Adjustment of Status in the United States, 13 Nova L.Rev. 165 (1988)--410

Briggs, V., Immigration Policy and the American Labor Force (1984)--208

Browning & Rodriguez, The Migration of Mexican Indocumentados as a Settlement Process: Implications for Work, in Hispanics in the U.S. Economy (G. Borjas & M. Tienda eds. 1985)--73

Brownstone, D., I. Franck & D. Brownstone, Island of Hope, Island of Tears (1979)--421

Bruck, Springing the Haitians, The American Lawyer, September 1982 at 36--720

Burdick, W., The Law of Crime (1946)--544

Business Necessity: A Year After Information Industries, 67 Interp.Rel. 253 (1990)--206

Bustamante & Martinez, Undocumented Immigration from Mexico: Beyond Borders but Within Systems, 33 J.Int'l Aff. 265 (1979)--73

Calavita, Employer Sanctions Violations: Toward a Dialectical Model of White-Collar Crime, 24 Law & Society Rev. 1041 (1990)--308-13

Calavita, The Immigration Policy Debate: Critical Analysis and Future Options, Mexican Migration to the United States: Origins, Consequences, and Policy Options (W. Cornelius & J. Bustamante, eds., 1989)--276-78

Calvo & Davis, Congress Nears Approval of Legislation to Protect Abused Aliens, 70 Interp.Rel. 1665 (1993)--187

Carens, Aliens and Citizens: The Case for Open Borders, 49 Rev. of Politics 251 (1987)--91

Census Bureau Releases Statistics on Foreign-Born Population in the U.S., 70 Interp. Rel. 1638 (1994)--146

Center for Immigration Studies, The Costs of Immigration: Assessing a Conflicted Issue (1993)--284

Chaos at the Gates, N.Y.Times, Sept. 11-14, 1994--102

Choper, J., Y. Kamisar & L. Tribe, The Supreme Court: Trends and Developments, 1980-1981 (1982)--606

Clark, R., J. Passel, W. Zimmermann, & M. Fix, Fiscal Impacts of Undocumented Aliens: Selected Estimates for Seven States (1994)--274, 283, 284-89, 287, 289

Commission for the Study of International Migration and Cooperative Economic Development, Unauthorized Migration: An Economic Development Response (1990)--101

Committee on Immigration and Nationality Law of the Association of the Bar of the City of New York, Visa Denials on Ideological Grounds: An Update, 8 Seton Hall Legis. J. 249 (1984-85)--352

Comprehensive study on the human rights issues related to internally displaced persons, United Nations Doc. E/CN.4/1993/35 (1993)--735

Congressional Research Service, 96th Cong., 2d Sess., History of the Immigration and Naturalization Service (Comm.Print 1980)--101

Congressional Research Service, 96th Cong., 2d Sess., Review of U.S. Refugee Resettlement Programs and Policies (Comm.Print, Senate Comm. on the Judiciary, 1980)--736

Coolidge, M., Chinese Immigration (1909)--3

Cornelius, Mexican Migration to the United States: Introduction, Mexican Migration to the United States: Origins, Consequences, and Policy Options 1 (W. Cornelius & J. Bustamante, eds., 1989)--289-92, 313-14

Cornelius, Mexican Migration to the United States: The View from Rural Sending Communities, Center for Int'l Studies, M.I.T., Discussion Paper c-77-11 (mimeo 1977)--73

Cornelius, The U.S. Demand for Mexican Labor, in Mexican Migration to the United States: Origins, Consequences, and Policy Options 25 (W. Cornelius & J. Bustamante, eds., 1989)--304

Cornelius, W., Mexican Migration to the United States: The Limits of Government Intervention (Working Papers in U.S.-Mexican Studies, 5: 1981)--278

Corwin, E., The Constitution and What It Means Today (H. Chase and C. Ducat, eds., 14th ed.1978)--19

Coudert, The Evolution of the Doctrine of Territorial Incorporation, 26 Colum.L.Rev. 823 (1926)--975

Cox, "Well-Founded Fear of Being Persecuted": The Sources and Application of a Criterion of Refugee Status, 10 Brooklyn J.Int'l Law 333 (1984)--778

Currie & Goodman, Judicial Review of Federal Administrative Action: Quest for the Optimum Forum, 75 Colum.L.Rev. 1 (1975)--926

Daniels, R., Coming to America: A History of Immigration and Ethnicity in American Life (1990)--66

Davis, D., The Problem of Slavery in the Age of Revolution, 1770-1823 (1975)--10

Davis, K., Administrative Law Treatise (2d. ed 1980)--865

Davis, K. & R. Pierce, Administrative Law Treatise (3d ed.1994)--685, 714

Davis, The Requirements of a Trial-Type Hearing, 70 Harv.L.Rev. 193 (1956)--402

Deffenbaugh, Resettlement as Protection: New Directions in the U.S. Refugee Program, Refugee Reports, Apr. 29, 1994, at 10-15--759

Dionne, Issue and Debate: Barring Aliens for Political Reasons, N. Y. Times, Dec. 8, 1983--355

Diver, The Optimal Precision of Administrative Rules, 93 Yale L.J. 65 (1983)--173, 681

Donner, R., The Regulation of Nationality in International Law (2d ed. 1994)--1059, 1060

Duvall, Expatriation Under United States Law, Perez to Afroyim: The Search for a Philosophy of American Citizenship, 56 Va.L.Rev. 408 (1970)--1046-49

Eliot, T.S., The Love Song of J. Alfred Prufrock--971

Elliott, Strategy and Tactics in Deportation Proceedings, 90-5 Imm.Briefings (1990)--595

Elliot's Debates (1881 ed.)--512-13

Employment Practices Guide (Commerce Clearing House 1985)--302

Endelman, How to Prevent Loss of Citizenship, 89-11 & 89-12 Imm. Briefings (1989)--1080

Enforcing Restraint: Collective Intervention in Internal Conflicts (L. Damrosch ed. 1993)--882

Eskridge, Interpreting Legislative Inaction, 87 Mich.L.Rev. 67 (1988)--497

Ethical Considerations in Immigration Cases, 4 Imm.L.Rep. 169 (1985)--181, 210

Ethical Issues in Immigration Practice: A Roundtable Discussion, 90-8 Imm. Briefings (Aug.1990)--181

Fallows, Immigration: How It's Affecting Us, The Atlantic Monthly, Nov. 1983, at 88--227

Fallows, No Hard Feelings?, The Atlantic Monthly, Dec. 1988, at 71--758

Feingold, H., The Politics of Rescue: The Roosevelt Administration and The Holocaust, 1938-1945 (1970)--735

Fitzpatrick & Pauw, Foreign Policy, Asylum and Discretion, 28 Willamette L.Rev. 751 (1992)--861

Foreign Investors: Strategies for Obtaining Residence, 4 Imm.Law Rep. 97-102 (1985)--224

Fragomen, Jr., A., A. Del Rey, Jr. & S. Bernsen, Immigration Law and Business (1994)--223, 245

Franck, T., Political Questions/Judicial Answers (1992)--403

Frankfurter, Some Reflections on the Reading of Statutes, 47 Colum.L.Rev. 527 (1947)--551

Frelick, B., & B. Kohnen, Filling the Gap: Temporary Protected Status (United States Committee for Refugees issue paper 1994)--896

Frelick, Haitian Boat Interdiction and Return: First Asylum and First Principles of Refugee Protection, 26 Cornell Int'l L.J. 675 (1993)--880-81

Friedland, J. & J. Rodriguez y Rodriguez, Seeking Safe Ground: The Legal Situation of Central American Refugees in Mexico (1987)--804

Friendly, H., Federal Jurisdiction: A General View (1973)--925

Friendly, Some Kind of Hearing, 123 U.Pa. L.Rev. 1267--629

Fullerton, Persecution Due to Membership in a Particular Social Group: Jurisprudence in the Federal Republic of Germany, 4 Geo.Imm.L.J. 381 (1990)--851

Fullerton, Restricting the Flow of Asylum-Seekers in Belguim, Denmark, the Federal Republic of Germany, and the Netherlands: New Challenges to the Geneva Convention relating to the Status of Refugees and the European Convention on Human Rights, 29 Va.J.Int'l L. 35 (1988)--719

Fullerton & Kinigstein, Strategies for Ameliorating the Immigration Consequences of Criminal Convictions: A Guide for Defense Attoneys, 23 Am. Crim. L. Rev. 425 (1986)--549

Gardner, The Informal Actions of the Federal Government, 26 Am.U.L.Rev. 799 (1977)--926

Gellhorn, W., C. Byse & P. Strauss, T. Rakoff & R. Schotland, Administrative Law: Cases and Comments (8th ed. 1987)--714

Gilboy, Administrative Review in a System of Conflicting Values, 13 Law & Soc. Inquiry 515 (1988)--590

Gilboy, Deciding Who Gets In: Decision-making by Immigration Inspectors, 25 Law & Soc'y Rev. 571 (1991)--103

Gilboy, Penetrability of Administrative Systems: Political "Casework" and Immigration Inspections, 26, Law & Soc'y Rev. 273 (1992)--103

Gilboy, Setting Bail in Deportation Cases: The Role of Immigration Judges, 24 San Diego L.Rev. 347 (1987)--110

Glazer, N. & D. Moynihan, Beyond the Melting Pot (1963)--229

Goldberg, Asylum Law and Gender-Based Persecution Claims, 94-9 Imm.Briefings (1994)--852

Goldie, Legal Aspects of the Refusal of Asylum by U.S. Coast Guard on 23 November 1970, 62 U.S. Naval War College Int'l L.Stud. 626--761

Gomez, The Consequences of Nonappearance: Interpreting New Section 242B of the Immigration and Nationality Act, 30 San Diego L.Rev. 75 (1993)--595

Goodwin-Gill, G., The Refugee in International Law (1983)--718, 778

Goodwin-Gill, Non-Refoulement and the New Asylum Seekers, 26 Va.J.Int'l L. 897 (1986)--885

Goodwin-Gill, The Future of International Refugee Law, Refugees, Oct. 1988 at 28--731

Gordon, Appellate Immigration Practice: Appeals to the BIA and AAU, 2 1992-93 Immigration & Nationality Handbook 522 (1992)--658

Gordon, C. & H. Rosenfield, Immigration Law and Procedure--458, 675, 783, 975

Gordon, C. & S. Mailman, Immigration Law and Procedure--21, 114, 117, 218, 931

Gordon, C. & S. Mailman & S. Yale-Loehr, Immigration Law and Procedure (1994)--244, 245, 250-53, 369, 544, 549, 559, 581, 582, 592-95, 649, 656, 678, 696, 712, 902, 931, 991, 993-1000, 1016

Gordon, Finality of Immigration and Nationality Decisions: Can the Government Be Estopped?, 31 U.Chi.L.Rev. 433 (1964)--432

Gordon, The Citizen and the State: Power of Congress to Expatriate American Citizens, 53 Geo.L.J. 315, 326-27 (1965)--1049

Gotcher, Review of Consular Visa Determinations, 60 Interp.Rel. 247 (1983)--368

Grahl-Madsen, A., supra note 1 (1966)--806

Grahl-Madsen, A., The Status of Refugees in International Law (2 vols. 1966)--718, 777-78

Grahl-Madsen, A., The Status of Refugees in International Law (2 vols. 1972)--718, 762

Graves, From Definition to Exploration: Social Groups and Political Asylum Eligibility, 26 San Diego L.Rev. 739 (1989)--851

Greenawalt, Speech and Crime, 1980 Am.Bar Found.Res.J. 645 (1981)--527

Guendelsberger, Implementing Family Unification Rights in American Immigration Law: Proposed Amendments, 25 San Diego L.Rev. 253-254 (1988)--190

Guendelsberger, The Right to Family Unification in French and United States Immigration Law, 21 Cornell Int'l L.J. 1 (1988)--190

Hadfield, Weighing the Value of Vagueness: An Economic Perspective on Precision in the Law, 82 Calif.L.Rev. 541 (1994)--558

Hailbronner, Non-Refoulement and "Humanitarian" Refugees: Customary International Law or Wishful Legal Thinking?, 26 Va.J.Int'l L. 857 (1986)--885

Hailbronner, Perspectives of a Harmonization of the Law of Asylum after the Maastricht Summit, 29 Common Mkt. L.Rev. 917 (1992)--804

Hake, Dual Representation in Immigration Practice: The Simple Solution is the Wrong Solution, 5 Geo.Imm.L.J. 581 (1991)--210

Hammar, Citizenship: Membership of a Nation and of a State, 24 Int'l Migration 735 (1986)--989

Hammar, Dual Citizenship and Political Integration; 19 Int'l Migration Rev. 438 (1985)--1060

Hand, L., The Bill of Rights (1958)--16

Handlin, O., The Uprooted (2d ed. 1973)--66

Hansen, N., The Border Economy: Regional Development in the Southwest (1981)--293

Harper, Jr., E. & R. Chase, Immigration Laws of the United States (3d ed.1975)--427, 713

Hart H. & A Sacks, The Legal Process 172 (Tent. ed. 1958)--687

Hart, H. & A. Sacks, The Legal Process: Basic Problems in the Making and Application of Law (W. Eskridge & P. Frickey, eds. 1994)--545, 551

Hart, The Power of Congress to Limit the Jurisdiction of the Federal Courts: An Exercise in Dialectic, 66 Harv.L.Rev. 1362 (1953)--364, 366, 397-400, 630, 902

Harvard Research in International Law, Nationality, 23 Am.J.Int'l L. 27-29 (Special Supp. 1929)--990

Harwood, E., In Liberty's Shadow: Illegal Aliens and Immigration Law Enforcement (1986)--101

Hathaway, A Reconsideration of the Underlying Premise of Refugee Law, 31 Harv.Int'l L.J. 129 (1990)--735

Hathaway, Harmonizing for Whom? The Devaluation of Refugee Protection in the Era of European Economic Integration, 26 Cornell Int'l L.J. 719 (1993)--804, 834, 846

Hathaway, J., The Law of Refugee Status (1991)--718, 735, 787, 792

Hathaway, Selective Concern: An Overview of Refugee Law in Canada, 33 McGill L.J. 676 (1988)--745

Heidt, The Conjurer's Circle: The Fifth Amendment Privilege in Civil Cases, 91 Yale L.J. 1062 (1982)--616

Heiserman & Pacun, Professional Responsibility in Immigration Practice and Government Service, 22 San Diego L.Rev. 971 (1985)--181

Helton, Persecution on Account of Membership in a Social Group as a Basis for Refugee Status, 15 Colum.Hum.Rts.L.Rev. 39 (1983)--851

Helton, Political Asylum under the 1980 Refugee Act: An Unfulfilled Promise, 17 U.Mich.J.L.Ref. 243 (1984)--748, 878

Helton, Stevic: The Decision and its Implications, 3 Imm.L.Rep. 49 (1984)--772

Helton, The Legality of Detaining Refugees in the United States, 14 N.Y.U.Rev.L. & Soc.Change 353 (1986)--877

Helton, The Proper Role of Discretion in Political Asylum Determinations, 22 San Diego L.Rev. 999 (1985)--795

Henkin, L., Foreign Affairs and the Constitution (1972)--12

Henkin, L., R. Pugh, O. Schachter, & H. Smit, International Law: Cases and Materials (3d ed.1993)--848

Henkin, The Constitution and United States Sovereignty: A Century of Chinese Exclusion and its Progeny, 100 Harv.L.Rev. 853 (1987)--40

Heyman, Redefining Refugee: A Proposal for Relief for the Victims of Civil Strife, 24 San Diego L.Rev. 449 (1987)--885

Hiatt, Zhirinovsky Gets Visa for Speech in U.S., Wash. Post, Nov. 2, 1994, at A29--360

Higham, J., Strangers in the Land: Patterns of American Nativism 1860-1925 (1955)--55, 66, 515-16

Hing, Beyond the Rhetoric of Assimilation and Cultural Pluralism: Addressing the Tension of Separatism and Conflict in an Immigration-Driven Multiracial Society, 81 Calif.L.Rev. 863 (1993)--229

Hing, B., Making and Remaking Asian America Through Immigration Policy, 1850-1990 (1993)--3

Hofmann, Asylum and Refugee Law, in The Legal Position of Aliens in National and International Law (J. Frowein & T. Stein eds. 1987)--731

Huddle, D., The Cost of Immigration in 1993 (1993)--284

Human Rights and Forced Repatriation, Int'l J. Refugee L. 137-171 (Special Issue, Sept. 1990)--757

Hurwitz, Motion Practice Before the Board of Immmigration Appeals, 20 San Diego L.Rev. 79 (1982)--658

Hutchinson, E., Legislative History of American Immigration Policy 1798-1965 (1981)--343

Immigrants Benefits Might Be Restricted in Welfare Reform Initiatives, 71 Interp.Rel. 521 (1994)--374-75

Immigration, Trade, and the Labor Market (Nat'l Bureau of Econ. Research, R. Freeman ed. 1988)--208

Immigration and the Politics of Citizenship in Europe and North America (W.R. Brubaker ed. 1989)--1060

INS Guidelines for Overseas Processing of Refugees Evaluated, Problems Identified, Refugee Reports, September 7, 1984, at 1-3--750-51

International Centre for Migration Policy Development, The Key to Europe--a Comparative Analysis of Entry and Asylum Policies in Western Countries (1994)--719

International Law of State Responsibility for Injuries to Aliens (R. Lillich ed.1983)--1059

James, Cult-Induced Renunciation of United States Citizenship: The Involuntary Expatriation of Black Hebrews, 28 San Diego L.Rev. 645 (1991)--1082

James, Expatriation in the United States: Precept and Practice Today and Yesterday, 27 San Diego L.Rev. 853 (1990)--1059

James, The Board of Appellate Review of the Department of State: The Right to Appellate Review of Administrative Determinations of Loss of Nationality, 23 San Diego L.Rev. 261 (1986)--1080

Johnson, Refugee Law Reform in Europe: The Belgian Example, 27 Colum.J. Transnat'l L. 589 (1989)--802

Johnson, Responding to the 'Litigation Explosion'': The Plain Meaning of Executive Branch Primacy Over Immigration, 71 N.C.L.Rev. 413 (1993)--842

Jones, M.A., American Immigration (1960)--44, 66

Kalin, Troubled Communications: Cross-Cultural Misunderstandings in the Asylum Hearing, 20 Int'l Migration Rev. 230 (1986)--866

Kamisar, Betts v. Brady Twenty Years Later: The Right to Counsel and Due Process Values, 61 Mich.L.Rev. 219 (1962)--564

Kamisar, Does (Did)(Should) the Exclusionary Rule Rest on a "Principled Basis" Rather than an "Empirical Proposition," 16 Creighton L.Rev. 565 (1983)--626

Kamisar, The Right to Counsel and the Fourteenth Amendment: A Dialogue on "The Most Pervasive Right" of an Accused, 30 U.Chi.L.Rev.1 (1962)--606

Kansas, S., United States Immigration Exclusion and Deportation, and Citizenship of the United States of America (2d ed.1940)--592

Kanstroom, Hello Darkness: Involuntary Testimony and Silence as Evidence in Deportation Proceedings, 4 Geo.Immig.L.J. 599 (1990)--616

Kelly, Anker & Beasley, Guidelines for Women's Asylum Claims, 71 Interp.Rel. 813 (1994)--859

Kelly, Dual Nationality, the Myth of Election, and a Kinder, Gentler State Department, 23 U.Miami Inter-Am.L.Rev. 421 (1991-92)--1057, 1082

Kennedy, Form and Substance in Private Law Adjudication, 89 Harv.L.Rev. 1685 (1976)--681

Kesselbrenner, Contesting Deportability, 92-5 Imm.Briefings (1992)--595

Kesselbrenner, D. & L. Rosenberg, Immigration Law and Crimes (1994)--549

Kettner, J., The Development of American Citizenship, 1608-1870 (1978)--9, 974

Killingsworth, Effects of Immigration Into the United States on the U.S. Labor Market: Analytical and Policy Issues, in U.S. Immigration and Refugee Policy (M. Kritz ed. 1983)--208

King, Immigration from Developing Countries: Some Philosophical Issues, Ethics, April 1983--75

Klasco, Proposed E Visa Regulations: No Treaty Between the INS and the State Department, 68 Interp.Rel. 1417 (1991)--259-60

Knauff, E., The Ellen Knauff Story (1952)--395, 402

Koh, Reflections on Refoulement and Haitian Centers Council, 35 Harv. Int'l L.J. 1 (1994)--881

Koh, The Human Face of the Interdiction Program, 33 Va. J. Int'l L. 483 (1993)--881

Kozinski, Sanhedrin II: the Case of Ivan Demjanjuk, The New Republic, Sept. 13, 1993, at 16--1084

Krieger, Labor Certification: Avoiding Notices of Findings, 13 Imm.L.Rep. 193 (1994)--195

Lai, H., G. Lim & J. Yung, Island: Poetry and History of Chinese Immigrants on Angel Island, 1910-1940 (1980)--421

Landis, A Note on "Statutory Interpretation", 43 Harv.L.Rev. 886 (1930)--551

Langbein, The Criminal Trial Before the Lawyers, 45 U.Chi.L.Rev. 263 (1975)--629

Langbein, The German Advantage in Civil Procedure, 52 U.Chi.L.Rev. 823 (1985)--109

Law and Force in the New International Order (L. Damrosch & D. Scheffer eds. 1991)--882

Lawyers Committee for Human Rights, Handbook on Obtaining Temporary Protected Status (1991)--894

Lawyers Committee for Human Rights, Refugee Refoulement: The Forced Return of Haitians Under the U.S.-Haitian Interdiction Agreement (1990)--878

Lee, L., Consular Law and Practice (2d ed. 1991)--115

Lee, The Immigration and Naturalization Service: In Search of the Necessary Efficiency, 6 Geo. Imm.L.J. 519 (1992)--101

Legal Immigration to the United States: A Demographic Analysis of Fifth Preference Visa Admissions (Comm.Print, S.Prt. 100-34, 1987)--191

Legomsky, Forum Choices for the Review of Agency Adjudication: A Study of the Immigration Process, 71 Iowa L.Rev. 1297 (1986)--111, 113, 899

Legomsky, Immigration, Equality, and Diversity, 31 Colum. J. Transnat'l L. 319 (1993)--229

Legomsky, Immigration Law and the Principle of Plenary Congressional Power, 1984 Sup.Ct.Rev. 255--12

Legomsky, Political Asylum and the Theory of Judicial Review, 73 Minn.L.Rev. 1205 (1989)--841

Legomsky, S., Immigration and the Judiciary (1987)--40, 368

Legomsley, The Haitian Interdiction Programme, Human Rights, and the Role of Judicial Protection, Int'l. J. Refugee L. 181 (Special Issue, Sept. 1990)--878-79, 926, 931

Leibowitz, A., Defining Status: A Comprehensive Analysis of United States Territorial Relations (1989)--975

Leidigh, Defense of Sham Marriage Deportations, 8 U.C.-Davis L.Rev. 309 (1975)--179

LeMay, M., From Open Door to Dutch Door: An Analysis of U.S. Immigration Policy Since 1820 (1987)--66

Letter from Sarah G. Epstein, Wash. Post, May 20, 1990, at A20--814

Levinson, A Specialized Court for Immigration Hearings and Appeals, 56 Notre Dame Law. 644 (1981)--111

Levy, Practitioner's Guide to Section 274C: Parts 1 & 2, 94-6 & 94-7 Imm.Briefings (1994)--540

Lewis, Cause for Justice, N.Y. Times, Sept. 20, 1993, at A13--530

Linde, "Clear and Present Danger", Reexamined: Dissonanc in the Brandenburg Concerto, 22 Stan.L.Rev. 1163 (1970)--527

Lippermann, W., Public Opinion (1960)--732

Lippman, Avalanche of Mail for a Trickle of Visas, Wash. Post, Oct 17, 1994, at A3--117

Llewellyn, K., The Brumble Bush (1960)--676

Loescher, G. & J. Scanlan, Calculated Kindness: Refugees and America's Half-Open Door, 1945-Present (1986)--736

Lofgren, United States v. Curtiss-Wright Export Corporation: An Historical Reassessment, 83 Yale L.J. 1 (1973)--15

Lopez, Undocumented Mexican Migration: In Search of a Just Immigration Law and Policy, 28 U.C.L.A.L.Rev. 615 (1981)--275, 339

Love, Equality in Political Asylum Law: For a Legislative Recognition of Gender-Based Persecution, 17 Harv. Women's L.J. 133 (1994)--852

Mailman, B-1 Visitors for Business Revisited, 71 Interp.Rel. 149 (1994)--270

Mailman, The New Adjustment of Status Law: Background and Analysis, 71 Interp.Rel. 1505 (1994)--442-43, 443

Mann, Asylum Denied: The Vigilant Incident, 62 U.S. Naval War College Int'l L.Stud. 598 (1980)--761, 879

Mann, A., The One and the Many: Reflections on the American Identity (1979)--229

Marks, A Practitioner's Guide to Suspension of Deportation, 93-6 Imm.Briefings (1993)--654

Martin, Comparative Policies on Political Asylum: Of Facts and Law, 9 In Defense of the Alien 105 (1987)--848

Martin, Due Process and Membership in the National Community: Political Asylum and Beyond, 44 U.Pitt.L.Rev. 165 (1983)--402-03, 507, 630-33, 636-38, 882

Martin, D., Major Issues in Immigration Law (1987)--295-96, 931

Martin, Effects of International Law on Migration Policy and Practice: The Uses of Hypocrisy, 23 Int'l Migration Rev. 547 (1989)--885

Martin, Judicial Review of Legalization Denials, 65 Interp.Rel. 757 (1988)--949-50

Martin, Mandel, Cheng Fan Kwok, and Other Unappealing Cases: The Next Frontier of Immigration Reform, 27 Va.J.Int'l L. 803 (1987)--370, 926, 955-57

Martin, Membership and Consent: Abstract or Organic?, 11 Yale J. Int'l L. 278 (1985)--990

Martin, Political Asylum in the West: Dying or Recuperating?,____(1995)--804, 897-78

Martin, P., Illegal Immigration and the Colonization of the American Labor Market (1986)--208

Martin, Reforming Asylum Adjudication: On Navigating the Coast of Bohemia, 138 U.Pa.L.Rev. 1247 (1990)--730-34, 762, 866-67, 871, 882

Martin, Strategies for a Resistant World: Human Rights Initiatives and the Need for Alternatives to Refugee Interdiction, 26 Cornell Int'l L.J. 753 (1993)--882

Martin, The End of De Facto Asylum: Toward a Humane and Realistic Response to Refugee Challenges, 18 Calif.W.Int'l L.J. 161 (1987-88)--768

Martin, The Refugee Act of 1980: Its Past and Future, in Transnational Lagal Problems of Refugees, 1982 Mich.Y.B. Int'l L.Stud. 91--721, 745-48, 863-64

Martin, The Refugee Concept: On Definitions, Politics, and the Careful Use of a Scarce Resource, in Refugee Policy: Canada and the United States (H. Adelman ed. 1991)--735

Mashaw, J., Bureaucratic Justice (1983)--112

Maslow, Recasting Our Deportation Law: Proposals for Reform, 56 Colum.L.Rev. 309 (1956)--511, 526

Massey, Goldring, & Durand, Continuities in Transnational Migration: An Analysis of Nineteen Mexican Communities, 99 Am. J. Soc. 1492 (1994)--278-83

Massey, Individual Responsibility for Assisting the Nazis in Persecuting Civilians, 71 Minn.L.Rev. 97 (1986)--580

Massey, Understanding Mexican Migration to the United States, 92 Am.J.Soc. 1372 (1987)--73

Matas, D., Justice Delayed: Nazi War Criminals in Canada (1987)--1083

McClain, The Chinese Struggle for Civil Rights in Nineteenth Century America: The First Phase, 1850-1870, 72 Cal.L.Rev. 529 (1984)--3, 4

McDougal, Lasswell, & Chen, Nationality and Human Rights: The Protection of the Individual in External Areas, 83 Yale L.J. 900 (1974)--1059

McGrory, I Miss Manners, Wash. Post, Jan. 2, 1994, at C1--360

McNeill, W., Polyethnicity and National Unity in World History (1986)--229

Meissner, Class II Refugees: An Answer to a Growing Need, World Refugee Survey: 1986 in Review (1987)--745

Meissner, Let the Contras Find a Haven Rebuilding Peace in Nicaragua, Not Living in the U.S., Los Angeles Times, Sept. 11, 1989, §2, at 5--755

Meissner, Reflections on the Refugee Act of 1980, in The New Asylum Seekers: Refugee Law in the 1980s (D. Martin ed. 1988)--767

Melander, Refugees in Orbit, 16 A.W.R. Bull. 59 (1978)--795

Merriam-Webster, Webster's New International Dictionary, Second Edition, unabridged (1957)--915

Miles, Blacks vs. Browns, The Atlantic Monthly Oct. 1992, at 54--292-93

Minorities: Community and Identity (C. Fried ed. 1983)--229

Miranda, An Agenda for the Commission on Immigration Reform, 29 San Diego L.Rev. 701 (1992)--876

Morris, M., Immigration--The Beleaguered Bureaucracy (1985)--101

Motomura, Haitian Asylum Seekers: Interdiction and Immigrants' Rights, 26 Cornell Int'l L.J. 695 (1993)--486, 879

Motomura, Immigration Law After a Century of Plenary Power: Phantom Constitutional Norms and Statutory Interpretation, 100 Yale L.J. 545 (1990)--40, 498, 499, 612

Motomura, The Curious Evolution of Immigration Law: Procedural Surrogates for Substantive Constitutional Rights, 92 Colum.L.Rev. 1625 (1992)--40, 404, 451-52, 404, 591, 635-36

Muller, T. & T. Espenshade, The Fourth Wave: California's Newest Immigrants (1985)--66

Nafziger, Review of Visa Denials by Consular Officers, 66 Wash.L.Rev. 1 (1991)--117, 368, 421

Nafziger, The General Admission of Aliens Under International Law, 77 Am.J.Int'l L. 804 (1983)--15

Nash, Contemporary Practice of the United States Relating to International Law: Diplomatic Asylum, 75 Am.J.Int'l L. 142 (1981)--762

National Association of Latino Elected Officials, New Citizens in Limbo?: One in Three Applicants for U.S. Citizenship Neither Pass Nor Fail (NALEO Background Paper # 8, mimeo 1988)--1015

National Asylum Study Project, An Assessment of the Asylum Process of the Immigration and Naturalization Service (1993)--865

National Immigration Project of the National Lawyers Guild, Bond Practice Manual, (1993-94 ed.)--588

National Interest Waivers in the EB-2 Category, 13 Imm.L.Rep. 69-70 (1994)--214

National Interest Waivers: The INS Grants an Array of Second Preference Cases Without Job Offers or Labor Certifications, 13 Imm.L.Rep. 73--214

Neuman, Back to Dred Scott?, 24 San Diego L.Rev. 485 (1987)--990

Neuman, Buffer Zones Against Refugees: Dublin, Schengen, and The German Asylum Amendment, 33 Va.J.Int'l L. 503 (1993)--804

Neuman, Justifying U.S. Naturalization Policies, 35 Va.J.Int'l L. 237 (1995)--989

Neuman, The Lost Century of American Immigration Law (1776-1875), 93 Colum.L.Rev. 1833 (1993)--1, 370

Neuman, Whose Constitution?, 100 Yale L.J. 909 (1991)--975

North, D., The Long Gray Welcome: A Study of the American Naturalization Program (1985)--1015

North, D. & M. Portz, Decision Factories: The Role of the Regional Processing Facilities in the Alien Legalization Programs (Report to the Administrative Conference of the U.S. 1989)--105

Note, Asylum for Unrecognized Conscientious Objectors to Military Service: Is There a Right not to Fight?, 31 Va.J.Int'l L. 447 (1991)--828

Note, Basing Asylum Claims on a Fear of Persecution Arisng from a Prior Asylum Claim, 56 Notre Dame Law. 719 (1981)--807

Note, Coercive Population Control Policies: The Need for a Conscientious Objector Provision for Asylum Seekers, 30 Va.J.Int'l L. 1007 (1990)--815

Note, Congressional Proposals to Revive Guilt by Association: An Ineffective Plan to Stop Terrorism, 8 Geo.Imm.L.J. 227 (1994)--362

Note, Constitutional Limits on the Power to Exclude Aliens, 82 Colum.L.Rev. 957 (1982)--15, 456

Note, Consular Discretion in Immigrant Visa-Issuing Process, 16 San Diego L.Rev. 87 (1978)--371

Note, Crimes Involving Moral Turpitude, 43 Harv.L.Rev. 117 (1929)--564

Note, Developments in the Law--Immigration Policy and the Rights of Aliens, 96 Harv. L.Rev. 1286 (1983)--109, 111, 616, 667, 677-78

Note, Diplomatic Asylum in the United States and Latin America: A Comparative Analysis, 13 Brooklyn J.Int'l L. 111 (1987)--762

Note, Ethical Problems in Representing Aliens Applying for Visas Based on Marriages to United States Citizens, 28 Santa Clara L.Rev. 709 (1988)--181

Note, Ex Post Facto Limitations on Legislative Power, 73 Mich.L.Rev. 1491 (1975)--533

Note, Extradition Reform and the Statutory Definition of Political Offenses, 24 Va. J.Int'l L. 419 (1984)--860

Note, First Amendment and the Alien Exclusion Power--What Standard of Review?, 4 Cardozo L.Rev. 457 (1983)--355

Note, From Treblinka to the Killing Fields: Excluding Persecutors from the Definition of "Refugee," 27 Va.J. Int'l L. 823 (1987)--764

Note, Immigration and the First Amendment, 73 Calif.L.Rev. 1889 (1985)--528

Note, Immigration for Investors: A Comparative Analysis of U.S., Canadian, and Australian Policies, 7 B.C. Int'l & Comp. L.Rev. 113 (1984)--224

Note, Judicial Review of Visa Denials: Reexamining Consular Nonreviewability, 52 N.Y.U.L.Rev. 1137 (1977)--352, 367

Note, Jurisdiction to Review Prior Orders and Underlying Statutes in Deportation Appeals, 65 Va.L.Rev. 403 (1979)--919

Note, Litigating as Law Students: An Inside Look at Haitian Centers Council, 103 Yale L.J. 2337 (1994)--881

Note, Open-ended Warrants, Employers and the Simpson-Rodino Act, 87 Colum.L.Rev. 817 (1987)--623

Note, Political Legitimacy in the Law of Political Asylum, 99 Harv.L.Rev. 450 (1985)--735

Note, Reexamining the Constitutionality of Workplace Raids After the Immigration Reform and Control Act of 1986, 100 Harv.L.Rev. 1979 (1987)--622

Note, Refugee Determinations: A Consolidation of Approaches to Actions by Nongovernmental Forces, 33 Va.J.Int'l L. 927 (1993)--821

Note, Temporary Safe Haven for De Facto Refugees from War, Violence, and Disasters, 28 Va.J.Int'l.L. 509 (1988)--894

Note, The Agony and the Exodus: Deporting Salvadorans in Violation of the Fourth Geneva Convention, 18 N.Y.U.J.Int'l L. & Pol. 703 (1986)--885

Note, The Birthright Citizenship Amendment: A Threat to Equality, 107 Harv. L.Rev. 1026 (1994)--990

Note, The Constitutional Rights of Excluded Aliens: Proposed Limitations on the Indefinite Detention of the Cuban Refugees, 70 Geo.L.J. 1303 (1982)--456

Note, The Constitutionality of the INS Sham Marriage Investigation Policy, 99 Harv. L.Rev. 1238 (1986)--183

Note, The Immigration and Naturalization Service and Racially Motivated Questioning: Does Equal Protection Pick Up Where the Fourth Amendment Left Off?, 86 Colum.L.Rev. 800 (1986)--622

Note, The Reconciliation of Prominence and Exceptional Ability: A Necessary Step Toward a Coordinated Immigration Policy, 30 Va.J.Int'l L. 977 (1990)--246

Note, The Right of Asylum under United States Law, 80 Colum.L.Rev. 1125 (1980)--761

Novotny, A., Strangers at the Door: Ellis Island, Castle Garden, and the Great Migration to America (1971)--413-21

Nozick, R., Anarchy, State and Utopia (1974)--76

O'Higgins, Disguised Extradition: The Soblen Case, 27 Mod. L.Rev. 521 (1964)--861

O'Keefe, Immigration Issues and Airlines, 59 J.Air L. & Comm. 357 (1993)--422

Office of the United Nations High Commissioner for Refugees, Handbook on Procedures and Criteria for Determining Refugee Status (2d ed. 1988; UN Sales No. HCR/IP/4/Eng.Rev.1)--786

Office of the United Nations High Commissioner for Refugees, The Handbook on Procedures and Criteria for Determining Refugee Status Under the 1951 Convention and the 1967 Protocol Relating to the Status of Refugees (1979)--777, 823

Orfield, The Legal Effects of Dual Nationality, 17 Geo.Wash.L.Rev. 427--1056

Orlow, Rescission--Rationalizing the Irrational, 6 Immig.J. 6 (1983)--445

Ort, International and U.S. Obligations Toward Stowaway Asylum Seekers, 140 U.Pa.L.Rev. 285 (1991)--433

Ortolan, Diplomatie de la Mer (4th ed.)--23

Paparelli & Haight, Avoiding or Accepting Risks in H-1B/LCA Practice, Parts I & II, 92-11 & 92-12 Imm.Briefings (1992)--219

Parker, Victims of Natural Disasters in United States Refugee Law and Policy, in Transnational Legal Problems of Refugees (1982)--737

Patrick, Tell it to the Judge--Judicial Review of Immigration Decisions, 88-10 Imm. Briefings (1988)--931

Pear, Clinton Will Seek Spending to Curb Aliens, Aides Say, N.Y. Times, Jan. 21, 1995, at 1--118

Perluss & Hartman, Temporary Refuge: Emergence of a Customary Norm, 26 Va. J.Int'l L. 551 (1986)--885

Pfeiffer, Credibility Findings in INS Asylum Adjudications: A Realistic Assessment, 23 Tex.Int'l L.J. 139 (1988)--866

Piatt, B., Only English?: Law and Language Policy in the United States (1990)--227

Piore, M., Birds of Passage: Migrant Labor and Industrial Societies (1979)--208

Pitkin, T., Keepers of the Gate: A History of Ellis Island (1975)--380, 421

Pivec, Observations on the Enforcement of the H-1B Labor Condition Application Requirements, 71 Interp.Rel. 705 (1994)--219, 247

Plender, Recent Trends in National Immigration Control, 35 Int'l & Comp.L.Q. 531 (1986)--423

Plender, R., International Migration Law (rev. 2d ed. 1988)--172

Plender, The Legal Basis of International Jurisdiction to Act with Regard to the Internally Displaced, 6 Int'l J.Ref.L. 345 (1994)--735

Population and Development: The Search for Selective Interventions (Ridker, R., ed., 1976)--80

Portes, A. & R. Rumbaut, Immigrant America: A Portrait (1990)--139

Portes, The Return of the Wetback, 11 Society 10 (1974)--538

Portes & Borocz, Contemporary Immigration: Theoretical Perspectives on its Determinants and Modes of Incorporation, 23 Int'l Migration Rev. 606 (1989)--70

President's Commission on Immigration and Naturalization, Whom We Shall Welcome (1953)--109, 116, 526

Preston, Jr., W., Aliens and Dissenters: Federal Suppression of Radicals, 1903-1933 (1963)--514

Radin, Statutory Interpretation, 43 Harv. L.Rev. 863 (1930)--551

Raskin, Legal Aliens, Local Citizens: The Historical, Constitutional and Theoretical Meanings of Alien Suffrage, 141 U.Pa. L.Rev. 1391 (1993)--1085

Rawitz, From Wong Yang Sung to Black Robes, 65 Interp.Rel. 453 (1988)--110

Rawitz, In the Hands of Congress: Suspension of Deportation and Private Bills, 57 Interp.Rel. 76 (1980)--713

Rawls, J., A Theory of Justice (1971)--76

Rees, Advice for the New INS Commissioner, 70 Interp. Rel. 1533 (1993)--102

Refugees or Prisoners?, Newsweek, February 1, 1982, at 28-29--720

Reimers, D., Still the Golden Door: The Third World Comes to America (2d ed. 1992)--66

Riggs, F., Pressures on Congress: A Study of Repeal of Chinese Exclusion (1950)--35

Roberts, et al., Shutting the Golden Door, 117 U.S. News & World Report 36 (Oct. 3, 1994)--284

Roberts, Proposed: A Specialized Statutory Immigration Court, 18 San Diego L.Rev. 1 (1980)--111, 925

Roberts, The Exercise of Administrative Discretion under the Immigration Laws, 13 San Diego L.Rev. 144 (1975)--109, 647, 679-81

Roberts & Yale-Loehr, Employers as Junior Immigration Inspectors: The Impact of the 1986 Immigration Reform and Control Act, 21 Int'l Lawyer 1013 (1987)--299

Robie, A Response to Professor Verkuil, 39 UCLA L.Rev. 1365 (1992)--110, 111

Robinson, Sins of Omission: The New Vietnamese Refugee Crisis, World Refugee Survey--1988 in Review (1989)--756, 758

Rodino, The Impact of Immigration on the American Labor Market, 27 Rutgers L.Rev. 245 (1974)--193

Rodriguez, R., Hunger of Memory (1981)--229

Rohter, Florida Takes Fight On Immigrant Policy To a New Battlefield, N.Y.Times, Feb. 11 1994, at A1, A8--323

Rosberg, Aliens and Equal Protection: Why Not the Right to Vote?, 75 Mich.L.Rev. 1092 (1977)--1085, 1085-89

Rosen, The War on Immigrants, The New Republic, Jan. 30, 1995, at 22--988-989

Rosenberg & Sabagh, A Practitioner's Guide to INA § 212(c), 93-4 Imm.Briefings (1993)--711

Rosenfield, Consular Non-Reviewability: A Case Study in Administrative Absolutism, 41 Amer.Bar Assoc.J. 1109 (1955)--364

Roth, A., International Law Applied to Aliens (1949)--446

Rousseau, The Social Contract--984

Royce, Visa Lookout Failed, Newsday, July 23, 1993, at 33--362

Rules and Procedures under the 1986 Marriage Fraud Act, 7 Imm.L.Rep. 97 (1988)--186-87, 189

Ruthizer, Administrative Appeals of Immigration Decisions: A Practitioner's Guide, 88-1 Imm. Briefings (1988)--114, 117, 899

Ryan, Jr., A., Quiet Neighbors: Prosecuting Nazi War Criminals in America (1984)--580, 1083

Safire, W., Freedom (1988)--833

Saltzburg, Habeas Corpus: The Supreme Court and the Congress, 44 Ohio St.L.J. 367 (1983)--902

Scanlan, Aliens in the Marketplace of Ideas: The Government, the Academy, and the McCarran-Walter Act, 66 Tex.L.Rev. 1481 (1988)--354

Scaperlanda, Justice Thurgood Marshall and the Legacy of Dissent in Federal Alienage Cases, 8 Geo.Imm.L.J. 1 (1994)--354

Schacknove, Who is a Refugee?, 95 Ethics 274 (1985)--735

Schauer, Free Speech and the Paradox of Tolerance in Values in Conflict: Life, Liberty, and the Rule of Law 228 (B. Leiser ed. 1981)--357

Schlesinger, Jr., A. The Disuniting of America: Reflections on a Multicultural Society (1992)--229

Schmidt, Detention of Aliens, 24 San Diego L.Rev. 305 (1987)--465, 877

Schoonover & Walker, Immigration Provisions of the North American Free Trade Agreement, 94-3 Imm.Briefings (1994)--270

Schuck, Membership in the Liberal Polity: The Devaluation of American Citizenship in Immigration and the Politics of Citizenship in Europe and North America 51 (W.R. Brubaker ed. 1989)--985-88

Schuck, P., & R. Smith, Citizenship Without Consent: Illegal Aliens in the American Polity (1985)--989-90

Schuck, The Messages of 187, The American Prospect, No. 21 (Spring 1995)--339

Schuck, The Transformation of Immigration Law, 84 Colum. L.Rev. 1 (1984)--40, 336-37, 890, 900

Schuck, When the Exception Becomes the Rule: Regulatory Equity and the Formulation of Energy Policy Through an Exceptions Policy, 1984 Duke L.J. 163--681

Schuck & Elliott, To the Chevron Station: An Empirical Study of Federal Administrative Law, 1990 Duke L.J. 984--173

Schuck & Smith, Membership and Consent: Actual or Mythic?--A Reply to David A. Martin, 11 Yale J. Int'l L. 545 (1986)--990

Schuck & Wang, Continuity and Change: Patterns of Immigration Litigation in the Courts, 1979-1990, 45 Stan.L.Rev. 115 (1992)--173

Schwartz, The Amorality of Consent, 74 Calif.L.Rev. 2143 (1986)--990

Select Commission on Immigration and Refugee Policy SCIRP§, Final Report (1981)--102, 117, 224-27, 581, 596, 605, 874-75, 925

Select Commission on Immigration and Refugee Policy SCIRP§, U.S. Immigration Policy and the National Interest Staff Report (1981)--41, 65, 171, 275, 294, 434

Sham Divorces Still Stump Judges, Las Vegas Sun, Dec. 10, 1982, at 21, col. 1--183

Shapiro, Ideological Exclusions: Closing the Border to Political Dissidents, 100 Harv. L.Rev. 930 (1987)--354

Shue, H., Basic Rights: Subsistence, Affluence, and U.S. Foreign Policy (1980)--96

Shusterman, The New DOL Nurse Regulations: Revisiting the 'A' Word, 94-4 Imm.Briefings (1994)--245

Sidgwick, Henry, Methods of Ethics (1907)--76

Sidgwick, Henry, The Elements of Politics (1897)--77

Simon, Auction the Right to Be an Immigrant, N.Y. Times, Jan. 28, 1986--98

Simpson, J., The Refugee Problem (1939)--735

Simpson, Legal Immigration Reform, 25 San Diego L.Rev. 215 (1988)--220, 225

Simpson, Policy Implications of U.S. Consular Operations, in The Consular Dimension of Diplomacy (M. Herz ed. 1983)--116

Singer & Singer, The Ethics of Refugee Policy, in Open Borders? Closed Societies?: The Ethical and Political Issues 111 (M. Gibney ed. 1988)--735

Smith & Hake, Evidence Issues in Asylum Cases, 90-10 Imm. Briefings (1990)--864

Smolla, The Re-emergence of the Right-Privilege Distinction in Constitutional Law: The Price of Protesting Too Much, 35 Stan.L.Rev. 69 (1982)--411, 529

Smyser, W., Refugees: Extended Exile (1987)--719

Sofaer, The Change of Status Adjudication: A Case Study of the Informal Agency Process, 1 J.Legal Studies 349 (1972)--438

Solomon, Priorities and Preferences: Keeping Place in the Immigrant Visa Line, 92-6 Imm. Briefings (1992)--219

Sontag, Analysis of Illegal Immigrants In New York Defies Stereotypes, N.Y.Times, Sep. 2, 1993, at A11--274

Spiro, Leave for Appeal: Departure as a Requirement for Review of Deportation Orders, 25 San Diego L.Rev. 281 (1988)--957

Start, Naturalization in the English Colonies in North America, in American Historical Assn., Annual Report for the Year 1893, at 319 (1894)--1088

Stoddard, Illegal Mexican Labor in the Borderlands: Institutionalized Support of an Unlawful Practice, 19 Pac.Soc.Rev. 175 (1976)--293

Strauss, Hong Kong Expulsions to Continue, Wash.Post, Dec. 13, 1989, at A27--757

Suhrke, A., Global Refugee Movements and Strategies of Response, U.S. Immigration and Refugee Policy: Global and Domestic Issues (M. Kritz ed. 1983)--724-28

Suhrke, Indochinese Refugees: The Law and Politics of First Asylum, 467 The Annals 102 (1983)--758

Suro, Chinese Smuggling Grows, Forcing U.S. Reassessment, Wash. Post, June 2, 1994, at A1--818

Suro, Guatemala Agrees to Facilitate Repatriation of Illegal Chinese Immigrants, Wash. Post, Apr. 29, 1994, at A3--768, 819

Suro, On Immigration, A Question of Fairness, Wash.Post, Dec. 20, 1994, at A3--819

Suro, R., Remembering the American Dream: Hispanic Immigration and National Policy (1994)--229

Suro, U.S. Policy Changed with Guantanamo Safe Havens, Wash. Post, Feb. 5, 1995, at A24--882

Symposium, 35 Va.J.Int'l L. 1 (1995)--1060

Symposium, Focus on the Comprehensive Plan of Action, 5 Int'l J. Refugee L. 507 (1993)--759

Symposium on Bilingual Education, 6 J.L. & Politics 573 (1990)--227

Symposium: Law and Community, 84 Mich. L.Rev. 1373 (1986)--989

Takaki, R., Strangers from a Different Shore: A History of Asian Americans (1989)--3

Teitelbaum, Political Asylum in Theory and Practice, 76 The Public Interest 74 (1984)--720

Temporary Suspension of Deportation of Certain Aliens, Hearing before the Subcomm. on Immigration, Refugees, and International Law, House Subcomm. on the Judiciary, 98th Cong., 2d Sess., at 44 (April 12, 1984)--893-94

The Case of Miroslav Medvid: Hearings on H.Res. 314 Before the House Comm. on Foreign Affairs, 99th Cong., 2d Sess. (1985)--761

The Federalist, No. 42 (J. Madison)--974

The Gateway: Immigration Issues and Policy (B. Chiswick ed. 1982)--208

The Immigration Reform and Control Act of 1983, Hearings Before the Subcomm. on Immigration, Refugees, and International Law of the House Comm. on the Judiciary, 98th Cong., 1st Sess. 955 (1983)--925

The New Asylum Seekers: Refugee Law in the 1980s (D. Martin ed. 1988)--719

The New Immigration (J. Appel ed. 1971)--421

The Preference System: Hearings Before the Subcomm. on Immigration and Refugee Policy of the Sen. Comm. on the Judiciary, 97th Cong., 1st Sess. 213 (1981)--191, 225

The Random House Dictionary of the English Language (2d ed. 1987)--856

The Unavoidable Issue: U.S. Immigration Policy in the 1980s (D. Papademetriou & M. Miller eds. 1983)--208

The Year of the Refugee, The Economist, Dec. 23, 1989 at 17--721

Tienda, Socioeconomic and Labor Force Characteristics of U.S. Immigrants: Issues and Approaches--208

Tien-La Li, Congressional Policy of Chinese Immigration (1916)--4

Time for Decision: The United States and Puerto Rico (J. Heine ed. 1984)--975

To Loose the Bands of Wickedness: International Intervention in Defense of Human Rights (N. Rodley ed. 1992)--882

Tome, Administrative Notice of Changed Country Conditions in Asylum Adjudication, 27 Colum. J.L. & Soc. Probs. 411 (1994)--873

Tribe, L., American Constitutional Law (2d ed. 1988)--558

Trillin, Making Adjustments, The New Yorker, May 28, 1984--105, 178, 196

Troeller, UNHCR Resettlement as an Instrument of International Protection, 3 Int'l J. Refugee L. 564 (1991)--739

Tuchman, B., The Proud Tower (1966)--343

Tucker, Assimilation to the United States: A Study of the Adjustment of Status and Immigration Marriage Fraud Statutes, 7 Yale L. & Policy Rev. 20 (1989)--186

United Nations High Commissioner for Refugees, Handbook on Procedures and Criteria for Determining Refugee Status (1979)--786, 805, 806, 815, 824, 832, 839, 856, 878

United Nations High Commissioner for Refugees Resettlement Section, Assessment of Global Resettlement Needs for Refugees in 1995 (Dec. 1994)--759

United States Commission on Civil Rights, The Tarnished Golden Door: Civil Rights Issues in Immigration (1981)--41, 102, 109, 111, 149

United States Commission on Immigration Reform, U.S. Immigration Policy: Restoring Credibility (1994)--315-17, 318-21, 338

United States Committee for Refugees, World Refugee Survey: 1986 in Review 3 (1987)--887

United States Committee for Refugees, World Refugee Survey: 1994 (1994)--723

United States Department of Commerce, Statistical Abstract of the United States, 1980--126

United States Department of Labor, 1992 H-2A Program Data (1994)--244

United States Department of Labor, Dictionary of Occupational Titles--197

United States Department of State, Bureau of Consular Affairs, 7 Visa Bulletin, No. 35, April 1994--130

United States Department of State, Country Reports on Human Rights Practices for 1983, (Jt.Comm.Print, 98th Cong., 2d Sess., February 1984)--822

United States Department of State, Country Reports on Human Rights Practices for 1985 (Jt.Comm.Print, 99th Cong., 2d Sess., 1986)--756, 810

United States Department of State, Country Reports on Human Rights Practices for 1987 (Jt.Comm.Print, 100th Cong., 2d Sess. 1988)--756, 810

United States Department of State, Country Reports on Human Rights Practices for 1988, at 637 (Jt.Comm.Print(S.Prt. 101-3), 101st Cong., 1st Sess., February 1989)--828

United States Department of State, Department of State Today 5-7 (Dept. of State, Bureau of Public Affairs, March 1988)--117

United States Department of State, Report of the Visa Office, 1992--369, 421, 423, 426

United States General Accounting Office, Immigration Control: Deporting and Excluding Aliens from the United States (1989)--588-89

United States General Accounting Office, Immigration Control: Immigration Policies Affect INS Detention Efforts (1992)--588, 597

United States General Accounting Office, Immigration Marriage Fraud: Controls in Most Countries Surveyed Stronger than in U.S. (July 1986)--184

United States General Accounting Office, Immigration Reform-Employer Sanctions and the Question of Discrimination (1990)--305-07

United States General Accounting Office, The Future Flow of Legal Immigration into the United States (GAO/PEMD-88-7, 1988)--191

United States House Committee on the Judiciary, Refugee Issues in Southeast Asia and Europe (Comm.Print 97th Cong., 2d Sess., 1982)--750

United States Immigration and Naturalization Service, Annual Report, 1986--103

United States Immigration and Naturalization Service, Asylum Adjudications: An Evolving Concept and Responsibility for the Immigration and Naturalization Service, 66-68 (Immigration and Naturalization Service Staff Study, mimeo, June 1982)--871, 886

United States Immigration and Naturalization Service, Asylum Division, Preliminary FY 1994 Statistical Package, Oct. 28, 1994--769-70

United States Immigration and Naturalization Service Fact Book: Summary of Recent Immigration Data (June 1994)--102, 103

United States Immigration and Naturalization Service, Immigration Reform and Control Act: Report on the Legalized Alien Population (1992)--296

United States Immigration and Naturalization Service, Office of General Counsel, The Law of Arrest, Search, and Seizure for Immigration Officers (1983)--624

United States Immmigration and Naturalizatin Service, Statistical Yearbook (1980)--126

United States Immigration and Naturalization Service, Statistical Yearbook (1981)--
1014, 1015, 1083
United States Immigration and Naturalization Service, Statistical Yearbook (1985)--
1083
United States Immigration and Naturalization Service, Statistical Yearbook (1987)--
439
United States Immigration and Naturalization Service, Statistical Yearbook (1989)--
103
United States Immigration and Naturalization Service, Statistical Yearbook (1992)--
126, 439, 975, 1014
United States Immigration and Naturalization Service, Statistical Yearbook (1993)--
63, 65, 126, 134, 138, 231, 232, 233, 249,
250, 260, 274, 296, 432, 439, 527, 536,
541, 587, 640, 713, 714, 768, 975, 1014
United States Senate Subcommittee on Immigration and Refugee Policy, The Miroslav Medvid Incident, October 24-29, 1985
(Comm.Print No. 99-179, 99th Cong., 2d
Sess., 1986)--761

Van Alstyne, The Demise of the Right-Privi-
lege Distinction in Constitutional Law, 81
Harv.L.Rev. 1439 (1968)--529
Van Deusen, National Interest Waivers, 13
Imm.L.Rep. 73 (1994)--213
Vattel, E., The Law of Nations (1865)--23
Vierdag, The Country of "First Asylum":
Some European Aspects, in The New Asy-
lum Seekers: Refugee Law in the 1980's
(D.Martin ed. 1988)--795
Vobejda, Births, Immigration Revise Census
View of 21st Century U.S., Wash. Post,
Dec. 4, 1992, p. A10--148

Walzer, M., Spheres of Justice: A Defense of
Pluralism and Equality (1983)--17, 85,
165, 730, 749-50, 989
Walzer, M., The Distribution of Membership,
in Boundaries: National Autonomy and its
Limits (P. Brown & H. Shue, eds. 1981)--
77, 85
Warren, R., Estimates of the Resident Illegal
Alien Population Residing in the United
States, by Country of Origin and State of
Residence: October, 1992 (United States
Immigration and Naturalization Service
Statistics Division 1993)--274, 296
Wasserman, Crimes Involving Moral Turpi-
tude, 1 INS Monthly Rev. 2 (1944)--549
Watkins, Streamlining Deportation Proceed-
ings: Self-Incrimination, Immunity from
Prosecution and the Duty to Testify in a
Deportation Context, 22 San Diego L.Rev.
1075 (1985)--617
Webber, Strategies for Avoiding Labor Certi-
fication, 93-12 Imm.Briefings (1993)--213
Webster's Ninth New Collegiate Dictionary
(1983)--1038

Webster's Third New International Dictionary of the English Language 1291 (unabridged ed. 1963)--169
Webster's Third New International Dictio-
nary (16th ed. 1971)--776
Weis, P., Nationality and Statelessness in In-
ternational Law (2d ed.1979)--1059
Weis, The Draft United Nations Convention
on Territorial Asylum, 50 Brit.Y.B.Int'l L.
151-71 (1979)--731
Weiss, A Day in the Life of an Immigration
Practitioner, The Florida Bar Journal,
May 1992, at 74-75--119
Weissbrodt, D., Immigration Law and Proce-
dure in a Nutshell (3d ed.1992)--107,
1002-07
Wernick, Consular Processing of Immigrant
Visas, 90-12 Imm. Briefings (Dec.1990)--
424
Westin, Stephen J. Field and the Headnote to
O'Neil v. Vermont: A Snapshot of the
Fuller Court at Work, 67 Yale L.J. 363
(1958)--37
Wettstein, Lawful Domicile for Purposes of
INA § 212(c): Can it Begin With Tempo-
rary Residence?, 71 Interp.Rel. 1273
(1994)--695
Wheeler, Alien Eligibility for Public Benefits,
Parts 1 & 2, 88-11, 88-12 Imm. Briefings
(Dec.1988)--882, 886
Wheeler, Until INS Do Us Part: A Guide to
IMFA, 90-3 Imm. Briefings (March 1990)--
185-86, 188, 189
Whelan, Citizenship and Freedom of Move-
ment: An Open Admission Policy? in
Open Borders? Closed Societies?: The Eth-
ical and Political Issues 3 (M. Gibney ed.
1988)--97
Why Isn't the "Green Card" Green?, 70 In-
terp.Rel. 1043 (1993)--426
Widgren, Migration Policies in the OECD
Area: Towards Convergence?, 10 In De-
fense of the Alien 50 (1988)--423
Wigmore, Evidence (3d ed. 1940)--609
Wildes, Review of Visa Denials: The Ameri-
can Consul as 20th Century Absolute
Monarch, 26 San Diego L.Rev. 887, 900-02
(1989)--368
Wildes, The Nonpriority Program of the Im-
migration and Naturalization Service
Goes Public: The Litigative Use of the
Freedom of Information Act, 14 San Diego
L.Rev. 42 (1976)--648-50
Wilson, Open Letter to the President of the
United States on Behalf of the People of
California, N.Y.Times, Aug. 10 1993, at
A11--338
Wolf, Entry and Residence, in The Legal Pos-
ititon of Aliens in National and Interna-
tional Law 1873 (J.Frowein & T. Stein
eds. 1987)--423
Wolf, Fraud and Materiality: Has the Su-
preme Court Redefined Immigration and

Naturalization Fraud?, 62 Temple L.Rev. 481 (1989)--1045

Women and the Workplace: The Implications of Occupational Segregation (M. Blaxall & B. Reagan eds. 1976)--207

Women's Work-- and Wages, Newsweek, July 9, 1984, at 22--207

Wright, Federal Immigration Law and the Case for Open Entry, 27 Loy.-L.A. L.Rev. 1263 (1994)--97

Wyman, D., Paper Walls: America and the Refugee Crisis, 1938-1941 (1968)--735

Yale-Loehr, An Overview of INA § 212(c), 95-2 Imm.Briefings (1995)--711

Yang, Immigrant-Worker Scheme Comes Under Fire, Business Week (Nov. 8, 1993)--247

Yanni, Business Investors: E-2 Nonimmigrants and EB-5 Immigrants, 92-8 Imm.Briefings (1992)--224

Young, Immigrant Worker Scheme Comes Under Fire, Business Week (Nov. 8, 1993)--247

Zolberg, A., A. Suhrke & S. Aguayo, Escape from Violence: Conflict and the Refugee Crisis in the Developing World (1989)--728-30

Zucker, N. & N. Zucker, The Guarded Gate: The Reality of American Refugee Policy--733, 736

Table of Statutes, Rules and Regulations

IMMIGRATION AND NATIONALITY ACT

Sec.	This Work Page
3	689
19	489
	689
Tit. I	930
101—106	929
101(a)(13)	474
	490
	538
101(a)(15)	107
	229
	695
101(a)(15)(B)	231
	260
	379
101(a)(15)(E)	250
101(a)(15)(F)	231
	342
101(a)(15)(H)	247
101(a)(15)(H)(i)(a)	219
101(a)(15)(J)	119
	231
101(a)(15)(L)	930
101(a)(15)(M)	240
101(a)(15)(O)	248
101(a)(15)(P)	248
101(a)(20)	696
101(a)(21)	974
101(a)(22)	974
101(a)(27)(A)	126
	193
	411
	427
101(a)(27)(C)—(a)(27)(J)	129
101(a)(29)	975
101(a)(33)	994
101(a)(42)	738
	743
	744
	764
	770
	860
101(a)(42)(A)	723
	741
	775
	792
	804
	817
	828
101(a)(42)(B)	721

IMMIGRATION AND NATIONALITY ACT

Sec.	This Work Page
101(a)(42)(B) (Cont'd)	741
101(a)(43)	447
	540
	560
	861
101(a)(44)	128
	249
101(a)(45)	259
101(b)	155
101(b)(1)	125
	166
	174
101(b)(1)(B)	160
101(b)(1)(D)	150
	161
	175
101(b)(2)	125
101(b)(4)	107
101(f)	550
	647
	1004
101(f)(6)	1040
	1045
102	229
103	100
	101
	930
103(a)	259
104	101
	116
	367
	368
	424
104(a)(1)	116
104(c)	763
104(d)	763
106	904
	906
	907
	908
	919
	935
	938
	940
	942
	953
	960
	971
106(a)	442

IMMIGRATION AND NATIONALITY ACT

Sec.	This Work Page
106(a) (Cont'd)	907
	908
	909
	915
	916
	919
	920
	924
	925
	926
	928
	930
	931
	933
	934
	941
	957
	959
	960
	971
	972
106(a)(1)	907
	908
	973
106(a)(3)	652
	908
	953
	957
	959
106(a)(4)	612
	908
106(a)(5)	908
	1080
106(a)(6)	958
106(a)(8)	953
106(a)(10)	907
	933
	960
	961
	962
	968
	969
	970
	971
	972
	973
106(b)	906
	930
106(c)	908
	935
	937
	938
	940
	953
	954
	955
	959
112	296
122(b)	195
123(b)	431
Tit. II	930
201	123
	135

IMMIGRATION AND NATIONALITY ACT

Sec.	This Work Page
201—293	929
	968
201(b)	125
	186
201(b)(1)	126
201(b)(1)(B)	132
201(b)(2)(A)	124
	125
201(b)(2)(A)(i)	425
201(b)(2)(B)	126
201(c)	131
201(c)(1)(B)(ii)	131
201(c)(2)	131
201(c)(3)	127
201(d)(2)	127
	131
202	134
	135
	531
202(a)(4)	134
202(b)	134
202(c)(3)(C)	133
202(e)	134
203	123
	135
203(a)	124
	125
	126
	166
203(a)(2)	132
203(a)(7)	737
203(b)	118
	124
	128
	193
	222
	223
203(b)(1)(A)	248
203(b)(1)(C)	249
203(b)(2)	223
203(b)(2)(B)	213
203(b)(3)	223
203(b)(5)	224
203(c)	124
	130
	225
203(c)(1)(E)(v)	135
203(c)(2)	131
203(d)	127
	128
	186
	191
203(e)(2)	131
203(f)	229
204	424
204—206	125
204(a)	129
204(a)(1)	424
204(a)(1)(A)(iii)	187
	425
204(a)(1)(A)(iv)	187
	425
204(a)(1)(B)(ii)	187

IMMIGRATION AND NATIONALITY ACT

Sec.	This Work Page
204(a)(1)(B)(ii) (Cont'd)	425
204(a)(1)(B)(iii)	187
	425
204(a)(1)(D)	129
204(a)(2)	185
204(a)(2)(A)	189
204(b)	129
	194
204(c)	185
204(e)	432
204(g)	185
	443
	444
204(h)	187
207	126
	695
	722
	738
	743
	754
	803
	804
	881
207(b)	742
207(c)	721
	743
207(c)(1)	744
	803
207(c)(3)	743
207(c)(4)	762
208	126
	678
	695
	716
	723
	762
	762
	764
	770
	772
	773
	785
	787
	791
	793
	794
	795
	796
	803
	807
	828
	833
	841
	845
	862
	885
	934
	972
208(b)	762
208(d)	861
208(e)	884
209	126
	738

IMMIGRATION AND NATIONALITY ACT

Sec.	This Work Page
209(a)	743
	744
	762
209(a)(1)	743
209(a)(2)	744
	763
209(b)	762
	763
209(b)(2)	763
209(b)(3)	762
	763
209(b)(4)	803
210	105
	126
	942
210(b)(3)	295
210(c)	295
210(e)	942
	951
210A	126
	296
210A(d)(5)	216
211	424
211(b)	427
211(c)	721
212	193
	340
	341
	379
	487
212(a)	122
	125
	126
	231
	340
	341
	354
	382
	427
	509
	743
212(a)(1)(A)(i)	340
212(a)(1)(A)(iii)	560
212(a)(2)(A)	504
212(a)(2)(A)(i)(II)	501
212(a)(3)	357
	359
	360
	361
	362
212(a)(3)(C)	357
	360
	361
212(a)(3)(D)	357
	527
212(a)(3)(E)	505
	580
212(a)(3)(E)(i)	764
212(a)(4)	371
	425
212(a)(5)(A)	129
	193
212(a)(5)(A)(i)(I)	217

IMMIGRATION AND NATIONALITY ACT

Sec.	This Work Page
212(a)(5)(A)(ii)	195
	213
212(a)(5)(C)	193
212(a)(6)	274
212(a)(6)(A)	432
	507
212(a)(6)(B)	441
	507
	561
	582
	642
212(a)(6)(C)	375
212(a)(6)(C)(i)	375
	378
	379
212(a)(6)(E)	377
	487
212(a)(6)(F)	539
212(a)(7)(A)(i)	706
212(a)(19)	375
212(a)(27)	355
	558
212(a)(27) (former)	357
212(a)(28)	345
	352
212(a)(28) (former)	343
	354
	357
212(a)(28)(D)	345
212(a)(28)(G)(v)	345
212(b)	341
212(c)	341
	504
	536
	654
	689
	690
	691
	694
	695
	696
	697
	704
	708
	709
	711
	716
	972
212(c)—(g)	341
212(d)(3)	340
	341
	345
212(d)(5)	380
	382
212(d)(5)(B)	383
	752
212(e)	119
	723
	816
	928
212(f)	341
212(g)	341
212(g)—(i)	341

IMMIGRATION AND NATIONALITY ACT

Sec.	This Work Page
212(h)	113
	341
212(i)	341
	375
	537
212(k)	341
212(m)	219
212(n)	219
	247
	341
212(o)	442
214	229
	423
214(a)(2)	248
214(b)	229
214(c)	244
	930
214(c)(2)(A)	249
214(c)(2)(B)	249
214(c)(2)(D)	250
214(c)(3)	248
214(c)(4)	248
214(d)	185
214(g)(1)(A)	248
214(g)(1)(B)	245
214(g)(2)	245
	248
214(g)(4)	248
214(i)	246
216	184
	185
	186
	189
	216
	224
216(b)(1)	184
216(b)(1)(A)(i)	189
216(b)(2)	184
216(c)	184
216(c)(2)	184
216(c)(3)	185
216(c)(4)	184
	185
	187
	188
216(c)(4)(A)	187
216(c)(4)(B)	187
	188
216(c)(4)(C)	187
216(d)(1)	184
216(e)	184
216A	129
	216
	224
216A(d)(1)	224
217	270
	423
217(b)(4)	627
218(a)(1)	243
218(b)(3)	244
218(b)(4)	243
218(c)(4)	244
221	115

IMMIGRATION AND NATIONALITY ACT

Sec.	This Work Page
221 (Cont'd)	424
221(a)—(b)	423
221(f)—(h)	423
221(g)	379
221(h)	340
	422
	432
222	115
	424
222(c)—(f)	423
222(f)	118
223	427
231—240	427
234	118
235	427
	474
235(b)	107
	431
	432
	448
235(c)	402
	403
	404
	411
	629
	766
235(d)	433
236	427
	474
236(a)	107
	108
236(b)	112
236(c)	901
236(d)	118
236(e)	447
237	448
237(a)	422
237(a)(1)	475
237(a)(2)	475
241	512
	535
	560
	697
241(a)	474
	527
	529
	536
241(a)(1)	274
	714
241(a)(1)(A)	36
	432
	504
	536
	537
	538
241(a)(1)(B)	537
	538
	539
	706
241(a)(1)(C)(i)	537
	539
241(a)(1)(D)	184
241(a)(1)(E)	486

IMMIGRATION AND NATIONALITY ACT

Sec.	This Work Page
241(a)(1)(E) (Cont'd)	717
241(a)(1)(H)	537
	717
241(a)(2)(A)	36
	542
	570
	628
241(a)(2)(A)(i)	500
	542
	544
	551
	580
241(a)(2)(A)(i)(1)	504
241(a)(2)(A)(ii)	542
	544
	551
241(a)(2)(A)(iii)	560
241(a)(2)(A)(iv)	570
241(a)(2)(B)	603
241(a)(2)(B)(i)	504
	559
	570
	697
241(a)(2)(B)(ii)	560
241(a)(2)(C)	534
	560
241(a)(3)(C)	539
241(a)(4)	527
	531
241(a)(4)(B)	530
	531
	629
241(a)(4)(D)	36
	505
	534
	572
	579
	580
	764
	808
241(a)(5)	339
	972
241(a)(11)(B)	599
	601
241(a)(19)	764
	764
241(a)(19) (former)	763
241(b)	552
241(b) (repealed)	540
242	592
	930
242(a)	475
	589
	876
242(a)(2)	540
	590
	591
242(b)	108
	109
	580
	596
	597
	606

IMMIGRATION AND NATIONALITY ACT

Sec.	This Work Page
242(b) (Cont'd)	612
	642
	643
	901
	904
	916
	919
	920
	921
	924
	972
242(c)	448
	475
242(d)	475
242(f)	582
	627
	642
242(i)	540
	627
242(j)	287
	541
242A	540
	627
242A(b)	540
	627
	628
242A(d)	716
242A(d)(2)	716
242B	589
	595
242B(a)	587
242B(b)(1)	587
242B(c)	908
242B(c)(4)	908
242B(e)	642
	653
242B(e)(4)	863
243(a)	475
	685
	927
243(h)	474
	475
	486
	580
	597
	678
	716
	723
	761
	763
	764
	770
	771
	772
	785
	786
	787
	791
	793
	794
	795
	797
	803

IMMIGRATION AND NATIONALITY ACT

Sec.	This Work Page
243(h) (Cont'd)	807
	828
	833
	841
	845
	862
	880
	885
	929
243(h)(2)	763
	764
	795
	860
	861
243(h)(2)(A)	763
	764
	860
243(h)(2)(B)	862
243(h)(2)(C)	860
244	171
	475
	504
	653
	654
	656
	658
	662
	666
	667
	676
	677
	678
	681
	685
	688
	694
	697
	764
	895
	901
	920
	972
244(a)	653
	697
	716
244(a)(1)	501
	550
	654
	655
	657
244(a)(2)	654
	655
	716
244(b)(2)	501
	654
244(c)(2)	920
	921
244(e)	550
	580
	642
	643
	647
	716

IMMIGRATION AND NATIONALITY ACT

Sec.	This Work Page
244(e)(2)	560
	642
244(f)	653
244A	894
	895
244A(c)(4)	501
244A(e)	654
244A(h)	894
245	125
	126
	186
	214
	424
	433
	434
	440
	441
	444
	475
	679
	704
	919
	934
245(a)	440
	442
245(b)	439
245(c)	442
245(c)(1)	440
245(c)(2)	440
245(c)(3)	440
245(c)(4)	440
245(d)	185
245(d)—(f)	442
245(e)	185
	443
245(e)(3)	185
	444
245(i)	440
	441
	442
	443
245A	105
	126
	295
	889
	950
245A(a)(3)(B)	501
245A(f)(1)	950
	951
245A(h)	339
246	110
	444
	919
246(a)	444
248	233
	422
	423
249	712
	713
	716
252(b)	627
261—266	426
262	617

IMMIGRATION AND NATIONALITY ACT

Sec.	This Work Page
264(d)	426
266	617
273	116
	422
	486
273(d)	433
274	486
	552
274—277	474
274A	115
	298
	299
274A(b)	300
274A(e)	298
274A(h)(2)	337
274A(j)—(n)	305
274B	115
	298
	299
274B(a)	298
274B(a)(2)	299
274B(a)(3)(B)(i)	307
274B(a)(4)	299
274B(a)(5)	307
274B(a)(6)	300
	307
274B(c)	115
274B(d)(2)	299
274B(e)—(h)	299
274B(g)(2)(B)	307
274B(i)	299
274B(k)	305
274B(l)	307
274C	115
	274
	539
	540
275	476
	510
	616
	617
275(a)	274
275(b)	185
275(c)	224
276	274
	582
	617
	642
	907
279	442
	929
	930
	931
	933
	934
	972
279(a)	938
287(a)	587
	620
287(a)(5)	621
287(e)	623
291	379
	474
	475

IMMIGRATION AND NATIONALITY ACT

Sec.	This Work Page
291 (Cont'd)	510
	613
	614
	615
292	597
301	296
301(b)	991
301(c)	993
	994
301(d)	993
301(e)	993
301(g)	993
	994
301(h)	993
	995
303(a)	894
308(2)	993
308(4)	993
309	993
310	1000
310(b)	1001
310(c)	1001
311	991
311—331	1002
312	1002
312(b)	1004
313	581
	1002
315(c)	1006
316	1002
316(a)	550
318	1000
319	1007
322	1003
	1007
324(d)	995
328	1007
329	1007
331—334	1000
332(h)	1001
335	1000
	1001
336	1000
336(a)	1001
336(b)	1001
337	995
	1002
	1082
337—348	1000
337(a)	1007
340(a)	1015
	1035
	1045
	1079
	1081
349(a)(1)	1082
349(a)(4)	1078
349(a)(5)	1079
349(a)(6)	1079
349(a)(16)	1076
351(a)	1079

IMMIGRATION AND NATIONALITY ACT

Sec.	This Work Page
356	1077
358	1080
360(a)	1080
360(b)	1080
360(c)	1080
411—414	744
	886
505	540
541(a)(3)	538
545(c)	658
545(d)	658
	958
601(c)	361
701(a)(2)	928

UNITED STATES

UNITED STATES CONSTITUTION

Art.	This Work Page
I	8
I, § 8, cl. 3	8
I, § 8, cl. 4	9
	974
I, § 8, cl. 11	10
I, § 9, cl. 1	10
I, § 9, cl. 2	902

Amend.	
1	15
	344
	352
	353
	356
	361
	514
	527
	528
	529
	530
	531
4	15
	587
	617
	620
	621
	622
	623
	626
	627
	975
5	15
	19
	20
	460
	461
	464
	528
	583
	587
	590
	598

UNITED STATES CONSTITUTION

Sec.	This Work Page
5 (Cont'd)	616
	617
	689
	1061
	1062
	1080
6	15
	528
	571
	583
	598
	1061
8	1060
10	4
14	3
	19
	20
	612
	989
	990
	991
	993
	1068
14, § 1	41

UNITED STATES CODE ANNOTATED

5 U.S.C.A.—Government Organization and Employees

Sec.	This Work Page
552	114
553	114
	904
556(e)	873
701	685
	687
701—706	362
	903
701(a)(2)	927
702	900
	928
703	900
704	934
706	687
3105	900
5372	900
7521	900

7 U.S.C.A.—Agriculture

Sec.	This Work Page
2014(i)	374
2015(f)	283

8 U.S.C.A.—Aliens and Nationality

Sec.	This Work Page
1153 note	124
1201a	427

UNITED STATES CODE ANNOTATED

8 U.S.C.A.—Aliens and Nationality

Sec.	This Work Page
1255b	723

15 U.S.C.A.—Commerce and Trade

Sec.	This Work Page
1	551

18 U.S.C.A.—Crimes and Criminal Procedure

Sec.	This Work Page
16	560
16(b)	560
3583(d)	628
3607	570

19 U.S.C.A.—Customs and Duties

Sec.	This Work Page
2432	751

22 U.S.C.A.—Foreign Relations and Intercourse

Sec.	This Work Page
8	722
2691 (repealed)	355

28 U.S.C.A.—Judiciary and Judicial Procedure

Sec.	This Work Page
1331	928
	929
	930
	931
	933
	934
	972
1331(a)	938
1343	923
2201	903
	1080
2241	970
	971
2241 et seq.	902
	907
2412	952
Ch. 158	907

42 U.S.C.A.—The Public Health and Welfare

Sec.	This Work Page
615	374
1382c	283
1392j	374

UNITED STATES CODE ANNOTATED

42 U.S.C.A.—The Public Health and Welfare

Sec.	This Work Page
2000e–2	298

50 U.S.C.A.—War and National Defense

Sec.	This Work Page
21—23	10
	511

STATUTES AT LARGE

Year	This Work Page
1798, June 25, c. 58, 1 Stat. 570	511
1798, July 6, c. 66, 1 Stat. 577	511
1807, Mar. 2, c. 22, 2 Stat. 426	10
1870, May 31, c. 114, § 16, 16 Stat. 144	3
1868, July 28, c. __, 16 Stat. 739	3
1875, Mar. 3, c. 141, 18 Stat. 477	2
1875, Mar. 3, c. 141, § 5, 18 Stat. 477	542
	759
1880, Nov. 17, 22 Stat. 826	4
1882, May 6, c. 126, 22 Stat. 58	4
1882, Aug. 3, c. 376, 22 Stat. 214	2
1882, Aug. 3, c. 376, § 2, 22 Stat. 214	370
1882, Aug. 3, c. 376, § 4, 22 Stat. 214	759
1885, Feb. 26, c. 164, 23 Stat. 332	192
	511
1887, Feb. 23, c. 220, 24 Stat. 414	192
	511
1888, Oct. 19, c. 1210, 25 Stat. 566	511
1891, Mar. 3, c. 551, § 1, 26 Stat. 1084	542
	760
1891, Mar. 3, c. 551, § 11, 26 Stat. 1086	512
	536
1892, May 5, c. 60, 27 Stat. 25	21
	37
1903, Mar. 3, c. 1012, § 2, 32 Stat. 1219	514
1903, Mar. 3, c. 1012, § 20, 32 Stat. 1218	582
1907, Feb. 20, c. 1134, 34 Stat. 898	760

STATUTES AT LARGE

Year	This Work Page
1907, Feb. 20, c. 1134, § 2, 34 Stat. 899	760
1907, Feb. 20, c. 1134, § 3, 34 Stat. 899–900	512
1907, Feb. 20, c. 1134, § 20, 34 Stat. 904	582
1917, Feb. 5, c. 29, 39 Stat. 874	760
1917, Feb. 5, c. 29, § 3, 39 Stat. 877	760
1917, Feb. 5, c. 29, § 19, 39 Stat. 889	515
	543
	582
1917, May 10, c. 174, § 1, 41 Stat. 593	533
1918, Oct. 16, c. 186, § 1, 40 Stat. 1012	515
1920, June 5, c. 251, § 1, 41 Stat. 1008	515
1934, Mar. 24, c. 84, § 8, 48 Stat. 462	975
1940, Oct. 14, c. 439, 54 Stat. 1137	518
1946, June 11, c. 404, 60 Stat. 237	900
1948, May 25, c. 338, § 1, 62 Stat. 268	526
1948, June 25, c. 647, 62 Stat. 1009	736
1950, Sept. 23, c. 1024, 64 Stat. 987	581
	760
1950, Sept. 23, c. 1024, Tit. I, 64 Stat. 987	526
1950, Sept. 23, c. 1024, 64 Stat. 1006	532
1950, Sept. 23, c. 1024, § 22, 64 Stat. 1006	526
1950, Sept. 23, c. 1024, § 23, 64 Stat. 1006	760
1950, Sept. 27, c. 1052, 64 Stat. 1048	592
1951 Mar. 28, c. 23, § 1, 65 Stat. 28	526
1952, June 27, c. 414, 66 Stat. 163	653
1952, June 27, c. 414, 66 Stat. 214	653
1953, Aug. 9, c. 336, 67 Stat. 400	736
1957, Sept. 11, P.L. 85–316, 71 Stat. 639	736
1957, Sept. 11, P.L. 85–316, § 13, 71 Stat. 642	723
1957, Sept. 11, P.L. 85–316, § 15, 71 Stat. 643–44	736
1958, July 25, P.L. 85–559, 72 Stat. 419	736
1960, July 14, P.L. 86–648, 74 Stat. 504	736
1961, Sept. 26, P.L. 87–301, § 5, 75 Stat. 651	906
1965, Oct. 1, P.L. 89–236,	

STATUTES AT LARGE

Year	This Work Page
79 Stat. 911	737
1965, Oct. 1, P.L. 89–236, § 3, 79 Stat. 913	737
1966, Nov. 2, P.L. 89–732, 80 Stat. 1161	736
	896
1976, Oct. 21, P.L. 94–574, § 2, 90 Stat. 2721	928
1978, Oct. 10, P.L. 95–432, 92 Stat. 1046	995
1980, Mar. 17, P.L. 96–212, 94 Stat. 102	722
1980, Dec. 1, P.L. 96–486, § 2(a), 94 Stat. 2369	928
1986, Nov. 6, P.L. 99–603, 100 Stat. 3359	62
	115
	627
1986, Nov. 6, P.L. 99–603, § 202, 100 Stat. 3359	889
1986, Nov. 6, P.L. 99–603, § 314, 100 Stat. 3359	130
1986, Nov. 6, P.L. 99–603, § 701, 100 Stat. 3445	627
1986, Nov. 10, P.L. 99–639, 100 Stat. 3537	62
	176
	184
1986, Nov. 14, P.L. 99–653, 100 Stat. 3655	1079
1987, Dec. 2, P.L. 100–204, § 901, 101 Stat. 1399	357
1988, Oct. 1, P.L. 100–461, § 555, 102 Stat. 2268	357
1988, Oct. 24, P.L. 100–525, 102 Stat. 2609	653
1988, Oct. 24, P.L. 100–525, § 2(q), 102 Stat. 2613	653
1988, Nov. 15, P.L. 100–658, § 2, 102 Stat. 3908	130
1988, Nov. 18, P.L. 100–690, 102 Stat. 4181	540
1988, Nov. 18, P.L. 100–690, § 1751(b), 102 Stat. 4181	559
1988, Nov. 18, P.L. 100–690, § 7347, 102 Stat. 4181	627
1989, Nov. 21, P.L. 101–167, 103 Stat. 1195	63
	753
1989, Nov. 21, P.L. 101–167, § 599D, 103 Stat. 1261	63
	753
1989, Nov. 21, P.L. 101–167, § 599E, 103 Stat. 1263	753
1989, Dec. 18, P.L. 101–238, 103 Stat. 2099	219
	245
1990, Feb. 16, P.L. 101–246, § 128, 104 Stat. 15	357
1990, Nov. 29, P.L. 101–649, 104 Stat. 4978	62
	123
1990, Nov. 29, P.L. 101–649, § 132, 104 Stat. 5000	124

STATUTES AT LARGE

Year	This Work Page
1991, Oct. 28, P.L. 102–138, § 127, 105 Stat. 647	361
1991, Oct. 28, P.L. 102–138, § 128, 105 Stat. 647	361
1991, Dec. 10, P.L. 100–204, § 902, 101 Stat. 1331	889
1992, Oct. 9, P.L. 102–404, 106 Stat. 1969	136
	817
	888
	240
1993, Dec. 8, P.L. 103–182, 107 Stat. 2057	270
1994, Feb. 12, P.L. 103–211, § 403, 108 Stat. 3	284
1994, Apr. 30, P.L. 103–236, 108 Stat. 382	754
1994, Apr. 30, P.L. 103–236, § 512, 108 Stat. 466	754
1994, Sept. 13, P.L. 103–322, 108 Stat. 1796	187
	287
	318
	541
	542
	582
	627
1994, Sept. 13, P.L. 103–322, § 130001, 108 Stat. 2023	582
1994, Sept. 13, P.L. 103–322, § 130002, 108 Stat. 2023	541
1994, Sept. 13, P.L. 103–322, § 130004, 108 Stat. 2026–27	627
1994, Sept. 13, P.L. 103–322, § 130006, 108 Stat. 2028–29	318
1994, Sept. 13, P.L. 103–322, § 130007, 108 Stat. 2029	541
1994, Sept. 13, P.L. 103–322, § 20301, 108 Stat. 1824	287
	542
1994, Oct. 25, P.L. 103–416, 108 Stat. 4305	716
1994, Oct. 25, P.L. 103–416, 108 Stat. 4321	561
1994, Oct. 25, P.L. 103–416, 108 Stat. 4305	628
1994, Oct. 25, P.L. 103–416, § 101(b)—(d), 108 Stat. 4305	995
1994, Oct. 25, P.L. 103–416, § 222, 108 Stat. 4305	561
1994, Oct. 25, P.L. 103–416, § 223, 108 Stat. 4322	628
1994, Oct. 25, P.L. 103–416, § 224, 108 Stat. 4322–23	716

POPULAR NAME ACTS

ADMINISTRATIVE PROCEDURE ACT

Sec.	This Work Page
10(c)	934
554	598
701	685
706	685

CIVIL RIGHTS ACT OF 1964

Tit.	This Work Page
VII	205
	298
	299

IMMIGRATION REFORM AND CONTROL ACT

Sec.	This Work Page
5	185

SECURITIES ACT OF 1934

Sec.	This Work Page
704	958

SHERMAN ANTITRUST ACT

Sec.	This Work Page
1	551

SOCIAL SECURITY ACT

Tit.	This Work Page
XX	284

EXECUTIVE ORDERS

No.	This Work Page
12711	888
12711, § 4	817
12807	880

CODE OF FEDERAL REGULATIONS

Tit.	This Work Page
1, § 305.85–4	899
8, § 1.1(*l*)	109
8, § 2.1	596
8, § 3.1(a)(1)	112
8, § 3.1(b)	114
8, § 3.1(b)(1)	112
8, § 3.1(b)(2)	112
8, § 3.1(b)(4)	113
8, § 3.1(b)(5)	113
8, § 3.1(b)(6)	113
8, § 3.1(b)(7)	113
8, § 3.1(b)(9)	113
8, § 3.1(h)	114
8, § 3.1(h)(1)(ii)	697
8, § 3.2	658
	659
	662
	663
	697
	953

CODE OF FEDERAL REGULATIONS

Tit.	This Work Page
	957
8, § 3.3(a)	953
	957
8, § 3.4	953
	957
8, § 3.6(a)	652
8, § 3.8(a)	658
8, §§ 3.12–3.41	110
8, § 3.19(b)	588
8, § 3.23(b)	957
8, § 3.23(b)(2)	957
8, § 103.1(f)	114
8, § 103.1(f)(2)(ii)	113
8, § 103.1(f)(2)(vi)	113
8, § 103.1(f)(2)(x)	113
8, § 103.3(c)	114
8, § 103.4	114
8, § 103.5	957
8, § 103.5(a)	658
8, § 103.6(a)(2)(ii)	589
8, § 103.9(a)	114
8, Pt. 108	929
8, § 204.2(c)	161
8, § 204.5(g)—(*l*)	213
8, § 204.5(h)	223
8, § 204.5(k)	223
8, § 204.5(k)(4)(ii)	213
8, § 205.1	424
8, § 205.1(a)(3)	424
8, § 207.1(b)	744
8, Pt. 208	762
	818
8, § 208.1(b)	765
8, § 208.1(c)	765
8, § 208.2(b)	113
	765
8, § 208.3	764
8, § 208.4	764
8, § 208.4(c)(4)	765
8, § 208.6	767
8, § 208.7	766
	869
	883
8, § 208.8(f)(1)	795
8, § 208.9	764
8, § 208.10	869
8, § 208.11	872
8, § 208.12	872
8, § 208.12(a)	765
	827
8, § 208.13	791
8, § 208.13(a)	864
8, § 208.13(b)(1)	793
8, § 208.13(b)(1)(i)	792
8, § 208.13(b)(1)(ii)	793
8, § 208.13(b)(2)	791
8, § 208.13(c)	860
8, § 208.14	796
	860
8, § 208.14(b)	766
8, § 208.14(b)(3)	766
8, § 208.14(b)(4)	766
8, § 208.14(d)(2)	803
8, § 208.14(e)	804

CODE OF FEDERAL REGULATIONS

Tit.	This Work Page
8, § 208.15	803
8, § 208.16	791
8, § 208.16(b)	864
8, § 208.16(c)(2)(i)	860
8, § 208.16(c)(2)(ii)	862
8, § 208.16(c)(4)	795
8, § 208.18(b)	113
	766
8, § 211.1(b)	411
	427
8, § 211.5	193
8, § 212.1(a)	423
8, § 212.5	382
	448
	876
8, § 212.5(a)	449
8, § 212.6	423
8, § 212.6(a)	423
8, § 212.8(b)	224
8, § 212.12	467
8, §§ 212.12–212.13	472
8, § 212.13	467
8, § 214.2(b)(5)	269
8, § 214.2(e)(1)	250
8, § 214.2(f)(15)	239
8, § 214.2(h)(4)(iii)(C)(4)	246
8, § 214.2(h)(6)(ii)	245
8, § 214.2(h)(6)(iv)	244
8, § 214.2(h)(8)	248
8, § 214.2(h)(9)(iii)	248
8, § 214.2(h)(9)(iii)(C)	245
8, § 214.2(h)(15)(ii)(B)	248
8, § 214.2(h)(15)(ii)(C)	245
8, § 214.2(h)(16)	248
8, § 214.2(j)(1)(v)	239
8, § 214.2(l)(1)(ii)(G)	249
8, § 214.2(l)(3)(v)	249
8, § 214.2(l)(3)(vi)	249
8, § 214.2(l)(7)	250
8, § 214.2(l)(15)(ii)	250
8, § 214.2(l)(16)	250
8, § 214.2(o)(13)	248
8, § 214.2(p)(15)	248
8, § 214.6(d)(7)(i)	270
8, Pt. 215	110
8, § 216.4	184
8, § 216.5	184
8, Pt. 217	423
8, § 217.7(a)	113
8, § 235.1(f)	423
8, § 235.1(g)	423
8, § 235.3	448
	876
8, § 236.2(c)	109
8, § 242.1	587
8, § 242.1(c)	587
	617
8, § 242.2	588
8, § 242.2(b)	588
8, § 242.2(c)(2)	617
8, § 242.2(h)	588
8, § 242.5(a)(1)	642
8, § 242.5(a)(2)(vi)(C)	643
8, § 242.5(a)(3)	643

CODE OF FEDERAL REGULATIONS

Tit.	This Work Page
8, § 242.9	109
	597
8, § 242.16(a)	597
8, § 242.16(c)	109
	597
8, § 242.17(a)	639
8, § 242.17(b)	642
8, § 242.21	112
8, § 242.22	658
	957
8, § 242.24	591
8, § 243.4	652
	658
	915
	957
8, § 244.1	642
8, § 245.1(c)(2)	440
8, § 245.2(a)(4)	441
	475
8, § 245.2(a)(5)(ii)	113
8, § 245a.4	889
8, § 245a.5	339
8, Pt. 246	444
8, § 248.3(g)	113
8, § 253.1(f)	766
8, Pt. 264	426
8, Pt. 274a	299
8, § 274a.9	298
8, § 274a.12	298
8, § 274a.12(a)(11)	885
8, § 287.3	587
	617
	639
8, Pt. 292	605
8, § 292.1(a)(2)	597
8, § 292.3(3)	180
8, § 316.4	581
8, § 316.11	581
8, § 336.2(b)	1001
8, § 656.30(a)	217
20, § 416.1618	284
20, § 655.102(b)(4)	244
20, § 655.102(b)(5)	244
20, § 655.102(b)(9)	244
20, § 655.102(d)	243
20, § 655.103(d)	243
20, § 655.103(f)	243
20, § 655.105	243
20, § 655.107	244
20, Pt. 656	194
	213
20, § 656.3	208
20, § 656.10	194
20, § 656.11	195
20, §§ 656.20–656.21	195
20, § 656.20(g)	195
20, § 656.20(h)	195
20, § 656.21(b)(2)	204
20, § 656.21a	195
20, § 656.22	194
20, § 656.23	195
20, §§ 656.24–656.25	195
20, § 656.26	118
20, §§ 656.26–656.27	196

CODE OF FEDERAL REGULATIONS

Tit.	This Work Page
20, § 656.27	118
20, § 656.30(c)	218
20, § 656.40	195
	206
22, Pt. 7	1080
22, § 7.3	1080
22, § 7.6	1080
22, Pt. 40	421
22, Pts. 40–53	118
22, Pt. 41	421
22, § 41.2	423
22, § 41.31(b)	269
22, § 41.31(b)(1)	260
22, § 41.51	259
22, § 41.121(c)	116
	368
22, Pt. 42	424
22, § 42.61	441
22, § 42.65(b)	425
22, § 42.81	426
22, § 42.81(c)	116
	368
22, § 50.41	1080
22, § 50.42	1080
22, § 50.50	1079
22, § 50.52	1080
28, Pt. 44	115
	299
28, § 44.200(a)(1)	299
28, Pt. 68	115
	298
28, § 68.53(b)	299
45, § 1626.4	597
45, § 1626.11	597

FEDERAL REGISTER

Vol.	This Work Page
32, p. 6260	618
34, p. 70621	761
37, p. 3447	761
42, p. 3440	194
44, p. 4652	618
44, p. 4654	618
44, pp. 36187–93	679
44, p. 65728	539
44, p. 75165	539
45, p. 83926	194
46, p. 9119	679
46, p. 25599	539
46, p. 48107	878
46, p. 48109	878
47, p. 30044	448
	876
47, p. 46493	876

FEDERAL REGISTER

Vol.	This Work Page
48, p. 8038	110
48, p. 8056	110
48, p. 43160	113
51, p. 34439	105
51, p. 44266	269
52, p. 5738	249
52, p. 5739	249
52, pp. 11217–11218	196
52, p. 48884	466
53, p. 2893	872
53, p. 15659	112
53, p. 21405	742
53, p. 45249	742
53, p. 52520	466
54, p. 861	105
54, p. 31493	742
54, p. 36753	161
54, p. 47586	426
54, p. 53493	117
	370
54, p. 53496	368
55, p. 2803	817
55, p. 13897	817
	888
55, p. 30674	63
	722
	764
55, p. 51778	467
56, p. 1566	12
56, p. 2484	340
56, p. 12745	895
56, p. 33371	239
57, p. 23133	880
58, p. 32157	895
58, p. 40024	270
58, p. 58982	270
58, pp. 61846–61850	322
59, p. 9997	895
59, p. 15298	130
59, p. 17920	225
59, pp. 26587–26593	224
59, p. 29368	958
59, p. 29386	659
	697
59, p. 29387	662
59, p. 29388	697
59, p. 29440	896
59, p. 47231	112
59, p. 51091	442
59, p. 62284	63
	722
	765
59, p. 62751	643
	895
59, p. 65646	247

IMMIGRATION:

PROCESS AND POLICY

Third Edition

*

Chapter One

FOUNDATIONS OF THE IMMIGRATION POWER

SECTION A. THE SOURCES OF THE FEDERAL IMMIGRATION POWER

This casebook will attempt to familiarize you with an exceedingly complex statute, the Immigration and Nationality Act, as well as expose you to current debates on American immigration and refugee law and policy. These debates are largely about how many and what kind of immigrants the United States should permit to enter each year. What the debates take for granted is the power of the Congress to enact laws that regulate which aliens may enter the United States and under what conditions those that enter may remain. It is with this issue—the source of Congress' immigration power—that we begin this book.

You may find it curious that the source of Congress' power could be an interesting question. Surely the Framers would have endowed Congress explicitly with a power as important as that of controlling immigration. Yet the Constitution of the United States includes no language that expressly grants Congress such authority. The Supreme Court did not address the question until the second century of this country's existence, primarily because Congress did not enact significant limits on immigration until the 1880's. For most of the nineteenth century, Congress permitted open borders in an attempt to provide the developing nation with labor and capital. What "immigration law" existed was the creation of the states. Many had laws that the modern eye may not readily recognize as immigration laws because they often restricted entry by other states' citizens as well by foreigners, and because they regulated specific concerns, for example public health. In substance, however, these laws had much in common with modern immigration laws. *See* Neuman, *The Lost Century of Immigration Law (1776–1875)*, 93 Colum. L. Rev. 1833 (1993).

Chinese Immigration

The first federal statutes limiting immigration, enacted in 1875 and 1882, prohibited the entry of criminals, prostitutes, idiots, lunatics, and persons likely to become a public charge. Act of March 3, 1875, Ch. 141, 18 Stat. 477; Act of August 3, 1882, Ch. 376, 22 Stat. 214. In 1882, 1884, 1888 and 1892, Congress enacted the so-called "Chinese exclusion laws," and these became the first federal immigration statutes to be subjected to judicial scrutiny. These statutes—like many later immigration laws—were the product of economic and political concerns laced with racism and nativism.

Large-scale Chinese immigration into the United States began during the California gold rush of 1848. Chinese laborers were also sought to help construct the Central Pacific Railroad, built between 1864 and 1869. In a time of labor shortage, the Chinese were welcomed on the West Coast.

With the end of the gold rush and the arrival of European immigrants in California due to the completion of the transcontinental railroad, the demand for, and toleration of, Chinese laborers declined. The Panic of 1873, drought and the depression of 1877 fostered extreme anti-alien fervor in the West. Nativist groups demanded legislation to force the Chinese out of California. Of particular note was the Workingmen's Party of California, led by fireballer Dennis Kearney. The Party's Manifesto, published in 1876, stated:

> To an American death is preferable to a life on a par with the Chinaman * * *. Treason is better than to labor beside a Chinese slave * * *. The people are about to take their own affairs into their own hands and they will not be stayed either by * * * state militia, [or] United States Troops.

Throughout the 1870's the Chinese were subject to virulent and often violent attacks. The Chinese were accused of being criminals, prostitutes and opium addicts, while at the same time they were assailed for their willingness to perform hard work at low wages. Justice Field, who had served as a Justice on the California Supreme Court before joining the United States Supreme Court in 1863, described the prevailing view of Chinese laborers as follows:

> [The Chinese laborers] were generally industrious and frugal. Not being accompanied by families, except in rare instances, their expenses were small; and they were content with the simplest fare, such as would not suffice for our laborers and artisans. The competition between them and our people was for this reason altogether in their favor, and the consequent irritation, proportionately deep and bitter, was followed, in many cases, by open conflicts, to the great disturbance of the public peace.
>
> The differences of race added greatly to the difficulties of the situation. * * * [T]hey remained strangers in the land, residing apart by themselves, and adhering to the customs and usages of their own country. It seemed impossible for them to assimilate

with our people or to make any change in their habits or modes of living. As they grew in numbers each year the people of the coast saw, or believed they saw, in the facility of immigration, and in the crowded millions of China, where population presses upon the means of subsistence, great danger that at no distant day that portion of our country would be overrun by them unless prompt action was taken to restrict their immigration.

Chinese Exclusion Case, 130 U.S. 581, 595, 9 S.Ct. 623, 626, 32 L.Ed. 1068 (1889). *See generally* B. Hing, Making and Remaking Asian America Through Immigration Policy, 1850–1990, at 19–26 (1993); R. Takaki, Strangers from a Different Shore: A History of Asian Americans 79–131 (1989).

The Chinese had been the victims of discriminatory legislation in California since the 1850's. They were subjected to entry, license and occupation taxes, originally to raise money for the California treasury and later as a means to deter immigration. Chinese were not allowed to vote, denied the right to testify in court and prohibited from attending public schools with white children. Most of these statutes were declared invalid, either as a violation of the Fourteenth Amendment or as conflicting with federal treaties.[1]

Federal Regulation of Chinese Immigration

At first, the federal government had welcomed Chinese immigration. Based on the desires to improve trade with China and provide cheap labor for completion of the railroads, the United States negotiated the Burlingame Treaty. July 28, 1868, United States–China, 16 Stat. 739, T.S. No. 48. The Treaty recognized "the inherent and inalienable right of man to change his home and allegiance, and also the mutual advantage of free migration and emigration of [American and Chinese] citizens * * * for purposes of curiosity, of trade or as permanent residents." It therefore guaranteed citizens of one country visiting or residing in the other "the same privileges, immunities and exemptions * * * as may be enjoyed by the citizens or subjects of the most favored nation."

The restrictionist and racist tide in California began to have an impact in national politics by the mid–1870's.[2] The demand for federal legislation

---

1. *See, e.g., Ho Ah Kow v. Nunan,* 5 Sawyer 552 (C.C.D.Cal.1879) (Mr. Justice Field on circuit) (invalidating San Francisco's "Queue Ordinance" which required that all prisoners have their hair cut to a maximum length of one inch); *People v. Downer,* 7 Cal. 170 (1857) (invalidating $50 tax on Chinese passengers); *Ling Sing v. Washburn,* 20 Cal. 534 (1862) (voiding capitation tax on Chinese). *See generally* M. Coolidge, Chinese Immigration (1909); McClain, *The Chinese Struggle for Civil Rights in Nineteenth Century America: The First Phase, 1850–1870,* 72 Cal.L.Rev. 529 (1984).

2. Although federal legislation grew increasingly restrictionist in the last quarter of the nineteenth century, it is interesting that the Reconstruction Congress enacted legislation that extended protection to Chinese immigrants against discrimination. Section 16 of the Voting Rights Act of 1870, 16 Stat. 144, guaranteed *"all persons"* the "same right to make and enforce contracts, to sue, be parties, give evidence, and to the full and equal benefits of all laws and proceedings for the security of persons and property as is enjoyed by white citizens * * *." Other provisions in the civil rights laws had defined the protected class simply as "citizens." The

was due, in part, to the court decisions that had struck down California statutes as unlawful discrimination against the Chinese. Adopting restrictionist legislation, however, would have threatened a breach of the spirit, if not the letter, of the Burlingame Treaty. Accordingly, Congress authorized a diplomatic trip to China to renegotiate the Treaty. A supplemental treaty was signed in November 1880. Treaty of November 17, 1880, United States–China, 22 Stat. 826, T.S. No. 49.

The Treaty of 1880 authorized the United States to "regulate, limit or suspend" immigration of Chinese laborers whenever their entry or residence in the United States "affects or threatens to affect the interests of that country, or to endanger the good order of [the United States] or of any locality within the territory thereof." The Treaty expressly stated that the authority to suspend immigration applied only to Chinese *laborers,* and that the suspension power did not include the authority to "absolutely prohibit" immigration. Importantly, the Treaty preserved the right of Chinese laborers already within the United States "to go and come of their own free will and accord."

Within a year of the ratification of the Treaty, Congress enacted the first of the Chinese exclusion laws. The Act of May 6, 1882, Ch. 126, 22 Stat. 58, suspended the immigration of Chinese laborers for 10 years. The statute did not alter the right of Chinese laborers who were residing in the United States at the time the Treaty was signed to leave and return to the United States. To help effectuate the suspension of new immigration without limiting the ability of resident Chinese to leave and return, the Act established a procedure for the issuance of "certificates of identity" which would entitle Chinese laborers to re-enter the United States after a trip abroad.

The certificate system created by the 1882 Act was not mandatory and led to dissatisfaction. It was claimed that Chinese arriving for the first time persuaded officials that they were returning to a prior lawful residence in the United States. Congress sought to prevent evasion of the 1882 Act by enacting legislation in 1884 which rendered the certificate "the only evidence permissible to establish [the alien's] right of entry."

The federal legislation did not end anti-Chinese agitation in the West. In 1885 and 1886, brutal violence against Chinese occurred in California, Washington and Oregon. In Rock Spring, Wyoming, a mob of white miners attacked Chinese who had refused to join a strike; 28 Chinese were killed.

The United States government again sought to modify the Burlingame Treaty, signing a treaty in 1888 which would have prohibited the immigration of Chinese laborers for an additional twenty years. When rumors reached Washington that China was not likely to ratify the treaty,[3] Congress passed a statute on October 1, 1888, that prohibited the return of all Chinese laborers who had left the United States, even if they had obtained a certificate before their departure under the procedure established by the

---

use of the phrase "all persons" was intended to bring Chinese aliens within the law's protection. *See* McClain, *supra* note 2; *Runyon v. McCrary,* 427 U.S. 160, 195–201, 96 S.Ct. 2586, 2606–09, 49 L.Ed.2d 415 (1976) (White, J., dissenting).

3. *See* Tien–La Li, Congressional Policy of Chinese Immigration 53–66 (1916).

1882 and 1884 Acts. It further provided that no more certificates would be issued. The statute stranded Chinese in China who had been residents of the United States. It also effectively prevented Chinese then residing in the United States from returning home for a visit: since no more certificates would be issued, once they left the United States they would not be able to re-enter. The statute thus conflicted with the provisions of the Burlingame Treaty and the Treaty of 1880 which had guaranteed the right of aliens "to go and come of their own free will."

Chae Chan Ping was a Chinese laborer who had entered the United States in 1875. He lived in San Francisco until 1887, when he left for a visit to China. Before departing, he obtained a certificate pursuant to the 1882 and 1884 Acts. He returned to California shortly after passage of the 1888 Act and was denied re-admission to the United States even though he possessed a certificate. Chae Chan Ping brought suit, alleging that the 1888 Act violated the Constitution and conflicted with the Burlingame and 1880 Treaties. The opinion of Justice Field, writing for a unanimous Supreme Court, follows.

CHINESE EXCLUSION CASE
(CHAE CHAN PING v. UNITED STATES)

Supreme Court of the United States, 1889.
130 U.S. 581, 9 S.Ct. 623, 32 L.Ed. 1068.

MR. JUSTICE FIELD delivered the opinion of the Court.

* * *

* * * It must be conceded that the act of 1888 is in contravention of express stipulations of the [Burlingame] treaty of 1868 and of the supplemental treaty of 1880, but it is not on that account invalid or to be restricted in its enforcement. The treaties were of no greater legal obligation than the act of Congress. By the Constitution, laws made in pursuance thereof and treaties made under the authority of the United States are both declared to be the supreme law of the land, and no paramount authority is given to one over the other. A treaty, it is true, is in its nature a contract between nations and is often merely promissory in its character, requiring legislation to carry its stipulations into effect. Such legislation will be open to future repeal or amendment. If the treaty operates by its own force, and relates to a subject within the power of Congress, it can be deemed in that particular only the equivalent of a legislative act, to be repealed or modified at the pleasure of Congress. In either case the last expression of the sovereign will must control.

* * *

There being nothing in the treaties between China and the United States to impair the validity of the act of Congress of October 1, 1888, was it on any other ground beyond the competency of Congress to pass it? If so, it must be because it was not within the power of Congress to prohibit Chinese laborers who had at the time departed from the United States, or should subsequently depart, from returning to the United States. Those laborers are not citizens of the United States; they are aliens. That the government of the United States, through the action of the legislative department, can exclude aliens from its territory is a proposition which we do not think open to controversy. Jurisdiction over its own territory to that extent is an incident of every independent nation. It is a part of its independence. If it could not exclude aliens it would be to that extent subject to the control of another power. As said by this court in the case of *The Exchange,* 7 Cranch, 116, 136, speaking by Chief Justice Marshall: "The jurisdiction of the nation within its own territory is necessarily exclusive and absolute. It is susceptible of no limitation not imposed by itself. Any restriction upon it, deriving validity from an external source, would imply a diminution of its sovereignty to the extent of the restriction, and an investment of that sovereignty to the same extent in that power which could impose such restriction. All exceptions, therefore, to the full and complete power of a nation within its own territories, must be traced up to the consent of the nation itself. They can flow from no other legitimate source."

While under our Constitution and form of government the great mass of local matters is controlled by local authorities, the United States, in their relation to foreign countries and their subjects or citizens are one nation, invested with powers which belong to independent nations, the exercise of which can be invoked for the maintenance of its absolute independence and security throughout its entire territory. The powers to declare war, make treaties, suppress insurrection, repel invasion, regulate foreign commerce, secure republican governments to the States, and admit subjects of other nations to citizenship, are all sovereign powers, restricted in their exercise only by the Constitution itself and considerations of public policy and justice which control, more or less, the conduct of all civilized nations. * * *

The control of local matters being left to local authorities, and national matters being entrusted to the government of the Union, the problem of free institutions existing over a widely extended country, having different climates and varied interests, has been happily solved. For local interests the several States of the Union exist, but for national purposes, embracing our relations with foreign nations, we are but one people, one nation, one power.

To preserve its independence, and give security against foreign aggression and encroachment, is the highest duty of every nation, and to attain these ends nearly all other considerations are to be subordinated. It matters not in what form such aggression and encroachment come, whether from the foreign nation acting in its national character or from vast hordes of its people crowding in upon us. The government, possessing the powers which are to be exercised for protection and security, is clothed with authority to determine the occasion on which the powers shall be called forth; and its determination, so far as the subjects affected are concerned, are necessarily conclusive upon all its departments and officers. If, therefore, the government of the United States, through its legislative department, considers the presence of foreigners of a different race in this country, who will not assimilate with us, to be dangerous to its peace and security, their exclusion is not to be stayed because at the time there are no actual hostilities with the nation of which the foreigners are subjects. The existence of war would render the necessity of the proceeding only more obvious and pressing. The same necessity, in a less pressing degree, may arise when war does not exist, and the same authority which adjudges the necessity in one case must also determine it in the other. In both cases its determination is conclusive upon the judiciary. If the government of the country of which the foreigners excluded are subjects is dissatisfied with this action it can make complaint to the executive head of our government, or resort to any other measure which, in its judgment, its interests or dignity may demand; and there lies its only remedy.

* * *

The exclusion of paupers, criminals and persons afflicted with incurable diseases, for which statutes have been passed, is only an application of the same power to particular classes of persons, whose presence is deemed injurious or a source of danger to the country. As applied to them, there has never been any question as to the power to exclude them. The power is constantly exercised; its existence is involved in the right of self-preservation. * * *

The power of exclusion of foreigners being an incident of sovereignty belonging to the government of the United States, as a part of those sovereign powers delegated by the Constitution, the right to its exercise at any time when, in the judgment of the government, the interests of the country require it, cannot be granted away or restrained on behalf of any one. The powers of government are delegated in trust to the United States, and are incapable of transfer to any other parties. They cannot be abandoned or surrendered. Nor can their exercise be hampered, when needed for the public good, by any considerations of private interest. The exercise of these public trusts is not the subject of barter or contract. Whatever license, therefore, Chinese laborers may have obtained, previous to the act of October 1, 1888, to return to the United States after their departure, is held at the will of the government, revocable at any time, at its pleasure. Whether a proper consideration by our government of its previous laws, or a proper respect for the nation whose subjects are affected by its action, ought to have qualified its inhibition and made it applicable only to persons departing from the country after the passage of the act, are not questions for judicial determination. If there be any just ground of complaint on the part of China, it must be made to the political department of our government, which is alone competent to act upon the subject.

* * *

Order affirmed.

Sources of the Immigration Power

1. Delegated Powers

A fundamental principle of American constitutional law is that the federal government "is one of enumerated powers"; it can exercise "only the powers granted to it" and powers "necessary and proper" to the execution of delegated powers. *McCulloch v. Maryland,* 17 U.S. (4 Wheat.) 316, 324, 4 L.Ed. 579 (1819).

What delegated powers does Justice Field rely upon to support the conclusion that Congress had the authority to pass the Chinese exclusion laws? To what other powers explicit in Article I of the Constitution might he have appealed? In recent years, as state laws (and state politicians) play an ever greater role in the national debate about immigration law and policy, it has become increasingly important to consider the limits of the federal government's power to control immigration, and the extent to which it displaces any analogous state power. In responding to these questions, consider the following.

a. *The Commerce Power.* Art. I, § 8, cl. 3, of the Constitution authorizes Congress "to regulate Commerce with foreign Nations, and among the several States." In the mid–1800's, the Supreme Court invalidated a number of state statutes that sought to regulate immigration through the imposition of taxes or other regulations on carriers. *See Chy Lung v. Freeman,* 92 U.S. (2 Otto) 275, 23 L.Ed. 550 (1876), discussed *infra; Henderson v. New York,* 92 U.S. (2 Otto) 259, 23 L.Ed. 543 (1876) (striking down New York requirement that ship masters pay $1.50 tax per passenger brought to New York or provide $300 bond to indemnify city for relief expenses for four years); *Passenger Cases,* 48 U.S. (7 How.) 283, 12 L.Ed. 702 (1849) (invalidating Massachusetts and New York taxes on immigrants). *Passenger Cases* yielded a 5–4 decision in which eight Justices wrote opinions. While it is difficult to discover a ground for the decision that a majority of the Court agreed upon, the commerce power received prominent attention in the opinions of Justices McLean, Wayne, Catron and Grier.

Professor Gerald Neuman has pointed out the considerable equivocality in these decisions. The view prevailed then that "some actions that might be regulated by Congress under its power over interstate or foreign commerce could also be regulated by a state under its power of police, so long as no actual conflict with federal legislation occurred." *See* Neuman, *supra,* at 1887. For example, states might exercise their police power through quarantine and health laws in ways that amounted to immigration control. According to Neuman, several lower court decisions understood the Supreme Court decisions as approving broad state authority over immigration.

Eventually, however, the combination of federal regulation and judicial interpretation of the Commerce Clause gradually extinguished state power to control immigration directly. Key in this regard was the Supreme Court's decision in the *Head Money Cases,* 112 U.S. 580, 5 S.Ct. 247, 28 L.Ed. 798 (1884). The Court there relied on Congress' Commerce Clause powers to uphold a *federal* statute, enacted in 1882, that imposed a tax of fifty cents on every alien arriving in the United States. Said the Court: "Congress [has] the power to pass a law regulating immigration as a part of commerce of this country with foreign nations." *Id.* at 600, 5 S.Ct. at 254.

Can the commerce power be relied upon to uphold the regulation of aliens who do not come to the United States for commercial purposes? Is the migration of children, refugees, poor people, or spouses of resident aliens "commerce"? The Supreme Court, in at least one case, has concluded that migration is commerce. In *Edwards v. California,* 314 U.S. 160, 62 S.Ct. 164, 86 L.Ed. 119 (1941), a California statute that made it a crime to bring an indigent person into the state was struck down as an unconstitutional interference with Congress' power to regulate interstate commerce. The Court, through Justice Byrnes, stated that "it is settled beyond question that the transportation of persons is 'commerce.'" In a footnote, he added: "It is immaterial whether or not the transportation is commercial in character." *Id.* at 172 n. 1, 62 S.Ct. at 166 n.1.[4] Four Justices concurred in the result of the Court on other grounds, including Justice Jackson who believed that the California statute violated the "privileges or immunities" clause of the Fourteenth Amendment. He expressed the following concern over the majority's reliance on the commerce clause: "[T]he migrations of a human being, of whom it is charged that he possesses no thing that can be sold and has no wherewithal to buy, do not fit easily into my notions of what is commerce. To hold that the measure of his rights is the commerce clause is likely to result eventually either in distorting the commercial law or in denaturing human rights." *Id.* at 182, 62 S.Ct. at 171.

b. *The Naturalization Power.* Art. I, § 8, cl. 4 of the Constitution grants Congress the power to "establish an uniform Rule of Naturalization." This power was expressly delegated to Congress to prevent the confusion and controversy that could arise from separate state laws bestowing citizenship. *See* J. Kettner, The Development of American Citizenship, 1608–1870, at 224–25 (1978).

Does the power to naturalize necessarily imply the power to regulate the admission of aliens who may eventually be eligible for naturalization? Not obviously. One might well distinguish between regulation of the *physical entry* of aliens into the *territory* of the United States and regulation of the entry into the *political community* of the United States through the extension of full political rights to naturalized citizens. Can the Constitution be read as granting Congress only the latter power while reserving the former power to the States?

Interestingly, in the early years of the Republic, Congress viewed the naturalization power as a way to regulate immigration. In most states, aliens could not own or inherit land, vote or hold office—disabilities that were removed upon naturalization. Congress could thus encourage or discourage immigration by altering the prerequisites (such as length of residence) for naturalization. *See, e.g.,* 1 Annals of Cong. 1109–1125 (1790) (debate on Naturalization Act of 1790).

---

4. *See also Caminetti v. United States,* 242 U.S. 470, 37 S.Ct. 192, 61 L.Ed. 442 (1917) (upholding convictions under the White Slave Traffic Act of men who had transported their mistresses across state lines, even though it was neither charged nor proved at trial that the transportation was for commercial purposes).

c. *The War Power.* Art.I, § 8, cl.11 grants Congress the power "to declare War." It is beyond dispute that the war power gives the federal government the authority to stop the entry of enemy aliens and to expel enemy aliens residing in the United States. This power was first granted to the President by one of the Alien and Sedition Acts and remains on the books today. *See* 50 U.S.C.A. §§ 21–23. The constitutionality of this provision has been consistently upheld. *See, e.g., Ludecke v. Watkins,* 335 U.S. 160, 68 S.Ct. 1429, 92 L.Ed. 1881 (1948). But is it possible to view the war power as authorizing the mass of statutes that presently regulate immigration—or even the statute challenged in the *Chinese Exclusion Case?*

d. *The Migration and Importation Clause.* Art.I, § 9, cl.1 of the Constitution provides:

> The Migration or Importation of such Persons as any of the States now existing shall think proper to admit, shall not be prohibited by the Congress prior to the Year one thousand eight hundred and eight.

The denial of power to Congress *before* 1808 seems to imply the existence of such power *after* that year. Thus, this clause, at first reading, appears to authorize congressional power to *prohibit* immigration after 1808, and probably—by reasonable implication—to regulate it as well.

Unfortunately things are not as clear as they seem. This clause is almost assuredly a veiled reference to an institution that the Founding Fathers could not bring themselves, in a charter of fundamental law, to recognize by name: slavery. *Passenger Cases,* 48 U.S. (7 How.) 283, 512–13, 12 L.Ed. 702 (1849) (opinion of Justice Daniel). Thus this clause has generally been interpreted as prohibiting congressional attempts to stop the slave trade before 1808.[5] *See generally,* D.B. Davis, The Problem of Slavery in the Age of Revolution, 1770–1823, at 119–31 (1975); Berns, *The Constitution and the Migration of Slaves,* 78 Yale L.J. 198 (1968).

Even recognizing that protection of the slave trade was the primary motivation for the clause, is there any good reason for so limiting its application? Note in particular that the clause refers to *"the migration and importation"* of persons. One might well ask why the Constitution would include the word "migration"—which sounds like voluntary movement of people—if the clause were intended to apply only to the slave trade. At least three answers are possible, each of which stops short of finding in the clause a general power to regulate immigration. The first two restrict the clause to regulation of the slave trade: (1) "migration" was intended to refer to movement of slaves among the States, while importation referred to the initial entrance of the slave into the United States; or (2) "migration" was used in addition to "importation" "to prevent * * * cavils" over whether slaves were persons or property. *The Passenger Cases,* 48 U.S. (7 How.) 283, 476, 12 L.Ed. 702 (1849) (opinion of Chief Justice Taney). The third interpretation, offered in a dictum by the

5. Congress passed a law prohibiting the importation of slaves on March 2, 1807, Ch. 22, 2 Stat. 426, which took effect January 1, 1808.

Supreme Court in 1883, goes beyond the slave trade but limits the clause to the regulation of immigration by blacks:

> There has never been any doubt that this clause had exclusive reference to persons of the African race. The two words "migration" and "importation" refer to the different conditions of this race as regards freedom and slavery. When the free black man came here, he migrated; when the slave came, he was imported.

People v. Compagnie Générale Transatlantique, 107 U.S. (17 Otto) 59, 62, 2 S.Ct. 87, 27 L.Ed. 383 (1883) (striking down New York State tax on immigrants).

e. *The Foreign Affairs Power.* In the *Chinese Exclusion Case,* Justice Field sought to associate the power to regulate immigration with the power to conduct foreign affairs: "[T]he United States, in their relation to foreign countries and their subjects or citizens, are one nation, invested with powers which belong to independent nations * * *. * * * [F]or national purposes, *embracing our relations with foreign nations,* we are but one people, one nation, one power." (Emphasis supplied.)

In modern constitutional terms, these words would be seen as an appeal to the foreign affairs power of the federal government. But like the immigration power, the foreign affairs power receives no explicit mention in the Constitution. Finding the constitutional basis of the power to conduct foreign relations has proven a vexing task, as Professor Louis Henkin, a leading scholar on foreign affairs and the Constitution, has described:

> The Constitution does not delegate a "power to conduct foreign relations" to the federal government or confer it upon any of its branches. Congress is given power to regulate commerce with foreign nations, to define offenses against the law of nations, to declare war, and the President the power to make treaties and send and receive ambassadors, but these hardly add up to the power to conduct foreign relations. Where is the power to recognize other states or governments, to maintain or break diplomatic relations, to open consulates elsewhere and permit them here, to acquire or cede territory, to give or withhold foreign aid, to proclaim a Monroe Doctrine or an Open–Door Policy, indeed to determine all the attitudes and carry out all the details in the myriads of relationships with other nations that are "the foreign policy" and "the foreign relations" of the United States? * * * Congress can regulate foreign commerce but where is the power to make other laws relating to our foreign relations—to regulate immigration, or the status and rights of aliens, or activities of citizens at home or abroad affecting our foreign relations? These "missing" powers, and a host of others, were clearly intended for and have always been exercised by the federal government, but where does the Constitution say that it shall be so?

* * *

The attempt to build all the foreign affairs powers of the federal government with the few bricks provided by the Constitution has not been accepted as successful. It requires considerable stretching of language, much reading between lines, and bold extrapolation from "the Constitution as a whole," and that still does not plausibly add up to all the power which the federal government in fact exercises.

L. Henkin, Foreign Affairs and the Constitution 16–18 (1972).

Does Justice Field adequately describe how the immigration power may be inferred from the (somewhat tenuously inferred) power to conduct foreign relations? Some immigration decisions are clearly part of the conduct of American foreign policy. For example, during the Iranian Hostage crisis of 1980–81, President Carter ordered all Iranian students in the United States to report to INS offices and demonstrate the lawfulness of their presence in the country. *See Narenji v. Civiletti,* 617 F.2d 745 (D.C.Cir.1979), *cert. denied,* 446 U.S. 957, 100 S.Ct. 2928, 64 L.Ed.2d 815 (1980). In January 1991, the Attorney General mandated the photographing and fingerprinting of virtually all nonimmigrants bearing Iraqi and Kuwaiti travel documents, before they would be allowed to enter the country—part of the U.S. response to Iraq's invasion of Kuwait. 56 Fed. Reg. 1566 (1991). But are all regulations of immigration intended as acts of foreign policy? *See* Legomsky, *Immigration Law and the Principle of Plenary Congressional Power,* 1984 Sup.Ct.Rev. 255, 261–69. Were the Chinese exclusion laws? Or were they passed *despite* foreign policy objectives of the United States?

The federal government's power to conduct foreign affairs, whether or not it justifies federal regulation of immigration, has led the courts to invalidate *state* statutes that attempt to regulate immigration. The classic statement of this position occurs in *Chy Lung v. Freeman,* 92 U.S. (2 Otto) 275, 23 L.Ed. 550 (1875). The case involved, in the Court's words, "a most extraordinary statute" that authorized the California Commissioner of Immigration to inspect aliens seeking to enter the United States. For any alien determined by the Commissioner to be deaf, dumb, blind, crippled, infirm, or a lunatic, idiot, pauper, convicted criminal or lewd or debauched woman, the master of the vessel was required to give a bond or pay an amount determined by the Commissioner to be sufficient to provide for the alien's care. In striking the statute down, the Court, through Justice Miller, relied in large part on the impact that such a regulation could have on American foreign policy.

Individual foreigners, however distinguished at home for their social, their literary, or their political character, are helpless in the presence of this potent commissioner. Such a person may offer to furnish any amount of surety on his own bond, or deposit any sum of money; but the law of California takes no note of him. It is the master, owner, or consignee of the vessel alone whose bond can be accepted; and so a silly, an obstinate, or a wicked commissioner may bring disgrace upon the whole country, the enmity of a powerful nation, or the loss of an equally powerful friend.

While the occurrence of the hypothetical case just stated may be highly improbable, we venture the assertion, that, if citizens of our own government were treated by any foreign nation as subjects of the Emperor of China have been actually treated under this law, no administration could withstand the call for a demand on such government for redress.

Or, if this plaintiff and her twenty companions had been subjects of the Queen of Great Britain, can any one doubt that this matter would have been the subject of international inquiry, if not of a direct claim for redress? Upon whom would such a claim be made? Not upon the State of California; for, by our Constitution, she can hold no exterior relations with other nations. It would be made upon the government of the United States. If that government should get into a difficulty which would lead to war, or to suspension of intercourse, would California alone suffer, or all the Union? If we should conclude that a pecuniary indemnity was proper as a satisfaction for the injury, would California pay it, or the Federal government? If that government has forbidden the States to hold negotiations with any foreign nations, or to declare war, and has taken the whole subject of these relations upon herself, has the Constitution, which provides for this, done so foolish a thing as to leave it in the power of the States to pass laws whose enforcement renders the general government liable to just reclamations which it must answer, while it does not prohibit to the States the acts for which it is held responsible?

The Constitution of the United States is no such instrument. The passage of laws which concern the admission of citizens and subjects of foreign nations to our shores belongs to Congress, and not to the States. It has the power to regulate commerce with foreign nations: the responsibility for the character of those regulations, and for the manner of their execution, belongs solely to the national government. If it be otherwise, a single State can, at her pleasure, embroil us in disastrous quarrels with other nations.

Id. at 279–80. *See also Hines v. Davidowitz,* 312 U.S. 52, 61 S.Ct. 399, 85 L.Ed. 581 (1941), which invalidated Pennsylvania's Alien Registration Act. The Court struck down the statute as conflicting with federal legislation, but at the same time it discussed at length the state statute's potential impact on the conduct of foreign relations.

2. Inherent Power

Justice Field writes in the *Chinese Exclusion Case* that "[t]he power of exclusion of foreigners [is] an incident of sovereignty belonging to the government of the United States, as a part of those sovereign powers delegated by the Constitution." Earlier in the opinion he states:

That the government of the United States * * * can exclude aliens from its territories is a proposition which we do not think open to controversy. Jurisdiction over its own territory to that extent is an incident of every independent nation. It is a part of its independence. If it could not exclude aliens, it would be to that extent subject to the control of another power.

Three years later, the Court's decision in *Nishimura Ekiu v. United States,* 142 U.S. 651, 12 S.Ct. 336, 35 L.Ed. 1146 (1892), upheld the immigration act of 1891, which codified existing exclusion laws and provided for exclusive inspection of aliens by the federal government. Justice Gray, writing for the Court, stated:

> It is an accepted maxim of international law, that every sovereign nation has the power, as inherent in sovereignty, and essential to preservation, to forbid the entrance of foreigners within its dominions, or to admit them only in such cases and upon such conditions as it may see fit to prescribe. In the United States, this power is vested in the national government, to which the Constitution has committed the entire control of international relations, in peace as well as in war.

These powerful and oft-cited passages mask deep and unanswered puzzles. If the federal government is one of delegated powers, how can it possess "inherent powers" that seem to owe their existence to sources outside the Constitution? Why should "maxims of international law" define the power of Congress? Isn't that what a (or at least our) Constitution is for? Even if we accept the idea that an attribute of sovereignty is the power to regulate immigration, why don't we discover that power in the States, which, under the Tenth Amendment, retain all powers not delegated to the federal government?

The Supreme Court has answered these questions in a different context in a manner that might surprise. In *United States v. Curtiss–Wright Export Co.,* 299 U.S. 304, 57 S.Ct. 216, 81 L.Ed. 255 (1936), the Court, through Justice Sutherland, expounded at length upon the source of the federal government's foreign affairs power. Oddly enough, it found the power to derive, not from the Constitution, but from the fact of independence itself:

> The broad statement that the federal government can exercise no power except those specifically enumerated in the Constitution, and such implied powers as are necessary and proper to carry into effect the enumerated powers, is categorically true only in respect of our internal affairs.

* * *

> As a result of the separation from Great Britain by the colonies acting as a unit, the powers of external sovereignty passed from the Crown not to the colonies severally, but to the colonies in their collective and corporate capacity as the United States of America.

* * *

The Union existed before the Constitution, which was ordained and established among other things to form "a more perfect Union."

* * *

It results that the investment of the federal government with the powers of external sovereignty did not depend upon the affirmative grants of the Constitution.

299 U.S. at 315–18, 57 S.Ct. at 218–20.

Under the reasoning of *Curtiss-Wright*, we need no longer scrutinize the Constitution to find the immigration powers. We need simply conclude that the power to regulate the flow of aliens over our borders is inherent in the concept of sovereignty.[6]

Curtiss-Wright has been seriously questioned on logical and historical grounds.[7] Its theory is particularly troubling in the immigration area. If the power to regulate immigration is extra-constitutional, is it subject to any limits within the Constitution? May aliens be excluded without a guarantee of due process? Are aliens living in the United States not entitled to the protections of the First, Fourth, Fifth and Sixth Amendments? The Supreme Court has repeatedly stated that they are.[8] But how can these constitutional limits be applied to a power that exists outside the Constitution?

3.   Constructional and Structural Arguments

Perhaps there is some source of power between delegated powers and extra-constitutional powers. Let us suggest two.

a.   *The Rule of Necessity.*   Judge Learned Hand has written:

For centuries it has been an accepted canon in interpretation of documents to interpolate into the text such provisions, though not expressed, as are essential to prevent the defeat of the venture at hand; and this applies with especial force to the interpretation of constitutions, which, since they are designed to cover a great

---

6. Indeed, Professor Henkin's view is that *Curtiss-Wright*, by viewing immigration power as extra-constitutional, goes beyond the *Chinese Exclusion Case.* The latter case, he asserts, did not view the immigration power as extra-constitutional. Rather, the *Chinese Exclusion Case* viewed the immigration power as one inherent in sovereignty and therefore vested in the federal government by the Constitution as supplementary to those powers expressly granted. Henkin, *supra,* at 22. Do you agree with Professor Henkin's reading of the *Chinese Exclusion Case?*

See also Nafziger, *The General Admission of Aliens Under International Law,* 77 Am. J.Int'l L. 804 (1983) (criticizing the view that "sovereign decisions concerning the general admission of aliens are * * * immune from legal appraisal" and arguing that interna-

tional law supplies a "qualified duty to admit aliens when they pose no danger to the public safety, security, general welfare, or essential institutions of a recipient state").

7. *See* Henkin, *supra,* at 23–26; Lofgren, United States v. Curtiss–Wright Export Corporation: *An Historical Reassessment,* 83 Yale L.J. 1 (1973); Note, *Constitutional Limits on the Power to Exclude Aliens,* 82 Col. L.Rev. 995 (1982).

8. *See, e.g., Bridges v. Wixon,* 326 U.S. 135, 65 S.Ct. 1443, 89 L.Ed. 2103 (1945); *United States v. Brignoni–Ponce,* 422 U.S. 873, 95 S.Ct. 2574, 45 L.Ed.2d 607 (1975); *Wong Yang Sung v. McGrath,* 339 U.S. 33, 70 S.Ct. 445, 94 L.Ed. 616 (1950); *Wong Wing v. United States,* 163 U.S. 228, 16 S.Ct. 977, 41 L.Ed. 140 (1896).

multitude of necessarily unforeseen occasions, must be cast in general language, unless they are constantly amended.

L. Hand, The Bill of Rights 14 (1958).

Is it possible to infer the immigration power using Hand's reasoning—"not [as] a logical deduction from the structure of the Constitution but only as a practical condition upon its successful operation"? *Id.* at 15. Justice Field hints at such a justification when he argues that if the federal government were not able to control immigration, the United States "would be to that extent subject to the control of another power." Unfriendly nations could send *agents provocateurs* to disrupt American institutions; developing nations could send workers to take advantage of American jobs; other countries could seek to solve their problems of overpopulation by "exporting" people to the United States. Perhaps to lose control of one's borders is to "defeat the venture at hand" by losing our ability to achieve the objects for which the Constitution was established: "to insure domestic Tranquility, provide for the common defense, promote the general Welfare."

How far can the Rule of Necessity take us? Must the government demonstrate some serious threat to the security or integrity of the nation before aliens may be excluded? Is this a question a court should answer, or is it one to be left to the political branches of government?

b. *A Structural Justification.* Charles Black, a leading constitutional scholar, has suggested that much of our constitutional law may be seen not as "the explication or exegesis of [a] particular textual passage," but rather as an "inference from the structures and relationships created by the constitution." C. Black, Structure and Relationship in Constitutional Law 7 (1969). Under this view, one does not focus on isolated clauses in the document; instead, the interpreter takes a step back and examines the shape of the Constitution as a whole: the institutions it creates and the relationships between those institutions.

The primary purpose of the Constitution is to establish a system of government for a nation, a nation encompassing territory and members ("citizens"). A system of government is the process by which citizens establish rules of conduct for persons within the territory. From these premises, two sorts of structural arguments may follow. First, borrowing from the previous discussion, to be a sovereign nation, a people must have control over their territory. A nation of open borders runs the risk of not being able to govern itself because its sovereignty, to some extent, is in the hands of the other nations of the world. It seems reasonable to believe that the persons who wrote and ratified the Constitution thought (or hoped) they were creating a nation that would be able to take its place among other nations as an equal; one that would possess the powers of sovereignty generally possessed by all other nations. If, as the Supreme Court stated in 1892, it was a well-established "maxim of international law" that all sovereign states had the power to regulate immigration, it is nearly inconceivable that such a power could not have been a part of the Founding Fathers' concept of "nationhood." One might almost conclude that the power was so plain it did not even need to be enumerated; it followed from the very act of creating a sovereign nation.[9] Certainly the powers written into the document support such a conclusion; the power to regulate foreign commerce, prohibit the slave trade after 1808, enter into treaties, and establish a uniform rule of naturalization may all be viewed as manifestations of an underlying principle that one aspect of the sovereign nation created by the Constitution is the power to regulate the admission of aliens.

A second structural argument may be based on the notion of citizenship and the relationship of the citizen to the nation. Citizens, through the process of government, argue about, protect and further values. This discussion of values is essentially a process of national self-definition. The regulation of immigration may be crucial to the process of self-definition. Not only do immigration decisions give citizens the ability to regulate who the participants in the discussion will be, such decisions themselves are an act of self-definition. By deciding whom we permit to enter the country, we say much about who we are as a nation. As the Chinese exclusion laws demonstrate, the process of self-definition can be ugly, short-sighted, wrong. But perhaps it is one power that every people must possess to be a sovereign people. As Michael Walzer has written:

> [T]he right to choose an admissions policy is * * * not merely a matter of acting in the world, exercising sovereignty, and pursuing national interests. At stake here is the shape of the community that acts in the world, exercises sovereignty, and so on. Admission and exclusion are at the core of communal independence. They suggest the deepest meaning of self-determination.

M. Walzer, Spheres of Justice: A Defense of Pluralism and Equality 61–62 (1983). Thus we have identified two kinds of structural arguments to justify the immigration power: one based on *self-preservation,* the other on *self-definition.*[10]

The Chinese Exclusion Laws and Equal Protection

In its first major examination of the Fourteenth Amendment, the Supreme Court stated that it "doubt[ed] very much whether any action of a

9. Compare the statement of Justice Holmes that: "It is admitted that sovereign states have inherent power to deport aliens, and seemingly that Congress is not deprived of this power by the Constitution of the United States." *Tiaco v. Forbes,* 228 U.S. 549, 557, 33 S.Ct. 585, 586, 57 L.Ed. 960 (1913).

10. To what extent are U.S. immigration admission and expulsion rules in fact based on concerns of community self-definition? Consider the following argument:

"[S]elf-definition" has rarely been a central aspect of immigration regulation. The vast majority of immigration decisions are not club membership rules carefully crafted to preserve a particular group identity. They are much closer to university admission policies than they are to rules regulating religious conver-

sions. We choose how many aliens to admit based on economic, social and moral considerations, attempting to screen out individuals who are likely to threaten the public health, welfare, or security. * * * To be sure, immigration regulations reflect deep social norms and understandings. For example, family reunification policies are based on prevailing American definitions of "nuclear family." But our immigration laws are not primarily concerned with the construction or maintenance of a particular kind of community.

Aleinikoff, *Citizens, Aliens, Membership and the Constitution,* 7 Const.Comm. 9, 33–34 (1990).

state not directed by way of discrimination against the negroes as a class, or on account of their race, will ever be held to come within the purview of [the equal protection clause]." *Slaughter-House Cases,* 83 U.S. (16 Wall.) 36, 21 L.Ed. 394 (1873). Yet in a case of major importance, decided thirteen years later—and three years before the *Chinese Exclusion Case*— the court held that the equal protection clause protected Chinese nationals against discriminatory enforcement of a San Francisco ordinance regulating laundries. Based on evidence that 200 Chinese laundries had been ordered closed while 80 similar laundries operated by non-Chinese had not, the Court struck down the ordinance as a violation of equal protection, concluding that "no reason for [the discrimination] exists except hostility to the race and nationality to which the petitioners belong." *Yick Wo v. Hopkins,* 118 U.S. 356, 374, 6 S.Ct. 1064, 1073, 30 L.Ed. 220 (1886). First, however, the Court had to address the question whether the plaintiffs could invoke the equal protection clause at all:

> The rights of the petitioners, * * * are not less, because they are aliens and subjects of the Emperor of China. * * *

> The Fourteenth Amendment to the Constitution is not confined to the protection of citizens. It says: "Nor shall any state deprive any person of life, liberty, or property without due process of law; nor deny to any person within its jurisdiction the equal protection of the laws." These provisions are universal in their application, to all persons within the territorial jurisdiction, without regard to any differences of race, of color, or of nationality; and the equal protection of the laws is a pledge of the protection of equal laws. * * * The questions we have to consider and decide in these cases, therefore, are to be treated as involving the rights of every citizen of the United States equally with those of the strangers and aliens who now invoke the jurisdiction of the court.

> * * *

> When we consider the nature and the theory of our institutions of government, the principles upon which they are supposed to rest, and review the history of their development, we are constrained to conclude that they do not mean to leave room for the play and action of purely personal and arbitrary power. Sovereignty itself is, of course, not subject to law, for it is the author and source of law; but in our system, while sovereign powers are delegated to the agencies of government, sovereignty itself remains with the people, by whom and for whom all government exists and acts. And the law is the definition and limitation of power. It is, indeed, quite true that there must always be lodged somewhere, and in some person or body, the authority of final decision; and in many cases of mere administration the responsibility is purely political, no appeal lying except to the ultimate tribunal of the public judgment, exercised either in the pressure of opinion, or by means of the suffrage. But the fundamental rights to life, liberty, and the pursuit of happiness, considered as individual possessions, are secured by those maxims of constitutional law which are the

monuments showing the victorious progress of the race in securing to men the blessings of civilization under the reign of just and equal laws, so that, in the famous language of the Massachusetts Bill of Rights, the government of the commonwealth "may be a government of laws and not of men." For, the very idea that one man may be compelled to hold his life, or the means of living, or any material right essential to the enjoyment of life, at the mere will of another, seems to be intolerable in any country where freedom prevails, as being the essence of slavery itself.

* * *

* * * [T]he facts shown establish an administration directed so exclusively against a particular class of persons as to warrant and require the conclusion, that, whatever may have been the intent of the ordinances as adopted, they are applied by the public authorities charged with their administration, and thus representing the State itself, with a mind so unequal and oppressive as to amount to a practical denial by the State of that equal protection of the laws which is secured to the petitioners, as to all other persons, by the broad and benign provisions of the Fourteenth Amendment to the Constitution of the United States. * * *

118 U.S. at 368–70, 373, 6 S.Ct. at 1070–71, 1073.

If the Fourteenth Amendment protected Chinese citizens operating laundries in San Francisco, why were not the Chinese exclusion laws similarly invalid—evidencing, as they did, hostility based on race and nationality?

The quick answer is that the Fourteenth Amendment applies only to the actions of the States, and not to the federal government. In the late 19th century, this formalistic answer probably explains why an equal protection challenge was not made in the *Chinese Exclusion Case*, but that answer cannot suffice today. In *Bolling v. Sharpe,* 347 U.S. 497, 74 S.Ct. 693, 98 L.Ed. 884 (1954), a companion case to *Brown v. Board of Education,* the court held that segregated schools in the District of Columbia violated the due process clause of the Fifth Amendment. Since *Bolling,* it has been taken as given that "[e]qual protection analysis in the Fifth Amendment area is the same as that under the Fourteenth Amendment."[11] Does this mean that the Chinese exclusion laws would be invalid today? Not quite.

A more fundamental difficulty with applying the reasoning of *Yick Wo* to challenge Chae Chan Ping's exclusion would have been that the *Chinese Exclusion Case* involved an immigration question—an alien's right to enter the United States. *Yick Wo* alleged discrimination against aliens in the United States but did not challenge a decision to exclude or expel them. This aspect of *Yick Wo* suggests a tension that runs throughout the constitutional materials in this book. On the one hand, the *Chinese*

11. *Buckley v. Valeo,* 424 U.S. 1, 93, 96 S.Ct. 612, 670, 46 L.Ed.2d 659 (1976) (per curiam). *See generally* Edward S. Corwin's The Constitution and What It Means Today, 370 (H. Chase and C. Ducat, eds., 14th ed. 1978).

Exclusion Case is a seminal case for the "plenary power doctrine"—which severely limits aliens' constitutional rights when it comes to entering and remaining in this country. In contrast, *Yick Wo* suggests that aliens and citizens receive similar (but not necessarily identical) constitutional treatment in *nonimmigration* matters. Put differently, our constitutional law relating to *immigration* may differ from our constitutional law relating to noncitizen *immigrants*.

Federal preemption adds another complication to applying *Yick Wo*'s reasoning to challenge Chae Chan Ping's exclusion. Besides distinguishing immigration law from discrimination against aliens, one might also distinguish the federal law in the *Chinese Exclusion Case* from the local law in *Yick Wo*. While the Supreme Court has vigorously scrutinized most state legislation that discriminates against aliens, *see, e.g., Graham v. Richardson*, 403 U.S. 365, 91 S.Ct. 1848, 29 L.Ed.2d 534 (1971), it has permitted Congress to "make rules that would be unacceptable if applied to citizens." *Mathews v. Diaz*, 426 U.S. 67, 80, 96 S.Ct. 1883, 1891, 48 L.Ed.2d 478 (1976). Would application of a *federal* statute that made it impossible for Chinese nationals to operate laundries have passed constitutional muster? As you study the constitutional materials in this book, consider to what extent federal preemption explains the contrast between the discrimination cases—the progeny of *Yick Wo*—and the plenary power cases—the progeny of the *Chinese Exclusion Case*.

The Supreme Court has made clear that the equal protection component of the Fifth Amendment is only a modest restraint on the federal immigration power. This is not to say that notions of equal protection do not apply at all to federal regulation of immigration. It simply means that the Court is not likely to demand that Congress provide a compelling justification for immigration laws that discriminate on the basis of nationality or alienage.

If Congress were to re-enact the Chinese exclusion laws today, could they survive even this lower level of scrutiny? Recall Justice Field's description of the American perceptions of the Chinese as unassimilable and a threat to American workers and political institutions. Are these adequate justifications for the laws? Or, do they represent precisely the kind of racism and stereotyping that the Fourteenth Amendment (as now reflected in the Fifth Amendment) was intended to prevent?

From Exclusion to Deportation

The *Chinese Exclusion Case* answered the question whether Congress could *exclude* aliens from the United States. "Exclusion," in immigration law, refers to the process of preventing aliens from making a formal entry into the country. The Chinese exclusion laws not only prevented new Chinese laborers from entering the United States, but also prohibited the *return* of Chinese who had been residents of the United States and had left with certificates valid under the 1882 and 1884 laws. Aliens, like these Chinese, who have lawfully obtained permanent residence in this country and have left for a short period of time, are usually referred to as "returning residents" when they seek to re-enter the United States.[12] Does the exclusion of first-time entrants raise distinct constitutional issues from the exclusion of returning residents? It is clear that the Court did not think so in the *Chinese Exclusion Case.*

In 1892, Congress again addressed the issue of Chinese immigration. Act of May 5, 1892, Ch. 60, 27 Stat. 25. The 1882 statute had imposed a ten-year "temporary suspension" of immigration by laborers. The 1892 statute extended the suspension for another ten years. More importantly, the 1892 Act provided for the *deportation* of aliens residing in the United States.

Here we should interject that "deportation" has two meanings in the immigration laws. Here, it means the removal of aliens already within the United States—in contrast to the "exclusion" of aliens at the border who are seeking entry. "Deportation," in this context, is often referred to as "expulsion." "Deportation" may also be used to mean the physical removal to another country of any alien whether inside or at the border of the United States. Thus it is sometimes said that aliens who arrive at a port of entry in the United States are "excluded and deported." To avoid confusion, in this book we will use "exclusion" to refer to a denial of entry and "deportation" or "expulsion" to refer to the removal of an alien who has entered the United States.

The 1892 Act authorized the deportation of any Chinese alien unlawfully in the United States. It further required all Chinese laborers then living in the United States to acquire a "certificate of residence" from the Collector of Internal Revenue within one year after passage of the Act. Under regulations promulgated pursuant to the Act, the government would issue a certificate only on the "affidavit of at least one credible witness," which was construed as a white witness. *See* 149 U.S. at 701 n.1, 703, 731. An alien who failed to obtain the certificate could "be arrested * * * and taken before a United States judge, whose duty it shall be to order that he be deported from the United States." He could escape deportation only upon a demonstration "that by reason of accident, sickness or other unavoidable cause, he has been unable to procure his certificate, * * * and by at least one credible white witness, that he was a resident of the United States at the time of the passage of [the Act]." 27 Stat. 25–26.

This statute was challenged on numerous constitutional grounds. The Supreme Court's decision follows.

FONG YUE TING v. UNITED STATES

Supreme Court of the United States, 1893.
149 U.S. 698, 13 S.Ct. 1016, 37 L.Ed. 905.

[Three Chinese laborers who were arrested and held by Federal authorities for not having certificates of residence petitioned for writs of

---

12. The status of "permanent resident alien"—and the right to return—may be lost by an alien who stays outside the United States too long, thereby indicating an intent to abandon residence here. *See* C. Gordon, S. Mailman & S. Yale-Loehr, Immigration Law and Procedure § 35.02[2][c] [hereinafter cited as "GM & Y"].

habeas corpus. The Circuit Court for the Southern District of New York denied relief, and the Supreme Court consolidated the cases on appeal. The facts of one of the cases are stated.]

* * * On April 11, 1893, the petitioner applied to the collector of internal revenue for a certificate of residence; the collector refused to give him a certificate, on the ground that the witnesses whom he produced to prove that he was entitled to the certificate were persons of the Chinese race and not credible witnesses, and required of him to produce a witness other than a Chinaman to prove that he was entitled to the certificate, which he was unable to do, because there was no person other than one of the Chinese race who knew and could truthfully swear that he was lawfully within the United States on May 5, 1892, and then entitled to remain therein; and because of such unavoidable cause he was unable to produce a certificate of residence, and was now without one. The petitioner was arrested by the marshal, and taken before the judge; and clearly established, to the satisfaction of the judge, that he was unable to procure a certificate of residence, by reason of the unavoidable cause aforesaid; and also established, to the judge's satisfaction, by the testimony of a Chinese resident of New York, that the petitioner was a resident of the United States at the time of the passage of the act; but having failed to establish this fact clearly to the satisfaction of the court by at least one credible white witness, as required by the statute, the judge ordered the petitioner to be remanded to the custody of the marshal, and to be deported from the United States, as provided in the act.

* * *

Mr. Justice Gray, after stating the facts, delivered the opinion of the court.

The general principles of public law which lie at the foundation of these cases are clearly established by previous judgments of this court, and by the authorities therein referred to.

* * *

The right of a nation to expel or deport foreigners, who have not been naturalized or taken any steps towards becoming citizens of the country, rests upon the same grounds, and is as absolute and unqualified as the right to prohibit and prevent their entrance into the country.

* * *

The statements of leading commentators on the law of nations are to the same effect.

Vattel says: "Every nation has the right to refuse to admit a foreigner into the country, when he cannot enter without putting the nation in evident danger, or doing it a manifest injury. What it owes to itself, the care of its own safety, gives it this right; and in virtue of its natural liberty, it belongs to the nation to judge whether its circumstances will or will not justify the admission of the foreigner." "Thus, also, it has a right to send them elsewhere, if it has just cause to fear that they will corrupt the manners of the citizens; that they will create religious disturbances, or occasion any other disorder, contrary to the public safety. In a word, it has a right, and is even obliged, in this respect, to follow the rules which prudence dictates." Vattel's Law of Nations, lib. 1, c. 19, §§ 230, 231.

Ortolan says: "The government of each state has always the right to compel foreigners who are found within its territory to go away, by having them taken to the frontier. This right is based on the fact that, the foreigner not making part of the nation, his individual reception into the territory is matter of pure permission, of simple tolerance, and creates no obligation. The exercise of this right may be subjected, doubtless, to certain forms by the domestic laws of each country; but the right exists none the less, universally recognized and put in force. In France, no special form is now prescribed in this matter; the exercise of this right of expulsion is wholly left to the executive power." Ortolan, Diplomatie de la Mer, lib. 2, c. 14, (4th ed.) p. 297.

* * *

The right to exclude or to expel all aliens, or any class of aliens, absolutely or upon certain conditions, in war or in peace, being an inherent and inalienable right of every sovereign and independent nation, essential to its safety, its independence and its welfare, the question now before the court is whether the manner in which Congress has exercised this right in * * * the act of 1892 is consistent with the Constitution.

The United States are a sovereign and independent nation, and are vested by the Constitution with the entire control of international relations, and with all the powers of government necessary to maintain that control and to make it effective. The only government of this country, which other nations recognize or treat with, is the government of the Union; and the only American flag known throughout the world is the flag of the United States.

The Constitution of the United States speaks with no uncertain sound upon this subject. That instrument, established by the people of the United States as the fundamental law of the land, has conferred upon the President the executive power; has made him the commander-in-chief of the army and navy; has authorized him, by and with the consent of the Senate, to make treaties, and to appoint ambassadors, public ministers and consuls; and has made it his duty to take care that the laws be faithfully executed. The Constitution has granted to Congress the power to regulate commerce with foreign nations, including the entrance of ships, the importation of goods and the bringing of persons into the ports of the United States; to establish a uniform rule of naturalization; to define and punish piracies and felonies committed on the high seas, and offences against the law of nations; to declare war, grant letters of marque and reprisal, and make rules concerning captures on land and water; to raise and support armies, to provide and maintain a navy, and to make rules for the government and regulation of the land and naval forces; and to make all laws necessary and proper for carrying into execution these powers, and all other powers vested by the Constitution in the government of the United States, or in any department or officer thereof. And the several States are expressly forbidden to enter into any treaty, alliance or confederation; to grant letters of marque and reprisal; to enter into any agreement or compact with another State, or with a foreign power; or to engage in war, unless actually invaded, or in such imminent danger as will not admit of delay.

In exercising the great power which the people of the United States, by establishing a written Constitution as the supreme and paramount law, have vested in this court, of determining, whenever the question is properly brought before it, whether the acts of the legislature or of the executive are consistent with the Constitution, it behooves the court to be careful that it does not undertake to pass upon political questions, the final decision of which has been committed by the Constitution to the other departments of the government.

* * *

In *Nishimura Ekiu's case*, it was adjudged that, although Congress might, if it saw fit, authorize the courts to investigate and ascertain the facts upon which the alien's right to land was made by the statutes to depend, yet Congress might intrust the final determination of those facts to an executive officer; and that, if it did so, his order was due process of law, and no other tribunal, unless expressly authorized by law to do so, was at liberty to re-ëxamine the evidence on which he acted, or to controvert its sufficiency.

The power to exclude aliens and the power to expel them rest upon one foundation, are derived from one source, are supported by the same reasons, and are in truth but parts of one and the same power.

* * *

Chinese laborers * * * like all other aliens residing in the United States for a shorter or longer time, are entitled, so long as they are permitted by the government of the United States to remain in the country, to the safeguards of the Constitution, and to the protection of the laws, in regard to their rights of person and of property, and to their civil and criminal responsibility. But they continue to be aliens, having taken no steps towards becoming citizens, and incapable of becoming such under the naturalization laws; and therefore remain subject to the power of Congress to expel them, or to order them to be removed and deported from the country, whenever in its judgment their removal is necessary or expedient for the public interest.

* * *

* * * Congress, under the power to exclude or expel aliens, might have directed any Chinese laborer, found in the United States without a certificate of residence, to be removed out of the country by executive officers, without judicial trial or examination, just as it might have authorized such officers absolutely to prevent his entrance into the country. But Congress has not undertaken to do this.

The effect of the provisions of * * * the act of 1892 is that, if a Chinese laborer, after the opportunity afforded him to obtain a certificate of residence within a year, at a convenient place, and without cost, is found without such a certificate, he shall be so far presumed to be not entitled to remain within the United States, that an officer of the customs, or a collector of internal revenue, or a marshal, or a deputy of either, may arrest him, not with a view to imprisonment or punishment, or to his immediate deportation without further inquiry, but in order to take him before a judge, for the purpose of a judicial hearing and determination of the only facts which, under the act of Congress, can have a material bearing upon the question whether he shall be sent out of the country, or be permitted to remain.

* * *

If no evidence is offered by the Chinaman, the judge makes the order of deportation, as upon a default. If he produces competent evidence to explain the fact of his not having a certificate, it must be considered by the judge; and if he thereupon appears to be entitled to a certificate, it is to be granted to him. If he proves that the collector of internal revenue has unlawfully refused to give him a certificate, he proves an "unavoidable cause," within the meaning of the act, for not procuring one. If he proves that he had procured a certificate which has been lost or destroyed, he is to be allowed a reasonable time to procure a duplicate thereof.

The provision which puts the burden of proof upon him of rebutting the presumption arising from his having no certificate, as well as the requirement of proof, "by at least one credible white witness, that he was a resident of the United States at the time of the passage of this act," is within the acknowledged power of every legislature to prescribe the evidence which shall be received, and the effect of that evidence, in the courts of its own government. * * * The competency of all witnesses, without regard to their color, to testify in the courts of the United States, rests on acts of Congress, which Congress may at its discretion modify or repeal. The reason for requiring a Chinese alien, claiming the privilege of remaining in the United States, to prove the fact of his residence here, at the time of the passage of the act, "by at least one credible white witness," may have been the experience of Congress, as mentioned by Mr. Justice Field in [the *Chinese Exclusion Case*], that the enforcement of former acts, under which the testimony of Chinese persons was admitted to prove similar facts, "was attended with great embarrassment, from the suspicious nature, in many instances, of the testimony offered to establish the residence of the parties, arising from the loose notions entertained by the witnesses of the obligation of an oath." 130 U.S. 598, 9 S.Ct. 627. And this requirement, not allowing such a fact to be proved solely by the testimony of aliens in a like situation, or of the same race, is quite analogous to the provision, which has existed for seventy-seven years in the naturalization laws, by which aliens applying for naturalization must prove their residence within the limits and under the jurisdiction of the United States, for five years next preceding, "by the oath or affirmation of citizens of the United States." * * *

The proceeding before a United States judge * * * is in no proper sense a trial and sentence for a crime or offence. It is simply the ascertainment, by appropriate and lawful means, of the fact whether the conditions exist upon which Congress has enacted that an alien of this class may remain within the country. The order of deportation is not a punishment for crime. It is not a banishment, in the sense in which that word is often applied to the expulsion of a citizen from his country by way of punishment. It is but a method of enforcing the return to his own country of an alien who has not complied with the conditions upon the performance of which the government of the nation, acting within its constitutional authority and through the proper departments, has determined that his continuing to reside here shall depend. He has not, therefore, been deprived of life, liberty or property, without due process of law; and the provisions of the Constitution, securing the right of trial by jury, and prohibiting unreasonable searches and seizures, and cruel and unusual punishments, have no application.

The question whether, and upon what conditions, these aliens shall be permitted to remain within the United States being one to be determined by the political departments of the government, the judicial department cannot properly express an opinion upon the wisdom, the policy or the justice of the measures enacted by Congress in the exercise of the powers confided to it by the Constitution over this subject.

* * *

In the [case stated above], the petitioner had, within the year, applied to a collector of internal revenue for a certificate of residence, and had been refused it, because he produced and could produce none but Chinese witnesses to prove the residence necessary to entitle him to a certificate. Being found without a certificate of residence, he was arrested by the marshal, and taken before the United States District Judge, and established to the satisfaction of the judge, that, because of the collector's refusal to give him a certificate of residence he was without one by unavoidable cause; and also proved, by a Chinese witness only, that he was a resident of the United States at the time of the passage of the act of 1892. Thereupon the judge ordered him to be remanded to the custody of the marshal, and to be deported from the United States, as provided in that act.

It would seem that the collector of internal revenue, when applied to for a certificate, might properly decline to find the requisite fact of residence upon testimony which, by an express provision of the act, would be insufficient to prove that fact at a hearing before the judge. But if the collector might have received and acted upon such testimony, and did, upon any ground, unjustifiably refuse a certificate of residence, the only remedy of the applicant was to prove by competent and sufficient evidence at the hearing before the judge the facts requisite to entitle him to a certificate. To one of those facts, that of residence, the statute, which, for the reasons already stated, appears to us to be within the constitutional authority of Congress to enact, peremptorily requires at that hearing the testimony of a credible white witness. And it was because no such testimony was produced, that the order of deportation was made.

Upon careful consideration of the subject, the only conclusion which appears to us to be consistent with the principles of international law, with the Constitution and laws of the United States, and with the previous decisions of this court, is that in each of these cases the judgment of the Circuit Court, dismissing the writ of *habeas corpus,* is right and must be

Affirmed.

Mr. Justice Brewer dissenting.

* * *

I rest my dissent on three propositions: First, that the persons against whom the penalties of * * * the act of 1892 are directed are persons lawfully residing within the United States; secondly, that as such they are within the protection of the Constitution, and secured by its guarantees against oppression and wrong; and, third, that [the Act] deprives them of liberty and imposes punishment without due process of law, and in disregard of constitutional guarantees, especially those found in the Fourth, Fifth, Sixth, and Eighth Articles of the Amendments.

And, first, these persons are lawfully residing within the limits of the United States. [Justice Brewer then discusses the Burlingame Treaty and the 1880 Treaty.]

* * *

While subsequently to [these treaties], Congress passed several acts to restrict the entrance into this country of Chinese laborers, and while the validity of this restriction was sustained in the *Chinese Exclusion case,* yet no act has been passed denying the right of those laborers who had once lawfully entered the country to remain, and they are here not as travellers or only temporarily. We must take judicial notice of that which is disclosed by the census, and which is also a matter of common knowledge. There are 100,000 and more of these persons living in this country, making their homes here, and striving by their labor to earn a livelihood. They are not travellers, but resident aliens.

But, further, [the Act] recognizes the fact of a lawful residence, and only applies to those who have such; for the parties * * * to be reached by its provisions, are "Chinese laborers within the limits of the United States at the time of the passage of this act, and who are entitled to remain in the United States." These appellants, therefore, are lawfully within the United States, and are here as residents, and not as travellers. They have lived in this country, respectively, since 1879, 1877, and 1874—almost as long a time as some of those who were members of the Congress that passed this act of punishment and expulsion.

That those who have become domiciled in a country are entitled to a more distinct and larger measure of protection than those who are simply passing through, or temporarily in it, has long been recognized by the law of nations. * * *

* * *

* * * [W]hatever rights a resident alien might have in any other nation, here he is within the express protection of the Constitution, especially in respect to those guarantees which are declared in the original amendments. It has been repeated so often as to become axiomatic, that

this government is one of enumerated and delegated powers, and, as declared in Article 10 of the amendments, "the powers not delegated to the United States by the Constitution, nor prohibited by it to the States, are reserved to the States respectively, or to the people."

It is said that the power here asserted is inherent in sovereignty. This doctrine of powers inherent in sovereignty is one both indefinite and dangerous. Where are the limits to such powers to be found, and by whom are they to be pronounced? Is it within legislative capacity to declare the limits? If so, then the mere assertion of an inherent power creates it, and despotism exists. May the courts establish the boundaries? Whence do they obtain the authority for this? Shall they look to the practices of other nations to ascertain the limits? The governments of other nations have elastic powers—ours is fixed and bounded by a written constitution. The expulsion of a race may be within the inherent powers of a despotism. History, before the adoption of this Constitution, was not destitute of examples of the exercise of such a power; and its framers were familiar with history, and wisely, as it seems to me, they gave to this government no general power to banish. Banishment may be resorted to as punishment for crime; but among the powers reserved to the people and not delegated to the government is that of determining whether whole classes in our midst shall, for no crime but that of their race and birthplace, be driven from our territory.

Whatever may be true as to exclusion, * * * I deny that there is any arbitrary and unrestrained power to banish residents, even resident aliens. What, it may be asked, is the reason for any difference? The answer is obvious. The Constitution has no extraterritorial effect, and those who have not come lawfully within our territory cannot claim any protection from its provisions. And it may be that the national government, having full control of all matters relating to other nations, has the power to build, as it were, a Chinese wall around our borders and absolutely forbid aliens to enter. But the Constitution has potency everywhere within the limits of our territory, and the powers which the national government may exercise within such limits are those, and only those, given to it by that instrument. Now, the power to remove resident aliens is, confessedly, not expressed. Even if it be among the powers implied, yet still it can be exercised only in subordination to the limitations and restrictions imposed by the Constitution. * * *

* * *

In the case of *Yick Wo v. Hopkins*, 118 U.S. 356, 369, 6 Sup. Ct. Rep. 1070, it was said: "The Fourteenth Amendment of the Constitution is not confined to the protection of citizens. It says: 'Nor shall any State deprive any person of life, liberty, or property without due process of law; nor deny to any person within its jurisdiction the equal protection of the laws.' These provisions are universal in their application to all persons within the territorial jurisdiction, without regard to any differences of race, of color, or of nationality; and the equal protection of the laws is a pledge of the protection of equal laws." * * *

If the use of the word "person" in the Fourteenth Amendment protects all individuals lawfully within the State, the use of the same word "person" in the Fifth must be equally comprehensive, and secures to all persons lawfully within the territory of the United States the protection named therein; and a like conclusion must follow as to the Sixth.

* * * [The Act] deprives of "life, liberty, and property without due process of law." It imposes punishment without a trial, and punishment cruel and severe. It places the liberty of one individual subject to the unrestrained control of another. Notice its provisions: It first commands all to register. He who does not register violates that law, and may be punished; and so the section goes on to say that one who has not complied with its requirements, and has no certificate of residence, "shall be deemed and adjudged to be unlawfully within the United States," and then it imposes as a penalty his deportation from the country. Deportation is punishment. It involves first an arrest, a deprival of liberty; and, second, a removal from home, from family, from business, from property.   * * *

* * * [I]t needs no citation of authorities to support the proposition that deportation is punishment. Every one knows that to be forcibly taken away from home, and family, and friends, and business, and property, and sent across the ocean to a distant land, is punishment; and that oftentimes most severe and cruel. * * *

But punishment implies a trial: "No person shall be deprived of life, liberty, or property, without due process of law." Due process requires that a man be heard before he is condemned, and both heard and condemned in the due and orderly procedure of a trial as recognized by the common law from time immemorial.   * * * And no person who has once come within the protection of the Constitution can be punished without a trial. It may be summary, as for petty offences and in cases of contempt, but still a trial, as known to the common law.   * * * But here, the Chinese are * * * arrested and, without a trial, punished by banishment.

Again, it is absolutely within the discretion of the collector to give or refuse a certificate to one who applies therefor. Nowhere is it provided what evidence shall be furnished to the collector, and nowhere is it made mandatory upon him to grant a certificate on the production of such evidence. It cannot be due process of law to impose punishment on any person for failing to have that in his possession, the possession of which he can obtain only at the arbitrary and unregulated discretion of any official. It will not do to say that the presumption is that the official will act reasonably and not arbitrarily. When the right to liberty and residence is involved, some other protection than the mere discretion of any official is required.   * * *

Again, a person found without such certificate may be taken before a United States Judge. What judge? A judge in the district in which the party resides or is found? There is no limitation in this respect. A Chinese laborer in San Francisco may be arrested by a deputy United States marshal, and taken before a judge in Oregon; and when so taken before that judge, it is made his duty to deport such laborer unless he proves his innocence of any violation of the law, and that, too, by at least one credible white witness. And how shall he obtain that witness? No provision is made in the statute therefor.   * * *

It is said that these Chinese are entitled, while they remain, to the safeguards of the Constitution and to the protection of the laws in regard to their rights of person and of property; but that they continue to be aliens, subject to the absolute power of Congress to forcibly remove them. In other words, the guarantees of "life, liberty, and property," named in the Constitution, are theirs by sufferance and not of right. Of what avail are such guarantees?

Once more: Supposing a Chinaman from San Francisco, having obtained a certificate, should go to New York or other place in pursuit of work, and on the way his certificate be lost or destroyed. He is subject to arrest and detention, the cost of which is in the discretion of the court, and judgment of deportation will be suspended a reasonable time to enable him to obtain a duplicate from the officer granting it. In other words, he cannot move about in safety without carrying with him this certificate. The situation was well described by Senator Sherman in the debate in the Senate: "They are here ticket-of-leave men; precisely as, under the Australian law, a convict is allowed to go at large upon a ticket-of-leave, these people are to be allowed to go at large and earn their livelihood, but they must have their tickets-of-leave in their possession." And he added: "This inaugurates in our system of government a new departure; one, I believe, never before practised, although it was suggested in conference that some such rules had been adopted in slavery times to secure the peace of society."

It is true this statute is directed only against the obnoxious Chinese; but if the power exists, who shall say it will not be exercised to-morrow against other classes and other people? If the guarantees of these amendments can be thus ignored in order to get rid of this distasteful class, what security have others that a like disregard of its provisions may not be resorted to?   * * *

* * *

In view of this enactment of the highest legislative body of the foremost Christian nation, may not the thoughtful Chinese disciple of Confucius fairly ask, Why do they send missionaries here?

Mr. Justice Field dissenting.

* * *

I had the honor to be the organ of the court in announcing [the] opinion and judgment [of the Court in the *Chinese Exclusion Case*]. I still adhere to the views there expressed in all particulars; but between legislation for the exclusion of Chinese persons—that is, to prevent them from entering the country—and legislation for the deportation of those who have acquired a residence in the country under a treaty with China, there is a wide and essential difference. The power of the government to exclude foreigners from this country, that is, to prevent them from entering it, whenever the public interests in its judgment require such exclusion, has been repeatedly asserted by the legislative and executive departments of our government and never denied; but its power to deport from the country persons lawfully domiciled therein by its consent, and engaged in the ordinary pursuits of life, has never been asserted by the legislative or executive departments except for crime, or as an act of war in view of existing or anticipated hostilities * * *.

* * *

[Justice Field then discusses the Alien and Sedition Acts of 1798, which among other things, authorized the President to remove aliens adjudged to be dangerous to the peace and safety of the United States.]

The duration of the act was limited to two years, and it has ever since been the subject of universal condemnation. In no other instance, until the law before us was passed, has any public man had the boldness to advocate the deportation of friendly aliens in time of peace. I repeat the statement, that in no other instance has the deportation of friendly aliens been advocated as a lawful measure by any department of our government. And it will surprise most people to learn that any such dangerous and despotic power lies in our government—a power which will authorize it to expel at pleasure, in time of peace, the whole body of friendly foreigners of any country domiciled herein by its permission, a power which can be brought into exercise whenever it may suit the pleasure of Congress, and be enforced without regard to the guarantees of the Constitution intended for the protection of the rights of all persons in their liberty and property. Is it possible that Congress can, at its pleasure, in disregard of the guarantees of the Constitution, expel at any time the Irish, German, French, and English who may have taken up their residence here on the invitation of the government, while we are at peace with the countries from which they came, simply on the ground that they have not been naturalized?

* * *

The purpose of [the 1892 law] was to secure the means of readily identifying the Chinese laborers present in the country and entitled to remain, from those who may have clandestinely entered the country in violation of its laws. Those entitled to remain, by having a certificate of their identification, would enable the officers of the government to readily discover and bring to punishment those not entitled to enter but who are excluded. To procure such a certificate was not a hardship to the laborers, but a means to secure full protection to them, and at the same time prevent an evasion of the law.

This object being constitutional, the only question for our consideration is the lawfulness of the procedure provided for its accomplishment, and this must be tested by the provisions of the Constitution and laws intended for the protection of all persons against encroachment upon their rights. Aliens from countries at peace with us, domiciled within our country by its consent, are entitled to all the guaranties for the protection of their persons and property which are secured to native-born citizens. The moment any human being from a country at peace with us comes within the jurisdiction of the United States, with their consent—and such consent will always be implied when not expressly withheld, and in the case of the Chinese laborers before us was in terms given by the treaty referred to—he becomes subject to all their laws, is amenable to their punishment and entitled to their protection. Arbitrary and despotic power can no more be exercised over them with reference to their persons and property, than over the persons and property of native-born citizens. They differ only from citizens in that they cannot vote or hold any public office. As men having our common humanity, they are protected by all the guaranties of the Constitution. To hold that they are subject to any different law or are less protected in any particular than other persons, is in my judgment to ignore the teachings of our history, the practice of our government, and the language of our Constitution. Let us test this doctrine by an illustration. If a foreigner who resides in the country by its consent commits a public offence, is he subject to be cut down, maltreated, imprisoned, or put to death by violence, without accusation made, trial had, and judgment of an established tribunal following the regular forms of judicial procedure? If any rule in the administration of justice is to be omitted or discarded in his case, what rule is it to be? If one rule may lawfully be laid aside in his case, another rule may also be laid aside, and all rules may be discarded. In such instances a rule of evidence may be set aside in one case, a rule of pleading in another; the testimony of eye-witnesses may be rejected and hearsay adopted, or no evidence at all may be received, but simply an inspection of the accused, as is often the case in tribunals of Asiatic countries where personal caprice and not settled rules prevail. That would be to establish a pure, simple, undisguised despotism and tyranny with respect to foreigners resident in the country by its consent, and such an exercise of power is not permissible under our Constitution. Arbitrary and tyrannical power has no place in our system. * * *

I utterly dissent from and reject the doctrine expressed in the opinion of the majority, that "Congress, under the power to exclude or expel aliens, might have directed any Chinese laborer found in the United States without a certificate of residence to be removed out of the country by executive officers, without judicial trial or examination, just as it might have authorized such officers absolutely to prevent his entrance into the country." An arrest in that way for that purpose would not be a reasonable seizure of the person within the meaning of the Fourth Article of the amendments to the Constitution. It would be brutal and oppressive. The existence of the power thus stated is only consistent with the admission that the government is one of unlimited and despotic power so far as aliens domiciled in the country are concerned. According to its theory, Congress might have ordered executive officers to take the Chinese laborers to the ocean and put them into a boat and set them adrift; or to take them to the borders of Mexico and turn them loose there; and in both cases without any means of support; indeed, it might have sanctioned towards these laborers the most shocking brutality conceivable. I utterly repudiate all such notions, and reply that brutality, inhumanity, and cruelty cannot be made elements in any procedure for the enforcement of the laws of the United States.

The majority of the court have, in their opinion, made numerous citations from the courts and the utterances of individuals upon the power of the government of an independent nation to exclude foreigners from entering its limits, but none, beyond a few loose observations, as to its power to expel and deport from the country those who are domiciled therein by its consent. * * *

The government of the United States is one of limited and delegated powers. It takes nothing from the usages or the former action of European governments, nor does it take any power by any supposed inherent sovereignty. There is a great deal of confusion in the use of the word "sovereignty" by law writers. Sovereignty or supreme power is in this country vested in the people, and only in the people. By them certain sovereign powers have been delegated to the government of the United States and other sovereign powers reserved to the States or to themselves. This is not a matter of inference and argument, but is the express declaration of the Tenth Amendment to the Constitution, passed to avoid any misinterpretation of the powers of the general government. That amendment declares that "The powers not delegated to the United States by the Constitution, nor prohibited by it to the States, are reserved to the States, respectively, or to the people." When, therefore, power is exercised by Congress, authority for it must be found in express terms in the Constitution, or in the means necessary or proper for the execution of the power expressed. If it cannot be thus found, it does not exist.

* * * [A Chinese laborer's] deportation is thus imposed for neglect to obtain a certificate of residence, from which he can only escape by showing his inability to secure it from one of the causes named. That is the punishment for his neglect, and that being of an infamous character can only be imposed after indictment, trial, and conviction. If applied to a citizen, none of the justices of this court would hesitate a moment to pronounce it illegal. Had the punishment been a fine, or anything else than of an infamous character, it might have been imposed without indictment; but not so now, unless we hold that a foreigner from a country at peace with us, though domiciled by the consent of our government, is withdrawn from all the guaranties of due process of law prescribed by the Constitution, when charged with an offence to which the grave punishment designated is affixed.

The punishment is beyond all reason in its severity. It is out of all proportion to the alleged offence. It is cruel and unusual. As to its cruelty, nothing can exceed a forcible deportation from a country of one's residence, and the breaking up of all the relations of friendship, family, and business there contracted. The laborer may be seized at a distance from his home, his family and his business, and taken before the judge for his condemnation, without permission to visit his home, see his family, or complete any unfinished business. Mr. Madison well pictures its character in his powerful denunciation of the alien law of 1798 in his celebrated report upon the resolutions, from which we have cited, and concludes, as we have seen, that *if a banishment of the sort described be not a punishment, and among the severest of punishments, it will be difficult to imagine a doom to which the name can be applied.*

Again, when taken before a United States judge, he is required, in order to avoid the doom declared, to establish clearly to the satisfaction of the judge that by reason of accident, sickness, or other unavoidable cause, he was unable to secure his certificate, and that he was a resident of the United States at the time, *by at least one credible white witness.* Here the government undertakes to exact of the party arrested the testimony of a witness of a particular color, though conclusive and incontestible testimony from others may be adduced. The law might as well have said, that unless the laborer should also present a particular person as a witness who could not be produced, from sickness, absence, or other cause, such as the archbishop of the State, to establish the fact of residence, he should be held to be unlawfully within the United States.

There are numerous other objections to the provisions of the act under consideration. Every step in the procedure provided, as truly said by counsel, tramples upon some constitutional right. Grossly it violates the Fourth Amendment * * *.

* * *

I will not pursue the subject further. The decision of the court and the sanction it would give to legislation depriving resident aliens of the guaranties of the Constitution fills me with apprehensions. Those guaranties are of priceless value to every one resident in the country, whether citizen or alien. I cannot but regard the decision as a blow against constitutional liberty, when it declares that Congress has the right to disregard the guaranties of the Constitution intended for the protection of all men, domiciled in the country with the consent of the government, in their rights of person and property. How far will its legislation go? The unnaturalized resident feels it to-day, but if Congress can disregard the guaranties with respect to any one domiciled in this country with its consent, it may disregard the guaranties with respect to naturalized citizens. What assurance have we that it may not declare that naturalized citizens of a particular country cannot remain in the United States after a certain day, unless they have in their possession a certificate that they are of good moral character and attached to the principles of our Constitution, which certificate they must obtain from a collector of internal revenue upon the testimony of at least one competent witness of a class or nationality to be designated by the government?

What answer could the naturalized citizen in that case make to his arrest for deportation, which cannot be urged in behalf of the Chinese laborers of to-day?

* * *

MR. CHIEF JUSTICE FULLER dissenting.

I also dissent from the opinion and judgment of the court in these cases.

If the protection of the Constitution extends to Chinese laborers who are lawfully within and entitled to remain in the United States under previous treaties and laws, then the question whether this act of Congress so far as it relates to them is in conflict with that instrument, is a judicial question, and its determination belongs to the judicial department.

However reluctant courts may be to pass upon the constitutionality of legislative acts, it is of the very essence of judicial duty to do so when the discharge of that duty is properly invoked.

* * *

The argument is that friendly aliens, who have lawfully acquired a domicil in this country, are entitled to avail themselves of the safeguards of the Constitution only while permitted to remain, and that the power to expel them and the manner of its exercise are unaffected by that instrument. It is difficult to see how this can be so in view of the operation of the power upon the existing rights of individuals; and to say that the residence of the alien, when invited and secured by treaties and laws, is held in subordination to the exertion against him, as an alien, of the absolute and unqualified power asserted, is to import a condition not recognized by the fundamental law. Conceding that the exercise of the power to exclude is committed to the political department, and that the denial of entrance is not necessarily the subject of judicial cognizance, the exercise of the power to expel, the manner in which the right to remain may be terminated, rest on different ground, since limitations exist or are imposed upon the deprivation of that which has been lawfully acquired. And while the general government is invested, in respect of foreign countries and their subjects or citizens, with the powers necessary to the maintenance of its absolute independence and security throughout its entire territory, it cannot, in virtue of any delegated power, or power implied therefrom, or of a supposed inherent sovereignty, arbitrarily deal with persons lawfully within the peace of its dominion. But the act before us is not an act to abrogate or repeal treaties or laws in respect of Chinese laborers entitled to remain in the United States, or to expel them from the country, and no such intent can be imputed to Congress. As to them, registration for the purpose of identification is required, and the deportation denounced for failure to do so is by way of punishment to coerce compliance with that requisition. No euphuism can disguise the character of the act in this regard. It directs the performance of a judicial function in a particular way, and inflicts punishment without a judicial trial. It is, in effect, a legislative sentence of banishment, and, as such, absolutely void. Moreover, it contains within it the germs of the assertion of an unlimited and arbitrary power, in general, incompatible with the immutable principles of justice, inconsistent with the nature of our government, and in conflict with the written Constitution by which that government was created and those principles secured.[a]

Notes

1.   Are Exclusion and Deportation Two Sides of the Same Coin?

Justice Gray states that "[t]he right of a nation to expel or deport foreigners, who have not been naturalized or taken any steps towards

a. The exclusion of Chinese was extended several times and not repealed until 1943. *See generally* F. Riggs, Pressures on Congress: A Study of Repeal of Chinese Exclusion (1950).—eds.

becoming citizens of the country, rests upon the same ground, and is as absolute and unqualified as the right to prohibit and prevent their entrance into the country." The dissents of Justices Brewer, Field and Fuller argue that the Constitution imposes limits on the *exercise* of the deportation power—limits that may not apply to the exclusion power. But do these Justices doubt the *existence* of the power to deport aliens? Do the constitutional sources of the exclusion power equally support a power to deport aliens who have entered the country?

Under current law, aliens may be deported (1) for conduct occurring prior to their entry (*e.g.,* INA § 241(a)(4)(D) (Nazis)); (2) if they were excludable at time of entry (INA § 241(a)(1)(A)); and (3) for conduct occurring after a lawful entry (*e.g.,* INA § 241(a)(2)(A) (conviction of a crime involving moral turpitude)). Does the apparent justification for the first two deportation categories—"delayed exclusion" of those who should not have been allowed to enter—apply to aliens in the third category? If not, what is an alternative rationale?

2.   The Dissenters

a. *Exclusion v. Deportation.* Justice Field wrote the opinion for the Court in the *Chinese Exclusion Case*—an opinion joined by Justice Brewer. (Chief Justice Fuller joined the Court after the *Chinese Exclusion Case* was decided.) On what grounds were these Justices not convinced that the exclusion case controlled the deportation case?

For Justice Brewer the answer was "obvious": "The Constitution has no extraterritorial effect, and those who have not come lawfully within our territory cannot claim any protection from its provisions. * * * But the Constitution has potency elsewhere within the limits of our territory * * *." Does this adequately distinguish the *Chinese Exclusion Case?* The alien in that case was detained upon a steamship within the port of San Francisco. How was he not "within our territory"? Nor does Brewer's second ground (unlawful entry) appear persuasive. Chae Chan Ping was returning to his prior lawful residence in this country.

Chief Justice Fuller seems to view deportation as different from exclusion because the former entails "deprivation of that which has been lawfully acquired." Does this adequately distinguish the *Chinese Exclusion Case?* Was not Chae Chan Ping being deprived of that which he had lawfully acquired? Does Fuller's analysis suggest that aliens who enter without inspection are not entitled to the same constitutional protections against deportation as aliens who enter lawfully?

We will see repeated efforts to draw a line between exclusion and deportation based on the *location* (Brewer's ground) or *stake* (Fuller's ground) of the alien. To foreshadow what will be a major theme of this book, we do not believe that the "location argument" makes sense. Furthermore, if one takes the "stake argument" seriously—which we do—it may require a fundamental rethinking of both the *Chinese Exclusion Case* and *Fong Yue Ting.* We will address these issues more fully after we have considered the current statutory provisions regarding exclusion and deportation.

b. *Framing the Constitutional Challenge.* The dissenters paid little attention to Congress' decision to single out laborers of Chinese origin. Why not, given the Court's willingness to strike down the discriminatory municipal ordinance in *Yick Wo*? What exactly did the dissenters find objectionable about the statute, and why did they apparently find that objection more persuasive than a national origin or racial discrimination challenge?

c. *Deportation and Punishment.* Each of the dissenters asserts that the statute imposes "punishment" on aliens who are ordered deported for failure to procure a certificate of residence. But consider the following characterization: The statute is an ordinary regulation of immigration. Aliens residing in this country are asked to demonstrate that they are here lawfully. Those who do so are given a certificate which protects them against deportation; those unable to demonstrate that they are entitled to a certificate are presumed to be here illegally (or deemed to be here illegally), and hence deported. Perhaps the method of determining lawfulness of status is troubling (maybe even a violation of due process), but that does not make the resulting deportation "punishment." Are you persuaded? Do the dissenters hold the view that any deportation would constitute "punishment"? What if Congress had adopted a statute requiring the deportation of all Chinese laborers in the United States?

d. *Field's Lingering Anger.* Justice Field remained so incensed over the decision in *Fong Yue Ting* that he even proposed a kind of court-packing plan to friends who were influential with President Cleveland. The story of his intrigues, and the bitter internal battle within the Court when he circulated his dissenting opinion, is told in Westin, *Stephen J. Field and the Headnote to* O'Neil v. Vermont: *A Snapshot of the Fuller Court at Work*, 67 Yale L.J. 363, 380–83 (1958).

3. Deportation and Punishment: *Wong Wing v. United States*

The majority opinion holds that an "order of deportation is not a punishment for crime"; therefore, "the provisions of the Constitution, securing the right of trial by jury, and prohibiting unreasonable searches and seizures, and cruel and unusual punishments, have no application." Does this mean that Congress could imprison aliens unlawfully residing in the United States without providing them the protections mandated by the Constitution in criminal proceedings?

The Supreme Court answered this question in the landmark case of *Wong Wing v. United States,* 163 U.S. 228, 16 S.Ct. 977, 41 L.Ed. 140 (1896), which struck down a section of the 1892 immigration act not considered in *Fong Yue Ting*. The section provided that any Chinese citizen judged to be in the United States illegally "shall be imprisoned at hard labor for a period of not exceeding one year and thereafter removed from the United States." Aliens charged under the section were not afforded a trial by jury. Act of May 5, 1892, Ch. 60, 27 Stat. 25. The Court struck down the provision:

The Chinese exclusion acts operate upon two classes—one consisting of those who came into the country with its consent, the other of those who have come into the United States without their consent and in disregard of the law. Our previous decisions have settled that it is within the constitutional power of Congress to deport both of these classes, and to commit the enforcement of the law to executive officers.

The question now presented is whether Congress can promote its policy in respect to Chinese persons by adding to its provisions for their exclusion and expulsion punishment by imprisonment at hard labor, to be inflicted by the judgment of any justice, judge or commissioner of the United States, without a trial by jury. * * *

We think it clear that detention, or temporary confinement, as part of the means necessary to give effect to the provisions for the exclusion or expulsion of aliens would be valid. Proceedings to exclude or expel would be vain if those accused could not be held in custody pending the inquiry into their true character and while arrangements were being made for their deportation. Detention is a usual feature of every case of arrest on a criminal charge, even when an innocent person is wrongfully accused; but it is not imprisonment in a legal sense.

So, too, we think it would be plainly competent for Congress to declare the act of an alien in remaining unlawfully within the United States to be an offence, punishable by fine or imprisonment, if such offence were to be established by a judicial trial.

But the evident meaning of the section in question, and no other is claimed for it by the counsel for the Government, is that the detention provided for is an imprisonment at hard labor, which is to be undergone before the sentence of deportation is to be carried into effect, and that such imprisonment is to be adjudged against the accused by a justice, judge or commissioner, upon a summary hearing. * * *

* * *

Our views, upon the question thus specifically pressed upon our attention, may be briefly expressed thus: We regard it as settled by our previous decisions that the United States can, as a matter of public policy, by Congressional enactment, forbid aliens or classes of aliens from coming within their borders, and expel aliens or classes of aliens from their territory, and can, in order to make effectual such decree of exclusion or expulsion, devolve the power and duty of identifying and arresting the persons included in such decree, and causing their deportation, upon executive or subordinate officials.

But when Congress sees fit to further promote such a policy by subjecting the persons of such aliens to infamous punishment at hard labor, or by confiscating their property, we think such legislation, to be valid, must provide for a judicial trial to establish the guilt of the accused.

No limits can be put by the courts upon the power of Congress to protect, by summary methods, the country from the advent of aliens whose race or habits render them undesirable as citizens, or to expel such if they have already found their way into our land and unlawfully remain therein. But to declare unlawful residence within the country to be an infamous crime, punishable by deprivation of liberty and property, would be to pass out of the sphere of constitutional legislation, unless provision were made that the fact of guilt should first be established by a judicial trial. It is not consistent with the theory of our government that the legislature should, after having defined an offence as an infamous crime, find the fact of guilt and adjudge the punishment by one of its own agents.

Id. at 234–37, 16 S.Ct. 979–81.

Both *Wong Wing* and *Yick Wo* involved immigrants but not immigration. We observed earlier that federal preemption complicates the direct application of *Yick Wo*'s reasoning to challenge the exclusion law in the *Chinese Exclusion Case*. *Wong Wing*, however, upheld a constitutional challenge to a federal statute, and in that respect it may stand more clearly than *Yick Wo* for the proposition that aliens are members of the constitutional community apart from their right to enter and remain in this country.

4. Modern Attacks on "Plenary Power"

Professor Henkin has harshly criticized the view that the Constitution imposes no limits on the "plenary" power of Congress to exclude or deport aliens.

The doctrine that the Constitution neither limits governmental control over the admission of aliens nor secures the right of admitted aliens to reside here emerged in the oppressive shadow of a racist, nativist mood a hundred years ago. It was reaffirmed during our fearful, cold war, McCarthy days. It has no foundation in principle. It is a constitutional fossil, a remnant of a prerights jurisprudence that we have proudly rejected in other respects. Nothing in our Constitution, its theory, or history warrants exempting any exercise of governmental power from constitutional restraint. No such exemption is required or even warranted by the fact that the power to control immigration is unenumerated, inherent in sovereignty, and extraconstitutional.

As a blanket exemption of immigration laws from constitutional limitations, *Chinese Exclusion* is a "relic from a different era." [47] That era was one in which constitutional restraints were deemed inapplicable to actions by the United States outside its

47. The Court in [*Reid v. Covert*, 354 U.S. 1, 12, 77 S.Ct. 1222, 1 L.Ed.2d 1148 (1957)], used this phrase to reject *Ross v. McIntyre*, 140 U.S. 453, 11 S.Ct. 897, 35 L.Ed. 581 (1891).

territory; when orotund generalities about sovereignty and national security were a substitute for significant scrutiny of governmental action impinging on individual rights; when the Bill of Rights had not yet become our national hallmark and the principal justification and preoccupation of judicial review. It was an era before United States commitment to international human rights; before enlightenment in and out of the United States brought an end both to official racial discrimination at home and to national-origins immigration laws; before important freedoms were recognized as preferred, inviting strict scrutiny if they were invaded and requiring a compelling public interest to uphold their invasion. Since that era, the Supreme Court has held that the Bill of Rights applies to foreign as well as to domestic affairs, in war as well as in peace, to aliens as well as to citizens, abroad as well as at home. The Court has left only immigration and deportation outside the reach of fundamental constitutional protections.

The power of Congress to control immigration and to regulate alienage and naturalization is plenary. But even plenary power is subject to constitutional restraints. I cannot believe that the Court would hold today that the Constitution permits either exclusion on racial or religious grounds or deportation of persons lawfully admitted who have resided peacefully here. * * *

Chinese Exclusion—its very name is an embarrassment—must go.

Henkin, *The Constitution and United States Sovereignty: A Century of* Chinese Exclusion *and its Progeny,* 100 Harv.L.Rev. 853, 862–63 (1987).

Several commentators have analyzed how in recent decades the plenary power doctrine has undergone significant erosion—both directly and indirectly—and courts have become more willing to hear constitutional claims. See S. Legomsky, Immigration and the Judiciary 177–222 (1987); Motomura, *The Curious Evolution of Immigration Law: Procedural Surrogates for Substantive Constitutional Rights,* 92 Colum.L.Rev. 1625 (1992); Motomura, *Immigration Law After a Century of Plenary Power: Phantom Constitutional Norms and Statutory Interpretation,* 100 Yale L.J. 545 (1990); Schuck, *The Transformation of Immigration Law,* 84 Colum. L.Rev. 1 (1984).

SECTION B.   A BRIEF HISTORY OF IMMIGRATION TO THE UNITED STATES

Writing in the Federalist Papers, John Jay observed: "Providence has been pleased to give this one connected country to one united people—a people descended from the same ancestors, speaking the same language, professing the same religion, attached to the same principles of government, very similar in their manners and customs." The Federalist No. 2. This statement, clearly false when written in 1787, cannot begin to describe the ethnic, racial, religious and political richness that two hundred years of immigration have brought the United States.

Our immigration history has shown America at its best and worst. Literally tens of millions of aliens have been welcomed to our shores. The United States has accepted more refugees for permanent settlement than any other country in the world. And in a time of growing restrictionism in most of the countries of the world, the United States currently admits for permanent residence well over half a million aliens a year. Unlike many of the Western industrialized nations, it is relatively easy for lawfully admitted aliens to attain citizenship; and any person born in the United States is an American citizen, irrespective of the nationality of her parents.[13]

But there is also a darker side to the history of American immigration policy—one that often has overshadowed the national symbol of the Statue of Liberty. "The image of the golden door," the United States Commission on Civil Rights has written, "is a tarnished one." United States Commission on Civil Rights, The Tarnished Golden Door: Civil Rights Issues in Immigration 1 (1981). Some federal laws have been blatantly racist, prohibiting immigration from China and Japan and favoring northern and western Europeans over southern and eastern Europeans. Persons have been excluded or deported for their political beliefs. Enforcement of the immigration laws has, at times, violated fundamental notions of fairness and decency. Aliens continue to be scapegoats for some of the problems of American society.

We will explore these conflicting perspectives in the chapters ahead. What follows is a brief history of American immigration. Note particularly the role that economic, political, and international events have played in the formulation of immigration policy.

SELECT COMMISSION ON IMMIGRATION AND REFUGEE POLICY [SCIRP], U.S. IMMIGRATION POLICY AND THE NATIONAL INTEREST

Staff Report 92, 93, 161–216 (1981).

IMMIGRATION AND U.S. HISTORY—THE EVOLUTION OF THE OPEN SOCIETY*

* * * The first inhabitants to the New World, scientists believe, came when the last great Ice Age lowered the level of the Pacific Ocean sufficiently to expose a land bridge between Asia and North America, enabling people to cross the ocean from Asia. Recent evidence suggests that the ancestors of the present-day native Americans settled in North America more than 30,000 years ago and by about 10,000 B.C. had expanded their settlement as far as the tip of South America.

Some 116 centuries later, migration to America occurred again, this time coming from the opposite direction. European monarchs and mer-

---

13. "All persons born or naturalized in the United States, and subject to the jurisdiction thereof, are citizens of the United States and of the State wherein they reside." U.S. Const. Amend. 14, § 1. The section's reference to "subject to the jurisdiction thereof" is intended to except from citizenship children born to representatives of foreign countries residing in this country. *See United States v. Wong Kim Ark,* 169 U.S. 649, 18 S.Ct. 456, 42 L.Ed. 890 (1898).

* Lawrence H. Fuchs and Susan S. Forbes, principal authors. [The footnotes have been renumbered—eds.]

chants—whether Spanish, Portuguese, French, English or Dutch—encouraged exploration and then settlement of the newly "discovered" lands of the Americas. The descendants of the occupants of these lands, native American Indians, sometimes joke that the "Indians had bad immigration laws." In fact, there were a variety of responses. In some cases, Indian tribes welcomed the new settlers, negotiating treaties, many of which were abrogated by the colonists. In other instances, the Indians fought newcomers who encroached upon their lands. Whatever the response, though, most tribes found themselves overwhelmed by the better-armed Europeans.

The continents of the Western Hemisphere soon became a microcosm of the European continent, peopled in the north by northern and western Europeans and in the south by the Spanish and Portuguese.

Because of the diversity of national origins, it was by no means certain at the time of English settlement that those who spoke the English language would dominate the development of the area that eventually became the United States. To the south of the British-occupied territories were Spanish colonies, to the north were the French, between were Dutch and Swedish settlements. By the second half of the eighteenth century, though, the French had been defeated and had withdrawn from Canada, a modus vivendi of sorts had been established with Spain and the small Dutch and Swedish settlements had been incorporated into the middle colonies of New York, New Jersey, Pennsylvania and Delaware. Hence, it was a certainty by the time of the Revolution that the newly formed republic would be one in which the English influence would prevail.

Despite Anglo–American dominance, however, the colonial period saw the establishment of a tendency towards ethnic pluralism that also was to become a vital part of U.S. life. At least a dozen national groups found homes in the area. Most came in search of religious toleration, political freedom and/or economic opportunity. Many, particularly some ancestors of those who later thought of themselves as "the best people," came as paupers, or as bond servants and laborers who paid for their passage by promising to serve employers, whom they could not leave for a specified number of years. Not all came of their own free will. Convicts and vagrants were shipped from English jails in the seventeenth century. Beginning in Virginia in 1619, some 350,000 slaves were brought from Africa until the end of the slave trade in 1807.

Non–English arrivals were treated with ambivalence, whether they were Dutch, German or even Scotch–Irish Presbyterians from Great Britain. The Germans who came to Pennsylvania, for example, had first learned of the colony through an advertising campaign designed by William Penn to attract their attention and migration. The earliest German settlers came in the hopes of finding liberty of conscience, and once their glowing reports were sent back to Germany, others of their nationality— seeking not only religious toleration but economic opportunity—followed. They were welcomed by many English colonists who applauded their industry and piety. Yet, they were attacked by others who questioned if they would ever assimilate.

This question asked about each successive wave of immigrants was to become a familiar refrain in U.S. history, but the ambivalence towards foreigners was by no means great enough during the colonial period to cause restrictions on immigration. In fact, the Declaration of Independence cites as one of the failings of King George III, and thus a justification for revolution, that "He has endeavored to prevent the Population of these States; for that purpose obstructing the Laws for Naturalization of Foreigners; refusing to pass others to encourage their migrations hither, and raising the conditions of new Appropriations of Lands."

After the revolution and the creation of a new government, Americans kept the gates of their new country open for several reasons. The land was vast, relatively rich and sparsely settled. At the time of the first census, taken in 1790, America had a recorded population of 3,227,000—all immigrants or descendants of seventeenth and eighteenth century arrivals.[1] The population density at that time was about 4.5 persons per square mile. Labor was needed to build communities as well as to clear farms on the frontier and push back the Indians. People were needed to build a strong country, strong enough to avoid coming once again under the rule of a foreign power. Moreover, many U.S. citizens thought of their new nation as an experiment in freedom—to be shared by all people, regardless of former nationality, who wished to be free.

Despite all of these reasons for a liberal immigration policy, some doubts still remained about its wisdom. Although people were needed to build the new nation, some feared that the entry of too many aliens would cause disruptions and subject the United States to those foreign influences that the nation sought to escape in independence.

With the signing of the Treaty of Paris in 1783, the United States was officially recognized as an independent nation and the history of official U.S. immigration policy began. * * *

Beginning in 1790, Congress passed a series of acts regulating naturalization. The first act permitted the liberal granting of citizenship to immigrants. After a heated debate—in which the losing side argued not only for strict naturalization requirements but also for barriers against the admission of "the common class of vagrants, paupers and other outcasts of Europe"—Congress required a two-year period of residence and the renunciation of former allegiances before citizenship could be claimed.

By 1795, though, the French Revolution, and the ensuing turmoil in Europe, had raised new fears about foreign political intrigue and influence. A new naturalization act, passed in 1795, imposed more stringent requirements including a five-year residency requirement for citizenship and the renunciation of not only allegiances but titles of nobility. Still, some thought U.S. standards for naturalization were too liberal, and, in 1798, another law was passed that raised the residency requirement to fourteen years. At the same time, the Alien Enemies Act and the Alien Friends Act

1. More than 75 percent of this population was of British origin, another eight percent was German and the rest were mainly Dutch, French or Spanish. In addition, approximately a half million black slaves and perhaps as many Native Americans lived within the borders of the United States.

gave the president powers to deport any alien whom he considered dangerous to the welfare of the nation. One proponent of these laws explained his support: "If no law of this kind was passed, it would be in the power of an individual State to introduce such a number of aliens into the country, as might not only be dangerous, but as might be sufficient to overturn the Government, and introduce the greatest confusion in the country."

The xenophobia that gave rise to the Alien Acts of 1798 passed with the transfer of power from the Federalist to the Republican Party in 1800. The [Alien Friends Act was] permitted to expire,[a] and, in 1802, a new Naturalization Act re-established the provisions of the 1795 Act—what was to become a permanent five-year residency requirement for citizenship. While the Republicans were by no means free of suspicion of foreigners, they were not sufficiently fearful of the consequences of immigration to impose any restraints on the entry or practices of the foreign born. Instead, they pursued a policy that has been aptly described by Maldwyn Allen Jones in his history, *American Immigration:*

> Americans had to some degree reconciled the contradictory ideas that had influenced the thinking of the Revolutionary generation and had developed a clearly defined immigration policy. All who wished to come were welcome to do so; but no special inducements or privileges would be offered them.

For the next 75 years, the federal government did little about the regulation of immigration. It did establish procedures that made the counting of a portion of all immigrants possible. In 1819 Congress passed a law requiring ship captains to supply to the Collector of Customs a list of all passengers on board upon arrival at U.S. ports. This list was to indicate their sex, occupation, age and "country to which they severally belonged." At first only Atlantic and Gulf port information was collected; Pacific ports were added after 1850. Immigration information from Hawaii, Puerto Rico and Alaska dates only from the beginning of the twentieth century, as does the recording of information across land borders with Canada and Mexico.

Although a fully accurate picture of the level of all immigration cannot be made, the data available have enabled historians to sketch the general composition and trend of U.S. immigration. These data show a steadily increasing level of immigration. Immigrants arriving between the end of the Revolutionary War and the passage of the 1819 act are estimated to have totaled about 250,000. During the next ten years, over 125,000 came, and between 1830 and 1860, almost 4.5 million European immigrants arrived in the United States. Never before had the United States had to incorporate so large a number of newcomers into its midst. At first, the new arrivals were greeted with enthusiasm. With a nation to be built, peasants from Norway were as welcome as skilled craftsmen from Great Britain and experienced farmers from western, Protestant Germany. The novelist Herman Melville characterized this spirit:

> There is something in the contemplation of the mode in which America has been settled, that, in a noble breast, should forever extinguish the prejudices of national dislikes.

a. The Alien Enemies Act is still on the books. 50 U.S.C.A. §§ 21–23.—eds.

Settled by the people of all nations, all nations may claim her for their own. You cannot spill a drop of American blood without spilling the blood of the whole world. . . .

We are the heirs of all time, and with all nations, we divide our inheritance. On this Western Hemisphere all tribes and people are forming into one federate whole; and there is a future which shall see the estranged children of Adam restored as to the old hearthstone in Eden.

Beginning in the 1830s, though, the composition of the groups entering the United States began to change, and few U.S. residents thought so romantically about the new immigrants.

Waves of Irish during the potato famines and German Catholic immigrants flowed into the country during the European depressions of the 1840s. These Catholics entered a country that was not only overwhelmingly Protestant, but that had been settled by some of the most radical sectarians, who prided themselves on their independence from the Pope's authority as well as from any king's. To begin with, U.S. residents had brought with them from Europe centuries of memories of the Catholic–Protestant strife that had so long dominated that continent's social and political life. Much anti-Irish feeling arose from these roots and was nourished by an oversimplified view of Catholicism which saw Catholics as unable to become good citizens—that is, independent and self-reliant—since they were subject to orders from the church. Even before the mass immigration of Catholics during the 1840s and 1850s, the xenophobic inventor Samuel F.B. Morse warned his fellow Americans:

How is it possible that foreign turbulence imported by shiploads, that riot and ignorance in hundreds of thousands of human priest-controlled machines should suddenly be thrown into our society and not produce turbulence and excess? Can one throw mud into pure water and not disturb its clearness?

It was easy to blame these new immigrants for many of the problems of the rapidly changing, increasingly urban nineteenth century U.S. society. Hostility against immigrants grew as they were accused of bringing intemperance, crime and disease to the new world. The first Select Committee of the House of Representatives to study immigration concluded:

that the number of emigrants from foreign countries into the United States is increasing with such rapidity as to jeopardize the peace and tranquility of our citizens, if not the permanency of the civil, religious, and political institutions of the United States. . . . Many of them are the outcasts of foreign countries; *paupers, vagrants,* and *malefactors* . . . sent hither at the expense of foreign governments, to relieve them from the burden of their maintenance.

A Protestant magazine sounded a further alarm by suggesting that "the floodgates of intemperance, pauperism and crime are thrown open by [immigrants], and if nothing be done to close them, they will carry us back to all of the drunkenness and evil of former times.["]

Out of these fears arose an alliance of those committed to saving the United States from the alleged dangers of immigration. Composed of social reformers who hoped to preserve the nation's institutions, some Protestant evangelicals who hoped to preserve the nation's morals and nativists who hoped to preserve the nation's ethnic purity, they formed associations, such as the secret Order of the Star–Spangled Banner, and political parties, such as the Know–Nothing Party.

These groups were committed to placing a curb on immigration itself and to ensuring that foreigners not be permitted to participate in the nation's political affairs. The naturalization statutes were a principal target of their concern. A pamphlet of the Know–Nothing Party warned of the inadequacy of these laws in protecting the nation against fraud:

> It is notorious that the grossest frauds have been practiced on our naturalization laws, and that thousands and tens of thousands have every year deposited votes in the ballot box, who could not only not read them, and knew nothing of the nature of the business in which they were engaged, but who had not been six months in the country, and, in many cases, hardly six days.

The party hoped to avoid these problems by eliminating the participation of even naturalized immigrants in the political process.

At its most vitriolic, nativism manifested itself in anti-Catholic riots against the Irish. New York, Philadelphia and Boston all saw such violence. Exposes revealing the "truth" about Catholic nunneries—that they were dens of iniquity and vice—precipitated the burning of convents and Catholic churches.[2] Although strident, nativist voices did not prevail. Attacks on ethnic groups usually came from a small, but vocal portion of the population that by no means represented the wishes of all Americans. Even during the times in which nativism reached its peak, there continued to be a variety of potent support for unlimited immigration. Economic needs, reinforced by the ideals of opportunity and freedom that were more deeply rooted in the country than was the anti-Catholic heritage or fears of foreign takeover, worked against restricting immigration or making requirements for citizenship or voting more stringent.

After the Civil War, the country's desire for immigrants seemed insatiable * * *. Railroads were being laid across the nation, thus opening vast lands for settlement. Labor was needed to gouge the earth for coal and iron, to work in rapidly developing mills and to build cities.

As demand for labor increased, so too did the number of immigrants. From 1860 to 1880, about 2.5 million Europeans entered this country each decade; during the 1880s the number more than doubled to 5.25 million. Another 16 million immigrants entered during the next quarter century, with 1.25 million entering in 1908.

Because the numbers of immigrants were so large, it appeared as if the United States had never before experienced immigration of this sort. Not

---

2. Not all convent-burning was indicative of anti-Catholicism per se. The burning of the Ursuline Convent at Charlestown, Massa- chusetts was due mainly to the local brick-makers' resentment of Irish economic competition.

only was there a change in the size of the flow, there was also a change, once more, in the source of immigration. The migration before the 1880s had been overwhelmingly from northern and western Europe. Even the hated Irish Catholics had come from a country where English was generally spoken and Irish immigration was now traditional. Less than three percent of the foreign-born population of the country had come from eastern or southern Europe. During the 1890s that pattern began to reverse itself, and during the first decade of the twentieth century, about 70 percent came from the new areas.

Just as the Irish and Germans had appeared to Americans to be more "foreign" than English Protestants, so too did the new immigrants appear to be more "foreign" than the old ones. In what may be an inevitable process, the old immigrants had become familiar and, therefore, respectable while the new ones were put under the closest possible scrutiny for signs of dissimilitude. And, alien characteristics are exactly what many Americans found—strange coloring, strange physiques, strange customs and strange languages.

The new immigrants were disliked and feared. They were considered culturally different and incapable of this country's version of self-government, and not because of their backgrounds but because they were thought to be biologically and inherently inferior. Influential professors of history, sociology and eugenics taught that some races could never become what came to be called "100 percent American."

A leading academic proponent of nativism, Edward Ross, wrote of Jews that they are "the polar opposite of our pioneer breed. Undersized and weak muscled, they shun bodily activity and are exceedingly sensitive to pain." He also lamented that it was impossible to make Boy Scouts out of them. Italians, he noted, "possess a distressing frequency of low foreheads, open mouths, weak chins, poor features, skewed faces, small or knobby crania and backless heads." According to Ross, Italians "lack the power to take rational care of themselves." He concluded that the new immigrants in general were undesirable because they "are beaten men from beaten races, representing the worst failures in the struggle for existence."

Even though * * * mortality statistics do not support the contention that the new immigrants were inherently diseased or biologically inferior, such sentiments began to take their toll. In 1882 the United States passed its first racist, restrictionist immigration law, the Chinese Exclusion Act. From 1860 to 1880, Chinese immigration had grown from 40,000 to over 100,000. Chinese labor had been welcomed to lay railway lines and work in mining. However, with the completion of the transcontinental railroad, which was followed by a depression in the 1870s, intense anti-Chinese feelings developed, particularly in the West, where hard-working and ambitious Chinese had made lives for themselves.

The attacks upon the Chinese often focused upon their inability, in the eyes of their opponents, to assimilate. In 1876, a California State Senate Committee described the Chinese as follows:

They fail to comprehend our system of government; they perform no duties of citizenship.... They do not comprehend or appreciate our social ideas.... The great mass of the Chinese ... are not amenable to our laws.... They do not recognize the sanctity of an oath.

The supposed criminality of the Chinese was of particular concern. Although the crime statistics of the period do not bear out the accusations, the Chinese were believed to be criminals nevertheless. The state senate committee complained that "the Pacific Coast has become a Botany Bay to which the criminal classes of China are brought in large numbers and the people of this coast are compelled to endure this affliction." The Chinese were especially accused of bringing gambling and prostitution to the region. In 1876, *Scribner's Magazine* noted that "no matter how good a Chinaman may be, ladies never leave their children with them, especially little girls." The legislative committee concluded that "the Chinese are inferior to any race God ever made ... [and] have no souls to save, and if they have, they are not worth saving."

Restrictionists—looking for justifications for closing other types of immigration—also eyed European immigrants as criminally inclined. The Police Commissioner of New York, Theodore Bingham, wrote in the *North American Review* that ["]85 percent of New York criminals were of exotic origin and half of them were Jewish." The author of an article in *Collier's Magazine* labeled Italians as "the most vicious and dangerous" criminals, and he suggested that "80 percent of the limited number of clever thieves" were Jewish.

Again, the crime statistics do not bear out the accusations. * * * The majority of immigrants were arrested for the petty crimes—vagrancy, disorderly conduct, breach of the peace, drunkenness—associated with poverty and difference in values. Immigrants were statistically more likely to commit minor offenses than were the native born who tended to commit property crimes and crimes of personal violence. According to the statistics, there was only one real cause for concern as far as immigrant crime was concerned. The children of the foreign born were the most likely group of all to commit crimes. Their crimes more often resembled those of the native born, though, than those of immigrants. This pattern indicates, more than anything else, that acculturation occurred even in the area of crime.

Despite the known evidence that immigrants were neither inherently criminal nor diseased, nativist arguments emphasizing the inferiority of immigrants were widely accepted. Restrictionists called for legislation that would decide whether the United States would be, as some put it, peopled by British, German and Scandinavian stock, or the new immigrants, "beaten men from beaten races; representing the worst failures in the struggle for existence."

Earlier, nativism had been offset by confidence that the United States had room for all, by a tradition of welcoming the poor and the oppressed and by belief that life in the New World would transform all comers into new Adams and Eves in the American Eden. At the end of the century, however, these ideas were affected by four historical developments:

- The official closing of the U.S. frontier;
- Burgeoning cities and increasing industrialization;
- The persistence of immigrants from southern and eastern Europe in maintaining their traditions; and
- The Catholic or Jewish religion of most of the new immigrants.

In the light of these developments, many Americans began to doubt the country's capacity to welcome and absorb the ever-increasing waves of new immigrants.

Evidence of this new feeling about European immigration could be seen as early as 1891. There had been earlier attempts at controlling the entry of immigrants to the United States—in the Act of 1875 that excluded prostitutes and alien convicts and in the Act of 1882 that barred the entry of lunatics, idiots, convicts and those liable to become a public charge—but these were not as comprehensive as the measure debated that year. One of the principal spokesmen for the bill, Henry Cabot Lodge, of Massachusetts, urged his fellow congressmen to establish new categories of admission to the United States in order to "sift ... the chaff from the wheat" and prevent "a decline in the quality of American citizenship." The 1891 bill added new categories of exclusion that mirrored the concerns about the biological inferiority of immigrants. Those suffering from loathsome or contagious diseases and aliens convicted of crimes involving moral turpitude were barred from entry. The bill also provided for the medical inspection of all arrivals.[3]

Both houses of Congress quickly passed the measure; in the Senate, noted the *New York Times,* "the matter did not even occupy ten minutes." The measure did not go far enough for the quantitative restrictionists, though, since it did not succeed in stemming the flow of new entrants. In their efforts to change immigration policy, these restrictionists began to center their arguments upon one area of regulation—literacy.

As early as 1887, economist Edward W. Bemis gave a series of lectures in which he proposed that the United States prevent the entry of all male adults who were unable to read and write their own language. He argued that such a regulation would reduce by half or more those who were poor and undereducated. As awareness of the nature of the new immigration grew, nativists realized that a literacy test would also discriminate between desirable and undesirable nationalities, not just individuals. The proponents of the test saw it as an effective method of nationality restriction because, unlike the other "proofs" of cultural inferiority, literacy could easily and readily be measured.

The new immigrants were often attacked for their attachments to their native languages and what was perceived to be a failure to learn English. In an editorial, the *Nation* magazine proposed that a literacy test was insufficient and that English-language ability should be a requirement of

---

3. Further grounds of exclusion similar in intent were added in 1903 and 1907.

entry. Recognizing that a proposal to make English a requirement of entry would effectively limit immigration to residents of the British Isles, the *Nation* declared in 1891 what other restrictionists believed—that "we are under no obligation to see that all races and nations enjoy an equal chance of getting here."

"literacy"
tests
(=English only)

A literacy bill was first introduced in the Congress in 1895, and under the leadership of Senator Lodge passed both houses. In the last days of his administration, President Cleveland vetoed it, suggesting that the test was hypocritical. The House overrode his veto, but the Senate took no action and the proposal died. In a new wave of xenophobia that followed the assassination of President McKinley by an anarchist mistakenly believed to be an immigrant, a new bill passed the House. Despite the support of the new president, Theodore Roosevelt, the bill's sponsors were unable to gain a favorable vote in the Senate, and it too died.

In 1906, new, comprehensive legislation was proposed that included a literacy test for admission and both a literacy and an English-language requirement for naturalization. The restrictionists, now aided by labor unions wary of competition, were opposed in their endeavors by newly organized ethnic groups as well as business leaders opposed to any elimination of new labor sources. In all but one area, the restrictionists were triumphant. Once again, though, they were unsuccessful in gaining passage of a literacy requirement for either entry or naturalization. English-language proficiency was made a basis for citizenship, though, since most congressmen agreed with Representative Bonynge that "history and reason alike demonstrate that you cannot make a homogeneous people out of those who are unable to communicate with each other in one common language."

In 1907, after the restrictionist attempt to impose a literacy requirement failed, immigration to the United States reached a new high—with the arrival of 1,285,000 immigrants—and an economic depression hit the country. That same year, Congress passed legislation to establish a joint congressional presidential Commission to study the impact of immigrants on the United States. Its members appointed in 1909, the Dillingham Commission, as it is usually known, began its work convinced that the pseudoscientific racist theories of superior and inferior peoples were correct and that the more recent immigrants from southern and eastern Europe were not capable of becoming successful Americans. Although their own data contradicted these ideas, the Commission nevertheless held on to them. The Commission's recommendations were published in 1911 with 41 volumes of monographs on specific subjects, including discussions of immigrants and crime, changes in the bodily form of immigrants and the industrial impact of immigration. In the view of the Commission, their findings all pointed to the same conclusions:

- Twentieth century immigration differed markedly from earlier movements of people to the United States;

- The new immigration was dominated by the so-called inferior peoples—those who were physically, mentally and linguistically different, and, therefore, less desirable than either the native-born or early immigrant groups; and

- Because of the inferiority of these people, the United States no longer benefited from a liberal immigration admissions policy and should, therefore, impose new restrictions on entry.

The Commission endorsed the literacy test as an appropriate mechanism to accomplish its ends.

The demand for large-scale restriction still did not succeed, though, because of the continuing demand for labor, the growing political power of the new immigrant groups and the commitment of the nation's leaders to preserving the tradition of free entry. In 1912, Congress once more passed a literacy test, but President Taft successfully vetoed it, extolling the "sturdy but uneducated peasantry brought to this country and raised in an atmosphere of thrift and hard work" where they have "contributed to the strength of our people and will continue to do so." Another veto, this time by President Woodrow Wilson, defeated the work of the restrictionists in 1915. According to Wilson, the literacy test "seeks to all but close entirely the gates of asylum which have always been open to those who could find nowhere else the right and opportunity of constitutional agitation for what they conceived to be the natural and inalienable rights of men."

After the United States entered World War I in 1917, Congress finally overrode the presidential veto and enacted legislation that made literacy a requirement for entry. The bill also codified the list of aliens to be excluded, and it virtually banned all immigration from Asia. The efforts of the restrictionists were finally successful, in large measure because World War I brought nervousness about the loyalty and assimilability of the foreign born to a fever pitch. The loyalty of immigrants became a hot political issue. Theodore Roosevelt, for example, stormed against "hyphenated Americans," as he voiced his concern that the country was becoming little more than a "poly-glot boarding house." A frenzy of activity against German Americans (who only a short while before were thought, along with the English, Scots and Scandinavians to be the best qualified to enter) led to the closing of thriving German-language schools, newspapers and social clubs. The Governor of Iowa took what may have been the strongest measures; he decreed that the use of any language other than English in public places or over the telephone would be prohibited.

This agitation against the foreign born culminated in two efforts: a movement to "Americanize" immigrants and the development of immigration restrictions based on national origins quotas. The Americanization movement had had its start in 1915 when two government agencies, operating independently of each other, began assessing the number and efficacy of immigrant education programs operating in the country. One of these agencies, the Bureau of Naturalization, undertook a letter-writing campaign aimed at learning the degree to which such programs existed. The following summer, the Bureau held a conference in Washington to discuss the information it collected and propose plans for speeding the acculturation of immigrants. In the meantime, though, the Bureau of Education convened its own conference, out of which came the National Committee of One Hundred—prominent citizens organized "for the purpose of assisting in a national campaign for the education of immigrants to fit them for American life and citizenship." With the efforts of these two agencies for guidance, hundreds of communities, private organizations and businesses embarked upon their own programs of Americanization. * * * Lobbying efforts by the Bureau of Education led many states—twenty between 1919 and 1921—to pass legislation establishing Americanization programs to ensure that all immigrants would learn English, the "language of America," as a California commission called it.

Industry also joined the movement. It was frequently asserted that "ignorance of English is a large factor in [job] turnover" and similarly that "there is an important connection between ignorance of English and illiteracy to economic loss." The National Association of Manufacturers encouraged Americanization programs among its members. Henry Ford set up classes within his plants and required attendance of his 5,000 non-English-speaking employees. The International Harvester Company produced its own lesson plans for the non-English-speaking workers in its plants. They clearly taught more than English itself. The first plan read:

I hear the whistle. I must hurry.

I hear the five minute whistle.

It is time to go into the shop. . . .

I change my clothes and get ready to work. . . .

I work until the whistle blows to quit.

I leave my place nice and clean.

I put all my clothes in the locker.

I must go home.

By 1923, the Bureau of Naturalization announced it had 252,808 immigrants in 6,632 citizenship-training courses around the nation. Of these, 4,132 were conducted in public school buildings, 1,256 in homes, 371 in factories and 873 at other locations.

The success of the Americanization program in enrolling immigrants was not enough to satisfy the opponents of immigration. Still convinced that racial differences precluded the full assimilation of the new immigrants, some nativists doubted the ability of Americanization classes to transform immigrants into "100 percent Americans." Some were convinced that all immigrants should be compelled to learn English, and if they could not, should be subject to deportation. Theodore Roosevelt proclaimed that "I would have the government provide that every immigrant be required to learn English, with instruction furnished free. If after five years he has not learned it let him be returned to the country from which he came." To Roosevelt and other nativists, failure to learn English represented some sort of disloyalty or a failure of will; both were clearly reasons for expelling the alien.

As the movement to compel assimilation of those already here progressed, those fearful of the consequences of immigration also sought new restrictions on entry. Restrictionists had learned that the literacy requirement which they believed held so much promise was not succeeding as had been expected. Immigration from southern and eastern Europe continued.

The literacy rates of European countries showed increasing numbers eligible for entry; Italy even established schools in areas of high emigration to teach peasants to be literate so that they could pass the new U.S. test for entry.

To quantitative restrictionists, new measures were needed. The suspension of all immigration—an idea never before of any great appeal in U.S. immigration history—began to gain support. The two groups most associated with it, organized labor and "100 percenters", had little else in common. Labor supported suspension of immigration because of the competition for jobs that occurred with the entry of aliens.

The 100 percenters feared that European people and ideas—whether "bestial hordes" from conquered Germany or the "red menace" of Bolshevism—would contaminate U.S. institutions and culture.

The extreme form of restrictionism proposed by those wishing to ban all immigration gained some support in the House of Representatives, where arguments that postwar immigration was composed largely of Jews who were "filthy, un-American, and often dangerous in their habits" were particularly effective, but failed to pass the Senate Committee on Immigration, which was dominated by easterners with large businesses and ethnic constituencies favorable to immigration.

Instead, the Senate proposed its own legislation to reduce overall immigration and to change the ethnic composition of those permitted entry. The goal of the bill—similar to one originally proposed by Senator Dillingham of the earlier Immigration Commission—was to ensure that northern and western Europeans still had access to the United States while southern and eastern European immigration would be restricted. In 1921, Congress passed and President Harding signed into law the Senate-proposed legislation—a provisional measure which introduced the concept of national origins quotas. This act established a ceiling on European immigration and limited the number of immigrants of each nationality to three percent of the number of foreign-born persons of that nationality resident in the United States at the time of the 1910 census.

This first quota act was extended for two more years, but in 1924 came the passage of what was heralded as a permanent solution to U.S. immigration problems. The Johnson–Reed measure, more commonly known as the National Origins Act,—provided for an annual limit of 150,000 Europeans, a complete prohibition on Japanese immigration, the issuance and counting of visas against quotas abroad rather than on arrival, and the development of quotas based on the contribution of each nationality to the overall U.S. population rather than on the foreign-born population. This law was designed to preserve, even more effectively than the 1921 law, the racial and ethnic status quo of the United States. The national origins concept was also designed, as John Higham wrote in his study of U.S. nativism, *Strangers in the Land,* to give "comfort to the democratic conscience" by counting everyone's ancestors and not just the foreign born themselves.

Recognizing that it would take some time to develop the new quotas, as a stopgap measure the bill provided for the admission of immigrants according to annual quotas of two percent of each nationality's proportion of the foreign-born U.S. population in 1890 until 1927—amended to 1929— when the national origins quotas were established. The use of the 1890 census had been criticized as a discriminatory measure since it seemed to change the rules of European entry solely to lower the number of the so-called "new" immigrants. Use of the 1890 census instead of that of 1910 meant a reduction in the Italian quota from 42,000 to about 4,000, in the Polish quota from 31,000 to 6,000 and in the Greek quota from 3,000 to 100. The proponents of the new legislation argued, however, that use of the 1910 Census was what was really discriminatory since it underestimated the number of visas that should go to those from northern and western Europe.

In preparing its report on the new legislation, the House Committee on Immigration relied heavily on an analysis prepared by John B. Trevor, an aide to Representative Johnson, which gave an estimated, statistical breakdown of the origins of the U.S. population. Trevor also calculated the quotas that would be derived from the use of the 1890 and 1910 census figures on the foreign born. He found that the 1890 census better approximated the national origins of the overall population. Trevor argued that about 12 percent of the U.S. population in 1890 derived from eastern and southern Europe, but on the basis of the 1910 census they were given about 44 percent of the total quota. Using the 1890 census they would have 15 percent of the immigrant numbers. The restrictionists were thus able to turn around the criticism aimed against them by arguing that previous policy favored the "new" immigrants at the expense of the older U.S. stock.

Despite the rhetoric of its supporters—and the exemption of members of the Western Hemisphere from its quotas—the Immigration Act of 1924 clearly represented a rejection of one of [the] longest-lived democratic traditions of the United States, represented by George Washington's view that the United States should ever be "an asylum to the oppressed and the needy of the earth." It also represented a rejection of cultural pluralism as a U.S. ideal. The Commissioner of Immigration could report, one year after this legislation took effect, that virtually all immigrants now "looked" exactly like Americans. Abraham Lincoln's fear that when the nativists gained control of U.S. policy they would rewrite the Declaration of Independence to read: "All men are created equal, except Negroes, and foreigners, and Catholics" seemed to be coming true.

Immigration to the United States suffered still another blow with the Great Depression. During the 1930s, only 500,000 immigrants came to the United States, less than one-eighth of the number that had arrived in the previous decade. Most reduced in number were members of those nations jointly affected by the national origins quotas, and by economic conditions that made impossible their usual pattern of temporary migration for the purposes of work. Temporary migration was a familiar pattern before the imposition of the new legislation. In fact, the prevalence among the "new" immigrants of "birds of passage"—accused of being unstable forces in society, prone to crime and disease and displacing U.S. citizens from jobs— had been one reason for passing restrictive legislation. Temporary migration can be measured through data on emigration, the number of immigrants who leave the country some time after arrival. Throughout most of the early twentieth century, according to official statistics that were collected beginning in 1908, emigration stood at a minimum of 20 percent of immigration and, more commonly, at 30 to 40 percent. In times of depression, the proportion of those who left the country as opposed to those who arrived increased still further; the temporary migrants returned home until conditions in this country improved. In 1932, at the height of the Great Depression, the emigration figure stood at 290 percent of legal immigration. While 35,576 entered the country, over 100,000 left.

Those most tragically affected by the U.S. policy of restrictive immigration (and the economic problems that made U.S. citizens unwilling to alter it) were the refugees who tried to flee Europe before the outbreak of World War II. Although some efforts were made to accommodate them—in 1940 the State Department permitted consuls outside of Germany to issue visas to German refugees because the German quota sometimes remained unfilled—these measures were too few and came too late to help most of the victims of Nazi persecution. In what may be the cruelest single action in U.S. immigration history, the U.S. Congress in 1939 defeated a bill to rescue 20,000 children from Nazi Germany, despite the willingness of U.S. families to sponsor them, on the grounds that the children would exceed the German quota. Those refugees who were able to come in under existing quotas were still subject to all of the other requirements of entry, and a significant number were refused visas because of the public charge provisions in the grounds for exclusion.

Although the quota system of the 1920s stood substantially intact until 1965, U.S. immigration policy was affected by the events of World War II—in particular the shock this country received when it learned most graphically of the fate of the refugees refused entry. Even before that knowledge came, the war challenged long-held notions about U.S. traditions and needs. The United States realized that it once more needed the labor of aliens, for example. This country and Mexico then negotiated a large-scale temporary worker program—the bracero program—designed to fill the wartime employment needs of the United States. Also, in large part because of the alliance of the United States with China, Congress repealed the ban on all Chinese immigration, making it possible for a small number of Chinese once again to enter the country as legal immigrants. Notions of the inherent inferiority of certain groups [were] dispelled when those same groups became allies in the fight against other groups that were proving to be much stronger enemies than expected.

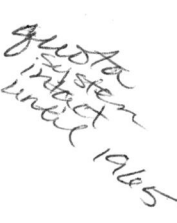

For a short period, the atmosphere was right for a liberalization of immigration policy. At the close of the war, especially after Americans learned of the Nazi atrocities, they seemed united in their appreciation of democracy and their commitment to renewing the U.S. role as a haven for the oppressed. An important first step was taken by President Harry S. Truman who issued a directive in December 1945 admitting 40,000 war refugees. Responding to the plight of U.S. soldiers who had married overseas, Congress passed the "War Brides Act" in 1946, which permitted 120,000 alien wives, husbands and children of members of the armed forces to immigrate to the United States.

In the years following the war, the executive branch continued to take an active role in reshaping immigration policy, even after the advent of the Cold War when public attitudes towards the issue turned more conservative. Most of these efforts, though, were in the area of refugee admissions and did not change the basic structure of U.S. immigration law. President Truman prodded the Congress to pass the Displaced Persons Act in 1948. After its expiration, Congress passed the Refugee Relief Act, under which 214,000 persons were admitted. Designed principally to expedite the admission of refugees fleeing Iron Curtain countries, the Act incorporated safeguards to prevent the immigration of undesirable aliens. Additional measures were passed in 1956 and 1957 to facilitate the entry of Hungarians displaced by the revolution in that country and "refugee-escapees" fleeing Communist or Communist-occupied or dominated countries and countries in the Middle East. In 1960, the Refugee Fair Share Law was passed to provide a temporary program for the admission of World War II refugees and displaced persons who remained in camps under the mandate of the United Nations High Commissioner for Refugees. This legislation gave the Attorney General a specific mandate to use his parole authority to admit eligible refugee-escapees. Although the statute was for a limited period of time, it was more comprehensive than other refugee admission programs and provided an ongoing mechanism to assist refugees.

Despite these strides in developing a policy that permitted refugees to escape from some of the restrictions of the national origins quota requirements, little else in the way of progress occurred in the immigration area until the 1960s. In fact the determination to preserve the quota system was so strong that the refugee measures provided that those entering under those provisions were to be charged to future quotas of their country of origin, as long as these did not exceed 50 percent of the quota of any one year. The refugee acts were seen as complements to the national origins policy; they made the 1924 law more responsive to emergencies but did not significantly alter immigration policy itself.

During the early 1950s, the climate was not ripe for any major liberalizing changes. Concern with communist expansion dominated U.S. thinking in the early 1950s, and the stand against communism often took the form of opposition to anything foreign. It was a period in which ethnic customs and values could easily be defined as "un-American."

It was in such an atmosphere that congressional hearings on a new immigration law took place. They were conducted under the leadership of Senator Patrick A. McCarran who, with his followers, believed that there were in the United States what he called "indigestible blocks" which would not assimilate into the American way of life. In 1952, the McCarran–Walter bill—passed into law as the Immigration and Nationality Act—consolidated previous immigration laws into one statute, but, in so doing, it preserved the national origins quota system. The Act also established a system of preferences for skilled workers and the relatives of U.S. citizens and permanent resident aliens, and tightened security and screening procedures.

It established a 150,000 numerical limitation on immigration from the Eastern Hemisphere; most Western Hemisphere immigration remained unrestricted, although it established a subquota for immigrants born in the colonies or dependent areas of the Western Hemisphere. Finally, the Act repealed Japanese exclusion and established a small quota for the Asia–Pacific Triangle under which Orientals would be charged.

Congress passed the McCarran–Walter Act over the veto of President Truman who favored the liberalization of the immigration statutes and the elimination of national origins quotas. In his veto message, he strongly reaffirmed U.S. ideals.

> Such a concept [national origins quota] is utterly unworthy of our traditions and ideals. It violates the great political doctrine of the Declaration of Independence that "all men are created equal." It denies the humanitarian creed inscribed beneath the Statue of Liberty proclaiming to all nations: "Give me your tired your poor, your huddled masses, yearning to breathe free...."

President Truman on September 4, 1952 appointed a commission to study and evaluate the immigration and naturalization policies of the United States. On January 1, 1953 the Commission issued its report, *Whom We Shall Welcome,* a statement of support for a nondiscriminatory, liberal immigration policy. The Commission summarized its findings:

> The Commission believes that our present immigration laws—
>
> > flout fundamental American traditions and ideals, display a lack of faith in America's future, damage American prestige and position among other nations, ignore the lessons of the American way of life.
>
> The Commission believes that laws which fail to reflect the American spirit must sooner or later disappear from the statute books.
>
> The Commission believes that our present immigration laws should be completely rewritten.

It was not until 1965 that major changes—some urged as early as the Truman Commission—were actually made in the Immigration and Nationality Act. The election of John F. Kennedy, a descendent of Irish immigrants and the first Catholic president of the United States, marked a turning point in immigration history and focused attention again on immigration policy. As a senator, Kennedy had written *A Nation of Immigrants,* a book denouncing the national origins quota system. Now, as President, he introduced legislation to abolish the 40–year-old formula.

That a Catholic could be elected president signified the extent to which the United States had changed since the 1920s. Across the country came a lessening in anti-Catholic, anti-Asian and anti-Semitic sentiment, in part the result of a new tolerance of racial and ethnic differences stimulated by the civil rights movement. By the mid–1960s, Congress was ready for proposals to liberalize immigration policy, particularly after the assassination of President Kennedy and the Lyndon Johnson presidential landslide of 1964. The effort to eliminate the national origins quotas—begun many years earlier—culminated in the passage of the Immigration and Nationality Act Amendments of 1965.

The amendments accomplished the following:

- Abolished the national origins formula, replacing it with a per-country limit of 20,000 on every country outside the Western Hemisphere, and an overall ceiling of 160,000 for those countries;

- Placed a ceiling of 120,000 on immigration from the Western Hemisphere with no country limits; and

- Established Eastern Hemisphere preferences for close relatives, as well as those who had occupational skills needed in the United States under a seven-category preference system.

In signing the new bill, President Lyndon Johnson said:

from this day forth, those wishing to emigrate into America shall be admitted on the basis of their skills and their close relationship to those already here.

The fairness of this standard is so self-evident . . . yet the fact is that for over four decades the immigration policy of the United States has been twisted and has been distorted like a harsh injustice of the national origins quota system . . . families were kept apart because a husband or a wife or a child had been born in the wrong place. Men of needed skill and talent were denied entrance because they came from southern or eastern Europe or from one of the developing continents. The system violated the basic principle of American democracy—the principle that values and rewards each man on the basis of his merit . . . it has been un-American.

The new amendments, as the President suggested, heralded in a new era in U.S. immigration policy. No longer would one nationality be given a larger quota than another in the Eastern Hemisphere. Preference would be given to reuniting families and to bringing those who had certain desirable or needed abilities. These were to be the goals of immigration policy, and the goal of preserving the racial and ethnic domination of northern and western Europe would no longer be an explicit part of U.S. immigration law.

The United States was, of course, far from free of prejudice at that time, and one part of the 1965 law reflected a change in policy that was in part due to antiforeign sentiments. Prejudice against dark-skinned people, particularly in social and economic life, remained strong. In the years after World War II, as the proportion of Spanish-speaking residents increased, much of the lingering nativism in the United States was directed against those from Mexico and Central and South America. The 1952 law—in keeping with the "Good Neighbor" policy, as it was described by Franklin Delano Roosevelt—had not placed any limitations on immigration from these regions, but by 1965 the pressure for such restrictions had mounted. Giving in to these pressures as a price to be paid for abolishing the national origins system, Congress put into the 1965 amendments a ceiling on immigration from the Western Hemisphere that was designed to close the last remaining open door of U.S. policy. This provision went into effect on July 1, 1968.

The legislation did not accomplish its goal regarding Western Hemisphere immigration without substantial costs. In 1976, the House Judiciary Committee reported on the effect of ending the Good Neighbor open door: a steadily increasing backlog of applicants from Latin America, with prospective immigrants waiting two years for a visa. The Committee, recognizing that the ceiling on Western Hemisphere migration had been part of a compromise in the passage of the 1965 amendments, noted:

> When repealing the national origins quota system, the 89th Congress did not provide an adequate mechanism for implementing the Western Hemisphere ceiling.... The result, completely unforeseen and unintended, has been considerable hardship for intending immigrants from this hemisphere who until 1968 enjoyed the privilege of unrestricted immigration.

In 1976 a new law was passed to make regulations regarding immigration the same for both hemispheres, applying to countries of the Western Hemisphere the 20,000–per-country limit and the preference system that was in effect in the Eastern Hemisphere. The only provision to cause any controversy in the 1976 Act was the application of the per-country ceiling provision to Mexico, which had exceeded the 20,000 limit every year since the enactment of the 1965 amendments. There was considerable support for the idea that special provisions should be permitted for contiguous countries, particularly Mexico, because of the special relationship that had developed as a result of shared borders. President Gerald Ford noted in his statement on signing the 1976 amendments into law that he would submit legislation to Congress to increase the immigration quotas for Mexicans desiring to come to the United States, and President Jimmy Carter endorsed similar legislation in 1977. No action, however, was taken to provide this special treatment for Mexico.

The 1976 law maintained two last vestiges of differential geographic treatment—the separate annual ceilings of 170,000 for the Eastern and 120,000 for the Western Hemisphere and the special ceiling (600 visas per year) assigned to colonies and dependencies. In 1978, new legislation combined the ceilings for both hemispheres into a worldwide total of 290,000 with the same seven-category preference system and per-country limits applied to both. Senator Edward Kennedy described the benefits accruing from the 1978 legislation:

> The establishment of a worldwide ceiling corrects an anomaly in the law, and is a logical step in consequence of the major immigration reforms Congress enacted in 1965—on which I served as floor manager at the time.

> In the long term, this reform makes more flexible the provisions of the preference system, and in the short run it has the likely effect of allowing the use of more nonpreference visas next year for the backlog in the Western Hemisphere and the use of more conditional entry visas for Indochina refugees—a need that is extraordinari-

ly urgent in Southeast Asia today. All this will not involve, however, any increase in the total annual immigration authorized under the law.

Concern about Indochinese conditional entries was an important consideration in the establishment of a worldwide ceiling. The 1965 amendments to the Immigration and Nationality Act had included a permanent statutory authority for the admission of refugees, called the conditional entry provision, patterned after earlier legislation, especially the Fair Share Refugee Act of 1960. The seventh preference category was designated for these admissions and was allocated six percent of the Eastern Hemisphere ceiling of 170,000 visas, one-half of which could be used for aliens in the United States who were adjusting their status. In 1976 the preference system was extended to the Western Hemisphere, under a separate numerical ceiling with its own proportion of seventh-preference slots. At the time of Senator Kennedy's remarks, it was apparent that Western Hemisphere seventh-preference numbers—applicable only to Cubans who were then unable to leave in sizeable numbers—were unused whereas Eastern Hemisphere demand was great. A worldwide ceiling would permit the visas to go where the refugee need was greatest without reference to hemisphere.

The 1978 amendments did not address the full range of issues raised by U.S. refugee policy, nor were they intended to do so. The working definition of a refugee—originally developed during the Cold War—still included considerations of national origins, even though the rest of immigration policy had dismissed this criteria.

In the Immigration and Nationality Act of 1952, a refugee was defined as a person [sic] who:

> (i) because of persecution or fear of persecution on account of race, religion, or political opinion * * * have fled (I) from any Communist or Communist-dominated country or area, or (II) from any country within the general area of the Middle East, and (ii) are unable or unwilling to return to such country or area on account of race, religion, or political opinion, and (iii) are not nationals of the countries or areas in which their application for conditional entry is made; or (B) that they are persons uprooted by catastrophic natural calamity as defined by the President who are unable to return to their usual place of abode.

This definition did not permit the entry of those fleeing noncommunist persecution unless they came from the Middle East.

Problems also arose because of the inadequacy of the conditional-entry provisions in dealing with large-scale emergencies. Although when these provisions were enacted Congress intended that they would be the means through which most refugees would be admitted, the parole provision of the Immigration and Nationality Act was actually the major authority for the entrance of large groups of refugees. Under the parole authority, the Attorney General has the discretion to parole any alien into the United States temporarily, under such conditions as the Attorney General may prescribe, in emergencies or for reasons deemed strictly in the public interest. During the 1960s, Cuban refugees were paroled into the United

States; between 1962 and the end of May 1979, over 690,000 Cubans entered this country under that authority. In 1975, two parole programs were adopted to aid the resettlement of refugees from Indochina. Other major programs permitted the parole of still more Indochinese between 1976 and 1979. In June 1979 President Carter announced that the number of Indochinese paroled into the country would be set at 14,000 per month. During the same period, the parole of about 35,000 Soviet refugees for the year was also authorized as was the entry of slightly more than a thousand Chilean and Lebanese parolees.

The parole authority had been used in these cases because the conditional entry provisions were too limited to deal with emergencies. Yet reliance on the parole authority seemed to be an inappropriate response to what were recurring situations. Attorney General Griffin B. Bell described one of the major problems with the use of the parole authority in refugee crises: "This . . . has the practical effect of giving the Attorney General more power than the Congress in determining limits on the entry of refugees into the country." He also noted that the use of parole authority prevented the country from giving clear signals to other nations about the extent of U.S. willingness and ability to respond to world refugee needs. Because of the absence of an ongoing policy for refugee admissions, the United States was unable to plan effectively, and, as Bell concluded, "individual refugees [were] hostage to a system that necessitates that their plight build to tragic proportions so as to establish the imperative to act."

The concerns about refugees led to legislative action in 1979 and 1980. The Refugee Act of 1980 was designed to correct the deficiencies of U.S. refugee policy by providing ongoing mechanisms for the admission and aid of refugees. The legislation broadened the definition of refugee by removing the geographic and ideological limitations of the earlier conditional-entry provisions. It also established an allocation of 50,000 for normal refugee admissions, through 1982, and provided procedures through which the President in consultation with Congress could increase this number annually in response to unforeseen circumstances. It further provided for a special conditional entry status with adjustment to permanent resident alien status after one year in the United States.

In addition to making changes in admissions policy, the Refugee Act of 1980 also established the ongoing responsibility of the federal government for the resettlement of refugees accepted under the Act. The legislation included provision for up to 100 percent reimbursement to states for cash and medical assistance provided to refugees during their first 36 months in this country and for grants to voluntary agencies for some of their costs incurred in resettlement.

Later Developments

Immigration legislation and policy have rarely been off the congressional agenda or the front pages of the newspapers in the 1980s and 1990s. In 1986, after years of debate, Congress enacted the most far-reaching immigration legislation since the 1950s—the Immigration Reform and Control Act (IRCA). Pub.L. No. 99–603, 100 Stat. 3359. IRCA was conceived as a multi-pronged attack on undocumented migration. Its major features were (1) imposition of penalties on employers who hire undocumented aliens ("employer sanctions"); (2) legalization of long-term undocumented aliens; (3) legalization of aliens who had performed agricultural labor in the United States ("Special Agricultural Workers" or "SAWs"); and (4) protection of U.S. citizens and permanent resident aliens from employment discrimination occasioned by employer sanctions. We will discuss these programs in Chapter Three.

Less noticed, but of significant importance, was another piece of legislation enacted in 1986—the Immigration Marriage Fraud Amendments (IMFA). Pub.L. No. 99–639, 100 Stat. 3537. IMFA provides a modified status and detailed procedures for aliens seeking to gain permanent residence on the basis of marriage. We will consider these provisions—and the controversy surrounding them—in Chapter Three.

While IRCA and IMFA took aim at unlawful migration, the Immigration Act of 1990, Pub.L. No. 101–649, 104 Stat. 4978, worked a major overhaul of the legal migration system. The Act substantially expanded employment-based immigration, provided additional visa numbers for some family-based categories, and created the new category of "diversity immigrants," meant to provide visas to aliens from "low admission" countries and regions. The 1990 Act also rewrote the exclusion and deportation grounds and adopted a number of provisions directed at ensuring the removal of criminal aliens.

Figure 1.1

Immigrants Admitted: Fiscal Years 1900–93

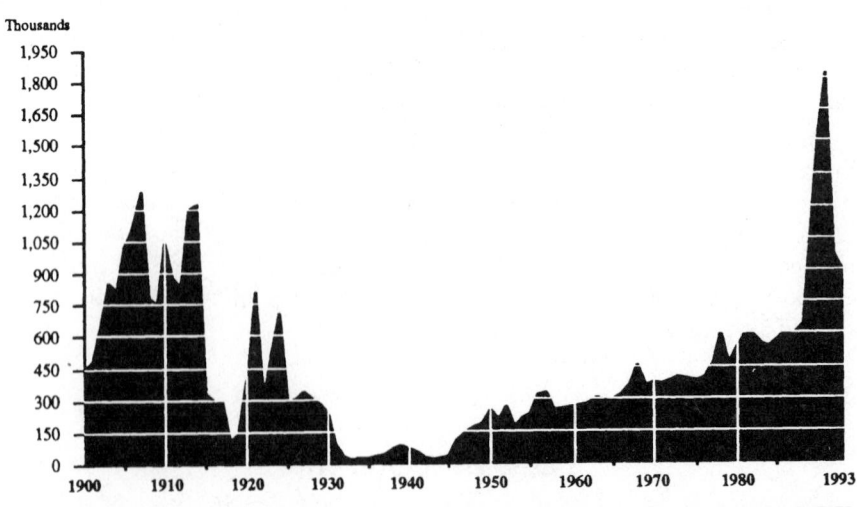

1993 INS Statistical Yearbook, Chart C.

Although refugees have remained a controversial subject throughout the 1980s and 1990s, and continue to attract considerable congressional attention, the basic structure of the Refugee Act has remained intact. But when the executive branch began, in 1988, to apply more stringent standards in evaluating the persecution claims of applicants in overseas refugee programs, Congress reacted strongly—particularly because of the policy's impact on Soviet nationals (who by then were able to emigrate far more readily). Temporary legislation passed, which has made much easier for Soviet and Indochinese applicants to qualify for inclusion in those refugee programs. Pub.L. No. 101–167, § 599D, 103 Stat. 1195, 1261 (1989). These provisions have been regularly renewed every two years since then, despite the end of the Cold War.

Controversy over asylum has also arisen, but Congress has made only minor adjustments by statute. The Justice Department, however, did bring significant changes to asylum processing by regulation, 55 Fed.Reg. 30674 (1990), creating a centralized corps of specialist asylum officers, supported by their own documentation center. Additional administrative reforms to streamline procedures and curb abuses were adopted in late 1994, 59 Fed.Reg. 62284 (1994), and Congress doubled the resources available to the system. And in the Immigration Act of 1990, Congress included a provision authorizing the Attorney General to grant "temporary protected status" (TPS) to aliens from countries experiencing civil war, environmental disaster or other conditions preventing the aliens' safe return. Ending years of political debate and agitation, another section of the 1990 Act created a specific TPS program for Salvadorans to run until mid–1992, and Presidents Bush and Clinton extended the period of protection through 1994.

Figure 1.2

Origins of U.S. Immigration, by Region, 1821–1990

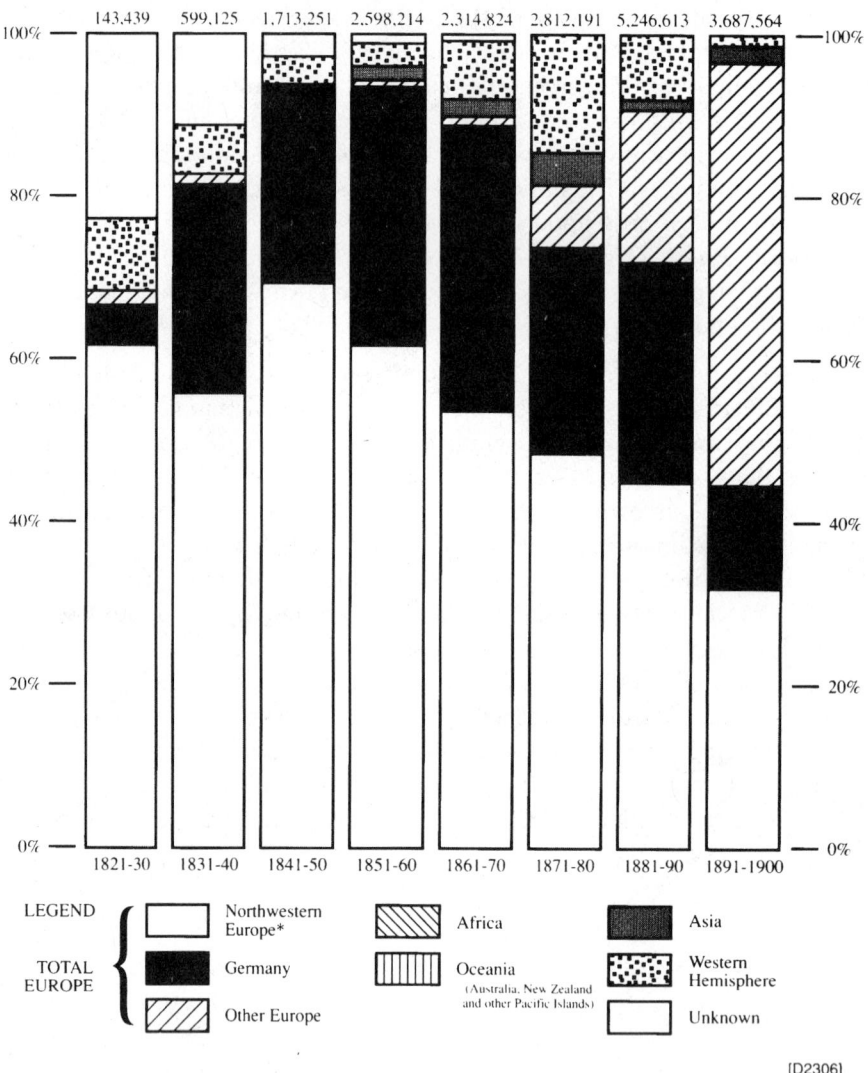

[D2306]

* Includes Germany after 1900.

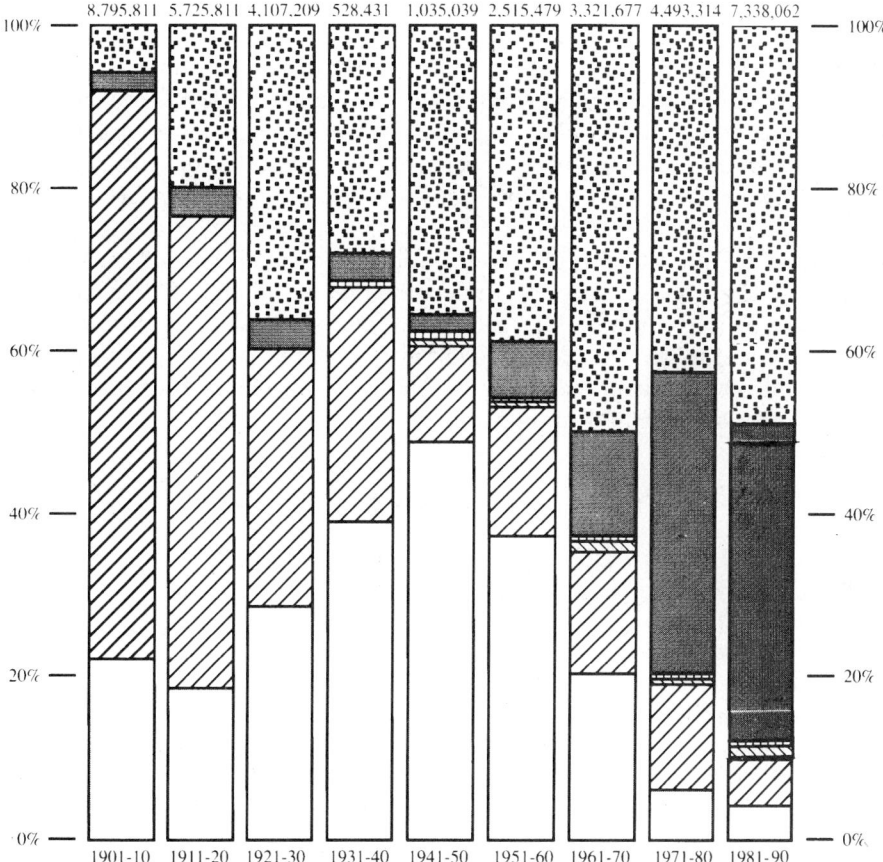

8,795,811 5,725,811 4,107,209 528,431 1,035,039 2,515,479 3,321,677 4,493,314 7,338,062

Source: SCIRP, Staff Report 172–73 (for 1821–1970); 1993 INS Statistical Yearbook, Table 2 (1971–90).

With the 1990 Act, Congress completed work on most of the reform agenda that had been debated since the 1970s. But given the scope of those reforms and continuing controversy over the effectiveness and fairness of many changes enacted over the last five years, it is not surprising that several major areas of legislative concern have emerged in the 1990s.

One is the deportation of "criminal aliens"—both legal aliens who have been convicted of crimes making them deportable, as well as undocumented aliens who are deportable by definition and who have committed crimes in addition. We will see in Chapter Six that Congress has made the removal of criminal aliens a top priority. This view has led to numerous statutory and regulatory changes, to both substantive deportation grounds and deportation procedures. A second goal of Congress has been control of undocumented immigration. Of course, this has been central theme of immigration law and policy since the 1980s and IRCA. More recently, however, control of "illegal" immigration has emerged as a core issue of domestic politics, a fixture on both the front page and the editorial page. A significant aspect of this concern has been a certain tension between the federal government and the states. One key issue is who pays the costs attributed to undocumented immigration, especially education, medical care, and the incarceration of undocumented criminals. An even more fundamental issue is how far states may go in trying to control costs by denying benefits to the undocumented. Chapter Three will discuss a number of recently adopted measures intended to address these and other aspects of undocumented immigration.[14]

SECTION C.   THEORIES OF MIGRATION

GEORGE J. BORJAS, FRIENDS OR STRANGERS: THE IMPACT OF IMMIGRANTS ON THE U.S. ECONOMY

7–18 (1990).

A unifying hypothesis of the research summarized in this book is that immigrants choose to come to the United States. The immigrant flow is composed of the pool of persons who are attracted by the earnings, employment, and welfare opportunities provided by the American economy, who are willing to incur the costs associated with immigration, and who are able to gain entry into the country. Changes in immigration policy, like changes in economic conditions and migration costs, alter the size and skill characteristics of the group of persons attracted to the United States; hence they change the role immigrants play in the U.S. economy.

In a sense, the United States competes with other countries, such as the home countries of migrants and other potential host countries, for the immigrant's human and physical capital. International trade involves not only the movement of goods and services among countries, but also the movement of people. Just as countries compete in a worldwide market in which goods and services are exchanged, they also compete in an immigration market. By presenting a specific set of economic opportunities and by pursuing an immigration policy that prevents the entry of some persons but encourages the entry of others, the United States makes a particular type of "offer" in the immigration market. The attractiveness of the American offer, relative to the offers of other countries, determines the size

14. For further general discussion of American immigration history, *see* R. Daniels, Coming to America: A History of Immigration and Ethnicity in American Life (1990); O. Handlin, The Uprooted (2d ed. 1973); J. Higham, Strangers in the Land: Patterns of American Nativism, 1860–1925 (1955); M.A. Jones, American Immigration (1960); M. LeMay, From Open Door to Dutch Door: An Analysis of U.S. Immigration Policy Since 1820 (1987); T. Muller & T. Espenshade, The Fourth Wave: California's Newest Immigrants (1985); D. Reimers, Still the Golden Door: The Third World Comes to America (2d ed. 1992).—eds.

and composition of the immigrant flow entering the United States. This approach to the study of immigration yields a number of new insights and results that can play a central role in the ongoing debate over immigration policy.

* * *

There are three sets of players in the immigration market: the people contemplating whether to leave their home countries, the governments of immigrants' home countries, and the governments of the various potential host countries. All of these players enter the immigration market with different objectives, and it is the interaction among them that leads to a particular sorting of immigrants among the various host countries.

Persons residing in any country of origin consider the possibility of remaining there or of migrating to one of a number of host countries. Individuals make the immigration decision by comparing the values of the various alternatives, and they choose the country that makes them best off considering the financial and legal constraints regulating the international migration process.

These constraints include the individual's financial resources. After all, international migration is costly. The costs include direct expenditures, such as the out-of-pocket expenses associated with the transportation of the immigrant and his family to their new home, along with indirect costs, such as the income losses associated with unemployment spells that occur as immigrants look for work in the new country. Because only persons who have accumulated sufficient wealth and savings can afford to migrate, the potential migrant's financial resources obviously influence the immigration decision.

Potential host countries are also important players in the immigration market, for they can encourage, discourage, or prevent the entry of certain groups of persons. In particular, potential host countries are characterized by a specific set of economic opportunities. These income and employment opportunities can be described in terms of the existing income distribution, whereby certain types of skills are highly rewarded and other types are not; whereby jobs are easily available in some industries but scarce in others; whereby some occupations are in high demand, but high levels of unemployment persist in others; whereby persons who experience relatively poor labor market outcomes are subsidized by the welfare state, while persons who experience favorable outcomes are heavily taxed. These differences in income and employment opportunities by skill, industry, and occupation imply that the attractiveness of the economic "offer" made by a host country will differ among potential migrants. Some will find the offers lucrative, others will not.

Host countries also regulate the size and composition of the immigrant flow by imposing restrictions on entry according to the potential migrant's skills, wealth, occupation, political background, moral rectitude, national origin, or family relationships with current residents. These regulations generate additional variations in migration costs among potential migrants. For example, current U.S. immigration policy makes immigration costs almost prohibitive for persons who do not already have relatives residing here. Other host countries, such as Australia and Canada, have a "point system" in which potential immigrants are screened and graded on the basis of their educational attainment, age, occupation, and other demographic characteristics, and only those individuals who score highly can enter the country. Immigration policies, by their very nature, impose different entry costs on different people and act as a screening device to filter out "undesirable" persons from the applicant pool.

* * *

The home countries of potential migrants are the last major players in the immigration market. Their economies also provide a certain set of income and employment opportunities to their residents, and their emigration policies regulate the size and skill composition of the outgoing flow. In some countries, like the United States, citizens are free to leave the country whenever they wish, for any duration, and for whatever reason. In other countries, emigration statutes impose large costs and penalties on potential emigrants and make it very difficult for residents to migrate elsewhere. Moreover, such restrictions often control not only the size but also the skill composition of the emigrant flow. For instance, the Soviet Union long prevented the exit of any persons who worked in sensitive government jobs, and Cuba prohibited the exit of persons in the age group subject to military service.

Economists typically assume that individuals behave in ways that maximize their well-being. In the context of the immigration market, this means that after potential migrants compare the feasible alternatives, they choose the country that provides the best economic opportunities. There exists a close analogy between the immigration market and the job market. Like persons looking for work, potential migrants enter the market, receive offers from competing host countries and their home country, compare the offers, and make a migration decision. The information gathered in the immigration market leads many to conclude that they are better off staying where they are. Others decide that conditions in some foreign country are better than at home, and these persons are the ones who make up international migration flows. A subset of these immigrants find that the U.S. offer was more attractive than the offers of competing host countries, and these make up the pool of foreign-born persons in the United States.

* * *

If we assume that individuals move in response to better economic opportunities, it is evident that differences in average income levels among countries are a prime determinant of the size and direction of immigrant flows. Immigrants tend to gravitate from low-income countries to high-income countries. Further, the greater the income differential between the countries, the larger the size of the population flow. For instance, the wage differential between Mexico and the United States is the largest income gap between any two contiguous countries in the world. It should not be too surprising, therefore, that large migration flows originate in

Mexico and move toward the United States, instead of the other way around.

* * *

The main determinant of the skill sorting generated by the immigration market is the fact that countries competing in this marketplace attach different values to workers' skills. For instance, in practically all countries, higher education levels are associated with higher earnings. College-educated persons are better paid than persons with a high school diploma, who in turn earn more than persons who only completed grammar school. But the rate at which earnings increase with additional schooling, or the rate of return to schooling, is not the same for all countries. In a well-known study of international differences in the rate of return to schooling, economist George Psacharopoulos reports that an additional year of higher education increases earnings by only 5 percent in Germany, by 15 percent in the United States, and by 29 percent in Mexico.

Because people migrate in search of better economic opportunities, highly educated workers have much to gain by moving to countries that pay a higher price for their skills. As long as income differentials among countries are large enough to justify migration, highly educated workers naturally gravitate to countries in which the rate of return to education is high. Workers with little schooling have little to gain by immigrating to such countries, and because immigration is costly they are much less likely to move there. Therefore, the sorting of persons in the immigration market leads to the allocation of highly educated workers to countries that have high rates of return to education.

* * *

Should highly skilled Swedes immigrate to the United States? They can choose to remain in their birthplace but find that their earnings opportunities are severely constrained by the fact that Sweden, relative to the United States, has an egalitarian income distribution. Put differently, highly skilled Swedes do not earn much more than those less skilled. In addition, because of the almost confiscatory tax rates at higher income levels, the income distribution in Sweden narrows even more relative to that in the United States. Therefore, highly skilled Swedes find that their earnings opportunities would increase substantially if they migrated to the United States. By the same token, unskilled Swedes find that their economy protects them from the poor labor market outcomes that would likely befall them if they were to migrate to the United States. Because the United States, relative to Sweden, does not insure unskilled workers against the possibility of low earnings, unskilled Swedes would experience a decline in their economic well-being if they were to migrate to the United States. Therefore, the self-selection of the immigrant pool ensures that the typical immigrant originating in Sweden is highly skilled.

* * *

Should a highly skilled Mexican immigrate to the United States? Mexico has substantially more income inequality than the United States.

Skilled Mexicans find that the Mexican income distribution greatly rewards those skills, while unskilled Mexicans have little protection from poor labor market outcomes. As long as they can afford to migrate, unskilled Mexicans have the most incentive to come to the United States and skilled Mexicans the least, so Mexicans in the United States are likely to be unskilled. This point suggests that the United States attracts relatively unskilled persons from countries that have highly disperse income distributions, because these countries reward skills more than we do.

ALEJANDRO PORTES & JÓZSEF BÖRÖCZ, CONTEMPORARY IMMIGRATION: THEORETICAL PERSPECTIVES ON ITS DETERMINANTS AND MODES OF INCORPORATION [a]

23 International Migration Review 606, 607–14 (1989).

ORIGINS

The most widely held approach to the origins of international migration—"push-pull" theories—see labor flows as an outcome of poverty and backwardness in the sending areas. Representatives of this perspective provide lists of "push factors"—economic, social and political hardships in the poorest parts of the world—and "pull factors"—comparative advantages in the more advanced nation-states—as causal variables determining the size and directionality of immigrant flows. These lists are invariably elaborated *post factum,* that is, after particular movements have already been initiated. The compilation of such lists is usually guided by two underlying assumptions: first, the expectation that the most disadvantaged sectors of the poorer societies are most likely to participate in labor migration; and second, the assumption that such flows arise spontaneously out of the sheer existence of inequalities on a global scale.

On the surface, these assumptions appear self-evident: workers migrate from Mexico to the United States and from Turkey to West Germany and not vice versa. However, the tendency of the push-pull model to be applied to those flows which are already taking place conceals its inability to explain why similar movements do not arise out of other equally "poor" nations or why sources of outmigration tend to concentrate in certain regions and not in others within the same sending countries.

Thus, the proclivity of these theories to the *post hoc* recitation of "obvious" causes makes them incapable of predicting the two principal differences in the origin of migration: 1) differences among collectivities— primarily nation-states—in the size and directionality of migrant flows; 2) differences among individuals within the same country or region in their propensities to migrate. The first question concerns macrostructural determinants of labor displacements while the second concerns their microstructural causes. The difference between these levels of analysis is also absent from most standard push-pull writings.

a. Certain references in the text have been moved to footnotes. Others have been omitted.—eds.

At the broader level of determination, the onset of labor flows does not arise out of invidious comparisons of economic advantage, but out of a history of prior contact between sending and receiving societies. History is replete with instances in which an absolute wage advantage in economically expanding areas has meant nothing to the population of more isolated regions; when their labor has been required, it has had to be coerced out of them. In general, the emergence of regular labor outflows of stable size and known destination requires the prior penetration by institutions of the stronger nation-state into those of the weaker sending ones. Political and economic conditions in the latter are then gradually molded to the point where migration to the hegemonic center emerges as a plausible option for the subordinate population. The process of external penetration and internal imbalancing of labor-exporting areas has taken very different forms, however, during the history of capitalism.

Conquest and the slave trade involved the partial penetration of outlying areas to the expanding capitalist world economy and resulted in coerced labor flows from them. This form of displacement required relatively large, high risk capital investment and active support by the colonizing power so that the labor of slave-releasing areas should be available to mines and plantations located elsewhere under the same colonial domain.

Migrant recruitment through economic inducements can be seen as the midpoint of an historical process that ranged from coerced labor extraction, as above, to the spontaneous initiation of flows on the basis of labor demand in the wealthier countries. The nineteenth to mid-twentieth century labor recruitment practices of the post-colonial nations of the Americas—from the United States to Argentina—were again costly in terms of capital input, but required only passive support from the coercive bodies of the receiving states. Deliberate recruitment through economic inducements has also been a common practice throughout the twentieth century with the goal of provoking labor displacements from nearby peripheries, for example from the relatively less developed countries of the Caribbean or the Mediterranean basin.

Self-initiated or spontaneous labor flows are more recent phenomena. They arise out of a change taking place in peripheral societies' consumption patterns which reflect more and more those being diffused from the advanced centers. The fulfillment of such expectations becomes increasingly difficult under the economies of scarcity of the periphery and growing cross-national ties make it possible for certain groups located there to seek a solution by migrating abroad. Thus, external penetration in its successive forms—from physical coercion to economic inducement to cultural diffusion—has been a precondition for the initiation of international labor flows under capitalism.

* * *

The various historical forms of penetration * * * form part of a progression guided by the initiatives of states at the center of the international economy and the changing interests of its dominant classes. The outcome of this progression has been to increase consistently the supply of pliable labor while decreasing its costs. The process has reached its culmination today when labor migrants assume the initiative and the full costs of the journey. This outcome is what economists now refer to as "inexhaustible supplies" of labor.

From the point of view of the population of less developed countries, labor migration has emerged as a viable solution to their own societies' immediately perceptible internal imbalances, which causes are often well-hidden in historical relationships of domination. While in appearance migration arises out of a series of "rational" economic decisions by individuals to escape their immediate situation, in reality its fundamental origin lies in the history of past economic and political contact and power asymmetries between sending and receiving nations.

STABILITY

A second difficulty with standard push-pull theories is their inability to account for individual differences in patterns of migration. Given the same set of expelling forces and external inducements, why is it that some individuals leave while others stay? Why, in particular, given the lopsided "differentials of advantage" in favor of the receiving society, do only a minority of the source populations migrate? Descriptions of Mexican, Dominican or West Indian migration—including those at an exclusively macrostructural level—suggest that "everyone is leaving", which is far from being the case.

A related shortcoming is the inability of conventional theories to explain the resilience of migrant flows once the original economic inducements have disappeared or have been significantly lessened. According to the underlying economic rationale of the push-pull approach, migration should reflect, with some lag, ups and downs in the "differential of advantage" which gives rise to the process in the first place. In reality, migration flows, once established, tend to continue with relative autonomy from such fluctuations.

Contrary to the assertion that international labor migration is basically an outcome of economic decisions governed by the law of supply and demand, we will argue that the phenomenon is primarily social in nature. Networks constructed by the movement and contact of people across space are at the core of the microstructures which sustain migration over time. More than individualistic calculations of gain, it is the insertion of people into such networks which helps explain differential proclivities to move and the enduring character of migrant flows.

Contemporary patterns of Mexican labor migration to the United States provide an illustration of this argument. Wage differentials between Mexico and the United States have been consistently poor predictors of the dynamics of the inflow. * * * Macrostructural origins of Mexican migration must be sought in a history of military conquest, economic penetration and internal imbalancing of this country by its more powerful neighbor. Yet this fact, by itself, does not suffice to explain the differential propensities of Mexican communities to export migrants nor the stability of the process over time.

A recent study of four Mexican communities found that a major predictor of the probability of labor migration was prior migrant experience by the individual and his or her kin.[1] Families apparently pass on their knowledge of the different aspects of the process and its expected rewards to younger generations. This mechanism helps explain the self-sustaining character of the flow as well as its selectivity of destinations. Several studies have documented the tendency of Mexican immigrants to go to certain places in the United States and not to others. Ties between specific sites of origin and destination are not exclusively economic, but also social as they depend on the continuing existence of supportive networks.[2]

Bustamante and Martinez[3] conclude their study of Mexican migrant workers in the United States by noting that the vast majority remain only for a limited period of time, between two and six months on the average. The process can be characterized as a cyclical pattern in which a greater number of past trips by self and kin increases the probability of new departures. Thus, as the social phenomenon of migration unfolds "the factors that originally spurred it become less relevant."[4] Contacts across space, "family chains" and the new information and interests which they promote become at least as important as calculations of economic gain in sustaining the cyclical movement.

Studies of newcomers on the United States side of the border support the same conclusions. Most recent arrivals from Mexico—including the undocumented—are reported to find jobs within a few days thanks to the assistance of family and kin. The same social networks serve as financial safety nets and as sources of cultural and political information.[5] These microstructures of migration not only permit the survival of recent arrivals, but constitute a significant undercurrent often running counter to broader economic trends. Through these arrangements, variations in wages and employment opportunities are evened out so that, over time, the size and destinations of the migrant flow become relatively insensitive to fluctuations in the economic cycle.

* * *

An important aspect of labor migration is the fact that the social channels which it creates open ways for entry and settlement of individuals who do not directly participate in the labor process. These dependent family members may enter the labor market subsequently. Opportunities

1. Massey, *Understanding Mexican Migration to the United States,* 92 Am.J.Soc. 1372 (1987).

2. Cornelius, *Mexican Migration to the United States: The View from Rural Sending Communities,* Center for Int'l Studies, M.I.T., Discussion Paper C–77–11 (mimeo 1977); Alba, *Mexico's International Migration as a Manifestation of Its Development Pattern,* 12 Int'l Migration Rev. 502 (1978).

3. Bustamante & Martinez, *Undocumented Immigration from Mexico: Beyond Borders but Within Systems,* 33 J.Int'l Aff. 265 (1979).

4. Massey, *supra* n.1.

5. Browning & Rodriguez, *The Migration of Mexican Indocumentados as a Settlement Process: Implications for Work,* in Hispanics in the U.S. Economy 277 (G. Borjas & M. Tienda eds. 1985).

may emerge, for example, for wives and for migrant children as they become of age. Occupationally inactive migrants continue to increase, however, the dependency ratios of foreign working class communities. In West Germany, even though entries of laborers from outside the EEC were banned in 1973, the numbers of foreign residents continued to grow due to family reunification. The latter has become the major legal entry category for foreign nationals. The average length of stay has also increased significantly and the composition of migrant communities has begun to approximate—except for the invariant absence of the elderly—that of their home societies. The consolidation of migrant networks across space and the emergence of ethnic communities in West Germany signal once again the failure of policies based on simple assumptions about individualistic economic behavior.

More than movement from one place to another in search of higher wages, labor migration should be conceptualized as a process of progressive network building. Networks connect individuals and groups distributed across different places, maximizing their economic opportunities through multiple displacements. Labor migration is thus a device through which individual workers and their households adapt to opportunities distributed unevenly in space. Hence, migration performs a dual function: for capital, it is a source of more abundant and less expensive labor; for the migrants, it is a means of survival and a vehicle for social integration and economic mobility.

Note

How should the arguments for and against certain theories of migration affect the formulation of specific immigration laws?

SECTION D.   THE EXERCISE OF THE IMMIGRATION POWER: THE MORAL CONSTRAINTS

Having read the *Chinese Exclusion Case* and *Fong Yue Ting,* you are aware that Congress has the constitutional authority to regulate immigration to the United States. This conclusion probably comes as little surprise to you. A much more difficult issue is how Congress should use its power. In beginning to answer that question we believe that it is important first to explore possible moral bases for, or constraints upon, exercise of the immigration power. If our presence in the United States is essentially an accident of birth, what gives us the right to keep others from entering? What is the nature of our moral claim to the territory of the United States? What is our responsibility to needy people living in other parts of the world? To needy people in the United States? The following materials are intended to help you focus on these questions.

TIMOTHY KING, IMMIGRATION FROM DEVELOPING COUNTRIES: SOME PHILOSOPHICAL ISSUES

Ethics, April 1983, 525–31.*

Suppose the government of some developed country to be trying to determine its policies on immigration from developing countries. Assume that the immigration in question is that of individuals whose skills, in comparison with both sending and receiving countries, are low—in other words, that we are not concerned with the so-called brain-drain. After inquiry, the government reaches the following conclusions: (1) the migration is into occupations which are domestically among the least well paid; (2) some domestic workers will remain in these occupations even though the incomes they now earn there have fallen. Others will move into occupations slightly higher up the premigration wage scale, depressing wages there; (3) most members of the domestic population, however, benefit economically from migration since they possess skills essential to their occupations which neither the migrants nor the displaced domestic workers possess, and they are now able to buy more cheaply the goods and services produced in the migrant-competing occupations; (4) the migrants are well informed about working and social conditions and come voluntarily; and (5) their departure raises average incomes in their countries of origin and does not lower and may raise the incomes of the poorest there.

* * *

The government sees its policy options as broadly threefold: (1) to prohibit immigration altogether; (2) to allow unlimited flows of immigrants with right to long-term residence; (3) to allow limited migration with tight control over its magnitude, length of stay, and conditions of employment.

Believing that these questions raise philosophical as well as practical administrative and political issues, the government has formed a committee of philosophers to advise it. I shall summarize their discussion * * *.

For Philosopher A, the issue was essentially one of global utilitarianism. He argued that once a reasoning human being lifted her sights above pure egoism and recognized the interests of others as well as of herself, she must eventually accept that all of humankind had equal claim to be considered.[3] There could be no objective reason for giving priority to the interests of a particular family, tribe, or nation. If this were accepted there could be little doubt that, however utilities were weighted and aggregated, the consequences of unrestricted immigration were superior to any alternative. It was clear that the number of people gaining from such a policy exceeded those who lost from it, and that while the gainers included some of the rich of the world, the poorest groups also gained.

3. *See, e.g.*, Peter Singer, *The Expanding Circle* (New York: Farrar, Strauss & Giroux, 1980), p. 131. It should be noted, however, that Singer later cautions against making the ethical code of society too heavily dependent on abstract moral reasoning.

B said that although he did not regard himself as a utilitarian, he came to the same conclusion. The issue was one of global social justice. Rawls had argued that social justice required maximizing the welfare of the least well-off (subject to the requirement of equal liberty), and although he had confined this principle to justice within nations, suggesting that the principles for international relations would be differently determined, B could see no justification for this.[4] If the [Rawlsian] "veil of ignorance" approach to questions of social justice was an attempt to eliminate morally arbitrary factors from judgments about the justice of particular social arrangements, there could be nothing more arbitrary than the wealth of the society in which one happened to have been born. Representatives of all societies meeting behind such a veil of ignorance would presumably adopt a global "maximin" principle on the same reasoning that Rawls had applied to national questions. Applying such a principle on a global basis, it was clear that the least well-off would benefit most from unrestricted migration.

C agreed that the right policy was unrestricted migration, though he considered the arguments advanced for this by A and B to be unacceptable. Both assumed that government policies could be selected simply by comparing the outcomes of policies in the light of some a priori criterion. But such an approach could lead to the unjustified disregard of the rights of individuals and minorities. In addition it involved looking at a snapshot of the current situation without consideration of the historical processes which had brought it about. Rather, the state should be seen as a protective association for a particular territory with a monopoly over the use of force in that territory and the obligation to protect the rights of everybody there.[5] This did not give it justification to interfere with the rights of individuals to trade with each other, including trade in labor services, even when their trading partners were members of other protective associations. Unrestricted migration ought therefore to be permitted.

D came to the same practical conclusion as the three preceding speakers but disagreed with all the arguments so far put forward. All had spoken as though national boundaries were irrelevant to the choice of policy and had maintained that the government should adopt principles which made no distinction between the welfare of its own citizens and those of other countries (except in the case of C, who had argued that it had to protect certain rights of its citizens). This was both unjustifiable and unrealistic. In the first place, it was natural for one to feel a diminishing level of concern for the welfare of others as they became increasingly remote from one's family and immediate friends.[6] Not only did this appeal to intuition; it was also efficient since it often meant that assistance could be given to the needy without cumbersome and expensive schemes of social welfare. A sense of family responsibility, a sense of

4. John Rawls, *A Theory of Justice* (Cambridge, Mass.: Harvard University Press, 1971), pp. 377–79; Brian Barry, *The Liberal Theory of Justice* (Oxford: Oxford University Press, 1973), pp. 128–33; Charles Beitz, *Political Theory and International Relations* (Princeton, N.J.: Princeton University Press, 1979), pp. 127–76.

5. Robert Nozick, *Anarchy, State and Utopia* (New York: Basic Books, 1974).

6. Henry Sidgwick, *Methods of Ethics* (1907; reprint ed., London: Macmillan, 1962), p. 246.

attachment to small community groups, and beyond these, loyalty to the nation were things to be encouraged rather than opposed.

Second, the question of the extent to which an individual had any moral obligation to come to the assistance of others at some cost to himself was a very difficult one. National boundaries were one contrivance for helping to define this. In general he believed that a nation had a duty to refrain from directly harming another nation but no obligation to assist it if this was detrimental to its own interests.

Third, national governments had responsibilities to their constituents, to consider their welfare rather than to pursue some abstract and little accepted ideals. There could be no doubt that there was nearly universal acceptance of the idea that a nation-state had a right to determine its own immigration policy. Although states had no right to coerce potential emigrants into remaining, they had no duty to admit emigrants from other states. In these circumstances, citizens had a right to expect that the government to which they gave allegiance would promote their own interests, rather than some global ideal.

D therefore argued that the issue collapsed into one of national economic policy. The total income of citizens would be higher with a policy of unrestricted immigration; those who gained, could, in principle, compensate those who lost, and they could not be bribed not to make the change. If the government wished to use fiscal mechanisms to make such transfers, it could. As an aside, however, he noted that he did not favor such transfers. Economic life, he observed, was unfair; trying to compensate piecemeal for some aspects of unfairness while others inevitably remained led governments arbitrarily to favor some individuals compared to others no less deserving.

E accepted most of what D had said but did not think that the issue should be judged by purely economic criteria. These gave greatest weight to those with the greatest economic strength, which was unjust. E would simply submit the issue to a referendum. Since those who gained from the policy of unrestricted migration greatly outnumbered those who lost, one might expect a referendum to reflect this.

F agreed that the interests of the inhabitants of the nation-state rather than the world as a whole should be decisive. In contrast to D, however, this led him to uncompromising opposition to all immigration of the type in question. He argued that membership in a human community was a primary good of the first importance.[7] This carried with it both a degree of security and some mutual obligation to assist fellow members. The world as a whole was not yet such a community; indeed it showed few tendencies in this direction. To foster cohesion within such a community, membership could not simply be kept open to anybody who wished to apply.[8] In the first place, this might destroy the loyalty of those who were hurt by immigration. Second, it would change the character of the community in ways that might be unattractive to existing members even if it was

7. Michael Walzer, "The Distribution of Membership," in *Boundaries: National Autonomy and Its Limits,* pp. 1–35.

8. Henry Sidgwick, *The Elements of Politics* (London: Macmillan, 1897), pp. 307–9.

economically advantageous to many of them. It was not certain that a referendum would favor immigration at all, and certainly not unrestricted immigration. In Britain and the United States, there was considerable evidence that continued immigration was unpopular and that the arguments were not simply economic. But in any case a referendum was not the right way to settle the issue, since those who would be hurt by immigration had some right to protection by the rest of the community. Since he did not feel that the world economy could seriously be regarded as the sort of scheme of social cooperation which underlay Rawls's approach to social justice, Rawlsian arguments should be applied at a national level. This would favor a policy of no immigration at all, unless there was a cast-iron policy of redistributing the gains from migration to the losers. Knowing how little income or wealth is actually redistributed by the fiscal system in practice in most countries, he found this highly implausible.

He also pointed out that population growth was much higher in developing countries than in developed countries, and that this contributed to employment problems, low wages, and pressures to migrate. Such population growth was thus imposing a cost to the societies in which it was occurring. Emigration let them pass some of this cost on to the rest of the world. Although many developing countries had policies to try to reduce population growth, these were not universal, and even where they existed on paper, they were often not vigorously implemented. Emigration reduced the pressure on governments to take action, and so increased the burden of population growth for the world as a whole.

Population growth in developing countries raised a practical question which it was impossible to ignore. Seventy-five percent of the world's population lived in developing countries, and it was impossible to reduce significantly population pressure in most countries by emigration from them, no matter how generous developed countries were in allowing immigration. Sooner or later every country would have to control immigration; virtually all now do so. Permitting immigration even for a short period meant increasing family ties across national boundaries, and growing expectations of future migration-ties which, sooner or later, would have to be weakened, expectations which would have to be dashed. Those suffering the severance of family ties and dashed expectations might well exceed the number of people benefiting from the migration. But in any case the number of people who could benefit from migration was trivially small in relation to those in need.

G was disturbed by the tendency of previous speakers to take an "all or nothing" stance on the issue. He felt that a good case could be made for limited, but not unrestricted, immigration. He would favor some sort of "guest-worker" program, admitting limited numbers of immigrants on a temporary basis into specific occupations. Although this would have an adverse economic effect on some people, their numbers would be limited, and the community could take steps to help and compensate them. Retraining and other assistance could be provided. In this way the rest of the community could obtain many of the benefits of unlimited immigration, while retaining control over the process. In other words, by permitting discrimination between citizens and noncitizens in the labor market, the country might obtain its goods and services at lower cost, while limiting the harm done to citizens.

H also favored limited migration. He agreed with F on the importance of community membership as a primary good. It was incorrect to see the state as simply an association to provide public goods—a better analogy was a club, or even an extended family. The decision to admit to membership was not to be taken lightly. But having taken it, immigrants should be admitted to full membership, not simply as live-in servants. Otherwise one had an exploited, disenfranchised class of individuals in the community, denied political rights and civil liberties, and subject to continual threat of deportation. But if human rights were truly universal, they should apply to everybody everywhere, not simply in their country of permanent citizenship. Furthermore, the need to enforce two classes of community members, through the actions of both the police and private employers, was bound to invade the privacy of all residents, including citizens. In addition the guest worker was separated from his dependents for long periods of time, causing considerable hardship to both. If guest workers were doing socially necessary work, they should be given the potential to become full members of society.

G retorted that giving full economic rights to immigrants would eliminate many of the alleged gains from migration. One might agree that aliens had a right to due process and basic liberties, without holding that they had the right to vote, or to equality with respect to labor legislation and social security. The economic and social rights set out in the Universal Declaration of Human Rights were much more controversial than, for example, the right not to be tortured.

A, the global utilitarian, said he was particularly disturbed by two of the arguments of later speakers. The notion of the modern nation state as a private club or a tightly knit scheme of social cooperation was absurd. National boundaries had often been arbitrarily determined by historical events and frequently failed to respect cultural or linguistic groupings. Nations differed enormously in size, power, wealth, and social cohesion. Not infrequently, national legislation forbade local communities, and possibly even private clubs, from discriminating on the basis of race, or national origin. Yet here it was being suggested that it was permissible for a nation, which was a much less tightly knit grouping, to do just that. This sort of argument had frequently been used to justify immigration policies that blatantly discriminated among different ethnic groups-for example White Australia policies, U.S. immigration quotas before 1965, and de facto immigration restrictions in Britain.

The other argument concerned the disparity of population growth rates in developed or developing countries and the inevitability of immigration restrictions. More immigration was not likely to lead to faster growth in the place of origin. There was plenty of evidence that the level of development was a very significant determinant of population growth rates, along with government population policy.[9] So if the effect of migration was

9. *See, e.g.,* Ronald G. Ridker, ed., *Population and Development: The Search for Selective Interventions* (Baltimore: Johns Hopkins University Press, 1976).

to lead to more rapid development of the countries of emigration, this would have a favorable effect on population growth. In either case, this was not likely to be very large in relation to the whole population problem.

However, the fact that the beneficiaries from migration were few in comparison with the size of the world's population and poverty problem was not a good argument for doing nothing. The fact that rescuers at a fire may be only able to rescue 1 percent of those caught in it is not an argument for failing to rescue that 1 percent. The fact that one could not give enough foreign assistance to eliminate world poverty was not an argument for giving none at all. Even if generous immigration policies imposed a cost on every citizen of the host country, he believed that their much more comfortable position would justify the imposition of the cost. But this was not even at issue here, since in general citizens of the host country would be better-off.

BRUCE ACKERMAN, SOCIAL JUSTICE IN THE LIBERAL STATE

89–95 (1980).*

[In this work of political philosophy, Professor Ackerman defends modern liberalism as having "its own inner coherence when understood as a sustained effort to achieve a power structure in which all members of a political community can engage in a distinctive form of dialogue with one another." (P.30.) That "distinctive dialogue," which Ackerman refers to as "Neutral Dialogue," is characterized by several principles, two of which are relevant here: (1) The Rationality Principle: "Whenever anybody questions the legitimacy of another's power, the power holder must respond not by suppressing the questioner but by giving a reason that explains why he is more entitled to the resource than the questioner is." (P.4.) (2) The Neutrality Principle: "No reason is a good reason if it requires the power holder to assert: (a) that his conception of the good is better than that asserted by any of his fellow citizens, *or* (b) that, regardless of his conception of the good, he is intrinsically superior to one or more of his fellow citizens." (P. 11.) Ackerman uses the device of the Neutral Dialogue—in which power holders are forced to provide neutral and consistent reasons for their control of resources—to generate principles of social justice. The dialogues below concern the first question that Ackerman must consider: who is entitled to participate in the Neutral Dialogue? Or, to put the matter more concretely, what moral claims does an individual have to membership (or citizenship) in a liberal society?]

Imagine * * * that there are two spaceships—Explorer and Apollo— engaged in the task of discovery. * * * The Explorer, however, lands first, and the Commander of that ship gives each member of her landing party a single grain of manna[a] with which to begin life. A split second later, the

---

a. "Manna," according to Ackerman's fantasy, is a resource that is "infinitely divisi-
ble and malleable, capable of transformation into any physical object a person may desire." However, "it is impossible to squeeze

Apollonians arrive and demand equal standing in the burgeoning liberal polity:

Apollonian: I want half your manna.

Explorer: Sorry, but I need all of it—and more—if I am to attain my ends in life.

Apollonian: But I need it too! If personal need is a good reason for your getting manna, why shouldn't it count in my case as well?

Explorer: Do I have to answer that question?

Apollonian: Absolutely. Rationality requires power wielders to answer the question of legitimacy whenever it is raised.

Explorer: But I want nothing from you!

Apollonian: That doesn't mean you're not exercising power over me. I want half the manna and you're trying to stop me. That's enough to establish a power relationship requiring justification.

Explorer: Look, I didn't ask you to come. Why don't you just go away?

Apollonian: I didn't ask you to come either. Why isn't that an equally good reason for you to go away and leave all the manna for me?

Explorer: Well, if you really must know, I'll come up with a serious answer.

Apollonian: I'm waiting.

Explorer: I should get the manna because I'm a citizen of the liberal state we Explorers have established, and you're not.

Apollonian: Progress at last. There's only one problem.

Explorer: What's that?

Apollonian: * * * [W]hy do you think you qualify as a citizen and I do not?

Explorer: Easy. I landed on the Explorer, hence I must be a citizen of the liberal state we Explorers have established.

Apollonian: That can't be right. After all, there are lots of things that landed on the Explorer that don't qualify as citizens. That hunk of metal, for example. (Pointing to the spaceship.)

Explorer: But I'm different from the hunk because I can justify my claims to power.

Apollonian: So can I. Why then don't I qualify as a citizen along with you?

* * *

Explorer: Because I landed in the hunk and you didn't!

an infinite quantity of a desired good from a single grain of the miracle substance." (P. 31.)—eds.

Apollonian: Awfully mysterious. This metal hunk doesn't even qualify as a citizen and yet it constitutes the decisive difference between you and me.

Explorer: But you don't deny the fact that, thanks to the Explorer, I got here ahead of you.

Apollonian: I don't deny the fact. I just want to know why the fact should count as a reason justifying your superior power position.

Explorer: Because people who arrive first are better than people who arrive second.

Apollonian: Reason at last! But this would plainly be an un-Neutral reason if given to a citizen of the liberal state.

Explorer: An irrelevant objection. I'm giving this as a reason for denying you citizenship. No Neutrality objections please; by its own terms, the [Neutrality] principle limits its protections to "citizens."

Apollonian: And what about your children? Will they ever qualify as citizens?

Explorer: Of course.

Apollonian: But they will arrive even later than I have.

Explorer: Do I have to respond to this point?

Apollonian: Absolutely. * * *

Explorer: Well, if you insist, I declare that the special superiority that I possess by virtue of my first arrival is passed down to my descendants forever and ever, while the special inferiority you possess taints your descendants as well.

Apollonian: And suppose that I deny your claim, asserting instead that true moral superiority resides with those with a high IQ or those with a particularly beautiful body or those who are born black or those—

Explorer: Then what you'd say would simply be wrong. True moral superiority resides with the first inhabitants and their descendants. Only a fool would think otherwise!

Apollonian: Aren't you troubled by the kinds of answers you're giving?

Explorer: An irrelevant question. * * * You've asked some hard questions, but I've answered them. Have I satisfied you?

Apollonian: Not at all. * * *

* * * [D]on't you agree that citizenship is the most fundamental right a person could have in a liberal state?

Explorer: Why do you think so?

Apollonian: After all, it is nothing less than to have conversational rights * * *. And what could be more fundamental than that?

Explorer: A good point.

* * *

Apollonian: If citizenship is the most fundamental right in liberal theory, how can you allow this right to be assigned for reasons you would never tolerate on less important questions?

* * *

Explorer: You know, I really do wish you'd go away.

Apollonian: I realize that. But I'm not going away. Like it or not, you are exercising power over me, and I shall continue to press my question of legitimacy. So tell me, isn't it obvious that citizenship is the most fundamental status question; after all, you're using it as the reason for denying me all my rights!

Explorer: Really, I have more important things to do with my time and manna than engage in such twaddle.

Apollonian: More important things! Do you imagine that you are some divinity whose claim to dominion over me is self-evident? Why don't you answer my question?

Explorer: Well, frankly, I do find it difficult to deny that citizenship is central. After all, in order to establish my own rights to scarce resources, I am constantly relying on my citizenship status.

Apollonian: Then you must concede the same to me.

Explorer: And if I do not?

Apollonian: Then you must abandon the claim that you Explorers have established an ideal liberal state. For the first principle of such a polity requires each of its citizens to provide rational and consistent answers to the question of legitimacy whenever asked. And you have just failed this minimal test.

* * *

* * * We can make sense of citizenship only by rooting it in more fundamental ideas of political community. In liberal theory, the polity achieves its distinctiveness by a commitment to a process by which questions are, in principle, followed by rational answers. Nor can answers take any form the power wielders find convenient. Instead, when faced with the question of legitimacy, *the challenged party cannot respond by asserting the moral inferiority of the questioner*. It is this basic idea that is particularized by Neutrality's guarantee to all "citizens" of the liberal state. Yet this basic idea also applies to the conversation that determines the citizenship status of persons capable of participating in a liberal polity. The liberal state is not a private club; it is rather a public dialogue by which each person can gain social recognition of his standing as a free and rational being. I cannot justify my power to exclude you without destroying my own claim to membership in an ideal liberal state.

* * *

But it is time to descend to earth. Quite unthinkingly, we have come to accept the idea that we have the right to exclude nonresidents from our midst. Yet, unless something further can be said, the dialogue between

Explorer and Apollonian applies equally to the conversation between a rich American and an impoverished Mexican who swims over the border for a talk. The American can no more declare the intrinsic superiority of the first occupant than the Explorer can. Instead, it is only a very strong empirical claim that can permit the American to justify exclusion of the foreign-born from "his" liberal state.

To simplify the argument, divide the world into two nation-states, the poor East and the rich West. Assume further that Western domestic institutions are organized in a liberalish way while the East is an authoritarian dictatorship in which a small elite explicitly declares its superiority over the masses they exploit. Assume, finally, that as part of its second-best response to this dark reality, the West has adopted a forthcoming immigration policy, admitting a large number, Z, of Easterners on a first-come, first-served basis. Indeed, Z is so large that it strains the capacity of Western institutions to sustain a liberal political conversation. Any more than Z and the West's standing as a liberal society will be endangered; the presence of so many alien newcomers will generate such anxiety in the native population that it will prove impossible to stop a fascist group from seizing political power to assure native control over the immigrant underclass. Nonetheless, the Easterners keep coming at an awesome rate; the scene takes place at the armed Western border:

Easterner: I demand recognition as a citizen of this liberal state.

Western Statesman: We refuse.

Easterner: What gives you the right to refuse me? Do you think I would fail to qualify as a citizen of an ideal liberal state?

Westerner: Not at all.

Easterner: Do you imagine you're better than me simply because you've been born west of this frontier?

Westerner: No. If that were all, I would not hesitate before admitting you.

Easterner: Well, then, what's the trouble?

Westerner: The fact is that we in the West are far from achieving a perfect technology of justice; if we admit more than Z newcomers, our existing institutions will be unable to function in anything but an explicitly authoritarian manner.

Easterner: But why am I being asked to bear the costs of imperfection?

Westerner: Sorry, we're doing everything we can. But Z is the limit on immigrants.

Easterner: But you're not doing everything. Why not expel some of your native-born Westerners and make room for me? Do you think they're better than I am?

Westerner: Z is the limit on our assimilative capacity only on the assumption that there exists a cadre of natives familiar with the operation of liberal institutions. If some of the natives were removed from the population, even Z would be too many.

Easterner: So what am I to do? I'll be dead before I get to the front of the line of immigrants.

Westerner: Go back among your own people and build your own liberal state. We'll try to help you out as best we can.

* * *

The *only* reason for restricting immigration is to protect the ongoing process of liberal conversation itself. Can our present immigration practices be rationalized on this ground?

MICHAEL WALZER, SPHERES OF JUSTICE: A DEFENSE OF PLURALISM AND EQUALITY
31–34, 37–40, 45, 47–49, 61–62 (1983).*

The idea of distributive justice presupposes a bounded world within which distributions [take] place: a group of people committed to dividing, exchanging, and sharing social goods, first of all among themselves. That world * * * is the political community, whose members distribute power to one another and avoid, if they possibly can, sharing it with anyone else. When we think about distributive justice, we think about independent cities or countries capable of arranging their own patterns of division and exchange, justly or unjustly. We assume an established group and a fixed population, and so we miss the first and most important distributive question: How is that group constituted?

I don't mean, How *was* it constituted? I am concerned here not with the historical origins of the different groups, but with the decisions they make in the present about their present and future populations. The primary good that we distribute to one another is membership in some human community. And what we do with regard to membership structures all our other distributive choices: it determines with whom we make those choices, from whom we require obedience and collect taxes, to whom we allocate goods and services.

* * *

* * * Since human beings are highly mobile, large numbers of men and women regularly attempt to change their residence and their membership, moving from unfavored to favored environments. Affluent and free countries are, like élite universities, besieged by applicants. They have to decide on their own size and character. More precisely, as citizens of such a country, we have to decide: Whom should we admit? Ought we to have open admissions? Can we choose among applicants? What are the appropriate criteria for distributing membership?

* (New York, N.Y.: Basic Books, Inc., 1983). Revised from Michael Walzer, *The Distribution of Membership*, in Peter G. Brown and Henry Shue, eds., Boundaries: National Autonomy and its Limits (Totowa, N.J.: Rowman and Littlefield © 1981). Reprinted by permission.

The plural pronouns that I have used in asking these questions suggest the conventional answer to them: we who are already members do the choosing, in accordance with our own understanding of what membership means in our community and of what sort of a community we want to have. Membership as a social good is constituted by our understanding; its value is fixed by our work and conversation; and then we are in charge (who else could be in charge?) of its distribution. But we don't distribute it among ourselves; it is already ours. We give it out to strangers. Hence the choice is also governed by our relationships with strangers—not only by our understanding of those relationships but also by the actual contacts, connections, alliances we have established and the effects we have had beyond our borders. * * *

* * * In a number of ancient languages, Latin among them, strangers and enemies were named by a single word. We have come only slowly, through a long process of trial and error, to distinguish the two and to acknowledge that, in certain circumstances, strangers (but not enemies) might be entitled to our hospitality, assistance, and good will. This acknowledgment can be formalized as the principle of mutual aid, which suggests the duties that we owe, as John Rawls has written, "not only to definite individuals, say to those cooperating together in some social arrangement, but to persons generally." Mutual aid extends across political (and also cultural, religious, and linguistic) frontiers. The philosophical grounds of the principle are hard to specify (its history provides its practical ground). * * *

It is the absence of any cooperative arrangements that sets the context for mutual aid: two strangers meet at sea or in the desert or, as in the Good Samaritan story, by the side of the road. What precisely they owe one another is by no means clear, but we commonly say of such cases that positive assistance is required if (1) it is needed or urgently needed by one of the parties; and (2) if the risks and costs of giving it are relatively low for the other party. Given these conditions, I ought to stop and help the injured stranger, wherever I meet him, whatever his membership or my own. This is our morality; conceivably his, too. It is, moreover, an obligation that can be read out in roughly the same form at the collective level. Groups of people ought to help necessitous strangers whom they somehow discover in their midst or on their path. But the limit on risks and costs in these cases is sharply drawn. I need not take the injured stranger into my home, except briefly, and I certainly need not care for him or even associate with him for the rest of my life. My life cannot be shaped and determined by such chance encounters. Governor John Winthrop, arguing against free immigration to the new Puritan commonwealth of Massachusetts, insisted that this right of refusal applies also to collective mutual aid: "As for hospitality, that rule does not bind further than for some present occasion, not for continual residence." Whether Winthrop's view can be defended is a question that I shall come to only gradually. Here I only want to point to mutual aid as a (possible) external principle for the distribution of membership, a principle that doesn't depend upon the prevailing view of membership within a particular society. The force of the principle is uncertain, in part because of its own vagueness, in part because it sometimes comes up against the internal force of social meanings. And these meanings can be specified, and are specified, through the decision-making processes of the political community.

* * * [S]o long as members and strangers are, as they are at present, two distinct groups, admissions decisions have to be made, men and women taken in or refused. Given the indeterminate requirements of mutual aid, these decisions are not constrained by any widely accepted standard. That's why the admissions policies of countries are rarely criticized, except in terms suggesting that the only relevant criteria are those of charity, not justice. It is certainly possible that a deeper criticism would lead one to deny the member/stranger distinction. But I shall try, nevertheless, to defend that distinction and then to describe the internal and the external principles that govern the distribution of membership.

* * *

* * * The same writers who defended free trade in the nineteenth century also defended unrestricted immigration. They argued for perfect freedom of contract, without any political restraint. International society, they thought, should take shape as a world of neighborhoods, with individuals moving freely about, seeking private advancement. In their view, as Henry Sidgwick reported it in the 1890s, the only business of state officials is "to maintain order over [a] particular territory . . . but not in any way to determine who is to inhabit this territory, or to restrict the enjoyment of its natural advantages to any particular portion of the human race." Natural advantages (like markets) are open to all comers, within the limits of private property rights; and if they are used up or devalued by overcrowding, people presumably will move on, into the jurisdiction of new sets of officials.

Sidgwick thought that this is possibly the "ideal of the future," but he offered three arguments against a world of neighborhoods in the present. First of all, such a world would not allow for patriotic sentiment, and so the "casual aggregates" that would probably result from the free movement of individuals would "lack internal cohesion." Neighbors would be strangers to one another. Second, free movement might interfere with efforts "to raise the standard of living among the poorer classes" of a particular country, since such efforts could not be undertaken with equal energy and success everywhere in the world. And, third, the promotion of moral and intellectual culture and the efficient working of political institutions might be "defeated" by the continual creation of heterogeneous populations. Sidgwick presented these three arguments as a series of utilitarian considerations that weigh against the benefits of labor mobility and contractual freedom. But they seem to me to have a rather different character. The last two arguments draw their force from the first, but only if the first is conceived in non-utilitarian terms. It is only if patriotic sentiment has some moral basis, only if communal cohesion makes for obligations and shared meanings, only if there are members as well as strangers, that state officials would have any reason to worry especially about the welfare of their own people (and of *all* their own people) and the success of their own culture and politics. For it is at least dubious that the average standard of living of the poorer classes throughout the world would decline under conditions of perfect labor mobility. Nor is there firm evidence that culture cannot thrive in cosmopolitan environments, nor that it is impossible to govern casual aggregations of people. As for the last of these, political theorists long ago discovered that certain sorts of regimes— namely, authoritarian regimes—thrive in the absence of communal cohesion. That perfect mobility makes for authoritarianism might suggest a utilitarian argument against mobility; but such an argument would work only if individual men and women, free to come and go, expressed a desire for some other form of government. And that they might not do.

Perfect labor mobility, however, is probably a mirage, for it is almost certain to be resisted at the local level. Human beings, as I have said, move about a great deal, but not because they love to move. They are, most of them, inclined to stay where they are unless their life is very difficult there. They experience a tension between love of place and the discomforts of a particular place. While some of them leave their homes and become foreigners in new lands, others stay where they are and resent the foreigners in their own land. Hence, if states ever become large neighborhoods, it is likely that neighborhoods will become little states. Their members will organize to defend the local politics and culture against strangers. Historically, neighborhoods have turned into closed or parochial communities (leaving aside cases of legal coercion) whenever the state was open: in the cosmopolitan cities of multinational empires, for example, where state officials don't foster any particular identity but permit different groups to build their own institutional structures (as in ancient Alexandria), or in the receiving centers of mass immigration movements (early twentieth century New York) where the country is an open but also an alien world—or, alternatively, a world full of aliens. The case is similar where the state doesn't exist at all or in areas where it doesn't function. Where welfare monies are raised and spent locally, for example, as in a seventeenth-century English parish, the local people will seek to exclude newcomers who are likely welfare recipients. It is only the nationalization of welfare (or the nationalization of culture and politics) that opens the neighborhood communities to whoever chooses to come in.

Neighborhoods can be open only if countries are at least potentially closed. Only if the state makes a selection among would-be members and guarantees the loyalty, security, and welfare of the individuals it selects, can local communities take shape as "indifferent" associations, determined solely by personal preference and market capacity. Since individual choice is most dependent upon local mobility, this would seem to be the preferred arrangement in a society like our own. The politics and the culture of a modern democracy probably require the kind of largeness, and also the kind of boundedness, that states provide. I don't mean to deny the value of sectional cultures and ethnic communities; I mean only to suggest the rigidities that would be forced upon both in the absence of inclusive and protective states. To tear down the walls of the state is not, as Sidgwick worriedly suggested, to create a world without walls, but rather to create a thousand petty fortresses.

The fortresses, too, could be torn down: all that is necessary is a global state sufficiently powerful to overwhelm the local communities. Then the result would be the world of the political economists, as Sidgwick described it—a world of radically deracinated men and women. Neighborhoods might maintain some cohesive culture for a generation or two on a voluntary basis, but people would move in, people would move out; soon the cohesion would be gone. The distinctiveness of cultures and groups depends upon closure and, without it, cannot be conceived as a stable feature of human life. If this distinctiveness is a value, as most people (though some of them are global pluralists, and others only local loyalists) seem to believe, then closure must be permitted somewhere. At some level of political organization, something like the sovereign state must take shape and claim the authority to make its own admissions policy, to control and sometimes restrain the flow of immigrants.

* * *

* * * To say that states have a right to act in certain areas is not to say that anything they do in those areas is right. One can argue about particular admissions standards by appealing, for example, to the condition and character of the host country and to the shared understandings of those who are already members. * * * Decisions of this sort are subject to constraint, but what the constraints are I am not yet ready to say. It is important first to insist that the distribution of membership in American society, and in any ongoing society, is a matter of political decision. The labor market may be given free rein, as it was for many decades in the United States, but that does not happen by an act of nature or of God; it depends upon choices that are ultimately political. What kind of community do the citizens want to create? With what other men and women do they want to share and exchange social goods?

* * *

Can a political community exclude destitute and hungry, persecuted and stateless—in a word, necessitous—men and women simply because they are foreigners? Are citizens bound to take in strangers? Let us assume that the citizens have no formal obligations; they are bound by nothing more stringent than the principle of mutual aid. The principle must be applied, however, not to individuals directly but to the citizens as a group, for immigration is a matter of political decision. Individuals participate in the decision making, if the state is democratic; but they decide not for themselves but for the community generally. And this fact has moral implications. It replaces immediacy with distance and the personal expense of time and energy with impersonal bureaucratic costs. Despite John Winthrop's claim, mutual aid is more coercive for political communities than it is for individuals because a wide range of benevolent actions is open to the community which will only marginally affect its present members * * *. * * * These actions probably include the admission of strangers, for admission to a country does not entail the kinds of intimacy that could hardly be avoided in the case of clubs and families. Might not admission, then, be morally imperative, at least for *these* strangers, who have no other place to go?

* * *

* * * [Wealth, resources and territory] can be superfluous, far beyond what the inhabitants of a particular state require for a decent life (even as they themselves define the meaning of a decent life). Are those inhabitants morally bound to admit immigrants from poorer countries for as long as superfluous resources exist? Or are they bound even longer than that, beyond the limits of mutual aid, until a policy of open admissions ceases to attract and benefit the poorest people in the world? Sidgwick seems to have opted for the first of these possibilities; he proposed a primitive and parochial version of Rawls's difference principle: immigration can be restricted as soon as failure to do so would "interfere materially ... with the efforts of the government to maintain an adequately high standard of life among the members of the community generally—especially the poorer classes." But the community might well decide to cut off immigration even before that, if it were willing to export (some of) its superfluous wealth. * * * [T]hey could share their wealth with necessitous strangers outside their country or with necessitous strangers inside their country. But just how much of their wealth do they have to share? Once again, there must be some limit, short (and probably considerably short) of simple equality, else communal wealth would be subject to indefinite drainage. The very phrase "communal wealth" would lose its meaning if all resources and all products were globally common. * * *

If we stop short of simple equality, there will continue to be many communities, with different histories, ways of life, climates, political structures, and economies. Some places in the world will still be more desirable than others, either to individual men and women with particular tastes and aspirations, or more generally. Some places will still be uncomfortable for at least some of their inhabitants. Hence immigration will remain an issue even after the claims of distributive justice have been met on a global scale-assuming, still, that global society is and ought to be pluralist in form and that the claims are fixed by some version of collective mutual aid. The different communities will still have to make admissions decisions and will still have a right to make them. If we cannot guarantee the full extent of the territorial or material base on which a group of people build a common life, we can still say that the common life, at least, is their own and that their comrades and associates are theirs to recognize or choose.

There is, however, one group of needy outsiders whose claims cannot be met by yielding territory or exporting wealth; they can be met only by taking people in. This is the group of refugees whose need is for membership itself, a non-exportable good. The liberty that makes certain countries possible homes for men and women whose politics or religion isn't tolerated where they live is also non-exportable: at least we have found no way of exporting it. These goods can be shared only within the protected space of a particular state. At the same time, admitting refugees doesn't necessarily decrease the amount of liberty the members enjoy within that space. The victims of political or religious persecution, then, make the most forceful claim for admission. If you don't take me in, they say, I shall be killed, persecuted, brutally oppressed by the rulers of my own country. What can we reply?

* * *

The distribution of membership is not pervasively subject to the constraints of justice. Across a considerable range of the decisions that are made, states are simply free to take in strangers (or not)—much as they are free, leaving aside the claims of the needy, to share their wealth with foreign friends, to honor the achievements of foreign artists, scholars, and scientists, to choose their trading partners, and to enter into collective security arrangements with foreign states. But the right to choose an admissions policy is more basic than any of these, for it is not merely a matter of acting in the world, exercising sovereignty, and pursuing national interests. At stake here is the shape of the community that acts in the world, exercises sovereignty, and so on. Admission and exclusion are at the core of communal independence. They suggest the deepest meaning of self-determination. Without them, there could not be *communities of character,* historically stable, ongoing associations of men and women with some special commitment to one another and some special sense of their common life.

But self-determination in the sphere of membership is not absolute. It is a right exercised, most often, by national clubs or families, but it is held in principle by territorial states. Hence it is subject both to internal decisions by the members themselves (*all* the members, including those who hold membership simply by right of place) and to the external principle of mutual aid. Immigration, then, is both a matter of political choice and moral constraint. * * *

JOSEPH H. CARENS, ALIENS AND CITIZENS: THE CASE FOR OPEN BORDERS
49 Review of Politics 251, 266–71 (1987).

* * * Walzer compares the idea of open states with our experience of neighborhoods as a form of open association. But in thinking about what open states would be like, we have a better comparison at hand. We can draw upon our experience of cities, provinces, or states in the American sense. These are familiar political communities whose borders are open. Unlike neighborhoods and like countries, they are formally organized communities with boundaries, distinctions between citizens and noncitizens, and elected officials who are expected to pursue policies that benefit the members of the community that elected them. They often have distinctive cultures and ways of life. Think of the differences between New York City and Waycross, Georgia, or between California and Kansas. These sorts of differences are often much greater than the differences among nation-states. Seattle has more in common with Vancouver than it does with many American communities. But cities and provinces and American states cannot restrict immigration (from other parts of the country). So, these cases call into question Walzer's claim that distinctiveness depends on the possibility of formal closure. What makes for distinctiveness and what erodes it is much more complex than political control of admissions.

This does not mean that control over admissions is unimportant. Often local communities would like to restrict immigration. The people of California wanted to keep out poor Oklahomans during the Depression. Now the people of Oregon would like to keep out the Californians. Internal migrations can be substantial. They can transform the character of communities. (Think of the migrations from the rural South to the urban North.) They can place strains on the local economy and make it difficult to maintain locally funded social programs. Despite all this, we do not think these political communities should be able to control their borders. The right to free migration takes priority.

Why should this be so? Is it just a choice that we make as a larger community (*i.e.*, the nation state) to restrict the self-determination of local communities in this way? Could we legitimately permit them to exclude? Not easily. No liberal state restricts internal mobility. Those states that do restrict internal mobility are criticized for denying basic human freedoms. If freedom of movement within the state is so important that it overrides the claims of local political communities, on what grounds can we restrict freedom of movement across states? This requires a stronger case for the *moral* distinctiveness of the nation-state as a form of community than Walzer's discussion of neighborhoods provides.

Walzer also draws an analogy between states and clubs. Clubs may generally admit or exclude whomever they want, although any particular decision may be criticized through an appeal to the character of the club and the shared understandings of its members. So, too, with states. This analogy ignores the familiar distinction between public and private, a distinction that Walzer makes use of elsewhere. There is a deep tension between the right of freedom of association and the right to equal treatment. One way to address this tension is to say that in the private sphere freedom of association prevails and in the public sphere equal treatment does. You can pick your friends on the basis of whatever criteria you wish, but in selecting people for offices you must treat all candidates fairly. Drawing a line between public and private is often problematic, but it is clear that clubs are normally at one end of the scale and states at the other. So, the fact that private clubs may admit or exclude whomever they choose says nothing about the appropriate admission standards for states. When the state acts it must treat individuals equally.

Against this, one may object that the requirement of equal treatment applies fully only to those who are already *members* of the community. That is accurate as a description of practice but the question is why it should be so. At one time, the requirement of equal treatment did not extend fully to various groups (workers, blacks, women). On the whole, the history of liberalism reflects a tendency to expand both the definition of the public sphere and the requirements of equal treatment. In the United States today, for example, in contrast to earlier times, both public agencies and private corporations may not legally exclude women simply because they are women (although private clubs still may). A white shopkeeper may no longer exclude blacks from his store (although he may exclude them from his home). I think these recent developments, like the earlier extension of the franchise, reflect something fundamental about the inner logic of liberalism. The extension of the right to immigrate reflects the same logic: equal treatment of individuals in the public sphere.

* * *

Any approach like Walzer's that seeks its ground in the tradition and culture of *our* community must confront, as a methodological paradox, the fact that liberalism is a central part of our culture. The enormous intellectual popularity of Rawls and Nozick and the enduring influence of utilitarianism attest to their ability to communicate contemporary understandings and shared meanings in a language that has legitimacy and power in our culture. These theories would not make such sense to a Buddhist monk in medieval Japan. But their individualistic assumptions and their language of universal, ahistorical reason makes sense to us because of *our* tradition, *our* culture, *our* community. For people in a different moral tradition, one that assumed fundamental moral differences between those inside the society and those outside, restrictions on immigration might be easy to justify. Those who are *other* simply might not count, or at least not count as much. But we cannot dismiss the aliens on the ground that they are other, because *we* are the products of a liberal culture.

* * *

* * * If my arguments are correct, the general case for open borders is deeply rooted in the fundamental values of our tradition. No moral argument will seem acceptable to *us,* if it directly challenges the assumption of the equal moral worth of all individuals. If restrictions on immigration are to be justified, they have to be based on arguments that respect that principle. Walzer's theory has many virtues that I have not explored here, but it does not supply an adequate argument for the state's right to exclude.

Free migration may not be immediately achievable, but it is a goal toward which we should strive. And we have an obligation to open our borders much more fully than we do now. The current restrictions on immigration in Western democracies—even in the most open ones like Canada and the United States—are not justifiable. Like feudal barriers to mobility, they protect unjust privilege.

Does it follow that there is *no* room for distinctions between aliens and citizens, no theory of citizenship, no boundaries for the community? Not at all. To say that membership is open to all who wish to join is not to say that there is no distinction between members and nonmembers. Those who choose to cooperate together in the state have special rights and obligations not shared by noncitizens. Respecting the particular choices and commitments that individuals make flows naturally from a commitment to the idea of equal moral worth. (Indeed, consent as a justification for political obligation is least problematic in the case of immigrants.) What is *not* readily compatible with the idea of equal moral worth is the exclusion of those who want to join. If people want to sign the social contract, they should be permitted to do so.

Open borders would threaten the distinctive character of different political communities only because we assume that so many people would move if they could. If the migrants were few, it would not matter. A few immigrants could always be absorbed without changing the character of the community. And, as Walzer observes, most human beings do not love to move. They normally feel attached to their native land and to the particular language, culture, and community in which they grew up and in which they feel at home. They seek to move only when life is very difficult where they are. Their concerns are rarely frivolous. So, it is right to weigh the claims of those who want to move against the claims of those who want to preserve the community as it is. And if we don't unfairly tip the scales, the case for exclusion will rarely triumph.

People live in communities with bonds and bounds, but these may be of different kinds. In a liberal society, the bonds and bounds should be compatible with liberal principles. Open immigration would change the character of the community but it would not leave the community without any character. It might destroy old ways of life, highly valued by some, but it would make possible new ways of life, highly valued by others. The whites in Forsythe County who want to keep out blacks are trying to preserve a way of life that is valuable to them. To deny such communities the right to exclude does limit their ability to shape their future character and destiny, but it does not utterly destroy their capacity for self-determination. Many aspects of communal life remain potentially subject to collective control. Moreover, constraining the kinds of choices that people and communities may make is what principles of justice are for. They set limits on what people seeking to abide by these principles may do. To commit ourselves to open borders would not be to abandon the idea of communal character but to reaffirm it. It would be an affirmation of the liberal character of the community and of its commitment to principles of justice.

Notes

1. In Professor Ackerman's first dialogue, do you think the Explorer has made her best argument in responding to the Apollonian's demand for manna? Imagine a different version of the dialogue.

Apollonian: I want half your manna.

Explorer: Sorry. In order to attain our goals in life, it is necessary for Explorers to adopt an admissions policy that preserves and furthers our culture and political institutions.

Apollonian: But I would like to join your community. Just give me some manna, and I'll show you what a productive member I can be.

Explorer: We Explorers are aware that you might well put the manna to good use. Nor do we question the moral worthiness of your goals. In fact, we might even export some manna to your home country to help you achieve your life plans. But your conception of the good may not be our conception of the good. Communities are more than distribution centers for resources. They are "ongoing associations of men and women with some special commitment to one another and some special sense of their common life." [Walzer, Spheres of Justice, *supra*, at 62.] Thus, while your need for manna is moving, it can grant you no right to enter our community.

Apollonian: But what did you do to deserve the manna you are keeping from me? You did not create it. By refusing me entry to your community you are saying I am not worthy of being a member. You are thus violating a basic tenet of liberalism by denying that I am at least as good as you.

Explorer: Not at all. We respect your right to establish and live in your own community according to whatever principles of membership you agree upon. But surely you can have no right to destroy our right of self-determination simply because your ship got you to our community. In a few years-once we have multiplied our manna and created the society we desire-we will take applications from Apollonians, Centaurians, Venutians, and other foreigners. Apply and we shall see what happens.

Apollonian: You are no liberal.

Explorer: But your liberalism appears inherently contradictory. You are violating your own rules by insisting that we run our community according to your principles. Are you not asserting that your idea of the good is better than ours? Are you not denying us the right to choose the kind of people and community we would like to be?

Does the Explorer sound more persuasive here? Persuasive enough?

2. The Apollonian–Explorer debates may seem a bit artificial because they concern a situation that we rarely see today: the settlement of newly discovered, unoccupied land. Suppose the Apollonians arrived several generations after the Explorers and in that time the Explorers had developed a thriving economy and rich culture. What different arguments might the Explorers make? Would they be more compelling? Would such arguments support a policy of the Explorers that gave preference to Explorers emigrating from the "old country" over the Apollonians?

Consider the defense of the Senate Judiciary Committee for retention of the national origins quota system in the McCarran–Walter Act of 1952:

> Without giving credence to any theory of Nordic Superiority, the subcommittee believes that the adoption of the national origins formula was a rational and logical method of numerically restricting immigration in such a manner as to best preserve the sociological and cultural balance in the population of the United States. There is no doubt that it favored the peoples of the countries of northern and western Europe over those of southern and eastern Europe, but the subcommittee holds that the peoples who had made the greatest contribution to the development of this country were fully justified in determining that the country was no longer

a field for further colonization, and henceforth, further immigration would not only be restricted but directed to admit immigrants considered to be more readily assimilable because of the similarity of their cultural background to those of the principal components of our population.

S.Rep. No. 1515, 81st Cong., 2d Sess. 455 (1950).

3. Note an ambiguity in Professor Ackerman's dialogue. Do the Apollonians wish to settle on the planet—and join the Explorer community—or simply take some of the manna back to their home country? Is the moral claim to manna (essentially a question of distributive justice) different from the moral claim to membership? Or, to put the question in more practical terms, what is and should be the relationship between American immigration and foreign aid policies ?[15]

4. Ackerman asserts that "[t]he *only* reason for restricting immigration is to protect the ongoing process of liberal conversation itself." Would Walzer agree? Do you? To what extent are the positions of Ackerman, Walzer, and Carens reflected in the earlier discussion of the source of congressional authority to restrict immigration? (Consider particularly the structural justifications based on self-preservation and self-determination.)

5. Consider a different sort of moral justification for control of immigration:

> In a world of many states, some may be despotisms, but it is unlikely that all will be despotic at the same time. The existence of nondespotic states offers the possibility of a refuge from the despotisms, and the possibility of the flight of skilled people from despotic to free societies (however much the despotic regime may try to prevent this) tends to temper despotic government. (This is an important liberal argument for free movement, especially emigration and asylum for refugees.) Moreover, the existence of the nondespotic states stands as a constant reproach to the despotisms, offering a model of something better and serving as a source of moral (and perhaps also material) support for reformers, revolutionaries, and dissidents in the oppressed society. From a world state, however, should it fall into the hands of a despotic government, there would be no escape. The memory of nondespotic ways of life would gradually fade away, and endogenous change in a liberal direction would be difficult without external bases of support. A world of numerous independent states with somewhat differing forms of government thus appears to offer the means of correcting abuses that may appear here and there in the system as a whole, much as a liberal constitution, with a separation of powers, is supposed to offer the means of self-correction in the face of institutional tendencies to corruption. If a world state could turn out to be the worst case (in liberal terms), whatever its possible merits, a cautious liberal might well choose to stick with

---

15. For discussions of normative principles in foreign policy and international distributive justice, *see* C. Beitz, Political Theory and International Relations (1979); H. Shue, Basic Rights: Subsistence, Affluence, and U.S. Foreign Policy (1980).

the state system, whatever its actual defects, as a framework within which the survival of liberal values seems more secure.

The second argument for a plurality of states arises from the typical liberal (Millian) view of the sources of progress. Economic productivity and cultural vitality flourish best when there is a large number of autonomous centers of decision, each seeking opportunities for the (locally) optimal employment of its particular set of resources and talents, their interactions with one another coordinated only informally by markets, emulation, rational persuasion, and the like. Beneficial innovations (which outweigh the occasional failures) are stimulated by the diversity that results when individuals are free to choose their own "plans of life." Even conflicts among the competing interests or ideals of independent agents are, to a point, healthy phenomena, a theme Kant developed in terms of the "unsocial sociability" of human beings. If this view is plausible with respect to a society of individuals, so it may be also with respect to the society of states: each state follows, or provides the political means by which its people follow, its own distinctive genius or program of political experimentation, thereby not only attaining the satisfaction that attends autonomy, but also making its own special contribution to the overall cultural resources of humanity.

Whelan, *Citizenship and Freedom of Movement: An Open Admission Policy?*, in Open Borders? Closed Societies?: The Ethical and Political Issues 3, 25–26 (M. Gibney ed. 1988). Do open borders necessarily mean the demise of nationalism? For an argument that they do not, see Wright, *Federal Immigration Law and the Case for Open Entry*, 27 Loy.-L.A. L.Rev. 1263 (1994).

6. Consider the following proposal for allocating immigrant visas:

The debate over immigration tends to focus on a narrow range of tired options, excluding more radical ideas. One idea that has received no attention is sale of the right to immigrate.

Such a system would be fairer and economically more beneficial to the United States and the people in poorer countries than the present system. With each passing year, admission to this country depends more upon whom you're related to and less upon what you can contribute to American society.

By contrast, visas would be allocated impartially by selling admission. Individuals with the most to gain economically would offer the highest prices. Inevitably, these people would have the most to contribute economically to all of us.

* * *

Would an auction mean only the wealthiest would get in? One way to prevent this is to allow "buyers" to enter now and pay later together with income tax. Failure to pay might result in deportation. * * *

* * *

The fees from the auction would put additional purchasing power into the hands of native Americans and provide a fund for foreign aid or scholarships in the United States for deserving foreign students.

Simon, *Auction the Right to Be an Immigrant,* New York Times, Jan. 28, 1986, at A25. For a similar proposal by Nobel Laureate economist Gary Becker, see *An Open Door for Immigrants—The Auction*, Wall St.J., Oct. 14, 1992, at A14.

7. The Senate Report that accompanied the Senate's immigration reform legislation in the 98th Congress included the following statement of the "national interest."

The Committee believes that the paramount obligation of any nation's government, indeed the very reason for its existence and the justification for its power, is to promote the national interest— the long-term welfare of the majority of its citizens and their descendants.

Consequently, we believe that the formulation of U.S. immigration policy must involve a judgment of what would promote the interests of American citizens—as they are at the present time and as they and their descendants are likely to be in the foreseeable future. An immigration policy which would be detrimental to the long-term well-being of the American people should not be adopted.

We certainly do not mean to suggest that charity and compassion should not play a role in U.S. immigration policy. Even if a particular charitable policy would not promote the national interest, as long as it would not be harmful to that interest and was supported by a majority of the American people, then it should of course be adopted.

Because the well-being of individuals is affected by both economic and noneconomic circumstances, an immigration policy which serves the national interest should be based on an analysis of both the economic and noneconomic impacts of immigration. Economic variables include unemployment, wages, working conditions, productivity and per capita Gross National Product. Noneconomic matters include population size, other demographic phenomena, and such cultural elements as values, customs, institutions, and degree of unity or of tension between subcultures.

There is an additional component of the national interest which a realistic analysis must not ignore. This is related to the ability of human beings to experience change without discomfort and it exists regardless of whether any objectively adverse impacts occur. Although the desire of immigrants from other lands to change their lives totally by coming to the United States is obviously greater than their reluctance to leave their homes, the ability of the American people to welcome aliens into their day-to-day life experiences has limits. These limits depend in part on the degree and kind of change which will be caused in their lives. We see evidence that if the newcomers to a community do not excessively disrupt or change the attributes of the community which make it familiar to its residents and uniquely their "home" (as compared with foreign areas, which they may respect highly but which are not "home" to them), then the newcomers may well be welcome, especially if they make positive contributions to the community's economic and general well-being. On the other hand, it is seen that if the newcomers remain "foreign," they may not be welcome, especially if they seek to carve out separate enclaves to embrace only their own language and culture and if their numbers and the areas of the community which they directly affect are great. This should not be so in the "ideal" world, but it is real.

S.Rep. No. 62, 98th Cong., 1st Sess. 3–4 (1983). Which (if any) of the moral theories explored above support the Senate Committee's view?

8. What does the way in which we exercise the "immigration" power imply for the rights and obligations of those who are admitted? Consider Michael Walzer's view:

One might insist, as I shall ultimately do, that the same standards apply to naturalization as to immigration, that every immigrant and every resident is a citizen, too—or at least, a potential citizen. That is why territorial admission is so serious a matter. The members must be prepared to accept, as their own equals in a world of shared obligations, the men and women they admit; the immigrants must be prepared to share the obligations.

Walzer, supra, at 52. *See also* Bosniak, *Membership, Equality and the Difference That Alienage Makes*, 69 N.Y.U.L.Rev. __ (1994).

Chapter Two

FEDERAL AGENCIES

A person who decides she wants to immigrate to the United States may well start the process by visiting the American official most easily accessible: the consular officer posted to her home country. If she looks carefully at the signs around the entrance of the consulate, she may learn that consuls are officers of the Department of State. And, in short order, if she pursues her application, she will come into contact with a rather bewildering variety of other U.S. agencies.

She will probably need an approved visa petition from the Immigration and Naturalization Service (INS), through a process initiated by a close family member already in the United States, or by a prospective employer. If an employer is involved, the Department of Labor may play an important role. If a family member's petition is denied, an appeal may take the case before the Board of Immigration Appeals (BIA), which is not part of INS, but is, like INS, located within the Department of Justice. Once a petition is approved, the action shifts back to the consulate for thorough screening before a visa issues. At the port of entry, she will again encounter the INS in the person of the immigration inspector, who is entitled to rethink the screening determination of the consul. At that stage, a representative of the Public Health Service might perform medical reviews. And several other potential governmental players may become involved as well.

In light of these complexities, we will detour briefly before launching our examination of the substantive provisions of the Immigration and Nationality Act (INA), in order to describe the agencies that administer those provisions. You may wish to refer back to this general map later, to help in determining why an issue was decided initially by one agency rather than another, for example, or why a dispute now in the courts went through the particular forms and stages of administrative and judicial review that it followed.

SECTION A. THE DEPARTMENT OF JUSTICE

Take a careful look at § 103 of the INA. That basic enabling provision places the principal authority for administering the Act, as well as enforcing its provisions against lawbreakers, in the Attorney General. But note that administering and enforcing can be quite different undertakings, each calling for distinct skills and orientation. Administering any complex statute (think of the Social Security Act or other public assistance measures) often requires the administrators to counsel affected individuals regarding their possible rights, liabilities and future actions—what forms to file, what benefits or exemptions to seek—and help guide them through the process. In large measure, these functions involve service to the public. Enforcement of a statute, however, particularly one that is frequently violated, might properly call forth an attitude of tough-mindedness and suspicion on the part of the officials involved. The two functions can coexist if the agency is carefully organized and the administrators are sensitive, skillful and well-trained, but there is inevitably tension between the tasks. Because the INA is both highly complex and notoriously violated on a broad scale, the tension here becomes particularly acute. The possibilities for (and reality of) conflicts and confusion of roles based upon these potentially incompatible tasks will often be apparent in the materials we consider throughout this book.[1]

1. THE IMMIGRATION AND NATURALIZATION SERVICE

A few powers relating to immigration are split off and reserved for the Secretary of State and for diplomatic and consular officers under § 104, but the Attorney General retains all residual authority under the statute and is plainly the key figure in its implementation. The Attorney General is authorized under § 103—and inescapably required—to delegate responsibilities to officers of "the Service" (meaning the Immigration and Naturalization Service, INS) and also to other officers or employees of the Department of Justice.[2] The Service, headed by the Commissioner of Immigration and Naturalization, is therefore expressly established by statute, but the INA says little about which of the Attorney General's delegated immigration powers must be lodged there, rather than in other units of the Justice

1. For further exploration of the problems afflicting our immigration agencies see, e.g., M. Morris, Immigration—The Beleaguered Bureaucracy (1985); E. Harwood, In Liberty's Shadow: Illegal Aliens and Immigration Law Enforcement 25–48, 168–92 (1986); Lee, *The Immigration and Naturalization Service: In Search of the Necessary Efficiency*, 6 Geo. Imm.L.J. 519 (1992) (summarizing recent critical studies of INS management). For a bold proposal that virtually all immigration-related functions now scattered among several units in the Departments of Justice and State be consolidated in a new independent agency, the Agency for Migration Affairs, see Unauthorized Migration: An Economic Development Response (Report of the Comm'n for the Study of Int'l Migration and Cooperative Economic Development 1990).

2. The Service has been part of the Justice Department only since 1940. Early federal regulation of immigration was under the authority of the Secretary of the Treasury,

who initially had to act through State officials, usually designated by State governors. In 1891, Congress decided that the divided authority under this scheme was unworkable. Legislation that year created the federal post of Superintendent of Immigration within the Treasury Department, and federal officials shortly assumed full responsibility for administering the immigration laws. In 1903, these functions were transferred to the Department of Commerce and Labor. When that Department was split in 1913, immigration functions moved to the new Department of Labor. There they remained until a general reorganization plan of 1940 transferred the Immigration and Naturalization Service (as it had been known since 1933) to the Department of Justice. A complete account appears in Congressional Research Service, 96th Cong., 2d Sess., History of the Immigration and Naturalization Service (Comm.Print 1980).

Department. Although most such powers in fact have been delegated to the Service, this statutory flexibility, permitting delegation to subordinates who are not part of INS, has led to some important changes over the years, to be discussed below.

Organizationally, INS is a constituent part of the Department of Justice, roughly equivalent, on the organization charts, to the Civil Rights or Antitrust Division, for example, or the Bureau of Prisons. The Commissioner is assisted by a Deputy Commissioner, four Executive Associate Commissioners, a General Counsel, and a host of other officers located in the INS Central Office in Washington, D.C. That central office is set up to deal largely with budgetary matters and with broad questions of law and policy. Street-level administration and enforcement take place primarily at INS district offices, regional service centers, and border patrol sectors. As controversies over migration policy have mounted in recent years, Congress has voted dramatic expansions in INS's staffing and budget. In fiscal year (FY) 1992, the agency had approximately 18,000 employees and a budget of $1.44 billion. In 1995 the staffing will exceed 20,000 and the budget will rise to $2.1 billion, a 25 percent increase over FY 1994.[3]

INS was once respected as a relatively well-run and efficient administrative agency, even by those who disagreed with many of the policies carried out. But those days are long in the past. As its tasks expanded and the statute and regulations became more complex, the agency's budget and staffing levels did not keep pace. Management systems became badly outmoded, and tales of long delays on routine matters, lost files, and poor morale among employees—often accompanied by testiness (and worse) toward the agency's clientele—became distressingly common.[4] Although INS has introduced several promising changes in recent years (especially to automate records and improve the adjudication system), it still rarely receives the benefit of the doubt in its many controversies—from the public, the Congress, the courts, or even from other parts of the executive branch.

A lawyer handling a matter involving an individual alien almost certainly would not go to the central office in Washington. Such questions have traditionally been dealt with in the district offices, the basic operating units of the Service, but an increasing proportion of applications instead are now filed by mail with one of four regional service centers. There are 32 district offices in this country and three located overseas, each headed by a district director. (The overseas offices have a limited and carefully defined set of functions; most overseas activity relating to immigration

3. INS Fact Book: Summary of Recent Immigration Data 34–37 (June 1994); 71 Interp. Rel. 1141–42 (1994); 72 *id.* 91–93 (1995). A substantial part of the recent increases goes toward improved computer systems, including a $300 million, five-year contract awarded in August 1994, the largest INS contract of its kind ever awarded. 72 *id.* 8 (1995).

4. *See* SCIRP, Final Report 238–44; U.S. Commission on Civil Rights, *The Tarnished* *Golden Door: Civil Rights Issues in Immigration* 31–34 (1980); Rees, *Advice for the New INS Commissioner*, 70 Interp. Rel. 1533, 1534 (1993) (article by recently departed INS General Counsel, commenting that the "institutional culture" of INS often makes it the "Anti–Immigration and Naturalization Service"); *Chaos at the Gates*, N.Y.Times, Sept. 11–14, 1994 (5–part article on corruption, insensitivity, and inefficiency in INS).

falls to the Department of State.) The 32 basic district offices cover all the territory of the United States, and suboffices exist within many of the districts.

Each district office is divided into units, some concerned principally with enforcement, others with adjudication and related service functions. For example, the Investigations staff concentrates on enforcement in the interior of the country—locating aliens who are illegally present, detecting fraud, investigating smuggling operations, and the like. The Detention and Deportation staff handles the logistics of taking custody of certain aliens in exclusion and deportation proceedings, assuring the presence of detained aliens in immigration court, and managing the ultimate removal of those (detained or not) who receive final exclusion or deportation orders. In addition, immigration inspectors are stationed at over 150 regularly staffed ports of entry; about half of these are land border posts, and most of the rest international airports. (Seaports now generate only about 2 percent of inspections.) The inspectors' function is to examine the documents, or other evidence of entitlement to enter, presented by arriving aliens and citizens alike. In fiscal year 1987, approximately 333 million persons were inspected and admitted, 59 percent of them aliens. By 1993 the number rose to 483 million, about 65 percent of them aliens; nearly 900,000 were denied entry after inspection. The admissions number doubtless includes multiple counting of people who made multiple entries.[5]

Another key enforcement arm is the Border Patrol, staffed by about 3200 officers as of 1986, and slated to expand to 5000 in 1995. It is a component part of INS, but Border Patrol officers are not under the supervision of the district directors. The Border Patrol has its own distinctive geographic and bureaucratic organization pattern, broken down into 21 "sectors" that ring the country. Although the sectors cooperate closely with the district offices, they report to the higher levels of the service through the regional directors. The Border Patrol performs enforcement functions exclusively, nearly all of its work focusing on locations between and around designated ports of entry.[6]

The major service function of INS involves adjudicating applications for various benefits available under the immigration laws. For example, when a grandfather from the old country who has come to visit decides he would like to stay a bit longer with his granddaughter, he must apply for an extension of stay as a tourist or, to use the technical term, a "temporary visitor for pleasure." When an alien who has come to this country as a nonimmigrant marries a citizen or permanent resident alien and decides to settle here (a not infrequent occurrence), she must apply for adjustment of her status to that of a lawful permanent resident. And when a citizen decides to help her brother come from abroad to resettle here as an

---

5. For useful empirical studies of INS's inspections work, see Gilboy, *Deciding Who Gets In: Decision-making by Immigration Inspectors*, 25 Law & Soc'y Rev. 571 (1991); Gilboy, *Penetrability of Administrative Systems: Political "Casework" and Immigration Inspections*, 26 *id.* 273 (1992).

6. For a more complete description of enforcement staffing and operations, including many of the statistics used in the text, *see* INS Fact Book, *supra* note 3, at 10; 1992 INS Statistical Yearbook 170–72 and *passim*; 1989 *id.* xli–xlv; 1987 *id.* xlii–xliii; 1986 INS Annual Report 5–7.

immigrant, the process does not start overseas where the brother is located. It begins instead with the citizen's filing a visa petition with INS. An examiner will review the petition in order to verify the claimed family relationship and establish prima facie qualification for preference immigration. Of course several other steps must be completed, many of them by U.S. consular officials in the brother's home country, before an immigrant visa will issue.

In each such case (and there are many other examples) the INS officer who passes on the petition or request must decide whether the application is complete and bona fide, whether it meets the requirements set forth in the statute and the regulations, and in many cases whether the applicant further merits a favorable exercise of the discretion that the law vests in the Attorney General, or, by delegation, in the district director or other Service officer. (Although the cases often speak of "the district director" as the decisionmaker on such matters, in fact most such adjudications are further delegated and are actually decided by lower-level immigration examiners.) These decisions amount to adjudication, but in most cases, this is not the kind of "adjudication" that lawyers tend to think of—a formal hearing involving two contestants battling out the issues before a relatively passive decisionmaker. Much of the time the applicant does not even see in person the officer who will make the decision. The case must instead be made in writing on one of dozens of prescribed forms that work their way through the INS bureaucracy by the thousands each day. When personal contact does occur, it usually takes the form of a rather informal interview conducted by an examiner. Quite often, the individual applicant is not represented by counsel. In FY 1993, INS adjudicated 4.3 million applications and petitions for benefits under the INA. 71 Interp.Rel. 522 (1994).

Traditionally, applicants went in person to a district office to file the various applications, and the adjudications were performed by examiners in the office where the filing took place. Beginning in the 1980s, however, the Service has been experimenting with various ways to improve the efficiency of its adjudication functions, and greater specialization and division of labor have resulted. Regulations in 1990, for example, reflected the judgment that asylum adjudications require unique skills and training, and should no longer be handled by regular examiners. Consequently, separate asylum offices were opened in seven (soon to be eight) cities around the country, staffed by over 150 asylum officers by 1993 (a number that should double in 1995).

Of wider impact was an adjudication initiative that began in 1985. That year INS created four Regional Adjudication Centers—now called Regional Service Centers (RSCs)—for centralized high-volume processing of certain designated types of applications. Originally the papers relating to such applications were forwarded to the RSCs after the applicant filed them in the district offices. Today in most cases the applicant mails the designated applications, with the required fee, directly to the Service Center having jurisdiction over the applicant's place of residence (varied in some instances depending on the type of application being made). These arrangements have been highly successful in improving productivity, largely because the centralization allows for data processing efficiencies and because RSC staff normally avoid the interruptions, caused by phone inquiries and client contact, that are standard in the district offices.

Originally the list of applications slated for the Service Centers included only those applications that could ordinarily be decided on the basis of the papers alone, without a personal interview. (If an interview proved necessary, the case was referred to the district office having jurisdiction over the residence of the petitioner.) But INS has gradually expanded the list of applications that go to the Centers, to the point that RSCs handled nearly 60 percent of INS filings by mid–1994. Further refinements and expansions of the system are continuing, but it is increasingly common now to require filing with the RSCs even of those applications (such as asylum applications) that clearly will entail a personal interview or hearing. In such cases the Center performs initial functions such as checking for completeness of the papers and inclusion of the appropriate fee, logging in the application and generating a receipt to be mailed back to the applicant, creating the administrative file, and scheduling the interview at the district office or asylum office, as appropriate.[7]

Though it was written before the invention of the RSCs, a 1984 article from *The New Yorker* provides some penetrating insights into the operations of an INS district office and the day-to-day practice of immigration law, insights that remain generally valid even with the increasing role of the RSCs.

CALVIN TRILLIN, MAKING ADJUSTMENTS

The New Yorker, May 28, 1984, at 50–52, 56–57.

[T]he agreement of May 17, 1982 * * * gave immigration lawyers their own line, on one side of the entrance [to the building housing the Houston District Office of INS.] Before that, they had to stand in line with the general public, across from the fish wholesaler. That line is let inside the gate in gulps of twenty or so; on mornings when it happened to have a couple of hundred people in it, a lawyer who hadn't arrived before dawn could spend most of his day outside the building.

* * *

Under the agreement of May 17, 1982, a lawyer can use the special lawyers' line and file papers with a special clerk on one predetermined day

---

7. *See* 71 Interp.Rel. 849 (1994); 54 Fed. Reg. 861 (1989); 51 *id.* 34439 (1986). In addition to the initial INS adjudication forums mentioned in the text, INS created two additional units to treat the special legalization programs created by the Immigration Reform and Control Act of 1986 (IRCA), described briefly in Chapter One. *See* INA §§ 210, 245A. Initial receipt of applications and interviewing was carried out in approximately 100 temporary Legalization Offices located throughout the country. These were separate from district offices, in part because of the strict confidentiality requirements of IRCA. Ultimate legalization decisions were made in Regional Processing Facilities, one for each of the four regions. A few years after the close of the legalization periods, the work of the RPFs was merged into the operations of the regular Regional Service Centers. *See generally* D. North & M. Portz, Decision Factories: The Role of the Regional Processing Facilities in the Alien Legalization Programs (Report to the Administrative Conference of the U.S. 1989).

of the week, according to the first letter of his last name. Wednesday is for people whose names begin with letters "H" through "P." On Wednesdays, Frank Halim, who studied law in Bombay as well as in New York, is almost always at Immigration. So is Patrick Murphy, a former English professor, who handles immigration matters for Fulbright & Jaworski, one of Houston's huge downtown firms. His business usually concerns the non-immigrant visas available for intracompany transfers—what I heard referred to at times as fat-cat visas. The Wednesday crowd also includes Richard Prinz, one of the few immigration lawyers in Houston who regularly go to court—defending someone accused of smuggling aliens into the country, for instance, or someone the I.N.S. is trying to deport under a provision of the law that permits the deportation of permanent residents who have been convicted of a serious crime.

* * *

A lawyer who has come to Immigration to accompany a client at an interview has another wait ahead of him inside the building, but that wait may be enlivened by the opportunity to buttonhole a passing immigration examiner and press for information on some other case. An immigration lawyer often has a case that he is particularly eager to have moved along quickly. An immigration lawyer always has a case that has been maddeningly, inexplicably delayed. The Houston office is thought of as more efficient than most I.N.S. district offices, but, considering the reputation of most I.N.S. district offices, that is not the sort of compliment that someone might be tempted to frame and hang on the wall. When people who deal regularly with the I.N.S. try to illustrate the depths of its inefficiency and obduracy, they often find themselves at a loss for American institutions to compare it with, and turn to foreign examples—the South Vietnamese Army, maybe, or the Bolivian Foreign Service. About the kindest remark that is ever made concerning the efficiency level of the Immigration and Naturalization Service is that the agency has been chronically underfinanced and overworked, and that is a remark usually made by an I.N.S. official.

Simply finding out, through the device of a shrewdly timed buttonholing, which examiner is handling which sort of visa applications is valuable in the immigration practice. So is knowing how to find him. * * * [Patrick Murphy] still carries among the papers in his briefcase a blueprint of the Houston District Office of the Immigration and Naturalization Service. "A blueprint of the building is the key to the practice of immigration law," he told me that rainy Wednesday.

"I beg to differ," a colleague said. "The key to the practice of immigration law is knowing that an immigration examiner who wants to go to the bathroom has to pass through the waiting room to get there."

* * *

"Have you ever won a suspension case?" I asked an immigration lawyer in Houston.

"It depends on what you mean by winning," he said.

Immigration lawyers win time. Given calendar delays and court appeals and bureaucratic lethargy, a suspension-of-deportation action might take years. The immigration judges in Houston have almost never granted asylum to a Salvadoran, so, strictly speaking, lawyers in Houston have almost never won a Salvadoran-asylum case. On the other hand, there is a backlog of eight thousand asylum cases to be heard in Houston, there are only two immigration judges to hear them, and there are three levels of appeal—so, speaking not very strictly, lawyers have won a lot of time in Salvadoran-asylum cases. In time, as immigration lawyers say, "something good could happen." The client might marry a citizen—giving him permanent-resident status unless Immigration decides that the marriage is a sham. The client might find a job that makes it possible to get permanent residence through labor certification. Congress might pass the Simpson–Mazzoli bill, which would legalize the presence of any alien who can demonstrate that he has lived in this country since before some specified date. The I.N.S. might lose the file. Meanwhile, the client is in the United States, and that is what he wanted in the first place. Nothing good is likely to happen to someone who is hanging around the American consulate in Karachi or Salonika waiting for an immigrant visa—one reason that, in the words of George Sellnau, "any immigration lawyer worth his salt would say, 'Get here first!' " [a]

The fact that an alien has been living in the United States for months, or even years, with no more documentation than an expired student visa does not prevent him from getting a green card [*i.e.*, obtaining permanent resident status] if, say, he manages to get labor certification before Immigration manages to deport him. One reason that lawyers are so eager to grab an immigration examiner as he walks through the waiting room is that they are often trying to juggle matters in a way that makes something good happen before something bad happens. Immigration lawyers are people who have an interest in seeing that some folders are on the top of the pile and some folders are on the bottom of the pile.

2. SPECIAL INQUIRY OFFICERS, a/k/a IMMIGRATION JUDGES

You may have noticed that we have not yet mentioned the kind of adjudication that probably generates the most drama and draws the greatest attention. Certainly it has the highest potential for an immediate impact on the right of an alien physically present in this country to remain. We are speaking, of course, of exclusion and deportation decisions.

Under the statute, proceedings to exclude or deport aliens must be conducted by "special inquiry officers," officials designated by the Attorney General as "specially qualified" to carry out this role. See INA § 101(b)(4) (definition); § 235(b), § 236(a) (exclusion proceedings); § 242(b) (deportation proceedings). Throughout most of our history, such officers were

---

a. Is this sound advice? Is it consistent with an attorney's ethical obligations? To secure a nonimmigrant visa, most applicants must satisfy the consul that they have "a residence in a foreign country which [they have] no intention of abandoning." INA § 101(a)(15). For a discussion of the ethical constraints on advising a client about the INA provision regarding a fixed intent to immigrate, *see* D. Weissbrodt, Immigration Law and Procedure in a Nutshell 446–49 (3d ed.1992).—eds.

simply experienced or senior immigration officers, designated to hold such hearings as part—but only part—of a range of responsibilities to administer and enforce the immigration laws. On one day they might have examined aliens at the border, on another investigated violations, on yet another marshalled the case against a deportable alien, and on still another served as a special inquiry officer to adjudicate the deportation of other aliens who had been investigated by their colleagues.

This mixture of roles prompted court challenges alleging that the use of adjudicators so closely involved in enforcement functions violated due process rights to a fair hearing. In 1950, the Supreme Court seemed to bring down the curtain on this practice and to require that officers conducting the hearing be separated from enforcement responsibilities. *Wong Yang Sung v. McGrath*, 339 U.S. 33, 70 S.Ct. 445, 94 L.Ed. 616 (1950). But while the Court's opinion hinted that such separation might be required by the Constitution, its holding rested squarely only on the (then relatively new) Administrative Procedure Act (APA). Congress re-acted quickly, attaching to an appropriations bill a rider that exempted immigration proceedings from the separation-of-functions requirements in the APA. Two years later, when earlier immigration laws were compre-hensively revised and codified to create the Immigration and Nationality Act of 1952, Congress preserved the possibility that enforcement officials could serve as special inquiry officers. In the congressional debates on the INA, supporters of the *Wong Yang Sung* decision argued for a more rigid separation of functions on due process grounds. In the end, however, they could not prevail against widespread congressional concerns about the expense and potential complications if the proceedings became more judi-cial in nature. A few of their opponents also suggested that the political and diplomatic implications of immigration policy precluded the use of fully insulated, quasi-judicial adjudicating officers. The congressional majority, however, did concede a few points to the critics. The INA expressly precludes any special inquiry officer from adjudicating the case of an alien as to whom he had earlier undertaken investigatory or prosecutorial functions. INA § 242(b). When the Supreme Court considered these new, watered-down separation-of-functions provisions contained in the INA, it found no due process violation. *Marcello v. Bonds*, 349 U.S. 302, 311, 75 S.Ct. 757, 762, 99 L.Ed. 1107 (1955). *See also Ardestani v. INS*, 502 U.S. 129, 112 S.Ct. 515, 116 L.Ed.2d 496 (1991) (reaffirming the *Marcello* holding that deportation hearings are not governed by the APA).

The current *statutory* provisions governing the role of special inquiry officers in exclusion and deportation proceedings (INA §§ 236(a), 242(b)), bear two striking features, largely unchanged since 1952. (Current prac-tice is a different matter, but we will come to that in a moment.) First, as we have noted, is the decided statutory tolerance for officers who some-times adjudicate and sometimes enforce. And second, the statutory frame-work for the hearings to be conducted by these special inquiry officers also departs significantly from the adversarial model familiar to Anglo–Ameri-can practice. These officers not only preside over the proceedings like judges, but the statute also expressly authorizes them to present or receive evidence, and also to interrogate, examine, and cross-examine witnesses, including the alien respondent. This broad authority for an active or "inquisitorial" role is based, at least in part, on a desire to permit a full development of the record even when neither party—the government or the alien—is represented by counsel, but it has drawn frequent condemnation.[8]

Due process concerns of this type failed to carry the day in Congress in 1952. But where those arguments fell short, over the years bureaucratic imperatives—including the division of labor, the felt need for increasing professionalization, and the Justice Department's drive for more rational and predictable decisionmaking—have largely succeeded in securing both types of changes the due process advocates had urged. Commingling of roles for these adjudicators is a thing of the past, and regulations have engrafted most features of trial-type hearings onto procedures that one would expect to be quite different, if one looked only at the bare provisions of the statute. The statute itself has not been changed. It merely *permitted* the old arrangements; it did not require them. And regulations have now accomplished some major alterations.

The seeds of this evolution were sown in the statute itself. In deportation proceedings, § 242(b) authorizes the Attorney General, if he finds it useful, to provide for the presence of another immigration officer to present the evidence on behalf of the government and to carry out cross-examination—thus freeing the special inquiry officer for a more passive, judge-like decisionmaking role. In 1956, the Service began to use this procedure regularly for contested cases. And beginning with administrative changes in 1962, INS has developed a specialized staff of "trial attorneys" to fulfill this function. The regulations now require that the government case in deportation proceedings be presented by a trial attorney unless the alien concedes deportability, 8 C.F.R. § 242.16(c), and in practice a trial attorney or other INS officer appears in virtually all deportation and exclusion proceedings, whatever the issues. *See id.* §§ 236.2(c), 242.9.

Parallel specialization and professionalization have taken place among the special inquiry officers themselves. Since 1956, INS has required that special inquiry officers have law degrees, and the Service generally has insulated them from other enforcement functions. Beginning in 1973, as a sign of their evolving status within the agency, a regulation was promulgated changing the designation of these officials to "immigration judges." *See* 8 C.F.R. § 1.1(*l*). (Do not be confused by this title. The statute still refers to these officials as "special inquiry officers"; the terms are fully synonymous.) Gradually a stronger *esprit de corps* developed among the immigration judges, who increasingly took their quasi-judicial role seriously and resisted what were regarded as efforts to hinder or control their functions emanating from elsewhere in the Service. *See* Rawitz, *From*

---

8. *See* The Tarnished Golden Door, *supra* note 4, at 37–43; *Developments, in the Law—Immigration Policy and the Rights of Aliens,* 96 Harv.L.Rev. 1286, 1363–66 (1983); *Whom We Shall Welcome: Report of the President's Commission on Immigration and Naturalization* 152–167 (1953). *See generally* Roberts, *The Exercise of Administrative Discretion under the Immigration Laws,* 13 San Diego L.Rev. 144, 147–48 (1975). For a general commentary much more favorable to nonadversarial procedures on the continental model, see Langbein, *The German Advantage in Civil Procedure,* 52 U.Chi.L.Rev. 823 (1985).

Wong Yang Sung *to Black Robes,* 65 Interp.Rel. 453 (1988); Robie, *A Response to Professor Verkuil,* 39 UCLA L.Rev. 1365, 1366 (1992).

Nevertheless, through the early 1980s, immigration judges remained subordinate in a significant way to the district directors in charge of the district where they held court—especially in matters of budget and administrative support. If the district director did not place a high priority on the adjudicative functions of the immigration judge, the judge might go for weeks without adequate secretarial services, and the tapes of deportation or exclusion hearings might languish for months before a typist was made available to transcribe the proceedings. These developments obviously magnified the possibility of delay, and they drew criticism from many quarters.

In January of 1983, the Department of Justice took important steps to remedy several of these problems. New regulations separated the corps of immigration judges from the Immigration and Naturalization Service and placed them in a new unit, known as the Executive Office of Immigration Review (EOIR), located in the Department of Justice and directly accountable to the Associate Attorney General. *See* 48 Fed.Reg. 8038, 8056 (1983). This does not mean that all the immigration judges moved to Washington; most remained physically in their old offices located in or near INS facilities throughout the country. Nevertheless, it is clear that EOIR now controls the budget available to immigration judges and provides directly for support services. Today, no immigration judge is answerable to anyone in the Service, and this different line of accountability provides a better structural assurance of adjudicative neutrality. Among the many improvements introduced by the new centralized leadership of the immigration judges is a set of uniform rules of practice, issued in early 1987 to replace diverse local customs and unwritten lore with a uniform standardized procedure. 8 C.F.R. §§ 3.12–3.41.

The major portion of an immigration judge's time is consumed with hearing exclusion and deportation cases—including passing upon a wide variety of applications for relief that may be made in such proceedings by aliens who concede that they are formally excludable or deportable. But a few other kinds of cases may also appear on the docket. Immigration judges also conduct proceedings, for example, to rescind an admitted immigrant's adjustment of status under INA § 246, and they may hear challenges brought by aliens ordered *not* to leave the country under the departure control provisions of 8 C.F.R. Part 215.

In fiscal year 1992, there were approximately 85 immigration judges, including the chief immigration judge and four assistant chief immigration judges. In that year, immigration judges logged 109,354 receipts in deportation and exclusion cases, issued 85,488 decisions (obviously many were summary orders; only about one-third required merits hearings), and recorded 24,814 other completions.[9] This total amounted to about 30

---

9. Source: Executive Office of Immigration Review. In addition, immigration judges received and decided over 10,000 bond rescission requests in FY 1992. *See generally* Gil- boy, *Setting Bail in Deportation Cases: The Role of Immigration Judges,* 24 San Diego L.Rev. 347 (1987).

completions per working week per judge.   In 1994 the number of immigration judges rose to 116, and the Department plans to increase that number by another 60 or so beginning in 1995, to reduce processing delays and to accommodate an expected surge in immigration court cases resulting from political asylum reform and enhanced immigration law enforcement.

The structural separation of adjudication from enforcement functions, now more clearly established with the creation of EOIR, is of course an important element of real independence and neutrality on the part of immigration judges, but it is not the only test.   The types of training and working instructions such officials receive are also significant, as are long-term career patterns.   That is, if a government employee could become an immigration judge only by serving several years in the Border Patrol or the enforcement units of the INS—or even several years as an INS trial attorney (historically a more common pattern)—then one would expect a quite different orientation on the part of the adjudicators, compared to a system where recruiting was more broadly based.   Critics have charged that an enforcement mentality pervades immigration-related agencies, including those separate from INS.   They have also argued that even structural independence like that now enjoyed by EOIR is inadequate, as immigration judges and the BIA remain ultimately answerable to the Attorney General, and she in turn remains the chief enforcement officer under the statute.[10]

As a result, arguments have been heard for a wholly separate adjudicative agency, divorced from the Department of Justice and perhaps set up as an Article I court.   *See, e.g.,* Roberts, *Proposed: A Specialized Statutory Immigration Court,* 18 San Diego L.Rev. 1 (1980); Levinson, *A Specialized Court for Immigration Hearings and Appeals,* 56 Notre Dame Law. 644 (1981).   But in its consideration of immigration reform bills in the 1980s, Congress remained noticeably cool to these proposals for complete independence.   Why should this be so?   Are there good arguments for keeping a higher degree of political sensitivity and accountability or control, in light of the nature of immigration adjudications and their possible links to foreign policy decisions?   For a most useful discussion of the adjudication and appeals system, including the system for judicial review, see Legomsky, *Forum Choices for the Review of Agency Adjudication: A Study of the Immigration Process,* 71 Iowa L.Rev. 1297 (1986) (based on a study done for the Administrative Conference of the United States).

To shift the focus, consider whether the mere fact of a formal chain of command running from adjudicators up to a Cabinet-level official who retains enforcement responsibilities (as is the case under the 1983 reforms creating EOIR) substantially undermines independence and neutrality. The answer probably cannot be given in the abstract, simply by consulting tables of organization.   Instead it depends significantly on the conception

10. *See Developments, supra* note 8, at 1363–66; *The Tarnished Golden Door, supra* note 4, at 42–43.   Hirings since the creation of EOIR, however, reveal a systematic effort at broader-based recruiting.   *See also* Robie, *supra,* 39 UCLA L.Rev. at 1367 (discussing independent study of federal administrative adjudication which found that only the Nuclear Regulatory Commission and the immigration judge corps displayed no "indicia" of lack of independence).

of their own role that the adjudicating officers develop and how they reinforce and protect that conception (for example, through training, publications, and union or professional organizations). It may also depend on how the supervisory officer exercises his or her authority. *See generally* J. Mashaw, Bureaucratic Justice 41–44 (1983). (The Mashaw book contains an excellent and thorough discussion of the often contradictory demands and expectations associated with any system requiring "mass justice" adjudications. Though the book's focus is the Social Security disability insurance system, many of its insights are useful for understanding immigration decisions.)

3. APPEALS

The Act expressly gives aliens ruled excludable by immigration judges a right of appeal to the Attorney General (INA § 236(b)), and deportable aliens have equivalent appeal rights by regulation. 8 C.F.R. § 242.21. Naturally a Cabinet officer cannot hear such pleas personally. In practice, therefore, appeals are heard by the Board of Immigration Appeals (BIA), a multi-member review body appointed by the Attorney General. Although the Board has existed since immigration responsibilities were first given to the Attorney General in 1940, it has never been recognized by statute; it is entirely a creature of the Attorney General's regulations.[11] Nevertheless, it is important to recognize that the Board has never been a part of INS. Instead, it has always been accountable directly to the Attorney General through a separate chain of command. Under the 1983 reorganization, the BIA is one of the constituent units of the Executive Office for Immigration Review in the Department of Justice.

Through most of its existence, the BIA has had five permanent members, including its chairman. Formerly they heard all cases en banc, although only a tiny proportion on the basis of oral argument. In 1988, however, bowing to increasing caseload pressures, the Attorney General authorized designation of up to two immigration judges to serve temporarily as additional members of the Board, ordinarily on a one-month rotation. *See* 53 Fed.Reg. 15659 (1988) (amending 8 C.F.R. § 3.1(a)(1)). The new system allowed most cases to be decided by panels of three, consisting of two full BIA members and a designated immigration judge. Important matters were still heard by the five full members, sitting en banc, however. In September 1994, the Department promulgated regulations that will expand the BIA's membership to nine. 59 Fed.Reg. 47231 (1994). The Board is also assisted by approximately 55 staff attorneys, due to be increased by another 20 or so in 1995, and by other support personnel.

The staple of the Board's jurisdiction consists of appeals from immigration judge decisions in exclusion and deportation cases. 8 C.F.R. § 3.1(b)(1), (2). But the Board also hears appeals, for example, from decisions relating to bonds, parole, and detention of deportable aliens, and

---

11. Since 1921, a Board of Review had existed in the Department of Labor, empowered to make recommendations to the Secretary regarding the disposition of appeals in exclusion and deportation cases. In 1940, following the transfer of immigration functions to the Department of Justice, new regulations changed the name to Board of Immigration Appeals and vested in it authority to issue final orders in such matters.

from decisions imposing administrative fines and penalties on aircraft and vessels. *Id.* § 3.1(b)(4), (7). The Board also reviews determinations on visa petitions for intending immigrants, but only if the basis for the petition is a family relationship, *id.* § 3.1(b)(5); petitions based on occupational preferences follow a different avenue of appeal. As you may have noted, not all adjudications reviewed by the Board come from immigration judges. Several provisions of the regulations authorize Board review of decisions made by INS officers on matters that have never been before an immigration judge. *See, e.g., id.* § 3.1(b)(5), (6), (9).[12]

What about all the other adjudications not reviewable by the BIA? A few are simply not appealable administratively—such as denials by district directors of applications to change from one nonimmigrant status to another (say, from student to tourist, or vice versa). *Id.* § 248.3(g). But a majority of decisions issued by district offices and Regional Service Centers are in fact appealable. For example, if an examiner denies a visa petition based on occupational grounds—for permanent workers under the employment based preference categories or for temporary workers or trainees in nonimmigrant category H—such decisions are reviewable within the INS hierarchy, and not by immigration judges or the Board. *Id.* § 103.1(f)(2)(ii), (x).[13]

For many years, such internal appeals went to the four regional commissioners of INS. This appeal structure, however, provided problems, equivalent to a split among federal circuit courts, as different regional commissioners sometimes reached contradictory results on the same legal question. In September 1983, INS therefore centralized all appellate authority previously vested in the regional commissioners. Such appeals now go directly from the INS examiner to the Associate Commissioner for Examinations, located in Washington, where they are actually decided by a centralized Administrative Appeals Unit (AAU), staffed by appellate examiners, who usually are not attorneys.[14]

Thus two main appellate tribunals or decisionmakers now exist within the Department of Justice: the BIA and the AAU.[15] We wish we could

12. The workload of the BIA is reflected in these statistics: In fiscal year 1992, the Board docketed 12,774 cases, up from 8,204 in 1987 and 3,630 in 1983. In 1992 it completed 11,546 cases, leaving a pending backlog of 13,266. Source: EOIR, 1993; 65 Interp. Rel. 487 (1988).

13. In addition, a few such decisions are not subject to administrative appeal, but the alien may renew the application once exclusion or deportation proceedings have begun, and the immigration judge then considers the application *de novo,* followed by possible appeal to the BIA. *See, e.g.,* 8 C.F.R. §§ 208.2(b), 208.18(b) (applications for asylum); *id.* § 245.2(a)(5)(ii) (application for adjustment of status to lawful permanent resident). Other such decisions are appealable within INS and subsequently can be renewed before the immigration judge, whose decision

can be appealed to the BIA. *See, e.g., id.* §§ 103.1(f)(2)(vi), 212.7(a); *Matter of Sanchez,* 17 I & N Dec. 218 (BIA 1980) (review of waivers of excludability under INA § 212(h)). For a comprehensive account, see Legomsky, *supra,* 71 Iowa L.Rev., at 1300–12.

14. *See* 48 Fed.Reg. 43160 (1983); Legomsky, *supra* note 13, at 1308, 1318–20. The AAU decided 3,943 appeals in FY 1993, up 46 percent from 1992. 71 Interp.Rel. 214 (1994). Appeals in IRCA legalization cases (see Chapter Three, *infra*) also go to the Associate Commissioner, where they are decided by the Legalization Appeals Unit (LAU), a branch of the AAU. A surprising number of such appeals (79,000) were still pending in 1994, even though the legalization application period ended in 1988. Some 16,-000 such cases were decided in 1993. *Id.* at 215.

present a rule of thumb that would allow an easy differentiation between the two zones of appellate jurisdiction, but we cannot. Although there are rough patterns, the actual line drawn between the categories seems to defy theory. Especially mystifying is the distinction between visa petitions based on family ties and those based on occupational grounds. Although both types of petitions are decided originally by the same class of adjudicating officers, appeals in occupational cases go to the AAU, but in family cases to the BIA (except petitions for orphans filed by adoptive parents, which go to the AAU!) .

We are therefore reduced to this advice: If you want to appeal an exclusion or deportation order issued by an immigration judge, go to the BIA. Beyond this, in order to appeal an adverse determination, consult the regulations to determine the forum. Do not assume you can guess which route is correct. But at the same time, you need not despair. It is not excessively difficult to determine the appropriate forum once you realize that you should scout the regulations to find a reference to the precise determination you wish to have reviewed. Title 8 C.F.R. §§ 3.1(b) and 103.1(f) are the most important such regulations. *See also* Ruthizer, *Administrative Appeals of Immigration Decisions: A Practitioner's Guide,* 88–1 Imm. Briefings (1988).

A large quantity of appellate decisions are handed down each month. Only a small fraction of these are designated as "precedent decisions," *see* 8 C.F.R. § 103.3(c), for inclusion in the official reports. Those that are designated appear first in slip opinion form as sequentially numbered "Interim Decisions" and later are published in the multi-volume set known as "Administrative Decisions Under Immigration and Nationality Laws of the United States" (I & N Dec.). *Id.* § 103.9(a). You will find there reported decisions from the BIA and the AAU, and also some decided by the Commissioner, the Deputy Commissioner, Regional Commissioners, and occasionally the Attorney General.[16]

---

15. There are also possibilities for "certification" of the case to the Commissioner, the Deputy Commissioner, or other appellate authority for an authoritative decision by one of those high officials, at the initiative of the reviewing official, or of the initial decision-maker, if the question is a complex or novel one. 8 C.F.R. § 103.4. In addition, cases before the BIA are "referred" to the Attorney General for a final authoritative decision by that Cabinet officer, either before or after an initial ruling by the Board, in three circumstances: when the Attorney General so directs; when the Chairman or a majority of the BIA decides that the case should be referred; or when the Commissioner requests referral. *Id.* § 3.1(h).

16. Immigration regulations are published by the INS (and to a much lesser extent by other Justice Department units) in Title 8 of the Code of Federal Regulations, usually after notice-and-comment rulemaking procedures

in accordance with the Administrative Procedure Act, 5 U.S.C.A. § 553. For guidance, INS officers also rely significantly on what are known as Operations Instructions, compiled in a thick volume updated and supplemented periodically without going through the APA rulemaking procedures. Although many OIs read like regulations, INS treats them more like an internal operating manual; there have been controversies over their exact function and status within the administrative scheme. For many years, the OIs were not released, but beginning in 1972, and in compliance with the Freedom of Information Act, 5 U.S.C.A. § 552, INS made nearly all of them public. *See* GM & Y § 3.24[2]. The current version appears in Volume 9 of the GM & Y treatise. INS also communicates guidance to its offices by means of a variety of policy wires, cables, and memoranda that are not necessarily incorporated into the OIs. The important ones, however, are

4. OTHER UNITS

Two other units in the Department of Justice should be mentioned, both brought into existence because of the passage of the Immigration Reform and Control Act of 1986 (IRCA), Pub.L. No. 99–603, 100 Stat. 3359. As indicated in Chapter One, IRCA created a system of employer sanctions to penalize those who knowingly hire undocumented aliens or fail to perform certain documentary verification before any hiring. INA § 274A. In an attempt to assure that this system did not increase discrimination against ethnic minorities, IRCA also added new provisions barring discrimination based on national origin or citizenship status. INA § 274B. Under the statute, allegations of employer violations of either of these provisions are to be heard by administrative law judges in the Department of Justice. Accordingly the Department added a new unit to EOIR, the Office of Chief Administrative Hearing Officer (OCAHO), with a corps of ALJs under his or her supervision, to carry out this function. See 28 C.F.R. Part 68. Later Congress also bestowed authority on the ALJs to impose civil penalties for document fraud under INA § 274C.

The principal investigation and charging responsibility under the employer sanctions and civil document fraud provisions rests with INS. But the statute created a new office in the Department of Justice, the Office of Special Counsel for Immigration Related Unfair Employment Practices, to fulfill these responsibilities under IRCA's antidiscrimination provisions. The Special Counsel is appointed by the President, subject to the advice and consent of the Senate. See INA § 274B(c); 28 C.F.R. Part 44.

SECTION B. THE DEPARTMENT OF STATE

For over 70 years, most persons wishing to travel to the United States, even for a short visit, have been required to secure preliminary documents known as visas from a U.S. official overseas.[17] State Department officials, called consular officers, are stationed at over 200 offices throughout the world to decide on applications for visas. *See* INA §§ 221, 222. They issue over 5 million visas annually.[18]

Securing a visa, as arduous a process as it may be for some, does not guarantee admission—and many of the relevant documents bear a warning to this effect. Visas do not constitute permission to enter the United States. They are more in the nature of permission to travel to the United States and apply for admission at the border. In other words, the admitting immigration officer is entitled to disagree with the consular officer and thus to detain a properly documented alien for an exclusion hearing. Fortunately, this disagreement does not happen often. Indeed, the system would break down if visas did not usually function to secure entry. But

carried in reporting services like Interpreter Releases, published by Federal Publications, Inc., or the Federal Immigration Law Reporter, published by the Washington Service Bureau, or Immigration Policy & Law, published by the Bureau of National Affairs, Inc.

17. Exceptions to the visa requirement, recently expanded, are described at p. 423 *infra.*

18. 1992 Report of the Visa Office 19 (1994). For a comprehensive discussion of the functions of consuls, see L. Lee, Consular Law and Practice (2d ed. 1991).

because airlines and other carriers are subject to substantial fines and other penalties if they bring aliens here without proper documents, INA § 273, a traveller probably cannot board unless the papers presented at the foreign ticket counter are all in order. A visa therefore constitutes an indispensable document for aliens wishing to come here from most other countries.

Although § 104 of the INA places these documentation responsibilities in officials of the Department of State, the formal authority of the Secretary of State is circumscribed. Note the curious language of § 104(a)(1), giving the Secretary broad authority, but excepting from that control "those powers, duties, and functions conferred upon the consular officers relating to the granting or refusal of visas." Can it really be intended to give consular officers autocratic power, immune to the supervision of their nominal superiors, to decide whether to issue documents indispensable to aliens who wish to come to this country? Critics have often charged that this is the way the system operates. *See, e.g.,* Whom We Shall Welcome: Report of the President's Commission on Immigration and Naturalization 147 (1953). But there is a different theory that underlies this provision: namely, that such separation insulates what are meant to be routine bureaucratic decisions on admissibility from the high politics that are the stock-in-trade of the Secretary of State and his subordinates on the diplomatic side of the Department.[19]

To be sure, this provision may occasionally function to fortify an American ambassador when she is explaining why the generalissimo's dissolute nephew was denied a visa and will not receive one whatever foreign policy consequences are threatened. But it remains a fair question whether this statutory explanation is convincing to the generalissimo or to the ambassador. Consular officers are members of the foreign service, ultimately dependent on their superiors for advancement in their profession. Indeed, many of the officers issuing visas are foreign service officers on their first assignment with the Department, hoping to move out of consular work and into future assignments as political or economic officers.

In any event, this putative insulating measure does serve to complicate moderately the normal bureaucratic business of review and supervision to assure timeliness, consistency of outcomes, and compliance with the statute and the regulations. Nevertheless, these bureaucratic imperatives have still found expression. The State Department has developed informal review mechanisms, crafted with delicate attention to § 104(a)(1). All visa refusals are supposed to be followed by review of the papers, carried out by a second consular officer, who may raise questions with the first. If the reviewing officer remains convinced that a visa should be issued, she may issue it herself. But she lacks authority, no matter how far she outranks the initial officer, to order the subordinate to issue that visa under his own name. Differences of opinion may also be referred to the Visa Office in Washington for what is labelled an "advisory opinion" on the dispute. 22 C.F.R. §§ 41.121(c), 42.81(c). Such opinions are binding only on legal

---

19. *See, e.g.,* Simpson, *Policy Implications of U.S. Consular Operations,* in The Consular   Dimension of Diplomacy 11 (M. Herz ed. 1983).

questions, while the determination of facts remains fully the responsibility of the consular officer.[20] Visa Office advice, however, is usually followed. Although denial of a visa may totally prevent an alien from travelling to the United States, courts usually deny judicial review of such decisions—especially at the behest of the alien.

As the statute indicates, visa issuance falls under the general responsibility of the Bureau of Consular Affairs, headed by an Assistant Secretary of State.[21] In addition to Visa Services, the Bureau contains two other major divisions, Passport Services and Overseas Citizens Services. Through regional Passport Agencies in the United States and through its posts abroad, the Bureau issues some 5 million passports to U.S. citizens each year. Overseas Services arranges for protection and assistance for Americans in foreign countries, responding to about two million such requests annually. (To give an idea of the scale of these responsibilities, in 1986, there were about two million U.S. residents abroad and 30 million travelers.) For example, consular officers search for missing Americans, visit those hospitalized or in prison, monitor the cases of those arrested, assist next of kin in the United States when relatives die abroad, process estate and property claims, and help citizens in financial difficulty, usually by arranging for a return home or for the transfer of funds from relatives or friends. In nonemergency situations, consular officers provide information on absentee voting, tax forms, and selective service registration, transmit travel advisories, notarize documents, arrange for the transfer of federal benefit payments, and manage the paperwork and occasional investigations required in connection with the acquisition and loss of American citizenship. In a typical year, consular officers record 46,000 births and 6000 deaths abroad of U.S. citizens.[22]

20. *See* Ruthizer, *Administrative Appeals of Immigration Decisions: A Practitioner's Guide*, 88–1 Imm. Briefings 9–11 (1988); Nafziger, *Review of Visa Denials by Consular Officers,* 66 Wash.L.Rev. 1, 16–25 (1991). Consider whether other arrangements for administrative review, including the possibility of explicitly binding rulings by an appellate administrative tribunal, would improve the functioning of the system. For various suggestions along these lines, *see* 54 Fed.Reg. 53493 (1989) (formal recommendations adopted by Administrative Conference for modest increase in administrative review of visa denials); SCIRP, Final Report 253–55 (1981) (rejecting proposals for a formal and independent review mechanism but suggesting improvements in the current informal system); H.R. 2567, 100th Cong., 1st.Sess. (1987) (bill introduced by Rep. Gonzalez to create a Visa Review Board within the Dept. of State).

21. The Department recently created a National Visa Center (NVC), based at a decommissioned military base in New Hampshire, to take over from consuls a few of the more routine functions involved in visa issuance. The Center, with a staff of about 200, mostly contract personnel, checks visa requests for accuracy and completeness, creates immigrant visa files and computer records, and mails necessary notices and requests for information to applicants or their attorneys, even when the actual visa will be issued at a consular post abroad. The NVC is expected to handle 680,000 cases a year and is capable of housing up to four million immigrant visa petitions (a storage capacity made necessary by the backlogs resulting from the quotas placed on most immigrant visa categories). Across the parking lot from the NVC, the Bureau has also established a new National Passport Center, where all passport renewal applications are now processed. *See* 71 Interp.Rel. 714; 68 *id.* 1269; Lippman, *Avalanche of Mail for a Trickle of Visas*, Wash. Post, Oct. 17, 1994, at A3.

22. *See The Department of State Today* 5–7 (Dept. of State, Bureau of Public Affairs, March 1988); GM & Y §§ 3.09–3.12. The State Department issues a Foreign Affairs Manual (FAM), certain chapters of which are devoted to interpretations and instructions relating to immigration and nationality questions, and amplifying the regulations appear-

SECTION C. OTHER FEDERAL AGENCIES

1. THE DEPARTMENT OF LABOR

The statute requires the Department of Justice to cooperate with the Labor Department in the process that leads to the granting of visas to persons who are subject to the labor certification requirement. Before such documents can be issued, the Labor Department, through its Employment and Training Administration, must certify that American workers in the applicant's field are unavailable in the locality of the applicant's destination and that the applicant's employment will not adversely affect wages and working conditions of American workers. The labor certification requirement applies to most immigrants who enter under the employment-based preference categories of INA § 203(b). If certification is initially denied by one of the Department's regional Certifying Officers, the employer may appeal to the Board of Alien Labor Certification Appeals (BALCA), a panel composed of seven Administrative Law Judges, which has authority to affirm, reverse, or remand. 20 C.F.R. §§ 656.26, 656.27. The Labor Department also has similar regulatory responsibilities in connection with several of the business-related categories for nonimmigrants. In addition to these adjudication functions, DOL's Wage and Hour Division enforces federal labor standards and is receiving additional funding and authority in 1995 to help enforce the immigration laws that affect employment.[23]

We will examine the complicated and specialized process of labor certification in some detail in Chapter Three.

2. THE PUBLIC HEALTH SERVICE

The Public Health Service (PHS), headed by the Surgeon General, is an agency in the Department of Health and Human Services. Because several grounds of exclusion relate to medical conditions, PHS doctors and other authorized medical officials play a role under the Immigration and Nationality Act, both at ports of entry and overseas. PHS doctors conduct medical examinations of arriving aliens, and some of their determinations are unreviewable by INS or any other body, save a special medical review panel established pursuant to the statute. *See* INA §§ 234, 236(d).

3. THE UNITED STATES INFORMATION AGENCY

The United States Information Agency (USIA) bears responsibility for the U.S. government's overseas information, educational exchange, and cultural programs. Most of its work is done abroad, through information and public affairs officers in U.S. diplomatic missions, the Voice of America radio service, and a variety of other videotape and film distribution net-

ing in 22 C.F.R. Parts 40–53. Portions of the Manual have been released to the public, and are now available in Volumes 10 and 11 of the GM & Y treatise. Many of the documents and records involved in visa process-

ing, however, are confidential under specific statutory direction. INA § 222(f).

23. Pear, *Clinton Will Seek Spending to Curb Aliens, Aides Say,* N.Y. Times, Jan. 21, 1995, at 1.

works. It also brings selected foreign visitors to this country under a variety of programs. For immigration-law purposes, the most important are educational exchange arrangements like the Fulbright program, which send Americans to other countries and bring several thousand foreign nationals here each year. A specific nonimmigrant status (known as J–1) exists for "exchange visitors" (see INA § 101(a)(15)(J)), who enter subject to particular requirements and restrictions. Although administration of exchange visitor arrangements is largely carried out by the participating programs, the USIA oversees their functioning, and also plays a crucial role in deciding whether some of the restrictions can be waived. See INA § 212(e).

———

For a further glimpse into the ways in which an immigration lawyer may have to interact with these agencies, consider the following article by an experienced Miami practitioner.

ELAINE WEISS, A DAY IN THE LIFE OF AN IMMIGRATION PRACTITIONER

The Florida Bar Journal, May 1992, at 74–75.

4:00 a.m.: I'm on the telephone to the U.S. Consulate in Copenhagen. It's taken jurisdiction of the immigration case of a Polish client currently in the U.S. By statute, he must pick up his green card at a U.S. Consulate abroad. The Consulate in Warsaw has mandatory jurisdiction, but my client refuses to return there. The Consulate in Copenhagen is the only U.S. consular office among the 40 that I surveyed that agreed to take discretionary jurisdiction. My client's wife and children—whom he hasn't seen since coming to the U.S. 10 years ago—will be meeting him in Copenhagen, hopefully for a successful permanent residence interview at the Consulate there. Organizing a reunion for the family in a third country is nerve-wracking; they could be stuck there if any of the documents I am readying is faulty or goes astray. Yet the case is exciting, too. * * *

With rare exception, there are people—not companies, not property—at the heart of immigration cases, and the life stories of these people—particularly the pro bono clients—are often compelling.[a]

* * *

7:15 a.m.: I'm on the road to the [INS district office] to attend a so-called "adjustment interview" for a Haitian man. If all goes right, he'll leave INS a permanent resident of the U.S.

9:30 a.m.: We're finally called for our 7:30 a.m. interview. The hearing will likely take only 10 minutes. Overworked and understaffed, the Miami INS office often runs an hour or two behind. * * * Case approved.

---

a. Relocated paragraph.—eds.

Noon: I attend an executive board meeting of the local chapter of the American Immigration Lawyers Association. * * *

[We] discuss our association's efforts to get the local U.S. Attorney's office to prosecute [a certain kind of fraud under one of the 1986 amnesty programs.] * * * The problem is that many aliens—frequently assisted by unscrupulous lawyers—are making fraudulent skeleton applications [as allowed by a court decision]. While these have the immediate effect of providing aliens with much sought after work authorizations, this "benefit" derives of material misstatement. When these same people come to reputable practitioners to make their immigration status right and permanent, we can promise nothing, since the statute takes a very dim view of fraud in obtaining immigration benefits. One way to discourage aliens from such fraud is by prosecuting the lawyers and others who promote it. Unfortunately, the already overburdened U.S. Attorney's office in Miami has not made [such] fraud a priority. Our board members grimly joke about limousines picking up aliens at Miami International Airport and driving them directly to INS to apply for [these] work authorizations—and, at best, immigration limbo.

2:00 p.m.: I meet with a prospective client. From the facts she presents, I tell her there is an excellent chance of fulfilling her goal of permanent residence based on a recent job offer. However, I tell her, the process will take no less than one to two years from start to finish. And, during this time, the process will accord her no interim work authorization. * * * I am singing a familiar refrain: I can likely get what you want, but not within your preferred timeframe.

* * *

3:00 p.m.: I am called by a senior partner in a Cleveland law firm. His son's girlfriend—an Italian national—has had difficulties with INS airport personnel in Detroit. The immigration inspectors accuse her of lying: they say she really intends to enter the U.S. to live permanently rather than merely visit as permitted by her visa. They have put her into exclusion proceedings. As an alleged "excludable alien," the girlfriend must now prove to an immigration judge that she is seeking to enter the U.S. for purposes consistent with the terms of her visitor's visa.

Many experienced lawyers unfamiliar with immigration law err in this situation, thinking that approaching INS with courtly manners and a reasonable story—or, perhaps, advising the alien to just get on an airplane and depart—will have the desired result of getting the alien unstuck at INS. They are in for a rude awakening: a false move and the alien may find it nearly impossible to visit the U.S. again.

* * *

5:20 p.m.: In a move that is virtually impossible to explain to aliens looking for logic in U.S. immigration policy, Congress recently established a series of annual green card lotteries to benefit natives of certain countries. The chances of obtaining residence this way are remote, but far better than the odds of winning the Florida jackpot. This afternoon, I get a call from a client for whom I managed to win this year's lottery. He has just returned from his trip to the U.S. Consulate in France where he successfully completed his processing for permanent residence. I am delighted for him: he has moved from nonimmigrant to U.S. resident in near record time of seven weeks.

* * *

Chapter Three

ADMISSION AND EXCLUSION: SUBSTANTIVE PROVISIONS

The American immigration system allows for the admission of two broad categories of aliens: immigrants and nonimmigrants. In general, immigrants, as the label suggests, come to take up permanent residence, whereas nonimmigrants enter for a specific purpose to be accomplished during a temporary stay. An alien in either group must show initially that he or she qualifies for admission by meeting certain categorical qualifying requirements, and must also demonstrate that none of the multiple grounds for exclusion appearing in § 212(a) of the INA renders him or her ineligible for entry.

In this Chapter, we will examine first the qualifying categories and then the exclusion provisions. We will also consider "parole," an administrative device that may permit the physical presence of an alien despite a failure to qualify otherwise for admission. In the next Chapter we will review the procedures used to decide the applicability of these various substantive provisions.

SECTION A. IMMIGRANTS

1. OVERVIEW

The story of the American immigrant admissions system is largely a story of numbers, along with the intricate substantive distinctions used to define the categories to which those numbers are assigned. Since 1921, the law has imposed annual numerical limitations on most immigrant categories.[1] The character of those limitations, as we have seen, changed considerably in 1965, when Congress abandoned the former national-origins

---

1. After admission, immigrants are also often referred to as lawful permanent residents (LPRs) or permanent resident aliens, until they obtain citizenship through naturalization. Permanent resident status means quite simply that they may stay as long as they wish (provided they do not engage in certain post-entry activities that render them deportable). Most immigrants who choose to apply for naturalization after meeting the residence requirement—ordinarily five years—qualify rather routinely, but there is no obligation to apply for naturalization. One may remain in LPR status indefinitely.

quota system in favor of a more neutral preference system. A variety of modest refinements occurred in succeeding years, before the Immigration Act of 1990, Pub. L. No. 101–649, 104 Stat. 4978, thoroughly rewrote the key immigrant admission provisions of the INA.

The current system essentially provides for four grand categories of immigrants, each governed by its own intricate rules and ceilings. They are: (1) family-sponsored immigrants; (2) employment-based immigrants; (3) diversity immigrants; and (4) refugees. The refugee provisions, largely unchanged since their enactment in 1980, provide for the fixing of an admission ceiling at the beginning of each fiscal year (subject to adjustment for emergencies), based on a judgment about likely refugee needs and feasible U.S. responses. Refugee admissions have run between 67,000 and 125,000 annually in recent years, but the totals are subject to wide variation and are independent of the developments in the other three categories. The refugee provisions therefore will be considered separately and in detail in Chapter Eight. The balance of this Section focuses on the other three grand categories.

4 categories of immigrants

The 1990 Act purports to establish all-embracing ceilings on the non-refugee admissions of immigrants to the United States.[2] INA § 201. We will see below that the nominal ceiling on family-sponsored immigration can be breached, leading to higher total immigration. Nevertheless, these ceilings, set forth in Table 3.1, are a useful starting point for beginning to understand the complex structure Congress adopted in 1990.

Table 3.1
Baseline Annual Immigration Ceilings, beginning FY 1995

Family-sponsored (immediate relatives and family preference immigrants)	480,000
Employment-based preferences	140,000
Diversity (low-admission countries)	55,000
TOTAL	675,000

Because immigration to the United States in the equivalent ordinary immigration categories had been running at or below 500,000 in the late 1980s, the 1990 Act reflects a congressional decision to increase immigration levels substantially. In debating the measure, key members of Congress expressed particular concern about using our immigration system to import skilled workers and entrepreneurs, to meet the needs of the U.S. economy in an increasingly competitive international market. Under the earlier system, only 54,000 admission spaces were available for employment-based immigrants, both skilled and unskilled, and a substantial portion of the admission numbers in those categories was used for the admission of family members, rather than the worker himself or herself.

---

2. The 1990 Act imposed a slightly different set of ceilings for fiscal years (FY) 1992–94, partly in order to facilitate the regularization, during those three years, of the status of certain family members of aliens who were legalized under the 1986 Immigration Reform and Control Act. INA §§ 201 and 203 reflect these complications. The text here sets forth only the permanent provisions, as effective October 1, 1994, the first day of FY 1995.

The provision in the 1990 Act of 140,000 admission spaces based on employment represents a 160 percent increase for this category of immigration (although, like the earlier system, some of these numbers will still be used by the immediate family members who immigrate with the occupational immigrant). These 140,000 numbers are to be parceled out among five employment-based preference categories, INA § 203(b).

For family-sponsored immigration, the subdivisions (four preference categories, plus a highly favored grouping for "immediate relatives" of U.S. citizens) are largely the same as those employed under earlier legislation. INA §§ 201(b)(2)(A), 203(a). What the 1990 Congress changed are the ways that numbers are assigned to each of the various subdivisions, although even here the end product (after sifting through statutory formulas that are unfortunately far more intricate than in earlier versions of the law) produces numerical results surprisingly similar to previous law. This system will be explored below.

The diversity provisions are meant, in part, to reflect a treasured national self-image—an image of a pluralistic America open to all comers with the pluck and fortuity to make a go of it in a new land. They establish lotteries to select immigrants from among people who meet the threshold requirements; several million applicants have applied each year. 1990 Act, § 132, 8 U.S.C.A. § 1153 note (transitional program for FY 1992–94); INA § 203(c) (permanent diversity provisions effective beginning FY 1995). The byzantine allocation rules of the permanent diversity provisions strongly favor applicants from Europe and Africa, at least in the early years of operation.

The U.S. immigrant selection scheme is quite complex, sometimes bewilderingly so. At times only subtle and easily missed differences distinguish one category from another. The following pages provide an introduction into these complexities, describing the general structure of the statutory system for the family, employment, and diversity categories. Before embarking on that review, however, a brief sketch of immigration procedures may be useful, to foster understanding of how the substantive categories described below are actually implemented. (Such procedures will be considered in detail in Chapter Four.)

Most American immigration today formally begins not with the action of the alien overseas who wishes to immigrate, but with a document called a *visa petition* filed by a person already in the United States—usually a family member or prospective employer—whose relation to the alien will become the basis for the alien's proof that he fits within a qualifying category. The family member or employer is known as the *petitioner;* the alien who wishes to immigrate is the *beneficiary.* For family categories, the family member typically files a visa petition with the INS, accompanied by proof (such as birth or marriage certificates) of the necessary relationship. For occupational categories, the process typically begins one stage earlier. The prospective employer first files documents with the Department of Labor in order to obtain "labor certification," *i.e.,* certification from the Department that the alien will not be taking a job for which qualified American workers (citizens or resident aliens) are available. After the certification is issued, the employer files a visa petition with INS, which verifies other qualifications, such as the prospective immigrant's identity and the employer's ability to pay the stated salary or wage. Once INS is satisfied that the relationship (either family or employment) is genuine and meets the legal requirements, it approves the visa petition and sends a copy to the consulate in the country the petitioner has designated as the place where the alien beneficiary will actually apply for the immigrant visa, usually the closest consular facility in the country of nationality. (The consul usually takes as a given the basic qualifying category; his or her main function is to apply the exclusion grounds of INA § 212(a), treated in Section D.) The statutory provisions for the petition procedures are set forth in INA §§ 204–206.[3]

a. Family–Sponsored Immigration

Aliens who obtain permanent residence in the United States based on a family relationship qualify either under one of the four preference categories assigned to family reunification, INA § 203(a), or a "immediate relatives" of U.S. *citizens*. INA § 201(b)(2)(A). You may find it useful to consult those sections of the INA at this point and refer back to them as you make your way through the following material. "Immediate relative" is defined to include spouses and children, and, if the petitioning citizen is over 21, parents as well.[4]

The statutory definition of "child," INA § 101(b)(1), is lengthy and precise. The subtle differences among the various family categories derive primarily from the specific terms of this definition, and the related definition of "parent" in § 101(b)(2). Those definitions merit very close attention. Note that a "child" must be under 21 and unmarried. The definition includes stepchildren and legitimated children, if the qualifying relationship was established before the child reached age 18, and it includes adopted children if the adoption occurred before age 16. With certain qualifications, it also includes illegitimate children. Status as a "parent" depends upon relationship to a "child" as defined in § 101(b)(1). The parent is not ineligible if the son or daughter is now over 21 or married, provided that the relationship was established while the offspring still satisfied the statutory definition of "child."

No quotas apply to immediate relatives. All who meet the qualitative requirements by showing the requisite family relationship qualify, making this perhaps the most highly favored of all immigration categories.[5] The

[handwritten margin note: "no quota for "immed.- relatives""]

---

3. We will also consider in Chapter Four an important and frequently used procedure, called adjustment of status (INA § 245), which allows an alien already in the country to obtain permanent resident status, under specified conditions, without leaving U.S. territory. The INS examiner then both examines the visa petition (to see if there is adequate proof of the claimed relationship) and also scrutinizes the alien's own qualifications—scrutiny that would have been performed by the consular officer if the alien were in a foreign country.

4. This qualifier on petitioning for parents was adopted in view of America's uniquely strong *jus soli* citizenship rules: virtually any child born in U.S. soil, even to parents illegally present, is a U.S. citizen. If not for the age 21 requirement, the newborns could immediately petition for permanent resident status for their parents.

5. INA § 201(b) lists other categories that are not subject to numerical limitation, but only a few are numerically significant, and even they do not enjoy the highly favored status of "immediate relatives." The numer-

number of such admissions has increased markedly over the last 20 years, as shown in Table 3.2.

Table 3.2

Immediate Relatives Admitted

Fiscal year	Number Admitted
1970	79,213
1975	85,871
1980	145,992
1985	204,368
1990	231,680
1991	237,103
1992	235,484
1993	255,059

Source: 1980 Statistical Abstract of the United States, Table 133 (for 1970–1975); 1980 INS Statistical Yearbook, Table 4 (for 1980); 1992 INS Statistical Yearbook, Table 4 (for 1985–92); 1993 INS Statistical Yearbook, Table 4 (for 1993).

In contrast to immediate relatives, the family-sponsored preference categories of INA § 203(a) are subject to annual numerical ceilings. When there are more applicants than admission spaces (a common condition, for all but the first preference, over the last few years), backlogs develop. Allocations are made within each family preference in chronological order, based on the time when the visa petition initiating the process was filed with the immigration authorities. The family-based preferences are as follows:

preference (after immed. relatives)

• The first preference provides 23,400 admissions for unmarried sons and daughters of U.S. citizens. Unmarried children of

ically significant portions of INA § 201(b)(1) are as follows:

(A) Special immigrants under § 101(a)(27)(A) are lawful permanent residents "returning from a temporary visit abroad." Several hundred thousand admissions occur each year in this category, but these are all readmissions of persons who went through the full immigrant screening in the past. Without this escape hatch, they would be double-counted against relevant quotas. (Returning resident aliens are also usually exempt from certain documentary requirements, but they can still be excluded when attempting reentry; the exclusion grounds of INA § 212(a) apply anew each time they cross the border. *See* Chapter Five.)

(B) Aliens admitted under § 207 or whose status is adjusted under § 209 are refugees and asylees. These admissions have numbered over 100,000 in recent years, but overseas refugees are subject to their own separate quotas established each year under § 207, and asylees must satisfy a fairly rigorous statutory test, INA § 208, to obtain this status. These provisions are covered in detail in Chapter Eight.

(C) The category of aliens who gain adjustment of status under §§ 210, 210A, or 245A includes the beneficiaries of special amnesty or farm-worker programs adopted in the Immigration Reform and Control Act of 1986. Nearly three million qualified under §§ 210 and 245 (§ 210A never took effect). Most of these people have now adjusted status, but because of litigation a few additional adjustments can be expected for many years to come.

In addition, § 201(b)(2)(B) exempts from numerical limitation those aliens "born to an alien lawfully admitted for permanent residence during a temporary visit abroad." These admissions typically run between 2,000 and 3,000 per year.

citizens, you will recall, can come in as immediate relatives, without quota limits. (Ask yourself: why then is this preference category necessary?)

SONS & DAUGHTERS OLDER THAN 21

● The second preference allows for a minimum of 114,200 admissions annually, of the spouses and unmarried sons and daughters of *lawful permanent resident aliens*. This category was a particular focus of reform efforts in the 1990 Act, for backlogs under the earlier law had resulted in separation of these close family members for a minimum of two years (and for as many as ten years for Mexican nationals, owing to per-country ceilings discussed below). The current ceiling for second preference reflects the addition in 1990 of over 40,000 numbers. At that time Congress also subdivided this preference into subparagraphs (A) and (B), to assure that a higher percentage of admissions would go to spouses and minor children (category 2–A)—those for whom lengthy separation is especially harsh—as opposed to offspring who had already reached age 21. These older offspring may not claim more than 23 percent of the admissions available under the second preference.

● The third preference provides 23,400 admissions for married sons and daughters of U.S. citizens—those who cannot qualify, because of marital status (and perhaps age), for the immediate relative category or for first preference.

● The fourth preference provides 65,000 admissions each year for brothers and sisters of U.S. citizens. The statutory definition of "child" is consulted to decide whether the requisite sibling relationship is satisfied.[6]

Consider the case of an alien who enters under the third family preference, as a married daughter of a U.S. citizen. What about her own husband and children, who do not personally meet the statutory requirements for third preference and have no other way of directly qualifying for admission to the United States? Must they wait until she enters and then wait still further until she successfully petitions for them under the second preference?

The answer is no. The statute takes an important step toward avoiding such separation of nuclear families. Section 203(d) (which also applies to employment-based and diversity immigration) provides that the spouse or child may be admitted in the same preference category and in the "same order of consideration" (*i.e.*, at the same spot on the waiting list,

---

6. The preference categories, both family-sponsored and employment-based, allow for "spill-down." That is, if there are not enough qualified aliens to use all 23,400 first-preference numbers, the balance spills down and becomes available for second preference that same year, and so on. Because demand is near the number available in the first preference and vastly exceeds supply in the remaining preferences, little spill-down occurs in the family categories. Under separate provisions, if not all employment-based numbers are used in a given year, the unused balance can be applied to family-sponsored immigration the following year (and vice versa). INA § 201(c)(3), (d)(2). Even in high demand years, some such cross-category carryover to the following fiscal year occurs simply because of the logistical complexity of the system; it is hard to make the numbers come out exactly even on September 30 of each year.

when there is a backlog) as the principal alien. Their admissions are then charged against the ceiling for the principal's preference category. Section 203(d) applies to accompanying family members and also those "following to join." Administrative practice treats aliens as "following to join" at any time after the migration of the principal, so long as the family member remains a spouse or child at the time of his or her admission. The benefits of § 203(d) are available, however, only when the specified family relationship existed at the time when the principal was admitted. "After-acquired" spouses and children of lawful permanent residents must use the second preference. Note also that § 203(d) does not apply to those who are admitted as immediate relatives.

b. *Employment-based Immigration*

As indicated, before the 1990 Act, only 54,000 admission spaces were available based on employment, divided between two preference categories. Qualification for these spots was established primarily through the process of labor certification, and lengthy backlogs had developed, owing to high demand.

The 1990 Act dramatically increased the numbers available based on employment, as divided among five more detailed employment-based preferences (INA § 203(b)):

• The first preference provides roughly 40,000 numbers[7] for "priority workers," a category that is further subdivided to include (1) aliens with "extraordinary ability," (2) outstanding professors and researchers, and (3) certain multinational executives and managers (these two terms are defined in INA § 101(a)(44)).

• The second preference provides roughly 40,000 admissions for professionals holding advanced degrees "or their equivalent" or who, "because of their exceptional ability in the sciences, arts, or business, will substantially benefit prospectively the national economy, cultural or educational interests, or welfare of the United States." Their services must be sought by an employer, unless this requirement is waived by the Attorney General "in the national interest."

• The third preference is for professionals having only baccalaureate degrees, and for skilled and unskilled workers who would fill positions for which there is a shortage of American workers. In the debates on the 1990 Act, some proposed eliminating admission of unskilled alien workers altogether, arguing that employers with a need for unskilled labor should be forced to train or

---

7. INA § 203(b) states the employment-based preference category totals in terms of percentages of the worldwide ceiling on employment-based admissions (normally 140,-000): 28.6 percent each for the first three categories, and 7.1 percent each for the fourth and fifth. In years when the 140,000 total is augmented because family admissions the previous year fell below the family ceiling (*see* note 6 *supra*), each employment-based category's quota rises proportionately. In contrast, all "extra" numbers for the family-sponsored preference categories are assigned to the second preference, destined for the nuclear family members of lawful permanent residents.

otherwise attract unemployed Americans. As a compromise, no more than 10,000 of the roughly 40,000 admissions available for this preference can be applied to unskilled workers; substantial backlogs have developed in the "other workers" subcategory for the unskilled.

• The fourth preference, with about 10,000 annual admissions, is for certain "special immigrants" as defined in INA § 101(a)(27)(C) through (J). These categories, which include religious workers, former long-time employees of the U.S. government or of international organizations, and a host of other miscellaneous provisions, used to be exempt from numerical ceilings, but demand is expected to remain below 10,000 for the foreseeable future.

• The fifth preference, a controversial one, provides 10,000 numbers for investors whose investments will create a minimum of 10 jobs in the U.S. economy. The baseline minimum investment is $1,000,000, but the required amount is lowered if the investment is in a rural area or a high unemployment area, and it is increased if the business is established in an area with low unemployment. Concerned about possible fraud in this category, Congress provided that fifth-preference immigrants will initially receive only conditional permanent residence status, under procedures that are designed to result in a careful review of the investment after two years. INA § 216A.

Under the 1990 Act, labor certification is required only for the second and third employment-based preferences, see INA §§ 204(b), 212(a)(5)(A). Also, aliens in the first preference—except those with "extraordinary ability," which requires "sustained national or international acclaim" (the House report suggests that a Nobel prize would suffice[8])—cannot ordinarily initiate the petitioning process themselves. As with second- and third-preference aliens, an employer interested in using their services usually must petition. INA § 204(a)(1)(D). Aliens with extraordinary ability and fourth- and fifth-preference aliens can petition for themselves. INA § 204(a).

c. Diversity Immigration

The immigration system Congress adopted in 1965 when it ended national origins quotas anticipated that preference immigrants would not use all the numbers potentially available. The excess would be open for "nonpreference" immigration, on a first-come first-served basis, to those who met certain minimal requirements. Such immigration did not require a petition by a family member here already; hence it could cover a more diverse population. But by 1978, demand in the preference categories exceeded the supply of numbers available under the overall preference ceiling, and nonpreference immigration therefore disappeared. By 1986, Congress was searching for ways to recapture some of the openness that

---

8. H.R.Rep. No. 101–723, pt. 1, at 59 (1990).

nonpreference immigration signaled, and also to ameliorate the steep reduction in European migration that had been an unexpected byproduct of the 1965 amendments. Supporters of new provisions most often voiced concern about reduced immigration opportunities from Ireland.

With the 1986 Immigration Reform and Control Act, Congress launched the first of several experiments in an effort to meet these ends. IRCA, Pub.L. No. 99–603, § 314, 100 Stat. 3359. That legislation provided 10,000 new admissions available over two years (later increased to 40,000 over four) for persons from countries "adversely affected" by the 1965 changes. It became known as the NP–5 program. The list of 36 such countries was disproportionately, but not exclusively, European. Immigrants were selected, in essence, by a lottery, and as it happened, Irish nationals turned out to be the biggest winners in this sweepstakes. In 1988 Congress provided another 20,000 admissions, spread over two years, but adopted a different method for parcelling them out. It opened them for persons from "underrepresented countries"—defined in such a way that it included all but the 13 leading immigrant-sending countries. Immigration Amendments of 1988, Pub.L. No. 100–658, § 2, 102 Stat. 3908 (establishing what became known as the OP–1 program). A differently structured random lottery this time attracted over 3 million applicants. Bangladeshis claimed nearly 5000 of the admissions, followed by natives of Pakistan, Poland, Turkey, and Egypt. *See* 66 Interp.Rel. 184, 251, 668, 1038, 1192 (1989).

The 1990 Act tried a different approach (albeit somewhat akin to the OP–1 program) toward increasing immigration from countries not currently well-represented in the immigrant population. INA § 203(c) establishes a permanent diversity program, which started with FY 1995.[9] It employs an extraordinarily intricate formula, based on the immigration statistics from the immediately preceding five-year period, to decide which countries can share in the 55,000 diversity admissions each year. People from "high admission countries" are not eligible. In 1995 this provision disqualified nationals of the following 12 countries: Canada, the Dominican Republic, El Salvador, India, Jamaica, Mexico, the People's Republic of China, the Philippines, South Korea, Taiwan, the United Kingdom, and Vietnam. Natives of all other countries can qualify, but their relative share of the total depends on whether their country of origin is in a high-admission or a low-admission region. The allocations for each region appear in Table 3.3. For a detailed look at the formulas and projections, see 68 Interp.Rel. 137 (1991) (you might want to brush up on your integral calculus first). For a description of the registration procedures used for FY 1995, see 7 Visa Bulletin, No. 35, April 1994. The regulations were published in 59 Fed. Reg. 15298 (1994).

9. Over the three years before the permanent diversity system went into effect in FY 1995, the 1990 Act provided for a transitional diversity program, essentially a high-powered version of the 1986 NP–5 program. The 40,000 visas available each year to persons from "adversely affected" countries went overwhelmingly to natives of Ireland and Poland.

Table 3.3

Allocation of Diversity Admissions for FY 1995

Africa:	20,200
Asia:	6,837
Europe:	24,549
North America:	8
South America:	2,589
Oceania:	817

Source: 71 Interp.Rel. 451 (1994).

Individuals must meet certain threshold requirements to qualify for these diversity visas. INA § 203(c)(2). They must (1) have a high school education or its equivalent, or (2) within five years preceding the application, have had at least two years of experience in an occupation that requires at least two years of training or experience. Aspirants for diversity immigration may file only one application per year, and a random lottery then selects the actual beneficiaries. INA § 203(e)(2). Winners can bring their immediate families, but they count against the total diversity ceiling. There will be a separate registration and a separate lottery each year. The State Department received over 8 million registrations for FY 1995 under the DV–1 program, as it is now known, but 1.5 million were quickly disqualified (*e.g.*, because the registration letter was in the wrong form, or because of identified multiple filings).

d. Ceilings and Floors

At first glance, INA § 201(c) appears to set a ceiling on all family-sponsored immigration, including immediate relatives, at the level of 480,-000 from FY 1995. A firm cap of this sort was in fact the intent of some early versions of the legislation that became the 1990 Act. Because those bills would still have assured unhindered admission of all immediate relatives of U.S. citizens, however (provided those numbers did not exceed the overall family cap), the effect would have been a steady shrinkage of admissions for the family preference categories as immediate relative admissions increased.

Other members of Congress, noting that all family preferences but the first are seriously backlogged, opposed such a fixed ceiling, and their views ultimately prevailed in the final version of the 1990 Act. Instead of simply repealing the family ceiling, however, Congress adopted the uniquely complex formula of INA § 201(c). It guarantees a floor for the family-sponsored preference categories—a minimum of 226,000 admissions every year. INA § 201(c)(1)(B)(ii). Thus if immediate relative admissions exceed 254,000, the ostensible family caps can be pierced the following fiscal year. (All the numerical adjustments of this sort take effect during the immediately following fiscal year. *See* INA § 201(c)(2), (d)(2).) The family ceiling thus came to be called, in the unlovely jargon of the trade, a "pierceable cap with a floor."

To take an illustrative hypothetical, assume that FY 1996 immediate relative admissions total 260,000.[10] If the family cap were firm and unyielding, family preference admissions for FY 1997 would have to be limited to 220,000. Instead, here the override provisions kick in and assure that the minimum of 226,000 spaces remain available for the family preferences. Thus FY 1997 admissions would be 226,000 for the family preferences, plus however many spouses and minor children of U.S. citizens happen to qualify for immediate relative status. If the latter group amounts to 260,000 again, total family admissions would be 486,000. (Or if that group happened to jump to 300,000, the total for family admissions would be 526,000.) The nominal family cap would be pierced, in order to assure a minimum of 226,000 for the preference categories. Of course, because all these adjustments occur in the *next* fiscal year, it could also happen that despite the working of the override provision to set the annual ceilings for FY 1997 in our hypothetical, actual family admissions could still fall below the nominal cap that year. That is, if demand for immediate relative admissions in FY 1997 fell to 240,000, for example, actual world-wide family admissions that year would amount to only 466,000.

What happens then for FY 1998? Following out this shortfall hypothetical enables us to work through the last wrinkles of this (depressingly) complex system. Because the 240,000 immediate relative admissions in our hypothetical for FY 1997 are 14,000 below the piercing level, there are extra family numbers available for the following fiscal year. Who gets this bounty? The answer is that all are assigned to the second preference, for spouses and unmarried sons and daughters of lawful permanent residents—a further sign of Congress's desire to reduce backlogs affecting these particularly close family relationships. Check INA § 203(a)(2). Under these assumptions, then, the family admission ceilings for FY 1998 would be as follows:

Table 3.4

Hypothetical Family Admission Ceilings, FY 1998

Immediate relatives	unlimited (depends entirely on demand from qualified aliens)
1st preference	23,400
2d preference	128,200 (at least 77% of these reserved for spouses and minor children)
3d preference	23,400
4th preference	65,000
Total, family preference categories only	240,000 (14,000 over the preference floor)

10. In order to simplify the calculations, all the hypotheticals in this section assume no aliens admitted in the category described in § 201(b)(1)(B) (aliens born to a lawful permanent resident during a temporary visit abroad). These persons, who in reality number about 2,000 to 3,000 a year, are not technically "immediate relatives," but the statute requires that their admissions be added to the number of immediate relatives before figuring how many family preference spaces will be available for the following year.

If immediate relative admissions in FY 1998 happen to be 250,000, then overall family admissions will actually total 490,000. But in that event, for FY 1999 the second preference would then enjoy the infusion of only 4,000 extra spaces, for a total of 118,200 second-preference numbers.

If all these calculations leave you confused, then you can join the chorus of those who think the 1990 Congress should simply have repealed the nominal cap on overall family admissions. De facto, most of the time family preference admission ceilings after FY 1995 are likely to be 226,000. This total will be augmented then by immediate relative admissions, which in reality remain unhindered by any quota limits. As it happens, the main effect of the 1990 formulas, ironically, is not to cap family admissions, but to allow for an increase in second-preference opportunities whenever immediate relative demand slackens.[11]

Table 3.5
Actual Admissions of Immigrants by Selected Categories
FY 1992–93
(excludes IRCA Legalizations)

Category	FY 1992		FY 1993	
Immediate relatives	235,484		255,059	
Family-sponsored preferences	213,123		226,776	
1st preference		12,486		12,819
2d preference		118,247		128,308
3d preference		22,195		23,385
4th preference		60,195		62,264
Employment-based preferences	116,198		147,012	
1st preference		5,456		21,114
2d preference		58,401		29,468
3d preference		47,568		87,689
4th preference		4,063		8,158
5th preference		59		583
pre–1992 employment preferences		651		—
Refugee and asylee adjustments	117,037		127,343	
Other (including transition diversity program)	128,793		123,824	
TOTAL	810,635		880,014	

Source: 1993 INS Statistical Yearbook, Table 4.

11. One other eventuality that can provide added second-preference family admissions should be noted, although the discussion in text to this point, for simplicity's sake, has ignored this possibility. If employment-based admissions fall below their ceiling of 140,000 in a given year, the unused numbers are added to the *family* totals for the following year. INA § 202(c)(3)(C). If employment admissions come to 125,000, for example, in FY 1996, there would be an additional 15,000 numbers carried over and added to the nominal family cap for FY 1997. In this hypothetical example, that cap would be 495,000 for FY 1997, and the floor for the family preferences would come into play only if immediate relative admissions in FY 1996 exceeded 269,000. Exactly this sort of scenario will result in roughly 25,000 additional second-preference admissions in FY 1995, even though there were roughly 259,500 immediate relative admissions in FY 1994, 5,500 over the ostensible piercing level. For more information on the calculations, including the preliminary figures for FY 1995 ad-

The calculation of annual category ceilings is complicated enough, but unfortunately, one other set of ceilings adds further complexity: per-country ceilings under INA § 202. Congress added such ceilings in 1965 when it repealed the national origins quotas. They were, in their own way, a kind of diversity provision, assuring that no one country received over 20,000 of the preference admissions in any one year. The ceilings had particularly harsh and unintended effects on Mexico and the Philippines, where, owing to geography or historical ties, demand for U.S. immigration is particularly strong; the backlogs of waiting preference immigrants in each country exceeded 400,000 by 1990.[12]

In the 1990 Act, Congress complicated the calculations, but retained the idea of per-country ceilings. You need not bother with the numbing complexity of § 202, but you should know that the ceiling will now be at least 25,620, and it will be somewhat higher whenever the number of immediate relatives falls below the "piercing" level described above or whenever there are carryovers resulting from admissions below the preference ceilings in the previous fiscal year. This per-country provision is sometimes misunderstood. It does not mean that each nation is entitled to send 25,000 preference immigrants each year. Instead it is an override provision that kicks in only if the normal operation of the worldwide preference system would happen to send more than the per-country ceiling in a given year, based on demand from qualifying aliens from that particular state.[13]

The per-country ceilings of INA § 202 apply only to preference immigration in the employment-based and family-sponsored categories. Immediate relatives are not affected by such ceilings, and even a massive use of immediate relative admissions by a particular state will not reduce the per-country ceiling available for preference immigrants from that country.[14]

missions in all preference categories, see 71 Interp.Rel. 1427–30 (1994). For the actual FY 1994 calculations, when the floor did come into play, see 71 id. 368–71.

12. As of January 1994 the State Department's waiting lists had grown to 983,966 for Mexico and 568,552 for the Philippines. Overall the Department had 3.6 million people registered and waiting for a visa, roughly 96 percent of them in the family categories—because the 1990 Act increased employment admissions enough to make most of the employment categories current. Over 45 percent of those on the lists were waiting for the family fourth preference, and 41.5 percent for the family second preference. For a highly detailed breakdown of the waiting list, see 71 Interp. Rel. 609–19 (1994) (reprinting data from the May 1994 Visa Bulletin).

13. Chargeability to a foreign state is based on location of birth, not nationality (although these usually coincide), with a few exceptions designed primarily to keep immigrating families together. INA § 202(b). Also, the statute provides special allocation rules for countries that are at the per-country ceiling, to assure that not all of that country's numbers are used up by the higher preferences. INA § 202(e).

14. Congress also exempted 75 percent of second-preference admissions of spouses and minor children (the so-called "2–A floor") from the per-country ceilings. INA § 202(a)(4). Again the calculations are incredibly intricate, but this provision had the intended effect of greatly easing the backlog of second-preference admissions from Mexico, where such family members previously had to wait as many as 10 years for legal admission.

Diversity immigrants are subject to their own separate per-country ceiling provision (seven percent of the 55,000 admissions, or 3,850).   INA § 203(c)(1)(E)(v).

Fortunately, most immigration lawyers never have to attempt the calculations required under §§ 201, 202, and 203.   That unhappy task falls to officials of the Visa Office of the Department of State, who prepare charts showing how far down the waiting list consular officers will reach in processing preference immigrant visas for a particular month.   Those charts—rather than the statutory sections—*are* frequently consulted by the immigration bar, particularly in order to advise clients about approximately when they can expect to immigrate in any category for which they might qualify.   They are published monthly in the State Department's Visa Bulletin and in various periodical reporting services like *Interpreter Releases*.

Table 3.6 reprints one of these charts, showing visa allocation priority dates for November 1994.   Use the table to familiarize yourself with this basic tool of immigration practice.   The chart also gives a useful indication of the lengthy backlogs that have developed under several of the categories and especially for those high-demand countries adversely affected by the per-country ceilings.

Table 3.6

Visa Preference Admissions for November 1994

	All chargeability areas except those listed	CHINA-mainland born	DOMINICAN REPUBLIC	INDIA	MEXICO	PHILIPPINES
FAMILY PREFERENCES						
1st	C	C	C	C	01MAR94	29OCT85
2A	15OCT91	15OCT91	15OCT91	15OCT91	22SEP91	15OCT91
2B	15JAN90	15JAN90	15JAN90	15JAN90	15JAN90	15JUL88
3rd	08MAY92	08MAY92	08MAY92	08MAY92	15FEB87	01AUG83
4th	08JAN85	08JAN85	08JAN85	08MAY83	01OCT83	12JUL77
EMPLOYMENT PREFERENCES						
1st	C	C	C	C	C	C
2nd	C	C	C	C	C	C
3rd	C	01JUL93	C	C	C	01JAN94
Other Workers	15JUN88	15JUN88	15JUN88	15JUN88	15JUN88	15JUN88
4th	C	C	C	C	C	19MAY93
5th	C	U	C	C	C	C
Targeted Employment Areas	C	U	C	C	C	C

Notes to Table 3.6

On the chart, "C" indicates that a category is current, and "U" indicates that visas are unavailable that month for that category.   The dates in the columns set forth visa allocation priority dates, which, roughly speaking, show an alien's position on the waiting list.   Preference visas are distributed, within each relevant classification, in chronological order of application. No immigrant subject to the quotas may receive a visa until his or her priority date has been reached. The immigrant's priority date is the date when the first relevant document was filed with the appropriate administrative agency (visa petition for the family categories and some employment categories; application for labor certification for those employment preferences subject to this requirement). Note that this is a date many months in advance of any determination by those agencies that the alien is in fact eligible. Naturally no visa will issue until all the eligibility determinations are concluded.[15]

To take an example of how priority dates are assigned, assume that an employer applies for labor certification for a stated position on April 1, 1994, and that the certification is issued by the U.S. Department of Labor on August 4. The employer then files with INS a visa petition for the appropriate employment-based preference category. It is approved on October 15, and the endorsed visa petition is sent, via the National Visa Center, to the consulate in the country where the alien is expected to apply for the actual visa. In these circumstances, the alien's visa allocation priority date is April 1, 1994.

As an example in a family-sponsored preference categories, assume that a U.S. citizen father petitions for his 26–year–old daughter, a Brazilian national, under the first preference, filing his visa petition with INS on July 7, 1993. Because of a controversy over the foreign birth certificate he submits, the petition is not approved until September 20, 1994, and it does not reach the U.S. consulate in Rio de Janeiro until October of that year. The daughter's visa allocation priority date is July 7, 1993. If she marries before admission to the United States, she becomes ineligible for the first preference, but she can still retain the same priority date for the category that now pertains: the third family-sponsored preference. Consider closely what effects both the marriage and the rule allowing her to retain the same priority date will have on the actual timing of her admission.

Problems

To sharpen your initial familiarity with the functioning of these preference categories, and your understanding of who may petition and who may benefit from a petition, work through the following problems. (As to some, you should remember that a lawful permanent resident qualifies for naturalization, in most cases, after five years' residence in this country.) In each, assume you are an attorney approached for advice. What do you recommend? What additional information must you develop, if any? There may be many ways to accomplish the client's aims; try to find the most expeditious one, paying attention to any backlogs in the preference categories for which your client may qualify.

15. Under the employment-based categories for the People's Republic of China, fifth-preference admissions were unavailable and third-preference admissions were backlogged because of certain special rules under the Chinese Student Protection Act, Pub.L.No. 102–404, 106 Stat. 1969 (1992). That legislation mortgaged future Chinese admissions in these categories in order to provide permanent resident status to Chinese nationals already in the United States at the time of the Tiananmen Square massacre and subsequent Chinese government crackdown in 1989–90.

1. Your client has been a lawful permanent resident of the United States since 1986. Last month in Nairobi he married a national of Kenya who has a six-year-old child by a previous marriage (which was properly terminated by a valid divorce action), and naturally he wants to bring his wife and her child to this country as soon as possible.

2. Your client is a lawful permanent resident alien who entered this country in that status in 1982. He wants to bring his brother here from Greece.

3. Your client, a citizen of the Philippines, entered as a lawful permanent resident alien two years ago under the third family-sponsored preference, for married sons and daughters of U.S. citizens. At the time he brought with him his wife and three of his four children, leaving behind his eldest, an 18-year-old daughter. This daughter had already entered college and believed at the time that she did not want to emigrate. Now she has changed her mind, and would like to immigrate to the United States and take up studies in this country as soon as possible.

4. You have been contacted by a 20-year-old Swiss national who wishes to immigrate to the United States. He has heard that family ties are the key to immigration, and he reports that he has an uncle in Chicago who is a U.S. citizen and would be willing to do any necessary paperwork. He also reports that he has worked as a researcher for a sociology professor at his university, where he is completing his basic degree with a major in sociology.

5. Your client, a high school dropout, is the principal shareholder and chief executive officer of a Brazilian software firm with annual gross receipts equivalent to several million dollars. For many years, he has been thinking of establishing sales outlets in a variety of other countries, possibly including the United States. In any event, whatever happens with the business, he wishes to take up permanent residence here. What do you advise? If he had finished high school, would this make a difference in his chances? If he had finished college? If he had a Ph.D. in mathematics?

e. *Changing Patterns of American Immigration*

The national-origins quota system, adopted in the 1920s, was an effort to freeze the ethnic composition of the American population. As Figure 1.2 in Chapter One indicates, it was not entirely successful in meeting this professed goal, largely because of the provisions allowing numerically unconstrained immigration from Western Hemisphere countries.

After the national origins system was abolished in 1965, some observers worried that its discriminatory effects would continue in a more disguised form, owing to the strong preference given to family reunification categories. Such immigration, after all, requires the presence in this country of family members who gained admission under the old system to initiate the process. If particular countries or ethnic groups were excluded earlier, there will be no base for using the family reunification provisions of the new, ostensibly more neutral system.

Figure 3.1

**Immigrants Admitted by Region of Birth:
Selected Fiscal Years 1955–93**

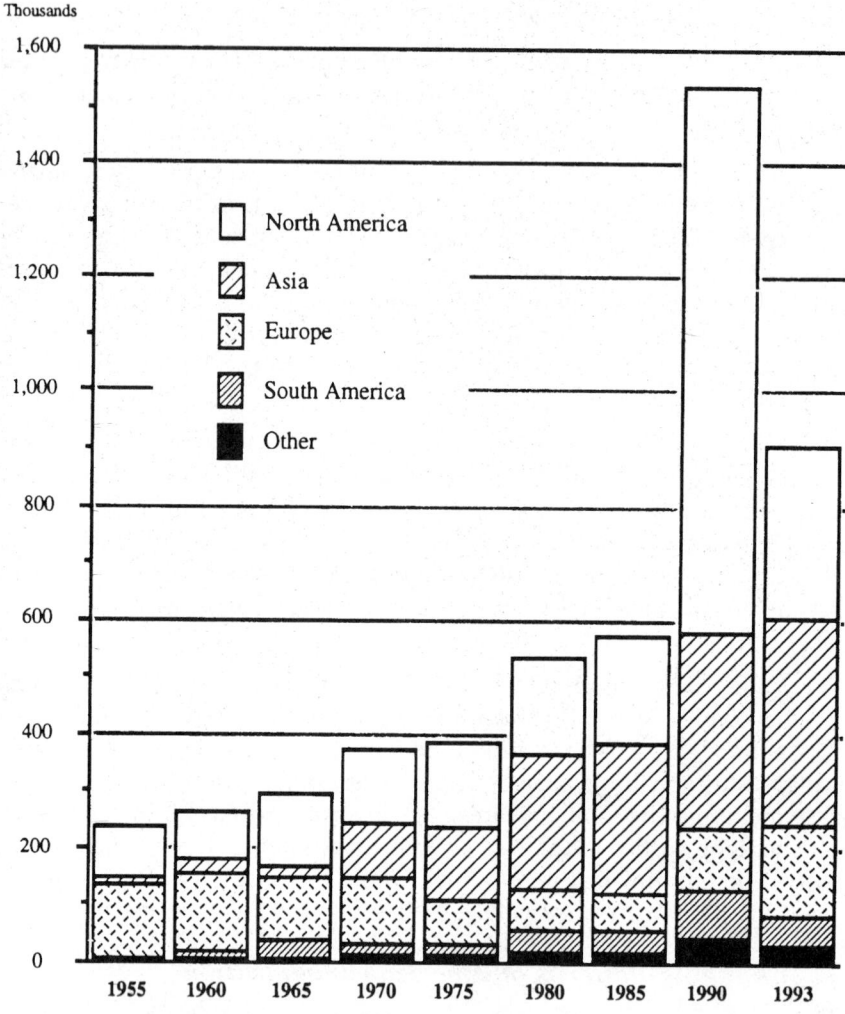

Source: 1993 INS Statistical Yearbook, Chart A, p. 12.

Figure 3.1 indicates, however, that the worst fears of perpetuating a discriminatory system have not been realized. For example, Asians, heavily disfavored under the Chinese exclusion acts, the "Gentleman's Agreement" with Japan, and the national origins laws, now fill a large proportion of immigration slots. Of course, there remain particular countries with low totals because of the absence of a family reunification base, and immigration from Africa still claims only a small proportion of annual numbers. But overall, the abolition of the national origins system, combined with entrepreneurial use of the occupational categories and significant refugee admission programs, has altered the racial and ethnic composition of immigration to the United States in the last several decades. The next readings provide insights into the ongoing effects of immigration on American demographics.

ALEJANDRO PORTES & RUBÉN G. RUMBAUT, IMMIGRANT AMERICA: A PORTRAIT

Pp. 6–27, 34–48 (1990).

After a lapse of half a century, the United States has again become a country of immigration. In 1980, the foreign-born population reached 14.1 million or 6.2 percent of the total. Although a far cry from the situation sixty years earlier, when immigrants accounted for 13.2 percent of the American population, the impact of contemporary immigration is both significant and growing. Numerous books and articles have called attention to this revival and sought its causes—first in a booming American economy and second in the liberalized provisions of the 1965 immigration act. A common exercise is to compare this "new" immigration with the "old" inflow at the turn of the century. Similarities include the predominantly urban destination of most newcomers, their concentration in a few port cities, and their willingness to accept the lowest paid jobs. Differences are more frequently stressed, however, for the "old" immigration was overwhelmingly European and white; but the present inflow is, to a large extent, nonwhite and comes from countries of the Third World.

The public image of contemporary immigration has been colored to a large extent by the Third World origins of most recent arrivals. Because the sending countries are generally poor, many Americans believe that the immigrants themselves are uniformly poor and uneducated. Their move is commonly portrayed as a one-way escape from hunger, want, and persecution and their arrival on U.S. shores as not too different from that of the tired, "huddled masses" that Emma Lazarus immortalized at the base of the Statue of Liberty. The "quality" of the newcomers and their chances for assimilation are sometimes portrayed as worse because of their non-European past and the precarious legal status of many.

The reality is very different. * * * Clearly, not all newcomers are doctors or skilled mechanics, and fewer still become politicians or millionaires. Still, these are not isolated instances. Underneath its apparent uniformity, contemporary immigration features a bewildering variety of origins, return patterns, and modes of adaptation to American society. Never before has the United States received immigrants from so many countries, from such different social and economic backgrounds, and for so many reasons. Although pre-World War I European immigration was by no means homogeneous, the differences between successive waves of Irish, Italians, Jews, Greeks, and Poles often pale by comparison with the current diversity. For the same reason, theories coined in the wake of the

Europeans' arrival at the turn of the century have been made obsolete by events during the last decades.

* * *

Many of the countries from which today's immigrants come have one of their largest cities in the United States. Los Angeles' Mexican population is next in size to Mexico City, Monterrey, and Guadalajara. Havana is not much larger than Cuban Miami, and Santo Domingo holds a precarious advantage over Dominican New York. This is not the case for all groups; others, such as Asian Indians, Laotians, Argentines, and Brazilians, are more dispersed throughout the country. Reasons for both these differences and other characteristics of contemporary immigrant groups are not well known—in part because of the recency of their arrival and in part because of the common expectation that their assimilation process would conform to the wellknown European pattern. But immigrant America is a different place today from the America that emerged out of Ellis Island and grew up in the tenements of New York and Boston.

The Origins of Immigration

Why do they come? A common explanation singles out the 1965 change in American immigration law as the principal factor. According to this view, today's immigrants come because they can, whereas before 1965 legal restrictions prevented them from doing so. Although the 1965 law certainly explains qualitative and quantitative changes in immigration during the last two decades, it is an insufficient explanation. Not everyone in even the major sending countries has immigrated or is planning to do so. Compared to the respective national populations, those who decide to migrate generally represent a minuscule proportion. The question can thus be reversed to ask not why many come, but why so few have decided to undertake the journey, especially with difficult economic and political conditions in many sending countries.

Moving to a foreign country is not easy, even under the most propitious circumstances. It requires elaborate preparations, much expense, giving up personal relations at home, and often learning a new language and culture. Not so long ago, the lure of higher wages in the United States was not sufficient by itself to attract foreign workers and had to be activated through deliberate recruitment. * * *

The question then remains, What are the factors motivating some groups but not others to seek entry into the United States at present? The most common answer is the desperate poverty, squalor, and unemployment of many foreign lands. * * *

These statements are made despite a mounting body of evidence that points in the exact opposite direction. Consider legal immigration. The proportion of professionals and technicians among occupationally active immigrants consistently exceeds the average among U.S. workers. During the last decade, immigrant professionals represented around 25 percent of the total, at a time when professionals and technicians amounted to no more than 18 percent of the American labor force. Although the gap may be somewhat exaggerated by the available immigration data, other sources confirm that recent immigrants are as well represented as the native American population at the higher educational and occupational levels. For 1980, the census reported the percentage completing four or more years of college as 16.3 percent for natives and 15.8 percent for the foreign born; the number in professional specialty occupations was the same for both groups: 12 percent. For this reason, the gap in median household incomes in favor of the native born did not exceed U.S. $3,000 in that year, despite the fact that over 40 percent of the foreign born had been in the United States for ten years or less.

But even if legal immigrants represent a select group from most sending countries, what about the illegals? The evidence here is more tentative because of the difficulty of investigating a surreptitious flow. However, the available studies coincide on two points: The very poor and the unemployed seldom migrate, either legally or illegally; and unauthorized immigrants tend to have above-average levels of education and occupational skills in comparison with their homeland populations. More important, they are positively self-selected in terms of ambition and willingness to work.

* * *

But if migrants do not come to escape unemployment or destitution, why do they come? Why, in particular, should middle-class professionals and skilled workers embark in a costly journey, sometimes surreptitiously, and sacrifice work, friends, and family back home? The basic reason is the gap between life aspirations and expectations and the means to fulfill them in the sending countries. Different groups feel this gap with varying intensity, but it clearly becomes a strong motive for action among the most ambitious and resourceful. Because relative, not absolute deprivation lies at the core of most contemporary immigration, its composition tends to be positively selected in terms of both human capital and motivation. The United States and the other industrialized countries play a double role in this process. First, they are the source of much of the modern culture of consumption and of the new expectations diffused worldwide. Second, the same process of global diffusion has taught an increasing number of people about economic opportunities in the developed world that are absent in their own countries.

* * *

IMMIGRANTS AND THEIR TYPES

Within this general picture, there are significant differences in migration goals and their relative fulfillment. Any typology implies simplification, but it is useful at this point to present a basic classification of contemporary immigrants to organize * * * analysis of their process of adaptation. * * *

Labor Migrants

Manual labor immigration corresponds most closely to popular stereotypes about contemporary immigration. The movement of foreign workers in search of menial and generally low paid jobs has represented the bulk of immigration, both legal and undocumented, in recent years. * * * [We note here] the principal ways manual labor immigration has materialized in recent years.

First, migrants can simply cross the border on foot or with the help of a smuggler or overstay a U.S. tourist visa. In official parlance, illegal border crossers have been labeled EWIs (entry without inspection); those who stay longer than permitted are labeled visa abusers. In 1987, the U.S. Immigration and Naturalization Service (INS) located 1.19 million deportable aliens, of which 1.17 million were EWIs. Predictably, the overwhelming majority of illegal border crossers—97 percent—were Mexicans.

A second channel of entry is to come legally by using one of the family reunification preferences of the immigration law (left untouched, for the most part, by the 1986 reform). This avenue is open primarily to immigrants who have first entered the United States without legal papers or for temporary periods and who have subsequently married a U.S. citizen or legal resident. Marriage automatically entitles the immigrant to a legal entry permit; spouses of U.S. citizens are given priority because they are exempt from existing quota limits. A study of 822 legal Mexican immigrants arriving during 1973–1974 found that about 70 percent of respondents had lived in the United States prior to legal entry, most for periods of six months or more. Forty-eight percent of this sample came with visas granted to spouses of U.S. citizens; another 45 percent came under the quota as spouses of U.S. legal residents. * * *

The last avenue is to come as a contract laborer [such as temporary workers admitted as H–2 nonimmigrants].

* * *

The men and women who come under these circumstances find in the modest entry jobs available on this side of the border the means to fulfill expectations blocked in their own countries. Some do stay and attempt to carve a new life in America. Many return, however, because although U.S. wages are higher, the "yield" of these wages in terms of consumption, investments, and social status is often greater back home. Having accumulated enough savings, most immigrants seek to reestablish or gain a position of social respectability, a goal more easily accomplished in their home communities. Manual labor immigration is thus not a one-way flow away from poverty and want, but rather a two-way process fueled by the changing needs and interests of those who come and those who profit from their labor.

Professional Immigrants

The third preference category of the U.S. visa allocation system [as it existed before the 1990 amendments] is reserved for "members of the professions of exceptional ability and their spouses and children." This category provides the main entry channel for the second type of immigrants. Unlike the first, these come legally and are not destined to the bottom layers of the American labor market. Labeled "brain drain" in the countries of origin, this flow of immigrants represents a significant gain of highly trained personnel for the United States. In 1987, 64,099 persons classified as professionals and managers arrived as permanent residents; the main contributors were the Philippines (8,512), India (5,712), Great Britain (3,344), mainland China (3,264), and Taiwan (2,924). The overall number and the principal contributors have changed little during the 1980s.

* * *

Because they do not come to escape poverty, but to improve their careers, immigrant professionals seldom accept menial jobs in the United States. However, they tend to enter at the bottom of their respective occupational ladders and to progress from there according to individual merit. This is why, for example, foreign doctors and nurses are so often found in public hospitals throughout the country. But in recent years, a number of foreign professionals—primarily of Asian origin—have had to turn to other pursuits because of new entry barriers to their respective careers in the United States. Common alternatives have been small business or even the unregulated practice of their profession while awaiting better times. Despite these difficulties, these immigrants' economic success has been remarkable. For example, immigration from India during the last two decades has been heavily skewed toward university-educated professionals and technical personnel. In 1980, the median household income of Indian immigrants was $25,644—$6,000 above the median for the U.S. population and $11,000 above the figure for the foreign born, despite the fact that almost 80 percent of these immigrants had been in the United States ten years or less.

An important feature of this type of immigration is its inconspicuousness. We seldom hear reference to a Filipino or an Indian immigration "problem," although there are over one million Filipinos and over five hundred thousand Indians living in this country. The reason is that professionals and technicians, heavily represented among these nationalities, seldom form tightly knit ethnic communities. * * * [P]rofessional immigrants are among the most rapidly assimilated—first because of their occupational success and second because of the absence of strong ethnic networks that reinforce the culture of origin. However, assimilation in this case does not mean severing relations with the home country. On the contrary, because successful immigrants have the means to do so, they attempt to bridge the gap between past and present through periodic visits and cultivating family and friends left behind. During the first generation at least, a typical pattern is the attempt to juggle two different social worlds. Although this is a difficult and expensive task, many foreign professionals actually succeed in it.

Entrepreneurial Immigrants

* * *

Entrepreneurial minorities are the exception in both turn-of-the-century and contemporary immigrations. Their significance is that they create an avenue for economic mobility unavailable to other groups. This avenue is open not only to the original entrepreneurs, but to later arrivals as well. The reason is that relations between immigrant employers and their co-ethnic employees often go beyond a purely contractual bond. When immigrant enterprises expand, they tend to hire their own for supervisory positions. Today Koreans hire and promote Koreans in New York and Los Angeles, and Cubans do the same for other Cubans in Miami, just as sixty years ago the Jews of Manhattan's Lower East Side and the Japanese of San Francisco and Los Angeles hired and supported those from their own communities.

A tightly knit ethnic enclave is not, however, the only manifestation of immigrant entrepreneurship. In other cities, where the concentration of these immigrants is less dense, they tend to take over businesses catering to low-income groups, often in the inner cities. In this role as "middleman minorities," entrepreneurial immigrants are less visible because they tend to be dispersed over the area occupied by the populations they serve. Koreatown in Los Angeles is not, for example, the only manifestation of entrepreneurship among this immigrant group. Koreans are also present in significant numbers in New York City, where they have gained increasing control of the produce market, and in cities like Washington, D.C., and Baltimore, where they have progressively replaced Italians and Jews as the principal merchants in low-income inner-city areas. Similarly, roughly two-thirds of Cuban-owned firms are concentrated in Miami, but they are also numerous in other cities like Los Angeles, Jersey City, and West New York. The percentage of firms per thousand Cuban population is actually higher in these secondary concentrations than in Miami.

The rise of ethnic enclaves and middleman minorities is generally fortuitous. * * * In general, entrepreneurial minorities come under preferences designated for other purposes. Koreans and Chinese, two of the most successful business-oriented groups, have availed themselves of the [employment-based] preference categories for professionals and skilled workers and, subsequently, of the family reunification provisions of the 1965 immigration law. Cubans came as political refugees and were initially resettled in dispersed localities throughout the country. It took these refugees more than a decade after initial arrival to start regrouping in certain geographic locations and begin the push toward entrepreneurship.

Refugees and Asylees

* * *

Major refugee groups living at present in the United States * * * tend to share strong anti-Communist feelings, although they are different in many other respects. Their entry into the American labor market, for example, has been heterogeneous, paralleling and even exceeding the diversity among regular immigrants. Political refugees are found today in low-paid menial work, as is the case with many Cambodians, Laotians, Afghans, Ethiopians, and 1980 Mariel Cubans. They are also found at the higher end of the labor market, in prominent and well-paid professional careers, as is often the case with Eastern Europeans. Others have veered toward business and self-employment after giving up hopes of returning to their countries. Cubans in south Florida and increasingly the Vietnamese, concentrated in Orange and Los Angeles counties, have followed this route. Finally, there is even the option of remaining out of work, made possible by the welfare provisions of the 1980 refugee act. Asian refugees with little education and work skills are commonly found in this situation.

The official label of refugee conceals differences not only between national groups but within each of them as well. Two categories are generally found in most refugee flows. First, there is an elite of former notables who left because of ideological and political opposition to their countries' regimes. They tend to be among the earlier arrivals and usually have little difficulty validating their claim of political persecution. Second, there is a mass of individuals and families of more modest backgrounds who left at a later date because of the economic exactions and hardships imposed by the same regimes. Depending on the relationship between their home country and the United States, they can be classified as bona fide refugees or as illegal aliens. This diversity in the origins of refugees and the interaction between the earlier elite arrivals and subsequent cohorts goes a long way toward explaining each group's economic and social adaptation.   * * *

* * *

CONTEMPORARY SETTLEMENT PATTERNS: A MAP OF IMMIGRANT AMERICA

These various processes have led to a settlement pattern among recent immigrants to the United States that combines two apparently contradictory outcomes: concentration, because a few states and metropolitan areas receive a disproportionate number of the newcomers, and diffusion, because immigrants are found in every state of the Union and because different immigrant types vary significantly in their locational decisions. In 1987, 71 percent of the 601,516 foreign persons admitted for legal permanent residence went to just six states: California (26.8 percent), New York (19.0 percent), Florida (9.1 percent), Texas (7.0 percent), New Jersey (5.1 percent), and Illinois (4.3 percent). At the other extreme, no state received fewer than two hundred immigrants, the least favored being Wyoming (261) and South Dakota (304).

[Table 3.7] portrays the national composition of immigrant flows to the six major receiving urban areas. Together these cities accounted for 42 percent of legal immigration during 1987. With small variations, this settlement pattern is representative of those registered throughout the 1980s.

PREFERRED PLACES

Immigration to the United States is today an urban phenomenon and one concentrated in the largest cities. In 1987, less than 7 percent of legal immigrants went to live in nonurban areas, and more than half settled in just ten metropolitan locations. In particular, recent years have seen the gradual end of what was a significant component of pre-World War I immigration: rural-bound groups coming to settle empty lands or work as farm laborers.

* * *

[Table 3.7]

Composition of Immigrant Flows to Six
Major Metropolitan Destinations, 1987

New York—97,510

Dominicans	15%
Jamaicans	11%
Guyanese	7%
Chinese	7%
Haitians	6%

Chicago—20,297

Mexicans	20%
Filipinos	11%
Indians	11%
Poles	9%
Koreans	6%

Los Angeles–Long Beach—64,453

Mexicans	23%
Filipinos	12%
Koreans	9%
Salvadorans	6%
Iranians	6%

Washington—17,936

Koreans	9%
Salvadorans	6%
Indians	6%
Filipinos	5%
Vietnamese	5%

Miami—37,887

Cubans	59%
Haitians	9%
Jamaicans	5%
Colombians	5%
Dominicans	2%

San Francisco—16,234

Chinese	24%
Filipinos	22%
Salvadorans	5%
Vietnamese	5%
Mexicans	4%

Note: Chinese include immigrants from mainland China only.

[Table data reorganized from Figure 1, p. 36, of the book.—eds.]

* * *

In the absence of deliberate recruitment or other ad hoc factors, entry jobs at the bottom of the respective ladders are more easily accessible in large urban agglomerations and in those experiencing processes of rapid economic growth. Once immigrants from a particular nationality "discover" the existence of such opportunities in an urban area, the process becomes self-perpetuating through the operation of ethnic networks. It is thus not surprising that the principal concentrations of the three largest immigrant groups at present are found in Los Angeles, a large metropolitan area that has experienced rapid economic expansion in recent years. It is not surprising either that Cubans concentrate in Miami, another fast growing city that has become the center of U.S. trade with Latin America. Washington, D.C., is also an attractive area of destination for entrepreneurially oriented groups because of the presence of a large inner-city minority population, along with a sizable segment of highly paid government workers.

* * *

CENSUS BUREAU RELEASES STATISTICS ON FOREIGN–BORN POPULATION IN THE U.S.

70 Interpreter Releases 1638 (1994).

The Commerce Department's Census Bureau has released a report on the nation's foreign-born population. * * * The following highlights, extracted from the report's 400 pages of statistical tables, provide comparisons between foreign-born groups and natives:

- In 1990, about 20 million of the nation's total population was foreign-born and 229 million native-born. About six percent of immigrants entering the country between 1987 and 1990 were naturalized, compared with 10 percent of those entering during 1985–1986, 19 percent during 1982–1984, 27 percent during 1980–1981, and 61 percent before 1980.

- One out of four immigrants who arrived after 1980 had a bachelor's degree or higher, and one out of five had a bachelor's degree among those entering before 1980, as compared with one out of five adults overall, whether foreign-born or native, who had a bachelor's degree or higher in 1990.

- About two-thirds of naturalized citizens had a high school diploma or more education in 1990, compared with slightly more than one-half of noncitizens.

- Nearly 90 percent of African-born residents had a high school education or higher, compared with 76 percent of Asian-born and 46 percent of Central American-born residents. The per capita income of African immigrants averaged $20,117 in 1989, compared with $16,661 for Asian immigrants and $9,446 for Central Americans.

- About 19 percent of families with a foreign-born household member (householder) had three or more workers in the family in 1990, compared with 13 percent among native-born families.

- Although the foreign-born had a higher per capita income than the native-born ($15,033 versus $14,367) in 1989, their median *family* income was almost $4,000 less than that of the native-born ($31,785 versus $35,508).

- The unemployment rate for foreign-born persons aged 16 and over was 7.8 percent in 1990, compared with 6.2 percent for the native-born. Immigrants who entered since 1980 had an unemployment rate of nearly 10 percent, while those entering before 1980 had a rate of 6.4 percent. The unemployment rate in 1990 for naturalized citizens (5.4 percent) was four percentage points lower than that for noncitizens (9.4 percent).

- About 15 percent of families with a foreign-born householder were living in poverty in 1989, compared with about 10 percent of families with a native-born householder. In 1990, the poverty rate of families with a naturalized householder (8.7 percent) was 12 percentage points lower than that of comparable noncitizens (20.7 percent).

- About eight out of 10 of the foreign-born (five years of age and older) speak a language other than English at home. Nearly nine out of 10 of those who have arrived since 1980 speak a language other than English at home, compared with seven out of 10 of those who arrived before 1980. About seven out of 10 naturalized citizens (five years and older) spoke a language other than English at home in 1990, compared with more than eight out of 10 noncitizens.

* * *

BARBARA VOBEJDA, BIRTHS, IMMIGRATION REVISE CENSUS VIEW OF 21ST CENTURY U.S.

The Washington Post, Dec. 4, 1992, p. A10.

An increase in births among American women coupled with massive immigration will add more people to the nation's population during the 1990s than any time since the baby boom decade of the 1950s, the Census Bureau projected in a report released today.

The new population projections also underscore the nation's rapidly changing ethnic profile: By the middle of the next century, virtually half of the population will be made up of blacks, Hispanics, Asians and American Indians and our terminology of "majority" and "minority" will become meaningless.

The Census Bureau, in revising its projections from those released in the late 1980s, was forced to take into account recent and far-reaching changes in society: Fertility rates are higher among American women than they were in the early '80s, illegal immigration remains high and new legislation will allow more legal immigrants into the country.

Together, these factors led the agency to forecast much higher population growth over the coming decades than previously assumed.

In the late 1980s, the bureau projected that the population would peak around 2038 and decline to about 300 million by 2050. But the revised figures add another 80 million to that figure and assume that population will not peak, but continue to grow into the late 21st century. * * *

The bureau, which for the first time broke out population changes by race and ethnic group, projects that the number of Hispanics will surpass that of blacks in two to three decades. And by the middle of the next century, the number of Hispanics will nearly quadruple to 81 million, or more than a fifth of the population.

Asians, including Pacific Islanders, will remain the fastest growing racial group, increasing from their current number of 9 million to 41 million by 2050. Over the same period, the number of black Americans will nearly double to 62 million, or 16 percent of the population.

And non-Hispanic whites will grow slowly in number but decrease rapidly as a fraction of the population, from three quarters now to just about half in the mid–21st century. * * *

Overall, the American population is expected to grow by about 50 percent from its current level of 255 million. And while some of that increase is driven by higher fertility rates, the overwhelming engine of growth is immigration.

The projections, which in the last decade assumed about 500,000 immigrants into the country each year, now include 880,000 a year.

That change reflects the recognition that the 1986 Immigration and Reform Act [sic] did not reduce undocumented immigration as much as expected. "In fact, there is no evidence of any reduction in the undocumented movement," wrote Jennifer Day, author of the Census Bureau report.

Also, the Immigration Act of 1990 increased by nearly 40 percent the number of immigrants allowed legal entry into the country each year.

Over time, the effects of immigration on population are multiplied by higher birth rates among immigrant groups. At the same time, fertility rates among all American women increased "dramatically" in the late 1980s, the report said, from 1.8 births per woman to almost 2.1 births.

* * *

Further Questions

The 1990 Act, as noted, implemented a significant increase in the total legal immigration permitted to this country—at a time when most other Western countries were seeking ways to reduce their own intake of foreigners. It passed during a somewhat quiet time in the politics of immigration in the United States, but that period did not last long. By the summer of 1993 the political climate had changed markedly, provoked by certain highly visible events such as the grounding of a smuggler's ship in New York harbor, and fed by a national recession that hit hardest in California, which is also the state with the highest population of immigrants, both legal and illegal. Immigration then figured prominently and angrily in many 1994 elections—again most visibly in California. There a ballot initiative known as Proposition 187, which gained 59 percent of the vote, enacted provisions to cut off schooling and all nonemergency services to undocumented aliens. (Implementation was initially blocked by litigation.) *See* Section C, *infra*.

Meantime, bills were introduced in the 103d Congress to undo many of the 1990 Act's provisions regarding legal migration. Some would have imposed a moratorium to limit admissions to no more than about half the current levels for five years (S.1884, H.R.3862). Others would have cut the migration ceilings permanently (to 300,000) (S.1351), or even eliminated nearly all permanent migration except for immediate relatives of U.S. citizens (H.R. 4934). None of these measures passed, but similar bills may pick up additional momentum in the 104th Congress, which convened in 1995 with a strikingly altered membership. Its deliberations may also be influenced by the work of the Commission on Immigration Reform, an 11-member body created by the 1990 Act and now headed by former Congresswoman Barbara Jordan. The Commission's preliminary report, U.S. Immigration Policy: Restoring Credibility (1994), focused primarily on suggested improvements in enforcement of the laws against illegal migration, but its final report, due in 1997, will assess the impact of the 1990 Act more fully and suggest "an immigration policy for the 21st century." 71 Interp.Rel. 1345–50 (1994).

In this new political atmosphere, should the changes made by the 1990 Act be reconsidered? Is the level of legal immigration too high? Should a comprehensive and nonpierceable admission cap be enacted? If so, should it include a comprehensive limit on refugee admissions and grants of asylum? Is the diversity admissions program worthwhile? What arguments support giving 55,000 valued admission spaces to strangers selected randomly, at a time when second preference spouses and minor children must now wait over three years to join a family member here? If you were advising the Commission, what further changes would you urge it to include in its final report? *See also* Accepting the Immigration Challenge: The President's Report on Immigration (1994) (summarizing the Clinton administration's immigration policy and recounting its "progress in reversing the course of past failures and [in] implementing a coherent, comprehensive immigration policy for the future").

2. CONSTITUTIONAL STANDARDS FOR EVALUATING ADMISSION CATEGORIES

The preference categories and the other provisions of the INA governing immigrant admissions inevitably draw a host of fine distinctions among categories of aliens who might wish to immigrate to the United States. Much room is left to dispute the fairness and desirability of such distinctions. Is it fair, for example, to burden citizens of Mexico or the Philippines with inordinately long waiting lists, solely because the country ceiling provisions fail to take account of the lengthy historical ties between the United States and those nations? Is it fair to hold the People's Republic of China, with over a billion people, to the same country ceiling as Belize? Why should marriage disqualify the offspring of permanent resident aliens?

Questions like these are the stuff of wide-ranging debates over legislative reform of the U.S. immigration system. But to what extent are questions like those presented above constitutional questions, subject to the policing of the federal courts? The Supreme Court considered these matters in the following case. The litigation presented a challenge to the definition of "child" in INA § 101(b)(1)(D) as it read before its amendment in 1986. At the time of the decision, the statute recognized only the relationship between illegitimate children and their natural mothers, excluding such relationships with the natural fathers.

FIALLO v. BELL

Supreme Court of the United States, 1977.
430 U.S. 787, 97 S.Ct. 1473, 52 L.Ed.2d 50.

Mr. Justice Powell delivered the opinion of the Court.

This case brings before us a constitutional challenge to §§ 101(b)(1)(D) and 101(b)(2) of the Immigration and Nationality Act of 1952 (Act).

I

The Act grants special preference immigration status to aliens who qualify as the "children" or "parents" of United States citizens or lawful permanent residents. Under § 101(b)(1), a "child" is defined as an unmarried person under 21 years of age who is a legitimate or legitimated child, a stepchild, an adopted child, or an illegitimate child seeking preference by virtue of his relationship with his natural mother. The definition does not extend to an illegitimate child seeking preference by virtue of his relationship with his natural father. Moreover, under § 101(b)(2), a person qualifies as a "parent" for purposes of the Act solely on the basis of the person's relationship with a "child." As a result, the natural father of an illegitimate child who is either a United States citizen or permanent resident alien is not entitled to preferential treatment as a "parent." [a]

The special preference immigration status provided for those who satisfy the statutory "parent-child" relationship depends on whether the immigrant's relative is a United States citizen or permanent resident alien. A United States citizen is allowed the entry of his "parent" or "child" without regard to *either* an applicable numerical quota *or* the labor certification requirement. On the other hand, a United States permanent resident alien is allowed the entry of the "parent" or "child" subject to numerical limitations but without regard to the labor certification requirement.

Appellants are three sets of unwed natural fathers and their illegitimate offspring who sought, either as an alien father or an alien child, a special immigration preference by virtue of a relationship to a citizen or resident alien child or parent. In each instance the applicant was informed that he was ineligible for an immigrant visa unless he qualified for admission under the general numerical limitations and, in the case of the alien parents, received the requisite labor certification.

* * *

At the outset, it is important to underscore the limited scope of judicial inquiry into immigration legislation. This Court has repeatedly emphasized that "over no conceivable subject is the legislative power of Congress more complete than it is over" the admission of aliens. Our cases "have long recognized the power to expel or exclude aliens as a fundamental sovereign attribute exercised by the Government's political departments largely immune from judicial control." *Shaughnessy v. Mezei,* 345 U.S. 206, 210, 73 S.Ct. 625, 628, 97 L.Ed. 956 (1953). Our recent decisions have not departed from this long-established rule. Just last Term, for example, the Court had occasion to note that "the power over aliens is of a political character and therefore subject only to narrow judicial review." *Hampton v. Mow Sun Wong,* 426 U.S. 88, 101 n. 21, 96 S.Ct. 1895, 1904–1905, 48 L.Ed.2d 495 (1976); accord, *Mathews v. Diaz,* 426 U.S. 67, 81–82, 96 S.Ct. 1883, 1892, 48 L.Ed.2d 478 (1976). And we observed recently that in the exercise of its broad power over immigration and naturalization, "Congress regularly makes rules that would be unacceptable if applied to citizens." *Id.,* at 80, 96 S.Ct., at 1891.

Appellants apparently do not challenge the need for special judicial

---

a. Before the 1976 amendments to the INA, most Western Hemisphere immigration was subject to an annual ceiling of 120,000, but the preference system did not apply. Aliens who were not excludable simply queued up for available numbers. All were subject to the labor certification requirement, however, unless it was waived because of specified family relationships. The Court treats the *Fiallo* case under pre–1976 law, but you should keep in mind that parents of permanent resident aliens—unlike parents of American citizens—no longer receive any special immigration benefits.—eds.

deference to congressional policy choices in the immigration context,[5] but instead suggest that a "unique coalescing of factors" makes the instant case sufficiently unlike prior immigration cases to warrant more searching judicial scrutiny.

Appellants first observe that since the statutory provisions were designed to reunite families wherever possible, the purpose of the statute was to afford rights not to aliens but to United States citizens and legal permanent residents. Appellants then rely on our border-search decisions in *Almeida-Sanchez v. United States,* 413 U.S. 266, 93 S.Ct. 2535, 37 L.Ed.2d 596 (1973), and *United States v. Brignoni–Ponce,* 422 U.S. 873, 95 S.Ct. 2574, 45 L.Ed.2d 607 (1975), for the proposition that the courts must scrutinize congressional legislation in the immigration area to protect against violations of the rights of citizens. At issue in the border-search cases, however, was the nature of the protections mandated by the Fourth Amendment with respect to Government procedures designed to stem the illegal entry of aliens. Nothing in the opinions in those cases suggests that Congress has anything but exceptionally broad power to determine which classes of aliens may lawfully enter the country.

Appellants suggest a second distinguishing factor. They argue that none of the prior immigration cases of this Court involved "double-barreled" discrimination based on sex and illegitimacy, infringed upon the due process rights of citizens and legal permanent residents, or implicated "the fundamental constitutional interests of United States citizens and permanent residents in a familial relationship." But this Court has resolved similar challenges to immigration legislation based on other constitutional rights of citizens, and has rejected the suggestion that more searching judicial scrutiny is required. In *Kleindienst v. Mandel* [408 U.S. 753 (1972), considered below, pp. 345–352], for example, United States citizens challenged the power of the Attorney General to deny a visa to an alien who, as a proponent of "the economic, international, and governmental doctrines of World communism", was ineligible to receive a visa under INA § 212(a)(28)(D) absent a waiver by the Attorney General. The citizen-appellees in that case conceded that Congress could prohibit entry of all aliens falling into the class defined by [that section]. They contended, however, that the Attorney General's statutory discretion to approve a waiver was limited by the Constitution and that their First Amendment rights were abridged by the denial of Mandel's request for a visa. The Court held that "when the Executive exercises this [delegated] power negatively on the basis of a facially legitimate and bona fide reason, the courts will neither look behind the exercise of that discretion, nor test it by balancing its justification against the First Amendment interests of those who seek personal communication with the applicant." 408 U.S., at 770, 92 S.Ct., at 2585. We can see no reason to review the broad congressional

---

5. The appellees argue that the challenged sections of the Act, embodying as they do "a substantive policy regulating the admission of aliens into the United States, [are] not an appropriate subject for judicial review." Our cases reflect acceptance of a limited judicial responsibility under the Constitution even with respect to the power of Congress to regulate the admission and exclusion of aliens, and there is no occasion to consider in this case whether there may be actions of the Congress with respect to aliens that are so essentially political in character as to be nonjusticiable.

policy choice at issue here under a more exacting standard than was applied in *Kleindienst v. Mandel,* a First Amendment case.[6]

Finally, appellants characterize our prior immigration cases as involving foreign policy matters and congressional choices to exclude or expel groups of aliens that were "specifically and clearly perceived to pose a grave threat to the national security," * * * "or to the general welfare of this country." * * * We find no indication in our prior cases that the scope of judicial review is a function of the nature of the policy choice at issue. To the contrary, "[s]ince decisions in these matters may implicate our relations with foreign powers, and since a wide variety of classifications must be defined in the light of changing political and economic circumstances, such decisions are frequently of a character more appropriate to either the Legislature or the Executive than to the Judiciary," and "[t]he reasons that preclude judicial review of political questions also dictate a narrow standard of review of decisions made by the Congress or the President in the area of immigration and naturalization." *Mathews v. Diaz,* 426 U.S., at 81–82, 96 S.Ct., at 1892.

* * *

III

As originally enacted in 1952, § 101(b)(1) of the Act defined a "child" as an unmarried legitimate or legitimated child or stepchild under 21 years of age. The Board of Immigration Appeals and the Attorney General

---

6. The thoughtful dissenting opinion of our Brother Marshall would be persuasive if its basic premise were accepted. The dissent is grounded on the assumption that the relevant portions of the Act grant a "fundamental right" to American citizens, a right "given only to the citizen" and not to the putative immigrant. The assumption is facially plausible in that the families of putative immigrants certainly have an interest in their admission. But the fallacy of the assumption is rooted deeply in fundamental principles of sovereignty.

We are dealing here with an exercise of the Nation's sovereign power to admit or exclude foreigners in accordance with perceived national interests. Although few, if any, countries have been as generous as the United States in extending the privilege to immigrate, or in providing sanctuary to the oppressed, limits and classifications as to who shall be admitted are traditional and necessary elements of legislation in this area. It is true that the legislative history of the provision at issue here establishes that congressional concern was directed at "the problem of keeping families of United States citizens and immigrants united." H.R.Rep. No. 1199, 85th Cong., 1st Sess., 7 (1957), U.S.Code Cong. & Admin.News, 1957, pp. 2016, 2020. See also H.R.Rep. No. 1365, 82d Cong., 2d Sess., 29 (1952), U.S.Code Cong. & Ad-

min.News 1952, pp. 1653, 1680 (statute implements "the underlying intention of our immigration laws regarding the preservation of the family unit"). To accommodate this goal, Congress has accorded a special "preference status" to certain aliens who share relationships with citizens or permanent resident aliens. But there are widely varying relationships and degrees of kinship, and it is appropriate for Congress to consider not only the nature of these relationships but also problems of identification, administration, and the potential for fraud. In the inevitable process of "line drawing," Congress has determined that certain classes of aliens are more likely than others to satisfy national objectives without undue cost, and it has granted preferential status only to those classes.

As Mr. Justice Frankfurter wrote years ago, the formulation of these "[p]olicies pertaining to the entry of aliens ... is entrusted exclusively to Congress". *Galvan v. Press,* 347 U.S., at 531, 74 S.Ct., at 743. This is not to say, as we make clear in n. 5, *supra,* that the Government's power in this area is never subject to judicial review. But our cases do make clear that despite the impact of these classifications on the interests of those already within our borders, congressional determinations such as this one are subject only to limited judicial review.

subsequently concluded that the failure of this definition to refer to illegitimate children rendered ineligible for preferential nonquota status both the illegitimate alien child of a citizen mother, and the alien mother of a citizen born out of wedlock. The Attorney General recommended that the matter be brought to the attention of Congress, and the Act was amended in 1957 to include what is now § 101(b)(1)(D). Congress was specifically concerned with the relationship between a child born out of wedlock and his or her natural mother, and the legislative history of the 1957 amendment reflects an intentional choice not to provide preferential immigration status by virtue of the relationship between an illegitimate child and his or her natural father.

This distinction is just one of many drawn by Congress pursuant to its determination to provide some—but not all—families with relief from various immigration restrictions that would otherwise hinder reunification of the family in this country. In addition to the distinction at issue here, Congress has decided that children, whether legitimate or not, cannot qualify for preferential status if they are married or are over 21 years of age. Legitimated children are ineligible for preferential status unless their legitimation occurred prior to their 18th birthday and at a time when they were in the legal custody of the legitimating parent or parents. Adopted children are not entitled to preferential status unless they were adopted before the age of 14 and have thereafter lived in the custody of their adopting or adopted parents for at least two years.[b] And stepchildren cannot qualify unless they were under 18 at the time of the marriage creating the stepchild relationship.

With respect to each of these legislative policy distinctions, it could be argued that the line should have been drawn at a different point and that the statutory definitions deny preferential status to parents and children who share strong family ties. But it is clear from our cases that these are policy questions entrusted exclusively to the political branches of our Government, and we have no judicial authority to substitute our political judgment for that of the Congress.

Appellants suggest that the distinction drawn in § 101(b)(1)(D) is unconstitutional under any standard of review since it infringes upon the constitutional rights of citizens and legal permanent residents without furthering legitimate governmental interests. Appellants note in this regard that the statute makes it more difficult for illegitimate children and their natural fathers to be reunited in this country than for legitimate or legitimated children and their parents, or for illegitimate children and their natural mothers. And appellants also note that the statute fails to establish a procedure under which illegitimate children and their natural fathers could prove the existence and strength of their family relationship. Those are admittedly the consequences of the congressional decision not to accord preferential status to this particular class of aliens, but the decision nonetheless remains one "solely for the responsibility of the Congress and wholly outside the power of this Court to control." *Harisiades v. Shaugh-*

---

b. Later amendments raised the age limit for adoption to 16 and deleted "thereafter" from the definition, thus recognizing two years' custody whether it occurred before or after formal adoption. See current INA § 101(b)(1)(E).—eds.

nessy, 342 U.S., at 597, 72 S.Ct., at 522 (Frankfurter, J., concurring). Congress obviously has determined that preferential status is not warranted for illegitimate children and their natural fathers, perhaps because of a perceived absence in most cases of close family ties as well as a concern with the serious problems of proof that usually lurk in paternity determinations.[8] In any event, it is not the judicial role in cases of this sort to probe and test the justifications for the legislative decision.[9] *Kleindienst v. Mandel,* 408 U.S., at 770, 92 S.Ct., at 2585.

IV

We hold that §§ 101(b)(1)(D) and 101(b)(2) of the Immigration and Nationality Act of 1952 are not unconstitutional by virtue of the exclusion of the relationship between an illegitimate child and his natural father from the preferences accorded by the Act to the "child" or "parent" of a United States citizen or lawful permanent resident.

Affirmed.

MR. JUSTICE MARSHALL, with whom MR. JUSTICE BRENNAN joins, dissenting.

Until today I thought it clear that when Congress grants benefits to some citizens, but not to others, it is our duty to insure that the decision comports with Fifth Amendment principles of due process and equal protection. Today, however, the Court appears to hold that discrimination among citizens, however invidious and irrational, must be tolerated if it occurs in the context of the immigration laws. Since I cannot agree that Congress has license to deny fundamental rights to citizens according to the most disfavored criteria simply because the Immigration and Nationality Act is involved, I dissent.

* * *

The definitions [in § 101(b)]cover virtually all parent-child relationships except that of biological father-illegitimate child. Thus while all American citizens are entitled to bring in their alien children without regard to either the numerical quota or the labor certification requirement, fathers are denied this privilege with respect to their illegitimate children. Similarly, all citizens are allowed to have their parents enter without regard to the labor certification requirement, and, if the citizen is over 21, also without

---

8. The inherent difficulty of determining the paternity of an illegitimate child is compounded when it depends upon events that may have occurred in foreign countries many years earlier. Congress may well have given substantial weight, in adopting the classification here challenged, to these problems of proof and the potential for fraudulent visa applications that would have resulted from a more generous drawing of the line. Moreover, our cases clearly indicate that legislative distinctions in the immigration area need not be as " 'carefully tuned to alternative considerations,' " * * * as those in the domestic area.

9. Appellants insist that the statutory distinction is based on an overbroad and outdated stereotype concerning the relationship of unwed fathers and their illegitimate children, and that existing administrative procedures, which had been developed to deal with the problems of proving paternity, maternity, and legitimation with respect to statutorily recognized "parents" and "children," could easily handle the problems of proof involved in determining the paternity of an illegitimate child. We simply note that this argument should be addressed to the Congress rather than the courts. Indeed, in that regard it is worth noting that a bill introduced in the 94th Congress would have eliminated the challenged distinction. H.R. 10993, 94th Cong., 1st Sess. (1975).

regard to the quota. Illegitimate children, however, are denied such preferences for their fathers.

The unfortunate consequences of these omissions are graphically illustrated by the case of appellant Cleophus Warner. Mr. Warner is a naturalized citizen of the United States who * * * petitioned the Attorney General for an immigrant visa for his illegitimate son Serge, a citizen of the French West Indies. Despite the fact that Mr. Warner acknowledged his paternity and registered as Serge's father shortly after his birth, has his name on Serge's birth certificate, and has supported and maintained Serge since birth, the special dispensation from the quota and labor certification requirements was denied because Serge was not a "child" under the statute. It matters not that, as the Government concedes, Serge's mother has abandoned Serge to his father and has, by marrying another man, apparently rendered impossible, under French West Indies law, Mr. Warner's ever legitimating Serge. Mr. Warner is simply not Serge's "parent."

* * *

This case, unlike most immigration cases that come before the Court, directly involves the rights of citizens, not aliens. "[C]oncerned with the problem of keeping families of United States citizens and immigrants united", H.R.Rep. No. 1199, 85th Cong., 1st Sess., 7 (1957), U.S.Code Cong. & Admin.News 1957, p. 2020, Congress extended to American citizens the right to choose to be reunited in the United States with their immediate families. The focus was on citizens and their need for relief from the hardships occasioned by the immigration laws. The right to seek such relief was given only to the citizen, not the alien. INA § 204. If the citizen does not petition the Attorney General for the special "immediate relative" status for his parent or child, the alien, despite his relationship, can receive no preference. It is irrelevant that aliens have no constitutional right to immigrate and that Americans have no constitutional right to compel the admission of their families. The essential fact here is that Congress did choose to extend such privileges to American citizens but then denied them to a small class of citizens. When Congress draws such lines among citizens, the Constitution requires that the decision comport with Fifth Amendment principles of equal protection and due process. The simple fact that the discrimination is set in immigration legislation cannot insulate from scrutiny the invidious abridgment of citizens' fundamental interests.

ILLEG. DADS

* * *

Once it is established that this discrimination among citizens cannot escape traditional constitutional scrutiny simply because it occurs in the context of immigration legislation, the result is virtually foreordained. One can hardly imagine a more vulnerable statute.

The class of citizens denied the special privilege of reunification in this country is defined on the basis of two traditionally disfavored classifications—gender and legitimacy. Fathers cannot obtain preferred status for their illegitimate children; mothers can. Conversely, every child except the illegitimate—legitimate, legitimated, step-, adopted—can obtain preferred status for his or her alien father. The Court has little tolerance for either form of discrimination.

* * *

In view of the legislation's denial of this right to these classes, it is clear that, whatever the verbal formula, the Government bears a substantial burden to justify the statute.

* * *

The legislative history, however, gives no indication of why these privileges were absolutely denied illegitimate children and their fathers. The Government suggests that Congress may have believed that "such persons are unlikely to have maintained a close personal relationship with their offspring." If so, Congress' chosen shorthand for "closeness" is obviously overinclusive. No one can dispute that there are legitimate, legitimated, step-, and adoptive parent-child relationships and mother-illegitimate child relationships that are not close and yet are accorded the preferential status. Indeed, the most dramatic illustration of the overinclusiveness is the fact that while Mr. Warner can never be deemed a "parent" of Serge, nevertheless, if he should marry, his wife could qualify as a stepparent, entitled to obtain for Serge the preferential status that Mr. Warner cannot obtain. *Andrade v. Esperdy,* 270 F.Supp. 516 (S.D.N.Y. 1967); *Nation v. Esperdy,* 239 F.Supp. 531 (S.D.N.Y.1965). Similarly, a man who, in an adulterous affair, fathers a child outside his marriage cannot be the "parent" of that child, but his wife may petition as stepparent. *Matter of Stultz,* 15 I & N Dec. 362 (1975).

That the statute is underinclusive is also undisputed. Indeed, the Government could not dispute it in view of the close relationships exhibited in appellants' cases, recognized in our previous cases, and established in numerous studies.

The Government suggests that Congress may have decided to accept the inaccurate classifications of this statute because they considered a case-by-case assessment of closeness and paternity not worth the administrative costs. This attempted justification is plainly inadequate. In *Stanley v. Illinois,* [405 U.S. 645, 92 S.Ct. 1208, 31 L.Ed.2d 551 (1972)], we expressed our low regard for the use of "administrative convenience" as the rationale for interfering with a father's right to care for his illegitimate child.

> "Procedure by presumption is always cheaper and easier than individualized determination. But when, as here, the procedure forecloses the determinative issues of competence and care, when it explicitly disdains present realities in deference to past formalities, it needlessly risks running roughshod over the important interests of both parent and child. It therefore cannot stand." 405 U.S., at 656–657, 92 S.Ct., at 1215.

This Court has been equally intolerant of the rationale when it is used to deny rights to the illegitimate child. While we are sensitive to " 'the lurking problems with respect to proof of paternity,' "we are careful not to allow them to be " 'made into an impenetrable barrier that works to shield otherwise invidious discrimination.' " We require, at a minimum, that the statute [be] " 'carefully tuned to alternative considerations' ", and not exclude all illegitimates simply because some situations involve difficulties of proof.

Given such hostility to the administrative-convenience argument when invidious classifications and fundamental rights are involved, it is apparent that the rationale is inadequate in the present case. As I observed earlier, since Congress gave no indication that administrative costs were its concern we should scrutinize the hypothesis closely. The likelihood of such a rationale is diminished considerably by the comprehensive and elaborate administrative procedures already established and employed by the INS in passing on claims of the existence of a parent-child relationship. All petitions are handled on a case-by-case basis with the petitioner bearing the burden of proof. Moreover, the INS is no stranger to cases requiring proof of paternity. When, for example, a citizen stepmother petitions for the entrance of her husband's illegitimate child, she must necessarily prove that her husband is the child's father. Indeed, it is ironic that if Mr. Warner marries and his wife petitions for Serge, her proof will, in fact, be one step more complex than his would be—not only must she prove his paternity, but she must also prove their marriage. Nevertheless, she would be entitled to an opportunity to prove those facts; he is not.

Nor is a fear of involvement with foreign laws and records a persuasive explanation of the omission. In administering the Act with respect to legitimated children, for example, the critical issue is whether the steps undertaken are adequate under local law to render the child legitimate, and the INS has become expert in such matters. I note, in this connection, that where a child was born in a country in which all children are legitimate, proof of paternity is the critical issue and the proof problems are identical to those involved with an illegitimate child.

Given the existence of these procedures and expertise, it is difficult indeed to give much weight to the hypothesized administrative-convenience rationale. Moreover, as noted previously, this Court will not allow concerns with proof to justify "an impenetrable barrier that works to shield otherwise invidious discrimination." As the facts of this case conclusively demonstrate, Congress has "failed to consider the possibility of a middle ground between the extremes of complete exclusion and case-by-case determination of paternity." Mr. Warner is a classic example of someone who can readily prove both paternity and closeness. Appellees concede this. The fact that he is denied the opportunity demonstrates beyond peradventure that Congress has failed to " 'carefully tun[e] [the statute] to alternative considerations.' " That failure is fatal to the statute.

When Congress grants a fundamental right to all but an invidiously selected class of citizens, and it is abundantly clear that such discrimination would be intolerable in any context but immigration, it is our duty to strike the legislation down. Because the Court condones the invidious discrimination in this case simply because it is embedded in the immigration laws, I must dissent.

Mr. Justice White also dissents, substantially for the reasons stated by Mr. Justice Marshall in his dissenting opinion.

Notes

1. Justice Marshall's dissent seems to suggest that the Court can apply more rigorous constitutional review to the classifications in *Fiallo* without necessarily having to apply such scrutiny in most other immigration cases. "This case," he writes, "unlike most immigration cases that come before the Court, directly involves the rights of citizens." He supports this claim by citing passages in the legislative history which demonstrate that Congress paid particular attention to citizens' interests in family reunification.

But does this factor really distinguish most immigration cases? The vast majority of permanent immigration today, except for refugees, begins with a petition filed with the INS by a U.S. citizen. (For the family-sponsored second preference, the petitioner need not be a citizen. That preference allows a permanent resident alien to petition, but the category of beneficiaries is more limited: spouse or unmarried son or daughter.) Even the employment-based preferences usually begin in this way, with a petition filed by the prospective American employer. Several nonimmigrant classifications follow a similar procedure. Moreover, do you doubt that the legislative history of most immigration provisions will contain speeches by members of Congress emphasizing their solicitude for the interests of *citizens?*

2. After *Fiallo*, could Congress amend the INA to make all but members of the Caucasian race ineligible for immigration? What standard should a court use in considering an equal protection challenge to such a statute? *Cf. Dunn v. INS,* 499 F.2d 856 (9th Cir.1974), *cert. denied,* 419 U.S. 1106, 95 S.Ct. 776, 42 L.Ed.2d 801 (1975) (using the "rational basis" test in denying an equal protection challenge to a provision rendering Mexican nationals ineligible to adjust status from nonimmigrant to immigrant while within the United States; the INA was later amended to remove this preclusion). Before the 1965 INA amendments abolished the national-origins quota system, courts rather easily disposed of constitutional challenges to the lines Congress had drawn. *See, e.g., Hitai v. INS,* 343 F.2d 466 (2d Cir.1965). *Hitai* even presented an aggravated example of purely racial theories as manifested in the INA at that time. Hitai was born in Brazil to naturalized Brazilian citizens. But because his parents had been born Japanese citizens, he came within the small Japanese quota under the INA as then written, rather than being treated like other citizens of Brazil. Even in this setting, the court sustained the constitutionality of the statute.

Against the background of cases like *Hitai,* it is somewhat surprising that the Supreme Court in *Fiallo* goes so far as to state (in footnote 5) that "[o]ur cases reflect acceptance of a limited judicial responsibility" to review Congress's line-drawing, rather than no responsibility at all. Perhaps the Court speaks of a "limited responsibility" precisely to preserve the possibility that it might strike down any modern immigration legislation that established preference categories based explicitly on racial distinctions.

Still, we need to consider the underlying question regarding the judicial role more carefully. It is virtually inconceivable in the 1990s that a statute drawing explicit racial lines that disadvantage nonwhite groups would issue forth from Congress. But arguably analogous provisions are within the realm of possibility in forms that might present knottier problems. Suppose, for example, that Congress responded to a new crisis in the Middle East by providing that no nationals of the following countries could be admitted to the United States: Morocco, Algeria, Libya, Egypt, Jordan, Syria, Saudi Arabia, Kuwait, and Iraq. If you were the judge, how would you analyze a case wherein the plaintiffs allege that the statute violates equal protection principles because it constitutes discrimination against Arabs as a racial group? In one sense of the term, the statute is based on "national origin" discrimination. Should such distinctions in the immigration sphere be considered wholly equivalent to "racial" discrimination and thus subject to "strict scrutiny"? Or is the statute to be upheld if it rests on a "rational basis" or—perhaps even less demanding—a "facially legitimate and bona fide reason"?

If the government claims that foreign policy concerns justify the use of these immigration restrictions, how should a court evaluate the genuineness and strength of such factors? Are courts institutionally capable of handling such review? *See, e.g., Narenji v. Civiletti,* 617 F.2d 745 (D.C.Cir. 1979), *cert. denied,* 446 U.S. 957, 100 S.Ct. 2928, 64 L.Ed.2d 815 (1980) (reversing a district court decision that struck down, on equal protection grounds, an INS regulation imposing special reporting and review requirements solely on Iranian students, adopted in wake of the seizure of U.S. diplomats in Tehran); *Yassini v. Crosland,* 618 F.2d 1356 (9th Cir.1980) (rejecting a due process challenge to a decision to end the deferred departure policy that had previously protected Iranian nationals against forced return, in part because of the decision's linkage to the President's response to the Tehran hostage seizure).

3. Justice Marshall states that if Cleophus Warner were now to marry, his wife could petition to bring in Serge Warner as her stepchild, citing *Andrade v. Esperdy,* 270 F.Supp. 516 (S.D.N.Y.1967). Some judicial decisions have indeed held that the statutory definition of stepchild, INA § 101(b)(1)(B), is to be applied in this literal fashion. But the Board of Immigration Appeals resisted such an interpretation, arguing that the statutory purpose could be fulfilled by granting petitions for stepchildren only where there is evidence of a pre-existing family unit or equivalent ties. In *Matter of Moreira,* 17 I & N Dec. 41, 46–47 (BIA 1979), the Board stated its approach as follows:

> [A] steprelationship will be recognized for immigration purposes only where the stepparent has shown an interest in the stepchild's welfare prior to that child's eighteenth birthday, either by permitting the child to live in the family home and caring for him as a parent, or, if the child did not live with the stepparent, by

demonstrating an active parental interest in the child's support, instruction, and general welfare.

In *Palmer v. Reddy,* 622 F.2d 463 (9th Cir.1980), the court explicitly rejected the *Moreira* standards and directed that the "stepchild" provision be construed literally, *i.e.,* to require only marriage to the natural parent, whether or not there was a showing of "active parental interest." For the Board's agonized response to *Palmer, see Matter of Bonnette,* 17 I & N Dec. 587 (BIA 1980). Which approach is more consistent with the congressional plan? Which better honors Justice Marshall's principle of "closeness"? Which makes more sense to you? The Board eventually decided, reluctantly, to apply the *Palmer* result nationwide. *Matter of McMillan,* 17 I & N Dec. 605 (BIA 1981).

4. In 1986 Congress amended the definition of "child" so that INA § 101(b)(1)(D) now reads:

> an illegitimate child, by, through whom, or on whose behalf a status, privilege, or benefit is sought by virtue of the relationship of the child to its natural mother or to its natural father if the father has or had a bona fide parent-child relationship with the person.

Should this amendment be considered a vindication of the majority's position in *Fiallo:* namely, that changes in arguably objectionable immigration provisions may satisfactorily be left to the political branches?

The subsection of IRCA containing the amendment to § 101(b)(1)(D) was titled "Equal Treatment of Fathers," but this caption is not quite accurate. What does the final clause, beginning with "if the father," mean? Why would Congress have added it? How should the immigration authorities apply it? See 54 Fed.Reg. 36753 (1989) (implementing regulations, amending 8 C.F.R. § 204.2(c)); *Matter of Pineda,* Int.Dec. 3112 (BIA 1989). The implementing regulations refer to sophisticated blood tests that had been developed between 1977 and 1986 allowing for far more reliable objective determinations of paternity. If the *Fiallo* case had arisen after those tests became available, should the court have approached the issue differently? Which institution—courts or Congress, with their different factfinding capabilities—is better positioned to act on the basis of such scientific developments?

5. In 1991 a federal district court found it possible (unconvincingly, in the view of the editors) to distinguish *Fiallo* in order to strike down, under the equal protection clause, certain citizenship provisions that distinguished between legitimate and illegitimate children born to U.S. citizen parents outside the United States. *LeBrun v. Thornburgh,* 777 F.Supp. 1204 (D.N.J.1991).

Constitutional Protection of Aliens After Admission

Chapter One noted how the Supreme Court, in the late nineteenth century, offset its severe rulings in *Fong Yue Ting* and the *Chinese Exclusion Case* with others that protected the rights of Chinese aliens while in the United States—particularly the landmark *Yick Wo* and *Wong Wing* decisions. *See* pp. 18, 37 *supra*. Similarly, in the 1970s, *Fiallo* and *Kleindienst* coincided with other decisions invalidating state legislation that disadvantaged resident aliens.

The fountainhead decision was *Graham v. Richardson*, 403 U.S. 365, 91 S.Ct. 1848, 29 L.Ed.2d 534 (1971). There the plaintiffs, lawful permanent residents, challenged Arizona and Pennsylvania laws that limited access to public assistance programs, one by requiring that recipients be citizens, the other requiring citizenship or more than 15 years' lawful residence. A unanimous court struck down the requirements:

> The appellants argue initially that the States, consistent with the Equal Protection Clause, may favor United States citizens over aliens in the distribution of welfare benefits. It is said that this distinction involves no "invidious discrimination" * * * for the State is not discriminating with respect to race or nationality.

> * * *

> Under traditional equal protection principles, a State retains broad discretion to classify as long as its classification has a reasonable basis. * * * But the Court's decisions have established that classifications based on alienage, like those based on nationality or race, are inherently suspect and subject to close judicial scrutiny. Aliens as a class are a prime example of a "discrete and insular" minority (see *United States v. Carolene Products Co.*, 304 U.S. 144, 152—153, n. 4, 58 S.Ct. 778, 783—784, 82 L.Ed. 1234 (1938)) for whom such heightened judicial solicitude is appropriate. Accordingly, it was said in *Takahashi* [*v. Fish & Game Comm'n*, 334 U.S. 410, 420,] that "the power of a state to apply its laws exclusively to its alien inhabitants as a class is confined within narrow limits."

Id. at 370–72, 91 S.Ct. at 1851–52. The States' justifications for their laws could not meet this heightened scrutiny:

> We agree with the [court below] that the "justification of limiting expenses is particularly inappropriate and unreasonable when the discriminated class consists of aliens. Aliens like citizens pay taxes and may be called into the armed forces. Unlike the short-term residents in *Shapiro* [*v. Thompson*, 394 U.S. 618 (1969), which struck down one-year state residency requirements for welfare benefits, in a suit filed by citizens who had recently moved from another part of the U.S.,] aliens may live within a state for many years, work in the state and contribute to the economic growth of the state." There can be no "special public interest" in tax revenues to which aliens have contributed on an equal basis with the residents of the State.

> Accordingly, we hold that a state statute that denies welfare benefits to resident aliens and one that denies them to aliens who have not resided in the United States for a specified number of years violate the Equal Protection Clause.

Id. at 376, 91 S.Ct. at 1854. The Court went on to announce as well an alternate ground for this result: pre-emption of such restrictions by federal laws dealing with admission and with aliens' access to welfare. *Id.* at 376–80, 91 S.Ct. at 1854–56.

Does *Graham* go too far? Are aliens as a class truly discrete? Are they insular? Does the possibility of diplomatic intervention by their home governments undercut the argument that they are politically powerless?

Not long after *Graham*, cases arose asking whether this strong equal protection doctrine also constrains federal action regarding the status and entitlements of resident aliens. The issue reached the Court in *Mathews v. Diaz*, 426 U.S. 67, 96 S.Ct. 1883, 48 L.Ed.2d 478 (1976), involving a challenge to a federal statute restricting aliens' access to Medicare unless they had been lawful permanent residents of the United States for five years. The district court applied strict scrutiny, because of the risk of unjustifiable discrimination in view of aliens' lack of representation in the political process. A unanimous Supreme Court reversed.

There are literally millions of aliens within the jurisdiction of the United States. The Fifth Amendment, as well as the Fourteenth Amendment, protects every one of these persons from deprivation of life, liberty, or property without due process of law. Even one whose presence in this country is unlawful, involuntary, or transitory is entitled to that constitutional protection.

The fact that all persons, aliens and citizens alike, are protected by the Due Process Clause does not lead to the further conclusion that all aliens are entitled to enjoy all the advantages of citizenship or, indeed, to the conclusion that all aliens must be placed in a single homogeneous legal classification. For a host of constitutional and statutory provisions rest on the premise that a legitimate distinction between citizens and aliens may justify attributes and benefits for one class not accorded to the other; and the class of aliens is itself a heterogeneous multitude of persons with a wide-ranging variety of ties to this country.

In the exercise of its broad power over naturalization and immigration, Congress regularly makes rules that would be unacceptable if applied to citizens. The exclusion of aliens and the reservation of the power to deport have no permissible counterpart in the Federal Government's power to regulate the conduct of its own citizenry. The fact that an Act of Congress treats aliens differently from citizens does not in itself imply that such disparate treatment is "invidious."

In particular, the fact that Congress has provided some welfare benefits for citizens does not require it to provide like benefits for *all aliens*. Neither the overnight visitor, the unfriendly agent of a hostile foreign power, the resident diplomat, nor the illegal entrant, can advance even a colorable constitutional claim to a share in the bounty that a conscientious sovereign makes available to its own citizens and *some* of its guests. The decision to share that bounty with our guests may take into account the character of the relationship between the alien and this country: Congress may decide that as the alien's tie grows stronger, so does the strength of his claim to an equal share of that munificence.

* * *

Since it is obvious that Congress has no constitutional duty to provide *all aliens* with the welfare benefits provided to citizens, * * * *some* durational requirement would certainly be appropriate. In short, it is unquestionably reasonable for Congress to make an alien's eligibility depend on both the character and the duration of his residence. Since neither requirement is wholly irrational, this case essentially involves nothing more than a claim that it would have been more reasonable for Congress to select somewhat different requirements of the same kind.

Id. at 77–83, 96 S.Ct. at 1890. The *Diaz* Court distinguished the *Graham* line of cases applying strict scrutiny to state statutes disadvantaging aliens (*id.* at 85):

[A] division by a State of the category of persons who are not citizens of that State into subcategories of United States citizens and aliens has no apparent justification, whereas, a comparable classification by the Federal Government is a routine and normally legitimate part of its business. Furthermore, whereas the Constitution inhibits every State's power to restrict travel across its own borders, Congress is explicitly empowered to exercise that type of control over travel across the borders of the United States.

Despite *Diaz*, the Court continued to use the *Graham* doctrine to strike down numerous state statutes, for example, those requiring citizenship of all state civil servants, *Sugarman v. Dougall*, 413 U.S. 634, 93 S.Ct. 2842, 37 L.Ed.2d 853 (1973), limiting bar admission to citizens, *In re Griffiths*, 413 U.S. 717, 93 S.Ct. 2851, 37 L.Ed.2d 910 (1973), and denying certain state-funded scholarships to aliens, *Nyquist v. Mauclet*, 432 U.S. 1, 97 S.Ct. 2120, 53 L.Ed.2d 63 (1977). *See also Plyler v. Doe*, 457 U.S. 202, 102 S.Ct. 2392, 72 L.Ed.2d 786 (1982) (Texas law limiting access of undocumented aliens to public schools violates equal protection), considered at length at p. 325 *infra*. Eventually the Court began to carve out an area, however, where states would be allowed to impose citizenship requirements, for example, in hiring state troopers, *Foley v. Connelie*, 435 U.S. 291, 98 S.Ct. 1067, 55 L.Ed.2d 287 (1978), or public school teachers, *Ambach v. Norwick*, 441 U.S. 68, 99 S.Ct. 1589, 60 L.Ed.2d 49 (1979). A divided court explained the distinctions in *Cabell v. Chavez–Salido*, 454 U.S. 432, 438–40, 102 S.Ct. 735, 739–40, 70 L.Ed.2d 677 (1982):

Since *Graham*, the Court has confronted claims distinguishing between the economic and sovereign functions of government. This distinction has been supported by the argument that although citizenship is not a relevant ground for the distribution of economic benefits, it is a relevant ground for determining membership in the political community. "We recognize a State's interest in establishing its own form of government, and in limiting participation in that government to those who are within 'the basic conception of a political community.' " *Sugarman*. While not retreating from the position that restrictions on lawfully resident aliens that primarily affect economic interests are subject to heightened judicial scrutiny, we have concluded that strict scrutiny is out of place when the restriction primarily serves a political function * * *. We have thus "not abandoned the general principle that some state functions are so bound up with the operation of the State as a governmental entity as to permit the exclusion from those functions of all persons who have not become part of the process of self-government." *Ambach*. And in those areas the State's exclusion of aliens need not "clear the high hurdle of 'strict scrutiny,' because [that] would 'obliterate all the distinctions between citizens and aliens, and thus depreciate the historic value of citizenship.' " *Foley*.

The exclusion of aliens from basic governmental processes is not a deficiency in the democratic system but a necessary consequence of the community's process of political self-definition. Self-government, whether direct or through representatives, begins by defining the scope of the community of the governed and thus of the governors as well: Aliens are by definition those outside of this community. Judicial incursions in this area may interfere with those aspects of democratic self-government that are most essential to it. This distinction between the economic and political functions of government has, therefore, replaced the old public/private distinction.

Has *Cabell* adequately explained the distinctions? Is the economic vs. political typology undercut by recognizing, as the opinion seems not to, that resident aliens are of course clearly included in the community of the governed? Can you construct a better rationale that would allow the states to exclude aliens from voting and holding high public office, yet retain a strong shield against oppressive state statutes?

Consider the following views of Michael Walzer, from his noted book *Spheres of Justice* (considered in Chapter One), at 60–61, expressed in a passage discussing the morality of guest-worker programs:

[T]he principle of political justice is this: that the processes of self-determination through which a democratic state shapes its internal life, must be open, and equally open, to all those men and women who live within its territory, work in the local economy, and are subject to local law. Hence second admissions (naturalization) depend on first admissions (immigration) and are subject only to certain constraints of time and qualification, never to the ultimate constraint of closure. When second admissions are closed, the political community collapses into a world of members and strangers, with no political boundaries between the two, where the strangers are the subjects of the members. Among themselves, perhaps, the members are equal; but it is not their equality but their tyranny that determines the character of the state. * * * No democratic state can tolerate the establishment of a fixed status between citizen and foreigner (though there can be stages in the transition from one of these political identities to the other). * * * Democratic citizens, then, have a choice: if they want to bring in new workers, they must be prepared to enlarge their own membership; if they are unwilling to accept new members, they must find ways within the limits of the domestic labor market to get socially necessary work done.

Naturalization is available to lawful permanent residents in the United States after five years of residence (three years for spouses of U.S. citizens). Do Walzer's views support or undercut *Graham? Cabell? See also* Bosniak, *Membership, Equality, and the Difference that Alienage Makes,* 69 N.Y.U.L.Rev. ___ (1994).

3. FAMILY REUNIFICATION CATEGORIES

The dominant feature of current arrangements for permanent immigration to the United States is family reunification. Immediate relatives of U.S. citizens, as we have seen, can immigrate without numerical limitation, and well over half of the numerically limited immigration spaces are reserved for family members who qualify under the family-sponsored preferences of INA § 203(a). The materials that follow explore some of the technical issues that can arise in implementing these provisions, and they also explore the extent of the authority of the administrative agencies to define "family" for immigration purposes, in the course of implementing the general definitions that Congress has supplied. Finally, they consider the backlogs that have developed in the family categories, which can seriously hinder the reunification even of spouses and minor children.

a. *Offspring*

In developing an operative understanding of the statutory definition of "child," the agencies must apply the subsections of INA § 101(b)(1) to the legal systems and cultural practices prevalent in every country in the world—a staggering variety. The next case reflects the competing policy judgments that affect that process.

DE LOS SANTOS v. INS

United States Court of Appeals, Second Circuit, 1982.
690 F.2d 56.

KEARSE, CIRCUIT JUDGE:

Plaintiff Domingo Antonio de los Santos ("Domingo"), a citizen of the Dominican Republic and a lawful permanent resident of the United States, appeals from a final judgment of the United States District Court for the Southern District of New York, Robert J. Ward, *Judge,* dismissing his complaint seeking reversal of a ruling by defendant Immigration and Naturalization Service ("INS") that denied preferential immigration status for Enmanuel de los Santos ("Enmanuel") as Domingo's son under §§ 101(b)(1)(C) and 203(a)(2) of the Immigration and Nationality Act

("Act"). Section 203(a)(2) grants preferential status to, *inter alios,* the legitimate and legitimated children of lawful permanent residents of the United States. Enmanuel, a citizen and resident of the Dominican Republic, was born in 1957 out of wedlock. On the basis of undisputed facts, the district court concluded that Enmanuel had not been legitimated within the meaning of § 101(b)(1)(C) of the Act and granted summary judgment dismissing Domingo's complaint. We affirm * * *.

BACKGROUND

Under the complex statutory scheme governing the admission of aliens seeking to immigrate to the United States, one of the groups given immigration priority is composed of "the spouses, unmarried sons or unmarried daughters of an alien lawfully admitted for permanent residence." INA § 203(a)(2).[a] Although the Act contains no definition of "son" or "daughter," these terms are construed to mean that the prospective immigrant must be the "child" of the permanent resident alien. *See, e.g., Lau v. Kiley,* 563 F.2d 543, 545 (2d Cir.1977). The statutory definition of "child" includes certain illegitimate offspring. Section 101(b)(1)(C) of the Act provides that an individual born out of wedlock is a "child" if he or she has been

> legitimated under the law of the child's residence or domicile, or under the law of the father's residence or domicile, whether in or outside the United States, if such legitimation takes place before the child reaches the age of eighteen years and the child is in the legal custody of the legitimating parent or parents at the time of such legitimation.

INS *[sic]* has interpreted the word "legitimated" to refer to a child born out of wedlock who has been accorded legal rights that are identical to those enjoyed by a child born in wedlock. *See, e.g., Matter of Reyes,* Interim Decision No. 2822 (BIA 1980); *Matter of Clahar,* Interim Decision No. 2643, 16 I & N 484 (BIA 1978); *Matter of Remy,* Interim Decision No. 2160, 14 I & N 183 (BIA 1972).

The law of the Dominican Republic provides two means by which the illegitimate status of a child born out of wedlock may be altered. First, in a process called "legitimate filiation," the child may be legitimated by the subsequent marriage of his parents if they have acknowledged the child prior to or in the act of their marriage:

> Children born out of wedlock who are not the offspring of incestuous or adulterous unions, may be legitimated by the subsequent marriage of their parents in the cases where they have legally acknowledged them prior to or in the act of their marriage.

Dominican Civil Code [DCC] art. 331. DCC art. 333 provides that children legitimated in this fashion "shall enjoy the same rights and benefits of legitimate children." Second, an illegitimate child may be "naturally filiated":

---

a. The exact language of INA § 203(a)(2) was changed by the 1990 Act, but the provision still covers the same basic class of family members, and the issues discussed in this case are not affected by the change.—eds.

With respect to the mother a natural filiation is established by the sole fact of birth.

With respect to the father, it is established by acknowledgment or by judicial decision.

Law 985 of Aug. 1, 1945, art. 2. However, Law 985 art. 1 provides as follows:

Natural filiation established pursuant to the provisions of the law produces the same effects as legitimate filiation *with the exception of the distinction made in matters concerning successions.*

(Emphasis added.) The exception referred to provides that in the event the parent also has a legitimate child or children and dies intestate, the naturally filiated child will inherit only one half the share attributable to a legitimate child. Law 985 art. 10.

In the present case, Domingo and Enmanuel's mother have never been married to each other, and Domingo does not contend that Enmanuel has been legitimated under DCC art. 331. Rather, he asserts that he "acknowledged" Enmanuel eight days after Enmanuel was born, thereby naturally filiating Enmanuel under Law 985 art. 1, and that Enmanuel was thus legitimated under Dominican law for purposes of the United States immigration laws.

INS rejected Domingo's petition, concluding, as it had previously in *Matter of Reyes, supra,* that natural filiation under Dominican law does not establish rights identical to those enjoyed by legitimate children, and hence a "naturally filiated" Dominican child cannot be deemed "legitimated" within the meaning of § 101(b)(1)(C) of the Act. Domingo challenges here, as he did in the district court, INS's interpretation of legitimation as unreasonable and unduly narrow.

DISCUSSION

* * *

First, there is no serious question of Dominican law that is unresolved in any material respect. The district court implicitly construed Dominican law as according to children naturally filiated under Law 985 rights that are less extensive than those of legitimate children and children legitimated under DCC art. 331. This determination, which we review as a question of law, Fed.R.Civ.P. 44.1, was eminently correct. Domingo recognizes that under Dominican law naturally filiated children do not enjoy inheritance rights as extensive as those of legitimate children. The only serious question he poses is whether the naturally filiated child's lesser right of inheritance is a permissible basis for INS's refusal to deem such a child legitimated within the meaning of the immigration laws.

As to the matter of the correct interpretation of § 101(b)(1)(C), while this too is a question of law subject to full review by the appellate court, in general we must give deference to the construction accorded to a statute by the agency charged with its administration. Thus, if INS's interpretation is reasonable, in that it is consistent with the statutory language, legislative history, and purpose of the statute, we will not invalidate it.

We agree with the district court that INS's interpretation of "legitimated" as requiring the acquisition of rights coextensive with those of a legitimate child is consistent with the language of the Act. The plain meaning of the word is discussed in greater detail in the district court's opinion, and need not be explored further here.[b] The district court also reviewed at length the legislative history of the Act and of related statutes, to determine whether INS's interpretation is consistent with Congress's intent. Although the legislative history is not dispositive, we see in it no indication that Congress intended the word "legitimated" to denote the acquisition of fewer rights than those enjoyed by a legitimate son or daughter. Accordingly, the history, to the extent that it sheds light on this question, supports the view that INS's interpretation is not inconsistent with Congress's intent.

The closest question is whether INS's interpretation, as applied in the present case, is consistent with the purpose of the statutory scheme. Immigration preference categories were created as a means of allocating visas when the demand for them exceeds the number lawfully available. In general, insofar as is pertinent here, the Act grants preferential status to close relatives of United States citizens and permanent residents in order to facilitate the reunification of families.

INS contends that since the number of available visas is limited, the goal of family reunification requires that the Act be strictly interpreted in order to minimize the number of successful fraudulent claims. INS's narrow interpretation is thus based on the belief that a claimant will be less likely to claim as his child a person with whom he does not have a bona fide parent/child relationship if he must confer full filial rights on that person than if he may successfully assert such a claim while conferring fewer rights. We think this belief farfetched as it is applied to the provisions of Dominican law at issue here. Here the difference between the rights of naturally filiated children and legitimate children is slight: if the parent of a naturally filiated child dies intestate, and if there are legitimate children, the naturally filiated child will inherit only half the share attributable to a legitimate child. It hardly seems likely that a rule based solely on such a small difference—especially one that disappears if the parent dies testate or without legitimate children—would have any efficacy in deterring fraud. *See, e.g., Reyes v. INS,* 478 F.Supp. 63, 66 (E.D.N.Y.1979); *Delgado v. INS,* 473 F.Supp. 1343, 1348 (S.D.N.Y.1979). INS's interpretation of "legitimated," however, is a general one requiring complete identity of rights, not one focusing solely on rights of inheritance.

---

b. The district court stated:

The ordinary meaning of the word at issue here, "legitimated," is easily ascertained. Given that a "legitimate" child is a child born in wedlock, it follows that an illegitimate child has been "legitimated" when it has been placed in the position of a child born in wedlock. See Webster's Third New International Dictionary of the English Language 1291 (unabridged ed. 1963) ("legitimate" means "born in wedlock" when used as an adjective, and means "to put (a bastard) in the position or state of a legitimate child" when used as a verb). Thus, if the Court were to give the word "legitimated" its plain meaning in interpreting Section 101(b)(1)(C), it would agree with the INS that an illegitimate child has been "legitimated" only if the law of the child's domicile has granted him or her all the rights that it grants a legitimate child.

525 F.Supp. at 661–62.—eds.

Further, the rule is designed for worldwide application; it has not been fashioned with reference to particular distinctions drawn by the laws of any one country. In the context of rights such as financial support and use of the family name, and indeed in the context of other differences in rights of inheritance, INS's interpretation may well have the effect of reducing fraud.

It is not the province of the courts to insist that INS's interpretations of the Act result in the perfect immigration scheme, or even that they be the best interpretations possible. Rather INS is given a fair amount of latitude to exercise its judgment as to what interpretations will best effectuate the goals of the Act. * * * Since INS's strict interpretation is consistent with the language and history of the Act and is, as a general matter, reasonably calculated to serve the purposes of the Act, it is entitled to deference, and we will not invalidate it because in the present instance its usefulness may be tenuous.

CONCLUSION

The judgment of the district court is affirmed.

Notes

1. In many countries, legitimation can occur only by the marriage of the natural father and the natural mother. Such a marriage is sometimes impossible—either because one party is unwilling or because of legal impediments—despite genuinely close ties between the father and the child. Having in mind barriers like this, as well as the relatively trivial inheritance differences under the law of the Dominican Republic, an earlier court decision on facts like those in *de los Santos* was highly critical of the Board's rule requiring full equality of rights:

> The rule adopted has no reasonable relation to preventing fraud, and it ignores "the foremost policy underlying the granting of preference visas under our immigration laws, the reunification of families * * * ".

Delgado v. INS, 473 F.Supp. 1343, 1348 (S.D.N.Y.1979), quoting *Lau v. Kiley,* 563 F.2d 543 (2d Cir.1977).

To say that the Board's rule interferes with family reunification is a powerful charge. But is this really an objection to the *Board's* interpretation? Isn't *Delgado* objecting to the underlying *statutory* policy that restricts the recognition of certain close ties which fathers may develop with their natural children, particularly if the plain meaning of the term "legitimated" supports the Board's ruling?

2. Besides relying on plain meaning, the Board, as the principal case shows, also justified its rule by reference to the statutory purpose of deterring fraud. The Second Circuit found this a close question, but ultimately deferred to the Board's judgment that a fixed rule requiring full equality of rights was best suited for worldwide application. If one assumes that Congress has left the agency some discretion, should the Board be so wedded to its bright-line test, or should it consider the likelihood of

fraudulent claims case by case? Case-by-case consideration might involve developing, over time, a list of countries where the differences in rights between legitimate children and illegitimate children formally acknowledged are so trivial as not to give rise to a significant risk of fraud. Alternatively, case-by-case determination might be done on an individual basis rather than country-by-country. For example, the Board (or the initial adjudicating officer) might simply require proof of some procedure formally acknowledging paternity, as well as other evidence demonstrating genuine family relationships between the father and child, sufficient to show that the acknowledgement was not meant for the sole (and hence fraudulent) purpose of conferring immigration benefits.

If we adopt this latter stance, we come near to the position Justice Marshall seemed to advocate in *Fiallo,* requiring the recognition of a relation for immigration purposes whenever the petitioner "can readily prove both paternity and closeness." But if we have come this far, why should we stop there? Why should *both* factors be required? Why shouldn't closeness alone be sufficient? After all, Justice Marshall is elsewhere quite critical of "Congress' chosen shorthand for 'closeness,'" finding the definitions used both overinclusive and underinclusive. Why shouldn't aunts, uncles, or cousins be given family reunification immigration benefits if the petitioner shows that in his ethnic group—or perhaps only in his particular family—such ties are as close as the average ties among members of the usual suburban American nuclear family? See SCIRP, Staff Report, at 371 (quoting the testimony of Father Joseph A. Cogo, urging immigration benefits for grandparents and "fireside relatives like an aunt who's not married * * * and living with the family. * * * [T]hey should not be subjected to a definition by other ethnic groups just because other ethnic groups have different definitions in their tradition.")

Indeed, why require biological relationships at all? Why not adopt a system allowing family reunification-type immigration benefits based on closeness alone—that is, based on proof of functional family ties, whatever the biological relationship? *See Kahn v. INS*, 36 F.3d 1412 (9th Cir.1994) (remanding BIA denial of discretionary relief for failure to consider "warm and continuing relationship" of unmarried couple living together as equivalent to "family ties"); *Antoine-Dorcelli v. INS,* 703 F.2d 19 (1st Cir.1983) (requiring the BIA to consider "family" ties between the Haitian housekeeper and an American family she had lived with for over 30 years, for purposes of determining whether deportation would cause "extreme hardship" within the meaning of § 244);[16] *cf. Adams v. Howerton,* 673 F.2d

---

16. In 1986 the Supreme Court disapproved an expansive approach to functional family relationships like that employed in *Antoine–Dorcelli.* In *INS v. Hector,* 479 U.S. 85, 107 S.Ct. 379, 93 L.Ed.2d 326 (1986) (per curiam), the Court held that the term "child" should be construed with literal exactness for purposes of relief under § 244, because "Congress has specifically identified the relatives whose hardship is to be considered, and then set forth unusually detailed and unyielding provisions defining each class of included relatives." In a strongly worded dissent from *Kahn v. INS, supra,* 36 F.3d at 1422–23, Judge Kozinski criticized the majority for imposing "monumental problems of administration" on INS. And he suggested that the "majority's touchy-feely theory of human relations" will require inquiry "into the hearts and minds of couples to see if they have the requisite 'close and deeply emotional' relationship," perhaps "even if the parties happen to be married."

1036 (9th Cir.1982), *cert. denied*, 458 U.S. 1111, 102 S.Ct. 3494, 73 L.Ed.2d 1373 (1982) (refusing to extend immigration benefits based on a homosexual marriage, even though the court assumed that the marriage was valid under state law). *See generally* R. Plender, International Migration Law 374–385 (rev. 2d ed. 1988) (describing other countries' family reunification provisions, some of which bestow benefits on "unmarried partners," persons in a "serious relationship," or "closely connected through relatives or in a similar manner").

3. Once we work our way through to these possible alternative schemes, however, we should pause to take stock of the administrative implications. Under the rule approved in *de los Santos,* immigration examiners considering petitions for allegedly legitimated children usually need only consult BIA decisions to see whether the particular procedure (such as natural filiation) in the country at issue has been held to constitute "legitimation" under the INA. Even if the petitioner is from a country whose legitimation laws have not been reviewed yet by the BIA, the issue remains fairly clearcut for the immigration examiner. Does the procedure result in *full* equality of rights? The inquiry is directed toward the legal system of the country, not into the details of family relationships. Thus the examiner has no substantial discretion, and is not required to make judgment calls about whether seemingly minor differences are so significant in the actual practice of the foreign country that they should result in disqualification from immigration benefits.

At the opposite extreme falls the hypothetical proposal allowing preferential treatment whenever the petitioner shows family-like "closeness." How would such a scheme be implemented? What kinds of evidence would be relevant in proving closeness? Do we want INS agents or consular officers asking about the intimate details of life around the family fireside in order to decide whether the relationship to an aunt is close enough to merit immigration benefits? Remember that immigration examiners are relatively low-level bureaucrats. Few have had significant training in psychology or sociology. Vast changes in recruitment patterns, compensation, educational requirements, and regular duties would be needed to create a system wherein examiners had such a background. These staffing realities may help account for decisions by the INS and the BIA to use bright-line tests (despite occasional outcomes that may seem arbitrary), rather than employ vague criteria expanding the inquiry into other areas. Case-by-case judgments of "closeness" or other elusive concepts (like the likelihood of fraud in the use of a particular legitimation procedure) would give rise to a related concern. They are much harder for supervisors— ultimately running all the way up to the Attorney General—to monitor, in order to assure that like cases are treated alike, and even to detect whether an officer has issued a decision in a given case because of corruption or other improper favoritism.

Of course, the question remains whether these benefits to sound administration from the use of bright-line tests are outweighed by the inevitability of arbitrary outcomes and their impact in the particular setting. Judging that balance can be a difficult task, and administrators may have incentives for erring in favor of fixed rules. But judges may similarly be too quick to dismiss as "administrative convenience" certain concerns that are far more complex than simply adding to the annual agency appropriation. A most useful discussion of these issues appears in Diver, *The Optimal Precision of Administrative Rules*, 93 Yale L.J. 65 (1983). *See also Fook Hong Mak v. INS*, 435 F.2d 728, 730 (2d Cir.1970) (Friendly, J.); *American Hospital Ass'n v. NLRB*, 899 F.2d 651, 660 (7th Cir.1990) (Posner, J.) ("The decision how much discretion to eliminate from the decisional process is itself a discretionary judgment, entitled to broad judicial deference.").

4. The Supreme Court's 1984 decision in *Chevron, U.S.A., Inc. v. Natural Resources Defense Council*, 467 U.S. 837, 104 S.Ct. 2778, 81 L.Ed.2d 694 (1984), has had a major impact in defining the respective roles of agencies and courts in implementing regulatory statutes. *See generally* Schuck & Elliott, *To the Chevron Station: An Empirical Study of Federal Administrative Law*, 1990 Duke L.J. 984; Schuck & Wang, *Continuity and Change: Patterns of Immigration Litigation in the Courts, 1979–1990*, 45 Stan.L.Rev. 115, 169–72 (1992). The Court stated (467 U.S. at 842–44, 104 S.Ct. at 2781–83):

> When a court reviews an agency's construction of the statute which it administers, it is confronted with two questions. First, always, is the question whether Congress has directly spoken to the precise question at issue. If the intent of Congress is clear, that is the end of the matter; for the court, as well as the agency, must give effect to the unambiguously expressed intent of Congress.[9] If, however, the court determines Congress has not directly addressed the precise question at issue, the court does not simply impose its own construction on the statute, as would be necessary in the absence of an administrative interpretation. Rather, if the statute is silent or ambiguous with respect to the specific issue, the question for the court is whether the agency's answer is based on a permissible construction of the statute.
>
> "The power of an administrative agency to administer a congressionally created ... program necessarily requires the formulation of policy and the making of rules to fill any gap left, implicitly or explicitly, by Congress." Morton v. Ruiz, 415 U.S. 199, 231, 94 S.Ct. 1055, 1072, 39 L.Ed.2d 270 (1974). If Congress has explicitly left a gap for the agency to fill, there is an express delegation of authority to the agency to elucidate a specific provision of the statute by regulation. Such legislative regulations are given controlling weight unless they are arbitrary, capricious, or manifestly contrary to the statute. Sometimes the legislative delegation to an agency on a particular question is implicit rather than explicit. In such a case, a court may not substitute its own

---

9. The judiciary is the final authority on issues of statutory construction and must reject administrative constructions which are contrary to clear congressional intent. * * * If a court, employing traditional tools of stat- utory construction, ascertains that Congress had an intention on the precise question at issue, that intention is the law and must be given effect.

construction of a statutory provision for a reasonable interpretation made by the administrator of an agency.

Such deference may also be defended on additional grounds. First, the agency works with the statute on a daily basis and is likely to have a better understanding of the operational implications of a narrow or broad construction of a statute. Second, the agency may have aided in the drafting of the statute and therefore may have greater insight than the courts into the intent of the language chosen and the purposes of the statutory provision. Finally, deference to agency interpretation may create greater uniformity in application of the statute than would be achieved under different opinions among courts of appeals. What counterarguments against agency deference on matters of statutory interpretation should be considered, particularly in the immigration context? Does the *Chevron* approach give too much authority to the administrators?

Consider whether *de los Santos* and the other cases in this Chapter (and indeed throughout the book) are consistent with the mandate of *Chevron*.

5. The court seems to suggest, in the second paragraph in *de los Santos,* that "son" or "daughter" means the same thing as "child" under the statute. This is not quite accurate. A "child" must be under 21 and unmarried; the statute refers to "son" or "daughter" when Congress wishes to include people enjoying the same basic familial relationship, but who may be over that age or married. The other stipulations of INA § 101(b)(1) do apply, however, in deciding whether or not an individual is a son or daughter.

> While neither of the terms "sons" or "daughters" is defined in the Act, it seems well established that in order to qualify as a "son" or "daughter" for the purposes of obtaining visa preference, one must once have qualified as a "child" under § 101(b)(1) of the Act * * *.

Lau v. Kiley, 563 F.2d 543, 545 (2d Cir.1977). *See also Nazareno v. Attorney General,* 512 F.2d 936 (D.C.Cir.1975) *cert. denied,* 423 U.S. 832, 96 S.Ct. 53, 46 L.Ed.2d 49 (1975) (reviewing the complicated statutory history to decide that the age ceiling on adoptions appearing in INA § 101(b)(1) applies in deciding whether an alien qualifies as a son or daughter; persons adopted at age 32 do not qualify).

6. As is evident, family relationship questions will often turn on foreign law, the law of petitioner's or beneficiary's domicile at the time of birth or other relevant event. This may present unique difficulties:

> Foreign law, and particularly the kind of nonstatutory, custom law with which this Board must often deal, is sometimes hard to ascertain. It is particularly difficult for the alien, who frequently finds that local consulates, or even his embassy, do not have appropriate legal help or may even be unsympathetic to his claims and hence not disposed to be helpful.

Matter of Lee, 16 I & N Dec. 305, 308 (BIA 1977) (Appleman, Member, dissenting).

The BIA has held that foreign law is a question of fact, and that the petitioner has the burden of proving any point of foreign law on which he relies to establish eligibility for an immigration benefit. *Matter of Annang,* 14 I & N Dec. 502 (BIA 1973). *Cf.* Fed.R.Civ.P. 44.1 (allowing for determination of foreign law through any relevant source, including testimony, but treating the determination as a ruling on a question of law); *Crespo v. United States,* 185 Ct.Cl. 127, 399 F.2d 191, 192 (1968) ("Although the law of a foreign jurisdiction may be proved as a fact, it is the function of the court and not that of a jury to determine the state of the foreign law from the proof presented on the issue."). But INS personnel and the Board of Immigration Appeals frequently resort as well to expert advice from the staff of the Library of Congress. *See, e.g., Matter of Lee, supra,* at 305; *id.* at 308 (Appleman, Member, dissenting) (suggesting that the petitioner should have been given an opportunity to comment on the Library of Congress memorandum before the Board relied on it).

7. Application of the family reunification provisions can be complicated not only by the need to interpret foreign law. It may also require difficult determinations about the interaction of state family law and federal immigration law. *See, e.g., Kaliski v. District Director,* 620 F.2d 214 (9th Cir.1980) (beneficiary treated as "legitimated" son under California law from before age 18, even though petitioner, now domiciled in California, and son both lived in Yugoslavia until son was 19); *Burgess v. Meese,* 802 F.2d 338 (9th Cir.1986) (in accord with decree of Washington state court, child held to be "legitimated" based on residence with father in Mexico).

8. The 1986 amendment to INA § 101(b)(1)(D), recognizing most relationships between fathers and illegitimate offspring for immigration purposes, should greatly reduce litigation like that presented in *de los Santos, Delgado, Kaliski, Andrade* and similar cases, because most such fathers will no longer have to try to squeeze their relationships into the statutory definitions of "stepchild" or "legitimated" child. But because there are still some qualifications on that recognition, such litigation will not disappear.

b. *Immigration Based on Marriage*

If an alien lacks family members in this country already in position to file a visa petition, and if he knows no U.S. employers willing to petition for him under the employment-based preferences, marriage to a U.S. citizen or permanent resident may appear as the only available option for securing admission as an immigrant. We will consider here how the law and the administrative agencies have dealt with the resulting tension between the objective of avoiding fraud or abuse and the highly valued objective of family unification.

The opening materials in this part, through *Dabaghian,* treat these matters as they appeared before 1986, when Congress adopted significant statutory changes. These cases provide a useful opening glimpse of the two-fold controversies Congress and the administrative agencies have confronted in trying to combat marriage fraud. First, it is a more complex matter than might be expected to specify conceptually just what constitutes a sham marriage. Second, even if we manage to settle these conceptual disputes, how can we most efficiently provide for effective detection and enforcement, while maintaining respect for human dignity and privacy? After grappling with those questions under earlier case law, we will be in a position to consider closely the solution Congress adopted in 1986, primarily to render enforcement more efficient, the Immigration Marriage Fraud Amendments of 1986 (IMFA), Pub.L. No. 99–639, 100 Stat. 3537.

BARK v. INS

United States Court of Appeals, Ninth Circuit, 1975.
511 F.2d 1200.

HUFSTEDLER, CIRCUIT JUDGE:

Petitioner was denied adjustment of status from student visitor to permanent resident, pursuant to section 245 of the Immigration and Nationality Act ("the Act"), and he seeks review. Respondent has conceded that the denial was based solely on the Immigration Judge's conclusion, affirmed by the Board of Immigration Appeals, that petitioner was ineligible for adjustment of status because the marriage upon which he based his application was a sham.

Petitioner and his wife had been sweethearts for several years while they were living in their native Korea. She immigrated to the United States and became a resident alien. Petitioner came to the United States in August, 1968, initially as a business visitor and then as a student. They renewed their acquaintance and were married in Hawaii in May 1969. Petitioner's wife filed a petition on his behalf to qualify him for status as the spouse of a resident alien pursuant to sections 203(a)(2) and 204 of the Act. Petitioner thereafter filed his own application for adjustment of status under section 245 of the Act.

Petitioner and his wife testified at the hearing on his application that they married for love and not for the purpose of circumventing the immigration laws; they admitted quarreling and separating. Their testimony about the time and extent of their separation was impeached by evidence introduced by the Service. The Immigration Judge discredited their testimony and held that the marriage was a sham, relying primarily (perhaps solely), on the evidence of their separation. In affirming the Immigration Judge's decision, the Board of Immigration Appeals stated: "Investigation revealed that [petitioner] and his wife lived in separate quarters. While both testified that their marriage was 'a good marriage,' their testimony as to how much time they actually spent together was conflicting."

Petitioner's marriage was a sham if the bride and groom did not intend to establish a life together at the time they were married. The concept of establishing a life as marital partners contains no federal dictate about the kind of life that the partners may choose to lead. Any attempt to regulate their life styles, such as prescribing the amount of time they must spend together, or designating the manner in which either partner elects to spend his or her time, in the guise of specifying the requirements of a bona fide marriage would raise serious constitutional questions. (*Cf.* Roe v. Wade (1973) 410 U.S. 113, 93 S.Ct. 705, 35 L.Ed.2d 147; Graham v. Richardson (1971) 403 U.S. 365, 91 S.Ct. 1848, 29 L.Ed.2d 534; Griswold v. Connecticut (1965) 381 U.S. 479, 85 S.Ct. 1678, 14 L.Ed.2d 510.) Aliens cannot be required to have more conventional or more successful marriages than citizens.

Conduct of the parties after marriage is relevant only to the extent that it bears upon their subjective state of mind at the time they were married. (Lutwak v. United States (1953) 344 U.S. 604, 73 S.Ct. 481, 97 L.Ed. 593.) Evidence that the parties separated after their wedding is relevant in ascertaining whether they intended to establish a life together when they exchanged marriage vows. But evidence of separation, standing alone, cannot support a finding that a marriage was not bona fide when it was entered. The inference that the parties never intended a bona fide marriage from proof of separation is arbitrary unless we are reasonably assured that it is more probable than not that couples who separate after marriage never intended to live together. Common experience is directly to the contrary. Couples separate, temporarily and permanently, for all kinds of reasons that have nothing to do with any preconceived intent not to share their lives, such as calls to military service, educational needs, employment opportunities, illness, poverty, and domestic difficulties. Of course, the time and extent of separation, combined with other facts and circumstances, can and have adequately supported the conclusion that a marriage was not bona fide.[1]

The administrative record discloses that the Immigration Judge and Board of the Immigration Appeals did not focus their attention on the key issue: Did the petitioner and his wife intend to establish a life together at the time of their marriage? The inquiry, instead, turned on the duration of their separation, which, as we have pointed out, is relevant to, but not dispositive of the intent issue. Moreover, the determination may have been influenced by the irrelevant fact, cited by respondent to support the Service, that "the wife could and did leave as she pleased when they were together." The bona fides of a marriage do not and cannot rest on either marital partner's choice about his or her mobility after marriage.

We decline to speculate about the conclusion that would have been reached if the Service had confined itself to evidence relevant to the parties' intent at the time of their marriage. The Service will have an opportunity

---

1. *E.g.*, Lutwak v. United States, *supra*, 344 U.S. 604, 73 S.Ct. 481, 97 L.Ed. 593, which involved criminal prosecutions stemming from an elaborate scheme to secure entry into the United States for two brothers and the former wife of one of them under the "War Brides Act." Female veterans were hired to marry the brothers, and the brothers' nephew (also a veteran) married the former wife. The parties agreed beforehand to separate as soon as possible, and none of them ever cohabited.

In United States v. Sacco (9th Cir.1970) 428 F.2d 264 the defendant claimed derivative citizenship based on his mother's marriage to a citizen. His mother's marriage was found a sham because she married solely to legitimate a child. She did not marry to circumvent the immigration laws, but the evidence was clear that she and her husband never intended to live together after marriage.

* * *

on remand to develop the record in accordance with the views herein expressed.

Reversed and remanded.

CALVIN TRILLIN, MAKING ADJUSTMENTS
The New Yorker, May 28, 1984, at 65, 71.

One of the procedures that Beaumont Martin often tells potential clients that they can carry out themselves is filing for a green card on the basis of having married an American citizen. If they are good at English and uncowed by bureaucrats, they might indeed file the papers themselves—although they might stand in line for hours, present documents to the clerk at the counter, and be told, perhaps not terribly politely, that some mistake or omission means that they have to go through the process all over again another day. Also, immigration lawyers can predict a good number of the questions an immigration examiner is likely to ask if he has reason to suspect that the marriage is a sham: Where does she put her shoes at night? What do his parents do for a living? What's his favorite food? Where did you meet her?

A lawyer is not allowed to coach his clients during the interview, but his presence can provide not just a sense of security but a sort of implied character witness. An immigration lawyer's practice depends to some extent on his reputation at Immigration, so it is obviously not in his best interest to become known as someone who shows up in the company of couples he suspects are attached only by the requirements necessary for a green card. Immigration examiners, many of whom began their career as border patrolmen, tend to be suspicious by nature, and most of them have seen their suspicions confirmed any number of times. True love hit Iranian students with a peculiar frequency a few years ago, when a lot of them had visa problems; Nigerian students are also known for being quick down the aisle. Any couple who seem far apart culturally or ethnically or linguistically obviously raise suspicions, even if they are accompanied by a pillar of the immigration bar. When the Turkish waiter Beaumont Martin was representing showed up with his new American wife outside Immigration one Wednesday, she turned out to be a nice-looking, exceedingly dark-skinned black woman. Ed Prud'homme looked the couple over, turned to Martin, and said, in the shorthand that allows old acquaintances to place bets with each other without much elaboration, "Three dollars."

* * *

At [a Houston immigration lawyers'] gathering I attended, Ed Prud'homme found out that he had not in fact won three dollars on the outcome of the Turkish waiter's interview. Beaumont Martin acknowledged, though, that the questioning had been unusually prolonged. The waiter, he reported, had almost destroyed his own case when he seemed to avoid giving a specific answer about the last gift he had received from his wife. Before the waiter was in the room, his wife had answered the same question by saying that she had given him some undershorts; apparently, he was embarrassed to mention such intimate apparel before strangers. "I finally started laughing," Martin said. "So did the examiner. It was so much like 'The Newlywed Game.'"

Sham Marriages and the Ethical Responsibilities of an Attorney

The discovery of fraudulent marriages is a difficult and time-consuming process for the INS, and investigation practices vary from district to district. *See* Leidigh, *Defense of Sham Marriage Deportations*, 8 U.C.–Davis L.Rev. 309, 315–16 (1975). Does an attorney who is representing an alien claiming to be married to a United States citizen have an ethical obligation to determine the *bona fides* of the client's marriage? Does the lawyer have some responsibility to help enforce the immigration laws? Consider the following (anonymous) letter, reprinted in 59 Interp.Rel. 144–45 (1982).

The firm at which I now work as an associate handles on the average about 100 spousal I–130's per year. Like any sensible practitioners, we do not induce clients to commit fraud; nor do we receive confessions from clients on the subject. Thus, in any given case, we never "know" that a sham marriage is involved. Yet, we are all quite certain that between 90 and 95% of these cases involve sham marriages. The circumstances make it completely obvious.

It is our experience that INS will never detect a sham marriage unless one of the parties to the conspiracy actually tells them outright that the marriage was contracted for immigration purposes (as, for revenge) or unless the client handles his arrangements in a completely idiotic fashion (*e.g.*, he fails to learn the name of his "wife," he gets an accomplice who is twice his age and can't speak his language, etc.). The record is fairly clear: in about 3 years, roughly 250 sham marriages have gone through this office. INS has detected nothing despite the fact that these clients have not taken extraordinary precautions to avoid detection and despite the fact that many secure dissolutions almost immediately after the Green Card issues.

So beneficial is the status of "spouse of a U.S. citizen," so simple is the procedure, so high the success rate, that it becomes more and more difficult to dissuade clients from taking this route to a Green Card. Recently, there is even a trend in the direction of respectable clients, who might well obtain labor certificates, going the marriage route simply for convenience and speed. Where an alien has little chance of qualifying for Permanent Residence in any other way, it is no easy matter to persuade them that a method that works well over 99% of the time should not be resorted to.[a]

---

a. This letter surely exaggerates the prevalence of marriage fraud in immigration proceedings. For example, preliminary results of an INS pilot study found reasons to suspect fraud in 30% of the spouse petitions intensively reviewed—far below 90%, but

What would you do if you were in the position of the attorney who wrote the letter? The immigration regulations allow the Department of Justice to suspend or disbar any attorney "[w]ho willfully misinforms or deceives an officer or employee of the Department of Justice concerning any material and relevant fact in connection with a case." 8 C.F.R. § 292.3(3). Would an attorney have an affirmative duty to disclose information suggesting a sham marriage? Or would disclosure jeopardize the lawyer-client relationship?

Rule 1.6 of the Model Rules of Professional Conduct (as adopted by the American Bar Association in 1983) states: "A lawyer shall not reveal information relating to representation of a client unless the client consents after consultation"—with certain narrow exceptions. The Comment to this rule makes clear that it "applies not merely to matters communicated in confidence by the client but also to all information relating to the representation, whatever its source." An earlier draft of the Model Rules permitted a lawyer to reveal information "to rectify the consequences of a client's criminal or fraudulent act in the commission of which the lawyer's services had been used." Model Rules of Professional Conduct, Rule 1.6(b)(3) ("final" draft, 1981). This language was deleted, however, from the version adopted by the ABA in 1983. The 1981 draft of Rule 1.2(d) of the Model Rules prohibited a lawyer from assisting a client "in conduct that the lawyer knows or reasonably should know is criminal or fraudulent." The final approved version, however, deletes the words "or reasonably should know" from the rule. Model Rules of Professional Conduct, Rule 1.2(d) (1983).

Despite the obvious effort of the ABA in 1983 to strengthen client confidentiality and reduce attorney obligations unilaterally to reveal or rectify questionable practices, some state bars seem to enforce a conception of ethical responsibility more in line with the 1981 draft. The following appeared in the Texas Bar Journal, and is reprinted from 61 Interp.Rel. 442 (1984):

> The District 10 Grievance Committee issued a private reprimand to an attorney of San Antonio on Dec. 22, 1983. The committee found that the attorney failed to undertake an adequate investigation into the marital status of his client before assisting him in an application for temporary status with the Immigration and Naturalization Service. The attorney knew, or should have known, that his client's marital status was questionable. Also, the attorney failed to timely advise the Immigration and Naturalization Service as to false information given to it at the time of the application for temporary status. Shortly thereafter, the attorney knew that false information had been given.

See also United States v. Zalman, 870 F.2d 1047 (6th Cir.1989) (sustaining attorney's conviction for fraud and failing to disclose sham marriages when clients applied for adjustment of status); United States v. Maniego, 710

hardly a statistic to inspire confidence. (That study too proved to be flawed, and INS later pulled back from even the 30 percent figure. See 65 Interp. Rel. 26 (1988), 66 id. 1011 (1989).)—eds.

F.2d 24 (2d Cir.1983) (per curiam) (sustaining lawyers' convictions on fraud charges growing out of major sham marriage operation); *Ethical Considerations in Immigration Cases*, 4 Imm.L.Rep. 169 (1985); Heiserman & Pacun, *Professional Responsibility in Immigration Practice and Government Service*, 22 San Diego L.Rev. 971 (1985); Note, *Ethical Problems in Representing Aliens Applying for Visas Based on Marriages to United States Citizens*, 28 Santa Clara L.Rev. 709 (1988); *Ethical Issues in Immigration Practice: A Roundtable Discussion*, 90–8 Imm. Briefings (Aug. 1990).

DABAGHIAN v. CIVILETTI

United States Court of Appeals, Ninth Circuit, 1979.
607 F.2d 868.

CHOY, CIRCUIT JUDGE:

Dabaghian appeals from the district court's judgment upholding a decision of the Immigration and Naturalization Service ("INS") which stripped him of permanent-resident status. We reverse and remand with instruction to enter judgment for Dabaghian.

Dabaghian is a native and citizen of Iran. He entered the United States as a visitor in 1967 and obtained student status in 1968. In September 1971 he married a United States citizen. In October 1971 he applied for adjustment of status to "alien lawfully admitted for permanent residence" under § 245 of the Immigration and Nationality Act. The adjustment of status was granted on January 13, 1972, a date on which there is contested evidence to show that he was separated from his wife. On January 28, 1972, Dabaghian filed for divorce, which was granted seven months later. In September 1973 he married an Iranian citizen.

In August 1974 the Attorney General moved under § 246 of the Act, to rescind the adjustment of status on the ground that Dabaghian had not in fact been eligible for it at the time it was granted. The Immigration Judge revoked Dabaghian's status as a permanent resident; a split Board of Immigration Appeals dismissed Dabaghian's appeal. His action for review and relief in the district court was then dismissed on summary judgment.

The INS, it is important to note, never has claimed or proved that Dabaghian's first marriage was a sham or fraud when entered. Instead, the INS moved to rescind on the ground that on January 13, 1972, when the adjustment of status was granted, his marriage was dead in fact even though it was still legally alive. Thus, says the INS, he was not the "spouse" of a United States citizen and was ineligible for the adjustment of status.

We reject the INS' legal position. If a marriage is not sham or fraudulent from its inception, it is valid for the purposes of determining eligibility for adjustment of status under § 245 of the Act until it is legally dissolved.

The INS contention has no support in any statute or federal decision. Indeed, it has been rejected time and again in recent immigration cases.

* * *

[After discussing *Bark* and other Ninth Circuit precedents, the court continued:]

In *Chan v. Bell,* 464 F.Supp. 125 (D.D.C.1978), the INS rejected an American wife's petition under § 204 of the Act to classify her alien husband as a "spouse" under § 201(b) of the Act. Such petitions are to establish eligibility, as in the present case, for an application for adjustment of status to that of a permanent resident. The INS denied the petition solely because the spouses had separated; the INS admitted the marriage was legally valid and not sham. The court rejected the INS position, noting that even the relevant INS regulation "quite appropriately conditions the revocation of a petition merely upon the 'legal termination' of the relationship of husband and wife, not upon any assumed dissolution of the marriage by reference to a standard not known to the law of domestic relations." 464 F.Supp. at 128.

The court in *Chan* stated that the INS "has no expertise in the field of predicting the stability and growth potential of marriages—if indeed anyone has—and it surely has no business operating in that field." *Id.* at 130. Moreover, the very effort to apply the "factually-dead" test would trench on constitutional values; it "would inevitably lead the INS into invasions of privacy which even the boldest of government agencies have heretofore been hesitant to enter." *Id.* at 130 n. 13.

* * *

Dabaghian's purported ineligibility turns upon whether he was the "spouse" of an American citizen at the time of adjustment of status. If he was, he was eligible then to receive permanent-resident status, not subject to any quota. The word "spouses" in § 201(b) includes the parties to all marriages that are legally valid and not sham. There is no exception for marriages that the INS thinks are "factually dead" at the time of adjustment. For the INS to give such an interpretation to "spouses" and for the Attorney General to be satisfied that Dabaghian was not a "spouse" are abuses of discretion. Since no other reason for ineligibility under § 245 of the Act has been alleged or proven, there can be no rescission of Dabaghian's permanent-resident status.

Reversed and Remanded to the district court with instruction to enter a judgment directing the INS to reinstate Dabaghian as a permanent resident.

Notes

1. INS and the Board have traditionally sought to deny visa petitions for alleged spouses in two distinct situations: (1) when the underlying marriage is sham or fraudulent—that is, when the parties "did not intend to establish a life together at the time they were married," *Bark v. INS, supra*—and (2) when the underlying marriage is nonviable or "factually dead" at the time when the immigration benefit is sought. The agencies persisted in using both grounds for denial for many years after the first court decisions ruling use of the second test invalid. In 1980, the Board

finally capitulated and ruled that, in the future, visa petitions will not be denied based solely on a finding that the underlying marriage is not viable. *Matter of McKee,* 17 I & N Dec. 332 (BIA 1980). It emphasized, however, that it still will scrutinize evidence of current separation in order to determine whether the initial marriage was sham or fraudulent; this position is consistent with *Bark* and *Dabaghian.* The Board has also stressed that petitions may not be granted on the basis of marriages *legally* terminated as of the date that the immigration benefit is to be conferred. *Matter of Boromand,* 17 I & N Dec. 450, 453 (BIA 1980). Nor may immigration benefits be granted when the spouses have legally separated under a formal, written separation agreement. *Matter of Lenning,* 17 I & N Dec. 476 (BIA 1980). *See generally Benefits for Spouses Under the Immigration and Nationality Act,* 1 Imm. Law Rep. 121 (1982).

2. All of 15 days elapsed between Dabaghian's adjustment of status and his filing for divorce from the U.S.-citizen wife who had petitioned for his adjustment. If the "foremost policy" of our permanent immigration provisions is family reunification, as the court stated in *Lau v. Kiley,* 563 F.2d 543, 547 (2d Cir.1977), why should Dabaghian benefit when his family manifestly has no interest in unifying? In other words, isn't the "factually dead" standard a sound way of implementing the statute, in light of Congress's overriding purpose?

3. One reason for the court's rejection of the "factually dead" test in *Dabaghian* appears to be the court's concern about the potential intrusiveness of the questioning INS might conduct to see if the marriage were still "alive." Yet, is not a similarly intrusive inquiry necessary to determine whether a marriage is a "sham"? Consider the questioning process as described by Trillin, *supra.* Further descriptions of, and reflections on, the investigation and interview process appear in *Horta-Ruiz v. United States Dep't of Justice,* 635 F.Supp. 1039, 1040 (S.D.N.Y.1986); *Pena-Urrutia v. INS,* 640 F.2d 242 (9th Cir.1981); Note, *The Constitutionality of the INS Sham Marriage Investigation Policy,* 99 Harv.L.Rev. 1238 (1986).

4. The BIA has also encountered sham divorces—formal dissolution of marriage bonds for the sole purpose of claiming benefits that are available only to unmarried persons, such as second preference visas for sons and daughters. Some Nevada officials fear that the practice is relatively common among aliens who file for divorce under that state's liberal divorce laws. *See Sham Divorces Still Stump Judges,* Las Vegas Sun, Dec. 10, 1982, at 21, col. 1.

In *Matter of Aldecoaotalora,* 18 I & N Dec. 430 (BIA 1983), the Board ruled that such a divorce would not be recognized for immigration purposes, where the former spouses continued to live together and to hold property jointly. It based this conclusion on its view that "the intent of Congress in providing for preference status for unmarried sons and daughters of lawful permanent residents was to reunite with their parents unmarried children who, although not minors, were still part of a family unit. * * * By her own admissions, the beneficiary has established that, although divorced from her husband, she has neither severed her relationship with him nor returned to the family unit of her parents." Is this an

accurate reading of congressional intent? Could INS deny second preference benefits to otherwise eligible persons who have never been married on
the grounds that they have long lived apart from the parents' family unit?

The Immigration Marriage Fraud Amendments of 1986

In 1986, Congress dramatically altered the INA provisions governing
immigration based on marriage, in order to deter and detect fraudulent
marriages more effectively. Immigration Marriage Fraud Amendments of
1986 (IMFA), Pub.L. No. 99–639, 100 Stat. 3537. Surprisingly the legislation passed both houses by voice vote with only perfunctory floor consideration. 63 Interp.Rel. 856, 907 (1986). *See generally* General Accounting
Office, *Immigration Marriage Fraud: Controls in Most Countries Surveyed
Stronger than in U.S.* (July 1986) (a briefing report prepared at the request
of Senator Simon, the main proponent of these changes in the Senate).

Under the most important provision added by IMFA, INA § 216, all
persons who obtain lawful permanent resident status based on a marriage
that is less than two years old at the time (whether under the second
preference or as an immediate relative) receive such status "on a conditional basis." The conditional period lasts for two years, unless INS acts
before that time to terminate the alien's resident status. The conditional
period counts fully toward the necessary residence period for naturalization, however. INA § 216(e). Within the last 90 days of the two-year
period, both spouses must take the initiative to petition INS, by filing Form
I–751 with the Regional Service Center, to have the conditional basis
"removed," although under certain circumstances the alien may secure a
waiver to the requirement of a joint filing. INA § 216(c)(4). INS has clear
statutory authority to call both spouses in to the district office for an
interview at this point, although the interview is usually waived, thus
reserving examiners' time for those cases where the papers raise a question
meriting further inquiry. 8 C.F.R. §§ 216.4, 216.5.

The terminology is somewhat confusing. INS *terminates* the permanent resident *status* if it finds during the two-year period that the underlying marriage was improper (as defined in the Act) or has been judicially
annulled or terminated. INA § 216(b)(1). *See also* § 216(c)(2) (termination for failure to file timely removal petition). After a termination, the
person is deportable under INA § 241(a)(1)(D). But INS *removes* the
conditional basis at the end of the two years, if it finds that the underlying
marriage was valid and has not ended. *Id.* § 216(c), (d)(1). Removal
signifies that the conditional period is over and the alien has graduated to
full permanent resident status. Aliens will want removal; they will hope
to avoid termination.

If removal is denied at the end of the two-year period (or if no petition
for removal is filed), the alien becomes deportable, but the relevant determinations are open for reconsideration in the deportation proceedings
before the immigration judge. Moreover, INS will bear the burden of
proof, under a "preponderance of the evidence" standard, on most such
issues—for example, to show that the marriage has been annulled or that a
fee was paid for the filing of the visa petition. *See* INA § 216(b)(2), (c)(2),

(c)(3). If the alien seeks a waiver of some of the provisions requiring a joint petition for removal, under § 216(c)(4), the alien bears the burden of proof. Waiver requests specifying which ground is invoked must first be presented to the RSC and may not be first introduced upon appearance before the immigration judge. (The BIA has been fairly generous in ordering continuances of IJ proceedings in order to allow the presentation of waiver claims first to the RSC.) On some of the details of procedure, including the burden of proof and the respective roles of the Regional Service Center, the immigration judge, and the BIA in the adjudications, *see Matter of Mendes*, Int.Dec. 3224 (BIA 1994); *Matter of Lemhammad*, Int.Dec. 3151 (BIA 1991).

Why would aliens come forward and petition for removal if the underlying marriage was questionable? Why not disappear into the system as they often did before IMFA? The most important incentive derives from the papers involved. Conditional permanent residents receive documents clearly marked to show that the status expires at the end of two years. Under the earlier system, in contrast, even if INS received information showing that a marriage was fraudulent from the inception, it often had difficulty locating the alien (and indeed in marshalling sufficient evidence to carry its burden in deportation proceedings). All the while the alien retained a resident alien card ("green card") of indefinite validity.

Congress also used IMFA as the occasion to stiffen a few other provisions meant to prevent and punish marriage fraud. For example, it tightened the requirements for the nonimmigrant category for fiancées and fiancés (the K category), INA §§ 214(d), 245(d); strengthened the restrictions on future immigration of persons who have ever been involved in marriage fraud, INA § 204(c) *see Salas–Velazquez v. INS*, 34 F.3d 705, 707–08 (8th Cir.1994); established criminal sanctions for involvement in marriage fraud, with penalties up to five years imprisonment and a fine of $250,000, INA § 275(b); made it more difficult for a person who immigrated on the basis of a first marriage to bring in a second spouse thereafter (following divorce from the first), INA § 204(a)(2); and rendered it considerably more difficult for aliens in deportation proceedings to cure their problems by means of "eleventh hour" marriages, entered into while deportation proceedings were pending. INA §§ 204(g), 245(e). These last-mentioned provisions, enacted in § 5 of IMFA, have sparked many complaints and considerable litigation, raising both technical questions of interpretation and due process challenges. Congress responded with an ameliorative amendment in 1990, adding INA § 245(e)(3), which applies retroactively. That section now permits the alien the benefit of the late marriage, despite its occurrence during deportation proceedings, if the alien proves its genuineness by clear and convincing evidence—a demanding burden of proof. We will consider the controversies raised by IMFA § 5 in more detail in Chapter Four, at pp. 443–44.

Use the following problems to familiarize yourself with the terms of IMFA. The most important section is INA § 216, which is awkwardly drafted and requires careful attention. But you may also need to refer to INA §§ 204(a)(2), (c), (g); 245(d), (e), all of which were added by IMFA. For useful commentary, see Wheeler, *Until INS Do Us Part: A Guide to*

IMFA, 90–3 Imm. Briefings (March 1990); *Rules and Procedures under the 1986 Marriage Fraud Act,* 7 Imm.L.Rep. 97 (1988); Tucker, *Assimilation to the United States: A Study of the Adjustment of Status and Immigration Marriage Fraud Statutes,* 7 Yale L. & Policy Rev. 20 (1989).

Problems

1. Alien A marries U.S. citizen B and is admitted as an immediate relative under INA § 201(b). Eighteen months later, A separates from B. Six months pass, and the couple has not reconciled. What happens?

2. Same facts, except that A and B are legally divorced after twenty months. What result? What if B instead had died after twenty months?

3. Alien C marries U.S. citizen D and enters as a permanent resident alien. Twenty-two months later, C catches pneumonia and is in bed for three months. What result?

4. Alien E marries U.S. citizen F and is admitted as an immediate relative. One year later, a child is born. Six months later, F walks out and refuses to help E in any further immigration proceedings. What result? Suppose instead that the child was born outside the United States after the marriage but before E's admission. Would this make any difference?

5. Alien G is admitted as a nonimmigrant and does not leave the United States at the end of her authorized stay. She is thus here illegally. INS locates her and begins deportation proceedings. G marries U.S. citizen H and asks H to file a petition on her behalf so that she may adjust her status under INA § 245. What result?

6. Same facts. H's petition is denied and G is deported. When may H and G live together again in the United States?

7. Alien J marries U.S. citizen K and is admitted as a permanent resident alien. Conditional status is removed two years later, but six months after that, J and K are divorced. One year later, J marries L, an alien not admitted to the United States, and files a second preference petition on L's behalf. What result?

8. Alien M, a permanent resident alien, married alien N, a native of Mexico, three years ago. N is still waiting for a second-preference visa. M has just become a U.S. citizen and now seeks to have N granted permanent resident status as an immediate relative of a U.S. citizen. Does INA § 216 apply?

9. Aliens P and Q (both living in Venezuela) were married one year ago. P has just been granted a visa under the employment-based third preference and plans to move with Q to the United States. Q is granted permanent resident status based on P's visa (see INA § 203(d)). Does INA § 216 apply?

Notes and Questions

1. Suppose that the resident or citizen spouse who initially petitioned for the alien's admission based on the marriage (whom we will call the anchor spouse) refuses to join in the joint petition ordinarily required for removal of the conditional basis at the end of the two-year period. It remains possible for the alien spouse to obtain a waiver under INA § 216(c)(4) and still have the conditional basis removed. Consider this statutory provision closely.

For purposes of § 216(c)(4)(A), what is "extreme hardship"? Suppose a child was born to the marriage. Should the child's birth lead to a finding of extreme hardship (a) if the anchor spouse has been awarded custody or joint custody; (b) if the alien spouse has been awarded custody? What if the child was born before the alien spouse's admission?

INA § 216(c)(4)(B), provides for a "good faith/not at fault" waiver. If a divorce was obtained in a state that provides for no-fault divorce, does this provision authorize, or even require, INS to reexamine the circumstances, to see whether the alien bore some fault for the conditions leading to the breakdown of the marriage? What should the couple do if they are in the process of obtaining a divorce, but final judicial proceedings will not occur until well after the two-year mark and the anchor spouse is willing to cooperate in the INS proceedings for removal of the conditional basis? For discussions of INS policy on several of these questions, see 65 Interp.Rel. 1219 (1988); 66 *id.* 1277–79, 1428–30 (1989); 68 *id.* 435–39 (1991); 69 *id.* 627–30 (1992). For reflections on these issues by experienced practitioners, see 7 Imm.L.Rep., *supra,* at 100–105. *See generally Matter of Balsillie,* Int.Dec. 3175 (BIA 1992).

The battered spouse or child waiver of § 216(c)(4)(C) was added in 1990. The 1990 amendment also mandated regulations to protect the confidentiality of information concerning abused spouses or children. Are any waivers authorized under that provision that would not be possible under one of the preceding subparagraphs? The crime bill enacted in 1994, Pub.L.No. 103–322, 108 Stat. 1796, contained provisions that originated in a proposed Violence Against Women Act, introduced in 1993 by Rep. Patricia Schroeder (D–Colo.). *See* Calvo & Davis, *Congress Nears Approval of Legislation to Protect Abused Aliens,* 70 Interp.Rel. 1665 (1993). The 1994 legislation further amended this paragraph of § 216(c)(4) to instruct the Attorney General to consider "any credible evidence" regarding the grounds for this waiver, but it then gives that official "sole discretion" to determine what is credible and what weight it deserves. Other related provisions enacted in the crime bill allow a battered alien spouse or child of a U.S. citizen or lawful permanent resident, under certain conditions, to self-petition for immigration benefits. INA § 204(a)(1)(A)(iii), (A)(iv), (B)(ii), (B)(iii). *Cf.* INA § 204(h) (limiting revocation of approved visa petitions granted to a battered spouse or child).

In fiscal year 1992, INS processed 92,483 cases involving conditional status removals and terminations. In 86,713 cases the conditional status was removed, and in 4,360 cases the status was terminated. (The rest were administratively closed.) Terminations resulted primarily from failure to file (3,196 cases); only 479 were terminated for cause, *i.e.,* because of a determination that the alien was ineligible for removal. 1992 INS Statistical Yearbook, Table 22. In FY 1993, 91,258 cases led to only 81,810 removals of conditional status. Of the 7,591 terminations, 6,342 were based on failure to file, and 508 were for cause. 1993 *id.,* Table 22.

2. Does IMFA reinstate a milder form of "viability" test to be applied to aliens' marriages—in the sense of a requirement that the marriage meet certain tests not only at the time when it is entered into but also at the time when immigration benefits are provided? If so, is this a bad thing? Does IMFA exacerbate or alleviate the problems that concerned the *Bark* and *Dabaghian* courts? Compare the kinds of investigation and questioning required before IMFA (as allowed by the two cases) to the kinds of inquiry required or facilitated by IMFA. *See generally* Wheeler, *supra,* 90–3 Imm. Briefings, at 11–12. If the spouses are still legally married at the two-year review, INS now acknowledges that nonviability is not a valid basis for refusing to remove the conditional status. Opinion of INS General Counsel, 69 Interp.Rel. 80–82 (1992). *See also Matter of Mendes,* Int.Dec. 3224, at 9–10 n. 3 (BIA 1994).

3. Section 216(c)(4) may not lead to waiver in all situations where the marriage was initially undertaken in good faith and was wholly valid under the *Bark* test but later fell apart. Whether waiver is available in such a situation depends on how INS examiners interpret the "not at fault" provision in subparagraph (B) and also on how INS exercises the discretion explicitly granted by § 216(c)(4).[17] Should the possibility of losing permanent residence in this fashion be considered a defect in the statute? Overly harsh? Consider the response of Senator Simpson (R–Wyo.), who chaired the key Senate subcommittee when IMFA was considered (quoted in 65 Interp.Rel. 1339 (1988)):

> With regard to the marriage fraud amendments, we realize that there could be cases in which the alien spouse was not primarily responsible for the failure of the marriage, and during debate, some pointed out that this would give rise to an opportunity for "unfairness." However, if we all understand that the only real purpose in giving the substantial immigration benefit our laws provide to an alien spouse is to keep the family together, then we would wish that all will further understand that if the marriage just simply doesn't work—for whatever reason—even when the alien spouse is not at fault, there is no longer a family to "keep together." Further, the immigration benefit which is lost to the alien spouse if the marriage fails, for whatever reason, was made available to that person only because of the marriage to an

17. Before its amendment in 1990, the second clause of § 216(c)(4)(B) read: "the qualifying marriage has been terminated (other than through the death of the spouse) *by the alien spouse for good cause.*" The 1990 Act deleted the italicized words. The former language probably made it much harder to obtain a waiver when the marriage simply did not work out. What did Congress intend by this amendment? What weight should this change carry in the exercise of the INS's discretion under § 216(c)(4)?

American citizen or resident. When that marriage no longer exists, there is no reasonable justification for the special immigration benefit to continue.

4. It is not only spouses who may obtain conditional permanent residence. Sometimes children from a prior marriage of the alien spouse will also fall into this category. Look closely at the language of § 216 to see why this is so. Issues concerning such children are examined in 7 Imm.L.Rep., *supra,* at 98–99.

5. INA § 204(a)(2)(A), added by IMFA, prevents an alien petitioner who gained lawful permanent resident status on the basis of an earlier marriage from successfully petitioning for a new spouse under the second preference unless (1) five years have passed since the petitioner attained resident status or (2) the alien "establishes to the satisfaction of the Attorney General by clear and convincing evidence that the prior marriage * * * was not entered into for the purpose of evading any provision of the immigration laws." What policy underlies the imposition of this stringent burden of proof? What kinds of evidence might be offered to satisfy it? *See Matter of Patel,* 19 I & N Dec. 774 (BIA 1988); *cf. Matter of Pazandeh,* 19 I & N Dec. 884 (BIA 1989).

How does the test here (which is quite similar to the basic test IMFA created for § 216; *see, e.g.,* § 216(b)(1)(A)(i)) differ from the sham marriage standard set forth in *Bark* and *Dabaghian*? (Hint: consider the facts of *United States v. Sacco,* described in the footnote to *Bark.*) Why is there a different test? Which is better?

c. *The Backlog Problem*

Until the mid–1970s, qualified immigrants in the preference categories usually had to wait only as long as the paperwork required before immigrating. Today's waiting lists in most categories, by contrast, are remarkably long. Look again at the information presented in Table 3.6 on p. 135 *supra.*

The per-country ceilings cause some of the distortions reflected in that Table. Their effects have been moderated by the 1990 Act, but should these ceilings simply be abolished? What purposes do they serve today, given that large categories of immigration are not included in the ceiling calculations? If they are not abolished, should they be modified for greater responsiveness to other factors? What other factors should count? Gross population of the source country? Historical ties to the United States? Proximity?

Beyond this, reformers have focused attention on the backlogs in the family-sponsored second and fourth preferences. Consider the following:

> [Several] provisions of American immigration law * * * impede the entry of immediate family members of permanent resident aliens. [Of particular concern are] the numerical limitations—the annual ceiling and the per-country ceiling on preference category visas—which force applicants from countries of high immigration demand to wait for long periods of time before visas

become available. As a result, spouses and minor children of some permanent resident aliens enter immediately, while those from countries like Mexico or the Philippines must wait as long as eight years. The inequities are exacerbated by the recently passed Immigration Reform and Control Act of 1986 (IRCA), under which as many as two million persons who entered illegally may become legal residents, while spouses or children of resident aliens who remained behind waiting for their visas to become available are afforded no relief.

* * * [F]amily unity is such an essential component of individual liberty that provisions of immigration law should interfere with that right no more than is necessary to meet compelling national interests. Although the nation has compelling interests in controlling the flow of immigration, analysis of the rationale for the quantitative limitations which cause prolonged separation of immediate family members of permanent resident aliens reveals that the national interests could be protected by means which do not impede family unity. * * * In particular, Congress should eliminate the numerical ceilings on entry of the spouses and minor children of permanent resident aliens.

Guendelsberger, *Implementing Family Unification Rights in American Immigration Law: Proposed Amendments,* 25 San Diego L.Rev. 253–254 (1988).[18] Do you agree? The author goes on to outline possible constitutional arguments supporting these conclusions, drawing importantly on *Moore v. City of East Cleveland,* 431 U.S. 494, 97 S.Ct. 1932, 52 L.Ed.2d 531 (1977), which struck down a city ordinance that interfered with the right of a grandmother to live with her two grandsons.

The 1990 Act, as we have seen, reduced some of the obstacles to reunifying the families of lawful permanent residents, and the second-preference delays suffered by nuclear families from high-demand countries were noticeably reduced. But thereafter, the delays are once again growing, because annual demand outstrips the number of second-preference admission spaces. By fall 1994 those being admitted applied over three years earlier. An early version of reform legislation championed in 1989 by Congressman Bruce Morrison (D–Conn.), then chairman of the House subcommittee, would have treated all spouses and minor children of perma-

---

18. *See also* Guendelsberger, *The Right to Family Unification in French and United States Immigration Law,* 21 Cornell Int'l L.J. 1 (1988). Although participants in the debate over second preference often speak of multiyear separations of aliens from spouses and minor children, a high proportion of these families in fact manage to reunify while waiting to clear the backlog. That is, the family members simply enter clandestinely and live with the principal alien in the United States, incurring all the difficulties inherent in undocumented status. When their place is finally reached on the waiting list, they have historically returned to the home country to pick up their visas. (Beginning with FY 1995, such people may adjust status without leaving the United States, upon payment of a much higher fee.) To the extent that this happens, the primary issue is not family separation, but the immigration law's role in inducing clandestine migration and forcing an underground existence on the spouse and children, as the only means to satisfy the understandable—indeed admirable—human impulse for a family to live together. Does this fact increase or decrease the urgency of reforms that will reduce second preference (and other) backlogs?

nent resident aliens as "immediate relatives" able to immigrate without numerical limit, thus essentially eliminating the second preference. Would you favor such an approach? What effect would it have on INA § 203(d)? Other proponents of family reunification urged adding large numbers to the second preference, clearing backlogs by increasing the supply of admissions. Still others focused on the demand side, proposing instead to reduce delays by disqualifying sons and daughters over age 26.

The preference for brothers and sisters suffers from even lengthier backlogs. The State Department in 1994 reported over 1.6 million active registrants who are already the beneficiaries of approved visa petitions and are simply waiting for an admission space in the family fourth preference. Table 3.6 shows that in November 1994 brothers and sisters were being admitted only if they had started the application nearly ten years earlier. The fourth preference is sometimes criticized, as well, for its alleged "visa multiplier" effect:

> Unlike the other categories, the allotment of visas based on "sibship" potentially leads to an unlimited demand for visas by *new* qualified applicants. For example, the admission of one immigrant who has foreign-born siblings or who marries an individual with foreign-born siblings automatically creates additional potentially qualified visa applicants, who, when admitted, can petition for the siblings of their spouses. Indeed, if the immigrant's parents are admitted, they can in turn petition for *their* brothers and sisters resulting potentially in the addition of the brother and sister in-laws, uncles, cousins, etc. of the original immigrant.

The Preference System: Hearings Before the Subcomm. on Immigration and Refugee Policy of the Sen. Comm. on the Judiciary, 97th Cong., 1st Sess. 213 (1981) (testimony of Professor Mark R. Rosenzweig). The extent to which this sort of "chain migration" really takes place is hotly disputed. *See generally* Staff Report: Legal Immigration to the United States: A Demographic Analysis of Fifth Preference Visa Admissions (Comm.Print, S.Prt. 100–34, 1987); General Accounting Office, The Future Flow of Legal Immigration into the United States (GAO/PEMD–88–7, 1988). Others testifying at the 1981 hearing countered that, for many ethnic groups, "brothers and sisters, whether or not they are married, are an integral part of the family reunion concept. Elimination of this preference category would violate a sacrosanct human right of an American citizen to live with his family according to his own traditional lifestyle." *The Preference System: Hearings, supra,* at 170 (testimony of Rev. Joseph A. Cogo).

In its consideration of immigration reform legislation in 1982, the Senate decided that the preference for brothers and sisters of U.S. citizens should be eliminated altogether. S. 2222, 97th Cong., 2d Sess., § 202. In 1983, examining the same issue, the Senate voted to make such immigration available only to *unmarried* brothers and sisters. S. 529, *supra,* § 202. In 1988 the Senate likewise restricted this preference to unmarried siblings, but it tried to compensate for the limitation by giving points toward qualifying for independent immigration (in categories that would have been governed by a point system) to siblings who would no longer fall within the preference. Even these changes evoked strongly negative reactions in a number of strong constituencies, however, and in the 1990 Act, Congress made no changes to the preference for brothers and sisters. At the same time it turned down proposals to add numbers to cope with the backlog; the annual ceiling for this preference under the 1990 Act is only 200 higher than before. What public objectives are served by a family unification policy that delays unification for ten years or more?

The saga of this preference in the Senate suggests some of the political difficulties that stand in the way of reform. Many diverse groups—ethnic, business, humanitarian—maintain intense interest in the small piece of immigration law that they care about deeply. But adjustments in many small pieces of once-comprehensive reform proposals can nibble broader policy objectives to death. It is hard to sustain the focus of the legislative process on the aims of broader systemic reform in the midst of such interest-group pressures.

4. LABOR CERTIFICATION AND EMPLOYMENT–BASED IMMIGRATION

a. *Labor Certification*

(i) *Background and Basic Procedures*

The impulse to protect American workers against allegedly unfair competition from immigrant laborers has long played a role in the shaping of our immigration laws. As we have seen, the first federal immigration controls were imposed in 1875. Just ten years later Congress adopted the first labor-related immigration measure, the Contract Labor Law of 1885. Act of February 26, 1885, Ch. 164, 23 Stat. 332. Its enforcement provisions were strengthened two years later. Act of Feb. 23, 1887, Ch. 220, 24 Stat. 414. As described by a later congressional committee, this law

> was aimed at the practice of certain employers importing cheap labor from abroad. This importation practice began in 1869. Advertisements were printed offering inducements to immigrants to proceed to this country, particularly to the coal fields, for employment. Many advertisements asserted that several hundred men were needed in places where there were actually no vacancies. The object was to oversupply the demand for labor so that the domestic laborers would be forced to work at reduced wages.
> * * *

> The alien contract labor law made it unlawful to import aliens or assist in importation or migration of aliens into the United States, its Territories, or the District of Columbia under contract, made previous to the importation or migration, for the performance of labor or service of any kind in the United States. The law made such contracts void [with certain exceptions] and provided certain penalties.

H.R.Rep. No. 1365, 82d Cong., 2d Sess. 12–13 (1952).

These provisions remained on the books until the major restructuring and codification of our immigration laws that took place with passage of the Immigration and Nationality Act in 1952. By then, opinion concerning foreign labor recruitment had changed considerably. In the view of many, the country needed at least selective efforts to fill gaps in the U.S. personnel pool with immigrant workers. And it was thought that other measures, such as the National Labor Relations Act and the Fair Labor Standards Act, afforded adequate protection against the earlier employer abuses. *See generally* Rodino, *The Impact of Immigration on the American Labor Market,* 27 Rutgers L.Rev. 245 (1974). The 1952 Act therefore repealed the 1885 law and adopted in its place the first labor certification provision of our immigration law. In its initial form, operative until 1965, this section permitted the Secretary of Labor to block the entry of aliens seeking to enter for the purpose of skilled or unskilled labor upon a finding that such entry would displace U.S. workers or "adversely affect" the wages and working conditions of U.S. workers similarly employed. The initiative rested with the Secretary of Labor to declare an occupation oversupplied, and he rarely bestirred himself to invoke the provision.

In 1965, responding to effective lobbying led by the AFL–CIO, Congress reversed the operation of the labor certification process. Since that date the law has essentially presumed that foreign workers are not needed; the alien and her intending employer must take the initiative to secure affirmative certification.[19] The current version of the labor certification provision appears in INA § 212(a)(5)(A), (C).

You might want to study that language closely at this point. How far must an employer search for U.S. workers? What if qualified workers are available in the state's largest city but they don't want to work at the employer's place of business 200 miles away? What if one worker would do so, provided he received a 25 percent boost in salary over the employer's initial offer? In what circumstances may the employer reject a U.S. applicant because he is not equally qualified with the alien, even though he is minimally qualified for the job? To what preference categories under INA § 203(b) do the "equally qualified" provisions correlate? (Compare the language closely.)

Although the basic labor certification provision appears in § 212, as part of the lengthy list of grounds of exclusion, it is more usefully conceptualized as a provision setting forth one of the initial grounds of qualification that most intending immigrants in the employment-based

19. The change did not bring to an end one anomalous practice, known as the "green card commuter" category, that some have vigorously challenged as a contravention of the protections the labor certification system is meant to provide for American workers. Several tens of thousands of such persons reside in Canada or Mexico and commute to the United States for daily or seasonal employment. They met the requirements for admission, including labor certification, only once—many of them years ago when nonpreference immigration was still available.

Thereafter, INS has accepted the fact of their foreign residence but has readmitted them, whatever their current occupation, as returning residents (and therefore numerically exempt special immigrants under INA § 101(a)(27)(A)). 8 C.F.R. § 211.5. When unions challenged this practice as a violation of the plain language of the statute, a divided Supreme Court decided to defer to the agency and permit its continuation. *Saxbe v. Bustos,* 419 U.S. 65, 95 S.Ct. 272, 42 L.Ed.2d 231 (1974).

preferences must fulfill. Section 204(b) makes this conceptual linkage more explicit. As that provision indicates, the labor certification requirement is a prerequisite that must be satisfied by every entering immigrant in the employment-based second and third preferences, which provide for roughly 80,000 admissions each year (plus any spill-down numbers from the first preference). Before an alien in these categories can become the beneficiary of an approved visa petition, then, labor certification must be secured from the Department of Labor. Certification establishes that a shortage of available and qualified workers exists in the alien's field at the place of intended employment, and that her hiring on the offered terms would not adversely affect the wages or working conditions of other workers. In sharp contrast, immigrants entering by virtue of a family relationship, either as immediate relatives or in one of the family-sponsored preferences, are not hindered by the labor certification requirement, even if they intend to compete with American workers in fields already well supplied.

The Department of Labor was not initially well-equipped to handle the new responsibility imposed in 1965; years passed before the agency developed detailed and well-structured procedures and regulations to implement these provisions. *See* 42 Fed.Reg. 3440 (1977) (adopting comprehensive regulations, codified in 20 C.F.R. Part 656); 45 Fed.Reg. 83926 (1980) (recodification with significant amendments). We will be examining these arrangements below, primarily in the context of *individual* labor certification—a procedure whereby a single employer, having a particular alien in mind, takes steps to secure the necessary Labor Department approval. But, to place these cases in context, you should understand that the Department of Labor has also managed to avoid the need for that complicated individual process with respect to several occupations by means of certain broad determinations embodied in the Department's Schedule A and Schedule B.

Schedule A lists occupations judged chronically short of qualified U.S. workers. It amounts to a blanket determination that anyone seeking that kind of work in the United States will not displace U.S. workers or adversely affect wages and working conditions. The Schedule has been reduced in recent years, because Congress has moved some of its former categories into the first or fourth employment-based preferences, which do not require labor certification. As of this writing, Schedule A includes only licensed nurses and physical therapists, and certain aliens "of exceptional ability" in the sciences or arts (but excluding the performing arts). 20 C.F.R. § 656.10. A qualified alien seeking to come to this country to work in those occupations can avoid processing at the Department of Labor altogether. He or she may file the relevant papers directly with the consular officer overseas, or with the INS if the applicant is already in this country and seeks adjustment of status from nonimmigrant to immigrant. *See* 20 C.F.R. § 656.22.

In contrast, Schedule B lists occupations in which the Department of Labor considers there are sufficient U.S. workers throughout the country and for which a labor certification will not be issued. Current examples include parking lot attendants, bartenders, cashiers, keypunch operators (yes—still on the list though not in anyone's offices any more), truck drivers, and many others. There are provisions for waivers of this Schedule B preclusion, but waivers are relatively rare. *See* 20 C.F.R. §§ 656.11, 656.23.

If the alien's occupation does not appear on either schedule, then the employer must initiate the individual certification process by filing Form ETA 750 and demonstrating that the manifold requirements for individual labor certification have been fulfilled. 20 C.F.R. §§ 656.20–656.21. In most cases, the employer must show, *inter alia*, that it has engaged in good-faith recruitment efforts aimed at qualified U.S. workers, including elaborately detailed advertising requirements; that it has interviewed interested U.S. workers and has rejected any such applicants for lawful, job-related reasons; that it has offered the "prevailing wage" as defined in *id.* § 656.40, and is capable of paying that wage; and that its job requirements (as set forth in the job descriptions used as the basis for U.S. recruitment) are not unduly restrictive. *See generally* Krieger, *Labor Certification: Avoiding Notices of Findings*, 13 Imm.L.Rep. 193 (1994); *Warmtex Enterprises v. Martin*, 953 F.2d 1133 (9th Cir.1992); *Production Tool Corp. v. Employment and Training Administration*, 688 F.2d 1161 (7th Cir.1982); *Posadas de Puerto Rico Associates, Inc. v. Secretary of Labor*, 698 F.Supp. 396 (D.P.R.1988).[20]

Applications for labor certification are filed by the employer with the local Job Service office, an arm of the state government, which also then participates in the attempt to find qualified U.S. workers, but the actual determinations are made by a regional "certifying officer," who is a federal official, part of the Employment and Training Administration of the Department of Labor. If the certifying officer believes that the employer's application does not meet the requirements, he or she issues a Notice of Findings—essentially, a preliminary determination that the certification should be denied. The employer may contest this preliminary determination and file additional information or take new steps to meet the objections.[21] If these are unsuccessful, the certifying officer issues a Final Determination denying certification. 20 C.F.R. §§ 656.24–656.25. The employer is entitled to administrative review, upon appropriate request, before a panel of the Board of Alien Labor Certification Appeals (BALCA)

20. Some cases are designated for "special handling" under the DOL regulations, especially positions for college or university teachers and aliens of "exceptional ability" in the performing arts. 20 C.F.R. § 656.21a. The special handling reflects the fact that in these fields (and a few others) an employer may reject U.S. workers who are minimally qualified for the position, if it can show that they were not "equally qualified" with the proposed alien worker. INA § 212(a)(5)(A)(ii). With regard to most other occupational fields, the availability of a minimally qualified U.S. worker, though not as talented or experienced as the alien, will defeat certification.

21. Section 122(b) of the 1990 Act, supported by organized labor, introduced the possibility of a more adversarial cast to at least some labor certification proceedings. It requires that at the time of filing, employers must give notice of the application to the bargaining representative in the occupation and area affected, or must post a notice to this effect, if there is no union. Moreover, any person may file "documentary evidence bearing on the application for certification," such as information on available workers, or on actual wages and working conditions at the work site. *See* 20 C.F.R. § 656.20(g), (h).

of the Department of Labor.[22] *Id.* §§ 656.26–656.27. Judicial review of a labor certification denial is available in federal district court under the Administrative Procedure Act, after the employer has exhausted the administrative remedies. *See, e.g., Reddy, Inc. v. Department of Labor*, 492 F.2d 538, 542–44 (5th Cir.1974).

If the certifying officer approves, he or she issues the formal labor certification. The employer is then responsible for filing that document with INS, accompanied by the employer's actual visa petition (Form I–140). INS approval of the visa petition following labor certification is not pro forma. Under current regulations, the Department of Labor's certification is conclusive regarding labor market conditions, but INS is entitled to question the alien's qualifications for the certified job or the employer's ability to pay the stated wage or salary, or otherwise to investigate fraud or misrepresentation by the alien or the employer, and to deny a visa petition on such grounds despite labor certification. *See, e.g., K.R.K. Irvine, Inc. v. Landon*, 699 F.2d 1006 (9th Cir.1983); *Madany v. Smith*, 696 F.2d 1008 (D.C.Cir.1983); *Joseph v. Landon*, 679 F.2d 113 (7th Cir.1982). If INS detects no such defects, its approval of the visa petition is then communicated, via the National Visa Center in New Hampshire, to a consular officer in the alien's country for the ultimate processing of the immigrant visa.

In FY 1993, the Department of Labor received 30,068 applications for permanent labor certification, down from 34,607 the previous year and a steep fall-off from 1989, when 71,652 applications were received. (The 1989 statistic includes applications for both temporary and permanent certification, but the overwhelming majority were for the latter.) The overall approval rate in 1993 was 62 percent, down from 94.5 percent four years earlier. 70 Interp.Rel. 1436 (1993). The decline in applications reflects a declining economy, reduced opportunities for unskilled workers after enactment of the 1990 Act, tougher DOL standards, and possibly the effects of a stricter DOL policy to report to INS all applications in which the beneficiary appears already to be working illegally in the United States. *See id.* at 291–92, 1436.

———

Helping clients navigate the intricacies of the labor certification process constitutes an important—and lucrative—part of the practice of immigration lawyers. Some idea of how the labor certification process looks from the perspective of the immigration bar can be derived from the following reading. It is reprinted from *The New Yorker* article excerpted previously, an account of the author's experiences spending a few weeks examining the practice of immigration law in Houston.

CALVIN TRILLIN, MAKING ADJUSTMENTS
The New Yorker, May 28, 1984, at 61–62, 65–66.

The process of getting labor certification amounts to staging a sort of sham employment offer. The lawyer writes a job description that complies

22. BALCA was created in 1987 to replace a system of appeals to single administrative law judges within the Department, a system that gave rise to problems with uniformity and consistency. *See* 52 Fed.Reg. 11217–18 (1987).

with the Department of Labor's standards, and the potential employer of the alien actually advertises such a job through the state employment commission. If someone shows up who is a citizen and has the qualifications outlined in the ad and is willing to work for the stated wage, the labor certification is not granted—although the employer has no obligation to give the citizen a job. If the lawyer who wrote the job description has been skillful, there is a good chance that no qualified citizen will show up. Writing job descriptions that pass the Department of Labor but attract no other potential employees is what Ed Prud'homme calls "one of the few art forms in the business," and Beaumont Martin is considered one of the artists. One of the Chinese students had managed to get a job in the accounting department of a small oil company, and, since the job required some computer expertise, Martin decided to write a job description that nudged her over a bit from accounting to computer analysis. ("There are a lot of people running around with accounting degrees.") When he had typed it up, he handed it to her:

SYSTEMS ANALYST 020.067–018

Conduct analyses of accounting, management, and operational problems and formulate mathematical models for solution by IBM computer system, using FORTRAN, COBOL, and PASCAL. Analyze problems in terms of management information. Write computer programs and devise and install accounting system and related procedures. Masters or equal in management information systems. $1667/month.

She read it over. "It's beautiful," she said.

* * *

Along with the forms and folders on the floor next to Beaumont Martin's lounge chair was a worn copy of a fourteen-hundred-page government book called Dictionary of Occupational Titles—known to immigration lawyers as the D.O.T. For anyone who wants to make labor certification into an art form, the D.O.T. is an essential piece of equipment. It contains one-paragraph descriptions of virtually every occupation practiced by anybody in the United States. It describes the task of a neurosurgeon and it describes the task of a fibre-glass-container-winding operator. In a consistently direct style, it says what a leak hunter does ("Inspects barrels filled with beer or whisky to detect and repair leaking barrels") and what a sponge buffer does ("Tends machine that buffs edges of household sponges to impart rounded finish") and what an airline pilot does ("Pilots airplane"). Using the D.O.T. as a guide, an immigration lawyer tries to give the client an occupational title in the least crowded field available and then describe the job in a paragraph that sounds pretty much like a paragraph in the D.O.T. but happens to describe almost nobody but the client in question. "Immigration law is taking a short-order cook and making him into an executive chef," Pete Williamson told me. "What we're talking about here is a matter of focus."

When I was discussing labor certification with Pete Williamson one afternoon, he mentioned a young woman he had seen that day who wanted to stay in the country but did not fall into any of the categories of family reunification. She obviously did not qualify for any of the non-immigrant visas available to businessmen or investors. She was already married—to someone who, as it happened, had more or less the same visa problems that she did. Her only hope for a green card was labor certification. Her only occupation was looking after the children of a neighbor.

I said that it didn't sound promising. A few days with immigration lawyers had greatly broadened my view of how the employment sections of the immigration law were actually used. I was no longer under the delusion that the law worked to bring to this country people who had rare skills or worked in fields where there were serious shortages of American workers. "It's a matter of nudging the client's situation over a bit one way or another in order to make it fit into a category that's eligible," one lawyer had told me. "And sometimes, if you want to stay in the United States, you have to shape your career to fit the immigration law." Williamson had explained that it was possible for, say, a South American shirt manufacturer who wanted to resettle here to come in on a visitor's visa or a business visa, establish a corporation, have the personnel department of the corporation file an application to have him labor-certified as the president of a shirt firm doing business with Latin America ("Must know Spanish. Must be familiar with South American cottons . . . "), apply for a green card through the labor certification, and settle in for life. Still, it seemed unlikely that being a mother's helper in Texas was a job "for which a shortage of employable and willing persons exists."

There were two other important elements in the case, Williamson said. The young woman in question was a college graduate. Also, both she and the children she looked after were Muslims—all from Pakistan. Williamson intended to nudge her over from a nanny to a tutor—a tutor qualified to instruct the children in their own culture and religion. He thought it unlikely that any citizen with similar qualifications would respond to the ad. Williamson takes some satisfaction in such focussing—enough, he says, to offset the repetitiousness of certain aspects of the practice and the frustrations of dealing with the Immigration and Naturalization Service. "It's a competent, involved, technical job in which, if you're successful, you can see the consequences of your actions," he told me when I asked what appealed to him about practicing immigration law. "Also, I don't like the government."

Notes

The withdrawal of President Clinton's first nominee for Attorney General, Zoe Baird, focused a brief spotlight on the labor certification provisions for nannies and other household employees in early 1993. It was revealed shortly before her confirmation hearings that she and her husband had hired an undocumented alien couple to care for their children and their home, and had failed to pay Social Security taxes on their wages. Baird had initiated the labor certification process in order eventually to regularize the employees' immigration status, but these steps did not propitiate the strong public reaction to what remained an illegal hiring, particularly since unskilled workers still had to wait many years for employment-based third-preference admission even after receiving certification. Some commentators began to question Congress's decision to impose such a low ceiling on unskilled admissions (no more than 10,000 per year, as a subset of the third employment-based preference, under the 1990 Act). They charged that this restriction unnecessarily hindered the hiring of needed childcare workers. Congress eventually eased the Social Security tax requirements applied to household help, but it did not change the third preference provisions. Should it have? What policy arguments justify the continuation of the low ceiling on importing unskilled alien labor?

In the meantime, the 10,000 ceiling and the resulting backlogs have sparked other creative initiatives, designed primarily to take advantage of the fact that virtually all other employment-based admission categories became current after the 1990 Act took effect. (*See* Table 3.6 *supra*.) For example, in 1993 a Washington, D.C., attorney filed an application with the DOL's Occupational Analysis Field Center in North Carolina, requesting the establishment of a job title, duties and standard vocational preparation (SVP—roughly a measure of the skill level required for the occupation) for the new category of "nanny," to be added to the D.O.T. The Field Center initially approved the request, with an SVP of 6, enough to count the occupation as "skilled." Shortly thereafter, DOL ordered the rescission of the new category, effective immediately, apparently fearing a flood of new applications. It stated that the earlier ruling rested on "insufficient factfinding and research" and promised further study of the childcare industry. For the time being, such work in private homes must continue to be classified under the D.O.T.'s categories for children's tutor and child monitor, with a lower SVP rating. 71 Interp.Rel. 488, 559 (1994).

(ii) Job Requirements and Employer's "Personal Preferences"

How can the Labor Department guard adequately against the obvious incentives, evident in the Trillin article, that employers and attorneys may have to tailor their job descriptions to make it nearly impossible that qualified American workers will be found? The following case, which arose before adoption of the Labor Department's more comprehensive regulations, describes early efforts by the agencies and courts to police against the intrusion of such "personal preferences" into the recruitment process. *Pesikoff* affords a useful starting point for considering the issues and the competing policies involved. The notes that follow then discuss contrary decisions by other courts, and also the response of the administrative agencies as they have tried to refine the standards to be applied to these questions.

PESIKOFF v. SECRETARY OF LABOR

United States Court of Appeals, District of Columbia Circuit, 1974.
501 F.2d 757, cert. denied, 419 U.S. 1038, 95 S.Ct. 525, 42 L.Ed.2d 315.

*Sec'y of labor
discretion*

J. SKELLY WRIGHT, CIRCUIT JUDGE:

Appellants seek review of a decision of the Secretary of Labor denying certification for appellant Quintero to enter the United States as an alien seeking to perform skilled or unskilled labor. Appellants filed in the District Court a complaint requesting, pursuant to 28 U.S.C. § 2201 (1970) and 5 U.S.C. § 704 (1970), a declaratory judgment that the Secretary's decision was an unlawful exercise of his authority under Section 212(a)(14) of the Immigration and Nationality Act.[a] The District Court dismissed the complaint for failure to state a cause of action, and this appeal followed. We find that the Secretary, in declining to grant certification, did not abuse the discretion vested in him by Section 212(a)(14) and affirm.

I

Appellant Pesikoff is a Houston child psychiatrist. His wife was a law student when this action was commenced. They are the parents of two preschool-age children. Because of the time demands on him and his wife, Dr. Pesikoff felt it important that he obtain help in caring for his household. He states he attempted to find such assistance through newspaper advertisements, employment agencies, and inquiries with friends. He learned from the latter source that appellant Quintero, a citizen of Mexico with experience in caring for children, was available to work as a live-in maid. Dr. Pesikoff entered into a contract with Ms. Quintero under which she was to be paid $70 per week plus room and board for providing washing, ironing, cooking, and care for the two Pesikoff children. Though Ms. Quintero was to live in, Dr. Pesikoff represented to the Secretary that her work day was to have been only from 8:00 a.m. to 12:00 noon and from 2:00 p.m. to 6:00 p.m.

On or about July 20, 1971 appellants submitted a request to the Department of Labor that the Secretary, pursuant to Section 212(a)(14), certify Ms. Quintero for immigration into this country for the purpose of being employed by the Pesikoffs as a live-in maid.

* * *

* * * A Department of Labor Manpower Administration officer in Dallas, Texas, to whom the Secretary's authority under this provision had been delegated, informed Dr. Pesikoff on July 28, 1971 that the Secretary could not issue for Ms. Quintero the certification required by Section 212(a)(14) because available job market information did not show that United States workers were unavailable for the job Ms. Quintero was to perform. Before denying Dr. Pesikoff's request the certifying officer had

---

a. Section 212 was thoroughly reorganized in 1990. Section 212(a)(14) was the statutory predecessor to current § 212(a)(5)(A), the labor certification provision. The slight changes in language effectuated by the 1990 Act are not material to the issues in this case.—eds.

been advised by the Texas Employment Commission that there were approximately 180 maids registered in the Commission's Houston office. The Employment Commission also advised that inquiries of employers and perusals of newspaper advertisements enabled it to estimate that in excess of 100 maids were available for work. The Commission indicated, however, that very few of the registered workers would accept jobs that required cooking and that none were willing to live in.

In affirming the certifying officer's decision, the Labor Department's Assistant Regional Manpower Administrator in Texas cited the Employment Commission's report on the general availability of maids in Houston. The Administrator stated that the absence in Houston of maids willing to live in was irrelevant to the Pesikoff application because "based on the job described and hours of work, the live-in requirement is a personal preference and not a necessity in the performance of the job." In March 1972 appellants filed in the District Court their complaint against the Secretary, dismissal of which we now review.

[The Court held that Dr. Pesikoff had standing to obtain judicial review of the Secretary's decision under the Administrative Procedure Act.]

* * *

* * * Dr. Pesikoff asserts that the Secretary's denial constituted an abuse of his discretion under Section 212(a)(14) because it was based on insufficient evidence. More specifically, Dr. Pesikoff argues that the Secretary should have presented evidence sufficient to prove that there were particular workers available, willing, able, and qualified to perform all the tasks Ms. Quintero had contracted to perform and to live in with the Pesikoffs while doing so.

Our evaluation of Dr. Pesikoff's position must commence with an analysis of the section and its legislative history. We first stress that the section is written so as to set up a presumption that aliens should not be permitted to enter the United States for the purpose of performing labor because of the likely harmful impact of their admission on American workers. This presumption, the statutory language makes clear, can be overcome only if the Secretary of Labor has determined that the two conditions set forth in parts (A) and (B) of the subsection are met. This structuring of the statute strongly indicates that the Secretary is not obligated to prove in the case of every alien seeking entry to perform labor that the conditions are not met. Given the presumption of the statute against admission, if the Secretary's consultation of the general labor market data readily available to him suggests that there is a pool of potential workers available to perform the job which the alien seeks, the burden should be placed on the alien or his putative employer to prove that it is not possible for the employer to find a qualified American worker.

This interpretation of the statute is supported by its legislative history. Before enactment of the 1965 amendments to the Immigration and Nationality Act, Section 212(a)(14) was structured to permit entry to aliens seeking to perform labor in the United States unless the Secretary of Labor certified that there were sufficient American workers available to perform such labor or that the employment of the aliens would adversely affect the wages and working conditions of American workers. The Senate and House reports on the 1965 amendments to the Act make clear that Congress, by restructuring Section 212(a)(14) to exclude such aliens unless the Secretary certified that there were *not* sufficient American workers available, intended to reverse the prior presumption favoring admission to strengthen the protection of the American labor market and to reduce the burden on the Secretary in implementing this protection.

cong. intent

* * *

In light of our interpretation of Section 212(a)(14) and the legislative history supporting this interpretation, we conclude that the Secretary's denial of Ms. Quintero's certification did not constitute an abuse of discretion. First, we find proper the Secretary's treatment of Dr. Pesikoff's live-in requirement for his maid as a personal preference irrelevant to determination of whether there was in Houston a pool of potential workers willing to perform the Pesikoffs' domestic tasks. If the Secretary were required to find an individual American worker who met all the personal specifications of the prospective employer of each alien seeking Section 212(a)(14) certification, the burden on him in performing his statutory duty to protect the American labor market would be much greater than Congress intended in passing the 1965 amendments to the Act. It is well within the Secretary's discretion to ignore employer specifications which he deems, in accordance with his labor market expertise, to be irrelevant to the basic job which the employer desires performed. The Secretary may, therefore, survey the available labor market for a class of workers who, while possibly not meeting the prospective employer's personalized job description, do provide the employer with the potential for getting his job accomplished. The Secretary's treatment and classification of Dr. Pesikoff's employee request as one for a general maid who could live in or out was an appropriate exercise of the above described discretion. Dr. Pesikoff's statement to the Labor Department that Ms. Quintero would work only from 8:00 a.m. to 12:00 noon and 2:00 p.m. to 6:00 p.m. indicates that her need to live in is not significantly different from that of millions of American workers who readily and adequately perform their duties without living at their employment site.

"personal preference" arg no good

pↄ: protect Am labor mkt

We think the Secretary's treatment of Dr. Pesikoff's live-in preference was appropriate for an additional reason. As set forth above, Section 212(a)(14) provides that in order to grant an alien labor certification the Secretary must determine, not only that there are not American workers available, but also that employment of the alien will not adversely affect American wages and working conditions. The Secretary could well predict that the wages and working conditions of American maids would be adversely affected if Americans seeking domestic help could import, at the prevailing wage for live-out daily maids, aliens to work as live-in maids who are almost continuously on call. There is nothing in the record which moves us to question Dr. Pesikoff's representation that Ms. Quintero would have limited working hours. However, if the Secretary were to deem relevant to his survey of the available American work force a live-in

adverse effect on working condtns

preference of an employer who represents that his maid will work limited daytime hours, an American employer intending to work an alien at least intermittently around the clock could, by simple misrepresentation, defeat one of the primary purposes of Section 212(a)(14). Our analysis above of the section and its legislative history indicates that the Secretary has discretion to protect the American labor market against such employers with prophylactic procedures such as the employer personal preference disposition he made here.

* * *

Affirmed.

[A separate opinion by Judge MacKinnon, dissenting as to the "personal preference" issue, is omitted.]

Notes

1. Labor certification applications for housekeepers, once a weighty component of DOL's caseload, have fallen off considerably in recent years. In FY 1989 more than 10,000 applications for housekeepers were approved; by 1993 that number dropped to 1,200. 70 Interp.Rel. 1437 (1993). Much of the decline probably results from the huge backlogs for the "other worker" or unskilled category under the employment-based third preference, resulting in a six-year wait (steadily expanding) as of late 1994. Most potential certification beneficiaries in this category are probably already working for their employers; the added paperwork and fees, with such a delayed payoff, may not seem worthwhile.

2. The *Pesikoff* majority recognizes substantial discretion in the Secretary of Labor to determine what constitutes "the basic job" that the employer seeks to have accomplished, and then to decide, in light of that judgment, whether the specific requirements set forth in the employer's job description are excessive. But how does one decide what constitutes the "basic job" and what constitutes mere "personal preference"? Isn't the employer in a far better position to know in detail what the job requires? Won't employers suffer whenever the Department decides to treat a newly developed line of work or specialty as merely something that ought to be shoehorned into one of its standardized categories of "basic jobs"? Does the statute authorize—or, on the other hand, require—such an intrusive role for the agency? Why or why not?

3. Several other courts have been far less deferential than *Pesikoff* to the Secretary of Labor on these issues. *Ratnayake v. Mack,* 499 F.2d 1207 (8th Cir.1974), is illustrative. In that case, the operators of a school devoted to the Montessori method of teaching sought labor certification for two well-trained Montessori-method teachers from Ceylon (now Sri Lanka). The Department's denial was based on labor market data showing a surplus of college-trained teachers who could, in the Department's view, do the essential job with a minimum of training in the Montessori method. The court ruled for the employer:

In reviewing the job requirements established by appellant schools, the mere fact that the prerequisite for employment is a lengthy and extensive training period does not automatically give the Secretary the power to disregard them as unreasonable. There must be some deference accorded employment qualifications for "[e]very employer is entitled to hire persons who have qualifications that can be utilized in a manner that will contribute to the efficiency and quality of the business." Acupuncture Center of Washington v. Brennan, 364 F.Supp. 1038, 1042 (D.D.C.1973). In *Acupuncture Center,* the court held that it was not unreasonable for the employer to demand that applicants speak three dialects of Chinese as well as have an understanding of acupuncture terminology and science. The First Circuit has recently asserted that the Secretary "should not have the privilege of determining the qualifications of any particular applicant for the job to be filled. Nor without proof, should he have the right to attack the good faith of an employer's personnel procedures." Digilab, Inc. v. Secretary of Labor, 495 F.2d 323, at 326 [(1st Cir.) cert. denied, 419 U.S. 840, 95 S.Ct. 70, 42 L.Ed.2d 67 (1974)]. The job requirements of an employer are not to be set aside if they are shown to be reasonable and tend to contribute to or enhance the efficiency and quality of the business.

499 F.2d, at 1212.

The *Ratnayake* case, on its facts, is not difficult to swallow. The Labor Department had decided, in essence, that the basic job was simply that of school teacher, and it apparently was not willing to allow the development of a new and separate job classification—Montessori teachers—at least not with the two-year training requirements that the school envisioned. But the standard the court employed to overturn the agency's ruling is quite broad. In this court's view, the employer's job requirements should be upheld if they are "reasonable and tend to contribute to or enhance the efficiency and quality of the business." Can't a clever lawyer always draft job specifications tailored so precisely to the background of the alien intended as a beneficiary that they exclude all other persons in the world, and then successfully defend such requirements as reasonably calculated to "enhance" the employer's business? (Consider in this connection the facts of the *Acupuncture Center* case, summarized in the *Ratnayake* excerpt above. The district court's decision cited there was eventually reversed on appeal, relying on *Pesikoff.* 543 F.2d 852 (D.C.Cir.), *cert. denied,* 429 U.S. 818, 97 S.Ct. 62, 50 L.Ed.2d 78 (1976).)

The Current Administrative Approach: Business Necessity

With respect to the "personal preference" issue, Labor Department regulations now provide (20 C.F.R. § 656.21(b)(2)):

The employer shall document that the job opportunity has been and is being described without unduly restrictive job requirements:

(i) The job opportunity's requirements, unless adequately documented as arising from business necessity:

(A) Shall be those normally required for the job in the United States;

(B) Shall be those defined for the job in the *Dictionary of Occupational Titles (D.O.T.)* including those for subclasses of jobs;

(C) Shall not include requirements for a language other than English.

Controversy continued for some time over how to interpret the business necessity test set forth here. Some cases applied the relaxed *Ratnayake* standard; others began employing a test derived from *Diaz v. Pan Am World Airways, Inc.,* 442 F.2d 385 (5th Cir.1971), *cert. denied,* 404 U.S. 950, 92 S.Ct. 275, 30 L.Ed.2d 267 (1971), a Title VII employment discrimination case. Under that test, business necessity would be found only "when the *essence* of the business operation would be undermined" by failing to include the challenged job requirement. *Id.* at 388 (emphasis in original). The *Diaz* test drew criticism, however, in part because it would probably make it impossible for large enterprises to include requirements more restrictive than those of the D.O.T. *See* Berlowitz, Beattie, & O'Brien, *Labor Certification: The Statutory and Regulatory Evolution of the Business Necessity Requirement—Part I,* 12 Imm.J. 1 (1989).

In 1989, the Board of Alien Labor Certification Appeals issued a decision meant to resolve these issues and set governing standards for "business necessity" in future labor certification cases. *Matter of Information Industries,* 1990 WL 103627, 6 Imm. L. & Proc. Rep. B3–182 (BALCA, Feb. 9, 1989).

> We hold that, to establish business necessity under § 656.21(b)(2)(i), an employer must demonstrate that the job requirements bear a reasonable relationship to the occupation in the context of the employer's business and are essential to perform, in a reasonable manner, the job duties as described by the employer. This standard, in assuring both that the job's requirements bear a reasonable relationship to the occupation and are essential to perform the job duties, gives appropriate emphasis to the Act's presumption that qualified U.S. workers are available. An employer cannot obtain alien labor certification by showing that the job requirements merely "tend to contribute to or enhance the efficiency and quality of the business." On the other hand, this standard is not impossible to meet. An employer has the discretion, within reason, to obtain certification for any job whose requirements are directly related to its business, and does not have to establish dire financial consequences if the job is not filled or is filled by a U.S. worker who is not fully qualified.

In a footnote, the Board offered an illustration:

> For example, for a position as a lawyer, a job requirement of the ability to play golf usually cannot be justified as a business necessity even if the employer listed playing golf as a job duty on the Form 750–A. Although it may "tend to contribute to or

enhance the efficiency and quality of the business" socially and perhaps even economically, playing golf generally does not bear a reasonable relationship to the occupation of practicing law.

Make sure you understand what the Board means by job requirements vs. job duties. For more on the meaning of these terms, and their interrelation in the labor certification context, see *Ashbrook–Simon–Hartley v. McLaughlin,* 863 F.2d 410, 415 (5th Cir.1989). Has BALCA succeeded, with the *Information Industries* decision, in providing workable and effective guidelines, consistent with the basic policies underlying the statute? BALCA cases since *Information Industries* have tended to show that the first prong of the test, requiring a "reasonable relationship" between job requirements and the occupation is relatively easy to satisfy. Of greater importance in most cases is the second prong, requiring a showing that the job requirements "are *essential* to perform, in a reasonable manner, the job duties." (Emphasis added.) *See Business Necessity: A Year After* Information Industries, 67 Interp.Rel. 253, 256 (1990).

(iii) The Prevailing Wage Requirement

The Labor Department's regulations, *see* 20 C.F.R. § 656.40, require employers to pay the certified alien at least the prevailing wage, even if she would be willing to work for less. They impose this requirement, in major part, to implement the statutory directive that employment of the alien not "adversely affect the wages and working conditions of the workers in the United States similarly employed." But what wage level is "prevailing"? What is the relevant group for comparison, and how much discretion should the Secretary have in making such decisions? The question is analogous to determining what constitutes the "basic job."

Golabek v. Regional Manpower Administration, 329 F.Supp. 892 (E.D.Pa.1971), involved an application for labor certification for an art teacher in a parochial school. The Department denied certification in part because the wage offered was below comparable wages paid in the local public schools. The district court reversed the determination, holding that parochial school wages should have been the standard for comparison. The court explained—rather unhelpfully—that the "classroom and school situation is different and there may be any number of reasons why a teacher would prefer to work in one school system rather than the other." *Id.* at 896. How should such issues be resolved in a way that affords reasonable protection against erosion of wage scales for U.S. workers?

In *Matter of Tuskegee University,* 5 Imm. L. & Proc. Rep. B3–172 (BALCA, Feb. 23, 1988), the DOL certifying officer initially denied certification for a position as associate professor of physics. He found that Tuskegee was not offering the prevailing wage as measured by the pay scales used at other nearby colleges. Tuskegee argued that the relevant standard for comparison was instead the 43 schools that were part of the United Negro College Fund; by this standard its proposed pay scale was well above the prevailing rate. A divided Board of Alien Labor Certification Appeals agreed with the university: "It is clear that it is not only the job titles, but the nature of the business or institution where the jobs are located—for example, public or private, secular or religious, profit or non-profit, multi-national corporation or individual proprietorship—which must be evaluated in determining whether the jobs are 'substantially comparable.' "

In 1994, however, BALCA revisited the issue and unanimously overruled *Tuskegee*, in a case involving a nonprofit treatment center for handicapped children that wanted to hire a "maintenance repairer." *Matter of Hathaway Children's Services*, 91–INA–388 (BALCA, Feb. 4, 1994), summarized in 71 Interp.Rel. 357 (1994). The center argued that the relevant standard for comparison was wages paid at other United Way nonprofit agencies, but the Board took a different view:

> [N]either the record in *Tuskegee*, nor the record before us today, suggests that the skills and knowledge required to perform the duties of the job opportunity being offered are any different depending on the employer's financial ability to pay the going rate. Specifically, there is no evidence to suggest that the duties of the job offered [in either case] differed as between charitable non-profit institutions and businesses operated for a profit.

The Board ruled that it could not allow Hathaway to pay substandard wages to its maintenance staff while telling "the Mom-and-Pop shop next door or around the corner" that the INA and the regulations allow no waivers of the prevailing wage requirement on the basis of the employer's hardship, citing *Matter of Norberto La Rosa*, 89–INA–287 (BALCA, March 27, 1991).

Should *Tuskegee* have been overruled? What policy is served if the job goes unfilled because Tuskegee or Hathaway cannot pay the DOL-determined prevailing wage?

The Department's "prevailing wage" approach raises deeper issues as well. Insisting on such wages prevents a *deterioration* of pay scales as currently provided in the relevant industry. But deterioration is not the only possible adverse effect that wages might suffer. Should the Department be equally concerned about retarding increases in wages that might otherwise occur in times of labor shortage?

Consider a concrete example. Professional nurses are in such short supply that licensed nurses are exempt from individual labor certification, under the provisions of Schedule A. In fact, however, there are large numbers of trained U.S. workers in the field who simply do not practice that profession; wages have traditionally been low, and many trained nurses find better opportunities for higher pay in other fields. Indeed, some claim that wages have remained low in the nursing field because it has traditionally been regarded as "women's work." *See Women's Work—and Wages,* Newsweek, July 9, 1984, at 22; *Lemons v. City and County of Denver,* 17 FEP Cas. 906 (D.Colo.1978), *affirmed,* 620 F.2d 228 (10th Cir.1980), *cert. denied,* 449 U.S. 888, 101 S.Ct. 244, 66 L.Ed.2d 114 (1980) (plaintiffs asserted that the city engaged in forbidden sex discrimination by paying nurses less than workers in male-dominated occupations; court refused to accept this "comparable worth" theory and ruled for defendants). *See generally Women and the Workplace: The Implications of*

Occupational Segregation (M. Blaxall & B. Reagan eds. 1976). If hospitals were unable to hire alien nurses at current wage scales, what would be likely to happen? If you conclude that employers would bid up wages, drawing many qualified workers back into the labor pool, and inducing more people to develop the necessary skills and training, consider what other conditions must hold for this conclusion to be sound. Would the same results occur in the restaurant or hotel business, in factories, in marginal small businesses, in agriculture?

The availability of foreign nurses under Schedule A may well interfere with improvements in wages. Should this result be considered an adverse effect? In other words, is the Department of Labor's time horizon too short or vision too restricted in light of the fundamental workings of a free-market system? On the other hand, should the Department's approach be seen instead as a valid measure to keep down hospital costs or to keep marginally profitable hospitals open and functioning? Is the Labor Department the appropriate agency to carry out this function? These questions just scratch the surface of a highly complex and contentious economic, social, and political debate. *See generally, e.g.,* Killingsworth, *Effects of Immigration Into the United States on the U.S. Labor Market: Analytical and Policy Issues, in* U.S. Immigration and Refugee Policy 249 (M. Kritz ed. 1983); Tienda, *Socioeconomic and Labor Force Characteristics of U.S. Immigrants: Issues and Approaches, id.,* at 211; R. Bach & D. Meissner, America's Labor Market in the 1990s: What Role Should Immigration Play? (1990); Immigration, Trade, and the Labor Market (Nat'l Bureau of Econ. Research, R. Freeman ed. 1988); P. Martin, Illegal Immigration and the Colonization of the American Labor Market 35–45 (1986); V. Briggs, Immigration Policy and the American Labor Force (1984); The Unavoidable Issue: U.S. Immigration Policy in the 1980s (D. Papademetriou & M. Miller eds. 1983); The Gateway: Immigration Issues and Policy (B. Chiswick ed. 1982); M. Piore, Birds of Passage: Migrant Labor and Industrial Societies (1979); and sources cited in Section C *infra.*

(iv) The Requirement of a Genuine Employment Relationship

The Department of Labor also has worried about other ways in which a genuine test of labor market conditions might be defeated in the labor certification process. For example, the regulations forbid labor certification for jobs that amount to self-employment. "Employment" is defined as "permanent full-time work by an employee for an employer *other than oneself.*" 20 C.F.R. § 656.3. The Department has applied this rule not only to solo practitioners, but also to persons who own a controlling share of the corporation seeking certification, under two circumstances: when the corporation is a sham or when the alien is indispensable or inseparable from the corporation. The court in *Hall v. McLaughlin,* 864 F.2d 868 (D.C.Cir.1989), explained these two tests:

> The "sham" question determines only whether the corporation was fraudulently established for the sole purpose of obtaining certification for the alien. The "inseparability" question considers whether the corporation, even if legitimately established, relies so heavily on the pervasive presence and personal attributes of the

alien that it would be unlikely to continue in operation without him. This latter question is appropriate because a company that depends so heavily on the alien that it would probably shut down without him is unlikely to make any real choice between him and a "qualified" United States worker.

Id. at 874–75. The dissent, however, found the "inseparability" test inappropriate: "[T]he insistence on the alien's being dispensable seems to directly *defeat* the statutory purpose. Proof that a worker is indispensable would seem to satisfy [the statutory] requirement of a showing that 'there are not sufficient workers in the United States who are able, willing, qualified, ... and available.' " *Id.* at 880.

In the wake of *Hall*, the Board of Alien Labor Certification Appeals reaffirmed and amplified the basic approach taken by the majority. *Matter of Lignomat USA, Ltd.*, 7 Imm.L. & Proc.Rep. B3–123 (BALCA, Oct. 24, 1989). The Ninth Circuit has also approved the doctrine, with these observations:

> As the district court correctly noted, "the DOL certification process is built around a central administrative mechanism: A private good faith search by the certification applicant for U.S. workers qualified to take the job at issue." * * * The two independent safeguards challenged by [the employer]—the ban on alien self-employment and the bona fide job requirement—make the good faith search process self-enforcing. These prophylactic rules permit the Department of Labor to process more than 50,000 permanent labor certification requests each year.

Bulk Farms, Inc. v. Martin, 963 F.2d 1286, 1288 (9th Cir.1992). Do you agree? Is the ban on self-employment good policy? Consistent with the statute? Should it be applied to situations where the corporation is bona fide and was validly established for purposes other than enabling the immigration of the principal owner?

(v) Labor Certification and an Attorney's Professional Responsibility

The Trillin article, *supra*, uses language in describing the certification process, such as "sham" employment offer, that obviously departs from the way most practicing attorneys would think of their role—or would want others to think of that role. (Those characterizations were Trillin's, not those of the attorneys he had observed, and the article was sharply criticized by the immigration bar.) Around the time that article appeared, INS and the Departments of Labor and State began an extensive investigation of possible fraud in labor certification and marriage cases. Several lawyers were indicted, but some of the government's investigative tactics, particularly interrogation of employer clients without notice to the attorneys, drew vigorous denunciation. A few of the highly publicized indictments were dropped, but others led to convictions of attorneys. Eventually some of the more questionable investigative techniques were abandoned. *See* 62 Interp.Rel. 416 (1985); 63 *id.* 392 (1986); 64 *id.* 1291 (1987); N.Y. Times, Oct. 21, 1985, at A1; *id.*, May 1, 1986, at A25.

These experiences prompted more explicit attention to ethical issues involved in the labor certification process. The following excerpts from a useful and wide-ranging article both warn of the pitfalls and provide revealing glimpses of the substantial practical problems confronting an attorney handling a labor certification case.[23]

ETHICAL CONSIDERATIONS IN IMMIGRATION CASES

4 Immigration Law Report 169 (Dec. 1985).

* * * One source of the significant ethical problems faced by immigration practitioners is the ambiguity and inconsistency in interpretation of the Immigration and Nationality Act, the statute governing the standards and procedures for obtaining immigration benefits for aliens. Another source is the aliens themselves, since obtaining an immigration benefit, particularly U.S. permanent residence, can be perceived by some aliens as virtually a matter of life and death for which they would not hesitate to fabricate facts or commit fraud.

Between the complexity of the law and the fervor with which the client desires to achieve his or her goal, unwary or simply incautious immigration practitioners can become enmeshed in a situation which may not only threaten their adherence to professional standards, but possibly lead to prosecution for perpetrating or abetting an immigration fraud.

* * *

STANDARDS IN THE CODE OF PROFESSIONAL RESPONSIBILITY

* * *

The most pertinent canon under the Code with regard to fraudulent conduct is Canon 7: "A lawyer should represent a client zealously within the bounds of the law." * * *

[Ethical Consideration (E.C.) 7–6] states: "Whether the proposed action of a lawyer is within the bounds of the law may be a perplexing question when his client is contemplating a course of conduct having legal consequences that vary according to the client's intent, motive, or desires at the time of the action. Often a lawyer is asked to assist his client at a particular time. He may properly assist his client in the development and preservation of evidence of existing motive, intent or desire; obviously, he may not do anything furthering the creation or preservation of false evidence. In many cases a lawyer may not be certain as to the state of mind of his client, and in those situations he should resolve reasonable doubts in favor of his client."

* * *

23. The article was written by attorneys from the experienced immigration firm of Fragomen, Del Rey & Bernsen, which produces the *Immigration Law Report* periodical. It refers to the American Bar Association's Model Code of Professional Responsibility, which has now been superseded in many states by the ABA's Model Rules of Professional Conduct (of particular relevance to the discussion here are Rules 1.2(d), 1.7, 3.1, 3.3). The basic points in the article are not affected by that change. *See also* Hake, *Dual Representation in Immigration Practice: The Simple Solution is the Wrong Solution,* 5 Geo.Imm.L.J. 581 (1991).

Labor Certification Cases

The ethical difficulties in marriage cases pale in comparison to the problems and pitfalls that a practitioner can encounter in a labor certification application. Probably no area of the immigration law fits more clearly within the circumstances described in E.C. 7–6, quoted above.

* * *

While the largest employers often have "canned" job descriptions and statements of minimum requirements for most positions in their corporate hierarchy, most employers do not have such sophisticated personnel operations. Even after an employer has filled the position in question by hiring the alien after an extensive recruitment and interview process, the employer's hiring agent may still have a difficult time verbalizing its minimum requirements in filling a position. It would not be unusual for an employer to have no minimum requirements, but rather a set of preferences which, however, could be replaced by the correct subjective elements, such as the "right" personality for the job or a desirable aggressiveness or flair. The practitioner in this situation is confronted with the daunting task of somehow translating the employer's criteria for the position into the quantifiable criteria demanded by the [Department of Labor (DOL)]. While the employer might not initially think of its criteria in terms of minimum requirements, it is obvious that not every person would be considered qualified by the employer.

It therefore becomes the role of the attorney, who is aware of the vocabulary and standards of the DOL, to aid the employer in verbalizing in acceptable form the "minimum requirements" which must be provided for labor certification purposes. The attorney who must engage in this process with the employer enters upon dangerous terrain, since the employer may be convinced that its actual requirements are nothing like the final result of the process and who therefore believes that the requirements have been manufactured by the attorney. The attorney, on the other hand, may be convinced that he or she has successfully translated those factors important to the employer in hiring the alien into a statement of the minimum requirements sufficient to satisfy the DOL. Given the disparity between the employer's and the attorney's perceptions, it is not surprising that attorneys who may be investigated for engaging in the perpetration of a fraud in framing the minimum requirements would consider the suggestion of fraud to be unfair. The reality of these investigations, however, requires the conscientious attorney to follow certain procedures, as much for self-preservation as for ethical considerations, which he or she may believe have not been transgressed.

The attorney must be certain that the employer is aware and understands that the labor certification application is the employer's application, not the alien's. The employer is responsible for the statements made in the certification and must be comfortable with all of the affirmations contained in it. If, after the attorney works with the employer to verbalize the employer's minimum requirements, the employer is not convinced that those requirements really underlie its hiring decision, the attorney should not file an application containing those requirements. The attorney has an obligation under the Code to inform the employer of the prospects of success in filing the labor certification application, and should inform the employer of the impact of failing to include certain requirements, but the attorney must be satisfied that the employer is not accepting a given statement of requirements simply because of the attorney's assessment of the likelihood of success without those requirements.

The difficulty of this situation is compounded when the attorney is retained to represent the alien. It may happen in this situation that the employer agrees to the attorney's representation of it but does not make its personnel representative sufficiently available to the attorney, apparently in the belief that the attorney is fundamentally representing the alien. Proceeding on this basis is a tremendous mistake, since the DOL expects the employer to take responsibility for the application and conduct the recruitment of U.S. workers without the involvement of the alien. The danger of the employer repudiating the certification application or recruitment results in this type of case should serve as sufficient deterrent to the practitioner faced with this arrangement.

* * *

The difficulty that can sometimes confront the practitioner when retained by the alien in the labor certification process is only one aspect of the larger ethical dilemma in representing both the employer and employee in the immigration setting. The interests of the two parties may be differing and result in a potential conflict of interest that can violate the Code's ethical considerations. The Code states that a lawyer is precluded from accepting or continuing employment that will adversely affect his or her judgment on behalf of a client, particularly when two clients have "differing interests," whether such interests be conflicting, inconsistent, diverse or otherwise discordant. E.C. 5–14. When an attorney is presented with potentially differing interests, the Code directs that he or she resolve all doubts against the propriety of the representation. E.C. 5–15. Particularly when a lawyer will represent both a corporate client and an individual employee, the Code directs that the lawyer may serve the individual only if the lawyer is convinced that differing interests are not present. E.C. 5–18. While two different lawyers are almost never involved in the representation of the alien and the employer in an immigration case, such dual representation might prevent some difficult problems that can arise with regard to such issues as the stated intention of the employee to seek or accept new employment upon conferral of permanent resident status.

(vi) Easing the Task of Labor Certification—or Avoiding it Altogether

As is evident from the earlier cases and discussion, individual labor certification is a time-consuming, highly technical, and expensive process. Moreover, there are some signs that DOL is tightening up its standards and rejecting employer statements of job requirements that previously passed muster. For these reasons, good immigration lawyers seek to avoid labor certification whenever that is possible. *See* Webber, *Strategies for Avoiding Labor Certification*, 93–12 Imm.Briefings (1993).

Exercise

An American university seeks to hire a promising young scientist from India for the physics department, with the rank of assistant professor. The university's interest was attracted by a "brilliant" article he published in an international journal. University officials have not decided just how much teaching they would want him to perform, because they are primarily interested in his joining a high-powered research team that they hope will win large foundation and government grants for the university. The employment-based second preference would seem to fit, but that category ordinarily requires labor certification.

The university has engaged you as its lawyer to speed the approval of his immigration papers. What would you advise? Consider first whether this case can be brought within the more favorable "equally qualified" provisions of INA § 212(a)(5)(A)(ii). Then decide whether labor certification can be avoided altogether. Is Schedule A a possibility? (Check the regulations governing permanent labor certification, 20 C.F.R. Part 656, reprinted in the Supplement.) "Priority workers" under the employment-based first preference also are not required to obtain labor certification. Can his case be made to fit any of those categories? Consider carefully in this connection 8 C.F.R. § 204.5(g)-(*l*), giving operational content to some of the vague terms used in the statute (*e.g.*, "outstanding," "extraordinary ability," "exceptional ability").[24] *See Buletini v. INS*, 860 F.Supp. 1222 (E.D.Mich.1994) (construing the INS regulations governing "extraordinary ability" in a manner highly favorable to the alien).

———

One previously overlooked technique for avoiding labor certification is attracting increasing interest. INA § 203(b)(2)(B) allows the Attorney General to waive the requirement that a second-preference alien's services be sought by an employer in the United States, when waiver is deemed "in the national interest." The regulations, without further elaboration of the "national interest" standard, provide that such a waiver also exempts the individual from labor certification. 8 C.F.R. § 204.5(k)(4)(ii).

Decisions by the INS's Administrative Appeals Unit (AAU) are beginning to provide more guidance, and they show, to date, a fairly generous stance. The AAU's standards consider whether the alien's admission: (1) will improve the U.S. economy; (2) will improve wages and working conditions of U.S. workers; (3) will improve educational and training programs for U.S. children and underqualified workers; (4) will improve

---

24. One writer has observed that many practitioners have "developed a warm and welcoming relationship with the extensive and detailed lists of qualifying criteria set out in [these] regulations. [They] provide a co- gent and well-directed road map which, if closely followed, should lead to eventual INS approval." Van Deusen, *National Interest Waivers,* 13 Imm.L.Rep. 73, 75–76 (1994).

health care; (5) will provide more affordable housing for young, aged, or poor U.S. residents; (6) will improve the U.S. environment and lead to more productive use of national resources; or (7) is requested by an interested U.S. government agency. This is quite a laundry list, but the AAU emphasized that the alien's presence must provide a benefit to the country beyond the prospective national benefit already required of second-preference immigrants. The burden is on the alien, and the stress is on close case-by-case review. *See National Interest Waivers in the EB–2 Category*, 13 Imm.L.Rep. 69–70 (1994) (summarizing AAU standards and illustrative case law); *National Interest Waivers: The INS Grants an Array of Second Preference Cases Without Job Offers or Labor Certifications, id.* at 73 (describing procedures and case law). Are these standards consistent with the statute? Do they reflect wise policy?

(vii) Other Problems With Labor Certification

YUI SING TSE v. INS

United States Court of Appeals, Ninth Circuit, 1979.
596 F.2d 831.

BROWNING, CIRCUIT JUDGE:

[The petitioner had sought adjustment of status under INA § 245, from nonimmigrant student to sixth preference immigrant under the old system (the preference for skilled and unskilled workers in a field and location suffering from a shortage of U.S. workers) based on a labor certification for a job as Chinese specialty cook. Adjustment was denied.]

At a hearing held July 24, 1975, petitioner disclosed that he had applied and been accepted for admission to dental school, and would enroll in the fall. He testified it would require four years to complete dental school, and that he intended to continue working as a full-time Chinese specialty cook to support himself and his family while attending school.

The immigration judge denied petitioner's request for an adjustment of status and ordered petitioner deported. The Board [of Immigration Appeals] affirmed on the ground that petitioner was ineligible for an adjustment of status because he planned to become a dentist rather than to continue to work as a cook.

* * *

Taken together, [the labor certification provision and the employment-based preference categories] are designed to permit aliens capable of performing jobs for which American workers are not available to come to this country, while protecting American workers from the competition of aliens entering the United States to take jobs American workers could fill.

The second and potentially conflicting interest involved is the interest of an alien granted permanent resident status in the opportunity to earn a living, to improve his economic circumstances, and to engage in common occupations, without unreasonable limitation or invidious discrimination. This interest was reflected in a regulation of the Department of Labor in effect when the Board rendered its decision in this case which provided that "[t]he terms and conditions of the labor certificate shall not be construed as preventing an immigrant properly admitted to the United States from subsequently changing his occupation, job, or area of residence." 29 C.F.R. § 60.5(f) (1976). Addressing the question of an alien's freedom to change occupations, the court in *Castaneda-Gonzalez v. INS,* 183 U.S.App.D.C. 396, 412, 564 F.2d 417, 433 n. 36 (1977), noted the previous existence of this regulation and said: "[a]ny other interpretation could raise serious constitutional issues as to the extent to which employment opportunities may be restricted on the basis of alienage."

In the present case, the Board looked solely to whether at the moment of entry the alien intended to change from the certificated employment, and concluded that petitioner was not entitled to preference as an immigrant because his intention at "entry" was to change employment, though only in the distant future and upon a condition that might not be satisfied. The standard applied by the Board was entirely subjective. It was both too narrow and too rigid to accommodate the interests to be protected.

It is appropriate to require that the alien intend to occupy the certificated occupation for a period of time that is reasonable in light both of the interest served by the statute and the interest in freedom to change employment. But to hold, as the Board did in this case, that an alien is not eligible for admission as a preference immigrant when his intention at entry is to engage in the certified employment unless and until he can complete the educational and other requirements for advancement to the profession of dentistry, a period of four years, fails to recognize that both the interest underlying the grant of preference and the interest in freedom of opportunity for self-improvement would be substantially served by petitioner's admission.

The Board's approach is not required either by the statute or by the Board's regulations.

* * *

Reversed and remanded.

WALLACE, CIRCUIT JUDGE, dissenting:

* * *

[The] question most emphatically is not whether an immigrant alien, once properly admitted, may change jobs. Rather, the question is whether an alien who applies for immigrant status, and who is thus considered as if he were initially entering the country, *see, e.g., Campos v. INS,* 402 F.2d 758, 760 (9th Cir.1968), may definitely intend, at the time that he makes his application, to change employment from that for which he acquires his labor certificate.

The Board did not forbid an immigrant alien from changing his mind in the future and improving his employment situation. The Board simply held that at the specific time the petitioner submits his application, he must have made a choice to work in the specific area for which he received the work certificate. When the petitioner admits that his desire to do that type of work is merely temporary (i.e., until he can secure some other type of work), he does not qualify.

* * *

The protection of the American work force, as underscored by section [212(a)(5)], specifically has to do with where an alien will compete in the job market. The ultimate intent of petitioner is not to work as a Chinese food cook but to work as a dentist. Granting him a labor certificate for what is obviously only temporary employment and closing the Board's eyes to his eventual employment desire would merely frustrate the basic purposes of the statute and prevent the Board from performing its statutorily mandated duty of protecting American labor.

* * *

Notes

1. Similar questions to those presented in the principal case arise when an alien enters on an employment-based visa, and either works for a very short time at the certified employment or fails to report for that job at all. The courts have generally been insistent that aliens are not deportable on such facts alone. The government must go further and prove that the alien willfully misrepresented his intent to take the certified work at the time of his entry. *See, e.g., Jang Man Cho v. INS,* 669 F.2d 936 (4th Cir.1982) (reversing and remanding deportation order for further proceedings, even though the alien never even reported for the certified employment); Annotation, 62 A.L.R.Fed. 402 (1983).

2. Suppose Congress explicitly rewrote the statute to require, as a prerequisite to visa issuance, a commitment from second- and third-preference immigrants that they remain in the certified employment for a minimum of, say, five years. It could, for example, initially give such aliens only conditional permanent residence, like the status received by alien spouses under § 216 and alien investors under § 216A. Consider the majority's dictum in *Yui Sing Tse.* Would there be constitutional problems with such a provision? Would such a change constitute sound policy? *Cf.* INA § 210A(d)(5) (provisions requiring "replenishment agricultural workers" to work a specified amount of time in agriculture over 3–5 years in order to avoid deportation and eventually to naturalize; the RAW program was never implemented, however).

(viii) The Future of Labor Certification

Under cases like *Yui Sing Tse* and *Jang Man Cho,* an alien may be able to secure labor certification and then, after a token stay in the certified employment—long enough to defeat deportation or prosecution based on bad faith or willful misrepresentation—enter any field of employment he wishes. That is, there is little guarantee that even those who do enter after complying with the complicated requirements of the occupational preferences will refrain from competing with American workers in fields where there is no labor shortage.

Consider, as well, other possible incentives created by the intricate provisions for individual labor certification.

In order to obtain a labor certification, the alien [generally] must have a specific job offer from a prospective employer. * * * Obviously, it is not easy for an alien to learn of a job opening, and to obtain an offer for it, while abroad. Still less likely is it that the prospective employer will be willing to file a set of papers with the Labor Department—and possibly haggle with them over job requirements and wages—on behalf of an alien whom he has never met, for a job to be taken two or three years later when the alien is finally admitted. As a result, * * * aliens by the thousands enter the United States with visitors' visas forbidding them to work, and then seek and obtain job offers and illegally fill those jobs while awaiting their immigrant visas. When the visa is available, they return home briefly to receive it from the consul, and are back at work here in the United States soon after. It therefore appears that the requirement that the alien have a specific job offer (rather than simply be qualified in a job area known to be short of personnel) and the long delays in obtaining a visa combine to make illegal immigration and employment helpful if not necessary steps in the pursuit of permanent residence in the United States.

Abrams & Abrams, *Immigration Policy—Who Gets In and Why?,* 38 The Pub.Int. 3, 14–15 (1975). Abrams & Abrams wrote in 1975. It was hoped that IRCA's employer sanctions scheme, adopted by Congress in 1986, would reduce some of the problems of which they warned, but employer sanctions have not been very successful, and the cycle still occurs. *See* Section C *infra.*

Other problems with labor certification would be highlighted, however, if the sanctions are someday made more effective. For example, before the 1990 Act, employers with certified jobs often had to wait years before the alien could legally immigrate, owing to lengthy backlogs for some categories and countries. Most of these backlogs were cleared when the 1990 Act more than doubled the number of employment-based admissions, but the unskilled worker category suffers from waits of over six years, and a few oversubscribed countries are likely to see backlogs in the next few years. If the employer can survive for several years without the employee, how real was the labor need on which the immigration opportunity was premised? [25]

Consider in this connection the remarkable durability of certifications. Under current regulations, a labor certification, once issued, is "valid indefinitely," at least for the employee first mentioned in the papers. 8 C.F.R. § 656.30(a). Is this provision consistent with the statute? Check carefully the language of INA § 212(a)(5)(A)(i)(I). Does indefinite validity render even more problematic the claim that the process supplies workers genuinely needed by American employers? For an aggravated example along these lines, see *Masonry Masters, Inc. v. Thornburgh,* 875 F.2d 898

---

25. This problem is partially ameliorated, or course, if the employer can legally obtain the alien's services in the meantime under the H or L nonimmigrant worker provisions, discussed in Section B *infra.* But such opportunities are rare for the unskilled.

(D.C.Cir.1989) (case remanded in 1989 for proper consideration of employer's ability to pay the prevailing wage *in 1979,* when it first applied for labor certification).

The Department of Labor has tried to reduce some of these anomalies by at least restricting the right of employers to substitute other alien workers on the certification or employment-based visa petition. (Substitution is highly valued because visa priority dates are currently established as of the date of the request for labor certification, not the date of the visa petition or the date when the individual alien first expresses interest in immigrating.) An early DOL guideline allowing substitution only in the first six months after certification was struck down by a court as exceeding DOL's authority, on the plausible theory that the no-substitution rule did not deal directly with the labor market, which is supposed to be DOL's focus of concern. *Medellin v. Bustos,* 854 F.2d 795 (5th Cir.1988). INS and DOL then tried new approaches, described in *Kooritzky v. Reich,* 17 F.3d 1509 (D.C.Cir.1994). In October 1991, DOL adopted new regulations (amending 20 C.F.R. § 656.30(c)) to forbid substitution of alien employees altogether, but a court invalidated them for failure to comply with the notice-and-comment rulemaking requirements of the APA. *Id.* As of late 1994, no new regulations have appeared on the subject, and the invalidated regulations remain in C.F.R.

In light of all these problems, is labor certification worth the trouble? *See, e.g.,* G & M § 2.40d (1989 ed.) (suggesting that "the labor certification program in its present form is a failure"). Should Congress give up on preference provisions tied so closely to specific job requirements? Should all immigration for permanent residence be based on family reunification or other personal characteristics specific to the alien, no matter what field of work he or she may ultimately choose? How would you craft such requirements?

In the debates that led up to enactment of the 1990 Act, proposals for reducing reliance on individual labor certification, which is inefficient and expensive, received considerable attention. Some legislators argued for a shift to more extensive use of broader labor market determinations (something like the current Schedules A and B) as the basis for decisions about which skilled people would be admitted. Others questioned whether such determinations could be reliably made in a country with a labor market as decentralized as that of the United States. Unlike Germany, for example, the United States has no central labor agency through which a high proportion of all hiring is channeled; thus it lacks sensitive indicators of developing scarcity or surplus of workers in particular fields. Even with better data, some argued, recruitment of foreigners, followed by the necessary documentation and admission process, would be a very cumbersome way to meet real labor market needs.

The version of the 1990 Act reported by the House Judiciary Committee would have streamlined the process of filling employment-based immigration slots by moving to a labor attestation system, rather than labor certification. The committee report (H.R.Rep. No. 101–723, Pt. 1, at 43) explained:

Many employers prefer to hire domestically and place much effort in the search for workers, yet are unable to find the technician or expert needed. Additionally, the current labor certification process required to prove that this search has occurred is fraught with time-consuming hurdles. In many parts of the country this part of the immigration process alone can take 15 months. The bill responds to this problem by allowing employers to file an attestation as to recruitment, payment of prevailing wages, and strike conditions, thus replacing the lengthy, adjudicatory, labor certification process with a process that allows attestations that have not been challenged to become effective. Attestations that have been challenged will go through a thorough administrative review procedure. This will focus Department of Labor resources on enforcement procedures, not on universal, routine and frequently unnecessary administrative screening and review activities.

If an employer were found guilty of misrepresentation or other misuse of the attestation system, the bill provided for civil monetary penalties, back pay (if pay had been below the prevailing wage), and one-year suspension of the privilege of importing foreign labor on a temporary or permanent basis.

The attestation system was modified before the bill passed the House, and then it was dropped in the House–Senate conference before final passage of the 1990 Act. The conferees did keep a limited version of attestation, applicable to nonimmigrant admissions in category H–1B. INA § 212(n), discussed at pp. 245–48 *infra*.[26] Would you favor changing to an attestation system? Would attestations provide adequate deterrence against misuse of the employment-based immigration provisions? Or on the other hand, do they provide too much deterrence, making employers fearful of using the provisions, since they might not know until long after the work starts that they are in violation, then incurring significant penalties? *See* Paparelli & Haight, *Avoiding or Accepting Risks in H–1B/LCA Practice, Parts I & II*, 92–11 & 92–12 Imm.Briefings (1992); Pivec, *Observations on the Enforcement of the H–1B Labor Condition Application Requirements*, 71 Interp.Rel. 705 (1994).

Consider also another recent and creative reform proposal, set forth in Solomon, *Priorities and Preferences: Keeping Place in the Immigrant Visa Line*, 92–6 Imm. Briefings 21–22 (1992), and which would seem to serve more closely the underlying purposes of the statutory scheme. Solomon's proposed reforms would allow aliens to self-petition for any employment category for which they qualify by education and experience; multiple filings would be allowed and the individual's visa allocation priority date would be the date of approval of this individual skills petition. Employers seeking to fill a vacancy would separately file labor certification applications with the DOL, without having to identify the expected alien employee. As Solomon argues, the DOL's decision would then focus "on the nonavailability of U.S. workers and an analysis of the terms and conditions offered

---

26. The first use of an attestation procedure (using quite different criteria) was adopted by the Immigrant Nursing Relief Act of 1989, Pub.L. No. 101–238, 103 Stat. 2099. These provisions appear in INA §§ 101(a)(15)(H)(i)(a), 212(m).

in the employment—not on the availability or qualifications of the alien. What difference does it make to this determination as to who the alien is who will fill this position if U.S. workers are not available, so long as the alien meets all the qualifications for the position that were required for U.S. workers?" *Id.* at 21. The employer could use an approved certification within a year by making an offer to an alien with an approved individual petition. (After a year the employer would have to make a new labor market test.) The alien would then go to a consulate with the offer and certification, and if his priority date is current based on his earlier self-petition, he could receive a visa. How do you answer the question posed in the quoted passage? Should this reform be adopted?

b. *The Employment–Based Preferences*

Perhaps the dominant feature of the reforms enacted in 1990 is the growth by 160 percent of admission numbers for employment-based immigration. In an article that predated the 1990 Act, Senator Simpson presented the arguments for such a change:

> Other immigrant-receiving countries do not focus so exclusively on family-connected immigration. As one scholar [David North] has noted, "I know of no nation roughly comparable to ours that places such an emphasis on family connections. Australia, Canada and New Zealand, for example, all welcome some foreign-born as immigrants, not as guestworkers. Each of these nations is interested in securing talented people and investors, in addition to family members. Each has a system designed to meet these goals—as we do not now. Each is better positioned, frankly, than we are to attract the restless talent of the world."

> There is no question that some of today's family-connected immigrants display "restless talents" and contribute to the nation's economy. However, it is also clear that some are less talented than others (or have talents less needed than others), and that given the tremendous worldwide interest in immigrating to the United States, our legal immigration system could do a more responsible job of selecting immigrants who serve the national interest.

Simpson, *Legal Immigration Reform,* 25 San Diego L.Rev. 215, 218–19 (1988). Others made the same points in stronger language:

> [T]he current system of family preference is nepotistic and no longer serving the national interest. * * * [W]e should select immigrants more on the basis of what needed talents and skills they bring. Not on the basis of "who they know." Certainly immigrants who enter * * * ought to be able to bring immediate relatives. But we must adopt a policy that judges people on the basis of individual merit rather than national origin, race, or "family connections."

Reform of Legal Immigration, Hearings before the Subcomm. on Immigration, Refugees and International Law, House Comm. on the Judiciary, 100th Cong., 2d Sess. 398 (Serial No. 101, 1988) [hereafter *Reform Hear-*

ings] (statement of Daniel A. Stein, Executive Director, Federation for American Immigration Reform).

Other observers took issue with this harsh assertion, stressing certain instrumental values served by families in the immigration process:

> A family reunification-based immigration policy recognizes that families serve as buffers and mediators between the individual immigrant and the host environment. Families are the facilitators of an immigrant's social, economic and, gradually, political integration and enhance the immigrant's ability to make a successful transition to the new community and society. Families also provide an important private social safety net, critical childcare, and information about the labor market. These are essential to an immigrant's successful adaptation.

Reform Hearings, supra, at 426 (statement of Doris Meissner, then Senior Associate at the Carnegie Endowment, appointed Commissioner of INS in 1993).

Meissner's testimony in those hearings summarized the results of an extensive examination of Canadian immigration, which attempts in a highly systematic way, through a point system, to orient about 40 percent of its immigration toward bringing in people who will serve Canada's economic objectives. (The Canadian point system has been used as a model by some who want to shift U.S. policy much further in this direction.) She found, however, that a surprisingly high percentage, 45 percent, of those who came in as selected workers also had family connections in Canada. "The conclusion to draw is not that Canada or point systems are unable or unwilling to tap independent flows; it is that family members remain the largest single source of applicants interested in immigrating and can and do serve to meet not only the family unification objectives of immigration policy but also the objectives of independent immigration policies." *Id.* at 421.

Which of the above positions do you find more persuasive?

The reform bill reported in 1990 by the House Judiciary Committee took an importantly different view (from that of Senator Simpson or Mr. Stein) of the real challenges to U.S. competitive success in the global economy, and it proposed a novel and controversial fee of $1000 per imported worker as a way of responding. The Committee report explained its understanding of both the problem and the remedy (H.R.Rep. No. 101–723, pt. 1, at 41–45):

> The U.S. labor market is now faced with two problems that immigration policy can help to correct. The first is the need of American business for highly skilled, specially trained personnel to fill increasingly sophisticated jobs for which domestic personnel cannot be found and the need for other workers to meet specific labor shortages. The second problem concerns the increasing skills gap in the current and projected U.S. labor pool. "Workforce 2000," which was prepared for the Department of Labor by the Hudson Institute, is one study among several that indicates

that the education and skills of the emerging U.S. labor force will be mismatched with labor market needs. Because it is unlikely that enough U.S. workers will be trained quickly enough to meet legitimate employment needs, and because such needs are already not being met, the Committee is convinced that immigration can and should be incorporated into an overall strategy that promotes the creation of the type of workforce needed in an increasingly competitive global economy without adversely impacting on the wages and working conditions of American workers.

* * *

The Committee believes, however, that immigration must be part of an overall human resources policy that recognizes the needs of members of our own society who have been left behind. As Deputy Assistant Secretary of Labor for Employment and Training David O. Williams stated, "We must guard against making a fundamental miscalculation and relying excessively on immigration. Doing so could place immigration policy in conflict with other national priorities ... by interfering with our resolve as a nation to bring into the economic mainstream some of those who are not now there: minority youth, the disabled, the disadvantaged, older Americans."

These challenges are met in this legislation by creation of a system under which certain employers who are granted permission to import foreign workers will be required to pay a fee that will be deposited in an account in the Department of Labor. Funds from this account will be used for education and training of U.S. workers as part of the broader linkage between immigration and labor policy.

* * *

By creating an Education and Training Fund as a component part of H.R. 4300, the Committee recognizes the need to balance the short term employment demands of employers with the need to train and educate the new generation of American workers. The Committee believes that increased immigration levels should not lead to a dependence on foreign workers, nor should they place training of unemployed U.S. citizens at risk. The fund established in the bill will supplement national efforts in assisting the unemployed and underemployed in obtaining the necessary skill levels to compete in today's market. Employers seeking foreign workers have a special obligation to ensure that obtaining workers from abroad is a last resort. Payment of fees by these employers into the fund for training American workers will assure that continuing effort.

The proposed fee did not survive into the final version of the 1990 Act. Should it have? Is there anything left in § 203(b) of the "overall strategy" the Committee envisioned? Some critics charge that the 1990 Act moves to the opposite pole from what the House Judiciary Committee envisioned, making dependency on foreign labor more likely, and in fact skimming the cream of well-trained and skilled personnel from less developed countries. Do you agree? If so, should U.S. policy be concerned about a brain drain from such countries?

Exercise

As a further exercise to acquaint yourself with the employment-based preferences, consider the situation of the alien involved in *Hall v. McLaughlin*, p. 208 *supra*, as described by the court, 864 F.2d, at 870–71:

Eric Hall, a Pakistani national, is a founder and corporate president of appellant Hall Enterprises, Inc. * * * [He] currently resides in the United States under an E–2 visa, which is a form of nonimmigrant visa that permits an alien to come to the United States to develop and direct the operations of a business enterprise in which he has invested a substantial amount of capital. * * * Eric Hall and his wife Marjorie established Hall Enterprises in August 1982, incorporating it under the laws of Maryland. Initially, each of the Halls owned 50 percent of the stock. The company is engaged in the business of importing and exporting Pakistani furniture, giftware and military spare parts. On December 12, 1982, Eric Hall sold 490 of his 500 shares of Hall Enterprises stock to Joseph J. Bernot, retaining an option to repurchase under certain conditions. Two weeks later, on December 29, 1982, Hall Enterprises applied for labor certification for Eric Hall, who was already serving as corporate president.

Under the Department of Labor's "inseparability" test, Hall was ruled ineligible for labor certification. But that case arose in 1982 and was finally resolved in the court of appeals in 1989. Under the revisions to INA § 203(b), as accomplished by the 1990 Act, what avenues are now open to him even without certification? Which categories appear most promising? If you were his attorney, what might you advise him to do to restructure his business or his hiring arrangements in order to maximize his chances for permanent resident status under these provisions? Now assume for a moment that the Department of Labor were to relax its standards for finding a genuine employment relationship—or reassessed the corporate structure of Hall Enterprises, so that Hall would not be precluded from labor certification. Under which category or categories of § 203(b)(2) or (b)(3) might he qualify? Consider closely with this exercise 8 C.F.R. § 204.5(h), (k), reprinted in the Supplement.

Investors as Immigrants

Until the 1990 Act, U.S. laws contained no specific provisions favoring the immigration of prospective investors in the American economy. When nonpreference numbers remained available, however, aliens could use their investment plans to secure one of the nonpreference admissions, because under INS regulations a qualifying investment was held to exempt the alien from the labor certification requirement otherwise applicable. The magnitude of the required investment varied over the years, but the latest version required commitment of $40,000 and a demonstration that the enterprise would employ at least one U.S. citizen or permanent resident other than the applicant and his or her family members. 8 C.F.R. § 212.8(b) (1990). When nonpreference admission became unavailable after 1978, these provisions became moot. Lawyers devised other possible strategies for admission, however, under the old third and sixth preferences. *See generally Foreign Investors: Strategies for Obtaining Residence,* 4 Imm.Law Rep. 97–102 (1985); Note, *Immigration for Investors: A Comparative Analysis of U.S., Canadian, and Australian Policies,* 7 B.C. Int'l & Comp.L.Rev. 113 (1984).

Ever since nonpreference immigration disappeared, some had advocated reinstating immigration options for investors. The arguments often followed this line: we provide preferences for those who come to *fill* jobs for which American workers are unavailable; why not provide a preference for aliens who would *create* jobs for American workers? The Select Commission on Immigration and Refugee Policy, which issued its report in 1981, was persuaded that we should do so. It recommended reserving a small number of admissions for substantial investors, suggesting a minimum investment of $250,000. SCIRP, Final Report 131–32. Father Theodore M. Hesburgh, the Commission's chair, dissented, commenting that "the rich should not be able to buy their way into this country." *Id.* at 336. Senator Bumpers led a fight against such provisions in the Senate for several years, arguing that such a provision "is odious, it is offensive, it flies right in the face of the national character of this country." 129 Cong.Rec. S6738 (daily ed. May 16, 1983).

Congress finally agreed to the addition of an investors provision in 1990 (under the label of "employment creation" visas), INA § 203(b)(5), establishing the fifth employment-based preference and giving it 10,000 admission spaces. It requires an investment that will create no fewer than 10 jobs for U.S. workers, not counting the investor and his or her family. The baseline investment is $1 million, but this can be reduced to $500,000 for "targetted employment areas"—rural communities or high-unemployment areas. Does such an admission provision represent good policy? What incentives does it create for unsound investments that may not be enduring? Does Congress's addition of a provision to criminalize "immigration related entrepreneurship fraud," INA § 275(c), adequately guard against such problems? As a further protection, all fifth-preference aliens and their families receive permanent residence on a conditional basis for two years under INA § 216A, which is closely modeled on INA § 216, the conditional residence provision for alien spouses. Consider carefully the criteria that must be satisfied when the alien petitions to have the conditional status removed at the end of the two-year period. INA § 216A(d)(1). *See* 59 Fed.Reg. 26587–93 (1994) (final regulations governing conditional residence for alien investors). *See also* Yanni, *Business Investors: E–2 Nonimmigrants and EB–5 Immigrants,* 92–8 Imm.Briefings (1992).

For all the stormy debate over these provisions, it turns out that interest in investment-based immigration has been quite modest. Between October 1, 1991, when the provision took effect, and March 31, 1994, INS received only 983 applications. It approved 437 and denied 202. The rest were still pending or had been cancelled. 71 Interp.Rel. 532 (1994). Some speculate that the U.S. provision is simply priced too high; investors can secure immigration rights in other countries, including Canada, for less than half the U.S. cost. Whatever the reason, Congress enacted a new pilot program in 1992 meant to ease the requirements in some circumstances. *See id.*; 59 Fed.Reg. 17,920 (1994) (final implementing regulations).

5. DIVERSITY IMMIGRATION

The concern for diversity among the aliens in our immigrant stream led to experimentation in the 1980s and finally the adoption of a permanent diversity provision in INA § 203(c). See pp. 129–31 *supra*. But the debates revealed that those who argued for diversity often harbored very different conceptions of that value. Is it a problem, as some implied, that so much of current immigration comes from Asia and Latin America? Or is this a welcome corrective to earlier discrimination? Some speak of diversity and emphasize restoring higher levels of European (especially Irish) immigration. *See, e.g., Reform Hearings, supra,* at 269, 542 (statements of Thomas Flatley and Donald Martin). Others invoke diversity and emphasize "new seed" immigrants from regions barely represented in current or historical migration. *Id.* at 242 (statement of Mr. Swartz).[27]

Underlying some of these positions are deeper concerns about sustaining national unity in a highly heterogeneous nation. Is unity a valid concern of government? Is unity more threatened today than in the past? If so, to what extent is immigration a cause? Can immigration reform help provide a cure? Consider the points made in the following readings.

STATEMENT OF SENATOR ALAN K. SIMPSON, COMMISSIONER, SELECT COMMISSION ON IMMIGRATION AND REFUGEE POLICY

SCIRP, Final Report 409–13 (1981).

Numbers. New *legal* entries of immigrants and refugees for fiscal years 1977–1980 totaled, respectively, about 400,000; 500,000; 525,000; 675,000. Emigration may be as high as 30% of the number of new immigrants (not counting refugees). Although the exact figure is unknown, net *illegal* immigration may well number in the hundreds of thousands per year.

In a 1980 study by Dr. Leon F. Bouvier, who served as research demographer on the Select Commission staff and now is with the Population Reference Bureau, Washington, D.C., "The Impact of Immigration on the Size of the U.S. Population," he estimates that even if (a) net immigration, illegal as well as legal, equals 750,000 per year; (b) the fertility rate of

---

27. Some manage to link both these objectives:

The focus of our system on family connections has effectively eliminated the opportunity of immigration from countries of "older" immigration, such as Europe, and for countries that have not significantly utilized our immigration system at all—such as Africa.

Simpson, *supra,* 25 San Diego L.Rev., at 225.

the existing population and its descendants remains at its present low level (which seems unlikely); and (c) the fertility rate of new immigrants and their descendants immediately declines to that of the present population as a whole (which seems even less likely); then the U.S. population in the year 2080 will be 300,000,000, one-third of which will consist of post–1979 immigrants and their descendants.

* * *

Ethnic Patterns

* * *

The present immigration flow differs from past flows in [a] * * * significant way. Immigration to the United States is now dominated to a high degree by persons speaking a single foreign language, Spanish, when illegal immigration is considered. The assimilation of the English language and other aspects of American culture by Spanish-speaking immigrants appears to be less rapid and complete than for other groups. A desire to assimilate is often reflected by the rate at which an immigrant completes the naturalization process necessary to become a U.S. citizen. A study by the Select Commission staff indicates that immigrants from Latin America naturalize to a lesser extent than those from other regions.* In part the apparently lower degree of assimilation may be due to the proximity to and the constant influx of new Spanish-speaking illegal immigrants from Latin America, many of whom regard their stay as only "temporary" and thus may not feel the need or desire to learn English or otherwise assimilate; and finally the greater tolerance for bilingualism and "biculturalism" in recent years, at least among a majority of legislators, who have adopted government policies which seem actually to promote linguistic and cultural separatism, policies such as the promotion of bilingual/"bicultural" education and foreign language ballots.

Under existing law and policies such patterns are likely to continue to be accentuated since the pressures for international migration are likely to increase over the coming decades, especially from regions which already dominate U.S. immigration flows.

Assimilation. Although the subject of the immediate economic impact of immigration receives great attention, assimilation to fundamental American public values and institutions may be of far more importance to the future of the United States. If immigration is continued at a high level and yet a substantial portion of the newcomers and their descendants do not assimilate, they may create in America some of the same social, political and economic problems which existed in the country which they have chosen to depart. Furthermore, as previously mentioned, a community with a large number of immigrants who do not assimilate will to some

---

* A sample of those granted permanent resident status in 1971 was examined. Of those of Mexican origin who remained in the U.S. at the end of 7 years, only 5% had naturalized. For the entire region of South America the rate was 24.6%, for Europe 42.6%, and for Asia 80.3% (excluding China, India, Korea, and the Philippines, whose rates were, respectively, 73.8%, 67.8%, 80.9%, and 67.6%). [Note that Canadians had naturalized at a rate of 5–6%—eds.]

degree seem unfamiliar to longtime residents. Finally, if linguistic and cultural separatism rise above a certain level, the unity and political stability of the nation will in time be seriously eroded.

————

The role of the English language in promoting American solidarity—or enforcing unwanted uniformity—remains a controversial issue, highlighted in recent years by proposals for making English the official language of a state or of the nation.[28] Consider the various additional views reported in the following article.

JAMES FALLOWS, IMMIGRATION: HOW IT'S AFFECTING US

The Atlantic Monthly, November 1983, at 88–89.

Hispanics are more acutely aware than most Anglos that, as a practical reality, English is the national language of commerce, government, and mobility. But some have suggested that, in principle, it should not be this way.

They invoke the long heritage of Mexican–Americans in the Southwest. As "Californios" or "Tejanos," the ancestors of some of these families lived on and owned the territory before the Anglo settlers. Others came across at the turn of the century, at a time of Mexican upheaval; still others came during the forties and fifties, as workers. They have paid taxes, fought in wars, been an inseparable part of the region's culture. Yet they were also subject to a form of discrimination more casual than the segregation of the Old South, but having one of the same effects. Because of poverty or prejudice or gerrymandered school districts, many Mexican–Americans were, in effect, denied education. One result is that many now in their fifties and sixties do not speak English well. Still, they are citizens, with the right of citizens to vote. How are they to exercise their right if to do so requires learning English? Do they not deserve a ballot printed in a language they can understand?

* * *

[As a result of court decisions and legislation during the 1970's,] ballots in parts of the country are printed in Spanish, or Chinese, or Tagalog, along with English. This is true even though anyone applying for naturalization must still pass an English-proficiency test, which consists of questions such as "What are the three branches of government?" and "How long are the terms of a U.S. Senator and member of Congress?" The apparent inconsistency reflects the linguistic reality that many native-born citizens have not learned the national language.

* * *

28. *See generally Hearing on English Language Constitutional Amendments,* Subcomm. on Civil and Const'l Rights, House Comm. on the Judiciary, 100th Cong., 2d Sess. (Serial No. 120, 1988); B. Piatt, Only English? : Law and Language Policy in the United States (1990); *Symposium on Bilingual Education,* 6 J.L. & Politics 573 (1990).

But there are those who feel that even the present arrangement is too onerous. Rose Matsui Ochi, an assistant to the mayor of Los Angeles, who served on the Select Commission, dissented from the commission's recommendation to keep the English-language requirement for citizenship. She wrote in her minority opinion, "Abolishing the requirement recognizes the inability of certain individuals to learn English." Cruz Reynoso, the first Mexican–American appointee to the California Supreme Court, was also on the Select Commission, and he too dissented. "America is a *political* union—not a cultural, linguistic, religious or racial union," he wrote. "Of course, we as individuals would urge all to learn English, for that is the language used by most Americans, as well as the language of the marketplace. But we should no more demand English-language skills for citizenship than we should demand uniformity of religion. That a person wants to become a citizen and will make a good citizen is more than enough."

Some Chicano activists make the same point in less temperate terms. Twice I found myself in shouting matches with Mexican–Americans who asked me who I thought I was to tell them—after all the homeboys who had died in combat, after all the insults they'd endured on the playground for speaking Spanish—what language they "should" speak.

That these arguments were conducted in English suggests the theoretical nature of the debate. Still, in questions like this, symbolism can be crucial. "I have sympathy for the position that the integrating mechanism of a society is language," Henry Cisneros [mayor of San Antonio] says, "The U.S. has been able to impose fewer such integrating mechanisms on its people than other countries, but it needs some tie to hold these diverse people, Irish, Jews, Czechs, together as a nation. Therefore, I favor people learning English and being able to conduct business in the official language of the country."

"The *unum* demands only certain things of the *pluribus*," Lawrence Fuchs [Executive Director of the Select Commission] says. "It demands very little. It demands that we believe in the political ideals of the republic, which allows people to preserve their ethnic identity." Most immigrants come from repressive regimes; we say, we're asking you to believe that government should *not* oppress you. Then it only asks one other thing: that in the wider marketplace and in the civic culture, you use the official language. No other society asks so little.

"English is not just an instrument of mobility. It is a sign that you really are committed. If you've been here five years, which you must to be a citizen, and if you are reasonably young, you should be able to learn English in that time. The rest of us are entitled to that."

Notes

1. Would promotion of naturalization alleviate some of these worries? In unofficial drafts of reform legislation in the 1980s, INS proposed steps to better promote naturalization, principally through reducing the residence requirement from five years to three and sharply limiting the right of long-time residents to petition for the immigration of family members if they did

not naturalize. (This benefit is thought to be a much stronger inducement than the political rights usually seen as the main result of naturalization.) *See* 65 Interp.Rel. 404 (1988); 66 *id.* 341 (1989).

2. For more on these issues, which have perhaps become even more controversial and important since Simpson and Fallows wrote the principal articles, *see, e.g.,* R. Suro, Remembering the American Dream: Hispanic Immigration and National Policy (1994); A. Schlesinger, Jr., The Disuniting of America: Reflections on a Multicultural Society (1992); W. McNeill, Polyethnicity and National Unity in World History (1986); Minorities: Community and Identity (C. Fried ed. 1983); R. Rodriguez, Hunger of Memory (1981); A. Mann, The One and the Many: Reflections on the American Identity (1979); N. Glazer & D. Moynihan, Beyond the Melting Pot (1963); Legomsky, *Immigration, Equality, and Diversity*, 31 Colum. J. Transnat'l L. 319 (1993); Hing, *Beyond the Rhetoric of Assimilation and Cultural Pluralism: Addressing the Tension of Separatism and Conflict in an Immigration–Driven Multiracial Society*, 81 Cal.L.Rev. 863 (1993).

SECTION B.   NONIMMIGRANTS

A nonimmigrant, generally speaking, is an alien who seeks entry to the United States for a specific purpose to be accomplished during a temporary stay. The qualifying categories for nonimmigrants are set forth, rather surprisingly, as part of the statutory definition of "immigrant." INA § 101(a)(15). But a close examination of § 214, which is captioned "Admission of nonimmigrants," will reveal the reason for this placement.

Section 214(b) establishes a presumption that is fundamental to the workings of the admission process. Under that section, almost every alien who wishes to come to the United States is presumed to be an "immigrant"—and therefore subject to the more restrictive requirements applicable to the latter category.[1] The alien applicant, then, must shoulder the burden of demonstrating that he or she is entitled to nonimmigrant status. Section 101(a)(15) simply mirrors this basic presumption in definitional form. It defines "immigrant," without further embellishment, as "every alien except" those who happen to fall within one of the carefully defined categories of nonimmigrants which § 101(a)(15) then proceeds to list.

The nonimmigrant categories range from tourists, who are now generally granted an entry period of six months (even if they intend a shorter visit); through students and various business-related categories, which may allow entry for longer periods; to diplomats and employees of foreign governments or affiliated with international organizations, whose stay may be extended indefinitely and who are exempted from several other requirements because of their official status. *See, e.g.,* INA § 102. The Visa Office of the Department of State has developed a set of visa symbols for the various nonimmigrant categories, generally tracking the alphabetical subparagraphs in § 101(a)(15), and sometimes subdividing the categories

---

1. Not only are aliens presumed to be immigrants, but they are also presumed, in essence, to be diversity immigrants—the least favorable immigrant category—until they show that they either qualify for a preference category or are quota-exempt. INA § 203(f).

even further than is suggested by the statutory language. For example, a tourist enters as a "temporary visitor for pleasure" on a B–2 visa. An alien here temporarily on business, perhaps to negotiate a contract with an American supplier, will enter on a B–1 visa, as a "temporary visitor for business." A student headed for an academic institution receives an F–1 visa; the student's spouse and children receive F–2 visas. INS employs the same symbols for nonimmigrant admission categories.

You can gain a sense of the wide array of the nonimmigrant categories and relative demand for them by examining Table 3.5.

Table 3.7
Nonimmigrant Classes and Admissions, Fiscal Year 1993

Visa Symbol	Class	Admission
A–1	Ambassador, public minister, career diplomat or consular officer, spouse and children	23,806
A–2	Other foreign government official or employee, spouse and children	76,427
A–3	Attendant, servant, or personal employee of A–1 or A–2 alien, spouse and children	1,940
B–1	Temporary visitor for business	2,961,775[2]
B–2	Temporary visitor for pleasure	16,900,459[3]
C–1	Alien in transit	177,505
C–2	Alien in transit to United Nations Headquarters	810
C–3	Foreign government official, spouse and children, attendant, servant, or personal employee, in transit	7,967
C–4	Transit without visa	150,736
E–1	Treaty trader, spouse and children (under a treaty between the U.S. and the alien's country)	65,465
E–2	Treaty investor, spouse and children	79,415
F–1	Student attending academic institution	253,048
F–2	Spouse and children of F–1 student	32,822
G–1	Principal resident representative of recognized foreign member government to international organization, his or her staff, spouse and children	9,052
G–2	Other representative of recognized foreign member government to international organization, spouse and children	8,967
G–3	Representative of nonrecognized or nonmember foreign government to international organization, spouse and children	361
G–4	International organization officer or employee, spouse and children	52,917
G–5	Attendant, servant, or personal employee of alien classified G–1, G–2, G–3, or G–4, spouse and children	1,537
H–1A	Temporary worker performing services as registered nurse	6,437

2. Not including 639,277 admissions under the Visa Waiver Pilot Program.

3. Not including 8,618,304 admissions under the Visa Waiver Pilot Program.

Visa Symbol	Class	Admission
H–1B	Temporary worker performing services in "specialty occupation"	93,069
H–2A	Temporary worker performing agricultural services unavailable in the U.S.	16,257
H–2B	Temporary worker performing services unavailable in the U.S.	15,038
H–3	Trainee	3,135
H–4	Spouse and children of H–1, H–2, or H–3 temporary worker	37,893
I	Representative of foreign information media, spouse and children	21,088
J–1	Exchange visitor	197,545
J–2	Spouse and children of J–1 exchange visitor	42,911
K–1	Fiancee or fiance of U.S. citizen	8,571
K–2	Child of fiancee or fiance of U.S. citizen	819
L–1	Intracompany transferee	82,781
L–2	Spouse and children of L–1 alien	49,642
M–1	Student in vocational or other recognized non-academic institution	4,382
M–2	Spouse and children of M–1 student	557
N–1 through 7	NATO officials, spouse and children	8,896
O–1	Alien with extraordinary ability in sciences, arts, education, business, or athletics	3,128
O–2	Aliens assisting in athletic or artistic performance of O–1 alien	977
O–3	Spouse and children of O–1, O–2 aliens	322
P–1	Internationally recognized entertainers and athletes	17,205
P–2	Artist or entertainer performing under exchange program	423
P–3	Artist or entertainer performing under a program that is culturally unique	4,103
P–4	Spouse and children of P–1, P–2, P–3 aliens	501
Q–1	Participant in international cultural exchange program	1006
R–1	Religious workers	4460
R–2	Spouse and children of R–1 religious workers	1048
	Total	21,446,993

Source: 1993 INS Statistical Yearbook, Table 40.

The statute places no fixed numerical limits on nonimmigrant admissions, except in the H–1B and H–2B categories, as discussed later. Control over nonimmigrant admissions is maintained by applying the qualitative requirements for each category and the exclusion grounds in INA § 212(a). For many of the nonimmigrant categories, the most important requirement is that the alien "has a residence in a foreign country which he has no intention of abandoning." *See, e.g.,* INA § 101(a)(15)(B),(F),(J). In deciding whether to issue nonimmigrant visas, State Department consular officers tend to be especially careful in this regard, particularly in countries known for a high incidence of visa abuse.

This care reflects the fear that the alien is not a bona fide nonimmigrant, but in fact intends to remain in the United States indefinitely. She might simply overstay her visa, for example. Nonimmigrant overstays apparently constitute roughly half of the undocumented population. 1993 INS Statistical Yearbook 182. Alternatively, soon after arrival the alien might follow the usual avenues toward permanent residency.

An alien is not a bona fide nonimmigrant if his intent from the beginning is to remain in the United States permanently by any means possible, legal or otherwise. But "a desire to remain in this country permanently in accordance with the law, should the opportunity to do so present itself, is not necessarily inconsistent with lawful nonimmigrant status." *Matter of Hosseinpour*, 15 I & N Dec. 191, 192 (BIA 1975). *See also Lauvik v. INS*, 910 F.2d 658, 660–61 (9th Cir.1990); *Bong Youn Choy v. Barber*, 279 F.2d 642, 645–46 (9th Cir.1960). This is the "dual intent" doctrine, which makes the permanent foreign residence requirement less rigid than it might be otherwise. The INA and/or regulations have expressly recognized the dual intent doctrine for some (but not most) nonimmigrant categories, thus making those categories significantly more attractive, as a practical matter, for bona fide nonimmigrants who would stay in the United States if they could lawfully. In principle, however, applicants for any nonimmigrant visa may have "dual intent."

There are also many nonimmigrants who enter the United States with no intent to remain in the United States, but later change their minds and decide to stay if they can. Many such bona fide nonimmigrants eventually become lawful permanent residents, though many find that they have complicated their pursuit of permanent residency by violating the terms of their nonimmigrant status. Often the violation could have been avoided through greater care (which the alien did not exercise precisely because she did not intend to stay permanently). One typical violation of nonimmigrant status is overstaying the allowed time period. Another is unauthorized employment. B–2 nonimmigrants, the most numerous, may not work; other categories usually may work only for a specific employer incident to their status, or with permission, which is usually granted only for a specific position.

For the vast majority of aliens, there are two basic procedural paths to a given nonimmigrant status in the United States. (Chapter Four will treat admission procedures more fully.) More typically, an alien who plans to enter the United States as a nonimmigrant applies for a visa at a consulate overseas. The visa serves to authorize travel to the United States in order to apply for admission at the port of entry, but it does not guarantee admission if the immigration officer at the border finds that the alien is not entitled to enter. After entry, the category and expiration date shown in the admission documents (form I–94) issued at the border, or later modified and/or extended at an INS office in the United States, determine the rights and limitations attached to the nonimmigrant entry, regardless of what might have been shown on the visa. The second procedural path is for an alien who has been lawfully admitted as a nonimmigrant, and who is maintaining that status, to change to a different nonimmigrant status under INA § 248. Whichever procedure is used, some nonimmigrant visas require supporting documentation before the alien can apply for the visa overseas or a change of nonimmigrant status in the United States. For some employment-related categories, the employer must file a preliminary petition with the INS. Prospective students and scholars must present documents from the school or exchange program. These supporting requirements are discussed more fully later in this section.

Our goal in this section is to provide a general overview of nonimmigrant visas and the basic issues that they raise. We leave the intricacies of the voluminous and detailed regulations to the many excellent practitioner texts available, some of which have contributed excerpts to this section.

1. NONIMMIGRANT VISAS FOR STUDENTS AND SCHOLARS

On average, about 260,000 aliens were admitted to the United States in each of the past five years to pursue studies at American institutions of higher education. 1993 INS Statistical Yearbook, Table 40. Most enter on F visas, although a substantial number obtain J nonimmigrant classification. To help focus your consideration of the materials that follow, assume that you are travelling abroad and have met a student pursuing graduate studies in applied physics who would very much like to continue her education at a leading American research university. She asks you the following questions: How do I go about applying for a visa, and which kind should I request? How long may I stay in the U.S.? May I bring my husband and young child? Will I be able to work while I am studying?

How would you respond?

AUSTIN T. FRAGOMEN, JR., ALFRED J. DEL REY, JR. & SAM BERNSEN, IMMIGRATION LAW AND BUSINESS
Vol. 1, §§ 2.4(a), 2.4(c) (1994).

STUDENT AND EXCHANGE VISITOR CATEGORIES

F Academic Students. Under § 101(a)(15)(F) of the INA, a qualified student may enter the United States as a nonimmigrant to pursue a full course of study at an established institution of learning, provided the institution has been approved by the INS after consultation with the Department of Education. The F nonimmigrant category covers the principal alien who is admitted in F–1 status, as well as the spouse and minor children, who are admitted in F–2 status. * * *

Section 101(a)(15)(F) sets out a number of specific requirements for an alien to qualify as a nonimmigrant student. First, the alien must have a residence in a foreign country which he or she has no intention of abandoning. Second, he or she must be a "bona fide student qualified to pursue a full course of study." Third, he or she must seek to enter the United States "temporarily and solely for the purpose of pursuing such a course of study at an established institution of learning or other recognized place of study in the United States." The statute provides that the institution at which the alien will study must be "particularly designated" by the student and approved by the Attorney General after consultation with the Department of Education. The statute also places certain obligations upon the institution or place of study, such as reporting to the Attorney General the termination of attendance of each nonimmigrant student. The statute provides that failure to make reports as required by the Attorney General shall result in the withdrawal of approval for the school to accept nonimmigrant alien students.

* * *

[T]he consular officer will not issue an F–1 visa unless the prospective student can demonstrate the intent to leave the United States after completing the course of study. 22 C.F.R. § 41.61(b)(1)(iv). Substantial evidence must be presented to the consular officer, particularly with regard to the alien's ties to his or her home country, in order to demonstrate that the alien intends to depart the United States after the completion of studies. Such evidence as the availability of employment in the alien's home country in the field in which he or she is undertaking studies is helpful in demonstrating that the alien will return to the home country upon completion of those studies. F.A.M. 41.61, note 12.3.

* * *

The regulations provide that a student is to be admitted for "duration of status." 8 C.F.R. 214.2(f)(1). "Duration of status" is defined by the regulation to cover any number of academic programs (e.g., bachelor's degree followed by master's degree), any authorized periods of practical training, plus sixty days to depart the United States. 8 C.F.R. § 214.2(f)(5)(i). * * *

* * *

* * * The current student employment program under the INS rules has five major components: (1) on-campus employment; (2) curricular practical training; (3) work authorization based on economic necessity; (4) employment under the pilot program established by the 1990 Act; and (5) optional practical training (which includes pre- and post-graduation practical training). * * *

On-campus employment has traditionally been viewed more liberally than other types of student employment. Such employment is often a part of the student's academic program or often involves work that will not displace a U.S. worker. Thus, under 8 C.F.R. § 214.2(f)(9)(i), on-campus employment that is pursuant to the terms of a scholarship, fellowship, or assistantship, or that will not displace a U.S. worker, is authorized by regulation; no application need be made to the INS; instead, employment authorization is authorized by the school but no specific endorsement is required by the foreign student advisor. Such employment must be limited to twenty hours a week (full-time during vacation periods), and cannot occur after completion of the course of study. * * *

Some schools have alternate work/study courses as a part of the regular curriculum, either for all students or for students in particular programs of study. Under this type of program (referred to as curricular practical training in the INS rules), the student is required to take academic courses for one term, followed by a term of work experience; in some instances, course work and work experience may coincide. Under the INS rules, a student may engage in off-campus employment that is required by a work/study or cooperative education program in which the student is enrolled, and explicit INS authorization is not required. * * * 8 C.F.R. § 214.2(f)(10)(i). * * *

* * *

* * * For a student to be eligible for employment authorization because of unforeseen economic necessity, the student must first show that he or she needs to work because of "severe economic hardship caused by unforeseen circumstances beyond the student's control." The rules highlight the following unforeseen circumstances: (1) loss of financial aid or on-campus employment without fault on the part of the student; (2) substantial fluctuations in the value of currency or exchange rate; (3) inordinate increases in tuition or living costs; (4) unexpected changes in the financial condition of the student's source of support; or (5) medical bills or other substantial and unexpected expenses. The student must also show that the 1990 Act program is unavailable or insufficient because of the unwillingness or inability of local employers to participate in the program, and that suitable on-campus employment is unavailable. In order to be eligible for work authorization based on unforeseen economic necessity, the rules also require that the student: (1) have completed one full academic year (nine months) in F–1 status; (2) be in good academic standing as determined by his or her foreign student advisor; (3) obtain a recommendation from the foreign student advisor in favor of work authorization; (4) obtain an employment authorization document from the INS; and (5) work no more than twenty hours per week when school is in session (full-time work is permissible during vacation periods).

* * *

* * * The 1990 Act established a three-year pilot program under which F–1 students may obtain employment authorization for off-campus work * * *.[a] * * *

Under the INS final rule, a foreign student may work off-campus for a specific employer, provided the employer meets the attestation requirement of § 221 of the 1990 Act. 8 C.F.R. § 214.2(f)(9)(ii) (1991). * * *

Few employers have filed attestations under the student employment program, and for almost two-thirds of those who have, the attestations have been rejected by the Department of Labor (DOL) because the employers failed to meet the complicated recruitment rules established by the

a. Notwithstanding a report from the INS and the Department of Labor recommending that the program be ended, the October 1994 Immigration Technical Corrections Act, 103–416, § 215, 108 Stat. 4315, extended the program to September 30, 1996.—eds.

DOL. In view of this record, few employment opportunities are likely to open up for foreign students under the 1990 Act program. * * *

* * *

* * * The employer must file an attestation with the DOL and the student's school stating that the employer has recruited for at least sixty days for the position and will pay the alien and similarly employed U.S. workers the prevailing wage rate for the occupation in the area of intended employment or the actual wage rate at the place of employment, whichever is higher.

* * *

Optional practical training includes training: (1) during the student's annual vacation and at other times when school is not in session, if the student is attending a college, university, seminary, or conservatory and is eligible to register for the next term or semester (and intends to do so); (2) during the school year, provided that employment does not exceed twenty hours per week while school is in session; (3) when the student is in a bachelor's, master's, or doctoral program and has completed all course requirements for the degree (excluding a thesis or its equivalent), and (4) when the student has completed his or her course of study. 8 C.F.R. § 214.2(f)(10)(ii)(A). * * * All optional practical training must be completed within a fourteen-month period following the completion of study. 8 C.F.R. § 214.2(f)(10)(ii)(A). Optional practical training is additional to a "curricular" practical training available to foreign students attending schools offering such curricular programs.

* * *

J Exchange Visitors. Under § 101(a)(15)(J) of the INA, aliens may enter the United States as nonimmigrants as participants in programs designated for that purpose by the director of the United States Information Agency (USIA). Section 101(a)(15)(J) requires that the alien have "a residence in a foreign country which he has no intention of abandoning," and that he be a "bona fide student, scholar, trainee, teacher, professor, research assistant, specialist, or leader in a field of specialized knowledge or skill, or other person of similar description." Among the acceptable purposes for participating in an exchange visitor program under § 101(a)(15)(J) are "teaching, instructing or lecturing, studying, observing, conducting research, consulting, demonstrating special skills, or receiving training." * * *

In addition to the principal alien, who is classified in the J–1 category, the alien's spouse and minor children of the principal who accompany or follow to join the principal are classified in the J–2 category.

The J nonimmigrant category is used predominantly by four groups: (1) students coming to the United States to study at a university; (2) scholars and other experts, often university professors in other countries, who come to U.S. universities or research organizations to undertake research or train other people in their skills; (3) foreign medical graduates coming to U.S. medical schools to receive graduate medical education, or to

U.S. hospitals or medical institutions to receive medical training in the form of internships and residencies; and (4) persons from business or industrial organizations, coming to the United States to receive training, which can consist of training in a particular occupational skill, a particular company's methods and techniques, or an introduction to U.S. business or industrial techniques. * * *

A special restriction exists with regard to exchange students and visitors under the J category which does not apply to other nonimmigrant categories. Under § 212(e) of the INA, certain aliens who are admitted to the United States as J nonimmigrants or who acquire that status after admission are subject to a two-year foreign residency requirement after completing their activities in J status. The two-year foreign residency requirement applies to those aliens who seek an immigrant visa or permanent residence, as well as those who seek H or L visas or a change of nonimmigrant classification to the H or L category after having spent any time in the United States in the J nonimmigrant category. Those aliens must establish that they have resided and have been physically present in the country of their nationality or last residence for an aggregate of at least two years following departure from the United States, if they fall into one of three classes: (1) an alien "whose participation in the program for which he came to the United States was financed in whole or in part, directly or indirectly, by an agency of the Government of the United States or by the government of the country of his nationality or his last residence"; (2) an alien "who at the time of admission or acquisition of status under section 101(a)(15)(J) was a national or resident of a country which the Secretary of State [now the director of the USIA] pursuant to regulations prescribed by him, had designated as clearly requiring the skills of persons engaged in the field of specialized knowledge or skill in which the alien was engaged ['the skills list']"; and (3) an alien "who came to the United States or acquired such status in order to receive graduate medical education or training."

These three classes of J nonimmigrants subject to the two-year foreign residence requirement may receive a waiver of that requirement under § 212(e) "upon the favorable recommendation of [the director of the USIA], pursuant to the request of an interested United States Government agency, or of the Commissioner of Immigration and Naturalization after he has determined that departure from the United States would impose exceptional hardship upon the alien's spouse or child (if such spouse or child is a citizen of the United States or a lawfully resident alien), or that the alien cannot return to the country of his nationality or last residence because he would be subject to persecution on account of race, religion, or political opinion." The waiver is adjudicated by the Attorney General and is limited to the cases of aliens whose admission to the United States "is found by the Attorney General to be in the public interest."

[A] waiver is also provided "upon the favorable recommendation of the Secretary of State [now the director of the USIA] . . . in any case in which the foreign country of the alien's nationality or last residence has furnished the Secretary of State a statement in writing that it has no objection to such waiver in the case of such alien." The no-objection waiver is barred by statute in the case of aliens coming to the United States in J nonimmigrant status to receive graduate medical education or training. 22 C.F.R. [§ 514.27(g)]. * * *

The special requirements with regard to the J nonimmigrant category derive from the inception of the exchange visitor program in the Information and Educational Exchange Act of 1948, 62 Stat. 6. The legislative intent behind the 1948 Act was to foster international relations by affording aliens opportunity to visit the United States and acquire skills that would be useful in their homelands. In line with the objective, Congress enacted § 212(e) in order to insure that exchange visitors would in fact return to their homeland to impart skills and knowledge acquired in the United States, and would be precluded from using their J visas to circumvent the normal immigration procedure. * * *

* * *

In February 1990, the General Accounting Office (GAO) issued a congressionally mandated report regarding the uses of the exchange visitor programs and USIA oversight of those programs. Concern had arisen in Congress regarding exchange programs that permit employment by foreign nationals in the United States. The immediate cause for concern was the "au pair" programs that have permitted the admission of young persons as child-care monitors in exchange for the opportunity to experience life in the United States and tour the country. The GAO concluded that particularly for programs in the business training and international visitor categories, employment often had little to do with "cultural exchange" and really constituted foreign worker programs that could be seen as displacing U.S. workers. Among the major areas of concern in the business training programs was hotel employment involving waiters, chefs, receptionists, and first-line managers. Another program involved automobile body repair and painting. International visitor programs permitting work, such as summer student travel/work programs, have included employment in fast food restaurants, summer resorts, and as camp counselors.

* * *

In response to the GAO's report, the USIA developed new regulations adopted in March 1993 to govern exchange visitor training programs. 58 Fed.Reg. 15180 (3/19/93).[b] * * *

* * *

b. In December 1994, the USIA published interim final regulations setting out new guidelines for J au pair programs. *See* 59 Fed.Reg. 64296 (1994).

Also, the 1990 Immigration Act created a new Q nonimmigrant category. INA § 101(a)(15)(Q). What kinds of programs do you think Congress was thinking about? Here is one view:

The Q visa status may have been created in response to concerns that the U.S. Information Agency (USIA) may soon restrict some J–1 exchange visitor programs. * * * Worried about a possible crackdown, the Walt Disney Company urged legislation to protect itself and other major J–1 program sponsors. Thus, for example, Disney will be able to use the new Q classification to obtain visas for aliens to work at the Epcot Center at Disneyworld in Florida.

67 Interp.Rel. 76 (1991).

* * * [E]xchange visitors are admitted by the INS for "duration of status," as indicated by the exchange program sponsor on Form IAP–66. * * *

* * *

* * * Employment that is incident to J classification, in that employment is permitted under the program sponsor's designation from the USIA, is evidenced by the exchange visitor's I–94 card and his or her Form IAP–66 indicating the type of employment inherent in the program. Employment may be undertaken only with the program sponsor, with the exception of occasional lectures or consultations with other employers, which may be considered incident to status as long as this activity falls within USIA guidelines set forth in 22 C.F.R. § 514.20(g)(1). * * *

When employment is not incident to status, in that it is not already indicated on Form IAP–66, explicit employment authorization must be sought from the INS through an application for an employment authorization document on Form I–765, with appropriate filing fee. This rule will apply to exchange visitor students seeking periods of practical training or employment based on economic necessity.

The current employment authorization procedures for dependents of exchange visitors in the J–2 category remain unchanged, with an application to the INS on Form I–765 required. The dependents of the principal J nonimmigrant may be granted employment authorization if such employment is for the support of the dependents alone, and not the support of the principal nonimmigrant. 8 C.F.R. § 214.2(j)(1).

Notes

J's older -- looking to settles.

1. The two-year foreign residency rule applies to some J visa holders, but not to Fs. What do you suppose accounts for the difference in treatment? *See Newton v. INS,* 736 F.2d 336 (6th Cir.1984); *Mendez v. Major,* 340 F.2d 128 (8th Cir.1965). Given the return requirement, why might an alien status seek J status? It may be that the government of the alien's home country will permit exit, or support the student, only if he or she accepts J status. (Why might that be?) On a policy level, if a J–1 exchange visitor wants to stay in the United States and we find it in our national interest to allow her to stay, why force her to return home?

2. Another reason to prefer a J–1 visa may be that the employment rules are more lenient for J–1 than for F–1 nonimmigrants. Spouses and children of J–1 nonimmigrants may ask the INS for work authorization, *see* 8 C.F.R. § 214.2(j)(1)(v), which is usually granted if the income will not be to support the J–1 alien, *see* 56 Fed.Reg. 33371 (1991). Spouses and children of F–1 students may not work, *see* 8 C.F.R. § 214.2(f)(15).

3. The J nonimmigrant classification introduces a new federal actor into our study of immigration law: the United States Information Agency. What might explain the USIA's role in approving exchange programs and making recommendations for waiver of the two-year foreign residency requirement rule? A number of federal appeals courts have held that an

unfavorable recommendation by USIA on a waiver request is not subject to judicial review. *E.g., Singh v. Moyer,* 867 F.2d 1035 (7th Cir.1989) (statute provides "no meaningful standard" for reviewing agency decision); *Dina v. Attorney General,* 793 F.2d 473 (2d Cir.1986). For a lone dissenting view, see *Chong v. Director, U.S.I.A.,* 821 F.2d 171 (3d Cir.1987).

4. In 1981, Congress created M visas for students pursuing vocational or other nonacademic studies. INA § 101(a)(15)(M). Such students were originally included in the F category. The amendment was intended to enable INS to keep tighter control on vocational students, whom Congress perceived as more likely to violate restrictions on employment and length-of-stay rules. H.Rep. No. 264, 97th Cong., 1st Sess. 18 (1981). The rules for M and F status are roughly parallel, but procedural controls for M status are more strict, and the terms of stay less generous. For example, F students may transfer schools without INS approval, while M students may not. F students have some on-campus and off-campus employment opportunities, while M students may work only in a practical training program.

5. Following the suppression of the "Democracy Movement" in China in 1989, Congress passed legislation extending the status of Chinese students in the U.S. on J–1 visas and waiving the two-year foreign residency requirement. President Bush vetoed the legislation, citing the need to preserve his "ability to manage foreign relations," 66 Interp.Rel. 1313 (1989). However, he directed the Department of Justice to provide nearly identical administrative relief to Chinese students. In May 1990, the INS instructed district offices to grant foreign residency waivers to any Chinese national "present in the United States on or after June 5, 1989, up to and including April 11, 1990," the date of the President's implementing order. 67 Interp.Rel. 558 (1990). The J–1 waivers were made irrevocable and exercisable until January 1, 1994, allowing J–1 visa holders to seek permanent residency status or adjust to another nonimmigrant status without returning to China.

These events were superseded in 1992 by the so-called Chinese Student Protection Act, Pub. L. No. 102–404, 106 Stat. 1969, which provided permanent resident status for Chinese nationals who arrived in the United States before April 11, 1990 and resided continuously in the United States since that date.

2. BUSINESS AND ENTREPRENEURIAL NONIMMIGRANTS

The United States economic system—the largest of any nation in the world—attracts literally millions of aliens a year interested in pursuing business opportunities here. Some come as temporary laborers, picking apples and lettuce, cutting sugar cane, even herding sheep. Others come to drum up business for foreign corporations. Multinational corporations send employees to receive training and manage American subsidiaries. Foreign investors may enter to investigate opportunities for purchasing U.S. businesses and property or opening businesses of their own. Professional athletes enter for the length of a sports season. Performers and entertainers may plan an American tour.

An increasingly interdependent world combined with significant waits for some employment-based immigrant visas has guaranteed an exceptionally high demand for nonimmigrant work-related visas. Naturally, this demand comes in large part from the nonimmigrants themselves, but it also comes at least as much from the many employers in the United States who believe that they have an inadequate domestic labor force at their disposal.

Much of modern immigration practice concerns the entry of these nonimmigrants seeking work or business opportunities and meeting the needs of U.S. employers. The array of categories—each with their own detailed rules of eligibility and conditions of stay—can appear perplexing (if not mind-numbing). The job of the immigration practitioner is to understand the needs of the client (the alien, the sponsoring organization or both) and to assess the availability and implications of the various possible avenues of entry. As you consider the following materials, try to resist the temptation to believe that categories are fixed, that they describe a set of natural relations (employer/employee; professional; investor), or that an immigration attorney merely matches a client with the appropriate nonimmigrant category. Quite to the contrary, the INA leaves important concepts and terms undefined; and administrative agencies and courts often disagree about the definition of the categories. Furthermore, it is not as if aliens walk into an attorney's office with "H–1" or "E–2" stamped on their heads. Commercial relations are extraordinarily complex and varied, and the sophisticated immigration lawyer will often need to spend a great deal of time defining the nature and terms of the alien's intended work in a way that both meets the needs of the client and the requisites of the INA. Throughout the discussion, of course, you should be digging for the underlying justifications for the categories (and testing those justifications against alternative policy considerations and other possible constructions of categories).

One fundamental policy tension runs through these materials on business and entrepreneurial nonimmigrants. American employers often seek to hire foreign employees. It is surely sensible national policy to permit the entry of aliens who are needed by domestic industry, as well as those who as entrepreneurs will create opportunities in the domestic economy. However, since the earliest immigration laws, immigration policy has sought to protect American labor from competition from foreign workers. For aliens seeking entry as immigrants, the labor certification process mediates these two goals. But the immigrant categories are often unsuitable for business and entrepreneurial nonimmigrants. First, the employer may need workers only temporarily, but the relatively complicated labor certification process can be expensive. Second, the employer may need workers immediately, but it takes time to process labor certification and immigrant visa applications, and visa categories may be backlogged. Thus the INA includes a number of nonimmigrant classifications that allow relatively quick entry for particular purposes and limited time periods. To ensure that employers and workers do not use nonimmigrant visas as a way around restrictions on immigrant admissions, the INS and the Department of State patrol the categories rather assiduously.

Exercise

To provide a concrete focus for the discussion of the nonimmigrant categories that follows, consider the following hypothetical:

Shoshi Productions, Inc. (SPI), a Japanese corporation based in Tokyo, manufactures computer microchips. Its subsidiary, Shoshi Foreign Distributions (SFD), is responsible for selling and distributing the parent's products outside of Japan. SPI owns fifty percent of SFD.

 SPI has recently purchased a small American computer company, New World Chips. To enable New World to make the microchips currently being produced in Japan, SPI would like its top engineer (who holds a degree from a first-rate Japanese engineering school) to come to the U.S. to supervise the retooling of New World's factory.

 SPI also seeks to have its Vice President for Personnel come to the U.S. to run New World temporarily while he trains New World supervisors and employees in Japanese-style management techniques. The Vice President, who began working for SPI ten years ago in the sales department, has no college degree. The Vice President has a spouse and two children (ages 13 and 16) who would like to accompany him to the U.S. His spouse is a concert violinist who has a national reputation within Japan, but whose work is not widely known outside her home country. The older child, who has graduated from high school in Japan, would like to enroll in a U.S. college, but feels she needs to visit a number of campuses before deciding where to apply. She also hopes to work for her father at New World while attending school.

 Finally, SPI would like to redesign the New World workspace, and has hired a Canadian industrial architecture firm to do the job. That firm has informed SPI that its architects will have to spend at least six months on site, drawing up blueprints and supervising the reconstruction.

 SFD wants to open a U.S. office from which it could sell and distribute SPI's microchips. SFD would like to send to the U.S. a three-person delegation that could scout out an appropriate location for the office. SFD hopes to assign some of its sales staff from its Japanese operations to work in the office on a temporary basis until U.S. workers can be found. SFD also would like to send salespeople to the U.S. to drum up new customers for SPI and New World and to locate talented American computer engineers who might like to work in the SPI design laboratories in Tokyo.

SPI and SFD have asked you for advice on U.S. immigration law. What nonimmigrant categories are available to each alien? Which category is best for each? What further information would you seek from your clients in order to be able to respond sensibly? Assume that each alien wants to remain permanently in the United States. How does that alter your judgment as to the appropriate nonimmigrant category for each alien?

Also: are there any *immigrant* categories available to these aliens? How much longer is it likely to take to secure admission as an immigrant under the employment-based preferences than it would to get a nonimmigrant visa?

a. H, O, and P Nonimmigrant Visas

H–2A. Agriculture provides the paradigmatic case of a need for short-term labor. Crops ripen and must be picked quickly; following the harvest, labor is not needed again until the next growing season. Not surprisingly, then, temporary worker programs have operated for decades in the agricultural industry. The best known example may be the Mexican *bracero* program, operative from 1942 to 1964. "Bracero" literally means one who works with his arms; the closest English equivalent is probably "field hand." Beginning in 1942 the United States entered into a series of agreements with Mexico for the employment of temporary agricultural workers, under a variety of statutes authorizing the practice. Between four and five million Mexican workers were employed under this "Bracero Program" before the special statutory authority was allowed to lapse in 1964. As explained more fully in section C *infra*, many observers believe that the bracero program contributed significantly to today's illegal immigration because the migration patterns established under the bracero program simply continued even after the legal authority ended.

In recent years, thousands of H–2 aliens have entered each year to cut sugar cane in Florida or pick apples on the east coast. (The H–2 program was rarely used by western and southwestern growers. Why?) In 1986, when Congress attempted to staunch the flow of undocumented labor with the imposition of employer sanctions, growers argued that without a large-scale temporary worker program crops would rot in the field. Some earlier versions of the legislation included a massive temporary worker program, but the statute as enacted rejected such approaches. What Congress did do was divide the H–2 category in two: H–2A for temporary workers in agriculture, and H–2B for temporary workers in other fields. The 1986 Act tried to assure growers of an adequate work supply through several provisions, including a streamlined set of procedures for the entry of H–2A temporary agricultural workers.[4]

To bring in H–2A agricultural workers, an employer must first file a labor certification application with the Department of Labor, to show that "(A) there are not sufficient workers who are able, willing and qualified, and who will be available at the time and place needed, to perform the [agricultural] labor or services involved in the petition, and (B) the employment of the alien in such labor or services will not adversely affect the wages and working conditions of workers in the United States similarly employed." INA § 218(a)(1). If the labor certification is granted, next the employer must have a petition approved by the INS before the individual workers can obtain visas for entry.

As with labor certification for some employment-based immigrant preferences, the employer must undertake recruitment efforts that are governed in some detail by the statute and regulations. *See* INA § 218(b)(4), 20 C.F.R. §§ 655.102(d), 655.103(d),(f), 655.105. These provi-

---

4. IRCA's other agricultural provisions are discussed in Section C *infra*.

sions have drawn some criticism, in part because recruitment of United States workers need not be as extensive as recruitment of H–2A workers. "[G]rowers send agents overseas months in advance of the need for workers to negotiate with foreign governments and select the alien help they want. They also have a travel system established to get foreign workers to the jobs. But they do not send agents to Florida to recruit any of the hundreds of unemployed U.S. farm workers there * * *." Yale–Loehr, *The H–2A Agricultural Worker*, in GM & Y § 20.09.

In agriculture, it can be especially hard to know if employment of H–2A workers would adversely affect the wages and working conditions of United States workers. Many farm workers are compensated at a piece rate and/or partly in-kind (*e.g.*, employer-provided housing). Moreover, some sectors of the agricultural labor market are notorious for substandard wages and working conditions. Accordingly, there are complex rules for determining what wage must be offered to H–2A workers in a given situation, *see* 20 C.F.R. §§ 655.102(b)(9), 655.107. Also, workers must be provided with free housing that complies with federal and local standards, *see* INA § 218(c)(4); meals or convenient cooking facilities, *see* 20 C.F.R. § 655.102(b)(4); return transportation, *see* 20 C.F.R. § 655.102(b)(5); and workers' compensation insurance or the equivalent, *see* INA § 218(b)(3).

The number of H–2A labor certifications granted increased steadily from the program's inception to a high of 25,702 in 1991, but then declined over 25 percent in 1992, to 18,939. Four categories accounted for over 87 percent of the applications: apple pickers in the Northeast and Middle Atlantic states (30 percent), tobacco harvesters (27 percent), Jamaican sugar cane workers in Florida (22 percent), and sheepherders (8.5 percent). *See* Department of Labor, 1992 H–2A Program Data (1994), *digested at* 71 Interp.Rel. 394 (1994).

————

H–2B. The definition of the H–2B temporary nonagricultural worker category includes a clause analogous to the labor certification requirement for some employment-based preferences; H–2B designation is available only "if unemployed persons capable of performing such service or labor cannot be found in this country." Section 214(c) of the INA (relating to the admission of nonimmigrants) instructs the Attorney General to consult with "appropriate agencies of the Government, upon petition of the importing employer" in deciding whether American labor is available. By regulation, the INS requires that petitioning employers have certification from the Department of Labor "that qualified persons in the United States are not available and that the alien's employment will not adversely affect wages and working conditions of similarly employed United States workers." 8 C.F.R. § 214.2(h)(6)(iv). The certification procedure is similar to the process for immigrant visas.

The definition of the H–2B category has a double requirement of "temporariness": the alien must be entering *temporarily* to fill a *temporary* job. Why does the statute demand that the job be temporary? Should it? In *Matter of Artee Corp.*, 18 I & N Dec. 366 (Comm'r 1982), the Commissioner ruled that "[i]t is not the nature or the duties of the position which must be examined to determine the temporary need. It is the nature of the need for the duties to be performed which determines the temporariness of the position." This interpretation, which was upheld in *Sussex Engineering v. Montgomery*, 825 F.2d 1084 (6th Cir.1987), *cert. denied*, 485 U.S. 1008, 108 S.Ct. 1473, 99 L.Ed.2d 702 (1988), has been codified in INS regulations. 8 C.F.R. § 214.2(h)(6)(ii).

To help work through the distinction, consider the following situation. A company provides highly skilled personnel to the nuclear power industry. It petitions for the entry of thirty nuclear start-up technicians, who will perform temporary services for nuclear power plants around the country. For the previous five years, the company had sought and received nonimmigrant labor certification from the Department of Labor for such technicians. Should H–2B status be granted?

How temporary is a "temporary" job? "As a general rule, the period of the petitioner's need must be a year or less." 8 C.F.R. § 214.2(h)(6)(ii). Also, the need must be "a one-time occurrence, a seasonal need, a peakload need, or an intermittent need." *Id.* These rules have made it very difficult to use the H–2B category for certain types of workers—nannies, for example. More generally, note the tension between the statutory demands that the job be temporary and that there be no U.S. workers available to perform it: "By demonstrating this unavailability, * * * the employer has also demonstrated some very good reasons why the need for such workers might persist and why the real intentions of the employer are permanent employment of alien workers." A. Fragomen, Jr., A. Del Rey, Jr., & S. Bernsen, Immigration Law and Business, § 2.5(b)(2) (1994).

H–2B nonimmigrants are admitted for up to one year at first, with one-year extensions possible up to a maximum of three years. *See* 8 C.F.R. § 214.2(h)(9)(iii)(C), 214.2(h)(15)(ii)(C). H–2B temporary workers are limited to 66,000 per fiscal year. INA §§ 214(g)(1)(B), (g)(2). This has easily covered recent demand; H–2B admissions were 21,485 in FY 1991, 18,029 in FY 1992, and 15,038 in FY 1993. 1993 INS Statistical Yearbook, Table 40. It is clear, however, that the demand would be much higher but for the double "temporariness" requirement.

H–1B.[5] Until the 1990 Act, H–1B visas were granted to aliens "of distinguished merit and ability" coming temporarily to the U.S. to perform services "of an exceptional nature requiring such merit and ability." Administrative case law had developed two ways to show "distinguished merit and ability": membership in a "profession," and "prominence" in one's field of endeavor. Of course, this gloss on the statutory language created a host of problems. Exactly what made an occupation a "profes-

---

5. We do not discuss here the H–1A nonimmigrant category, aliens "coming temporarily to the United States to perform services as a registered nurse," which was added by the Immigration Nursing Relief Act of 1989, Pub.L. 101–238, 103 Stat. 2099. A noteworthy feature of the H–1A category is that employers must attest that they have taken steps not only to recruit United States workers as nurses, but also to retain United States workers already employed as nurses by improving wages and working conditions. *See generally* GM & Y § 20.07[2][d][ii]; Shusterman, *The New DOL Nurse Regulations: Revisiting the "A" Word*, 94–4 Imm.Briefings (1994).

sion" was not always clear. Nor did the term "prominence" suggest any more definite standards than "distinguished merit and ability." *See generally* Note, *The Reconciliation of Prominence and Exceptional Ability: A Necessary Step Toward a Coordinated Immigration Policy,* 30 Va.J.Int'l L. 977 (1990). In January 1990, the INS adopted detailed regulations that for the first time set out specific standards for determining H–1B status. 55 Fed.Reg. 2606 (1990).

In the 1990 Immigration Act, Congress rewrote the H–1B classification to cover aliens coming temporarily to the United States to provide services in a "specialty occupation." The category, despite the change in terminology, closely tracks the INS regulations' definition of "profession" under the old H–1B. The "prominence" prong of the old H–1B classification was deleted. Those who would have qualified under it must now apply in the new O and P nonimmigrant categories (discussed below), except for fashion models of distinguished merit and ability, whom Congress added back into the H–1B category in 1991. The definition of "specialty occupation" and the ways in which an alien can show membership in such an occupation are specified in INA § 214(i). Crucial to the definition is that the occupation requires the equivalent of a United States bachelor's or higher degree in the specialty. The statute thus declined to follow several court decisions that had recognized certain occupations as "professions" even though entry into the occupation did not require a college degree. *See, e.g., Hong Kong T.V. Video Program, Inc. v. Ilchert,* 685 F.Supp. 712 (N.D.Cal.1988) (president and chief executive officer of a business constitutes a "profession"). Is this a sensible policy? What is the magic of a college degree? Why might Congress have rejected a more flexible definition of "specialty occupation"? Can business careers qualify as "specialty occupations"? If not, are there other nonimmigrant classifications available?

An alien applying for H–1B classification must demonstrate that she is qualified to work in a specialty occupation. This is usually shown by possession of the requisite college degree. Qualification may also be established by licensure, or by experience in the specialty equivalent to the completion of such a degree and "recognition of expertise in the specialty through progressively responsible positions relating to the specialty." 8 C.F.R. § 214.2(h)(4)(iii)(C)(4).

Before the 1990 Act, eligibility for H–1B status did not require a showing that an alien would be filling a position for which U.S. workers were unavailable. But the legislative history reflects concern that the lack of any kind of labor certification requirement produced "heavy use and abuse of the H–1 category, particularly because at present employers are not required to test the U.S. labor market as a prerequisite to petition approval." H.Rep. No. 101–723, at 67 (1990). While unwilling to impose a full labor certification process on H–1Bs, the 1990 Act did mandate that an employer seeking approval of an H–1B petition file a Labor Condition Application ("LCA"), also known as an "attestation," with the Department of Labor.

The employer must attest, among other things, that it has notified the appropriate "bargaining representative" of its employees of the petition or posted notice of its filing "in conspicuous locations at the place of employment." (But ask yourself how many positions that qualify for H–1B treatment will be unionized.) The employer must also attest that the job is being offered at the prevailing wage or actual wage paid to similar individuals (whichever is greater), and that it will provide working conditions for the alien that will not adversely affect the working conditions of similarly employed workers. Note that these new rules do not require that the employer undertake recruitment efforts in the U.S.

The attestation requirement, a procedure first established in the 1989 legislation creating H–1A status for registered nurses, is clearly a compromise measure intended to protect (somewhat) U.S. workers without reducing (too much) the flexibility and speed of H–1 designation. Is it likely to accomplish either goal? A number of regulations implementing the requirement drew strong criticism for being too inflexible and time-consuming. In 1991, Congress responded by reversing some of the agency interpretations that critics had found most burdensome. For example, now a prospective H–1B employer need only show that it has filed an attestation; DOL "approval" is not required. *See* INA §§ 101(a)(15)(H), 212(n). But the attestation requirement continues to draw criticism. Employers complain that they cannot accurately predict what the government will ultimately determine is the "prevailing wage," and that the government makes those determinations neither expeditiously nor accurately. The employer who makes what turns out to be an incorrect determination may suffer serious consequences. If the DOL finds a violation, the employer will owe backpay, it may be fined up to $1000 per violation, and it may be precluded from filing any immigrant or nonimmigrant labor petition for one year. *See* INA § 212(n). These difficulties have led a leading practitioner to lament, "I am not convinced that the benefits of the H–1B process are worth the risks." Pivec, *Observations on the Enforcement of The H–1B Labor Condition Application Requirements*, 71 Interp.Rel. 705, 711 (1994).

At the same time, other critics have charged that the H–1B program has failed to protect United States workers adequately. Recent enforcement actions by the Department of Labor have targeted a number of "job shops," staffed by underpaid H–1B workers, especially in computer programming and physical therapy. *See An Immigrant–Worker Scheme Comes Under Fire*, Business Week, at 40 (Nov. 8, 1993); 70 Interp.Rel. 1325 (1993). In December 1994, the DOL published new final regulations governing attestations. In general terms, these regulations will make it more difficult for employers to hire H–1B workers, at least when the DOL believes that highly skilled U.S. workers would be harmed. *See* 59 Fed. Reg. 65646 (1994); 72 Interp.Rel. 1 (1995).

Why shouldn't labor certification be required for members of a "specialty occupation"? Does it not seem likely that many qualifying professionals (for example, accountants, pharmacists, lawyers) might well be in competition for jobs with American professionals? Or is a somewhat overinclusive category untroubling for a nonimmigrant classification established for temporary employment? Note that in contrast to H–2B workers, H–1B workers may come "temporarily" to fill a job that is itself permanent.

H–1B nonimmigrants can be admitted for up to three years initially, extendable to a maximum authorized stay not exceeding six years. *See* INA § 214(g)(4), 8 C.F.R. § 214.2(h)(9)(iii), 8 C.F.R. § 214.2(h)(15)(ii)(B). The 1990 Act eliminated the requirement that an H–1B nonimmigrant have "a foreign residence which he has no intention of abandoning," and under the regulations an alien may legitimately come to the United States as an H–1B nonimmigrant and, "at the the same time, lawfully seek to become a permanent resident." 8 C.F.R. § 214.2(h)(16). What is the effect of eliminating the foreign residence requirement? Why might Congress have done so?

H–1B temporary workers are limited to 65,000 per fiscal year. INA § 214(g)(1)(A), (g)(2), 8 C.F.R. § 214.2(h)(8). For each of the past several years, the number has approached the cap: 60,179 in FY 1994, *see* 71 Interp.Rel. 1450 (1994). This trend, combined with the possibility (discussed shortly) that some nonimmigrants who had been admitted as B–1 business visitors will need to enter as H–1B temporary workers, has caused some concern that H–1B admissions would be unavailable near the end of the fiscal year.

O and P nonimmigrants. As mentioned above, aliens who had attained "prominence" in their field of endeavor could formerly be admitted as H–1B nonimmigrants under the (now repealed) "distinguished merit and ability" statutory standard. The primary beneficiaries of this gloss on the statutory language were entertainers and athletes. The 1990 Act limited H–1B to members of "specialty occupations," keyed to the requirement of a bachelor's or higher degree. While this eliminated many previously eligible performing artists and athletes from the H–1B category, Congress created two new nonimmigrant classifications to accommodate them.

Take a close look at INA § 101(a)(15)(O) and (P). What other occupations qualify for the O and P classifications? The O category requires "extraordinary ability * * * which has been demonstrated by sustained national or international acclaim." You have seen that language somewhere before. (*See* INA § 203(b)(1)(A).) Does either classification have any kind of labor certification or attestation requirement? (*See* INA § 214(c)(3), (4).) For what periods of time may Os and Ps be admitted? (*See* INA § 214(a)(2).) Do the categories favor famous, established performers over "cutting edge" artists who are well-respected by the cognoscenti but have not yet received the public attention they deserve? Under the regulations, an alien may legitimately come to the United States as an O or P nonimmigrant and, "at the same time, lawfully seek to become a permanent resident." 8 C.F.R. § 214.2(o)(13), (p)(15). In contrast to the H–1B visas, there is no numerical limit on O or P nonimmigrants.

b. L Nonimmigrant Visas

In 1970, Congress acknowledged the growing importance of multinational corporations to the U.S. economy by creating L nonimmigrant visas for aliens seeking transfer from a firm overseas to its operations in the United States. Aliens granted L visas are generally referred to as "intracompany transferees." The category was originally designed to help domestic corporations with foreign operations bring employees to the U.S. for management training. But with the penetration of the U.S. economy by foreign-based corporations, the L classification is extensively used today by foreign corporations to transfer executive level employees to this country to oversee operations of a firm's American branch or subsidiary. In FY 1993, more than 82,000 aliens entered on L–1 visas, bringing with them more than 49,000 immediate relatives on L–2 visas. 1993 INS Statistical Yearbook, Table 40.

Crucial to the L classification is the INA's requirement that the alien "render his services * * * in a capacity that is managerial, executive, or involves specialized knowledge." The definitions of "managerial" and "executive" capacity are in INA § 101(a)(44). (Note that these definitions also apply to the employment-based immigrant category for managers and executives. INA § 203(b)(1)(C).) "Specialized knowledge" is defined as "special knowledge of the company product and its application in international markets or * * * an advanced level of knowledge of processes and procedures of the company." INA § 214(c)(2)(B). The statute stipulates that an alien seeking L classification must have been employed by the sponsoring firm for at least one year within the three years preceding the date of his application for entry. Note that no such requirement applies to the H categories.

The motivation behind creation of the L visa was to aid multinational corporations interested in transferring employees to U.S. operations. However, nothing in the express language of the INA limits the category to large firms, and the INS and the courts have recognized that the statute does not exclude sole proprietorships or partnerships from using L visas to bring personnel to the United States. Yet the Service believes that the classification is being misused by investors and entrepreneurs. The INS has stated that "[t]he L classification was not created for self-employed persons to enter the United States to continue self-employment, unless they are otherwise qualified for L classification." 52 Fed.Reg. 5738, 5739 (1987). The Service seems concerned about the following kind of practice: an alien who owns a small business overseas could buy or start up a small U.S. firm; the firm would then file an L–1 petition on behalf of its sole stockholder/manager. Accordingly, the regulations impose special requirements if the alien is being transferred to the United States to open or work in a new office. See 8 C.F.R. § 214.2(*l*)(3)(v), (vi). The regulations also require that the foreign entity continue doing business during the alien's stay in the U.S. See 8 C.F.R. § 214.2(*l*)(1)(ii)(G). This prevents the entrepreneur from liquidating the place of employment to which he supposedly would have returned. Would the language of the statute prohibit an L visa in these situations? Should U.S. policy provide this route of entry for entrepreneurs?

L nonimmigrant visas require that the employer file a preliminary petition with the INS. INS regulations allow large corporations meeting certain requirements relating to size and prior L–1 usage to be granted blanket L–1 petitions, rather than petitions for individual aliens. INA § 214(c)(2)(A).

L nonimmigrants may be granted an authorized stay of up to one or three years, extendable to a maximum of seven years for managers and executives and five years for those with "specialized knowledge." *See* INA § 214(c)(2)(D), 8 C.F.R. § 214.2(*l*)(7), 8 C.F.R. § 214.2(*l*)(15)(ii). An L–1 alien is not required to have a foreign residence that he has no intention of abandoning. An alien may legitimately come to the United States as an L–1 nonimmigrant and, "at the the same time, lawfully seek to become a permanent resident." 8 C.F.R. § 214.2(*l*)(16).

c. E Nonimmigrant Visas

pursuant to a grand btw US + alien's country of origin

The discussion of H visas started from the assumption that an employer in the United States sought the labor of foreign workers. L visas suggest, however, that much of the demand for nonimmigrant visas comes from foreign enterprises that seek to create or exploit business and investment opportunities here. As international trade and investment opportunities in the United States have grown, E status has become a prominent vehicle for nonimmigrant admissions. In FY 1993, more than 140,000 principal aliens and family members entered on E visas. 1993 INS Statistical Yearbook, Table 40.

Examine closely the language of INA § 101(a)(15)(E). You will note that the statute provides for two distinct E classifications. The category for a "treaty trader" is designated E–1; the category for a "treaty investor" is designated E–2. Crucial for each is an international agreement between the United States and the alien's country of origin under whose terms an E nonimmigrant seeks to carry on activities in this country.

An E nonimmigrant is typically admitted for one year initially, with two-year extensions, *see* 8 C.F.R. § 214.2(e)(1), and may remain in the United States as long as he or she continues to undertake the activities for which entry was initially granted. Thus, E status offers a distinct advantage over H–1B and L classifications, which are subject to a five, six, or seven-year cap. Another advantage over the H and L categories is that an E visa does not require a preliminary petition by a sponsoring entity in the United States. The alien initiates the process by applying for an E visa at a consular office overseas, or by applying for a change of nonimmigrant status in the United States. Like H–1B and L nonimmigrants, however, E visa holders need not retain a foreign residence that they do not intend to abandon. *See* 70 Interp.Rel. 1444 (1993).

The basics of the E category are explained in the following excerpt.

CHARLES GORDON, STANLEY MAILMAN & STEPHEN YALE–LOEHR, IMMIGRATION LAW AND PROCEDURE

§§ 17.01–17.06 (1994).*

A nonimmigrant classification which most closely approximates the status of an immigrant is that of treaty trader (E–1) or treaty investor (E–

2). * * * So long as eligibility continues, "E" status not only permits the alien to engage in the qualifying trade or investment, but permits incidental activities, as well, and a stay of indefinite duration. It also allows the spouse and children to join the principal alien in the same status * * *. An indispensable requirement, however, is that the principal alien be a national of a country with which the United States has a treaty of commerce and navigation, providing for the trade or investor activity. The nationality of the accompanying spouse or children is immaterial to their "E" status.

The treaty trader must carry on trade of a substantial nature that is international in scope and principally between the United States and the treaty country. The treaty investor must have invested or be in the process of investing a substantial amount of capital in an enterprise which he or she will develop and direct and which will not be a marginal enterprise entered into solely to earn a living.

Employees of qualified treaty persons or business organizations may be classified as treaty traders or investors if they have the treaty nationality. They must be engaged, however, in an executive or supervisory capacity, or have special qualifications essential to the enterprise. An agent of a qualified foreign person or organization, may also qualify for E–1.

* * *

The statute specifies that the agreement, under which the alien may enter for the specified trade or investor purposes, is to be "a treaty of commerce and navigation." The agreements recognized by the State Department as treaties of "friendship, commerce, and navigation" (FCN) and listed in the Visa Office, Foreign Affairs Manual are by and large so entitled or similarly named.[1] Not all such agreements, however, are strictly FCNs. * * * Authorization for treaty status (E–1 and E–2) was accomplished, in the case of the Philippines and Canada by diplomatic agreements that are not formally treaties, after specific statutory authorization.

Bilateral investment treaties (BITs) negotiated by the United States with other countries are also recognized as FCNs, but only for purposes of conferring E–2 authorization. * * *

Still another means of conveying treaty trader/investor rights was employed by the Immigration Act of 1990. Under the indirect language of that statute, the nationals of Australia and Sweden may enjoy E–1/E–2 benefits provided reciprocal benefits are extended to Americans. Although not an FCN, the reciprocal action required by the statute could be viewed as an international agreement.

Prototypical of FCN language authorizing both treaty trader and treaty investor classification is the text of the 1953 treaty with Japan, at Article I, paragraph 1:

---

1. *See* 9 FAM, 22 C.F.R. §§ 41.51, Exhibit I * * * .

"Nationals of either Party shall be permitted to enter the territories of the other Party and to remain therein: (a) for the purpose of carrying on trade between the territories of the two Parties and engaging in related commercial activities; (b) for the purpose of developing and directing the operations of an enterprise in which they have invested, or in which they are actively in the process of investing, a substantial amount of capital; and (c) for other purposes subject to the laws relating to the entry and sojourn of aliens."[8]

As the language of a given treaty may differ, any doubts as to its meaning should be resolved by consulting its text.

Agreements with the following countries are recognized by the State Department as authorizing both treaty trader (E–1) and treaty investor (E–2) classifications to their nationals, or simply treaty trader issuance (those preceded by an asterisk being limited to E–1, and those preceded by two asterisks being limited to E–2):

Argentina, Australia, Austria, **Bangladesh, Belgium, *Bolivia, *Brunei (Borneo), **Cameroon, Canada, China (Taiwan), Colombia, Costa Rica, **Czech Republic, *Denmark, **Egypt, *Estonia, Ethiopia, Finland, France, Germany, *Greece, **Grenada, Honduras, Iran, Ireland, *Israel, Italy, Japan, Korea, *Latvia, Liberia, **Luxembourg, Morocco, Netherlands, Norway, Oman, Pakistan, **Panama, Paraguay, Philippines, **Senegal, **Slovak Republic, Spain, **Sri Lanka, Suriname, Sweden, Switzerland, Thailand, Togo, **Tunisia, Turkey, United Kingdom, Yugoslavia, **Zaire.

Bilateral investment treaties (BITs) negotiated with some countries authorize only E–2 classification. The exchange of instruments of ratification will soon permit E–2 but not E–1 status for nationals of Poland under an economic treaty, and for nationals of the Congo and Russia under BITs signed with these countries. (The Senate has already given its advice and consent to these treaties.)[a] Should the North American Free Trade Agreement be ratified, E–1 and E–2 visas will become available to Mexico on January 1, 1994, as they are now to Canadians under the U.S.-Canada Free–Trade Agreement.[b] * * *

* * *

Although the treaty trader (E–1) and treaty investor (E–2) classifications are identical in most of their characteristics, inherent in their definition are marked differences. Distinguishing the treaty trader, in terms of the required commercial activity, is the operative phrase "solely to carry on substantial trade, including trade in services or trade in technology, principally between the United States and the foreign state of which he

8. 4 U.S.T. 2063, 2066 (1953).

a. In addition, BIT's have recently entered into force between the United States and Bulgaria, Kazakhstan, Krygyzstan, Romania. Also, the United States has signed BIT's (that have not yet entered into force) with Haiti, Armenia, Moldova, Ecuador, Belarus, Jamaica, Ukraine, Georgia, Estonia, Trinidad and Tobago, and Mongolia.—eds.

b. NAFTA was ratified, as discussed later in this Section.—eds.

is a national...." Under a rule that is both old and questionable, the trade must already exist at the time classification is sought; this means binding contracts, that "call for the immediate exchange of qualifying items of trade," not merely negotiations.

The concept of "trade," which had been largely restricted in the past to transactions involving goods and certain few quasi-services, has recently been expanded by regulation to include services more generally and by statute to include services and technology. The Immigration Act of 1990 further solidified this expansion by specifically including "trade in services or trade in technology" within the definition of a treaty trader at INA § 101(a)(15)(E)(i). What is meant by "substantial trade" has never been defined by regulation, but interpretations have emphasized a regularity of transactions in amounts sufficient to support the trader and his or her family. Under a 1990 amendment, the Secretary of State must establish an amount of trade for this purpose after consulting with other government agencies. More than half of the trade must be between the United States and the treaty country. The trade must constitute an exchange; it must be international in scope; and it must involve qualifying activities.

* * *

The statutory language which speaks directly to the E–2 investor is: "solely to develop and direct the operations of an enterprise in which he has invested, or of an enterprise in which he is actively in the process of investing, a substantial amount of capital...." Issues suggested by this language relate to the extent the investment must be committed before status is granted, the nature of the capital investment permitted, the meaning of "substantial" in this context and the special significance, if any, of the phrase "solely to develop and direct the operations...."

* * *

In the State Department's view, a hallmark of the investment intended by the statute is the placing of funds or other capital assets at risk to generate a profit. The nature of the asset invested ordinarily does not matter so long as it is subject to loss. According to the 1952 House report, Congress contemplated investments in "commercial enterprises," and that the new status would be for "aliens who will be engaged in ... a real operating enterprise and not a fictitious paper operation." E–2 classification was not designed for retirees, for philanthropists as such, or for the employees of non-profit organizations.

Being "actively in the process of investment" involves something more than a mere intention to invest. How much more can be hard to assess. According to the State Department, "the alien must be close to the start of actual business operations, not merely in the stage of signing contracts (which may be broken) or scouting for suitable locations and property."
* * *

MATTER OF WALSH AND POLLARD

Board of Immigration Appeals, 1988.
Int. Dec. 3111.

On March 2, 1987, the Chief Immigration Judge found the applicants admissible as treaty investor employees under section 101(a)(15)(E)(ii) of the Immigration and Nationality Act. He ordered that the exclusion proceedings be terminated and that the applicants be admitted pursuant to their "E–2" visas. The Immigration and Naturalization Service has appealed from that decision. The appeal will be dismissed.

The applicants are natives and citizens of Great Britain, ages 59 and 25 years old, who are automotive design engineers. They attempted to enter the United States as nonimmigrants on September 18, 1985, by presenting "E–2" visas. They are employees of IAD Modern Design, Ltd. ("IAD, Ltd."), a British-owned corporation, which is the treaty investor in this case.[1] They are coming to the United States pursuant to a contract between IAD, Ltd. and General Motors ("GM") to provide experienced automotive design engineers to GM for the purpose of redesigning GM's line of cars in a smaller, more European fashion. The less experienced man is a transmission designer with a Higher National Certificate, indicating extensive post-secondary education, and with special training in computer-aided design. The more senior man is also to be employed in the United States as a transmission designer. He has approximately 30 years of varied automotive design experience and a Higher National Certificate. It was stipulated that there are not sufficient numbers of United States automotive design engineers to fill the present needs of the automotive industry. IAD, Ltd. expects in the future to bring as many as 300 designers and other related workers to the United States to meet the demands of United States automotive manufacturers.

Under the present arrangement these two designers would report to a GM subsidiary, Hydra-matic, to work on projects as assigned. They would be paid an hourly wage and a daily living allowance plus bonuses by IAD, Ltd. GM reimburses IAD, Ltd. for the applicants' services by purchase order at a higher hourly rate than the applicants receive from their employer. The applicants do not receive any fringe benefits from GM but remain employees of IAD, Ltd.[2] The applicants in question began work for IAD, Ltd. just before being sent to the United States. A representative from IAD, Ltd. testified that the applicants would be offered other work with IAD, Ltd. upon their return to England.

In order to facilitate and expand contract relationships between IAD, Ltd. and American automobile manufacturers, the British corporation

1. The parent corporation of IAD Modern Design, Ltd. is IAD (UK) Ltd., formerly Tigergraph, Ltd. The parent company is a substantial business specializing in automotive design with branches or affiliates in several countries.

2. In similar cases involving a request for permission to bring alien workers to the United States to work for United States firms pursuant to a contract between an American firm and the petitioning firm, it has been held that the foreign workers are employees of the petitioning firm. *Sussex Engineering, Ltd. v. Montgomery*, 825 F.2d 1084 (6th Cir. 1987); *Matter of Artee Corporation*, 18 I & N Dec. 366 (Comm.1982) (both involving denials of "H–2" visa petitions).

formed a Michigan corporation, IAD Modern Design, Inc. ("IAD, Corp."), which is a wholly owned subsidiary. The corporation also assists the British workers in their relocation and business relationships with GM. This corporation was established by renting offices, purchasing office furniture, and hiring two United States citizen employees. This corporation has a bank account of approximately $15,000. Expansion is expected as business increases.

The Chief Immigration Judge found that the British company qualified as a treaty investor based on the investment in IAD, Corp. He further found that the applicants were highly skilled individuals in a responsible position, whose skills were necessary to the IAD, Ltd. investment in the United States. He concluded that they were essential to the IAD, Ltd. investment because American design engineers were not available to be hired to enable IAD, Ltd. to fulfill its contract with GM. He therefore granted them admission.

The Service contends that the British company has not made a substantial investment in the United States as required by section 101(a)(15)(E) of the Act. It also states that the applicants are not entitled to enter the United States as employees of the treaty investor because they are not coming to develop and direct the investment of the treaty investor. The Service argues that it is its policy to require employees of treaty traders to meet the "develop and direct" test.

* * *

* * * There are two main issues in this case: whether the British company qualifies as a treaty investor by reason of its investment in IAD, Corp. and whether the applicants qualify for "E–2" visas as employees of a treaty investor. * * *

It is the responsibility of the [Department of State (DOS)] to accept applications for treaty investor status and to issue the visa to the treaty investor or to its qualified employees. Section 221(a)(2) of the Act. It is the responsibility of the Service to determine admissibility of an alien who applies for admission at the border. Sections 103(a), 221(h) of the Act; 8 C.F.R. §§ 214.1(a), 235.1(d)(1) (1988).

Nothing in Title 8 of the regulations or the Immigration and Naturalization Service Operations Instructions ("O.I.") relates to the issue of "substantiality" of the investment. Since "substantial" is not defined in the statute, reference must be made to the DOS regulations for clarification. The definition in those regulations of investing a "substantial amount of capital" is "investing capital in a bona fide enterprise" as contrasted with "investment of a small amount of capital in a marginal enterprise solely for the purpose of earning a living." 22 C.F.R. § 41.51(b)(1) (1988). The DOS Foreign Affairs Manual ("FAM") notes to 22 C.F.R. § 41.41 (the State Department regulations and instructions relating to treaty investor visas) amplify the concept of a "bona fide enterprise" by requiring "a real and active commercial or entrepreneurial undertaking, producing some service or commodity. It cannot be a paper organization or an idle speculative investment held for potential appreciation in value...." Vol. 9, Foreign Affairs Manual, Part II, 22 C.F.R. § 41.51 note 5.2 (hereinafter cited as FAM). In regard to the concept of investment, the FAM provides:

> No minimum investment amount is required for E–2 status; however, the investment must be substantial. Using a "proportionality test," the consular officer should weigh the amount invested against either 1) the total value of the particular enterprise in question, or 2) the amount normally considered necessary to establish a viable enterprise of the nature contemplated. The alien need only satisfy the requirement of "substantiality" in one of the above ways, not both.

Id. at note 5.3–1.

> The concept of "substantiality" is further amplified as follows:

> [T]he amount normally considered necessary to establish a viable enterprise is less susceptible to precise calculation. Here, the consular officer must draw on personal knowledge of the U.S. business scene to judge whether the amount the alien proposes to invest is reasonable for that type of business....

Id. at note 5.3–2.

> In small to medium-sized businesses, the term "substantial" necessarily connotes an investment of more than half the value of the enterprise, or an amount normally considered necessary to establish an enterprise....

Id. at note 5.3–3.

A Service memorandum in the record from the Assistant Commissioner, Adjudications, dated June 14, 1985, to the regional and district office cites this DOS interpretation with approval. However, in this case the Service argues that if only a minimum amount is invested, it would not qualify the alien for treaty investor status.

* * *

We find that the statute itself does not explain the term "substantial" and it does not address the requirements to be met by employees of treaty investor companies or corporations. The DOS has drafted the regulations which must be applied in this case. Under its regulations, the DOS issued the visas at issue. The replies to the interrogatories propounded by the DOS Visa Office indicate that the officials of that office find no error in the issuance of the "E–2" visas. As a general matter, great deference should be accorded to an agency's construction of a statute which it administers and the agency's interpretation of regulations it has drafted. The Service contends that a minimum dollar amount is required to meet the substantiality test and that employees of the treaty trader must be coming to directly or indirectly develop and direct the treaty trader's investment in the United States. In opposition to the DOS interpretation, the Service has placed only an unpublished "policy," one aspect of which recently has been publicly contradicted by the official of the Service responsible for these policy issues.[3] The Service's requirement of a minimal investment, likewise, is not published or reflected in any written material. We cannot give weight to these alleged policies of the Service in the face of the DOS regulations and the Service's history of acquiescence with them. *See* OI 214.2(e), 248.6. If the Service disagrees with the regulations of the DOS, it should take advantage of existing mechanisms of inter-agency consultation to convince the DOS to change its regulations.[4] *See* section 104(e) and 105 of the Act.

In applying the DOS guidelines and regulations to the present case, we note that the employing company must first qualify as a treaty investor. In order to qualify as a treaty investor the company must have invested, or be actively in the process of investing, a substantial amount of capital. When Congress enacted the Immigration and Nationality Act of 1952, it enlarged the "E" visa class to include the "E–2" category. The only discussion of the substantiality issue was that the investment must be in "a real operating enterprise and not a fictitious paper operation." H.R.Rep. No. 1365, 82d Cong., 2d Sess., *reprinted in* 1952 U.S.Code Cong. & Ad.News 1653, 1697. The DOS regulations require a bona fide enterprise. The legislative history and the DOS regulations both fail to impose a dollar amount requirement for "substantiality" and adopt a definition that envisions a bona fide, viable business.

Since the present case involves an investment in a new business in the United States, the "amount normally considered necessary to establish a viable enterprise of the nature contemplated" test is applicable. FAM at § 41.51 note 5.3–1. In this case, the investment required to establish a viable and profitable business is not large. The evidence indicates the amount thus far actually invested and in the process of being invested is sufficient to accomplish its purpose. The business is in operation and is engaged in business activity on behalf of its parent company. Thus, the business created is a viable one. We find the present investment is sufficient to establish a profitable and viable business in the United States. As all of this amount has been provided by the treaty investor, the proportionality test is met.

Finally, the DOS regulation requires that the investment not be "in a marginal enterprise solely for the purpose of earning a living." 22 C.F.R. § 41.51(b)(1) (1988). The gloss on this language in the FAM is that "[a]n applicant is not entitled to E–2 classification if the investment, even if substantial, will return only enough income to provide a living for the applicant and family." FAM at § 41.51 note 5.4. The note goes on to provide examples of ways to determine marginality, any of which are sufficient proof of meeting this requirement. The testimony indicates that, based on its like experience in other countries, the investor in this case

3. Mr. Richard Norton, the Service Associate Commissioner for Examinations, stated in response to a question posed at a public conference that the Service agrees with the DOS that an employee of a treaty investor was not required to be in the United States to develop and direct the treaty investor's investment in the United States.

4. The witness from the Service Central Office, the Deputy Assistant Commissioner, Adjudications, testified that the present DOS regulations were developed in close consultation with Service over a period of time.

reasonably expects substantial revenues from its investment far above a living wage. Moreover, it was established by testimony of the chief economist in the Michigan Department of Commerce that the investment is expected to expand job opportunities in the State of Michigan.

The next issue is whether the applicants fit within the category of employees of a treaty investor company qualified to come to the United States with an "E–2" visa. Nothing in the Service regulations relates to this issue. The only language in O.I. 214.2(e) relating to an employee of a treaty investor is that the applicant must have "special qualifications necessary for the firm's efficient operation." The applicable law, as found in 22 C.F.R. § 41.41(a)(3) (1987), formerly required that the alien be employed by a treaty investor in a responsible capacity. The regulations presently state that an applicant must have special qualifications that make his services essential to the efficient operation of the enterprise. 22 C.F.R. § 41.51 (1988).

The standards for managerial personnel and for highly trained and specially qualified ("essential") personnel are basically the same for "E–1" and "E–2" visas. * * * [T]he FAM note 3.4–3(a) lists factors to be considered in determining whether an alien possesses "specific qualifications" that are "essential" to the firm's United States operations such as: the degree of proven expertise, uniqueness of the specific skills, length of experience with the firm, the period of training, and the salary. There was considerable testimony at the hearing as to the skill and importance of the job performed by an automotive design engineer, as well as evidence regarding the high qualifications of the applicants. It was shown that even if one has an engineering degree, approximately 10 years are required to train an automotive design engineer. The one applicant has 30 years of experience. The computer skills of the younger applicant are unique. We agree with the Chief Immigration Judge that each of the applicants is to be employed in a highly creative job involving independent judgment and is thus occupying a very responsible position. They have special qualifications. Their employment is also essential to the treaty investor, as it could otherwise not meet its contract obligations.

As the applicants meet the requirements of the applicable regulations promulgated and interpreted by the DOS, they should be admitted.

* * *

Notes

1. Put yourself in the shoes of the INS. It sees in *Walsh and Pollard* a clever scheme by GM and a British corporation to take advantage of a treaty between the U.S. and U.K. and to avoid the pitfalls of the H–1B, H–2B or B–1 categories. IAD (UK) Ltd. notices that there is substantial demand for British automotive design engineers in the U.S. It therefore forms a subsidiary (IAD Modern Design, Ltd.) which will hire such engineers (Walsh and Pollard), and enters into a contract with GM whereby the British subsidiary is compensated for providing the services of the two aliens. To qualify as a "treaty investor," the British corporation estab-

lishes a wholly owned subsidiary in Michigan (IAD, Corp.) which will assist the British workers in relocating in the U.S. and working with GM. The entry of Walsh and Pollard is not intended to help the British company pursue its (rather meager) U.S. investment, *viz.*, IAD Corp. In fact, it is the other way around: the U.S. "investment" will allegedly help the aliens perform their labor contracts. Furthermore, while the transaction is carefully structured so that Walsh and Pollard remain employees of the British company, it is clear—is it not?—that they will essentially be performing labor for GM much as any H–1B or H–2B alien would. In such a case, is not the INS justified in not recognizing the investment, which for all the world appears to be orchestrated simply to provide a hook upon which to hang an ordinary contract for the services of alien workers? That is, does not this arrangement seem rather far afield from the concept of "treaty investor" provided by the statute (which appears to anticipate entry of an alien for the purpose of developing and directing an enterprise which infuses "a substantial amount of capital" into the U.S. economy)?

Now take the perspective of the foreign firm, General Motors, and Walsh and Pollard. As the Board's opinion notes, it was stipulated that "there are not sufficient numbers of the United States automotive design engineers to fill the present needs of the automotive industry." Given the importance of the industry to the U.S. economy, the importance of design engineers to the success of the industry, and the conceded shortage of design engineers, what justifies INS' unsympathetic reading of the statute? Can it not be plausibly argued that the arrangement is fully consistent with congressional intent to facilitate entry of aliens who will benefit the U.S. economy from nations with which we have treaties of friendship and commerce?

2. Under what other nonimmigrant categories might Walsh and Pollard have sought entry? With what likelihood of success? What other facts might you need to know to answer these questions intelligently? *See Sussex Engineering, Ltd. v. Montgomery*, 825 F.2d 1084 (6th Cir.1987) (upholding INS denial of H–2 status to automotive design engineers because petitioners' needs were not "temporary").

3. At the heart of *Matter of Walsh and Pollard* seems to be a dispute between the Departments of State and Justice. Recall that the aliens were granted visas overseas, but refused entry by the INS at the U.S. border. Why does the Board adopt the State Department interpretation instead of INS's? Note that INA § 103(a) describes the responsibilities of the Justice and State Departments and provides "that determination and ruling by the Attorney General with respect to all questions of law shall be controlling." Does the fact that E status is based on a treaty provide sufficient justification? Or is it simply that INS had not promulgated its interpretation in a formal policy statement or rule?

In 1990, Congress took steps to settle the interagency dispute over the meaning of "substantial" by adding the "definition" that now appears in INA § 101(a)(45). Who won? (The implementing regulations are at 22 C.F.R. § 41.51.) *See generally* Klasko, *Proposed E Visa Regulations: No*

Treaty Between the INS and the State Department, 68 Interp.Rel. 1417 (1991).

d. B Nonimmigrant Visas

We have saved the largest category of business-related nonimmigrants for last, B–1 aliens who are "visiting the United States temporarily for business." In FY 1993, almost 3 million aliens entered on B–1 visas. 1993 INS Statistical Yearbook, Table 40.

From the perspective of the alien, B–1 classification offers advantages over other business nonimmigrant categories. An alien initiates the process overseas; no petition on his or her behalf need be filed with the INS in the U.S. And no labor certification is required.

One can easily imagine a wide range of business activities that would qualify for B–1 classification. Individual entrepreneurs and representatives of foreign corporations may seek to enter to find U.S. customers, investigate potential investments, look for locations to establish a U.S. subsidiary, arrange international deals, or negotiate contracts. The B–1 category has been interpreted to embrace numerous other activities as well. Indeed, it has become a catch-all provision, used by the INS to admit nonimmigrant aliens for business-related purposes when other nonimmigrant classifications are not applicable. Thus, categories for which INS Operations Instructions permit B–1 classification (provided the alien receives no salary from a U.S. source other than reimbursement for expenses incident to the temporary stay) include the following: missionaries; aliens coming to the U.S. to attend an executive seminar; aliens seeking an investment which would qualify for E–2 status; aliens coming to open or be employed at a new branch or subsidiary which will qualify them for L–1 status; foreign sports teams. For a complete list, see OI 214.2b. *See also* FAM § 41.31.

Importantly, the statute excludes from the B–1 category aliens "coming for the purpose * * * of performing skilled or unskilled labor." INA § 101(a)(15)(B). Similarly, State Department regulations provide: "The term 'business,' as used in INA 101(a)(15)(B), refers to conventions, conferences, consultations and other legitimate activities of a commercial or professional nature. It does not include local employment or labor for hire." 22 C.F.R. § 41.31(b)(1). Yet this conceptual distinction between B–1s and H–2s is sometimes hard to apply in the real world. Consider, for example, a foreign corporation that intends to send its employees to the U.S. to help perform a contract in the U.S. For the reasons mentioned above, the firm is likely to prefer B–1 classification to H–1B or H–2B. How should the INS decide which nonimmigrant category is appropriate in such a case? Should it view the aliens as employees of the foreign corporation whose labor in the U.S. enables the overseas firm to enter into such contracts (in which case B–1 might be a sensible classification), or should it see the aliens as undertaking labor in the United States that domestic workers might be able to perform (in which case utilizing H–2B and its labor certification process might be advisable)? The next case explores these difficult questions of definition and the sometimes conflicting goals behind nonimmigrant classifications.

INTERNATIONAL UNION OF BRICKLAYERS AND ALLIED CRAFTSMEN v. MEESE

United States District Court for the Northern District of California, 1985.
616 F.Supp. 1387.

LEGGE, DISTRICT JUDGE.

Plaintiff International Union of Bricklayers and Allied Craftsmen ("International Union") represents approximately 100,000 masonry craftsmen working in the construction industry in the United States. Plaintiff Local No. 7, California, International Union of Bricklayers and Allied Craftsmen ("Local 7") is affiliated with plaintiff International Union in Northern California, and represents masonry craftsmen working in Lake County, California.

Defendants Edwin Meese III ("Attorney General"), George P. Schultz ("Secretary of State"), and the Immigration and Naturalization Service ("INS") are charged with the administration and enforcement of the immigration laws in the United States.[1] Defendant-intervenor Homestake Mining Company of California ("Homestake") is a California corporation, and the owner of the McLaughlin Gold Project in Lake County, California.

* * *

II.

* * *

Homestake began construction in early 1984 on its McLaughlin Gold Project in order to open a new gold mine. Due to metallurgical problems in the Lake County region, Homestake concluded that it was necessary to employ technology not used previously in the gold mining industry. Davy McKee Corporation ("Davy McKee"), Homestake's construction manager, therefore conducted a search to locate the appropriate technology.

On behalf of Homestake, Davy McKee agreed to purchase a newly-designed gold ore processing system from Didier–Werke ("Didier"), a West German manufacturing company. Although the purchase agreement required Didier to supply an integrated processing system, it was not possible to premanufacture the entire system in West Germany. The purchase agreement was therefore made contingent upon Didier's West German employees completing the work on the system at the project site in Lake County.

In September 1984, Didier submitted B–1 "temporary visitor for business" visa petitions on behalf of ten of its West German employees to United States consular officers in Bonn, West Germany. Relying upon INS Operations Instruction 214.2(b)(5), consular officers approved the petitions

---

1. Defendants Attorney General, Secretary of State, and INS are collectively referred to herein as the "federal defendants."

and issued B–1 visas to the West Germans.[5] In January 1985, the West Germans entered the United States to work on the processing system. The work involves the installation of the interior linings of the system's autoclaves, and requires certain technical bricklaying skills.

* * *

Plaintiffs allege that the federal defendants' practice of issuing B–1 "temporary visitor for business" visas under the authority of INS Operations Instruction 214.2(b)(5) violates two provisions of the Act. First, plaintiffs allege that the practice violates section 101(a)(15)(B) of the Act, because the issuance of B–1 visas to aliens coming to the United States to perform skilled or unskilled labor is expressly prohibited by section 101(a)(15)(B). Second, plaintiffs allege that the practice violates section 101(a)(15)(H)(ii) of the Act, because aliens have been permitted to bypass the labor certification requirements contained in the regulations under section 101(a)(15)(H)(ii).

Plaintiffs therefore ask this court to declare that INS Operations Instruction 214.2(b)(5) violates the Act; to permanently enjoin the federal defendants from issuing B–1 visas under the authority of the Operations Instruction; and to order the federal defendants to reclassify the visa status of all B–1 "temporary visitor for business" alien nonimmigrants who are currently performing skilled or unskilled labor in the United States.

* * *

IV.

The Validity of the Operations Instruction Under the Act

* * *

In testing the Operations Instruction against the Act, the court's task is to interpret the Act in light of the purposes Congress sought to achieve in enacting it. The starting point must be the language employed by Congress. *I.N.S. v. Phinpathya,* 464 U.S. 183, 189, 104 S.Ct. 584, 589, 78 L.Ed.2d 401 (1984). Absent a clearly expressed legislative intention to the contrary, the statutory language is to be regarded as conclusive.

A.

The Language of the Act and the Operations Instruction

* * *

INS Operations Instruction 214.2(b)(5) provides that an alien may be classified as a "temporary visitor for business" nonimmigrant if:

> *he/she is* to receive no salary or other remuneration from a United States source (other than an expense allowance or other reimbursement for expenses incidental to the temporary stay) ... [and is] *coming to install, service, or repair commercial or industrial equipment*

---

5. Neither the West Germans nor their employer was required to seek labor certification from the Secretary of Labor, because the certification procedures only govern the issuance of H–2 "Temporary worker" visas.

or machinery purchased from a company outside the U.S. or to train U.S. workers to perform such service. . . .

INS Operations Instruction 214.2(b)(5) (emphasis added).

A comparison of the language of section 101(a)(15)(B) of the Act with the language of INS Operations Instruction 214.2(b)(5) demonstrates that the Operations Instruction contravenes that section of the Act. Section 101(a)(15)(B) unequivocally excludes from the B–1 "temporary visitor for business" classification an alien who is "coming for the purpose of . . . performing skilled or unskilled labor." That exclusion is reinforced by the federal defendants' own regulations. In this regard, the Secretary of State has promulgated a regulation defining "business" for purposes of section 101(a)(15)(B): "The term 'business' . . . refers to legitimate activities of a commercial or professional character. *It does not include purely local employment or labor for hire.*" 22 C.F.R. § 41.25(b) (1985) (emphasis added).[9]

INS Operations Instruction 214.2(b)(5), however, does not contain an exclusion for an alien seeking to enter the United States to perform skilled or unskilled labor. The Operations Instruction provides that an alien may be classified as a "temporary visitor for business" if the alien is "coming to install, service, or repair commercial or industrial equipment or machinery." The effect of this language is to authorize the issuance of a B–1 visa to an alien coming to this country to perform skilled or unskilled labor. In the present case, for example, the West Germans undeniably are performing labor—whether it be deemed skilled or unskilled—in connection with the installation of the gold ore processing system at the McLaughlin Gold Project.

Similarly, a comparison of the language of section 101(a)(15)(H)(ii) of the Act with the language of INS Operations Instruction 214.2(b)(5) shows that the Operations Instruction also contravenes that section of the Act. Section 101(a)(15)(H)(ii) classifies an H–2 "temporary worker" as an alien "coming . . . to perform temporary services or labor, if unemployed persons capable of performing such service or labor cannot be found in this country." Because the Act requires the Attorney General to consult other agencies of the government concerning "temporary worker" visas, *see* INA § 214(c), the Attorney General has established H–2 labor certification procedures. Thus, an H–2 visa petition cannot be approved unless the alien's employer obtains either *"[a] certification from the Secretary of Labor . . .* stating *that qualified persons in the United States are not available and that the employment* of the beneficiary *will not adversely affect wages and working conditions of workers in the United States* similarly employed . . . [or] notice that such certification *cannot* be made." 8 C.F.R. § 214.2(h)(3) (1985) (emphasis added).

---

9. Further, the Secretary of State's regulation provides that "[a]n alien seeking to enter as a nonimmigrant for *employment or labor pursuant to a contract* or other prearrangement *shall be required to qualify . . . [for H–2 'temporary worker' status*]." 22 C.F.R. § 41.25(b) (1985) (emphasis added).

It is again important to note that an alien cannot qualify for H–2 "temporary worker" status until his employer has sought labor certification from the Secretary of Labor regarding the availability of qualified American workers.

In contrast, INS Operations Instruction 214.2(b)(5) does not require an alien to seek labor certification prior to obtaining a nonimmigrant visa. More importantly, the Operations Instruction authorizes the issuance of a nonimmigrant visa to a person performing skilled or unskilled labor, though qualified Americans may be available to perform the work involved. The Operations Instruction therefore lacks the safeguards contained in section 101(a)(15)(H)(ii) of the Act and the regulation promulgated under that section. Again, the present case illustrates this point, because the parties have stipulated that neither the West Germans nor their employer was required to seek labor certification from the Secretary of Labor prior to the issuance of the visas to the West Germans.

* * *

B.

The Intent of Congress

Having determined that INS Operations Instruction 214.2(b)(5) is expressly inconsistent with the relevant sections of the Act, the court will also examine the congressional intent underlying those sections. As noted above, however, the scope of the court's inquiry is quite limited. Absent a clearly expressed legislative intention to the contrary, the language of the Act is to be regarded as conclusive.

The current substantive versions of sections 101(a)(15)(B) and 101(a)(15)(H)(ii) of the Act were enacted in 1952.[10] Congress, however, demonstrated its concern for the protection of American workers as early as 1885. In the Act of Feb. 26, 1885, 23 Stat. 332, Congress enacted legislation prohibiting the entry of contract laborers. Contract laborers generally were unskilled aliens who received minimal wages in return for passage to the United States. The importation of those laborers was intended "to oversupply the demand for labor so that the domestic laborers would be forced to work at reduced wages." H.R.Rep. No. 1365, 82d Cong., 2d Sess., *reprinted in* 1952 U.S.Code Cong. & Ad.News 1653, 1662 (discussion of 1885 Act in House Report accompanying 1952 Act). In the 1885 Act, Congress therefore sought to protect American labor from an influx of cheaper foreign competition.

In the Immigration Act of 1924, Pub.L. No. 68–139, 43 Stat. 153, Congress enacted a "temporary visitor for business" nonimmigrant provision in section 3(2) that was very similar to section 101(a)(15)(B) of the current Act. Section 3(2) was construed by the Supreme Court in *Karnuth v. United States ex rel. Albro*, 279 U.S. 231, 49 S.Ct. 274, 73 L.Ed. 677 (1929). *Karnuth* involved a challenge to a regulation providing that an alien's entry into the United States to perform "labor for hire" did not constitute "business" within the meaning of the "temporary visitor for business" class in section 3(2) of the Act.[11] In the specific case before the

---

10. Certain technical changes not relevant to this dispute were made in 1970, 1976, and 1981.

11. Although section 3(2) of the 1924 Act closely resembled section 101(a)(15)(B) of the current Act, section 3(2) did not contain a specific *exclusion* concerning skilled or un-

Court, the regulation had been applied to prohibit aliens from crossing the Canadian border to perform labor in the United States. The Supreme Court upheld the regulation. In reaching that conclusion, the Court relied primarily on its interpretation of the congressional intent underlying section 3(2):

> [T]he case ... is narrowed to the simple inquiry whether the word "business," as used in the statute, includes ordinary work for hire....
>
> The various acts of Congress since 1916 evince a progressive policy of restricting immigration. The history of this legislation points clearly to the conclusion that one of its great purposes was to protect American labor against the influx of foreign labor....
>
> In view of this definite policy, it cannot be supposed that Congress intended, by admitting aliens temporarily for business, to permit their coming to labor for hire in competition with American workmen, whose protection it was one of the main purposes of the legislation to secure.

Id. at 243–44, 49 S.Ct. at 278–79 (citations omitted). The Court therefore concluded that aliens temporarily visiting the United States for the purpose of performing labor for hire were not entitled to nonimmigrant visas under section 3(2).

Significant changes in the immigration laws were enacted by Congress in the Immigration and Nationality Act of 1952, Pub.L. No. 82–414, 66 Stat. 163. Congress amended section 101(a)(15)(B) of the Act—the successor to section 3(2) of the 1924 Act—to include a specific provision *excluding* an alien from the B–1 "temporary visitor for business" class who comes to the United States "for the purpose of ... performing skilled or unskilled labor." Further, Congress enacted section 101(a)(15)(H)(ii) of the Act, thereby establishing the H–2 "temporary worker" class.

In taking these actions, Congress evidenced a continuing concern for the protection of American workers from unnecessary foreign competition. The House Report accompanying the 1952 Act explained that the purpose of section 101(a)(15)(H)(ii) was to:

> grant the Attorney General sufficient authority to admit *temporarily certain alien workers,* industrial, agricultural, or otherwise, *for the purpose of alleviating labor shortages as they exist or may develop* in certain areas or certain branches of American productive enterprises....

H.R.Rep. No. 1365, 82d Cong., 2d Sess., *reprinted in* 1952 U.S.Code Cong. & Ad.News 1653, 1698 (emphasis added).

Similarly, in discussing the 1952 version of the Act, the Senate Report noted:

> While the present classes of nonimmigrants would be retained, ...
> the subcommittee has made recommendations with respect to each

---

skilled labor. In the 1952 version of the Act, Congress responded to the Supreme Court's holding in *Karnuth* by adding that specific exclusion to section 101(a)(15)(B).

class of nonimmigrants which it believes will permit more effective control of aliens permitted to enter for temporary periods. *Under the proposed legislation, the nonimmigrant classes of admissible aliens will include* ... *aliens seeking to enter temporarily* to furnish services of an exceptional nature or *to furnish services or labor if unemployed persons capable of performing such services or labor cannot be found in this country. Of particular significance is the extension of the nonimmigrant classification to temporary workers who seek* to furnish services involving exceptional skill or *to furnish noncompetitive services or labor.* The admission of aliens as temporary workers has created many problems and it is believed that by ... [the proposed legislation], many of the problems will be prevented or more effectively minimized.

S.Rep. No. 1515, 81st Cong., 2d Sess. 1, 590 (1950) (emphasis added).

The foregoing legislative history demonstrates that one of Congress' central purposes in the Act was the protection of American labor. The legislative history also demonstrates that sections 101(a)(15)(B) and 101(a)(15)(H)(ii) of the Act were intended to restrict the influx of aliens seeking to perform skilled or unskilled labor in the United States. Thus, to the extent that INS Operations Instruction 214.2(b)(5) permits aliens to circumvent the restrictions enacted by Congress in those sections, the Operations Instruction is inconsistent with both the language and the legislative intent of the Act.

C.

Defendants' Arguments

Defendants contend that INS Operations Instruction 214.2(b)(5) should be upheld because it embodies a reasonable administrative interpretation of the Act.

Defendants' argument centers on the purposes Congress sought to achieve in sections 101(a)(15)(B) and 101(a)(15)(H)(ii) of the Act. Defendants contend that those sections evidence Congress' intent to foster multiple purposes. Although defendants acknowledge that one such purpose was the protection of American labor, they argue that another was the promotion of international commerce. Further, defendants assert that the language in sections 101(a)(15)(B) and 101(a)(15)(H)(ii) reveals a tension between American labor interests and international commerce interests; that the Operations Instruction seeks to minimize the tension; and that the Operations Instruction is therefore consistent with the multiple purposes in the Act.

Defendants rely primarily upon the decision of the Board of Immigration Appeals in *Matter of Hira,* 11 I. & N.Dec. 824 (BIA 1966). In *Hira,* an alien employed by a Hong Kong custom-made clothing manufacturer had entered the United States under the authority of a B–1 "temporary visitor for business" visa. While in this country, the alien took orders on behalf of his employer from prospective customers, and took the measurements of those customers. Prior to the expiration of the alien's visa, the INS commenced deportation proceedings against him. The INS concluded that the alien's activities involved the performance of skilled labor, and ordered that the alien be deported for failure to maintain his B–1 "temporary visitor for business" status. On appeal, the Board of Immigration Appeals focused its analysis on the term "business" within section 101(a)(15)(B) of the Act. Adopting the Supreme Court's definition from an earlier version of the Act, the Board held that "business," for purposes of section 101(a)(15)(B) of the Act, "contemplate[s] only 'intercourse of a commercial character.'" *Id.* at 827 (quoting *Karnuth v. United States ex rel. Albro,* 279 U.S. 231, 49 S.Ct. 274, 73 L.Ed. 677 (1929)). In support of that definition, the Board alluded to prior administrative cases in which aliens were found eligible for "temporary visitor for business" status because "there was involved international trade or commerce and the employment was a necessary incident thereto." *Id.* at 830 (citations omitted). The Board also elaborated upon the underlying requirements for eligibility as a "temporary visitor for business" nonimmigrant:

> The significant considerations to be stressed are that there is a clear intent on the part of the alien to continue the foreign residence and not to abandon the existing domicile; the principal place of business and the actual place of eventual accrual of profits, at least predominantly, remains in the foreign country; the business activity itself need not be temporary, and indeed may long continue; the various entries into the United States made in the course thereof must be individually or separately of a plainly temporary nature in keeping with the existence of the two preceding considerations.

Id. at 827 (footnote omitted).

Applying those principles the Board in *Hira* concluded that the alien's business was intercourse of a commercial character, even though he took prospective customers' measurements in connection with the business. Thus, the Board held that the alien was entitled to B–1 "temporary visitor for business" status. The Attorney General subsequently affirmed the Board's decision, and certified it as controlling.

Defendants argue that *Hira* controls the result in this case, since the principles underlying INS Operations Instruction 214.2(b)(5) and *Hira* are nearly identical. Defendants focus on the portion of *Hira* that permits the issuance of B–1 "temporary visitor for business" visas to an alien coming to the United States to engage in "intercourse of a commercial character," or coming to work as a "necessary incident" to international trade or commerce. *Hira, supra,* 11 I. & N.Dec. at 827, 830. Defendants argue that here the West Germans came to this country only as a necessary incident to the purchase and sale of the gold-ore processing system, rather than as individuals hired expressly as laborers. Further, defendants contend that it must be presumed that Congress has acquiesced in the policies underlying the Operations Instruction, because Congress has been aware of those policies for many years but has failed to take action.

Defendants' arguments are answered primarily by the language of the Act. It is important to reemphasize that in matters of statutory interpretation, a court must interpret the statute in light of the purposes Congress sought to achieve in enacting it. And absent a clearly expressed legislative intention to the contrary, the statutory language is regarded as conclusive. Under those principles, the language of section 101(a)(15)(B) of the Act which *excludes* an alien "coming for the purpose of ... performing skilled or unskilled labor," precludes defendants' purported distinction between business and labor in this case; so does the expressed congressional intent of protecting American labor.

Similarly, there is no indication that Congress has acquiesced in the policies underlying INS Operations Instruction 214.2(b)(5). The current substantive versions of sections 101(a)(15)(B) and 101(a)(15)(H)(ii) were enacted in 1952. The Operations Instruction was not promulgated until 1972. And there is no suggestion from legislative history that Congress considered either the specific holding of the Board of Immigration Appeals in *Hira* in 1966, or *Hira* 's impact on other types of foreign labor performed in the United States.

The interpretation of a federal statute by the officials responsible for its administration is entitled to deference. A court, however, must reject an administrative interpretation "that [is] inconsistent with the statutory mandate or that frustrate[s] the policy that Congress sought to implement." *Securities Industry Ass'n v. Board of Governors*, 468 U.S. 137, 143, 104 S.Ct. 2979, 2983, 82 L.Ed.2d 107 (1984).

The court concludes from both the language and legislative intent of the Act that the federal defendants' interpretation embodied in the Operations Instruction contravenes the Act. The court therefore decides that INS Operations Instruction 214.2(b)(5) violates sections 101(a)(15)(B) and 101(a)(15)(H)(ii) of the Act.

* * *

ORDER

* * *

2. INS Operations Instruction 214.2(b)(5) is declared unlawful and in violation of sections 101(a)(15)(B) and 101(a)(15)(H)(ii) of the Immigration and Nationality Act.

3. Defendants Edwin Meese III, George P. Schultz, and the Immigration and Naturalization Service, and their agents, successors and assigns, and all persons acting with or in concert with them, are permanently enjoined from issuing B–1 "temporary visitor for business" visas under the authority of INS Operations Instruction 214.2(b)(5).

* * *

Notes

1. Would *Bricklayers* have come out differently if the OI had expressly excluded "purely local employment or labor for hire," as the Department of State's regulation did?

2. Does *Bricklayers* distinguish or overrule *Matter of Hira*?

3. An appeal in the *Bricklayers* litigation was dropped when the parties reached agreement on a new regulation regarding the entry of building and construction workers. In its announcement of the amended rule, the INS reported the reaction of foreign countries and corporations to the court's opinion:

> Following the District Court's order, which precluded the admission of even the most highly specialized technicians, the Service and the Department of State received communications from U.S. industries and foreign governments which indicated a problem of crisis proportions. Industry predicted that equipment under warranty would not be repaired or serviced, with resultant losses of investment and lay-offs of American workers, and that access to state-of-the-art foreign technology would be limited with resultant losses of competitive position. Foreign governments generally viewed this new restriction as a constraint on trade and hinted at reciprocal actions.

51 Fed.Reg. 44266 (1986).

> The post-litigation regulation promulgated by the INS provides:

> Aliens seeking to enter the country to perform building or construction work, whether on-site or in-plant, are not eligible for classification or admission as B–1 nonimmigrants * * *. However, alien nonimmigrants otherwise qualified as B–1 nonimmigrants may be issued visas and may enter for the purpose of supervision or training of others engaged in building or construction work, but not for the purpose of actually performing any such building or construction work themselves.

8 C.F.R. § 214.2(b)(5). The State Department has adopted regulations to the same effect. *See* 22 C.F.R. § 41.31(b).

The new rule complies with a narrow reading of the court's opinion—that is, that the decision extends no further than the situation of building or construction workers. But does not the reasoning of the case put in doubt the validity of a number of the categories for which INS and the State Department allow B–1 admissions?

2. A Canadian railroad clerk employed by a Canadian railroad seeks to enter the U.S. on a daily basis in order to clear his employer's railroad cars for transport from the U.S. to Canada. His time in the U.S. constitutes about one-third of his work day. Is he eligible for a B–1 visa?

3. In November 1992, the National Association of Computer Consultant Businesses challenged the use of B–1 visas, alleging that United States companies arrange with foreign subsidiaries, especially in India, Australia, and the United Kingdom, for computer programmers to enter the United States on B–1 visas for long-term consulting and software development projects. The argument is that these programmers are paid less than the prevailing wage that would be required if they entered properly as H–1B temporary workers. *See B–1 in Lieu of H–1 Visas: A Brouhaha Brews*, 69 Interp.Rel. 1495 (1992). (Recall that the use of H–1B visas for computer programmers has also been criticized as displacing United States workers.)

In 1993, both the Department of State and INS proposed regulations that would limit this use of B–1 visas in lieu of H–1B visas. *See* 58 Fed.Reg. 40024 (1993) (State); 58 Fed.Reg. 58982 (1993) (INS). *See generally* Mailman, *B–1 Visitors for Business Revisited*, 71 Interp.Rel. 149 (1994).

4. Since 1986, INA § 217 has authorized a visa waiver pilot program that allows nationals of selected countries (with low visa refusal rates and reciprocal privileges) to visit the United States for up to 90 days without a B visa. *See* Chapter Four *infra*.

e.   *The North American Free Trade Agreement (NAFTA)*

The North American Free Trade Agreement, which took effect January 1, 1994, brought Mexico into the free trade zone that had existed since 1988 by virtue of the U.S.-Canadian Free Trade Agreement (FTA), 27 I.L.M. 293 (1988). NAFTA makes no provision for permanent immigration, but it does allow four categories of Canadian and Mexican citizens to enter the United States as nonimmigrants if they are "businesspersons"— defined as those "engaged in trade in goods, the provision of services or the conduct of investment activities." NAFTA, ch. 16, Annex 1603. These categories are labeled "business visitors," "traders and investors," "intra-company transferees," and "professionals." The first three categories roughly correspond to the B–1, E–1 and E–2, and L–1 categories, respectively. The "professionals" category appears to correspond to the H–1B category, but consists of a carefully negotiated list of specifically eligible occupations.

For business visitors and intra-company transferees, entry under NAFTA is accommodated under the existing INA sections. For E visas, an amendment to the INA allows access by Canadians and Mexicans. The implementing legislation also created a new "TN" category for professionals. *See* Pub. L. No. 103–182, 107 Stat. 2057 (1993). The procedure for TN aliens parallels that for H–1Bs, except that Canadian citizens need not file a labor attestation nor a preliminary petition with the INS. Also, "TN" professionals are not subject to the 65,000 cap on H–1B visas. Mexican TN nonimmigrants are limited to 5,500 annually, *see* 8 C.F.R. § 214.6(d)(7)(i). The United States and Mexico can raise this limit, and in any case it expires in ten years (or earlier by mutual agreement). *See generally* Schoonover & Walker, *Immigration Provisions of the North American Free Trade Agreement*, 94–3 Imm.Briefings (1994).

SECTION C.   UNDOCUMENTED ALIENS IN THE UNITED STATES

So far, we have been primarily concerned with lawful immigration to the United States. We have explored the family reunification and occupational categories for immigrants and the provisions for nonimmigrant admissions. We may well be vulnerable, however, to the accusation that we have exalted legal procedures over the true picture, for we have not touched upon illegal immigration.

BILL BARICH, A REPORTER AT LARGE: LA FRONTERA

The New Yorker, December 17, 1990, at 72–74.

The most heavily travelled border in the world is a strip of scrubby California desert that runs for fifteen miles between the United States and Mexico, starting at the Pacific Ocean and ending at a thriving yet isolated spot called Otay Mesa. A chain-link fence follows the border for much of its course, but it is torn in many places and trampled in many others, and in some places it has fallen down. Where the fence is still standing, you find litter on both sides of it which illegal aliens have left behind—beer and soda cans, cigarette packs, diapers, syringes, candy wrappers, and even comic-book *novelas* that feature cautionary tales about the perils of a trip to *El Norte*. These *novelas* tell of dishonest employers, horrible living conditions, and the corruptive power of American dollars. In their most dramatic stories, families come apart, brothers murder brothers, and lovers' hearts are broken beyond mending. The stories offer a liberal blend of truth and fiction, but that is an accurate reflection of the border, where nothing is ever absolute.

Between the ocean and the mesa, the only town of any size is San Ysidro, California, just across from Tijuana. About forty-three million people pass through its legal port of entry every year, in vehicles, on bicycles, and on foot, but nobody knows for certain how many undocumented migrants slip illegally over *la frontera*. An educated guess would be about five thousand every day. They come primarily from Mexico and Central America, and they carry their most precious belongings with them in knapsacks or plastic supermarket bags. The Border Patrol, in its San Diego Sector—a territory roughly as big as Connecticut—apprehends about a third of them, logging almost fifteen hundred arrests every twenty-four hours, but the others drift on to Los Angeles or San Francisco or Sacramento, or to farms in the great Central Valley, staying with relatives and friends while they look for work. If they fail to be hired anywhere, they go farther north, to Oregon and Washington, ready to pick fruit or to gut salmon in a packinghouse, willing to do anything to earn their keep.

Like many border towns, San Ysidro is conducive to paranoia. Set in the midst of sagebrush and dry, brown mountains covered with chaparral, it has the harmless look of an ordinary suburb, but this is deceptive and does not hold up under close inspection. For instance, there is a blood bank on the edge of its largest mall, and all day you can watch donors come out the door with balls of cotton pressed to their forearms, bound for a shopping spree at a nearby K mart before going home to Tijuana. The sky above San Ysidro is often full of ravens and buzzards, and skulls of small animals turn up in its playgrounds. Its population is mostly Hispanic, but more and more Anglos—retired people, and people who commute to San Diego—are buying property in the tile-roofed housing tracts that are devouring the last farms and ranches, and they get very angry the first time some illegal aliens dash through their back yards, trampling the shrubbery and pausing to drink from garden hoses.

The Border Patrol is the uniformed arm of the Immigration and Naturalization Service, and it is supposed to control the flow of uninvited foreigners into the States. In California, as in Texas, its stations are understaffed and underfunded, and are asked to perform a nearly impossible task. In the San Diego Sector, agents must police all of San Diego County, as well as substantial parts of Orange and Riverside Counties, scouring not only the canyons and the backwoods but also the teeming barrios in cities, where aliens frequently seek shelter. Although the sector captures more illegal aliens than any other sector in the country—more than four hundred and seventy thousand in fiscal year 1990, almost half the United States total—this record does little for the morale of the agents, since there is no real penalty imposed on those who are apprehended, unless they have some contraband or resist arrest. Mexicans are given a brief interview, then returned to Tijuana, sometimes so quickly that they get caught crossing again on the same night.

The law isn't the only obstacle that the Border Patrol faces in dispatching its duty. It used to be easy for agents to spot new arrivals because they dressed like field hands and looked dirty and frightened, but now the aliens disguise themselves in clothes fresh off the rack, relying on such items as bluejeans, Reeboks, and L.A. Dodgers caps for protective coloration. The business of providing goods and services to migrants has grown enormously, forming a closed economy worth millions, and they have an elaborate network of support, which often involves extended families and functions in the manner of an underground railroad. Then, too, illegal aliens are always testing agents by devising new tricks for sneaking into California. On a hot summer day, they like to put on bathing suits and wander up the coast, or they dive from a boat and swim to shore. They wade through raw sewage in the Tijuana River and slip into Imperial Beach, just north of San Ysidro. They jam themselves into car trunks and into boxcars, and they ride across the border spread-eagled on top of freight trains. The boldest ones merely sprint through the backed-up traffic at the port of entry, defying the Border Patrol to chase them.

Once illegal aliens get by this first line of defense, they can relax and blend into the crowd of legal Hispanics in San Ysidro. They treat the town as a sort of flea market, making connections and buying Stateside necessities, usually on the sly. If they require fake documents—anything from birth certificates to green cards—they seek out a dealer in such papers and begin negotiations. A high-quality document might cost more than a thousand dollars. Only an expert can detect that it's a forgery, while a so-called "fifty-footer" looks bad even at that distance and can be bought without much haggling. If migrants have some pesos to be laundered, they speak to the fellows hanging around the pay phones by the United States Customs gate. Those phones, supplied by half a dozen different companies, are the conduit through which a fortune in drug profits—from the sale of cocaine, marijuana, and methamphetamines—is annually rerouted. The men who smuggle in aliens use the phones, too, arranging transportation for their customers. The smugglers are known as *coyotes,* on account of their predatory habits, and they flourish on the border, where expediency is the rule of thumb.

In San Ysidro, there are also safe houses, where, for a price, a migrant can hole up for a while. The safe houses look like the houses around them, but everybody on a given block can point them out. As it happens, secrecy tends to play a very limited role in illegal immigration. Anyone who wants to see how openly aliens cross the border, even in broad daylight, can take a drive on Dairy Mart Road, which winds from the outskirts of town through beanfields, pastures, and fallow land scattered with junked farm machinery. On any morning or afternoon, in any season, you'll have to brake to a halt as people streak by in front of your car, speeding from one hiding place to another. For the most part, they are young men in their late teens and early twenties, and they never seem the slightest bit afraid. They emerge from arroyos, from stands of bamboo and pampas grass, from copses of trees, and from vacant buildings. One morning as I cruised on Dairy Mart Road, I counted twenty-two people in a two-hour period.

The action at night is even more spectacular, and it occurs on a much larger scale. At dusk, you start hearing sirens and whistles all over San Ysidro, as if several robberies were in progress, and then comes the chopping sound of helicopter blades slashing up the clouds. Step outside your motel room and you notice beams from above shining down on a Carl's, Jr., restaurant, on kids in baseball uniforms and elderly folks out for an evening stroll. Sometimes a beam illuminates a drainage ditch, and a human form scampers away, like a rabbit rousted from its burrow. It's disconcerting to find normal life going on in what appears to be a suburban war zone. If you walk to a weedy field near the blood bank, you can look toward the concrete levee of the Tijuana River, where, in the glare of I.N.S. floodlights and in full view of the Border Patrol, more than five hundred people will be congregated in little bands, waiting for an opportune moment to begin their journey to the United States.

Notes

1. Crossing the border surreptitiously—also known as "entry without inspection" (or "EWI")—accounts for roughly half of undocumented aliens. Almost all of the rest entered as nonimmigrants and overstayed. A third, much smaller group consists of permanent residents who have not complied with a deportation order or grant of voluntary departure.[1]

2. Most undocumented aliens apprehended by the government agree to depart the United States "voluntarily" without being formally deported. If, however, they are deported from the United States, that deportation may make them excludable or deportable if they later attempt to return.

---

1. The terms "illegal aliens," "undocumented aliens," and "undocumented immigrants" are all in common usage. Some object to "illegal aliens" by noting that they may obtain discretionary relief, and in any event that the United States has tolerated and even encouraged their presence. But others counter that "undocumented" is a euphemism for entry and continuing presence that violate federal law. For the first time, a Supreme Court majority consistently used "undocumented alien" in *McNary v. Haitian Refugee Center*, 498 U.S. 479, 111 S.Ct. 888, 112 L.Ed.2d 1005 (1991) (upholding district court jurisdiction to hear challenges to INS policies). The dissent consistently used "illegal alien."

See, e.g., INA §§ 212(a)(6), § 241(a)(1).[2] Illegal entry, fraud and misuse of visas, and similar acts are also criminal offenses. *See, e.g.,* INA §§ 274C, 275(a), 276. In practice, however, prosecutions are infrequent and generally reserved for organized smuggling operations.

3. In 1994, the INS took several significant steps to make surreptitiously entry on the southern border significantly more difficult. These measures included a shift in emphasis from apprehension after illegal entry to prevention of illegal entry in the first place, improved physical barriers at the border, and better recordkeeping to identify those who repeat attempts to cross. We will discuss strategies for improving border enforcement later in this Section.

––––––––

It should hardly surprise you that there is little consensus on the number of undocumented aliens in the United States. Those who would reach scientifically sound estimates face a number of daunting problems. The number of border apprehensions may provide a very rough estimate of successful crossings and thus of EWIs. However, EWIs stay for varying lengths of time; some settle permanently, others come and go seasonally, and others commute daily but do not reside in the United States. This uncertainty complicates extrapolation from estimates of the number of EWIs. Moreover, these EWI-based estimates overemphasize Mexico, which accounts for over 60 percent of EWIs but only about 40 percent of the entire undocumented population.[3] *See* R. Warren, Estimates of the Resident Illegal Alien Population Residing in the United States, by Country of Origin and State of Residence: October 1992, at 14, 27 (INS Statistics Division 1993). Estimates of visa overstays depend on records of nonimmigrant departures. Researchers must also subtract the estimated number of undocumented aliens who leave the United States, acquire legal status, or die.

Considering all of these obstacles, the best figures currently available are probably those from the INS Statistics Division, which estimated an October 1992 undocumented population of about 3.4 million and an annual growth rate of about 300,000 (about one-third of the total immigrant flow). *See* 1993 INS Statistical Yearbook 183; R. Warren, *supra,* at 13.[4] But bear in mind that as we examine the issues raised in this Section, we will be

2. Exclusion and deportation grounds are treated in Section D *infra* and Chapter Six *infra,* respectively.

3. This varies from region to region, of course. A 1993 study by the New York City Planning Department found that the three largest undocumented nationality groups in New York state (which is the second largest in the country, after only California) were from Ecuador, Italy, and Poland. Undocumented immigration from Mexico barely showed up in the statistics. *See* Sontag, *Analysis of Illegal Immigrants In New York Defies Stereotypes,* N.Y.Times, Sep. 2, 1993, at A11.

4. For an analysis of different estimates of the undocumented population—by the INS, the Census Bureau, the General Accounting Office, and the nongovernmental Center for Immigration Studies—and the conclusion that the INS estimate is "clearly preferable to the other estimates," see R. Clark, J. Passel, W. Zimmermann, & M. Fix, Fiscal Impacts of Undocumented Aliens: Selected Estimates for Seven States 4, 17–33 (1994). We will consider this study's other findings later in this Section.

confronted at every point by a dismaying lack of information and a confusing array of contradictory theories, explanations, and projections. There is no scholarly agreement concerning the number of undocumented aliens presently in the United States, the effect of such workers on the employment of legal residents and citizens, the burdens that undocumented aliens impose on public services and programs, or the efficacy of employer sanctions.

1. WHY DO UNDOCUMENTED ALIENS ENTER THE UNITED STATES?

Aliens enter the United States unlawfully for a number of reasons. Some come to join family members, some to flee persecution in their homeland, some to go to school. These motivations are normally referred to as "push" and "pull" factors. "Push" factors are those considerations that lead an alien to want to leave his or her home country; "pull" factors are those considerations that lead an alien to choose the United States as their destination.

Virtually all scholars agree that economic factors provide the most common incentive for illegal entry and residence. *See* SCIRP, Staff Report 490–99. America offers jobs to unemployed or underemployed laborers from less developed nations and wages that are generally substantially above prevailing wages in the aliens' countries of origin (even if the wages the aliens receive here are below wages normally paid to U.S. citizens or legal immigrants).

It is doubtful, however, that these factors alone can explain the massive amount of unlawful migration that the United States has witnessed throughout this century. As Gerald Lopez points out:

> There have been numerous instances * * * where economic disparity between nations—even adjoining nations—exists but mass migration is absent. In other words, economic disparity is necessary but not sufficient for migration. * * * [E]conomic disparity [does not] account for the pattern of Mexican migration. Primary Mexican source regions for today's undocumented migration are areas that provided labor earlier in this century. Yet the economic disparity between these source regions and the United States is no greater than that existing between numerous other regions in Mexico and this country.

Lopez, *Undocumented Mexican Migration: In Search of a Just Immigration Law and Policy,* 28 UCLA L.Rev. 615, 640 (1981). Accordingly, Lopez offers the following hypothesis as an alternative to the conventional "push-pull" explanation:

> Where there is substantial economic disparity between two adjoining countries and the potential destination country promotes *de jure* or *de facto* access to its substantially superior minimal wage, that promotion encourages migrants reasonably to rely on the continuing possibility of migration, employment, and residence, until a competitive economic alternative is made available in the source country.

Id. at 640–41.

Lopez' hypothesis forces us to consider the role that public and private actors in this country have played in encouraging, or at least tolerating, unlawful immigration. Examination of history, federal statutes and regulations, and enforcement practices reveals a complex set of federal policies toward undocumented labor—policies that, over the years, may have promoted illegal migration much more than was commonly acknowledged by federal decisionmakers.

KITTY CALAVITA, THE IMMIGRATION POLICY DEBATE: CRITICAL ANALYSIS AND FUTURE OPTIONS

Mexican Migration to the United States: Origins, Consequences, and Policy Options 151, 155–59 (W. Cornelius & J. Bustamante, eds., 1989).

MEXICAN MIGRATION AS A BACKDOOR LABOR SOURCE

Mexican immigration to the United States gained momentum in the pre-World War I period, as policymakers and even some employers reassessed the costs versus the benefits of European immigration. The European immigrant was a reputed troublemaker who frequently became a permanent member of American society and was increasingly the backbone of labor strikes. In 1911, the Dillingham Commission, responding to these concerns, noted the special advantages of Mexican migration:

> Because of their strong attachment to their native land ... and the possibility of their residence here being discontinued, few become citizens of the United States. The Mexican migrants are providing a fairly adequate supply of labor.... While they are not easily assimilated, this is of no very great importance as long as most of them return to their native land. In the case of the Mexican, he is less desirable as a citizen than as a laborer.

The most significant restrictions of the early twentieth century exempted Mexicans from their orbit. A response to warnings from Southwestern growers that successful harvests depended on abundant Mexican labor excluded Mexicans from the literacy test requirement of 1917 for the duration of the war. As World War I came to a close, the labor secretary and immigration commissioner extended the exemptions. As a result of these policies and employers' recruitment efforts, legal immigration from Mexico soared from eleven thousand in 1915 to fifty-one thousand in 1920. Industries as far north as Chicago drew labor from this back door. By 1926, 35 percent of Chicago Inland Steel's labor force was Mexican.

The passage of the quotas in the 1920s again exempted Mexicans. The argument against restricting Mexican immigration was strong:

> The Mexican, they pointed out, was a vulnerable alien living just a short distance from his homeland.... He, unlike Puerto Ricans or Filipinos ... could easily be deported. No safer or more economical unskilled labor force was imaginable.

The shift from European to Mexican migration as a source of labor did enhance flexibility, as evidenced by the repatriation of thousands of Mexican workers and their families during the depression of the 1930s. As World War II refueled the U.S. economy, the United States again needed and used Mexican contract laborers imported through the Bracero Program, whose formal and informal policies contributed to the rise of the undocumented nature of Mexican migration that characterizes the contemporary period. The program attempted to institutionalize the primary virtue of this labor supply, its flexibility.

The Bracero Agreement of 1949 provided that "illegal workers, when they are located in the United States, shall be given preference under outstanding U.S. Employment Service Certification." Illegals, or "wetbacks," were "dried out" by the U.S. Border Patrol which escorted them to the Mexican border, had them step to the Mexican side, and brought them back as braceros. Employers often accompanied their undocumented workers back to the border and contracted them there as legal workers. In some cases, the border patrol "paroled" illegals directly to employers. In 1951 the President's Commission on Migratory Labor estimated that between 1947 and 1949 the United States legalized more than 142,000 undocumented Mexicans in this way, while recruiting only 74,600 new braceros from Mexico.

In addition to these more or less official policies of encouraging illegal migration, Immigration and Naturalization Service (INS) district chiefs enhanced, at their discretion, the supply of undocumented workers for seasonal employment. The chief inspector at Tucson, for example, reported to the President's Commission on Migratory Labor that he "received orders from the District Director at El Paso each harvest to stop deporting illegal Mexican labor." In other cases, Border Patrol officials told agents to stay away from designated ranches and farms in their district. The implicit message from Congress to the Border Patrol was consistent with this laissez-faire approach. Congress was "splendidly indifferent" to the rising number of illegals during the bracero period, reducing the budget of the Border Patrol just as undocumented migration increased.

By the time the United States terminated the Bracero Program in 1964, the symbiosis between Mexican migrants and employers in the Southwest was well entrenched, the product of over fifty years of formal and informal policy-making. Almost five million Mexican workers had been brought to the United States as braceros; more than five million illegal aliens were apprehended during the same period.

While policies associated with the Bracero Program were instrumental in enhancing the appeal of illegal migration from the migrants' point of view, a key congressional decision immunized employers from any risk involved in their employment. In 1952, the McCarran–Walter Act made it illegal to "harbor, transport, or conceal illegal entrants." An amendment to the provision, referred to as the Texas Proviso after the Texas growers to whom it was a concession, excluded employment per se from the category of "harboring." Whether or not "knowing" employment of undocumented workers would constitute harboring remained ambiguous despite congressional discussion. Nonetheless, the amendment was interpreted by the INS as carte blanche to employ undocumented workers.

Of course, the U.S. attitude toward Mexican migrants has not been unequivocal. Mass expulsions and roundups of Mexican workers and their families during Operation Wetback in 1954 and 1955 were reminiscent of the depression policies of the 1930s. In part, these mass deportations reflected the militaristic approach of the new INS commissioner, Joseph Swing, a former U.S. Army general known within the INS bureaucracy as "The General," in apparent reference both to his former military career and to his leadership style. More generally, however, they represented the long-held view of Mexican labor as eminently flexible—welcomed during periods of high demand and deported when the demand had waned. In any case, such periodic deportations neither significantly interrupted the now-institutionalized patterns of migration nor reflected any fundamental change in the perception of Mexico as a backdoor source of labor.

———

Given the historical pattern, the following excerpt provides a model for understanding how, as one leading scholar put it, "Mexican migration to the United States represents a deeply institutionalized, multigenerational social process." W. Cornelius, Mexican Migration to the United States: The Limits of Government Intervention 2–4 (Working Papers in U.S.-Mexican Studies, 5; 1981).

DOUGLAS S. MASSEY, LUIN GOLDRING, AND JORGE DURAND, CONTINUITIES IN TRANSNATIONAL MIGRATION: AN ANALYSIS OF NINETEEN MEXICAN COMMUNITIES

99 American Journal of Sociology 1492, 1496–1502 (1994).*

Transnational labor migration may originate for a variety of complementary reasons. Migrants may observe wage differentials between origin and destination areas and respond to expected positive returns to foreign labor. Households may seek to diversify risks to their economic well-being by sending family members to work in different regional labor markets, one of which is foreign. Migrants may be recruited by foreign employers seeking to import workers for specific tasks. People may be impelled to move because structural transformations in the local economy eliminate traditional sources of sustenance or because political upheavals cause people to fear for their physical safety.

No matter how international migration begins, the first migrants from a community are likely to experience it as a very costly and risky enterprise, both in monetary and psychological terms. They have little or no knowledge of conditions in the host country and are ignorant of its culture, language, and ways of life. In most cases, they incur the expenses of the trip and absorb the opportunity costs of income forgone while moving and looking for work. They arrive having to pay off these overhead expenses and are thus relatively dependent on their first employer. Given their lack of knowledge about prevailing wage rates, work habits, legal conventions, and social expectations, they are vulnerable to exploitation and mistreatment, especially if they are undocumented and do not speak the language of the host country.

Given these costs and risks, the first transnational labor migrants usually come not from the bottom of the socioeconomic hierarchy but from the lower middle ranges. Such people have enough resources to absorb the costs and risks of the trip but are not so affluent that foreign labor is unattractive.

* * *

[T]he earliest migrants leave their families and friends behind and strike out for solitary work in an alien land. Most transnational migrants begin as target earners, seeking to earn as much money as possible as quickly as possible in order to recoup their initial investment, attain a predetermined income goal, and return home to family and friends. They have little interest in permanent settlement abroad.

Once one or more people have come and gone in this fashion, however, the situation in the sending community does not return to the status quo ante. Each act of migration generates a set of irreversible changes in individual motivations, social structures, and cultural values that alter the context within which future migration decisions are made. These changes accumulate across time to create conditions that make additional migration more likely. * * *

At the individual level, participation in a high-wage economy induces changes in tastes and motivations that turn people away from target earning and toward persistent migration. Satisfaction of the wants that originally led to migration creates new wants. Access to high wages and the goods they buy creates new standards of material well-being, and first-hand experience in an affluent society raise expectations and create new ambitions for upward mobility. As migrants earn high wages and alter their consumption patterns, they adopt new lifestyles and local economic pursuits become less attractive.

The first-hand experience gained from migration makes the satisfaction of these new wants increasingly feasible. Once someone has migrated and returned, that person has direct knowledge of employment opportunities, labor-market conditions, and ways of life in the destination country; they use these understandings to migrate again with fewer risks and costs than before. Once it has been experienced, therefore, migration becomes a familiar and reliable socioeconomic resource that can be employed again and again as new needs arise and motivations change.

Empirical research in Mexico shows conclusively that once a man has migrated to the United States, the odds are extremely high that he will migrate again. Indeed, the probability of taking an additional trip rises monotonically as the number of trips increases. The more a man migrates, the more he is likely to continuing migrating, a pattern that has proved to be remarkably persistent in the face of restrictive immigration policies.

Given their status as target earners, during the first few trips and in the early history of migration from a community, migrants tend to live under rather spartan conditions, sleeping in barracks or sharing apartments with other men and sleeping in shifts to save money. They work long hours and have little social life. In some cases they work two eight-hour shifts in the same day. Most of their earnings are repatriated in the form of savings or remittances. Migrants see themselves as members of their home communities and not as participants in the host society.

As migrants spend increasing time abroad, however, this form of social life becomes more and more problematic. As stays abroad lengthen and the number of trips rises, pressure from family members wanting to migrate grows. The first relatives to accompany a married migrant are typically unmarried sons of working age, since they have the greatest earnings potential after the father and their migration is consistent with prevailing gender roles. Over time, however, unmarried working-age daughters, wives, and younger children are likely to accompany him as well. Other relatives, such as nephews, nieces, and cousins, eventually join experienced migrants. As increasing numbers of young men acquire migrant experience, they also begin to travel north in groups based on friendship as well as kinship. As a result, the demographic base of migration steadily widens and the mean age of migration drops.

The act of migration not only induces changes within individual migrants that make further movement more likely, it also initiates changes in social structures that spread migration through the community. Each migrant is inevitably linked to a set of nonmigrants through a variety of social ties that carry reciprocal obligations for assistance based on shared understandings of kinship, friendship, and common community origin. Given the expectations and practices associated with kinship and friendship, each act of migration creates a set of people with social ties to the receiving country. Nonmigrants draw upon these ties to gain access to employment and assistance abroad, substantially reducing the costs and risks of movement compared to earlier migrants.

Every new migrant thus reduces the costs and risks and increases the attractiveness and feasibility of migration for a set of friends and relatives. With these lowered costs and risks, additional people are induced to migrate for the first time, which further expands the set of people with ties abroad. This additional migration reduces costs and risks for a new set of people, causing some of them to migrate, and so on. Once the number of network connections reaches a critical threshold, migration becomes self-perpetuating because each act of movement creates the social structure necessary to sustain it. Empirical studies in Mexico clearly show that having network connections greatly increases the likelihood of international movement.

As migrants make successive trips, they accumulate foreign experience and knowledge that render ties to them increasingly valuable. As information about the destination country and its socioeconomic resources accumulates in the population, the costs of migration steadily drop to make the cost-benefit calculation positive for an increasingly large set of people, while the risks of movement steadily fall to render migration a feasible risk-diversification strategy for a growing number of households. Over time, therefore, migration becomes progressively less selective and more representative of the community as a whole.

Migration also changes the cultural context within which decisions are made, and international movement becomes increasingly attractive for reasons that are not purely economic. Migrants evince a widely-admired lifestyle that others are drawn to emulate. Although some of its attractiveness is material—based on the ability to consume goods and purchase property—the lifestyle also acquires a strong normative component. In communities where foreign wage labor has become fully integrated into local values and expectations, people contemplating entry into the labor force literally do not consider other options: they expect to migrate frequently in the course of their lives and assume they can go whenever they wish.

As migration assumes a greater role in the community, it becomes increasingly important as a rite of passage for young men, providing an accepted means of demonstrating their worthiness, ambition, and manhood to others. Moreover, as women become more integrated within postindustrial society, they begin to push for more egalitarian gender roles and encourage activities that lead to longer stays abroad, such as investing in household goods and buying property in the destination country.

Over time and with extensive movement back and forth, communities of origin and destination increasingly come to comprise transnational circuits—social and geographic spaces that arise through the constant circulation of people, money, goods, and information. As these circuits develop, practices and values that once demarcated distinct societies begin to have a transformative influence on each other. Over time, migrant communities become culturally "transnationalized," incorporating ideologies, practices, expectations, and political claims from both societies to create a "culture of migration" that is distinct from the culture of both the sending and receiving nation.

As migration is increasingly taken for granted, the demographic composition and socioeconomic role of the place of origin undergo a dramatic transformation. In many places, women, children, and older people dominate a reduced population except during the few weeks or months when migrants return for holidays and celebrations. In economically marginal agricultural areas, farming and other traditional activities lose importance. As the place of origin becomes a site of rest and recreation, in sharp contrast to the routine of work abroad, its social meaning undergoes changes. Migrants spend money collectively on infrastructure and other community projects aimed at transforming the landscape into a place of leisure, a place where migrants and their families can display their status and exercise political claims and power.

The first migrants from a community typically go to a specific niche in the destination country's political economy, yielding little diversity with respect to destination, occupation, or strategies of movement. Early migrants follow the path of the first migrant because that is where the costs and risks of migration are lowest and the chances of success greatest. Once they have identified a promising migrant worker, moreover, labor recruiters and contractors tend to use them as vehicles to recruit additional workers from their circle of friends and relatives. As experience in the host country accumulates, however, and as more people are drawn into the process, some migrants inevitably seek out better opportunities in new places and occupations. In this way the diversity of foreign destinations, jobs, and strategies increases.

As the migration process proceeds, however, typically someone from the sending community achieves a position of responsibility that enables him or her to channel employment, housing, and other resources to fellow townspeople. The position may be a crew boss in a railroad, a foreman in a factory, a union representative in a company, a majordomo in a restaurant, a labor contractor for a grower, or perhaps even a business owner. Although it is impossible to predict where or how it will occur, sooner or later someone attains such a position and begins to recruit fellow townspeople for work.

At this point, the migration stream begins to focus more narrowly and the diversity of jobs, destinations, and strategies begins to constrict, a process Jones has called "channelization." This concentration does not necessarily involve a single foreign location for a particular labor-exporting community, but the overall pattern of early diversity followed by increasing concentration in one or more sites is a general feature of the process by which migrants establish branch communities in receiving societies.

As migrants make repeated trips and accumulate more time abroad, as wives and children join the migrant workforce, as more people become involved in the migration process, and as stronger links are formed with specific employers in particular locations, a growing number of migrants and families settle in the host society. They acquire informal ties to its inhabitants and establish formal links with institutions such as banks, government, and schools. They learn the host-country language and become permanent legal residents. Empirical studies show that the probability of settlement rises steadily as migrant experience increases.

As families settle around specific places of employment, branch communities of long-term and permanent out-migrants begin to form. These communities anchor the networks and further reduce the costs and risks of movement by providing a secure and familiar environment within which new migrants can arrive, find housing and employment, and learn the ropes in the receiving country. Increasingly, migration is channeled to these communities and the diversity of destinations associated with a place of origin is further reduced.

As migrants become part of established communities in the host country, they adapt themselves to the local setting. Whether or not they have legal documents, they send their children to school, learn a minimum of the host country's language, and use financial institutions and social services. Over time the local landscape of the receiving community is transformed. Whether or not they are immigrant entrepreneurs, the migrants contribute to the creation and growth of a market for specialized foods, entertainment, and cultural products. The formation of ethnic neighborhoods represents a process of socioeconomic adaptation and transformation that permits many "foreign" practices to be maintained in the new setting.

2. IMPACT OF ILLEGAL MIGRATION IN THE UNITED STATES

Undocumented labor may affect the employment opportunities and wages of U.S. citizens and legal aliens. Also, undocumented aliens may affect state and local finances—contributing tax dollars, using public services and participating in social programs. Other effects are less obvious. For example, the money that undocumented workers send home to their families is a significant form of unofficial foreign aid.[5]

There is consensus on one key fact: that the impact is highly concentrated in a few states. Responding to concerns raised by some of these states, the federal government asked the Urban Institute to undertake a study, published in September 1994, which by way of introduction summarized the geographical pattern:

> * * * 86 percent of undocumented immigrants in the United States reside in the seven states [California, Florida, Texas, New York, Illinois, Arizona, and New Jersey] that are the focus of this study. Undocumented immigrants represent a larger share of the population of these states than others—2.8 percent of the combined population of the seven states is undocumented versus 0.3 percent for the rest of the states. California stands out even among these seven states because it has both the largest absolute number of undocumented immigrants (1.4 million, or 43 percent of the national total) and the highest concentration (4.6 percent of the state's population).

R. Clark, J. Passel, W. Zimmermann, & M. Fix, Fiscal Impacts of Undocumented Aliens: Selected Estimates for Seven States 6 (1994).

a. Impact on Social Services

The major federally-funded public benefits programs are limited to citizens, lawful permanent resident aliens, and aliens who are "otherwise permanently residing in the United States under color of law" ("PRUCOL"). Programs thus off-limits to undocumented aliens include Aid to Families with Dependent Children, Supplemental Security Income, nonemergency Medicaid, public housing, legal services, unemployment compensation, postsecondary financial aid, and job training. See, e.g., 7 U.S.C.A. § 2015(f) (food stamps); 42 U.S.C.A. § 1382c (SSI).[6] Eligibility for public

---

5. One study concluded that Mexican workers in the United States sent home about $3.2 billion in 1990. See F.L. Ascencio, Bringing It Back Home: Remittances to Mexico from Migrant Workers in the United States (A. Yanez, trans. 1993). El Salvador's Central Bank estimates that Salvadorans in the United States will remit $840 million in FY 1994, more than the total income from coffee, the country's largest single export. See 71 Interp.Rel. 1324 (1994).

6. "PRUCOL" is defined somewhat differently for different programs, but it generally excludes undocumented aliens, except under some programs they may be eligible if they are in the United States "with the knowledge and permission of the Immigration and Naturalization Service and the agen-

benefits have been similarly restricted on an ad hoc basis. For example, the $11 billion federal appropriation to aid victims of the January 1994 Southern California earthquake allowed undocumented aliens to receive emergency but not long-term aid (for example, Department of Housing and Urban Development eighteen-month housing vouchers). *See* § 403, Pub. L. 103–211, 108 Stat. 3.

Other public services are available to the undocumented. The 1982 Supreme Court decision in *Plyler v. Doe*, 457 U.S. 202, 102 S.Ct. 2382, 72 L.Ed.2d 786 (1982), p. 325 *infra*, established that states may not deny undocumented alien children access to public elementary and secondary education. Other federal programs open to undocumented aliens include: the Special Supplemental Food Program for Women, Infants, and Children (WIC), community and migrant health centers, the school lunch program, and social service programs authorized under Title XX of the Social Security Act. State Medicaid plans must provide emergency medical services (including childbirth).

The literature includes many studies on the fiscal impact of immigrants in general, but few studies have focused on *undocumented* immigrants. The 1994 Urban Institute study, like others before it, will generate controversy, but it is likely to set the terms of debate because it is recent, detailed, and in key respects unique. The study analyzed cost estimates by the seven states with 86 percent of the undocumented population.[7] While the Urban Institute concluded that many of the states' estimates were too high, it generally supported the view that undocumented aliens impose substantial fiscal costs on states and localities.[8] In the following excerpts, consider not only its substantive conclusions but also its treatment of methodology.

One part of the study discussed the cost of public elementary and secondary education for undocumented aliens:

> The total cost of providing public education to undocumented aliens depends on two components: the number of undocumented aliens enrolled in public schools and the per pupil costs of providing public education. Because there are no direct data on the enrollment of undocumented aliens in public schools, we estimated enrollment by multiplying together the following three factors:
>
> 1. The number of undocumented aliens in each state. * * *
>
> 2. The percentage of undocumented aliens of school age.
>   * * *

---

cy does not contemplate enforcing [their] departure." 20 C.F.R. § 416.1618 (SSI).

7. Arizona, California, Florida, New Jersey and Texas have sued the federal government for reimbursement. *See* 15 Refugee Reports 2 (Dec. 31, 1994); Roberts, *et al., Shutting the Golden Door*, 117 U.S. News & World Report 36 (Oct. 3, 1994); 71 Interp.Rel. 894 (1994).

8. Other studies have reached higher (sometimes substantially higher) cost estimates. *See, e.g.,* D. Huddle, The Cost of Immigration in 1993 (1993); Center for Immigration Studies, The Costs of Immigration: Assessing a Conflicted Issue (1993).

3. The percentage of undocumented alien children enrolled in public primary and secondary schools. * * *

* * * If there are errors in our estimates of the number of undocumented aliens enrolled in public schools, the estimates are more likely to overstate enrollment rather than understate it. However, since there are no direct measures of the age structure and public school enrollment of undocumented aliens, we have no objective basis on which to determine whether, and if so how much, to reduce our estimates. More importantly, comparisons of our estimates with counts of total school enrollment from official government data indicate that our methodology under- rather than over-counts. * * *

* * * Urban Institute estimates of undocumented immigrants enrolled in public schools are significantly *higher* than estimates from Arizona, Florida, Illinois and Texas, even though our estimates of the total undocumented population are much lower for Illinois and Texas. Our estimates are essentially equal to the estimate from New York and somewhat lower than the estimate from New Jersey. California is the only state providing an estimate of undocumented alien enrollment that substantially surpasses our estimate.

* * *

The costs attributable to undocumented aliens enrolled in public school were calculated by multiplying the estimated number of undocumented alien students by the estimated per student costs. The per student costs estimates are based on state-specific data on current expenditures from the National Center for Education Statistics (NCES). These NCES data permit us to standardize cost estimates across states.

Our cost data do not take into account two important factors affecting the cost of educating undocumented aliens. First, as noted, OMB [Office of Management and Budget] asked us to use average cost per student in our calculations. Undocumented aliens are probably more expensive to educate on average than other students because the undocumented students are more likely to be poor and less likely to speak English well. Second, although we believe that undocumented aliens are more likely than other students to live in urban areas where per student expenses are relatively high, we were unable to take the geographic distribution of undocumented aliens into account in our calculations. The necessary data—estimates of the intrastate geographic distribution of undocumented aliens and uniformly-defined estimates of state and local per student costs for individual school districts—do not exist.

* * * *The estimated total current expenditures for providing public education to undocumented aliens across the seven states for FY 1993 was $3.1 billion.* In Arizona, Florida, Illinois and Texas,

our estimates exceed the states' estimates. In New Jersey, the estimates are nearly identical and in New York, our estimate is only 11 percent lower than the state's. Only in California is our estimate substantially lower than the state's estimate.   * * *

R. Clark, *et al.*, *supra*, at 9–11. The states' estimates for public education totaled about $3.5 billion, or about 15 percent over the Urban Institute estimates. *Id.* at 11.

The Urban Institute encountered different problems in addressing the costs of emergency Medicaid coverage:

> * * * State administrative records on services provided under [the Omnibus Budget Reconciliation Act of 1986] are potentially the best data for calculating the Medicaid costs attributable to undocumented aliens. However, problems with the states' data, such as the inclusion of persons who are not undocumented aliens, raise questions about the accuracy of the states' reported costs.
>
> Data are not available to develop reliable alternative estimates of Medicaid costs for undocumented aliens. We, therefore, assess the quality of states' estimates by: evaluating the states' data collection procedures or estimating methodologies; evaluating the completeness of the states' reported costs; and comparing the state's reported costs to a range of benchmarks developed using a uniform methodology for all states. These benchmarks use Medicaid data on eligible legalized aliens (ELAs)—formerly undocumented aliens who became legal U.S. residents under IRCA.   * * * Given that undocumented aliens are probably less likely to use Medicaid services than ELAs, we expect our benchmarks to represent an approximate upper-bound on undocumented alien Medicaid costs.

Id. at iii-iv. The seven states estimated that Medicaid for undocumented aliens cost about $445 million in 1993, well over both of the Urban Institute's aggregate benchmarks, which were $209.4 million ("low") and $313.9 million ("high"). *Id.* at 13.

The Urban Institute also addressed the state costs of incarcerating undocumented aliens:

> We estimated the total number of incarcerated illegal aliens from data supplied by the states on all foreign-born prisoners incarcerated in state prisons as of mid-March 1994. The immigration status of these prisoners was determined by matching them to INS records or through interviews conducted with the prisoners by INS. The total costs to the states are calculated by multiplying the estimated number of illegal alien prisoners by state-specific estimates of average annual prisoner costs from the Census of State Prisons.
>
> Our major findings are:
>
> - 21,395 illegal aliens were incarcerated in the seven states as of March 1994;

- $471 million is the estimated total 1994 cost for incarcerating illegal aliens in state prisons in the seven states;

- California has a disproportionate share of the incarcerated illegal aliens in the seven states—43 percent of the undocumented aliens but 71 percent of the incarcerated illegal aliens; and

- California's annual cost of incarcerating illegal aliens is much larger than the other states ($368 million)—the next highest state is New York ($45 million) * * *.

Id. at ii-iii. The states' estimates (not including New Jersey, for which data was unavailable) totaled about $533 million, about 13 percent over the Urban Institute's. *Id.* at 8.[9]

On revenues from undocumented aliens, the Urban Institute concluded:

> There are no direct measures of tax payments by undocumented aliens. Consequently, we rely on indirect methods of estimation to estimate state income taxes, state sales taxes, and state and local property taxes paid by undocumented immigrants. * * * Just as state expenditures on public schools, prisons, and Medicaid are only a fraction of total costs of undocumented immigrants, these three taxes do not reflect the total revenue generated by undocumented aliens. In fact, these taxes represent only about 40 percent of state and local revenue.

Our major findings are:

- $1.9 billion was collected from undocumented aliens in the seven states for the three taxes:

  $1.1 billion in sales taxes;

  $700 million in property taxes; and

  $100 million in state income taxes;

- The share of tax revenues paid by undocumented aliens is far less than their share of the population in each state, largely because of the lower-than-average incomes of undocumented aliens;

- In California, for example, undocumented aliens paid an estimated $732 million in taxes, or 1.7 percent of all the taxes collected, but they represent 4.6 percent of the state's population.

Id. at iv.

The Urban Institute study also provided an illuminating account of its own limitations:

---

9. Under new INA § 242(j), added by the 1994 Crime Act, upon request by a state the Attorney General must either compensate the state or local authorities for the costs of incarcerating undocumented criminal aliens or take federal custody of them. The Crime Act also authorized $1.8 billion over six years for these reimbursements. *See* Pub.L. 103–322, § 20301, 108 Stat. 1796, 1824.

The scope of this study is narrowly defined. First, we were asked to make estimates only for undocumented aliens—foreign-born persons who entered the United States without inspection or who entered the United States legally as non-immigrants, but whose period of authorized stay has expired. Other groups, including citizen children of undocumented aliens and legal non-immigrants, are beyond the scope of this project. Second, we provide estimates of the costs of providing three types of services and revenues generated by three types of taxes. Other services and sources of revenue are not considered. Third, we make no attempt to measure how undocumented aliens indirectly affect the economy, as members of the labor force, business owners, or consumers. * * *

Our cost estimates for education and incarceration do not necessarily represent the amount of money that would be saved if undocumented aliens could no longer receive public education or were no longer incarcerated in state prisons. Potential cost savings from preventing undocumented aliens from using a service can only be estimated from *marginal cost* data—in this case, the amount saved, on average, when a user is dropped. At the request of OMB, we based our estimates on *mean costs*—total expenditures for a service divided by the total number of users. To our knowledge, all assessments of costs of immigrants, including those provided by the states, have been based on mean costs. Mean costs may be greater than marginal costs because mean costs include both variable costs, which are affected by the number of individuals using the service, and fixed costs—such as interest payments on bonds used to finance already existing buildings and certain administrative costs—which are not. But mean costs may also be less than marginal costs. High marginal costs can be associated with the addition of *any* users—for example, adding students to a system where new schools must be built immediately because existing schools are already filled to capacity. They can also be associated specifically with undocumented aliens. For example, if undocumented aliens in a school district are less likely to speak English fluently and are more likely to be poor than other students—and are therefore more likely to use bilingual education, school lunch and other programs—the costs of adding a given number of undocumented aliens to that school district would be greater than the cost of adding the same number of students who are not undocumented aliens.

The estimates from this study cannot be used to calculate the *net* costs of undocumented immigrants because many sources of revenues generated by undocumented aliens and services used by these aliens are not considered. A full assessment of the fiscal impacts of undocumented aliens is beyond the scope of this study. Indeed, such an assessment has never been undertaken and would require a complete accounting of government costs imposed by undocumented aliens, as well as the costs that would be imposed if currently provided services were withdrawn. It would also require a detailed analysis of indirect impacts of undocumented aliens. These include job creation and job loss caused by undocumented aliens, the further effects of spending by these aliens on the economy, trade impacts, and job retention effects. The assessment should also include estimates of net costs to each level of government and of funding flows between levels of government. Taxes from undocumented aliens, like taxes from other groups, flow mainly to the federal government, but the presence of undocumented aliens increases the level of intergovernmental funding determined by the size of the total or low-income population in an area. The costs of enforcing reductions in the flow of undocumented immigrants across the borders, of increasing removals of undocumented aliens already in the United States, and of withdrawing services from undocumented aliens are rarely considered, but obviously could be significant. A full assessment might also include the long-term impacts of today's undocumented aliens— services these aliens and their children will use in the future, taxes paid by these aliens as they improve their economic positions, and revenue streams generated by their children. All existing studies of impacts of immigrants, legal or otherwise, omit at least some of the important fiscal impacts listed here.

Id. at 2–3.

b. *Impact on the Labor Market*

WAYNE A. CORNELIUS, MEXICAN MIGRATION TO THE UNITED STATES: INTRODUCTION

Mexican Migration to the United States: Origins, Consequences, and Policy
Options 1, 4–8 (W. Cornelius & J. Bustamante, eds., 1989).

It is popularly believed that undocumented immigrant workers toil in the informal or "underground" economy, where employers pay sub-minimum wages and escape government regulation of labor standards. Some immigrants do—especially recent arrivals who lack social networks in the United States that can assist them in job-seeking. But field research in California and Illinois has found that most *indocumentados* work in relatively small or medium-sized "formal sector" firms that are very much part of the mainstream economy. They tend to concentrate in firms and industries that are under intense foreign and/or domestic competitive pressures and that suffer from sharp fluctuations in demand for the goods or services they produce.

For such firms, the principal advantage of undocumented immigrant labor is not its cheapness but its *flexibility* (or *disposability,* in the more critical view of many academics and labor-union leaders). The immigrant work force is more willing than U.S.-born workers to accept high variability in working hours, working days per week, and months per year, and low job security. These same conditions, combined with relatively low wage scales, make employment in such firms unattractive to U.S.-born workers. Immigrant workers are ideal "shock absorbers," enabling businesses to adapt more quickly and easily to rapidly changing market conditions and consumer preferences. They can be brought on board quickly when needed, in periods of peak product or service demand, and disposed of just as easily when demand slackens.

Thus, the U.S. labor markets in which Mexican undocumented workers typically participate are not so much *illegal* as they are *fluid* and *volatile*. Mexican labor gives U.S. employers the flexibility they need to cope with an increasingly competitive, frequently global market. For many firms and industries affected by restructuring in the U.S. and world economies, the availability of immigrant labor has had a cushioning effect, helping them adjust to changes in production techniques and spreading the costs of adjustment over a longer period of time.

In recent decades there has been a trend toward greater sectoral and geographic dispersion of the Mexican immigrant work force within the U.S. economy. According to the best-informed estimates, agriculture now employs no more than 15 percent of Mexican labor in California, Texas, and Arizona. Between 1981 and 1987, the percentage of farmworkers among the total of "deportable Mexican aliens" located by the U.S. Immigration and Naturalization Service averaged only 7 percent. Most Mexican immigrants—both legal and undocumented—are now being absorbed into the labor-intensive urban service and retail sector, light manufacturing, and construction. In short, the U.S. demand for Mexican labor has become much more diversified, and this trend is likely to persist. Agriculture will continue to be a major employer of Mexican labor (mainly in the Southwest and the Pacific Northwest); but in relative terms, Mexican migrants will find far more employment opportunities in the nonagricultural sectors of the U.S. economy. The service sector—where Mexicans now work primarily as janitors, dishwashers and busboys, gardeners, hotel workers, maintenance and laundry workers in hospitals and convalescent homes, car washers, house cleaners, and child-care providers—will be particularly important in absorbing future migrants.

While the destinations for Mexican migrants to the United States are increasingly dispersed—extending from southern California to the Pacific Northwest, Chicago, the New York City metropolitan area, and the deep South—most Mexicans continue to gravitate to the same places favored by their fathers and grandfathers. California alone absorbs at least half (and perhaps as much as 60 percent) of the total flow of both legal and illegal immigrants from Mexico. It is highly probable that the distribution of undocumented Mexican immigrants is very similar, since most are part of extended family networks "anchored" by legal immigrants with long residence in the United States.

IMPACTS ON U.S.-BORN WORKERS

Are U.S.-born workers helped or hurt by the availability of Mexican immigrant labor—especially undocumented workers? What impact does the immigrant presence in U.S. labor markets have on wages and working conditions? These are the questions concerning Mexican immigration that have been debated most intensely in the United States since the early 1970s.

Virtually all available evidence suggests that the *macroeconomic* impact of Mexican immigration—and of immigration more generally—on the United States is positive. The availability of this labor source helps to hold down prices of many consumer goods and services, makes it possible for labor-intensive industries to expand more rapidly, and stimulates employment growth through consumer spending by the immigrants themselves and their families. But the *microeconomic* impacts of undocumented immigration—particularly on U.S.-born minorities and other disadvantaged workers—have been the subject of considerable controversy.

The deceptively simple questions about "labor market impact" require complex answers, which fail to satisfy either politicians or the general public. In-depth field studies of specific industries and labor markets have found that the impact of undocumented Mexican immigration on U.S.-born workers varies widely. Undocumented immigrants can be either substitutes (competitors) or complements for U.S.-born workers, depending on the industry, the region, type of firm, vigilance of government agencies (in regard to wage and labor standards), and other conditions. Some domestic workers—particularly those employed in "immobile" industries where large numbers of undocumented immigrants have clustered, such as agriculture and building maintenance—are adversely affected. Other U.S.-born workers are benefited, especially in potentially mobile or "footloose" industries that face strong foreign competition, such as garment and shoe manufacturing, and electronics. For firms in these industries, the availability of Mexican labor to perform lower-level production jobs or to fill jobs in the firm's subcontractors (resulting in lower-cost inputs) enables management to keep at least some production operations in the United States rather than moving them "offshore," thereby preserving jobs for U.S.-born workers.

Other industries (e.g., full-service restaurants) that provide jobs for large numbers of U.S.-born workers could not have expanded so rapidly in recent years without the immigrant labor pool. In some firms and industries, Mexican immigrants play a "key ingredient" role: Even where they do not constitute a majority of the work force, they perform key tasks in the production process, and their removal would force drastic restructuring and cause significant employment losses for U.S.-born workers.

Considerable evidence contradicts the simplistic notion of one-to-one job competition between Mexicans (especially the undocumented) and U.S.-born workers. When immigrants displace native workers, such displacement usually occurs *indirectly*—not as a result of direct competition between natives and migrants for the same jobs. For example, firms that hire mostly undocumented Mexican workers can often underbid firms (especially unionized ones) that hire mainly U.S.-born workers; as a result, immigrant-using firms expand while other firms in the industry lose business and lay off U.S.-born workers. It is through this mechanism—the expansion of some types of (immigrant-dependent) firms and the contraction of other kinds (low or non-users of immigrant labor)—that "displacement" most commonly occurs.

Today, competition for jobs in industries where Mexican immigrants cluster most often pits one subclass of immigrants against another segment of the immigrant population (e.g., newly arrived "illegals" vs. long-staying undocumented immigrants, or those who have legalized themselves through IRCA-mandated "amnesty" programs). U.S.-born workers no longer seek these jobs; and most employers who now rely on immigrants to fill them—tired of extremely high turnover among the very few non-immigrants who apply for such jobs—have given up on recruiting U.S.-born workers.

Real wages in many immigrant-dependent industries have not risen in recent years, and wages for low-skill jobs in some sectors (e.g., Los Angeles manufacturing industries) have declined in relation to national and other regional averages, leading researchers to conclude that the influx of undocumented immigrants is depressing wage scales in these sectors of the economy. It is true that immigrant workers—especially those most recently arrived and those still lacking any kind of legal status in the United States—are usually willing to accept wage scales lower than the average U.S.-born person would demand for similar work. However, the weight of the evidence suggests that immigration per se is not the most important factor affecting wages and labor standards in these and other sectors of the U.S. economy. Far more influential are technological changes affecting the labor content of products, foreign competition (the changing international factor price of labor), and the declining strength of the U.S. labor movement—a decline which is largely unrelated to the growing presence of immigrant workers.

In most parts of the United States that are impacted by immigration from Mexico, the objective complementarities between the Mexican labor supply and U.S. needs probably increased during the 1980s. These complementarities are likely to be strengthened in the 1990s, as the U.S. "baby bust" and the restructuring of the U.S. and global economies continue. This does not mean, however, that public perceptions will mirror the realities of the situation. On the contrary, recent public opinion polls and a rising chorus of protests from residents of urban neighborhoods close to the street-corner labor markets where recently arrived undocumented migrants congregate suggest that a majority of Americans will continue to view Mexican immigrants as having a net negative impact on the U.S. economy and society. And some U.S. politicians and other opinion leaders will continue to insist that, despite a looming domestic labor shortage, there are still substantial pockets of unemployment in the United States (e.g., legally admitted refugees living on welfare), and such people can fill jobs now being taken by undocumented immigrants.

Note

Consider the quite different perspective offered by a Los Angeles Times editor:

> If you live here, you don't need the General Accounting Office to
> bring you the news. The almost total absence of black gardeners,

busboys, chambermaids, nannies, janitors, and construction workers in a city with notoriously large pool of unemployed, unskilled
black people leaps to the eye. According to the U.S. Census, 8.6
percent of South Central Los Angeles residents sixteen years old
and older were unemployed in 1990, but an additional 41.8 percent
were listed as "not in the labor force." If Latinos were not around
to do that work, nonblack employers would be forced to hire
blacks—but they'd rather not. They trust Latinos. They fear or
disdain blacks. The result is unofficial but widespread preferential hiring of Latinos—the largest affirmative-action program in
the nation, and one paid for, in effect, by blacks.

Miles, *Blacks vs. Browns*, The Atlantic Monthly 54 (Oct.1992).

3. CONTROLLING UNDOCUMENTED MIGRATION: THE IRCA RESPONSE

Professor Niles Hansen has written:

> The informal undocumented migration system continues to
> operate largely because it benefits all parties concerned, at least so
> long as each party looks only at its own situation and what it
> would be if undocumented migration were strictly curtailed. A
> key factor in the system is that most undocumented Mexicans are
> in the United States on a temporary basis. The United States
> gains relatively cheap labor willing to perform tasks that citizen
> workers are reluctant to undertake. The available evidence shows
> that undocumented Mexican workers do not use social services to
> any significant extent, though they do pay numerous taxes. For
> demographic reasons, in the near future fewer Americans will be
> available to take low-wage, entry-level jobs, so the issue of the
> displacement of American workers by undocumented Mexicans is
> likely to decline in importance. Mexico exports some of its unem-
> ployment and gains foreign exchange that workers send or bring
> home as well as some technical skills when workers return home.
> The migrants gain higher incomes and, frequently, better working
> conditions than in Mexico. These phenomena explain why undoc-
> umented Mexican workers have long been a "normal, functioning
> ingredient" of the southwest borderlands, where they have been
> encouraged and utilized "with the approval and support of social
> and cultural institutions of the region with the tacit cooperation of
> border control agencies and legal authorities."

N. Hansen, The Border Economy: Regional Development in the Southwest
158–59 (1981), quoting Stoddard, *Illegal Mexican Labor in the Borderlands:
Institutionalized Support of an Unlawful Practice*, 19 Pac.Soc.Rev. 175
(1976).

If Hansen has correctly described undocumented migration, is there a
problem at all? Perhaps the first question is whether undocumented aliens
do serious economic harm to the United States. But arguably, the issue
goes well beyond economics. The 1981 Staff Report to the Select Commission on Immigration and Refugee Policy stated:

The long-term social consequences of a growing undocumented/illegal alien population seem clear:

- Expansion of an underground population with negative consequences for public health, education and the U.S. criminal justice system;

- Promotion of the idea that certain kinds of labor are fit only for foreigners and a growing U.S. dependence on foreign labor for the performance of those jobs;

- Institutionalization of a double standard of legal due process and equal protection for a growing alien population, with concomitant litigation growing out of that ambiguity; and

- Growing disrespect for the law generally and a specific lack of regard for an immigration law which penalizes those who obey it and wait their turn to enter the United States legally.

SCIRP, Staff Report 532–33.

The Immigration Reform and Control Act (IRCA) of 1986 announced a national policy dedicated to staunching the flow of undocumented immigration. According to the House Report:

While there is no doubt that many who enter illegally do so for the best of motives—to seek a better life for themselves and their families—immigration must proceed in a legal, orderly, and regulated fashion. As a sovereign nation, we must secure our borders.

H.Rep. No. 682(I), 99th Cong., 2d Sess. 46 (1986).

How were we to gain control of our borders? IRCA adopted a multi-prong strategy: legalization of undocumented aliens; the H–2A program for admitting temporary agricultural workers; increased INS enforcement; sanctions on employers who hire undocumented aliens; and provisions to minimize discrimination caused by employer sanctions. Section B *supra* discussed the H–2A program. We focus now on legalization, employer sanctions, and the antidiscrimination provisions.

a. *Legalization*

Proposals to legalize the status of long-term undocumented aliens had been part of immigration reform discussions for more than a decade before IRCA. The House Report on IRCA summarized the reasons for a legalization program:

The United States has a large undocumented alien population living and working within its borders. Many of these people have been here for a number of years and have become a part of their communities. Many have strong family ties here which include U.S. citizens and lawful residents. They have built social networks in this country. They have contributed to the United States in myriad ways, including providing their talents, labor and tax dollars. However, because of their undocumented status, these people live in fear, afraid to seek help when their rights are violated, when they are victimized by criminals, employers or landlords or when they become ill.

Continuing to ignore this situation is harmful to both the United States and the aliens themselves. However, the alternative of intensifying interior enforcement or attempting mass deportations would be both costly, ineffective, and inconsistent with our immigrant heritage.

The Committee believes that the solution lies in legalizing the status of aliens who have been present in the United States for several years, recognizing that past failures to enforce the immigration laws have allowed them to enter and to settle here.

H.Rep. No. 682(I), 99th Cong., 2d Sess. 49 (1986).

Congress believed (hoped?) that legalization, coupled with employer sanctions, would solve the problem of undocumented immigration: undocumented aliens in the United States would either legalize or go home (because employer sanctions would prevent them from working), and increased border patrol and employer sanctions would dissuade new illegal entries. Congress also thought it quite important to bill legalization as a one-time amnesty, lest more undocumented aliens arrive to take advantage of an anticipated future legalization program.

IRCA's general legalization program was limited to aliens who had been residing unlawfully in the United States since January 1, 1982—nearly five years preceding enactment. *See* INA § 245A. Excluded were the many undocumented aliens who entered after that date, as well as those whose presence was legal—for example, as a nonimmigrant—until after that date. Those eligible had one year (May 1987 to May 1988) to apply for "temporary resident status," which lasted for eighteen months, after which they had three years to apply for permanent resident status.[10]

IRCA also legalized "special agricultural workers" (SAWs)—aliens who had resided in the United States and worked at least 90 days in "seasonal agricultural services" between May 1985 and May 1986. SAW legalization paralleled the general program but was more liberal. Recognizing that growers and labor contractors often fail to keep accurate employment (including payroll) records, Congress relaxed the proof requirements. *See* INA § 210(b)(3),(c). Legalized SAWs were not required to remain in agricultural labor, but the program's proponents expected that a high proportion of them would do so anyway.

SAW legalization reflected IRCA's delicate political background. Before 1986, agricultural interests had blocked immigration reform legislation out of concern that their farm labor needs would go unmet. "If [those provisions] seem remarkably generous to certain farmworkers and to the growers who will employ them, one must keep in mind that this generosity

---

10. Permanent residency required that applicants (1) maintain continuous residence in the United States, (2) remain free of criminal convictions, and (3) demonstrate a minimal understanding of the English language and a knowledge and understanding of the history and government of the United States (or that they are satisfactorily pursuing a course of study to this end). This "basic citizenship skills" requirement was waivable for applicants over sixty-five years of age.

was the price that had to be paid to resolve the impasse and achieve passage of any kind of immigration reform legislation." D. Martin, Major Issues in Immigration Law 125 (1987).[11]

Neither legalization program granted derivative status to family members who were ineligible because, for example, they arrived after the cutoff date. Since February 1990, however, undocumented spouses and minor children who entered by May 5, 1988 and live with legalized aliens have received voluntary departure (and work authorization) for renewable one-year periods under a "Family Unity" policy. *See* Immigration Act of 1990, § 301. Also, § 112 of the 1990 Act provided up to 55,000 visas for FY 1992, 1993, and 1994 to spouses and minor children of legalized aliens. Of course, relatives have also been able, eventually, to immigrate in the preference categories, once their priority dates were reached, or as immediate relatives if the principal alien naturalizes.

Almost 1.7 million aliens have obtained lawful status under the general legalization program. *See* INS, Immigration Reform and Control Act: Report on the Legalized Alien Population (1992). Largely due to the cutoff date, the legalized population is not a cross-section of the undocumented population as a whole. Seventy percent of the legalized aliens are from Mexico; the next largest groups are Salvadorans (8%), Guatemalans (3%), Colombians (1.5%), and Filipinos (1.1%). Thirty-five percent of the legalized aliens applied from in the Los Angeles–Long Beach area, 55 percent from California. Texas, Illinois, and New York combined to account for another 31 percent. Approximately 75 percent had entered without inspection.

More than 1.3 million aliens applied for SAW status—far more than anticipated by the drafters and the INS. Over 80 percent of the applicants were Mexican, with the next largest groups from Haiti, El Salvador, Guatemala, India, and Pakistan. SAW processing has been slower because of a higher incidence of suspected fraud, but the 93 percent approval rate of cases completed thus far has been very close to the 94 percent rate for the general program.

Together, the general and SAW programs legalized over 60 percent of the pre-IRCA undocumented population. *See* 1993 INS Statistical Yearbook 183; R. Warren, *supra*, at 14. The final outcome of both programs will have to await the resolution of a large number of SAW cases still awaiting initial decision, plus about 79,000 (as of 1994) pending appeals in both programs. *See* 71 Interp.Rel. 215 (1994). In addition, several pending lawsuits challenge INS interpretations of eligibility rules and application procedures. *See, e.g., Reno v. Catholic Social Services*, 509 U.S. ___, 113 S.Ct. 2485, 125 L.Ed. 38 (1993); *McNary v. Haitian Refugee Center*, 498 U.S. 479, 111 S.Ct. 888, 112 L.Ed.2d 1005 (1991). Although legalization has become generally unavailable, court decisions or settlements in these lawsuits may yet allow many aliens to reopen their cases after an initial denial or even file for the first time.

11. IRCA also authorized a Replenishment Agricultural Worker (RAW) program to admit new immigrants in FY 1990–93 if an agricultural labor shortage developed according to a formula in INA § 210A (which never happened).

b. *Employer Sanctions*

The reasoning behind employer sanctions is straightforward: (1) the imposition of penalties on employers of undocumented aliens will deter the hiring of such aliens; and (2) because securing employment is the primary reason for illegal entry and residence, this will reduce incentives for illegal entry. The Senate Report on an earlier version of the bill that became IRCA made the case for employer sanctions as follows:

There are only two types of solutions available to the problem of illegal immigration.

The first is direct enforcement: (A) to physically prevent illegal entry into the United States, for example through border control, fences, and interdiction, and (B) to find and deport those who are successful in entering illegally, as well as those who enter legally and then violate the terms of their visa.

The second type of solution involves reducing the incentives to enter.

Reliance on direct enforcement alone would require massive increases in enforcement in the interior—in both neighborhoods and work places—as well as at the border. This would be more costly and intrusive, as well as less effective, than a program which combines direct enforcement at reasonable levels with a reduction in the incentives to enter the United States.

At the present time there is a substantial disparity in job opportunity between the United States and Third World countries—a disparity which may well continue or even widen as a result of political and social conditions in those countries. Such disparity exists not only in rates of unemployment, but in wages and working conditions. Even if the unemployment rates were reduced, a difficult task in light of the high birth rates in these countries, the disparity in wages and working conditions would remain.

As long as greater job opportunities are available to foreign nationals who succeed in physically entering this country, intense illegal immigration pressure on the United States will continue. This pressure will decline only if the availability of United States employment is eliminated, or the disparity in wages and working conditions is reduced, through improvement in the Third World or deterioration in the United States.

The United States should, of course, assist Third World development, but the achievement of substantially higher living standards there is a prospect only for the long run, and in the short run Third World development may actually increase migration to the United States. Since deterioration in the United States is certainly not an attractive resolution, only one approach remains: To prohibit the knowing employment of illegal aliens.

S.Rep. No. 62, 98th Cong., 1st Sess. 7–8 (1983).

You should now study INA § 274A, which (1) prohibits the hiring of "unauthorized aliens"[12]; and (2) requires that employers use form I–9 (reprinted in the Statutory Supplement) to verify the lawful status of all new hires. The INS may initiate a proceeding on either type of violation before an administrative law judge within the Office of the Chief Administrative Hearing Officer (OCAHO), which is within the Executive Office of Immigration Review (EOIR). An employer who loses before the ALJ may seek a limited form of discretionary review by the Chief Administrative Hearing Officer; judicial review lies in the federal courts of appeals. *See generally* INA § 274A(e); 8 C.F.R. § 274a.9; 28 C.F.R. Part 68.

The debate over employer sanctions was long and intense. Some members of Congress argued that the program might place an undue burden on employers. Not only would all employers be subject to new paperwork obligations; but a regime of employer sanctions also raised the spectre that employers would have to become experts in immigration law in order to identify which categories of aliens were authorized to work. Another area of special concern was the question of what kind of documentation would suffice to establish eligibility for employment. Congress was aware of the huge market that exists in fraudulent documents, and some proponents argued that a form of counterfeit-proof documentation ought to be devised to ensure the effectiveness of the program. The risk that this might lead to a "national identity card," however, caused many members of Congress to shy away from such a requirement. The final version of the legislation responded to many of these issues.

c. *Antidiscrimination Provisions*

One major concern was that employer sanctions would lead to employment discrimination against Hispanic–Americans, Asian–Americans, or others who "looked foreign," and that existing fair employment laws would provide no remedy. For example, Title VII of the Civil Rights Act of 1964, 42 U.S.C.A. § 2000e–2, applies only to employers with fifteen or more full-time employees. Moreover, Title VII bars "national origin" discrimination but not discrimination based solely on alienage. *See Espinoza v. Farah Manufacturing Co.*, 414 U.S. 86, 94 S.Ct. 334, 38 L.Ed.2d 287 (1973).

As a result, Congress adopted new INA § 274B, which established a "Special Counsel for Immigration–Related Unfair Employment Practices" in the Department of Justice to investigate and pursue charges of employment discrimination based on "national origin" or "citizenship status." As to the latter, § 274B covers "citizenship status" discrimination only against citizens and certain classes of aliens, *viz.* lawful permanent resident aliens, newly legalized aliens, refugees, and asylees. Lawful permanent residents are not covered if they fail to initiate the naturalization process within six months after satisfying the residency requirement for citizenship. INA § 274B(a). Nonimmigrants (even those authorized to work) and parolees are not covered.

---

12. The categories of aliens authorized to work, either incident to status or by specific permission, are listed in 8 C.F.R. § 274a.12.

There are several other exceptions. Employers with fewer than four employees are not covered. Moreover, INA § 274B covers national origin discrimination only where Title VII does not. IRCA thus covers national origin discrimination only by an employer with at least the four employees required for IRCA coverage but not the fifteen required for Title VII. IRCA permits discrimination based on citizenship status when lawfully required under federal, state, or local governmental authority. And an employer may hire a U.S. citizen in preference to an alien if the two are "equally qualified." INA § 274B(a)(2),(4). Also, IRCA, unlike Title VII, applies only to hiring, referral for a fee, and firing, and thus offers no remedy for discrimination on the job. *See Ortega v. Vermont Bread*, 3 O.C.A.H.O. 475 (1992).

A sharp dispute over the coverage of the new § 274B surfaced on the first day of IRCA's existence. Title VII may be violated by actions motivated by discriminatory intent *or* by practices having a disparate impact on different groups. When President Reagan signed IRCA, he carefully included in his signing statement his interpretation that IRCA reaches only discriminatory intent, not disparate impact. Statement by the President, *reprinted in* 63 Interp.Rel. 1036, 1037 (1986). Representative Barney Frank, the primary sponsor of the antidiscrimination provisions, promptly denounced this reading as "mean-spirited" and incorrect. N.Y.Times, Nov. 7, 1986, at A12. The implementing regulations adopt President Reagan's view. 28 C.F.R. § 44.200(a)(1). Executive branch officials have stated that they have difficulty conceiving of employer practices, covered by IRCA rather than Title VII, that could have discriminatory effects without discriminatory intent. But what about an English language requirement, or a requirement of five years residence in the community? Are these policies lawful under a disparate impact test? An intent test?

If the Special Counsel has not filed a complaint within 120 days after receiving an allegation of unlawful discrimination, a private party may also initiate an enforcement action. INA § 274B(d)(2). Administrative law judges hear complaints and may impose civil penalties, order equitable relief, and award attorneys fees. *See* § 274B(e)-(h), 28 C.F.R. Part 44. There is no administrative review, but the ALJ's order is subject to review in the federal courts of appeals. *See* INA § 274B(i), 28 C.F.R. § 68.53(b).

In order to understand exactly what Congress wrought in §§ 274A and 274B, work your way through the following questions. You will need to consult both the statute and the implementing regulations in 8 C.F.R. Part 274a.[13]

Questions on Employer Sanctions and Discrimination

You have XYZ Widget Co. as a client. The President of XYZ has come to you for advice. How would you answer the following questions:

13. For a helpful summary of the provisions, see Roberts & Yale–Loehr, *Employers as Junior Immigration Inspectors: The Im-* *pact of the 1986 Immigration Reform and Control Act*, 21 Int'l Lawyer 1013 (1987).

1.   "I need to hire three new employees this year. What does the law require me to do? Doesn't it just apply to aliens?"

2.   "How long do I have to keep the I–9 forms?"

3.   "Is a draft card sufficient for proof of identification?"

4.   "Suppose I hire someone who later turns out to be an illegal alien who showed phony identification documents. Do I have to fire him? Can I be held liable for having hired him?"

5.   "Maybe one way to protect myself would be to require all new hires to post a bond in an amount equal to the penalty I can be hit with if they turn out to be illegal. Can I do this?"

6.   "I think that illegal aliens are harder workers and more reliable than U.S. citizens. So, I may hire a few, and if I get caught I'll treat the penalty as a tax. How much could it cost me?" [Would you have any ethical qualms about answering this question?]

7.   "I hear that my state also has a law prohibiting the hiring of illegal aliens (although apparently it's never enforced). Can I be penalized under both the state and federal statutes?"

8.   Suppose I hire an employee sent to me by a head-hunting firm. Do I have to verify the status of the employee? Does the head-hunter?

9.   "Do I have to ask you for identification before hiring you as my lawyer?"

————

An employer may not knowingly hire an alien who lacks work authorization, but a diligent verification effort may unlawfully discriminate. The Office of Special Counsel, attempting to provide guidance, has advised that an employer with "constructive knowledge" that an alien lacks work authorization must inquire further, notwithstanding the antidiscrimination provisions. *See* 70 Interp.Rel. 906 (1993). But if the employer lacks "constructive knowledge," further inquiry risks unlawful discrimination under INA § 274B(a)(6), which provides that it is a violation to request documents different from or additional to those required to comply with INA § 274A(b). *See, e.g., United States v. Louis Padnos Iron & Metal Co.,* 1 O.C.A.H.O. 414 (1992).

When does an employer have "constructive knowledge"? Consider the following case.

COLLINS FOODS INTERNATIONAL, INC. v. U.S. INS

United States Court of Appeals, Ninth Circuit, 1991.
948 F.2d 549.

CANBY, CIRCUIT JUDGE:

* * *

Ricardo Soto Gomez (Soto), an employee at a Phoenix Sizzler Restaurant, is authorized to hire other Sizzler employees for that location. Soto extended a job offer to Armando Rodriguez in a long-distance telephone conversation; Soto was in Phoenix and Rodriguez was in California. Rodriguez said nothing in the telephone conversation to indicate that he was not authorized to work in the United States. Rodriguez was working for Sizzler in California at the time Soto extended the offer of employment in Phoenix.

When Rodriguez came to Phoenix, he reported to Sizzler for work. Before allowing Rodriguez to begin work, Soto asked Rodriguez for evidence of his authorization to work in the United States. Rodriguez informed Soto that he did not have the necessary identification with him. At that point, Soto did not let Rodriguez begin work, but sent him away with the understanding that he would return with his qualifying documents.

Rodriguez returned with a driver's license and what appeared to be a Social Security card. Soto looked at the face of the documents and copied information from them onto a Form I–9. Soto did not look at the back of the Social Security card, nor did he compare it with the example in the INS handbook. After Soto completed the necessary paperwork, Rodriguez began work at the Sizzler in Phoenix. Rodriguez, it turned out, was an alien not authorized to work in the United States, and his "Social Security card" was a forgery.

DISCUSSION

The INS charged Collins Foods with one count of hiring an alien, knowing him to be unauthorized to work in the United States, in violation of INA § 274A(a)(1)(A). * * * Inasmuch as it was uncontroverted that Rodriguez was unauthorized to work in the United States, the only issue to be decided at the hearing was whether Collins Foods knew that Rodriguez was unauthorized at the time of hire. The ALJ declined to decide that Collins Foods had actual knowledge of the fact that Rodriguez was an illegal alien, but decided instead that it had "constructive knowledge." The ALJ based his "constructive knowledge" conclusion on two facts: first, that Soto offered the job to Rodriguez over the telephone without having seen Rodriguez' documentation; and, second, that Soto failed to compare the back of the Social Security card with the example in the INS manual. While we do not disturb the factual determinations made by the ALJ, we hold that these two facts cannot, as a matter of law, establish constructive knowledge under INA § 274A(a)(1)(A).

I. Job Offer Prior to Verification of Documents

The first of these facts, as a matter of law, cannot support a finding of constructive knowledge. Nothing in the statute prohibits the offering of a job prior to checking the documents; indeed, the regulations contemplate just such a course of action.

The statute that Collins Foods is charged with violating prohibits "a person or other entity [from] hir[ing] for employment" an alien not authorized to work. INA § 274A(a)(1)(A). The Regulations define "hiring" as "the actual commencement of employment of an employee for wages or other remuneration." 8 C.F.R. § 274a.1(c). As Rodriguez had not commenced employment for wages at the time Soto extended a job offer to him over the telephone, Rodriguez was not yet "hired" for purposes of section 274A. Soto was therefore not required to verify Rodriguez' documentation at that time.

Another regulation addresses the issue of the timeliness of verification, and it suggests the same result. Under 8 C.F.R. § 274a.2(b)(ii), employers are required to examine an employee's documentation and complete Form I–9 "within three business days of the hire." Because Soto had examined Rodriguez' documents and completed the necessary paperwork by the time Rodriguez began work for wages, Soto was not delinquent in verifying Rodriguez' documentation.

There are additional, highly cogent reasons for rejecting the ALJ's reliance on the fact that Soto "told Rodriguez he would be hired long before Soto ever saw, or had any opportunity to verify, *any* evidence of Rodriguez' work authorization." To hold such a failure of early verification against the employer, as the ALJ did, places the employer in an impossible position. Pre-employment questioning concerning the applicant's national origin, race or citizenship exposes the employer to charges of discrimination if he does not hire that applicant. The Equal Employment Opportunity Commission has held that pre-employment inquiries concerning a job applicant's race, color, religion, national origin, or citizenship status "may constitute evidence of discrimination prohibited by Title VII." EEOC, *Pre–Employment Inquiries* (1981), *reprinted in* 2 Employment Practices Guide ¶ 4120, 4163 (CCH 1985). An employer who makes such inquiries will have the burden of proving that the answers to such inquiries "are not used in making hiring and placement decisions in a discriminatory manner prohibited by law." Id. ¶ 4120 at 4166. For that reason, employers attempting to comply with the Immigration Reform and Control Act of 1986 ("IRCA"), are well advised not to examine documents until after an offer of employment is made * * *.

The ultimate danger, of course, is that many employers, faced with conflicting commands from the EEOC and the INS, would simply avoid interviewing any applicant whose appearance suggests alienage. The resulting discrimination against citizens and authorized aliens would frustrate the intent of Congress embodied in both Title VII of the Civil Rights Act of 1964, 42 U.S.C. § 2000e et seq., and the 1986 Immigration Reform Act itself. We discuss below some of the legislative history of the latter Act. The legislative history cannot be squared with the ruling of the ALJ regarding Soto's telephone offer of employment to Rodriguez.

* * *

II. *Verification of Documents*

The portion of the statute that Collins Foods allegedly violated prohibits the hiring of an alien while "knowing" the alien is not authorized to work. The statute also prohibits the hiring of an individual without complying with the verification requirements outlined in the statute at INA § 274A(b)(1)(A). These two actions, failing properly to verify an employee's work-authorization documents, and hiring an alien knowing him to be unauthorized to work, constitute separate offenses under the IRCA. Nevertheless, the INS argues, and the ALJ held, that Collins Foods' failure to comply with the verification provisions of the statute establishes the knowledge element of subsection (a)(1)(A), hiring an alien knowing him to be unauthorized. We need not decide, however, whether a violation of the verification requirement establishes the knowledge element of section (a)(1)(A); Collins Foods complied with the verification requirement.

The statute, at INA § 274A(b)(1)(A), provides that an employer will have satisfied its verification obligation by examining a document which "reasonably appears on its face to be genuine." Soto examined the face of both Rodriguez' false Social Security card and his genuine driver's license, but failed to detect that the Social Security card was invalid. But as the ALJ acknowledged, even though Rodriguez was spelled "Rodriquez" on the front of the social security card, at a glance the card on its face did not appear to be false.

* * * [T]he ALJ held that Collins Foods did not satisfy its verification obligation because Soto did not compare the back of Rodriguez' social security card with the example in the INS handbook. We can find nothing in the statute that requires such a comparison. Moreover, even if Soto had compared the card with the example, he still may not have been able to discern that the card was not genuine. The handbook contains but one example of a Social Security card, when numerous versions exist. The card Rodriguez presented was not so different from the example that it necessarily would have alerted a reasonable person to its falsity. * * *

* * *

Congress carefully crafted INA § 274A to limit the burden and the risk placed on employers. The ALJ's holding in this case places on employers a verification obligation greater than that intended by Congress and beyond that outlined in the narrowly-drawn statute.

In addition, the ALJ's holding extends the constructive knowledge doctrine far beyond its permissible application in IRCA employer sanction cases. IRCA, as we have pointed out, is delicately balanced to serve the goal of preventing unauthorized alien employment while avoiding discrimination against citizens and authorized aliens. The doctrine of constructive knowledge has great potential to upset that balance, and it should not be expansively applied. * * * When the scope of liability is expanded by the doctrine of constructive knowledge, the employer is subject to penalties for a range of undefined acts that may result in knowledge being imputed to him. To guard against unknowing violations, the employer may, again, avoid hiring anyone with an appearance of alienage. To preserve Congress' intent in passing the employer sanctions provisions of IRCA, then, the doctrine of constructive knowledge must be sparingly applied.

* * *

Notes

1. A research team asked California employers in 1987–88 what they would do if they suspected that a document presented by a job applicant was fraudulent. Here are a few representative responses:

> I'd put it in the file and say, I hope it's not [fake].

> If it's a flagrant fake I.D., then we obviously would turn it down; but we're not responsible for being professional identification checkers.

> I would just try to get them to get something that wasn't so fraudulent looking. If it doesn't look right, go get a right one for me.

> It's not our business [to check]. We're an employer, not a policeman. Blatantly fraudulent documents we don't accept—and we've had some miserable reproductions. Some of the forgeries are absolutely magnificent, however, and we don't question them.

> The technology of falsification is far more advanced than the technology of detection. . . . They show me the stuff, and it's wrong, and there's nothing I can do about it.

> The compliance procedures are not that difficult. You don't have to verify the person's documents are valid, so there's no hazard in hiring someone with fraudulent documents.

> It's so easy for these guys to get the fake IDs. . . . I think that's one of the reasons we haven't had any problems getting employees. You ask them for IDs and they don't have any. Three days later, they do.

Cornelius, *The U.S. Demand for Mexican Labor*, in Mexican Migration to the United States: Origins, Consequences, and Policy Options 25, 43–44 (W. Cornelius & J. Bustamante, eds., 1989).

2. Several cases have involved the relationship between IRCA's antidiscrimination provisions and nonimmigrant visas for temporary workers. In *United States v. McDonnell–Douglas Corp.*, 2 O.C.A.H.O. 351 (1991), the Office of Special Counsel charged McDonnell with rejecting or discouraging applications by qualified United States workers so that McDonnell could hire H–2B nonimmigrants from the United Kingdom (based on a labor certification that there were insufficient qualified United States workers). The ALJ ruled that compliance with the H–2B visa process would not excuse any discrimination by McDonnell, and that the Special Counsel's burden was "simply to prove that the preference existed and that discrimination of U.S. workers occurred as a result." The parties later settled, *see* 70 Interp.Rel. 618 (1993).

d. The Impact of IRCA

(i) Discrimination

As noted above, during congressional consideration of employer sanctions a number of legislators expressed strong concern that the program would increase discrimination against some U.S. citizens and lawful resident aliens. Other members of Congress thought that employer sanctions could impose unreasonable burdens on small businesses. To garner the political support necessary for enactment, the statute included an elaborate monitoring provision requiring the General Accounting Office to prepare and transmit to Congress three annual reports on these concerns and on whether the program had been implemented satisfactorily. If the final GAO report found that a "widespread pattern of discrimination" resulted from implementation of employer sanctions, then the sanction program would terminate if Congress enacted a joint resolution stating that it approved the GAO findings. INA § 274A(j)-(n). Congress also enacted a sunset provision, INA § 274B(k), which would terminate the antidiscrimination provisions if (1) employer sanctions are repealed based on a finding of discrimination, or (2) if the final GAO report determined that employer sanctions had resulted in "no significant discrimination," and Congress adopted a joint resolution approving such findings.

The GAO issued its final report in March 1990. It was based largely on a survey of over 9400 employers, which statistically projected to a universe of about 4.6 million employers. The GAO also conducted "hiring audits" in San Diego and Chicago, in which "pairs of persons matched closely on job qualifications applied for jobs with 360 employers in two cities. One member of each pair was a 'foreign-appearing, foreign-sounding' Hispanic and the other was an Anglo with no foreign accent." General Accounting Office, Immigration Reform—Employer Sanctions and the Question of Discrimination 3 (1990).

The GAO summarized its findings on discrimination as follows:

Employers Reported Discriminatory Practices Resulting From the Law

GAO's survey results indicate that national origin discrimination resulting from IRCA, while not pervasive, does exist at levels that amount to more than "just a few isolated cases" and constitutes "a serious pattern of discrimination." GAO estimates that 461,000 (or 10 percent) of the 4.6 million employers in the survey population nationwide began one or more practices that represent national origin discrimination. The survey responses do not reveal whether the persons affected by the discrimination were eligible to work. However, given that these employers hired an estimated 2.9 million employees in 1988, GAO believes it is reasonable to assume that many eligible workers were affected.

An estimated 227,000 employers reported that they began a practice, as a result of IRCA, not to hire job applicants whose foreign appearance or accent led them to suspect that they might be unauthorized aliens. Also, contrary to IRCA, an estimated 346,000 employers said that they applied IRCA's verification system only to persons who had a "foreign" appearance or accent. Some employers began both practices.

Employers reported that they engaged in practices which under the law would be classified as discriminatory verification and hiring practices. They were in a variety of industries and areas of the Nation and included firms of various sizes. The levels of discrimination ranged by geographical location from 3 to 16 percent and were higher in areas having high Hispanic and Asian populations.

These employer responses specifically related the discriminatory hiring and verification practices to IRCA. Therefore, they represent "new" national origin discrimination that would not have occurred without IRCA. There is no evidence that would lead GAO to believe that employers who said they discriminated as a result of IRCA did not. But even if some employers did not report accurately, the remaining group would be substantial.

Since these data meet the criteria in the law and its legislative history, GAO concluded that the national origin discriminatory practices reported do establish a widespread pattern of discrimination. On the basis of the information GAO has, GAO determined that it is more reasonable to conclude that a substantial amount of these discriminatory practices resulted from IRCA rather than not.

Finally, GAO's hiring audit of 360 employers in Chicago, Illinois, and San Diego, California, showed that the "foreign-appearing, foreign-sounding" Hispanic member of the matched pairs was three times more likely to encounter unfavorable treatment than the Anglo non-foreign-appearing member of the pairs. For example, the Anglo members received 52 percent more job offers than the Hispanics. These results, taken together with the survey responses, show a serious problem of national origin discrimination that GAO believes IRCA exacerbated.

Employers Reported Other Forms of Discriminatory Practices

While GAO's statutory determination is limited to national origin discrimination that can be linked directly to IRCA's sanctions section, GAO's survey results indicate that the law also resulted in citizenship discrimination.

GAO estimates that an additional 430,000 employers (9 percent) said that because of the law they began hiring only persons born in the United States or not hiring persons with temporary work eligibility documents. These practices are illegal and can harm people, particularly those of Hispanic and Asian origin.

Adding these employers to those who began national origin discrimination, GAO estimates that 891,000 (19 percent) of the 4.6 million employers in the survey population nationwide began one or more discriminatory practices as a result of the law.

Id. at 5–7.

While "[a]bout 78 percent of employers said they wanted a simpler or better verification system," *id.* at 7, the GAO concluded that IRCA did not burden employers unnecessarily. On the link between the discrimination and burden issues, the GAO commented:

GAO identified three possible reasons why employers discriminated: (1) lack of understanding of the law's major provisions, (2) confusion and uncertainty about how to determine eligibility, and (3) the prevalence of counterfeit and fraudulent documents that contributed to employer uncertainty over how to verify eligibility.

Id. at 8.

Note

Following publication of the GAO's report, Congress did not adopt a joint resolution approving its findings, and employer sanctions were not terminated. The Immigration Act of 1990, however, included a number of provisions that sought to make the antidiscrimination prohibition more effective, including new INA § 274B(a)(6), under which an employer discriminates unlawfully by requesting documents in addition to or different from those required by the statute, or by refusing to honor documents that appear on their face to be genuine. The 1990 Act also provided increased fines for violators, INA § 274B(g)(2)(B), anti-retaliation protection for complainants, *id.* (a)(5), extension of antidiscrimination protection to "special agricultural workers" legalized under IRCA, *id.* (a)(3)(B)(i), and a new educational program for employers and employees, *id.* (*l*).

(ii) Effects on Undocumented Immigration

Have employer sanctions effectively deterred undocumented immigration? The GAO concluded:

> Nearly all the evidence suggests that IRCA has reduced illegal immigration and employment. * * * While INS interviews of unauthorized aliens apprehended at work showed many had fraudulent or counterfeit documents, the data in this chapter suggest that many other unauthorized aliens without such documents were unable to find work because of the law's verification system.

General Accounting Office, *supra*, at 102. The GAO based this conclusion on a number of sources, including interviews of employers who said that IRCA changed their hiring patterns; interviews of undocumented aliens who said that employers had had refused to hire them because they could not show work authorization documents; surveys of towns and cities in Mexico where many residents said IRCA discouraged them from going to the United States; and a 35 percent decline in border apprehensions between November 1986 and September 1988.

The next two selections reach conclusions different from the GAO's, and in so doing analyze some of the adaptive behavior and other fundamental changes that may be attributable to IRCA.

KITTY CALAVITA, EMPLOYER SANCTIONS VIOLATIONS:
TOWARD A DIALECTICAL MODEL OF
WHITE–COLLAR CRIME

24 Law & Society Review 1041, 1046–55, 1057, 1060 (1990).

* * *

The data for the study come primarily from research carried out in 1987 and 1988 on 103 "immigrant-dependent" firms in Los Angeles, Orange, and San Diego counties. * * *

The sectors represented in the sample—garment, construction, electronics, hotels, restaurants, food processing, and building and landscape maintenance—are those in which undocumented workers traditionally have been concentrated. Agriculture was excluded, as growers were not susceptible to fines under employer sanctions until December 1988. The firms in the sample tend to be small and medium-sized, with the average size being one hundred employees. At least 25 percent of the workforce of each firm in the sample was Hispanic, mostly Mexican, and the average proportion of Hispanic workers was 52 percent. * * *

* * *

* * * Because of the constraints of the sampling techniques and the nature of the study itself, the findings are clearly not generalizable to all employers, or even to all immigrant-dependent employers. In addition to the underrepresentation of very small firms and underground employers is the obvious geographical limitation. There is of course no pretense that employers in other regions of the United States respond to employer sanctions in exactly the same way as the immigrant-dependent firms in this southern California sample. Indeed, the southern California location was chosen not to be representative of the country as a whole—which it clearly is not—but because it provided a showcase through which to examine the interconnections between legal formulations and risk-free employer violations. To the extent that employers in other regions of the country may be less immigrant-dependent, compliance rates will probably tend to be higher. The primary purpose here, however, is not to estimate compliance rates but to expose the substantial incentives for violation and to trace those incentives to their source in the legal process. The focus on these three southern California counties, which receive the greatest influx of immigrant workers in the United States, seems well-suited for this purpose.

* * *

During the debates preceding the enactment of employer sanctions, its advocates in Congress and within the INS maintained that most employers would voluntarily comply with the law. Admitting that the INS would be able to monitor only a tiny fraction of the nation's approximately seven million employers each year, employer sanctions proponents argued that this was of little consequence. The deterrent effect of the law, this argument went, would be based on voluntary compliance and the example set by a few well-publicized fines.

After passage of employer sanctions, INS Commissioner Alan Nelson stated that most employers were abiding by the law simply because it was the law. INS District Counsel in San Diego Martin Soblick spoke enthusiastically of "the success we've had across the board in securing voluntary compliance from employers nationwide". The Western Regional Commissioner of the INS, Harold Ezell, insisted that the fines imposed under employer sanctions operated as a deterrent on those few employers who might not otherwise comply voluntarily.

The data derived from our interviews paint quite a different picture. About 48 percent of the employers interviewed said that they "thought" they had undocumented workers on their work force.[13] Close to half of these (45 percent) estimated that 25 percent or more of their work force was undocumented. Another 11 percent said they "did not know" whether any of their workers were undocumented. Eighty percent of respondents said that the new law has not affected "in any way" the type of workers they currently hire, and twelve employers (11 percent) volunteered that they *knew* that they had hired undocumented workers since employer sanctions went into effect. Seventy-eight percent anticipate no future changes in the way they hire workers.

Interviews with workers tend to validate these findings. Fifty-eight percent of the sample said that they thought there were undocumented workers at their work place. Thirty percent were themselves undocumented at the time of the interview (another 30 percent were in the process of applying for amnesty), and fifty-one of these, or 35 percent, had purchased or borrowed fraudulent documents in order to secure employment. Six of the undocumented workers reported having been told by their *employer* to obtain false papers. Furthermore, these undocumented workers were not confined to firms that had been subject to INS raids in the past. Of the workers interviewed, 17 percent reported that their work place had been raided in the preceding year. In these "raided" firms, 26 percent of the workers interviewed were undocumented; in the firms that had not been subject to a raid, 31 percent of the respondents were undocumented. Overall, 15 percent of the undocumented workers interviewed worked in firms that had been raided in the previous years, while 85 percent worked for employers who had not been subject to a raid.

Several employers were outspoken in their intentions to continue to hire undocumented workers as they are needed. The owner of a landscaping company said matter of factly, "The majority of people who do this work don't have papers, but . . . I will employ them eventually when I need

13. Because of the potentially sensitive nature of this information, the question was posed in this way: "I realize you have no way of knowing this for sure, but do you think that some of your employees may be undocumented immigrants?" In most cases, these employers appeared to be remarkably candid with the interviewer. A few employers even volunteered information, once the tape recorder was turned off, about additional illegal activity regarding their employment of undocumented workers. It is of course likely that some under-reporting occurred, in which case the statistics presented here represent conservative estimates of actual violations.

them." And later, "People have a need to work and we need workers; sooner or later we will employ them [the undocumented] again."

* * *

The employers I studied are well aware of the benefits of using [an undocumented alien] work force. A number of employers spoke glowingly of the immigrants' "work ethic." A restaurant manager told us, for example, that "[a]liens have a strong work ethic; they need a job; they are good workers. . . . Other workers will be less motivated." The vice president of a light assembly operation claimed, "it's been proven to us that an ethnic workforce works better than we do. . . . I don't care what you call it, reverse prejudice or whatever; they work better." Another employer concurred, "When you hire undocumented workers, you can get more out of them."

* * *

Many employers recognize that the jobs they are offering are not particularly desirable and that were it not for immigrant labor, it would be difficult for them to maintain a work force. The general manager of a food-processing firm described work at his plant and the difficulties of attracting a domestic work force:

> These girls come in at four o'clock in the morning, and it's cold out there in the room that they're working in. There's chicken meat all over the place, and it's not real desirable work. . . . It's hard to find people that will do that. All the girls that we have out there are either resident aliens or of Mexican heritage, and . . . ah . . . they're willing to do it. Consequently, if that's the type of people we have to get to do that type of work . . . we would have to hire them to get the work done.

A garment shop owner, noting the competitive pressure to violate the employer sanctions law, complained, "When you have someone who's bidding against you and using illegals and paying them under the table, it's not really right." Another said simply, "There's a lot of pressure right here not to comply." Indicative of this pressure, over half (57 percent) of the employers interviewed said that they think "other firms in this line of work use undocumented workers."

The apparent benefits of undocumented labor contrast markedly with its perceived costs. Most employers who continued to hire the undocumented expressed very little fear of getting caught. The personnel director of an electronics firm, who earlier had admitted that he still employed some undocumented workers, was unconcerned: "I think the whole thing is a lot of hype about nothing." A food-processing company executive said nonchalantly, "We'll continue to go about hiring those people [Mexican immigrants] the way we always have." Another echoed the sentiment, "I'm open to hiring anyone looking for work. Why not?"

Why not, indeed. Thirty-two percent of these employers are convinced that the INS does not have the ability to enforce the law. A number of employers cited the lack of INS resources, reasoning, as one restaurant manager did, "It's going to be a nightmare for them [the INS]. I suspect that they will probably spotcheck ... There are just too many companies that use undocumented workers."

Such perceptions are at least partially validated by enforcement statistics. In its first report to Congress on employer sanctions, the U.S. General Accounting Office (GAO) noted that the INS expected to audit approximately 20,000 employers in fiscal year 1988—in other words, one-third of 1 percent of the approximately seven million employers in the United States. INS records showed that it fell short of even this goal, having completed 12,319 inspections, or less than one-fifth of 1 percent of the nation's employers. Nor has the pace picked up: In the first five months of fiscal year 1989, the INS conducted 5,000 inspections, almost exactly replicating the 1988 figures. The selection procedure for inspections reduces even further the chances of an offending employer being detected. In order to "demonstrate that the Service is not engaging in selective enforcement of the law", a substantial portion of inspections is initiated on the basis of a random selection process (referred to as the General Administrative Plan, or GAP) generated by a listing of five million employers across the country. By early 1989, 25 percent of employer sanctions had been based on this random procedure, while 75 percent were based on leads that suggested the possibility of employer violations. By 1990, the proportion of GAP inspections had risen to 35 percent. Even though the GAP procedure nets far fewer offenders than lead-based inspections, the goal is to increase to 40 percent the number of inspections based on random selection.

Even in the face of these inspection statistics, it could be argued that the threat of substantial fines might be enough to deter employers of illegal aliens. But the violators in this study expressed very little fear of potential fines. Usually, this lack of fear was tied to a (probably realistic) perception of their slim chances of being caught. However, a few employers added that, given the size of potential fines, violations were an acceptable risk. According to the general manager of a restaurant, "the fines are a reprimand, not a serious threat." The owner of a garment shop in Los Angeles said light-heartedly that if he were caught in a violation, "they're [the INS] going to hit my hands and say I've been naughty." Summarizing this mentality, a personnel director likened the situation to that of a freeway speeder:

> [It's] like saying if you go 56 on the freeway and the speed limit's 55, you're in violation of the law. No foolin'. But, everyday I go 70 until I get caught and when I get caught I say, "Well, I've been doing this for two years and I got nailed for a $100 fine. That's not too bad. That's ten cents a day. I'll continue to go 70."

This employer's analysis of the costs attached to violations is substantiated by the low rate and size of INS fines in the three years following the law's enactment. By September 1989, the INS had recorded 39,594 violations of employer sanctions—36,354 of which were for "paperwork" offenses. The overwhelming majority of these cases resulted in a warning or citation, with fines actually imposed on 3,532 employers. While the average fine initially assessed was approximately $4,840, extensive use of out-of-court settlements has reduced the average to less than $2,500 per employer. Furthermore, fines vary substantially from region to region, with the high-impact western and southern regions imposing the lowest average fines. Although IRCA provides for criminal sanctions in cases of a "pattern or practice" of knowingly hiring unauthorized aliens, criminal prosecutions have been extremely rare.

The final, and most potent, ingredient in employers' risk analyses is their perception of the protection accorded them by the I–9 form. This component goes far beyond the simple mathematical calculation of the chances of being inspected, times the size of a potential fine, and adds a dimension to violators' sense of security that virtually ensures widespread violations. Remember that IRCA requires employers to request documentation from all new hires and to fill out I–9 forms attesting to having seen these documents. All but five of the employers interviewed systematically request such documentation and complete the required paperwork. Rather than seeing the paperwork requirement as burdensome, many of these employers view the I–9 form as an effective barrier between violations and prosecution. The director of human resources at a large plant who later told the interviewer, "Evidently, we have people who are illegal," pointed out that "It [the I–9] would help protect us."

These employers have tapped the source of a paradox that lies at the heart of this analysis. As we have seen, almost half of these employers suspect that they employ undocumented workers, and 11 percent admit outright that they have violated the law. Yet, not only is it unlikely that either group will be subject to fines under employer sanctions, but those who have completed the paperwork (the vast majority) are for all practical purposes labeled "compliers." A garment shop personnel director who confided to the interviewer that he had instructed his undocumented workers to "fix" their patently false documents, explained the paradox this way: "The I–9," he said, "takes a lot of responsibility off of me and puts it back on the employee."

* * *

[In formulating the employer sanctions program, immigration] policymakers faced an apparently irresolvable dilemma grounded in [a] political-economic contradiction * * *. Confronted on one hand by the political pressure for an employer sanctions law, and on the other by the impossibility of passing such a law over the objection of employers who derived significant economic benefits from undocumented migration, the outcome was an employer sanctions law that would be easy to comply with. * * *

* * *

The move to make compliance easy for the employer was based on political necessity and justified on the grounds that "most employers, as generally law-abiding citizens, will uphold the law." This assumption of the law-abiding nature of employers not only made it important to protect the employer through the affirmative defense provision in order to minimize discrimination; it also apparently made it unnecessary to worry lest this protection become a loophole through which offending employers could avoid detection—a possibility that was left virtually unexplored through five years of congressional debate. The employer sanctions law that resulted, grounded as it was in assumptions about voluntary compliance, guaranteed widespread employer violations. Facing a contradiction between political and economic forces, legislators produced a law whose effect was to be solely symbolic. The point here is not simply that Congress passed a toothless law by making compliance easy through the incorporation of loopholes. Rather, the law in effect made *violations* "pragmatically easy." Through the affirmative defense and good faith provisions, Congress guaranteed that conformity with the paperwork requirements would be taken as an indication of compliance, thereby ensuring that violations of the "knowing hire" provision—the real meat of the law— would be virtually risk-free.

WAYNE A. CORNELIUS, MEXICAN MIGRATION TO THE UNITED STATES: INTRODUCTION

Mexican Migration to the United States: Origins, Consequences, and Policy Options 1, 11–14 (W. Cornelius & J. Bustamante, eds., 1989).

Mexico has not had to cope with massive return migration by long-absent workers who suddenly found themselves jobless in the United States as a result of employer sanctions. On the contrary, recent field studies have found that migratory flows from traditional sending communities in Mexico remain unchanged or may actually have increased since IRCA's passage. In communities that have long depended on income earned in the United States, most people continue to have an essentially positive view of the U.S. opportunity structure: not as wide open as before IRCA's passage, but still accessible to those with determination and, even more importantly, family contacts in the United States.

Nevertheless, INS statistics on apprehensions of illegal entrants along the U.S.-Mexico border show a 40 percent drop compared with the 1986 fiscal year, before enactment of IRCA. INS authorities consider this decline indisputable proof of IRCA's deterrent effect on would-be illegal immigrants. Researchers at the Urban Institute, reporting the results of a sophisticated though technically flawed regression analysis of the INS statistics, have argued that "the new legislation *has* slowed the rate of undocumented migration across the southern border of the United States, but this reduction is not as large as many have claimed." Meanwhile, another team of researchers, based at the Rand Corporation, analyzing the same data base, conclude that IRCA did cause a significant decline in illegal entries in Fiscal Year 1987 but had little or no impact on illegal border crossings in Fiscal Year 1988, after the effects of legalization programs and enhanced border enforcement by the INS are taken into account.

Resolving the conflicting claims and evidence concerning the deterrent impact of IRCA's employer sanctions is beyond the scope of this essay. Interpreting changes in INS apprehension statistics has been rendered vastly more complicated and ambiguous by IRCA's amnesty programs, which have made it possible for more than three million persons to cross the border legally, no longer at risk of being apprehended by the Border Patrol. Similarly, employer sanctions, coupled with stepped-up border enforcement, undoubtedly have made some heretofore "short-stay" undocumented migrants already in the United States reluctant to leave, for fear that they will find it too difficult to come back or to find regular employment in the United States again. These temporarily or permanently grounded "shuttle" migrants are no longer at risk of being apprehended at the border either. Clearly, several more years of data—collected through different methodologies—will be needed before any definitive assessment of IRCA's efficacy in halting new illegal migration can be made. In any event, it is premature to conclude that the employer sanctions component of the law is "working"—at least in the way the U.S. Congress intended.

Today, the vast majority of U.S. employers are complying with their legal obligation under IRCA—a relatively simple paperwork requirement. But quite obviously, the supply of jobs available to undocumented Mexican immigrants has not dried up. Most critics of employer sanctions legislation predicted that its principal consequence would be to create a bonanza for false document makers, and gradually this prophecy is coming to pass. Field research findings reported elsewhere in this volume suggest that large numbers of undocumented migrants are successfully using bogus documents—purchased or borrowed—to gain employment in the United States. And employers, not required by IRCA to verify the authenticity of documents presented by job applicants, are either unable or unwilling to go beyond their obligations under the law.

While IRCA may not, in the long run, drastically reduce the overall *level* of Mexican migration to the United States, its effects on the *social composition* and *dynamics* of the flow could be both significant and enduring. The sudden legalization of a large portion of the migratory flow from Mexico to the United States has shifted it toward greater permanence: relatively less short-term, shuttle migration; more "settling out" in the United States. The migration of women and children has increased since IRCA's enactment, both to take advantage of the amnesty programs and for family reunification. Male family heads who secured amnesty for themselves quickly began sending for their wives and children in Mexico, whether or not these dependents themselves could qualify for legalization, using *coyotes* to guide them across the border.

Given the increased problems associated with crossing the border, there is now a stronger incentive for whole family units to migrate together. The presence of more complete immigrant families in U.S. receiving communities will inevitably be reflected in heavier utilization of education, health care, and other social services. On the Mexican side, it will mean fewer dollars remitted by migrants employed in the United States. More generally, to the extent that IRCA's legalization programs reduce shuttle migration and encourage permanent settlement in the United States, the law is likely to have a negative impact on remittance flows in the long term.

Note

Starting about the time the preceding two excerpts were published, the INS began to place greater emphasis on enforcement of employer sanctions, although not necessarily in ways that address all of the limitations identified by Calavita and Cornelius. In 1991, the INS stopped first visiting employers to educate them about IRCA before issuing a Notice of Intent to Fine. It also began to conduct more investigations based on leads rather than random selection. And to maximize deterrence, INS investigators now give priority to large penalties for large-scale violations. *See* Memorandum from Commissioner McNary, Jan. 2, 1992, *reprinted at* 69 Interp.Rel. 267 (1992); Memorandum from Commissioner McNary, Apr. 1, 1991, *reprinted at* 68 Interp.Rel. 445 (1992). Such efforts have resulted in a $260,000 settlement with Disneyland, where a 1993 investigation found 1,156 paperwork violations and numerous counterfeit work documents. The INS has also issued Notices of Intent to Fine of over $1.1 million against Lane Packing Co., a Georgia peach harvester, and $1.2 million against Honeycutt Tearoff Inc., a roofing company in Orange County, California. *See* 71 Interp.Rel. 1150 (1994).

4. AFTER IRCA: THE FUTURE OF IMMIGRATION CONTROL

Even if increased border enforcement and employer sanctions reduce the number of new illegal entries, many more thousands of undocumented aliens will enter the United States each year for the foreseeable future. Does this mean that IRCA should be declared a failure? Or should any reduction in the entry and residence of undocumented aliens be seen as a positive gain for the United States? More generally, what policies ought we adopt to deal with the large number of undocumented aliens residing in the United States?

The 1990 Immigration Act established the 11–member Commission on Immigration Reform and required it to report on several major policy issues, including control of undocumented immigration. In September 1994, the Commission, chaired by former Congresswoman Barbara Jordan, issued its first report.

a. *Border Enforcement*

U.S. COMMISSION ON IMMIGRATION REFORM, U.S. IMMIGRATION POLICY: RESTORING CREDIBILITY

49–52 (1994).

* * * Traditional policy, focused on apprehension of illegal aliens, has many shortcomings. For example, too many illegal aliens are able to elude the Border Patrol; too many violent confrontations occur between the Border Patrol and those suspected of being illegal aliens as officers pursue and aliens attempt to evade capture; and the border is a revolving door with apprehended aliens attempting a new entry within hours of release. Further, when Border Patrol operations focus on apprehensions, coordina-

tion with inspections operations suffers. Yet, the resulting barriers to legal entry may be a factor in causing illegal movements. Because the waits at bridges and other ports of entry on the southern border are sometimes hours long, even some Mexican residents with valid Border Crossing Cards [BCCs] cross the border illegally to avoid the delay in entry.

The Commission believes that the prevention strategy, such as that utilized by "Operation Hold the Line," holds many advantages over such an apprehension approach and recommends that it be the prevalent form of border enforcement along the southern border.

The Commission was favorably impressed with the pilot "Operation Hold the Line" program in El Paso. Originally conceived by Border Patrol Sector Chief Silvestre Reyes, this two-week pilot program was tested on the El Paso, Texas and the Ciudad Juarez, Mexico border as "Operation Blockade." In the twenty-mile section of the Rio Grande River that separates the two cities, the Border Patrol stationed 450 agents—triple the normal number—on an around-the-clock watch. This new strategy, which began in September 1993, saturated the border with Border Patrol agents to prevent entries without inspection. Previously, the strategy in El Paso (as is the case in many border areas) was to allow movement across the border and to apprehend illegal crossers once they were in the country. The old strategy took advantage of the rugged terrain around El Paso that makes it difficult for long-distance migrants to move to interior destinations but allowed easy access to El Paso for local illegal migrants. The new strategy substantially reduced illegal crossings and, thereby, substantially reduced the need for Border Patrol apprehension operations.

Following the expiration of the two week operation, the Border Patrol decided to continue the strategy but renamed the operation in response to criticism of the negative connotation of the term "Blockade." The strategy continued as "Operation Hold the Line." Increased Border Patrol presence on the border was made possible by posting agents normally stationed in the interior at the border, although the number of agents on the line was less than the 450 deployed during the initial operation.

The Commission funded a University of Texas study on the effects of "Operation Hold the Line" on El Paso/Juarez from September 1993 through April 1994. The study used a wide variety of quantitative and qualitative methods to gauge the operation's scope and effectiveness. The quantitative evidence includes border crossing and apprehensions data, police and crime data, birth and hospital data, education and school attendance statistics, and sales tax and general sales data. The qualitative evidence includes ethnographic and in-depth interviews and provides information about motivations and other factors not evident from official statistics on either illegal or legal crossings.

The study found that "Operation Hold the Line" affected the immediate border area in three ways. First, it substantially deterred illegal crossings into El Paso, thereby eliminating the cycle of voluntary return and reentry that has characterized unlawful border crossings. Second, due to reduced interaction between the Border Patrol and would-be crossers, the number of charges of Border Patrol human rights violations declined substantially. Third, seizures of illegal drugs, illegal agricultural products, and other contraband increased. The Operation had a number of beneficial side effects, particularly for the downtown El Paso area. There was a reduction in illegal workers engaging in street vending in downtown El Paso and a substantial decrease in criminal activity. Decreases in petty crime appeared directly linked to reductions in the number of illegal alien entries; decreases in more serious crime occurred because police were able to redirect their resources towards investigation of these crimes.

Although many people in the business communities on both sides of the border feared that "Operation Hold the Line" would affect their livelihood, the study found that business activity in El Paso and Juarez was not substantially harmed. Other effects were small declines in school enrollment and in the number of reported births.

Although no independent surveys of public opinion were undertaken during this period, interviews by University of Texas researchers with residents of El Paso generally indicated high levels of public support for the operation. Elected officials reported that many residents supported the operation because it signaled a reduction in petty crime and the removal of street vendors from downtown El Paso. Additionally, the respondents agreed that the operation greatly diminished complaints of Border Patrol and police harassment of Mexican Americans and legal Mexican residents and that daily illegal crossings were disrupted.

However, the Commission's investigation indicated that some improvements are needed for the type of prevention strategy embodied in "Operation Hold the Line" to work nationally. Foremost, a strategy of this type will not work in isolation. Border management must be comprehensive in its approach. The study of "Operation Hold the Line" showed that unless a similar strategy is utilized across the entire border, illegal crossings will move to other sections. * * *

The evaluation further affirms that a prevention strategy must be combined with an effective work deterrent as employment is the primary magnet for people wanting to cross illegally. Those who cross to work may extend their stays instead of taking the chance of crossing back and forth. Illegal workers with valid crossing documents for entering the U.S. are even more free to work illegally because of decreased Border Patrol presence in the city of El Paso. * * *

The evaluation further demonstrated that relying on staff alone to "hold the line" has diminishing returns because of growing boredom of Border Patrol agents undertaking this type of guard duty and, thus, the need both for retraining of Border Patrol officers to meet the new challenges of a prevention strategy and for new performance measures. * * *

Notes

1. In September 1994, the Border Patrol began "Operation Gatekeeper" in Southern California and "Operation Safeguard" near Nogales, Arizona, also designed to prevent illegal crossings by deploying Border Patrol agents along the border and erecting new fences and lights. *See* 71

Interp.Rel. 1470 (1994). Even before Operation Gatekeeper, the INS had replace most of the chain-link fencing near San Ysidro with solid metal fencing, fashioned from obsolete military "landing mats" used for temporary runways. In October 1994, the INS added new computerized fingerprinting equipment that will allow better identification of those who repeat crossing attempts. The system is eventually to operate nationwide and may lay the groundwork for stiffer penalties for these repeaters.

2. Congress has supported efforts to strengthen border enforcement by authorizing and appropriating funds for additional Border Patrol personnel. The INS budget increased seven percent in FY 1994 and over 25 percent in FY 1995, with the increases devoted in large part to border enforcement. *See* 71 Interp.Rel. 1546–47 (1994); 71 *id.* 1141–42 (1994); 70 *id.* 1434 (1993). The 1994 Crime Bill authorized $675 million over four years for additional Border Patrol agents (1000 more each year) and investigations and deportation resources. Of this amount, $228 million is for FY 1995 alone. Pub.L. 103–322, § 130006, 108 Stat. 1796, 2028–29. For a summary of FY 1995 resource allocations, see 72 Interp.Rel. 91 (1995).

b. *Employer Sanctions*

U.S. COMMISSION ON IMMIGRATION REFORM, U.S. IMMIGRATION POLICY: RESTORING CREDIBILITY

90–101 (1994).

Current worksite enforcement mechanisms have proved less effective than anticipated in deterring illegal immigration and the hiring of unauthorized workers, as well as in preventing unfair immigration-related employment practices. This has been demonstrated by the rise in the estimated number of illegal aliens to nearly pre-IRCA levels, despite IRCA's legalization of 2.7 million aliens, and the documentation of government and private studies of discriminatory practices against foreign-sounding and foreign-looking applicants for employment. (These studies do not have baseline data on pre-employer sanctions discrimination, however, and debate continues about the extent to which the discriminatory patterns result from immigration policy or other factors.) Additionally, employers have found the verification process time-consuming and confusing. Further reasons for the apparent failure include lack of a comprehensive, simple, and realistic worksite enforcement plan, ineffective enforcement of potentially viable laws, and an inefficient use of resources.

Based on these problems with employer sanctions, some critics have urged the law's repeal. While the Commission agrees that these problems do need to be addressed, it has concluded that the best way to do so is through improving the system, not repealing it. The Commission believes that the credibility of the immigration system depends on reducing employment opportunities for unauthorized workers, thus encouraging those who are here illegally to leave and discouraging others from entering. The Commission further believes that employer sanctions could be a viable mechanism for reducing the employment magnet and that the Commission's recommendations will enhance the effectiveness of the system and remedy its current deficiencies.

* * *

The sheer number of documents available for use in verification * * * presents challenges for effective implementation of employer sanctions. Some efforts are underway to correct this situation. INS has proposed regulatory changes that would reduce the number of documents to be used for verifying work authorization for aliens. The Commission believes that these efforts will not solve the problems inherent in the current verification process for several reasons. Reducing the long list of documents by a few documents would still leave too many documents for effective verification; it would also be unlikely to reassure employers sufficiently about the security of the system and may even add to employer confusion and lead to a potential increase in differential treatment. Counterfeiting or the fraudulent use of documents would still continue.

The Commission reviewed options that would reduce the number of acceptable documents even more stringently. The proposals that all aliens use an INS-issued document and all citizens present one of a limited number of documents, such as a passport, birth certificate, social security card, and/or driver's licenses, still contain a basic flaw: the employee would still have to self-identify as an alien or citizen. Such proposals would continue to permit considerable amounts of fraud if illegal aliens declare themselves to be citizens and present counterfeited documents. They also would potentially permit perpetuation or increase of current levels of differential treatment if employers question whether foreign-looking or -sounding citizens are citizens and require an INS-issued document.

Recognizing the problems inherent in strategies to reduce documentation but not to change the overall system of verification, the Commission set a number of criteria by which it measured the potential impacts of more comprehensive reform.

First, a new system would have to be potentially more reliable and less susceptible to unfair immigration-related employment practices than the present one. Any solution would have to take into account that most documents can now be counterfeited within a relatively short time and for a cost that would be recoverable from the sale of the counterfeit documents. Employers generally do not have sufficient expertise to recognize counterfeit documents and, therefore, require a simple, effective means of validating the information presented by new workers. Moreover, the new system would need to apply not only to aliens, but also to U.S. citizens; otherwise, problems of fraud could continue (illegal aliens could claim to be U.S. citizens) and/or unfair immigration-related employment practices may increase (employers could set different documentation standards for all foreign-looking and -sounding individuals).

Second, the new system would have to meet civil liberties and privacy standards. The new verification process should provide protection against use of the system for purposes other than those specified in law. The verification system should protect the privacy of the information to be used in verifying work authorization.

Third, the system would have to lessen the time, resources, and paperwork spent by employers in verifying work authorization. The Commission is persuaded that the current I–9 process requires excessive commitment of time and resources because of the complexity of the verification process. Any new system should be simple to use and require as little paperwork as possible for employers. It should also be simple in overall design, so that enforcement may focus on substantive violations and not become preoccupied with paperwork violations rather than knowing hire of unauthorized workers.

Fourth, the new system would have to be as cost-effective as possible. Given that illegal aliens represent at most a very small portion of the total U.S. labor force, the Commission does not think it appropriate to recommend strategies with costs out of proportion to the problem to be solved. To improve verification without undue costs is possible, we believe, if a new verification system builds to the extent possible on the existing responsibilities, capabilities, and data systems of federal agencies rather than if it were to create new mechanisms that would be used only for verification of immigration-related work authorization.

Fifth, more effective verification likely would require a companion initiative for improvements in the integrity of the underlying or "breeder documents" (such as birth certificates) used to establish identity in this country. Birth certificates are easily counterfeited or easily obtained through counterfeit means. As counterfeiting operations have become multimillion dollar businesses, meaningful penalties would be needed to deter the counterfeiting of documents. New enforcement measures, commensurate with the scale of these operations, are needed to identify and destroy the counterfeiting rings.

* * *

Having assessed dozens of options for verification of work authorization, the Commission believes that the proposed computerized registry best meets the criteria described above. As envisioned by the Commission, the computerized registry would be used to verify that a social security number is valid and has been issued to the individual who is being hired. This database would be created and updated from SSA and INS files, but not connected to either. From SSA would come a limited set of data: name; social security number; and several other identifiers, such as date of birth and mother's maiden name. From INS would come information about the immigration status of lawfully admitted immigrants, nonimmigrants, and other aliens permitted to remain temporarily or permanently in the United States. The INS data would also contain information about the duration of work authorization for aliens granted temporary employment permits.

The Commission believes *the key to this process is the social security number.* For decades, all workers have been required to provide employers with their social security number. The computerized registry would add only one step to this existing requirement: an employer check that the social security number is valid and has been issued to someone authorized to work in the United States.

* * *

Under the proposed verification system, the employer would not ask individuals if they are citizens or aliens. Instead, the individuals would be asked for a name and social security number. This information could then be verified with the computerized registry. The employer would be given a confirmation number if the information given by the employee matches the database information. This verification number would be kept by the employer and could be used as an affirmative defense if the employer is accused of knowingly hiring an illegal alien. If, for any reason, a match is not found within the system, the employer would receive acknowledgement that the verification process was carried out but that, as confirmation could not be made within the system, the employee should check with the local Social Security office to correct the problem. It would not be necessary—or possible—for the inquiry to give to the employer information about the reason why a match was not effected.

Also under this approach, in situations where the worker has temporary authorization to work, the employer could be told the individual has work authorization but to reverify as of a particular date when the eligibility expires. By the time of reverification, the information would be updated to include the individual's current employment eligibility status. The computer registry could also verify that an alien granted authorization to work for a specific employer, for example, under certain nonimmigrant visas, is not seeking employment elsewhere. Some of the costs of the new system may be offset by savings if the computer system allows extension of work eligibility to be done through updating of the database rather than through issuance of a new INS employment authorization document [EAD].

The Commission believes a computerized registry based on the social security number is the most promising option for verification because it holds great potential for accomplishing the following:

- *Reduction in the potential for fraud.* Using a computerized registry rather than only documents, as in the I–9 process, guards against counterfeiting. It provides more reliable information about work authorization.

- *Reduction in the potential for discrimination* based on national origin and citizenship status, as well as inappropriate demands for specific or additional documents, given that employers will not be required to ascertain whether a worker is a citizen or an immigrant and will have no reason to reject documents believed to be counterfeit. The only relevant question will be: "What is your social security number?"

- *Reduction in the time, resources, and paperwork* spent by employers in complying with the Immigration Reform and Control Act of 1986 and corresponding redirection of enforcement activities from paperwork violations to knowing hire of unauthorized workers. Through use of this system, employer confusion will be greatly reduced as employers will not need to rely on faulty documents.

Notes

1. The Commission recommended "that the President immediately initiate and evaluate pilot programs using the proposed computerized verification system in the five states with the highest levels of illegal immigration as well as several less affected states." *Id.* at 101. A bill introduced in January 1995 by Senator Alan Simpson would require three-year pilot programs in five states. The programs would be at least partly based on a new database to be created from current INS and Social Security Administration records. *See* S. 269, 104th Cong., 1st Sess. (1995).

2. Commissioners Warren Leiden and Nelson Merced issued a concurring statement with the following reservations:

> * * * [I]t is far from certain whether, in the real world, such a system can be made affordable, accurate, reliable, and politically acceptable with regard to civil liberties and individual privacy. Thus, our concurrence in recommending the initiation of pilot programs to test the proposed computerized verification system is solely for the purpose of examining whether such a verification system can measure up to the factors that would warrant a subsequent determination that such a system should be publicly implemented and relied upon. * * *

> * * * Until a final analysis and evaluation has been completed, the proposed verification system should not be relied upon to deny employment to any individual, nor should it be integrated with other systems that could allow for its misuse in other circumstances.

Id. at Appendix.

3. In October 1994, the Clinton Administration issued a report, *Accepting the Immigration Challenge: The President's Report on Immigration*, which did not mention the Jordan Commission's verification proposal.[14] Instead, the President's report emphasized a Telephone Verification System (TVS), which would allow employers to verify work authorization by telephoning a centralized computer database. TVS is currently only a pilot program that is planned to expand to 200 employers in FY 1995 and 500 employers in FY 1996, *see* 71 Interp.Rel. 1471 (1994). The INS has also proposed reducing the number of acceptable work authorization documents from 29 to 16, *see* 58 Fed. Reg. 61846–50 (1993), with the possibility of eventually reducing the number to two: the "green card" for permanent residents and a new, standardized work authorization document for all other aliens. *See* 71 Interp.Rel. 1293 (1994).

---

14. In testimony before the House immigration subcommittee in October 1994, INS Commissioner Doris Meissner refuted suggestions by subcommittee members that the Clinton Administration was lukewarm about the Jordan Commission report. She "expressed amazement that the administration was falsely reported to have been uninterested in the Commissions's recommendations." 71 Interp.Rel. 1474 (1994). In his State of the Union address on January 24, 1995, President Clinton endorsed in general terms the Commission's proposal "to better identify illegal aliens in the workplace."

c. *Public Benefits*

A number of states and localities have enacted laws restricting undocumented aliens' access to public benefits and other government services. Part of the thinking is predominantly fiscal. There is also growing support for the view that benefits and services attract illegal immigration (and perhaps legal immigration as well), and that denying access is therefore part of any effective control strategy. For example, in 1994 Florida began to deny foster care to undocumented children. *See* Rohter, *Florida Takes Fight On Immigrant Policy To a New Battlefield*, N.Y.Times, Feb. 11, 1994, at A1, A8. Starting March 1, 1994, California limited driver's licenses and identification cards to those whose presence in the United States is "authorized under federal law." *See* Cal.Veh.Code § 12801.5 (West 1994).

In November 1994, California passed Proposition 187, the so-called "Save Our State" Initiative, with almost 60 percent of the vote. Proposition 187 restricts undocumented aliens' access to public services, including education and nonemergency health care. It also creates substantial criminal penalties for the manufacture, distribution, sale, or use of false citizenship or permanent residence documents. And it requires state and local law enforcement officials to cooperate with the INS in identifying and apprehending undocumented aliens.

The preamble to Proposition 187 reads as follows:

SECTION 1.   Findings and Declaration.

The People of California find and declare as follows:

That they have suffered and are suffering economic hardship caused by the presence of illegal aliens in this state.

That they have suffered and are suffering personal injury and damage caused by the criminal conduct of illegal aliens in this state.

That they have a right to the protection of their government from any person or persons entering the country unlawfully.

Therefore, the People of California declare their intention to provide for cooperation between their agencies of state and local government with the federal government, and to establish a system of required notification by and between such agencies to prevent illegal aliens in the United States from receiving benefits or public services in the State of California.

With regard to nonemergency medical services and elementary and secondary education, Proposition 187 provides:

SECTION 6.   Exclusion of Illegal Aliens from Publicly Funded Health Care.

* * *

[A new § 130 is added to the Health and Safety Code:]

Section 130. (a) In order to carry out the intention of the People of California that, excepting emergency medical care as required by federal law, only citizens of the United States and aliens lawfully admitted to the United States may receive the benefits of publicly-funded health care, and to ensure that all persons employed in the providing of those services shall diligently protect public funds from misuse, the provisions of this section are adopted.

(b) A person shall not receive any health care services from a publicly-funded health care facility, to which he or she is otherwise entitled until the legal status of that person has been verified as one of the following:

(1) A citizen of the United States.

(2) An alien lawfully admitted as a permanent resident.

(3) An alien lawfully admitted for a temporary period of time.

(c) If any publicly-funded health care facility in this state from whom a person seeks health care services, other than emergency medical care as required by federal law, determines or reasonably suspects, based upon the information provided to it, that the person is an alien in the United States in violation of federal law, the following procedures shall be followed by the facility:

(1) The facility shall not provide the person with services.

(2) The facility shall, in writing, notify the person of his or her apparent illegal immigration status, and that the person must either obtain legal status or leave the United States.

(3) The facility shall also notify the State Director of Health Services, the Attorney General of California, and the United States Immigration and Naturalization Service of the apparent illegal status, and shall provide any additional information that may be requested by any other public entity.

* * *

SECTION 7. Exclusion of Illegal Aliens From Public Elementary and Secondary Schools.

Section 48215 is added to the Education Code to read:

Section 48215. (a) No public elementary or secondary school shall admit, or permit the attendance of, any child who is not a citizen of the United States, an alien lawfully admitted as a permanent resident, or a person who is otherwise authorized under federal law to be present in the United States.

(b) Commencing January 1, 1995, each school district shall verify the legal status of each child enrolling in the school district for the first time in order to ensure the enrollment or attendance only of citizens, aliens lawfully admitted as permanent residents, or persons who are otherwise authorized to be present in the United States.

(c) By January 1, 1996, each school district shall have verified the legal status of each child already enrolled and in attendance in the school district in order to ensure the enrollment or attendance only of citizens, aliens lawfully admitted as permanent residents, or persons who are otherwise authorized under federal law to be present in the United States.

(d) By January 1, 1996, each school district shall also have verified the legal status of each parent or guardian of each child referred to in subdivisions (b) and (c), to determine whether such parent of guardian is one of the following:

(1) A citizen of the United States.

(2) An alien lawfully admitted as a permanent resident.

(3) An alien admitted lawfully for a temporary period of time.

(e) Each school district shall provide information to the State Superintendent of Public Instruction, the Attorney General of California, and the United States Immigration and Naturalization Service regarding any enrollee or pupil, or parent or guardian, attending a public elementary or secondary school in the school district determined or reasonably suspected to be in violation of federal immigration laws within forty-five days after becoming aware of an apparent violation. The notice shall also be provided to the parent or legal guardian of the enrollee or pupil, and shall state that an existing pupil may not continue to attend the school after ninety calendar days from the date of the notice, unless legal status is established.

(f) For each child who cannot establish legal status in the United States, each school district shall continue to provide education for a period of ninety days from the date of the notice. Such ninety day period shall be utilized to accomplish an orderly transition to a school in the child's country of origin. Each school district shall fully cooperate in this transition effort to ensure that the educational needs of the child are best served for that period of time.

———

Apart from a policy assessment of Proposition 187, is it constitutional? Consider the following case.

PLYLER v. DOE

Supreme Court of the United States, 1982.
457 U.S. 202, 102 S.Ct. 2382, 72 L.Ed.2d 786.

JUSTICE BRENNAN delivered the opinion of the Court.

The question presented by these cases is whether, consistent with the Equal Protection Clause of the Fourteenth Amendment, Texas may deny to undocumented school-age children the free public education that it provides to children who are citizens of the United States or legally admitted aliens.

I

Since the late 19th century, the United States has restricted immigration into this country. Unsanctioned entry into the United States is a crime, and those who have entered unlawfully are subject to deportation. But despite the existence of these legal restrictions, a substantial number of persons have succeeded in unlawfully entering the United States, and now live within various States, including the State of Texas.

In May 1975, the Texas Legislature revised its education laws to withhold from local school districts any state funds for the education of children who were not "legally admitted" into the United States. The 1975 revision also authorized local school districts to deny enrollment in their public schools to children not "legally admitted" to the country. Tex.Educ.Code Ann. § 21.031 (Vernon Supp.1981). These cases involve constitutional challenges to those provisions.

* * * [8]

II

* * * Appellants argue at the outset that undocumented aliens, because of their immigration status, are not "persons within the jurisdiction" of the State of Texas, and that they therefore have no right to the equal protection of Texas law. We reject this argument. Whatever his status under the immigration laws, an alien is surely a "person" in any ordinary sense of that term. Aliens, even aliens whose presence in this country is unlawful, have long been recognized as "persons" guaranteed due process of law by the Fifth and Fourteenth Amendments. *Shaughnessy v. Mezei,* 345 U.S. 206, 212, 73 S.Ct. 625, 629, 97 L.Ed. 956 (1953); *Wong Wing v. United States,* 163 U.S. 228, 238, 16 S.Ct. 977, 981, 41 L.Ed. 140 (1896); *Yick Wo v. Hopkins,* 118 U.S. 356, 369, 6 S.Ct. 1064, 1070, 30 L.Ed. 220 (1886). Indeed, we have clearly held that the Fifth Amendment protects aliens whose presence in this country is unlawful from invidious discrimination by the Federal Government. *Mathews v. Diaz,* 426 U.S. 67, 77, 96 S.Ct. 1883, 1890, 48 L.Ed.2d 478 (1976).

* * *

III

* * * In applying the Equal Protection Clause to most forms of state action, we thus seek only the assurance that the classification at issue bears some fair relationship to a legitimate public purpose.

But we would not be faithful to our obligations under the Fourteenth Amendment if we applied so deferential a standard to every classification. The Equal Protection Clause was intended as a restriction on state legislative action inconsistent with elemental constitutional premises. Thus we have treated as presumptively invidious those classifications that disadvantage a "suspect class," or that impinge upon the exercise of a "fundamental right." With respect to such classifications, it is appropriate to enforce the mandate of equal protection by requiring the State to demonstrate that its classification has been precisely tailored to serve a compelling governmental interest. In addition, we have recognized that certain forms of legisla-

---

8. Appellees * * * continue to press the argument that § 21.031 is pre-empted by federal law and policy. In light of our disposi- tion of the Fourteenth Amendment issue, we have no occasion to reach this claim.

tive classification, while not facially invidious, nonetheless give rise to recurring constitutional difficulties; in these limited circumstances we have sought the assurance that the classification reflects a reasoned judgment consistent with the ideal of equal protection by inquiring whether it may fairly be viewed as furthering a substantial interest of the State. * * *

Sheer incapability or lax enforcement of the laws barring entry into this country, coupled with the failure to establish an effective bar to the employment of undocumented aliens, has resulted in the creation of a substantial "shadow population" of illegal migrants—numbering in the millions—within our borders. This situation raises the specter of a permanent caste of undocumented resident aliens, encouraged by some to remain here as a source of cheap labor, but nevertheless denied the benefits that our society makes available to citizens and lawful residents. The existence of such an underclass presents most difficult problems for a Nation that prides itself on adherence to principles of equality under law.

The children who are plaintiffs in these cases are special members of this underclass. Persuasive arguments support the view that a State may withhold its beneficence from those whose very presence within the United States is the product of their own unlawful conduct. These arguments do not apply with the same force to classifications imposing disabilities on the minor *children* of such illegal entrants. At the least, those who elect to enter our territory by stealth and in violation of our law should be prepared to bear the consequences, including, but not limited to, deportation. But the children of those illegal entrants are not comparably situated. Their "parents have the ability to conform their conduct to societal norms," and presumably the ability to remove themselves from the State's jurisdiction; but the children who are plaintiffs in these cases "can affect neither their parents' conduct nor their own status." *Trimble v. Gordon*, 430 U.S. 762, 770, 97 S.Ct. 1459, 1465, 52 L.Ed.2d 31 (1977). Even if the State found it expedient to control the conduct of adults by acting against their children, legislation directing the onus of a parent's misconduct against his children does not comport with fundamental conceptions of justice. * * *

Of course, undocumented status is not irrelevant to any proper legislative goal. Nor is undocumented status an absolutely immutable characteristic since it is the product of conscious, indeed unlawful, action. But § 21.031 is directed against children, and imposes its discriminatory burden on the basis of a legal characteristic over which children can have little control. It is thus difficult to conceive of a rational justification for penalizing these children for their presence within the United States. Yet that appears to be precisely the effect of § 21.031.

Public education is not a "right" granted to individuals by the Constitution. But neither is it merely some governmental "benefit" indistinguishable from other forms of social welfare legislation. Both the importance of education in maintaining our basic institutions, and the lasting impact of its deprivation on the life of the child, mark the distinction. * * * [E]ducation provides the basic tools by which individuals might lead economically productive lives to the benefit of us all. In sum, education has a fundamental role in maintaining the fabric of our society. We cannot ignore the significant social costs borne by our Nation when select groups are denied the means to absorb the values and skills upon which our social order rests.

In addition to the pivotal role of education in sustaining our political and cultural heritage, denial of education to some isolated group of children poses an affront to one of the goals of the Equal Protection Clause: the abolition of governmental barriers presenting unreasonable obstacles to advancement on the basis of individual merit. Paradoxically, by depriving the children of any disfavored group of an education, we foreclose the means by which that group might raise the level of esteem in which it is held by the majority. But more directly, "education prepares individuals to be self-reliant and self-sufficient participants in society." *Wisconsin v. Yoder, supra*, 406 U.S., at 221, 92 S.Ct., at 1536. Illiteracy is an enduring disability. The inability to read and write will handicap the individual deprived of a basic education each and every day of his life. The inestimable toll of that deprivation on the social, economic, intellectual, and psychological well-being of the individual, and the obstacle it poses to individual achievement, make it most difficult to reconcile the cost or the principle of a status-based denial of basic education with the framework of equality embodied in the Equal Protection Clause. What we said 28 years ago in *Brown v. Board of Education*, 347 U.S. 483, 74 S.Ct. 686, 98 L.Ed. 873 (1954), still holds true:

> " * * * In these days, it is doubtful that any child may reasonably be expected to succeed in life if he is denied the opportunity of an education. Such an opportunity, where the state has undertaken to provide it, is a right which must be made available to all on equal terms."

These well-settled principles allow us to determine the proper level of deference to be afforded § 21.031. Undocumented aliens cannot be treated as a suspect class because their presence in this country in violation of federal law is not a "constitutional irrelevancy." Nor is education a fundamental right; a State need not justify by compelling necessity every variation in the manner in which education is provided to its population. But more is involved in these cases than the abstract question whether § 21.031 discriminates against a suspect class, or whether education is a fundamental right. Section 21.031 imposes a lifetime hardship on a discrete class of children not accountable for their disabling status. The stigma of illiteracy will mark them for the rest of their lives. By denying these children a basic education, we deny them the ability to live within the structure of our civic institutions, and foreclose any realistic possibility that they will contribute in even the smallest way to the progress of our Nation. In determining the rationality of § 21.031, we may appropriately take into account its costs to the Nation and to the innocent children who are its victims. In light of these countervailing costs, the discrimination contained in § 21.031 can hardly be considered rational unless it furthers some substantial goal of the State.

IV

* * * [I]n the State's view, Congress' apparent disapproval of the presence of these children within the United States, and the evasion of the

federal regulatory program that is the mark of undocumented status, provides authority for its decision to impose upon them special disabilities. Faced with an equal protection challenge respecting the treatment of aliens, we agree that the courts must be attentive to congressional policy; the exercise of congressional power might well affect the State's prerogatives to afford differential treatment to a particular class of aliens. But we are unable to find in the congressional immigration scheme any statement of policy that might weigh significantly in arriving at an equal protection balance concerning the State's authority to deprive these children of an education.

The Constitution grants Congress the power to "establish an uniform Rule of Naturalization." Art. I., § 8, cl. 4. Drawing upon this power, upon its plenary authority with respect to foreign relations and international commerce, and upon the inherent power of a sovereign to close its borders, Congress has developed a complex scheme governing admission to our Nation and status within our borders. The obvious need for delicate policy judgments has counseled the Judicial Branch to avoid intrusion into this field. But this traditional caution does not persuade us that unusual deference must be shown the classification embodied in § 21.031. The States enjoy no power with respect to the classification of aliens. This power is "committed to the political branches of the Federal Government." *Mathews*, 426 U.S., at 81, 96 S.Ct., at 1892. Although it is "a routine and normally legitimate part" of the business of the Federal Government to classify on the basis of alien status, *id.*, at 85, 96 S.Ct., at 1894, and to "take into account the character of the relationship between the alien and this country," *id.*, at 80, 96 S.Ct., at 1891, only rarely are such matters relevant to legislation by a State.

As we recognized in *De Canas v. Bica*, 424 U.S. 351, 96 S.Ct. 933, 47 L.Ed.2d 43 (1976), the States do have some authority to act with respect to illegal aliens, at least where such action mirrors federal objectives and furthers a legitimate state goal. In *De Canas*, the State's program reflected Congress' intention to bar from employment all aliens except those possessing a grant of permission to work in this country. In contrast, there is no indication that the disability imposed by § 21.031 corresponds to any identifiable congressional policy. The State does not claim that the conservation of state educational resources was ever a congressional concern in restricting immigration. More importantly, the classification reflected in § 21.031 does not operate harmoniously within the federal program.

To be sure, like all persons who have entered the United States unlawfully, these children are subject to deportation. But there is no assurance that a child subject to deportation will ever be deported. An illegal entrant might be granted federal permission to continue to reside in this country, or even to become a citizen. In light of the discretionary federal power to grant relief from deportation, a State cannot realistically determine that any particular undocumented child will in fact be deported until after deportation proceedings have been completed. It would of course be most difficult for the State to justify a denial of education to a child enjoying an inchoate federal permission to remain.

We are reluctant to impute to Congress the intention to withhold from these children, for so long as they are present in this country through no fault of their own, access to a basic education. In other contexts, undocumented status, coupled with some articulable federal policy, might enhance state authority with respect to the treatment of undocumented aliens. But in the area of special constitutional sensitivity presented by these cases, and in the absence of any contrary indication fairly discernible in the present legislative record, we perceive no national policy that supports the State in denying these children an elementary education. * * * We therefore turn to the state objectives that are said to support § 21.031.

V

Appellants argue that the classification at issue furthers an interest in the "preservation of the state's limited resources for the education of its lawful residents." Of course, a concern for the preservation of resources standing alone can hardly justify the classification used in allocating those resources. *Graham v. Richardson*, 403 U.S. 365, 374–375, 91 S.Ct. 1848, 1853, 29 L.Ed.2d 534 (1971). The State must do more than justify its classification with a concise expression of an intention to discriminate. Apart from the asserted state prerogative to act against undocumented children solely on the basis of their undocumented status—an asserted prerogative that carries only minimal force in the circumstances of these cases—we discern three colorable state interests that might support § 21.031.

First, appellants appear to suggest that the State may seek to protect itself from an influx of illegal immigrants. While a State might have an interest in mitigating the potentially harsh economic effects of sudden shifts in population,[23] § 21.031 hardly offers an effective method of dealing with an urgent demographic or economic problem. There is no evidence in the record suggesting that illegal entrants impose any significant burden on the State's economy. To the contrary, the available evidence suggests that illegal aliens underutilize public services, while contributing their labor to the local economy and tax money to the state fisc. The dominant incentive for illegal entry into the State of Texas is the availability of employment; few if any illegal immigrants come to this country, or presumably to the State of Texas, in order to avail themselves of a free education. Thus, even making the doubtful assumption that the net impact of illegal aliens on the economy of the State is negative, we think it clear that "[c]harging tuition to undocumented children constitutes a ludicrously ineffectual attempt to stem the tide of illegal immigration," at least when compared with the alternative of prohibiting the employment of illegal aliens. 458 F.Supp., at 585.

---

23. Although the State has no direct interest in controlling entry into this country, that interest being one reserved by the Constitution to the Federal Government, unchecked unlawful migration might impair the State's economy generally, or the State's ability to provide some important service. Despite the exclusive federal control of this Nation's borders, we cannot conclude that the States are without any power to deter the influx of persons entering the United States against federal law, and whose numbers might have a discernible impact on traditional state concerns. See *De Canas v. Bica*, 424 U.S., at 354–356, 96 S.Ct., at 935–936.

Second, * * * appellants suggest that undocumented children are appropriately singled out for exclusion because of the special burdens they impose on the State's ability to provide high-quality public education. But the record in no way supports the claim that exclusion of undocumented children is likely to improve the overall quality of education in the State. * * * Of course, even if improvement in the quality of education were a likely result of barring some *number* of children from the schools of the State, the State must support its selection of *this* group as the appropriate target for exclusion. * * *

Finally, appellants suggest that undocumented children are appropriately singled out because their unlawful presence within the United States renders them less likely than other children to remain within the boundaries of the State, and to put their education to productive social or political use within the State. Even assuming that such an interest is legitimate, it is an interest that is most difficult to quantify. The State has no assurance that any child, citizen or not, will employ the education provided by the State within the confines of the State's borders. In any event, the record is clear that many of the undocumented children disabled by this classification will remain in this country indefinitely, and that some will become lawful residents or citizens of the United States. It is difficult to understand precisely what the State hopes to achieve by promoting the creation and perpetuation of a subclass of illiterates within our boundaries, surely adding to the problems and costs of unemployment, welfare, and crime. It is thus clear that whatever savings might be achieved by denying these children an education, they are wholly insubstantial in light of the costs involved to these children, the State, and the Nation.

* * *

JUSTICE MARSHALL, concurring.

While I join the Court's opinion, I do so without in any way retreating from my opinion in *San Antonio Independent School District v. Rodriguez*, 411 U.S. 1, 70–133, 93 S.Ct. 1278, 1315–1348, 36 L.Ed.2d 16 (1973) (dissenting opinion). I continue to believe that an individual's interest in education is fundamental, and that this view is amply supported "by the unique status accorded public education by our society, and by the close relationship between education and some of our most basic constitutional values." *Id.*, at 111, 93 S.Ct., at 1336. * * * It continues to be my view that a class-based denial of public education is utterly incompatible with the Equal Protection Clause of the Fourteenth Amendment.

JUSTICE BLACKMUN, concurring.

* * *

* * * Children denied an education are placed at a permanent and insurmountable competitive disadvantage, for an uneducated child is denied even the opportunity to achieve. * * * Other benefits provided by the State, such as housing and public assistance, are of course important; to an individual in immediate need, they may be more desirable than the right to be educated. But classifications involving the complete denial of education are in a sense unique, for they strike at the heart of equal protection values

by involving the State in the creation of permanent class distinctions. In a sense, then, denial of an education is the analogue of denial of the right to vote: the former relegates the individual to second-class social status; the latter places him at a permanent political disadvantage.

* * *

* * * [T]he structure of the immigration statutes makes it impossible for the State to determine which aliens are entitled to residence, and which eventually will be deported. Indeed, any attempt to do so would involve the State in the administration of the immigration laws. * * * [T]he statute at issue here sweeps within it a substantial number of children who will in fact, and who may well be entitled to, remain in the United States. Given the extraordinary nature of the interest involved, this makes the classification here fatally imprecise. * * *

* * *

JUSTICE POWELL, concurring.

* * *

Our review in a case such as these is properly heightened. The classification at issue deprives a group of children of the opportunity for education afforded all other children simply because they have been assigned a legal status due to a violation of law by their parents. These children thus have been singled out for a lifelong penalty and stigma. A legislative classification that threatens the creation of an underclass of future citizens and residents cannot be reconciled with one of the fundamental purposes of the Fourteenth Amendment. In these unique circumstances, the Court properly may require that the State's interests be substantial and that the means bear a "fair and substantial relation" to these interests.

* * * [T]he interests relied upon by the State would seem to be insubstantial in view of the consequences to the State itself of wholly uneducated persons living indefinitely within its borders. By contrast, access to the public schools is made available to the children of lawful residents without regard to the temporary nature of their residency in the particular Texas school district. * * * [T]he exclusion of appellees' class of children from state-provided education is a type of punitive discrimination based on status that is impermissible under the Equal Protection Clause.

In reaching this conclusion, I am not unmindful of what must be the exasperation of responsible citizens and government authorities in Texas and other States similarly situated. Their responsibility, if any, for the influx of aliens is slight compared to that imposed by the Constitution on the Federal Government. So long as the ease of entry remains inviting, and the power to deport is exercised infrequently by the Federal Government, the additional expense of admitting these children to public schools might fairly be shared by the Federal and State Governments. But it hardly can be argued rationally that anyone benefits from the creation within our borders of a subclass of illiterate persons many of whom will remain in the State, adding to the problems and costs of both State and National Governments attendant upon unemployment, welfare, and crime.

CHIEF JUSTICE BURGER, with whom JUSTICE WHITE, JUSTICE REHNQUIST, and JUSTICE O'CONNOR join, dissenting.

Were it our business to set the Nation's social policy, I would agree without hesitation that it is senseless for an enlightened society to deprive any children—including illegal aliens—of an elementary education. I fully agree that it would be folly—and wrong—to tolerate creation of a segment of society made up of illiterate persons, many having a limited or no command of our language. However, the Constitution does not constitute us as "Platonic Guardians" nor does it vest in this Court the authority to strike down laws because they do not meet our standards of desirable social policy, "wisdom," or "common sense." We trespass on the assigned function of the political branches under our structure of limited and separated powers when we assume a policymaking role as the Court does today.

The Court makes no attempt to disguise that it is acting to make up for Congress' lack of "effective leadership" in dealing with the serious national problems caused by the influx of uncountable millions of illegal aliens across our borders. The failure of enforcement of the immigration laws over more than a decade and the inherent difficulty and expense of sealing our vast borders have combined to create a grave socioeconomic dilemma. It is a dilemma that has not yet even been fully assessed, let alone addressed. However, it is not the function of the Judiciary to provide "effective leadership" simply because the political branches of government fail to do so.

* * *

The dispositive issue in these cases, simply put, is whether, for purposes of allocating its finite resources, a state has a legitimate reason to differentiate between persons who are lawfully within the state and those who are unlawfully there. The distinction the State of Texas has drawn—based not only upon its own legitimate interests but on classifications established by the Federal Government in its immigration laws and policies—is not unconstitutional.

The Court acknowledges that, except in those cases when state classifications disadvantage a "suspect class" or impinge upon a "fundamental right," the Equal Protection Clause permits a state "substantial latitude" in distinguishing between different groups of persons. Moreover, the Court expressly—and correctly—rejects any suggestion that illegal aliens are a suspect class, or that education is a fundamental right. Yet by patching together bits and pieces of what might be termed quasi-suspect-class and quasi-fundamental-rights analysis, the Court spins out a theory custom-tailored to the facts of these cases.

* * *

The Court first suggests that these illegal alien children, although not a suspect class, are entitled to special solicitude under the Equal Protection

Clause because they lack "control" over or "responsibility" for their unlawful entry into this country. Similarly, the Court appears to take the position that § 21.031 is presumptively "irrational" because it has the effect of imposing "penalties" on "innocent" children. However, the Equal Protection Clause * * * protects against arbitrary and irrational classifications, and against invidious discrimination stemming from prejudice and hostility; it is not an all-encompassing "equalizer" designed to eradicate every distinction for which persons are not "responsible."

The Court does not presume to suggest that appellees' purported lack of culpability for their illegal status prevents them from being deported or otherwise "penalized" under federal law. Yet would deportation be any less a "penalty" than denial of privileges provided to legal residents? Illegality of presence in the United States does not—and need not—depend on some amorphous concept of "guilt" or "innocence" concerning an alien's entry. Similarly, a state's use of federal immigration status as a basis for legislative classification is not necessarily rendered suspect for its failure to take such factors into account.

* * * This Court has recognized that in allocating governmental benefits to a given class of aliens, one "may take into account the character of the relationship between the alien and this country." *Mathews v. Diaz,* 426 U.S. 67, 80, 96 S.Ct. 1883, 1891, 48 L.Ed.2d 478 (1976). When that "relationship" is a federally prohibited one, there can, of course, be no presumption that a state has a constitutional duty to include illegal aliens among the recipients of its governmental benefits.[7]

* * *

The importance of education is beyond dispute. Yet we have held repeatedly that the importance of a governmental service does not elevate it to the status of a "fundamental right" for purposes of equal protection analysis. * * * Moreover, the Court points to no meaningful way to distinguish between education and other governmental benefits in this context. Is the Court suggesting that education is more "fundamental" than food, shelter, or medical care?

* * *

The central question in these cases, as in every equal protection case not involving truly fundamental rights "explicitly or implicitly guaranteed by the Constitution," *San Antonio Independent School Dist., supra,* 411 U.S., at 33–34, 93 S.Ct., at 1296–1297, is whether there is some legitimate basis for a legislative distinction between different classes of persons. The fact that the distinction is drawn in legislation affecting access to public education—as opposed to legislation allocating other important governmental benefits, such as public assistance, health care, or housing—cannot make a difference in the level of scrutiny applied.

---

7. It is true that the Constitution imposes lesser constraints on the Federal Government than on the states with regard to discrimination against lawfully admitted aliens. * * * However, the same cannot be said when Congress has decreed that certain aliens should not be admitted to the United States at all.

Once it is conceded—as the Court does—that illegal aliens are not a suspect class, and that education is not a fundamental right, our inquiry should focus on and be limited to whether the legislative classification at issue bears a rational relationship to a legitimate state purpose.

The State contends primarily that § 21.031 serves to prevent undue depletion of its limited revenues available for education, and to preserve the fiscal integrity of the State's school-financing system against an ever-increasing flood of illegal aliens—aliens over whose entry or continued presence it has no control. Of course such fiscal concerns alone could not justify discrimination against a suspect class or an arbitrary and irrational denial of benefits to a particular group of persons. Yet I assume no Member of this Court would argue that prudent conservation of finite state revenues is *per se* an illegitimate goal. Indeed, the numerous classifications this Court has sustained in social welfare legislation were invariably related to the limited amount of revenues available to spend on any given program or set of programs. The significant question here is whether the requirement of tuition from illegal aliens who attend the public schools—as well as from residents of other states, for example—is a rational and reasonable means of furthering the State's legitimate fiscal ends.[10]

Without laboring what will undoubtedly seem obvious to many, it simply is not "irrational" for a state to conclude that it does not have the same responsibility to provide benefits for persons whose very presence in the state and this country is illegal as it does to provide for persons lawfully present. By definition, illegal aliens have no right whatever to be here, and the state may reasonably, and constitutionally, elect not to provide them with governmental services at the expense of those who are lawfully in the state. In *De Canas v. Bica*, 424 U.S. 351, 357, 96 S.Ct. 933, 937, 47 L.Ed.2d 43 (1976), we held that a State may protect its "fiscal interests and lawfully resident labor force from the deleterious effects on its economy resulting from the employment of illegal aliens." * * *

It is significant that the Federal Government has seen fit to exclude illegal aliens from numerous social welfare programs, such as the food stamp program, the old-age assistance, aid to families with dependent children, aid to the blind, aid to the permanently and totally disabled, and supplemental security income programs, the Medicare hospital insurance benefits program, and the Medicaid hospital insurance benefits for the aged and disabled program. Although these exclusions do not conclusively demonstrate the constitutionality of the State's use of the same classification for comparable purposes, at the very least they tend to support the rationality of excluding illegal alien residents of a state from such programs so as to preserve the state's finite revenues for the benefit of lawful residents.

The Court maintains—as if this were the issue—that "barring undocumented children from local schools would not necessarily improve the

---

10. The Texas law might also be justified as a means of deterring unlawful immigration. While regulation of immigration is an exclusively federal function, a state may take steps, consistent with federal immigration policy, to protect its economy and ability to provide governmental services from the "deleterious effects" of a massive influx of illegal immigrants. *De Canas v. Bica*, 424 U.S. 351, 96 S.Ct. 933, 47 L.Ed.2d 43 (1976). * * *

quality of education provided in those schools." However, the legitimacy of barring illegal aliens from programs such as Medicare or Medicaid does not depend on a showing that the barrier would "improve the quality" of medical care given to persons lawfully entitled to participate in such programs. Modern education, like medical care, is enormously expensive, and there can be no doubt that very large added costs will fall on the State or its local school districts as a result of the inclusion of illegal aliens in the tuition-free public schools. The State may, in its discretion, use any savings resulting from its tuition requirement to "improve the quality of education" in the public school system, or to enhance the funds available for other social programs, or to reduce the tax burden placed on its residents; each of these ends is "legitimate." * * *

* * *

Notes

1. Justice Brennan relies in part on the "[s]heer incapability or lax enforcement of the laws barring entry into this country, coupled with the failure to establish an effective bar to the employment of undocumented aliens," 457 U.S. at 218, 102 S.Ct. at 2395. Quoting the district court, Brennan adds that "[c]harging tuition to undocumented children constitutes a ludicrously ineffectual attempt to stem the tide of illegal immigration," at least when compared with the alternative of prohibiting the employment of illegal aliens. 457 U.S. at 228–29, 102 S.Ct. at 2401. And he notes "[t]here is no evidence in the record suggesting that illegal entrants impose any significant burden on the State's economy." 457 U.S. at 228 102 S.Ct. at 2400. Do all of these observations remain valid today? If not, what follows?

2. Consider the following comment on *Plyler* by Professor Peter Schuck:

> If those to whom we have refused entry are entitled by their mere presence—together with the presence of their children—to claim not only constitutional procedural protections, but also the significant substantive entitlements that legislatures grant to lawful residents, then immigration law's ideal of national community has also been transformed. In the classical view, the political branches of government defined the boundaries of that community and the consequences of exclusion. That definition, responsive to the political values, local interests and policy concerns that animate Congress, has tended to exclude those whose entry was believed to threaten these interests. The most important meaning of *Plyler* may be that the courts are beginning to assert a coordinate, if not supervisory, role in defining the dimensions and meaning of national community in the immigration context. Courts are expositors of a constitutional tradition that increasingly emphasizes not the parochial and the situational, but the universal, transcendant values of equality and fairness imminent in the due process and equal protection principles. In that capacity, they

have also asserted a larger role in the creation and distribution of opportunities and status in the administrative state. In *Plyler*, the Supreme Court moved boldly on both fronts. In doing so, the Court seems to have begun to redefine the community to include all those whose destinies have somehow, even in violation of our law, become linked with ours.

Schuck, *The Transformation of Immigration Law*, 84 Colum. L.Rev. 1, 58 (1984).

3. Figuring prominently in both the *Plyler* majority and dissent is *De Canas v. Bica*, 424 U.S. 351, 96 S.Ct. 933, 47 L.Ed.2d 43 (1976), in which the Supreme Court (in an unanimous opinion by Justice Brennan) upheld the constitutionality of a California state statute that provided that "[n]o employer shall knowingly employ an alien who is not entitled to lawful residence in the United States if such employment would have an adverse effect on lawful resident workers." According to the Court, employment is a traditional area of state law concern, and the California law was consistent with federal immigration policy. 424 U.S. at 356–63, 96 S.Ct. at 936–40. Is *Plyler* consistent with *De Canas*? (Note that IRCA expressly preempted state laws of the type at issue in *De Canas*, *see* INA § 274A(h)(2).) Why does depriving undocumented children of an education differ from depriving their parents of a job?

4. To what extent do the *Plyler* majority's reasoning and result follow from *Graham v. Richardson*, p. 162 *supra*, a case that involved lawful permanent residents?

5. Is the majority correct in treating the Texas law as a "denial of education" to undocumented children or as imposing lifetime illiteracy? Are there no schools in Mexico? Regarding tuition payments, consider the material earlier in this Section on the earnings of undocumented immigrants. Should the Court have required case-by-case challenges rather than striking down the statute on its face?

6. The proponents of Proposition 187 were well aware that *Plyler* posed a major obstacle to implementation of § 7 relating to public elementary and secondary education, but they hoped that passage of Proposition 187 would eventually prompt a new Supreme Court decision with a different result. What about the other provisions of Proposition 187? Will they pass constitutional muster?

The day after Proposition 187 passed, eight lawsuits to block its implementation were filed in federal and state courts in California. Several temporary restraining orders and preliminary injunctions followed, which, as we go to press, have kept all but the document fraud provisions from taking effect.

7. Could the federal government, relying on *Mathews v. Diaz*, discussed p. 163 *supra*, bar undocumented aliens from federally funded educational programs?

8. Apart from citing *Plyler*, the Jordan Commission stayed away from the issue of public education for undocumented aliens. However, it did comment on public benefits generally:

The Commission recommends that federal legislation should clearly permit states and localities to limit benefit eligibility for illegal aliens on the same criteria as the federal government. Due to various judicial decisions, states and localities are presently prohibited from making alienage an eligibility factor in their benefit programs. Thus, restrictions on illegal alien use of federal assistance programs can shift costs to states and localities. However, if the authority to limit eligibility is extended to states and localities, the use and the cost of such benefits for illegal immigrants can be reduced. Implementation of this recommendation will mean that illegal aliens may not be eligible for any public assistance benefits—federal, state, or local. For illegal aliens who require assistance, their only recourse should be return to their countries of origin.

* * *

* * * It is not entirely clear whether federal legislation granting states authority to limit the eligibility of illegal aliens for benefits consistent with federal policies would be sufficient to overcome the 14th Amendment's equal protection clause. However, previous court rulings imply that, where it is established that national interests are supported by such delegation of authority, Congress can delegate specific authority to states to determine benefit eligibility—if any—for illegal aliens.

U.S. Commission on Immigration Reform, U.S. Immigration Policy: Restoring Credibility 155–56 (1994).

9. The significance of Proposition 187 goes beyond its substantive prohibitions to the imposition of a duty on benefits and services providers (school districts, hospitals, etc.) to verify immigration status. In the same vein, in March 1994 Rep. Dana Rohrabacher (R–Cal) unsuccessfully tried to amend a federal elementary and secondary education authorization bill to require, as a condition of federal funding, that school districts report on the number of students who are undocumented or who have one undocumented parent. *See* 71 Interp.Rel. 345 (1994). Imposing this duty on nongovernmental actors takes immigration law enforcement further in the direction pioneered by IRCA when it imposed an analogous duty on employers.

10. As discussed in Chapter Ten, persons born in the United States are automatically citizens and therefore fully eligible for public benefits, regardless of their parents' immigration law status. In 1993, California Governor Wilson, a staunch supporter of Proposition 187, proposed an amendment to the United States Constitution that would deny citizenship to children born in the United States to undocumented parents. He asked: "Why does the U.S. government reward illegal immigrants who successfully violate the law and manage to have a child born on U.S. soil?" *Open Letter to the President of the United States on Behalf of the People of California*, N.Y.Times, Aug. 10, 1993, at A11. *See also* H.J.Res. 56, 104th Cong., 1st Sess. (1995) (proposing constitutional amendment to same effect), and Chapter Ten, pp. 989–90 *infra*.

11. Responding to concerns about the costs of state and federal assistance to newly legalized permanent residents, IRCA allowed states and localities to exclude legalized aliens from means-tested financial assistance. And to reimburse states for these costs, IRCA appropriated funds for "state legalization impact-assistance grants" (or "SLIAG" funds). To limit federal expenditures, INA § 245A(h) disqualified legalized aliens from most but not all federal means-tested benefit programs for five years from the grant of temporary resident status.[15] An alien is thus eligible for benefits only after residing in the United States for a considerable period of time, perhaps a decade—in unlawful status since January 1982 plus five years after legalization. In contrast, a permanent resident alien who has just arrived in the United States may be eligible for some forms of assistance immediately.[16] Perhaps relying on *Mathews v. Diaz*, 426 U.S. 67, 80, 96 S.Ct. 1883, 1891, 48 L.Ed.2d 478 (1976), p. 163 *supra*, Congress apparently felt under little obligation to consider seriously whether this aspect of IRCA is constitutional. *See* H.Rep. No. 682(I), 99th Cong., Sess. 74–75 (1986).

Some recent welfare reform proposals would curtail access of any lawful permanent residents to federal public benefits. The Republican Welfare Reform bill takes one possible approach: to limit eligibility outright. *See* H.R. 4, 104th Cong., 1st Sess. (1995) (over 50 programs barred to aliens except refugees within six years of arrival and lawful permanent residents over 75 years of age who have resided in the United States for at least five years). Another approach is to deem the income of anyone who signs an affidavit of support to be the alien's income in determining eligibility. The Clinton Administration's proposal in 1994 would have extended the period for such "deeming." *See* H.R. 4605, 103d Cong., 2d Sess. (1994). Senator Simpson has proposed extending the deeming period all the way to naturalization. *See* S. 269, 104th Cong., 2d Sess. (1995).

12. For an analysis of Proposition 187, see Schuck, *The Messages of 187*, The American Prospect, No. 21 (Spring 1995). For thoughtful arguments for recognizing resident undocumented aliens as members of the U.S. community, see Bosniak, *Exclusion and Membership: The Dual Identity of the Undocumented Worker under United States Law*, 1988 Wisc. L.Rev. 955; Lopez, *Undocumented Mexican Migration: In Search of a Just Immigration Law and Policy*, 28 U.C.L.A.L.Rev. 615 (1981).

SECTION D. GROUNDS FOR EXCLUSION

1. OVERVIEW

All aliens who wish to come to this country must first fit themselves within one of the qualifying categories canvassed in Sections A and B of this Chapter. But that is only part of the story. They must also avoid any

---

15. Legalized aliens are excluded from Aid to Families with Dependent Children, Food Stamps and Medicaid (except emergency services and aid to pregnant women), but eligible for school lunch aid, Headstart, job training, and supplemental security income. *See* 8 C.F.R. § 245a.5.

16. This difference is somewhat undercut by INA § 241(a)(5), which renders deportable an alien who "within five years after the date of entry, has become a public charge from causes not affirmatively shown to have arisen since entry."

determination of excludability under INA § 212(a). Section 212(a) lists "classes of excludable aliens who are ineligible to receive visas and who shall be excluded from admission into the United States." This language reflects the dual exclusion screening potentially applicable to all who wish to migrate to the United States. Ordinarily the exclusion grounds are applied first and most importantly by the consular officer considering issuance of a visa, but the INS inspector at the border or port of entry has full authority to consider anew the application of all the exclusion grounds, even if the alien bears a visa duly issued by a consul. *See* INA § 221(h).

Before 1990, the INA contained 33 separate grounds of exclusion, a list that had grown haphazardly since 1952 as Congress added categories of undesirable conduct or status. The grounds covered quite a range, from clearly understandable and legitimate requirements to others that provoked controversy and sparked widespread calls for reform. Congress finally used the occasion of the Immigration Act of 1990 to rewrite the exclusion grounds, effective June 1, 1991, but it made relatively little substantive change in most of them. Its major contribution was to regroup the grounds under nine major headings, with numerous detailed subclasses. The new arrangement is more logical, if more cumbersome, than the old, and much of the previous caselaw remains relevant because of the substantive continuity with the previous provisions. Nevertheless, the 1990 Act did remove a few of the former grounds, for example, those applicable to homosexuals[1] or to "paupers, professional beggars, or vagrants." It also modified others, especially those relating to national security, which we will examine more closely in subsection 2 *infra,* and those relating to communicable diseases.[2]

INA § 212(a) contains the actual exclusion grounds themselves. The balance of § 212 consists primarily of waiver provisions that cut back in intricate and hard-to catalogue ways on the exclusion grounds of subsection

---

1. The earlier provisions barring homosexuals had been sustained against constitutional challenge in *Boutilier v. INS,* 387 U.S. 118, 87 S.Ct. 1563, 18 L.Ed.2d 661 (1967). But when the American Psychiatric Association in 1974 removed homosexuality from its listing of mental disorders, new questions arose about the enforceability of this exclusion ground, which was included among the statute's medical grounds. The circuits split on the question, *see Matter of Longstaff,* 716 F.2d 1439 (5th Cir.1983), *cert. denied,* 467 U.S. 1219, 104 S.Ct. 2668, 81 L.Ed.2d 373 (1984); *Hill v. INS,* 714 F.2d 1470 (9th Cir. 1983), but the 1990 amendments have obviated final Supreme Court resolution.

2. The outbreak of AIDS (acquired immune deficiency syndrome) prompted a panicky congressional rider to an appropriations bill in 1987 that led to regulations excluding virtually all aliens having AIDS or the associated HIV (human immunodeficiency virus) infection. During passage of the 1990 Act, cooler heads prevailed, and Congress rewrote the health-related exclusion grounds to block admission only of those aliens having communicable diseases "of public health significance." In response the Department of Health and Human Services proposed new regulations to remove AIDS and several other diseases from the exclusion list, because they cannot be spread by casual contact, leaving only infectious tuberculosis as the basis for exclusion under this provision. 56 Fed.Reg. 2484 (1991). These steps proved to be highly controversial, however, and Congress again intervened in early 1993 by attaching another rider to an unrelated bill. It added a clause to INA § 212(a)(1)(A)(i) requiring that the HHS regulations "include infection with the etiologic agent for acquired immune deficiency syndrome."

This ground of exclusion is waivable in some circumstances, however, particularly for nonimmigrants under § 212(d)(3). INS and the State Department have wrestled with the issue of what standards should govern waivers for persons with HIV infection or AIDS; strict limits are often placed on the duration of admission under a waiver.

(a).[3] After the 1990 Act, all of these are discretionary waiver provisions. That is, merely meeting the statutory prerequisites (which can themselves be quite daunting; *see, e.g.,* INA § 212(h) allowing waiver of certain criminal grounds) is not enough. One must also receive a favorable exercise of discretion from the Attorney General or her delegate.

You are not expected to commit the exclusion grounds to memory, but you should become familiar with the general structure of § 212, and know where to look to answer specific questions a hypothetical client might pose to you. The problems appearing below will help establish that familiarity, both with the exclusion grounds and the available waiver provisions. Read carefully § 212(a) and also the following, which are the most important waivers for our purposes: § 212(c) through (e), (g) through (i), and (k).

A few further generalizations about the waivers may be useful before embarking on the problems. Section 212(d)(3) provides the Attorney General with discretionary power to waive nearly all the exclusion grounds for those who intend to enter the United States as nonimmigrants. The only other waiver provision that approaches section 212(d)(3) in breadth applies only to long-resident immigrants: Section 212(c) grants the Attorney General discretion to waive nearly all exclusion grounds for lawful permanent residents who are returning to an unrelinquished domicile of at least seven consecutive years.[4] For unexplained reasons, the handful of nonwaivable exclusion grounds are not quite the same under section 212(c) as under section 212(d)(3). Arriving aliens who are neither nonimmigrants nor longtime returning residents have far fewer opportunities to obtain waivers. Those who have a spouse, child, or parent who is a U.S. citizen or lawful permanent resident retain the best chances. Such aliens may qualify for discretionary waiver of the exclusion grounds based on criminal behavior (§ 212(h)), certain health-related conditions (§ 212(g)), or prior visa fraud (§ 212(i)). Each such waiver provision differs slightly, and each also contains its own precise set of eligibility standards.

Problems

Section 212 is extraordinarily long and complex. Test your initial ability to find your way through it by hunting down the answers to the following questions. In each one, what paragraphs of § 212(a) might apply? What waiver provisions from the later subsections might relieve the alien of the application of such exclusion grounds? What other factual

3. Other portions of the later subsections set forth additional requirements that must be met to avoid exclusion in certain defined circumstances. *See, e.g.,* § 212(n) (describing the attestation process necessary for H–1B nonimmigrants). In addition, § 212(b) contains a requirement, added in 1990, directing the provision of certain information to the alien when he or she is denied a visa or excluded at the border. And § 212(f) gives the President extensive authority to issue a proclamation suspending the entry of specific classes of aliens or all aliens, when he or she

finds that entry "would be detrimental to the interests of the United States." *See, e.g.,* Proclamation 6685 of May 7, 1994, 59 Fed. Reg. 24337, barring the entry of certain Haitian officials (as part of the escalating international sanctions meant to bring down the Cédras regime).

4. Because § 212(c) has been ruled applicable in deportation proceedings—and is far more heavily used in that setting, we will defer detailed consideration to Chapter Seven.—eds.

information might you need to develop? What other statutory provisions or case law might you have to consult to arrive at an answer?

1.   Your client qualifies for the family-sponsored first preference, but was convicted of petty larceny seven years ago and sent to prison for a total of three months. Is she excludable? What if she had been convicted of two counts of petty larceny? What if the conviction was for grand theft? What if it was for possession of 150 grams of marijuana?

2.   A consular officer considering the issuance of a student visa under section 101(a)(15)(F) is told by the CIA of solid intelligence information linking the alien to a clandestine organization believed to be responsible for recent bombings in the alien's home country. A check with local police authorities there, however, reveals no convictions or even arrests for any offenses. Can this alien be excluded? On what ground?

3.   A national of Colombia is apprehended on the beach at night, tugging a small boat up away from the waterline. Undaunted, he tells the Border Patrol officers that he is glad to see them and wishes to apply for admission as a tourist. He has a passport. Is he excludable? On what ground?

4.   Your client, a U.S. citizen, wishes to bring his father in for a three-month visit from his home in Yugoslavia, but the father suffers from tuberculosis. Will he be able to secure a nonimmigrant visa? What if the father is healthy but was convicted of narcotics trafficking and served a two-year sentence, ending 12 years ago? What if the conviction was for burglary? Under each factual assumption—tuberculosis, narcotics trafficking, burglary—could the father secure entry as an immigrant?

5.   Your client, a Honduran national, recently married an American citizen in Tegucigalpa, but she had been deported from the United States three years ago for overstaying her student visa. Is she excludable? Suppose she also reveals that she has been active in the sanctuary movement, assisting church groups in the United States to move undocumented Salvadorans across the southern border in an effort to find a haven in this country. Does that complicate matters?

6.   Your client, who seeks to come as an F–1 nonimmigrant student, admits that he entered the United States without inspection twice over the last six years. Is he excludable? What if he helped smuggle his brother into the country along with him at the time of his second entry?

7.   Your client was a member of the Communist party in Czechoslovakia until the Communist regime collapsed in late 1989. He now seeks to enter the United States as an F–1 student. Is he excludable? What if he seeks to enter for permanent residence under one of the employment-based preferences? Would it make a difference if instead he had been a member of the Communist party in Cuba, going into exile two years ago? What if he seeks to enter in the family-sponsored fourth preference?

8.   A German national employed in the U.S. consulate in Frankfurt recognizes an individual who comes in to apply for a B–2 visa. She takes the consular officer aside and says that the applicant is well known on the streets for running an illegal gambling operation in the region; she

wouldn't be surprised if he means to set up a similar operation in Minneapolis, where he says he will visit friends. Is he excludable? Should he be?

9. Your client used a bogus green card to secure entry into the United States one time eight years ago. Now he has developed a substantial international import-export business and seeks to enter the United States lawfully as a nonimmigrant E–1 treaty trader. Is he excludable? He also has a daughter who is now a U.S. citizen. They are estranged and he is not sure whether she would petition for his permanent residence. If she will, would that make any difference in his possible admissibility?

2. EXCLUSION BASED ON NATIONAL SECURITY AND THE SEARCH FOR SUBSTANTIVE CONSTITUTIONAL CONSTRAINTS ON EXCLUSION GROUNDS

In 1903, in the wake of the 1901 assassination of President McKinley by an anarchist mistakenly believed to be an alien, Congress added to the grounds of exclusion a provision rendering anarchists ineligible for admission. (For a gripping account of the assassin, Leon Czolgosz, and of the anarchist milieu in which he devised his plans, see B. Tuchman, The Proud Tower 122–24 (1966).) In succeeding years, and particularly during times of war or other national emergency, Congress expanded and elaborated the grounds of exclusion based on activities, beliefs, and affiliations which it viewed as subversive. *See* E. Hutchinson, Legislative History of American Immigration Policy 1798–1965, at 423–27 (1981).

By 1952, the list was quite lengthy. Although some people made an effort to cut back on these provisions in the debate that year over the proposed Immigration and Nationality Act, Congress chose to perpetuate them in an especially prolix and expansive form. The old section 212(a)(28) provided in part (and only in part) that the following aliens would be excludable:

(A) Aliens who are anarchists;

(B) Aliens who advocate or teach, or who are members of or affiliated with any organization that advocates or teaches, opposition to all organized government;

(C) Aliens who are members of or affiliated with (i) the Communist Party of the United States, (ii) any other totalitarian party of the United States, (iii) the Communist Political Association, (iv) the Communist or any other totalitarian party of any State of the United States, of any foreign state, or of any political or geographical subdivision of any foreign state, (v) any section, subsidiary, branch, affiliate, or subdivision of any such association or party, or (vi) the direct predecessors or successors of any such association or party, regardless of what name such group or organization may have used, may now bear, or may hereafter adopt: *Provided,* That nothing in this paragraph, or in any other provision of this Act, shall be construed as declaring that the Communist Party does not advocate the overthrow of the Government of the United States by force, violence, or other unconstitutional means;

(D) Aliens not within any of the other provisions of this paragraph who advocate the economic, international, and governmental doctrines of world communism or the establishment in the United States of a totalitarian dictatorship, or who are members of or affiliated with any organization that advocates the economic, international, and governmental doctrines of world communism or the establishment in the United States of a totalitarian dictatorship, either through its own utterances or through any written or printed publications issued or published by or with the permission or consent of or under the authority of such organization or paid for by the funds of, or funds furnished by, such organization;

* * *

(G) Aliens who write or publish, or cause to be written or published, or who knowingly circulate, distribute, print, or display, or knowingly cause to be circulated, distributed, printed, published, or displayed, or who knowingly have in their possession for the purpose of circulation, publication, distribution, or display, any written or printed matter, advocating or teaching opposition to all organized government, or advocating or teaching (i) the overthrow by force, violence, or other unconstitutional means of the Government of the United States or of all forms of law; or (ii) the duty, necessity, or propriety of the unlawful assaulting or killing of any officer or officers (either of specific individuals or of officers generally) of the Government of the United States or of any other organized government, because of his or their official character; or (iii) the unlawful damage, injury, or destruction of property; or (iv) sabotage; or (v) the economic, international, and governmental doctrines of world communism or the establishment in the United States of a totalitarian dictatorship;

Are these provisions consistent with the First Amendment? The Supreme Court considered the constitutional validity of some of them in 1971, in the *Mandel* case, which follows. Certain background information may be useful as you read *Mandel*. The Court has long struggled to fashion doctrines for judging what limits the First Amendment places on government efforts to restrict or punish subversive activities or advocacy of unlawful action. Justice Holmes' "clear and present danger" test, first announced in *Schenck v. United States,* 249 U.S. 47, 39 S.Ct. 247, 63 L.Ed. 470 (1919), was one such attempt. Just two years before *Mandel,* however, the court seemed to have reached an important landmark clarifying applicable doctrine and providing the tightest limits yet on government action in this realm. In *Brandenburg v. Ohio,* 395 U.S. 444, 89 S.Ct. 1827, 23 L.Ed.2d 430 (1969) (per curiam), the court ruled that the First Amendment forbids government action proscribing unlawful advocacy "except where such advocacy is directed to inciting or producing imminent lawless action and is likely to incite or produce such action." This doctrinal evolution caused some to think that the court was prepared to make substantial inroads into § 212(a)(28) when the *Mandel* case appeared on its docket.

KLEINDIENST v. MANDEL

Supreme Court of the United States, 1972.
408 U.S. 753, 92 S.Ct. 2576, 33 L.Ed.2d 683.

Mr. Justice Blackmun delivered the opinion of the Court.

[Ernest Mandel was a well-known Belgian author who described himself as "a revolutionary Marxist" but not a member of the Communist party. His writings and activities rendered him excludable under the pre-1990 version of INA §§ 212(a)(28)(D) and (G)(v), reprinted above, as one who advocates or teaches "the economic, international, and governmental doctrines of world communism." He had visited the United States twice before filing the unsuccessful visa application that led to this litigation. Both times, apparently unbeknownst to him, he was the beneficiary of a waiver, in accordance with INA § 212(d)(3), of his excludability under § 212(a)(28). In 1969, he applied for a nonimmigrant visa to attend conferences in the United States. He was informed of his excludability, and after several rounds of correspondence, he was told that the Attorney General would not grant a waiver this time, because, in the Attorney General's view, he had violated the terms of his earlier admissions by deviating from the stated purposes of those trips. Mandel and several of those who had invited him to this country filed suit. The District Court ruled for the plaintiffs.]

* * *

II

Until 1875 alien migration to the United States was unrestricted. The Act of March 3, 1875, 18 Stat. 477, barred convicts and prostitutes. Seven years later Congress passed the first general immigration statute. Act of Aug. 3, 1882, 22 Stat. 214. Other legislation followed. A general revision of the immigration laws was effected by the Act of Mar. 3, 1903, 32 Stat. 1213. Section 2 of that Act made ineligible for admission "anarchists, or persons who believe in or advocate the overthrow by force or violence of the Government of the United States or of all government or of all forms of law." By the Act of Oct. 16, 1918, 40 Stat. 1012, Congress expanded the provisions for the exclusion of subversive aliens. Title II of the Alien Registration Act of 1940, 54 Stat. 671, amended the 1918 Act to bar aliens who, at any time, had advocated or were members of or affiliated with organizations that advocated violent overthrow of the United States Government.

In the years that followed, after extensive investigation and numerous reports by congressional committees, see *Communist Party v. Subversive Activities Control Board,* 367 U.S. 1, 94 n. 37, 81 S.Ct. 1357, 1409 n. 37, 6 L.Ed.2d 625 (1961), Congress passed the Internal Security Act of 1950, 64 Stat. 987. This Act dispensed with the requirement of the 1940 Act of a finding in each case, with respect to members of the Communist Party, that the party did in fact advocate violent overthrow of the Government. These provisions were carried forward into the Immigration and Nationality Act of 1952.

We thus have almost continuous attention on the part of Congress since 1875 to the problems of immigration and of excludability of certain defined classes of aliens. The pattern generally has been one of increasing control with particular attention, for almost 70 years now, first to anarchists and then to those with communist affiliation or views.

III

It is clear that Mandel personally, as an unadmitted and nonresident alien, had no constitutional right of entry to this country as a nonimmigrant or otherwise. *United States ex rel. Turner v. Williams,* 194 U.S. 279, 292, 24 S.Ct. 719, 723, 48 L.Ed. 979 (1904); *United States ex rel. Knauff v. Shaughnessy,* 338 U.S. 537, 542, 70 S.Ct. 309, 312, 94 L.Ed. 317 (1950); *Galvan v. Press,* 347 U.S. 522, 530–532, 74 S.Ct. 737, 742–743, 98 L.Ed. 911 (1954); *see Harisiades v. Shaughnessy,* 342 U.S. 580, 592, 72 S.Ct. 512, 520, 96 L.Ed. 586 (1952).

The appellees concede this. Indeed, the American appellees assert that "they sue to enforce their rights, individually and as members of the American public, and assert none on the part of the invited alien." "Dr. Mandel is in a sense made a plaintiff because he is symbolic of the problem."

The case, therefore, comes down to the narrow issue whether the First Amendment confers upon the appellee professors, because they wish to hear, speak, and debate with Mandel in person, the ability to determine that Mandel should be permitted to enter the country or, in other words, to compel the Attorney General to allow Mandel's admission.

Issue

IV

In a variety of contexts this Court has referred to a First Amendment right to "receive information and ideas":

> "It is now well established that the Constitution protects the right to receive information and ideas. 'This freedom [of speech and press] ... necessarily protects the right to receive....'"

* * *

In the present case, the District Court majority held:

> "The concern of the First Amendment is not with a non-resident alien's individual and personal interest in entering and being heard, but with the rights of the citizens of the country to have the alien enter and to hear him explain and seek to defend his views; that, as *Garrison* [*v. Louisiana,* 379 U.S. 64, 85 S.Ct. 209, 13 L.Ed.2d 125 (1964)] and *Red Lion* [*Broadcasting Co. v. FCC,* 395 U.S. 367, 89 S.Ct. 1794, 23 L.Ed.2d 371 (1969)] observe, is of the essence of self-government." 325 F.Supp., at 631.

The Government disputes this conclusion on two grounds. First, it argues that exclusion of Mandel involves no restriction on First Amendment rights at all since what is restricted is "only action—the action of the alien in coming into this country." Principal reliance is placed on *Zemel v. Rusk*, 381 U.S. 1, 85 S.Ct. 1271, 14 L.Ed.2d 179 (1965), where the Government's refusal to validate an American passport for travel to Cuba was upheld. The rights asserted there were those of the passport applicant himself. The Court held that his right to travel and his asserted ancillary right to inform himself about Cuba did not outweigh substantial "foreign policy considerations affecting all citizens" that, with the backdrop of the Cuban missile crisis, were characterized as the "weightiest considerations of national security." *Id.*, at 13, 16, 85 S.Ct., at 1279. The rights asserted here, in some contrast, are those of American academics who have invited Mandel to participate with them in colloquia debates, and discussion in the United States. In light of the Court's previous decisions concerning the "right to receive information," we cannot realistically say that the problem facing us disappears entirely or is nonexistent because the mode of regulation bears directly on physical movement.

* * *

The Government also suggests that the First Amendment is inapplicable because appellees have free access to Mandel's ideas through his books and speeches, and because "technological developments," such as tapes or telephone hook-ups, readily supplant his physical presence. This argument overlooks what may be particular qualities inherent in sustained, face-to-face debate, discussion and questioning. While alternative means of access to Mandel's ideas might be a relevant factor were we called upon to balance First Amendment rights against governmental regulatory interests—a balance we find unnecessary here in light of the discussion that follows in Part V—we are loath to hold on this record that existence of other alternatives extinguishes altogether any constitutional interest on the part of the appellees in this particular form of access.

V

Recognition that First Amendment rights are implicated, however, is not dispositive of our inquiry here. In accord with ancient principles of the international law of nation-states, the Court in *The Chinese Exclusion Case*, 130 U.S. 581, 609, 9 S.Ct. 623, 631, 32 L.Ed. 1068 (1889), and in *Fong Yue Ting v. United States*, 149 U.S. 698, 13 S.Ct. 1016, 37 L.Ed. 905 (1893), held broadly, as the Government describes it, that the power to exclude aliens is "inherent in sovereignty, necessary for maintaining normal international relations and defending the country against foreign encroachments and dangers—a power to be exercised exclusively by the political branches of government...." Since that time, the Court's general reaffirmations of this principle have been legion. The Court without exception has sustained Congress' "plenary power to make rules for the admission of aliens and to exclude those who possess those characteristics which Congress has forbidden." *Boutilier v. Immigration and Naturalization Service*, 387 U.S. 118, 123, 87 S.Ct. 1563, 1567, 18 L.Ed.2d 661 (1967). "[O]ver no conceivable subject is the legislative power of Congress more complete than it is over" the admission of aliens. *Oceanic Navigation Co. v. Stranahan,* 214 U.S. 320, 339, 29 S.Ct. 671, 676, 53 L.Ed. 1013 (1909).

* * *

We are not inclined in the present context to reconsider this line of cases. Indeed, the appellees, in contrast to the *amicus,* do not ask that we do so. The appellees recognize the force of these many precedents. In seeking to sustain the decision below, they concede that Congress could enact a blanket prohibition against entry of all aliens falling into the class defined by §§ 212(a)(28)(D) and (G)(v), and that First Amendment rights could not override that decision. But they contend that by providing a waiver procedure, Congress clearly intended that persons ineligible under the broad provision of the section would be temporarily admitted when appropriate "for humane reasons and for reasons of public interest." S.Rep.No. 1137, 82d Cong., 2d Sess., 12 (1952). They argue that the Executive's implementation of this congressional mandate through decision whether to grant a waiver in each individual case must be limited by the First Amendment rights of persons like appellees. Specifically, their position is that the First Amendment rights must prevail, at least where the Government advances no justification for failing to grant a waiver. They point to the fact that waivers have been granted in the vast majority of cases.[7]

Appellees' First Amendment argument would prove too much. In almost every instance of an alien excludable under § 212(a)(28), there are probably those who would wish to meet and speak with him. The ideas of most such aliens might not be so influential as those of Mandel, nor his American audience so numerous, nor the planned discussion forums so impressive. But the First Amendment does not protect only the articulate, the well known, and the popular. Were we to endorse the proposition that governmental power to withhold a waiver must yield whenever a bona fide claim is made that American citizens wish to meet and talk with an alien excludable under § 212(a)(28), one of two unsatisfactory results would necessarily ensue. Either every claim would prevail, in which case the plenary discretionary authority Congress granted the Executive becomes a nullity, or courts in each case would be required to weigh the strength of

7. The Government's brief states: "The Immigration and Naturalization Service reports the following with respect to applications to the Attorney General for waiver of an alien's ineligibility for admission under Section 212(a)(28):

"Year	Total Number of Applications for Waiver of Section 212(a)(28)	Number of Waivers Granted	Number of Waivers Denied
1971	6210	6196	14
1970	6193	6189	4
1969	4993	4984	9
1968	4184	4176	8
1967	3860	3852	8"

Brief for Appellants 18 n. 24. These cases, however, are only those that, as § 212(d)(3)(A) provides, come to the Attorney General with a positive recommendation from the Secretary of State or the consular officer. The figures do not include those cases where these officials had refrained from making a positive recommendation.

the audience's interest against that of the Government in refusing a waiver to the particular alien applicant, according to some as yet undetermined standard. The dangers and the undesirability of making that determination on the basis of factors such as the size of the audience or the probity of the speaker's ideas are obvious. Indeed, it is for precisely this reason that the waiver decision has, properly, been placed in the hands of the Executive.

Appellees seek to soften the impact of this analysis by arguing, as has been noted, that the First Amendment claim should prevail, at least where no justification is advanced for denial of a waiver. The Government would have us reach this question, urging a broad decision that Congress has delegated the waiver decision to the Executive in its sole and unfettered discretion, and any reason or no reason may be given. This record, however, does not require that we do so, for the Attorney General did inform Mandel's counsel of the reason for refusing him a waiver. And that reason was facially legitimate and bona fide.

* * *

In summary, plenary congressional power to make policies and rules for exclusion of aliens has long been firmly established. In the case of an alien excludable under § 212(a)(28), Congress has delegated conditional exercise of this power to the Executive. We hold that when the Executive exercises this power negatively on the basis of a facially legitimate and bona fide reason, the courts will neither look behind the exercise of that discretion, nor test it by balancing its justification against the First Amendment interests of those who seek personal communication with the applicant. What First Amendment or other grounds may be available for attacking exercise of discretion for which no justification whatsoever is advanced is a question we neither address or decide in this case.

Reversed.

Mr. Justice Douglas, dissenting.

Under *The Chinese Exclusion Case*, 130 U.S. 581, 9 S.Ct. 623, 32 L.Ed. 1068, rendered in 1889, there could be no doubt but that Congress would have the power to exclude any class of aliens from these shores. The accent at the time was on race. Mr. Justice Field, writing for the Court, said: "If, therefore, the government of the United States, through its legislative department, considers the presence of foreigners of a different race in this country, who will not assimilate with us, to be dangerous to its peace and security, their exclusion is not to be stayed because at the time there are no actual hostilities with the nation of which the foreigners are subjects." *Id.*, at 606, 9 S.Ct., at 630.

An ideological test, not a racial one, is used here. But neither, in my view, is permissible, as I have indicated on other occasions. Yet a narrower question is raised here.

* * *

As a matter of statutory construction, I conclude that Congress never undertook to entrust the Attorney General with the discretion to pick and choose among the ideological offerings which alien lecturers tender from our platforms, allowing those palatable to him and disallowing others. The discretion entrusted to him concerns matters commonly within the competence of the Department of Justice—national security, importation of drugs, and the like.

I would affirm the judgment of the three-judge District Court.

MR. JUSTICE MARSHALL, with whom MR. JUSTICE BRENNAN joins, dissenting.

* * *

I * * * am stunned to learn that a country with our proud heritage has refused Dr. Mandel temporary admission. I am convinced that Americans cannot be denied the opportunity to hear Dr. Mandel's views in person because their Government disapproves of his ideas. Therefore, I dissent from today's decision and would affirm the judgment of the court below.

* * *

Today's majority apparently holds that Mandel may be excluded and Americans' First Amendment rights restricted because the Attorney General has given a "facially legitimate and bona fide reason" for refusing to waive Mandel's visa ineligibility. I do not understand the source of this unusual standard. Merely "legitimate" governmental interests cannot override constitutional rights. Moreover, the majority demands only "facial" legitimacy and good faith, by which it means that this Court will never "look behind" any reason the Attorney General gives. No citation is given for this kind of unprecedented deference to the Executive, nor can I imagine (nor am I told) the slightest justification for such a rule.

Even the briefest peek behind the Attorney General's reason for refusing a waiver in this case would reveal that it is a sham. The Attorney General informed appellees' counsel that the waiver was refused because Mandel's activities on a previous American visit "went far beyond the stated purposes of his trip ... and represented a flagrant abuse of the opportunities afforded him to express his views in this country." But, as the Department of State had already conceded to appellees' counsel, Dr. Mandel "was apparently not informed that [his previous] visa was issued only after obtaining a waiver of ineligibility and therefore [Mandel] may not have been aware of the conditions and limitations attached to the [previous] visa issuance." There is *no* basis in the present record for concluding that Mandel's behavior on his previous visit was a "flagrant abuse"—or even willful or knowing departure—from visa restrictions. For good reason, the Government in this litigation has *never* relied on the Attorney General's reason to justify Mandel's exclusion. In these circumstances, the Attorney General's reason cannot possibly support a decision for the Government in this case. But without even remanding for a factual hearing to see if there is *any* support for the Attorney General's determination, the majority declares that his reason is sufficient to override appellees' First Amendment interests.

Even if the Attorney General had given a compelling reason for declining to grant a waiver under § 212(d)(3)(A), this would not, for me, end the case. As I understand the statutory scheme, Mandel is "ineligible" for a visa, and therefore inadmissible, solely because, within the terms of § 212(a)(28), he has advocated communist doctrine and has published writings advocating that doctrine. The waiver question under § 212(d)(3)(A) is totally secondary and dependent, since it is triggered here only by a determination of (a)(28) ineligibility.

* * *

Accordingly, I turn to consider the constitutionality of the sole justification given by the Government here and below for excluding Mandel— that he "advocates" and "publish[es] . . . printed matter . . . advocating . . . doctrines of world communism" within the terms of § 212(a)(28).

Still adhering to standard First Amendment doctrine, I do not see how (a)(28) can possibly represent a compelling governmental interest that overrides appellees' interests in hearing Mandel. Unlike (a)(27) or (a)(29), (a)(28) does not claim to exclude aliens who are likely to engage in subversive activity or who represent an active and present threat to the "welfare, safety, or security of the United States." Rather, (a)(28) excludes aliens solely because they have advocated communist doctrine. Our cases make clear, however, that government has no legitimate interest in stopping the flow of ideas. It has no power to restrict the mere advocacy of communist doctrine, divorced from incitement to imminent lawless action. *Noto v. United States,* 367 U.S. 290, 297–298, 81 S.Ct. 1517, 1520–1521, 6 L.Ed.2d 836 (1961); *Brandenburg v. Ohio,* 395 U.S. 444, 447–449, 89 S.Ct. 1827, 1829–1831, 23 L.Ed.2d 430 (1969). For those who are not sure that they have attained the final and absolute truth, all ideas, even those forcefully urged, are a contribution to the ongoing political dialogue. The First Amendment represents the view of the Framers that "the path of safety lies in the opportunity to discuss freely supposed grievances and proposed remedies; and that the fitting remedy for evil counsels is good ones"—"more speech." *Whitney v. California,* 274 U.S., at 375, 377, 47 S.Ct., at 648, 649, 71 L.Ed. 1095 (Brandeis, J., concurring).

* * *

The heart of Appellants' position in this case * * * is that the Government's power is distinctively broad and unreviewable because "[t]he regulation in question is directed at the admission of aliens." Thus, in the appellants' view, this case is no different from a long line of cases holding that the power to exclude aliens is left exclusively to the "political" branches of Government, Congress, and the Executive.

These cases are not the strongest precedents in the United States Reports, and the majority's baroque approach reveals its reluctance to rely on them completely. They include such milestones as *The Chinese Exclusion Case,* 130 U.S. 581, 9 S.Ct. 623, 32 L.Ed. 1068 (1889), and *Fong Yue Ting v. United States,* 149 U.S. 698, 13 S.Ct. 1016, 37 L.Ed. 905 (1893), in which this Court upheld the Government's power to exclude and expel Chinese aliens from our midst.

But none of these old cases must be "reconsidered" or overruled to strike down Dr. Mandel's exclusion, for none of them was concerned with the rights of American citizens. All of them involved only rights of the excluded aliens themselves. At least when the rights of Americans are involved, there is no basis for concluding that the power to exclude aliens is absolute. "When Congress' exercise of one of its enumerated powers clashes with those individual liberties protected by the Bill of Rights, it is our 'delicate and difficult task' to determine whether the resulting restriction on freedom can be tolerated." *United States v. Robel*, 389 U.S. 258, 264, 88 S.Ct. 419, 424, 19 L.Ed.2d 508 (1967).

* * *

I do not mean to suggest that simply because some Americans wish to hear an alien speak, they can automatically compel even his temporary admission to our country. Government may prohibit aliens from even temporary admission if exclusion is necessary to protect a compelling governmental interest.[6] Actual threats to the national security, public health needs, and genuine requirements of law enforcement are the most apparent interests that would surely be compelling. But in Dr. Mandel's case, the Government has, and claims, no such compelling interest. Mandel's visit was to be temporary. His "ineligibility" for a visa was based solely on § 212(a)(28). The only governmental interest embodied in that section is the Government's desire to keep certain ideas out of circulation in this country. This is hardly a compelling governmental interest. Section (a)(28) may not be the basis for excluding an alien when Americans wish to hear him. Without any claim that Mandel "live" is an actual threat to this country, there is no difference between excluding Mandel because of his ideas and keeping his books out because of their ideas. Neither is permitted.

* * *

Notes

1. Some commentators treat *Mandel* as deciding only the applicability of the First Amendment to the waiver scheme. In this view, the case left open the constitutional validity of § 212(a)(28) itself. *See, e.g.*, Note, *Judicial Review of Visa Denials: Reexamining Consular Nonreviewability*, 52 N.Y.U.L.Rev. 1137, 1149 (1977); Committee on Immigration and Nationality Law of the Association of the Bar of the City of New York, *Visa Denials on Ideological Grounds: An Update*, 8 Seton Hall Legis. J. 249 (1984–85). Is this an accurate reading of the somewhat elliptical treatment of First Amendment issues in Part V of the majority opinion? Isn't Justice Marshall correct when he states that the waiver question "is totally secondary and dependent"—meaning that the majority, despite the way it avoids direct discussion of the issue, has inescapably decided that paragraph (28) is consistent with the First Amendment?

6. I agree with the majority that courts should not inquire into such things as the "probity of the speaker's ideas." Neither should the Executive, however. Where Americans wish to hear an alien, and their claim is not a demonstrated sham, the crucial question is whether the *Government's* interest in excluding the alien is compelling.

Part of the difficulty stems from the curious construction, to say the least, of the majority opinion. The court seems to go out of its way to find that a First Amendment issue exists, only to reach an ultimate result extremely deferential to the political branches of the government, an outcome hardly characteristic of most other First Amendment cases. The majority finds a free speech issue despite its apparent acceptance of the notion that *Mandel,* "as an unadmitted and nonresident alien," would have no First Amendment rights to assert. But even on the majority's view that the First Amendment grants the other plaintiffs a right to "receive information and ideas," aren't the government defendants correct that information and ideas are not restricted by the visa denial—that the denial does not abridge speech, for it merely affects conduct or action?

The court's answer to this question is not entirely straightforward. But in any event, the majority does refuse to use the defendants' suggested analysis as a way of evading the free speech issues. Having decided to confront such issues, however, the court then resolves them by sustaining government immigration decisions whenever they are based on "a facially legitimate and bona fide reason." Is this outcome functionally similar to saying that there will be no First Amendment scrutiny in the immigration field?

2. If we are to be critical of the majority opinion, however, perhaps we should also cast a critical eye on the dissents. Justice Douglas would overturn the visa denial based solely on his reading of the statute and the underlying congressional intent. Apparently he would find that the Attorney General, under the statute, *must* waive excludability unless he finds that the alien's presence would raise concerns "commonly within the competence of the Department of Justice—national security, importation of drugs, and the like." Can this possibly have been the intent of Congress in enacting paragraph (28) and making it waivable under subsection (d)(3)? Why would Congress even add paragraph (28) when other subsections address security and criminal concerns directly?

3. Justice Marshall does not pretend to find such an improbable congressional intent, but instead bases his dissent squarely on constitutional grounds. He believes he can distinguish all the "old cases" recognizing plenary power in the political branches over the exclusion of aliens, because none of those cases, he says, involved the rights of citizens. But isn't this fact a mere accident of litigation? If Justice Marshall's views became the governing doctrine, wouldn't nearly every excluded alien be in a position to find U.S. citizens who wish to speak with him or her and who could join as co-plaintiffs? Naturally, not all excluded individuals would find so distinguished a group as Mandel found, but Marshall surely would agree with the majority that First Amendment rights do not depend on the stature or number of the would-be listeners.

Justice Marshall goes on to remind us that not all plaintiffs who wish to speak with an alien denied a visa would win under his test. But if the government must show a *compelling* interest to sustain any particular exclusion, perhaps Marshall's opinion portends far wider consequences than just an occasional overturning of denials under paragraph (28). Is there a compelling interest, tied to the factors Marshall lists—national security, public health, or law enforcement—in excluding people a consul believes are likely to become public charges? People who plan to work but have not secured labor certification? Who don't have passports good for six months? What compelling interest supports a numerical ceiling of 675,000 annually, if the ceiling is challenged by an alien who could show that he would be admitted this year under a ceiling set at 900,000? We assume of course, that he is supported by citizens who want to hear him speak—or perhaps more potently, supported by lawful permanent resident family members who want to reunite the family as well as engage in political discussions. *See Moore v. East Cleveland,* 431 U.S. 494, 503–505, 97 S.Ct. 1932, 1937–38, 52 L.Ed.2d 531 (1977) (plurality opinion) ("the Constitution protects the sanctity of the family," including the extended family). Does Marshall's theory leave any room at all for numerical ceilings? At what number do the interests supporting ceilings become compelling?

For other (and more favorable) reflections on Marshall's opinion in this case and related cases, see Scaperlanda, *Justice Thurgood Marshall and the Legacy of Dissent in Federal Alienage Cases,* 8 Geo.Imm.L.J. 1, 5–8 (1994).

4. Objections to exclusions under former INA § 212(a)(28) ran not only to the character of the persons who might be excluded thereunder, but also to the very process required to administer the section. A thoughtful article on these exclusion grounds, Scanlan, *Aliens in the Marketplace of Ideas: The Government, the Academy, and the McCarran–Walter Act,* 66 Tex.L.Rev. 1481, 1499 (1988), quotes a letter from an official of a British association of teachers declining an invitation to a U.S. conference:

> The record of actual refusals [of visas under these sections] is small, not because of the liberal attitude of the United States Government, but because many of our members, as a matter of principle, consider it anathema to have to attest to their political views and affiliations; thus, many academics will not apply because they do not wish to place themselves in the position of signing declarations to that effect.

See also Shapiro, *Ideological Exclusions: Closing the Border to Political Dissidents,* 100 Harv.L.Rev. 930 (1987).

Later Developments

If *Mandel* is properly read as holding that the Constitution places few, if any, constraints on the choice of substantive exclusion grounds, that is hardly the end of the issue. It simply means that any objections to such grounds have to be pressed in a political forum, rather than the judicial forum. Amelioration might come either through executive action—widely employing available waiver provisions—or through legislative action to amend the statute.

After the Reagan Administration took office in 1981, it began using the national security provisions of INA § 212(a) on a wider scale. Visas were denied to Hortensia Allende, the widow of Salvador Allende, a Marxist and former President of Chile; Tomas Borge, Interior Minister of Nicaragua under the Sandinista government; Roberto d'Aubuisson, the right-wing President of the Salvadoran Constitutional Assembly; General Nino Pasti, a former member of the Italian Senate and critic of U.S. deployment of nuclear missiles in Europe; and many others. *See* Note, *First Amendment and the Alien Exclusion Power—What Standard of Review?,* 4 Cardozo L.Rev. 457 (1983); Dionne, *Issue and Debate: Barring Aliens for Political Reasons,* The New York Times, Dec. 8, 1983. Administration officials cited "foreign policy reasons," and occasionally stated they did not want to provide "a propaganda platform" in the United States for the excluded individuals. Secretary of State George Shultz remarked on the Borge visa denial: "As a general proposition I think we have to favor freedom of speech, but it can get abused by people who do not wish us well, and I think we have to take some reasonable precautions about that." Atkinson, *Congressmen, Others Denounce Denial of Visas to U.S. Critics,* The Washington Post, Dec. 3, 1983, at A12.

Some of these denials were carried out under paragraph (28), but the Administration made increasing use of former paragraph (27), which provided for exclusion of persons seeking to enter "to engage in activities which would be prejudicial to the public interest, or endanger the welfare, safety, or security of the United States." Indeed, paragraph (27) was used in several instances where paragraph (28) might also have been available— leading some critics to charge that (27) was employed in order to avoid certain potential waiver provisions applicable to paragraph (28), which required detailed reporting to Congress (22 U.S.C.A. § 2691 (1988), repealed by the 1990 Act). Litigants challenged most of these visa denials. Many courts ruled against the government. The following survey of those cases reflects the major controversies that led Congress to rewrite the national security exclusion grounds in 1990.

In *Allende v. Shultz,* 605 F.Supp. 1220 (D.Mass.1985), *related decision affirmed,* 845 F.2d 1111 (1st Cir.1988), reviewing a visa denial under paragraph (27) to Hortensia Allende, the district court initially denied the government's motion for summary judgment. It ruled that the "facially legitimate and bona fide reason" test applied, but held that the explanation must meet this standard "not only in a general sense, but also within the context of the specific statutory provision on which the exclusion is based." *Id.* at 1224. Viewed in this light, the government's two arguments were insufficient. First, the government could not rely on her membership in Communist-affiliated organizations, because that matter was expressly covered by paragraph (28), a provision not invoked in the original denial. Second, the court ruled, "vague notions of foreign policy do not provide a sufficient basis for the invocation of [§ 212(a)(27)]." *Id.* at 1225. The court also declined to examine the *in camera* submissions of the defendants, at least at this stage of the case.

In *Harvard Law School Forum v. Shultz,* 633 F.Supp. 525 (D.Mass. 1986), *vacated without published opinion,* 852 F.2d 563 (1st Cir.1986), the court relied on *Allende* in issuing a preliminary injunction against certain State Department travel restrictions. The restrictions would have prevented a representative of the Palestine Liberation Organization (PLO) from going to Boston to participate in a public debate on Middle Eastern politics. The court held that the *Mandel* test was applicable, but it found that the government's reasons were not facially legitimate under the First Amendment, because they were based on the content of the proposed discussions and were "directly related to the suppression of a political debate with American citizens." *Id.* at 531.

In *Abourezk v. Reagan,* 785 F.2d 1043 (D.C.Cir.1986), the district court had sustained the challenged visa denials on the basis of its *in camera* examination of a classified affidavit submitted by the State Department. The court of appeals vacated and remanded for further proceedings. It first held, in apparent contrast to the district court in *Allende,* that "foreign policy concerns [do] rank among the national interests whose protection would justify exclusion of an alien under subsection (27)." *Id.* at 1053. But it went on to express doubt about the State Department's application of this provision based on mere *entry* or *presence* of the alien, rather than on expected *activities* after entry. Such a question might well turn, the court ruled, on whether there had been a consistent administrative practice applying the provision as the State Department was then urging. Because the record was insufficient to judge such practice, a remand was necessary.

Moreover, the court ruled that "when an alien is a member of a proscribed organization, so that subsection (28) applies, the government may bypass that provision and proceed under subsection (27) only if the reason for the threat to the 'public interest[,] * * * welfare, safety, or security' is *independent of* the fact of membership in or affiliation with the proscribed organization. Only if such an independent reason exists will the use of subsection (27) leave intact the congressionally mandated restrictions on subsection (28)"—principally the requirement of a report to Congress whenever such waivers were refused. *Id.* at 1058 (emphasis in original, footnote omitted). The court also expressed "grave concern" that the district court considered *in camera ex parte* evidence, and it placed severe limits on such consideration on remand. *Id.* at 1060–61. Judge Bork filed a lengthy dissent. The Supreme Court granted certiorari, but the Justices divided evenly, and so affirmed the court of appeals without opinion. 484 U.S. 1, 108 S.Ct. 252, 98 L.Ed.2d 1 (1987).

The remand to the district court in *Abourezk* ultimately resulted in numerous rulings, largely against the government. They are summarized in a later decision in this litigation, recaptioned *City of New York v. Baker,* 878 F.2d 507, *rehearing denied,* 888 F.2d 134 (D.C.Cir.1989). In later stages of the *Allende* case, the courts accepted the basic approach of the D.C. Circuit in *Abourezk* and ruled in favor of Mrs. Allende's cause. *See Allende v. Shultz,* 845 F.2d 1111 (1st Cir.1988).

In *Rafeedie v. INS,* 795 F.Supp. 13 (D.D.C.1992), INS sought to exclude under subsections (27) and (28) a returning lawful permanent resident apparently believed to be a high official of the Popular Front for the Liberation of Palestine. The court held that this alien could invoke full First Amendment protection and that the subsections were unconstitutional for overbreadth and vagueness.

Congressional Action

Beginning in the mid–1980s, Congress began serious consideration of proposals to change the former INA §§ 212(a)(27) and (28), to eliminate some of their more troubling applications. After enacting temporary provisions that eased the restrictions,[5] Congress finally used the occasion of the enactment of the Immigration Act of 1990 to recast completely the security-related exclusion grounds. Review INA § 212(a)(3). How did Congress choose to resolve the various issues that arose in *Allende, Abourezk,* and other recent cases? Which exclusion grounds remain potentially troubling?

Note that Congress cut back considerably on the possibility of excluding past or present members of the Communist party. The remaining exclusion ground designed for these purposes, INA § 212(a)(3)(D), applies only to immigrants. Why would Congress differentiate between immigrants and nonimmigrants in applying this exclusion ground? What theories of free speech and membership in the national community underlie such a distinction? Can a society based on tolerance validly bar prospective members based solely on past affiliation with a disapproved organization or on a disapproved ideology? On the other hand, may democratic societies legitimately be intolerant of those who do not accept the basic principle of tolerance itself? *See* Schauer, *Free Speech and the Paradox of Tolerance* in *Values in Conflict: Life, Liberty and the Rule of Law* 228 (B. Leiser ed.1981). Does the answer vary depending on how serious a threat the alternative ideology happens to be at the time?

An especially sensitive issue for Congress's consideration was the provision for foreign policy exclusions, § 212(a)(3)(C). Much of the following excerpt from the conference committee report accompanying the 1990 Act is devoted to explaining that subparagraph. After reading this excerpt and reviewing the language of all of paragraph (3), answer the questions that follow.

> Under current law there is some ambiguity as to the authority of the Executive Branch to exclude aliens on foreign policy grounds * * *. The foreign policy provision in this title would establish a single clear standard for foreign policy exclusions (which is designated as 212(a)(3)(C) of the INA). The conferees believe that granting an alien admission to the United States is not a sign of approval or agreement and the conferees therefore expect that, with the enactment of this provision, aliens will be excluded not merely because of the potential signal that might be sent because of their admission, but when there would be a clear negative foreign policy impact associated with their admission.
>
> This provision would authorize the executive branch to exclude aliens for foreign policy reasons in certain circumstances.

---

5. Pub.L. No. 100–204, § 901, 101 Stat. 1399 (1987), *modified,* Pub.L. No. 100–461, § 555, 102 Stat. 2268 (1988), Pub.L. No. 101– 246, § 128, 104 Stat. 15 (1990). *See* 67 Interp.Rel. 201 (1990).

Specifically, under this provision, an alien could be excluded only if the Secretary of State has reasonable ground to believe an alien's entry or proposed activities within the United States would have potentially serious adverse foreign policy consequences. However, there are two exceptions to this general standard.

First, an alien who is an official of a foreign government or a purported government, or who is a candidate for election to a foreign government office (and who is seeking entry into the United States during the period immediately prior to the election) would not be excludable under this provision solely because of any past, current or expected beliefs, statements or associations which would be lawful in the United States. The word "solely" is used in this provision to indicate that, in cases involving government officials, the committee intends that exclusions not be based merely on, for example, the possible content of an alien's speech in this country, but that there be some clear foreign policy impact beyond the mere fact of the speech or its content, that would permit exclusion.

In particular, the conferees expect that the authority to exclude aliens with a government connection would apply primarily to senior government officials (or candidates for senior government posts). While, as a general matter, admitting foreign government officials is not necessarily a signal of approval, the conferees recognize that in cases involving senior officials it may be difficult to avoid conveying that impression.

The second exception, which applies to all other aliens, would prevent exclusion on the basis of an alien's past, current or expected beliefs, statements or associations which would be lawful within the United States unless the Secretary of State personally determines that the alien's admission to the United States would compromise a compelling United States foreign policy interest, and so certifies to the relevant Congressional Committees. It is the intent of the conference committee that this authority would be used sparingly and not merely because there is a likelihood that an alien will make critical remarks about the United States or its policies.

Furthermore, the conferees intend that the "compelling foreign policy interest" standard be interpreted as a significantly higher standard than the general "potentially serious adverse foreign policy consequences standard." In particular, the conferees note that the general exclusion standard in this provision refers only to the "potential" for serious adverse foreign policy consequences, whereas exclusion under the second exception (under which an alien can be excluded because of his beliefs, statements or associations) must be linked to a "compelling" foreign policy interest. The fact that the Secretary of State personally must inform the relevant Congressional Committees when a determination of excludability is made under this provision is a further indication that the conferees intend that this provision be used only in unusual circumstances.

With regard to the second exception, the following include some of the circumstances in which exclusion might be appropriate: when an alien's mere entry into the United States could result in imminent harm to the lives or property of United States persons abroad or to property of the United States government abroad (as occurred with the former Shah of Iran), or when an alien's entry would violate a treaty or international agreement to which the United States is party.

* * *

[Further, it] is the intent of the conferees that aliens who would previously have been excludable under section 212(a)(28) because of membership in or affiliation with the Communist party, but who are no longer excludable for that reason because of the changes made in this provision, would not be excludable under the new foreign policy grounds established by this legislation merely because of such membership or affiliation.

* * *

For the purposes of this legislation, the conferees consider a "terrorist organization" to be one whose leadership, or whose members, with the knowledge, approval or acquiescence of the leadership, have taken part in terrorist activities. In making determinations for the purpose of establishing excludability, the Department of State (or the Immigration Service when appropriate) should take into account the best available information from the intelligence community. A group may be considered a terrorist organization even if it has not conducted terrorist operations in the past several years, but there is reason to believe it still has the capability and inclination to conduct such operations.

H.R.Rep. No. 101–955, at 128–131 (1990).

Notes

1. Assume that Vladimir Zhirinovsky, the bellicose ultranationalist member of the Russian parliament who is often given to anti-Semitic remarks, is now running for election as Russian President. He applies for a B visa to travel to New York to speak to supporters there and perhaps to raise funds for his campaign. The Assistant Secretary of State with responsibility for Europe does not want to do anything that might suggest, to the U.S. public or to the Russian voters, that the United States supports his candidacy. He also wants to exclude Zhirinovsky as an expression of U.S. human rights policy. Should the Russian be excludable? Can he be excluded under the current version of INA § 212(a)(3)? Would it be harder or easier to exclude him if he were neither a candidate nor a government official?

In late 1993, several west European countries in fact barred Zhirinovsky from entry or forced him to leave abruptly, owing to his political positions or the inflammatory speeches he had been giving. These actions by the immigration authorities there drew praise from some American journalists not terribly sympathetic to earlier "ideological exclusions." One wrote:

> And who has stepped up to set the example for dealing with a slavering bigot? Hold your hats. It is Germany[, which] * * * took action against the antisemite of the year, Vladimir Zhirinovsky. On his post-election tour of Europe, the "Liberal Democrat" Russian fascist made a stop in Munich to meet with a former SS man. But when he applied for a visa to return, the Germans turned him down. * * * "The German government," went the official statement, "has no interest in having Zhirinovsky make his extreme right-wing statements in Germany." That was well said [sic].

McGrory, *I Miss Manners*, Wash. Post, Jan. 2, 1994, at C1.

As it happened, Zhirinovsky did schedule a speaking trip to the United States in October 1994, and he received a visa rather routinely. The consulate in Moscow stated that it found his views "anathema," but that the visa was issued under this country's "long and respected tradition of allowing freedom of speech to all persons." Hiatt, *Zhirinovsky Gets Visa for Speech in U.S.*, Wash. Post, Nov. 2, 1994, at A29. Was the U.S. right and Germany wrong? Or vice versa?

2. Could § 212(a)(3) be used to deny a U.S. visitor's visa to Raoul Cédras, ruler of Haiti after a coup that ousted the elected president in September 1991, who was himself exiled after the U.S.-led intervention in September 1994? Would it make a difference whether he wished to come for a vacation or instead to give speeches and raise money from supporters among Haitian exiles in this country? Could his wife (who apparently played an important behind-the-scenes role during the military's rule) be denied a visitor's visa?

3. How would § 212(a)(3) apply to an alien avowedly coming to the United States to raise funds for the nonviolent community organizing and child-care activities of a radical group closely affiliated with the Red Brigades of Italy (the group responsible in 1978 for the kidnapping and eventual murder of former Italian Prime Minister Aldo Moro)? Should such a person be excludable? Would it depend on the government's information about the actual use of the funds? How would the government know how the funds were to be used? How should its information be tested, particularly if it comes from classified sources or from individuals who have infiltrated the organization and would be severely endangered if their role in providing the information were somehow traceable?

4. The Conference report suggests that the Shah of Iran could have been excluded from the United States (his entry in 1979 after his government fell triggered the seizure of U.S. diplomats as hostages in Tehran). Is that result consistent with the language of § 212(a)(3)(C)? Wouldn't any concern about the repercussions of his entry have been based on associa-

tions—associations that would have been lawful in the United States because of the First Amendment?

5. Section 212(a)(3)(C) links its protections to a judgment about what "beliefs, statements or associations would be lawful within the United States." This language is evidently meant to incorporate constitutional standards under the First Amendment. But most First Amendment judgments are highly contextual; look again at the *Brandenburg* test, *supra* p. 344. Earlier tests employed by the Supreme Court are even more closely linked to context and circumstance: Was the theater crowded or empty? When he shouted "fire," was the shout an obvious jest? In applying § 212(a)(3) to the statements or associations of aliens undertaken in foreign countries, how much of the foreign country's context do we import for our comparison? For example, if the statements that prompt the U.S. government to attempt exclusion were made by a supporter of the Sendero Luminoso in Peru (a violent Maoist guerrilla organization), do we test them against our Constitution on the assumption that Maoist terrorism has spread through our countryside? (We will return to some of these questions in Chapter Six in connection with the *Harisiades* case, pp. 518–26.)

Implementation

In amending the national security exclusion provisions in 1990, Congress was concerned lest the procedures used to implement the earlier grounds continue to hamper the entry of aliens no longer covered. It therefore added § 601(c) to the 1990 Act (not codified in the INA), directing the Attorney General and the Secretary of State to develop "protocols and guidelines for updating lookout books and the automated visa lookout system and similar mechanisms." The new guidelines had to ensure that aliens whose names were in the system would either have their names removed upon request or upon applying for entry, if no longer covered because of the amendments to the exclusion grounds, or else would be informed that they had been found still excludable under the new grounds. Even stronger provisions to require purging of the State Department's system within three years and to protect against ill-founded exclusions on terrorist or foreign policy grounds were included in the Foreign Relations Authorization Act for FY 1992–93, Pub.L.No. 102–138, §§ 127, 128, 105 Stat. 647 (1991). For the State Department's report on its efforts in this regard, see 69 Interp.Rel. 576 (1992).

In 1993 concern over the automated visa lookout system (AVLOS) shifted sharply, however—away from worries about improperly excluding people and toward worries about failing to exclude dangerous individuals. Much of the concern was prompted by the admission of Sheik Omar Ahmed Abdel Rahman for permanent residence in 1991, via Khartoum. Rahman is a blind Egyptian cleric and leader of a fundamentalist Islamic sect. Some of his followers were allegedly responsible for bombing the World Trade Center in New York. Although Rahman's name was in the lookout system, the consulate in Khartoum was not equipped to use the computerized database, and the consular officer failed to find his name on the crude microfiche system in place there. The problem likewise went unnoticed at the time of Rahman's actual admission. In the subsequent furor over these errors, the State Department initiated a round of reforms, and Congress eventually appropriated extra money to upgrade the lookout system. *See* Royce, *Visa Lookout Failed*, Newsday, July 23, 1993, at 33. For the litigation over Rahman's own status in this country, see *Ali v. Reno*, 829 F.Supp. 1415 (S.D.N.Y.1993).

In the investigations prompted by the World Trade Center bombing, it also was revealed that several individuals convicted in earlier years in Cairo of involvement in terrorism were not placed in the lookout system. A State Department official explained that this was because "mere membership in or affiliation with a terrorist organization, except in the case of the PLO, does not constitute a ground for ineligibility" under the Immigration Act of 1990. Congressman Lantos, chair of the House international security subcommittee, called this a "totally insane interpretation." Royce, *supra*. Another official stated that even some persons convicted of terrorist acts may receive visas unless there is reason to believe they would commit such acts in the U.S. And those who appeal or who were convicted in absentia are usually not listed. *Id.* Review INA § 212(a)(3). Are these interpretations wrong, or has the congressional wind simply shifted?

These episodes have also renewed congressional interest in making the security-related exclusion grounds more stringent. *See* Note, *Congressional Proposals to Revive Guilt by Association: An Ineffective Plan to Stop Terrorism*, 8 Geo.Imm.L.J. 227, 240–45 (1994). What changes would you favor, if any, to cope more effectively with terrorist activity?

———

Judgments about the drafting and application of security-related exclusion grounds may be affected by an assessment of the government officials who will be involved in applying them. In particular, some of these grounds, arguably impairing First Amendment rights, might be more tolerable if ultimately applied by judges, rather than by consular officers. We therefore pause to consider the availability of judicial review of visa denials.

3. A BRIEF DIGRESSION: JUDICIAL REVIEW OF CONSULAR VISA DENIALS

In cases construing and applying the Administrative Procedure Act (APA), 5 U.S.C.A. §§ 701–706, the Supreme Court has held that agency action today is presumptively reviewable in the courts, absent clear signals from the Congress making judicial review inapplicable. *See Lincoln v. Vigil*, ___ U.S. ___, ___, 113 S.Ct. 2024, 2030, 124 L.Ed.2d 101 (1993); *Abbott Laboratories v. Gardner*, 387 U.S. 136, 140–41, 87 S.Ct. 1507, 1510–12, 18 L.Ed.2d 681 (1967).[6] But consular decisions made overseas are still generally held to be beyond the reach of the courts, largely because of the way that lower courts have construed the holding of *Kleindienst v. Mandel*.

6. The Court has been more willing in recent years, however, to find that the totality of the statutory scheme precludes or narrowly channels judicial review. *See, e.g., Thunder Basin Coal Co. v. Reich*, 114 S.Ct. 771 (1994).

This doctrine applies not only to a person seeking a visa for a short vacation or business trip to the United States, but also to a person seeking an immigrant visa based on his or her relation to a U.S. citizen or permanent resident alien.

PENA v. KISSINGER

United States District Court, Southern District of New York, 1976.
409 F.Supp. 1182.

POLLACK, DISTRICT JUDGE.

Plaintiff seeks review of the allegedly capricious decision of the American Consul in Santo Domingo denying an immigrant visa to her husband, Francisco A. Pena, a Dominican Republic, Western Hemisphere citizen who intends to work in the United States. Plaintiff is also a native and citizen of the Dominican Republic, but is a lawful permanent resident of the United States.

Mr. Pena applied for the visa as the spouse of a lawful permanent resident of the United States. The Consul, a defendant herein, denied his application on the ground that Pena's marriage to the plaintiff was a sham and undertaken to facilitate his immigration to the United States.

Plaintiff sues for a declaratory judgment that her marriage to Pena is a valid one, and for a direction to the Consul to process Pena's visa application on that basis.   * * *

The defendants, officials of the State Department and a consulate employee, have moved pursuant to Fed.R.Civ.P. 56 for summary judgment on the grounds that the plaintiff lacks standing to sue, that a consul's denial of a visa application is not subject to judicial review, and that mandamus jurisdiction may not be invoked against consular officials in regard to the processing of visas.

While the outcome might be different if this Court were "writing on a clean slate," *Galvan v. Press,* 347 U.S. 522, 530, 74 S.Ct. 737, 742, 98 L.Ed. 911, 921 (1954) (Frankfurter, J.), the defendants' motion for summary judgment must be granted partially and the complaint dismissed insofar as it seeks declaratory and injunctive relief.

* * *

C. JUDICIAL REVIEW

Notwithstanding plaintiff's standing to bring suit, the government maintains that the decision of an American consul to deny a visa to an alien is not subject to review in the courts. The precedents do appear to distinguish between a decision to deport an alien who is already in the United States and a decision to exclude or deny admission to an alien who remains outside; review is permitted of the former even where the alien initially gained admission illegally, but denied of the latter. *See, e.g., United States ex rel. Knauff v. Shaughnessy,* 338 U.S. 537, 543, 70 S.Ct. 309, 312, 94 L.Ed. 317, 324 (1950); *Shaughnessy v. United States ex rel. Mezei,* 345 U.S. 206, 73 S.Ct. 625, 97 L.Ed. 956 (1953).

Thus, there is substantial support in the cases for the government's position that consular decisions in regard to the issuance of visas are unreviewable. In *United States ex rel. London v. Phelps,* 22 F.2d 288 (2d Cir.1927), *cert. denied,* 276 U.S. 630, 48 S.Ct. 324, 72 L.Ed. 741 (1928), the Second Circuit declared:

> Whether the consul has acted reasonably or unreasonably is not for us to determine. Unjustifiable refusal to visé a passport may be ground for diplomatic complaint by the nation whose subject has been discriminated against.... It is beyond the jurisdiction of the court. 22 F.2d at 290.

A similar view was expressed in *United States ex rel. Ulrich v. Kellogg,* 58 App.D.C. 360, 30 F.2d 984, *cert. denied,* 279 U.S. 868, 49 S.Ct. 482, 73 L.Ed. 1005 (1929). These cases have been cited as authority in more recent decisions which find such consular decision-making immune from judicial scrutiny. *See Loza–Bedoya v. INS,* 410 F.2d 343 (9th Cir.1969); *Licea-Gomez v. Pilliod,* 193 F.Supp. 577 (N.D.Ill.1960).

As a consequence, American Consuls appear free to act arbitrarily or even maliciously in their conduct toward foreign nationals seeking entrance into the United States. This result has been labelled "brutal," and a "trivializ[ation] [of] the great guarantees of due process," Hart, *The Power of Congress to Limit the Jurisdiction of Federal Courts: An Exercise in Dialectic,* 66 Harv.L.Rev. 1362, 1395 (1953), as well as "an astonishing anomaly in American jurisprudence," Rosenfield, *Consular Non–Reviewability: A Case Study in Administrative Absolutism,* 41 Amer.Bar Assoc.J. 1109, 1110 (1955).

The law has undergone considerable change since the decisions were rendered in *London, Ulrich, Knauff* and *Mezei.* The rights afforded to aliens have been expanded, whether they are in the United States lawfully, or interacting with American officials outside the United States. Similarly, the Courts have adopted a more favorable attitude to the reviewability of administrative action under the Administrative Procedure Act. Since that Act applies to action by the State Department involving immigration matters, *see Rusk v. Cort,* 369 U.S. 367, 82 S.Ct. 787, 7 L.Ed.2d 809 (1962), it might have been expected that the "astonishing anomaly" of consular non-reviewability would also undergo change.

Indeed, while the Supreme Court asserted in *Knauff* that "it is not within the province of any court, *unless expressly authorized by law,* to review the determination of the political branch of the Government to exclude a given alien," 338 U.S. at 543, 70 S.Ct. at 312 (emphasis added), it subsequently declared in *Rusk v. Cort, supra,* that exceptions to the APA's presumption of reviewability of decisions made under the Immigration and Nationality Act would not be made "in the absence of clear and convincing evidence that Congress so intended." 369 U.S. at 380, 82 S.Ct. at 794. Thus, it appears true that "the courts have liberalized the standard governing reviewability" of administrative action in the immigration area.

Nonetheless, the Supreme Court in *Kleindienst v. Mandel,* 408 U.S. 753, 92 S.Ct. 2576, 33 L.Ed.2d 683 (1972), has recently reaffirmed the older authorities which restrict the reviewability of decisions by immigration officials. It appears that if plaintiff's claim to review here is controlled by *Mandel,* the defendants are entitled to summary judgment on the issue discussed.

* * *

[In *Mandel,* the] Supreme Court recognized that "First Amendment rights are implicated," but held that judicial review was unavailable where the government had acted on "the basis of a facially legitimate and bona fide reason." In reaching that conclusion the Court relied upon—and explicitly declined to reconsider—an 1895 opinion in which the Court had declared:

> The power of congress to exclude aliens altogether from the United States, or to prescribe the terms and conditions upon which they may come to this country, and to have its declared policy in that regard enforced exclusively through executive officers, *without judicial intervention,* is settled by our previous adjudications. 408 U.S. at 766, 92 S.Ct. at 2583 (emphasis added), citing *Lem Moon Sing v. United States,* 158 U.S. 538, 547, 15 S.Ct. 967, 970, 39 L.Ed. 1082, 1085.

Consequently, the Court concluded that it was unnecessary to balance the plaintiffs' First Amendment rights against the government's interest in excluding Mandel.

In holding that the Courts may not "look behind the exercise" of an official's discretionary authority to deny admission to an alien, the *Mandel* Court has seemingly precluded Mrs. Pena's ability to invoke judicial scrutiny of the Consul's denial of a visa to her husband. That result might be different were it possible to characterize the review sought here as involving only the Consul's decision concerning the *bona fides* of plaintiff's marriage, and not the visa denial. Such a characterization would be disingenuous, however, since the status of the marriage is merely an element in Mr. Pena's eligibility for a visa. The Consul's determination regarding the marriage is the "facially legitimate and bona fide reason" which is the basis for the discretionary decision on the visa application; as such, *Mandel* interdicts Court examination of the Consul's determination.

This result may seem anomalous, since the Courts are not reluctant to review the validity of marriages, even in the immigration context, where the challenged decision has been made by an official of the Immigration and Naturalization Service as distinguished from a Consul in the employ of the State Department. Moreover, judicial review is common of agency determinations—involving the denial of a labor certification—made pursuant to * * * the very statute under which the defendants here acted when they determined that Mr. Pena was subject to the labor requirement because his marriage was spurious.[a]

---

a. Before the 1990 amendments, the labor certification requirement presumptively applied to all aliens seeking to enter "for the purpose of performing skilled or unskilled labor." The alien could rebut the presumption, in essence, by showing that he qualified for family-sponsored immigration. In the *Pena* case, once the consul determined that the marriage was a sham, he invoked the presumption. He did not follow an alterna-

It is thus arguable that the plaintiff should nonetheless be entitled to judicial review here to assure, at a minimum, that her constitutional right to procedural due process has been satisfied by the Consul's decision-making procedures. As a resident legal alien, plaintiff is entitled to the full panoply of constitutional protection. Consequently, while "[w]hatever the procedure authorized by Congress is, it is due process as far as an alien denied entry is concerned," *United States ex rel. Knauff v. Shaughnessy, supra,* 338 U.S. at 544, 70 S.Ct. at 313, 94 L.Ed. at 325, it may not be due process as far as it affects an American citizen or permanent resident alien who has standing, as does the plaintiff here, to challenge it. Furthermore, it is settled that agency action which is committed to the agency's discretion and thus otherwise foreclosed from judicial review is nevertheless reviewable if it allegedly exceeds constitutional bounds. * * * Accordingly, this analysis suggests that Mrs. Pena is entitled to a review of the Consul's assessment of the status of her marriage to determine if his decision was reached so arbitrarily and capriciously as to violate her right to procedural due process.

However appealing this argument may be, it appears to run afoul of *Mandel.* In that case, the plaintiffs were Americans who sought to interpose the Constitution between themselves and a discretionary exercise of power by the Attorney General which affected them while acting directly upon an alien abroad; the Supreme Court decided that the constitutional interests recognized there were not susceptible of judicial protection in the face of the "plenary congressional power to make policies and rules for exclusion of aliens...." 408 U.S. at 769, 92 S.Ct. at 2585, 33 L.Ed.2d at 696. Since it would be outside the province of a District Court to disregard this lesson from the High Court, *but see Hart, supra,* 66 Harv.L.Rev. at 1396 ("when justices ... write opinions in behalf of the Court which ignore the painful forward steps of a whole half century of adjudication, making no effort to relate what then is being done to what the Court has done before, they write without authority for the future"), plaintiff is not entitled to judicial review of the Consul's decision.

* * *

Notes

1. Despite Judge Pollack's obvious reluctance to reach this result, hasn't he misread *Mandel?* Here he concludes that Ms. Pena "is not entitled to judicial review of the Consul's decision," but isn't this quite different from the outcome in *Mandel?* Didn't Mandel or, more precisely, Mandel's U.S. citizen coplaintiffs, obtain judicial review of that consular decision—simply losing on the merits according to a test that is highly favorable to the government? Of course, Judge Pollack also observes that the consul's stated ground for decision here was facially legitimate and

tive course that was available and is now the more common practice: sending the case back to INS for INS to consider revoking the approved visa petition in light of whatever new evidence had come to the consul's attention. A revocation by INS of the approved visa petition would almost surely be judicially reviewable under the APA.—eds.

bona fide, but he still casts his ultimate ruling as a judgment that he lacks jurisdiction to review the consul's action.

Perhaps it makes little difference to losing plaintiffs whether they lose "on the merits" according to a test that provides so little penetration of the government's stated justification or lose instead because the courts consider themselves without jurisdiction to hear the case. But it may make some difference to the ultimate development of a sound body of law. Consider this: Some observers have regarded the *Mandel* case as significant not for its deference to the government but rather for suggesting, for the first time, that the courts might have any role at all in reviewing immigration decisions of this type. *See, e.g.,* Note, *Judicial Review of Visa Denials: Reexamining Consular Nonreviewability,* 52 N.Y.U.L.Rev. 1137, 1148–49 (1977). (This view was given a mild boost in 1977, in an analogous setting, when the Court stated in *Fiallo v. Bell,* 430 U.S. 787, 793 n. 5, 97 S.Ct. 1473, 1478 n. 5, 52 L.Ed.2d 50 (1977) that past cases "reflect acceptance of a limited judicial responsibility under the Constitution even with respect to the power of Congress to regulate the admission and exclusion of aliens.")

If the courts are at least hearing the cases, perhaps further progress could be made in refining the substantive test without intruding unduly on immigration decisions or upsetting U.S. foreign relations. Even the "facially legitimate and bona fide reason" test contains the seeds of growth. Dissenting in *Fiallo v. Bell, supra* p. 150, Justice Marshall read *Mandel* as rejecting a government claim of "unfettered discretion" in visa decisions. He went on to restate the *Mandel* review standard as follows: There must be a finding that the denial "was based on a 'legitimate and bona fide' reason." *Id.* at 807, 97 S.Ct. at 1486. Consider the impact such a slight amendment of the formula would have on the role of reviewing courts. Indeed, would such an amendment go too far?

In any event, the *Mandel* substantive test, deferential as it is, at least seems to place on the government the burden of coming forth with some statement of reasons for visa denials. *Burrafato v. Department of State,* 523 F.2d 554, 556 (2d Cir.1975), *cert. denied* 424 U.S. 910, 96 S.Ct. 1105, 47 L.Ed.2d 313 (1976), illustrates how the court's understanding of *Mandel* might be decisive for the outcome of the case. The court there relied on *Mandel* in holding that the district court lacked subject matter jurisdiction, even though the State Department, contrary to its own regulations, had failed to state any reasons for denying a visa to the citizen plaintiff's husband.

2. Even if *Mandel* permits Congress to exempt visa decisions (and indeed all denials of admission, whether taking place in a consulate overseas or at the border) from judicial review, has Congress chosen to do so? Where is that choice expressed?

Recall from Chapter Two that an unusual provision in § 104 of the INA exempts individual visa determinations from the supervision and control of the Secretary of State. Does it follow, *a fortiori,* that Congress also wanted such determinations insulated from the review of the courts? *See Shen v. U.S. Consulate General,* 866 F.Supp. 779 (S.D.N.Y.1994). Or, on the contrary, should we find that the case for judicial review is made stronger by § 104? Since there is no administrative appeal from visa denials, isn't it plausible that Congress either would have left open the chance for judicial review or would have denied such review explicitly? After all, § 104 says nothing expressly, one way or the other, about review by any governmental official or body except the Secretary of State. *See* Nafziger, *Review of Visa Denials by Consular Officers,* 66 Wash.L.Rev. 1, 30, 56 (1991); Gotcher, *Review of Consular Visa Determinations,* 60 Interp.Rel. 247 (1983) (arguing that the doctrine of consular nonreviewability is unfounded). Is this second argument undercut by the existence of the de facto State Department review mechanism described in Chapter Two? (Under that mechanism, *see* 22 C.F.R. §§ 41.121(c), 42.81(c), all denials are supposed to be reviewed by a senior officer in the consulate. In some busy posts, however, such review appears to be done only on a spot-check basis. *See* 54 Fed.Reg. 53496 (1989) (report and recommendations of the Administrative Conference of the U.S.).)

In any event, whatever problems we might have with *Pena's* reading of *Mandel,* its conclusion that consular decisions are unreviewable has been widely accepted. *See, e.g., Li Hing of Hong Kong, Inc. v. Levin,* 800 F.2d 970 (9th Cir.1986); *Rivera de Gomez v. Kissinger,* 534 F.2d 518 (2d Cir.1976) *(per curiam), cert. denied* 429 U.S. 897, 97 S.Ct. 262, 50 L.Ed.2d 181; *Romero v. Consulate of the United States,* 860 F.Supp. 319 (E.D.Va. 1994); *Hermina Sague v. United States,* 416 F.Supp. 217 (D.P.R.1976). Some courts have found jurisdiction, however, to consider underlying questions regarding the constitutionality of the statute under which the consul acted, despite the consular nonreviewability doctrine. *See, e.g., Martinez v. Bell,* 468 F.Supp. 719 (S.D.N.Y.1979) (sustaining the government on the merits). And in *Abourezk v. Reagan, supra,* 785 F.2d 1043 (D.C.Cir.1987), *affirmed by an equally divided court,* 484 U.S. 1, 108 S.Ct. 252, 98 L.Ed.2d 1 (1987), the court of appeals gave the back of the hand to the government's claim that the court lacked jurisdiction to consider a visa denial. Noting that *Mandel* was a disposition on the merits, not on jurisdictional grounds, the court applied standard APA doctrine, including its presumption of reviewability, to find that plaintiffs were entitled to judicial review. Several commentators reach a similar conclusion despite lower-court cases like *Pena:* the consular nonreviewability doctrine, they maintain, should not be held to have survived the enactment of the APA. *See, e.g.,* S. Legomsky, Immigration and the Judiciary 144–51 (1987); Nafziger, *supra;* Wildes, *Review of Visa Denials: The American Consul as 20th Century Absolute Monarch,* 26 San Diego L.Rev. 887, 900–02 (1989).

Standing and Visa Denials

In many settings, courts have used a different basis—standing doctrine—for refusing to reach the merits of challenges to immigration decisions, including visa denials, filed by aliens who are not present in the United States.[7] Some of these decisions support this result by citing

---

7. Aliens in the United States, even after an illegal entry, have usually had little trouble surmounting the standing barrier and securing judicial review of immigration decisions affecting them, either under the Administrative Procedure Act, *see Reddy, Inc. v.*

Mandel; they read Part III of that decision as a ruling on standing. (Recheck that Part of the opinion. Is this a fair reading? One case has taken issue with this interpretation of *Mandel's* impact on standing determinations. *Mendelsohn v. Meese,* 695 F.Supp. 1474, 1479 n. 5 (S.D.N.Y. 1988).)

Several cases outside the immigration field speak of a "general rule that non-resident aliens have no standing to sue in United States Courts." *Berlin Democratic Club v. Rumsfeld,* 410 F.Supp. 144, 152 (D.D.C.1976). Although there are exceptions to this rule (and a possible trend toward relaxing these standing limitations), *see Cardenas v. Smith,* 733 F.2d 909 (D.C.Cir.1984), standing remains a major obstacle to the hearing of challenges to visa denials. *See* GM & Y § 81.01[3]; *Chinese American Civic Council v. Attorney General,* 396 F.Supp. 1250 (D.D.C.1975), *affirmed on other grounds,* 566 F.2d 321 (D.C.Cir.1977). There are a few cases that recognize standing in nonresident aliens outside the United States to challenge immigration decisions, but they involved alien plaintiffs who had been in the United States shortly before bringing the lawsuit, *Estrada v. Ahrens,* 296 F.2d 690 (5th Cir.1961); *Jaimez-Revolla v. Bell,* 598 F.2d 243 (D.C.Cir.1979), or aliens who were part of a plaintiff class composed primarily of aliens present in the country, *see Silva v. Bell,* 605 F.2d 978 (7th Cir.1979).

Standing determinations involve both constitutional limitations and prudential considerations tied to conceptions about the appropriate role of the courts. *See Warth v. Seldin,* 422 U.S. 490, 498, 95 S.Ct. 2197, 2204, 45 L.Ed.2d 343 (1975). Clearly most aliens outside the United States challenging visa denials or other negative immigration decisions would satisfy the constitutional requirements. They can demonstrate "injury in fact" fairly traceable to the actions of the United States government, giving them the necessary personal stake in the controversy. *See id.* at 498–99, 95 S.Ct. at 2204–05; *Larson v. Valente,* 456 U.S. 228, 238–39, 102 S.Ct. 1673, 1680, 72 L.Ed.2d 33 (1982); *Lujan v. Defenders of Wildlife,* 504 U.S. 555, ___, 112 S.Ct. 2130, 2137, 119 L.Ed.2d 351 (1992).

Denial of standing to nonresident aliens not physically present thus rests on prudential considerations. As one court phrased the matter: denial of standing is based on "the policy reasons against affording a Federal forum for a person anywhere in the world challenging denial of entry or immigration status." *Chinese-American Civic Council, supra,* at 1251. Consular officers worldwide issued 5.4 million nonimmigrant visas in FY 1992 and found 1.6 million applications ineligible (about 15% of the ineligibility findings are later "overcome" administratively by the submission of additional evidence or the grant of a waiver). 1992 Report of the Visa Office, Tables I, XX. As of 1994, there were only 649 authorized federal district court judgeships.

Are judges justified on prudential grounds in fearing a flood of litigation if review of visa determinations were allowed? Is this the real concern underlying the strained readings of *Mandel* to find that jurisdiction is

Department of Labor, 492 F.2d 538 (5th Cir. 1974), or under the special provisions for   judicial review set forth in the INA and examined in Chapter Nine.

lacking? If so, should courts be more candid about the real reasons? (After all, that prudential concern carries some genuine persuasive power.[8]) Finally, if we are relying on counsels of prudence in limiting the judicial review of visa denials, would it be possible for the courts to allow review of applications for immigrant visas, where the stakes are higher, even while denying review in the more numerous nonimmigrant cases? (If so, Ms. Pena's case was much more deserving of review than was Mandel's.) *See generally* Martin, *Mandel, Cheng Fan Kwok and Other Unappealing Cases*, 27 Va.J. Int'l L. 803 (1987).

4. THE PUBLIC CHARGE PROVISION

Concern about an influx of paupers underlay many of the earliest attempts—then carried out by the state governments—to impose broad-scale restrictions on immigration. *See, e.g., Mayor of the City of New York v. Miln,* 36 U.S. (11 Pet.) 102, 9 L.Ed. 648 (1837); *The Passenger Cases,* 48 U.S. (7 How.) 283, 12 L.Ed. 702 (1849). (For an excellent account of state regulation during this period, see Neuman, *The Lost Century of American Immigration Law (1776–1875),* 93 Colum.L.Rev. 1833, 1846–59 (1993).) In 1882, Congress enacted the first federal provision barring from entry "any person unable to take care of himself or herself without becoming a public charge." Act of Aug. 3, 1882, Ch. 376, § 2, 22 Stat. 214.

The Supreme Court considered the public charge provision in *Gegiow v. Uhl,* 239 U.S. 3, 36 S.Ct. 2, 60 L.Ed. 114 (1915). There the immigration commissioner had initially excluded certain Russian immigrants on this ground, reciting these reasons for the exclusion: "That they arrived here with very little money, * * * and are bound for Portland, Oregon, where the reports of industrial conditions show that it would be impossible for these aliens to obtain employment; that they have no one legally obligated here to assist them." *Id.* at 8, 36 S.Ct. at 2. The Supreme Court struck down this attempt to make the public charge provision a crude form of labor certification.

> The single question on this record is whether an alien can be declared likely to become a public charge on the ground that the labor market in the city of his immediate destination is over-stocked. In the [statute] determining who shall be excluded, 'Persons likely to become a public charge' are mentioned between paupers and professional beggars, and along with idiots, persons dangerously diseased, persons certified by the examining surgeon to have a mental or physical defect of a nature to affect their ability to earn a living, convicted felons, prostitutes and so forth. The persons enumerated in short are to be excluded on the ground of permanent personal objections accompanying them irrespective

8. In 1989 the Administrative Conference of the United States considered the entire system for review of visa denials. Although its consultant, Professor James Nafziger, had urged at least limited and selective judicial review, the plenary Conference removed from its final recommendations all reference to a role for the courts. 54 Fed.Reg. 53493 (1989); 67 Interp.Rel. 37 (1990). *See also Romero v. Consulate of the United States,* 860 F.Supp. 319, 324 (E.D.Va.1994) ("Were the rule to be otherwise, federal courts would be inundated with claims of disappointed and disgruntled off-shore aliens seeking review of consular officers' denials of their requests for nonimmigrant visitor's visas.").

of local conditions unless the one phrase before us is directed to different considerations than any other of those with which it is associated. Presumably it is to be read as generically similar to the others mentioned before and after.

Id. at 9–10, 36 S.Ct. at 3.

As thus limited, this venerable provision of the statutes continues to play an important role in excluding applicants for visas. It was continued virtually without change in the 1990 revisions. INA § 212(a)(4). A 1978 study describes its significance as follows:

> The public charge provision of the Act is responsible for the greatest number of immigrant visa refusals. In 1975, after taking into account refusals overcome, consular officers relied on the public charge provision to deny visas in almost sixty percent of all refusals. During the period from July, 1976, through June, 1977, the public charge provision accounted for sixty-one percent of all initial refusals in Mexico but only eleven percent of all initial refusals in Canada.

> On its face, the public charge provision of the Act represents a broad grant of discretion. Ineligibility includes "[a]liens who, *in the opinion of the consular officer* at the time of application for a visa, ... are likely at any time to become public charges."

> [State Department] regulations attempt to structure this discretion. A sworn job offer from an employer in the United States, for example, may establish eligibility. However, these regulations provide that consular officers must presume ineligible aliens who rely solely on expected income that falls below the income poverty guidelines.

> The interpretative and procedural notes to the Departmental regulations attempt more detailed structuring of the public charge provision. These notes contain Departmental policy governing acceptable types of public charge evidence. A partial list of such evidence includes bank deposits, pre-arranged employment, affidavits of support, and bonds posted.

> Departmental policy places a high priority on flexibility in the evaluation of evidence regarding sufficient funds to meet the public charge provision. According to the *Foreign Affairs Manual,* consular officers should consider a variety of factors, including the applicant's age, his physical condition, his family status, and economic conditions in the United States. Moreover, stated policy prohibits consular officers from using "a fixed sum of money as the sole criterion for judging a prospective immigrant's ability to meet the public charge requirement of the law."

Note, *Consular Discretion in Immigrant Visa–Issuing Process,* 16 San Diego L.Rev. 87, 113–14 (1978) (emphasis in original).

MATTER OF KOHAMA

Associate Commissioner, Examinations, 1978.
17 I & N Dec. 257.

This matter is before the Associate Commissioner, Examinations on certification as provided by 8 C.F.R. 103.4 for review of the District Director's decision denying the motion to reconsider his previous decision denying the applications for status as permanent residents under section 245 of the Immigration and Nationality Act.

The applicants are husband and wife, natives and citizens of Japan, 73 and 65 years of age. They last entered the United States as nonimmigrant visitors for pleasure on December 10, 1975, and were authorized to remain until March 16, 1976.

On March 23, 1976, immediate relative visa petitions were filed in their behalf by their naturalized United States citizen daughter. Concurrent with these petitions, the applicants filed applications to adjust their status to that of permanent residents pursuant to section 245 of the Immigration and Nationality Act, as amended. Satisfactory evidence of the claimed daughter-parent relationship was presented and the petitions were approved May 1976. By virtue of their approved visa petitions and their admission to the United States as nonimmigrant visitors, they were statutorily eligible to file the application for adjustment of status.

The applicants are unemployed and do not have savings or independent means of support. They rely, instead, on support from their daughter and son-in-law, both of whom are employed. As evidence of this support they presented affidavits executed by the daughter and son-in-law, along with evidence of their combined income of approximately $34,000 per year.

Following interviews in connection with the pending applications for adjustment of status on June 22, 1976, the applicants were advised that it would be necessary for them to post bonds each in the amount of $5,000 in order to insure that they would not become public charges. The applicants' son-in-law advised the Service by letter dated September 15, 1976, that it would be difficult for him and his spouse to post the bonds due to the charges imposed by the bonding company. In this letter the Service was requested to grant a period of 2 or 3 months to allow for the location of a suitable bonding company.

The record contains no evidence that the bonds were posted, and on March 17, 1977, the applications were denied by the District Director on the grounds that the applicants were likely to become public charges, pursuant to section 212(a)(15) of the Act.[a] In his decision the District Director concluded that the affidavits of support presented by the daughter and son-in-law were not acceptable and bases this conclusion on two court decisions, *County of San Diego* [*v. Viloria*, 276 Cal.App.2d 350, 80 Cal.Rptr. 869 (1969)] and *Department of Mental Hygiene of California v. Renal*, 173 N.Y.S.2d 231 (1957). The District Director states that these court deci-

---

a. Now recodified at INA § 212(a)(4).—
eds.

sions hold that the affidavit of support is a moral obligation and does not create any legal obligation to support the beneficiaries of the affidavit. The District Director also relied upon the *Matter of Harutunian,* 14 I & N Dec. 583 (R.C.1974). This decision also related to an applicant for adjustment of status pursuant to section 245 who was of advanced age, without means of support and with no one responsible for her support. This decision set forth criteria to be taken into consideration in determining the applicability of section 212(a)(15). The alien's age, incapability of earning a livelihood, a lack of sufficient funds for self-support, and a lack of persons in this country willing and able to assure that the alien will not need public support.

Following the denial of the applications, a motion to reopen and reconsider was filed April 22, 1977. The motion, which was prepared by the son-in-law set forth the following facts: He and his wife, the applicants' daughter, have been responsible for virtually all the wife's family's support since 1961. The motion describes a closely knit family, each doing their portion to see that the others did not want for the necessities of life. Three other children, one of whom is now married, are now employed and self-sufficient and also able to provide support to their parents. Attached to the motion are copies of numerous checks as well as bank records which reflect that the applicants' daughter and son-in-law have contributed several thousands of dollars to the parents' support over the last 10 or more years.

The motion to reopen and reconsider was considered by the District Director on June 10, 1977, who concluded that no new facts or evidence had been presented and accordingly affirmed his previous denial.

Despite the two State court decisions cited by the District Director, it is not believed the affidavits of support, although not legal obligations, are without weight in determining whether a person is likely to become a public charge. 8 C.F.R. 103.2(b)(1), which sets forth the requirement of evidence in support of applications, states in part: "Form I–34 may be used if an affidavit of support would be helpful in resolving any public charge aspect." In light of this regulation, the Service must give the affidavits due consideration consistent with the deponents' ability to provide the promised support. In the case at hand, the deponents have presented evidence of support over the past several years, as well as their ability to do so into the foreseeable future.

In the matter of *Harutunian, supra,* cited by the District Director, the circumstances are not parallel to the case at hand. In *Harutunian, supra,* the applicant was without any evidence of support, either of her own or by another person. In addition, she had a history of being dependent on the State of California for old age assistance; in the contrast, the present applicants have not received public assistance.

It is my conclusion that the applicants, although not self-supporting, have presented sufficient evidence that they will be supported if granted permanent resident status in the United States and are not likely to become public charges and are not, therefore, subject to the exclusion provisions of section 212(a)(15) of the Immigration and Nationality Act, as amended.

In view of the foregoing, it is determined that the record establishes the applicants' eligibility for the benefits sought under section 245 of the Act. Accordingly, the District Director's decision to deny the motion to reopen and reconsider is hereby withdrawn and the motion is granted.

* * *

Note

For many years Congress has manifested concern over the possible implications of state court decisions holding that affidavits of support are not legally enforceable. In 1980 it amended the statute establishing Supplemental Security Income (a federal program for the aged, blind, and disabled) to provide that, for three years—later extended to five years—after entry, the income and assets of the sponsor signing such an affidavit shall be deemed to be available to the alien beneficiaries, for purposes of determining eligibility for SSI. There are exemptions for refugees and for those whose disability necessitating assistance developed only after arrival in the United States. 42 U.S.C.A. § 1382j. In succeeding years, similar "deeming" provisions were added to the legislation governing other assistance programs. *See, e.g.,* 42 U.S.C.A. § 615 (Aid to Families with Dependent Children); 7 U.S.C.A. § 2014(i) (food stamp program). *See generally Aziz v. Sullivan,* 800 F.Supp. 1374 (E.D.Va.1992).

With regard to the SSI program, the bill that initially passed the Senate in 1980 would have made affidavits of support legally enforceable as a matter of federal law. The conference committee decided against that approach, however, substituting instead the deeming provisions, and also providing for notification to potential sponsors that their income would be deemed to the aliens in this fashion and that they would have to provide information on their assets and income when aliens applied for public assistance. *See* H.R.Conf.Rep. No. 96–944, 96th Cong., 2d Sess., at 70–72 (1980); 1980 U.S.Code Cong. & Ad.News 1392, 1417–19. Why would Congress have chosen the deeming approach? Which should it have chosen? What recourse does an alien denied public assistance now have if her sponsor has lost interest?

Concern over the use of welfare by aliens spawned numerous reform proposals in the 103d Congress. Much of the alarm focused on the use by illegal migrants of the few programs, such as emergency medical care or the Supplemental Food Program for Women, Infants, and Children (WIC), that are open to the undocumented. But some of the proposals reached further and would deny access to public assistance programs to all aliens, even if they were lawful permanent residents and had been present for many years. Should this latter change be made? Some proponents saw this measure as an inducement to naturalize; what might be the flaws with such a view? None of the bills passed before Congress adjourned in 1994, but the issue will probably figure prominently in the welfare reform debate that is likely in 1995. For a good summary, see *Immigrant's Benefits*

Might Be Restricted in Welfare Reform Initiatives, 71 Interp.Rel. 521 (1994).

5. FRAUD AND WILLFUL MISREPRESENTATION OF MATERIAL FACTS

Before 1986, INA § 212(a)(19) rendered ineligible for visas and excludable at entry:

> "any alien who seeks to procure, or has sought to procure, or has procured a visa or other documentation, or seeks to enter the United States, by fraud, or by willfully misrepresenting a material fact."

Under this language, fraud or misrepresentation might have very different consequences, depending upon the circumstances under which it occurred. Aliens who committed fraud or willful misrepresentation in seeking to procure a visa or "other documentation" were considered permanently barred from entry (subject to the extremely limited waiver provisions of the statute). But aliens who did the same only at the border or port of entry— the point where they were seeking to enter—were disqualified from entry on that application, but not from future admission. (Review the statutory language carefully to be sure you understand why the pre–1986 statute was read to provide this one-time-only prohibition in the latter circumstances.)

Whatever the underlying policy such a distinction served, Congress reconsidered when it passed the Immigration Marriage Fraud Amendments of 1986. Section 212(a)(19) was rewritten to apply a permanent bar for fraud or willful misrepresentation in either setting, again subject to limited possibilities for waiver. In 1990 this section was recodified, without substantive change, as INA § 212(a)(6)(C)(i), while the waiver provision in § 212(i) was liberalized. *See Matter of Y–G–*, Int.Dec. 3219 (BIA 1994). The amended section still presents difficult issues of interpretation and implementation.

The following reading contains relevant sections of the Foreign Affairs Manual, the manual that provides more precise guidance for consular officers in carrying out their functions under the INA. The passages below have not yet been revised to account for the 1990 Act, and they still refer to the provision using the old numbering (INA § 212(a)(19)). The 1990 Act, however, did not change the substance of the provision, and a headnote to this section of the FAM makes it clear that this guidance applies in implementing current INA § 212(a)(6)(C). (The Supreme Court has also struggled with the issue of deciding what misrepresentations and concealments are "material." For its latest (unfortunately fragmented) decision on these questions, see *Kungys v. United States,* 485 U.S. 759, 108 S.Ct. 1537, 99 L.Ed.2d 839 (1988), covered in Chapter Ten, p. 1029.) After considering these passages, try your hand at resolving the issues set forth in the Problems immediately following.

U.S. DEPARTMENT OF STATE, FOREIGN AFFAIRS MANUAL

Section 40.63, Notes,[9] as amended through 1993

* * *

APPLICATION OF SECTION 212(A)(19).

Intent of Congress. Section 212(a)(19) constitutes a ground of ineligibility which was not included in legislation prior to 1952. The adoption of this provision expresses the concern with which Congress viewed cases of aliens resorting to fraud or willful misrepresentations for the purpose of obtaining visas or otherwise effecting unauthorized entry into the United States. The section is intended to prevent aliens from attempting to secure entry into this country by fraudulent means and then, when the falsity is discovered, proceeding with an application as if nothing had happened.

Not a Substitute for Other INA 212(a) Ineligibility. INA 212(a)(19) was not intended by Congress, on the other hand, to be a substitute for the other grounds of ineligibility provided by the INA—nor for grounds that do not exist in the INA. It should not be used to accomplish indirectly that which cannot be accomplished directly. The section was not intended to permit—and must not become a device for—entrapment of aliens whom the consular officer might suspect to be ineligible on some other ground(s) for which there is not sufficient evidence to sustain a finding of ineligibility. Although consular officers should always bear in mind all INA provisions governing the eligibility or exclusion of certain specifically described classes, it must also be borne in mind that aliens may not be denied visas simply because they do not seem to be particularly desirable individuals as either immigrants or nonimmigrants.

Nature of Penalty. In applying the provisions of Section 212(a)(19), consular officers should keep in mind the severe nature of the penalty the alien incurs: permanent ineligibility. When imposing such a dire penalty, the consular officer should keep in mind the words quoted by the Attorney General in his landmark opinion on this matter (The Matter of S–and B–C, 9 I & N Dec. 436, at 446):

> "Shutting off the opportunity to come to the United States actually is a crushing deprivation to many prospective immigrants. Very often it destroys the hopes and aspirations of a lifetime, and it frequently operates not only against the individual immediately but also bears heavily upon his family in and out of the United States."

ELEMENTS SUPPORTING A FINDING UNDER SECTION 212(A)(19) OF THE INA.

Different Standards for Findings of "Fraud" or "Willfully Misrepresenting a Material Fact." The fact that Congress used the terms "fraud"

9. The internal numbering system for headings and subheadings has been omitted here.—eds.

and "willfully misrepresenting a material fact" in the alternative indicates an intent to set a lower standard than is required in making a finding of what is known in the law as fraud. Nearly all cases brought under section 212(a)(19) are cases of willful misrepresentation.

Criteria for Finding of Ineligibility. In order to find an alien ineligible to receive a visa under the provisions of section 212(a)(19), it must be determined that:

    (a) there has been misrepresentation made by the applicant;

    (b) the misrepresentation was willfully made, and

    (c) the fact misrepresented is material.

INTERPRETATION OF THE TERM "MISREPRESENTATION."

Misrepresentation Defined. As used in section 212(a)(19), a misrepresentation is an assertion or manifestation not in accordance with the facts. Misrepresentations can be made in oral interviews, written applications, or by submitting evidence containing false information.

Differentiation Between Misrepresentation and Failure to Volunteer Information. In determining whether a misrepresentation has been made, it is necessary to distinguish between what information was misrepresented and what was merely concealed by the alien's silence. Silence or failure to volunteer information does not in itself constitute a misrepresentation for the purpose of section 212(a)(19).

Misrepresentation Must Have Been Before U.S. Official. For a misrepresentation to fall within the purview of section 212(a)(19), it must have been practiced on an official of the United States Government; generally speaking, a consular officer or an officer of the Immigration and Naturalization Service.

Misrepresentation Must Be Made in Alien's Own Application. The misrepresentation must have been made by the alien with respect to his/her own visa application. Misrepresentations made in connection with some other person's visa application do not fall within the purview of section 212(a)(19), but may be considered in light of section 212(a)(31) [the predecessor to current § 212(a)(6)(E)].

Misrepresentation Made by Applicant's Attorney or Agent. The fact that an alien pursues a visa application through an attorney or travel agent does not serve to insulate the alien from liability for misrepresentations made by such agents if it is established that the alien was aware of the action being taken in furtherance of the application. This standard also applies in cases where a travel agent has executed a visa application on the alien's behalf by mail.

Timely Retraction. A timely retraction will serve to purge a misrepresentation and remove it from further consideration. Whether a retraction is timely depends on the circumstances of the particular case, but in general, it should be made at the first opportunity and in the course of the same proceedings or hearing at which the misrepresentation was made. For this reason, aliens being interviewed should be warned of the penalties of section 212(a)(19).

Misrepresentation Not Necessarily Present Where Alien's Activities in United States Differ From Statements Made in Visa Application. In determining whether a misrepresentation has been made, some of the most difficult questions arise from cases involving aliens in the United States who conduct themselves in a manner inconsistent with representations they made to consular officers concerning their intentions at the time of visa application. These types of cases occur most frequently with respect to aliens who, after having obtained visas as nonimmigrants either (a) apply for adjustment of status to permanent resident or (b) fail to maintain their nonimmigrant status by engaging in employment. The fact that an alien's subsequent actions are other than as stated at the time of visa application does not in itself prove, *ex post facto,* that the alien misrepresented his intent at the time of the application. As to those who adjust their status, it should be borne in mind that for a number of valid and lawful reasons as an alien may change his plans after obtaining a visa. As to those who fail to maintain status, in order to substantiate a finding under section 212(a)(19), it must be factually established that a misrepresentation has occurred.

INTERPRETATION OF THE TERM "WILLFULLY."

"Willfully" Defined. The term "willfully" as used in section 212(a)(19) of the INA is interpreted to mean knowingly and intentionally, as distinguished from accidentally, inadvertently, or in an honest belief that the true facts are otherwise. In order to find the element of willfulness, it must be determined that the alien was fully aware of the nature of the information sought and knowingly, intentionally, and deliberately made an untrue statement.

Misrepresentation Is Alien's Responsibility. An alien who acts on the advice of another is considered to be exercising his own will in accepting or rejecting such advice. It is no defense for an alien to say that he made a misrepresentation because someone else advised him to do so unless it is found that the alien lacked the capacity to formulate his own will.

Problems

1. Alien X, a high-school teacher from Istanbul, presents a fraudulent Turkish passport, bearing his picture and what appears to be a B–2 visa (nonimmigrant visitor for pleasure), upon arrival at Dulles International Airport in Washington. X states that he obtained it for a fee from someone who held himself out as a travel agent, that he never appeared before a U.S. consular officer, that he believed this procedure to be the proper way to obtain a passport and visa, and that he thought his documents were perfectly valid. Should X be barred from entry under INA § 212(a)(6)(C)(i)? Would it make a difference if X were instead a farmer from rural Turkey who had only a fourth-grade education?

2. (a) Alien Y, a Korean national, arrived at San Francisco Airport two years ago with a duly issued B–2 visa stamped in his passport. The border inspector, however, found a large amount of cash in his briefcase. Suspecting that Y was intending to stay indefinitely, the inspector sent him

to secondary inspection for further inquiry into his admissibility. Y then withdrew his application for admission and returned to Korea via the next available flight, never having left the international lounge of the airport. Now he is back at the U.S. consulate in Seoul, applying for another B–2 visa. You are the consular officer. Is Y excludable under § 212(a)(6)(C)(i)?

(b) Same facts, but instead of withdrawing the application for admission two years ago, Y insisted on an exclusion hearing. There, after questioning regarding the cash and other circumstances of his trip, the immigration judge ruled him inadmissible for failure to carry his burden (see INA § 291) of showing that he was qualified for admission category B–2. Specifically, the immigration judge found that Y had not carried his burden of demonstrating that he had a "residence in a foreign country which he has no intention of abandoning." INA § 101(a)(15)(B). Y then returned to Korea, without appealing to the BIA. Again you are the consular officer two years later. Does § 212(a)(6)(C)(i) disqualify him? Consider also § 221(g) for a further statement of the standard of proof a consular officer is to apply.

3. Alien Z was questioned extensively at Kennedy Airport when she arrived from Bolivia on a B–2 visa. Her English is limited, however, and no interpreter was present. After the questioning, she signed a paper typed by the immigration inspector. It stated that, when applying for her visa and during the initial part of her questioning at the airport, she had misrepresented her employment in Bolivia, claimed bank accounts that she did not in fact have, and purported to be married with two children when in fact she is single and childless. Because she was unwilling to withdraw her application for admission, Z was then held for an exclusion hearing, with excludability charged under INA § 212(a)(6)(C)(i).

Before the exclusion hearing, she engages a lawyer, who now challenges the admissibility of the signed statement, noting that it was procured without an interpreter and in the absence of an attorney. She also puts on evidence otherwise meant to demonstrate her admissibility. The border inspector, however, testifies that their conversation took place in both English and Spanish and that he placed in the typed statement only information that she had first stated in the interview. You are the immigration judge. How do you rule?

SECTION E. PAROLE

Suppose an intending immigrant is detained at the border and ultimately ruled excludable on a ground that is not waivable under § 212. What happens if she becomes gravely ill before removal can be effected? Can the district director send her to the hospital without permitting an entry and thus violating the Act? Must the district director condemn a portion of the hospital and make it a part of the INS detention facility?

Not surprisingly, immigration authorities early found ways to cope with such circumstances without initiating costly condemnation proceedings and without directly violating the exclusion laws. They developed the *def .*

concept of parole, under which an alien is allowed to travel away from the border and the detention facilities and yet remain subject to exclusion proceedings, rather than the more cumbersome and protective deportation proceedings, when it comes time to test out the alien's ultimate right to remain. In the eyes of the law, an alien paroled into the country near San Diego remains constructively at the border, even if she is authorized to travel all the way to Omaha in the center of the country. Technically, a parolee has made no "entry." (We will explore the intricacies of entry and its consequences in Chapter Five.) In a way, then, parole would serve to make the hospital bed of the gravely ill alien mentioned above a functional extension of the border detention facilities, but without having to transfer title to the hospital into the government's name.

At first, parole was fashioned by administrative ingenuity alone, without statutory sanction. But the 1952 Act codified the practice in § 212(d)(5). The Attorney General is now expressly authorized to parole aliens "temporarily under such conditions as he may prescribe for emergent reasons or reasons deemed strictly in the public interest." The statute also makes clear that at the end of the parole the alien returns "to the custody from which he was paroled and thereafter his case shall continue to be dealt with in the same manner as that of any other applicant for admission to the United States."

A 1952 congressional committee report explained the intent of this provision:

> The provision in the instant bill represents an acceptance of the recommendation of the Attorney General with reference to this form of discretionary relief. The committee believes that the broader discretionary authority is necessary to permit the Attorney General to parole inadmissible aliens into the United States in emergency cases, such as the case of an alien who requires immediate medical attention before there has been an opportunity for an immigration officer to inspect him, and in cases where it is strictly in the public interest to have an inadmissible alien present in the United States, such as, for instance, a witness or for purposes of prosecution.

H.R.Rep. No. 1365, 82nd Cong., 2d Sess., at 52; 1952 U.S.Code Cong. & Ad.News 1653, 1706. Congress plainly contemplated that parole might be used either before or after a final determination of excludability.

When the Justice Department decided to close Ellis Island and other border processing and detention facilities in 1954, *see* T. Pitkin, *Keepers of the Gate: A History of Ellis Island* 176–77 (1975), parole thereafter was used primarily to permit the temporary release of aliens in exclusion processing, pending a final decision on their admissibility. As it happened, some aliens might be on parole in this fashion for several years, establishing equities that made their case for remaining more sympathetic. Long-time parolees also began to assert an entitlement based on their lengthy physical presence, free of restraints, to certain forms of relief technically available under the INA only to aliens in deportation rather than exclusion proceedings. The Supreme Court ultimately held that such benefits are not available to parolees, in a case that discusses the history and policy underlying parole. *Leng May Ma v. Barber,* 357 U.S. 185, 78 S.Ct. 1072, 2 L.Ed.2d 1246 (1958). Excerpts follow:

> [O]ur immigration laws have long made a distinction between those aliens who have come to our shores seeking admission, such as petitioner, and those who are within the United States after an entry, irrespective of its legality. In the latter instance the Court has recognized additional rights and privileges not extended to those in the former category who are merely "on the threshold of initial entry."

> * * *

> For over a half century this Court has held that the detention of an alien in custody pending determination of his admissibility does not legally constitute an entry though the alien is physically within the United States. * * * Our question is whether the granting of temporary parole somehow effects a change in the alien's legal status. In § 212(d)(5) of the Act, generally a codification of the administrative practice pursuant to which petitioner was paroled, the Congress specifically provided that parole "shall not be regarded as an admission of the alien," and that after the return to custody the alien's case "shall *continue* to be dealt with in the same manner as that of any other applicant for admission to the United States." (Emphasis added.) * * *

> The Court previously has had occasion to define the legal status of excluded aliens on parole. In *Kaplan v. Tod,* 267 U.S. 228, 45 S.Ct. 257, 258, 69 L.Ed. 585 (1925), an excluded alien was paroled to a private Immigrant Aid Society pending deportation. The questions posed were whether the alien was "dwelling in the United States" within the meaning of a naturalization statute, and whether she had "entered or [was] found in the United States" for purpose of limitations. Mr. Justice Holmes disposed of the problem by explicitly equating parole with detention:

>> "The appellant could not lawfully have landed in the United States * * *, and until she legally landed 'could not have dwelt within the United States.' Moreover while she was at Ellis Island she was to be regarded as stopped at the boundary line and kept there unless and until her right to enter should be declared. When her prison bounds were enlarged by committing her to the custody of the Hebrew Society, the nature of her stay within the territory was not changed. She was still in theory of law at the boundary line and had gained no foothold in the United States." 267 U.S., at page 230, 45 S.Ct., at page 257.

> * * *

> The parole of aliens seeking admission is simply a device through which needless confinement is avoided while administrative proceedings are conducted. It was never intended to affect an alien's

status, and to hold that petitioner's parole placed her legally "within the United States" is inconsistent with the congressional mandate, the administrative concept of parole, and the decisions of this Court. Physical detention of aliens is now the exception, not the rule, and is generally employed only as to security risks or those likely to abscond. Certainly this policy reflects the humane qualities of an enlightened civilization. The acceptance of petitioner's position in this case, however, with its inherent suggestion of an altered parole status, would be quite likely to prompt some curtailment of current parole policy—an intention we are reluctant to impute to the Congress.

357 U.S. at 187–90, 78 S.Ct. at 1073–75. (The "humane" and "enlightened" policy favoring release while exclusion proceedings were underway was significantly restricted in 1981, *see* 8 C.F.R. Part 212.5, principally because the executive branch believed the release policy attracted too many asylum-seekers who could usually avoid detention and accept employment here while adjudication of asylum dragged on. We will consider the detention controversy in Chapter Four.)

As it had evolved, parole thus became an outstandingly flexible tool in the hands of the executive branch, permitting the physical presence of selected aliens despite other disqualifications—whether those be the application of the exclusion grounds of § 212(a) or the lack of an admission number under the national-origins quotas, or later, under the preference system. Presidents eventually began to take vigorous—and controversial—advantage of this flexibility, to bring in large groups of aliens in compelling circumstances. The first such episode occurred when the Soviet Union sent tanks into Hungary to put down a revolution there in 1956. Hungarian quotas were full, but the Eisenhower administration came under increasing pressure to admit large numbers of Hungarian refugees. The President ultimately decided to make innovative use of the parole power to bring some 30,000 refugees to this country.

Thus began a long and controversial practice of paroling in refugees when ordinary statutory provisions proved inadequate. People fleeing Cuba and Indochina, among others, were later beneficiaries. Many in Congress protested. Parole, they insisted, was supposed to be temporary, whereas the refugees were clearly here for an indefinite stay, and it was supposed to be used in individual cases, not for large groups. Nevertheless, the practice continued until Congress rewrote the refugee provisions comprehensively in the Refugee Act of 1980. When Congress did so, it closed the refugee-parole loophole permanently by adding subparagraph (B) to § 212(d)(5). That provision forbids the paroling of refugees except in isolated individual cases for individually compelling reasons. (Chapter Eight traces these developments in more detail.)

But that amendment did not spell the end of paroles of large groups. Soon after enactment of the Refugee Act, approximately 125,000 Cubans arrived directly—and chaotically—by boat in south Florida in the span of a few months, after Cuban Premier Fidel Castro opened the port of Mariel to permit their exit. The arriving Marielitos were excludable for lack of documents (and many on other grounds), and the political asylum claims most of them were filing would take months or years to process. But INS was obviously unable to detain such a large number. The answer? Parole, freeing most of the arrivals to sponsors. This release was technically consistent with § 212(d)(5)(B) because the aliens had not been determined to be refugees when they were paroled, and they were not being paroled as part of an official refugee program.[10] Indeed, especially because Cuba adamantly refused, for over three years, to cooperate in the return of any of the Marielitos, there really was no alternative to a parole on this scale. Later the Attorney General formalized the parole category used for this group (as well as that of some 30,000 Haitians who arrived during this period) with the label "Cuban/Haitian entrant—status pending." Congress acquiesced by providing funding to assist the parolees (again, there was no realistic alternative). Several thousand of the Marielitos, however, remained in detention several years after arrival, largely because of criminal activity either in the United States or in Cuba before their departure. Their cases have posed difficult due process questions, to be considered in Chapter Four.

A new wide-scale and controversial use of parole for Cubans was initiated in September 1994, in response to a sudden and dangerous exodus of rafters from Cuba that began in August and exceeded 3,000 per day at one point. The Clinton administration negotiated an agreement whereby Cuban authorities would restrict raft departures, using "persuasive means," and in return the United States would guarantee that at least 20,000 Cubans could come to the United States annually through regular channels. This latter program will require significant use of the parole power, including parole of an estimated 5,000–6,000 Cubans who win a lottery to be conducted annually. 71 Interp.Rel. 1213, 1409 (1994).

Parole can thus be used for a wide variety of purposes, either before or after an administrative finding of excludability: to permit medical treatment, to allow appearance in litigation or a criminal prosecution, to prevent inhumane separation of families or for other humanitarian reasons,[11] or to permit release pending adjudication of an exclusion case. But parole may be granted only by the Attorney General and a rather select list of his delegates, principally the district directors. Neither immigration judges

10. The Justice Department revived this approach eight years later. The Department began in 1988 to apply more rigorous scrutiny to refugee claims filed worldwide by persons who seek resettlement through the U.S. overseas refugee program. It sought, however, to mollify some adverse domestic reaction by offering to parole all Soviet Union nationals who were excluded from the refugee program because of failure to demonstrate refugee status under these more demanding tests. Several thousand persons came to the United States in this manner. But because parolees do not qualify for the financial assistance or certain other benefits provided to recognized refugees, the controversy continued. See Chapter Eight, pp. 751–55.

11. The Office of Refugees, Asylum and Parole in the INS Central Office (CORAP) grants several hundred requests for "humanitarian parole" each year, primarily to allow family members with approved visa petitions to enter before their place on the waiting list has been reached, owing to individually compelling circumstances. For the guidelines concerning humanitarian parole, see 69 Interp.Rel. 1099 (1992); 70 *id.* 1071, 1296 (1993). This centralized procedure for humanitarian parole is quite separate from the authority exercised by district directors—for example to release aliens pending completion of exclusion proceedings.

nor the BIA have authority to order parole. *Matter of Conceiro,* 14 I & N Dec. 278 (BIA 1973), *petition for habeas corpus dismissed, Conceiro v. Marks,* 360 F.Supp. 454 (S.D.N.Y.1973). A district director's denial of parole is judicially reviewable for abuse of discretion, but courts have generally been quite deferential in applying this test. *See, e.g., Bertrand v. Sava,* 684 F.2d 204 (2d Cir.1982); *Marczak v. Greene,* 971 F.2d 510 (10th Cir.1992). Some cases have applied an even more deferential standard of review to the Attorney General's exercise of discretion whether or not to parole aliens pending completion of exclusion proceedings. They have used the "facially legitimate and bona fide reason" approach derived from *Kleindienst v. Mandel, supra. See, e.g., Amanullah v. Nelson,* 811 F.2d 1, 10 (1st Cir.1987); *Mason v. Brooks,* 862 F.2d 190 (9th Cir.1988). For cases applying more intrusive review of parole decisions, however, see, e.g. *Moret v. Karn,* 746 F.2d 989 (3d Cir.1984) (reversing parole revocation where INS failed to follow its own internal procedures); *Li v. Greene,* 767 F.Supp. 1087 (D.Colo.1991); *Noorani v. Smith,* 810 F.Supp. 280 (W.D.Wash.1993).

Chapter Four

ADMISSION AND EXCLUSION: PROCEDURES

The efforts of agencies and courts to implement the complicated substantive provisions outlined in Chapter Three have resulted in an elaborate set of admission and exclusion procedures and a distinctive due process jurisprudence. No doubt you have gained some acquaintance with the procedures from the previous readings. Here we will set forth those procedures more comprehensively. We begin, however, by considering the constitutional framework for admission procedures.

SECTION A. DUE PROCESS IN EXCLUSION PROCEEDINGS

Since 1950, the due process rights of aliens in exclusion proceedings might well be summarized in one famous (and rather chilling) sentence written by Justice Minton: "Whatever the procedure authorized by Congress is, it is due process as far as an alien denied entry is concerned." *United States ex rel. Knauff v. Shaughnessy*, 338 U.S. 537, 544, 70 S.Ct. 309, 313, 94 L.Ed. 317 (1950). *Knauff* has never been overruled; hence you might expect this section of the casebook to be exceedingly short. Instead we will spend several pages examining *Knauff* and a 1953 case, *Mezei,* which accomplished the improbable feat of rendering the *Knauff* outcome even more severe. We do so precisely because we view the *Knauff-Mezei* doctrine as extreme. It has provoked a steady stream of critical academic commentary, and there are signs in some more recent decisions, including the Supreme Court's *Plasencia* opinion, reprinted below, that modification of the doctrine may be possible.

Part of the criticism rests on the way the doctrine assigns excludable aliens to constitutional limbo. Part of it also rests on the odd way the court of the 1950s seemed to draw the lines between the aliens who fall into this disfavored class and those who manage to get more complete due process protection (traditionally, those who are in deportation rather than exclusion proceedings). We will introduce these due process questions here, but we will still be discussing them at various places through

Chapters Five and Six, as we move away from the border and consider constitutional limitations on deportation proceedings.

UNITED STATES EX REL. KNAUFF v. SHAUGHNESSY

Supreme Court of the United States, 1950.
338 U.S. 537, 70 S.Ct. 309, 94 L.Ed. 317.

MR. JUSTICE MINTON delivered the opinion of the Court.

May the United States exclude without hearing, solely upon a finding by the Attorney General that her admission would be prejudicial to the interests of the United States, the alien wife of a citizen who had served honorably in the armed forces of the United States during World War II? The District Court for the Southern District of New York held that it could, and the Court of Appeals for the Second Circuit affirmed. We granted certiorari to examine the question especially in the light of the War Brides Act of December 28, 1945.

Petitioner was born in Germany in 1915. She left Germany and went to Czechoslovakia during the Hitler regime. There she was married and divorced. She went to England in 1939 as a refugee. Thereafter she served with the Royal Air Force efficiently and honorably from January 1, 1943, until May 30, 1946. She then secured civilian employment with the War Department of the United States in Germany. Her work was rated "very good" and "excellent." On February 28, 1948, with the permission of the Commanding General at Frankfurt, Germany, she married Kurt W. Knauff, a naturalized citizen of the United States. He is an honorably discharged United States Army veteran of World War II. He is, as he was at the time of his marriage, a civilian employee of the United States Army at Frankfurt, Germany.

On August 14, 1948, petitioner sought to enter the United States to be naturalized. On that day she was temporarily excluded from the United States and detained at Ellis Island. On October 6, 1948, the Assistant Commissioner of Immigration and Naturalization recommended that she be permanently excluded without a hearing on the ground that her admission would be prejudicial to the interests of the United States. On the same day the Attorney General adopted this recommendation and entered a final order of exclusion. To test the right of the Attorney General to exclude her without a hearing for security reasons, *habeas corpus* proceedings were instituted in the Southern District of New York, based primarily on provisions of the War Brides Act. The District Court dismissed the writ, and the Court of Appeals affirmed.

The authority of the Attorney General to order the exclusion of aliens without a hearing flows from the Act of June 21, 1941, amending § 1 of the Act of May 22, 1918 (55 Stat. 252, 22 U.S.C. § 223). By the 1941 amendment it was provided that the President might, upon finding that the interests of the United States required it, impose additional restrictions and prohibitions on the entry into and departure of persons from the United States during the national emergency proclaimed May 27, 1941. Pursuant to this Act of Congress the President on November 14, 1941, issued Proclamation 2523. This proclamation recited that the interests of the United States required the imposition of additional restrictions upon the entry into and departure of persons from the country and authorized the promulgation of regulations jointly by the Secretary of State and the Attorney General. It was also provided that no alien should be permitted to enter the United States if it were found that such entry would be prejudicial to the interests of the United States.

Pursuant to the authority of this proclamation the Secretary of State and the Attorney General issued regulations governing the entry into and departure of persons from the United States during the national emergency. Subparagraphs (a) to (k) of § 175.53 of these regulations specified the classes of aliens whose entry into the United States was deemed prejudicial to the public interest. Subparagraph (b) of § 175.57 provided that the Attorney General might deny an alien a hearing before a board of inquiry in special cases where he determined that the alien was excludable under the regulations on the basis of information of a confidential nature, the disclosure of which would be prejudicial to the public interest.

It was under this regulation § 175.57(b) that petitioner was excluded by the Attorney General and denied a hearing. We are asked to pass upon the validity of this action.

At the outset we wish to point out that an alien who seeks admission to this country may not do so under any claim of right. Admission of aliens to the United States is a privilege granted by the sovereign United States Government. Such privilege is granted to an alien only upon such terms as the United States shall prescribe. It must be exercised in accordance with the procedure which the United States provides. *Nishimura Ekiu* v. *United States,* 142 U.S. 651, 659, 12 S.Ct. 336, 338, 35 L.Ed. 1146; *Fong Yue Ting* v. *United States,* 149 U.S. 698, 711, 13 S.Ct. 1016, 1021, 37 L.Ed. 905.

Petitioner contends that the 1941 Act and the regulations thereunder are void to the extent that they contain unconstitutional delegations of legislative power. But there is no question of inappropriate delegation of legislative power involved here. The exclusion of aliens is a fundamental act of sovereignty. The right to do so stems not alone from legislative power but is inherent in the executive power to control the foreign affairs of the nation. When Congress prescribes a procedure concerning the admissibility of aliens, it is not dealing alone with a legislative power. It is implementing an inherent executive power.

Thus the decision to admit or to exclude an alien may be lawfully placed with the President, who may in turn delegate the carrying out of this function to a responsible executive officer of the sovereign, such as the Attorney General. The action of the executive officer under such authority is final and conclusive. Whatever the rule may be concerning deportation of persons who have gained entry into the United States, it is not within the province of any court, unless expressly authorized by law, to review the determination of the political branch of the Government to exclude a given alien. *Nishimura Ekiu* v. *United States,* 142 U.S. 651, 659–660, 12 S.Ct. 336, 338, 35 L.Ed. 1146; *Fong Yue Ting* v. *United States,* 149 U.S. 698,

713–714, 13 S.Ct. 1016, 1022, 37 L.Ed. 905; *Ludecke* v. *Watkins,* 335 U.S. 160, 68 S.Ct. 1429, 92 L.Ed. 1881. *Cf. Yamataya* v. *Fisher,* 189 U.S. 86, 101, 23 S.Ct. 611, 614, 47 L.Ed. 721. Normally Congress supplies the conditions of the privilege of entry into the United States. But because the power of exclusion of aliens is also inherent in the executive department of the sovereign, Congress may in broad terms authorize the executive to exercise the power, *e.g.,* as was done here, for the best interests of the country during a time of national emergency. Executive officers may be entrusted with the duty of specifying the procedures for carrying out the congressional intent. What was said in *Lichter* v. *United States,* 334 U.S. 742, 785, 68 S.Ct. 1294, 1316, 92 L.Ed. 1694, is equally appropriate here:

> "It is not necessary that Congress supply administrative officials with a specific formula for their guidance in a field where flexibility and the adaptation of the congressional policy to infinitely variable conditions constitute the essence of the program.... Standards prescribed by Congress are to be read in the light of the conditions to which they are to be applied. 'They derive much meaningful content from the purpose of the Act, its factual background and the statutory context in which they appear.'"

Whatever the procedure authorized by Congress is, it is due process as far as an alien denied entry is concerned. *Nishimura Ekiu* v. *United States, supra; Ludecke* v. *Watkins, supra.*

In the particular circumstances of the instant case the Attorney General, exercising the discretion entrusted to him by Congress and the President, concluded upon the basis of confidential information that the public interest required that petitioner be denied the privilege of entry into the United States. He denied her a hearing on the matter because, in his judgment, the disclosure of the information on which he based that opinion would itself endanger the public security.

We find no substantial merit to petitioner's contention that the regulations were not "reasonable" as they were required to be by the 1941 Act. We think them reasonable in the circumstances of the period for which they were authorized, namely, the national emergency of World War II. * * * We reiterate that we are dealing here with a matter of *privilege.* Petitioner had no vested *right* of entry which could be the subject of a prohibition against retroactive operation of regulations affecting her status.

Affirmed.

MR. JUSTICE JACKSON, whom MR. JUSTICE BLACK and MR. JUSTICE FRANKFURTER join, dissenting.

I do not question the constitutional power of Congress to authorize immigration authorities to turn back from our gates any alien or class of aliens. But I do not find that Congress has authorized an abrupt and brutal exclusion of the wife of an American citizen without a hearing.

* * *

[JUSTICE FRANKFURTER's dissenting opinion is omitted. JUSTICE DOUGLAS and JUSTICE CLARK took no part in deciding the case.]

SHAUGHNESSY v. UNITED STATES EX REL. MEZEI

Supreme Court of the United States, 1953.
345 U.S. 206, 73 S.Ct. 625, 97 L.Ed. 956.

MR. JUSTICE CLARK delivered the opinion of the Court.

This case concerns an alien immigrant permanently excluded from the United States on security grounds but stranded in his temporary haven on Ellis Island because other countries will not take him back. The issue is whether the Attorney General's continued exclusion of respondent without a hearing amounts to an unlawful detention, so that courts may admit him temporarily to the United States on bond until arrangements are made for his departure abroad. After a hearing on respondent's petition for a writ of habeas corpus, the District Court so held and authorized his temporary admission on $5,000 bond. The Court of Appeals affirmed that action, but directed reconsideration of the terms of the parole. Accordingly, the District Court entered a modified order reducing bond to $3,000 and permitting respondent to travel and reside in Buffalo, New York. Bond was posted and respondent released. Because of resultant serious problems in the enforcement of the immigration laws, we granted certiorari.

Respondent's present dilemma springs from these circumstances: Though, as the District Court observed, "[t]here is a certain vagueness about [his] history", respondent seemingly was born in Gibraltar of Hungarian or Rumanian parents and lived in the United States from 1923 to 1948. In May of that year he sailed for Europe, apparently to visit his dying mother in Rumania. Denied entry there, he remained in Hungary for some 19 months, due to "difficulty in securing an exit permit." Finally, armed with a quota immigration visa issued by the American Consul in Budapest, he proceeded to France and boarded the *Ile de France* in Le Havre bound for New York. Upon arrival on February 9, 1950, he was temporarily excluded from the United States by an immigration inspector acting pursuant to the Passport Act as amended and regulations thereunder [the same statute and regulations applied in the *Knauff* case].

Pending disposition of his case he was received at Ellis Island. After reviewing the evidence, the Attorney General on May 10, 1950, ordered the temporary exclusion to be made permanent without a hearing before a board of special inquiry, on the "basis of information of a confidential nature, the disclosure of which would be prejudicial to the public interest." That determination rested on a finding that respondent's entry would be prejudicial to the public interest for security reasons. But thus far all attempts to effect respondent's departure have failed: Twice he shipped out to return whence he came; France and Great Britain refused him permission to land. The State Department has unsuccessfully negotiated with Hungary for his readmission. Respondent personally applied for entry to about a dozen Latin American countries but all turned him down. So in June 1951 respondent advised the Immigration and Naturalization Service that he would exert no further efforts to depart. In short, respondent sat on Ellis Island because this country shut him out and others were unwilling to take him in.

Asserting unlawful confinement on Ellis Island, he sought relief through a series of habeas corpus proceedings. After four unsuccessful efforts on respondent's part, the United States District Court for the Southern District of New York on November 9, 1951, sustained the writ. The District Judge, vexed by the problem of "an alien who has no place to go", did not question the validity of the exclusion order but deemed further "detention" after 21 months excessive and justifiable only by affirmative proof of respondent's danger to the public safety. When the Government declined to divulge such evidence, even *in camera,* the District Court directed respondent's conditional parole on bond. By a divided vote, the Court of Appeals affirmed. Postulating that the power to hold could never be broader than the power to remove or shut out and that to "continue an alien's confinement beyond that moment when deportation becomes patently impossible is to deprive him of his liberty", the court found respondent's "confinement" no longer justifiable as a means of removal elsewhere, thus not authorized by statute, and in violation of due process. Judge Learned Hand, dissenting, took a different view: The Attorney General's order was one of "exclusion" and not "deportation"; respondent's transfer from ship to shore on Ellis Island conferred no additional rights; in fact, no alien so situated "can force us to admit him at all."

* * *

It is true that aliens who have once passed through our gates, even illegally, may be expelled only after proceedings conforming to traditional standards of fairness encompassed in due process of law. *The Japanese Immigrant Case (Kaoru Yamataya v. Fisher),* 1903, 189 U.S. 86, 100–101, 23 S.Ct. 611, 614, 47 L.Ed. 721; *Wong Yang Sung v. McGrath,* 1950, 339 U.S. 33, 49–50, 70 S.Ct. 445, 453–454, 94 L.Ed. 616; *Kwong Hai Chew v. Colding,* 1953, 344 U.S. 590, 598, 73 S.Ct. 472, 478. But an alien on the threshold of initial entry stands on a different footing: "Whatever the procedure authorized by Congress is, it is due process as far as an alien denied entry is concerned." *United States ex rel. Knauff v. Shaughnessy, supra.* And because the action of the executive officer under such authority is final and conclusive, the Attorney General cannot be compelled to disclose the evidence underlying his determinations in an exclusion case; "it is not within the province of any court, unless expressly authorized by law, to review the determination of the political branch of the Government". *United States ex rel. Knauff v. Shaughnessy.* In a case such as this, courts cannot retry the determination of the Attorney General.

Neither respondent's harborage on Ellis Island nor his prior residence here transforms this into something other than an exclusion proceeding. Concededly, his movements are restrained by authority of the United States, and he may by habeas corpus test the validity of his exclusion. But that is true whether he enjoys temporary refuge on land, or remains continuously aboard ship. In sum, harborage at Ellis Island is not an entry into the United States. For purposes of the immigration laws, moreover, the legal incidents of an alien's entry remain unaltered whether he has been here once before or not. He is an entering alien just the same, and may be excluded if unqualified for admission under existing immigration laws.

To be sure, a lawful resident alien may not captiously be deprived of his constitutional rights to procedural due process. *Kwong Hai Chew v. Colding*, 1953, 344 U.S. 590, 601, 73 S.Ct. 472, 479; cf. *Delgadillo v. Carmichael*, 1947, 332 U.S. 388, 68 S.Ct. 10, 92 L.Ed. 17. Only the other day we held that under some circumstances temporary absence from our shores cannot constitutionally deprive a returning lawfully resident alien of his right to be heard. *Kwong Hai Chew v. Colding, supra.* Chew, an alien seaman admitted by an Act of Congress to permanent residence in the United States, signed articles of maritime employment as chief steward on a vessel of American registry with home port in New York City. Though cleared by the Coast Guard for his voyage, on his return from four months at sea he was "excluded" without a hearing on security grounds. On the facts of that case, including reference to § 307(d)(2) of the Nationality Act of 1940, we felt justified in "assimilating" his status for constitutional purposes to that of continuously present alien residents entitled to hearings at least before an executive or administrative tribunal. Accordingly, to escape constitutional conflict we held the administrative regulations authorizing exclusion without hearing in certain security cases inapplicable to aliens so protected by the Fifth Amendment.

But respondent's history here drastically differs from that disclosed in Chew's case. Unlike Chew who with full security clearance and documentation pursued his vocation for four months aboard an American ship, respondent, apparently without authorization or reentry papers,[9] simply left the United States and remained behind the Iron Curtain for 19 months. Moreover, while § 307 of the 1940 Nationality Act regards maritime service such as Chew's to be continuous residence for naturalization purposes, that section deems protracted absence such as respondent's a clear break in an alien's continuous residence here. In such circumstances, we have no difficulty in holding respondent an entrant alien or "assimilated to [that] status" for constitutional purposes. That being so, the Attorney General may lawfully exclude respondent without a hearing as authorized by the emergency regulations promulgated pursuant to the Passport Act. Nor need he disclose the evidence upon which that determination rests. *United States ex rel. Knauff v. Shaughnessy*, 1950, 338 U.S. 537, 70 S.Ct. 309, 94 L.Ed. 317.

There remains the issue of respondent's continued exclusion on Ellis Island. Aliens seeking entry from contiguous lands obviously can be turned back at the border without more. While the Government might keep entrants by sea aboard the vessel pending determination of their admissibility, resulting hardships to the alien and inconvenience to the carrier persuaded Congress to adopt a more generous course. By statute it authorized, in cases such as this, aliens' temporary removal from ship to

---

9. * * * Of course, neither a reentry permit, issuable upon proof of prior lawful admission to the United States, nor an immigration visa entitles an otherwise inadmissible alien to entry. An immigrant is not unaware of this; [the statute] directs those facts to be "printed conspicuously upon every immigration visa." * * *

shore. But such temporary harborage, an act of legislative grace, bestows no additional rights. Congress meticulously specified that such shelter ashore "shall not be considered a landing" nor relieve the vessel of the duty to transport back the alien if ultimately excluded. And this Court has long considered such temporary arrangements as not affecting an alien's status; he is treated as if stopped at the border.

Thus we do not think that respondent's continued exclusion deprives him of any statutory or constitutional right. It is true that resident aliens temporarily detained pending expeditious consummation of deportation proceedings may be released on bond by the Attorney General whose discretion is subject to judicial review. *Carlson v. Landon*, 1952, 342 U.S. 524, 72 S.Ct. 525, 96 L.Ed. 547. By that procedure aliens uprooted from our midst may rejoin the community until the Government effects their leave. An exclusion proceeding grounded on danger to the national security, however, presents different considerations; neither the rationale nor the statutory authority for such release exists. Ordinarily to admit an alien barred from entry on security grounds nullifies the very purpose of the exclusion proceeding; Congress in 1950 declined to include such authority in the statute. That exclusion by the United States plus other nations' inhospitality results in present hardship cannot be ignored. But, the times being what they are, Congress may well have felt that other countries ought not shift the onus to us; that an alien in respondent's position is no more ours than theirs. Whatever our individual estimate of that policy and the fears on which it rests, respondent's right to enter the United States depends on the congressional will, and courts cannot substitute their judgment for the legislative mandate.

Reversed.

MR. JUSTICE BLACK, with whom MR. JUSTICE DOUGLAS concurs, dissenting.

Mezei came to this country in 1923 and lived as a resident alien in Buffalo, New York, for twenty-five years. He made a trip to Europe in 1948 and was stopped at our shore on his return in 1950. Without charge of or conviction for any crime, he was for two years held a prisoner on Ellis Island by order of the Attorney General. Mezei sought habeas corpus in the District Court. He wanted to go to his wife and home in Buffalo. The Attorney General defended the imprisonment by alleging that it would be dangerous to the Nation's security to let Mezei go home even temporarily on bail. Asked for proof of this, the Attorney General answered the judge that all his information was "of a confidential nature" so much so that telling any of it or even telling the names of any of his secret informers would jeopardize the safety of the Nation. Finding that Mezei's life as a resident alien in Buffalo had been "unexceptional" and that no facts had been proven to justify his continued imprisonment, the District Court granted bail. The Court of Appeals approved. Now this Court orders Mezei to leave his home and go back to his island prison to stay indefinitely, maybe for life.

MR. JUSTICE JACKSON forcefully points out the danger in the Court's holding that Mezei's liberty is completely at the mercy of the unreviewable discretion of the Attorney General. I join MR. JUSTICE JACKSON in the belief that Mezei's continued imprisonment without a hearing violates due process of law.

* * *

MR. JUSTICE JACKSON, whom MR. JUSTICE FRANKFURTER joins, dissenting.

Fortunately it still is startling, in this country, to find a person held indefinitely in executive custody without accusation of crime or judicial trial. Executive imprisonment has been considered oppressive and lawless since John, at Runnymede, pledged that no free man should be imprisoned, dispossessed, outlawed, or exiled save by the judgment of his peers or by the law of the land. The judges of England developed the writ of habeas corpus largely to preserve these immunities from executive restraint.

Under the best tradition of Anglo–American law, courts will not deny hearing to an unconvicted prisoner just because he is an alien whose keep, in legal theory, is just outside our gates. Lord Mansfield, in the celebrated case holding that slavery was unknown to the common law of England, ran his writ of habeas corpus in favor of an alien, an African Negro slave, and against the master of a ship at anchor in the Thames.

I.

What is our case?[2] In contemplation of law, I agree, it is that of an alien who asks admission to the country. Concretely, however, it is that of a lawful and law-abiding inhabitant of our country for a quarter of a century, long ago admitted for permanent residence, who seeks to return home. After a foreign visit to his aged and ailing mother that was prolonged by disturbed conditions of Eastern Europe, he obtained a visa for admission issued by our consul and returned to New York. There the Attorney General refused to honor his documents and turned him back as a menace to this Nation's security. This man, who seems to have led a life of unrelieved insignificance, must have been astonished to find himself suddenly putting the Government of the United States in such fear that it was afraid to tell him why it was afraid of him. He was shipped and reshipped to France, which twice refused him landing. Great Britain declined, and no other European country has been found willing to open its doors to him. Twelve countries of the American Hemisphere refused his applications. Since we proclaimed him a Samson who might pull down the pillars of our temple, we should not be surprised if peoples less prosperous, less strongly established and less stable feared to take him off our timorous hands. With something of a record as an unwanted man, neither his efforts nor those of the United States Government any longer promise to find him an abiding place. For nearly two years he was held in custody of the immigration authorities of the United States at Ellis Island, and if the Government has its way he seems likely to be detained indefinitely, perhaps for life, for a cause known only to the Attorney General.

2. I recite facts alleged in the petition for the writ. Since the Government declined to try the case on the merits, I think we must consider the question on well-pleaded allegations of the petition. Petitioner might fail to make good on a hearing; the question is, must he fail without one?

Is respondent deprived of liberty? The Government answers that he was "transferred to Ellis Island on August 1, 1950 for safekeeping," and "is not being detained in the usual sense, but is in custody solely to prevent him from gaining entry into the United States in violation of law. He is free to depart from the United States to any country of his choice." Government counsel ingeniously argued that Ellis Island is his "refuge" whence he is free to take leave in any direction except west. That might mean freedom, if only he were an amphibian! Realistically, this man is incarcerated by a combination of forces which keeps him as effectually as a prison, the dominant and proximate of these forces being the United States immigration authority. It overworks legal fiction to say that one is free in law when by the commonest of common sense he is bound. Despite the impeccable legal logic of the Government's argument on this point, it leads to an artificial and unreal conclusion. We must regard this alien as deprived of liberty, and the question is whether the deprivation is a denial of due process of law.

The Government on this point argues that "no alien has any constitutional right to entry into the United States"; that "the alien has only such rights as Congress sees fit to grant in exclusion proceedings"; that "the so-called detention is still merely a continuation of the exclusion which is specifically authorized by Congress"; that since "the restraint is not incidental to an order [of exclusion] but is itself the effectuation of the exclusion order, there is no limit to its continuance" other than statutory, which means no limit at all. The Government all but adopts the words of one of the officials responsible for the administration of this Act who testified before a congressional committee as to an alien applicant, that "He has no rights."

The interpretations of the Fifth Amendment's command that no person shall be deprived of life, liberty or property without due process of law, come about to this: reasonable general legislation reasonably applied to the individual. The question is whether the Government's detention of respondent is compatible with these tests of substance and procedure.

II.   Substantive Due Process.

* * *

Due process does not invest any alien with a right to enter the United States, nor confer on those admitted the right to remain against the national will. Nothing in the Constitution requires admission or sufferance of aliens hostile to our scheme of government.

Nor do I doubt that due process of law will tolerate some impounding of an alien where it is deemed essential to the safety of the state.

* * *

I conclude that detention of an alien would not be inconsistent with substantive due process, provided—and this is where my dissent begins—he is accorded procedural due process of law.

III. PROCEDURAL DUE PROCESS.

Procedural fairness, if not all that originally was meant by due process of law, is at least what it most uncompromisingly requires. Procedural due process is more elemental and less flexible than substantive due process. It yields less to the times, varies less with conditions, and defers much less to legislative judgment. Insofar as it is technical law, it must be a specialized responsibility within the competence of the judiciary on which they do not bend before political branches of the Government, as they should on matters of policy which compromise substantive law.

If it be conceded that in some way this alien could be confined, does it matter what the procedure is? Only the untaught layman or the charlatan lawyer can answer that procedures matter not. Procedural fairness and regularity are of the indispensable essence of liberty. Severe substantive laws can be endured if they are fairly and impartially applied. Indeed, if put to the choice, one might well prefer to live under Soviet substantive law applied in good faith by our common-law procedures than under our substantive law enforced by Soviet procedural practices. Let it not be overlooked that due process of law is not for the sole benefit of an accused. It is the best insurance for the Government itself against those blunders which leave lasting stains on a system of justice but which are bound to occur on *ex parte* consideration. *Cf. United States ex rel. Knauff v. Shaughnessy*, 338 U.S. 537, 70 S.Ct. 309, 94 L.Ed. 317, which was a near miss, saved by further administrative and congressional hearings from perpetrating an injustice. *See* Knauff, *The Ellen Knauff Story* (New York) 1952.

Our law may, and rightly does, place more restrictions on the alien than on the citizen. But basic fairness in hearing procedures does not vary with the status of the accused. If the procedures used to judge this alien are fair and just, no good reason can be given why they should not be extended to simplify the condemnation of citizens. If they would be unfair to citizens, we cannot defend the fairness of them when applied to the more helpless and handicapped alien. This is at the root of our holdings that the resident alien must be given a fair hearing to test an official claim that he is one of a deportable class. *Wong Yang Sung v. McGrath*, 339 U.S. 33, 70 S.Ct. 445, 94 L.Ed. 616.

The most scrupulous observance of due process, including the right to know a charge, to be confronted with the accuser, to cross-examine informers and to produce evidence in one's behalf, is especially necessary where the occasion of detention is fear of future misconduct, rather than crimes committed.

* * *

Because the respondent has no right of entry, does it follow that he has no rights at all? Does the power to exclude mean that exclusion may be continued or effectuated by any means which happen to seem appropriate to the authorities? It would effectuate his exclusion to eject him bodily into the sea or to set him adrift in a rowboat. Would not such measures be condemned judicially as a deprivation of life without due process of law?

Suppose the authorities decide to disable an alien from entry by confiscating his valuables and money. Would we not hold this a taking of property without due process of law? Here we have a case that lies between the taking of life and the taking of property; it is the taking of liberty. It seems to me that this, occurring within the United States or its territorial waters, may be done only by proceedings which meet the test of due process of law.

Exclusion of an alien without judicial hearing, of course, does not deny due process when it can be accomplished merely by turning him back on land or returning him by sea. But when indefinite confinement becomes the means of enforcing exclusion, it seems to me that due process requires that the alien be informed of its grounds and have a fair chance to overcome them. This is the more due him when he is entrapped into leaving the other shore by reliance on a visa which the Attorney General refuses to honor.

It is evident that confinement of respondent no longer can be justified as a step in the process of turning him back to the country whence he came. Confinement is no longer ancillary to exclusion; it can now be justified only as the alternative to normal exclusion. It is an end in itself.

The Communist conspiratorial technique of infiltration poses a problem which sorely tempts the Government to resort to confinement of suspects on secret information secretly judged. I have not been one to discount the Communist evil. But my apprehensions about the security of our form of government are about equally aroused by those who refuse to recognize the dangers of Communism and those who will not see danger in anything else.

Congress has ample power to determine whom we will admit to our shores and by what means it will effectuate its exclusion policy. The only limitation is that it may not do so by authorizing United States officers to take without due process of law the life, the liberty or the property of an alien who has come within our jurisdiction; and that means he must meet a fair hearing with fair notice of the charges.[9]

It is inconceivable to me that this measure of simple justice and fair dealing would menace the security of this country. No one can make me believe that we are that far gone.

9. The trial court sought to reconcile due process for the individual with claims of security by suggesting that the Attorney General disclose *in camera* enough to enable a judicial determination of the legality of the confinement. The Attorney General refused. I do not know just how an *in camera* proceeding would be handled in this kind of case. If respondent, with or without counsel, were present, disclosures to them might well result in disclosures by them. If they are not allowed to be present, it is hard to see how it would answer the purpose of testing the Government's case by cross-examination or counter-evidence, which is what a hearing is for. The questions raised by the proposal need not be discussed since they do not call for decision here.

HENRY HART, THE POWER OF CONGRESS TO LIMIT THE JURISDICTION OF THE FEDERAL COURTS: AN EXERCISE IN DIALECTIC

66 Harv.L.Rev. 1362, 1389–96 (1953).

Q. How then can aliens have any rights to assert in habeas corpus? I thought they came and stayed only at the pleasure of Congress.

A. The Supreme Court seemed to think so, too, at first. In its earliest decisions the Court started with the premise of plenary legislative power and on that basis seemed to be prepared to take the word "final" in the statutes literally and to decline any review whatever, even in deportation cases.[84]

Before long, however, it began to see that the premise needed to be qualified—that a power to lay down general rules, even if it were plenary, did not necessarily include a power to be arbitrary or to authorize administrative officials to be arbitrary. It saw that, on the contrary, the very existence of a jurisdiction in habeas corpus, coupled with the constitutional guarantee of due process, implied a regime of law. It saw that in such a regime the courts had a responsibility to see that statutory authority was not transgressed, that a reasonable procedure was used in exercising the authority, and—seemingly also—that human beings were not unreasonably subjected, even by direction of Congress, to an uncontrolled official discretion.[85]

Under the benign influence of these ideas, the law grew and flourished, like Egypt under the rule of Joseph. Thousands of cases were decided whose presence in the courts cannot be explained on any other basis. But what the status of many of these cases is now is not altogether clear.

Q. Why?

A. There arose up new justices in Washington which knew not Joseph. Citing only the harsh precepts of the very earliest decisions, they began to decide cases accordingly, as if nothing had happened in the years between.

---

84. The Chinese Exclusion Case, 130 U.S. 581 (1889) (admission); Nishimura Ekiu v. United States, 142 U.S. 651 (1892) (admission);. Fong Yue Ting v. United States, 149 U.S. 698 (1893) (deportation); Lem Moon Sing v. United States, 158 U.S. 538 (1895) (admission); Li Sing v. United States, 180 U.S. 486 (1901) (deportation); Fok Yung Yo v. United States, 185 U.S. 296 (1902) (admission); Lee Lung v. Patterson, 186 U.S. 168 (1902) (admission).

85. The turning point was the Japanese Immigrant Case (Yamataya v. Fisher), 189 U.S. 86 (1903), involving an immigrant taken into custody for deportation four days after her landing. After referring to earlier cases cited in note 84, *supra,* the Court said:

> But this court has never held, nor must we now be understood as holding, that administrative officers, when executing the provisions of a statute involving the liberty of persons, may disregard the fundamental principles that inhere in "due process of law" as understood at the time of the adoption of the Constitution. One of these principles is that no person shall be deprived of his liberty without opportunity, at some time, to be heard, before such officers, in respect of the matters upon which that liberty depends. ... No such arbitrary power can exist where the principles involved in due process of law are recognized.
>
> This is the reasonable construction of the acts of Congress here in question, and they need not be otherwise interpreted. ... An act of Congress must be taken to be constitutional unless the contrary plainly and palpably appears. *Id.* at 100–01.

Compare Justice Holmes' formulation in *Chin Yow* [v. *United States,* 208 U.S. 8, 12 (1908),] an admission case: "The decision of the Department is final, but that is on the presupposition that the decision was after a hearing in good faith, however summary in form."

* * *

In the *Knauff* case, Justice Minton said that, "Whatever the rule may be concerning deportation of persons who have gained entry into the United States, it is not within the province of any court, unless expressly authorized by law, to review the determination of the political branch of the Government to exclude a given alien." Since Congress has never expressly authorized any court to review an exclusion order, this statement either ignores or renders obsolete every habeas corpus case in the books involving an exclusion proceeding.

On the procedural side, Justice Minton went so far as to say that, "Whatever the procedure authorized by Congress is, it is due process as far as an alien denied entry is concerned," a patently preposterous proposition.

Justice Clark repeated and applied both statements in the *Mezei* case.

Q. Then we're back where we started half a century ago?

A. Oh no. The aberrations have been largely confined to admission cases. In deportations, for the most part, the Court has adhered to the sound and humane philosophy of the middle period. In some respects it has even extended its applications.

What is happening is what so often happens when there has been a development in the law of which the judges are incompletely aware. Some decisions follow the earlier precedents and some the later, until the conflict of principle becomes intolerable, and it gets ironed out.

Q. Do you mean to say that you don't think there are any material differences between the case of an alien trying to get into the country and the case of one whom the Government is trying to put out?

A. No. Of course there are differences in these alien cases—not only those simple ones but many others.[92] But such differences are material only in determining the content of due process in the particular situation. What process is due always depends upon the circumstances, and the Due Process Clause is always flexible enough to take the circumstances into account.

The distinctions the Court has been drawing recently, however, are of a different order. They are distinctions between when the Constitution applies and when it does not apply at all. Any such distinction as that produces a conflict of basic principle, and is inadmissible.

Q. What basic principle?

92. For example, if the alien is applying for admission, the force of his claim may vary according to whether he is coming for the first time or seeking to resume a permanent residence previously authorized. If he is coming for the first time, it may make a difference whether he is a stowaway or in possession of a duly authorized visa. If he has a visa, it may make a difference whether it is one for permanent residence or only for a temporary visit. If he is seeking to resume a previously authorized residence, it may make a difference whether he carries a reentry permit, border crossing card, or other document purporting to facilitate reentry.

Similarly, if the alien is resisting expulsion, the force of his claim may vary according to whether he entered legally or illegally. If he entered legally, it may make a difference whether he was duly admitted for permanent residence or came in only as a seaman, student, or other temporary visitor for business or pleasure.

A. The great and generating principle of this whole body of law—that the Constitution always applies when a court is sitting with jurisdiction in habeas corpus. For then the court has always to inquire, not only whether the statutes have been observed, but whether the petitioner before it has been "deprived of life, liberty, or property, without due process of law," or injured in any other way in violation of the fundamental law.

That is the premise of the deportation cases, and it applies in exactly the same way in admission cases. The harsh early decisions announcing a contrary premise applied such a contrary premise without distinction in both deportations and admissions. Indeed, Justice Minton cited early admission and deportation precedents indiscriminately in *Knauff*, without noticing that the principle which had compelled repudiation of the deportation precedents required repudiation also of the others.

That principle forbids a constitutional court with jurisdiction in habeas corpus from ever accepting as an adequate return to the writ the mere statement that what has been done is authorized by act of Congress. The inquiry remains, if *Marbury v. Madison* still stands, whether the act of Congress is consistent with the fundamental law. Only upon such a principle could the Court reject, as it surely would, a return to the writ which informed it that the applicant for admission lay stretched upon a rack with pins driven in behind his finger nails pursuant to authority duly conferred by statute in order to secure the information necessary to determine his admissibility. The same principle which would justify rejection of this return imposes responsibility to inquire into the adequacy of other returns.

Granting that the requirements of due process must vary with the circumstances, and allowing them all the flexibility that can conceivably be claimed, it still remains true that the Court is obliged, by the presuppositions of its whole jurisdiction in this area, to decide whether what has been done is consistent with due process—and not simply pass back the buck to an assertedly all-powerful and unimpeachable Congress.

Q. Would it have made any difference in *Knauff* and *Mezei* if the Court had said that the aliens were entitled to due process and had got it, instead of saying that they weren't entitled to it at all?

A. At least the opinions in that case might have been intellectually respectable. Whether the results would have been different depends upon subtler considerations. Usually, however, it *does* make a difference whether a judge treats a question as not properly before him at all, or as involving a matter for decision.

Take *Knauff*, for example. Remember that the War Brides Act was highly ambiguous on the point in issue of whether exclusion without a hearing was authorized. If one approaches such a question on the assumption that it is constitutionally neutral, as Justice Minton declared it to be, it is at least possible to resolve the doubt as he resolved it. But if one sees constitutional overtones, the most elementary principles of interpretation call for the opposite conclusion. Note how crucially important constitutional assumptions have been in the interpretation of statutes throughout this whole area.

Again, take the facts of *Mezei,* in comparison with its *dicta.* The *dicta* say, in effect, that a Mexican wetback who sneaks successfully across the Rio Grande is entitled to the full panoply of due process in his deportation. But the holding says that a duly admitted immigrant of twenty-five years' standing who has married an American wife and sired American children, who goes abroad as the law allows to visit a dying parent, and who then returns with passport and visa duly issued by an American consul, is entitled to nothing—and, indeed, may be detained on an island in New York harbor for the rest of his life if no other country can be found to take him.

I cannot believe that judges adequately aware of the foundations of principle in this field would permit themselves to trivialize the great guarantees of due process and the freedom writ by such distinctions. And I cannot believe that judges taking responsibility for an affirmative declaration that due process has been accorded would permit themselves to arrive at such brutal conclusions.

Q. But that is what the Court has held. And so I guess that's that.

A. No, it isn't.

The deepest assumptions of the legal order require that the decisions of the highest court in the land be accepted as settling the rights and wrongs of the particular matter immediately in controversy. But the judges who sit for the time being on the court have no authority to remake by fiat alone the fabric of principle by which future cases are to be decided. They are only the custodians of the law and not the owners of it. The law belongs to the people of the country, and to the hundreds of thousands of lawyers and judges who through the years have struggled, in their behalf, to make it coherent and intelligible and responsive to the people's sense of justice.

And so, when justices of the Supreme Court sit down and write opinions in behalf of the Court which ignore the painful forward steps of a whole half century of adjudication, making no effort to relate what then is being done to what the Court has done before, they write without authority for the future. The appeal to principle is still open and, so long as courts of the United States sit with general jurisdiction in habeas corpus, that means an appeal to them and their successors.

* * *

T. ALEXANDER ALEINIKOFF, ALIENS, DUE PROCESS AND "COMMUNITY TIES": A RESPONSE TO MARTIN

44 U.Pitt.L.Rev. 237, 258–59 (1983).

It is not hard to imagine the potential harshness that *Knauff* and *Mezei* can work on the alien at the border. But I would argue that it has been the immigration policymakers and enforcement officials who have suffered the most under the hands-off approach of *Knauff* and *Mezei* in recent years.

In most areas of law, constitutional due process has developed as a dialogue between the courts and the other branches of government. As notions of what constitutes fundamental fairness have evolved over time, the courts have "persuaded" legislators and administrators to add procedural protections when important liberty or property interests are at stake. Even in immigration law, the Court's demand for due process in deportation hearings has produced a steady conversation between the Congress and the courts.

This growth of process is less likely when the Supreme Court announces that it has no role to play. Such is the situation of the alien at the border. The clear signal of *Knauff* and *Mezei* is that the government is free—at least as to initial entrants and undocumented aliens at the border—to provide the procedures it deems appropriate. Given the perceived crush of aliens at the gates, the cost of process, and the difficulty of patrolling tens of thousands of miles of land and sea borders, it is not unreasonable to assume that Congress will opt for less rather than more process. More importantly, the border officials will search for ways to avoid the procedures that Congress mandates.

Recent cases involving the deportation, exclusion and detention of aliens from Haiti and El Salvador indicate that this predictable response to a hands-off approach from the courts has in fact occurred. Not only has due process, up until now, withered on the vine at the border, but the government in such cases continues to argue that the courts have no authority to intervene at all because the cases involve "political questions" and issues of international relations.

Lower courts will obey *Knauff* and *Mezei* for a long time, leading government officials down the garden path. But when the government conduct becomes so outrageous, so obviously unfair, federal judges will put a stop to it. In attempting to do so, however, they will not be able to simply add another flower in the garden of due process, because due process has never taken root at the border. Thus the courts are forced to leap in with both feet, demanding costly and intrusive procedures that make control of the borders and deportation of aliens considerably more difficult.

This is hardly a healthy way for due process to grow; and the results have ramifications beyond the domain of immigration law. If notions of due process reflect judgments of our society about fairness and the importance of procedural regularity, these norms should have their source in as broad a range of human experience as possible. * * *

Notes

1. Congressional and public pressure eventually secured the release of both Knauff and Mezei. Ellen Knauff was ultimately granted a full hearing at which the adverse information was revealed. Although the special inquiry officer ruled against her, the BIA reversed that result on appeal and admitted her to the United States, in a lengthy opinion setting forth in detail the slender evidence that had formed the basis for the

Justice Department's initial judgment that she was dangerous. The BIA opinion is reprinted as an appendix to the book she wrote about her experience. E. Knauff, *The Ellen Knauff Story* (1952). Ignatz Mezei secured his release under a special clemency measure after he had spent nearly four years in detention on Ellis Island. Unlike Knauff, he was paroled rather than formally admitted. *See Trop v. Dulles,* 356 U.S. 86, 102 n. 36, 78 S.Ct. 590, 599 n. 36, 2 L.Ed.2d 630 (1958); Davis, *The Requirements of a Trial–Type Hearing,* 70 Harv.L.Rev. 193, 251 (1956).

2. In 1952, Congress provided explicit statutory authority for the kinds of secret procedures that were employed against Knauff and Mezei on the authority of regulations alone. Section 235(c) of the INA, virtually unchanged since 1952, now permits the Attorney General to order exclusion without a hearing if he acts on the basis of "information of a confidential nature, the disclosure of which * * * would be prejudicial to the public interest, safety, or security." It is invoked far less frequently today than it was in the 1950s, but it is still employed on occasion. *See, e.g., El–Werfalli v. Smith,* 547 F.Supp. 152 (S.D.N.Y.1982) (court sustains exclusion, based on confidential information, of Libyan student coming to attend classes in aircraft training, under exclusion ground banning aliens believed likely to "engage in activities which would be prejudicial to the public interest, or endanger the welfare, safety, or security of the United States"); *Avila v. Rivkind,* 724 F.Supp. 945 (S.D.Fla.1989) (sustaining summary exclusion of long-time opponent of Fidel Castro (Orlando Bosch), who had often been involved in violence).

3. Professor Hart reads *Mezei* as stating, in dicta, that clandestine entrants ("Mexican wetbacks") receive the full panoply of due process rights in deportation proceedings. If so, the case creates an obvious inducement to enter without inspection, for the alien then winds up in a better constitutional position than the unfortunate soul who does as he is supposed to do and presents himself for inspection at the port of entry. Such a result is at best ironic, as several courts have noted. *See, e.g., Louis v. Nelson,* 544 F.Supp. 973, 977 (S.D.Fla.1982), *affirmed in part sub nom. Jean v. Nelson,* 727 F.2d 957 (11th Cir.1984), *modified,* 472 U.S. 846, 105 S.Ct. 2992, 86 L.Ed.2d 664 (1985); *Fernandez v. Wilkinson,* 505 F.Supp. 787, 790 (D.Kan.1980), *affirmed on other grounds sub nom. Rodriguez–Fernandez v. Wilkinson,* 654 F.2d 1382 (10th Cir.1981); *Sannon v. United States,* 427 F.Supp. 1270, 1276 (S.D.Fla.1977), *vacated and remanded on other grounds,* 566 F.2d 104 (5th Cir.1978).

But does *Mezei* have to be read that way? The Court describes the constitutionally preferred class as "aliens who have once passed through our gates, even illegally." Aliens who enter without inspection would seem to have jumped the fence, rather than passing through the gates. Maybe the Court meant to protect only those who were inspected at entry and who are later brought into deportation proceedings because of some defect— some illegality—that comes to light thereafter, revealing that the original entry was illegal, despite compliance with the formalities of inspection. The *Yamataya* and *Wong Yang Sung* cases cited in *Mezei* right after the quoted line can be read as supporting such a distinction. *See* Martin, *Due Process and Membership in the National Community: Political Asylum and*

Beyond, 44 U.Pitt.L.Rev. 165, 231–32 n. 234 (1983). Should such a distinction be made?

In any event, the traditional understanding of *Mezei* has read the case as Hart read it in 1953. See the lower court cases cited earlier in this note. Under the prevailing understanding, an alien's entitlement to due process is to be determined by whether she stands at the border trying to get in (even if she has been here before), or instead has already made an entry and must be removed. In other words, due process depends on whether the alien is in exclusion or deportation proceedings—on location, rather than on the stakes involved for the alien. We ask you to consider, both here and in later chapters, whether this application of the Constitution makes sense, and—a more difficult and important question—what alternative due process doctrines might be more satisfactory.

4. *Kwong Hai Chew v. Colding,* 344 U.S. 590, 73 S.Ct. 472, 97 L.Ed. 576 (1953), decided only a few months before *Mezei* and described therein, presents an odd contrast with the latter case. How should the dividing line be drawn between protected permanent resident aliens like Chew and unprotected aliens like Mezei—length of absence, nature of activities while outside the United States, types of preclearance before departure? Justice Clark's opinion in *Mezei* refers to several factors but fails to reveal which was decisive. The BIA ultimately decided that, at least for purposes of allocating the burden of proof in removal proceedings of any kind, an alien would be treated like Chew whenever he presented "a colorable claim to returning lawful resident alien status." *Matter of Kane,* 15 I & N Dec. 258, 264 (BIA 1975), relying on *Kwong Hai Chew v. Rogers,* 257 F.2d 606 (D.C.Cir.1958) (upon remand after the Supreme Court's decision). *See also Matter of Huang,* 19 I & N Dec. 749, 754 (BIA 1988) (in such a case, INS must establish excludability by clear, unequivocal and convincing evidence—the same standard applied in deportation proceedings). Is this a reasonable reading? Can it possibly account for what happened to Mezei?

5. In his footnote 9 in *Mezei,* Justice Jackson suggests that *in camera* revelation of the evidence would afford no solution to the underlying problem. Do you agree? In many settings, Congress evidently does not. In statutes passed during the 1970s, it often provided for *in camera* court review of sensitive information, as a kind of substitute for the full adversarial testing process. *See Ray v. Turner,* 587 F.2d 1187 (D.C.Cir.1978) (discussing *in camera* review procedures under the Freedom of Information Act) and *United States v. Belfield,* 692 F.2d 141 (D.C.Cir.1982) (discussing similar procedures under the Foreign Intelligence Surveillance Act). *See generally* Thomas Franck, Political Questions/Judicial Answers 137–53 (1992). Furthermore, in sharp contrast to its practices during the 1950s, the Justice Department now appears willing to share with the court *in camera* the sensitive information on which exclusion decisions are based, in those infrequent instances when INA § 235(c) is employed to bar a full hearing. And some courts have developed techniques for dealing with such materials appropriately. For example, in *El-Werfalli v. Smith,* 547 F.Supp. 152 (S.D.N.Y.1982), the court suggested that the information on the public record might not sustain the exclusion order or visa denial, but went on to approve the government decisions after reviewing confidential information

in camera. In *Azzouka v. Sava,* 777 F.2d 68 (2d Cir.1985), *cert. denied,* 479 U.S. 830, 107 S.Ct. 115, 93 L.Ed.2d 62 (1986), the Second Circuit approved the *in camera* judicial consideration of confidential information, as was done in *El-Werfalli.* *See also Azzouka v. Meese,* 820 F.2d 585 (2d Cir.1987) (after remand, court approves denial of asylum as well on the basis of the § 235(c) procedures).[1] Other decisions, however, are to the contrary. The court of appeals opinion in *Abourezk v. Reagan,* 785 F.2d 1043, 1060–61 (D.C.Cir.1986), *affirmed mem. by an equally divided court,* 484 U.S. 1, 108 S.Ct. 252, 98 L.Ed.2d 1 (1988), was sharply critical of the district court's decision to examine the government's *ex parte* submissions *in camera.* *See also Naji v. Nelson,* 113 F.R.D. 548 (N.D.Ill.1986) (citing *Abourezk,* court orders limited discovery of documents the government submitted *in camera*).

6. Justice Jackson's resistance to *in camera* procedures may stem from his uniquely inflexible view of the requirements of procedural due process. As part III of his *Mezei* dissent reveals, he seems to regard due process requirements as a rather fixed set, apparently defined by the usual elements of the traditional adversarial model familiar to us from its use, for example, in criminal trials. Whatever the merits of this view, the Supreme Court has not accepted it. The Court initiated a major reconceptualization of due process analysis in 1970:

> This fundamental transformation [of procedural due process as applied to civil cases] occurred in the "due process revolution" that began with the Supreme Court's 1970 decision in *Goldberg v. Kelly*[, 397 U.S. 254, 90 S.Ct. 1011, 25 L.Ed.2d 287 (1970)]. In that line of cases, the Court moved beyond the restrictive due process doctrines that guaranteed procedural safeguards only for traditional forms of property. * * * The Court rejected wooden reliance on the right-privilege distinction in the context of a procedural due process claim. Instead, it interpreted procedural due process much more broadly to include statutory "entitlements" or other forms of "new property," such as welfare benefits.

> *Goldberg* and its progeny established a two-step analysis for procedural due process claims, in which the Court first asks whether a claimant possesses a "liberty" or "property" interest under the Fifth Amendment's Due Process Clause. Given [such] an "entitlement," the second analytical step is to decide on a case-by-case basis exactly what procedural protections due process requires.

Motomura, *The Curious Evolution of Immigration Law: Procedural Surrogates for Substantive Constitutional Rights,* 92 Colum.L.Rev. 1625, 1651–52 (1992).

---

1. Courts have also sustained the use of confidential information in deportation proceedings, but only if the information bears on discretionary relief from deportation, not on the underlying question of deportability itself. *See Suciu v. INS,* 755 F.2d 127 (8th Cir.1985) (reluctantly considering that *Jay v. Boyd,* 351 U.S. 345, 357 n. 21, 360–61, 76 S.Ct. 919, 926 n. 21, 928, 100 L.Ed. 1242 (1956), which so held, remains good law on the due process requirements).

Modern due process cases, in striking contrast to Justice Jackson's views, stress the flexibility of the concept; procedures acceptable in some settings may be wholly unacceptable in others. What process is due now depends on a three-part balancing test set forth in the landmark case of *Mathews v. Eldridge*, 424 U.S. 319, 96 S.Ct. 893, 47 L.Ed.2d 18 (1976). The test requires the court to consider (1) the interests at stake for the individual, (2) the interest of the government in using the existing procedures, and (3) the gain to accurate decisionmaking that can be expected if one adds the procedural protection for which the individual is arguing. The *Plasencia* case, which follows, discusses *Eldridge* and reflects the current approach. Ask yourself, as you read it, just how much of the *Knauff-Mezei* doctrine survives.

LANDON v. PLASENCIA

Supreme Court of the United States, 1982.
459 U.S. 21, 103 S.Ct. 321, 74 L.Ed.2d 21.

JUSTICE O'CONNOR delivered the opinion of the Court.

* * *

I

Respondent Maria Antonieta Plasencia, a citizen of El Salvador, entered the United States as a permanent resident alien in March, 1970. She established a home in Los Angeles with her husband, a United States citizen, and their minor children. On June 27, 1975, she and her husband travelled to Tijuana, Mexico. During their brief stay in Mexico, they met with several Mexican and Salvadoran nationals and made arrangements to assist their illegal entry into the United States. She agreed to transport the aliens to Los Angeles and furnished some of the aliens with alien registration receipt cards that belonged to her children. When she and her husband attempted to cross the international border at 9:27 on the evening of June 29, 1975, an INS officer at the port of entry found six nonresident aliens in the Plasencias' car. The INS detained the respondent for further inquiry pursuant to § 235(b) of the Immigration and Nationality Act of 1952. In a notice dated June 30, 1975, the INS charged her under § 212(a)(31) of the Act, which provides for the exclusion of any alien seeking admission "who at any time shall have, knowingly and for gain, encouraged, induced, assisted, abetted, or aided any other alien to enter or to try to enter the United States in violation of law," [a] and gave notice that it would hold an exclusion hearing at 11:00 a.m. on June 30, 1975.

An immigration law judge [*sic*] conducted the scheduled exclusion hearing. After hearing testimony from the respondent, her husband, and three of the aliens found in the Plasencias' car, the judge found "clear, convincing and unequivocal" evidence that the respondent did "knowingly

---

a. In 1990, Congress amended this exclusion ground to eliminate the "for gain" requirement. The ground now appears as INA § 212(a)(6)(E), and is subject to a discretionary waiver under § 212(d)(11) if only close family members were smuggled in.—eds.

and for gain encourage, induce, assist, abet, or aid nonresident aliens" to enter or try to enter the United States in violation of law.

* * *

[Plasencia first argued that, as a returning resident absent only briefly, she should have been placed in deportation proceedings rather than exclusion proceedings under the statute. The Court rejected this contention.]

IV

* * * Plasencia [also] argued * * * that she was denied due process in her exclusion hearing. We agree with Plasencia that under the circumstances of this case, she can invoke the Due Process Clause on returning to this country, although we do not decide the contours of the process that is due or whether the process accorded Plasencia was insufficient.

This Court has long held that an alien seeking initial admission to the United States requests a privilege and has no constitutional rights regarding his application, for the power to admit or exclude aliens is a sovereign prerogative. See, *e.g., United States ex rel. Knauff v. Shaughnessy,* 338 U.S. 537, 542, 70 S.Ct. 309, 312, 94 L.Ed. 317 (1950); *Nishimura Ekiu v. United States,* 142 U.S. 651, 659–660, 12 S.Ct. 336, 338, 35 L.Ed. 1146 (1892). Our recent decisions confirm that view. See, *e.g., Fiallo v. Bell,* 430 U.S. 787, 792, 97 S.Ct. 1473, 1477, 52 L.Ed.2d 50 (1977); *Kleindienst v. Mandel,* 408 U.S. 753, 92 S.Ct. 2576, 33 L.Ed.2d 683 (1972). As we explained in *Johnson v. Eisentrager,* 339 U.S. 763, 770, 70 S.Ct. 936, 939, 94 L.Ed. 1255 (1950), however, once an alien gains admission to our country and begins to develop the ties that go with permanent residence his constitutional status changes accordingly. Our cases have frequently suggested that a continuously present resident alien is entitled to a fair hearing when threatened with deportation, and, although we have only rarely held that the procedures provided by the executive were inadequate, we developed the rule that a continuously present permanent resident alien has a right to due process in such a situation.

The question of the procedures due a returning resident alien arose in *Kwong Hai Chew v. Colding,* [344 U.S. 590, 73 S.Ct. 472, 97 L.Ed. 576 (1953)]. There, the regulations permitted the exclusion of an arriving alien without a hearing. We interpreted those regulations not to apply to Chew, a permanent resident alien who was returning from a five-month voyage abroad as a crewman on an American merchant ship. We reasoned that, "For purposes of his constitutional right to due process, we assimilate petitioner's status to that of an alien continuously residing and physically present in the United States." Then, to avoid constitutional problems, we construed the regulation as inapplicable. Although the holding was one of regulatory interpretation, the rationale was one of constitutional law. Any doubts that *Chew* recognized constitutional rights in the resident alien returning from a brief trip abroad were dispelled by *Rosenberg v. Fleuti,* [374 U.S. 449, 83 S.Ct. 1804, 10 L.Ed.2d 1000 (1963),] where we described *Chew* as holding "that the returning resident alien is entitled as a matter of due process to a hearing on the charges underlying any attempt to exclude him."

If the permanent resident alien's absence is extended, of course, he may lose his entitlement to "assimilat[ion of his] status," *Kwong Hai Chew v. Colding, supra,* 344 U.S., at 596, 73 S.Ct., at 477, to that of an alien continuously residing and physically present in the United States. In *Shaughnessy v. United States ex rel. Mezei,* 345 U.S. 206, 73 S.Ct. 625, 97 L.Ed. 956 (1953), this Court rejected the argument of an alien who had left the country for some twenty months that he was entitled to due process in assessing his right to admission on his return. We did not suggest that no returning resident alien has a right to due process, for we explicitly reaffirmed *Chew.* We need not now decide the scope of *Mezei;* it does not govern this case, for Plasencia was absent from the country only a few days, and the United States has conceded that she has a right to due process.

The constitutional sufficiency of procedures provided in any situation, of course, varies with the circumstances. * * * In evaluating the procedures in any case, the courts must consider the interest at stake for the individual, the risk of an erroneous deprivation of the interest through the procedures used as well as the probable value of additional or different procedural safeguards, and the interest of the government in using the current procedures rather than additional or different procedures. *Mathews v. Eldridge,* 424 U.S. 319, 334–335, 96 S.Ct. 893, 902–903, 47 L.Ed.2d 18 (1976). Plasencia's interest here is, without question, a weighty one. She stands to lose the right "to stay and live and work in this land of freedom." Further, she may lose the right to rejoin her immediate family, a right that ranks high among the interests of the individual. The government's interest in efficient administration of the immigration laws at the border also is weighty. Further, it must weigh heavily in the balance that control over matters of immigration is a sovereign prerogative, largely within the control of the executive and the legislature. The role of the judiciary is limited to determining whether the procedures meet the essential standard of fairness under the Due Process Clause and does not extend to imposing procedures that merely displace congressional choices of policy. Our previous discussion has shown that Congress did not intend to require the use of deportation procedures in cases such as this one. Thus, it would be improper simply to impose deportation procedures here because the reviewing court may find them preferable. Instead, the courts must evaluate the particular circumstances and determine what procedures would satisfy the minimum requirements of due process on the re-entry of a permanent resident alien.

Plasencia questions three aspects of the procedures that the government employed in depriving her of these interests. First, she contends that the immigration law judge placed the burden of proof upon her. In a later proceeding in *Chew,* the Court of Appeals for the District of Columbia Circuit held, without mention of the Due Process Clause, that, under the law of the case, Chew was entitled to a hearing at which the INS was the moving party and bore the burden of proof. *Kwong Hai Chew v. Rogers,* 257 F.2d 606 (CADC 1958). The BIA has accepted that decision, and although the Act provides that the burden of proof is on the alien in an exclusion proceeding, § 291, the BIA has followed the practice of placing the burden on the government when the alien is a permanent resident alien. *See, e.g., In re Salazar,* [17 I & N Dec. 167, 169 (BIA 1979);] *In re Kane,* 15 I & N Dec. 258, 264 (BIA 1975); *In re Becerra–Miranda,* 12 I & N Dec. 358, 363–364, 366 (BIA 1967). There is no explicit statement of the placement of the burden of proof in the Attorney General's regulations or in the immigration law judge's opinion in this case and no finding on the issue below.

Second, Plasencia contends that the notice provided her was inadequate. She apparently had less than eleven hours' notice of the charges and the hearing. The regulations do not require any advance notice of the charges against the alien in an exclusion hearing, and the BIA has held that it is sufficient that the alien have notice of the charges at the hearing, *In re Salazar, supra,* at 169. The United States has argued to us that Plasencia could have sought a continuance. It concedes, however, that there is no explicit statutory or regulatory authorization for a continuance.

Finally, Plasencia contends that she was allowed to waive her right to representation,[8] without a full understanding of the right or of the consequences of waiving it. Through an interpreter, the immigration law judge informed her at the outset of the hearing, as required by the regulations, of her right to be represented. He did not tell her of the availability of free legal counsel, but at the time of the hearing, there was no administrative requirement that he do so. 8 CFR § 236.2(a) (1975). The Attorney General has since revised the regulations to require that, when qualified free legal services are available, the immigration law judge must inform the alien of their existence and ask whether representation is desired. 44 Fed.Reg. 4654 (Jan. 23, 1979) (codified at 8 CFR § 236.2(a) (1982)). As the United States concedes, the hearing would not comply with the current regulations.

If the exclusion hearing is to ensure fairness, it must provide Plasencia an opportunity to present her case effectively, though at the same time it cannot impose an undue burden on the government. It would not, however, be appropriate for us to decide now whether the new regulation on the right to notice of free legal services is of constitutional magnitude or whether the remaining procedures provided comport with the Due Process Clause. Before this Court, the parties have devoted their attention to the entitlement to a deportation hearing rather than to the sufficiency of the procedures in the exclusion hearing.[9] Whether the several hours' notice

---

8. The statute provides a right to representation without expense to the government. Section 292. Plasencia has not suggested that she is entitled to free counsel.

9. Thus, the question of Plasencia's entitlement to due process has been briefed and argued, is properly before us, and is sufficiently developed that we are prepared to decide it. Precisely what procedures are due, on the other hand, has not been adequately developed by the briefs or argument. The dissent undertakes to decide these questions, but, to do so, must rely heavily on an argument not raised by Plasencia: to wit, that

she was not informed at the hearing that the alleged agreement to receive compensation and the meaningfulness of her departure were critical issues. Also, the dissent fails to discuss the interests that the government may have in employing the procedures that it did. The omission of arguments raised by the parties is quite understandable, for neither Plasencia nor the government has yet discussed what procedures are due. Unlike the dissent, we would allow the parties to explore their respective interests and arguments in the Court of Appeals.

gave Plasencia a realistic opportunity to prepare her case for effective presentation in the circumstances of an exclusion hearing without counsel is a question we are not now in a position to answer. Nor has the government explained the burdens that it might face in providing more elaborate procedures. Thus, although we recognize the gravity of Plasencia's interest, the other factors relevant to due process analysis—the risk of erroneous deprivation, the efficacy of additional procedural safeguards, and the government's interest in providing no further procedures—have not been adequately presented to permit us to assess the sufficiency of the hearing. We remand to the Court of Appeals to allow the parties to explore whether Plasencia was accorded due process under all of the circumstances.

Accordingly, the judgment of the Court of Appeals is

Reversed and remanded.

JUSTICE MARSHALL, concurring in part and dissenting in part.

I agree that the Immigration and Nationality Act permitted the INS to proceed against respondent in an exclusion proceeding. The question then remains whether the exclusion proceeding held in this case satisfied the minimum requirements of the Due Process Clause. While I agree that the Court need not decide the precise contours of the process that would be constitutionally sufficient, I would not hesitate to decide that the process accorded Plasencia was insufficient.

The Court has already set out the standards to be applied in resolving the question. Therefore, rather than just remand, I would first hold that respondent was denied due process because she was not given adequate and timely notice of the charges against her and of her right to retain counsel and to present a defense.[2]

While the type of hearing required by due process depends upon a balancing of the competing interests at stake, due process requires "at a minimum ... that deprivation of life, liberty or property by adjudication be preceded by notice and opportunity for hearing." *Mullane v. Central Hanover Bank & Trust Co.,* 339 U.S. 306, 313, 70 S.Ct. 652, 656, 94 L.Ed. 865 (1950). Permanent resident aliens who are detained upon reentry into this country clearly are entitled to adequate notice in advance of an exclusion proceeding.

To satisfy due process, notice must "clarify what the charges are" in a manner adequate to apprise the individual of the basis for the government's proposed action. Notice must be provided sufficiently in advance of the hearing to "give the charged party a chance to marshal the facts in his defense." * * *

Respondent was not given notice sufficient to afford her a reasonable opportunity to demonstrate that she was not excludable. The immigration judge's decision to exclude respondent was handed down less than 24 hours after she was detained at the border on the night of June 29, 1975. By notice in English dated June 30, 1975, she was informed that a hearing would be conducted at eleven o'clock on the morning of that same day, and

2. Because Plasencia did not receive constitutionally sufficient notice, I find it unnec- essary to address the other constitutional deficiencies she asserts.

that the government would seek to exclude her on the ground that she had "wilfully and knowingly aided and abetted the entry of illegal aliens into the United States in violation of the law and for gain." It was not until the commencement of the hearing that she was given notice in her native language of the charges against her and of her right to retain counsel and to present evidence.

The charges against Plasencia were also inadequately explained at the hearing itself. The immigration judge did not explain to her that she would be entitled to remain in the country if she could demonstrate that she had not agreed to receive compensation from the aliens whom she had driven across the border. Nor did the judge inform respondent that the meaningfulness of her departure[b] was an issue at the hearing.

These procedures deprived Plasencia of a fair opportunity to show that she was not excludable under the standards set forth in the Immigration and Nationality Act. Because Plasencia was not given adequate notice of the standards for exclusion or of her right to retain counsel and present a defense, she had neither time nor opportunity to prepare a response to the government's case. The procedures employed here virtually assured that the Government attorney would present his case without factual or legal opposition.

When a permanent resident alien's substantial interest in remaining in this country is at stake, the Due Process Clause forbids the Government to stack the deck in this fashion. Only a compelling need for truly summary action could justify this one-sided proceeding. In fact, the Government's haste in proceeding against Plasencia could be explained only by its desire to avoid the minimal administrative and financial burden of providing her adequate notice and an opportunity to prepare for the hearing. Although the various other government interests identified by the Court may be served by the exclusion of those who fail to meet the eligibility requirements set out in the Immigration and Nationality Act, they are not served by procedures that deny a permanent resident alien a fair opportunity to demonstrate that she meets those eligibility requirements.

I would therefore hold that respondent was denied due process.

Notes

1. *Plasencia* distinguishes *Mezei;* it does not purport to overrule the latter case. But at least the Court has now removed much of the threat that *Mezei* seemed to pose to permanent resident aliens who travel. Henceforth, full due process entitlement seems to be the norm for nearly all such persons, even if they are validly placed in exclusion proceedings, and *Mezei* marks out an ill-defined exception.

But how should we go about drawing the line that distinguishes these exceptional cases? The Court says only that an alien may lose her

b. Under *Rosenberg v. Fleuti*, 374 U.S. 449, 83 S.Ct. 1804, 10 L.Ed.2d 1000 (1963), to be considered at length in Chapter Five, if a permanent resident alien's departure was not "meaningfully interruptive" of her residence here, she is not considered to make an "entry" upon return to the border and therefore would not be excludable.—eds.

protected status if her "absence is extended." In future cases should the one-year rule that governs for some purposes under the immigration laws be employed? For example, a returning resident loses the right to rely on her Alien Registration Receipt Card (familiarly known as the "green card") as a reentry permit if her absence extends beyond one year. 8 C.F.R. § 211.1(b). Or should the test take more subjective factors into account? That is, rather than relying mechanically on length of absence, should a court try to determine whether the alien *intended* to abandon his residence status? (The BIA now uses a multiple factor test to determine whether an alien has intended to abandon residence here and thus no longer qualifies as a special immigrant under INA § 101(a)(27)(A). *See Matter of Kane,* 15 I & N Dec. 258, 262–64; *Chavez-Ramirez v. INS,* 792 F.2d 932 (9th Cir.1986).)

If any subjective intent test is ultimately employed, the Court probably could not avoid a de facto overruling of *Mezei.* According to the facts as Mezei pleaded them, he had no intention of making a lengthy journey, much less of abandoning his U.S. home. And the fact that his family remained behind in Buffalo while he travelled lends a strong measure of plausibility to Mezei's argument.

In *Rafeedie v. INS,* 880 F.2d 506 (D.C.Cir.1989), *on remand,* 794 F.Supp. 13 (D.D.C.1992), the court of appeals applied *Plasencia* and held that a permanent resident alien had substantial due process rights, even though the government claimed he had been involved in "nefarious" activities (allegedly a gathering of a Palestinian terrorist organization) during his absence of several weeks. Noting the "stake in the United States" that permanent residents have, the court held that Rafeedie could not be subjected to the summary exclusion proceedings ordinarily held under INA § 235(c).

2. The Court has often proclaimed the death of the old right-privilege distinction that used to play a major role in deciding due process controversies. *See, e.g., Goldberg v. Kelly,* 397 U.S. 254, 262, 90 S.Ct. 1011, 1017, 25 L.Ed.2d 287 (1970); *Board of Regents v. Roth,* 408 U.S. 564, 571, 92 S.Ct. 2701, 2706, 33 L.Ed.2d 548 (1972). But the Court in *Plasencia* explains the denial of due process rights to first-time applicants for admission by asserting that such a person "requests a privilege and has no constitutional rights regarding his application." Is this an accurate characterization? Should any government action be free of due process scrutiny? *See generally* Smolla, *The Re-emergence of the Right–Privilege Distinction in Constitutional Law: The Price of Protesting Too Much,* 35 Stan.L.Rev. 69 (1982).

In *Roth, supra,* the court placed new emphasis on a careful threshold assessment of the nature of the individual interest at stake. The Due Process Clause protects only against deprivations of "life, liberty, or property," the Court stressed, and not all government actions negatively affecting individuals deprive them of such interests.

> To have a property interest in a benefit, a person clearly must
> have more than an abstract need or desire for it. He must have

more than a unilateral expectation of it. He must, instead, have a legitimate claim of entitlement to it. * * *

Property interests, of course, are not created by the Constitution. Rather, they are created and their dimensions are defined by existing rules or understandings that stem from an independent source like state law * * *.

408 U.S. at 577, 92 S.Ct. 2709.

Liberty, according to *Roth,* enjoys a more expansive conception. (Later cases may have cut back on its extent, however. *See, e.g., Connecticut Board of Pardons v. Dumschat,* 452 U.S. 458, 101 S.Ct. 2460, 69 L.Ed.2d 158 (1981); *Paul v. Davis,* 424 U.S. 693, 96 S.Ct. 1155, 47 L.Ed.2d 405 (1976); *Arnett v. Kennedy,* 416 U.S. 134, 94 S.Ct. 1633, 40 L.Ed.2d 15 (1974) (opinion of Rehnquist, J.).) *Roth* states: "In a Constitution for a free people, there can be no doubt that the meaning of 'liberty' must be broad indeed." 408 U.S. at 572, 92 S.Ct. at 2707. *Roth* also quotes from *Meyer v. Nebraska,* 262 U.S. 390, 399, 43 S.Ct. 625, 626, 67 L.Ed. 1042 (1923):

Without doubt [liberty] denotes not merely freedom from bodily restraint but also the right of the individual to contract, to engage in any of the common occupations of life, to acquire useful knowledge, to marry, establish a home and bring up children, to worship God according to the dictates of his own conscience, and generally to enjoy those privileges long recognized ... as essential to the orderly pursuit of happiness by free men.

If you are beginning to think that *Knauff* was wrongly decided, ask yourself just what sort of a liberty or property interest Ellen Knauff had at stake there. In other words, can her claim, as a first-time applicant for admission, be brought within the *Roth* framework? To be sure, exclusion imposed bodily restraints on her freedom of movement, but do all aliens in the world who might happen to present themselves at our borders for the first time have a legitimate claim of entitlement to free movement in this very potent sense? If we think of Knauff's claim under the "property" rubric, did she have more than a unilateral expectation or hope that she would be permitted to enter the United States? If you think the War Brides Act provides the independent source for a "legitimate claim of entitlement," would that approach permit us to distinguish Knauff's situation from the case of any other first-time applicant for admission who has a visa and believes that he meets the admission requirements set forth in the INA, but nonetheless finds himself enmeshed in exclusion proceedings upon arrival at the port of entry? What if he had no visa? Can we afford to provide due process to everyone in the world who simply presents himself or herself at a port of entry? If so, how much process? If not, how do we decide when due process rights attach?

SECTION B. ADMISSION PROCEDURES: A GLANCE BACKWARD

Ellis Island, for many years the principal port of entry for immigrants to the United States, has become a fixture in American folklore. Before we examine modern procedures, it may be worthwhile to look closely at the procedures employed at that facility.

The following passages paint a composite picture of immigrant processing at Ellis Island in 1907, the year that still holds the record for the highest number of immigrants admitted. Keep in mind that this was before the national-origins quotas were adopted. Indeed, no numerical ceilings applied at all, but each alien had to satisfy various qualitative exclusion criteria.

ANN NOVOTNY, STRANGERS AT THE DOOR: ELLIS ISLAND, CASTLE GARDEN, AND THE GREAT MIGRATION TO AMERICA

10–23 (1971).

Soon after dawn the next day, there was a sudden change in the ship's motion and a different sound from the engine. The harbor pilot from Ambrose Lightship had just come aboard. Early risers up on deck cried out in different languages as they caught sight of a gray strip of land (the Long Island, someone said it was called) emerging on the horizon as the sun burned off the morning mist. One word was the same on all tongues: "America!" Many of those peering at the coast broke into tears. Down in steerage there was frenzied excitement as immigrants jostled around bunks, arranging bundles for the last time, washing hands and faces in basins of cold, salty water, combing unwashed hair or smoothing creases out of the prettiest apron, saved for this occasion—all in an attempt to look their best for the American inspectors. Money was counted for the hundredth time, then secreted away in some safe inner pocket. The deck became more and more crowded as baggage was carried up and added to the mounting piles of battered suitcases, wicker baskets, cooking pots tied in old blankets and bulky goose-feather pillows bound together with thin rope. Then there was nothing to do for a while except find a place to sit and rehearse once again the best answers to all the questions the inspectors might ask about health, money, work and friends.

* * *

Heads on deck turned as a small cutter came alongside. A ladder was raised against the ship's rail, and two men and a woman in uniforms climbed aboard and pushed their way quickly through the crowd of immigrants toward the second cabin-class area. A murmur of apprehension ran through the watching crowd, but the officers barely glanced at the immigrants. Their business was with cabin-class passengers only, and the immigrants' turn would come later, at Ellis Island. In the saloon, the immigration inspector asked two or three brief questions of each waiting second-cabin passenger, while the other man, a doctor from the U.S. Public Health Service, looked quickly at their eyes as they filed past. Full information about these travelers was listed, as required by law, on the ship's official passenger list or "manifest." Because the shipping companies had made a great fuss when regular inspections in this class had begun about five years earlier, the inspector did his job as quickly as possible. He hardly looked at a small hunchbacked Polish woman from Danzig, who said that her husband and children would meet her at the pier; he did not know or care that this woman had been deported from Ellis Island because of her deformity two years earlier, when the whole family had arrived in steerage, and that her husband had finally saved enough money to bring her into the country this easy way. If the woman could afford to travel in style, she would obviously never become a public charge. When the last second-cabin passenger had been passed, the inspector ran his eyes down the first-cabin list of Americans and wealthy foreign visitors who were coming to tour or settle in this country (no one ever called *them* "immigrants"), and simply muttered, "Okay, that'll do." The Public Health Service officer was chatting with the ship's doctor, making sure that there had been no cases of epidemic diseases such as cholera, yellow fever or typhoid. If any serious contagious illnesses had been reported, the patients would have been taken at once on the quarantine boat, the *James W. Wadsworth,* to hospital wards on Hoffman Island, while other passengers would have been held in strict isolation on nearby Swinburn Island until the danger of their developing symptoms had passed. As it was, the doctor said the ship's hospital contained only one second-cabin woman with suspected appendicitis. This patient, in the care of the matron, was led down to the cutter and the small launch headed straight for Ellis Island's hospital.

The liner had been moving slowly north into the Upper Bay while this inspection was taking place. As the enormous harbor came into view, expressions of wonder and awe could be heard on the steerage deck, and people in the center pushed and craned to get a better look at the spectacular sight. Mothers lifted small children into the air to see. There on the left was the towering Statue of Liberty, lifting her torch of freedom to the sky. The bay itself was filled with other steamships, tugs and paddle-wheeled ferries crossing in all directions; an excursion boat passed, carrying a happy crowd to Coney Island. Rising on the skyline five miles away were the office buildings of lower Manhattan, taller than anything in Hamburg; so tall, in fact, that they looked like a ridge of small hills. The highest one of all, the new Singer Building, would reach forty-seven stories when it was finished the next year. Also on the left of their view, just beyond the Statue of Liberty, were the red brick buildings of Ellis Island where the immigrants would be taken. They had all heard of the Island and knew its name. That was the famous Island of Tears—*Tranen Insel* to the Germans, *Isola delle Lacrime* to the Italians—where those whom the inspectors judged too weak, old or poor to support themselves would be detained, then deported back to Europe to rebuild a broken life there.

* * *

[The steamer discharged its passengers at a pier in Manhattan. Cabin-class passengers were allowed to proceed to their destination, but the other immigrants were ushered onto a tightly packed ferry-boat or barge for the trip to Ellis Island. They might spend several hours aboard, waiting just off the crowded docks at the island before landing space became available. After disembarking, there was more waiting, in groups clustered according to big numbers on the tags tied to their coats.]

* * * Then the shouting began once more and, one by one, groups of thirty people at a time moved slowly forward, through the big door into dark tiled corridors, then—jostling two or three abreast—up a steep flight of stairs.

Their eyes blinking in the sudden bright light, they paused for a moment at the top. Sunshine streamed through the arched windows of the largest room they had ever seen. An unbelievable crowd of men, women and children was on all sides—enough to populate ten villages back home—and the hall was so huge that it might have contained their farm animals as well.

* * *

The immigrants at the top of the stairs were not given any more time to stand and stare. "This way! Hurry up!" an interpreter shouted in several languages, and they were pushed along one of the dozens of metal railings which divided the whole floor into a maze of open passageways. Although they did not realize it, they were already passing their first test as they hastened down the row in single file. Twenty-five feet away a doctor, in the smart blue uniform of the U.S. Public Health Service, was watching them carefully as they approached him. All children who looked over two years old were taken from their mothers' arms and made to walk.

It took only a few moments for the immigrants to reach the doctor, but that was time enough for his sharp eyes to notice one man who was breathing too heavily, a woman who was trying to hide her limp behind a big bundle, and a young girl whose shuffle and bewildered gaze might have been symptoms of a feeble mind. As each immigrant paused in front of him, the doctor looked hard at his face, hair, neck and hands; at the same time, with an interpreter at his side to help, he asked short questions about the immigrant's age or work to test his alertness. When a mother came up with children, each child in turn, starting with the oldest, was asked his name to make sure that he was not deaf or dumb.

In the doctor's hand was a piece of chalk; on the coats of about two out of every ten or eleven immigrants who passed him he scrawled a large white letter—"H" for possible heart trouble, "L" for lameness, a circled "X" for suspected mental defects, or "F" for a bad rash on the face. Then the immigrants filed on to a second doctor who was looking for diseases specifically mentioned in the law as reasons for deportation: signs of tuberculosis, leprosy, or a contagious skin disease of the scalp called *favus*.

* * *

At the end of the aisle interpreters waved immigrants whose coats were unmarked back toward the main part of the Registry Hall. But those whose coats bore chalk letters were pushed aside into a "pen," an area enclosed by a wire screen, to wait for more detailed medical examinations by other doctors. If they had any of the diseases proscribed by the immigration laws, or seemed too ill or feeble-minded to earn their living, they would be deported. One sobbing mother was pushed into the enclosure to wait with her little girl of eight or nine. The law said a parent had to accompany any very young child who was deported; but children of ten or older were sent back to Europe alone and simply released in the port from which they had sailed. Several weeping families in the hall were trying to make a terrible decision—"Shall we all go back together? Who will stay?"

Those immigrants waiting on benches for their final test talked anxiously and rehearsed for the last time their answers to probable questions about jobs, cash and relatives. Some said it was best to answer questions as fully as possible. Others said that inspectors were just like lawyers, always trying to trip you up, and it was best to keep your mouth shut and just say "Yes" and "No" so they couldn't muddle you. Could American officials be bribed with a gold coin or two? You had to be very, very careful. You had to show some money, but perhaps it wasn't safe to show it all. The waiting time, often an hour or two on busy days like these, seemed endless to the nervous immigrants; many of them leaned against their bundles in exhaustion and tried to sleep.

At last an interpreter moved them into the adjoining row. He made sure that they all had the same big number pinned on their coats. At the end of the aisle sat an inspector, on whose desk lay the manifest headed by that number. This large sheet of paper had been prepared by the shipping company and contained answers to questions about each of the thirty immigrants listed on it. As the first immigrant from the group approached the high desk, the inspector peered at the tag on his coat, noted the smaller "1" in its bottom corner, put his finger against that man's name on the first line of the form, and wearily prepared to start the questioning again.

* * *

* * * Before this long day was over, the interpreter would have helped the inspector question between four and five hundred immigrants, so that between them the two officials had only about two minutes in which to decide whether each immigrant was "clearly and beyond a doubt entitled to land," as the law specified. Every doubtful case was detained for further questioning.

The rapid queries, designed to verify the most important of the twenty-nine bits of information about each immigrant on the manifest, began: "What work do you do?" "Do you have a job waiting for you?" "Who paid for your passage here?" "Is anyone meeting you?" "Where are you going?" "Can you read and write?" "Have you ever been in prison?" "How much money do you have?" "Show it to me now." "Where did you get it?"

Nearly all of the immigrants quickly got curt nods from the inspector, who handed them landing cards, and sudden friendly smiles from the interpreter. They were in! "Praise God," murmured an elderly Ruthenian farmer, bending suddenly over the desk and kissing the back of the inspector's hand in gratitude. For most of the group, the ordeal was over. After only three or four hours on Ellis Island, they were free to go.

* * *

But the beginning was delayed, perhaps forever, for the unfortunate immigrants who were kept behind at Ellis Island. As one manifest group passed, for example, the inspector singled out a pretty Swedish girl who said she was going to Chicago alone to get married; he ordered her detained until her fiancé or a representative from the Lutheran Pilgrim House came to get her. Immigration officials refused to send single women alone into the streets of strange cities. If the Swedish girl's boy friend came East to meet her, an interpreter would probably escort the young couple to City Hall to be married on the spot to prevent any deception (in earlier days hundreds of marriages were performed on Ellis Island itself to combat "white slavery"). A second detained immigrant was an old Russian Jew whose threadbare pockets contained only seventy-five cents. His American relatives in Rhode Island would send him money for a train ticket, he said. Terrified that the inspector was not going to admit him, he began to sob out the story of his family's murder in the 1905 *pogrom,* wailing that the Americans might as well kill him then and there as send him back. A man from the Hebrew Immigrant Aid Society came running up at the sound of the commotion. He soothed the old man, saying that he would send a telegram at once to his relatives, and that the old man would be well looked after on the Island until the money arrived. A few minutes later, a nervous young Italian, sweating with excitement, answered pressing questions about the work he could do by waving a well-thumbed letter under the inspector's nose. An Italian uncle in Pittsfield—"See, right here"—had promised him a job on a construction gang. A frown passed over the inspector's face as he ordered the young man detained for the Board of Special Inquiry. "But why? Why?" the young man shouted. As the interpreter said that the Contract Labor Law would be explained at the hearing, the young man's heart sank. He had forgotten! He had been warned to lie about this! Immigrants had to show that they were strong and clever enough to find work easily, but it was against the law for them to have agreed before they left home to take a specific job in exchange for their passage. This law had been in effect for over twenty years. It was meant to protect immigrants from slave-like labor, and to protect American workers from gangs of European laborers imported by a "boss" to break strikes or keep wages low. If this young man had sailed with several friends, all of whom were bound for Pittsfield, the inspector would have felt sure that the padrone system was at work, and the whole group would probably have been sent back to Italy together.

The Swedish girl, the old Russian and the unlucky Italian were typical of those immigrants (about two out of every ten) who were held at the Island for more than a few hours. More than half of them, like the girl and the old man, were detained for two or three days for their own protection. The others, such as the young Italian, who faced more questioning before a Board of Special Inquiry, rarely numbered more than one out of every ten people admitted. Immigrants were brought before the board for many different reasons, including violations of the Contract Labor Law. A telegram from Europe might have brought word that an immigrant was a criminal wanted by the police in his own country; perhaps a man's wife had reported that he was deserting her. Sometimes inspectors felt that an immigrant was really a pauper who had been given a steamship ticket and a suit of clothes by a foreign government eager to get him off its charity rolls. Unfortunate people physically or mentally handicapped in earning a living would be deported if they seemed "likely to become public charges." The law ordered deportation for anyone who was a criminal, a prostitute, or suffering from insanity or a contagious disease. A few immigrants were sent back because of their political or religious beliefs: they were usually anarchists who wanted to overthrow organized government, or polygamists who believed that a man should have several wives.

A detained immigrant went into a small side office to face the Board of Special Inquiry, made up of three inspectors and an interpreter sitting behind a long desk. He swore on the Bible or a crucifix to tell the truth, then answered questions about his right to land, as a stenographer recorded his words. No lawyers were present, but an immigrant's friends and relatives were often brought to the Island to testify in his behalf. The votes of two out of the three inspectors decided a case, but if the third inspector or the immigrant himself felt that a sentence of deportation was unfair, he could appeal the decision to the Secretary of Commerce and Labor in Washington. At this stage, the immigrant was allowed to hire a lawyer to help him. In fact, the secretary often sustained an immigrant's appeal, or ordered a new hearing to be held if fresh evidence was presented. Sometimes the immigrant would be admitted after a bond was posted guaranteeing that he would not become dependent on public charity. Inspectors who were chosen by Ellis Island's commissioner to serve on the Boards of Special Inquiry, like their colleagues in the Registry Hall, worked under great pressure in these busy years and had to rely mainly on their common sense. In a single year, seventy thousand or more cases would be heard. The system was not too cruel: about five out of every six immigrants whose cases were heard were admitted by the boards after careful questioning. The greatest number of exclusions happened in 1911, when about thirteen thousand immigrants (just over two per cent of the 650,000 who arrived that year) were sent back to their homelands.

* * *

The shipping companies, who were supposed to screen out all "undesirables" in Europe, had to transport the immigrants home without charge and to pay for the cost of keeping them on the Island until their next ships arrived.

The job of housing and feeding all the detained immigrants was almost too much for the officials at Ellis Island. There wasn't enough room even for the immigrants who passed through without delay. The architects who designed the buildings in 1897 had planned them to accommodate no more than 500,000 foreigners in one year—they had believed that the flood tide of immigration was over. No one guessed that the high point of the greatest mass movement in history was just about to begin. For inspectors and immigrants alike, it was a nightmare * * *.

The Evolution of the Visa Requirement

Seven years later the outbreak of World War I slowed the immigrant flow to a mere trickle. After the war immigration picked up again, but in 1921 Congress changed the legal requirements significantly. Enormous confusion resulted, as administrators struggled to make a system that was designed to perform qualitative screening serve also to impose quantitative ceilings. The Novotny book describes the transition (*id.* at 127–130):

> The First Quota Law, or Johnson Act, which went into effect on June 3, 1921, specified that no more than twenty per cent of a nation's quota could be filled in any one month. Officials of the shipping companies were close to panic; during the last few days of grace they organized a mad dash to land thousands of immigrants in American ports before the deadline. Any ship that could make the transatlantic passage was crammed with passengers and some vessels racing through the Narrows actually collided in their haste. During June, once the new system was in effect, steamships still raced to land their passengers on Ellis Island as soon as possible, and within the first few days of the month the specified twenty per cent of all national quotas had been filled. Then the first scenes of a human tragedy began. Some ten thousand aliens arrived at Ellis Island to be told that their quotas had been filled for June—there was no room for them in America. It was an impossible situation that no one, apparently, had foreseen. Puzzled officials held the surplus immigrants on their ships and asked Washington for instructions; the answer came back that the immigrants were to be admitted on bond, and their numbers subtracted from July's quotas.

> But in July, and during the first days of every succeeding month, the same thing happened, as the steamships continued their race to grab as large a share as possible of the quotas for their own passengers. Whole shiploads of immigrants were now turned back to Europe in scenes of terrible anguish described by one Public Health Service doctor as "one of my most painful reminiscences of service at the Island." She recalled one particular group of five hundred southeastern Europeans who had sold their homes and possessions and traveled four thousand miles to start a new life, only to hear after they had passed the Statue of Liberty that they were inadmissible. "They screamed and bawled and beat about like wild animals, breaking the waiting-room furniture and attacking the attendants, several of whom were severely hurt. It was a pitiful spectacle...." The immigrants were helpless victims of the steamship lines, and the immigration inspectors were helpless too, in the face of the new law. Commissioner Wallis complained bitterly to Washington in October, 1921, that "our nation is committing a gross injustice." He urged that immigrants be examined by American consuls in European ports,

to save all this "indescribable" suffering "that would melt a heart of granite."

* * *

* * * The restrictive law and the sad tales of rejection which were taken back to Europe reduced the volume of arrivals; physical improvements were made; and the staff was better organized. The First Quota Law, never intended to be more than a temporary measure, was replaced in July, 1924, by a second, more restrictive, act based on the same principle. The basis for the quotas was moved back from the population census of 1910 to that of 1890—cutting still further the proportion of "new" immigrants (who in 1890 were just starting to arrive). The percentage of admissible immigrants from any nation was reduced from three per cent to two per cent of its population in this older census, and the overall ceiling was slashed from 358,000 to 164,000 people a year. Italy's quota, under this arrangement, was cut from 42,057 under the First Quota Law to a mere 3,845 per year. The second law's most important provision, as far as Ellis Island's history is concerned, was a rule that all immigrants were to be inspected at the American consular offices in Europe, where visas would be issued to those found acceptable. Consuls would slowly fill the national quotas, issuing no more than ten per cent of the available visas in one month, in an attempt to end the first-come-first-served system used by the steamships and the inevitable disappointments in American ports.

As soon as the second law went into effect, the Secretary of Labor visited Ellis Island and boasted that the place looked "like a 'deserted village'." Immigrants were still examined there, but they arrived in an evenly-spaced flow over the months, and very few of those who had been judged acceptable by the consuls had to be detained. There was now enough time and space for physical conditions on the Island to be rapidly improved: iron bunks were moved out to make room for proper beds with mattresses, and modern plumbing replaced what one magazine writer called the "ancient exhibits." Ellis Island looked like a different place—and it was, because its role was completely changing. In 1926 and 1927, immigration inspectors and Public Health Service doctors were stationed at American consulates over most of Europe, and the primary inspection of the immigrants—once the Island's function—was finished before the immigrants even set sail. Possession of an American visa was almost a guarantee of admission. Inspectors in New York needed only to make a final check of all passengers as the ships sailed into the Upper Bay, and they held only a few doubtful cases—eventually about one per cent of all arrivals—for questioning before Boards of Inquiry or for medical treatment. By 1926, much of Ellis Island's staff had been disbanded. Dust began to settle in the empty rooms. In 1928 officials in Washington were acknowledging it to be "something of an economic problem."

Other useful accounts of Ellis Island appear in D. Brownstone, I. Franck, D. Brownstone, Island of Hope, Island of Tears (1979); T. Pitkin, Keepers of the Gate: A History of Ellis Island (1975); and The New Immigration (J. Appel ed. 1971) (reprinting an essay by Jacob Riis reporting on his 1903 visit to Ellis Island; the essay is notable for the intriguing mixture of sympathy and aversion toward the immigrants displayed by Riis, a former immigrant himself, who had passed through Castle Garden, Ellis Island's predecessor, many years earlier). Procedures at San Francisco's harsher equivalent of Ellis Island, known as Angel Island, are movingly reflected in H. Lai, G. Lim, J. Yung, Island: Poetry and History of Chinese Immigrants on Angel Island 1910–1940 (1980).

SECTION C. MODERN PROCEDURES AND DOCUMENTS

1. NONIMMIGRANT ADMISSIONS

From most countries in the world, those who want to come to the United States for a temporary stay must first secure a nonimmigrant visa from a U.S. consular officer in a foreign country. Application may be made in person at the American consulate, but the personal appearance requirements can be waived for a range of categories, and a great many nonimmigrant visas, particularly for B–1 and B–2 visitors, are applied for and issued by mail. The most recent available statistics show issuance of nearly 5.4 million nonimmigrant visas and roughly 1.3 million final findings of ineligibility during fiscal year 1992. 1992 Report of the Visa Office, Tables I, XX.

The alien bears the burden of proving qualification for the visa, and the most important issue in the high-demand categories (B–1 and B–2 visitors, F and M students, and J exchange visitors) will often be whether the alien truly has a home in the foreign country to which he or she intends to return. The consular officer has discretion to require any kind of documentary support deemed necessary. A few of the nonimmigrant categories, such as H, L, and K, require advance clearance from INS, secured by means of a petition filed by the alien's expected employer or intended spouse, as the case may be.

If the visa application is approved, the consular officer stamps a nonimmigrant visa into the applicant's passport. The stamp will show a visa number, date and place of issue, expiration date, and visa classification. Unless otherwise specified, the visa is good for any number of entries before its expiration. The basic regulations governing the nonimmigrant visa process appear at 22 C.F.R. Parts 40, 41. Useful insights into actual administrative practice, based in part on interviews and site visits at U.S. consulates on three continents, appear in Nafziger, *Review of Visa Denials by Consular Officers,* 66 Wash.L.Rev. 1 (1991).

Without a visa (or a showing that he or she is exempt from the visa requirement), an alien probably will not be able to board a plane or other vessel for the United States; carriers are subject to fines and other

expenses for bringing aliens without adequate documentation. *See* INA
§§ 237(a), 273; O'Keefe, *Immigration Issues and Airlines*, 59 J.Air L. &
Comm. 357 (1993). But the visa does not guarantee admission. Immigration officers at the border are not bound by the consul's decisions on
admissibility and may seek to exclude an alien despite the possession of the
visa. INA § 221(h).

Aliens coming to the United States are typically asked to fill out a
Form I–94 card, the Arrival–Departure Record, before the plane lands, and
to carry it with them through inspection. It asks for basic personal
information and provides spaces for the INS inspector to record key
information reflecting the processing, such as a routine admission stamp,
or data regarding a referral to secondary inspection (where more extensive
questioning can be carried out in those cases prompting initial suspicion).
Upon admission, the inspector keeps the upper portion of the I–94 card and
gives to the nonimmigrant the bottom portion, stamped and endorsed to
show the classification in which the alien is admitted (usually, but not
always, the same as the visa classification), the time allowed for the alien to
remain in the United States, and any other specific conditions of entry.
This card is usually stapled into the passport, and is meant to be surrendered upon departure from the United States. It is a highly important
document, usually the first item that should be checked if a nonimmigrant
has questions about his status. Take a look now at the blank Form I–94
and the sample of endorsed Forms in the Statutory Supplement.

Until recently, if a nonimmigrant received INS's permission to work
(most do not), this permission was usually manifested in an appropriate
stamp or endorsement on the I–94. Because these notations were easily
counterfeited, however, INS began in 1989 to issue a uniform and counter-
feit-resistant Employment Authorization Document (EAD), Form I–688B
(see Supplement), in the form of a laminated card with a photograph, to
most categories of nonimmigrant aliens granted permission to work. The
EAD must be applied for separately (on Form I–765), with a separate fee.
A "green card," which is a document issued only to lawful permanent
residents, is thus not the only valid proof of work authorization.

Although people commonly speak of an alien's being here "on a tourist
visa" or "on a student visa," this usage is technically incorrect—and
potentially misleading. The visa serves only to help move the alien to the
port of entry. The type and length of her actual entry are controlled by the
I–94. If the I–94 states admission in B–2 status until March 1, 1996, the
alien must leave by then. On March 2, it will do no good to point to a visa
expiration date of September 1, 1996. Of course, she could leave in late
February and use the visa to journey back to the United States on August
30. If the admitting officer determines that the new visit is bona fide, she
may then receive a new I–94 valid, for example, for another six months'
visit here. After her entry, the visa's expiration makes no difference to her
continued right to stay. While still in status on the first entry, she could
also have applied to INS for an extension of her admission period, or for a
change under INA § 248 from one nonimmigrant classification to another,
for example, from B–2 tourist to F–1 student. If permission is granted, she
need not have the visa amended, at least not if she plans no further travel

outside the United States before the new admission period expires. The change will be reflected adequately on the I–94.[3] You may wish to read through the most important statutory provisions relating to nonimmigrant admission procedures (INA §§ 214; 221(a)–(b), (f)–(h); 222(c)–(f), 248) to confirm your understanding of how the procedures operate.

Before 1986, visas were required of all nonimmigrants except for a few narrowly defined classes. Chief among the exceptions were Mexican nationals who presented border crossing cards (Form I–186 or I–586, issued by INS), see 8 C.F.R. §§ 212.6, 235.1(f), (g), and Canadian nationals, for whom the visa requirement was waived altogether, provided they were entering for a temporary stay. Id. § 212.1(a). (Canadians also sometimes obtain border crossing cards, for convenience. Id. § 212.6(a).) If you have traveled to Europe in recent years, you probably realize that many other Western countries waive visa requirements for U.S. citizens, and for nationals of many other countries, on a far wider scale than has the United States.[4] This lack of reciprocity was a sore spot for some Europeans, and in any event this country's blanket visa requirement was seen by some as generating unnecessary paperwork.

In 1986, Congress included in IRCA an authorization for a visa waiver pilot program, covering temporary visitors (up to 90 days) from selected countries with low visa abuse rates. Special arrangements between the U.S. government and participating air carriers are necessary. The visitor who enters under this program waives all rights to extend her stay or to change her status once she is in the United States (except as an immediate relative of a U.S. citizen). She also waives her right to any review of a finding of admissibility or deportability, except that she may apply for asylum. INA § 217; 8 C.F.R. Part 217; 22 C.F.R. § 41.2. These waivers were sustained against a limited range of constitutional challenges in *Nose v. Attorney General*, 993 F.2d 75 (5th Cir.1993) and *McGuire v. INS*, 804 F.Supp. 1229 (N.D.Cal.1992). In FY 1993, the program admitted 9.5 million people from the 22 qualifying countries, roughly 45 percent of total nonimmigrant admissions. *See* 71 Interp.Rel. 1059, 1311 (1994). As a result, the workload of the consulates has dropped considerably, from 8.7 million nonimmigrant visas issued in FY 1988 to 5.4 million in FY 1992. 1992 Report of the Visa Office, Table I. The State Department hoped to gain a permanent authorization for the visa waiver program in 1994, but instead Congress simply extended it through September 1996.

3. In some cases the Form I–797, Notice of Approval, has been used to memorialize changes in nonimmigrant status. INS is now in the process of implementing a modified system for issuing I–797s on special security paper, and the newer versions will have a replacement I–94 on a tear-off slip at the bottom, to be removed and kept with the alien's passport. *See* 71 Interp.Rel. 317, 600 (1994).

4. For a useful comparison of the "insular/Western Hemispheric" model of immigration control, which relies heavily on front-end screening through visas, and the "continental" model, which relies more on residence and work authorization controls after entry, see Plender, *Recent Trends in National Immigration Control*, 35 Int'l & Comp.L.Q. 531 (1986); Wolf, *Entry and Residence*, in The Legal Position of Aliens in National and International Law 1873 (J. Frowein & T. Stein eds. 1987). For an account of how the two types of systems are gradually converging, taking pages from each other's practice books, see Widgren, *Migration Policies in the OECD Area: Towards Convergence?*, 10 In Defense of the Alien 50 (1988).

2. IMMIGRANT VISAS AND VISA PETITIONS

The process of securing status as a lawful permanent resident alien in the United States is more elaborate and time-consuming than what is involved in securing nonimmigrant admission. In the remainder of this section we will look at the immigrant visa process, then consider procedures at the border, and finally examine adjustment of status under § 245. In connection with the following, you may want to review INA §§ 104, 204, 211, 221, and 222. The relevant regulations appear in 22 C.F.R. Part 42. A detailed and helpful description of the process, prepared by an experienced immigration attorney, appears in Wernick, *Consular Processing of Immigrant Visas*, 90–12 Imm. Briefings (Dec.1990).

The process for obtaining an immigrant visa typically begins with the filing of a visa petition, usually by mail to the INS Regional Service Center. This petition is meant to verify the family or employment relationship that underlies the alien's claim to preference or immediate relative status. Family petitions are filed on Form I–130. Petitions for occupational preference are filed on Form I–140, and the employer often must have secured labor certification from the Labor Department before presenting the I–140 to INS. Upon approval, an INS examiner endorses the visa petition and forwards it to the State Department's National Visa Center, which creates a case file and handles the preliminary paperwork needed before scheduling an interview with the U.S. consul in the alien's country. If the petition indicates, however, that the alien is in the United States and wishes to obtain residence through adjustment of status, rather than through the visa process, the approved petition will be sent to the appropriate INS office instead of the State Department. Approval of the visa petition does not mean that INS has found the alien generally admissible; that issue must be decided by the consul—or by the INS examiner considering an adjustment application. *See De Figueroa v. INS,* 501 F.2d 191 (7th Cir.1974).

The family member or employer who files the visa petition is known as the petitioner; the alien overseas who wants to immigrate is known as the beneficiary.[5] The labels indicate who remains in command of the process at this stage: the petitioner. That individual can withdraw the petition at any time, without the beneficiary's consent, and certain events, such as the petitioner's death, may result in automatic revocation. 8 C.F.R. § 205.1. The beneficiary receives no vested rights based merely on the approval of a petition. If, at the time of revocation, the beneficiary has not already traveled to the United States under the immigrant visa, or been accorded an adjustment of status based on the petition, the revocation will be effective to block the beneficiary's immigration. *See Wright v. INS,* 379 F.2d 275 (6th Cir.1967); *Amarante v. Rosenberg,* 326 F.2d 58 (9th Cir. 1964). The Attorney General may make an exception, on humanitarian grounds, to automatic revocation based on the death of the petitioner. 8 C.F.R. § 205.1(a)(3). *See generally Sanchez–Trujillo v. INS,* 632 F.Supp. 1546 (W.D.N.C.1986). An amendment made by the 1990 Act also specifies

---

5. For a few employment-based categories, such as special immigrants (fourth preference), investors (fifth), or aliens of extraordinary ability (the first subcategory in the first preference), the alien himself or herself can petition directly. *See* INA § 204(a)(1).

that spouses of U.S. citizens, if they had been married for two years, are to be counted as "immediate relatives" for visa petitioning purposes for a full two years after the death of the citizen spouse, if the petition had already been approved. *See Dodig v. INS*, 9 F.3d 1418 (9th Cir.1993). In these circumstances the alien can file the petition on his or her own behalf. INA § 201(b)(2)(A)(i). A further amendment in 1994 allows battered spouses and children to self-petition under certain conditions. INA § 204(a)(1)(A)(iii), (A)(iv), (B)(ii), (B)(iii).

When the approved visa petition is received at the National Visa Center, an officer checks to see if it is complete and technically correct, creates an electronic file, and notifies the consulate where the alien is expected to apply for the visa. If a visa is not immediately available,[6] the officer notifies the alien that the petition has been received and will be held until a visa is available. If the alien's visa allocation priority date is current, however, the alien is sent Packet 3.

Packet 3 contains instructions, a summary biographical form, and detailed information about the rest of the necessary documentation and how to obtain it. The regulations require aliens to provide a police certificate or certificates; a certified copy of any prison record, military record, and record of birth; and certified copies of "all other records or documents which the consular officer considers necessary." 22 C.F.R. § 42.65(b). Police certificates show what, if anything, the local police records contain concerning the individual. They must be obtained from any jurisdiction where the alien has resided for at least one year, and the consular officer can demand them from other locations as well. The alien must also gather "evidence of support," to show that he is not likely to become a public charge (INA § 212(a)(4)). Any documents not in English must be accompanied by a certified translation.

The alien is supposed to return the completed biographical data sheet immediately, and then to notify the consulate when he has gathered the other documentation, perhaps weeks or months later. That notification triggers the final stages of the process. The alien is then scheduled for a visa interview, typically two to four months after completion of packet 3, and packet 4 is mailed to him. This packet contains the letter with the visa appointment notification, the actual visa application form, as well as instructions regarding the required medical examination by an approved physician. Usually the medical appointment is scheduled directly by the consulate for the day of the interview.

At the interview the consular officer makes sure that all the information has been correctly supplied on the application form and then proceeds to question the applicant, especially on any matters that raise doubts about admissibility. In this setting, the applicant formally executes the application and swears to it or affirms it before the officer. If the consul finds that any of the exclusion grounds apply, she may deny the visa. Denial is

---

6. It will be available if either the visa allocation priority date is current (meaning that processing in that preference category has already reached the date marking the alien's place on the waiting list; see Table 3.6) or if the alien is an immediate relative, to which no quotas—and thus no waiting lists—apply.

subject to a limited form of review by another officer at the post, and, under some circumstances, referral to the Department of State's Visa Office for an advisory opinion. 22 C.F.R. § 42.81. If the applicable exclusion ground is subject to waiver, however, the consul usually assists the alien in completing a waiver application, to be forwarded to the INS for adjudication, along with the consul's report of any pertinent information bearing on the waiver and developed during the interview. (Waivers are usually in the discretion of the Attorney General, not the Secretary of State.) A revealing and engaging description of the real-life functioning of a busy consulate, including the problems of crowd control, the role of guards, document checkers, cashiers, and even hot-dog vendors, appears in a State Department cable captioned "Just Another Tijuana Sunrise: Coping with IMMACT 90 on the Border" and reprinted in 69 Interp.Rel. 509 (1992). The State Department issued 447,229 immigrant visas in FY 1991, and 526,770 in FY 1992. 1992 Report of the Visa Office, Table I.

If the consul finds the alien admissible, she issues an immigrant visa, valid for four months. The visa is not stamped into the alien's passport. It consists instead of a separate set of documents, with attachments, meant to be presented in a special envelope to the admitting immigration officer at the port of entry. If that officer finds no disqualifications upon his inspection, he will keep the immigrant visa, make a notation of admission as a lawful permanent resident in the alien's passport, and forward the necessary papers to an INS facility for ultimate issuance of the Alien Registration Receipt Card, Form I–551. Issuance may require several additional months. The alien's file is sent on to the INS district office having jurisdiction over the place of his intended residence in the United States.

The I–551 is the celebrated "green card," although in recent years it has been issued in a version closer to light pink in color. *See Why Isn't the "Green Card" Green?*, 70 Interp.Rel. 1043 (1993). Before 1976, a truly green card, Form I–151, was used as the alien registration receipt card. That version was replaced with the current, machine-readable I–551 when new technology became available, and the old cards are being phased out. In 1989, INS introduced further refinements in its ongoing efforts to promote automation and defeat counterfeiting. The new I–551 cards are valid for only 10 years and contain optical patterns difficult to duplicate. The new system also allows INS computers to store and transmit images of the photo, fingerprint and signature placed on the card, to thwart impostors claiming to have lost an earlier card. *See* 66 Interp.Rel. 869, 1305 (1989); 54 Fed.Reg. 47586 (1989).

The green card is usually thought of as a permit for employment in the United States. It does fulfill that purpose and also many others, but as its official name suggests, it was adopted principally to serve as evidence of compliance with the alien fingerprinting and registration requirements of INA §§ 261–266. *See* especially § 264(d) and 8 C.F.R. Pt. 264. (INS appears to be trying to change the official name to "Resident Alien Card." *See* 54 Fed. Reg. 47586 (1989).) The I–94 usually serves a similar function for nonimmigrants, evidencing compliance with applicable registration provisions, although many nonimmigrants are exempt from fingerprinting under reciprocal arrangements with their countries of nationality. *See* 8 U.S.C.A. § 1201a. When the federal government adopted its comprehensive alien registration scheme in 1940, its action served to preempt similar requirements then being imposed by the states. *See Hines v. Davidowitz,* 312 U.S. 52, 61 S.Ct. 399, 85 L.Ed. 581 (1941).

If a permanent resident alien plans to leave this country temporarily, he may do so and then return as a "special immigrant" under INA §§ 101(a)(27)(A), 211(b). (Make sure you understand why such aliens are treated as special immigrants under the Act.) But for purposes of return, it is important for the alien to take along documentation clearly demonstrating that he or she is a returning resident. If the alien will be gone from the country no longer than 12 months, the I–551, the Alien Registration Receipt Card, may be used as the needed re-entry permit. 8 C.F.R. § 211.1(b). *See* INA § 223, governing reentry permits. But as we will examine in Chapter Five, in nearly all circumstances such a return to the United States constitutes a new "entry" under the Act, making all the exclusion grounds of § 212(a) applicable afresh. Possession of a green card thus will not *assure* re-entry; it merely dispenses with certain documentary requirements.

3. AT THE BORDER

After securing a visa and traveling to the United States, intending immigrants and nonimmigrants encounter an immigration inspector at the border checkpoint or port of entry. Most are admitted after a few quick and routine questions. A small percentage undergo more thorough processing, and some are placed in exclusion proceedings before an immigration judge, the ultimate forum (subject to administrative and judicial review) for testing the applicant's right to enter.

In connection with the following material, you should review INA §§ 231–240 and read §§ 235 and 236 with care.

ELIZABETH J. HARPER, IMMIGRATION LAWS OF THE UNITED STATES

487–92 (3d ed. 1975).

§ 1. Summary

Whether an alien is admissible to the United States when he arrives at a port of entry is determined by the Immigration and Naturalization Service. The fact that an alien is in possession of an immigrant or nonimmigrant visa in itself does not entitle him to enter the United States if he is found inadmissible by the Immigration and Naturalization Service. (Sections 221(h), 235). The burden of proof that he is admissible rests upon the applicant for admission. (Section 291).

The initial examination of an arriving alien, called primary inspection, is conducted by an inspecting immigration officer. He can admit but not exclude the alien. If the inspecting immigration officer, also referred to as primary inspector, believes that the cause of the alien's excludability can be readily removed by the exercise of discretionary authority he may refer the case to the district director. If the district director exercises discretionary authority the primary inspector may admit the alien. However, if an alien is not clearly entitled to land he must be detained and the case referred for further inquiry to a special inquiry officer. The special inquiry officer conducts a formal hearing. The decision of the special inquiry officer must be based on the evidence of record and, with certain exceptions, may be appealed to the Board of Immigration Appeals. Special rules apply if an alien is excluded on physical or mental grounds. Limited judicial review of the final administrative decision in exclusion proceedings is available by habeas corpus.

§ 2. Inspection and Admission of Aliens

INSPECTION AT PORTS OF ENTRY

Every alien, whether immigrant or nonimmigrant, arriving at a port of the United States, is examined by one or more immigration officers in order to determine whether he is entitled to land. Immigration officers are authorized to board and search any vessel, aircraft, railway car or other vehicle in which they believe aliens are being brought into the United States. (Section 235(a))

[PRE-EXAMINATION]

* * * [In some circumstances, including] aircraft proceeding from Guam, Puerto Rico, or the Virgin Islands of the United States * * * [or] directly from foreign contiguous territory or adjacent islands to the continental United States, the examination may be made immediately prior to the departure of the aircraft or vessel. The examination of aliens under these circumstances has the same effect as though made at the destined port of entry into the United States.

GENERAL QUALIFICATIONS

Every alien asking admission into the United States may be required to state under oath the purpose for which he comes and the length of time he intends to remain in the United States. He can be required to give any other information necessary for determining whether he belongs to any of the excludable classes. The following general qualifications and requirements must be met by any alien seeking to enter the United States as an immigrant or nonimmigrant:

(1) He must apply for admission in person at a place designated as a port of entry for aliens;

(2) He must apply for admission at a time the immigration office at the port is open for inspection;

(3) He must make his application in person to an immigration officer;

(4) He must present whatever documents are required, and

(5) He has to establish that he is not subject to exclusion under the immigration laws, Executive orders or Presidential proclamations. (8 CFR 235.1)

ADMISSION

If the inspecting immigration officer finds an alien admissible he will insert in the alien's passport, if one is required, the word "admitted" and the date and place of admission. The same information will be inserted on the immigrant visa, re-entry permit, or the Arrival–Departure Card (Form I–94), presented by, or prepared for, an alien who is admitted. (8 CFR 235.4)

DETENTION AND REFERRAL

If the examining immigration officer finds that an alien is not clearly entitled to land, or if his decision to admit him is challenged by another immigration officer, the alien is detained for further inquiry by a special inquiry officer. However, if the examining officer has reason to believe that the cause of an alien's excludability can readily be removed by:

(1) the posting of a bond,

(2) the exercise of discretionary authority vested in the Attorney General to waive certain grounds of ineligibility or to waive jointly with the Secretary of State certain documentary requirements, or

(3) the exercise of discretionary authority by the Attorney General for the admission of otherwise inadmissible returning resident aliens,

he may, instead of detaining the alien, refer his case to the district director within whose district the port is located. In such case further examination is deferred until the district director has decided whether the alien should be admitted by granting administrative relief as indicated above. (Section 236(a); 8 CFR 235.7)

If the examining immigration officer detains the alien for further inquiry before a special inquiry officer, the alien must be promptly informed by the delivery of Form I–122, "Notice to Alien detained for Hearing by Special Inquiry Officer." (8 CFR 235.6)

§ 3. Special Inquiry

SPECIAL INQUIRY OFFICER

A special inquiry officer, also referred to as an immigration judge (8 CFR § 1.1(1)), is an immigration officer whom the Attorney General deems specially qualified to conduct special inquiries and who is designated and selected by the Attorney General individually or by regulations to conduct such proceedings. No immigration officer is permitted to act as a special inquiry officer in any case in which he has engaged in investigative or prosecuting functions. (Sections 101(b)(4), 236(a))

RESPONSIBILITIES

The special inquiry officer determines whether an alien detained on inspection is to be excluded and deported from the United States or whether he will be permitted to enter. Hearings before the special inquiry officer are not open to the public unless the alien requests that the public, including the press, be admitted and states for the record that he is waiving the requirement that the hearing be closed. The decision of a special inquiry officer in exclusion proceedings must be rendered only on the evidence produced in the hearing and is final unless it is reversed on appeal. (Section 236(a), (b)). In exclusion proceedings the special inquiry officer rules on objections, introduces material and relevant evidence on behalf of the Government and the alien and regulates the course of the hearing. (8 CFR 236.2(b))

HEARING

In exclusion proceedings the alien may be represented by an attorney or representative who is permitted to examine the alien. The attorney or representative or the alien himself is permitted to examine any witness offered in the alien's behalf and to cross-examine any witness called by the Government, to offer evidence and to make objections. (8 CFR 236.2)

TRIAL ATTORNEY

The district director may assign an immigration officer to the exclusion proceedings as a trial attorney for the Government. The responsibilities of a trial attorney include the presentation of evidence and the interrogation, examination, and cross-examination of the applicant and other witnesses. (8 CFR 236.2(c))

RECORD OF HEARING

Exclusion hearings are recorded verbatim except for statements made off the record with the permission of the special inquiry officer. The record of the hearing including the testimony and exhibits, the special inquiry officer's decision and all written orders, motions, and appeals constitute the record in the case. (8 CFR 236.2(e))

DECISION

The special inquiry officer will either admit or exclude the alien. His decision may be oral or written. If made orally the alien, at his request, is furnished with a transcript of the decision. (8 CFR [236.5])

APPEAL

* * *

The decision of the special inquiry officer excluding the alien may be appealed to the Board of Immigration Appeals [by either the alien or the Service, within 10 calendar days after service of the decision (13 days if mailed). Appeals are taken by filing a notice of appeal, Form EOIR–26, with the office of the immigration judge having administrative jurisdiction over the case. Briefs may be filed along with the notice or within a further time established by the immigration judge. (8 CFR 3.3, 3.38)]

Notes

1. As is evident from this reading, in the ordinary case an alien held for exclusion proceedings has fairly extensive procedural rights under the statute and implementing regulations. The alien enjoys a right to counsel (at no expense to the government), an opportunity to present his case by written or oral evidence, as he chooses, and the chance to cross-examine opposing witnesses. The decision must be based exclusively on the record

compiled in the administrative proceedings, and the immigration judge must set forth the reasons for the decision, which is then subject to both administrative and judicial review.

Some versions of the Simpson–Mazzoli bills, forerunners of IRCA, would have cut back on the procedural entitlements of one class of excludable aliens, those who arrive without documents. The Senate bill was the more restrictive. S. 529, 98th Cong., 1st Sess., § 121, 129 Cong.Rec. S6970 (daily ed. May 18, 1983), would have replaced the first sentence of INA § 235(b) with, *inter alia,* the following:

> (b)(1) If an examining immigration officer at the port of arrival determines that an alien does not have the documentation required to obtain entry into the United States, does not have any reasonable basis for legal entry into the United States, and has not applied for asylum under section 208, such alien shall not be admissible and shall be excluded from entry into the United States without further inquiry or hearing.

Section 123(b) of the bill ostensibly precluded judicial review of such summary exclusion decisions.

What exactly would this change (which was not enacted) accomplish? Would it be constitutional under the tests the Supreme Court developed in *Mathews v. Eldridge?* Does the Constitution require some avenue of appeal? Or is the summary procedure appropriately tailored in light of the limited range of factual issues an alien subject to it under S.529 could be expected to raise? *Cf. Califano v. Yamasaki,* 442 U.S. 682, 696–97, 99 S.Ct. 2545, 2555–56, 61 L.Ed.2d 176 (1979). Would the proposed change be good policy?

In 1993, interest in summary exclusion revived, in the wake of media reports on abuse of the procedure for applying for asylum by aliens arriving at international airports. Many bills were introduced. The Clinton administration prepared legislation that would have permitted expedited exclusion by an immigration officer, without reference to an immigration judge, when the alien presented no documents on arrival, presented documents determined by the officer to be fraudulent, or arrived aboard a ship intercepted by U.S. authorities at sea. No administrative appeal was allowed, and judicial review was highly restricted as well. S.1333, 103d Congress, 1st Sess. (1993). Unlike Simpson–Mazzoli, however, a simple request for asylum would not take the alien outside this expedited procedure. Instead his asylum claim would be initially screened by an experienced asylum officer to decide whether the alien had a "credible fear" of persecution. If so, he would gain access to the regular exclusion hearing process, and his asylum claim would be finally adjudicated by the immigration judge. If not, summary exclusion could proceed. Is this version better or worse than the 1983 proposal? What are your criteria for judging? No summary exclusion bill was adopted in 1993–94, but the idea is likely to attract considerable attention in the 104th Congress. We will consider some features of the 1993 bill more closely in Chapter Eight.

2. As Harper points out, the possession of a visa does not guarantee that the alien will be admitted. The immigration inspector may reach his

own conclusions about the alien's admissibility. (Indeed, even if he decides to admit, the government may still retry the question of admissibility years later, by bringing deportation proceedings alleging that the alien was excludable at the time of entry. INA § 241(a)(1)(A), to be discussed in Chapter Six.) Why should this be so? Hasn't the U.S. consul, a government official sworn to uphold the laws and expert in the application of the immigration provisions, already determined, after inquiry, that the alien meets the requirements for admission to the United States? Shouldn't principles of *res judicata* or estoppel prevent such redeterminations?

Part of the answer lies in the explicit directive from Congress that admissibility is to remain open to wholesale reconsideration. INA §§ 204(e), 221(h). But the Supreme Court also held, relatively early in the history of federal immigration controls, that principles of *res judicata* did not have to be applied in such proceedings. *Pearson v. Williams*, 202 U.S. 281, 26 S.Ct. 608, 50 L.Ed. 1029 (1906). *See* Gordon, *Finality of Immigration and Nationality Decisions: Can the Government Be Estopped?*, 31 U.Chi.L.Rev. 433 (1964). In any event, significant practical problems would arise if administrative *res judicata* were held to apply here, for in that event the agencies would doubtless develop procedures far more cumbersome and painstaking than anything we now experience. Most border processing can be quick and routine, even perfunctory, precisely because an admission decision is not binding on the government for the indefinite future.

For an account of the growing acceptance of administrative *res judicata* in some settings, and a suggestion, in dictum, that it might apply to some determinations under the immigration and nationality laws, *see Cartier v. Secretary of State*, 506 F.2d 191, 195–98 (D.C.Cir.1974), *cert. denied* 421 U.S. 947, 95 S.Ct. 1677, 44 L.Ed.2d 101 (1975). For application of *res judicata* or similar principles in limited immigration-related settings, see *Medina v. INS*, 993 F.2d 499 (res judicata applies to block deportation when earlier exclusion proceeding was terminated on ground that respondent was a U.S. citizen), *reh'g denied, with opinion*, 1 F.3d 312 (5th Cir.1993); *Choe v. INS*, 11 F.3d 925 (9th Cir.1993) (earlier decision to adjust status precludes deportation on ground that preconceived intent to immigrate invalidated the original nonimmigrant admission).

3. Section 235(b) provides that every alien who does not appear to be "clearly and beyond a doubt entitled to land" shall receive an exclusion hearing. But in fact relatively few aliens receive such hearings: 4,411 were excluded after a formal hearing in FY 1993, measured against the 483 million admissions (which included U.S. citizens) recorded that year. A far greater number of aliens, however, is functionally excluded at the border, but without ever seeing an immigration judge, because aliens believed excludable are usually given an opportunity to withdraw their applications for admission (thus avoiding the one-year preclusion on return of § 212(a)(6)(A)). *See generally Matter of Gutierrez*, 19 I & N Dec. 562 (BIA 1988) (withdrawal may not be invoked as of right). In FY 1993, 275,315 aliens withdrew their applications during the primary inspection process, and another 602,474 withdrew during secondary inspection, a total of 877,789. 1993 INS Statistical Yearbook 157, 175. (Secondary inspection is

the more detailed questioning typically handled in the office area of the port of entry, after referral from a border inspector who detects a problem with admissibility that cannot be cleared up at the initial inspection booth.) Some commentators have expressed concern about this process. *See* Bernsen, *Withdrawal of Applications for Admission*, 71 Interp.Rel. 441 (1994).

4. In addition to withdrawal of the application, there are two other situations in which a formal exclusion hearing will not be held, under exceptions enumerated in the statute. The first we have already encountered. The INA precludes a hearing when an alien is deemed excludable based on confidential information, in accordance with § 235(c). The second is based on § 273(d), and it allows for summary exclusion of stowaways, without a hearing before an immigration judge. But, as you might expect, there are also exceptions to this exception. Stowaways who appear to be returning residents may be entitled to a full hearing. *Matter of B.*, 5 I & N Dec. 712 (BIA 1954). And it has been held that stowaways who apply for political asylum must be given a full hearing on the asylum issue, under the Refugee Act of 1980. *Yiu Sing Chun v. Sava*, 708 F.2d 869 (2d Cir.1983). *See generally* Ort, *International and U.S. Obligations Toward Stowaway Asylum Seekers*, 140 U.Pa.L.Rev. 285 (1991).

4. ADJUSTMENT OF STATUS

For many years, the only avenue for gaining immigrant status required the issuance of an immigrant visa, and visas were not—and still are not—issued in the United States. They must be obtained from U.S. consular officers posted abroad, usually in the country of the alien's nationality or residence. The Immigration Service found itself faced increasingly with aliens in this country in nonimmigrant status, however, who could show that they qualified for permanent immigration and who wished to avoid a costly trip overseas. One might easily say that such "nonimmigrants" deserve no special favors, as their new immigration plans reveal that they were not legitimate nonimmigrants from the start. Suspicion about such concealed intentions lingers, but the administrators eventually concluded that many who sought an easier way to change status had honestly undergone a change of heart after arrival here—often associated with marriage to a U.S. citizen or permanent resident.

In 1935 the agency therefore developed a "pre-examination" process that simplified matters somewhat. Under it, clearly qualified aliens could complete most of the necessary paperwork while in this country, and then travel briefly (and less expensively) to a U.S. consulate in Canada to secure the actual immigrant visa. This administrative reform built pressure for Congress to amend the statute and allow even greater simplification.

In 1952, with the new Immigration and Nationality Act, Congress finally made the change. It adopted § 245, which authorizes "adjustment of status" from nonimmigrant to immigrant for aliens who meet certain requirements. This whole process can be carried out by the INS, and the alien need never leave the United States. Congress periodically has changed the qualifications—sometimes loosening them, sometimes tightening them, in response to increasing or declining concern about possible abuses by the nonimmigrants who might seek those benefits. Indeed, controversy continues over whether the availability of the adjustment option encourages fraud by nonimmigrant visa applicants. Some claim that this mechanism induces people to conceal their intent to immigrate in order to secure nonimmigrant admission and then, after entry, establish the family ties or employment relationships necessary to adjust status. *See, e.g.,* SCIRP, Appendix G 35–38, 47.

The following case arose under the version of INA § 245 operative before 1986, when Congress tightened a few of the requirements. (These changes will be examined in the Notes.) Nevertheless, it sets forth many of the principal policy issues, illustrates the procedural framework still used, and suggests the interplay between threshold requirements of statutory eligibility and the Attorney General's exercise of the discretion explicitly granted by the statute.[7]

JAIN v. INS

United States Court of Appeals, Second Circuit, 1979.
612 F.2d 683, cert. denied, 446 U.S. 937, 100 S.Ct. 2155, 64 L.Ed.2d 789 (1980).

FEINBERG, CIRCUIT JUDGE:

Om Prakash Jain, a citizen of India in this country on a nonimmigrant business visa, petitions for review of a decision of the Board of Immigration Appeals, which denied his application for adjustment of status under section 245 of the Immigration and Nationality Act. The Board based its denial, in the exercise of its discretion, on a finding that petitioner entered the United States with a preconceived intent to remain permanently in this country. Petitioner's principal claim is that this is an improper reason for denying relief under section 245. For reasons given below, we reject this contention, along with petitioner's other arguments. We therefore deny the petition for review and affirm the decision of the Board.

I

The facts, as they appear in the record before us, may fairly be summarized as follows. This is petitioner Jain's third stay in the United States. The first began in June 1974, when he was 23 years old and was admitted on a nonimmigrant visa as a visitor for business. Jain had obtained that visa as the proprietor and business representative of a company located in Jaipur, India, which exported gems, beads and semi-precious stones. Jain remained here for four to five weeks looking for customers, but left without success. A little over a year later, Jain returned in the same capacity as before, and again found no customers. After staying in this country a month, Jain again departed. While he was here, however, Jain apparently conceived the idea of creating a company within the United States to import beads and jewelry from India and keep an inventory here. This would allow Jain to guarantee quick delivery to potential customers, thus overcoming the difficulty he had earlier encoun-

---

7. We will consider issues of discretion in greater detail in Chapter Seven, for this interplay of eligibility and discretion is a common feature of most forms of relief from deportation.

tered in seeking to sell his goods. Before he left this country on this second visit, Jain retained an attorney, created a new import company supposedly located in the room at the hotel where he stayed, filed a certificate of doing business under the assumed name of Asian Imports and obtained a social security number for himself.

Upon his return to India, Jain quickly liquidated his export firm in Jaipur by turning it over to his brother. Thereafter, he reentered the United States in January 1976 on a nonimmigrant business visa good for four months, as the representative of his former export business. The true reason for his return, however, was to run Asian Imports, his newly established enterprise here. Within a month, Jain also applied to the Immigration and Naturalization Service for adjustment of his status to that of permanent resident alien. The basis of the application was his alleged status as an investor, a term of art in this context more fully described below.[a]

Two years later, the District Director of the Service denied Jain's application for adjustment of status because of his lack of good faith in applying for his nonimmigrant visa abroad. After Jain failed to depart voluntarily, the Service began deportation proceedings. Before an immigration judge, Jain conceded his deportability, but again sought adjustment of status as an investor and, in the alternative, applied for reinstatement of voluntary departure status. After a hearing, the immigration judge held in August 1978 that Jain did not qualify as an investor and, alternatively, that even if he did, his application would be denied on discretionary grounds because Jain last entered this country with a preconceived intent to remain permanently. On appeal, the Board in July 1979 affirmed the decision of the immigration judge on the second, discretionary ground, and granted Jain again the privilege of voluntary departure. Jain's petition to us for review allows him to enjoy the automatic stay of deportation that accompanies such action, and almost four years have now elapsed since Jain's entry in January 1976 on a four-month business visa.

II

* * *

The Act presumes that entering aliens seek to do so as immigrants. Consequently, nonimmigrants—those aliens seeking entry only for a limited time and purpose—bear the burden of demonstrating to the United States consular officials abroad and the immigration authorities in this country that they are bona fide nonimmigrants. Jain, like many nonimmigrants, obtained entry under a nonimmigrant visa for business. Such a visa allows an alien to conduct business in the United States for a foreign employer for a limited period. 8 C.F.R. 214.2(b). However, in order to establish his bona fide nonimmigrant status and thereby qualify for such a visa, a nonimmigrant is required to demonstrate to the satisfaction of the

a. Until 1990 there was no preference under § 203 for investors, but in 1976 an adequate investment might exempt an alien from the labor certification requirement, and thus make it possible for him to enter in the nonpreference category. Nonpreference became unavailable after 1978. See the discussion of Investors as Immigrants, *supra* pp. 223–25—eds.

immigration authorities that he has a foreign residence that he has no intention of abandoning and that he will depart voluntarily at the end of his authorized stay.

Under earlier versions of the Act, nonimmigrant aliens who sought to adjust their status to that of immigrants were required to leave the country and seek reentry as immigrants. To ameliorate this hardship, the Immigration and Naturalization Service devised an administrative procedure, known as pre-examination, under which nonimmigrant aliens were examined by immigration officials in the United States and were issued an immigrant visa by the consular office in Canada if their admissibility as immigrants was established. This procedure was used extensively for many years. In 1952, Congress enacted section 245 of the Act, to obviate the need for the pre-examination procedure. The current version of the statute provides in pertinent part:

> (a) The status of an alien, other than an alien crewman, who was inspected and admitted or paroled into the United States may be adjusted by the Attorney General, in his discretion and under such regulations as he may prescribe, to that of an alien lawfully admitted for permanent residence if (1) the alien makes an application for such adjustment, (2) the alien is eligible to receive an immigrant visa and is admissible to the United States for permanent residence, and (3) an immigrant visa is immediately available to him at the time his application is approved.[b]

Thus, a nonimmigrant alien may now adjust his status to that of an immigrant without leaving the country if he is admissible for permanent residence and is eligible for an immigrant visa, which is "immediately available" to him. However, even if the nonimmigrant satisfies these express statutory requirements, the Service has discretion under section 245 to deny the application for adjustment of status. Furthermore, the alien bears the burden of persuading the Service to exercise its discretion favorably, since adjustment of status under section 245 is considered to be extraordinary relief.

The deceptively brief statutory requirements of section 245 nonetheless pose complex administrative problems. One major obstacle facing section 245 applicants is to demonstrate that an immigrant visa is "immediately available." The law governing the availability of visas is complicated, and if a nonimmigrant cannot establish an exemption from the numerical limitations applicable to certain categories of immigrant visas, he must await the chronological distribution of such visas. Furthermore, certain categories of immigrant visas are unavailable unless the applicant either obtains a certification from the Secretary of Labor that his employment in this country will not affect the American labor market adversely or establishes an exemption from this certification requirement. Jain apparently was eligible only for this type of visa and therefore attempted to establish an exemption from the certification requirement as an investor in a domestic enterprise. The investor exemption, at the time Jain applied,

b. An amendment in 1976 changed the last word to "filed"—a far more demanding requirement. See GM & Y § 51.03[4][f].— eds.

allowed waiver of the certification requirement if the alien had invested over $10,000 in an enterprise that he managed and that directly created domestic job opportunities. *Mehta v. Immigration and Naturalization Service,* 574 F.2d 701 (2d Cir.1978). While Jain's investment in Asian Imports apparently satisfied the requisite amount, the immigration judge found that Jain was ineligible for the investor exemption because his enterprise had "failed to expand job opportunities for anyone in this country." Relying on the authority of *Mehta,* supra, the judge therefore found that Jain had failed to demonstrate that an immigrant visa was "immediately available." Although this determination of statutory ineligibility seems amply supported by the record, the Board of Immigration Appeals affirmed the denial of section 245 relief on the second rationale offered by the immigration judge—that Jain's application did not warrant a favorable exercise of discretion. We now turn to this issue.

III

The immigration judge ruled that even if Jain were "statutorily eligible" for adjustment of status, relief would be denied as a discretionary matter. Because Jain had already liquidated his business in India and made plans to operate Asian Imports in this country, the judge concluded that Jain had "not been candid" with the immigration authorities when he last entered the country on a nonimmigrant visa for business and that his application presented no "outstanding or unusual equities" warranting a favorable exercise of discretion. The Board of Immigration Appeals adopted this ground for decision, holding that the evidence supported "the immigration judge's conclusion that [Jain] entered the United States with a preconceived intent to remain permanently" and that such a finding would support a discretionary denial of status adjustment.

Petitioner now argues that his preconceived intent to remain permanently in this country after entering on a temporary nonimmigrant visa was an improper basis for denying discretionary relief. The issue is an important one, and apparently has not been addressed in a published opinion of this court. However, a number of other circuits have considered whether the good faith of an alien's entry as a nonimmigrant is a proper consideration in the exercise of discretion under section 245. The most extensive discussion of the issue is by the Third Circuit, sitting en banc in *Ameeriar v. Immigration and Naturalization Service,* 438 F.2d 1028 (3d Cir.1971). Both the majority opinion and the dissent of Judge Gibbons rely heavily upon the legislative history of section 245, although their interpretations differ. The original version of section 245 enacted in 1952 to replace the pre-examination procedure authorized the Attorney General, through the Service, to grant relief "under such regulations as he may prescribe to insure the application of this paragraph solely to the cases of aliens who entered the United States in good faith as nonimmigrants." 66 Stat. 217. Therefore, good faith entry as a nonimmigrant was apparently regarded as a condition precedent to the favorable exercise of discretion. This requirement was deleted in the 1960 amendments to the Act in order to enlarge the Service's discretion to act favorably on behalf of nonimmigrants who were otherwise eligible for admission as immigrants. However, the Service thereafter took the position that the absence of good faith entry, even though no longer a statutory bar to section 245 relief, was nonetheless a factor relevant to the favorable exercise of discretion. See Sofaer, The Change of Status Adjudication: A Case Study of the Informal Agency Process, 1 J. Legal Studies 349, 374–76 (1972). The majority in *Ameeriar,* as well as the other circuits that have considered the issue, adopted this view.

* * *

While the statutory question is not free from doubt, we nonetheless believe that the majority view is more persuasive.

* * *

Furthermore, allowing the Service the discretion to deny section 245 relief to nonimmigrant aliens who enter in bad faith appears to comport with the proper administration of the statute. As previously noted, the Act distinguishes between immigrants and nonimmigrants and specifically requires those seeking nonimmigrant status to establish that they have no intention of abandoning their foreign residence and that they will depart voluntarily at the end of their authorized stay. We do not know whether Jain would have received an immigrant visa had he applied for one in India with a true statement of his intent. But had the true facts been known, he clearly would not have received a nonimmigrant visa because he would not have been entitled to one. Jain did not seek entry into the United States to represent a foreign employer for a limited period; he instead sought entry to remain permanently and to run his own business here. To require the Service to disregard this misrepresentation by Jain would effectively undercut the Act's requirement that nonimmigrants demonstrate their bona fide status. In contrast, permitting the Service to deny section 245 relief based on the nonimmigrant's lack of good faith protects the integrity of the consular procedures established by the Act.

Finally, it should be noted that denial of section 245 relief, when coupled with a grant of voluntary departure, is a lenient disposition of what might possibly be regarded as fraud. Although denied an adjustment of status, Jain is not precluded from seeking entry as an immigrant through the normal process established by the Act.

* * *

Thus, we are content to adopt the majority view espoused in *Ameeriar,* knowing full well that in this area Congress legislates frequently and can correct us if we are wrong. On this reading of section 245, it is clear that the Board's decision was not an abuse of discretion.

* * *

IV

Jain also argues on appeal that he was denied due process because he was unable to appeal the original denial of his section 245 application directly and could only do so in the context of deportation proceedings. We find this argument to be without merit. Although the regulations do preclude a direct administrative appeal from the denial by a district director of a section 245 application, the alien is entitled to a de novo review of his application in the context of deportation proceedings. We consider this dual opportunity to present a section 245 application to provide ample process, particularly in light of the discretionary nature of section 245 relief. The fact that the second consideration of the application takes place within the context of a deportation proceeding is irrelevant. Petitioner's argument to the contrary assumes that Jain could have avoided deportation proceedings simply by choosing not to renew his section 245 application. However, since Jain's deportability as an overstay was clear, the initiation of deportation proceedings was a matter over which he had no control.

Accordingly, the petition for review is denied.

Notes on Adjustment of Status

1. Adjustment of status has become increasingly popular over the years since its adoption in 1952. In FY 1987, a total of 100,656 adjustments were recorded, as against 468,699 total admissions, for preference category admissions and immediate relatives (21.5%). By FY 1992, the data were maintained in somewhat different form, but 181,829 adjustments were recorded as against 693,598 total admissions, for all categories except refugees and IRCA legalization (26.2%). This figure includes an estimated 155–160,000 adjustments in the categories comparable to the 1987 totals. Of these, approximately 57,000 were in the employment-based second and third preferences, and approximately 92,000 were for immediate relatives. 1987 INS Statistical Yearbook, Table 4; 1992 *id.*, Table 5. Adjustment of status for one who qualifies in one of the preference categories is not a numerical add-on; it counts against the annual total in that category for the current fiscal year. INA § 245(b).

2. The *Jain* case sketches the applicable procedures for adjustment of status. In its purest form, adjustment simply provides a replacement for traveling overseas to obtain an immigrant visa in the classic fashion, from a consular officer. Adjustment does not supersede the need for a visa petition in those immigration categories to which the petition requirement applies (on Form I–130 for family preferences and I–140 for occupational preferences). Sometimes these can be submitted simultaneously with the application for adjustment on Form I–485, but increasingly the visa petition must first be submitted to the Regional Service Center, and the adjustment application can be filed only after that petition is approved. The alien may be scheduled for an interview before adjustment is granted, but interviews are now usually waived except when the petition is based on a recent marriage.

In passing on the actual application for adjustment of status based on the information supplied on the I–485 (as distinguished from deciding the merits of a visa petition—an INS function in virtually all cases), the INS examiner makes all the same determinations as a consular officer. She must assure that the applicant is qualified for the immigrant category claimed, and must go on to judge whether any of the grounds of exclusion might apply. For purposes of this process, the applicant for adjustment, although physically within the United States, is considered as though he were at the border applying for initial entry. *See Yui Sing Tse v. INS,* 596 F.2d 831, 834 (9th Cir.1979).

3. As the *Jain* case also makes clear, the INS examiner considering an adjustment application has to make several determinations beyond those required of a consular officer. In particular, the INS officer must decide whether the applicant meets the special requirements imposed by the core provisions of § 245. (Note that after October 1, 1994, those who fail some of these requirements but nevertheless qualify for immigrant admission may still adjust status upon paying a high fee; the new subsection providing this option, INA § 245(i), is discussed immediately following these Notes.)

The most important core requirements of § 245 are the following: (1) The alien must have been inspected and admitted or paroled. INA § 245(a). This means that adjustment is available almost exclusively to people present in the United States on nonimmigrant visas; until late 1994 it could not be claimed under any circumstances by those who entered without inspection. (2) The alien must have been admitted in some status other than that of alien crewman (§ 245(c)(1)), "transit without visa" (§ 245(c)(3)), or beneficiary of the visa waiver pilot program (§ 245(c)(4)) (except for such beneficiaries who are immediate relatives of U.S. citizens). (3) The alien must not have worked without INS authorization as a nonimmigrant. *See Pei–Chi Tien v. INS,* 638 F.2d 1324 (5th Cir.1981). This final limitation, imposed under § 245(c)(2), does not apply, by its terms, to adjustment applicants who are the immediate relatives of U.S. citizens.

The 1986 immigration legislation made significant changes in § 245. Section 245(c)(2), which formerly disqualified aliens only on the basis of unauthorized employment, now applies as well to certain violations of status by people admitted as nonimmigrants. As amended, it renders ineligible for ordinary adjustment any alien (other than an immediate relative of a U.S. citizen) who "is in unlawful immigration status on the date of filing the application for adjustment of status or who has failed (other than through no fault of his own or for technical reasons) to maintain continuously a lawful status since entry into the United States." Does this amendment effectively eliminate adjustment in deportation proceedings? Under what circumstances might § 245 relief still be available in that setting? Suppose a nonimmigrant goes out of status while waiting for INS action on an extension request. Should he be disqualified from adjustment? The answer is no; the regulations consider this a failure to maintain status "through no fault of his own or for technical reasons." 8 C.F.R. § 245.1(c)(2).

4. Beyond the preclusions discussed in Note 3, the district director must be sure that an immigrant visa is immediately available to the applicant as of the date when the Form I–485 is filed. If the applicant seeks to qualify in one of the numerically limited preference categories, availability can usually be determined by consulting the chart in the most

recent Visa Office Bulletin—*see* Table 3.6, p. 135 *supra,* for a sample. In short, if there is a two year backlog for aliens in this applicant's preference category, the theory of § 245 is that the alien should pass that time in his home country and eventually come in, if he is still interested, through the regular immigrant visa process.

One last factor has traditionally been quite significant in § 245 adjudications: the application of the "Attorney General's" discretion. *Jain* suggests the difficulties in managing such discretion and in submitting it to meaningful judicial review. *See Matter of Blas,* 15 I & N Dec. 626 (BIA 1974, AG 1976). Issues concerning the exercise and review of such discretion will be examined at length in Chapter Seven.

5. It is important to remember that an alien denied adjustment on one of the grounds described in the two preceding Notes is not necessarily disqualified from permanent resident alien status; he will simply have to use the usual immigrant visa process (or the new avenue opened by § 245(i), discussed below) if he wishes to obtain permanent residence. For example, if an adjustment application is denied because the alien entered without inspection, he can probably return to his home country and apply for an immigrant visa from there. In practice, earlier clandestine entries do not bar the issuance of an immigrant visa if all the other qualifications are met—at least if the applicant left this country voluntarily and not under a deportation order (*see* INA § 212(a)(6)(B)).

Such aliens were ordinarily expected, at least until the enactment of § 245(i), to return to their home countries to pick up their visas at the U.S. consulate there. In limited circumstances, however, aliens may persuade a consulate elsewhere to process the case and issue the visa, particularly if they risk persecution or other danger in their homeland or if the United States offers no visa services there. *See* 22 C.F.R. § 42.61 (1990); 64 Interp.Rel. 1094 (1987); 66 *id.* 458 (1989). Such cases are often known as "orphan visa" or "homeless visa" cases.

6. If the applicant is denied adjustment of status by INS, as Jain was, on either statutory or discretionary grounds, no administrative appeal is allowed. 8 C.F.R. § 245.2(a)(4). Instead, the regulations provide that the application for adjustment may be renewed before the immigration judge conducting the alien's deportation proceedings. The immigration judge is not bound in any way by the earlier adjudication in the district office or regional service center, but instead applies the statutory grounds and exercises the Attorney General's discretion anew, based on any information in the appropriate forms or developed at the deportation hearing. In this latter setting, adjustment functions more like the other provisions for relief from deportation to be covered in Chapter Seven, rather than as the replacement for immigrant visa processing we have been examining in this chapter. Adjustment may also be sought from the immigration judge during proceedings even if the alien had not earlier requested it by means of an application to INS.[8]

8. If the alien is already in proceedings by the time he decides he wishes to apply for adjustment, he may not present the application to INS; his only forum at that point is the immigration court.

Ordinarily there is no judicial review of a denial of adjustment until after a renewal in the deportation hearing has proved unsuccessful. In that event, review is sought di-

The Special Adjustment Provisions of INA § 245(i)

As part of an appropriations bill passed in August 1994, Congress introduced a significant liberalization of the adjustment provisions, operative on a trial basis for a three-year period. One commentator called the measure "the most sweeping change in the checkered history of adjustment." Mailman, *The New Adjustment of Status Law: Background and Analysis*, 71 Interp.Rel. 1505 (1994). Most people previously barred from adjustment, but who are nonetheless eligible for an immigrant visa and do not fall within any of the exclusion grounds, will now be able to adjust, provided they pay a penalty fee of five times the normal adjustment fee (in 1994: $650 on top of the normal $130 fee for filing the I–485). INA § 245(i).[9] In these cases, adjustment is available even if the alien entered without inspection (disqualified under § 245(a)), or would otherwise be ineligible under the provisions of INA § 245(c). See Note 3 above. (Immigration lawyers must remain familiar with the rules described in that Note, however, in order to determine whether clients owe the higher fee.) The new adjustment provision, however, does not waive the disqualifications imposed by § 245(d)-(f), which derive from concerns about fraudulent marriages or fraudulent use of the immigrant investor provisions.

People previously disqualified from adjustment rarely abandoned their efforts to immigrate; they simply had to travel back home to obtain a visa. (Consider, however, whether this course was open to Jain.) In this light, the 1994 change could be seen as Congress's way of diverting funds from airlines into the coffers of the U.S. Treasury. In fact, Congress added an ancillary provision in the same legislation to make it even more attractive for such persons to pay the higher fee and adjust, rather than travel home for a visa without the $650 fee. Under new INA § 212(*o*), a person who has been physically present in this country but was not in a lawful status at the time of departure may not receive an immigrant visa from a consulate until he or she has spent 90 days outside the United States.

Besides avoiding travel, adjustment also carries other advantages for the alien over the visa process, including the right to be accompanied by counsel during the procedure, and far more ample appeal rights (remember the consular nonreviewability doctrine). For the interim INS regulations implementing the requirements of § 245(i), see 59 Fed.Reg. 51091 (1994).

rectly in the court of appeals as part of the statutory review procedure under INA § 106(a), which brings to the court all issues tried in the actual deportation proceedings. The *Jain* case exemplifies this avenue of review. But occasionally an alien has secured immediate judicial review in the district court, under § 279, of the district director's denial of adjustment, without waiting for the commencement of a deportation proceeding. *See Nasan v. INS,* 449 F.Supp. 244 (N.D.Ill. 1978).

9. In the rush to adjournment in late 1994, Congress actually passed two provisions designated as INA § 245(i). A technical correction is expected in 1995.

Previously disqualified aliens can also now adjust without paying the higher fee if (1) they are under 17 years old and unmarried, or (2) are covered by the "family unity" program for certain family members of IRCA legalization beneficiaries who entered before May 5, 1988.

State Department instructions are reprinted in 71 Interp.Rel. 1188 (1994). The workload at many U.S. consulates should decrease noticeably under this change, and that for INS offices increase.

The full significance of § 245(i) has yet to be worked out, but now that Congress appears to be affirmatively promoting adjustment (sometimes at a premium price), much of the earlier doctrine based on suspicions about nonimmigrants' preconceived intent may have to be revised. *See* Mailman, *supra*, at 1509–10. Now that EWIs (entrants without inspection) and unauthorized workers may adjust, would it still make sense to deny adjustment in the exercise of discretion in situations similar to *Jain*? Would § 245(i) allow aliens thus denied to adjust anyway by paying a higher fee? (Look closely at the wording of the subsection.) INS has tacitly recognized that the new provision may carry important implications for discretionary denials, by requiring all such denials by INS officers now to be certified to the Administrative Appeals Unit for further review. INS Memorandum, reprinted in 71 Interp.Rel. 1309 (1994).

Adjustment Based on Marriage

The possibility to ask an immigration judge for adjustment during deportation proceedings remains an important tool that immigration lawyers can sometimes use to help their clients remain in the United States. But the availability of such relief at that stage may also trigger abuses by individuals who see no other way to prevent their expulsion. In 1986, Congress sought to block one such potential abuse, by adding subsection (e) to INA § 245, as part of the Immigration Marriage Fraud Amendments (IMFA). In its original form this subsection totally precluded adjustment based on a marriage entered into during the pendency of deportation proceedings.[10] And Congress went even further in manifesting its suspicion of aliens who marry under such circumstances. Another provision adopted at the same time prohibited the granting of an immediate relative or preference petition based on such a marriage "until the alien has resided outside the United States for a 2–year period beginning after the date of the marriage." INA § 204(g). (The eleventh-hour marriages of concern here were those to American citizens, although the statute is phrased more broadly. Why, as a practical matter, wouldn't such a marriage to a lawful permanent resident raise the same issues?)

This provision clearly would end all temptation to enter into a sham marriage as a way of defeating deportation through adjustment. But it was overinclusive. It also imposed a harsh disability (two years' separation or joint exile) on some couples whose marriage might be wholly genuine. Many unsuspecting aliens caught in its toils challenged its validity. Most courts upheld its constitutionality under the highly deferential standard of review established by the Supreme Court in *Kleindienst v. Mandel* and *Fiallo v. Bell. See, e.g., Azizi v. Thornburgh*, 908 F.2d 1130 (2d Cir.1990); *Anetekhai v. INS*, 876 F.2d 1218 (5th Cir.1989). Two courts, however,

10. In *Matter of Enriquez*, 19 I & N Dec. 554 (BIA 1988), the Board ruled that the relevant time period does not end with the issuance of a deportation order; the proceedings are still "pending" until the alien departs from the United States.

found constitutional defects. *Escobar v. INS*, 896 F.2d 564 (D.C.Cir.1990), *vacated pending rehearing en banc, appeal dismissed as moot (after statutory change), and opinion withdrawn from bound volume*, 925 F.2d 488 (D.C.Cir.1991); *Manwani v. U.S. Dept. of Justice*, 736 F.Supp. 1367 (W.D.N.C.1990).

Responding to these concerns, Congress acted in 1990 to ameliorate the harshness of this IMFA provision. It added paragraph (3) to INA § 245(e), with a corresponding change to § 204(g). What kind of evidence can an alien offer to meet the enhanced burden of proof established by this provision? What course of action would you advise to a visa-overstaying client who has just been served with charging papers initiating deportation proceedings, but has been living with a U.S. citizen for two years, and now deeply regrets that they did not get married earlier as they had often discussed? If you were a member of Congress, would you have voted for the 1990 amendment? Consider the pros and cons of this hypothetical alternative: eliminate the two-year foreign residency requirement altogether (§ 204(g)) but keep the adjustment provision in its original form (before the addition of § 245(e)(3)), thus requiring aliens who enter into eleventh-hour marriages to use the visa process.

Rescission of Adjustment of Status

The last sentence of INA § 246(a) provides for rescission of adjustment of status acquired under § 245 if "it shall appear to the satisfaction of the Attorney General that the person was not in fact eligible for such adjustment of status." *See generally Kim v. Meese*, 810 F.2d 1494 (9th Cir.1987); *Zaoutis v. Kiley*, 558 F.2d 1096 (2d Cir.1977). Contested rescission actions are heard by immigration judges, and are appealable to the BIA. 8 C.F.R. Part 246. The government bears the burden of establishing by clear, unequivocal, and convincing evidence that the adjustment was improperly granted. *Baria v. Leno*, 849 F.Supp. 750 (D.Hawaii 1994).

Note that § 246 rescissions are subject to a five-year statute of limitations. This is a curious provision, because in 1952, when the adjustment procedure was created, along with § 246, Congress was busy *removing* nearly all statutes of limitation that had previously restricted the deportation of aliens whose initial entry was later revealed to be defective. *See* H.R.Rep. No. 2096, 82d Cong., 2d Sess. 129 (1952); 98 Cong.Rec. 4302 (1952) (remarks of Rep. Walter). The five-year limitation in § 246(a) is so curious, in fact, that the Justice Department has tried to explain it away as "a historical anomaly or the result of an accident in the legislative process." Quoted in *Oloteo v. INS*, 643 F.2d 679, 683 n. 8 (9th Cir.1981). (We will examine the broader issue of statutes of limitation for deportation more closely in Chapter Six.)

Is there any reason why an alien whose status was adjusted should enjoy greater immunity after five years than does an alien who entered on an immigrant visa? We are hard put to come up with a policy justification. Nevertheless, the Board of Immigration Appeals, in various encounters with § 246(a), has steadfastly attempted to give real meaning to the apparent congressional choice to favor adjustment beneficiaries. In two significant cases, the Board read the section as providing, in essence, immunity to removal for an adjusted alien after five years had passed. In both instances, however, the Attorney General took referral of the cases and reversed the Board's decision. *Matter of S.,* 9 I & N Dec. 548 (BIA 1961; AG 1962), and *Matter of Belenzo,* 17 I & N Dec. 374 (BIA 1980; AG 1981). The Attorney General held that even after the five years have passed, the alien remains fully subject to deportation (or exclusion if he has traveled abroad and seeks readmission), whether the ground for deportation or exclusion relates to a defect in the original entry prior to adjustment (*Matter of S.*) or to a defect in the adjustment itself (*Matter of Belenzo*). As a result, if INS seeks to remove an adjusted alien *within* five years, it must always commence rescission proceedings first and then, if successful, launch deportation proceedings. *See Matter of Saunders,* 16 I & N Dec. 326 (BIA 1977). After five years, INS may go directly to deportation proceedings. The lapse of time furnishes no immunity on the bottom-line issue of removal. *See* Orlow, *Rescission—Rationalizing the Irrational,* 6 Immig.J. 6 (1983).

Doesn't this approach effectively read the five-year limitation out of the statute? The Attorney General believed that he had not wholly transgressed the congressional intent: "the limitations period is designed to assure that, if no other action to obtain rescission is taken within 5 years, the Attorney General may not use the procedural mechanism for rescission, but must instead seek deportation, a route that offers special statutory safeguards to the alien." *Belenzo, supra,* at 383–84. Do you find this a convincing explanation?

Given the absence of statutes of limitation applicable to most immigrants, probably either outcome—the Board's or the Attorney General's—leads to unsatisfactory and distasteful results. In light of this dilemma, do you regard the Attorney General's decisions as a creative response to a congressional accident, assuring equal treatment of two classes of aliens (those who adjust and those who enter on an immigrant visa) who are similarly situated in every functional respect? Or do these decisions amount to a flouting of congressional intent to treat adjusted aliens as a preferred class, a choice which, however hard to justify, is evident from the plain language of the statute?

SECTION D.   DUE PROCESS REVISITED: DETENTION OF EXCLUDABLE ALIENS

In *Shaughnessy v. United States ex rel. Mezei,* 345 U.S. 206, 73 S.Ct. 625, 97 L.Ed. 956 (1953), the Supreme Court clearly approved indefinite detention of an excludable alien, without any judicial testing of the substantive merits or even the procedural validity of the detention order. This doctrine is of course limited, to some extent, by the continuing validity of *Wong Wing v. United States,* 163 U.S. 228, 16 S.Ct. 977, 41 L.Ed. 140 (1896), reprinted in part in Chapter One, pp. 37–39, which found unconstitutional a statute that provided for up to a year's imprisonment, at hard labor, of persons found by executive officials to be in the country illegally. Incarceration for violating the immigration laws could be imposed, the Court ruled, but "such legislation, to be valid, must provide for a judicial trial to establish the guilt of the accused." *Id.* at 237, 16 S.Ct. at 981. On the other hand, "temporary confinement, as part of the means necessary to give effect to the provisions for the exclusion or expulsion of aliens, would be valid." *Id.* at 235, 16 S.Ct. at 980.

The *Mezei* decision provoked harsh criticism in the press and in academic commentary, as we have seen. But succeeding years presented few opportunities to rethink the result in that case. In part, the absence of such opportunities reflects the relative rarity of a case like Mezei's; most of the time an excludable alien has somewhere to go. Indeed, it is usually recognized under international law that a nation has an obligation to permit the return of its nationals. *See, e.g.,* A. Roth, International Law Applied to Aliens 39–44 (1949); *Universal Declaration of Human Rights,* art. 13(2), UNGA Res. 217 (III), UN Doc. A/801 (1948), ("Everyone has the right to leave any country, including his own, and to return to his country."). And beyond this, the government simply began to detain aliens less frequently. Not only was the McCarthy era subsiding (bringing a reduction in security-based exclusions), but perhaps more importantly, the Justice Department decided to close Ellis Island and other detention facilities in 1954, largely as an economy measure. Thereafter, the overwhelming majority of aliens in exclusion proceedings were freed on parole, unless there was some significant reason to regard them as dangerous or as likely to abscond before the hearing.

Marielitos

In 1980 this situation changed. Beginning in April and continuing until September, thousands of undocumented Cubans arrived directly in the United States from the port of Mariel, opened by the Cuban government with an invitation to relatives in the United States to come pick up their family members. But the returning boats brought not only relatives. Cuban officials also forced them to carry thousands of others whom the Cubans wished to remove. As it turned out, a small percentage (but a sizable number) of the 125,000 Marielitos had criminal records in Cuba. For this reason, although the vast majority of the Cubans were paroled shortly after arrival, the government chose to detain many based on their criminal records. Others committed criminal offenses after arrival, leading to a revocation of the initial parole. The detainees were given hearings and nearly all were held excludable. But the Cuban government refused to take them back. Not wishing to incur the expense of lengthy detentions, but also not wanting to release dangerous criminals, the government undertook various screening measures to decide who among this riskier group could be released.

At about the same time, a boat flow of longer standing was beginning to peak. Since the early 1970s, Haitians had been coming to Florida by small boat and very often filing for political asylum upon encountering INS. The numbers of Haitian asylum applicants exceeded 1000 per month during much of 1980. These numbers were low compared to the Cuban flow at the time, but they did place additional strain on INS resources and on several agencies of the state of Florida, where most of them landed.

Shortly after taking office, the Reagan administration began extensive review of the problem of immigration control. The release policy followed since 1954 came to be seen as one cause of the increase in the number of asylum-seekers, making it more attractive for excludable aliens to come to the United States. Even if meritless, an asylum claim would purchase several months or years in this country, free of restraints and usually with permission to work. After mid–1981, the 1954 release policy was ended, although there is some controversy about when and how the new detention policy came into existence. Detention pending exclusion hearings became the norm thereafter, at least for aliens who arrived without documents.[11] Several lawsuits challenged these new detention practices. The most important cases involved Haitians, even though other groups, such as Salvadorans and Guatemalans, were also affected.

Detention thus posed due process questions in two different but related settings, and it is hard to know which is the more poignant. Cubans believed to have criminal records faced confinement of indefinite duration; for all anyone could tell at the time, it might be permanent. The prospects for release seemed to be entirely dependent on the uncertainties of diplomacy between two feuding and mutually suspicious nations. On the other hand, restrictive measures of some sort are more easily justified in the case of individuals who have committed serious crimes in the past. Moreover, these Cuban detainees had been ruled excludable, and most of those exclusion orders were final by the time the due process litigation reached decision in the courts.

The Haitians were in a different situation. Any who found confinement intolerable did not have to await the outcome of diplomatic maneuvering to secure release. They could simply return to Haiti. But of course, most were resisting such return based on the claim that they would be persecuted if they did so. Moreover, they had not yet been ruled excludable; asylum applications were still pending in the administrative system or in the courts. Some might yet prove to have perfectly valid entitlements to remain. Nevertheless, unlike the Cubans, they did not face the prospect of endless confinement. One way or another, detention would end, either with deportation to Haiti or release into the United States with status as an asylee, as soon as the asylum claims were finally adjudicated.

The first significant rulings on the constitutionality of detention appeared in Cuban cases involving Cubans. *Rodriguez-Fernandez v. Wilkinson*, 654 F.2d 1382 (10th Cir.1981), ordered the release of a Marielito who had been detained in federal penitentiaries. The court distinguished *Mezei*, because that case was based on national security risks, the government had been continuing its efforts to deport Mezei, and the conditions of confinement at Ellis Island were less severe than the petitioner faced here. The court also invoked *Wong Wing* and *Yick Wo v. Hopkins*, 118 U.S. 356, 6 S.Ct. 1064, 30 L.Ed. 220 (1886) (summarized in Chapter One at pp. 18, 37), and even international human rights doctrine, but ultimately resolved the case on the basis of statutory construction. Although the INA authorizes

---

11. The 1990 Act also mandated the systematic detention of excludable aliens who have been convicted of an "aggravated felony" as defined in INA § 101(a)(43). They may be released only in very limited circumstances. INA § 236(e).

temporary detention pending removal, it does not "permit indefinite detention as an alternative to exclusion." Unless the government could carry its burden of showing that detention was still "temporary pending expulsion," the petitioner had to be released. (The court opined, somewhat implausibly, that this did not necessarily require release into the United States.)

After *Rodriguez-Fernandez*, other courts considered similar issues and reached disparate results. In *Palma v. Verdeyen,* 676 F.2d 100 (4th Cir.1982), the court found that the statute authorized the indefinite detention of excludable aliens. It pointed in particular to the absence from INA § 237 of any language limiting the length of detention that would be comparable to the limitations imposed in the deportation setting by § 242(c). Citing *Knauff* and *Mezei,* the court also found few constitutional limitations on such detention. Nevertheless, it insisted that the Attorney General had to abide faithfully by the limitations Congress imposed, and it went on to review the denial of parole under an abuse-of-discretion standard. Because of the petitioner's serious record of misbehavior in the detention facilities, in addition to his conviction of theft offenses in Cuba, the court found no abuse of discretion. It authorized continued detention, "pending further review of his suitability for parole in accordance with the Justice Department's plan." The Second Circuit reached a similar result, reversing a district court decision that ordered release of several detained Haitians. *Bertrand v. Sava,* 684 F.2d 204 (2d Cir.1982) (emphasizing the narrow scope of judicial review of the district director's parole decisions).

The next important decision occurred in a case brought by Haitian detainees who still had asylum claims pending. In *Louis v. Nelson,* 544 F.Supp. 973 (S.D.Fla.1982), the court ruled that the new detention policy put into effect in 1981 was invalid for failure to comply with the notice-and-comment rulemaking procedures required by the Administrative Procedure Act (APA). It also held, after lengthy consideration, that the plaintiffs' claim of national-origin discrimination, allegedly committed by INS and directed invidiously against black Haitians, could be heard under the Constitution, despite their excludable status. But it found against the plaintiffs on the facts of the case, ruling that intentional discrimination had not been proven.

The Justice Department responded to the APA-based ruling with quick promulgation of interim detention regulations, published "under protest" for notice and comment, but made effective immediately. 47 Fed.Reg. 30044 (1982) (amending 8 C.F.R. §§ 212.5, 235.3). The notice stated: "The Administration has determined that a large number of Haitian nationals and others are likely to attempt to enter the United States illegally unless there is in place a detention and parole regulation meeting the approval of the District Court. Such a large scale influx would clearly be contrary to the public interest." The notice emphasized the drafters' belief that the statutory mandate makes detention the norm (quoting the language of INA § 235(b)), and went on to summarize the only exceptions for undocumented aliens awaiting an exclusion hearing. The new regulations permitted release under these circumstances: "(1) serious medical conditions; (2) pregnant women; (3) certain juveniles; (4) aliens with close family relatives in the United States; (5) other unusual situations warranting parole." (With minor changes these regulations still govern. 8 C.F.R. § 212.5(a).)

Meanwhile, both sides sought review of the district court's decision in *Louis v. Nelson*. In 1982, a panel of the Eleventh Circuit affirmed the APA ruling, and went ahead to reverse the finding of no discrimination. *Jean v. Nelson,* 711 F.3d 1455 (11th Cir.1983). But the panel's ruling was shortly vacated, 714 F.2d 96 (11th Cir.1983), when the entire court agreed to rehear the case en banc. (We reprint the en banc decision below.)

In the meantime, important developments had occurred in the Cuban cases. In *Fernandez-Roque v. Smith,* 567 F.Supp. 1115 (N.D.Ga.1983), *reversed* 734 F.2d 576 (11th Cir.1984), the court issued the most ambitious decision yet, protecting the due process rights of excludable aliens. The case was a habeas corpus class action brought on behalf of over 1000 Marielitos detained in the Atlanta Federal Penitentiary. By this time, INS had developed a well-defined Status Review Plan for considering the release of the detained Cubans:

> The plan created a review panel selected from officials of the different divisions of the Department of Justice. Under the plan, the panel initially examines the file of the detainee. To recommend release, the panel must conclude that "(1) the detainee is presently a nonviolent person, (2) the detainee is likely to remain nonviolent, and (3) the detainee is unlikely to commit any criminal offenses following his release." If the panel decides in favor of parole, its recommendation is forwarded to the Commissioner of the Immigration and Naturalization Service (Commissioner) for approval.
>
> If the Commissioner rejects the panel's recommendation or if the panel is unable to make a determination based solely on the detainee's file, the alien is personally interviewed by the panel. Written notice of the interview is furnished to the alien at least seven days in advance. At the interview, the detainee may be assisted by a person of his choice. He may examine the documents and may submit either written or oral information supporting his release.
>
> After the interview, the panel forwards its recommendation to the Commissioner. If the Commissioner grants release, he may impose "such special conditions as considered appropriate by the Commissioner." If parole is denied, the alien remains in custody. In either case, the detainee is notified of the Commissioner's final decision in English and Spanish. The plan provides for at least annual reviews of an alien's case as long as he remains in detention.
>
> Parole may be revoked if the alien is convicted in the United States of a felony or a serious misdemeanor. An alien who poses a clear and imminent danger to the community or himself may also be returned to custody. Finally, parole may be revoked if an alien released to a special placement project violates the conditions of his parole. Upon revocation of parole, the alien is returned to

detention and any further petition for release is processed under the plan.

Fernandez-Roque v. Smith, 734 F.2d 576, 579 (11th Cir.1984).

At the trial level in *Fernandez-Roque,* the district court first determined, in disagreement with *Rodriguez-Fernandez,* that the INA granted authority to the Attorney General to detain excludable aliens indefinitely. But the court went on to rule that the Constitution places important limitations on the exercise of that authority:

> Once an excludable alien's detention can no longer be justified merely as a means to his exclusion, *i.e.,* once detention is no longer justifiable simply on the basis of excludability, then a legitimate expectation arises that the detention will end unless some new justification for continuing the detention is established. The basis for this expectation is simply the fundamental principle inherent in our constitutional system that all persons are entitled to their liberty absent some legally sufficient reason for detaining them. An alien's excludability provides such a reason so long as the detention reasonably serves as an aid to the alien's exclusion. After this initial period of time, however, the individual's basic entitlement to liberty once again comes to the fore. Thus, even though the government is authorized to detain excludable aliens indefinitely where immediate exclusion is impracticable, the excludability determination itself provides the essential predicate for the exercise of this authority only for an initial, temporary period of time. Thereafter, a liberty interest arises on behalf of the alien detainee requiring that the continued exercise of the detention power be justified on the basis of a procedurally adequate finding that the detainee, if released, is likely to abscond, to pose a risk to the national security, or to pose a serious and significant threat to persons or property within the United States.

567 F.Supp. at 1128. The court distinguished *Mezei* on the grounds that *Mezei's* detention was founded on a wartime emergency measure, and also based on its reading that *Mezei* sought formal admission to the country, not parole. *Id.* at 1129. In this latter understanding, the court relied on the exact wording of a passage from *Landon v. Plasencia,* 459 U.S. 21, 103 S.Ct. 321, 329, 74 L.Ed.2d 21 (1982), which stated that "an alien seeking initial admission to the United States requests a privilege and has no constitutional rights *regarding his application* " (emphasis supplied). Since petitioners here were not seeking formal admission, they were not asking a court to find constitutional rights regarding an application for admission. Instead, they sought only parole pending arrangements for return to Cuba.

Having found a cognizable liberty interest, the court went on to spell out what process was due the petitioners. Although the court acknowledged the "superficial adequacy" of exclusion hearings in procedural terms, it nevertheless suggested that the procedural safeguards are "largely illusory." 567 F.Supp., at 1128. Moreover, it considered the Status Review Plan inadequate, even though the procedures were similar to those judged acceptable by the Supreme Court for use by a state parole board deciding on the release of those serving criminal sentences. Such procedures might be adequate in that setting, the district court ruled, because the original deprivation of liberty was based on a criminal trial with a wide range of procedural protections not accorded in a determination of excludability. 567 F.Supp., at 1131–32.

Although the court rejected the petitioners' claim that they were entitled to procedures equivalent to those available at a criminal trial, it went on to mandate a lengthy list of procedural protections: (1) prior written notice of the factual allegations supporting continued detention, and access to the underlying information in government files; (2) right to compulsory attendance of witnesses; (3) right to confrontation and cross-examination of adverse witnesses, unless good cause related to prison discipline is shown; (4) a neutral decisionmaker who will decide based solely on the evidence adduced at the hearing and who will produce a written statement of the reasons for his decision (and whose decision would not be reviewable by any other government official); (5) protection against self-incrimination; (6) counsel provided at government expense; and (7) a requirement that the government carry the burden of proof, according to a "clear and convincing evidence" standard, that the detainee "will be likely to abscond, to pose a risk to the national security, or to pose a serious threat to persons or property in the United States." *Id.* at 1145.

Notes

1. What is the source of the liberty interest the district court in *Fernandez-Roque* discovers? What are its contours? Notice that the ruling here covers more than merely *procedural* due process. The court would not consider adequate a jury trial with full safeguards if the only factual determination leading to continued incarceration were whether the alien arrived without documents. The court requires certain substantive findings. What is the source of these latter requirements?

2. Consider the following comment. What is the proper relationship between procedural and substantive review in immigration cases?

> [*Rodriguez-Fernandez* and *Fernandez-Roque*] demonstrate the manner in which "procedural" interests in "liberty" have been used to bring mainstream procedural due process analysis into immigration law, where it can serve as a surrogate for "substantive" constitutional challenges to admission and exclusion categories. The Marielitos seemed to raise "procedural" claims in that they challenged the government's provisional treatment of detainees, and because their formal complaints were not directed against the statute that made them ineligible for admission. *Rodriguez-Fernandez* tried to maintain the fiction that the decision left substantive admission and exclusion categories undisturbed. It did so by emphasizing that ordering the INS to release the detainees did not necessarily mean ordering their release within the United States. But of course, the detainees could hardly be released anywhere else, so this result—freedom from restraint in

the United States—was close to what a successful substantive claim would have accomplished. It was not quite the same result, because parole is not lawful permanent resident status. In a broader sense, however, judicially ordered release touched on admission and exclusion. This "substantive" impact was the basis for the Court's refusal in *Mezei* to regard detention as independently significant for constitutional purposes. In other words, the apparently "procedural" parole remedy operated as a surrogate for judicial review of a limited substantive claim to a form of admission to the United States.

Motomura, *The Curious Evolution of Immigration Law: Procedural Surrogates for Substantive Constitutional Rights*, 92 Colum.L.Rev. 1625, 1668–69 (1992).

———

The district court's decision in *Fernandez-Roque* was ultimately reversed by the Court of Appeals, holding that "excludable aliens cannot challenge either admission or parole decisions under a claim of constitutional right." *Fernandez-Roque v. Smith*, 734 F.2d 576, 582 (11th Cir. 1984). But this reversal was clearly foreshadowed a few months earlier when the higher court, sitting en banc, issued its decision in *Jean v. Nelson*, the Haitian detainee litigation.

JEAN v. NELSON

United States Court of Appeals, Eleventh Circuit, en banc, 1984.
727 F.2d 957, modified, 472 U.S. 846, 105 S.Ct. 2992, 86 L.Ed.2d 664 (1985).

VANCE, CIRCUIT JUDGE:

[The court first vacated, on the grounds of mootness, that portion of the district court's judgment finding noncompliance with the APA, owing to the release of most of the original class members and the promulgation of the 1982 regulations.]

* * *

B. THE CONSTITUTIONAL RIGHTS OF EXCLUDABLE ALIENS

Any analysis of the constitutional rights of aliens in the immigration context must begin by taking note of the fundamental distinction between the legal status of excludable or unadmitted aliens and aliens who have succeeded in effecting an "entry" into the United States, even if their presence here is completely illegal. The Supreme Court originally indicated that the powers of the political branches with respect to the exclusion and expulsion of aliens are equally broad, *see Fong Yue Ting*, 149 U.S. at 713–14, 13 S.Ct. at 1022, but it soon recognized that "an alien who has entered the country, and has become subject in all respects to its jurisdiction, and a part of its population" is entitled to due process under the fifth amendment and cannot be deported "without giving him all opportunity to be heard upon the questions involving his right to be and remain in the

United States." *Kaoru Yamataya v. Fisher [The Japanese Immigrant Case]*, 189 U.S. 86, 101, 23 S.Ct. 611, 615, 47 L.Ed. 721 (1903). While resident aliens, regardless of their legal status, are therefore entitled to at least limited due process rights, aliens "who have never been naturalized, nor acquired any domicile of residence within the United States, nor even been admitted into the country pursuant to law" stand in a very different posture: "As to such persons, the decisions of executive or administrative officers, acting within powers expressly conferred by congress, are due process of law." *Nishimura Ekiu,* 142 U.S. at 660, 12 S.Ct. at 339.

In the eighty years since the Court first recognized this distinction between the rights of excludable and deportable aliens, it has become engrained in our law. * * *

* * *

This principle was reiterated by the Court last Term in *Landon v. Plasencia,* 459 U.S. 21, 32, 103 S.Ct. 321, 329, 74 L.Ed.2d 21 (1982), in which Justice O'Connor noted that

> an alien seeking admission to the United States requests a privilege and has no constitutional rights regarding his application, for the power to admit or exclude aliens is a sovereign prerogative.... [H]owever, once an alien gains admission to our country and begins to develop the ties that go with permanent residence his constitutional status changes accordingly.

Aliens seeking admission to the United States therefore have no constitutional rights with regard to their applications and must be content to accept whatever statutory rights and privileges they are granted by Congress. The INA does in fact contain a number of provisions that collectively guarantee at least limited due process protection for excludable aliens. Under § 236(a), an alien seeking entry is entitled to a hearing on the validity of his application for admission before an immigration judge. At the hearing the alien is permitted the assistance of counsel, § 292, and has the right to present evidence in his own behalf, to examine and object to evidence against him, and to cross-examine witnesses presented by the government. 8 C.F.R. § 236.2(a). If the immigration judge determines that the alien is not entitled to admission, this decision may be appealed to the Board of Immigration Appeals (BIA). INA § 236(b); 8 C.F.R. § 236.7. An alien may also challenge a final order of exclusion in the federal courts by filing a petition for a writ of habeas corpus. INA § 106(b).

* * *

There is no question that the Haitian plaintiffs in this case are excludable aliens and have not been formally admitted into the United States. Since an alien's legal status is not altered by detention or parole under the entry doctrine fiction, it seems clear that plaintiffs here can claim no greater rights or privileges under our laws than any other group of aliens who have been stopped at the border. The district court, however, concluded that the entry doctrine and the precedents cited above were inapplicable because the Haitian plaintiffs here are challenging their continued incarceration *pending* a determination of admissibility, rather than seeking to compel the government to grant them admission in a legal sense. Likewise, the panel distinguished *Mezei* and other immigration decisions on the grounds that those cases concerned "immigration procedures" rather than "the discretionary exercise of the Executive's parole power." *Jean,* 711 F.2d at 1484–85. The panel also considered the entry doctrine inapplicable because "its purpose [is] to limit the procedural rights of an excludable alien 'regarding his application' for admission," *id.* at 1484 (quoting Plasencia, 459 U.S. at 31, 103 S.Ct. at 329), and therefore concluded that the Haitian plaintiffs had equal protection rights on the basis of their physical presence within the territorial limits of the United States. *See id.* 1484–85.

Although the distinction between parole and admission drawn by the panel and the district court is not an implausible one, we conclude that it cannot be reconciled with the Supreme Court's jurisprudence in this area. In particular, we believe that the Court's decision in *Mezei* is controlling on this issue and that a close examination of the facts at issue in *Mezei* forecloses us from relying on the arguments that the panel and the district court found persuasive. Thus, we cannot accept appellees' argument that *Mezei* is not on point because "the alien was challenging non-admissibility, not incarceration." The gravamen of Mezei's complaint was clearly not the government's right to exclude him—a permanent exclusion order had already been entered in his case, and he did not contest it in his habeas petition—but the power of the government to continue to detain him without a hearing pending his deportation. *See Mezei,* 345 U.S. at 207, 73 S.Ct. at 627. Justice Clark stated explicitly in his majority opinion that "[t]he issue is whether the Attorney General's continued exclusion of respondent without a hearing *amounts to an unlawful detention,* so that courts may admit him *temporarily* to the United States on bond until arrangements are made for his departure abroad." *Id.* (emphasis added).

* * * We therefore conclude that *Mezei* compels us to hold that the Haitian plaintiffs in this case cannot claim equal protection rights under the fifth amendment, even with regard to challenging the Executive's exercise of its parole discretion.

We realize, of course, that *Mezei*—like its predecessor, *Knauff*—has been heavily criticized by academic commentators. As an intermediate appellate court, however, we cannot properly question the continued authority of this Supreme Court precedent—a precedent that the Court cited without reconsideration as recently as last Term. *See Plasencia,* 459 U.S. at 32, 103 S.Ct. at 329. With regard to the key issue here—whether the grant or denial of parole is an integral part of the admissions process—*Mezei* is fully in accord with other, less controversial precedents. * * *

These decisions reflect policy imperatives and fundamental principles of national sovereignty that cannot be easily dismissed, regardless of the individual merits of the Court's decisions in *Knauff* and *Mezei.*[19] The

19. It is worth pointing out in this context that much of the criticism of *Mezei* and *Knauff* has focussed on the fact that the aliens who were ordered excluded without a hearing in those cases had strong personal or family ties to the United States. *See Mezei,* 345 U.S. at 216–17, 73 S.Ct. at 631–32 (Black, J., dissenting); *Knauff,* 338 U.S. at

reason that Congress has passed legislation regulating the admission of aliens is its concern about how their entry will affect the economic, political, and social well-being of this nation. The grant of parole is subject to certain restrictions and is theoretically of a short-term character, but it does permit the physical entry of the alien into the midst of our society and implicates many of the same considerations—such as employment and national security concerns—that justify restrictions on admission. Parole is an act of extraordinary sovereign generosity, since it grants temporary admission into our society to an alien who has no legal right to enter and who would probably be turned away at the border if he sought to enter by land, rather than coming by sea or air. * * *

* * *

Of course, there are certain circumstances under which even excludable aliens are accorded rights under the Constitution.

* * *

For example, those with the status of deportable aliens are constitutionally entitled to rights in the deportation context that are inapplicable to exclusion proceedings. Illegal or resident aliens may also claim other rights under the fifth and fourteenth amendments. *See, e.g., Plyler v. Doe,* 457 U.S. 202, 102 S.Ct. 2382, 72 L.Ed.2d 786 (1982); *Hampton v. Mow Sun Wong,* 426 U.S. 88, 96 S.Ct. 1895, 48 L.Ed.2d 495 (1976); *Graham v. Richardson,* 403 U.S. 365, 91 S.Ct. 1848, 29 L.Ed.2d 534 (1971); *Yick Wo v. Hopkins,* 118 U.S. 356, 6 S.Ct. 1064, 30 L.Ed. 220 (1886).

The courts have also recognized that aliens can raise constitutional challenges to deprivations of liberty or property outside the context of entry or admission, when the plenary authority of the political branches is not implicated. Aliens seized by United States officials for suspected involvement in criminal activity are entitled to the same constitutional rights that normally apply in such proceedings. *See, e.g., Wong Wing,* 163 U.S. at 238, 16 S.Ct. at 981 ("[A]liens shall not be held to answer for a capital or other infamous crime, unless on a presentment or indictment of a grand jury, nor be deprived of life, liberty, or property without due process of law."); *United States v. Henry,* 604 F.2d 908, 914 (5th Cir.1979) ("[A]n alien who is within the territorial jurisdiction of this country, whether it be at the border or in the interior, in a proper case and at the proper time, is entitled to those protections guaranteed by the Fifth Amendment in criminal proceedings which would include the *Miranda* warning."). The courts have further ruled that aliens who are the victims of unconstitutional government action abroad are protected by the Bill of Rights if the government seeks to exploit fruits of its unlawful conduct in a criminal proceeding in the United States. *United States v. Demanett,* 629 F.2d 862, 866 (3d Cir.), *cert. denied,* 450 U.S. 910, 101 S.Ct. 1347, 67 L.Ed.2d 333 (1980); *United States v. Toscanino,* 500 F.2d 267, 280 (2d Cir.1974); *cf.*

539, 70 S.Ct. at 310. Most excludable aliens have far weaker claims to enjoying the benefits of admission into this country, however, and the harsh results of *Knauff* and *Mezei* should not obscure the compelling policy justifications that support the entry doctrine fiction and the general principle that excludable aliens have no rights with regard to their applications for admission or parole.

United States v. Tiede, 86 F.R.D. 227, 242–44 (U.S. Ct. for Berlin 1979) (protections of Bill of Rights apply to friendly aliens in the American sector of West Berlin). The Supreme Court has also recognized that even non-resident aliens are entitled to the protection of the fifth amendment's prohibition on unlawful takings. *Russian Volunteer Fleet v. United States,* 282 U.S. 481, 489, 491–92, 51 S.Ct. 229, 232, 75 L.Ed. 473 (1931).

These authorities, however, do not mandate the conclusion that excludable aliens such as the Haitian plaintiffs can claim equal protection rights under the fifth amendment with regard to parole. *Russian Volunteer Fleet* can be distinguished because it clearly does not implicate in any way the powers of the national government over immigration. When the government seizes the property of foreign nationals within this country, its actions do not fall within a sphere of plenary executive and legislative authority, and it therefore cannot claim that the aliens involved are entitled only to the degree of due process that Congress is prepared to extend them as a matter of grace.

Similar considerations apply in the context of criminal prosecutions. When the government subjects an alien to the criminal process it is plainly no longer seeking to effectuate its power to control admission into the United States by removing the alien from this country. The arrests of the aliens in *Wong Wing* and *Henry* may have grown out of the Executive's efforts to control the entry of foreigners into the United States, but the decision by government officials to subject them to criminal prosecution or punishment, rather than deportation, completely changed the nature of the proceedings. From that point forward any action taken by the government derived not from its power to control admission into this country, but from the powers of the Executive over law enforcement. The government's actions in prosecuting Henry and imprisoning Wong Wing therefore fell outside the plenary power to control immigration that justifies the extraordinary executive and congressional latitude in that area.

* * *

Some courts and commentators have suggested that when an exercise of the government's power to exclude results in an indefinite detention of an excludable alien, at some point the continued imprisonment becomes punishment, regardless of the legal justifications or fictions involved. These authorities contend that at this juncture the government should be required to make some justification to continue to detain the alien. *See, e.g., Rodriguez–Fernandez v. Wilkinson,* 654 F.2d 1382, 1387 (10th Cir. 1981); *Soroa-Gonzalez v. Civiletti,* 515 F.Supp. 1049, 1056 n. 6 (N.D.Ga. 1981); *Fernandez-Roque v. Smith,* 91 F.R.D. 239, 243 (N.D.Ga.1981), *appeal dismissed,* 671 F.2d 426 (11th Cir.1982); Note, *Constitutional Limits on the Power to Exclude Aliens,* 82 Colum.L.Rev. 957, 980 (1982); Note, *The Constitutional Rights of Excluded Aliens: Proposed Limitations on the Indefinite Detention of the Cuban Refugees,* 70 Geo.L.J. 1303, 1306 (1982).

* * *

We could distinguish *Rodriguez-Fernandez* from this case on the grounds that the former involved an alien against whom an exclusion order had already been entered and who was clearly unable to return to his country of origin.[26] Indeed, the tenth circuit placed no time limits on the government's ability to detain excludable aliens pending the admission decision. *Id.* at 1389. Nevertheless, we detect two significant problems that prevent us from endorsing the tenth circuit's reasoning. The first— which is controlling from our point of view—is that it cannot be reconciled with the Supreme Court' decision in *Mezei,* which held that an excludable alien could not challenge his continued detention without a hearing. The second difficulty is that if the prospect of indefinite detention is held to be sufficient to require the government to meet some judicially-imposed standard to continue to detain an alien, the plenary authority of the political branches in the exclusion area is largely rendered nugatory. The prospect of indefinite confinement, after all, can be raised by the refusal of an excludable alien to return home, or the refusal of his country of origin or any other country to accept him.

This is the critical flaw with the second circuit's decision in *Mezei* and the tenth circuit's decision in *Rodriguez-Fernandez,* each of which based the alien's right to challenge his continued confinement on whether or not he had a foreseeable chance of being able to go elsewhere. At first glance, this is an attractive solution. It seems both humane and eminently realistic, because it does not turn on legal fictions and distinctions that appear to lack practical substance. Unfortunately, this approach would ultimately result in our losing control over our borders. A foreign leader could eventually compel us to grant physical admission via parole to any aliens he wished by the simple expedient of sending them here and then refusing to take them back. In the probable absence of any reliable information about such aliens beyond what they cared to provide, could the government meet its burden under some judicially-imposed standard of showing that indefinite detention was justified? It seems unlikely.

Mindful of the Supreme Court's warning that "[a]ny rule of constitutional law that would inhibit the flexibility of the political branches of government to respond to changing world conditions should be adopted only with the greatest caution," *Mathews v. Diaz,* 426 U.S. 67, 81, 96 S.Ct. 1883, 1892, 48 L.Ed.2d 478 (1976), we conclude that we must resist the temptation to tamper with the authority of the Executive by ruling that excludable aliens have constitutional rights in this area, even with regard to their applications for parole.

C. Judicial Review of Executive Discretion

Although we hold that the Haitian plaintiffs cannot challenge the refusal of executive officials to parole them on the basis of the fifth amendment's equal protection guarantee, this is not the end of our inquiry. That the authority of the political branches in this area is plenary does not mean that it is wholly immune from judicial review. As two leading

---

26. Haiti has indicated that it is willing to accept the return of these aliens. Although plaintiffs contend that they fear prosecution if they return to Haiti, its government has denied that they would be subject to any reprisals.

commentators have noted, the Executive's discretionary authority concerning parole decisions "is broad, but not unlimited. It may be subjected to judicial scrutiny on a charge that discretion was arbitrarily exercised or withheld." 1 C. Gordon & H. Rosenfield, *supra,* at § 2.54. This principle has been recognized by our colleagues on the second and fourth circuits, who have held that an executive official's decision to deny parole to an unadmitted alien may be subject to judicial review for abuse of discretion. *Bertrand v. Sava,* 684 F.2d 204, 210 (2d Cir.1982); *Palma v. Verdeyen,* 676 F.2d 100, 105 (4th Cir.1982).

* * *

The discretionary decisions of executive officials in the immigration area are therefore subject to judicial review, but the scope of that review is extremely limited. * * *

* * *

Thus, under the approach taken by the Supreme Court in *Kleindienst v. Mandel* and adopted by the second circuit in *Bertrand,* the critical question a court must answer when reviewing an alien's challenge to the denial of his request for parole is whether the immigration officials involved were acting within the scope of their delegated powers. * * * Congress has delegated remarkably broad discretion to executive officials under the INA, and these grants of statutory authority are particularly sweeping in the context of parole. * * * In view of these provisions, immigration officials clearly have the authority to deny parole to unadmitted aliens if they can advance "a facially legitimate and bona fide reason" for doing so.

The Haitian plaintiffs contend that such a reason was lacking in this case, submitting that they were the victims of national origin discrimination. Plaintiffs and the district court both stressed that the challenged actions here were those of executive officials rather than Congress, apparently believing that the Executive is clearly prohibited from adopting policies on its own motion that discriminate on the basis of national origin in the immigration field while Congress is just as clearly permitted to do so. Because the government has contended throughout this case that its new detention policy does not discriminate on the basis of national origin, resolution of this question is not essential to our holding; however, we believe that responsible executive officials such as the President or Attorney General possess this authority under the INA.[30] Nevertheless, since

---

30. In view of the Supreme Court's repeated emphasis on the concurrent nature of executive and legislative power in this area and the sweeping congressional delegations of discretionary authority to the Executive under the INA, there is little question that the Executive has the power to draw distinctions among aliens on the basis of nationality. This issue was squarely presented to the D.C. Circuit in *Narenji v. Civiletti,* 617 F.2d 745 (D.C.Cir.1979), *cert. denied,* 446 U.S. 957, 100 S.Ct. 2928, 64 L.Ed.2d 815 (1980), in which the court upheld a regulation requiring nonimmigrant alien post-secondary school students of Iranian citizenship or birth to provide information to the INS concerning their residence and academic status. The court held that the challenged regulation was within the Attorney General's authority under INA § 103(a), which permits the Attorney General to "perform such other acts as he deems necessary" for carrying out his responsibility to administer and enforce the immigration laws, and concluded that "[d]is-the discretion of lower-level immigration officials is circumscribed not only by legislative enactments but also by the instructions of their superiors in the executive branch, our conclusion that the Executive's policy is consistent with the power delegated by Congress does not end the process of judicial inquiry here. The district court must still determine whether the actions of lower-level officials in the field conform to the policy statements of their superiors in Washington. For as the second circuit correctly noted in *Bertrand:*

> [T]he constitutional authority of the political branches of the federal government to adopt immigration policies based on criteria that are not acceptable elsewhere in our public life would not permit an immigration official, in the absence of such policies, to "apply neutral regulations to discriminate on [the basis of race and national origin]."

684 F.2d at 212 n. 12 (quoting *Vigile v. Sava,* 535 F.Supp. 1002, 1016 (S.D.N.Y.1982)).

The district court on remand should conduct such proceedings as are necessary to determine whether there exists a facially legitimate and bona fide reason for the government's decision to deny parole to the class members presently in detention, remembering that it is not the court's proper role "to disregard the [stated criteria employed] or to substitute its own policy preferences for those of the official vested by law with discretionary authority to act on requests for parole." *Id.* at 217. The district court should consider (1) whether local immigration officials in fact exercised their discretion under § 212(d)(5)(A) to make individualized determinations and (2) whether the criteria employed in making those determinations were consistent with the statutory grant of discretion by Congress, the regulations promulgated by the agencies involved, and the policies which had been established by the President and the Attorney General. If the court should find that low-level immigration officials have discriminated on the basis of national origin despite the adoption of a contrary policy by their superiors in the executive branch, such conduct would constitute an abuse of discretion that would justify appropriate relief. Without expressing any opinion on this score, we note that the district court may wish to reconsider whether class treatment is still an appropriate vehicle for making the determinations set forth above. We therefore remand for further proceedings in light of this opinion.

TJOFLAT, concurring in part and dissenting in part: [omitted]

tinctions on the basis of nationality may be drawn in the immigration field by the Congress or the Executive. [Citations omitted]. So long as such distinctions are not wholly irrational they must be sustained." 617 F.2d at 747.

Although Congress significantly altered the system of nationality-based quotas for the issuance of immigration visas in 1965, it has not disturbed a variety of administrative provisions that distinguish among aliens on the basis of national origin. *See, e.g.,* 8 C.F.R. § 101.1 (presumption of lawful admission for certain national groups); *id.* § 212.1 (documentary requirements for nonimmigrants of particular nationalities); *id.* § 252.1 (relaxation of inspection requirements for certain British and Canadian crewmen). The courts have generally viewed such classifications as within the permissible scope of executive discretion.

KRAVITCH, CIRCUIT JUDGE, specially concurring in part and dissenting in part with whom JOHNSON, HATCHETT and CLARK, CIRCUIT JUDGES, join.

* * *

* * * My objection to the majority's reading of the INA is the conclusion that the Attorney General may invidiously discriminate in the granting of parole merely because the Executive decides, without rational reason, that aliens from a certain country should be denied temporary parole.

Nor does such a view create the possibility that the United States would "lose control over our borders." The scenario that the majority describes of a foreign leader sending over citizens of his country and "compel[ling] us to grant physical admission via parole ...," is both irrelevant to the holding and unnecessarily alarmist.

First, here we are concerned only with the discriminatory denial of temporary parole prior to deportation or exclusion proceedings; hence, the constitutionality of "indefinite detention" is not properly before us. Second, to the extent pre-deportation parole is relevant, such a de facto invasion envisioned by the majority would present a rational basis for the Attorney General to deny temporary parole. Third, the President has the capability of preventing any such crisis under INA § 212(f) (cited by the majority as an example of the Executive's broad powers) and § 215(a), which gives the President broad powers to act during a national emergency or time of war; moreover, such an "attack" on our borders would likely fall under the Executive's foreign affairs power. Finally, the majority's prime concern—ensuring that excludable aliens could be detained indefinitely *without a justifiable reason*—would extend the holdings of those cases cited by the majority beyond their intended scope and meaning.

* * *

Notes

How should the Haitian and Cuban detainee cases in this Section have been decided? Would it have been possible to reverse the district court's procedurally demanding decision in *Fernandez-Roque* without declaring excludable aliens so far beyond the reach of the Fifth Amendment? Has the *Jean* court properly understood what the Supreme Court intended in *Plasencia?*

Is it appropriate to detain asylum applicants at all? What if they arrive in exceedingly large numbers, as they did in Florida in mid–1980? How long may such detention last? Is detention permissible if it is adopted for deterrent purposes, that is, explicitly to discourage more asylum-seekers from coming by making more severe the conditions experienced by the first arrivals? How does a court develop standards for judging when conditions permit—or require—release? We shall return to some of these questions when we consider the law of political asylum in Chapter Eight.

Jean v. Nelson in the Supreme Court

The Supreme Court granted certiorari in *Jean v. Nelson* to decide whether unadmitted aliens may claim the safeguards of the Fifth Amendment, in particular its equal protection component. But the majority concluded that this long-debated constitutional question need not be reached, and thus it did not use the occasion to revisit *Knauff* and *Mezei.* The Supreme Court agreed with what it took to be the court of appeals' construction of the governing statute and regulations: neither permitted lower level officials to discriminate on the basis of race or national origin. In order to hold any discrimination proven on remand to be unlawful, then—and thus to grant the Haitian plaintiffs the relief they sought—no court would have to reach the constitutional questions. Therefore, the Supreme Court held, under longstanding doctrine dictating the avoidance of unnecessary constitutional holdings, the court of appeals should not have reached and decided the parole question on constitutional grounds. That court should simply have remanded (as it ultimately did) to the district court to decide whether INS officials discriminated in violation of the statute, regulations, and governing INS policy. *Jean v. Nelson,* 472 U.S. 846, 105 S.Ct. 2992, 86 L.Ed.2d 664 (1985).

Justice Marshall, joined by Justice Brennan, filed a lengthy dissent. He argued that the general language of the statute, the regulations, and Justice Department policy statements could not be read as provisions forbidding national origin discrimination. Hence the Court could not avoid the constitutional question. Reviewing the facts of *Knauff, Mezei,* and *Kwong Hai Chew v. Colding,* Justice Marshall proceeded to sketch out his own position:

> I agree that broad dicta in *Mezei* might suggest that an undocumented alien detained at the border does not enjoy *any* constitutional protections, and therefore cannot invoke the equal protection guarantees of the Fifth Amendment's Due Process Clause. See also *United States ex rel. Knauff v. Shaughnessy,* 338 U.S. 537, 544, 70 S.Ct. 309, 313, 94 L.Ed. 317 (1950); *Kwong Hai Chew v. Colding,* 344 U.S. 590, 601, 73 S.Ct. 472, 479, 97 L.Ed. 576 (1953). This broad dicta [*sic*], however, can withstand neither the weight of logic nor that of principle, and has never been incorporated into the fabric of our constitutional jurisprudence. Moreover, when stripped of its dicta, *Mezei* stands for a narrow proposition that is inapposite to the case now before the Court.

* * *

The narrow question decided in *Knauff* and *Mezei* was that the denial of a hearing in a case in which the Government raised national security concerns did not violate due process. The question decided in *Chew* was that the alien's due process rights *had* been violated. The broad notion that " 'excludable' aliens ... are not within the protection of the Fifth Amendment," *Kwong Hai Chew v. Colding,* 344 U.S., at 600, 73 S.Ct., at 479, on which the

Government heavily relies in this case, is therefore clearly dictum, and as such it is entitled to no more deference than logic and principle would accord it. Under this standard, the broad dictum in question deserves no deference at all.

Our case law makes clear that excludable aliens do, in fact, enjoy Fifth Amendment protections [discussing *Wong Wing v. United States*, 163 U.S. 228, 16 S.Ct. 977, 41 L.Ed. 140 (1896), and *Russian Volunteer Fleet v. United States*, 282 U.S. 481, 51 S.Ct. 229, 75 L.Ed. 473 (1931)].

* * *

[A]ny limitations on the applicability of the Constitution within our territorial jurisdiction fly in the face of this Court's long-held and recently reaffirmed commitment to apply the Constitution's due process and equal protection guarantees to all individuals within the reach of our sovereignty. "These provisions are universal in their application, to all persons within the territorial jurisdiction, without regard to any differences of race, of color, or of nationality." *Yick Wo v. Hopkins*, 118 U.S. 356, 369, 6 S.Ct. 1064, 1070, 30 L.Ed. 220 (1886). Indeed, by its express terms, the Fourteenth Amendment prescribes that "[n]o State . . . shall deprive any person of life, liberty, or property without due process of law; nor deny to any person within its jurisdiction the equal protection of the laws." In *Plyler v. Doe*, 457 U.S. 202, 102 S.Ct. 2382, 72 L.Ed.2d 786 (1982), we made clear that this principle applies to aliens, for "[w]hatever his status under the immigration laws, an alien is surely a 'person' in any ordinary sense of that term." *Id.*, at 210, 102 S.Ct., at 2391; see also *Mathews v. Diaz*, 426 U.S. 67, 77, 96 S.Ct. 1883, 1890, 48 L.Ed.2d 478 (1976). Such emphasis on universal coverage is not surprising, given that the Fourteenth Amendment was specifically intended to overrule a legal fiction similar to that undergirding *Knauff*, *Chew*, and *Mezei*—that freed slaves were not "people of the United States." *Scott v. Sandford*, 19 How. 393, 404, 15 L.Ed. 691 (1857).

Therefore, it cannot rationally be argued that the Constitution provides no protections to aliens in petitioners' position. Both our case law and pure logic compel the rejection of the sweeping proposition articulated in the *Knauff–Chew–Mezei* dicta. To the extent that this Court has relied on *Mezei* at all, it has done so only in the narrow area of entry decisions. See, *e.g.*, *Landon v. Plasencia*, 459 U.S. 21, 32, 103 S.Ct. 321, 329, 74 L.Ed.2d 21 (1982); *Kleindienst v. Mandel*, 408 U.S. 753, 766, 92 S.Ct. 2576, 2583, 33 L.Ed.2d 683 (1972). It is in this area that the Government's interest in protecting our sovereignty is at its strongest and that individual claims to constitutional entitlement are the least compelling. But even with respect to entry decisions, the Court has refused to characterize the authority of the political branches as wholly unbridled. Indeed, "[o]ur cases reflect acceptance of a limited judicial responsibility under the Constitution even with respect to the power of Congress to regulate the admission and exclusion of aliens." *Fiallo v. Bell,* 430 U.S. 787, 793, n. 5, 97 S.Ct. 1473, 1478, n. 5, 52 L.Ed.2d 50 (1977).

* * * The proper constitutional inquiry must concern the scope of the equal protection and due process rights at stake, and not whether the Due Process Clause can be invoked at all.

* * *

[W]hatever *Mezei* may have held about procedural due process rights in connection with parole requests is not applicable to the separate constitutional question whether the Government may establish a policy of making parole decisions on the basis of race or national origin without articulating any justification for its discriminatory conduct. As far back as *Yick Wo,* the Court recognized that even decisions over which the Executive has broad discretion, and which the Executive may make without providing notice or a hearing, cannot be made in an invidiously discriminatory manner.

* * *

This dissent is not the place to determine the precise contours of petitioners' equal protection rights, but a brief discussion might clarify what is at stake. It is clear that, consistent with our constitutional scheme, the Executive enjoys wide discretion over immigration decisions. Here, the Government would have a strong case if it showed that (1) refusing to parole Haitians would slow down the flow onto United States shores of undocumented Haitians, and that (2) refusing to parole other groups would not have a similar deterrent effect. Then, its policy of detaining Haitians but paroling other groups might be sufficiently related to the valid immigration goal of reducing the number of undocumented aliens arriving at our borders to withstand constitutional scrutiny. Another legitimate governmental goal in this area might be to reduce the time it takes to process applications for asylum. If the challenged policy serves that goal, then arguably it should be upheld, provided of course that it is not too underinclusive.

It is also true that national origin can sometimes be a permissible consideration in immigration policy. But even if entry quotas may be set by reference to nationality, national origin (let alone race) cannot control every decision in any way related to immigration. For example, that the Executive might properly admit into this country many Cubans but relatively few Haitians does not imply that, when dealing with aliens in detention, it can feed Cubans but not feed Haitians.

In general, national-origin classifications have a stronger claim to constitutionality when they are employed in connection with decisions that lie at the heart of immigration policy. *Cf. Hampton v. Mow Sun Wong,* 426 U.S. 88, 116, 96 S.Ct. 1895, 1911, 48 L.Ed.2d 495 (1976) ("due process requires that [an agency's] decision to impose [a] deprivation of an important liberty ... be justified by reasons which are properly the concern of that agency"). When central immigration concerns are not at stake, however, the Executive must recognize the individuality of the alien, just as it must recognize the individuality of all other persons within our borders. If in this case the Government acted out of a belief that Haitians (or Negroes for that matter) are more likely than others to commit crimes or be disruptive of the community into which they are paroled, its detention policy certainly would not pass constitutional muster.

Notes

1. If Justice Marshall's views had prevailed in *Jean,* could the Mariel Cuban detainees successfully challenge their long-term detention under the Fifth Amendment?

2. Consider the following comment on the Supreme Court majority's approach in *Jean.*

> * * * *Jean v. Nelson* interpreted the asylum statute and regulations to bar race and national origin discrimination. This reading sidestepped the asylum seekers' constitutional challenge, which the plenary power doctrine seemed plainly to bar. In fact, the asylum statute and regulations said nothing about race and national origin discrimination. The Court's reading of the statute and regulations in *Jean* reflected a background constitutional norm—forbidding race and national origin discrimination—which is engrained beyond serious question in mainstream constitutional law. In immigration law, the same antidiscrimination norm remains a "phantom"—not real enough to govern explicitly constitutional decisions in the face of the plenary power doctrine, but real enough to influence the reading of a statute. By allowing such "phantom" constitutional norms to guide statutory interpretation, some courts have reached results similar to those that might have emerged from a more explicit scheme of substantive judicial review.

Motomura, *supra*, 92 Colum.L.Rev. at 1698–99.

3. Several other cases have considered and rejected challenges to detention filed by allegedly excludable aliens—usually asylum seekers awaiting adjudication of their applications. *See, e.g., Clark v. Smith,* 967 F.2d 1329 (9th Cir.1992); *Amanullah v. Nelson,* 811 F.2d 1 (1st Cir.1987); *Ishtyaq v. Nelson,* 627 F.Supp. 13 (E.D.N.Y.1983); *Singh v. Nelson,* 623 F.Supp. 545 (S.D.N.Y.1985). Others have found even lengthy detention sometimes justified after the order is final but before physical removal can be arranged. *Bruce v. Slattery,* 781 F.Supp. 963 (S.D.N.Y.1991). *But see Marczak v. Greene,* 971 F.2d 510 (10th Cir.1992) (remanding parole denial to district director because of "frail" statement of reasons); *Li v. Greene,* 767 F.Supp. 1087 (D.Colo.1991) (requiring new hearing on request for parole because district director did not give adequate reasons for denial);

Lynch v. Cannatella, 810 F.2d 1363, 1373–74 (5th Cir.1987) (due process clause protects excludable stowaways against physical abuse during detention pending removal; case remanded for further consideration of damage claims against detaining officials); *Medina v. O'Neill*, 589 F.Supp. 1028 (S.D.Tex.1984) (finding that conditions of detention imposed on excludable stowaways violated due process), *reversed*, 838 F.2d 800 (5th Cir.1988). *See generally* Schmidt, *Detention of Aliens*, 24 San Diego L.Rev. 305 (1987).

The Cuban Detainees: Later Developments

Although the Supreme Court ruled that the court of appeals should not have reached the constitutional questions in *Jean v. Nelson*, the lower court's *en banc* decision in *Jean* still states the governing law for the Eleventh Circuit concerning the constitutional rights of excludable aliens. This became clear a few weeks after the Supreme Court ruled, when the court of appeals decided *Garcia–Mir v. Smith*, 766 F.2d 1478 (11th Cir. 1985), *cert. denied sub nom. Marquez–Medina v. Meese*, 475 U.S. 1022, 106 S.Ct. 1213, 89 L.Ed.2d 325 (1986). *Garcia–Mir* constituted another in the line of Cuban detainee cases.

By this time, several important political developments had taken place. In December 1984, Cuba and the United States, after lengthy negotiation, had agreed to the phased return of 2,746 Marielitos, in return for the resumption of regular U.S. immigration processing in Havana. The White House announcement of the accord specified that the returnees would be individuals who had committed serious crimes in Cuba or the United States, or who "suffer from severe mental disorders." Despite litigation, actual removals began in early 1985. Meantime, because repatriation was in prospect, the Justice Department halted all further releases under the Status Review Plan. It also began much more systematically to take into federal custody those released Marielitos who had committed crimes in this country, following completion of their regular criminal sentences in state or local prisons.

The repatriation process did not last long. After roughly 200 people had been flown back to Havana, in May 1985 Fidel Castro suspended further returns in retaliation for the beginning of broadcasts to Cuba over the U.S. government–funded Radio Marti. But because the U.S. government hoped to negotiate a revival of the returns, it maintained the moratorium on further use of the Status Review Plan (a moratorium which lasted until June 1987, although a few ad hoc paroles were granted in the meantime). The population of detainees grew apace. See 61 Interp.Rel. 1080 (1984); 64 id. 740, 1307 (1987).

It was in this bleak context that the Eleventh Circuit considered, in *Garcia–Mir*, the plaintiffs' plea for constitutional scrutiny of further detention of the Cubans then held in the Atlanta federal prison. Nevertheless the court reaffirmed the doctrine promulgated in its *en banc* ruling in *Jean*. Unadmitted aliens "continue to 'have no constitutional rights with regard to their applications, and must be content to accept whatever statutory rights and privileges they are granted by Congress.' *Jean*, 727 F.2d at 968. Furthermore, the contours of those rights that they do have are to be largely left to the discretion of the political branches." The court continued: "These legal realities may be harsh, but they are that way by design." 766 F.2d at 1484.

A few months later, the court of appeals considered yet another in the series of class action challenges to the Atlanta detention of Marielitos. In *Garcia–Mir v. Meese,* 788 F.2d 1446 (11th Cir.1986), *cert. denied sub nom. Ferrer–Mazorra v. Meese,* 479 U.S. 889, 107 S.Ct. 289, 93 L.Ed.2d 263 (1986), the court of appeals held inapplicable several other possible nonconstitutional grounds for relief, including claims under international human rights law, that the detainees sought to use as the basis for challenges to detention. The court displayed some weariness with the continuing string of cases and the parade of new arguments that regularly had found favor in the district court in Atlanta only to be overturned on appeal. The court wrote (788 F.2d at 1455):

> [W]ith today's decision we have rejected all legal theories, constitutional and otherwise, advanced by the appellees. They have exhausted all claims for relief available in the federal court system at all levels save that of the Supreme Court. Accordingly, it is our judgment that, unless the appellees elect to seek, and the United States Supreme Court elects to grant, a petition for writ of *certiorari,* these cases have reached the terminal points and shall be DISMISSED. *Interest reipublicae ut sit finis litium.*

The Cuban plaintiffs petitioned for certiorari in the Supreme Court. Despite the lower court's virtual invitation, despite the six-year incarceration that some class members had endured, and despite the clarity of the constitutional questions presented in this case (the clearest form since *Mezei,* and the very questions the Court had seemed ready to reach in *Jean*), the Supreme Court denied the petition, over the dissents of two Justices. *Ferrer–Mazorra v. Meese,* 479 U.S. 889, 107 S.Ct. 289, 93 L.Ed.2d 263 (1986).

As indicated above, despite this ruling, in June 1987 the Justice Department finally reinstated the review program that enabled some of the detainees to gain release on a showing that they posed minimal threats to the community. But in November of that year, the White House announced that it had arranged with the Cuban government to resume returns to Cuba under the 1984 agreement. Violent riots ensued in two detention facilities—the Atlanta federal prison and INS's new alien detention center in Oakdale, Louisiana. The rioting detainees took hostages and eventually caused millions of dollars in property damage (including virtual destruction of the Oakdale facility). Delicate negotiations with the detainees finally won release of the hostages, on the government's promise to institute more protective procedures to decide just who would be repatriated to Cuba, and also to review all cases of those not repatriated, with a view toward their possible parole. *See* 64 Interp.Rel. 1307 (1987); 65 *id.* 1, 10 (1988).

The Justice Department promptly established the promised review procedures, essentially a somewhat more elaborate version of the earlier Status Review Plan. *See* 52 Fed.Reg. 48884 (1987), modified, 53 Fed.Reg.

52520 (1988), 55 Fed. Reg. 51778 (1990) (repatriation review program); 8 C.F.R. §§ 212.12, 212.13 (release review program). But the process is cumbersome, and returns to Cuba have proceeded at a very slow pace. *See* 66 Interp.Rel. 1260 (1988) (first five Cubans returned in December 1988). As of 1990, several thousand Marielitos were still detained, including at least 60 who had been in detention continuously since arrival in 1980. 11 *Refugee Reports* 1 (1990). As of early 1993, 942 Cubans had been repatriated under the agreement. *In re Mariel Cuban Habeas Corpus Petitions*, 822 F.Supp. 192, 194 (M.D.Pa.1993). Meantime the federal government spends millions of dollars each year detaining Marielitos.

In the early 1990s, a host of additional cases were brought, challenging the continued detention of Marielitos. In nearly all the courts approved continued confinement. *See, e.g., id.; Rodriguez v. Thornburgh*, 831 F.Supp. 810 (D.Kan.1993); *Alvarez-Mendez v. Stock*, 941 F.2d 956 (9th Cir.1991), *cert. denied*, ___ U.S. ___, 113 S.Ct. 127, 121 L.Ed.2d 82 (1992). One district court, however, did order that a group of Cuban petitioners was entitled to appointed counsel under the Criminal Justice Act to help pursue their habeas petitions. *Saldina v. Thornburgh*, 775 F.Supp. 507 (D.Conn.1991). And a panel of the Ninth Circuit found that a Marielito detained for eight years had to be released. *Barrera-Echavarria v. Rison*, 21 F.3d 314 (1994), *vacated pending rehearing en banc*, 35 F.3d 436 (9th Cir.1994). Judge Noonan explained the panel majority's position:

> Barrera is not a citizen; he is not a resident alien; he is an excluded alien, who in a legal sense has not entered this country. It is not disputed that he is a person. He is a person within our jurisdiction. As a person he is protected by the Fifth Amendment to the Constitution of the United States. *Yick Wo v. Hopkins*, 118 U.S. 356, 6 S.Ct. 1064, 30 L.Ed. 220 (1886).

> It is also common ground between the parties that neither Barrera nor any other person may be punished by the United States without a conviction following a trial. *Wong Wing v. United States*. The first question, then, for decision is whether the prolonged incarceration in federal prisons to which he has been subjected constitutes punishment. Common sense says yes, but common sense is not always right. The government argues that he is being subjected to preventive detention, a detention only imposed because it is the only way to achieve the object of the immigration laws that bar from the country excluded aliens. Drop the detention, says the government, and you will in effect have permitted Barrera to have made himself at home here in mockery of our immigration law and policy. You will also have made it easy for any foreign dictator to deposit on our shores his country's undesirables and, by refusing to take them back, to force us to keep them and make them ours.

> The government's contentions are not without force. The government has not proceeded maliciously or without reason in finding Barrera, a man who has already served time for state

convictions of burglary and robbery in Florida, to be a potential danger to society. * * * The government, moreover, backs up its argument with one undisputed authority, *Shaughnessy v. United States ex rel. Mezei*, which found nothing unconstitutional in an excluded alien, who would not be taken back by his country of origin, being held at Ellis Island for over two years. A detainee's life in the 1950's on this small island in sight of the Statue of Liberty was regimented; he slept in a dormitory and spent the day in the great Passenger Hall. But he was free to read and write as he chose, and his companions were not felons. Not explicitly taking up whether confinement on Ellis Island was punishment, the Court simply found that the petitioner's "continued exclusion" did not deprive him "of any statutory or constitutional right."

Detention, however, is permissible only if not "excessive in relation to the regulatory goal." *United States v. Salerno*, 481 U.S. 739, 747, 107 S.Ct. 2095, 2101, 95 L.Ed.2d 697 (1987). Excessive is what is disproportionate. What the government has lost sight of is the sense of proportion that must inform any governmental intrusion on liberty.

* * * [The U.S. Penitentiary at] Leavenworth, where Barrera presently resides, has a rated capacity of 951 and had a population of 1,597 in 1991. The overcrowded prison features a massive wall with gun towers at each corner. Not the Bastille, it is a formidable fortress. The Bureau of Prisons, the administrator of all four facilities [where Barrera has been held], describes them as "correctional" and their inhabitants as "offenders"; the administrator's announced aim is "a balance between punishment, deterrence, incapacitation, and rehabilitation." No indication is given by the record here that the purpose of punishment is less vigorously pursued by the Bureau of Prisons when one of the inmates in its charge happens to be an excluded alien.

Since his incarceration began in 1985, Barrera has been outside of a federal prison for only six months in 1992. For over eight years he has been a federal prisoner in the fullest sense * * *.

* * *

In sustaining statutes in the very few and limited situations in which preventive detention is permissible in the United States, the Supreme Court has stressed the crucial role of time. * * *

In contrast, the government in this case insists that it has the power to hold Barrera in close physical confinement indefinitely. There is no time limit. The situation is most analogous to that presented by *Foucha v. Louisiana*, ___ U.S. ___, 112 S.Ct. 1780, 118 L.Ed.2d 437 (1992). There, too, a unit of government argued that it could hold a person indefinitely because he had "an antisocial personality that sometimes leads to aggressive conduct" and his disorder was one "for which there is no effective treatment." In short, the contention was that for an indefinite period preventive detention was both appropriate and constitutional because the purpose was not to punish but to guard the community against a probable danger for which there was no apparent remedy. The Court held confinement under this statutory scheme to violate substantive due process.

Garcia-Mir v. Meese, 788 F.2d 1446 (11th Cir.), *cert. denied, Ferrer–Mazorra v. Meese,* 479 U.S. 889, 107 S.Ct. 289, 93 L.Ed.2d 263 (1986); and *Palma v. Verdeyen,* 676 F.2d 100 (4th Cir.1982) applied *Mezei* literally to the Mariels. These cases did not have *Foucha* for guidance. *Gisbert v. Attorney General,* 988 F.2d 1437, 1441 n. 6 (5th Cir.1993), *amended on other grounds,* 997 F.2d 1122 (5th Cir.1993), inadequately distinguishes it as involving a citizen in a psychiatric facility. *Foucha* established that while purpose is relevant in determining if detention is preventive, purity of purpose is not enough to exonerate governmental conduct that cuts excessively into liberty.

It is argued that the cases on pretrial detention and civil commitment do not have a generality that makes them applicable by analogy to confinement of an alien. On the contrary, Chief Justice Burger has written for a unanimous Supreme Court "that civil commitment *for any purpose* constitutes a significant deprivation of liberty that requires due process protection." *Addington v. Texas,* 441 U.S. 418, 425, 99 S.Ct. 1804, 1809, 60 L.Ed.2d 323 (1979) (emphasis supplied).

In determining whether Barrera is being subjected to punishment we must then turn to apply a standard of excessiveness that is objective. Is he being deprived by the government of a good to which any person is entitled and is the deprivation of such duration that it is excessive? Freedom to move outside a limited physical space, freedom to select one's companions, freedom to choose one's meals, freedom to attend to such studies or recreations as one likes, sexual freedom, freedom not to obey the directions of a warden—all of these goods are among those of which Barrera is denied by his confinement to a federal prison. The deprivation has gone on for over eight years. It can no longer be fictionally characterized as exclusion from the country. It is imprisonment within the country. We need not draw the line exactly as to when attempted exclusion becomes imprisonment. * * * Over eight years of such deprivations constitute punishment.

If we had to decide this case as one in which the validity of a statute was challenged as contrary to the Constitution of the United States, we would not hesitate to say that the Constitution had been violated. We do hesitate, however, to impute to Congress an intention to violate the Constitution. Consequently, we do not find in the ambiguous statutory scheme any authority to imprison Barrera indefinitely.

The government, to begin with, argues that the Attorney General is given implicit authority because once an alien has been determined excludable, the only way the alien may physically enter the United States is by parole granted by the Attorney General. But of course this contention is not helpful. Physically Barrera has entered the United States. The question to be decided is under what conditions is he to stay in the United States. The question remains as to whether his excluded status may be converted into imprisonment for an unlimited duration by virtue of anything in the statute.

The government notes the statute does specify that an alien excluded under this Act "shall be immediately deported . . . unless the Attorney General . . . concludes that immediate deportation is not practicable or proper." INA § 237(a). The dissent takes this undisputed statutory right of the Attorney General to deport or postpone the deportation of an excluded alien, combines it with vague language from INA § 212(d)(5)(A) dealing with parole and § 237(a)(1) dealing with the costs of detention, and determines that the statutory scheme gives the Attorney General the right to detain an alien indefinitely. A gap, however, exists between the statutory powers to deport, parole and detain and the power to imprison indefinitely. Congress has said nothing here about imprisoning in perpetuity. Implicit in the statutory scheme is the power of the Attorney General to detain for a period. It is not unusual for a duration proper when limited in time to become improper and excessive when the confinement becomes excessive.

* * *

The attempt is made to justify the government's action by focusing on the past of Barrera. It is not persuasive. Barrera was an Havana pickpocket awaiting trial when he became a Mariel refugee. He then committed the crimes for which he was punished in Florida. Since 1985 he has not been convicted of any state or federal crime. It is fanciful to suppose him more dangerous than any other ex-felon. * * * The government owes to those it governs the duty of protection. That duty is betrayed when the government uses illegitimate means to provide protection, when, for example, as here, the government imprisons a person it deems dangerous without charge, trial, or conviction. The infamous lettres de cachet of the King of France, a device for confining persons on the royal say-so, began as an extraordinary political measure and eventually became a routinized method of preserving order, employed in thousands of cases. * * * Some evils are too great for any margin to be given them. The practice of administratively imprisoning persons indefinitely is not a process tolerable in use against any person in any corner of our country.

* * *

The Attorney General's zeal for the protection of society is laudable. But all government officials present their actions as zealous for the welfare and protection of society. Even the royal letters de cachet consigning persons to the Bastille were normally executed with a virtuous sense of the danger being prevented by such expeditious means. In our society no person may be imprisoned for many years without prospect of termination. The rights of the human person must be vindicated as part of the common good of our society. Barrera has been punished too long without statutory warrant. The judgment of the district court issuing the Great Writ is affirmed.

Judge Sneed dissented:

The majority has given us an opinion from which we hear, in the distance, the clash of ideas and arms that characterized the Age of Enlightenment and the accompanying American and French Revolutions. However, I am not moved to conclude that the incarceration of Barrera–Echavarria has violated, or presently does violate, the Eighth Amendment of the Constitution. Moreover, this incarceration is explicitly authorized by an act of Congress.

* * *

[T]he overall statutory and regulatory structure of the immigration laws * * * [gives] the Attorney General three alternatives: deportation, detention, and parole. Congress * * * has expressed a preference for the first, but generally has delegated the ultimate choice to the Attorney General.

* * *

Nor can the mere length of detention, without more, guarantee an excluded alien's parole into the United States. To hold otherwise would reward the intractability of nations like Cuba who engage in thrusting their undesirables upon their enemies. The Constitution requires no such absurd result.

* * *

Barrera–Echavarria arrived in the United States on May 29, 1980. Thereafter, he was arrested four times for various crimes. * * * On July 11, 1982, petitioner was arrested for armed robbery. After his conviction in state court on March 1, 1983, he was sentenced to 230 days in prison, most of which he had served by the March 1 date.

No more than two months thereafter, May 26, 1983, Barrera–Echavarria was arrested for burglary and theft, and sentenced to two years in state prison. Less than two years later, January 29, 1985, the immigration authorities revoked petitioner's parole and assigned him to federal prison effective February 13, 1985. Thus, Barrera–Echavarria was not under direct control of the Immigration and Naturalization Service for almost five years following his arrival in this country. The loss of that status was attributable to his own misconduct while in this country for which he was punished by state authorities primarily.

* * * [W]hile in prison, Barrera–Echavarria has been disciplined for numerous acts of misconduct. * * *

During his federal detention, he has received six parole reviews [by INS in accordance with the special parole procedures for Mariel Cubans set forth in 8 C.F.R. §§ 212.12–.13,] roughly on an annual basis. The last was in February, 1993. In 1992 he was paroled to a halfway house, but on June 8, 1992, he was arrested on charges of sexual assault and apparently detained by state authorities to May 28, 1993, when in due course he was transferred to the federal prison in Terre Haute, Indiana.

In light of this record, does continued incarceration of Barrera–Echavarria violate the Eighth Amendment? I think not. Petitioner, like his fellow Mariel Cubans, has received every opportunity to earn the parole he now claims as his right.

* * *

[T]he majority frames the issue solely in terms of the petitioner's rights, inaccurately described. The rights of the public are treated as of substantially unequal and subordinate value. In that manner it finds "punishment" when in fact the sovereign has no interest in either subjecting the alien to retribution or to reform, but only in protecting the public during his uninvited and unwanted presence. * * *

Petitioner should, of course, continue his efforts to secure parole so as to ensure that he may again be paroled at the point where such parole would be reasonably safe for the community. The immigration officials should assume some risks in order to avoid crossing the line into retribution or reform. This court should stand ready to review the propriety of later parole decisions. But I cannot judicially impose a procrustean time limit on this process. I must, therefore, respectfully dissent.

Questions

1. What does Judge Noonan mean by an objective standard of excessiveness, to be used in deciding whether Barrera's detention amounts to punishment? Would a subjective standard be more appropriate? Is this what Judge Sneed envisions? How should a subjective standard for deciding whether this detention is preventive or punitive be framed?

2. Is the panel decision in *Barrera* a constitutional or a statutory ruling? In the panel's view, is the government's default procedural or substantive?

The *en banc* court ultimately agreed with Judge Sneed and upheld the continued detention of Barrera, aligning itself with every other circuit that has considered the ongoing detention of Marielitos—with the possible exception of the Tenth Circuit in the 1981 case of *Rodriguez-Fernandez*. The court emphasized the annual review of Barrera's continued confinement: "When viewed in this light, as a series of one-year periods of detention followed by an opportunity to plead his case anew, we have no difficulty concluding that Barrera's detention is constitutional under *Mezei*." *Barrera-Echavarria v. Rison*, 44 F.3d 1441, ___ (9th Cir.1995) (*en banc*).

A few final words to bring the Cuban developments up to date through early 1995 may be useful. The Clinton administration, early in its tenure, tried to reenergize the process of returning Marielitos who had criminal records, but it enjoyed only limited success. Then in August 1994, a new boat crisis developed, this time involving Cubans sailing by small home-made rafts toward the United States. Some raft traffic had been underway for many years, and rafters had hitherto been rescued by the U.S. Coast Guard and taken to Florida, where most were released and eventually given permanent resident status under the Cuban Adjustment Act of 1966. The raft traffic soared in August, however, to as many as 3000 persons per day, when Fidel Castro ceased patrolling the beaches, in response to domestic unrest. In a significant change of policy, the U.S. government then announced that rafters would henceforth be taken to safe havens in the region, rather than to the United States, and eventually the raft traffic slackened. The immediate crisis was largely resolved with a limited agreement between Cuba and the United States on September 9. Cuba agreed to halt the dangerous departures "using mainly persuasive methods," and in return the United States agreed to assure the admission of at least 20,000 Cubans per year after selection and processing through the U.S. diplomatic facilities in Havana. *See* 71 Interp.Rel. 1213, 1236–37 (1994). Over 20,000 Cubans are indefinitely housed in a "safe haven" at the U.S. Naval base at Guantanamo; several hundred have voluntarily returned to Cuba. The two governments also agreed to continue discussion of the return of Marielitos, but apparently the discussions still focus only on the remaining individuals from the original 1984 list, not the hundreds of additional Cubans detained after later criminal convictions in the United States.

If you were the Attorney General, what would you do about the Mariel Cuban detainees, now that a decade and a half have elapsed since the boatlift? To what extent is your answer dependent on your acceptance or rejection of the *Barrera* panel's views about your statutory and constitutional authority?

Chapter Five

ENTRY

SECTION A. THE DEFINITION OF "ENTRY" AND ITS RELEVANCE

The concept of "entry" into the United States plays a crucial, and somewhat curious, role in immigration law. For an alien whom the government seeks to send home, "entry" is the difference between exclusion and deportation: aliens who have "entered" the United States are entitled to deportation hearings; aliens who have not "entered" are placed in exclusion hearings. This distinction is not made explicit in the statute, but it may be inferred from INA §§ 235, 236 and 291. Furthermore, numerous grounds of deportation are keyed to "entry," *see* INA § 241(a); and illegal entry is the core of several criminal provisions in the statute. *See* INA §§ 274–77.

"Entry" is defined in INA § 101(a)(13), which you should now read.

Suppose the United States establishes an inspection center just below its northern border. Alien C, who seeks permanent residence in this country, crosses the Canadian border and presents herself at the INS facility for inspection. Has she "entered" the United States? Or, to ask the question in its most relevant way: if the INS believes C should be sent home, is she entitled to an exclusion hearing or a deportation hearing? A literal reading of the definition would indicate that C had "entered"; she clearly has come into the United States from a foreign place. But this reading cannot be correct. Since inspection centers are usually located on this side of the border, such an interpretation would effectively read exclusion out of the statute. Thus it has been well-established that mere physical presence in the United States is not enough to constitute "entry."

The insufficiency of mere physical presence also follows from the concept of parole as explained in *Leng May Ma v. Barber,* 357 U.S. 185, 78 S.Ct. 1072, 2 L.Ed.2d 1246 (1958), which you should recall from Chapter Three. That case concerned an alien who was detained for over a year after arrival in the United States and then released on parole pending determination of her admissibility. When the government ruled she was not entitled to enter, she applied for withholding of deportation under INA § 243(h) on the ground that she would be persecuted if returned to her native China. At that time, § 243(h) relief was available only if the alien was "within the United States." The Court, in a 5–to–4 decision, concluded that because the alien's detention and parole into the United States did not constitute "entry," she was not "within the United States" and thus could not invoke § 243(h). While the Refugee Act of 1980 has superseded *Leng May Ma*'s restrictive implications for § 243(h), *see* Chapter Eight *infra,* the Court's conclusion that an alien paroled into the United States has not "entered" is still good law.

The notion that paroled aliens have not "entered" is carried one step further in the following situation. Alien G has applied for adjustment of status under INA § 245. Under INS regulations, an alien who departs the United States during the pendency of a § 245 petition is deemed to have abandoned the application. This result may be avoided by requesting "advance parole" from the INS prior to departure. 8 C.F.R. § 245.2(a)(4). Assume that G has been granted advance parole, leaves the United States for a two-month trip and is permitted to cross the border after inspection upon return. Eventually her adjustment petition is denied and the INS begins removal proceedings. According to INS regulations, "[i]f the [§ 245] application of an individual granted advance parole is subsequently denied, the applicant will be subject *to the exclusion provisions of section 236* of the [INA]." *Id.* (emphasis supplied). Note that G is now in the interior of the country, and many months have elapsed. What is the reason for the INS regulation? Is it sensible? Should the fact that INS calls her re-admission "parole" determine which kind of removal proceeding she will receive? Should it make a difference whether her previous nonimmigrant status had expired before her departure?

The Difference Between Exclusion and Deportation Proceedings

Some of the reasons why the alien might prefer a deportation proceeding are found in the INA: (1) The burden of proof is on the alien in an exclusion proceeding to show she is not subject to exclusion; in a deportation proceeding, the government must prove deportability. INA § 291. (2) An alien who has been in the United States for at least seven years may apply for a form of relief in a deportation hearing (INA § 244) that is not available to an alien in an exclusion hearing. (3) An alien in a deportation hearing may designate the country to which he prefers to be sent, INA § 243(a); an excluded alien must be returned to the country in which he boarded the carrier that brought him here. INA § 237(a)(1).[1] (4) An alien in a deportation proceeding may appeal bond determinations, INA § 242(a); no similar provision exists for aliens in exclusion proceedings. (5) Aliens detained after an order of deportation generally must be released after six months if removal cannot be accomplished before then, INA § 242(c), (d); no similar statutory provisions protect aliens detained following exclusion. Besides these statutory differences, aliens in deportation hearings will find it easier to raise constitutional claims, particularly procedural due process

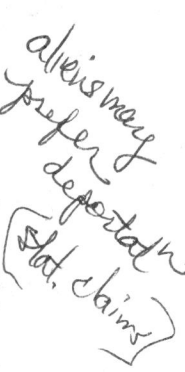

alien's may prefer deport'n (std. claim)

(const'l claim)

---

1. If that country will not accept the alien, the statute provides the Attorney General with other options for returning the excluded alien. INA § 237(a)(2).

claims, than aliens in exclusion hearings. This remains true in spite of recent indications that the deportation-exclusion line is no longer entirely dispositive for constitutional purposes, *see Landon v. Plasencia*, at p. 405 *supra*.

The "entry" issue usually arises because the alien prefers deportation proceedings to exclusion proceedings, for the reasons discussed above. But because illegal entry is a criminal offense under INA § 275, an alien arrested near the border may prefer to argue that she had *not* entered the United States at the time of her apprehension. If she prevails, she faces an exclusion hearing but avoids a possible criminal charge.

Defining "Entry"

Rejecting the test of physical presence may be necessary, but fashioning an acceptable alternative has proven rather difficult. Consider the next two opinions, one from the BIA and the other from a federal district court. Has either developed a coherent, common-sense meaning for "entry?"

MATTER OF G–

Board of Immigration Appeals, 1993.
Int. Dec. 3215.

* * *

The applicant is a 29–year-old married, male native and citizen of the People's Republic of China, who attempted to enter the United States on June 6, 1993. The applicant was taken into custody by the Immigration and Naturalization Service and detained for exclusion proceedings. * * *

* * *

* * * [W]e must first resolve the issue of whether the applicant "entered" the United States within the meaning of section 101(a)(13) of the Act, for if an "entry" occurred, the question of the applicant's continued presence here may only be adjudicated in deportation proceedings commenced under section 242(b) of the Act.

General Facts of Ship's Arrival

The record reflects the applicant arrived in the United States on Sunday, June 6, 1993, aboard a cargo freighter named the *Golden Venture*. The applicant was one of a cargo of some 300 passengers when the vessel, piloted by a crew of 13 Indonesian nationals, ran aground on a sandbar off the coast of New York. The grounding took place 100 to 200 yards offshore of the Fort Tilden military reservation located on the Rockaway Peninsula in the Gateway National Recreation Area of Queens, New York.

According to the record, at about 1:45 a.m. on that Sunday, two officers of the United States Department of Interior Park Police were patrolling the Gateway National Recreation Area when they observed the distressed ship and a number of its passengers swimming in the water or running on the beach. The officers spotted life preservers bobbing in the water and heard people yelling. At 1:58 a.m., the officers placed an emergency call for help to the New York City Police Department and other authorities and then proceeded to assist several of the ship's passengers out of the water.

The Coast Guard dispatched boats and helicopters to the scene of the reported shipwreck to observe and rescue persons aboard the disabled vessel.

At 2:19 a.m., officers from the New York City Police Department arrived on the beach at Fort Tilden; 2 minutes later, the New York City Fire Department was alerted. Police canine units and New York State police helicopters equipped with searchlights also were deployed to search for passengers on shore or still in the water. Officers from the various law enforcement agencies involved—the New York City Police Department, the Park Police, the Jacob Riis Park Police, and the Coast Guard—waded into the harbor to assist people to shore.

During these early morning hours, a portion of the Fort Tilden beach—about ¼ to ½–mile-long and extending 600 yards inland from the water line—was ultimately cordoned off and controlled by enforcement officers of these various organizations to prevent passengers who reached shore from leaving the area.

According to newspaper accounts of several passengers interviewed, pandemonium erupted on board when the ship grounded. Passengers began spewing out of the cargo hold of the ship, where they had been forced to stay during their 3–month-long voyage. They crowded the ship's deck, only to be told by the ship's crew to jump overboard.

Over the next several hours as rescue personnel assembled in the area, about 200 passengers fled the ship by leaping blindly into the surf or descending a ladder on the side of the boat. Ignoring police and Coast Guard pleas to remain on the vessel, many swam and waded to shore clutching plastic bags of belongings while others used plastic jugs as makeshift floats.

An armada of small vessels, rafts, and cutters fished many of these 200 out of the 53–degree waters and brought them to shore.[3] Other passengers managed to reach dry land on their own only to be apprehended on the beach or within the perimeter of the cordoned-off area. Many of the ship's occupants who swam to shore suffered from hypothermia and simply collapsed on reaching the beach. A few, however, eluded capture by fleeing through the thick-brushed dunes into the surrounding neighborhoods. Several of these survivors were reported seen knocking on the doors of homes in several nearby communities, offering money in exchange for the use of a telephone. Three men, for example, were found in a construction site in the neighboring town of Breezy Point after having offered a resident $100 to use his telephone. Local police later apprehended 26 other men near a shopping center in the town of Huntington Beach after receiving an anonymous telephone call that several Asian men were seen leaving a tan van.

---

3. The Coast Guard recovered the bodies of four passengers who had drowned in the choppy waters. Three other passengers plucked from the 53–degree waters died later.

More than 100 passengers, however, remained on board and awaited the arrival of rescue personnel.

In an effort to detain those passengers apprehended, a building in the Fort Tilden military reservation was used to house passengers not in need of medical treatment; these individuals were subsequently transferred to detention facilities for immigration processing. Police escorted about 30 other passengers to local hospitals for treatment; these passengers were later released to the immigration authorities.

By 3:30 a.m., when the first immigration officials arrived, 200 to 300 rescue personnel were at the scene. Swimmers were still being pulled from the water and passengers were still being rescued from the boat.

Understandably under the circumstances, no attempt was made to differentiate and keep track of those persons rescued from the deck of the *Golden Venture*, plucked from the water, intercepted within the cordoned-off area, or taken to medical facilities. Immigration officials processed all detainees as one large group.

By the evening of June 6, 1993, 273 of the 300 passengers reported to have been aboard the vessel had been accounted for while some 30 remained at large. Law enforcement authorities took the captain of the freighter and his crew of 12 off the ship and arrested them pending criminal prosecution on smuggling charges.[4]

THE ISSUE OF ENTRY

In relevant part, an "entry" for immigration purposes is defined as "any coming of an alien into the United States, from a foreign port or place or from an outlying possession, whether voluntary or otherwise." Section 101(a)(13) of the Act. Over time, caselaw has led to the formulation of a more precise definition of that term, requiring: (1) a crossing into the territorial limits of the United States, i.e., physical presence; (2)(a) inspection and admission by an immigration officer, or (b) actual and intentional evasion of inspection at the nearest inspection point; and (3) freedom from official restraint.

The definitional "entry" requirements at issue in this case are those of evasion of inspection and freedom from official restraint. It is this latter requirement, however, which is the principal focus of the parties on appeal.

Regarding the requirement of freedom from official restraint, we note at the outset that, in circumstances such as those now before us, there can be no certainty as to when and under what precise circumstances during those few critical hours immediately following the *Golden Venture's* grounding each and every individual alien landed on shore. Viewing the situation in its totality, however, it is clear that some passengers of the Golden Venture arrived in the United States free from official restraint, while others did not.

---

4. According to newspaper accounts, the *Golden Venture* sailed from Thailand with its cargo of illegal Chinese immigrants as part of an elaborate multimillion-dollar smuggling operation. Many passengers paid more than $20,000 or agreed to pay off a portion of the fee by agreeing to be indentured servants in this country.

For example, although the exact number may never be known, several of the ship's occupants, presumably the first to jump ship, did reach dry land before the vessel was spotted by the two Park Police officers who first observed the disabled ship at 1:45 a.m. According to the record, the officers witnessed "numerous" individuals running "to avoid detection." These passengers were clearly free from any official restraint. Similarly, other evidence in the record suggests that several passengers were found, possibly hours later, in neighboring communities. These aliens were not only free from any restraint, but were in fact mixing with the general population.

In contrast, for those 100 or more passengers who were escorted off the ship—as well as the many others who were pulled from the water by rescue personnel or who landed in the cordoned-off area after it was secured—we would not find that their physical presence here was coupled with "freedom from official restraint." The movements of these aliens were restricted to the immediate vicinity of the beach cordoned-off by the scores of law enforcement personnel at the scene. These aliens were never free to leave the area. They were never at liberty in the United States, and, under these circumstances, clearly lacked the freedom to go at large and mix with the general population.

Thus, some passengers of the *Golden Venture* were clearly in this country free from official restraint, while others were not. However, in circumstances such as those which occurred on the morning of June 6, 1993, the facts of each individual case may never be clearly determinable for various reasons. For one, it could never be definitively established at what precise point the cordoned-off area of the beach at Fort Tilden was finally secured. Secondly, even if that time theoretically could be established, e.g. at 3:49 a.m., many aliens—even if testifying fully and truthfully—would not know exactly when they reached shore. Finally, particularly where saving lives was the primary concern of the government officials on the scene, one would not expect those officials to be recording specific data on the identities of each passenger or on the times when and circumstances under which each was taken into custody. Indeed, in many cases, particularly those involving aliens who managed to swim to shore, there likely will never be any certainty as to exactly when and under what circumstances they made it onto the beach.

If aliens can establish the specific circumstances of their arrivals, their cases can be resolved on the facts. For example, if an alien can show that he was one of the first passengers to disembark the ship and reach shore, or that he managed to arrive at a neighboring town, freedom from official restraint would be found.

On the other hand, in cases where there is no clear evidence of the facts determinative of the entry issue, those cases ultimately must be resolved on where the burden of proof lies. Accordingly, since it is the alien, with a limited exception not relevant here, who bears the burden of showing that exclusion proceedings are improper, it is he who must prove that his arrival on land constituted an "entry" into the United States within the scope of section 101(a)(13) of the Act. Section 291 of the Act.

* * * [T]he applicant testified that he was in (what appears to have been) the cargo hold of the ship when the vessel ran aground. According to the applicant, he made his way to the deck of the ship and was told by those in the front to jump. He did so and swam to shore clutching a plastic bag containing his personal belongings. He admittedly did not know how long he was in the water, but found himself cold and dizzy as he reached the shore.

Once on the beach, he quickly changed his clothes and went searching for a road in the dark. He did not recall being chased. He recounted having passed two roadways, but could not explain how far from the beach he had walked or in what direction he was walking when apprehended. He did not testify with any clarity as to any of the time frames involved. All he was certain of was that he was in New York. As he entered what he described as a "forest," he encountered two police officers who escorted him back to the beach and instructed him to lie on his stomach. Eventually, the Service took the applicant into custody and detained him for exclusion proceedings. The applicant paid a down payment of 3,000 yuan for this voyage to the United States.

* * *

We observe that nowhere in the record is there evidence suggesting that the applicant deliberately surrendered himself to the authorities for immigration processing, or that, once ashore, he sought them out, voluntarily awaited their arrival, or otherwise acted consistently with a desire to submit himself for immigration inspection. In fact, given the circumstances under which the *Golden Venture* landed, the applicant's payment of money to a smuggling operation for passage to the United States, his lack of travel documents entitling him to enter this country, and his conduct once he came ashore, we find that the requisite intent to evade can be sufficiently gleaned from the record.

As to the second requirement—freedom from official restraint—the applicant points out on appeal that some passengers did manage to make their way into neighboring towns, thereby proving he too was "free from official restraint."

As noted above, the applicant is correct in his assertion that several passengers from the *Golden Venture* were found in nearby communities. However, the applicant does not allege nor can we find any evidence to suggest that he was one of those passengers. In this regard, it is incumbent upon the applicant to prove that his physical presence in the United States was coupled with "freedom from official restraint." From the applicant's testimony, however, it is not clear where in the continuum of events on the morning of June 6, 1993, he actually reached shore. No evidence was presented suggesting that he was one of the first passengers to reach dry land or that the beach was deserted when he landed, from which one might conclude that he was free from official restraint. We note that he did not have a watch and could not explain how long he was in the water or how many minutes passed before he was caught. He admittedly did not know where he was when he was apprehended, in what direction he was walking, or how far from the beach he had travelled. Consequently, we do not find that the applicant has presented clear evidence that he was ever free from official restraint. As such, we do not find that he has met the burden, which he alone must bear, of demonstrating that he made an entry into the United States. Accordingly, we find that these exclusion proceedings are proper.

* * *

IN THE MATTER OF THE APPLICATION OF PHELISNA

United States District Court, Eastern District of New York, 1982.
551 F.Supp. 960.

NICKERSON, DISTRICT JUDGE.

* * *

Petitioner arrived without a visa in the United States on July 5, 1981, in a boat carrying some two hundred Haitians, who disembarked on a Florida beach near Miami. A report of the officers of the Public Safety Department of Dade County, Florida, shows that they apprehended the Haitians on Rickenbaker Causeway one quarter of a mile south of "Sundays Restaurant" and turned them over to the Service.

On July 28, 1981, the Service, claiming that petitioner had made no "entry" into the United States, instituted exclusion proceedings against her pursuant to INA § 236. When the hearing began on September 2, 1981, petitioner's counsel moved to convert it into one for "deportation"—technically, expulsion—on the ground that petitioner had "entered" the United States before being apprehended. Petitioner testified that she had arrived by boat, entered the United States on July 5, 1981, and did not know where she was. The immigration judge, who announced at the inception of the hearing that he would permit only "several questions" of petitioner and would limit "severely" the testimony, refused to subpoena the arresting officer, announced that "[t]he burden is on the applicant" to establish the impropriety of exclusion proceedings, and denied the motion to convert the hearing into one for deportation.

When the exclusion hearing was resumed on December 1, 1981, petitioner's counsel moved for reconsideration of the motion to change the proceeding to one for deportation and offered in evidence "a police report from Miami, Dade County." The immigration judge denied the motion for reconsideration, declined to accept the report in evidence, declined an offer of proof as to what the evidence would be, and found petitioner excludable under INA § 212(a)(20). After the hearing the immigration judge denied asylum and ordered petitioner excluded.

Petitioner appealed to the Board, which dismissed the appeal, holding that (1) petitioner had the burden of showing that she had made an "entry"; (2) intentional evasion of inspection is an element of "entry"; and (3) petitioner had "failed to prove" that element. The present petition followed, asking that petitioner "be restored to a deportation proceeding."

* * *

The government contends that petitioner is "excludable" under INA § 212(a) which provides that among the aliens who "shall be excluded from admission into the United States" are those who when they apply for "admission" do not have a valid visa or other entry document. Petitioner contends that when she landed on the beach she had made an "entry" and should not be "excluded" but is entitled to be deported under INA § 241(a) which provides that an alien shall be "deported" who "at the time of entry" was within a class of aliens "excludable by the law existing at the time of such entry." The term "entry" is defined in INA § 101(a)(13) to encompass, so far as pertinent, "any coming of an alien into the United States, from a foreign port or place, ... whether voluntarily or otherwise."

* * *

Petitioner contends that she made an "entry," by "coming ... into the United States" from a foreign place within the meaning of INA § 101(a)(13). She urges that "entry" occurred when she was present in the United States free from restraint. Quite patently the statute cannot be read to mean that mere presence in the United States is enough to show an entry. The inspection stations at which the United States determines whether aliens are admissible are per force inside the nation's borders. Congress could not have meant that an alien had come "into" the United States when he arrived at one of the usual points where the government is prepared to process applications for admission.

But if the alien crosses the border where there are no inspection facilities, for example, somewhere along the Mexican or Canadian borders or the coast line of the United States, common sense suggests that ordinarily the alien has "entered" the United States. Even under those circumstances the cases have made an exception where the alien has established that he had an intent to be inspected. Thus, in *Thack v. Zurbrick,* 51 F.2d 634 (6th Cir.1931), aliens, long time residents of the United States, returned to Poland for a visit without obtaining certificates entitling them to reentry here within a year. They came back across the Canadian border and headed for the nearest inspection station at Newport, Vermont. On arrival at the station they were arrested and charged with illegal entry. Later they were ordered deported. The court held that an alien who "merely follows the ordinary path from the international line to the nearest inspection point and presents himself for inspection" has not made an "entry" so as to be guilty of "an offense for which Congress intended he should be sent to his former foreign residence and forbidden ever to try to return to this country." 51 F.2d at 635. The court explained that had the aliens "not intended to go to an inspection point" or had they been apprehended "in the effort to evade doing so" the question would be different. *Id.* at 636.

The government and the Board seize on these decisions to argue that petitioner, in order to prove that she had "entered," must demonstrate that when she arrived on the beach she had an intent to "evade" inspection. Aside from the question of burden of proof, this court does not believe that the above cases prescribe as an element of "entry" an intent to evade inspection. It would be enough that the alien had no intention, whether through ignorance or otherwise, to follow the usual path to an inspection station.

But in any event in this court's opinion the Board was not correct in imposing on petitioner more than the burden of proving that she came physically into the United States at some point not in the vicinity of an inspection station. If the government wishes to exclude an alien landing at a point far distant from such a station on the theory that the alien had the particular intent to submit himself to inspection and was on the way to doing so, the government must prove it.

The allocation of the burden of persuasion is, of course, a matter of substantive policy, which Congress may set. But where Congress has not specifically addressed itself to the question and legislative intent is not otherwise apparent, we may assume that the issue has been left to the judiciary for resolution. * * *

The government contends that Congress intended to impose the burden on petitioner and points to language in INA § 291, providing that when a person "makes application for admission, or otherwise attempts to enter the United States, the burden of proof shall be upon such person to establish that he ... is not subject to exclusion." The government asserts that petitioner was "obviously a person 'attempt[ing] to enter the United States.'" But that simply begs the question. The issue is whether "entry" was accomplished. One who is attempting to enter has by hypothesis not yet entered and must show he is entitled to do so. But one who has entered is no longer attempting to do so.

There is thus no express statutory provision allocating the burden of proving "entry," and the court must apply traditional criteria in deciding the question. Plainly what is at stake both for petitioner and for the government is relevant. * * * [U]nder the statutory scheme "entry" is the criterion on which the acquisition of important rights depends. At risk for the alien is the loss of those rights, one of which is regarded by petitioner as literally vital, namely, the right to designate a country to which she is to be sent. At issue for the government is something far less critical, that is, some degree of administrative convenience.

The government argues that the burden of proving petitioner's intent should rest with her since the pertinent evidence on that matter is more accessible to her than to the government. But the significant proof may well be not the self serving declarations of the alien but documentary evidence such as arrest reports and testimony by third persons as to the objective facts from which an inference as to intent may be drawn. The government is ordinarily more likely to have ready access to this evidence than the alien. For example, in this case the government had the resources and the ability to obtain testimony from those who observed the Haitians land on the shore and proceed along the highway and to the local police officers who apprehended them.

Moreover, to impose on petitioner the burden of showing more than the time, place and manner in which she came within the borders of the United States on the beaches of Florida would hardly be the appropriate method of narrowing the issues for decision. If the government contends that an alien had a peculiar intent, not ordinarily inferable from the physical facts, it is not unfair to ask the government to assert that contention and to prove it.

The Board, in addition to imposing on petitioner the burden of proving an intent to evade inspection, also said in its opinion that petitioner "was looking for immigration officials to test her status." There is no evidence in the record to support the supposition that as of the time that petitioner landed on the beach she was seeking out the immigration officials. The only conceivable support for such a finding is the following statement in her later application for asylum: "When we came to the beach in Miami, Florida, we met other Haitians who said that we should see the immigration officials." This language is equally consistent with a lack of intent at the time of landing to seek inspection. Indeed, the statement can scarcely be taken as evidence of the formulation of such an intent even after the landing. It speaks of what others said to her, not what she decided.

* * *

The matter is remanded to the Service for further proceedings consistent with this opinion. So ordered.

Notes

1. In another Golden Venture case, the BIA found, as in *Matter of G-*, that the alien had the burden to show freedom from official restraint, that he had failed to meet that burden, and that therefore he had not "entered." On review, the district court reversed, citing *Phelisna*. *See Xin–Chang v. Slattery*, 859 F.Supp. 708, 714 (S.D.N.Y.1994) ("The government is clearly in a better position to prove official restraint than an alien."). Another district court has adopted the BIA's position that the alien has the burden to show freedom from official restraint. *See Chen v. Carroll*, 858 F.Supp. 569, 573 (E.D.Va.1994).

2. Consider the following situation:

[The alien] arrived in the Houston Intercontinental Airport on September 7, 1990, and presented an Indian passport and an Employment Authorization Card (Form I–688A) to the immigration inspector. The immigration inspector processed the applicant and stamped his passport: "ADMITTED, SEP 07 1990, CLASS: I–688A." The applicant was not referred to secondary inspection and proceeded directly to customs for an inspection of his baggage and personal effects.

In the customs area of the airport, the applicant presented his passport and customs form to the customs officer. Finding the applicant's passport suspicious, the customs officer returned the applicant to the immigration section to verify his documentation. A computer check revealed the applicant's passport to be a fraudulent one, and he was accordingly served with a Notice to Applicant for Admission Detained for Hearing before Immigration Judge (I–122) and placed in exclusion proceedings.

Is the alien entitled to a deportation hearing instead?

3. In *Matter of Ching and Chen,* 19 I & N Dec. 203 (BIA 1984), the record disclosed the following facts:

> The applicants are a 22–year-old female and an 18–year-old male, natives and citizens of the People's Republic of China, each of whom also holds a valid Hong Kong identification card and a Taiwanese passport. They were among a group of five aliens traveling from Hong Kong to Guatemala via Tokyo and Los Angeles on a commercial airline. Upon arrival at Los Angeles International Airport on July 20, 1984, the carrier (airline) presented the group for inspection and admission under the transit without visa (TRWOV) privilege. *See* 8 C.F.R. §§ 212.1(e)(1) and 214.2(c)(1). The examining immigration officer denied the five aliens entry as TRWOVs and issued to the carrier a Form I–259 (Notice to Detain, Deport, Remove, or Present Aliens), formally directing that they be detained by the carrier pending their removal on the carrier's next available return flight to Hong Kong. *See* 8 C.F.R. § 235.3(d). The aliens apparently made no attempt to obtain a further determination of their admissibility as TRWOVs at a continued or deferred inspection, or to pursue their applications for admission at an exclusion hearing before an immigration judge, but agreed to abide by the examining immigration officer's decision and return to Hong Kong. They then apparently were kept in isolation in a waiting area or lounge within the airport until their final removal by the carrier could be effected. While in this carrier custody, the instant two applicants surreptitiously left the detention lounge and the Los Angeles International Airport, abandoning their passports, airline tickets, and baggage. Two days later they were apprehended on board an eastbound commercial bus at the border patrol check point at Sierra Blanca, Texas.

Are the aliens entitled to an exclusion hearing or a deportation hearing?

The BIA concluded that *Ching and Chen* was analogous to *Matter of A-,* 9 I & N Dec. 356 (BIA 1961), which had found an "entry" where an alien detained aboard a ship as a stowaway had escaped and managed to land. In both cases the aliens' "inspections and applications for admission were completed and a final determination was made refusing to admit them and ordering them removed." In effect, Ching and Chen "made two separate attempts to enter the United States: their first failed when they were rejected for admission as TRWOVs; their second succeeded when they slipped away from the detention lounge, evading detection by either carrier or Service authorities and fleeing into the country's interior."

The BIA distinguished *Matter of Lin,* 18 I & N Dec. 219 (BIA 1982), which found no "entry" by an alien who escaped from detention pending exclusion proceedings and was apprehended two days later in New York City. The BIA is certainly correct that *Lin can* be distinguished from *Ching and Chen:* in *Lin* the INS had not completed exclusion proceedings.

But why *should* such a distinction be drawn? How does such a distinction serve the theory underlying the concept of "entry"?

4. The multi-part definition of "entry" applied by the BIA in *Matter of G-* stems from the Board's decision in *Matter of Pierre*, 14 I & N Dec. 467, 468 (BIA 1973). Building on that test, can we construct a rule that adequately accounts for the results in the cases described thus far in this Chapter? Can, for example, *Matter of G-* and *Phelisna* be reconciled with each other? More fundamentally, should we construct such a harmonizing rule? Is it sensible to have an adjudication system that rewards surreptitious entrants over those who present themselves to border authorities?

5. Several early cases under the criminal statutes punishing illegal entry held that aliens who were apprehended after crossing the border without inspection had not "entered" because they were on their way to an inspection point (and thus had not intended to evade inspection). *E.g., Thack v. Zurbrick*, 51 F.2d 634 (6th Cir.1931). These decisions avoided the harshness of a literal reading of the criminal statutes. In *Phelisna*, however, the government unsuccessfully tried to turn this ameliorative shield into a sword by asserting that an alien claiming "entry" must show that she intended to evade inspection.

6. Aliens who are interdicted in United States territorial waters before reaching shore clearly have not "entered." But are they even entitled to exclusion hearings? No, according to a Department of Justice memorandum, which reasoned that the language and structure of the INA contemplate exclusion hearings only for those who arrive at the "ports" of the United States. *See* 71 Interp.Rel. 381 (1994). *Cf. Sale v. Haitian Centers Council, Inc.*, ___ U.S. ___, ___, 113 S.Ct. 2549, 2558–62, 125 L.Ed.2d 128 (1993) (interdicted aliens may not invoke withholding of deportation under INA § 243(h)). *Cf.* Motomura, *Haitian Asylum Seekers: Interdiction and Immigrants' Rights*, 26 Cornell Int'l L.J. 695, 709–14 (1993) (suggesting that interdicted aliens should be treated as having reached the "functional equivalent of the border"). We will treat interdiction more fully in Chapter Eight.

SECTION B. THE RE–ENTRY DOCTRINE

[handwritten margin note: makes possible the exclusion & sometime deportat[ion] at ports]

Alien T enters the United States in 1984 and establishes lawful permanent residence. In 1990, without leaving this country, T helps an alien illegally enter the United States. Since entering, T has never left the United States. Although § 241(a)(1)(E) makes aiding illegal entry a ground for deportation, the deportation provision is limited to acts committed *within five years* after any entry. Because the conduct occurred six years after T's first and only entry, he is not deportable under subsection (a)(1)(E) (although he is subject to criminal sanctions under INA §§ 273 and 274).

Now assume that T takes a two-month trip to the South Pacific. Upon his return to the United States, he is stopped at the border and told that he will not be able to re-enter because he aided the unlawful entry of an alien in 1990. When T wonders out loud how he can be excluded for an act for which he could not be deported, the INS official reads him § 212(a)(6)(E). It requires exclusion of "[a]ny alien who at any time knowingly has * * * aided any other alien to enter * * * the United States in violation of law."

Can the INS be correct? Is a permanent resident alien subject to the grounds of exclusion every time he leaves and returns to the United States? May the fact that a permanent resident alien has taken a vacation mean that he will lose his residence in the United States for conduct for which he could not have been deported? The answer to all these questions is yes; and the term used to describe these phenomena is the "re-entry doctrine." Essentially the doctrine holds that the word "entry" in the INA refers to any coming into the United States, not simply the *first* entry of the alien.[2]

In the situation just described, the re-entry doctrine makes possible the *exclusion* of returning residents. As the next case demonstrates, the re-entry doctrine may also trigger the *deportation* of a resident alien where an element of the deportable conduct is that it occur within a certain number of years "after entry."

UNITED STATES EX REL. VOLPE v. SMITH

Supreme Court of the United States, 1933.
289 U.S. 422, 53 S.Ct. 665, 77 L.Ed. 1298.

MR. JUSTICE McREYNOLDS delivered the opinion of the Court.

In 1906, when sixteen years old, petitioner, Volpe, entered the United States from Italy as an alien. He has resided here continuously since that time, but has remained an alien.

In 1925 he pleaded guilty and was imprisoned under a charge of counterfeiting obligations of the United States—plainly a crime involving moral turpitude.

During June, 1928, without a passport, he made a brief visit to Cuba. Returning, he landed from an airplane at Key West, Florida, and secured admission by Immigrant Inspector Phillips.

December 15, 1930, Volpe was taken into custody under a warrant issued by the Secretary of Labor which charged him with being unlawfully in this country because "he has been convicted of, or admits the commission of a felony, or other crime or misdemeanor, involving moral turpitude, to-wit: possessing and passing counterfeit U.S. War Savings Stamps, prior to his entry into the United States."

* * *

The only substantial point which we need consider is this:—Was the petitioner subject to deportation because he reëntered the United States from a foreign country after conviction, during permitted residence in the United States, of a crime committed therein which involved moral turpitude? Relevant provisions of the Act of 1917 are in the margin.*

---

2. Note that some aliens snared by the re-entry doctrine may be able to avail themselves of waivers of excludability provided in

INA § 212.

* Sec. 1. That the word "alien" wherever used in this Act shall include any person not

Upon this question federal courts have reached diverse views. The cases are cited in the opinion announced below in the present cause.

We accept the view that the word "entry" in the provision of § 19 which directs that "any alien who was convicted, or who admits the commission, prior to entry, of a felony or other crime or misdemeanor involving moral turpitude; ... shall, upon the warrant of the Secretary of Labor, be taken into custody and deported," includes any coming of an alien from a foreign country into the United States whether such coming be the first or any subsequent one. And this requires affirmance of the challenged judgment.

[margin handwriting: "entry" can apply to 1st and any subseq- entrances]

* * *

An examination of the Immigration Act of 1917, we think, reveals nothing sufficient to indicate that Congress did not intend the word "entry" in § 19 should have its ordinary meaning. Aliens who have committed crimes while permitted to remain here may be decidedly more objectionable than persons who have transgressed laws of another country.

It may be true that if Volpe had remained within the United States, he could not have been expelled because of his conviction of crime in 1925, more than five years after his original entry; but it does not follow that after he voluntarily departed he had the right of reëntry. In sufficiently plain language Congress has declared to the contrary.

The judgment is affirmed.

Note

Justice McReynolds attempts to make the result in *Volpe* appear noncontroversial. But does not his interpretation of the "sufficiently plain" statutory language make mincemeat of the statutory structure? To see this we must distinguish between two types of deportation grounds: those that help enforce exclusion provisions (*i.e.*, grounds based on conduct prior to entry) and those that concern post-entry conduct following a lawful admission.

a native-born or naturalized citizen of the United States; ...

Sec. 3. That the following classes of aliens shall be excluded from admission into the United States: ... persons who have been convicted of or admit having committed a felony or other crime or misdemeanor involving moral turpitude; ...

Sec. 19. That at any time within five years after entry, any alien who at the time of entry was a member of one or more of the classes excluded by law; any alien who shall have entered or who shall be found in the United States in violation of this Act, or in violation of any other law of the United States; ... except as hereinafter provided, any alien who is hereafter sentenced to im-

prisonment for a term of one year or more because of conviction in this country of a crime involving moral turpitude, committed within five years after the entry of the alien to the United States, or who is hereafter sentenced more than once to such a term of imprisonment because of conviction in this country of any crime involving moral turpitude, committed at any time after entry; ... any alien who was convicted, or who admits the commission, prior to entry, of a felony or other crime or misdemeanor involving moral turpitude; at any time within three years after entry, any alien ... who enters without inspection, shall, upon the warrant of the Secretary of Labor, be taken into custody and deported: ...

Conviction of a crime involving (moral turpitude) first entered the immigration laws as a ground of exclusion in (1875.) In 1903 Congress enacted a general deportation provision that required the deportation, within two years following entry, of aliens who were excludable at time of entry. This provision, accordingly, provided for the deportation of aliens who had committed crimes involving moral turpitude prior to entry but who had not been excluded at time of entry.

The 1917 Act did two things—both of which are reflected in § 19 (reprinted in the footnote to *Volpe*)—in response to demands for tougher laws against alien criminals. First, while it increased the general statute of limitations relating to application of exclusion grounds at time of admission from two to five years, it eliminated the statute of limitations altogether for crimes involving moral turpitude committed prior to entry. Second, for the first time it provided for the deportation of aliens who committed crimes after a lawful admission to the United States. The new ground required the deportation of an alien who had been "convicted in this country of a crime involving moral turpitude committed within five years after [entry, or two such convictions] committed at any time after entry."

The structure established by the 1917 Act seems plain. Aliens who committed crimes involving moral turpitude prior to their entry into the United States were excludable; and if they managed to evade exclusion at time of entry, they were deportable if caught any time after entry. Aliens convicted of such crimes in this country were treated differently. They were deportable if the conviction occurred within five years of entry; aliens who had lived here more than five years would have to be convicted twice before becoming deportable. This distinction appears to be an obvious compromise between the view that dangerous criminals should be deported and the recognition that deportation of long-term residents can work serious hardship on the alien and other persons in the United States.

Justice McReynolds' interpretation of the statute undermines this structure. By reading "entry" to mean any entry (not simply the alien's initial entry), he transforms a deportation ground intended to cover aliens excludable for acts committed prior to establishing residence in the United States into a ground that penalizes post-entry conduct. This conflicts with Congress' decision, as reflected in § 19, that aliens who have resided in the United States for more than five years should be allowed one wrongful act without triggering deportation. Justice McReynolds may be correct that "[a]liens who have committed crimes while permitted to remain here may be decidedly more objectionable than persons who have transgressed laws of another country." But he has neglected Congress' apparent conclusion that factors other than the simple commission of a crime are relevant in determining whether or not an alien should be deported. In short, the Court's creation of the re-entry doctrine undermines Congress' decision to give some protection to long-term resident aliens.

The tenuousness of the reasoning of *Volpe,* as well as the harsh consequences of the re-entry doctrine, led to calls for legislative repeal of the doctrine. Congress, however, expressly ratified the doctrine (with two exceptions discussed in the next case) when it defined "entry" in the 1952

Act to mean "*any* coming of an alien into the United States." § 101(a)(13) (emphasis supplied). As the next case demonstrates, however, "any" doesn't quite mean "any."

ROSENBERG v. FLEUTI

Supreme Court of the United States, 1963.
374 U.S. 449, 83 S.Ct. 1804, 10 L.Ed.2d 1000.

MR. JUSTICE GOLDBERG delivered the opinion of the Court.

Respondent Fleuti is a Swiss national who was originally admitted to this country for permanent residence on October 9, 1952, and has been here continuously since except for a visit of "about a couple hours" duration to Ensenada, Mexico, in August 1956. The Immigration and Naturalization Service, of which petitioner Rosenberg is the Los Angeles District Director, sought in April 1959 to deport respondent on the ground that at the time of his return in 1956 he "was within one or more of the classes of aliens excludable by the law existing at the time of such entry." In particular, the Service alleged that respondent had been "convicted of a crime involving moral turpitude" before his 1956 return, and had for that reason been excludable when he came back from his brief trip to Mexico. A deportation order issued on that ground, but it was discovered a few months later that the order was invalid, because the crime was a petty offense not of the magnitude encompassed within the statute. The deportation proceedings were thereupon reopened and a new charge was lodged against respondent: that he had been excludable at the time of his 1956 return as an alien "afflicted with psychopathic personality," § 212(a)(4),[a] by reason of the fact that he was a homosexual. Deportation was ordered on this ground and Fleuti's appeal to the Board of Immigration Appeals was dismissed, whereupon he brought the present action for declaratory judgment and review of the administrative action. It was stipulated that among the issues to be litigated was the question whether § 212(a)(4) is "unconstitutional as being vague and ambiguous." The trial court rejected respondent's contentions in this regard and in general, and granted the Government's motion for summary judgment. On appeal, however, the United States Court of Appeals for the Ninth Circuit set aside the deportation order and enjoined its enforcement, holding that as applied to Fleuti § 212(a)(4) was unconstitutionally vague in that homosexuality was not sufficiently encompassed within the term "psychopathic personality." 302 F.2d 652.

The Government petitioned this Court for certiorari, which we granted in order to consider the constitutionality of § 212(a)(4) as applied to respondent Fleuti. Upon consideration of the case, however, and in accordance with the long-established principle that "we ought not to pass on questions of constitutionality ... unless such adjudication is unavoidable," *Spector Motor Service, Inc. v. McLaughlin*, 323 U.S. 101, 105, 65 S.Ct. 152, 154, 89 L.Ed. 101; we have concluded that there is a threshold issue of statutory interpretation in the case, the existence of which obviates deci-

---

a. This ground of exclusion was repealed by the Immigration Act of 1990.—eds.

sion here as to whether § 212(a)(4) is constitutional as applied to respondent.

That issue is whether Fleuti's return to the United States from his afternoon trip to Ensenada, Mexico, in August 1956 constituted an "entry" within the meaning of § 101(a)(13) of the Immigration and Nationality Act of 1952, such that Fleuti was excludable for a condition existing at that time even though he had been permanently and continuously resident in this country for nearly four years prior thereto. * * * The question we must consider, more specifically, is whether Fleuti's short visit to Mexico can possibly be regarded as a "departure to a foreign port or place ... [that] was not intended," within the meaning of the exception to the term "entry" created by the statute. Whether the 1956 return was within that exception is crucial, because Fleuti concededly was not excludable as a "psychopathic personality" at the time of his 1952 entry.[2]

The definition of "entry" as applied for various purposes in our immigration laws was evolved judicially, only becoming encased in statutory form with the inclusion of § 101(a)(13) in the 1952 Act. In the early cases there was developed a judicial definition of "entry" which had harsh consequences for aliens. This viewpoint was expressed most restrictively in *United States ex rel. Volpe* v. *Smith* * * *. Although cases in the lower courts applying the strict re-entry doctrine to aliens who had left the country for brief visits to Canada or Mexico or elsewhere were numerous, many courts applied the doctrine in such instances with express reluctance and explicit recognition of its harsh consequences, and there were a few instances in which district judges refused to hold that aliens who had been absent from the country only briefly had made "entries" upon their return.

Reaction to the severe effects produced by adherence to the strict definition of "entry" resulted in a substantial inroad being made upon that definition in 1947 by a decision of the Second Circuit and a decision of this Court. The Second Circuit, in an opinion by Judge Learned Hand, refused to allow a deportation which depended on the alien's being regarded as having re-entered this country after having taken an overnight sleeper from Buffalo to Detroit on a route lying through Canada. *Di Pasquale* v. *Karnuth,* 158 F.2d 878. Judge Hand recognized that the alien "acquiesced in whatever route the railroad might choose to pull the car," *id.,* at 879, but held that it would be too harsh to impute the carrier's intent to the alien, there being no showing that the alien knew he would be entering Canada. "Were it otherwise," Judge Hand went on, "the alien would be subjected without means of protecting himself to the forfeiture of privileges which may be, and often are, of the most grave importance to him." *Ibid.* If there were a duty upon aliens to inquire about a carrier's route, it "would in practice become a trap, whose closing upon them would have no

2. The 1952 Act became effective on December 24, 1952, and Fleuti entered the country for permanent residence on October 9, 1952, a fact which is of significance because the Act only commands the deportation of aliens "excludable by the law existing at the time of such entry...." Hence, since respondent's homosexuality did not make him excludable by any law existing at the time of his 1952 entry, it is critical to determine whether his return from a few hours in Mexico in 1956 was an "entry" in the statutory sense. If it was not, the question whether § 212(a)(4) could constitutionally be applied to him need not be resolved.

rational relation to anything they could foresee as significant. We cannot believe that Congress meant to subject those who had acquired a residence, to the sport of chance, when the interests at stake may be so momentous." *Ibid.* Concluding, Judge Hand said that if the alien's return were held to be an "entry" under the circumstances, his "vested interest in his residence" would

> "be forfeited because of perfectly lawful conduct which he could not possibly have supposed would result in anything of the sort. Caprice in the incidence of punishment is one of the indicia of tyranny, and nothing can be more disingenuous than to say that deportation in these circumstances is not punishment. It is well that we should be free to rid ourselves of those who abuse our hospitality; but it is more important that the continued enjoyment of that hospitality once granted, shall not be subject to meaningless and irrational hazards." *Ibid.*

Later the same year this Court, because of a conflict between *Di Pasquale* and *Del Guercio* v. *Delgadillo,* 159 F.2d 130 (C.A. 9th Cir.1947), granted certiorari in the latter case and reversed a deportation order affecting an alien who, upon rescue after his intercoastal merchant ship was torpedoed in the Caribbean during World War II, had been taken to Cuba to recuperate for a week before returning to this country. *Delgadillo* v. *Carmichael,* 332 U.S. 388, 68 S.Ct. 10, 92 L.Ed. 17. The Court pointed out that it was "the exigencies of war, not his voluntary act," *id.,* at 391, which put the alien on foreign soil, adding that "[w]e might as well hold that if he had been kidnapped and taken to Cuba, he made a statutory 'entry' on his voluntary return. Respect for law does not thrive on captious interpretations." *Ibid.* Since "[t]he stakes are indeed high and momentous for the alien who has acquired his residence here," *ibid.,* the Court held that

> "[w]e will not attribute to Congress a purpose to make his right to remain here dependent on circumstances so fortuitous and capricious as those upon which the Immigration Service has here seized. The hazards to which we are now asked to subject the alien are too irrational to square with the statutory scheme." *Ibid.*

* * *

It was in light of all of these developments in the case law that § 101(a)(13) was included in the immigration laws with the 1952 revision. As the House and Senate Committee Reports * * * make clear, the major congressional concern in codifying the definition of "entry" was with "the status of an alien who has previously entered the United States and resided therein. . . ." This concern was in the direction of ameliorating the harsh results visited upon resident aliens by the rule of *United States ex rel. Volpe* v. *Smith, supra,* as is indicated by the recognition that "the courts have departed from the rigidity of . . . [the earlier] rule," and the statement that "[t]he bill . . . [gives] due recognition to the judicial precedents." It must be recognized, of course, that the only liberalizing decisions to which the Reports referred specifically were *Di Pasquale* and *Delgadillo,* and that there is no indication one way or the other in the legislative history of what Congress thought about the problem of resident aliens who leave the country for insignificantly short periods of time. Nevertheless, it requires but brief consideration of the policies underlying § 101(a)(13), and of certain other aspects of the rights of returning resident aliens, to conclude that Congress, in approving the judicial undermining of *Volpe, supra,* and the relief brought about by the *Di Pasquale* and *Delgadillo* decisions, could not have meant to limit the meaning of the exceptions it created in § 101(a)(13) to the facts of those two cases.

The most basic guide to congressional intent as to the reach of the exceptions is the eloquent language of *Di Pasquale* and *Delgadillo* themselves, beginning with the recognition that the "interests at stake" for the resident alien are "momentous," 158 F.2d, at 879, and that "[t]he stakes are indeed high and momentous for the alien who has acquired his residence here," 332 U.S., at 391, 68 S.Ct. at 12. This general premise of the two decisions impelled the more general conclusion that "it is ... important that the continued enjoyment of ... [our] hospitality once granted, shall not be subject to meaningless and irrational hazards." 158 F.2d, at 879. See also *Delgadillo, supra,* at 391. Coupling these essential principles of the two decisions explicitly approved by Congress in enacting § 101(a)(13) with the more general observation, appearing in *Delgadillo* as well as elsewhere, that "[d]eportation can be the equivalent of banishment or exile," it is difficult to conceive that Congress meant its approval of the liberalization wrought by *Di Pasquale* and *Delgadillo* to be interpreted mechanistically to apply only to cases presenting factual situations identical to what was involved in those two decisions.

The idea that the exceptions to § 101(a)(13) should be read nonrestrictively is given additional credence by the way in which the immigration laws define what constitutes "continuous residence" for an alien wishing to be naturalized. Section 316 of the 1952 Act, 66 Stat. 242–243, 8 U.S.C. § 1427, which liberalized previous law in some respects, provides that an alien who wishes to seek naturalization does not begin to endanger the five years of "continuous residence" in this country which must precede his application until he remains outside the country for six months, and does not damage his position by cumulative temporary absences unless they total over half of the five years preceding the filing of his petition for naturalization. This enlightened concept of what constitutes a meaningful interruption of the continuous residence which must support a petition for naturalization, reflecting as it does a congressional judgment that an alien's status is not necessarily to be endangered by his absence from the country, strengthens the foundation underlying a belief that the exceptions to § 101(a)(13) should be read to protect resident aliens who are only briefly absent from the country. Of further, although less specific, effect in this regard is this Court's holding in *Kwong Hai Chew* v. *Colding,* 344 U.S. 590, 73 S.Ct. 472, 97 L.Ed. 576, that the returning resident alien is entitled as a matter of due process to a hearing on the charges underlying any attempt to exclude him, a holding which supports the general proposition that a resident alien who leaves this country is to be regarded as retaining certain basic rights.

Given that the congressional protection of returning resident aliens in § 101(a)(13) is not to be woodenly construed, we turn specifically to construction of the exceptions contained in that section as they relate to resident aliens who leave the country briefly. What we face here is another harsh consequence of the strict "entry" doctrine which, while not governed directly by *Delgadillo,* nevertheless calls into play the same considerations which led to the results specifically approved in the Congressional Committee Reports. It would be as "fortuitous and capricious," and as "irrational to square with the statutory scheme," *Delgadillo, supra,* at 391, to hold that an alien may necessarily be deported because he falls into one of the classes enumerated in § 212(a) when he returns from "a couple hours" visit to Mexico as it would have been to uphold the order of deportation in *Delgadillo.* Certainly when an alien like Fleuti who has entered the country lawfully and has acquired a residence here steps across a border and, in effect, steps right back, subjecting him to exclusion for a condition for which he could not have been deported had he remained in the country seems to be placing him at the mercy of the "sport of chance" and the "meaningless and irrational hazards" to which Judge Hand alluded. *Di Pasquale, supra,* at 879. In making such a casual trip the alien would seldom be aware that he was possibly walking into a trap, for the insignificance of a brief trip to Mexico or Canada bears little rational relation to the punitive consequence of subsequent excludability. There are, of course, valid policy reasons for saying that an alien wishing to retain his classification as a permanent resident of this country imperils his status by interrupting his residence too frequently or for an overly long period of time, but we discern no rational policy supporting application of a re-entry limitation in all cases in which a resident alien crosses an international border for a short visit. Certainly if that trip is innocent, casual, and brief, it is consistent with all the discernible signs of congressional purpose to hold that the "departure ... was not intended" within the meaning and ameliorative intent of the exception to § 101(a)(13). Congress unquestionably has the power to exclude all classes of undesirable aliens from this country, and the courts are charged with enforcing such exclusion when Congress has directed it, but we do not think Congress intended to exclude aliens long resident in this country after lawful entry who have merely stepped across an international border and returned in "about a couple of hours." Such a holding would be inconsistent with the general purpose of Congress in enacting § 101(a)(13) to ameliorate the severe effects of the strict "entry" doctrine.

We conclude, then, that it effectuates congressional purpose to construe the intent exception to § 101(a)(13) as meaning an intent to depart in a manner which can be regarded as meaningfully interruptive of the alien's permanent residence. One major factor relevant to whether such intent can be inferred is, of course, the length of time the alien is absent. Another is the purpose of the visit, for if the purpose of leaving the country is to accomplish some object which is itself contrary to some policy reflected in our immigration laws, it would appear that the interruption of residence thereby occurring would properly be regarded as meaningful. Still another is whether the alien has to procure any travel documents in order to make his trip, since the need to obtain such items might well cause the alien to consider more fully the implications involved in his leaving the country. Although the operation of these and other possibly relevant factors remains to be developed "by the gradual process of judicial inclusion and exclusion," *Davidson* v. *New Orleans,* 96 U.S. 97, 104, 24 L.Ed. 616, we declare today simply that an innocent, casual, and brief excursion by a resident alien outside this country's borders may not have been "intended" as a departure disruptive of his resident alien status and therefore may not subject him to the consequences of an "entry" into the country on his return. The more civilized application of our immigration laws given recognition by Congress in § 101(a)(13) and other provisions of the 1952 Act protects the resident alien from unsuspected risks and unintended consequences of such a wholly innocent action. Respondent here, so far as appears from the record, is among those to be protected. However, because attention was not previously focused upon the application of § 101(a)(13) to the case, the record contains no detailed description or characterization of his trip to Mexico in 1956, except for his testimony that he was gone "about a couple hours," and that he was "just visiting; taking a trip." That being the case, we deem it appropriate to remand the case for further consideration of the application of § 101(a)(13) to this case in light of our discussion herein. If it is determined that respondent did not "intend" to depart in the sense contemplated by § 101(a)(13), the deportation order will not stand and adjudication of the constitutional issue reached by the court below will be obviated. The judgment of the Court of Appeals is therefore vacated and the case remanded with directions that the parties be given leave to amend their pleadings to put in issue the question of "entry" in accordance with the foregoing, and for further proceedings consistent herewith.

So ordered.

Mr. Justice Clark, with whom Mr. Justice Harlan, Mr. Justice Stewart and Mr. Justice White join, dissenting.

I dissent from the Court's judgment and opinion because "statutory construction" means to me that the Court can *construe* statutes but not that it can *construct* them. The latter function is reserved to the Congress, which clearly said what it meant and undoubtedly meant what it said when it defined "entry" for immigration purposes * * *. * * * That this definition of "entry" includes the respondent's entry after his brief trip to Mexico in 1956 is a conclusion which seems to me inescapable. The conclusion is compelled by the plain meaning of the statute, its legislative history, and the consistent interpretation by the federal courts. Indeed, the respondent himself did not even question that his return to the United States was an "entry" within the meaning of § 101(a)(13). Nonetheless, the Court has rewritten the Act *sua sponte,* creating a definition of "entry" which was suggested by many organizations during the hearings prior to its enactment but which was rejected by the Congress. I believe the authorities discussed in the Court's opinion demonstrate that "entry" as defined in § 101(a)(13) cannot mean what the Court says it means, but I will add a few words of explanation.

The word "entry" had acquired a well-defined meaning for immigration purposes at the time the Immigration and Nationality Act was passed in 1952. The leading case was *United States ex rel. Volpe* v. *Smith.* * * *

The federal courts in numerous cases were called upon to apply this definition of "entry" and did so consistently, specifically recognizing that the brevity of one's stay outside the country was immaterial to the question of whether his return was an "entry." A related but obviously distinguishable question did create difficulties for the courts, however, leading to conflicting opinions among the Circuits as to whether a resident alien makes an "entry" when he had no intent to leave the country or did not leave voluntarily. It was decided by this Court in *Delgadillo* v. *Carmichael*, 332 U.S. 388, 68 S.Ct. 10, 92 L.Ed. 17 (1947), which held that an alien whose ship had been torpedoed and sunk, after which he was rescued and taken to Cuba for a week, did not make an "entry" on his return to the United States. The Court discussed the *Volpe* case but distinguished it and others on the ground that "those were cases where the alien plainly expected or planned to enter a foreign port or place. Here he was catapulted into the ocean, rescued, and taken to Cuba. He had no part in selecting the foreign port as his destination." *Id.,* at 390, 68 S.Ct. at 12. The Court specifically relied on *Di Pasquale* v. *Karnuth*, 158 F.2d 878 (C.A. 2d Cir.1947), where an alien who had ridden a sleeping car from Buffalo to Detroit, without knowledge that the train's route was through Canada, was held not to have made an "entry" upon his arrival in Detroit.

These cases and others discussed by the Court establish the setting in which the Immigration and Nationality Act was passed in 1952. The House and Senate reports quoted by the Court show that the Congress recognized the courts' difficulty with the rule that "any coming" of an alien into the United States was an "entry," even when the departure from the country was unintentional or involuntary. The reports discuss the broad rule of the *Volpe* case and the specific limitations of the *Di Pasquale* and *Delgadillo* cases, citing those cases by name. * * *

Thus there is nothing in the legislative history or in the statute itself which would exempt the respondent's return from Mexico from the definition of "entry." Rather, the statute in retaining the definition expressed in *Volpe* seems clearly to cover respondent's entry, which occurred after he knowingly left the United States in order to travel to a city in Mexico. That the trip may have been "innocent, casual, and brief" does not alter the fact that, in the words of the Court in *Delgadillo*, the respondent "plainly expected or planned to enter a foreign port or place." 332 U.S., at 390, 68 S.Ct. at 12.

It is true that this application of the law to a resident alien may be harsh, but harshness is a far cry from the irrationality condemned in *Delgadillo, supra*, at 391, 68 S.Ct. at 12. There and in *Di Pasquale* contrary results would have meant that a resident alien, who was not deportable unless he left the country and reentered, could be deported as a result of circumstances either beyond his control or beyond his knowledge. Here, of course, there is no claim that respondent did not know he was leaving the country to enter Mexico and, since one is presumed to know the law, he knew that his brief trip and reentry would render him deportable. The Congress clearly has chosen so to apply the long-established definition, and this Court cannot alter that legislative determination in the guise of statutory construction. Had the Congress not wished the definition of "entry" to include a return after a brief but voluntary and intentional trip, it could have done so. The Court's discussion of § 316 of the Act shows that the Congress knows well how to temper rigidity when it wishes. Nor can it be said that the Congress was unaware of the breadth of its definition. Even aside from the evidence that it was aware of the judicial precedents, numerous organizations unsuccessfully urged that the definition be narrowed to accomplish what the Court does today. Thus, it was urged that the Act's definition of "entry" "should, we believe, be narrowed so that it will not be applicable to an alien returning from abroad, after a temporary absence, to an unrelinquished domicile here." Other groups complained also that "[t]he term 'entry' is defined to mean any coming of an alien into the United States. It is recommended that this be narrowed to provide that a return, after a temporary absence, to an unrelinquished domicile, shall not constitute a new entry." Despite such urging, however, the Congress made no change in the definition. * * *

All this to the contrary notwithstanding, the Court today decides that one does not really intend to leave the country unless he plans a long trip, or his journey is for an illegal purpose, or he needs travel documents in order to make the trip. This is clearly contrary to the definition in the Act and to any definition of "intent" that I was taught.

What the Court should do is proceed to the only question which either party sought to resolve: whether the deportation order deprived respondent of due process of law in that the term "afflicted with psychopathic personality," as it appears in § 212(a)(4) of the Act, is unconstitutionally vague. Since it fails to do so, I must dissent.

Notes

1. Should *Fleuti* be seen as an embarrassment to the United States Supreme Court? Isn't the dissent clearly correct that the majority rewrote the statute along the lines of proposals made to, but rejected by, Congress?

What do you make of the fact that Congress has not overturned the Court's interpretation of the statute in *Fleuti?* Does it indicate acquiescence or unconcern? What is the legal effect of a subsequent Congress' acquiescence in an incorrect decision by the Court as to a prior Congress' intent? May a subsequent Congress, in effect, amend the statute by not acting? *See generally* Eskridge, *Interpreting Legislative Inaction,* 87 Mich. L.Rev. 67 (1988).

2. What do you think motivated the decision of the Court: An appreciation of how Congress, if it had thought about the situation, would have wanted the statute to be interpreted? Concern for the particular alien? Adherence to the principle in *Fong Haw Tan?* Unhappiness with the underlying ground of exclusion? Belated unhappiness with the reentry doctrine?

Consider Hiroshi Motomura's analysis of *Fleuti*:

[T]he majority's *Fleuti* opinion * * * evinces sympathy for the view that immigration law inadequately recognized a permanent resident's stake in remaining in the United States. This observation explains several aspects of the opinion: the focus on the harshness of the leading reentry doctrine case, *United States* ex rel. *Volpe v. Smith,* and on the hardships that Fleuti would suffer if deported, citation to *Chew* for the observation that "a resident alien who leaves this country is to be regarded as retaining certain basic rights"; and the call for "more civilized application of our immigration laws. . . ." But * * * the constitutional norm that guided *Fleuti* 's reading of "entry" was a phantom, which in turn explains why the Court decided the case by interpreting "entry" in the statute, rather than by striking down the statute as unconstitutional. No decision of the Court had openly recognized procedural due process rights for an alien seeking entry, not even for a returning permanent resident. Indeed, *Mezei* had suggested and perhaps even held to the contrary. Still, the phantom norm of procedural due process for returning permanent residents was close enough to the constitutional horizon that it is unsurprising that the Court adopted it as a guide to statutory interpretation. Using this norm, the Court construed "entry" to recognize stake, even if prevailing doctrine did not permit a direct constitutional holding.

This interpretation of *Fleuti,* Motomura concludes, renders the case a milestone in the shift in constitutional doctrine from *Mezei* to *Landon v. Plasencia,* which recognized due process rights on behalf of returning resident aliens. Motomura, *Immigration Law After a Century of Plenary Power: Phantom Constitutional Norms and Statutory Interpretation,* 100 Yale L.J. 545, 577 (1990). Do you agree?

3. A related explanation for the result in *Fleuti* is that the Court read the statute as it did in order to avoid having to rule on the *substantive* constitutional issue in the case—*i.e.,* whether the exclusion ground was unconstitutionally vague. As Justice Goldberg notes in *Fleuti,* it is a well-established principle that the court will not consider a constitutional issue when the case may be decided on a nonconstitutional ground:

This Court has said repeatedly that it ought not pass on the constitutionality of an act of Congress unless such adjudication is unavoidable. This is true even though the question is properly presented by the record. If two questions are raised, one of non-constitutional and the other of constitutional nature, and a decision of the non-constitutional question would make unnecessary a decision of the constitutional question, the former will be decided.

Alma Motor Co. v. Timken–Detroit Axle Co., 329 U.S. 129, 136, 67 S.Ct. 231, 234, 91 L.Ed. 128 (1946).

Should the Court adopt a preference for nonconstitutional grounds of decision? Usually, such a rule is defended on the grounds that constitutional decisions implicate separation of powers concerns and are harder to change. A holding of unconstitutionality may also jeopardize other similar state and federal legislation. Does a rule favoring nonconstitutional grounds of decision justify the result in *Fleuti?* Is the process of legislation always better served by a nonconstitutional answer (which may well distort congressional intent) than a constitutional one? *See generally* Motomura, *supra,* at 600–13.

Interestingly, the Supreme Court considered the constitutional issue avoided in *Fleuti* four years later in *Boutilier v. INS,* 387 U.S. 118, 87 S.Ct. 1563, 18 L.Ed.2d 661 (1967). It ruled, in a 6–to–3 decision written by Justice Clark, that the statutory provision was not unconstitutionally vague.[3] The membership of the Court in 1967 was the same as in 1963, except Justice Goldberg had been succeeded by Justice Fortas. Does this cast doubt on the *bona fides* of the *Fleuti* majority's use of the canon of construction that constitutional issues are to be avoided? It seems, does it not, that a majority of the Court was not prepared to hold the statute unconstitutional, yet a majority desired to rule in the alien's favor; this led the Court to adopt a dubious interpretation of the statute which it then purported to justify on the ground that it was avoiding a constitutional issue. In fact, however, under then-prevailing constitutional doctrine, both the procedural due process and void-for-vagueness issues really did not exist, and were in fact were based on "phantom norms." *See* Motomura, *supra*, at 577–78.

Applying *Fleuti*

1. While the preceding discussion raises important issues of statutory interpretation, they are largely academic as far as *Fleuti* goes. Whether or not it is possible to defend the decision, its exception to the re-entry doctrine has become firmly imbedded in the law. Indeed, INS Operations Instructions regarding inspection of returning residents provide that interrogation of a "returning resident alien suspected of being inadmissible * * * shall cover, but not be limited to: (1) length of absence and frequency of prior absences, if any; (2) reason for absence; (3) documentation required or obtained; (4) itinerary, and (5) alien's understanding as to his immigration status and admissibility." INS Operations Instruction 235.1k.

2. *Fleuti* raised more questions than it answered. How does one decide whether a trip across the border was "meaningfully interruptive of the alien's permanent residence"? Justice Goldberg recommended some guidelines at the end of the opinion, each of which has spawned extensive litigation. The results are diverse and difficult to predict.

With the *Fleuti* issue decided on a case-by-case basis, abstract statements of guiding principles are no substitute for working with specific facts. Consider the following situations (the first three are drawn from published opinions with the names unchanged):

---

3. Even in the deportation context, constitutional void-for-vagueness challenges have been unsuccessful, as Chapter Six will examine more fully.

a. Munoz had been a lawful permanent resident for thirteen years when went to Mexico on a trip for which he had planned and saved for five years. He traveled to Durango, a distance of about 1000 miles into the interior of Mexico, where he visited his parents and a sister who was ill. He was absent from the United States for about one month. Five months after his return, he was convicted of a crime. Does Munoz' trip fit within the *Fleuti* exception? If not, he will be deportable under INA § 241(a)(2)(A)(i).

b. Four years ago, Jubilado, a citizen of the Philippines, was admitted to the United States as a permanent resident, along with two of his children. About fifteen months later, Jubilado left for the Philippines to bring his wife and four remaining children to the United States. He returned with them about three months later. Nine months after his return, he was convicted of a crime that he committed before his trip to the Philippines. He served all of a nine-month sentence. Does Jubilado's trip fit within the *Fleuti* exception?

c. Vargas, 41–year-old Mexican national, was admitted to the United States as a permanent resident seven years ago. Since then, he has lived in Colorado with his wife and four children, the youngest of whom is a native-born United States citizen. Vargas traveled to Juarez, Mexico, for two days to pay a condolence call on the family of a cousin who had recently passed away. Before departing Mexico, Vargas was approached by four Mexicans who sought his help in entering without inspection and procuring transportation to Chicago. Vargas accepted money from the four and made arrangements for them to be assisted by others in their journey northward. The group was apprehended by immigration officers after crossing the border surreptitiously. Does Vargas' trip fit within the *Fleuti* exception?

d. Now assume that Vargas did not become involved in alien smuggling. Instead, he saw the long lines on the bridge from Juarez to El Paso, Texas, and to avoid them he simply crossed the border by wading the Rio Grande. Does Vargas' trip fit within the *Fleuti* exception?

3. Fleuti was a permanent resident alien. Does the *Fleuti* exception apply to nonimmigrants as well? The BIA has consistently said no. *Matter of Chavez–Calderon*, Int.Dec. 3212 (1993); *Matter of Mundell,* 18 I & N Dec. 467 (BIA 1983). *Accord, Mendoza v. INS*, 16 F.3d 335, 337 (9th Cir.1994). *But cf. Campos v. Smith*, 791 F.Supp. 262, 264–65 (W.D.Wash. 1991) (applying *Fleuti* exception to legalization applicant).

The Ripples of *Fleuti*

Congress, as mentioned above, has shown no inclination to overturn *Fleuti*. Indeed, it has applied *Fleuti*'s concept of a "meaningful interruption" of an alien's residence to other immigration contexts. For example, Congress required that aliens applying for lawful status under IRCA's general legalization program establish continuous physical presence in the United States since November 6, 1986 (the date of IRCA's enactment). The statute provided, however, that "brief, casual, and innocent absences from the United States" are not considered to breach the continuous physical presence requirement. INA § 245A(a)(3)(B). *See also* § 244A(c)(4) ("brief, casual and innocent absences" do not violate continuous presence requirement for "temporary protected status").

Section 244(a)(1) of the INA, discussed in detail in Chapter Seven, provides relief from deportation for certain deportable aliens who have been "physically present in the United States for a continuous period" of seven years. In *INS v. Phinpathya,* 464 U.S. 183, 104 S.Ct. 584, 78 L.Ed.2d 401 (1984), the Supreme Court rejected lower court holdings that the section's continuous physical presence requirement is subject to *Fleuti's* exception for "brief, casual, and innocent" absences. The Court held that any absence, no matter how brief, would end the running of the seven year period. Congress, however, overturned the Court's decision, adding the following language to § 244(b)(2):

> An alien shall not be considered to have failed to maintain continuous physical presence * * * if the absence from the United States was brief, casual, and innocent and did not meaningfully interrupt the continuous physical presence.

These legislative developments seem to lend congressional support to the Court's reasoning and result in *Fleuti.* Can such post-legislation (and post-judicial decision) history help to justify a ruling purportedly based on the intent of an earlier Congress?

Where Is the *Fleuti* Question Resolved?

The re-entry doctrine's harsh consequences—and the possibility of rescue by *Fleuti*—can arise in either exclusion or deportation. To illustrate the exclusion scenario, assume that permanent resident Alien V, returning from an overseas trip, is stopped at the border due to a drug conviction. She has not made an "entry" back into the United States under *Matter of Pierre.* If the INS successfully argues that the trip was "meaningfully interruptive" of her permanent residence, V is excludable under INA § 212(a)(2)(A)(i)(II). Similarly, if Volpe had been stopped at the border when he returned from Cuba in 1928, he would have been excluded for his 1925 conviction.

In this scenario, does keeping V in exclusion to decide the *Fleuti* issue illogically assume what must be proved? The Supreme Court considered this question in *Landon v. Plasencia,* 459 U.S. 21, 103 S.Ct. 321, 74 L.Ed.2d 21 (1982), a case which we have already examined in the consideration of due process in exclusion proceedings.

Recall that Plasencia was a returning resident alien stopped at the border after a brief trip to Mexico. The INS discovered six undocumented aliens in her car, and subsequently sought to exclude her for aiding the illegal entry of an alien. Plasencia asserted that she was entitled to have the issue of whether her trip to Mexico came within the *Fleuti* exception to the re-entry doctrine determined in a deportation proceeding. The Supreme Court disagreed:

> Our analysis of whether [Plasencia] is entitled to a deportation rather than an exclusion hearing begins with the language of the

Act. Section 235 of the Act, permits the INS to examine *"[a]ll aliens"* who seek "admission or *readmission* to" the United States and empowers immigration officers to take evidence concerning the privilege of any person suspected of being an alien "to enter, *reenter,* pass through, or reside" in the United States. *Ibid.* (emphasis added). Moreover, "every alien" who does not appear "to be clearly and beyond a doubt entitled to land shall be detained" for further inquiry. *Ibid.* If an alien is so detained, the Act directs the special inquiry officer to determine whether the arriving alien "shall be allowed to enter or shall be excluded and deported." Section 236(a). The proceeding before that officer, the exclusion hearing, is by statute "the sole and exclusive procedure for determining admissibility of a person to the United States...." *Ibid.*

The Act's legislative history also emphasizes the singular role of exclusion hearings in determining whether an alien should be admitted. The reports of both the House and Senate state:

> The special inquiry officer is empowered to determine whether an alien detained for further inquiry shall be excluded and deported or shall be allowed to enter after he has given the alien a hearing. The procedure established in the bill is made the sole and exclusive procedure for determining the admissibility of a person to the United States.

S.Rep. No. 1137, 82d Cong., 2d Sess., 29 (1952); H.R.Rep. No. 1365, 82d Cong., 2d Sess., 56 (1952).

The language and history of the Act thus clearly reflect a congressional intent that, whether or not the alien is a permanent resident, admissibility shall be determined in an exclusion hearing. Nothing in the statutory language or the legislative history suggests that the respondent's status as a permanent resident entitles her to a suspension of the exclusion hearing or requires the INS to proceed only through a deportation hearing. Under the terms of the Act, the INS properly proceeded in an exclusion hearing to determine whether respondent was attempting to "enter" the United States and whether she was excludable.

To avoid the impact of the statute, the respondent contends, and the Court of Appeals agreed, that unless she was "entering," she was not subject to exclusion proceedings, and that prior decisions of this Court indicate that she is entitled to have the question of "entry" decided in deportation proceedings.

The parties agree that only "entering" aliens are subject to exclusion. That view accords with the language of the statute, which describes the exclusion hearing as one to determine whether the applicant "shall be allowed to *enter* or shall be excluded and deported." Section 236(a) (emphasis added). But the respondent's contention that the question of entry can be determined only in deportation proceedings reflects a misconception of our decisions.

* * *

The Court of Appeals [below] viewed *Fleuti* as a deportation case rather than an exclusion case and therefore not relevant in deciding whether the question of "entry" could be determined in exclusion proceedings. For guidance on that decision, the Court of Appeals turned to *Kwong Hai Chew v. Colding,* 344 U.S. 590, 73 S.Ct. 472, 97 L.Ed. 576 (1953), which it read to hold that a resident alien returning from a brief trip "could not be excluded without the procedural due process to which he would have been entitled had he never left the country"—*i.e.,* in this case, a deportation proceeding. The court concluded that Plasencia was entitled to litigate her admissibility in deportation proceedings. It would be "circular" and "unfair," thought the court, to allow the INS to litigate the question of "entry" in exclusion proceedings when that question also went to the merits of the respondent's admissibility.

We disagree. The reasoning of *Chew* was only that a resident alien returning from a brief trip has a right to due process just as would a continuously present resident alien. It does not create a right to identical treatment for these two differently situated groups of aliens. As the Ninth Circuit seemed to recognize, if the respondent here was making an "entry," she would be subject to exclusion proceedings. It is no more "circular" to allow the immigration judge in the exclusion proceeding to determine whether the alien is making an entry than it is for any court to decide that it has jurisdiction when the facts relevant to the determination of jurisdiction are also relevant to the merits. Thus, in *United States v. Sing Tuck,* 194 U.S. 161, 24 S.Ct. 621, 48 L.Ed. 917 (1904), this Court held that an immigration inspector could make a determination whether an applicant for admission was an alien or a citizen, although only aliens were subject to exclusion. *Cf. Land v. Dollar,* 330 U.S. 731, 739, 67 S.Ct. 1009, 1013, 91 L.Ed. 1209 (1947) (district court has jurisdiction to determine its jurisdiction by proceeding to a decision on the merits). Nor is it in any way "unfair" to decide the question of entry in exclusion proceedings as long as those proceedings themselves are fair. Finally, the use of exclusion proceedings violates neither the "scope" nor the "spirit" of *Fleuti.* As the Court of Appeals held, that case only defined "entry" and did not designate the forum for deciding questions of entry. The statutory scheme is clear: Congress intended that the determinations of both "entry" and the existence of grounds for exclusion could be made at an exclusion hearing.

Id. at 27–32, 103 S.Ct. at 325–29. Although Justice Marshall dissented from other portions of the Court's opinion, he concurred in the conclusion that the INA authorized the INS to proceed against Plasencia in an exclusion proceeding.

Suppose the exclusion hearing contemplated in *Plasencia* determines that V's trip was within the *Fleuti* exception and therefore she did not re-enter. V has avoided exclusion, but she will live happily ever after only if there is no deportation ground for drug convictions. But there is, and it applies whether or not V re-entered; V is deportable under § 241(a)(2)(B)(i).

The re-entry doctrine and the *Fleuti* issue can also arise in deportation. Assume permanent resident Alien T has committed a crime; he is convicted and serves time in prison. Later, T takes a month-long vacation in France; he flies home and is inspected and admitted at the port of entry. T has "entered" under *Matter of Pierre*, so it is too late for the INS to exclude him. Now assume further that the INS initiates deportation proceedings and persuades the immigration judge that T's trip was not within the *Fleuti* exception and therefore his return was a re-entry. Now T faces two potential problems.

First, if T was excludable under INA § 212(a)(2)(A) when he returned from France, he is deportable under INA § 241(a)(1)(A), as having been excludable at entry, even he was not excludable at any earlier time that he entered the United States. Similarly, if Fleuti's trip had "meaningfully interrupted" his permanent residency, then his return in 1956 would have been a re-entry, and he would have deportable as having been excludable at that time. (When Fleuti first came to the United States in 1952, there was no exclusion ground for homosexuality.)

Second, assume that T's crime did not involve moral turpitude. He would then not have been excludable when he returned from France, so he is not now deportable under INA § 241(a)(1)(A). T's re-entry still restarts the time period under the deportation ground for crimes of moral turpitude within five years after entry. *See* INA § 241(a)(2)(A)(i)(1). If T commits a crime involving moral turpitude four years later, T may become deportable, even if more than five years would have elapsed since T's original admission as a permanent resident. This would have been Volpe's problem if he had committed his offense three years after his return from Cuba instead of three years before.

Can these results be defended? If T had taken his vacation in Montana, he would not be deportable.

To close out the deportation scenario, assume instead that the immigration judge finds that T's trip is within the *Fleuti* exception and therefore his return is not a re-entry. If there is no analogous deportation ground, T lives happily ever after. In *Fleuti*, for example, there was no deportation ground for homosexuality, so Fleuti was able to stay. If, however, there is an analogous deportation ground that is not time-limited, T remains deportable.

The harshness of these results can be ameliorated by INA § 244, which grants, under certain circumstances, suspension of deportation to long-term residents; or by INA § 212(c), which allows waiver of certain grounds of deportability for long-term permanent resident aliens. These provisions will be discussed more fully in Chapter Seven.

Proposals to Modify the Re–Entry Doctrine

1. Although the *Fleuti* decision has blunted some of the criticism, the re-entry doctrine remains controversial. In its 1981 report, an eight-member majority of the Select Commission on Immigration and Refugee Policy recommended that the doctrine be modified so that returning permanent residents would not be subject to exclusion grounds, except for criminal exclusion grounds for convictions while abroad, political exclusion grounds, entry without inspection, and engaging in persecution. Three members voted to amend current law only to include a detailed statutory definition of what constitutes innocent, casual, and brief trips abroad. Two members voted to eliminate the re-entry doctrine entirely.

2. Had you been a Commissioner, how would you have voted? Why? Before you leap to the conclusion that the doctrine should be discarded in its entirety, consider the following situations:

(a) Alien E is a permanent resident. E takes a two week trip to Costa Rica and commits a crime involving moral turpitude.

(b) Alien N, after attaining lawful permanent resident status, leaves the United States and re-enters without inspection.

(c) Alien T, a nonimmigrant student, leaves the United States for spring vacation. The FBI learns that T is making plans to return with arms and plans for terrorist activity in the United States.

(d) Alien R, a permanent resident alien, was a Nazi and is deportable under § 241(a)(4)(D). R leaves the country for a few weeks. If his return is deemed to be an entry, he is excludable under § 212(a)(3)(E).

(e) Alien Y is a lawful permanent resident. During a vacation in the Sahara, Y contracts a deadly communicable disease for which there is no known cure in the United States.

If the re-entry doctrine is abolished, each of these aliens may not be excludable at the border, and some are not even deportable. (Which ones?) Do these hypotheticals affect your opinion of the re-entry doctrine, or are there other ways to deal with the problems they raise?

3. In 1986, Representative Mazzoli introduced legislation that would have eliminated the re-entry doctrine for returning permanent resident aliens. H.R. 4823, § 101, 99th Cong., 2d Sess. (1986). The House passed the measure, but the Senate did not consider it. Would you support or oppose the Mazzoli proposal?

SECTION C. A CONCLUDING CONVERSATION

Cynic: The entry cases and the re-entry doctrine represent the worst about legal thinking. The cases draw meaningless distinctions that defy common sense, and the doctrine produces intolerable consequences.

Believer: Nonsense. They represent the beauty of legal thought: the ability to reason from clear and supportable premises to fair results.

Cynic: What "clear and supportable premises" are you referring to?

Believer: First, the United States is entitled to distinguish between aliens seeking entry to this country and aliens who have already entered.

Cynic: O.K.

Believer: Second, entry cannot simply mean physical presence, or the government would be forced to establish all its inspection offices on foreign soil.

Cynic: So far so good.

Believer: Third, it is expensive to detain aliens while determining whether or not they are entitled to enter; thus, the government should be able to allow them to stay in the United States temporarily while their admissibility is being decided. Furthermore, since the alien, *ex hypothesi,* has not yet been lawfully admitted, the government's decision to enlarge her "prison bounds" [1] should not grant her any additional benefits. The alien is "still in theory of law at the boundary line and ha[s] gained no foothold in the United States." [2]

Cynic: I think that sounds all right.

Believer: · Fourth, aliens may choose to cross the border far from a designated port of entry. Some, if they are responsible, will try to locate the nearest inspection location. These people should be treated no differently than aliens who arrive at an official border crossing.

Cynic: I agree.

Believer: Well, there you have it.

Cynic: Funny, I don't see it.

Believer: You have just accepted the results in all the above cases.

Cynic: What about *Lin?* I didn't hear anything about aliens escaping detention.

Believer: Sure you did. The alien in *Lin* who escaped detention originally presented himself to immigration authorities at the border. Surely he should not be treated differently—indeed better—than the alien who waits in detention.

Cynic: True, but why should he be treated worse than an alien who never presented herself to authorities?

Believer: Because she never presented herself to authorities.

Cynic: Is there an echo?

Believer: No. You simply speak more wisdom than you know. I take it that an alien who has surreptitiously landed by boat in Southern Florida or Queens and travelled to Chattanooga has "entered" the country within any reasonable meaning of that word.

---

1. *Kaplan v. Tod,* 267 U.S. 228, 230, 45 S.Ct. 257, 69 L.Ed. 585 (1925).

2. *Id.*

Cynic: I would have thought so, but common sense does not appear to be of great advantage when interpreting the INA.

Believer: If you grant me that, then how can we distinguish the alien in Chattanooga from the alien in *Phelisna*—so long as there is no proof that Phelisna was on her way to an inspection post?

Cynic: But you're still saying that someone who violates our laws by willfully evading inspection gets benefits that a law abiding alien who presents himself to authorities does not.

Believer: First of all, I'm not so sure all aliens would prefer a deportation hearing. As you know, aliens who are deported may not re-enter the United States for five years without the consent of the Attorney General.[3] Aliens who are excluded need such authorization only for a year.[4]

Secondly, it is not I who am saying this, it is the statute.

Cynic: Then let's change the statute. Even if we can find a set of rules that explains the results, that doesn't make the results right.

Believer: Why would you want to? Just a minute ago you accepted all my initial premises.

Cynic: I'm not so sure, now that I think about it. You said at first that the United States "is entitled" to distinguish between aliens who have entered and those who are arriving at the border. Maybe the government is *entitled to,* but why should it?

Believer: What would you propose instead?

Cynic: I think we should first ask ourselves why we have two different procedures for exclusion and deportation.

Believer: Since 1952, the statute has provided for exclusion and deportation hearings; and it has used the notion of "entry" to determine who gets which. This is how it should be. Congress, under *Knauff* and *Mezei,* is given much more freedom to structure proceedings at the border (*i.e.,* exclusion hearings). This flexibility is needed if we are to maintain control over our borders. Aliens who have already entered and who have established ties to this country are entitled to greater protections before they are sent home.[5] Thus the distinction between exclusion and deportation is perfectly sensible.

Cynic: Doesn't your analysis founder on the re-entry doctrine? Under that doctrine aliens who have established all the ties you mention are subject to the lesser protections you have just defended.

---

3. INA § 212(a)(6)(B).

4. INA § 212(a)(6)(A). [Although this is technically correct, Believer is neglecting to point out that the vast majority of aliens arrested for entry without inspection are permitted to depart voluntarily from the United States without a deportation hearing; thus the five-year ban on readmission without permission would not apply. Aliens may also avoid the one-year bar following exclusion by withdrawing their applications for admission before the exclusion hearing is held.—eds.]

5. Compare Martin, *Due Process and Membership in the National Community: Political Asylum and Beyond,* 44 U.Pitt.L.Rev. 165 (1983) *with* Aleinikoff, *Aliens, Due Process and "Community Ties": A Response to Martin, id.* at 237.

Believer: Maybe so. But that only argues for getting rid of the re-entry doctrine; not for obliterating the distinction between exclusion and deportation.

Cynic: Well, at least we've taken a first step toward sensible reform. Let's go a bit further. To me, the entry cases have produced a set of distinctions that may charitably be described as highly artificial. If we take your reformulation—one that appears to turn on the "stake" of the alien, not "location"—we could of course distinguish between first-time entrants and aliens admitted for lawful permanent residence. But what about aliens who have entered without inspection?

Believer: They may have established some ties in the United States, but these were not lawfully acquired. Thus, we need not respect them.

Cynic: Precisely. So under your theory they are entitled only to an exclusion proceeding.[6]

Believer: I suppose so.

Cynic: But that conclusion runs directly counter to the entry cases, which clearly establish that surreptitious entrants are entitled to deportation proceedings. Either your theory or some of the cases it purports to explain must go. My own view is that you are on to something, but it has nothing to do with entry, as that term is defined in the statute.

Believer: What do you recommend?

Cynic: It seems to me that the fundamental (and functional) difference between exclusion and deportation proceedings is that in the former the alien is explaining why he or she has the right to enter and in the latter the government is asserting that the alien has no right to remain. This is what seems to underlie tying the two proceedings to the border/interior distinction.

Believer: So what's wrong with that?

Cynic: The problem is that the border/interior line is not always a useful proxy for the right-to-enter/no-right-to-remain line. An alien who entered surreptitiously, even though inside the United States, has never demonstrated that he is entitled to be here. I think that a different concept would better capture the distinction between exclusion and deportation proceedings: that of *admission after inspection.*

Believer: How would that work?

Cynic: First, it would recognize the obligation of an alien to demonstrate *at least once* her right to enter or reside in the United States. The burden should be on the alien to show this entitlement. Once an alien has been admitted by proper authorities, she should be presumed to be here lawfully until the government demonstrates otherwise.

Believer: How would this apply to aliens who enter without inspection?

Cynic: I think they should be treated as if they were first time entrants. They have never demonstrated to anyone their right to be here. Under this reasoning we avoid the absurd result that aliens who enter

---

6. *See* Martin, *supra,* at 230–34.

by intentionally evading inspection receive benefits not extended to aliens who obey the law and present themselves for inspection at the border.

Believer: And aliens like Lin?

Cynic: Under my theory, *Lin* is an easy case. Lin was never inspected or admitted. He therefore must demonstrate his right to be here.

Believer: And Phelisna and the alien in *Matter of G-*?

Cynic: Same result. Notice that this conclusion is reached without tortured reasoning about the intent of the alien or whether the alien or the government has the burden of proof on that issue. Furthermore, it avoids the rather unseemly spectacle created by the current law. In order for an alien like Phelisna to get what she wants (namely, a deportation hearing), she must argue that she had no intention of presenting herself to immigration authorities when she arrived in this country. Why should we reward such an intention?

Believer: Where would this "demonstration" take place? In an exclusion or deportation hearing?

Cynic: Neither. I would establish a new single proceeding. Let's call it an immigration hearing.

In the hearing, once the government presents a *prima facie* case of the person's alienage,[a] the burden would be on the alien to demonstrate either (a) a prior admission after inspection as a permanent resident or (b) a present right to enter or remain. To establish a right to enter, the alien would have to present proper documentation (*e.g.*, a valid visa) and also show that he is not excludable under § 212(a).

Believer: That's just an exclusion proceeding with a different name.

Cynic: Fair enough. But the crucial point is that it applies to any alien— no matter where located—who has not previously been inspected and admitted.

Believer: As in *Matter of G-, Phelisna,* and *Lin*?

Cynic: Exactly. To continue, if an alien can demonstrate that she has been inspected and admitted before as a permanent resident alien, then the burden is on the government to demonstrate (a) that the prior entry was unlawful, or (b) that the alien, following a prior entry after inspection, has committed a deportable act.[7] Note that since we have already agreed (haven't we?) that the re-entry doctrine should be abolished, the "prior entry" I am referring to is the alien's initial admission after inspection.

Believer: But what about an alien who is lawfully admitted, then leaves the country and re-enters without inspection? If the re-entry doctrine is gone, the alien is not deportable.

---

a. We will discuss this evidentiary burden in the Chapter Six. *See* pp. 613–16 *infra.*— eds.

7. The government should also be able to show that an alien who had been admitted as a permanent resident and then left the Unit- ed States for a long period of time has been out of the country so long that she has abandoned resident status. Such an alien would effectively be a new entrant and would have to demonstrate a right to enter.

Cynic: I am not at all sure that our deportation laws ought to banish a person who has been lawfully admitted and is otherwise entitled to remain simply because he or she fails to be re-inspected upon return to a lawful residence.

Believer: But surely a requirement that aliens submit themselves for inspection each time they cross the border is sensible policy. It would help us regulate and measure the flow of people across our borders and perhaps prevent the unlawful entry of other aliens whom returning residents assist in entering surreptitiously.

Cynic: Maybe you're right. But why make violation of such a requirement a ground for deportation? INA § 275 already makes it a crime to "elude[ ] examination or inspection by immigration officers."

Believer: I note that so far you have just been talking about aliens admitted for permanent residence. What about nonimmigrant aliens?

Cynic: I'd have to think more about that. My initial reaction is that if we are primarily concerned with the "stake" of the alien, then most nonimmigrants rank fairly low by any measure. Furthermore, applying the proposed procedures to nonimmigrants might produce curious results. For example, suppose an alien receives a multiple-entry visa as a business visitor and enters the United States for a one-week business trip. Then suppose he seeks re-entry for another trip two years later. I don't think the initial admission should immunize him from the grounds of exclusion.

Believer: Then you are keeping the re-entry doctrine for nonimmigrants?

Cynic: It looks that way.

Believer: What else would the merger of exclusion and deportation proceedings accomplish?

Cynic: It could make available to "entering" aliens benefits currently available only in deportation proceedings—such as the right of the alien to designate a country of deportation. It would also, of course, end the embarrassment of the present entry cases and make the Supreme Court's decision in *Plasencia* (as to where the *Fleuti* decision should be made) of no import.[b]

Believer: So far you have talked only about a statutory scheme. What happened to the Constitution? Doesn't your proposal destroy the well-established constitutional difference between exclusion and deportation proceedings in terms of the process that Congress may provide?

Cynic: I believe my proposal comports fully with the constitutional requirements of due process under the existing case law. However, I should add that I firmly believe that the border/interior line should be jettisoned in due process analysis. Development of that, however, requires a look at deportation procedures. Let's talk again at the end of Chapter Six.

---

b. One other potential benefit is that putting the burden on the alien to prove an entitlement to enter or a prior admission after inspection would end the game currently played under INA § 291. *See* pp. 613–16 *infra.*—eds.

Chapter Six

DEPORTATION

Deportation, or expulsion, is the removal of an alien who has entered the United States—either legally or illegally. Deportation statutes are nearly as old as the Republic. The Alien and Sedition Acts of 1798 authorized the President to deport (1) resident aliens who were citizens of nations at war with the United States (alien enemies) and (2) aliens whom the President judged "dangerous to the peace and safety of the United States." Act of June 25, 1798, Ch. 58, 1 Stat. 570; Act of July 6, 1798, Ch. 66, 1 Stat. 577. The latter section was apparently never invoked and was allowed to expire two years later, but the Alien Enemy Act remains on the books today. 50 U.S.C.A. §§ 21–23.

For most of the nineteenth century, the federal government had no general deportation statute.[1] Aliens who entered the country were permitted to remain as long as they wished. Deportation statutes began to flourish with the increased federal involvement in the regulation of immigration in the late 1800's. As the government began to impose restrictions on who could enter, it recognized the need to remove those who had entered in violation of these restrictions. Thus, at first, deportation statutes were viewed primarily as a supplement to the exclusion laws. For example, in 1885 and 1887 Congress passed "contract labor laws," which prohibited the "importation or migration" of aliens who had pre-existing contracts to perform most kinds of labor or services in the United States. Act of February 26, 1885, Ch. 164, 23 Stat. 332; Act of February 23, 1887, Ch. 220, 24 Stat. 414.[2] These acts were amended in 1888 to authorize the *deportation* of an immigrant who had been "allowed to land contrary to the prohibition" in the earlier laws. Act of Oct. 19, 1888, Ch. 1210, 25 Stat. 566.[3]

---

1. For a brief history of deportation statutes, *see* Maslow, *Recasting Our Deportation Law: Proposals for Reform*, 56 Colum.L.Rev. 309, 311–14 (1956).

2. The statutes did not apply to skilled jobs for which American workers could not be found, domestic servants, professional actors, artists, singers or lecturers.

3. Similarly, the 1892 statute at issue in *Fong Yue Ting v. United States*, p. 21 *supra*, which authorized the deportation of Chinese laborers who failed to obtain certificates of residence, was enacted to help enforce the earlier Chinese exclusion laws.

The 1891 revision and codification of the immigration laws provided a number of new grounds for exclusion. Concomitantly, it broadened the deportation provision of the 1888 Act to encompass "any alien who shall come into the United States in violation of law." Act of March 3, 1891, Ch. 551, § 11, 24 Stat. 1086.

In 1907, Congress amended the immigration laws to authorize deportation of an alien who was a prostitute "at any time within three years after she shall have entered the United States." Act of February 20, 1907, Ch. 1134, § 3, 34 Stat. 899–900. This statute, like the Alien and Sedition Acts, authorized the deportation of an alien based on that alien's conduct in the United States *after* he or she had made a lawful entry. Congress has since added considerably to the list of post-entry acts that render a lawfully admitted alien deportable. *See* INA § 241.

We have previously considered the constitutional sources of Congress' power to deport aliens as well as the substantive and procedural limits on Congress' power to exclude. As the following cases demonstrate, the Supreme Court has established essentially no limits on Congress' authority to define classes of deportable aliens. This parallels the doctrine developed by the Court in exclusion cases. On procedural matters, however, the Court has drawn a line between due process guarantees in exclusion and deportation proceedings. This Chapter is divided into two Sections. The first examines Congress' substantive power to deport aliens, and the second considers deportation procedures.

SECTION A.   THE DEPORTATION POWER

1.   CONSTITUTIONAL PERSPECTIVES

In a case upholding the constitutionality of the deportation of prostitutes under the 1907 Act, as amended in 1910, Justice Holmes wrote:

> It is thoroughly established that Congress has power to order the deportation of aliens whose presence in the country it deems hurtful. The determination by facts that might constitute a crime under local law is not a conviction of crime, nor is the deportation a punishment; it is simply a refusal by the Government to harbor persons whom it does not want.

Bugajewitz v. Adams, 228 U.S. 585, 591, 33 S.Ct. 607, 608, 57 L.Ed. 978 (1913). It is doubtful that Holmes could really have meant that deportation is not punishment, if by "punishment" we mean the imposition of harm or sanctions for misconduct or violation of law. James Madison forcefully made this point long ago in arguing against the Alien and Sedition Acts:

> If the banishment of an alien from a country into which he has been invited as the asylum most auspicious to his happiness,—a country where he may have formed the most tender connections; where he may have invested his entire property, and acquired property of the real and permanent, as well as the movable and temporary kind; where he enjoys, under the laws, a greater share

of the blessings of personal security, and personal liberty, than he can elsewhere hope for; * * *—if a banishment of this sort be not a punishment, and among the severest of punishments, it will be difficult to imagine a doom to which the name can be applied.

4 Elliot's Debates 555 (Philadelphia, J.B. Lippincott & Co., 1881 ed.). Rather, it seems clear that Holmes was making a technical distinction in order to protect congressional exercise of the immigration power from the substantive and procedural limits the Constitution places on criminal proceedings.

The Court's distinction between "deportation" and "punishment" can best be seen in the contrast between the landmark cases of *Fong Yue Ting v. United States*, 149 U.S. 698, 13 S.Ct. 1016, 37 L.Ed. 905 (1893), and *Wong Wing v. United States*, 163 U.S. 228, 16 S.Ct. 977, 41 L.Ed. 140 (1896), pp. 21, 37 *supra*. You will recall that *Fong* upheld the deportation of Chinese aliens under the 1892 immigration statute for lack of a residence certificate obtainable only with a white witness, while *Wong Wing* struck down a provision of the same statute that provided for imprisonment, without a judicial trial, of aliens found deportable. In *Wong Wing*, the Court sharply distinguished "deportation" from "punishment":

> No limits can be put by the courts upon the power of Congress to protect, by summary methods, the country from the advent of aliens whose race or habits render them undesirable as citizens, or to expel such if they have already found their way into our land and unlawfully remain therein. But to declare unlawful residence within the country to be an infamous crime, punishable by deprivation of liberty and property, would be to pass out of the sphere of constitutional legislation, unless provision were made that the fact of guilt should first be established by a judicial trial.

Id. at 237.

In this Section we will see that the Supreme Court has gone quite far in immunizing the federal deportation power from substantive constitutional constraints. *Fong Yue Ting* established that the constitutional protection against cruel and unusual punishment does not apply to deportation. 149 U.S. at 730, 13 S.Ct. at 1028. You will see later in this Section that the courts have also rejected claims that deportation for past conduct which was legal when undertaken violates the Constitution's prohibition against *ex post facto* laws, that deportation statutes are unconstitutional bills of attainder, or that they deny equal protection of the law.

The classic statement of the Supreme Court's reluctance to invalidate congressional deportation decisions is *Harisiades v. Shaughnessy*, which follows. Although the case was decided in 1952, it cannot be dismissed simply as a product of the Cold War and the McCarthy era. The Supreme Court continues to cite *Harisiades* as sound doctrine. *See, e.g., Fiallo v. Bell*, 430 U.S. 787, 792–99, 97 S.Ct. 1473, 1477–81, 52 L.Ed.2d 50 (1977).

A Brief Note on the Deportation of "Subversives"

Harisiades involved the deportation of aliens for their prior membership in the Communist Party. Since 1903, Congress has enacted numerous statutes that mandate exclusion or deportation of aliens deemed to be "subversive" on the basis of their political beliefs and activities. These statutes must be viewed in their historical contexts, coinciding with nativist reaction to Chinese immigration, the growth of a radical labor movement in the late 1880's and earlier 1900's, the assassination of President McKinley in 1901, the Russian Revolution, massive migration of Southern and Eastern Europeans in the first decades of this century, and opposition to American involvement in World War I. Anarchists, Communists, labor organizers, and pacifists all became linked in the public mind with "aliens." "The basic conservatism of the peasant immigrant, with his yearning for tradition, status, and authority," writes William Preston, Jr., "had little influence against nativist fears of foreign extremism. Nor did the alien's overt and steadfast repudiation of various radical movements soften the stereotype." W. Preston, Jr., Aliens and Dissenters: Federal Suppression of Radicals, 1903–1933, at 4 (1963). In short, aliens were often scapegoats for American hysteria over labor and political movements that called into question the basic organization of the American economic and political systems.[1]

The view that aliens were the root of civil disorder is evidenced by the 1903 Act which, for the first time, established subversiveness as a ground of exclusion. Passed in the wake of Leon F. Czolgosz' assassination of President McKinley, the Act excluded "anarchists, or persons who believe in or advocate the overthrow by force or violence of the Government of the United States * * * or the assassination of public officials." Act of March 3, 1903, Ch. 1012, § 2, 32 Stat. 1219.[5] That Czolgosz' heinous act could produce an immigration statute excluding anarchists is somewhat curious; he had only vague ties with the anarchist movement and was a native-born American citizen.

In 1917, the deportation grounds were extended to include *post-entry* subversive conduct of aliens. Thus "any alien who at any time after entry shall be found advocating or teaching [subversion]" could be deported.

---

4. Pinning the blame on foreigners also probably helped deny the legitimacy—or even possibility—of indigenous radical movements. *See, e.g.,* S.Rep. No. 1515, 81st Cong., 2d Sess. 782 (1950):

> Communism is, of necessity, an alien force. It is inconceivable that the people of the United States would, of their own volition, organize or become part of a conspiracy to destroy the free institutions to which generations of Americans have devoted themselves. The tremendous political freedom and the corollary standard of living of the United States have given the people of this country a national entity and heritage far superior to anything which human society has created elsewhere.

> * * *

> In the light of these facts, it is not strange that the vast majority of those who would establish a Communist dictatorship in this country come from alien lands; and it is easy to see that the forces of world communism must have or find ways and means for getting their minions into this country if they are to maintain the effectiveness of their organization here.

> The Comintern realizes that it cannot rely on native Americans because to do so involves the constant risk of having its work impeded or exposed. It is to be expected that the loyalty of a native American or of a citizen of long standing would occasionally reassert itself, despite the most intensive Communist indoctrination.

5. The Act was upheld against a First Amendment challenge in *United States ex rel. Turner v. Williams,* 194 U.S. 279, 24 S.Ct. 719, 48 L.Ed. 979 (1904).

Immigration Act of 1917, Ch. 29, § 19, 39 Stat. 889. World War I occasioned further expansions. Aliens who were "members of or affiliated with any organization that entertains a belief in" violent overthrow of the government or anarchism, Anarchist Act of 1918, Ch. 186, § 1, 40 Stat. 1012, as well as aliens who wrote, published, circulated or possessed subversive literature, Act of June 5, 1920, Ch. 251, § 1, 41 Stat. 1008, were made deportable.

The War also brought the Palmer Raids, a repressive campaign directed by the Attorney General of the United States to deport aliens affiliated with allegedly subversive organizations. Thousands of aliens were imprisoned, and over five hundred were eventually deported. What follows is a portion of historian John Higham's account of the Raids.

A new Attorney General, A. Mitchell Palmer, took over * * * in March 1919. Palmer's bulldog jaw belied his simple, placid face. Once the implacable opponent of the political bosses and liquor interests in Pennsylvania, he approached the war against Germany with the same crusading belligerence. * * * He was an ambitious man as well: his eye rested lovingly on the White House. The failure of Palmer's agents to find the perpetrators of several bombing episodes in April must have exasperated him considerably, and when another infernal machine battered the front of his own home in June, Palmer was ready to go with the current. He appealed to Congress for a special appropriation, telling the frightened legislators that he knew exactly when the Reds were planning "to rise up and destroy the Government at one fell swoop." The appropriation became available during the summer, and with it Palmer created a new division of the Bureau of Investigation for the war against radicalism. In anticipation of a peacetime sedition law, the division proceeded to assemble data on all revolutionary activities * * *. * * * [T]he Union of Russian Workers * * * was chosen as the first target.

On November 7, 1919, the second anniversary of the Bolshevik régime in Russia, Palmer's men descended on Russian meeting places in eleven cities and seized hundreds of members of the organization. Screening for once was swift. Little more than a month later 249 aliens, most of them netted in the November raids, were on a specially chartered transport en route to Finland. From there they traveled overland to Russia through snows and military lines. Some had to leave behind in America their wives and children, at once destitute and ostracized.

* * *

Basking in the popularity of his anti-Russian raid, Palmer now prepared a mightier blow. On January 2 the Department of Justice, aided by local police forces in thirty-three cities, carried out a vast roundup of alien members of the two communist parties. Officers burst into homes, meeting places and pool rooms, as often as not seizing everyone in sight. The victims were loaded into trucks, or sometimes marched through the streets handcuffed and chained to one another, and massed by the hundreds at concentration points, usually police stations. There officials tried to separate out the alien members of radical organizations, releasing the rest or turning them over to the local police. Many remained in federal custody for a few hours only; some lay in crowded cells for several weeks without a preliminary hearing. For several days in Detroit eight hundred men were held incommunicado in a windowless corridor, sleeping on the bare stone floor, subsisting on food which their families brought in, and limited to the use of a single drinking fountain and a single toilet. Altogether, about three thousand aliens were held for deportation, almost all of them eastern Europeans.

J. Higham, Strangers in the Land: Patterns of American Nativism 1860–1925, at 229–31 (1955).

The January 1920 raids in Boston and other New England towns netted approximately 1000 persons. Twenty aliens who had been arrested and subsequently ordered deported brought suit challenging the legality of the proceedings. The federal district court, in setting aside the deportation of most of the aliens on due process grounds, described the raids and their aftermath:

> * * * Pains were taken to give spectacular publicity to the raid, and to make it appear that there was great and imminent public danger, against which these activities of the Department of Justice were directed. The arrested aliens, in most instances perfectly quiet and harmless working people, many of them not long ago Russian peasants, were handcuffed in pairs, and then, for the purposes of transfer on trains and through the streets of Boston, chained together. The Northern New Hampshire contingent were first concentrated in jail at Concord and then brought to Boston in a special car, thus handcuffed and chained together. On detraining at the North Station, the handcuffed and chained aliens were exposed to newspaper photographers and again thus exposed at the wharf where they took the boat for Deer Island. The Department of Justice agents in charge of the arrested aliens appear to have taken pains to have them thus exposed to public photographing.

> Private rooms were searched in omnibus fashion; trunks, bureaus, suit cases, and boxes broken open; books and papers seized. I doubt whether a single search warrant was obtained or applied for. * * *

>   * * *

> At Deer Island the conditions were unfit and chaotic. No adequate preparations had been made to receive and care for so large a number of people. Some of the steam pipes were burst or disconnected. The place was cold; the weather was severe. The cells were not properly equipped with sanitary appliances. There was no adequate number of guards or officials to take a census of

and properly care for so many. For several days the arrested aliens were held practically incommunicado. There was dire confusion of authority as between the immigration forces and the Department of Justice forces, and the city officials who had charge of the prison. Most of this confusion and the resultant hardship to the arrested aliens was probably unintentional * * *. Undoubtedly it did have some additional terrorizing effect upon the aliens. Inevitably the atmosphere of lawless disregard of the rights and feelings of these aliens as human beings affected, consciously or unconsciously, the inspectors who shortly began at Deer Island the hearings, the basis of the records involving the determination of their right to remain in this country.

In the early days at Deer Island one alien committed suicide by throwing himself from the fifth floor and dashing his brains out in the corridor below in the presence of other horrified aliens. One was committed as insane; others were driven nearly, if not quite, to the verge of insanity.

After many days of confusion, the aliens themselves, under the leadership of one or two of the most intelligent and most conversant with English, constituted a committee, and represented to Assistant Commissioner Sullivan that, if given an opportunity, they would themselves clean up the quarters and arrange for the orderly service of food and the distribution of mail. This offer was wisely accepted, and thereupon the prisoners created a government of their own, called, ironically, I suppose, "The Soviet Republic of Deer Island." Through the assistance of this so-called Soviet government, conditions orderly, tolerable, not inhumane, were created after perhaps 10 days or 2 weeks of filth, confusion, and unnecessary suffering. It is not without significance that these aliens, thus arrested under charges of conspiracy to overthrow our government by force and violence, were, while under arrest, many of them illegally, found to be capable of organizing amongst themselves, with the consent of and in amicable cooperation with their keepers, an effective and democratic form of local government.

Colyer v. Skeffington, 265 Fed. 17, 44–45 (D.Mass.1920), *reversed in part sub nom. Skeffington v. Katzeff,* 277 Fed. 129 (1st Cir.1922).

The Supreme Court played a minor role throughout this period.[6] However, in 1939, it dropped a bombshell on Congress with its decision in *Kessler v. Strecker,* 307 U.S. 22, 59 S.Ct. 694, 83 L.Ed. 1082 (1939). There, by a seven-to-two vote, it held that an alien who had been a member of the Communist Party after entering the United States but had left the Party prior to his arrest was not deportable under the 1918 Act. Not surprising-

---

6. *See, e.g., United States ex rel. Tisi v. Tod,* 264 U.S. 131, 44 S.Ct. 260, 68 L.Ed. 590 (1924) and *United States ex rel. Vajtauer v. Commissioner of Immigration,* 273 U.S. 103, 47 S.Ct. 302, 71 L.Ed. 560 (1927) (upholding deportation of aliens under 1920 statute and rejecting claims of violations of due process).

ly, following *Kessler,* radical organizations "expelled" their alien members in an attempt to immunize them from deportation for subversion.

Congress, upset with the Court's interpretation and the clever action of the proscribed organizations, overruled *Kessler* in the Alien Registration Act of 1940. That statute amended the 1918 Act to provide for deportation of any alien who had been a member of a subversive group "at any time" after entering the United States. The statute specifically applied to aliens "irrespective of the time of their entry into the United States." Alien Registration Act of 1940, Ch. 439, § 23(b), 54 Stat. 673. As stated by the Senate Report on the bill, the amendment was intended to apply to all aliens who were associated with subversive organizations "for no matter how short a time or how far in the past." S.Rep. No. 1796, 76th Cong., 3d Sess. 3 (1940).

The constitutionality of the 1940 amendments to the 1918 Act was challenged in *Harisiades.*

HARISIADES v. SHAUGHNESSY

Supreme Court of the United States, 1952.
342 U.S. 580, 72 S.Ct. 512, 96 L.Ed. 586.

Mr. Justice Jackson delivered the opinion of the Court.

The ultimate question in these three cases is whether the United States constitutionally may deport a legally resident alien because of membership in the Communist Party which terminated before enactment of the Alien Registration Act, 1940.

Harisiades, a Greek national, accompanied his father to the United States in 1916, when thirteen years of age, and has resided here since. He has taken a wife and sired two children, all citizens. He joined the Communist Party in 1925, when it was known as the Workers Party, and served as an organizer, Branch Executive Committeeman, secretary of its Greek Bureau, and editor of its paper "Empros." The party discontinued his membership, along with that of other aliens, in 1939, but he has continued association with members. He was familiar with the principles and philosophy of the Communist Party and says he still believes in them. He disclaims personal belief in use of force and violence and asserts that the party favored their use only in defense. A warrant for his deportation because of his membership was issued in 1930 but was not served until 1946. The delay was due to inability to locate him because of his use of a number of aliases. After hearings, he was ordered deported on the grounds that after entry he had been a member of an organization which advocates overthrow of the Government by force and violence and distributes printed matter so advocating. * * *

Mascitti, a citizen of Italy, came to this country in 1920, at the age of sixteen. He married a resident alien and has one American-born child. He was a member of the Young Workers Party, the Workers Party and the Communist Party between 1923 and 1929. His testimony was that he knew the party advocated a proletarian dictatorship, to be established by force and violence if the capitalist class resisted. He heard some speakers advocate violence, in which he says he did not personally believe, and he was not clear as to the party policy. He resigned in 1929, apparently because he lost sympathy with or interest in the party. A warrant for his deportation issued and was served in 1946. After the usual administrative hearings he was ordered deported on the same grounds as Harisiades. * * *

Mrs. Coleman, a native of Russia, was admitted to the United States in 1914, when thirteen years of age. She married an American citizen and has three children, citizens by birth. She admits being a member of the Communist Party for about a year, beginning in 1919, and again from 1928 to 1930, and again from 1936 to 1937 or 1938. She held no office and her activities were not significant. She disavowed much knowledge of party principles and program, claiming she joined each time because of some injustice the party was then fighting. The reasons she gives for leaving the party are her health and the party's discontinuance of alien memberships. She has been ordered deported because after entry she became a member of an organization advocating overthrow of the Government by force and violence. * * *

* * *

I.

These aliens ask us to forbid their expulsion by a departure from the long-accepted application to such cases of the Fifth Amendment provision that no person shall be deprived of life, liberty or property without due process of law. Their basic contention is that admission for permanent residence confers a "vested right" on the alien, equal to that of the citizen, to remain within the country, and that the alien is entitled to constitutional protection in that matter to the same extent as the citizen. Their second line of defense is that if any power to deport domiciled aliens exists it is so dispersed that the judiciary must concur in the grounds for its exercise to the extent of finding them reasonable. The argument goes on to the contention that the grounds prescribed by the Act of 1940 bear no reasonable relation to protection of legitimate interests of the United States and concludes that the Act should be declared invalid. Admittedly these propositions are not founded in precedents of this Court.

For over thirty years each of these aliens has enjoyed such advantages as accrue from residence here without renouncing his foreign allegiance or formally acknowledging adherence to the Constitution he now invokes. Each was admitted to the United States, upon passing formidable exclusionary hurdles, in the hope that, after what may be called a probationary period, he would desire and be found desirable for citizenship. Each has been offered naturalization, with all of the rights and privileges of citizenship, conditioned only upon open and honest assumption of undivided allegiance to our Government. But acceptance was and is not compulsory. Each has been permitted to prolong his original nationality indefinitely.

So long as one thus perpetuates a dual status as an American inhabitant but foreign citizen, he may derive advantages from two sources of law—American and international. He may claim protection against our Government unavailable to the citizen. As an alien he retains a claim upon the state of his citizenship to diplomatic intervention on his behalf, a patronage often of considerable value. The state of origin of each of these aliens could presently enter diplomatic remonstrance against these deportations if they were inconsistent with international law, the prevailing custom among nations or their own practices.

The alien retains immunities from burdens which the citizen must shoulder. By withholding his allegiance from the United States, he leaves outstanding a foreign call on his loyalties which international law not only permits our Government to recognize but commands it to respect.   * * *

Under our law, the alien in several respects stands on an equal footing with citizens,[9] but in others has never been conceded legal parity with the citizen.[10] Most importantly, to protract this ambiguous status within the country is not his right but is a matter of permission and tolerance. The Government's power to terminate its hospitality has been asserted and sustained by this Court since the question first arose.[11]

* * *

That aliens remain vulnerable to expulsion after long residence is a practice that bristles with severities. But it is a weapon of defense and reprisal confirmed by international law as a power inherent in every sovereign state. Such is the traditional power of the Nation over the alien and we leave the law on the subject as we find it.

This brings us to the alternative defense under the Due Process Clause—that, granting the power, it is so unreasonably and harshly exercised by this enactment that it should be held unconstitutional.

In historical context the Act before us stands out as an extreme application of the expulsion power. There is no denying that as world convulsions have driven us toward a closed society the expulsion power has been exercised with increasing severity, manifest in multiplication of grounds for deportation, in expanding the subject classes from illegal entrants to legal residents, and in greatly lengthening the period of residence after which one may be expelled. This is said to have reached a point where it is the duty of this Court to call a halt upon the political branches of the Government.

9. This Court has held that the Constitution assures him a large measure of equal economic opportunity. *Yick Wo v. Hopkins,* 118 U.S. 356, 6 S.Ct. 1064, 30 L.Ed. 220; *Truax v. Raich,* 239 U.S. 33, 36 S.Ct. 7, 60 L.Ed. 131; he may invoke the writ of habeas corpus to protect his personal liberty, *Nishimura Ekiu v. United States,* 142 U.S. 651, 660, 12 S.Ct. 336, 338, 35 L.Ed. 1146; in criminal proceedings against him he must be accorded the protections of the Fifth and Sixth Amendments, *Wong Wing v. United States,* 163 U.S. 228, 16 S.Ct. 977, 41 L.Ed. 140; and, unless he is an enemy alien, his property cannot be taken without just compensation. *Russian Volunteer Fleet v. United*

States, 282 U.S. 481, 51 S.Ct. 229, 75 L.Ed. 473.

10. He cannot stand for election to many public offices. For instance, Art. I, § 2, cl. 2, § 3, cl. 3, of the Constitution respectively require that candidates for election to the House of Representatives and Senate be citizens. See Borchard, Diplomatic Protection of Citizens Abroad, 63. The states, to whom is entrusted the authority to set qualifications of voters, for most purposes require citizenship as a condition precedent to the voting franchise.

11. *Fong Yue Ting v. United States,* 149 U.S. 698, 707, 711–714, 730, 13 S.Ct. 1016, 1019, 1021–1022, 1028, 37 L.Ed. 905.

It is pertinent to observe that any policy toward aliens is vitally and intricately interwoven with contemporaneous policies in regard to the conduct of foreign relations, the war power, and the maintenance of a republican form of government. Such matters are so exclusively entrusted to the political branches of government as to be largely immune from judicial inquiry or interference.[16]

These restraints upon the judiciary, occasioned by different events, do not control today's decision but they are pertinent. It is not necessary and probably not possible to delineate a fixed and precise line of separation in these matters between political and judicial power under the Constitution. Certainly, however, nothing in the structure of our Government or the text of our Constitution would warrant judicial review by standards which would require us to equate our political judgment with that of Congress.

Under the conditions which produced this Act, can we declare that congressional alarm about a coalition of Communist power without and Communist conspiracy within the United States is either a fantasy or a pretense? This Act was approved by President Roosevelt June 28, 1940, when a world war was threatening to involve us, as soon it did. Communists in the United States were exerting every effort to defeat and delay our preparations. Certainly no responsible American would say that there were then or are now no possible grounds on which Congress might believe that Communists in our midst are inimical to our security.

Congress received evidence that the Communist movement here has been heavily laden with aliens and that Soviet control of the American Communist Party has been largely through alien Communists. It would be easy for those of us who do not have security responsibility to say that those who do are taking Communism too seriously and overestimating its danger. But we have an Act of one Congress which, for a decade, subsequent Congresses have never repealed but have strengthened and extended. We, in our private opinions, need not concur in Congress' policies to hold its enactments constitutional. Judicially we must tolerate what personally we may regard as a legislative mistake.

We are urged, because the policy inflicts severe and undoubted hardship on affected individuals, to find a restraint in the Due Process Clause. But the Due Process Clause does not shield the citizen from conscription and the consequent calamity of being separated from family, friends, home and business while he is transported to foreign lands to stem the tide of Communism. If Communist aggression creates such hardships for loyal citizens, it is hard to find justification for holding that the Constitution requires that its hardships must be spared the Communist alien. When citizens raised the Constitution as a shield against expulsion from their homes and places of business, the Court refused to find hardship a cause for judicial intervention.[17]

16. *United States v. Curtiss–Wright Corp.*, 299 U.S. 304, 319–322, 57 S.Ct. 216, 220–222, 81 L.Ed. 255.

17. *Hirabayashi v. United States*, 320 U.S. 81, 63 S.Ct. 1375, 87 L.Ed. 1774 (1943); *Korematsu v. United States*, 323 U.S. 214, 65 S.Ct. 193, 89 L.Ed. 194 (1944). [These cases upheld discriminatory wartime measures taken against American citizens of Japanese descent on the West Coast.—eds.]

We think that, in the present state of the world, it would be rash and irresponsible to reinterpret our fundamental law to deny or qualify the Government's power of deportation. However desirable world-wide amelioration of the lot of aliens, we think it is peculiarly a subject for international diplomacy. It should not be initiated by judicial decision which can only deprive our own Government of a power of defense and reprisal without obtaining for American citizens abroad any reciprocal privileges or immunities. Reform in this field must be entrusted to the branches of the Government in control of our international relations and treaty-making powers.

We hold that the Act is not invalid under the Due Process Clause. These aliens are not entitled to judicial relief unless some other constitutional limitation has been transgressed, to which inquiry we turn.

II.

The First Amendment is invoked as a barrier against this enactment. The claim is that in joining an organization advocating overthrow of government by force and violence the alien has merely exercised freedoms of speech, press and assembly which that Amendment guarantees to him.

The assumption is that the First Amendment allows Congress to make no distinction between advocating change in the existing order by lawful elective processes and advocating change by force and violence, that freedom for the one includes freedom for the other, and that when teaching of violence is denied so is freedom of speech.

Our Constitution sought to leave no excuse for violent attack on the status quo by providing a legal alternative-attack by ballot. To arm all men for orderly change, the Constitution put in their hands a right to influence the electorate by press, speech and assembly. This means freedom to advocate or promote Communism by means of the ballot box, but it does not include the practice or incitement of violence.[18]

True, it often is difficult to determine whether ambiguous speech is advocacy of political methods or subtly shades into a methodical but prudent incitement to violence. Communist governments avoid the inquiry by suppressing everything distasteful. Some would have us avoid the difficulty by going to the opposite extreme of permitting incitement to violent overthrow at least unless it seems certain to succeed immediately. We apprehend that the Constitution enjoins upon us the duty, however difficult, of distinguishing between the two. Different formulae have been applied in different situations and the test applicable to the Communist Party has been stated too recently to make further discussion at this time profitable.[19] We think the First Amendment does not prevent the deportation of these aliens.

III.

The remaining claim is that this Act conflicts with Art. I, § 9, of the Constitution forbidding *ex post facto* enactments. An impression of retro-

---

18. *Dennis v. United States,* 341 U.S. 494,   **19.** *Ibid.*
71 S.Ct. 857, 95 L.Ed. 1137.

activity results from reading as a new and isolated enactment what is actually a continuation of prior legislation.

During all the years since 1920 Congress has maintained a standing admonition to aliens, on pain of deportation, not to become members of any organization that advocates overthrow of the United States Government by force and violence, a category repeatedly held to include the Communist Party. These aliens violated that prohibition and incurred liability to deportation. They were not caught unawares by a change of law. There can be no contention that they were not adequately forewarned both that their conduct was prohibited and of its consequences.

In 1939, this Court decided *Kessler v. Strecker,* 307 U.S. 22, 59 S.Ct. 694, 83 L.Ed. 1082, in which it was held that Congress, in the statute as it then stood, had not clearly expressed an intent that Communist Party membership remained cause for deportation after it ceased. The Court concluded that in the absence of such expression only contemporaneous membership would authorize deportation.

The reaction of the Communist Party was to drop aliens from membership, at least in form, in order to immunize them from the consequences of their party membership.

The reaction of Congress was that the Court had misunderstood its legislation. In the Act here before us it supplied unmistakable language that past violators of its prohibitions continued to be deportable in spite of resignation or expulsion from the party. It regarded the fact that an alien defied our laws to join the Communist Party as an indication that he had developed little comprehension of the principles or practice of representative government or else was unwilling to abide by them.

However, even if the Act were found to be retroactive, to strike it down would require us to overrule the construction of the *ex post facto* provision which has been followed by this Court from earliest times. It always has been considered that that which it forbids is penal legislation which imposes or increases criminal punishment for conduct lawful previous to its enactment. Deportation, however severe its consequences, has been consistently classified as a civil rather than a criminal procedure. Both of these doctrines as original proposals might be debatable, but both have been considered closed for many years and a body of statute and decisional law has been built upon them. *Bugajewitz v. Adams,* 228 U.S. 585, 591, 33 S.Ct. 607, 608, 57 L.Ed. 978 * * *.

* * *

It is contended that this policy allows no escape by reformation. We are urged to apply some doctrine of atonement and redemption. Congress might well have done so, but it is not for the judiciary to usurp the function of granting absolution or pardon. We cannot do so for deportable ex-convicts, even though they have served a term of imprisonment calculated to bring about their reformation.

When the Communist Party as a matter of party strategy formally expelled alien members en masse, it destroyed any significance that discontinued membership might otherwise have as indication of change of heart by the individual. Congress may have believed that the party tactics threw upon the Government an almost impossible burden if it attempted to separate those who sincerely renounced Communist principles of force and violence from those who left the party the better to serve it. Congress, exercising the wide discretion that it alone has in these matters, declined to accept that as the Government's burden.

We find none of the constitutional objections to the Act well founded. * * *

MR. JUSTICE CLARK took no part in the consideration or decision of these cases.

MR. JUSTICE FRANKFURTER, concurring.

It is not for this Court to reshape a world order based on politically sovereign States. In such an international ordering of the world a national State implies a special relationship of one body of people, *i.e.*, citizens of that State, whereby the citizens of each State are aliens in relation to every other State. Ever since national States have come into being, the right of people to enjoy the hospitality of a State of which they are not citizens has been a matter of political determination by each State. (I put to one side the oddities of dual citizenship.) Though as a matter of political outlook and economic need this country has traditionally welcomed aliens to come to its shores, it has done so exclusively as a matter of political outlook and national self-interest. This policy has been a political policy, belonging to the political branch of the Government wholly outside the concern and the competence of the Judiciary.

Accordingly, when this policy changed and the political and law-making branch of this Government, the Congress, decided to restrict the right of immigration about seventy years ago, this Court thereupon and ever since has recognized that the determination of a selective and exclusionary immigration policy was for the Congress and not for the Judiciary. The conditions for entry of every alien, the particular classes of aliens that shall be denied entry altogether, the basis for determining such classification, the right to terminate hospitality to aliens, the grounds on which such determination shall be based, have been recognized as matters solely for the responsibility of the Congress and wholly outside the power of this Court to control.

The Court's acknowledgment of the sole responsibility of Congress for these matters has been made possible by Justices whose cultural outlook, whose breadth of view and robust tolerance were not exceeded by those of Jefferson. In their personal views, libertarians like Mr. Justice Holmes and Mr. Justice Brandeis doubtless disapproved of some of these policies, departures as they were from the best traditions of this country and based as they have been in part on discredited racial theories or manipulation of figures in formulating what is known as the quota system. But whether immigration laws have been crude and cruel, whether they may have reflected xenophobia in general or anti-Semitism or anti-Catholicism, the responsibility belongs to Congress. Courts do enforce the requirements imposed by Congress upon officials in administering immigration laws * * *. But the underlying policies of what classes of aliens shall be allowed to enter and what classes of aliens shall be allowed to stay, are for Congress exclusively to determine even though such determination may be deemed to offend American traditions and may, as has been the case, jeopardize peace.

In recognizing this power and this responsibility of Congress, one does not in the remotest degree align oneself with fears unworthy of the American spirit or with hostility to the bracing air of the free spirit. One merely recognizes that the place to resist unwise or cruel legislation touching aliens is the Congress, not this Court.

I, therefore, join in the Court's opinion in these cases.

MR. JUSTICE DOUGLAS, with whom MR. JUSTICE BLACK concurs, dissenting.

There are two possible bases for sustaining this Act:

(1) A person who was once a Communist is tainted for all time and forever dangerous to our society; or

(2) Punishment through banishment from the country may be placed upon an alien not for what he did, but for what his political views once were.

Each of these is foreign to our philosophy. We repudiate our traditions of tolerance and our articles of faith based upon the Bill of Rights when we bow to them by sustaining an Act of Congress which has them as a foundation.

The view that the power of Congress to deport aliens is absolute and may be exercised for any reason which Congress deems appropriate rests on *Fong Yue Ting v. United States,* 149 U.S. 698, 13 S.Ct. 1016, 37 L.Ed. 905, decided in 1893 by a six-to-three vote. That decision seems to me to be inconsistent with the philosophy of constitutional law which we have developed for the protection of resident aliens. We have long held that a resident alien is a "person" within the meaning of the Fifth and the Fourteenth Amendments. * * * He is entitled to habeas corpus to test the legality of his restraint, to the protection of the Fifth and Sixth Amendments in criminal trials, and to the right of free speech as guaranteed by the First Amendment.

An alien, who is assimilated in our society, is treated as a citizen so far as his property and his liberty are concerned. He can live and work here and raise a family, secure in the personal guarantees every resident has and safe from discriminations that might be leveled against him because he was born abroad. Those guarantees of liberty and livelihood are the essence of the freedom which this country from the beginning has offered the people of all lands. If those rights, great as they are, have constitutional protection, I think the more important one—the right to remain here—has a like dignity.

The power of Congress to exclude, admit, or deport aliens flows from sovereignty itself and from the power "To establish an uniform Rule of Naturalization." U.S. Const., Art. I, § 8, cl. 4. The power of deportation is therefore an *implied* one. The right to life and liberty is an *express* one. Why this *implied* power should be given priority over the *express* guarantee of the Fifth Amendment has never been satisfactorily answered. * * *

The right to be immune from arbitrary decrees of banishment certainly may be more important to "liberty" than the civil rights which all aliens enjoy when they reside here. Unless they are free from arbitrary banishment, the "liberty" they enjoy while they live here is indeed illusory. Banishment is punishment in the practical sense. It may deprive a man and his family of all that makes life worth while. Those who have their roots here have an important stake in this country. Their plans for themselves and their hopes for their children all depend on their right to stay. If they are uprooted and sent to lands no longer known to them, no longer hospitable, they become displaced, homeless people condemned to bitterness and despair.

This drastic step may at times be necessary in order to protect the national interest. There may be occasions when the continued presence of an alien, no matter how long he may have been here, would be hostile to the safety or welfare of the Nation due to the nature of his conduct. But unless such condition is shown, I would stay the hand of the Government and let those to whom we have extended our hospitality and who have become members of our communities remain here and enjoy the life and liberty which the Constitution guarantees.

Congress has not proceeded by that standard. It has ordered these aliens deported not for what they are but for what they once were. Perhaps a hearing would show that they continue to be people dangerous and hostile to us. But the principle of forgiveness and the doctrine of redemption are too deep in our philosophy to admit that there is no return for those who have once erred.

Statutory Developments After *Harisiades*

The Cold War brought a substantial broadening of the statutory grounds. *See, e.g.,* Act of May 25, 1948, Ch. 338, § 1, 62 Stat. 268. Under prior statutes, the government had been required to demonstrate in the deportation hearing that the organization to which the alien belonged advocated the violent overthrow of the government. The Subversive Activities Control Act (Title I of the Internal Security Act of 1950, Ch. 1024, 64 Stat. 987), sought to overcome this obstacle by identifying the Communist Party by name and making mere membership in, or affiliation with, the Party a ground of deportation. Ch. 1024, § 22, 64 Stat. 1006 (1950).[7] The McCarran–Walter Act of 1952 (the INA) codified the numerous deportation grounds for subversive activities then found in the law. The legislation was enacted over President Truman's veto; he objected, among other things, to the breadth and vagueness of the deportation grounds relating to subversion.[8]

7. In 1951, Congress amended the statute to protect immigrants who had fled Communist regimes in Eastern European countries. It provided that "membership" and "affiliation" did not include involuntary membership occasioned by being under 16 years old, operation of law or the necessity of obtaining a job, food or other essentials of living. Act of March 28, 1951, Ch. 23, § 1, 65 Stat. 28.

8. Veto Statement of President Truman, June 25, 1952, *reprinted in* President's Commission on Immigration and Naturalization, Whom We Shall Welcome 281–82 (1953). *See generally* Maslow, *supra* note 1, at 333–38.

Despite the broad grounds of deportation for subversion, these sections were rarely used. From 1971 to 1980, only 18 aliens were deported for subversive activities; the INS Statistical Yearbook no longer publishes these figures separately. 1993 INS Statistical Yearbook, Table 58. In the Immigration Act of 1990, Congress finally repealed provisions of § 241(a) mandating the deportation of anarchists, members of the Communist Party and other totalitarian parties, and other classes of subversive aliens. Recall, however, that some of these remain grounds of exclusion applicable to immigrants, and so might have some application in conjunction with the re-entry doctrine. *See* INA § 212(a)(3)(D). What other grounds of deportation might still be used to expel "subversive" aliens? *See* § 241(a)(4).

Constitutionally Protected Liberties and the Deportation Power

The aliens in *Harisiades* claimed that the 1940 Alien Registration Act violated the First Amendment because it subjected them to deportation for the expression of political views. Justice Jackson gave cursory treatment to the First Amendment issue. He seems to say that the "speech" engaged in by the aliens was not protected and thus deportation based on such speech could not offend the First Amendment.

Jackson's opinion relies heavily upon *Dennis v. United States,* decided the year before *Harisiades. Dennis* sustained the criminal convictions of Communist organizers under the Smith Act, a 1940 statute (passed as a rider to the statute in *Harisiades*) that prohibited knowingly or willfully advocating the overthrow of the United States government. *Dennis* held that speech is not protected by the First Amendment "where there is a 'clear and present danger' of the substantive evil which the legislature had the right to prevent." 341 U.S. 494, 515, 71 S.Ct. 857, 870, 95 L.Ed. 1137 (1951). Subsequent case law has cast substantial doubt on the continuing vitality of *Dennis.* In particular, *Brandenburg v. Ohio,* 395 U.S. 444, 89 S.Ct. 1827, 23 L.Ed.2d 430 (1969) (*per curiam*), struck down a statute similar to the Smith Act by applying a standard less deferential to the government. Under *Brandenburg,* the government may not "proscribe advocacy of the use of force or of law violation except where such advocacy is directed to inciting or producing imminent lawless action and is likely to incite or produce such action."[9] 395 U.S. at 447, 89 S.Ct. at 1829.

If the Supreme Court were to announce that *Dennis* is overruled, would it necessarily overrule *Harisiades*? That is, may Congress deport aliens for engaging in protected speech? Could Congress pass a law today ordering the deportation of any alien who marches in a parade supporting a nuclear freeze or who joins the Ku Klux Klan?

The Supreme Court has never directly confronted these issues. It has made clear that aliens in the United States are protected by the Bill of Rights, but in immigration law contexts different from *Harisiades.* For

9. *See also Hess v. Indiana,* 414 U.S. 105, 108, 94 S.Ct. 326, 328, 38 L.Ed.2d 303 (1973) (*per curiam*); Linde, *"Clear and Present Danger" Reexamined: Dissonance in the* Brandenburg *Concerto,* 22 Stan.L.Rev. 1163 (1970); Greenawalt, *Speech and Crime,* 1980 Am.Bar Found.Res.J. 645, 716–29 (1981).

example, under *Yamataya v. Fisher,* 189 U.S. 86, 23 S.Ct. 611, 47 L.Ed. 721 (1903), p. 583 *infra,* the Fifth Amendment's guarantee of due process applies in a deportation hearing, but *Yamataya* did not address substantive deportation grounds. *Kleindienst v. Mandel,* 408 U.S. 753, 92 S.Ct. 2576, 33 L.Ed.2d 683 (1972), p. 345 *supra,* rejected First Amendment claims by United States citizens, but in an exclusion context. *Wong Wing v. United States,* 163 U.S. 228, 16 S.Ct. 977, 41 L.Ed. 140 (1896), p. 37 *supra,* afforded Fifth and Sixth Amendment protections to aliens, but only with respect to criminal sanctions, not immigration proceedings.

Consider the following comments of Justice Murphy:

> The Bill of Rights is a futile authority for the alien seeking admission for the first time to these shores. But once an alien lawfully enters and resides in this country he becomes invested with the rights guaranteed by the Constitution to all people within our borders. Such rights include those protected by the First and the Fifth Amendments and by the due process clause of the Fourteenth Amendment. None of these provisions acknowledges any distinction between citizens and resident aliens. They extend their inalienable privileges to all "persons" and guard against any encroachment on those rights by federal or state authority. * * *

> Since resident aliens have constitutional rights, it follows that Congress may not ignore them in the exercise of its "plenary" power of deportation. * * * [T]he First Amendment and other portions of the Bill of Rights make no exception in favor of deportation laws or laws enacted pursuant to a "plenary" power of the Government. Hence the very provisions of the Constitution negative the proposition that Congress, in the exercise of a "plenary" power, may override the rights of those who are numbered among the beneficiaries of the Bill of Rights.

> Any other conclusion would make our constitutional safeguards transitory and discriminatory in nature. Thus the Government would be precluded from enjoining or imprisoning an alien for exercising his freedom of speech. But the Government at the same time would be free, from a constitutional standpoint, to deport him for exercising that very same freedom. The alien would be fully clothed with his constitutional rights when defending himself in a court of law, but he would be stripped of those rights when deportation officials encircle him. I cannot agree that the framers of the Constitution meant to make such an empty mockery of human freedom.

Bridges v. Wixon, 326 U.S. 135, 161–62, 65 S.Ct. 1443, 1455–56, 89 L.Ed. 2103 (1945) (Murphy, J., concurring). *See generally* Note, *Immigration and the First Amendment,* 73 Calif.L.Rev. 1889 (1985).

Do you agree with Justice Murphy that if the First Amendment prohibits the government from imprisoning an alien for protected speech, it also must prohibit the government from deporting the alien? The answer to this question would seem to depend in part upon one's view of the source and nature of the deportation power. Furthermore, if immigration decisions are intimately linked to the process of national self-definition, why should the nation not be able to deny aliens membership on political grounds even if it is unable to control the conduct of present members? Finally, cannot one distinguish imprisonment from deportation on the grounds that the latter is not "punishment," but simply the withdrawal of a privilege to remain in the United States ?[10]

Relying on doctrinal developments in First Amendment law and the force of Justice Murphy's reasoning in *Bridges v. Wixon,* a federal district court in 1989 held unconstitutional several parts of § 241(a) mandating deportation for certain kinds of "subversive" speech. *American-Arab Anti–Discrimination Committee v. Meese,* 714 F.Supp. 1060 (C.D.Cal.1989). To our knowledge, the court's decision was the first in American history to invalidate a deportation ground on constitutional grounds.

The court rejected the government's claim that "Congress' plenary power over immigration" justified a lower First Amendment standard for aliens in the deportation context:

> [I]t is impossible to adopt for aliens a lower degree of First Amendment protection solely in the deportation setting without seriously affecting their First Amendment rights outside that setting. Under a lower First Amendment standard, and without the constitutional protection against ex post facto laws, the Government could conceivably pass a law allowing for the deportation of aliens for statements made several decades earlier. An alien would have no way of knowing whether his or her speech would someday become a ground for deportation and consequently would be chilled from speaking at all.

> Simply stated, the Government's view is that aliens are free to say whatever they wish but the Government maintains the ability to deport them for the content of their speech. To state the proposition is to reject it. * * * Since aliens enjoy full First Amendment protection outside the deportation setting, we decline to adopt a lesser First Amendment test for use within that setting.

Id. at 1081–82. As to the government's claim that *Harisiades* provided strong support for its position that the deportation grounds were constitutional, the court stated:

> In addressing the aliens' First Amendment argument, the *Harisiades* Court dealt directly with the question of whether aliens have First Amendment rights in deportation matters. The Gov-

---

10. Assuming that admission of an alien is a "privilege," may Congress attach *any* condition it wants to a privilege it creates? Although this was once the prevailing view, it is now commonplace to say that the "rights/privilege distinction" is dead. *See, e.g., Sherbert v. Verner,* 374 U.S. 398, 404, 83 S.Ct. 1790, 1794, 10 L.Ed.2d 965 (1963); *Keyishian v. Board of Regents,* 385 U.S. 589, 605–06, 87 S.Ct. 675, 684–85, 17 L.Ed.2d 629 (1967); *Graham v. Richardson,* 403 U.S. 365, 374–75, 91 S.Ct. 1848, 1853, 29 L.Ed.2d 534 (1971). *See generally* Van Alstyne, *The Demise of the Right–Privilege Distinction in Constitutional Law,* 81 Harv.L.Rev. 1439 (1968). The funeral services, however, may have been premature; the distinction continues to be viewed as useful and inescapable in some settings. *See Landon v. Plasencia,* 459 U.S. 21, 32, 103 S.Ct. 321, 329, 74 L.Ed.2d 21 (1982); Smolla, *The Reemergence of the Right–Privilege Distinction in Constitutional Law: The Price of Protesting Too Much,* 35 Stan.L.Rev. 69 (1982).

ernment, as in this case, urged the Court to find that the First Amendment does not apply "to the political decision of Congress to expel a class of aliens whom it deems undesirable residents." The Court rejected this argument, ruling that it had the duty of distinguishing between aliens' constitutionally protected "advocacy of political methods" and their unprotected "methodical but prudent incitement to violence." To make this distinction, the Court explicitly employed the then prevailing test from *Dennis v. United States*. Although the Court found that the First Amendment did not prevent the resident aliens' deportation, the importance of its ruling for the instant case is that the Court applied the same First Amendment standard to aliens' claims that then applied to United States citizens' First Amendment challenges.

   * * * Had the *Harisiades* Court found that the Government's plenary immigration power required the same degree of judicial deference in *all* deportation challenges, it could have summarily dismissed the First Amendment attack in a sentence or two with a citation to its previous substantive due process discussion.

Id. at 1077–78.

Under this analysis, *Harisiades* helps the aliens rather than the government because of developments in First Amendment law since *Dennis* that have significantly expanded protection for political speech. Thus the district court could conclude that "no searching inquiry" was necessary to hold that the challenged provisions were "substantially overbroad" and therefore unconstitutional under current First Amendment doctrine.

On appeal, the Ninth Circuit reversed and remanded on the ground that the case was not yet ripe for judicial review. *American–Arab Anti–Discrimination Committee v. Nelson*, 970 F.2d 501 (9th Cir.1992). The Ninth Circuit noted that a full factual record had not yet been developed, and that Congress had repealed the deportation grounds that the INS had invoked. The INS has kept on with its efforts to deport the eight aliens— six nonimmigrants for overstays and other violations of their status, and two permanent residents under new INA § 241(a)(4)(B) for "terrorist" activity. In January 1994, Judge Wilson (the district judge in *American–Arab Anti–Discrimination Committee*) preliminarily enjoined deportation proceedings against the six nonimmigrants as unlawful selective prosecution based on their political associations. He found that he lacked jurisdiction to enjoin deportation proceedings against the two permanent residents. As we go to press, these rulings are on appeal to the Court of Appeals for the Ninth Circuit. In the pending deportation proceedings against the two permanent residents, the INS is asserting that § 241(a)(4)(B) covers any alien who has raised money or otherwise supported any organization that has ever engaged in terrorist activity. *See Matter of Hamide and Shehadeh*, Nos. A19 262 560 and A30 660 528. Both groups of aliens are making First Amendment claims similar to those endorsed earlier by Judge Wilson. *See generally* 71 Interp.Rel. 325 (1994). The INS position has prompted some sharp public criticism from the academy and the press. *See* Lewis, *Cause for Justice*, N.Y. Times, Sept. 20, 1993, at A13 (INS has an "especially dubious" case that goes "beyond common sense and the language of the statute").

A bill now pending in Congress may clarify the scope of INA § 241(a)(4)(B). S.390, 104th Cong., 2d Sess., proposing The Omnibus Counterterrorism Act of 1995, would expand the present exclusion and deportation grounds for terrorist activity. Among other things, under S.390 the determination that an alien is an excludable or deportable "representative" of a terrorist organization would be unreviewable in any court, and the definition of "terrorist organization" would include "any organization engaged, or which has a significant subgroup which engages, in terrorism activity, regardless of any legitimate activities conducted by the organization or its subgroups." *Id.*, § 202.

American-Arab Anti–Discrimination Committee is not the only recent decision to conclude that the First Amendment protects permanent residents and citizens equally. In *Rafeedie v. INS*, 795 F.Supp. 13, 22 (D.D.C.1992), the district court concluded that a permanent resident "is entitled to the same First Amendment protections as United States citizens, including the limitations imposed by the overbreadth and vagueness doctrines." *Rafeedie* is even more noteworthy because it concerned *exclusion* of a returning permanent resident, not deportation.

Do you think the Supreme Court would agree with the district court's analysis in *American-Arab Anti–Discrimination Committee*? Is new § 241(a)(4) constitutional as the INS is interpreting it? Should a different result be reached as to nonimmigrant aliens? What if the issue is not deportation or exclusion as such? In *Flemming v. Nestor,* 363 U.S. 603, 80 S.Ct. 1367, 4 L.Ed.2d 1435 (1960), the Supreme Court upheld the constitutionality of a statute that terminated the payment of social security benefits to aliens deported as subversives. For a treatment of similar issues in the naturalization context, see *Price v. INS*, 962 F.2d 836 (9th Cir.1992), *cert. denied,* ___ U.S. ___, 114 S.Ct. 683, 126 L.Ed.2d 650 (1994), p. 1010 *infra.*

Congress' Power to Discriminate

Consider Justice Frankfurter's remarks in his concurring opinion in *Harisiades:* "[T]he underlying policies of what classes of aliens shall be allowed to enter and what classes of aliens shall be allowed to stay, are for Congress exclusively to determine even though such determination may be deemed to offend American traditions and may, as has been the case, jeopardize peace." Can this be correct? How if at all does Justice Jackson's majority opinion adopt a different approach? Could Congress order the deportation of all black aliens or Jewish aliens? Did the cases upholding the Chinese exclusion laws answer this question? Did *Fiallo v. Bell?*

Deportation Statutes and the *Ex Post Facto* Clause

The case law makes clear that an alien may be deported for conduct that did not render the alien deportable at the time the act was committed.

In constitutional law terms, the prohibition against *ex post facto* laws does not apply to deportation statutes. For example, in *Galvan v. Press,* 347 U.S. 522, 74 S.Ct. 737, 98 L.Ed. 911 (1954), the Supreme Court considered the constitutionality of retroactive application of the Subversive Activity Control Act, Ch. 1024, 64 Stat. 1006 (1950), which ordered the deportation of any alien who at any time after entry had been a member of the Communist Party. Galvan, an alien of Mexican birth, had entered the United States in 1918. At Galvan's deportation hearing in 1950, the INS Hearing Officer found that he had been a member of the Communist Party between 1944 and 1946. Thus Galvan was ordered deported even though, as pointed out by the dissent of Justice Black (joined by Justice Douglas), at the time of his membership "[Communist] Party candidates appeared on California election ballots, and no federal law then frowned on Communist Party political activities." *Id.* at 532, 74 S.Ct. at 743.

Justice Frankfurter, writing for the Court, rejected Galvan's constitutional claims:

> In light of the expansion of the concept of substantive due process as a limitation upon all powers of Congress, * * * much could be said for the view, were we writing on a clean slate, that the Due Process Clause qualifies the scope of political discretion heretofore recognized as belonging to Congress in regulating the entry and deportation of aliens. And since the intrinsic consequences of deportation are so close to punishment for crime, it might fairly be said also that the *ex post facto* Clause, even though applicable only to punitive legislation, should be applied to deportation.

> But the slate is not clean. As to the extent of the power of Congress under review, there is not merely "a page of history," *New York Trust Co. v. Eisner,* 256 U.S. 345, 349, 41 S.Ct. 506, 507, 65 L.Ed. 943, but a whole volume. Policies pertaining to the entry of aliens and their right to remain here are peculiarly concerned with the political conduct of government. * * * [T]hat the formulation of these policies is entrusted exclusively to Congress has become about as firmly imbedded in the legislative and judicial tissues of our body politic as any aspect of our government. And whatever might have been said at an earlier date for applying the *ex post facto* Clause, it has been the unbroken rule of this Court that it has no application to deportation.

Id. at 530–31, 74 S.Ct. at 742.

Justices Black and Douglas dissented: "For joining a lawful political group years ago—an act which he had no possible reason to believe would subject him to the slightest penalty—[Galvan] now loses his job, his friends, his home, and maybe even his children, who must choose between their father and their native country." *Id.* at 533, 74 S.Ct. at 744 (Black, J., dissenting).

Are the statutes in *Harisiades* and in *Galvan* truly *ex post facto* laws? Or do they simply restate other deportation grounds that existed when the aliens undertook the conduct which subsequently resulted in deportation?

Recall Justice Jackson's comment in *Harisiades* that "[d]uring all the years since 1920 Congress has maintained a standing admonition to aliens, on pain of deportation, not to become members of any organization that advocates overthrow of the United States Government by force and violence, a category repeatedly held to include the Communist Party." Is the *ex post facto* claim stronger in *Galvan,* where the Subversive Activity Control Act dispensed with proof of the violent purposes of the Communist Party (proof that was required under the 1918 and subsequent statutes)?

Perhaps a clearer example of an *ex post facto* law appears in *Mahler v. Eby,* 264 U.S. 32, 44 S.Ct. 283, 68 L.Ed. 549 (1924). In 1920, Congress added as a deportation ground violation of the Selective Draft Act or the Espionage Act, both of which were enacted in 1917. Act of May 10, 1917, Ch. 174, § 1, 41 Stat. 593. Herbert Mahler was convicted of violating both Acts in 1918 and sentenced to five years in the federal penitentiary at Leavenworth. He was ordered deported in 1921 under the 1920 statute, even though at the time of his conviction in 1918 violations of the Acts were not grounds for deportation. (Furthermore, the criminal statutes had been repealed before the deportation proceeding.) The Court rejected the *ex post facto* claim: "Congress by the Act of 1920 was not increasing the punishment for the crimes of which [Mahler] had been convicted, by requiring [his] deportation if found [an] undesirable [resident]. It was, in the exercise of its unquestioned right, only seeking to rid the country of persons who had shown by their career that their continued presence here would not make for the safety or welfare of society." 264 U.S. at 39, 44 S.Ct. at 286. *See also Marcello v. Bonds,* 349 U.S. 302, 75 S.Ct. 757, 99 L.Ed. 1107 (1955) (rejecting *ex post facto* claim). Is it sensible to limit application of the *ex post facto* clause to criminal legislation, or do the values underlying the clause support scrutiny of non-criminal statutes that impose substantial burdens on individuals for past conduct? *See* Note, *Ex Post Facto Limitations on Legislative Power,* 73 Mich.L.Rev. 1491 (1975).

Even were we to conclude that a deportation statute is not punishment and therefore not condemned by the *ex post facto* clause, our inquiry would not be ended. The Supreme Court has made clear that it will scrutinize, under the due process clause, legislation that imposes new civil duties or liabilities based on past acts. *See, e.g., Pension Benefit Guaranty Corp. v. R.A. Gray & Co.,* 467 U.S. 717, 104 S.Ct. 2709, 81 L.Ed.2d 601 (1984); *Usery v. Turner Elkhorn Mining Co.,* 428 U.S. 1, 96 S.Ct. 2882, 49 L.Ed.2d 752 (1976). Since the New Deal, however, the Court has been quite hesitant to strike down retroactive impositions of burdens on industry. *See id.,* 428 U.S. at 17, 96 S.Ct. at 2893 (upholding sections of Federal Coal Mine Health and Safety Act of 1969 that require mine operators to provide compensation for former employee's death or disability due to black lung disease, even if employee had terminated employment before Act was passed).

Should this judicial deference apply with equal force in the deportation context? If we swallow the fiction that deportation is not punishment, what interests does the government serve by sending someone home for committing an act for which she could not have been deported at the time of the act's commission? Consider the observation in *Mahler v. Eby, supra,* that deportation for past bad acts seems no different from a law prohibiting persons convicted of a felony from practicing medicine. 264 U.S. at 39, 44 S.Ct. at 286.

There are two distinct issues that might concern us about the retroactive application of deportation statutes. The first is the obvious point that it is unfair to impose harsh sanctions upon a person for conduct which was lawful when undertaken. The second issue, which seems to be more at stake in *Harisiades,* is the justness of deporting a person who made a mistake long ago but since has lived a peaceful and productive life in the United States. Justice Douglas has described this problem as "the absence of a rational connection between the imposition of the penalty of deportation and the *present* desirability of the alien as a resident in this country." *Marcello v. Bonds,* 349 U.S. 302, 321, 75 S.Ct. 757, 767, 99 L.Ed. 1107 (1955) (Douglas, J., dissenting) (emphasis in original). Do you agree?

In 1978, Congress added a deportation ground, now in INA § 241(a)(4)(D), directed at former Nazis who had "ordered, incited, assisted, or otherwise participated" in the persecution of others between 1933 and 1945. The provision is known as the "Holtzman Amendment," named after its sponsor, Representative Elizabeth Holtzman. The courts and the BIA have rejected the claim that the new ground is an unconstitutional *ex post facto* law. *See Artukovic v. INS,* 693 F.2d 894 (9th Cir.1982); *Matter of Kulle,* 19 I & N Dec. 318 (BIA 1985). As discussed later in this Section, § 241(a)(4)(D) has also withstood arguments that it is an unconstitutional bill of attainder.

Similar issues have arisen from Congress' recent efforts to stiffen the deportation consequences of criminal activity by adding new deportation grounds and extending the scope of existing ones. *Ex post facto* challenges to the retroactive application of these changes have consistently failed. *See, e.g., United States v. Yacoubian,* 24 F.3d 1, 9–10 (9th Cir.1994) (deportation ground for firearms offenses applies retroactively); *Campos v. INS,* 16 F.3d 118, 122 (6th Cir.1994) (bar to waiver of deportation for aggravated felons applies retroactively); *United States v. Bodre,* 948 F.2d 28, 31–35 (1st Cir.1991) (repeal of judicial recommendations against deportation applies retroactively), *cert. denied,* 503 U.S. 941, 112 S.Ct. 1487, 117 L.Ed.2d 628 (1992).

Of course, courts need not decide constitutional *ex post facto* challenges unless they first construe a statute to apply retroactively. In 1994, the Supreme Court addressed retroactivity as a statutory interpretation issue in two cases involving the Civil Rights Act of 1991. According to the Court, retroactivity is a disfavored construction: "If the statute would operate retroactively, our traditional presumption teaches that it does not govern absent clear congressional intent favoring such a result." *Landgraf v. USI Film Products,* 511 U.S. ___, ___, 114 S.Ct. 1483, 1505, 128 L.Ed.2d 229 (1994). *Accord, Rivers v. Roadway Express, Inc.,* 511 U.S. ___, ___, 114 S.Ct. 1510, 1519, 128 L.Ed.2d 274 (1994). For a case holding that the deportation ground for firearms offenses, INA § 241(a)(2)(C), applies retroactively, see *Lopez–Amaro v. INS,* 25 F.3d 986, 988 (11th Cir.1994), *cert. denied,* ___ U.S. ___, 115 S.Ct. 1093, 130 L.Ed.2d 1062 (1995).

On the Construction of Immigration Statutes

Although (or perhaps, because) the Supreme Court has supplied no constitutional check on Congress' power to designate deportable classes of aliens, the Court has generally read deportation statutes quite narrowly. Justice Douglas penned the classic statement of this canon of interpretation:

> We resolve the doubts in favor of that construction [urged by the alien] because deportation is a drastic measure and at times the equivalent of banishment or exile * * *. It is the forfeiture for misconduct of a residence in this country. Such a forfeiture is a penalty. To construe this statutory provision less generously to the alien might find support in logic. But since the stakes are considerable for the individual, we will not assume that Congress meant to trench on his freedom beyond that which is required by the narrowest of several possible meanings of the words used.

Fong Haw Tan v. Phelan, 333 U.S. 6, 10, 68 S.Ct. 374, 376, 92 L.Ed. 433 (1948). In *Fong Haw Tan,* the government sought to deport a permanent resident alien on the basis of a criminal record; the Supreme Court ultimately interpreted the statute not to establish deportability. Should *Fong Haw Tan* 's rule of statutory interpretation apply in deportation cases involving nonimmigrants?

Does the Court's reading of the Constitution appear contradictory to its reading of immigration statutes? Or, does it demonstrate the Court's appreciation of the separation of powers that underlies our form of government? That is, the Supreme Court recognizes broad congressional authority but, because of the harsh consequences of deportation, will insist that Congress state with clarity what conduct shall render the alien deportable. This "clear statement" rule of statutory construction serves at least two purposes: imposition of a duty on Congress to consider carefully the scope of the grounds of deportation, and notice to aliens as to the specific acts that are condemned.

2. GROUNDS OF DEPORTATION

Section 241 of the INA lists the grounds of deportation. Like the exclusion grounds, they are an historical collection of traits and acts that various United States Congresses over the past century have deemed undesirable. The Immigration Act of 1990 lent some semblance of order to the deportation grounds, reorganizing and pruning the list. It also repealed a few of the more outdated grounds (including those mandating the deportation of prostitutes and persons institutionalized at public expense because of mental disease).

Table 6.1 indicates the frequency with which the various grounds of deportation have resulted in the removal of aliens over the last 13 years.

Table 6.1

Aliens Deported By Cause, Fiscal Years 1981–93

Year	Total	Convictions for criminal or narcotics violations	Related to criminal or narcotics violations	Entered without inspection	Violation of non-immigrant status	Other	Unknown
1981-93	315,916	79,052	5,027	199,743	18,586	12,786	722
1981-90	212,269	30,464	1,948	154,898	15,906	8,711	342
1981	16,720	310	54	13,601	1,959	776	20
1982	14,518	413	64	11,554	1,796	679	12
1983	18,232	863	93	14,318	1,958	994	6
1984	17,607	981	80	14,082	1,702	760	2
1985	21,334	1,544	150	16,943	1,916	775	6
1986	22,225	1,695	165	17,746	1,858	697	64
1987	22,233	4,091	265	15,759	1,268	848	2
1988	22,963	5,432	302	15,224	988	971	46
1989	30,346	7,003	341	20,588	1,236	1,101	77
1990	26,091	8,132	434	15,083	1,225	1,110	107
1991-93	103,647	48,588	3,079	44,845	2,680	4,075	380
1991	28,759	12,502	715	13,199	1,040	1,164	139
1992	38,202	17,216	1,201	17,190	982	1,482	131
1993	36,686	18,870	1,163	14,456	658	1,429	110

Source: 1993 INS Statistical Yearbook, Table 66.

Note that some of the grounds apply to conduct before entry (*e.g.*, (4)(D) (Nazis)); before or after entry (*e.g.*, (1)(E) (aiding illegal entry)); any time after entry (*e.g.*, (2)(A)(ii) (multiple criminal convictions)); or within a certain number of years after entry (*e.g.*, (5) (public charge within five years of entry from causes not arising after entry)). What accounts for these differences? Is it simply historical happenstance, or is there an underlying set of principles that explains the differences?

The following material is selective; it does not cover all deportation grounds, just the most important, and it does not cover waivers of specific deportation grounds. Please note also that waiver of deportation may also be available under INA § 212(c), discussed in Chapter Seven *infra*.

As you consider these deportation materials, assume that you are a member of Congress considering legislation that would rework the deportation grounds in the INA. Which of the grounds of deportation now included in § 241(a) would you vote to maintain or delete? What grounds would you *add*? Aliens who are child-abusers? Who do not naturalize within a certain number of years? Who violate civil rights laws?

What underlying principles and values guide your choices? Would you deport an alien for conduct (or a trait) which is not unlawful if done (or possessed) by an American citizen—*e.g.*, drug addiction or poverty? To state this question more abstractly, should we insist that those who have joined the American community by immigrating have fewer faults or be less of a burden on society than persons who are born here? Is Congress using the immigration laws, in part, to protect its image of ideal members of our community—an ideal that citizens sometimes fail to fulfill?

a. *Immigration Control Grounds*

(i) *Excludable at Time of Entry*

Section 241(a)(1)(A), a direct descendant of an early deportation provision, Act of March 3, 1891, § 11, 26 Stat. 1086, subjects an alien to deportation if he or she was excludable at time of entry or adjustment of status. The obvious purpose of the paragraph is to enable the government to expel aliens who had no right to enter the country. It is, as the leading authorities describe it, "delayed exclusion." GM & Y § 71.04[1]. There is no statute of limitations attached to this provision. Nor does the fact that the alien passed through inspection at the border prevent the government from subsequently deporting her. *See Pearson v. Williams*, 202 U.S. 281, 26 S.Ct. 608, 50 L.Ed. 1029 (1906).

Because of the re-entry doctrine, an alien who was not deportable when he left the United States may be deportable under § 241(a)(1)(A) after his re-entry where his conduct prior to leaving is a ground of exclusion. Recall *United States ex rel. Volpe v. Smith*, p. 487 *supra*.

Recognizing the potential harshness of § 241(a)(1)(A), Congress has provided a waiver for aliens, excludable for fraud or misrepresentation in obtaining an immigrant visa or entry, who have close relatives in the United States. INA § 241(a)(1)(H). Eligibility for this waiver is easier to establish than for the related exclusion waiver in § 212(i). Is this a sensible policy?

(ii) Entry Without Inspection or Presence in the United States in Violation of Law

By far the most frequently invoked ground of deportation is INA § 241(a)(1)(B): "entered the United States without inspection * * * or * * * is in the United States in violation of this Act." This provision embraces most of the aliens we commonly think of as "undocumented" or "illegal"—those who entered the United States surreptitiously by evading inspection ("EWI's") and those who entered lawfully with nonimmigrant visas (as students or visitors, for example) and stayed beyond the time authorized. (It should be stressed, however, that only one or two percent of the apprehended EWI's go through deportation proceedings. The rest avail themselves of "voluntary departure"—a procedure, discussed in Chapter Seven *infra*, that permits the alien to leave the United States at her own expense within a certain period of time.) Section 241(a)(1)(B) also applies to aliens who present themselves at the border and falsely claim American citizenship. The Supreme Court has held that such conduct "so significantly frustrate[s] the process for inspecting incoming aliens" that it renders the alien deportable under § 241(a)(1)(B) as having evaded inspection. *Reid v. INS*, 420 U.S. 619, 624, 95 S.Ct. 1164, 1168, 43 L.Ed.2d 501 (1975).

Note the overlap between deportation grounds. Nonimmigrants who violate the conditions of their admission are also deportable under INA § 241(a)(1)(C)(i). Also, ask yourself to what extent §§ 241(a)(1)(A) and (1)(B) overlap. Are all aliens who were excludable at time of entry also in the United States in violation of law? Suppose P, a permanent resident alien, had been convicted of a crime involving moral turpitude in his home country but did not disclose that fact to consular officials when applying for a visa or to INS officers at the time of his admission. Is he deportable under (1)(A) and/or (1)(B)?

Is every alien deportable under § 241(a)(1)(B) also deportable under (1)(A)? Is an alien who surreptitiously crosses the border deportable under (1)(A)? What about a nonimmigrant who stays beyond the time authorized at the time of admission?

Does § 241(a)(1)(B) apply to returning residents who enter without inspection or who enter without inspection and subsequently enter properly? Suppose permanent resident R leaves the United States to help alien S enter this country unlawfully. R and S cross the border surreptitiously but are apprehended five days later. R is charged under § 241(a)(1)(B) with entry without inspection. R's deportation hearing is scheduled for some months in the future. While he is waiting, he leaves the United States and re-enters by showing his green card to INS border officials. At the deportation hearing, R claims that his *last* entry was lawful and thus he can no longer be deemed deportable under § 241(a)(1)(B). What result?

The BIA considered such a claim in *Matter of Ruis,* 18 I & N Dec. 320 (BIA 1982). It held:

> [Section 241(a)(1)(B)] of the Act relates to any entry made by an alien who fails to submit to inspection. Consequently, we find that the respondent's deportability for entering without inspection is not prevented by the mere fact that he departed and returned with his Form I–151. To hold otherwise would be to thwart the policies underlying the Act and to provide an opportunity for aliens to violate our immigration laws with impunity.
>
> We need not decide at this time whether an alien who has entered the United States without inspection will be forever subject to deportation in all circumstances.[2]

Id. at 322–23. *See also Gunaydin v. United States INS,* 742 F.2d 776, 777–78 (3d Cir.1984) (following *Ruis*).

The result in *Ruis* may well strike you as correct, given the particular facts of the case. But what about the conclusion of the BIA that an entry without inspection is not erased by a subsequent lawful entry? Suppose alien B surreptitiously enters the United States to live with a relative, pending approval of a family preference visa. When the visa is approved, B returns home, picks up the visa and enters as a permanent resident alien.[11] Does B's prior illegal entry and residence subject him to deportation under § 241(a)(1)(B)? *Cf. Matter of R.G.,* 8 I & N Dec. 128 (BIA 1958) (prior conviction for attempting entry by misrepresenting self as U.S. citizen does not bar subsequent admission as lawful permanent resident and would not subject alien to immediate deportation after lawful entry under § 241(a)(3)). Or suppose that alien Q, a returning resident, was unaware that she was required to undergo inspection and thus neglected to do so.

2. We would note in this regard that the Service has prosecutorial discretion to decline to pursue the deportation of an alien who has entered the United States without inspection despite his possession of documents. *See* Operations Instructions 235.9; *see also* section 101(a)(13) of the Act. [Footnote by the BIA.]

11. This situation is hardly fanciful. *See generally* Portes, *The Return of the Wetback,* 11 Society 40, 41 (1974) ("The vast majority of new male adult Mexican immigrants have already lived in the United States * * *.")

Is Q deportable under § 241(a)(1)(B)? *Cf. Ex parte Callow,* 240 Fed. 212 (D.Colo.1916) (alien who had properly entered U.S. several times deportable for entry without inspection even though unaware of requirement of inspection).

Perhaps these types of situations led the BIA expressly to leave open the implications of its decision and to mention the INS Operations Instruction. Can you formulate a rule that would extend coverage of § 241(a)(1)(B) to appropriate situations and not others? What principles underlie your conclusions as to what an "appropriate situation" is?

(iii) Failure to Maintain Nonimmigrant Status

INA § 241(a)(1)(C)(i) provides for the deportation of nonimmigrants who fail to maintain their status or violate the conditions of their entry. This ground is primarily applied to nonimmigrants who stay beyond the time authorized at their admission. It would also cover, for example, nonimmigrants who work without authorization, students who leave school, and temporary workers who abandon their employment. *E.g., Olaniyan v. District Director,* 796 F.2d 373 (10th Cir.1986) (unauthorized employment). Nonimmigrants who are out of status or violate conditions on their stay are also deportable under INA § 241(a)(1)(B), because they are deemed to be in this country in violation of law.

In the midst of the Iranian hostage crisis, Attorney General Civiletti ordered all Iranians admitted as nonimmigrant students to report to INS district offices to demonstrate that they were in a lawful status (*e.g.,* still in the school they were authorized to attend). 44 Fed.Reg. 65728 (1979), *amended,* 44 Fed.Reg. 75165 (1979), *rescinded,* 46 Fed.Reg. 25599 (1981). This unprecedented regulation of nonimmigrants was challenged as beyond the Attorney General's authority and a violation of equal protection. A panel of the Court of Appeals for the District of Columbia rejected the claims. *Narenji v. Civiletti,* 617 F.2d 745 (D.C.Cir.1979), *cert. denied,* 446 U.S. 957, 100 S.Ct. 2928, 64 L.Ed.2d 815 (1980). Although the vast majority of the more than 50,000 Iranian students who reported to INS offices were found to be lawfully in the United States, those nonimmigrants who were out of status were ordered deported. *E.g., Shoaee v. INS,* 704 F.2d 1079 (9th Cir.1983).

(iv) Document Fraud

In 1990, Congress added § 274C, which you should now read. It imposes civil and criminal penalties on persons and entities that engage knowingly in various types of fraud in connection with immigration-related documents. Section 241(a)(3)(C) makes deportable any alien subject to a final order under § 274C. (Section 212(a)(6)(F) provides for exclusion as well.) The government can prove a civil violation of § 274C with just a preponderance of the evidence. There is no automatic hearing on the charges. Rather, the respondent must request a hearing or else a final order will issue automatically. In August 1994, a class action lawsuit was filed in federal district court in Seattle, claiming that the INS is enforcing § 274C without providing adequate notice of the nature and consequences of the proceedings. *Walters v. Reno*, No. C–94–1204 (W.D.Wash. Aug. 15, 1994).

The INS has concentrated its enforcement efforts on documents that employees offer to show work authorization in connection with I–9 forms. There is some question, however, as to whether § 274C covers documents in this context. On this issue and § 274C generally, see Levy, *A Practitioner's Guide to Section 274C: Parts 1 & 2*, 94–6 & 94–7 Imm.Briefings (1994).

b. Crime-Related Grounds

One of the most important trends in immigration law and policy over the past decade has been the growing emphasis on the swift deportation of aliens with criminal convictions. Congress has enacted a number of statutory provisions toward this end, and the INS has followed in the same direction. The statutory amendments include more restrictive substantive deportation grounds (discussed immediately following), swifter deportation procedures (discussed in Section B *infra*), and restrictions on relief from deportation (discussed in Chapter Seven *infra*). For now, we offer just a brief overview.

On the substantive side, Congress has added new deportation grounds for criminal activity and made aliens with convictions ineligible for certain forms of relief from deportation. Key has been the growing reliance on the term "aggravated felony," added by the Anti–Drug Abuse of 1988, Pub.L. No. 100–690, 102 Stat. 4181, and defined in INA § 101(a)(43). Congress has expanded the definition several times since. Also, § 505 of the 1990 Act repealed INA § 241(b), which had provided for judicial recommendations against deportation ("JRADs"). Contrary to the implication of the term "recommendation," JRADs were binding judicial determinations in criminal cases that convictions for crimes of moral turpitude would not visit negative immigration consequences upon the alien, *e.g.*, deportation or future exclusion.

Congress has also streamlined deportation procedures for criminal aliens. In 1986, it added what is now INA § 242(i), which requires the Attorney General to begin deportation proceedings "as expeditiously as possible" after conviction for a deportable crime. In 1988, § 242A established expedited deportation procedures for aliens with aggravated felony convictions, and § 242(a)(2) provided for their detention pending deportation. The 1994 Crime Act established an administrative deportation procedure, which avoids proceedings before an immigration judge, for aliens who are aggravated felons without permanent resident status and who are not eligible for any relief from deportation. *See* INA § 242A(b).

Congress has also focused on agency implementation. In 1990, while Congress was deliberating on the proposed Comprehensive Crime Control bill, the House Judiciary Committee stated in a sharply worded report that it was

> deeply disturbed that INS has not placed a higher priority on the criminal alien problem. Although the budget authority of INS in [FY] 1989 exceeded $1 billion, less than $50 million was expended

investigating, detaining and deporting criminal aliens. The Committee is convinced that among the classes of aliens deserving of deportation no class should receive greater attention than aliens convicted of serious criminal offenses. * * *

* * * According to a 1986 GAO report, approximately one out of every ten felony arrests in the New York City area involved an alien. The Department of Correctional Services for the State of New York reports that as of April 1988, foreign-born inmates in their custody comprised 11 percent of the total inmate population and represented 103 different countries of birth. * * *

In California, San Diego County's concern that illegal aliens were committing an increasing share of the crime led to a survey in which the Police Department found 16 percent of all felony arrests and 10 percent of misdemeanor arrests involved illegal aliens. The Sheriff's Department found that 30 percent of those arrested were undocumented aliens. The Santa Ana Narcotics Task Force reported that approximately 95 percent of the individuals they arrested, primarily on drug-trafficking charges, were illegal aliens.

H.Rep. No. 101–681, pt.1, at 145–46 (1990).

In response to these concerns, INS has in place a "Alien Criminal Apprehension Program" to identify and remove criminal aliens, primarily by exchanging information with federal, state, and local law enforcement agencies. A key element is the Institutional Hearing Program ("IHP"), *i.e.,* deportation hearings for convicted alien felons while they are still in prison, so that their deportation orders can be carried out as soon as they have served out their sentences. The 1994 Crime Act also required the INS to establish a Criminal Alien Tracking Center to notify law enforcement agencies if individuals arrested for crimes are aliens. *See* Pub.L. 103–322, § 130002, 108 Stat. 1796, 2023. To enhance information flow in the other direction, the 1990 Immigration Act requires states to send certified court records of all aliens with state law convictions to the INS. The number of aliens deported for criminal convictions has increased steadily in the past several years, from 8,132 in FY 1990 up to 18,870 in FY 1993. 1993 INS Statistical Yearbook, Table 67. The 1994 Crime Act supported these efforts by authorizing $55 million in appropriations to identify and remove criminal aliens in the federal prison system upon their release from incarceration. *See* Pub.L. 103–322, § 130007, 108 Stat. 1796, 2029.

These efforts have drawn attention to the substantial number of deportable aliens in the incarcerated population. A number of states have demanded financial reimbursement from the federal government for incarceration costs, particularly for undocumented criminal aliens. The 1994 Crime Act responded with new INA § 242(j), which provides that upon request by a state, the Attorney General must either compensate the state or local authorities for incarceration costs or take federal custody of the alien. The Crime Act also authorized $1.8 billion over six years for federal reimbursements to states. *See* Pub.L. 103–322, § 20301, 108 Stat. 1796, 1824; 71 Interp.Rel. 1356 (1994).

(i) Crimes Involving Moral Turpitude: A Discussion of the Meaning of Statutes

In spite of the substantial amount of new legislation, the principal crime-related deportation ground focuses on "crimes of moral turpitude." Please study INA § 241(a)(2)(A). Before we continue, make sure you fully understand this provision by answering the following questions. Assume all of the crimes mentioned in these questions are crimes of moral turpitude but not aggravated felonies.

Is a permanent resident alien deportable under § 241(a)(2)(A)(i) or (ii) who:

(a) entered the United States in 1960, was convicted in 1962 of larceny and given a six-month jail sentence.

(b) entered in 1970, committed and was convicted of forgery in 1976 and extortion in 1978, and received probation both times.

(c) entered in 1976, committed and was convicted of blackmail in 1977, and was sentenced to six months to two years in prison, with all but six months of the sentence suspended.

(d) entered in 1971 and was convicted in 1979 of four counts of tax fraud in the filing of a 1978 federal tax return.

(e) entered in 1974, travelled abroad for one month in 1980, committed a burglary in 1982, was convicted a year later and sentenced to 4 years in jail.

(f) entered in 1975, was convicted in 1982 for two burglaries of the same warehouse within two days of each other, and was sentenced to 4 years. Both crimes were committed during a prolonged period of drunkenness spanning both burglaries.

Why might the provision distinguish between crimes committed within five years of entry and those committed thereafter? Is this a sensible distinction?

The Statutory History of "Moral Turpitude"

An 1875 statute provided for the exclusion of "persons who are undergoing a sentence for conviction in their own country of felonious crimes." Act of March 3, 1875, Ch. 141, § 5, 18 Stat. 477. The provision was based on the widespread belief that European nations were shipping convicted criminals to America. *See, e.g.,* H.R.Rep. No. 359, 34th Cong., 1st Sess. (1856). "Moral turpitude" first entered the immigration statutes in 1891. The 1891 Act expanded the 1875 exclusion ground to deny entry to aliens convicted of a "felony or * * * crime or misdemeanor involving moral turpitude." Act of March 3, 1891, Ch. 551, § 1, 26 Stat. 1084. Neither the Act nor the accompanying House and Senate reports attempted to define what crimes were deemed to involve moral turpitude. *See* S.Rep.

No. 2165, 61st Cong., 2d Sess. (1891); H.R.Rep. No. 3807, 51st Cong., 2d Sess. (1891).

Once the federal government exercised its power to exclude criminals it began to think about deporting aliens in the United States who committed crimes. The Dillingham Commission Report of 1911 stated that a "serious, and * * * inexcusable, defect" in the immigration laws "is the fact that aliens admitted to this country * * * may pursue a criminal career without danger of deportation." The Commission thus recommended the deportation of criminals, although it added that "[I]t is not believed that the practice of deportation should be sufficiently extended to include minor offenses." Reports of the [Dillingham] Immigration Commission, vol. 1, S.Doc. No. 747, 61st Cong., 3d Sess. 34 (1911). The Commission also recommended that the new deportation ground have a statute of limitations to ensure that the aliens' "tendency to commit crimes cannot be attributed to conditions arising subsequent to their entry into this country." *Id.* The Commission's report was followed by other congressional reports that advocated deportation of aliens who committed serious criminal offenses. *E.g.,* S.Rep. No. 355, 63d Cong., 2d Sess. 11 (1914).

These recommendations reached fruition in the Immigration Act of 1917. Primarily remembered for its adoption of a literacy requirement, the Act also provided for the deportation of any alien who was sentenced to a prison term of a year or more because of conviction in the United States "of a crime involving moral turpitude committed within five years after * * * entry" or sentenced more than once to such a term because of conviction "of any crime involving moral turpitude, committed at any time after entry." Ch. 29, § 19, 39 Stat. 889. Again the legislative history says almost nothing about Congress' understanding of what constituted a crime of moral turpitude.

It is interesting that even though the provision was carefully scrutinized on the floor of the House, no one objected to the vagueness of the phrase or to its inclusion in the deportation laws. During debate on the bill, members of Congress repeatedly referred to the phrase "crimes involving moral turpitude," and never stated a concern with the coverage of the phrase. Our best reading of the legislative history is that "crimes involving moral turpitude" was a term that presented no definitional difficulties for the members of Congress. They appear to have thought that it had acquired a commonly known meaning over time and were content to let continuing interpretation by immigration officials and judges control.

In 1950, the Senate Judiciary Committee conducted a massive review of the immigration process and made a set of recommendations that formed the basis of the McCarran–Walter Act of 1952. In a discussion of the provision of the 1917 Act that excluded aliens who had committed crimes involving moral turpitude, the Committee observed that "[t]he term 'moral turpitude' has not been definitely and conclusively defined by the courts." S.Rep. No. 1515, 81st Cong., 2d Sess. 351 (1950). The Report went on to describe proposals for reform suggested by officials who enforced the immigration laws:

The American consul at Marseille, France, stated that while the visa instructions define moral turpitude as an act which in itself is one of baseness, vileness, or depravity, the applicability of the excluding provision often depends on what the individual officer considers to be baseness, vileness, or depravity. He suggested that there be a listing of crimes and circumstances comprehended within the meaning of moral turpitude.

An immigration inspector voiced similar objections citing instances where the purpose of the law had been ignored by including petty crimes, such as theft of a newspaper. He suggested a statute of limitations on petty crimes as far as immigration considerations are concerned.

Id. at 353. However, the Committee did not recommend a change in the statutory language. Rather, it seemed satisfied with the suggestion of another INS official that, "although it might be desirable to have the crimes specifically set forth, difficulties might be encountered in getting a phrase that would be broad enough to cover the various crimes contemplated within the law and yet easier to comprehend than the present phrase." *Id.*

The 1952 Act adopted the version of the deportation ground that now appears as § 241(a)(2)(A)(i) and (ii). The Senate and House reports accompanying the legislation reveal no discussion of the meaning of "moral turpitude."

The lesson of the legislative history, such as it is, is that Congress quite simply never attempted to define the meaning of "moral turpitude." The phrase had ancient lineage and application outside the immigration laws when it was included in the statute. *See, e.g.,* W. Burdick, The Law of Crime § 87 (1946) (identifying concept in Roman Law). No doubt Congress assumed that its meaning in other areas would be imported into the 1891 immigration law. By the time the 1917 statute was under consideration, the Chairman of the House Committee on Immigration and Naturalization could comment: "[T]he Supreme Court has determined what crimes are crimes involving moral turpitude under the federal law, and if so, that would control, I should think."

Administrative and Judicial Interpretation of "Moral Turpitude"

Complete the following sentence: A crime involving moral turpitude is a crime _____. If you have difficulty completing the sentence you are not alone. As the leading immigration treatise reports, "[a]ttempts to arrive at a workable definition of moral turpitude never have yielded entire satisfaction. * * * [T]his term defies precise definition, since its limits are charted by human experience." GM & Y § 71.05[1][d][i].

Various formulations have become commonplace in the administrative and judicial decisions. Most popular is the definition borrowed from Black's Law Dictionary: "an act of baseness, vileness, or depravity in the private and social duties which a man owes to his fellow men, or to society in general, contrary to the accepted and customary rule of right and duty between man and man."[12] Other definitions include: "an act that was at common law intrinsically and morally wrong;"[13] and "[a]nything done contrary to justice, honesty, principle or good morals."[14]

To what extent can these abstract definitions decide concrete cases? Take a look at the following list of crimes. Mark in the margin whether they do or do not "involve moral turpitude." (The administrative and judicial answers are in footnote 21 on p. 551.)

1. voluntary manslaughter

2. involuntary manslaughter

3. breaking and entering

4. failure to report for induction

5. tax evasion

6. escape from prison

7. carrying a concealed weapon

8. possessing stolen property

9. sale and possession of LSD

10. aiding alien to enter unlawfully

11. consensual heterosexual anal intercourse

12. possession of an altered immigration document

13. making a false statement in an application for federal student financial aid

How should an immigration official or judge go about deciding whether a particular crime involves moral turpitude? What sources should she examine? How does she determine prevailing social views on the depravity of an offense? Consider the following decision in thinking about these questions.

12. *See, e.g., United States v. Smith,* 420 F.2d 428, 431 (5th Cir.1970). Regarding the use of dictionary definitions consider the comments of Professors Hart and Sacks:

A dictionary, it is vital to observe, never says what meaning a word *must* bear in a particular context. Nor does it ever purport to say this. An unabridged dictionary is simply an historical record, not necessarily all-inclusive, of the meanings which words in fact *have* borne, in the judgment of the editors, in the writings of reputable authors. The editors make up this record by collecting examples of uses of the word to be defined, studying each use *in context,* and then forming a judgment about the meaning in that con-

text. A good dictionary always gives examples of the use of the word *in context* in each of the meanings ascribed to it.

H. Hart & A. Sacks, The Legal Process: Basic Problems in the Making and Application of Law 1190 (W. Eskridge & P. Frickey, eds. 1994) (emphasis in original).

13. *Tillinghast v. Edmead,* 31 F.2d 81, 83 (1st Cir.1929) (theft of $15 constitutes moral turpitude).

14. *Guarneri v. Kessler,* 98 F.2d 580, 581 (5th Cir.1938), *cert. denied,* 305 U.S. 648, 59 S.Ct. 229, 83 L.Ed. 419 (1938) (conspiracy to smuggle alcohol is crime of moral turpitude).

GOLDESHTEIN v. INS

United States Court of Appeals, Ninth Circuit, 1993.
8 F.3d 645.

CANBY, CIRCUIT JUDGE.

Issue

These consolidated cases present the question whether structuring financial transactions with domestic financial institutions to avoid currency reports, in violation of 31 U.S.C. §§ 5324(a)(3) and 5322(b), is a crime involving moral turpitude within the meaning of the Immigration and Nationality Act ("INA"). * * *

I. FACTUAL & PROCEDURAL BACKGROUND

Nir Goldeshtein is a native and citizen of Israel; he last entered the United States in June 1984. In December 1984, he married Zoe Lawton; she is a United States citizen. On May 30, 1985, on the basis of his marriage, Goldeshtein became a lawful permanent resident of the United States. In March 1989, Goldeshtein pleaded guilty to one count of conspiracy to violate federal currency laws, in violation of 18 U.S.C. § 371, and two counts of structuring financial transactions with domestic financial institutions to avoid currency reports, in violation of 31 U.S.C. §§ 5324(a)(3) and 5322(b) and 18 U.S.C. § 2. Goldeshtein was sentenced to concurrent forty-month prison terms on each count. He served his sentence and was released in February 1991.

lpr
While in prison here, deport. proceedings instituted by INS

Meanwhile, on August 20, 1990, the Immigration and Naturalization Service ("INS") instituted deportation proceedings against Goldeshtein. The INS alleged that Goldeshtein was deportable under section 241(a)(4) of the INA, because he had been convicted of a crime involving moral turpitude within five years after entry and had been sentenced to prison for more than a year.[2] The INS further alleged that Goldeshtein was deportable under section 241(a)(4)(B) of the INA, because he had been convicted of an aggravated felony.[3] In October and November 1990, and January 1991, deportation hearings were held before an immigration judge ("IJ"). Goldeshtein admitted his convictions, but denied an allegation that the money involved in the offenses had come from drug sales. On January 28, 1991, the IJ ruled that Goldeshtein was deportable under section 241(a)(4) of the INA because the offense of structuring financial transactions to avoid currency reports was a crime involving moral turpitude. The IJ ruled, however, that the INS had failed to establish deportability under section 241(a)(4)(B) of the INA because the evidence was insufficient to prove that Goldeshtein's offense was drug-related. Finally, the IJ denied Goldeshtein's request for a discretionary waiver of deportation under section 212(h) of the INA. The IJ ordered Goldeshtein deported to Israel. Goldeshtein appealed to the BIA. In August 1991, the BIA affirmed the IJ's decision and dismissed the appeal. In September 1991, Goldeshtein filed a petition for review.

II. ANALYSIS

A. *Statutory Definition of the Crime*

Goldeshtein contends that he is not deportable because structuring financial transactions to avoid currency reports does not constitute a crime

---

2. This provision is now codified at INA § 241(a)(2)(A)(i).

3. This provision is now codified at INA § 241(a)(2)(A)(iii).

involving moral turpitude within the meaning of INA § 241(a)(2)(A)(i). We agree.

Our prior decisions have made it quite clear that the question whether a crime is one of moral turpitude must be answered categorically. "Whether a crime is one with intent to defraud as an element, thereby making it a crime involving moral turpitude, is determined by the statutory definition or by the nature of the crime not by the specific conduct that resulted in the conviction." *McNaughton v. INS*, 612 F.2d 457, 459 (9th Cir.1980). For a crime to involve moral turpitude within the meaning of the INA, the crime " 'must *necessarily* involve moral turpitude.' " *Chu Kong Yin*, 935 F.2d at 1003 (quoting *Tseung Chu v. Cornell*, 247 F.2d 929, 935 (9th Cir.), *cert. denied*, 355 U.S. 892, 78 S.Ct. 265, 2 L.Ed.2d 190 (1957)) (emphasis in *Tseung Chu*).

The first question we must face, then, is whether, by its definition, the crime of structuring financial transactions with domestic financial institutions to avoid the filing of currency reports necessarily involves moral turpitude. The resolution of this question turns on whether evil intent—in this case intent to defraud—is an essential element of the crime.

The statute under which Goldeshtein was convicted provides in pertinent part:

No person shall for the purpose of evading the reporting requirements of section 5313(a) ... with respect to such transaction—

* * *

(3) structure or assist in structuring, or attempt to structure or assist in structuring, any transaction with one or more domestic financial institutions.

31 U.S.C. § 5324(a)(3) (1988).[5] The penalties for "willfully violating" this provision are set forth in 31 U.S.C. § 5322(b) (1988). Thus, the language of these statutes does not make intent to defraud the government an essential element of the offense.[6]

Indeed, in this circuit a defendant may be convicted of violating section 5324 without even having known that it is a crime to structure financial transactions to avoid currency reports. *United States v. Ratzlaf*, 976 F.2d 1280, 1283–87 (9th Cir.1992), *cert. granted*, ___ U.S. ___, 113 S.Ct. 1942, 123 L.Ed.2d 648 (1993). * * *[7] We recognize that the Supreme Court will be reviewing the scienter issue in *Ratzlaf*, but even if that Court decides that the crime of structuring currency transactions includes an element of knowledge of illegality,[a] it would not affect our conclusion on the issue of

---

5. Pursuant to 31 U.S.C. § 5313(a) (1988) and 31 C.F.R. § 103.22 (1992), financial institutions must report currency transactions that involve more than $10,000.

6. Goldeshtein also pleaded guilty to conspiracy to violate 31 U.S.C. §§ 5322(b) and 5324(a)(3). The conspiracy conviction, however, does not form an independent basis for the charge of deportability; a conspiracy to commit an offense involves moral turpitude

only when the underlying substantive offense is a crime involving moral turpitude. * * *

7. Similarly, here, Goldeshtein testified at the deportation hearing that he did not know that his conduct was unlawful.

a. The Supreme Court so concluded in *Ratzlaf v. United States*, 114 S.Ct. 655, 657 (1994)—eds.

moral turpitude. As we have pointed out, section 5324 requires no intent to defraud the government (or the financial institutions) of anything. It does not require any false statements to be made or used. The statute requires only structuring to avoid a reporting requirement. That act is not inherently fraudulent. If the Supreme Court were to add a requirement of scienter, that construction would not of itself convert the crime into one of moral turpitude. A crime that involves no element of fraud is not made fraudulent by the mere fact that the violator knew of the illegality. Because "evil intent, such as an intent to defraud" is not necessarily an element of the crime of which Goldeshtein was convicted, and his offense is not of the gravest character, we conclude that this crime does not involve moral turpitude.

The INS argues that evil intent exists if a conviction requires proof that a defendant did a forbidden act "willfully." This court previously has rejected this argument. Accordingly, conviction of willful conduct within the meaning of section 5322 does not establish the evil intent required for a crime of moral turpitude.

A review of the indictment reinforces our conclusion that Goldeshtein was not convicted of a crime involving moral turpitude. The two substantive counts of the indictment to which Goldeshtein pleaded guilty simply track the language of 31 U.S.C. §§ 5322(b) and 5324(a)(3).[8] Thus, the government was not required to prove intent to defraud to convict him of the offenses defined in the indictment.

B. Nature of the Crime

Even if intent to defraud is not explicit in the statutory definition, a crime nevertheless may involve moral turpitude if such intent is "implicit in the nature of the crime." *Winestock v. INS*, 576 F.2d 234, 235 (9th Cir.1978). The INS asserts that, despite the absence of intent to defraud in the statutory definition of Goldeshtein's offense, such intent is part of its "essential nature." We disagree.

The INS essentially reiterates the analysis propounded by the BIA in its decision. Fraud is inherent in the offense, concluded the BIA, because structuring financial transactions to avoid currency reports has the effect of depriving the government of information regarding currency transactions. Unlike the alien in [*Matter of Flores*, 17 I & N Dec. 225, 229 (BIA 1980)], however, Goldeshtein did not obtain anything from the government by deceit, graft, trickery, or dishonest means. The other cases upon which the INS and the BIA rely are subject to the same distinction; they all

---

8. Count seven of the indictment charged that Goldeshtein, his codefendants, "and others knowingly, willfully, and for the purpose of evading the reporting requirements of Title 31, United States Code, Section 5313(a), structured, assisted in the structuring of, and attempted to structure and assist in the structuring of financial transactions with domestic financial institutions by purchasing or causing to be purchased forty-four money orders, totalling approximately $46,748.00, each of which was in an amount of less than $10,000.00[.]" Count nine charged that Goldeshtein and his codefendants "knowingly, willfully, and for the purpose of evading the reporting requirements of Title 31, United States Code, Section 5313(a), structured, assisted in the structuring of, and attempted to structure and assist in the structuring of financial transactions with domestic financial institutions by causing a total of $32,675 in cash to be deposited in amounts of less than $10,000[.]"

involve some false or deceitful conduct through which the alien obtained something from the government. The offense of structuring financial transactions to avoid currency reports, in contrast, does not involve the use of false statements or counterfeit documents, nor does the defendant obtain anything from the government. Instead, the offense requires only that the defendant conduct cash transactions in amounts of less than $10,000 with the intent to prevent reporting. True, the government is deprived of information, but that is only a consequence of conduct that is not of a fraudulent character. We conclude that fraud is not inherent in the nature of this offense.

Finally, in each of the other cases cited in the BIA's decision, either fraud or intent to defraud was explicit in the statutory definition of the alien's crime. Goldeshtein was charged neither with fraud nor with conspiracy to defraud the United States. As we already have pointed out, fraud is not part of the statutory definition of the crime of structuring financial transactions to avoid currency transaction reports. Accordingly, proof of intent to defraud was not required to convict Goldeshtein.

III. CONCLUSION

Because Goldeshtein was not convicted of a crime involving moral turpitude, he is not deportable under INA § 241(a)(2)(A)(i). * * *

* * *

Notes

1.   The common law method has developed a number of rules that are regularly applied to decide whether crimes involve moral turpitude. *Goldeshtein* applies two such rules: (1) what matters is the "inherent nature" of the offense, not the particular conduct of the alien, *Matter of R-*, 6 I & N Dec. 444, 447–48 (BIA 1954); and (2) crimes with an element of fraud are crimes involving moral turpitude, *e.g., McNaughton v. INS*, 612 F.2d 457 (9th Cir.1980) (securities fraud); *Matter of Khalik*, 17 I & N Dec. 518 (BIA 1980) (issuing check with insufficient funds).

Authorities also publish long lists which place crimes into "involving" and "not involving" moral turpitude categories. *E.g.,* GM & Y § 71.05[1][d][iii]; D. Kesselbrenner & L. Rosenberg, Immigration Law and Crimes App. E (1994); Fullerton & Kinigstein, *Strategies for Ameliorating the Immigration Consequences of Criminal Convictions: A Guide for Defense Attorneys*, 23 Am. Crim. L. Rev. 425, 433–36 (1986). Indeed, a member of the BIA wrote in 1944 that the phrase moral turpitude "has evolved into a definitive workable guide." Wasserman, *Crimes Involving Moral Turpitude,* 1 INS Monthly Rev. 2, 8 (1944). Thus for most crimes there is broad agreement as to whether they "involve moral turpitude." But as *Goldeshtein* illustrates, questions of first impression will arise.

2.   Regarding the rule that the particular circumstances surrounding the commission of the crime have no weight in deciding whether it involves moral turpitude, the Board has advanced the following rationale: "The rule set forth exists because a standard must be supplied to administrative

agencies; it eliminates the burden of going into the evidence in a case; it eliminates the situation where a nonjudicial agency retries a judicial matter; and it prevents the situation occurring where two people convicted under the same specific law are given different treatment because one indictment may contain a fuller or different description of the same act than the other indictment; and makes for uniform administration of law." *Matter of R-, supra*, 6 I & N Dec. at 448 n.2.

Are you persuaded? Should the need for administrative efficiency, convenience, and uniformity condemn to deportation an alien whose particular crime did not involve moral turpitude? Should an alien who commits a serious crime with "evil" intent escape deportation simply because some conduct condemned by the statute would not constitute a crime involving moral turpitude? What about an alien who pleads guilty to a lesser offense? Should deportability turn on the "inherent nature" of the lesser crime, or the degree of turpitude evidenced by the alien's actual conduct? For a critical analysis, see *Marciano v. INS*, 450 F.2d 1022, 1031 (8th Cir.1971) (Eisele, J., dissenting).

3. An alien must establish that she is "a person of good moral character" to be eligible for several important immigration benefits, among them naturalization, *see* INA § 316(a), and certain forms of relief from deportation, *see, e.g.,* INA §§ 244(a)(1) (suspension of deportation), 244(e) (voluntary departure). Yet what constitutes "good moral character" is no more clear than what conduct involves "moral turpitude." INA § 101(f) only gives examples of what is *not* good moral character. What should be the relationship between crimes of moral turpitude and good moral character? Although INA § 101(f) states that any person whose income comes primarily from illegal gambling or who has been convicted of two or more gambling offenses shall not be deemed to have established "good moral character," the BIA has held that violation of gambling statutes does not constitute an act involving moral turpitude. *E.g., Matter of Gaglioti,* 10 I & N Dec. 719 (BIA 1964); *Matter of S,* 9 I & N Dec. 688 (BIA 1962).

4. "Moral turpitude" is a phrase that provides a standard of conduct in other areas of law. These include disbarment of attorneys,[15] revocation of licenses,[16] impeachment of witnesses,[17] and termination of municipal employment.[18] What relevance should the term's use in these contexts have in immigration law? [19]

---

15. *See, e.g., In re Giddens,* 30 Cal.3d 110, 177 Cal.Rptr. 673, 635 P.2d 166 (1981).

16. *See, e.g., Yurick v. Commonwealth,* 43 Pa.Cmwlth. 248, 402 A.2d 290 (1979) (revocation of osteopathy license).

17. *See, e.g., United States v. Gloria,* 494 F.2d 477, 481 (5th Cir.1974).

18. *See, e.g., Fortman v. Aurora Civil Service Commission,* 37 Ill.App.3d 548, 346 N.E.2d 20 (1976) (discharge of sanitation worker).

19. *See, e.g., Gonzales v. Barber,* 207 F.2d 398 (9th Cir.1953), *affirmed on other grounds,* 347 U.S. 637, 74 S.Ct. 822, 98 L.Ed. 1009 (1954) (assault with a deadly weapon is crime involving moral turpitude for purposes of federal immigration law, even if not for purposes of attorney disbarment); *Matter of R,* 4 I & N Dec. 644, 647 (BIA 1952) (unlawful disposal of narcotic drug is not a crime involving moral turpitude in immigration cases since narcotic law does not require presence of intent, motive or knowledge, even though it is a crime involving moral turpitude in nonimmigration cases).

5. How did Congress intend the courts and agencies to pour content into the phrase "moral turpitude"? Did it believe that they should look to the meaning of "moral turpitude" prevailing in 1891 or 1917, or contemporary moral standards? The latter view seems more likely: if the purpose of the provision is to rid the nation of aliens who commit particularly deplorable acts, one would expect that Congress intended "moral turpitude" to reflect current notions of deplorableness. If this interpretation is correct, Congress has essentially delegated legislative authority to the courts and agencies to determine what crimes involve moral turpitude. To give meaning to the phrase moral turpitude, they must adopt a common law approach to the interpretation of § 241(a)(2)(A)(i) and (ii).

This understanding of statutory interpretation is hardly confined to the immigration field. A prime example of a common law approach to a statute is judicial interpretation of § 1 of the Sherman Antitrust Act, 15 U.S.C.A. § 1, which prohibits combinations "in restraint of trade." However, the understanding deviates significantly from traditional ways of thinking about statutory construction. Legal theory normally ascribes to the judge the function of carrying out the will of the legislature by applying a statute whose meanings, aims, or purposes the legislature has fixed at the time of enactment. Courts are to share that power with administrative agencies, where, as with the INA, the statutory scheme so contemplates. Thus it has become well-established that a court should generally defer to an agency's construction of a statute where the statute is silent or ambiguous with respect to the precise question at issue. *See Chevron, U.S.A., Inc. v. Natural Resources Defense Council,* 467 U.S. 837, 104 S.Ct. 2778, 81 L.Ed.2d 694 (1984), discussed pp. 173–74 *supra.* In these ways, so the usual argument runs, courts and agencies recognize institutional limits on their competence and do not usurp the role of the legislature. Of course, the court or agency will apply the statute in situations not considered or imagined by the drafters. But in doing so, their task is generally described as remaining true to the intent of the legislature or the underlying purposes of the statute.[20]

Under § 241(a)(2)(A)(i) and (ii), however, Congress has apparently invited (or commanded) the courts and agencies to legislate. Although on a very general level, perhaps, Congress has provided some direction (*i.e.,* condemn conduct that violates norms of decency), it is clear, is it not, that under the statute a court or agency may (is free to?) reach decisions contrary to those that would have been reached by the Congress that enacted the provision. The task of the court or agency, then, is not one of discovery and application, but rather one of creation. Is it desirable for Congress to write a statute in this fashion? [21]

20. *See, e.g.,* Hart & Sacks, *supra,* Ch.VII; Frankfurter, *Some Reflections on the Reading of Statutes,* 47 Colum.L.Rev. 527 (1947); Landis, *A Note on "Statutory Interpretation,"* 43 Harv.L.Rev. 886 (1930). For the "realist" critique of this position, *see* Radin, *Statutory Interpretation,* 43 Harv.L.Rev. 863 (1930).

21. In considering the following answers to the questions on p. 545 *supra,* recall that each determination depends on the language of the statute in question:

(1) Yes. *E.g., Matter of Rosario,* 15 I & N Dec. 416 (BIA 1975) (intentional killing even without malice).

(2) Yes. *Matter of Franklin,* Int.Dec. 3228 (BIA 1994).

"Void for Vagueness"

It is not surprising that the use of the phrase "moral turpitude" has been challenged on the constitutional ground that it does not adequately warn aliens what conduct would subject them to deportation.

JORDAN v. DE GEORGE

Supreme Court of the United States, 1951.
341 U.S. 223, 71 S.Ct. 703, 95 L.Ed. 886.

MR. CHIEF JUSTICE VINSON delivered the opinion of the Court.

This case presents only one question: whether conspiracy to defraud the United States of taxes on distilled spirits is a "crime involving moral turpitude" within the meaning of § 19(a) of the Immigration Act of 1917.

Respondent, a native and citizen of Italy, has lived continuously in the United States since he entered this country in 1921. In 1937, respondent was indicted * * * for conspiring with seven other defendants to violate twelve sections of the Internal Revenue Code. The indictment specifically charged him with possessing whiskey and alcohol "with intent to sell it in fraud of law and evade the tax thereon." He was further accused of removing and concealing liquor "with intent to defraud the United States of the tax thereon." After pleading guilty, respondent was sentenced to imprisonment in a federal penitentiary for a term of one year and one day.

Respondent served his sentence under this conviction, and was released from custody. Less than a year later, he returned to his former activities and in December 1939, he was indicted again with eight other defendants for violating the same federal statutes. He was charged with conspiring to "unlawfully, knowingly, and willfully defraud the United

(3) Trick question. Depends upon object of unlawful entry. Compare Matter of M, 2 I & N Dec. 721 (A.G.1946) (no moral turpitude where evidence does not disclose that alien intended to permanently deny owner possession of property) with Matter of Moore, 13 I & N Dec. 711 (BIA 1971) (intent to commit larceny involves moral turpitude).

(4) No. E.g., Matter of S, 5 I & N Dec. 425 (BIA 1953) (conviction does not require "depraved mind or purpose" or fraud).

(5) Yes. Tseung Chu v. Cornell, 247 F.2d 929 (9th Cir.1957), cert. denied, 355 U.S. 892, 78 S.Ct. 265, 2 L.Ed.2d 190 (1957). But cf. Matter of S, 9 I & N Dec. 688 (BIA 1962) (no moral turpitude in failure to file tax return in absence of fraud or evil intent).

(6) No. Manzella v. Zimmerman, 71 F.Supp. 534 (E.D.Pa.1947) (statute comprehends escapes in which moral turpitude does not inhere in that an escape may involve the "least imaginable force" and "spring from the basic desire of the human being for liberty of action and freedom from restraint").

(7) No. Andreacchi v. Curran, 38 F.2d 498 (D.C.N.Y.1926).

(8) Yes. Okoroha v. INS, 715 F.2d 380 (8th Cir.1983); Wadman v. INS, 329 F.2d 812 (9th Cir.1964).

(9) No. Matter of Abreu–Semino, 12 I & N Dec. 775 (BIA 1968) (violation of regulatory legislation, where evil intent is not an element, does not involve moral turpitude).

(10) No. Matter of Tiwari, 19 I & N Dec. 875 (BIA 1989), distinguishing United States v. Raghunandan, 587 F.Supp. 423 (W.D.N.Y. 1984) (conviction for smuggling aliens in violation of INA § 274 constitutes a crime of moral turpitude for the purposes of INA § 241(b)).

(11) Yes. Velez-Lozano v. INS, 463 F.2d 1305 (D.C.Cir.1972) (per curiam).

(12) No. Matter of Serna, Int.Dec. 3188 (BIA 1992) (conviction requires knowledge of alteration, but not intent to use document to defraud government).

(13) Yes. Kabongo v. INS, 837 F.2d 753 (6th Cir.1988).

States of tax on distilled spirits."[5] After being tried and found guilty in 1941, he was sentenced to imprisonment for two years.

While serving his sentence under this second conviction, deportation proceedings were commenced against the respondent under § 19(a) of the Immigration Act [of 1917] which provides:

> " ... any alien ... who is hereafter sentenced more than once to such a term of imprisonment [one year or more] because of conviction in this country of any crime involving moral turpitude, committed at any time after entry ... shall, upon the warrant of the Attorney General, be taken into custody and deported...."

After continued hearings and consideration of the case by the Commissioner of Immigration and Naturalization and by the Board of Immigration Appeals, respondent was ordered to be deported in January 1946, on the ground that he had twice been convicted and sentenced to terms of one year or more of crimes involving moral turpitude. Deportation was deferred from time to time at respondent's request until 1949, when the District Director of Immigration and Naturalization moved to execute the warrant of deportation.

Respondent then sought habeas corpus in the District Court, claiming that the deportation order was invalid because the crimes of which he had been convicted did not involve moral turpitude. The District Court held a hearing, and dismissed the petition. The Court of Appeals reversed the order of the District Court and ordered that the respondent be discharged. The Court of Appeals stated that "crimes involving moral turpitude," as those words were used in the Immigration Act, "were intended to include only crimes of violence, or crimes which are commonly thought of as involving baseness, vileness or depravity. Such a classification does not include the crime of evading the payment of tax on liquor, nor of conspiring to evade that tax." 183 F.2d at 772. We granted certiorari to review the decision, as conflicting with decisions of the courts of appeals in other circuits.

* * *

The term "moral turpitude" has deep roots in the law. The presence of moral turpitude has been used as a test in a variety of situations, including legislation governing the disbarment of attorneys and the revocation of medical licenses. Moral turpitude also has found judicial employment as a criterion in disqualifying and impeaching witnesses, in determining the measure of contribution between joint tort-feasors, and in deciding whether certain language is slanderous.

In deciding the case before the Court, we look to the manner in which the term "moral turpitude" has been applied by judicial decision. Without exception, federal and state courts have held that a crime in which fraud is an ingredient involves moral turpitude. In the construction of the specific

---

5. The record establishes that respondent was a large-scale violator engaged in a sizable business. The second indictment alone charged him with possessing 4,675 gallons of alcohol and an undetermined quantity of distilled spirits. At the rate of $2.25 a gallon then in effect, the tax on the alcohol alone would have been over $10,000.

section of the Statute before us, a court of appeals has stated that fraud has ordinarily been the test to determine whether crimes not of the gravest character involve moral turpitude.

In every deportation case where fraud has been proved, federal courts have held that the crime in issue involved moral turpitude. This has been true in a variety of situations involving fraudulent conduct: obtaining goods under fraudulent pretenses, conspiracy to defraud by deceit and falsehood, forgery with intent to defraud, using the mails to defraud, execution of chattel mortgage with intent to defraud, concealing assets in bankruptcy, issuing checks with intent to defraud. In the state courts, crimes involving fraud have universally been held to involve moral turpitude.[13]

* * *

In view of these decisions, it can be concluded that fraud has consistently been regarded as such a contaminating component in any crime that American courts have, without exception, included such crimes within the scope of moral turpitude. It is therefore clear, under an unbroken course of judicial decisions, that the crime of conspiring to defraud the United States is a "crime involving moral turpitude."

But it has been suggested that the phrase "crime involving moral turpitude" lacks sufficiently definite standards to justify this deportation proceeding and that the statute before us is therefore unconstitutional for vagueness. Under this view, no crime, however grave, could be regarded as falling within the meaning of the term "moral turpitude." The question of vagueness was not raised by the parties nor argued before this Court.

It is significant that the phrase has been part of the immigration laws for more than sixty years.[14] As discussed above, the phrase "crime involving moral turpitude" has also been used for many years as a criterion in a variety of other statutes. No case has been decided holding that the phrase is vague, nor are we able to find any trace of judicial expression which hints that the phrase is so meaningless as to be a deprivation of due process.

* * *

The essential purpose of the "void for vagueness" doctrine is to warn individuals of the criminal consequences of their conduct. This Court has repeatedly stated that criminal statutes which fail to give due notice that an act has been made criminal before it is done are unconstitutional deprivations of due process of law. It should be emphasized that this statute does not declare certain conduct to be criminal. Its function is to

---

13. State decisions have held that the following crimes involve moral turpitude: passing a check with intent to defraud, using the mails to defraud, obtaining money and property by false and fraudulent pretenses, possessing counterfeit money with intent to defraud. One state court has specifically held that the wilful evasion of federal income taxes constitutes moral turpitude.

14. The term "moral turpitude" first appeared in the Act of March 3, 1891, 26 Stat. 1084, which directed the exclusion of "persons who have been convicted of a felony or other infamous crime or misdemeanor involving moral turpitude." Similar language was reenacted in the Statutes of 1903 and 1907. § 2, Act of March 3, 1903, 32 Stat. 1213; § 2, Act of Feb. 20, 1907, 34 Stat. 898. * * *

apprise aliens of the consequences which follow after conviction and sentence of the requisite two crimes.

Despite the fact that this is not a criminal statute, we shall nevertheless examine the application of the vagueness doctrine to this case. We do this in view of the grave nature of deportation. The Court has stated that "deportation is a drastic measure and at times the equivalent of banishment or exile.... It is the forfeiture for misconduct of a residence in this country. Such a forfeiture is a penalty." *Fong Haw Tan v. Phelan*, [333 U.S. 6, 10, 68 S.Ct. 374, 376, 92 L.Ed. 433 (1948)].

We shall, therefore, test this statute under the established criteria of the "void for vagueness" doctrine.

We have several times held that difficulty in determining whether certain marginal offenses are within the meaning of the language under attack as vague does not automatically render a statute unconstitutional for indefiniteness. Impossible standards of specificity are not required. The test is whether the language conveys sufficiently definite warning as to the proscribed conduct when measured by common understanding and practices.

is m.t. vague?
No

We conclude that this test has been satisfied here. Whatever else the phrase "crime involving moral turpitude" may mean in peripheral cases, the decided cases make it plain that crimes in which fraud was an ingredient have always been regarded as involving moral turpitude. We have recently stated that doubt as to the adequacy of a standard in less obvious cases does not render that standard unconstitutional for vagueness. But there is no such doubt present in this case. Fraud is the touchstone by which this case should be judged. The phrase "crime involving moral turpitude" has without exception been construed to embrace fraudulent conduct. We therefore decide that Congress sufficiently forewarned respondent that the statutory consequence of twice conspiring to defraud the United States is deportation.

Reversed.

MR. JUSTICE JACKSON, dissenting.

* * *

Except for the Court's opinion, there appears to be universal recognition that we have here an undefined and undefinable standard. The parties agree that the phrase is ambiguous and have proposed a variety of tests to reduce the abstract provision of this statute to some concrete meaning.

It is proposed by respondent, with strong support in legislative history, that Congress had in mind only crimes of violence. If the Court should adopt this construction, the statute becomes sufficiently definite, and, of course, would not reach the crimes of the respondent.

The Government suggests seriousness of the crime as a test and says the statute is one by which it is "sought to reach the *confirmed criminal, whose criminality has been revealed in two serious penal offenses.*" (Italics supplied.) But we cannot, and the Court does not, take seriousness as a test of turpitude. All offenses denounced by Congress, prosecuted by the Executive, and convicted by the courts, must be deemed in some degree "serious" or law enforcement would be a frivolous enterprise. However, use of qualifying words must mean that not all statutory offenses are subject to the taint of turpitude. The higher degrees of criminal gravity are commonly classified as felonies, the lower ones as misdemeanors. If the Act contemplated that repetition of any serious crime would be grounds for deportation, it would have been simple and intelligible to have mentioned felonies. But the language used indicates that there are felonies which are not included and perhaps that some misdemeanors are. We cannot see that seriousness affords any standard of guidance.

Respondent suggests here, and the Government has on other occasions taken the position, that the traditional distinction between crimes *mala prohibita* and those *mala in se* will afford a key for the inclusions and exclusions of this statute. But we cannot overlook that what crimes belong in which category has been the subject of controversy for years. This classification comes to us from common law, which in its early history freely blended religious conceptions of sin with legal conceptions of crime. This statute seems to revert to that practice.

The Government, however, offers the *mala prohibita, mala in se* doctrine here in slightly different verbiage for determining the nature of these crimes. It says: "Essentially, they must be measured against the moral standards that prevail in contemporary society to determine whether the violations are generally considered essentially immoral."

Can we accept "the moral standards that prevail in contemporary society" as a sufficiently definite standard for the purposes of the Act? This is a large country and acts that are regarded as criminal in some states are lawful in others. We suspect that moral standards which prevail as to possession or sale of liquor that has evaded tax may not be uniform in all parts of the country, nor in all levels of "contemporary society." How should we ascertain the moral sentiments of masses of persons on any better basis than a guess?

The Court seems no more convinced than are we by the Government's attempts to reduce these nebulous abstractions to a concrete working rule, but to sustain this particular deportation it improvises another which fails to convince us. Its thesis is (1) that the statute is sixty years old, (2) that state courts have used the same concept for various purposes, and (3) that fraud imports turpitude into any offense.

1. It is something less than accurate to imply that in any sense relevant to this issue this phrase has been "part of the immigration laws for more than sixty years."

But, in any event, venerability of a vague phrase may be an argument for its validity when the passing years have by administration practice or judicial construction served to make it clear as a word of legal art. To be sure, the phrase in its present context has been on the statute books since 1917. It has never before been in issue before this Court. * * * There have, however, been something like fifty cases in lower courts which applied this phrase. No one can read this body of opinions and feel that its application represents a satisfying, rational process. If any consistent pattern of application or consensus of meaning could be distilled from judicial decision, neither the Government nor the Court spells it out. * * *

2. The use of the phrase by state courts for various civil proceedings affords no teaching for federal courts. The Federal Government has no common-law crimes and the judges are not permitted to define crimes by decision, for they rest solely in statute. Nor are we persuaded that the state courts have been able to divest the phrase of its inherent ambiguities and vagueness.

3. The Court concludes that fraud is "a contaminating component in any crime" and imports "moral turpitude." The fraud involved here is nonpayment of a tax. The alien possessed and apparently trafficked in liquor without paying the Government its tax. That, of course, is a fraud on the revenues. But those who deplore the traffic regard it as much an exhibition of moral turpitude for the Government to share its revenues as for respondents to withhold them. Those others who enjoy the traffic are not notable for scruples as to whether liquor has a law-abiding pedigree. So far as this offense is concerned with whiskey, it is not particularly un-American, and we see no reason to strain to make the penalty for the same act so much more severe in the case of an alien "bootlegger" than it is in the case of a native "moonshiner." I have never discovered that disregard of the Nation's liquor taxes excluded a citizen from our best society and I see no reason why it should banish an alien from our worst.

But it is said he has cheated the revenues and the total is computed in high figures. If "moral turpitude" depends on the amount involved, respondent is probably entitled to a place in its higher brackets. Whether by popular test the magnitude of the fraud would be an extenuating or an aggravating circumstance, we do not know. We would suppose the basic morality of a fraud on the revenues would be the same for petty as for great cheats. But we are not aware of any keen sentiment of revulsion against one who is a little niggardly on a customs declaration or who evades a sales tax, a local cigarette tax, or fails to keep his account square with a parking meter. But perhaps what shocks is not the offense so much as a conviction.

We should not forget that criminality is one thing—a matter of law—and that morality, ethics and religious teachings are another. Their relations have puzzled the best of men. Assassination, for example, whose criminality no one doubts, has been the subject of serious debate as to its morality. This does not make crime less criminal, but it shows on what treacherous grounds we tread when we undertake to translate ethical concepts into legal ones, case by case. We usually end up by condemning all that we personally disapprove and for no better reason than that we disapprove it. In fact, what better reason is there? Uniformity and equal protection of the law can come only from a statutory definition of fairly stable and confined bounds.

* * *

Notes

1. Justice Jackson's rather witty dissent is disarmingly persuasive, is it not? Indeed, does not the fact that there was a split in the circuits over whether the offense in *De George* was a crime involving moral turpitude almost speak for itself on the issue of vagueness?

2. Under the "void for vagueness" doctrine the Court has struck down statutes whose indefiniteness "runs afoul of due process concepts which require that persons be given fair notice of what to avoid, and that the discretion of law enforcement officials, with the attendant dangers of arbitrary and discriminatory enforcement, be limited by explicit legislative standards." L. Tribe, American Constitutional Law § 12–31 at 1033 (2d ed. 1988). Furthermore, as noted in a classic study, the doctrine "has been used by the Supreme Court almost invariably for the creation of an insulating buffer zone of added protection at the peripheries of several of the Bill of Rights freedoms." Amsterdam, *The Void–For–Vagueness Doctrine in the Supreme Court*, 109 U.Pa.L.Rev. 67, 75 (1960). *See, e.g., Baggett v. Bullitt*, 377 U.S. 360, 84 S.Ct. 1316, 12 L.Ed.2d 377 (1964) (striking down state statutes requiring state employees to take loyalty oaths where the vagueness of the oath operated to inhibit Free Speech); *Papachristou v. City of Jacksonville*, 405 U.S. 156, 92 S.Ct. 839, 31 L.Ed.2d 110 (1972) (voiding city vagrancy ordinance which made criminal "activities which by modern standards are normally innocent"). But consider the view that vagueness has value because finding the ideal legal rule may require more information that a legislature can afford to gather and process. Vagueness may also encourage diversity in behavior, thus providing courts and agencies with more information to use in refining the law. *See* Hadfield, *Weighing the Value of Vagueness: An Economic Perspective on Precision in the Law*, 82 Calif.L.Rev. 541 (1994).

3. In *Rafeedie v. INS*, 795 F.Supp. 13 (D.D.C.1992), discussed p. 531 *supra*, the district court struck down as unconstitutionally vague pre–1990 INA § 212(a)(27), which excluded "[a]liens who the consular officer or the Attorney General knows or has reason to believe seek to enter the United States solely, principally, or incidentally to engage in activities which would be prejudicial to the public interest, or endanger the welfare, safety or security of the United States." Citing *DeGeorge*, the court explained that "[t]he undefined terms of the statute—'activities,' 'prejudicial,' 'endanger'—are so broad and vague as to deny plaintiff a reasonable opportunity to know what he may or may not say or do." *Id.* at 23.

4. Few would argue that "moral turpitude" is a phrase that adequately advises aliens of the kinds of crimes the commission of which would render them deportable. But is the vagueness issue in *De George* distinct from the issue involving statutes that inhibit protected or generally accepted conduct? Here, after all, the alien has been convicted of a major crime. Is not the criminal statute itself not only adequate warning to the alien that serious consequences will follow from its violation but also an adequate check on administrative arbitrariness? Does Justice Jackson consider these questions? Should he? Or is the degree of punishment imposed

by deportation—often more severe than imprisonment for a term of years—substantial enough to warrant invalidation of indefinite deportation statutes?

5. Does the body of case law defining "moral turpitude" vindicate the Supreme Court's decision in *De George*—that is, that the term "moral turpitude" has been rendered acceptably definite through administrative and judicial adjudications? The answer to this question depends upon the reasons for the constitutional principle that vague statutes violate due process. As we mentioned earlier, there are at least three values that are served by clear, definitive statutory commands: notice to regulated parties, control of non-uniform or arbitrary enforcement, and protection of liberty. We believe it is doubtful that the case law concretizing the meaning of "moral turpitude" has contributed much to either the first or third values. It is unlikely that aliens are aware of which crimes have been deemed to involve moral turpitude. Consider *Velez-Lozano v. INS,* 463 F.2d 1305, 1306 (D.C.Cir.1972) (per curiam) (alien not aware that conviction for act of consensual sodomy would render him deportable). Furthermore, the underlying criminal laws themselves both give notice and circumscribe freedom of action; adjudications limiting the application of the deportation laws are not likely to have much additional effect on decisions to undertake the forbidden conduct.

One hundred years of interpretation, however, have probably substantially achieved the second goal—restraining arbitrariness in enforcement. Perhaps recognizing that few people are fully aware of legal rules and prohibitions, the Supreme Court has recently stated: "The more important aspect of vagueness doctrine 'is not actual notice, but the other principal element of the doctrine—the requirement that a legislature establish minimal guidelines to govern law enforcement.'" *Kolender v. Lawson,* 461 U.S. 352, 358, 103 S.Ct. 1855, 1858, 75 L.Ed.2d 903 (1983), *quoting Smith v. Goguen,* 415 U.S. 566, 574, 94 S.Ct. 1242, 1247, 39 L.Ed.2d 605 (1974).

6. Recall the *Fong Yue Ting* dissenters and their greater receptivity to "procedural" constitutional challenges. Is a void-for-vagueness challenge "procedural"?

(ii) Drug Offenses, Aggravated Felonies, and Firearms Offenses

For more than half a century, the INA has mandated the deportation of persons convicted of drug offenses. The current version of this deportation ground is INA § 241(a)(2)(B)(i), which you should now read. Gordon, Mailman & Yale-Loehr have noted that "[t]he inflexibility of the statute in prescribing automatic deportation for minor offenses, without opportunity for amelioration, has been deplored, and statutory amendments to authorize reasonable flexibility have been urged." GM & Y § 71.05[4][c].

Congress (like the country), however, seems in no mood to soften the deportation ground. The Anti–Drug Abuse Act of 1988 broadened it to cover any conviction "relating to a controlled substance." Pub.L. No. 100–690, § 1751(b), 102 Stat. 4181. In 1990, Congress amended the deportation ground for any "narcotic drug addict" to include any alien who is a "drug abuser or addict," whether or not there has been criminal conviction. INA § 241(a)(2)(B)(ii). In explaining a parallel new exclusion ground, § 212(a)(1)(iii), the House Report noted:

> Drug abuse continues to be a national concern, both as a health matter and as a criminal matter. * * * This change reflects recognition that certain drugs, like cocaine, are not considered to be narcotic, but can be addictive, and that abuse of drugs— even without addiction—can have a harmful impact on our society and pose a danger to residents of the United States.

H.Rep. No. 101–723, pt.1, at 55 (1990). Does either the statute or the legislative history provide adequate guidance to the immigration authorities as to what constitutes drug abuse? Is an abuser of alcohol a drug abuser?

In addition to addressing drug convictions directly, the Anti–Drug Abuse Act of 1988 added a definition of "aggravated felony" in INA § 101(a)(43) (initially directed largely at crimes committed by participants in the drug trade, including murder, drug trafficking and trafficking in firearms). It amended § 241 to provide for the deportation of aliens "convicted of an aggravated felony at any time after entry," *see* § 241(a)(2)(A)(iii). The legislation also amended what is now § 241(a)(2)(C) to include convictions for possession of certain firearms, destructive devices, and automatic and semiautomatic weapons. *See Matter of Lopez–Amaro*, Int.Dec. 3202 (BIA 1993) (firearms offense includes any conviction for which the use of firearm is element of offense).

The 1990 Immigration Act expanded the definition of "aggravated felony" by including money laundering and any "crime of violence" (not including a "purely political offense") for which the term of imprisonment imposed is at least five years, and by clarifying that state and some foreign offenses come within the statutory definition. *See* INA § 101(a)(43). "Crime of violence" is defined in 18 U.S.C.A. § 16 as:

> (a) an offense that has as an element the use, attempted use, or threatened use of physical force against the person or property of another, or

> (b) any other offense that is a felony and that, by its nature, involves a substantial risk that physical force against the person or property of another may be used in the course of committing the offense.

See, e.g., Matter of Alcantar, Int.Dec. 3220 (BIA 1994) (involuntary manslaughter is "crime of violence" under 18 U.S.C. § 16(b)).

Thus, while the new deportation grounds for aggravated felonies and firearms offenses originated with the war on drugs, by 1990 they had assumed their present role as a deportation ground for aliens convicted of serious crimes. Moreover, aliens with aggravated felony convictions have become ineligible for most other forms of relief. For example, the 1988 Act made aggravated felons ineligible for voluntary departure under INA § 244(e)(2). (Was such an amendment necessary?) It also barred aliens deported for conviction of an aggravated felony from reapplying for admission for ten years without the consent of the Attorney General. *See* § 212(a)(6)(B). The 1990 Act raised the time bar to 20 years.

The 1994 Technical Corrections Act continued this trend by adding over sixteen new crimes to the definition of "aggravated felony." Among the additions: any theft or burglary offense for a which a five-year term of imprisonment is imposed, certain offenses relating to child pornography, and fraud or deceit involving losses to the victim(s) exceeding $200,000. Pub.L. 103–416, § 222, 108 Stat. 4305, 4321. H.R. 668, 104th Cong., 1st Sess., which passed the House on February 10, 1995, would further expand the definition of "aggravated felony" to include, for example, serious offenses involving commercial bribery, counterfeiting, forgery, or trafficking in stolen vehicles.

The following case shows one of these new statutes in action.

FLORES-ARELLANO v. INS

United States Court of Appeals, Ninth Circuit, 1993.
5 F.3d 360.

REINHARDT, CIRCUIT JUDGE:

Jaime Salvador Flores–Arellano challenges the finding that he is deportable on the basis of a misdemeanor state conviction of being under the influence of amphetamine/methamphetamine. Because we conclude that section 241(a)(2)(B)(i) of the Immigration and Nationality Act (INA) plainly reaches under-the-influence convictions for controlled substances other than marijuana, we deny Flores' petition for review.

I

Flores, now 29 years old, entered the United States as a permanent resident on April 16, 1990. Although this is the official date of his legal immigrant entry to the United States, Flores lived in this country for many years prior to 1990. All of Flores' parents and siblings are legal permanent residents, and he has two United States citizen children.

On August 13, 1990, Flores pleaded guilty in San Diego Municipal Court to using and being under the influence of amphetamine and methamphetamine on January 8, 1989, in violation of Cal. Health & Safety Code § 11550. On January 20, 1991, the Immigration & Naturalization Service (INS) issued an order to show cause charging Flores with deportability on the basis of his under-the-influence conviction. The Immigration Judge found Flores deportable on August 15, 1991, and he appealed. The Board of Immigration Appeals (BIA) dismissed his appeal on February 4, 1992. Flores petitions for review.

II

* * *

The plain language of section 241(a)(2)(B)(i) reaches under-the-influence convictions. The ordinary meaning of the phrase "any law ... relating to a controlled substance" encompasses laws proscribing use or being under the influence of a controlled substance. The provision is not ambiguous, nor does its plain language lead to absurd results or internal statutory inconsistencies. Flores' arguments that we should abandon this plain meaning in interpreting section 241(a)(2)(B)(i) are unpersuasive.

Flores relies on cases from the federal courts and the BIA interpreting a prior version of the statute as not reaching under-the-influence convictions. The previous version interpreted by these cases limited deportability to aliens convicted of trafficking or possession offenses. In the Anti–Drug Abuse Act of 1986, Congress substituted the broader language now in the statute. Flores argues that Congress did not intend the amendment to overrule precedent excluding under-the-influence convictions from the deportability statute. However, the legislative history surrounding the 1986 amendment of the deportability statute is inconclusive, lacking the clear indication of a contrary intention necessary to overcome the plain meaning of the post-amendment statute.

Looking to the structure of the statute, Flores argues that the inclusion of "drug abusers" as an independent deportable class under section 241(a)(2)(B)(ii) demonstrates that Congress did not intend aliens convicted of drug "use" crimes to be deportable under section 241(a)(2)(B)(i). Flores' contention rests on the conclusion that if drug "use" convictions render an alien deportable, then the provision regarding drug "abuse," involving more sustained use of controlled substances, would be superfluous. Flores' argument overlooks the conviction requirement in subsection (i), which renders the grounds for deportability specified in subsections (i) and (ii) logically distinguishable. Subsection (ii) reaches alien drug "abusers" who have not been convicted of a controlled substance offense while subsection (i) reaches all aliens convicted of controlled substance violations, including the use of drugs.

Finally, Flores contends that the legislature's specified exclusion of single offenses involving possession of a personal-use quantity of marijuana and its omission of a similar exclusion for actual use of marijuana leads to the incongruous result that one conviction of the less serious offense of marijuana use would lead to deportation while one conviction of possession would not. To avoid imputing such irrationality to our lawmakers, Flores argues that Congress did not interpret the section as reaching any under-the-influence offenses and therefore had no reason to specify an exception for marijuana use.

While the argument has some superficial appeal, there is a much more logical interpretation of section 241(a)(2)(B)(i) that avoids the paradoxical result suggested by Flores: the exception for a single conviction involving personal-use marijuana possession includes an implicit exception for a single conviction of actual personal use of marijuana. Such an interpretation of the statute makes absolute logical sense, but does not affect aliens, like Flores, who are convicted of being under the influence of controlled substances other than marijuana. The inclusion of a limited exception for a single conviction of marijuana possession does not contradict the plain meaning of section 241(a)(2)(B)(i) as encompassing under-the-influence convictions.

* * *

REINHARDT, CIRCUIT JUDGE, specially concurring:

* * * I write this special concurrence only to emphasize two points.

The first is that this is one of those rare occasions when our statutory interpretation rests almost entirely upon the legal fiction that Congress' language embodies its intent. Under the established approach to statutory interpretation, we rely on plain language in the first instance, but always look to legislative history in order to determine whether there is a clear indication of contrary intent. In the usual case, of course, the history provides further support for the plain-language interpretation. That is not surprising and explains in part why the presumption in favor of interpretations conforming to ordinary meaning makes sense. However, on some occasions, there is nothing in the congressional discussions to support the plain-language interpretation. This is such a case.

Neither party has identified anything in the legislative history that demonstrates that any legislator, much less a majority of them, thought about whether a lawful resident alien convicted of use or being under the influence should be deportable as one convicted of violating "any law ... relating to a controlled substance." The previous version of the statute had been consistently interpreted not to reach "use" convictions, and there is no indication, aside from its text, that the 1986 amendment was designed to overturn this longstanding interpretive precedent. Indeed, the INS agrees that the preeminent concerns in amending the section were apparently to simplify the statute and to broaden it to reach unspecified "designer drugs," but not to expand the provision to reach under-the-influence convictions. Thus, just as it lacks the clarity necessary to enforce the petitioner's argued departure from the ordinary meaning of the plain language, the legislative history offers no support for the government's position.

Ordinarily, where the legislative history fails to further support the plain-language interpretation of a statute, that interpretation is at least more consistent than the alternative with the apparent purpose of the legislation. Here, I am unsure that deporting lawfully resident aliens convicted of a single use of a controlled substance is consonant with the purpose of the deportation provision—whether that purpose be to discourage drug trafficking or to punish serious law violators. If the provision's purpose is to deter drug trafficking, deporting a few occasional users seems unlikely to so impact the demand for illicit drugs as to discourage traffickers. If the purpose is to punish serious lawbreakers, deporting one-time convicted drug users is at best a most dubious way of going about it.

That raises my second point—that the result dictated by the legislature's plain language is draconian. Federal efforts to decrease demand for illicit drugs have generally been non-punitive, in part out of recognition of the addictive nature of most controlled substances. Ordinarily, we look to *treat* drug users rather than to *punish* them. Although many states, such as California, continue to address drug use through the criminal justice system, the federal government generally has not chosen that approach. Leaving aside, however, the habitual drug user or drug addict, deportation for a single under-the-influence conviction is obviously an egregious form of federal *punishment* for what is normally no more than a misdemeanor offense. In my view, such punishment is self-evidently harsh and excessive, if not vindictive. We are concerned here with lawful resident aliens, many of whom have been in the United States for a number of years and have close family ties to this country. Some of these family ties, including those of parent and child, may be severed irrevocably simply because a person unwisely took drugs on one or even several occasions. I find this punitive approach to illicit drug use, visited upon lawful resident aliens, to be most unsettling and ungenerous. It is hardly consistent with the vision that we Americans have of our nation's policies.

* * *

Note

A student Note in the 1929 Harvard Law Review commented as follows on Congress' reliance on the phrase "crime of moral turpitude":

> [It] seems inevitable that in the classification of crimes it is perilous and idle to expect an indefinite statutory term to acquire precision by the judicial process of exclusion and inclusion. The legislature can ordinarily better accomplish its purpose by enumerating the proscribed offenses, or by dividing them on the basis of penalty imposed. Either method would replace with a uniform standard the apocalyptic criteria of individual judges.

Note, *Crimes Involving Moral Turpitude,* 43 Harv.L.Rev. 117, 121 (1929).

You have seen that the deportation grounds for drug offenses and aggravated felonies reflect variations on the two approaches mentioned in the Harvard Note. If you were a member of Congress, would you support legislation to amend the "crime of moral turpitude" deportation grounds in similar ways? Should Congress define "moral turpitude," much as it has defined "aggravated felony"? Should that definition list specific crimes or types of crimes? Or should Congress simply replace "crime of moral turpitude" with "felony"?[22] Now shift your focus to the deportation grounds for drug offenses and aggravated felonies. Should Congress draft these provisions with less specificity?

Try drafting statutory deportation grounds for criminal activity that you would prefer to those now on the books.

(iii) What Is a Conviction?

Crucial to the criminal deportation grounds—and to ineligibility for certain forms of relief—is that an alien be *convicted.* It may seem that the existence of a conviction should be a rather easy fact to determine—usually we imagine that a criminal is tried, convicted and sentenced. But a variety

---

22. *See Burr v. INS,* 350 F.2d 87, 90 (9th Cir.1965), *cert. denied,* 383 U.S. 915, 86 S.Ct. 905, 15 L.Ed.2d 669 (1966) (use of "felony" as touchstone of deportability would have subjected federal law to "niceties and nuances" of state law). *Cf.* Kamisar, Betts v. Brady *Twenty Years Later: The Right to Counsel and Due Process Values,* 61 Mich. L.Rev. 219, 266–67 (1962) (need for federal definition of crimes triggering right to counsel beyond crimes defined as felonies by the States).

of state procedures and programs create surprising problems. Consider, for example, state statutes that authorize expungement of criminal records for first-time or youthful offenders, or authorize probation before entering a final judgment of guilt. These kinds of statutes are based on the humanitarian desire to save a defendant believed likely to reform from a record-staining conviction. Should the federal government (namely, the INS) be bound by state definitions of "conviction"?

The following decision by the Board grapples with these issues.

MATTER OF OZKOK

Board of Immigration Appeals, 1988.
19 I & N Dec. 546.

In a decision dated September 13, 1985, the immigration judge found the respondent deportable * * * as an alien convicted of a narcotics violation, and ordered him deported from the United States. On October 18, 1985, the immigration judge certified his decision for our review. * * *

The respondent is a 32-year-old native and citizen of Turkey who was admitted to the United States as a lawful permanent resident on October 9, 1967. The record reflects that he pleaded guilty on August 20, 1981, to unlawful possession with intent to distribute cocaine in the Circuit Court for Baltimore County, Maryland. On October 23, 1981, the court stayed judgment and placed the respondent on probation for 3 years pursuant to the provisions of Article 27, section 641 of the Annotated Code of Maryland.[3] The judge further ordered the respondent to perform 100 hours of volunteer community service and to pay a fine of $1,500 plus court costs.

* * *

---

3. The statute in effect at that time provided in pertinent part:

(a) *Probation after plea or finding of guilt; power of court to provide terms and conditions; waiver of right to appeal from judgment of guilt.*—(1)(i) Whenever a person accused of a crime pleads guilty or nolo contendere or is found guilty of an offense, a court exercising criminal jurisdiction, if satisfied that the best interests of the person and the welfare of the people of the State would be served thereby, and with the written consent of the person after determination of guilt or acceptance of a nolo contendere plea, may stay the entering of judgment, defer further proceedings, and place the person on probation subject to reasonable terms and conditions as appropriate. The terms and conditions may include ordering the person to pay a fine or pecuniary penalty to the state, or to make restitution, but before the court orders a fine, pecuniary penalty, or restitution the person is entitled to notice and a hearing to determine the amount of the fine, pecuniary penalty, or restitu-

tion, what payment will be required, and how payment will be made. The terms and conditions also may include any type of rehabilitation program or clinic, or similar program, or the parks program or voluntary hospital program.

. . .

(2) By consenting to and receiving a stay of entering of the judgment as provided by this subsection, the person waives the right to appeal from the judgment of guilt by the court at any time. Prior to the person consenting to the stay of entering of the judgment, the court shall notify the person that by consenting to and receiving a stay of entry of judgment, he waives the right to appeal from the judgment of guilt by the court at any time.

(b) *Violation of probation.*—Upon violation of a term or condition of probation, the court may enter judgment and proceed with disposition of the person as if the person had not been placed on probation.

The question of what state action constitutes a conviction with sufficient finality for purposes of the immigration laws is one with which the Board has wrestled for many years. * * * Recognizing the need for a federal standard for a final conviction, the Board analyzed the possible courses of action by a court that could result in a conviction in *Matter of O-,* 7 I & N Dec. 539 (BIA 1957). We concluded there that a final conviction existed where, after a finding of guilt was made, a fine or sentence to imprisonment was imposed or either the execution or imposition of a sentence was suspended. We also found that if the court postponed further consideration of the case so that it was still pending for imposition of some sentence, an examination * * * would be necessary to determine if the conviction had achieved sufficient finality to support a deportation order.

A few years later the Board enunciated the three-pronged test which has been the standard we have applied since then to determine whether a conviction exists for immigration purposes. *Matter of L–R-,* 8 I & N Dec. 269 (BIA 1959).[4] During this same period, the Attorney General also examined the effect of expunction procedures on convictions for narcotics offenses, concluding that Congress did not intend for a narcotics violator to escape deportation as a result of a technical erasure of his conviction by a state. *Matter of A–F-,* 8 I & N Dec. 429 (BIA, A.G.1959). In so finding, the Attorney General noted the federal policy to treat narcotics offenses seriously and determined that it would be inappropriate for an alien's deportability for criminal activity to be dependent upon "the vagaries of state law." *Id.* at 446. He further pointed out that in 1959, when his decision was rendered, only a few states had expunction procedures, concluding that it was unfair to give preferential treatment to only a few aliens who were convicted in those jurisdictions.

It is apparent from a review of our decisions published since the Attorney General's opinion in *Matter of A–F-, supra,* that most states now employ some method of ameliorating the consequences of a conviction. The procedures vary from state to state and include provisions for annulling or setting aside the conviction, permitting withdrawal of the plea, sealing the records after completion of a sentence or probation, and deferring adjudication of guilt with dismissal of proceedings following a probationary period. Many states have more than one ameliorative provi-

(c) *Fulfillment of terms of probation.*— Upon fulfillment of the terms and conditions of probation, the court shall discharge the person from probation. The discharge is final disposition of the matter. Discharge of a person under this section shall be without judgment of conviction and is not a conviction for purposes of any disqualification or disability imposed by law because of conviction of crime.

Md.Ann.Code art. 27, § 641 (1982).

4. According to our definition as set forth in *Matter of L–R-, supra,* a conviction exists for immigration purposes where all of the following elements are present:

(1) there has been a judicial finding of guilt;

(2) the court takes action which removes the case from the category of those which are (actually, or in theory) pending for consideration by the court-the court orders the defendant fined, or incarcerated or the court suspends sentence, or the court suspends the imposition of sentence;

(3) the action of the court is considered a conviction by the state for at least some purpose.

sion, some applying only to youthful or first offenders, and others being available to the convicted population at large.

* * * [T]he Board has attempted over the years to reconcile its definition of a final conviction with the evolving criminal procedures created by the various states. Having reviewed our decisions in this regard, we must acknowledge that the standard which we have applied to the many variations in state procedure may permit anomalous and unfair results in determining which aliens are considered convicted for immigration purposes. For example, alien A, who has been found guilty of a narcotics violation by a jury or judge, but against whom no formal judgment has been entered by the judge, and who was placed on probation, fined, and even incarcerated as a special condition of probation, but who has no right to appeal and is subject to automatic entry of a judgment upon violation of probation, would not be considered "convicted" under our three-pronged test because there has been no judicial adjudication of guilt. On the other hand, we would find a conviction in the case of alien B, who pleaded nolo contendere to the same charge and against whom a formal judgment was entered by the court, but whose sentence was deferred with no other penalty imposed, so long as the state also considered him convicted for some purpose.

We find no rational or legal reason for according these two aliens different immigration status based on the criminal procedures of the states where they committed a crime. Under the approach we have taken in the past, form has been placed over substance, and aliens who are clearly guilty of criminal behavior and whom Congress intended to be considered "convicted" have been permitted to escape the immigration consequences normally attendant upon a conviction. We therefore find that a revision of our standard for a final conviction has become necessary.

As in the past, we shall consider a person convicted if the court has adjudicated him guilty or has entered a formal judgment of guilt. Since such a judicial action is generally deemed a final conviction in both federal and state jurisdictions, it will be sufficient to constitute a conviction for immigration purposes without consideration of the other two factors of our former test.[6]

Where adjudication of guilt has been withheld, however, further examination of the specific procedure used and the state authority under which the court acted will be necessary. As a general rule, a conviction will be found for immigration purposes where all of the following elements are present:

> (1) a judge or jury has found the alien guilty or he has entered a plea of guilty or nolo contendere or has admitted sufficient facts to warrant a finding of guilty;

---

6. The third prong of the standard set forth in *Matter of L–R–, supra,* required that the state also consider the court action a conviction. We note, however, in regard to our current change, a long-standing rule that whether a conviction exists for purposes of a federal statute is a question of federal law and should not depend on the vagaries of state law.

(2) the judge has ordered some form of punishment, penalty, or restraint on the person's liberty to be imposed (including but not limited to incarceration, probation, a fine or restitution, or community-based sanctions such as a rehabilitation program, a work-release or study-release program, revocation or suspension of a driver's license, deprivation of nonessential activities or privileges, or community service); and

(3) a judgment or adjudication of guilt may be entered if the person violates the terms of his probation or fails to comply with the requirements of the court's order, without availability of further proceedings regarding the person's guilt or innocence of the original charge.[7]

We are aware that this standard represents a significant departure from many of our previous decisions. For this reason it is necessary to overrule the following cases to the extent they relied on our former test for conviction and are inconsistent with the standard enunciated by the Board today: *Matter of Garcia*, [Int. Dec. No. 2995 (BIA 1985)]; *Matter of Zangwill*, [18 I & N Dec. 22 (BIA 1981)]; *Matter of Seda*, [17 I & N Dec. 550 (BIA 1980)]; *Matter of Robinson*, 16 I & N Dec. 762 (BIA 1979); *Matter of Varagianis*, [16 I & N Dec. 48 (BIA 1976)]; *Matter of Pikkarainen*, 10 I & N Dec. 401 (BIA1963); *Matter of L–R–, supra.*

We note that a conviction for a crime involving moral turpitude may not support an order of deportation if it has been expunged. We shall continue in this regard to follow the rule which was set forth by the Attorney General in *Matter of G–*, [9 I & N Dec. 159 (BIA 1960; A.G. 1961)], and subsequently reaffirmed in *Matter of Ibarra–Obando*, 12 I & N Dec. 576 (BIA 1966; A.G.1967), and *Matter of Gutnick*, 13 I & N Dec. 672 (BIA 1971). Furthermore, it is the policy of the Service to defer institution of deportation proceedings until an alien who is eligible to have his conviction for a crime involving moral turpitude expunged has had a reasonable opportunity to apply for expunction. *Matter of Tinajero*, 17 I & N Dec. 424 (BIA 1980); Immigration and Naturalization Service Operations Instructions 242.1(a)(29). However, pursuant to the Attorney General's determination in *Matter of A–F–, supra,* a conviction for a narcotics or marihuana violation is final regardless of the possibility of expunction.

Applying our new standard to the respondent's case, we look first to the record of conviction, which indicates that the respondent pleaded guilty to unlawful possession of cocaine in sufficient quantity to reasonably indicate an intent to distribute the drug. It further reflects that the judge stayed entry of the judgment pursuant to Article 27, section 641 of the Annotated Code of Maryland and placed the respondent on probation for 3 years. In addition, he ordered the respondent to donate 100 hours of volunteer community service and to pay a $1,500 fine plus court costs. Since the respondent entered a plea of guilty and the judge imposed several

---

7. It is well established that a conviction does not attain a sufficient degree of finality for immigration purposes until direct appellate review of the conviction has been exhausted or waived. *Marino v. INS.* 537 F.2d 686 (2d Cir.1976); *Aguilera-Enriquez v. INS.* 516 F.2d 565 (6th Cir.1975), *cert. denied*, 423 U.S. 1050 (1976); *Will v. INS.*, 447 F.2d 529 (7th Cir.1971). * * *

forms of punishment, the first two parts of our test for a conviction have been met.

We must next examine the statutory authority under which the judge acted to determine whether the third element is satisfied. According to subsection (b) of section 641, the court may enter judgment and proceed with disposition of the person upon violation of probation as if the person had not been placed on probation. It is clear from the statute that, if a violation of probation occurs, judgment may be automatically entered without further review of the question of guilt. This third requirement of our test having been met, we conclude that the respondent's conviction is sufficiently final to support an order of deportation. Accordingly, we shall affirm the September 13, 1985, decision of the immigration judge to the extent that the respondent was found deportable on the basis of his conviction. * * *

ORDER: The September 13, 1985, decision of the immigration judge is affirmed in part.

Notes

1. As compared with *Matter of L–R*, is the definition of "conviction" provided in *Ozkok* more or less favorable to an alien guilty of a criminal offense? (Would Ozkok have been considered "convicted" under the Board's old standard? Look at the Maryland statute reprinted in note 3 of *Ozkok*.)

2. After Alien M pleaded guilty to forgery, the court deferred adjudication rather than entering a formal finding or judgment of guilt. The court ordered M to serve three years of probation and to pay a fine and court costs. The relevant state statute provides:

(a) When in its opinion the best interest of society and the defendant will be served, the court may, after receiving a plea of guilty or a plea of nolo contendere, hearing the evidence, and finding that it substantiates the defendant's guilt, defer further proceedings without entering an adjudication of guilt, and place the defendant on probation on reasonable terms and conditions as the court may require and for a period as the court may prescribe not to exceed 10 years. However, upon written motion of the defendant requesting final adjudication filed within 30 days after entering such plea and the deferment of adjudication, the court shall proceed to final adjudication as in all other cases.

(b) On violation of a condition of probation imposed under Subsection (a) of this section, the defendant may be arrested and detained as provided in Section 8 of this Article. The defendant is entitled to a hearing limited to the determination by the court of whether it proceeds with an adjudication of guilt on the original charge. No appeal may be taken from this determination. After an adjudication of guilt, all proceedings, including assessment of punishment, pronouncement of sentence, granting of probation, and defendant's appeal continue as if the adjudication of guilt had not been deferred.

Has there been a "conviction" under *Ozkok?*

3. Reread the final paragraph of the Board's opinion. Does *Ozkok* accomplish the Board's goal of establishing a federal definition of "conviction" not dependent on the vagaries of state law? If not, does it matter?

4. In announcing a new definition of "conviction," the Board overrules a number of its prior cases and also affects the interpretation of a number of other sections of the INA dealing with criminal convictions. What is the basis for the Board's change of course? Is there any discussion of the intent of the Congress that enacted (a)(2)(B) or its predecessors? Should there be? Note that Congress has amended the statute frequently but has never dealt with the definition of "conviction." Might it have relied upon the earlier administrative interpretation, or, indeed, be deemed to have ratified it? What theory of statutory interpretation underlies the Board's action? *See Martinez–Montoya v. INS,* 904 F.2d 1018, 1022 (5th Cir.1990) (dictum suggesting that *Ozkok* may be inconsistent with congressional intent).

5. The *Ozkok* opinion notes that the Attorney General has ruled that the expungement of a conviction for a crime involving moral turpitude protects an alien from deportation under § 241(a)(2)(A). But *Ozkok* also indicates that expungement does not ameliorate the effects of a conviction for a narcotics offense under (a)(2)(B)(i)—even for simple possession of a small amount of a controlled substance. *See, e.g., Chong v. INS,* 890 F.2d 284 (11th Cir.1989) (per curiam) (accepting *Ozkok* with little discussion). Similarly, INA § 241(a)(2)(A)(iv) recognizes pardons for crimes of moral turpitude and aggravated felonies, but apparently not controlled substances or firearms offenses. Are these differences in treatment justified?

6. By way of exception, expungement under the Federal First Offender Act, 18 U.S.C. § 3607, or a state equivalent *does* erase a drug conviction for § 241(a)(2)(B)(i) purposes. The BIA has not recognized expungement where the state statute allowed expungement of drug offenses more serious than the mere possession covered in the federal statute. *See Matter of Deris,* Int.Dec. 3102 (BIA 1989). But in *Garberding v. INS,* 30 F.3d 1187 (9th Cir.1994), the court ruled that the requirement of a state equivalent violated equal protection:

> Here, there is no rational basis for treating Garberding differently. Had she possessed her marijuana in Michigan, Virginia or Wisconsin, she would not have been subject to deportation. These states have expungement statutes which are the exact counterpart of the FFOA. Garberding had the bad luck or poor judgment to possess her marijuana in Montana. The state legislature in Montana has seen fit to extend the privilege of expungement to persons who are convicted of drug offenses more serious than Garberding's simple first time possession. It is this fortuitous circumstance, not Garberding's conduct, which the INS used to distinguish her for deportation. This may indeed reflect a policy of harsh treatment of aliens who commit drug offenses, but distinguishing Garberding

for deportation because of the breadth of Montana's expungement statute, not because of what she did, has no logical relation to the fair administration of the immigration laws or the so-called "war on drugs."

Id. at 1990–91.

7. An alien may try to withdraw a guilty plea, arguing that it was involuntary because she did not understand the deportation consequences. A leading case rejecting this argument is *United States v. Parrino*, 212 F.2d 919, 921–22 (2d Cir.1954), which reasoned that because deportation is a mere "collateral consequence" of conviction, failure to understand does not support withdrawal. *People v. Pozo*, 746 P.2d 523, 528 (Colo.1987), allowed withdrawal, but on a different argument: that an alien has been deprived of his Sixth Amendment right to effective assistance of counsel if (1) defense counsel knew or should have known that the defendant was an alien, (2) counsel did not advise of deportation consequences, and (3) prejudice resulted. Other courts have accepted this argument, more readily if counsel affirmatively misinforms about deportation, *see, e.g., United States v. Nagaro-Garbin*, 653 F.Supp. 586, 590–91 (E.D.Mich.1987); sometimes if counsel mentions the possibility but fails to investigate, *see, e.g., People v. Soriano*, 194 Cal.App.3d 1470, 1478–82, 240 Cal.Rptr. 328, 333–36 (1987), and sometimes if counsel says nothing, *see, e.g., People v. Padilla*, 151 Ill.App.3d 297, 303, 104 Ill.Dec. 522, 526, 502 N.E.2d 1182, 1186 (1986). Other courts have rejected the ineffective assistance argument altogether. *See, e.g., United States v. Del Rosario*, 902 F.2d 55, 59 (D.C.Cir.1990). Of course, withdrawing a guilty plea merely reopens the criminal proceedings; the ultimate result may be harsher than under the plea bargain.

8. At least twelve states—California, Connecticut, Florida, Hawaii, Massachusetts, Montana, North Carolina, Ohio, Oregon, Texas, Wisconsin, and Washington—and the District of Columbia have statutes or court rules requiring that trial courts, before accepting a plea of guilty (or nolo contendere in most states), inform defendants that if they are not United States citizens a criminal conviction may lead to their deportation.

9. INS Operations Instruction 242.1(a)(28) gives an alien a reasonable opportunity to apply for expungement before the INS starts deportation proceedings. Otherwise, a stay of deportation while an alien pursues a pardon or any other post-conviction remedy is discretionary, and in fact may be very difficult to obtain. An alien cannot collaterally attack the conviction's validity in a deportation hearing. *See, e.g., De la Cruz v. INS*, 951 F.2d 226, 228 (9th Cir.1991). And as footnote 7 in *Ozkok* suggests, a conviction is "final" enough to support deportation even if the alien is still challenging the conviction through a discretionary appeal or through habeas corpus proceedings. *See, e.g., Morales–Alvarado v. INS*, 655 F.2d 172, 175 (9th Cir.1981).

c. Participants in Nazi Persecution

LINNAS v. INS

United States Court of Appeals, Second Circuit, 1986.
790 F.2d 1024.

ALTIMARI, CIRCUIT JUDGE:

Petitioner, Karl Linnas, seeks review of an order of the Board of Immigration Appeals ("BIA") determining that petitioner must be deported to the Soviet Union. The BIA ordered Linnas deported under section [241(a)(4)(D)] of the Immigration and Nationality Act ("INA"), because of Linnas' active participation in the Nazi persecution of Estonian Jews during World War II. The Soviet Union was designated as the country of deportation pursuant to section 243(a) of the INA.

Linnas now seeks review of the determination of the BIA on the ground that sections [241(a)(4)(D)], 243(h) and 244(e) of the INA [commonly referred to as the Holtzman amendment] constitute a bill of attainder in violation of Article I, section 9 of the Constitution of the United States. Alternatively, Linnas argues that his deportation to the Soviet Union would violate his rights to due process and equal protection.

BACKGROUND

Karl Linnas was born in Estonia in 1919 and entered the United States in 1951 under the auspices of the Displaced Persons Act ("DPA"), Pub.L. No. 80–774, 62 Stat. 1009 (1948), *amended by* Pub.L. No. 81–555, 64 Stat. 219 (1950). In order to gain admittance to the United States as a displaced person, Linnas informed members of the Army Counter Intelligence Corps that he had been a university student during the years 1940 to 1943. In May 1951 Linnas signed an immigration form stating that he had "never advocated or assisted in the persecution of any person because of race, religion or national origin." Upon entering the United States some three months later, Linnas swore to the truth of that statement. The New York State Supreme Court (Suffolk County) admitted Linnas to citizenship in 1960.

In 1979, the government began an action to revoke Linnas' certificate of naturalization on the grounds that it had been "illegally procured" and "procured by concealment of a material fact or by willful misrepresentation." *See* INA § 340(a). * * *

The evidence presented at Linnas' denaturalization trial before District Judge Jacob Mishler was overwhelming and largely uncontroverted. The government presented eyewitness testimony that Linnas was chief of the Nazi concentration camp in Tartu, Estonia during the time period that Linnas later claimed to have been a university student.

Linnas' duties as a concentration camp chief were such as to offend the decency of any civilized society. Eyewitnesses testified that Linnas supervised the transportation of prisoners from his camp to a nearby antitank ditch. On such occasions innocent Jewish women and children were tied by their hands and brought in their underwear to the edge of the ditch where they were forced to kneel. The guards then opened fire. The ditch became a mass grave.

There was also eyewitness testimony that Linnas on at least one occasion announced his victims' death sentence at the side of the ditch and gave the order to fire. Linnas was also said to have then personally approached the edge of the ditch, and fired into it. Another eyewitness recounted having seen Linnas help direct Jews out of a school and onto a schoolbus. That witness recalled that Linnas helped a small child with a doll onto the bus, and that the doll was later placed in a storage area for the personal effects of those who had been killed.

The government also introduced documents signed "Karl Linnas, Chief of Concentration Camps," and "Chief of Tartu Concentration Camp." Documentary evidence was also introduced showing that Linnas later joined the 38th Estonian Police Battalion under the command of a senior colonel of the SS and was wounded in battle on August 30, 1944.

From the evidence presented at trial, Judge Mishler concluded that it was "beyond dispute that defendant, Karl Linnas, 'assisted the enemy in persecuting civil populations of countries'.... The inescapable conclusion is that defendant unlawfully entered the country because of the willful misrepresentations he made." That conclusion was affirmed by this court on January 25, 1982. The horrific facts of Linnas' past exemplify what this court has described as the clearest case of involvement in persecution: one in which "an individual, often while employed at a concentration camp, has personally arrested, or fired upon detained civilians, or has ordered others to do so." *United States v. Sprogis,* 763 F.2d 115, 122 (2d Cir.1985) (citing *United States v. Linnas,* 527 F.Supp. 426 (E.D.N.Y.1981)).

Following Linnas' denaturalization, the government began deportation proceedings under section 242 of the INA. Immigration Judge Howard I. Cohen ruled on May 19, 1983 that Linnas was deportable. Linnas had designated "the free and independent Republic of Estonia" as the country to which he wished to be deported. The independent Republic of Estonia was forcibly incorporated into the Soviet Union following World War II. Linnas apparently intended his designation to mean the office building in New York currently housing the representatives of the independent Republic of Estonia. Immigration Judge Cohen, however, apparently took Linnas' designation to mean that geographic territory historically associated with the Republic of Estonia and currently incorporated in the Soviet Union. In attempting to comply with § 243 of the INA, Immigration Judge Cohen ordered that Linnas be deported from the United States to Estonia, but that if Estonia was unwilling to accept Linnas he was to be deported to the Soviet Union. The Soviet Union, which had tried Linnas in absentia and sentenced him to death for his war crimes, was the only country which had expressed a willingness to accept Linnas. Linnas' request for discretionary relief was denied on the ground that such relief is not available to Nazi persecutors * * *.

Linnas filed a timely appeal to the BIA. On July 31, 1984 the BIA affirmed the decision of the immigration judge except as to the country of deportation. The BIA remanded the case to the immigration judge with instructions to consider the effect of the United States' non-recognition of the Soviet annexation of Estonia and to articulate a statutory basis for the designation of a country of deportation.

On remand, Immigration Judge Cohen reviewed the three step process delineated in § 243(a) of the INA for designation of a country of deportation. Step one, the designation of a country by the deportee, was ruled inapplicable because of Linnas' designation of an office building in New York. Step two, the designation of a country of which the deportee is a citizen, was also held inapplicable. Linnas claimed to be a citizen of the Republic of Estonia, but that country no longer exists as an independent geographic territory. Under step three, the immigration judge may designate deportation to any country which falls within one of seven categories. Immigration Judge Cohen, therefore, considered deportation:

> (1) to the country from which such alien last entered the United States;

> (2) to the country in which is located the foreign port at which such alien embarked for the United States or for foreign contiguous territory;

> (3) to the country in which he was born;

> (4) to the country in which the place of his birth is situated at the time he is ordered deported;

> (5) to any country in which he resided prior to entering the country from which he entered the United States;

> (6) to the country which had sovereignty over the birthplace of the alien at the time of his birth; or

> (7) if deportation to any of the foregoing places or countries is impracticable, inadvisable, or impossible, then to any country which is willing to accept such alien into its territory.

On April 9, 1985, after considering a letter from the Legal Advisor of the Department of State to the effect that Linnas' deportation to the Soviet Union would not violate the nonrecognition policy, Immigration Judge Cohen held that Linnas should be deported to the Soviet Union under either category (4) or (7). Linnas once again appealed to the BIA, which, in a decision dated October 16, 1985, affirmed the immigration judge's decision based on § 243(a)(7).

* * *

DISCUSSION

I. Bill of Attainder

Article I, section 9 of the United States Constitution provides in unequivocal terms that "[n]o Bill of Attainder or ex post facto Law shall be passed." The wisdom of that constitutional command has been held in universally high esteem throughout the history of American jurisprudence. The issue now before this court is whether the legislation in question constitutes a bill of attainder.

A bill of attainder is defined as "a legislative act which inflicts punishment without a judicial trial." *United States v. Lovett,* 328 U.S. 303, 315, 66 S.Ct. 1073, 1078, 90 L.Ed. 1252 (1946) (quoting *Cummings v. Missouri,* 71 U.S. (4 Wall.) 277, 323, 18 L.Ed. 356 (1866)). Such bills are condemned in the Constitution largely because they represent a legislative encroachment on powers more properly exercised by the judiciary. A bill of attainder, "assumes, in the language of the textbooks, judicial magistracy; it pronounces upon the guilt of the party, without any of the forms or safeguards of trial." *Cummings v. Missouri,* 71 U.S. (4 Wall.) at 323. Historically, bills of attainder carried a death penalty while bills of pains and penalties carried lesser punishments. The bill of attainder clause of the Constitution, however, has been consistently construed to apply to bills of pains and penalties as well as bills carrying a death penalty.

* * *

Linnas argues that the Holtzman amendment is a legislative enactment directed at a small group of individuals, Nazi war criminals, for the purpose of punishing those persons without judicial trial. Linnas contends that such a statute constitutes a prohibited bill of attainder. The Holtzman amendment, in essence, requires the deportation of persons shown to have participated in Nazi persecution during World War II, and eliminates the Attorney General's power to grant such persons discretionary relief. The deportation of Nazi persecutors is required even though the deportee's life or freedom might be threatened as a result.

Applying the elements of a bill of attainder to the Holtzman amendment, it is readily apparent that the challenged provisions are a legislative act. In determining whether that act constitutes punishment the court must consider: "(1) whether the challenged statute falls within the historical meaning of legislative punishment; (2) whether the statute, 'viewed in terms of the type and severity of burdens imposed reasonably can be said to further nonpunitive legislative purposes'; and (3) whether the legislative record 'evinces a congressional intent to punish.' " *Selective Service System v. Minnesota Public Interest Research Group,* 468 U.S. 841, 852, 104 S.Ct. 3348, 3355, 82 L.Ed.2d 632 (1984) (quoting *Nixon v. Administrator of General Services,* 433 U.S. 425, 473, 97 S.Ct. 2777, 2805, 53 L.Ed.2d 867 (1977)).

Linnas contends that the Holtzman amendment is within the historical meaning of legislative punishment because deportation is the equivalent of banishment. Banishment is a punishment often associated with bills of attainder. Exclusion of a citizen of the United States has at times been held to constitute punishment equivalent to banishment. Deportation of noncitizens from the United States, however, has generally been held not to constitute punishment. Linnas is not a citizen of the United States. This case presents little reason for breaking with the traditional rule that deportation, although often severely burdensome, is not punishment. The exclusion of Linnas from ever entering the country would certainly not fit any historical meaning of punishment. To say that his deportation becomes punishment by virtue of his current presence in the United States, a presence fraudulently attained in 1951, would grant Linnas additional protection under the law as a result of his having sworn to untrue statements.

In order to determine whether the Holtzman amendment can be said to further a nonpunitive purpose the court must consider the type and severity of the burdens imposed. It is beyond cavil that deportation generally, and in this case particularly, imposes a severe burden on the deportee. Severity, however, does not in itself make a burden a punishment. Deportation furthers the nonpunitive legislative purpose of protecting the citizenry from persons harmful to the public good. In the case of Nazi persecutors, it borders on sophistry to deny the legitimate legislative purposes of excluding known mass murderers from the United States. It was certainly reasonable for the citizens of the United States, through their elected representatives, to conclude that they did not wish to share their communities with persons who ordered the wholesale extermination of innocent men, women and children. It is also reasonable for the United States, apart from any punitive intent, to wish not to be known in the family of civilized nations as a haven for the refuse of the Nazi abomination.

There is little indication in the legislative record of any Congressional intent to use the Holtzman amendment to punish. Although one Representative did comment that the Holtzman amendment would provide a device for bringing the culpable "to justice," 124 Cong.Rec. H31648 (daily ed. September 26, 1978) (statement of Rep. Gilman), the legislative record as a whole evinces only an intent to exclude from the United States those persons who committed crimes against humanity in the name of Nazism. Congress' goals in passing the Holtzman amendment appear to have been the need to "put our Government squarely on record as denying sanctuary in the United States to Nazi War criminals," and to "reaffirm our commitment to human rights." 124 Cong.Rec. H31647 (daily ed. September 26, 1978) (statements of Rep. Holtzman).

The Ninth Circuit Court of Appeals faced the issue now before this court in *Artukovic v. Immigration and Naturalization Service* and concluded that the Holtzman amendment is not a bill of attainder because deportation is not punishment. 693 F.2d 894, 897 (1982). We now reach the same conclusion. Because the Holtzman amendment is not punishment and, therefore, not a bill of attainder, we need not consider whether Linnas was deported without a judicial trial. We note, however, that Linnas did in fact receive extensive judicial review.

II. *Equal Protection and Due Process*

Linnas claims that his deportation to the Soviet Union is in fact a disguised extradition. Linnas was convicted *in absentia* in the Soviet Union and sentenced to death for his war crimes. Linnas contends that the Soviet trial was a sham and that deporting him to the Soviet Union is in fact extradition in the absence of an extradition treaty. Linnas argues that to deport him under these circumstances will deprive him of his life without due process.

The irony of Karl Linnas objecting to execution without due process is not lost on this court. The right to due process is, of course, essential to the American system of ordered liberty, and must be extended to all persons in the United States. The fact that Linnas enjoys the right to due process has enabled him to remain in the United States until 1986 even though the government began the denaturalization process in 1979. The considerable length of time that Linnas has been able to remain in the United States after the discovery of his heinous past is a small price to pay for a system of law which separates our government from the government that Linnas served as Chief of the Tartu concentration camp. We now, therefore, examine the merits of the petitioner's due process claim.

Linnas' argument centers on the proposition that a noncitizen has a right not to be extradited in the absence of an extradition treaty. We need not address this novel question, however, because no extradition has taken place in this case. Extradition may be applied to either a citizen or noncitizen, whereas deportation applies only to noncitizens such as Linnas. Extradition is initiated by a foreign state. While the Soviet Union may have an interest in the trial of Nazi war criminals, the impetus for the denaturalization and removal of Linnas appears to have come from the government of the United States. The legislative history of the Holtzman amendment indicates that the Congress intended to rid this nation of Nazi war criminals, not to court favor with nations having no extradition treaties with the United States. Ruling this procedure to be an extradition would greatly reduce the ability of this nation to deport those who have committed crimes of moral turpitude in their own countries.

In addition, Linnas was given the same opportunity given to any deportee to designate a country to which he wished to be sent. Linnas designated an office building in New York, thus wasting the opportunity to choose a proper place of deportation. The fact that such an opportunity was offered, however, strongly undercuts his contention that his deportation was a disguised attempt to extradite him to the Soviet Union. The record also indicates that the government made at least some attempt to find a country other than the Soviet Union which would accept Linnas. There is no support in the record for Linnas' claim that the government's efforts in this regard were a mere facade. Linnas' own failure to designate a country of deportation lends credence to the immigration judge's finding that no country other than the Soviet Union would accept him. Accordingly, there was no abuse of discretion in designating the Soviet Union as the country of deportation under INA § 243(a)(7). That designation did not transform the deportation of Linnas into an extradition.

Congress has broad authority over the status of aliens, and there is no substantive due process right not to be deported. Linnas' procedural due process rights have been meticulously observed throughout the denaturalization and deportation proceedings. As to Linnas' claim that he will be denied due process in the Soviet Union, the jurisdiction of this court obviously does not extend beyond the borders of the United States. It is well established that the federal judiciary may not require that persons removed from the United States be accorded constitutional due process.

We are not, however, deaf to Linnas' protestations concerning the fate which may await him in the Soviet Union. In *Gallina v. Fraser* this court permitted the extradition of a man convicted *in absentia* in a foreign country. 278 F.2d 77, 78–79 (2d Cir.), *cert. denied,* 364 U.S. 851, 81 S.Ct. 97, 5 L.Ed.2d 74 (1960). The *Gallina* court hypothesized, however, that there could arise a situation in which the person to be removed from the United States would be subjected to "procedures or punishment so anti-pathetic to a federal court's sense of decency" as to require judicial intervention. *Id.* at 79. This is not such a case.

The foundation of Linnas' due process argument is an appeal to the court's sense of decency and compassion. Noble words such as "decency" and "compassion" ring hollow when spoken by a man who ordered the extermination of innocent men, women and children kneeling at the edge of a mass grave. Karl Linnas' appeal to humanity, a humanity which he has grossly, callously and monstrously offended, truly offends this court's sense of decency.

Finally, we turn to Linnas' equal protection argument. The essence of that argument appears to be that Congress should not be permitted to treat Nazi war criminals differently from anyone else.

Nazi war criminals are not a class of persons entitled to enhanced scrutiny under the equal protection clause. The legislative system of excluding and deporting such persons will, therefore, "not be set aside as the denial of equal protection of the laws if any state of facts reasonably may be conceived to justify it." *Metropolitan Casualty Insurance Company v. Brownell,* 294 U.S. 580, 584, 55 S.Ct. 538, 540, 79 L.Ed. 1070 (1935). The rationality standard is not a difficult standard to meet. In this instance, we are convinced that a rational relationship exists between the deportation of Nazi war criminals and a legitimate legislative purpose. Petitioner's equal protection argument is, therefore, without merit.

CONCLUSION

The petition for review is denied.

Notes

1. The deportation of Karl Linnas to the Soviet Union in April 1987 was front-page news. Ethnic groups representing Baltic and Ukrainian emigres opposed deportation, and they were joined by conservative members of the Reagan Administration. Apparently more than a dozen countries had turned down Linnas' request for admission.

In July 1987, the Soviet press agency Tass reported that Linnas had died in a Leningrad hospital of heart and kidney disease. Tass said that Linnas had been awaiting action on an appeal for a pardon after judicial authorities had concluded that there were no grounds for a new trial.

2. Do you find credible the court's conclusion that the Holtzman Amendment was not intended to punish former Nazis? Suppose Congress' action was motivated by several concerns, including both those identified by the court and a desire to punish. Should the deportation ground be invalidated?

3. To be deportable, an alien must have "ordered, incited, assisted or otherwise participated" in the persecution of others. How broadly ought this statutory language to be read? Consider *Matter of Kulle,* 19 I & N Dec. 318 (BIA 1985), involving a former member of the Waffen SS who had been a guard, supervisor and trainer of other guards at the Gross–Rosen concentration camp:

> Deportability under * * * of the Act does not require specific evidence that [Kulle] engaged in acts of brutality against the prisoners. Section [241(a)(4)(D)] makes an alien deportable if he merely "assisted" in the persecution of others. Based on the testimony of the Government's witnesses, which the immigration judge found credible, the record clearly establishes that persecution was systematic and ongoing at Gross–Rosen and that [Kulle] knew about it.

> Similarly, [Kulle's] deportability * * * is not defeated by his contention that his service at the camp was involuntary because he was denied a transfer from Gross–Rosen and that he merely obeyed orders. Congress intended that all who assisted the Nazis in persecuting others must be deported regardless of the degree of voluntariness of such assistance. We have already held that the actions of a Ukrainian prisoner of war who was forced by the Nazis to guard the perimeter of a concentration camp constituted assistance in persecution within the meaning of the Act because his actions would have aided the Nazis in their confinement of the prisoners at the camp. [*Matter of Fedorenko,* 19 I & N Dec. 57 (BIA 1984).] * * * Therefore, [Kulle's] duty as a perimeter guard to prevent prisoners escaping from their slave labor at Gross–Rosen is sufficient to establish his assistance to the Nazi regime's persecution of these prisoners. * * * [His] involvement in supervising and training prison guards at the Gross–Rosen concentration camp also clearly constituted assistance in persecution * * * because his actions would have significantly aided the Nazis in their confinement of the prisoners at the camp.

The Board's decision was affirmed on appeal. *Kulle v. INS,* 825 F.2d 1188 (7th Cir.1987), *cert. denied,* 484 U.S. 1042, 108 S.Ct. 773, 98 L.Ed.2d 860 (1988).

Contrast with *Matter of Kulle* the Ninth Circuit's opinion in *Laipenieks v. INS,* 750 F.2d 1427, 1431 (9th Cir.1985). Laipenieks had been a member of the Latvian Political Police during the Nazi occupation of Latvia and was responsible for the investigation and interrogation of persons suspected of having participated in atrocities during the Soviet occupation of Latvia in 1940–41. The court held that "active personal involvement in persecutorial acts needs to be demonstrated" for deportability under § 241(a)(4)(D); "mere acquiesence or membership in an organization [that persecutes] is insufficient." The court reversed the BIA's finding of deportability on the ground that the government had not established that Laipenieks had personally assisted or participated in the persecution of others because of their political beliefs. Also consider *Petkiewytsch v. INS*, 945 F.2d 871, 880–81 (6th Cir.1991):

> Although Petkiewytsch wore a uniform and carried a rifle, the Board found that he was at all times a reluctant civilian guard, once himself imprisoned for failing to perform his guard duties diligently. The camp where he served was the least punitive of all types of Nazi camps. The Board also found that the petitioner served under duress and that he was told he would be shot if he attempted to escape. He never personally engaged in acts of persecution, and was released by the British authorities, who interned him as a suspected war criminal, upon a finding that the charges could not be sustained. His "particular conduct" just does not fit the description of a "Nazi war criminal" or a "person[ ]who engaged in war crimes," repeatedly described as the class sought to be made deportable by the Holtzman Amendment.

For a thoughtful analysis of the cases and the problem of defining "assistance," see Massey, *Individual Responsibility for Assisting the Nazis in Persecuting Civilians,* 71 Minn.L.Rev. 97 (1986).

4. In 1979, the Department of Justice established the Office of Special Investigations to investigate and prosecute former Nazis living in the U.S. An account of the office's efforts to locate and remove former Nazis is provided by its first director Allan A. Ryan, Jr. in Quiet Neighbors: Prosecuting Nazi War Criminals in America (1984).

5. Section 241(a)(4)(D) makes deportable not only any alien who assisted in Nazi persecution but also of any alien who has engaged in genocide. Both groups are excludable, *see* § 212(a)(3)(E), ineligible for voluntary departure, *see* §§ 242(b), 244(e), and withholding of deportation, *see* § 243(h).

d. Deportation Statutes and "Statutes of Limitations"

Recall the facts in *Harisiades v. Shaughnessy,* p. 518 *supra*. Harisiades had joined the Communist Party nine years after entering the United States. Mascitti had terminated his membership in the subversive organizations 17 years before deportation proceedings were initiated against him. In neither case was the length of time between entry and commission of the act or between commission of the act and initiation of deportation proceedings relevant to the alien's deportability. Both these issues are often loosely discussed under the name of "statutes of limitations" in immigration law, but they raise distinct issues of law and policy.

Time between Entry and the Commission of a Deportable Act

INA § 241(a)(2)(A)(i) makes deportable an alien who "is convicted of a crime involving moral turpitude committed *within five years after entry* and either sentenced to confinement or confined therefor in a prison or corrective institution, for a year or more." (Emphasis supplied.) Should the same notion—that acts should no longer be the basis for deportation after the alien has been in the United States for a certain period of time—be applied to other deportation grounds as well? For some grounds of deportation (*e.g.*, becoming a public charge), but not others (*e.g.*, committing crime of moral turpitude)? At some point, is it fair to say that an alien who has resided for a long period of time in the United States has become a product of American society? What about children who enter at a very young age and commit a crime in their twenties?

One response to these slightly slanted questions is that long-term residents have an easy way to avoid deportation: become citizens. Is this a good answer to the aliens in *Harisiades*? Justice Jackson seems to suggest that it is; but note that the Nationality Act of 1940, Ch. 876, 54 Stat. 1137, precluded the naturalization of aliens who belonged to organizations advocating the violent overthrow of the United States government, and the Internal Security Act of 1950, § 25, 64 Stat. 987, specifically barred naturalization of members of the Communist Party. *See* INA § 313, 8 C.F.R. §§ 316.4, 316.11; *see also* GM & Y § 95.04[2][c]. Similarly, the Chinese who challenged their deportation in *Fong Yue Ting* could not become citizens; in fact, various statutes barred naturalization by Asian immigrants until 1952.

A more basic response might be that permanent residency is a privilege. Consider Senator Simpson's views on this issue:

> In the criminal law, a statute of limitations prevents prosecution and punishment after a certain period of time following the past act which constitutes the offense. Deportation is not a penalty, which is intended to punish for past offense. Deportation represents a judgment that certain persons are unacceptable for presence in the U.S., because they *currently* represent a threat or because they are otherwise regarded as *currently* undesirable by the American people. Past behavior may well be relevant to both of these reasons for such a judgment.

SCIRP, Final Report 418. Under this view, discretionary relief, which Chapter Seven will consider, may be a more appropriate way to deal with long-term permanent residents facing deportation.

Time between Commission of Act and Initiation of Proceedings

So far we have been considering a "statute of limitations" as a bar to deportation of long-time residents who commit acts a number of years *after entry*. This is not the usual way people think about a "statute of limitations." In the criminal law, a statute of limitations normally begins running at the time a crime has been committed. One could envisage adopting a similar rule in immigration law that would prohibit initiation of deportation proceedings a certain number of years after commission of the act constituting the ground for deportation.

In fact, early immigration laws applied a statute of limitations to the deportation ground of excludable at entry. The 1903 Act provided that:

"any alien who shall come into the United States in violation of law * * * shall be deported * * * at any time within two years after arrival." Act of March 3, 1903, Ch. 1012, § 20, 32 Stat. 1218. Subsequent acts extended the limitation period to three years, Act of February 20, 1907, Ch. 1134, § 20, 34 Stat. 904, and then five years, Immigration Act of 1917, Ch. 29, § 19, 39 Stat. 889. When the 1952 Act eliminated the limitation, the Senate Judiciary Committee explained: "If the cause for exclusion existed at the time of entry, it is believed that such aliens are just as undesirable at any subsequent time as they are within the five years after entry." S.Rep. No. 1515, 81st Cong., 2d Sess. 389 (1950).

If you were a member of Congress, would you support this kind of statute of limitations for all grounds of deportation? Some grounds and not others?

Several rationales are generally cited as underlying the use of statutes of limitations in criminal law: (1) the desirability that prosecutions be based on fresh evidence; (2) the likelihood that a person who has refrained from further criminal activity for a period of time has reformed; (3) the decline of the retributive impulse over time; (4) the desirability of lessening the possibility of blackmail based on a threat to prosecute or disclose evidence to law enforcement officials; and (5) the promotion of repose. American Law Institute, Model Penal Code and Commentaries, Comment Part I § 1.06 (1985). Do these justifications equally support a statute of limitations in immigration law?

3. THE CONSEQUENCES OF DEPORTATION

Deportation imposes several disabilities (besides expulsion itself) on an alien who seeks to re-enter the United States or does re-enter. She may not enter for five years (20 years for aggravated felons) without the Attorney General's permission. INA § 212(a)(6)(B). If she enters without permission she is subject to summary deportation and criminal punishment. INA §§ 242(f), 276. Deportation also terminates residence for registry and naturalization purposes, and it may end her social security benefits. See GM & Y 71.01[6][c]. And in addition, the 1994 Crime Act enacted stiff penalties for aliens who fail to depart after a final deportation order. Pub.L. 103–322, § 130001, 108 Stat. 1796, 2023.

SECTION B.   DEPORTATION PROCEDURES

1. THE CONSTITUTIONAL REQUIREMENT OF DUE PROCESS

We have previously discussed the general unwillingness of the Supreme Court to scrutinize the procedures Congress establishes for the *exclusion* of aliens. "Whatever the procedure authorized by Congress is," the Court stated in *Knauff* and *Mezei*, "it is due process as far as the alien denied entry is concerned." We have already seen that in 1982 the Supreme Court softened its stance somewhat in *Landon v. Plasencia*, p. 405 *supra*, at least for exclusion cases involving returning lawful permanent residents. *Plasencia* notwithstanding, *Knauff* and *Mezei* continue to cast a large shadow for all other excludable aliens.

Perhaps it will strike you as odd that the Court has read the Constitution quite differently when examining the deportation process. The "constitutionalization" of deportation procedures has not occurred through constitutional provisions normally invoked to guarantee criminal defendants full and fair judicial proceedings (such as the Sixth Amendment). This is because the courts have steadfastly stuck to their description of deportation proceedings as "civil" in nature. *E.g., INS v. Lopez–Mendoza,* 468 U.S. 1032, 1938, 104 S.Ct. 3479, 3483, 82 L.Ed.2d 778 (1984) (Fourth Amendment exclusionary rule not applicable), p. 623 *infra*. Rather, the Constitution has been brought to the deportation setting through the due process clause of the Fifth Amendment. The landmark case that began this process follows.

THE JAPANESE IMMIGRANT CASE
(YAMATAYA v. FISHER)

Supreme Court of the United States, 1903.
189 U.S. 86, 23 S.Ct. 611, 47 L.Ed. 721.

[Kaoru Yamataya, a citizen of Japan, landed at Seattle on July 11, 1901. Four days later an immigration inspector, after investigation, decided that she was deportable because she had been excludable at time of entry as a pauper and a person likely to become a public charge. Yamataya asserted that the investigation had been inadequate because she did not understand English, did not realize that the investigation involved her deportability, was not assisted by counsel, and had not had an opportunity to show she was not deportable.]

MR. JUSTICE HARLAN * * * delivered the opinion of the Court.

* * *

The constitutionality of the legislation in question, in its general aspects, is no longer open to discussion in this court. That Congress may exclude aliens of a particular race from the United States; prescribe the terms and conditions upon which certain classes of aliens may come to this country; establish regulations for sending out of the country such aliens as come here in violation of law; and commit the enforcement of such provisions, conditions and regulations exclusively to executive officers, without judicial intervention, are principles firmly established by the decisions of this court. *Nishimura Ekiu v. United States,* 142 U.S. 651, 35 L.Ed. 1146, 12 Sup.Ct.Rep. 336; *Fong Yue Ting v. United States,* 149 U.S. 698, 37 L.Ed. 905, 13 Sup.Ct.Rep. 1016.

* * *

What was the extent of the authority of the executive officers of the Government over the petitioner after she landed? * * * [T]he Secretary of the Treasury, under the * * * act of October 19, 1888, c. 1210, was authorized, within one year after an alien of the excluded class entered the country, to cause him to be taken into custody and returned to the country whence he came. Substantially the same power was conferred by the act of March 3, 1891, c. 551, by the eleventh section of which it is provided that the alien immigrant may be sent out of the country, "as provided by law," at any time within the year after his illegally coming into the United States. Taking all its enactments together, it is clear that Congress did not intend that the mere admission of an alien, or his mere entering the country, should place him at all times thereafter entirely beyond the control or authority of the executive officers of the Government. On the contrary, if the Secretary of the Treasury became satisfied that the immigrant had been allowed to land contrary to the prohibition of that law, then he could at any time within a year after the landing cause the immigrant to be taken into custody and deported. The immigrant must be taken to have entered subject to the condition that he might be sent out of the country by order of the proper executive officer if within a year he was found to have been wrongfully admitted into or had illegally entered the United States. * * *

It is contended, however, that in respect of an alien who has already landed it is consistent with the acts of Congress that he may be deported without previous notice of any purpose to deport him, and without any opportunity on his part to show by competent evidence before the executive officers charged with the execution of the acts of Congress, that he is not here in violation of law; that the deportation of an alien without provision for such a notice and for an opportunity to be heard was inconsistent with the due process of law required by the Fifth Amendment of the Constitution.

Leaving on one side the question whether an alien can rightfully invoke the due process clause of the Constitution who has entered the country clandestinely, and who has been here for too brief a period to have become, in any real sense, a part of our population, before his right to remain is disputed, we have to say that the rigid construction of the acts of Congress suggested by the appellant are not justified. Those acts do not necessarily exclude opportunity to the immigrant to be heard, when such opportunity is of right. It was held in *Murray's Lessee v. Hoboken Land & Improvement Co.,* 18 How. 272, 280, 281, 283, 15 L.Ed. 372, 376, 377, that "though 'due process of law' generally implies and includes *actor, reus, judex,* regular allegations, opportunity to answer and a trial according to some course of judicial proceedings, yet this is not universally true;" and that "though, generally, both public and private wrong are redressed through judicial action, there are more summary extra-judicial remedies for both." Hence, it was decided in that case to be consistent with due process of law for Congress to provide summary means to compel revenue officers— and in case of default, their sureties—to pay such balances of the public money as might be in their hands. Now, it has been settled that the power to exclude or expel aliens belonged to the political department of the Government, and that the order of an executive officer, invested with the power to determine finally the facts upon which an alien's right to enter this country, or remain in it, depended, was "due process of law, and no other tribunal, unless expressly authorized by law to do so, was at liberty to reexamine the evidence on which he acted, or to controvert its sufficiency." *Fong Yue Ting v. United States,* 149 U.S. 698, 713, 37 L.Ed. 905, 913, 13 Sup.Ct.Rep. 1016. But this court has never held, nor must we now be understood as holding, that administrative officers, when executing the provisions of a statute involving the liberty of persons, may disregard the fundamental principles that inhere in "due process of law" as understood at the time of the adoption of the Constitution. One of these principles is that no person shall be deprived of his liberty without opportunity, at some time, to be heard, before such officers, in respect of the matters upon which that liberty depends—not necessarily an opportunity upon a regular, set occasion, and according to the forms of judicial procedure, but one that will secure the prompt, vigorous action contemplated by Congress, and at the same time be appropriate to the nature of the case upon which such officers are required to act. Therefore, it is not competent for the Secretary of the Treasury or any executive officer, at any time within the year limited by the statute, arbitrarily to cause an alien, who has entered the country, and has become subject in all respects to its jurisdiction, and a part of its population, although alleged to be illegally here, to be taken into custody and deported without giving him all opportunity to be heard upon the questions involving his right to be and remain in the United States. No such arbitrary power can exist where the principles involved in due process of law are recognized.

This is the reasonable construction of the acts of Congress here in question, and they need not be otherwise interpreted. In the case of all acts of Congress, such interpretation ought to be adopted as, without doing violence to the import of the words used, will bring them into harmony with the Constitution. An act of Congress must be taken to be constitutional unless the contrary plainly and palpably appears. The words here used do not require an interpretation that would invest executive or administrative officers with the absolute, arbitrary power implied in the contention of the appellant. Besides, the record now before us shows that the appellant had notice, although not a formal one, of the investigation instituted for the purpose of ascertaining whether she was illegally in this country. The traverse to the return made by the Immigration Inspector shows upon its face that she was before that officer pending the investigation of her right to be in the United States, and made answers to questions propounded to her. It is true that she pleads a want of knowledge of our language; that she did not understand the nature and import of the questions propounded to her; that the investigation made was a "pretended" one; and that she did not, at the time, know that the investigation had reference to her being deported from the country. These considerations cannot justify the intervention of the courts. They could have been presented to the officer having primary control of such a case, as well as upon an appeal to the Secretary of the Treasury, who had power to order another investigation if that course was demanded by law or by the ends of justice. It is not to be assumed that either would have refused a second or fuller investigation, if a proper application and showing for one had been made by or for the appellant. Whether further investigation should have been ordered was for the officers, charged with the execution of the statutes, to determine. Their action in that regard is not subject to judicial review. Suffice it to say, it does not appear that appellant was denied an opportunity to be heard. And as no appeal was taken to the Secretary from the decision of the Immigration Inspector, that decision was final and conclusive. If the appellant's want of knowledge of the English language put her at some disadvantage in the investigation conducted by that officer, that was her misfortune, and constitutes no reason, under the acts of Congress, or under any rule of law, for the intervention of the court by *habeas corpus*. We perceive no ground for such intervention—none for the contention that due process of law was denied to appellant.

The judgment is affirmed.

MR. JUSTICE BREWER and MR. JUSTICE PECKHAM dissented.

Notes

1. Can you construct a coherent interpretation of the Constitution that accounts for the results in the exclusion due process cases, *Knauff* and *Mezei* (pp. 386, 389 *supra*), and *Yamataya?* Does your interpretation also account for the differences in the Court's reasoning in *Yamataya* and *Fong Yue Ting*? Does your interpretation also answer the question reserved by Justice Harlan—whether an alien who entered without inspection and had been in the United States only a short time can invoke the due process clause in challenging deportation procedures?

We suggest you think about these difficult, but crucial, questions throughout this Section. We will spell out our views on these issues at the close of the Chapter.

2. Why should the Supreme Court (or any court, for that matter) distinguish procedural from substantive constitutional challenges and provide closer judicial scrutiny for the former?

3. *Yamataya* stands for the proposition that deportation procedures must conform to the dictates of the due process clause of the Constitution. But note that Yamataya's deportation was *upheld* in that case even though she had had no formal hearing, alleged that she could neither speak nor understand English, and claimed that she was unaware of the reason for her being questioned. Could such a "proceeding" be considered "due process of law" today?

Under current judicial interpretations of the constitutional mandate, aliens must be informed of the nature of the proceeding and the grounds of deportation at issue[1] and must be provided with an interpreter when they cannot understand English.[2] The current practice is to provide translation only of those questions directed at witnesses who cannot speak English. In *El Rescate Legal Services, Inc. v. EOIR*, 959 F.2d 742, 752 (9th Cir.1992), the court accepted that due process may require portions to be translated, but it declined to find that hearings must be translated in their entirety. *Cf. United States v. Leon–Leon*, 35 F.3d 1428, 1431–32 (9th Cir.1994) (failure to translate crucial parts of deportation hearing violated due process but no prejudice resulted).

1. *See, e.g., Hirsch v. INS*, 308 F.2d 562, 566–67 (9th Cir.1962); *Matter of Rios–Carrillo*, 10 I & N Dec. 291 (BIA 1963).

2. *See, e.g., Tejeda–Mata v. INS*, 626 F.2d 721, 726 (9th Cir.1980), *cert. denied*, 456 U.S. 994, 102 S.Ct. 2280, 73 L.Ed.2d 1291 (1982).

2. INITIATION OF PROCEEDINGS

a. *Arrest and the Order to Show Cause*

Until 1956, proceedings to deport an alien began with the arrest of the alien. Today, deportation proceedings begin with the filing of an Order to Show Cause ("OSC")—so called because it requires an alien to "show cause" why he or she should not be deported—on Form I–221 with the Office of Immigration Judge. 8 C.F.R. § 242.1. The OSC—which must be in English and Spanish—informs the alien of the nature of the proceedings, the factual allegations underlying the charge of deportability and the statutory provisions alleged to have been violated. The OSC requires the alien to appear before an immigration judge for a hearing at a designated time and place. INA § 242B(a). In order to give the alien a chance to obtain counsel, the hearing cannot be scheduled (unless she consents) earlier than fourteen days after the OSC is served. See INA § 242B(b)(1).

The OSC may be served by mail or in person. When an immigration officer serves the order, he is required by regulation to explain the order and advise the alien that anything the alien says may be used against her (but not that the she has the right to remain silent). The officer must also inform the alien that she has a right to be represented by an attorney (at no expense to the government); if the alien cannot afford an attorney, the officer must advise her of free legal services available in the district. 8 C.F.R. § 242.1(c).

While arrest no longer formally commences deportation proceedings and in fact many OSC's are filed and served without the alien first being arrested, the power of arrest remains. INA § 287(a) gives immigration officers the authority to arrest an alien whom the officer believes is in the country in violation of the law and is likely to escape before a warrant can be obtained. An alien arrested under this section must be brought before an immigration officer for an examination. If the examining officer is satisfied that a *prima facie* case exists that the alien is illegally in the United States, formal deportation proceedings are initiated by filing an OSC (unless the alien is permitted to depart the country voluntarily). By regulation, the decision to begin deportation proceedings must be made within 24 hours of the arrest. 8 C.F.R. § 287.3.

The arrest and search powers of immigration officers are subject to the requirements and restrictions of the Fourth Amendment. However, the exclusionary rule does not apply in deportation proceedings, and courts have not read the Constitution to require "*Miranda* warnings" in the deportation context. We will discuss these and other Fourth and Fifth Amendment issues later in this Section.

The vast majority of aliens served with an order to show cause or arrested for illegal presence in the United States do not go through a deportation hearing. In FY 1993, more than 1.3 million aliens were apprehended, yet only about 100,000 hearings were held. 1993 INS Statistical Yearbook, Table 59. Most apprehended aliens avoid a deportation hearing by agreeing to leave the United States voluntarily. ("Voluntary departure" is discussed in Chapter Seven *infra*.) The INS may also choose to defer deportation proceedings if an alien has applied for an immigration benefit that will regularize her status (such as adjustment of status), if she has applied for asylum, or if the INS deems the violation of law trivial or the enforcement of the statute inhumane under the particular circumstances. Cases in this latter category are sometimes given "deferred action status," also discussed in Chapter Seven *infra*.

b. Bond and Detention

Whether or not the alien was ever in custody before being served with an OSC, the next question is whether the INS detains the alien while the deportation proceeding is pending. The INS may detain an arrested alien, release her under specific conditions, or set bond. Aliens have the right to apply to an immigration judge for release from custody, change in the conditions of release, or reduction in bond. 8 C.F.R. § 242.2. Bond redetermination applications may be made by telephone, when authorized by the immigration judge. 8 C.F.R. § 3.19(b). Both the alien and the INS are entitled to appeal the judge's decision to the BIA. 8 C.F.R. § 242.2(b). An alien arrested pending determination of deportability should "be detained or required to post bond [only] * * * upon a finding that he is a threat to the national security * * * or that he is a poor bail risk." *Matter of Patel,* 15 I & N Dec. 666 (BIA 1976). Factors to be considered include the alien's employment history, length of residence in the community, existence of family ties, record of appearance or nonappearance at prior court proceedings, and previous criminal or immigration law violations. *Matter of Sugay,* 17 I & N Dec. 637 (BIA 1981); 8 C.F.R. § 242.2(h). *See generally* National Immigration Project of the National Lawyers Guild, Bond Practice Manual, (1993–94 ed.).

These are the basic rules, but understanding INS detention practices requires looking at different groups of detainees. A 1992 GAO study found a chronic shortage of detention space. *See* General Accounting Office, Immigration Control: Immigration Policies Affect INS Detention Efforts (1992). The INS uses 16 detention facilities, which can hold about 99,000 aliens per year at the current average stay of 23 days. This is only one-fifth of the aliens subject to detention and one-tenth of the aliens apprehended annually. Space being limited, the top INS priority is to detain deportable aggravated felons and other criminal aliens. The next major priority is to detain undocumented excludable aliens, but many are not detained. Aliens deportable for entry without inspection and other non-criminal reasons are typically released on their own recognizance or following the posting of bond. Overall, the GAO found that whether and how long an alien is detained varies greatly by nationality and by space available in a given location.

While bond and detention are mechanisms aimed at ensuring that aliens served with orders to show cause appear at their deportation hearings, many of these aliens subsequently fail to appear. A 1989 study by the General Accounting Office estimated a nonappearance rate of 27 percent, owing in part to the failure of INS to properly notify aliens of the time or place of their hearings and in part to the absence of serious consequences (other than forfeiture of bond) for failure to appear. General Accounting Office, Immigration Control: Deporting and Excluding Aliens from the United States 3 (1989). These findings led Congress in 1990 to add INA § 242B, which you should now read. What measures did Congress take to deal with the high level of absconding? What are the sanctions for failure to appear? Are they appropriate? How effective do you think they are likely to be?

Section 242(a) of the INA permits an alien to file a habeas corpus action in a federal district court challenging the government's detention or bond decision. Note that the section grants courts the power to "review or revise" bond determinations only "upon a conclusive showing * * * that the Attorney General is not proceeding with such reasonable dispatch as may be warranted by the particular facts and circumstances * * * to determine deportability." Some courts, however, have read the provision as authorizing an "abuse of discretion" test which would allow a broader review of the grounds for, and amount of, the bond. *See, e.g., Caporali v. Whelan,* 582 F.Supp. 217 (D.Mass.1984); *Application of Maringolo,* 303 F.Supp. 1389 (S.D.N.Y.1969). Is such review consistent with the statute?

In 1983, INS adopted a regulation requiring that all bonds in deportation cases include a rider barring the alien from working unless the District Director determined that employment was appropriate. 8 C.F.R. § 103.6(a)(2)(ii) (1984). After lengthy litigation, the Supreme Court considered the validity of this regulation in *INS v. National Center for Immigrants' Rights,* 502 U.S. 183, 112 S.Ct. 551, 116 L.Ed.2d 546 (1991). First interpreting the regulation not to apply to aliens who were otherwise authorized to work, the Court upheld it against a facial challenge as within the Attorney General's statutory authority.

An empirical study of the Chicago district office found a marked difference in bond setting by the INS and upon de novo review by immigration judges. Bond redetermination hearings resulted in an average reduction of over two-thirds of the original INS bonds. The study suggests that at the heart of the "interinstitutional differences" lies a "value dissensus":

> The bail area contains two conflicting values—effective immigration law enforcement and protection of the liberty interests of individuals. * * *

* * *

> * * * Immigration enforcement emphasizes the importance of the removal of deportable aliens. Bail emerges as an important enforcement tool in this task. Its importance in part is heightened by the INS enforcement function but also by the difficult environment in which INS investigators see themselves operating—one that contains immigration court delays and BIA appeals, extensive reliance on aliens leaving the country voluntarily on their own, and limited resources for locating absconders.

> Immigration judges do not face the same pressures, constraints, and responsibilities. * * * The practical day-to-day concerns of the INS in meeting its enforcement goals * * * are not those of the immigration judge. The perceived high bail of the

INS resulting from such pressures and interests leads judges to evaluate the INS's bail decisions in an unfavorable light.

As a result of the differing institutional valuation of the system's competing goals, there is pronounced interagency conflict and extreme decisional disparity. Since no agreement exists between reviewer and reviewed on the values to inform their decisionmaking, de novo review has little norm enforcement function and it flounders in its potential role as a mechanism of control over agency action.

Gilboy, *Administrative Review in a System of Conflicting Values,* 13 Law & Soc. Inquiry 515, 523–25 (1988).* If the author's findings for Chicago reflect a nationwide "dissensus" between INS bond-setters and immigration judges, should the present system be changed? How?

INS detention facilities have also come under scrutiny, some of it quite critical. For example, the American Civil Liberties Union's study of one detention facility in New York concluded:

[D]etainees are imprisoned in large dormitories without any access to fresh air or sunlight, with no opportunity for outdoor exercise, and with minimal activities to occupy their time. They are denied meaningful access to legal representation and are subject to arbitrary and punitive segregation. Even if they are found deportable, they are oftentimes detained for many additional months or years solely because of INS' inability to obtain travel documents and execute their departures.

ACLU Immigrants' Rights Project, Justice Detained: Conditions at the Varick Street Immigration Detention Center (1993).

The government's bond and detention practices have been subject to constitutional challenge. One group of decisions involves the version of INA § 242(a)(2) that Congress added in 1988 to effect the removal of aggravated felons after they have served their prison sentences. INA § 242(a)(2) required the Attorney General to detain aggravated felons pending deportation hearings. Several federal courts held that § 242(a)(2) violated the Fifth Amendment's due process clause because it deprived aliens of liberty without a hearing. *E.g., Kellman v. District Director,* 750 F.Supp. 625 (S.D.N.Y.1990); *Agunobi v. Thornburgh,* 745 F.Supp. 533 (N.D.Ill.1990). Other lower courts found § 242(a)(2) constitutional as a valid exercise of Congress's plenary power over immigration. *E.g., Morrobel v. Thornburgh,* 744 F.Supp. 725 (E.D.Va.1990).

In 1990, Congress amended § 242(a)(2) to allow the release of *permanent resident aliens* who completed sentences for aggravated felonies, if the Attorney General determined that they would not to be a threat to the community and not likely to abscond. In 1991, Congress once again amended § 242(a)(2), which you should now read. The current language puts the burden on the aggravated felon to demonstrate that he is not a threat to the community and not likely to abscond. The 1991 amendment also extended the possibility of bond under this standard to "any lawfully admitted alien." According to some congressional opponents, this extension was added to help Bob Probert of the Detroit Red Wings, who had been admitted to the United States as a nonimmigrant to play hockey. After Probert finished serving time on a cocaine charge, the INS invoked § 242(a)(2) to place him in mandatory detention pending deportation. *See* 68 Interp.Rel. 1677, 1679 (1991). Has Congress cured the constitutional problems of § 242(a)(2)? Does the mandatory detention of some aliens who commit aggravated felonies offend due process?

One recent Supreme Court case involving detention also deserves mention. *Reno v. Flores*, 507 U.S. ___, 113 S.Ct. 1439, 123 L.Ed.2d 1 (1993), was a class action that challenged INS policy regarding detention of minor children pending deportation. Under 8 C.F.R. § 242.24, detained minors in deportation proceedings may normally be released only to their parents, close relatives, or legal guardians. If none of these is available, minors are detained in juvenile care facilities, rather than released to the custody of "other responsible adults," as plaintiffs sought. The Supreme Court majority rejected the suit's facial challenge to the regulation as violating substantive and procedural due process, and as exceeding the Attorney General's statutory authority. Key to the majority's constitutional holding was its characterization of the right at issue not as freedom from detention, but as merely the right "to be placed in the custody of a willing-and-able private custodian rather than that of a government-operated or government-selected child-care institution." 507 U.S. at ___, 113 S.Ct. at 1447. That right did not amount to a constitutional imperative, especially in view of the traditional deference to the political branches in immigration law. *Id.* at ___, 113 S.Ct. at 1446–51. Justices O'Connor and Souter concurred, finding that there is "a constitutionally protected interest in freedom from institutional confinement," *id.* at 1454, but that the INS policy satisfied due process. Justices Stevens and Blackmun dissented, maintaining that Congress did not authorize a presumption that all unrelated adults are unsuitable custodians. They would have declared the regulation unconstitutional; in their view, the right at stake was the "not the right of detained juveniles to be released to one particular custodian rather than another, but the right not to be detained in the first place." *Id.* at ___, 113 S.Ct. at 1468.

Are constitutional challenges to the government's detention of deportable aliens subject to procedural due process review under *Yamataya* because they question INS procedures to implement substantive admission and deportation decisions? Or does the plenary power doctrine insulate detention policies and practices from constitutional challenge because release amounts to de facto admission and is therefore "substantive"? *See generally* Motomura, *supra*, 92 Colum.L.Rev. at 1665–73.

3. THE DEPORTATION HEARING

a. *The Conduct of a Deportation Hearing*

The earliest immigration statutes included no specific deportation procedures; they simply stated that aliens unlawfully in the United States were subject to deportation. By regulation, the executive branch provided an informal hearing with an administrative appeal.[3] It was not until 1952 that deportation procedures were written into a statute.[4] They currently are spelled out in INA § 242.

The following selection describes deportation proceedings and the mechanics of appealing an immigration judge's decision.

CHARLES GORDON, STANLEY MAILMAN & STEPHEN YALE-LOEHR, IMMIGRATION LAW AND PROCEDURE

§§ 72.04[5][b], 72.07[3] (1994).*

It is now customary to conduct the deportation hearing in two stages. The first is called the Master Calendar Hearing. This is a preliminary inquiry, similar to a calendar call in a civil case or an arraignment in a criminal case. Its purpose is to ascertain whether a further hearing is required to dispose of factual issues.

Many cases may be completed at the Master Calendar hearing. This may occur when the respondent appears at the hearing and states to the Court that he admits the allegations in the order to show cause and deportability and waives any right to relief except voluntary departure. In such case the IJ's order granting voluntary departure, coupled with a waiver of the right to appeal, may complete the proceeding.

In other situations, usually in cases involving border violations, a combined Master Calendar hearing may involve a number of border violations. Such mass hearings may be acceptable, but due process requirements will be satisfied only if the record demonstrates that each respondent's concessions and waivers were knowing and intelligent. An individual respondent's concessions or waivers will not be assumed from his silence in response to a general question regarding such concessions or waivers addressed to a group of respondents.

At the outset of the Master Calendar Hearing, the immigration judge determines whether an interpreter is needed, and ascertains whether respondent is represented by counsel. If so, counsel's identity is noted in

---

3. *See generally* C. Bouvé, A Treatise on the Laws Governing the Exclusion and Expulsion of Aliens in the United States 614–681 (1912); S. Kansas, United States Immigration Exclusion and Deportation, and Citizenship of the United States of America 235–243 (2d ed. 1940) (reprinting regulations relating to deportation). Interestingly, the Chinese exclusion laws provided substantially different procedures, including a hearing before a United States Commissioner or Judge. Bouvé, *supra*, at 628–53.

4. Before and after the enactment of the 1952 statute, Congress and the Supreme Court engaged in a colloquy over the applicability of the Administrative Procedure Act to deportation hearings. In *Wong Yang Sung v.*

McGrath, 339 U.S. 33, 70 S.Ct. 445, 94 L.Ed. 616 (1950), the Court construed the APA, enacted in 1946, to apply to deportation proceedings. Congress quickly overturned the decision, passing a statute exempting deportation hearings from the procedural dictates of the APA. Act of Sept. 27, 1950, Ch. 1052, 64 Stat. 1048. Following the specification of procedures in the 1952 Immigration Act, the Court was again asked to find the APA's procedural requirements applicable. It refused. *Marcello v. Bonds,* 349 U.S. 302, 75 S.Ct. 757, 99 L.Ed. 1107 (1955).

the record. If not, the IJ advises respondent of his right to representation by counsel, of his own choice at no expense to the Government, informs respondent of the availability of free legal services programs in the district where the deportation hearing is being held, ascertains whether respondent has received a list of such programs and a copy of Form I–618 (Written Notice of Appeal Rights), and informs him that he will have a reasonable opportunity to examine and object to the evidence against him, to present evidence in his own behalf, and to cross-examine witnesses presented by the Government. Much of this advice is unnecessary if respondent is already represented by counsel. After completing these preliminary inquiries, the respondent is placed under oath, and the order to show cause is entered as an exhibit in the record. If the respondent is not represented by counsel the IJ reads and explains it to him.

The respondent is then required to answer the charges. This is the "pleading" procedure inaugurated in February, 1956 and it requires respondent to state at the threshold of the hearing whether he admits or denies the factual allegations and deportability under the charges enumerated in the order to show cause, and he is asked to state what, if any, discretionary relief he seeks. This response is not made in a written document and consequently is not like an answer in a civil court action. Rather it is an oral statement incorporated in the hearing record, and it thus resembles the plea of guilty or not guilty in a criminal case. Such admissions or denials can be made by counsel representing respondent at the Master Calendar Hearing. However, the immigration judge may not accept an admission of deportability from an unrepresented respondent who is incompetent or under 16 and is not accompanied by a guardian, relative, or friend, nor from an officer of an institution in which a respondent is an inmate or patient.

* * *

In practice, many cases are disposed of at the Master Calendar Hearing, when the respondent admits the factual allegations and legal conclusion of deportability and seeks only the grant of voluntary departure.[a] The grant or denial of this relief usually can be decided at the Master Calendar Hearing. However, if there are disputed issues of fact or deportability, or if discretionary relief other than voluntary departure is sought, the next step is an individual hearing on the merits. It is usually not possible to conduct such a hearing at the Master Calendar, which generally involves many cases. Therefore, the individual hearing is usually set for a future date.

At the individual hearing, attended by respondent and his attorney, and any witnesses, the IJ hears the evidence on any facts not admitted by respondent and on any other matters he deems relevant and in due course renders a decision on any issues not resolved by admissions during the pleading. A trial attorney represents the INS at the hearing. The trial attorney conducts cross-examination and introduces evidence to the extent he deems necessary. Moreover, it is not inherently improper for him to conduct discussions off the record, which are sanctioned by the regulations.

* * *

a. An IJ who grants voluntary departure will typically enter an alternate order of deportation, which takes effect only if the alien has not departed within the time granted for voluntary departure.—eds.

The hearing normally is conducted on the charges recited in the order to show cause. However, errors or omissions in the order to show cause do not necessarily invalidate the proceedings if the correct facts are developed at the hearing and are reflected in the ultimate decision. Thus, an incorrect recital in the order to show cause as to the respondent's date of entry will not be fatal if the correct date of entry was sufficiently established in the ensuing proceedings. But a deportation order cannot be premised on a charge not set forth in the order to show cause, unless the additional charge was lodged at the hearing, in the manner described below.

During the hearing of a contested case the trial attorney may lodge additional charges of deportability against the respondent and develop evidence relating to such charges. The lodged charges must be accompanied by factual allegations like those required to support an order to show cause. Copies of the additional factual allegations and charges must be submitted in writing for service on the respondent and entry as an exhibit in the record. However, if additional charges are lodged the immigration judge must explain them to the respondent, must advise him again of his right to representation by counsel, and must offer respondent added time to meet the charges. The practice of lodging new charges at the hearing, when deemed necessary, has been in effect for many years and has been approved by the courts, provided sufficient opportunity to meet such charges is offered. * * *

The immigration judge is authorized to grant various types of discretionary relief from deportation. Indeed, in a majority of cases, deportability is conceded, and the application for some discretionary dispensation may present the only issue for decision. Even where deportability is contested, the respondent's eligibility for discretionary relief is often the crucial aspect of the case.

* * *

Notice of appeal must be filed in triplicate with the Office of the Immigration Judge on Form EOIR–[26] within ten days after the service of a summary decision or the mailing of a written decision or the stating of an oral decision. If the decision is served by mail the time to appeal is extended an additional three days. * * *

* * *

The notice of appeal must state the reasons for appeal. Failure to complete the notice of appeal in conformity with the instructions on Form EOIR–[26] may result in dismissal of the appeal. Respondent may, if he desires, submit a brief with the notice of appeal or within a reasonable period allowed after the date of filing, usually ten days, and this time may be extended, for good cause, by the immigration judge or the Board. The appeal can be withdrawn in writing at any time, and the departure from the United States of the person involved is deemed a withdrawal of the appeal.

If an appeal is taken the entire record is forwarded to the Board of Immigration Appeals, upon timely receipt of the brief or upon expiration of the time to submit briefs. The respondent has no part in the preparation of the record, which is assembled by the immigration judge and forwarded by him to the Board. The organization and completeness of the record is apparently the responsibility of the immigration judge. Execution of the order is stayed during the time an appeal may be filed, unless appeal is waived, and during consideration of the appeal. However, there is no stay upon appeal from denial of a motion of reconsideration, unless a stay is granted by the immigration judge, the Board or the district director. * * *

Notes

1. For strategies for contesting deportation, see Kesselbrenner, *Contesting Deportability*, 92–5 Imm.Briefings (1992); Elliott, *Strategy and Tactics in Deportation Proceedings,* 90–5 Imm.Briefings (1990).

2. Under INA § 242B, which you should now read, an alien who fails to appear at a deportation proceeding after receiving the notice prescribed by statute may be ordered deported *in absentia*. "Notice" includes written notice sent to his last known address, whether or not actually received. To rescind an *in absentia* deportation order, the alien must move to reopen by showing (1) he was in state or federal custody, (2) lack of notice, or (3) "exceptional circumstances." "Exceptional circumstances" means "serious illness of the alien or death of an immediate relative of the alien," or other circumstances that are "not less compelling" and "beyond the control of the alien." Aliens ordered deported *in absentia* are ineligible for relief from deportation for five years. *See generally* Gomez, *The Consequences of Nonappearance: Interpreting New Section 242B of the Immigration and Nationality Act*, 30 San Diego L.Rev. 75 (1993).

3. Another key development has been a dramatic expansion in the use of special procedures, discussed near the end of this Chapter, for certain groups of deportable aliens. For now, we only point out that not every deportable alien has her fate decided in the standard deportation procedures discussed in the preceding excerpt and the material that follows this note.

b. Constitutional and Statutory Rights in Deportation Hearings

The following discusses the most important (but not all) procedural due process issues in deportation proceedings. As you study these pages, consider which issues would be most important for you to resolve favorably if you were representing an alien in deportation, and which would be most important if you were representing the government. Also, are the prevailing approaches to the various issues consistent enough with each other (and with the general principles covered thus far in this Section)?

(i) An Independent Decisionmaker

For most of this century, federal officials who conducted deportation hearings were employees of the immigration service. Shortly after the passage of the McCarran–Walter Act of 1952, the Supreme Court summarily rejected a constitutional challenge to the adjudicator's dependence on the INS:

> [T]he only complaint which petitioner can urge concerning the hearing procedures in this case is the objection that the special inquiry officer was subject to the supervision and control of officials in the Immigration Service charged with investigative and prosecuting functions. Petitioner would have us hold that the presence of this relationship so strips the hearing of fairness and impartiality as to make the procedure violative of due process. The contention is without substance when considered against the long-standing practice in deportation proceedings, judicially approved in numerous decisions in the federal courts, and against the special considerations applicable to deportation which the Congress may take into account in exercising its particularly broad discretion in immigration matters.

Marcello v. Bonds, 349 U.S. 302, 311, 75 S.Ct. 757, 762, 99 L.Ed. 1107 (1955).

Marcello notwithstanding, criticism continued. In 1981, the Select Commission on Immigration and Refugee Policy found that "INS does not provide adequate support service to immigration judges, contributing to long delays in the administrative adjudication process," and that "[i]mmigration judges are administratively dependent upon officials (INS district directors) who are involved in an adversary capacity in proceedings before the judges." SCIRP, Final Report 246. In 1983, this arrangement finally ended with the creation of the Executive Office for Immigration Review (EOIR). *See* pp. 107–10 *supra.* Now, immigration judges are under the general supervision of the Director of the EOIR and expressly excepted from the control of the INS Commissioner. 8 C.F.R. §§ 2.1, 3.0.

Another objection often lodged against the deportation procedure in the INA was directed at the combination of prosecutive and adjudicative functions in the immigration judge. Section 242(b) provides that an immigration judge "shall administer oaths, present and receive evidence, interrogate, examine, and cross-examine the alien or witnesses, and ... shall make determinations, including orders of deportation." This subsection also prohibits an immigration judge from conducting a hearing "in any case * * * in which he shall have participated in investigative functions or in which he shall have participated (except as provided in this subsection) in prosecuting functions." Does this adoption of an inquisitorial model—conferring both prosecuting and judging functions on an immigration judge—violate due process?[5] Compare the new administrative deportation

5. The Supreme Court appeared to give an affirmative answer to this question in *Wong Yang Sung v. McGrath,* 339 U.S. 33, 46, 70 S.Ct. 445, 452, 94 L.Ed. 616 (1950), where, in order to avoid a difficult constitutional issue, it interpreted the APA hearing requirements to apply to deportation proceedings. Yet, when Congress reversed the Court's holding by exempting the INA from the APA, the Court, somewhat surprisingly, upheld the procedures it had so seriously questioned five years earlier. *Marcello v. Bonds,* 349 U.S. 302, 75 S.Ct. 757, 99 L.Ed. 1107 (1955). *Cf. Richardson v. Perales,* 402 U.S. 389, 408–10, 91 S.Ct. 1420, 1430–31, 28 L.Ed.2d 842 (1971) (rejecting such a due pro-

procedure for certain aggravated felons, discussed at p. 627 *infra*, which takes place without an immigration judge hearing at all.

In any event, this statutory scheme too has been ameliorated by regulation. In any hearing in which the alien does not admit deportability the judge must request the assignment of a trial attorney to present the government's case. 8 C.F.R. § 242.16(c). In practice, today a trial attorney represents the government in virtually all contested cases in immigration court, including those where deportability is admitted and the only issue is some form of relief from deportation. *See* 8 C.F.R. § 242.9.

(ii) Counsel

The INA, in two separate sections, provides that an alien in a deportation proceeding "shall have the privilege of being represented (at no expense to the Government) by such counsel, authorized to practice in such proceedings, as he shall choose." INA §§ 242(b), 292. By regulation, law students directly supervised by a faculty member or attorney in a legal aid program or law school clinic, and appearing without direct or indirect remuneration, may represent an alien in a deportation hearing with the immigration judge's consent. 8 C.F.R. § 292.1(a)(2).

Aliens who cannot afford a lawyer must be informed of the free legal service programs available in the district. 8 C.F.R. § 242.16(a). Note that detention, particularly in remote locations, can severely restrict access to volunteer lawyers. The 1992 GAO study of INS detention practices found that only 22 percent of the detainees in its sample had legal representation; this percentage was lower in remote locations. *See* General Accounting Office, Immigration Control: Immigration Policies Affect INS Detention Efforts 45–53 (1992).

Since 1983, Congress has imposed restrictions on the representation of aliens with funds appropriated for the Legal Services Corporation (LSC). Recipients of LSC funds may represent only permanent resident aliens, immediate relatives of U.S. citizens who have applied for adjustment of status, aliens granted refugee status or asylum, and aliens granted withholding of deportation under INA § 243(h). 45 C.F.R. § 1626.4. Thus, it may happen that many undocumented aliens, aliens applying for asylum, nonimmigrants and parolees will not be represented. In contrast, IRCA provided that aliens admitted as temporary H–2A agricultural workers are eligible for legal assistance in cases relating to wages, housing, transportation, and other employment-related rights. IRCA § 305; 45 C.F.R. § 1626.11. Are there good reasons for this disparate treatment of classes of aliens? Is the need for legal assistance less pressing for asylum applicants than for temporary H–2A agricultural workers?

One partial alternative to free legal services might have been the Equal Access to Justice Act (EAJA). Under EAJA, a person who is a "prevailing party" in an "adversary adjudication" against the government is entitled to recover attorneys' fees if the government's legal position was "not substantially justified." In *Ardestani v. INS*, 502 U.S. 129, 112 S.Ct. 515, 116 L.Ed.2d 496 (1991), the Supreme Court held that EAJA does not apply to

cess challenge to social security disability hearings).

deportation hearings. The Court reasoned that EAJA defines "adversary adjudication" as "an adjudication under section 554" of the Administrative Procedure Act, which in turn means an adjudication *governed* by § 554. Deportation hearings are not governed by § 554 even though they are identical in key respects to administrative hearings that are; therefore EAJA does not cover deportation hearings. The Court added: "We have no doubt that the broad purposes of the EAJA would be served by making the statute applicable to deportation proceedings. We are mindful that the complexity of immigration procedures, and the enormity of the interests at stake, make legal representation in deportation proceedings especially important." 502 U.S. at 538, 112 S.Ct. at 521. The Court concluded, however, that such a step should be left for Congress.

Given a statutory right to counsel at no expense to the government, the issue sometimes arises whether an alien has waived that right. Consider *Castro-O'Ryan v. INS,* 821 F.2d 1415 (9th Cir.1987), where the following discussion took place between the alien and immigration judge:

Q.: "You are here today by yourself, that is you don't have an attorney with you. Does that mean that you intend to speak for yourself today?"

A.: "Yes, I do."

Q.: "All right."

Upon review of the immigration judge's denial of Castro–O'Ryan's asylum claim, the Court of Appeals ruled: "Castro's laconic answer to Judge Nail was not an intelligent, voluntary waiver of counsel. The opportunity to obtain counsel was prevented." *Id.* at 1420. *Cf. Reyes–Palacios v. United States INS,* 836 F.2d 1154, 1155 (9th Cir.1988) (due process violation on similar facts).

Related issues arose in connection with a "sting" operation that the San Diego District Office of the INS conducted in July 1993. The INS sent letters to 608 aliens subject to outstanding deportation orders, making bogus offers of amnesty and employment authorization cards to lure them to the district office. About 60 aliens responded; many of these were deported immediately. Lawyers on record as representing these aliens were not notified. *See* Benson, *By Hook or by Crook: Exploring the Legality of an INS Sting Operation,* 31 San Diego L.Rev. 813 (1994).

Does the Constitution require the government to provide counsel to indigent aliens? Recall that the Sixth Amendment's guarantee of appointed counsel is not available to aliens in deportation hearings since the Supreme Court is unwilling to view them as criminal proceedings. Thus, a right to government-provided counsel, if it exists, must be found in the due process clause of the Fifth Amendment. While the following case predates *Mathews v. Eldridge, see* p. 405 *supra,* which established the prevailing test for deciding what defendant requires, it remains a leading discussion of the constitutional right to counsel in deportation hearings.

AGUILERA-ENRIQUEZ v. INS

United States Court of Appeals, Sixth Circuit, 1975.
516 F.2d 565, cert. denied, 423 U.S. 1050, 96 S.Ct. 776, 46 L.Ed.2d 638 (1976).

CELEBREZZE, CIRCUIT JUDGE.

Petitioner, Jesus Aguilera–Enriquez, seeks reversal of a deportation order on the ground that he was constitutionally entitled to but was not afforded the assistance of counsel during his deportation hearing. * * *

A thirty-nine-year-old native and citizen of Mexico, Petitioner has resided in the United States since December 18, 1967, when he was admitted for permanent residence. He is a married farm worker, living with his wife and three daughters in Saginaw, Michigan.

In December 1971, Petitioner traveled to Mexico for a vacation. An officer of the Saginaw, Michigan Police Department notified federal customs officers at the Mexican border that he had reason to believe that Petitioner would be returning with a quantity of heroin. When Petitioner crossed the border on his return, he was subjected to a search which produced no heroin but did reveal two grams of cocaine.

On April 12, 1972, Petitioner pleaded guilty in the United States District Court for the Western District of Texas, on one count of knowingly possessing a quantity of cocaine, a Schedule II controlled substance, in violation of 21 U.S.C. § 844(a) (1970). Petitioner received a suspended one-year sentence, was placed on probation for five years, and was fined $3,000, to be paid in fifty-dollar monthly installments over the five-year probationary period. Neither Petitioner's appointed counsel nor the District Court informed him that a narcotics conviction would almost certainly lead to his deportation.

On December 7, 1972, the Immigration and Naturalization Service issued an Order to Show Cause and Notice of Hearing, charging that because of his narcotics conviction, Petitioner should be deported under section 241(a)(11) of the Immigration and Nationality Act.

On February 6, 1973 Petitioner appeared before the Immigration Judge and requested appointed counsel. The Immigration Judge refused this request. After a hearing Petitioner was ordered deported and was not afforded the option of voluntary departure.

Shortly after the Immigration Judge's ruling, Petitioner engaged as counsel a Michigan legal assistance attorney, who in turn secured the services of a Texas attorney.

On February 14, 1973, Petitioner filed an appeal to the Board of Immigration Appeals, stating that the validity of the Texas conviction was being challenged.

On May 23, 1973, Petitioner's Texas counsel filed a motion to withdraw his guilty plea under Rule 32(d), F.R.Crim.P. The motion asserted that the District Court had not followed Rule 11 in accepting the plea because it had not properly determined that there was a factual basis for the plea and that the plea was made with a full understanding of the probable consequences.

On February 1, 1974, after full briefing and oral argument by counsel for Petitioner and the Government, the Board of Immigration Appeals dismissed Petitioner's appeal. A petition for review was timely filed in this Court.

The issue Petitioner raises here is whether an indigent alien has the right to appointed counsel in a deportation proceeding. He attacks the constitutional validity of INA § 242(b)(2), which gives an alien facing deportation proceedings "the privilege of being represented (at no expense to the Government) by such counsel, authorized to practice in such proceedings, as he shall choose."[1] The Immigration Judge held that this section prevented appointment of counsel at Government expense. Since he could not afford to hire a lawyer, he did not have one before the Immigration Judge.

The courts have been vigilant to ensure that aliens receive the protections Congress has given them before they may be banished from our shores. As this Circuit noted in United States ex rel. Brancato v. Lehmann, 239 F.2d 663, 666 (6th Cir.1956),

> Although it is not penal in character, * * * deportation is a drastic measure, at times the equivalent of banishment or exile, for which reason deportation statutes should be given the narrowest of the several possible meanings.

The Supreme Court has held that once an alien has been admitted to lawful residence, "not even Congress may expel him without allowing him a fair opportunity to be heard." Kwong Hai Chew v. Colding, 344 U.S. 590, 598, 73 S.Ct. 472, 478, 97 L.Ed. 576 (1953). Thus, if procedures mandated by Congress do not provide an alien with procedural due process, they must yield, and the constitutional guarantee of due process must provide adequate protection during the deportation process. Yamataya v. Fisher (The Japanese Immigrant Case), 189 U.S. 86, 100, 23 S.Ct. 611, 47 L.Ed. 721 (1903).

The test for whether due process requires the appointment of counsel for an indigent alien is whether, in a given case, the assistance of counsel would be necessary to provide "fundamental fairness—the touchstone of due process." Gagnon v. Scarpelli, 411 U.S. 778, 790, 93 S.Ct. 1756, 1763, 36 L.Ed.2d 656 (1973).[3]

---

1. *See also* INA § 292; 8 C.F.R. § 242.16.

3. The Supreme Court's holdings in Gagnon, Morrissey v. Brewer, 408 U.S. 471, 92 S.Ct. 2593, 33 L.Ed.2d 484 (1972), and In re Gault, 387 U.S. 1, 87 S.Ct. 1428, 18 L.Ed.2d 527 (1967), have undermined the position that counsel must be provided to indigents only in criminal proceedings. Decisions such as Tupacyupanqui–Marin v. Immigration and Naturalization Service, 447 F.2d 603 (7th Cir. 1971), and Murgia–Melendrez v. Immigration and Naturalization Service, 407 F.2d 207 (9th Cir.1969), which contain dictum appearing to set forth a *per se* rule against providing counsel to indigent aliens facing deportation, rested largely on the outmoded distinction between criminal cases (where the Sixth Amendment guarantees indigents appointed counsel) and civil proceedings (where the Fifth Amendment applies). Where an unrepresented indigent alien would require counsel to present his position adequately to an immigration judge, he must be provided with a lawyer at the Government's expense. Otherwise, "fundamental fairness" would be violated.

In Petitioner's case the absence of counsel at his hearing before the Immigration Judge did not deprive his deportation proceeding of fundamental fairness.

Petitioner was held to be deportable under section 241(a)(11) of the Immigration and Nationality Act, which states in relevant part:

(a) Any alien in the United States ... shall, upon the order of the Attorney General, be deported who—

. . .

(11) ... at any time has been convicted of a violation of ... any law or regulation relating to the illicit possession of or traffic in narcotic drugs....

Before the Immigration Judge, Petitioner raised no defense to the charge that he had been convicted in April 1972 of a violation of 21 U.S.C. § 844(a). Thus, he was clearly within the purview of section 241(a)(11) of the Act, and no defense for which a lawyer would have helped the argument was presented to the Immigration Judge for consideration. After the decision of the Immigration Judge, Petitioner moved to withdraw his guilty plea in the Texas District Court under Rule 32(d), F.R.Crim.P. He then urged before the Board of Immigration Appeals that this motion took him outside the reach of section 241(a)(11), because the likelihood of success on that motion meant that he had not been "convicted" of a narcotics offense. He was effectively represented by counsel before the Board, and his argument was considered upon briefing and oral argument. The lack of counsel before the Immigration Judge did not prevent full administrative consideration of his argument. Counsel could have obtained no different administrative result. "Fundamental fairness," therefore, was not abridged during the administrative proceedings, and the order of deportation is not subject to constitutional attack for a lack of due process.

* * *

The petition for review is denied.

DeMascio, District Judge (dissenting).[a]

A deportation proceeding so jeopardizes a resident alien's basic and fundamental right to personal liberty that I cannot agree due process is guaranteed by a "fundamental fairness" analysis on a case-by-case basis. Gagnon v. Scarpelli, 411 U.S. 778, 93 S.Ct. 1756, 36 L.Ed.2d 656 (1973). I think a resident alien has an unqualified right to the appointment of counsel. In re Gault, 387 U.S. 1, 87 S.Ct. 1428, 18 L.Ed.2d 527 (1967). When the government, with plenary power to exclude, agrees to allow an alien lawful residence, it is unconscionable for the government to unilaterally terminate that agreement without affording an indigent resident alien assistance of appointed counsel. Expulsion is such lasting punishment that meaningful due process can require no less. Assuredly, it inflicts punish-

---

a. [Hon. Robert E. DeMascio, U.S. District Judge for the Eastern District of Michigan, sitting by designation.]

ment as grave as the institutionalization which may follow an In re Gault finding of delinquency. A resident alien's right to due process should not be tempered by a classification of the deportation proceeding as "civil", "criminal", or "administrative." No matter the classification, deportation is punishment, pure and simple.

In *Gagnon,* the Supreme Court acknowledged that it was affording parolees and probationers less due process than it afforded juveniles in In re Gault. It reached this result because a parolee or probationer is in that position solely because he was previously convicted of a crime. The court reasoned that parolees and probationers should be required to demonstrate that an attorney would serve a useful purpose prior to compelling the government to provide counsel at government expense. But, in a deportation proceeding, the respondent need not necessarily be before the immigration judge because of a prior conviction.[2] The fact of conviction is only one of numerous grounds for deportation outlined in the statute. Similar to the juvenile, an alien may only stand accused of an offense.

As noted in *Gagnon,* the function of the probation or parole officer is not to "compel conformance to a strict code of behavior" but to "supervise a course of rehabilitation." 411 U.S. 784, 93 S.Ct. 1760. Insertion of counsel into such a "predictive and discretionary" proceeding could inadvertently circumscribe the officer's flexibility. However, no such justification for the exclusion of counsel exists in deportation proceedings where the sole duty of the immigration law judge is to determine whether a deportable offense has occurred. INA § 241(a).

Further, a probation revocation hearing is a non-adversary proceeding. The government is not represented by a prosecutor. There are no procedural rights which may be lost as in a criminal trial. A deportation hearing on the other hand is always an adversary proceeding.[3] *Gagnon* does not go so far as to hold that in adversary proceedings due process may be afforded on a case-by-case basis by retrospective determination that the hearing was characterized by "fundamental fairness."

The court today has fashioned a test to resolve whether a resident alien's due-process right requires appointment of counsel. That test is whether " . . . in a given case, the assistance of counsel would be necessary

---

2. If the court wishes to extend *Gagnon,* perhaps a better approach is to limit the case-by-case appointment of counsel to proceedings where respondent is being deported because he has a previous conviction and is, therefore, entitled to less due process. In all other instances, counsel should be appointed as a matter of right under the due process clause. The court suggests an indigent alien is entitled to appointed counsel only when it is necessary " . . . to present his position adequately to an immigration judge. . . ." (*See* fn. 3, *supra.*)

3. A reading of INA § 242(b) makes it apparent that the special inquiry officer [now an immigration judge by regulation] functions as a prosecutor, defense lawyer, finder of facts, and judge. While the statute does not provide for the appointment of a government trial attorney, a regulation does. 8 CFR § 242.16(c) provides that if an alien does not admit he is deportable the immigration judge shall appoint a government trial attorney to establish the facts justifying deportation. At the hearing, the rules of evidence do not apply. Hearsay evidence is admissible. During such an adversary hearing, the indigent resident alien stands alone. He does not have a lawyer to meaningfully participate in making a record, a record upon which the Appeals Board and this court will determine whether the order of deportation was supported by evidence that is clear and convincing.

to provide 'fundamental fairness—the touchstone of due process.' " *Gagnon, supra.* The majority concludes that lack of counsel before the immigration judge did not prevent full consideration of petitioner's sole argument and no different result would have been obtained had counsel been appointed. Accordingly, the court holds the hearing was fundamentally fair.[4] These conclusions are reached by second guessing the record—a record made without petitioner's meaningful participation.

In my view, the absence of counsel at respondent's hearing before the immigration judge inherently denied him fundamental fairness. Moreover, I do not believe that we should make the initial determination that counsel is unnecessary; or that lack of counsel did not prevent full administrative consideration of petitioner's argument; or that counsel could not have obtained a different administrative result. We should not speculate at this stage what contentions appointed counsel could have raised before the immigration judge. For example, a lawyer may well have contended that [§ 241(a)(2)(B)] is an unconstitutional deprivation of the equal protection of the laws by arguing that alienage was the sole basis for the infliction of punishment, additional to that imposed by criminal law; that since the government elected to rely upon the criminal law sanctions, it may not now additionally exile petitioner without demonstrating a compelling governmental interest.

I do not intend to imply such a contention has validity. I cite this only to emphasize the danger of attempting to speculate at this stage whether counsel could have obtained a different result and to show that it is possible that the immigration judge did not fully consider all of petitioner's arguments.

Because the consequences of a deportation proceeding parallels punishment for crime, only a per se rule requiring appointment of counsel will assure a resident alien due process of law. In this case, the respondent, a resident alien for seven years, committed a criminal offense. Our laws require that he be punished and he was. Now, he must face additional punishment in the form of banishment. He will be deprived of the life, liberty, and pursuit of happiness he enjoyed by governmental consent.[6] It may be proper that he be compelled to face the consequences of such a proceeding. But, when he does, he should have a lawyer at his side and one at government expense, if necessary. When the government consents to grant an alien residency, it cannot constitutionally expel unless and until it affords that alien due process. Our country's constitutional dedication to freedom is thwarted by a watered-down version of due process on a case-by-case basis.

4. The Second Circuit has similarly held that where the respondent admits the allegations in the order to show cause and it does not appear that an attorney would affect the outcome, lack of appointed counsel does not violate due process. Henriques v. Immigration & Naturalization Service, 465 F.2d 119, 121 (2nd Cir.1972), cert. denied, 410 U.S. 968, 93 S.Ct. 1452, 35 L.Ed.2d 703.

6. Of course, what I have said applies only to a resident alien. I readily agree that an alien who enters illegally is entitled to less due process, if any at all. It is interesting to note that the Immigration Act seems to treat all aliens alike.

I would reverse and remand for the appointment of counsel before the immigration judge.

Notes

1. In *Lassiter v. Department of Social Services,* 452 U.S. 18, 101 S.Ct. 2153, 68 L.Ed.2d 640 (1981), the Supreme Court, in a five-to-four decision, rejected the claim that indigent defendants in a proceeding to terminate their parental status have a right to appointed counsel. Recognizing that due process applies to such proceedings, the Court adopted the approach of *Gagnon v. Scarpelli,* 411 U.S. 778, 93 S.Ct. 1756, 36 L.Ed.2d 656 (1973): the right to appointed counsel should be decided on a case-by-case basis depending upon the particular facts and circumstances and the dictates of "fundamental fairness."

Explaining its decision, the Court summarized its prior decisions on the right to counsel as follows:

> The pre-eminent generalization that emerges from this Court's precedents on an indigent's right to appointed counsel is that such a right has been recognized to exist only where the litigant may lose his physical liberty if he loses the litigation.

Lassiter, 452 U.S. at 25, 101 S.Ct. at 2158. Is deportation a loss of physical liberty, or is it simply an order that aliens pursue their liberty in their home countries?

Potential loss of liberty appears to be a necessary, but not sufficient, reason for requiring appointment of counsel.[6] Which of the following factors might also be considered in determining whether a right to appointed counsel obtains: the adversarial nature of the proceedings, the formality of the hearing, the complexities of the legal standards and issues involved, the fact that the government is usually represented in such proceedings? Do these factors distinguish deportation proceedings from parole and probation revocations or voluntary commitment of minors?

In *Lassiter,* once the Court concluded that a loss of physical liberty was not at issue, it resorted to the due process balancing test in *Mathews v. Eldridge,* 424 U.S. 319, 96 S.Ct. 893, 47 L.Ed.2d 18 (1976), *see* p. 405 *supra*, to decide whether a right to appointed counsel should be found. The Court stated that the "new balance" of the *Eldridge* calculus must then be weighed against "the presumption that there is a right to appointed counsel only where the indigent, if he is unsuccessful, may lose his personal freedom." *Lassiter,* 452 U.S. at 27, 101 S.Ct. at 2159.

2. Note Judge DeMascio's statement in footnote 6 of his dissent that "an alien who enters illegally is entitled to less due process [than a resident alien], if any at all." (You will recall that Justice Harlan in *Yamataya* makes a similar suggestion.) What do these dicta mean?

---

6. *See Morrissey v. Brewer,* 408 U.S. 471, 92 S.Ct. 2593, 33 L.Ed.2d 484 (1972) (parole revocation); *Gagnon v. Scarpelli,* 411 U.S. 778, 93 S.Ct. 1756, 36 L.Ed.2d 656 (1973) (probation revocation); *Parham v. J.R.,* 442 U.S. 584, 99 S.Ct. 2493, 61 L.Ed.2d 101 (1979) (parent-initiated civil commitment of minors).

3. Assume that you are representing an alien appealing an order of deportation entered after a deportation hearing at which counsel was not present. How would you use *Lassiter* and *Eldridge* to argue that the absence of a right to appointed counsel is a denial of due process generally, irrespective of the facts in your client's particular case?

Assume you are a judge on a federal court of appeals hearing the appeal. How would you rule? If you do not believe that *Lassiter* answers the question, how would you (can you) evaluate and balance the factors identified by the court in *Eldridge?*

Assume you are a member of Congress rewriting the immigration code. Would you provide for appointed counsel for all indigent aliens? Is there additional information you would like to know before reaching a decision? Is it possible to identify particular types of deportation cases in which counsel should automatically be appointed—*e.g.*, claims of U.S. citizenship, permanent residence, or asylum? The Select Commission on Immigration and Refugee Policy recommended that counsel be provided to indigent "legal permanent resident aliens in deportation or exclusion proceedings." SCIRP Final Report, Recomm. VIII.B.2. Do you agree? What about a different approach—broadening the categories set out in 8 C.F.R. Pt. 292 of those authorized to represent aliens?

4. The statute guarantees an alien the "privilege" of having an attorney at a deportation hearing. Thus, all aliens who can afford to do so have the right to be represented. Does an indigent alien have a good claim that the statutory structure denies her equal protection? *Compare Douglas v. California,* 372 U.S. 353, 83 S.Ct. 814, 9 L.Ed.2d 811 (1963) (state must provide attorney for indigent defendant for first appeal after a criminal conviction) *and Boddie v. Connecticut,* 401 U.S. 371, 91 S.Ct. 780, 28 L.Ed.2d 113 (1971) (state cannot require court fees and costs in order to sue for divorce) *with United States v. Kras,* 409 U.S. 434, 93 S.Ct. 631, 34 L.Ed.2d 626 (1973) (upholding $50 fee for discharge in bankruptcy) *and Ortwein v. Schwab,* 410 U.S. 656, 93 S.Ct. 1172, 35 L.Ed.2d 572 (1973) (*per curiam*) (upholding $25 filing fee for indigent seeking judicial review of reduction in welfare payments).

5. Can a court exercise reasonable review of the immigration judge's case-by-case determination of whether counsel was needed at the hearing? How can a court rely on the record established at a hearing *without a lawyer* to answer the question of whether a lawyer was needed at that hearing?

Consider the remarks of Professor Yale Kamisar on *Lassiter:*

I cringe a bit when a court says, as the *Lassiter* Court did—on the basis of a record made *without* the assistance of counsel—that "the case presented no especially troublesome points of law, either procedural or substantive." * * * [A] record made *without* the assistance of counsel cannot establish that. It can only *fail* to establish *on its face* that the defendant was not seriously disadvantaged. What does it prove that the record reads well? How would it have read if the defendant had had counsel? What facts might have been uncovered if competent investigations had been made?

What defenses might have been advanced if competent legal research had been done? We do not know—at least we cannot be sure.

J. Choper, Y. Kamisar & L. Tribe, The Supreme Court: Trends and Developments, 1980–1981, at 174–75 (1982) (emphasis in original). *See generally* Kamisar, *The Right to Counsel and the Fourteenth Amendment: A Dialogue on "The Most Pervasive Right" of an Accused,* 30 U.Chi.L.Rev. 1 (1962).

(iii) Evidence: Quality

As with most administrative proceedings, the formal rules of evidence do not apply in deportation hearings. Hearsay and unauthenticated documents may be admitted if they are deemed probative and reliable by the immigration judge. *See, e.g., Bustos–Torres v. INS,* 898 F.2d 1053, 1055–56 (5th Cir.1990) (form on which INS official recorded alien's statements is admissible, as it is probative and "its use is fundamentally fair so as not to deprive the alien of due process"); *Guzman–Guzman v. INS,* 559 F.2d 1149, 1150 (9th Cir.1977) (other aliens' written statements admissible, as they are not "so infirm as to be unable to clear" the "modest" standard of fundamental fairness and probativeness). However, courts will occasionally order the exclusion of evidence if its admission would be unfair, or set aside a deportation order based on unauthenticated documents. *See, e.g., Cunanan v. INS,* 856 F.2d 1373, 1374–75 (9th Cir.1988) (fundamentally unfair to rely on affidavit of alien's wife where INS had not attempted to produce her as witness); *Iran v. INS,* 656 F.2d 469 (9th Cir.1981) (ruling inadmissible unauthenticated INS form and letter from consulate). Why do you think that deportation hearings are not run according to the Federal Rules of Evidence? Should they be?

(iv) Evidence: Standard of Proof

What is the burden of proof at a deportation hearing and who must carry it? INA § 242(b) provides in part that "no decision of deportability shall be valid unless it is based upon reasonable, substantial and probative evidence." Does this language establish the standard of proof that an immigration judge must apply in a deportation proceeding or the standard for judicial review of a deportation decision?

The Supreme Court answered this question in the following opinion.

WOODBY v. INS

Supreme Court of the United States, 1966.
385 U.S. 276, 87 S.Ct. 483, 17 L.Ed.2d 362.

MR. JUSTICE STEWART delivered the opinion of the Court.

The question presented by these cases is what burden of proof the Government must sustain in deportation proceedings. We have concluded that it is incumbent upon the Government in such proceedings to establish the facts supporting deportability by clear, unequivocal, and convincing evidence.

* * *

* * * [T]he petitioner is a resident alien who was born in Hungary and entered the United States from Germany in 1956 as the wife of an American soldier. Deportation proceedings were instituted against her on the ground that she had engaged in prostitution after entry. A special inquiry officer and the Board of Immigration Appeals found that she was deportable upon the ground charged.

At the administrative hearing the petitioner admitted that she had engaged in prostitution for a brief period in 1957, some months after her husband had deserted her, but claimed that her conduct was the product of circumstances amounting to duress. Without reaching the validity of the duress defense, the special inquiry officer and the Board of Immigration Appeals concluded that the petitioner had continued to engage in prostitution after the alleged duress had terminated. The hearing officer and the Board did not discuss what burden of proof the Government was required to bear in establishing deportability, nor did either of them indicate the degree of certainty with which their factual conclusions were reached. The special inquiry officer merely asserted that the evidence demonstrated that the petitioner was deportable. The Board stated that the evidence made it "apparent" that the petitioner had engaged in prostitution after the alleged duress had ended, and announced that "it is concluded that the evidence establishes deportability...."

In denying a petition for review, the Court of Appeals for the Sixth Circuit did not explicitly deal with the issue of what burden of persuasion was imposed upon the Government at the administrative level, finding only that "the Board's underlying order is 'supported by reasonable, substantial, and probative evidence on the record considered as a whole....'" We granted certiorari.

In the prevailing opinion in [a companion case, *Sherman v. INS*, 350 F.2d 894 (2d Cir.1965)], the Court of Appeals for the Second Circuit stated that "[i]f the slate were clean," it "might well agree that the standard of persuasion for deportation should be similar to that in denaturalization, where the Supreme Court has insisted that the evidence must be 'clear, unequivocal, and convincing' and that the Government needs 'more than a bare preponderance of the evidence' to prevail.... But here," the court thought, "Congress has spoken...." 350 F.2d at 900. This view was based upon two provisions of the Immigration and Nationality Act which use the language "reasonable, substantial, and probative evidence" in connection with deportation orders. The provisions in question are § 106(a)(4) of the Act which states that a deportation order, "if supported by reasonable, substantial, and probative evidence on the record considered as a whole, shall be conclusive," and § 242(b)(4) of the Act which provides *inter alia* that "no decision of deportability shall be valid unless it is based upon reasonable, substantial, and probative evidence."

It seems clear, however, that these two statutory provisions are addressed not to the degree of proof required at the administrative level in deportation proceedings, but to quite a different subject—the scope of judicial review. The elementary but crucial difference between burden of proof and scope of review is, of course, a commonplace in the law. The difference is most graphically illustrated in a criminal case. There the prosecution is generally required to prove the elements of the offense beyond a reasonable doubt. But if the correct burden of proof was imposed at the trial, judicial review is generally limited to ascertaining whether the evidence relied upon by the trier of fact was of sufficient quality and substantiality to support the rationality of the judgment. In other words, an appellate court in a criminal case ordinarily does not ask itself whether it believes that the evidence at the trial established guilt beyond a reasonable doubt, but whether the judgment is supported by substantial evidence.

That § 106(a)(4) relates exclusively to judicial review is made abundantly clear by its language, its context, and its legislative history. Section 106 was added to the Act in 1961 in order "to create a single, separate, statutory form of judicial review of administrative orders for the deportation and exclusion of aliens from the United States." The section is entitled "Judicial Review of Orders of Deportation and Exclusion," and by its terms provides "the sole and exclusive procedure for" the "judicial review of all final orders of deportation." Subsection 106(a)(4) is a specific directive to the courts in which petitions for review are filed.

It is hardly less clear that the other provision upon which the Court of Appeals for the Second Circuit relied, § 242(b)(4) of the Act, is also addressed to reviewing courts, and, insofar as it represents a yardstick for the administrative factfinder, goes, not to the burden of proof, but rather to the quality and nature of the evidence upon which a deportation order must be based. The provision declares that "reasonable, substantial, and probative evidence" shall be the measure of whether a deportability decision is "valid"—a word that implies scrutiny by a reviewing tribunal of a decision already reached by the trier of the facts. The location of this provision in a section containing provisions dealing with procedures before the special inquiry officer has little significance when it is remembered that the original 1952 Act did not itself contain a framework for judicial review—although such review was, of course, available by habeas corpus or otherwise. And whatever ambiguity might be thought to lie in the location of this section is resolved by its legislative history. The Senate Report explained § 242(b)(4) as follows: "The requirement that the decision of the special inquiry officer shall be based on reasonable, substantial and probative evidence means that, where the decision rests upon evidence of such a nature that it cannot be said that a reasonable person might not have reached the conclusion which was reached, the case may not be reversed because the judgment of the appellate body differs from that of the administrative body."

We conclude, therefore, that Congress has not addressed itself to the question of what degree of proof is required in deportation proceedings. It is the kind of question which has traditionally been left to the judiciary to resolve, and its resolution is necessary in the interest of the evenhanded administration of the Immigration and Nationality Act.

The petitioners urge that the appropriate burden of proof in deportation proceedings should be that which the law imposes in criminal cases—the duty of proving the essential facts beyond a reasonable doubt. The

Government, on the other hand, points out that a deportation proceeding is not a criminal case, and that the appropriate burden of proof should consequently be the one generally imposed in civil cases and administrative proceedings—the duty of prevailing by a mere preponderance of the evidence.

To be sure, a deportation proceeding is not a criminal prosecution. *Harisiades v. Shaughnessy,* 342 U.S. 580, 72 S.Ct. 512, 96 L.Ed. 586. But it does not syllogistically follow that a person may be banished from this country upon no higher degree of proof than applies in a negligence case. This Court has not closed its eyes to the drastic deprivations that may follow when a resident of this country is compelled by our Government to forsake all the bonds formed here and go to a foreign land where he often has no contemporary identification. * * *

In denaturalization cases the Court has required the Government to establish its allegations by clear, unequivocal, and convincing evidence. The same burden has been imposed in expatriation cases. That standard of proof is no stranger to the civil law.[18]

No less a burden of proof is appropriate in deportation proceedings. The immediate hardship of deportation is often greater than that inflicted by denaturalization, which does not, immediately at least, result in expulsion from our shores. And many resident aliens have lived in this country longer and established stronger family, social, and economic ties here than some who have become naturalized citizens.

We hold that no deportation order may be entered unless it is found by clear, unequivocal, and convincing evidence that the facts alleged as grounds for deportation are true.[19] Accordingly, in each of the cases before us, the judgment of the Court of Appeals is set aside, and the case is remanded with directions to remand to the Immigration and Naturalization Service for such further proceedings as, consistent with this opinion, may be deemed appropriate.

It is so ordered.

MR. JUSTICE CLARK, whom MR. JUSTICE HARLAN joins, dissenting.

The Court, by placing a higher standard of proof on the Government, in deportation cases, has usurped the legislative function of the Congress and has in one fell swoop repealed the long-established "reasonable, substantial, and probative" burden of proof placed on the Government by specific Act of the Congress, and substituted its own "clear, unequivocal, and convincing" standard. This is but another case in a long line in which the Court has tightened the noose around the Government's neck in immigration cases.

18. This standard, or an even higher one, has traditionally been imposed in cases involving allegations of civil fraud, and in a variety of other kinds of civil cases involving such issues as adultery, illegitimacy of a child born in wedlock, lost wills, oral contracts to make bequests, and the like. See 9 Wigmore, Evidence § 2498 (3d ed. 1940).

19. This standard of proof applies to all deportation cases, regardless of the length of time the alien has resided in this country. It is perhaps worth pointing out, however, that, as a practical matter, the more recent the alleged events supporting deportability, the more readily the Government will generally be able to prove its allegations by clear, unequivocal, and convincing evidence.

I.

I agree that § 106(a)(4), the 1961 amendment to the Immigration and Nationality Act of 1952, relates to judicial review of administrative orders of the Immigration Service but, with due deference, I cannot see how "It is hardly less clear" that § 242(b)(4) of the Act, as the Court says, likewise applies exclusively to judicial review. Indeed, on the contrary, the latter section was specifically enacted as the only standard of proof to be applied in deportation cases.

Before § 242(b) was enacted the immigration laws contained no detailed provision concerning the burden of proof in deportation cases. In *Wong Yang Sung v. McGrath*, 339 U.S. 33, 70 S.Ct. 445, 94 L.Ed. 616 (1950), this Court extended the provisions of the Administrative Procedure Act to deportation proceedings. Congress immediately exempted such proceedings from the Administrative Procedure Act and in 1952 established in § 242(b) an exclusive procedural system for deportation proceedings.

In essence that section, § 242(b), provides for notice and a hearing before a "special inquiry officer" of the Immigration Service; sets the standard of proof in such cases as "reasonable, substantial, and probative evidence"; and authorizes the Attorney General to issue regulations. In issuing those regulations the Attorney General established a Board of Immigration Appeals. The Board's relationship to the orders of the special inquiry officer is similar to the relationship an agency has to the orders of a hearing examiner under the Administrative Procedure Act. The section also specifically provides that the regulations shall include requirements that "no decision of deportability shall be valid unless it is based upon reasonable, substantial, and probative evidence" and that this standard shall be the "sole and exclusive procedure for determining the deportability of an alien under this section." This was the first time in our history that Congress had expressly placed a specific standard of proof on the Government in deportation cases. And the language Congress used made it clear that this standard related to the "burden of proof" as well as "the quality and nature of the evidence." The requirement of "reasonable" evidence cannot be meant merely to exclude "unreasonable" or "irrational" evidence but carries the obvious connotation from history and tradition of sufficiency to sustain a conclusion by a preponderance of the evidence.[1] Congress in overruling *Wong Yang Sung, supra,* carved deportation proceedings from the judicial overtones of the Administrative Procedure Act and established a *built-in* administrative procedure.

This is made crystal clear by the reports of both Houses of Congress on § 242(b). The Committee Reports, S.Rep. No. 1137, 82d Cong., 2d Sess., 30; H.R.Rep. No. 1365, 82d Cong., 2d Sess., 57, state in simple, understandable language that:

---

1. Thus the judicial review provision of the Administrative Procedure Act, 5 U.S.C. § 1009(e)(5), limits the scope of review to a determination of support by "substantial evidence," and 5 U.S.C. § 1006 limits the agencies to acting on "reliable, probative, and substantial evidence." This pattern has traditionally been held satisfied when the agency decides on the preponderance of the evidence.

"The requirement that the decision of the special inquiry officer shall be based on reasonable, substantial, and probative evidence means that, where the decision rests upon evidence of such a nature that it cannot be said that a reasonable person might not have reached the conclusion which was reached, the case may not be reversed because the judgment of the appellate body differs from that below."

The courts consistently applied the standard of "reasonable, substantial and probative" evidence after the adoption of § 242(b).

The Court, however, in *Shaughnessy v. Pedreiro,* 349 U.S. 48, 75 S.Ct. 591, 99 L.Ed. 868 (1955), once again extended the Administrative Procedure Act's provision respecting judicial review to deportation cases. The reaction of the Congress was identical to that of 1952 when it overruled *Wong Yang Sung, supra.* It enacted, in 1961, § 106(a)(4) of the Act. Just as § 242(b) was the first statutory standard of proof, § 106(a)(4) was the first express statutory standard of judicial review. It provided:

" . . . the petition [for review] shall be determined solely upon the administrative record upon which the deportation order is based and the Attorney General's findings of fact, if supported by reasonable, substantial, and probative evidence on the record considered as a whole, shall be conclusive."

Why Congress passed § 106(a)(4) if judicial review, as the Court holds, was already exclusively covered by § 242(b) is beyond my comprehension— unless it was engaged in shadow boxing. I cannot believe that it was.

The Court says that both the special inquiry officer and the Board of Immigration Appeals failed to state what the burden of proof was in these cases. Fault is found in the officer's use of the phrase "solidarity" of proof "far greater than required." This language was apparently patterned after this Court's opinion in *Rowoldt* [*v. Perfetto,* 355 U.S. 115, 78 S.Ct. 180, 2 L.Ed.2d 140 (1957)], where the phrase "solidity of proof" was used. The findings of both the officers and the Board in these cases show specifically that the burden of proof followed in each case was that required of the Government in § 242(b) and the Regulations of the Attorney General, *i.e.,* by "reasonable, substantial, and probative evidence." This standard has been administratively followed by the Immigration Service in a long and unbroken line of cases.

The Court now extends the standard of *Schneiderman v. United States,* 320 U.S. 118, 63 S.Ct. 1333, 87 L.Ed. 1796 (1943), in denaturalization cases, *i.e.,* "clear, unequivocal, and convincing evidence," to deportation cases. But denaturalization and expatriation are much more oppressive cases than deportation. They deprive one of citizenship which the United States had previously conferred. The *Schneiderman* rule only follows the principle that vested rights can be canceled only upon clear, unequivocal, and convincing proof; it gives stability and finality to a most precious right—citizenship. An alien, however, does not enjoy citizenship but only a conditional privilege extended to him by the Congress as a matter of grace. Both petitioners, the record shows, knew this, yet they remained in this country for years. * * * Still, neither made any effort to obtain citizenship.

* * *

I regret that my powers of persuasion with my Brethren are not sufficient to prevent this encroachment upon the function of the Congress which will place an undue and unintended burden upon the Government in deportation cases. I dissent.

Notes

1. As Justice Clark's dissent asks, why did Congress pass § 106(a)(4) if judicial review was already exclusively covered by § 242(b)?

2. Is *Woodby* a constitutional decision, or may Congress establish a lower standard of proof in deportation proceedings—*e.g.,* "preponderance of the evidence"? *Compare Vance v. Terrazas,* 444 U.S. 252, 100 S.Ct. 540, 62 L.Ed.2d 461 (1980) (upholding preponderance of the evidence standard in expatriation proceeding; *Woodby* did not purport to be constitutional holding) *with Santosky v. Kramer,* 455 U.S. 745, 102 S.Ct. 1388, 71 L.Ed.2d 599 (1982) (due process clause of Fourteenth Amendment requires clear and convincing evidence standard in proceeding to terminate parental rights; *Woodby* seemingly characterized as case based on constitutional notions of fundamental fairness).

> Consider Hiroshi Motomura's comment on the reasoning in *Woodby*:
>
> While the Court's opinion claimed to turn solely on a statute, the Court * * * relied heavily on constitutional considerations of the kind that the Court would recognize in the procedural due process revolution that began a few years afterwards with the Court's 1970 decision in *Goldberg v. Kelly.* * * * In particular, the *Woodby* Court noted the harsh consequences of deportation and that many permanent residents had strong ties to this country. Guided by a strong constitutional due process norm, the Court interpreted the immigration statute to require more procedural due process than was available in an ordinary civil proceeding. [T]hat norm was a phantom. Earlier cases starting with *Yamataya* had suggested some procedural due process minimum, but in fact the strictest real norm had imposed only the most modest requirements that have never begun to approach the constitutional protections of criminal procedure.

Motomura, *Immigration Law After a Century of Plenary Power: Phantom Constitutional Norms and Statutory Interpretation,* 100 Yale L.J. 545, 572 (1990).

3. Where does the majority's standard come from? Precedent? A cost-benefit analysis of the standard of proof in deportation proceedings? John Rawls?

4. Assuming that Congress is free to choose the standard of proof it desires and that you are a member of Congress, what standard would you support?

In thinking about this question, it is important to recognize that opting for a heightened standard of proof does more than simply ensure that fewer aliens are wrongfully deported. It also means that more aliens who should be deported will not be deported because the government will not be able to meet the higher level of proof. Justice Harlan has explained this trade-off as follows:

> In a lawsuit between two parties, a factual error can make a difference in one of two ways. First, it can result in a judgment in favor of the plaintiff when the true facts warrant a judgment for the defendant. The analogue in a criminal case would be the conviction of an innocent man. On the other hand, an erroneous factual determination can result in a judgment for the defendant when the true facts justify a judgment in plaintiff's favor. The criminal analogue would be the acquittal of a guilty man.
>
> The standard of proof influences the relative frequency of these two types of erroneous outcomes. If, for example, the standard of proof for a criminal trial were a preponderance of the evidence rather than proof beyond a reasonable doubt, there would be a smaller risk of factual errors that result in freeing guilty persons, but a far greater risk of factual errors that result in convicting the innocent. Because the standard of proof affects the comparative frequency of these two types of erroneous outcomes, the choice of the standard to be applied in a particular kind of litigation should, in a rational world, reflect an assessment of the comparative social disutility of each.

In re Winship, 397 U.S. 358, 370–71, 90 S.Ct. 1068, 1075–76, 25 L.Ed.2d 368 (1970) (Harlan, J., concurring).

How would you allocate the risk of error in the deportation context? Making a reasonable decision requires consideration of a number of issues, including: (1) by how much will wrongful non-deportations increase and proper non-deportations decrease by imposition of a higher standard of proof?; (2) how do we value a wrongful deportation as compared to a wrongful non-deportation?; and (3) how might other procedural protections—such as provision of counsel—affect the error rate?

The *Woodby* Standard in Action

A major distinction between exclusion and deportation proceedings, it is often said, is that the alien has the burden of proof in the former while the government has the burden of proof in the latter. INA § 291. This difference, although important, oversimplifies. As *Woodby* makes clear, the government must meet a high burden of proof in a deportation proceeding. But the statute specifically places upon the alien in the hearing the burden of showing "the time, place and manner of his entry into the United States." If this burden is not sustained, the alien "shall be presumed to be in the United States in violation of law." *Id.* Generally the courts have required the government first to present a *prima facie* case of alienage, such as a foreign birth certificate or a statement by the alien made at time of arrest. Once that is established, the burden is shifted to the alien to present evidence of time, place and manner of entry.

The burden shift and presumption in § 291 are particularly important in proving entry without inspection. Without these devices, the government would have to show that the alien had entered unlawfully—a task made difficult if the alien refuses to answer questions at the deportation hearing.

The effect of § 291 can be seen in the following case describing a deportation hearing where the charge was entry without inspection.

> At their deportation hearings, the petitioners admitted their true names and stipulated that the orders to show cause related to them; however, when confronted with questions regarding their nationality, places of birth and dates of birth, they claimed Fifth Amendment privileges and remained silent. At that point in both hearings, the Government offered and the Immigration Judge accepted into evidence properly authenticated Mexican birth certificates recording the births of individuals with names identical to the petitioners. The petitioners continued their silence in response to questions concerning whether the birth certificates related to them. The Government presented no further evidence.

Corona-Palomera v. INS, 661 F.2d 814, 815 (9th Cir.1981). You be the judge. Has the government met its burden of establishing deportability by clear, unequivocal and convincing evidence? (Note that there is no evidence, other than the aliens' names, linking the aliens before the judge to the particular birth certificates; nor is there any evidence about how the aliens entered the country.)

The immigration judge found the aliens deportable and the court of appeals affirmed. The court held that "identity of names [in the birth certificates and as stated at the hearing by the aliens] is sufficient to prove identity of persons where no effort is made to rebut such proof," and "[e]vidence of foreign birth gives rise to a presumption that the person so born is an alien." Therefore it was

> * * * proper for the Immigration Judge to have shifted the burden to petitioners for them to demonstrate the time, place, and manner of their entry into the United States per [INA § 291]. At that point, the additional presumption of illegal entry was in existence by virtue of [§ 291] and it remained unrebutted.

* * *

> Based upon the foregoing, it is our view that the record contains reasonable, substantial, and probative evidence to support the Immigration Judge's determination of deportability.

Id. at 816, 818. Are you persuaded?

Assume that in *Corona-Palomera* the government had not introduced Mexican birth certificates with the aliens' names on them (and therefore presented no evidence regarding the respondents' alienage). Could the judge find deportability?   Consider the following facts from the BIA's opinion in *Matter of Guevara,* Int.Dec. 3143 (BIA 1990):

> [T]he respondent * * * appeared before the immigration judge, and was called as a witness by the general counsel for the [INS]. However, the respondent refused to answer any questions other than as to his identity, asserting, as a basis for such refusal, his privilege against self-incrimination * * *.   The Service presented no evidence to establish the respondent's alienage and deportability other than the respondent's silence in the face of questioning. * * * [The immigration judge] drew an adverse inference from the respondent's silence, and found that the respondent was an alien as alleged.   He further determined that the burden of proof shifted to the respondent under [INA § 291], noted that the respondent had not established the time, place or manner of his entry, and consequently found the respondent deportable as charged.

TRIAL

Read the facts again.   Note that the government produced *no* evidence of any kind.   Do *Woodby* and the INA permit the immigration judge to find deportability?   The BIA thought not:

> We note at the outset that under certain circumstances, an adverse inference may indeed be drawn from a respondent's silence in deportation proceedings. * * * Thus, it is clear that when confronted with evidence of, for example, the respondent's alienage, the circumstances of his entry, or his deportability, a respondent who remains silent may leave himself open to adverse inferences, which may properly lead in turn to a finding of deportability against him.
>
> However, this proposition, and the cases which support it, are not controlling in the instant case. They do not relate to the situation at the outset of a hearing, prior to introduction of evidence by the government.   Therefore, they by no means mitigate the clear requirement [of *Woodby*]* * * that the burden of proof in deportation proceedings is upon the Service to establish the alienage of respondent, and ultimately his deportability, by evidence that is clear, unequivocal, and convincing.

* * *

> The legal concept of a "burden of proof" requires that the party upon whom the burden rests carry such burden by presenting evidence.   If the only evidence necessary to satisfy this burden were the silence of the other party, then for all practical purposes, the burden would actually fall upon the silent party at the outset. * * *

APPEAL

> * * * We find therefore that under the circumstances, the determination of the respondent's deportability was not properly made.

We salute the BIA's unwillingness to allow the government to make something out of (literally) nothing.   But return, then, to *Corona-Palomera.* Why was the "something" there (foreign birth certificates bearing the same name given by the respondents, coupled with the respondents' silence) enough to satisfy *Woodby*? Did the government *prove* anything? Are the various presumptions applied by the court consistent with the letter or spirit of *Woodby*? Or can the case be defended as demonstrating a better appreciation of the reality of the immigration process than the Supreme Court displayed in *Woodby*? *See generally* Kanstroom, *Hello Darkness: Involuntary Testimony and Silence as Evidence in Deportation Proceedings,* 4 Geo.Immig.L.J. 599 (1990).

Silence and Adverse Inferences

Aliens have a Fifth Amendment right to refuse to answer questions in a deportation hearing that could be used against them in a criminal proceeding. (Note that unlawful entry is a criminal offense as well as ground for deportation, INA § 275.) Accordingly, if an alien asserts a Fifth Amendment privilege in a deportation hearing but is ordered to respond without having been granted immunity from criminal prosecution, any statement she makes may not be used to establish her deportability. *Tashnizi v. INS,* 585 F.2d 781, 782 (5th Cir.1978) (per curiam); *Valeros v. INS,* 387 F.2d 921, 922 (7th Cir.1967).

Suppose the government introduces its *prima facie* case (*cf. Guevara, supra*) and the alien remains silent. Should an immigration judge be able to draw an "adverse inference" from this refusal to answer questions? Justice Brandeis, writing for the Court in *United States ex rel. Bilokumsky v. Tod,* 263 U.S. 149, 153–54, 44 S.Ct. 54, 55–56, 68 L.Ed. 221 (1923), gave the classic answer: "Conduct which forms a basis for inference is evidence. Silence is often evidence of the most persuasive character. * * * [T]here is no rule of law which prohibits officers charged with the administration of the immigration law from drawing an inference from the silence of one who is called upon to speak." Similarly, in *Cabral-Avila v. INS,* 589 F.2d 957, 959 (9th Cir.1978), *cert. denied,* 440 U.S. 920, 99 S.Ct. 1245, 59 L.Ed.2d 472 (1979), the court held:

> Petitioners' decision to remain mute during the deportability phase of the hearing was an appropriate exercise of their Fifth Amendment privilege, but by doing so they do not shield themselves from the drawing of adverse inferences that they are not legally in this country and their silence cannot be relied upon to carry forward their duty to rebut the Government's *prima facie* case.

This conclusion has been criticized. *See, e.g., Developments in the Law—Immigration Policy and the Rights of Aliens,* 96 Harv.L.Rev. 1286, 1388–89 (1983). Yet the commentators appeared not to be aware of *Baxter v. Palmigiano,* 425 U.S. 308, 316–20, 96 S.Ct. 1551, 1557–59, 47 L.Ed.2d 810 (1976), which allowed the drawing of an adverse inference from a prisoner's silence after invocation of the Fifth Amendment in a prison disciplinary proceeding. *See generally* Heidt, *The Conjurer's Circle: The Fifth Amendment Privilege in Civil Cases,* 91 Yale L.J. 1062, 1109–14 (1982).

Former Immigration Judge Henry Watkins has developed an interesting proposal for handling the "many genuine and complicated self-incrimination issues [that] exist in current deportation proceedings." Observing that he has been "unable to discover one instance where a respondent's answers in deportation proceedings have been used against the respondent in subsequent criminal proceedings," Judge Watkins recommends that

> the Attorney General promulgate a policy granting respondents in deportation proceedings immunity from prosecution for immigration law violations. Alternatively, immunity should be granted, at a minimum, for the offenses of entry without inspection [INA § 275], reentry after deportation [INA § 276], and failure to register as an alien [INA §§ 262, 266]. * * *

> Immunization from prosecution obliges the respondent to answer questions concerning alienage or any right to remain in the United States. An adverse inference is properly drawn where a respondent wrongfully refuses to answer. Significantly, such immunity obviates the need of immigration judges, the INS, and respondents to address these time-consuming and often difficult questions. Moreover, this grant of immunity requires no alteration of the government's *de facto* policy of not using statements obtained in deportation proceeding[s] for subsequent prosecution of immigration law violations. The formalization of this policy would eliminate many claimed constitutional violations, as well as procedural and evidentiary problems.

Watkins, *Streamlining Deportation Proceedings: Self–Incrimination, Immunity from Prosecution and the Duty to Testify in a Deportation Context,* 22 San Diego L.Rev. 1075, 1077–78 (1985). Judge Watkins' proposal may well simplify deportation proceedings, but is it consistent with Congress' express intent that certain violations of the immigration laws be prosecuted as criminal offenses? Furthermore, does compelling aliens to answer questions after a grant of immunity (or drawing adverse inferences from a refusal to testify) comport with notions of fundamental fairness? Does it, in effect, allow the government to shift the burden of proof to aliens in deportation proceedings?

(v) Evidence: Fifth and Fourth Amendment Exclusionary Rules

Fifth Amendment: *"Miranda* Warnings"

In three situations during the deportation process, current regulations require that aliens be informed of the nature of the deportation charges and told that anything they say may be used against them: (1) when served with an order to show cause, 8 C.F.R. § 242.1(c); (2) after arrest and a determination by an immigration officer to initiate deportation proceedings, 8 C.F.R. § 287.3; and (3) when arrested after the initiation of a deportation proceeding, 8 C.F.R. § 242.2(c)(2).

These three situations leave a gap in coverage. Recall the discussion, pp. 587–588 *supra,* of the initiation of deportation proceedings. If an alien is arrested without a warrant and brought to an INS office for questioning before an order to show cause is issued, will he be immediately advised of his rights?

In 1967, INS amended its regulations to require that aliens arrested without a warrant be advised of their rights. 32 Fed.Reg. 6260 (1967). In 1979, the regulations were changed, pushing back the time for advice of rights until "[a]fter the examining officer has determined that formal [exclusion or deportation hearings] will be instituted." 44 Fed.Reg. 4654 (1979). The gain to law enforcement occasioned by this change should be obvious. Aliens interrogated by INS officials without being told that they may be represented by a lawyer or that anything they say may be used against them often admit alienage, unlawful entry, unauthorized employment or other facts which provide the basis for a deportation charge. Such admissions may also serve as crucial (if not the only) evidence in the deportation proceeding, particularly when an alien refuses to answer questions in that setting.[7] The INS' position is that valuable, reliable evidence would be lost if an alien were given warnings or if a lawyer were present during the initial interrogation.

The 1979 change in the regulations brought vociferous objections from immigration attorneys. The INS responded:

> There is no statutory or constitutional mandate that advice be given to an alien during his interrogation. To safeguard the alien's procedural due process right, the advice concerning his right to counsel, including free legal services will be given to the alien at that stage in the interrogation when the immigration officer has determined that formal proceedings will be instituted.

44 Fed.Reg. 4652 (1979).

Under the famous case of *Miranda v. Arizona*, 384 U.S. 436, 86 S.Ct. 1602, 16 L.Ed.2d 694 (1966), failure to inform the individual of her rights renders any statements she makes during a custodial interrogation inadmissible in her criminal trial. The courts have not read the Constitution to require such warnings in the deportation context. Failure to give warnings would mean any admissions by the alien could be excluded from subsequent criminal proceedings. *See, e.g., United States v. Segovia–Melgar*, 595 F.Supp. 753 (D.D.C.1984). But the admissions would not be excluded automatically from the deportation proceeding itself. *E.g., Bustos–Torres v. INS*, 898 F.2d 1053, 1056–57 (5th Cir.1990); *Matter of Baltazar*, 16 I & N Dec. 108, 109 (BIA 1977). Again, this conclusion (as well as many others in this section) relies heavily on the characterization of deportation proceedings as "civil" rather than "criminal," as well as on the following considerations:

> A principal purpose of the *Miranda* warnings is to permit the suspect to make an intelligent decision as to whether to answer the government agent's questions. In deportation proceedings,

7. *See, e.g., Trias–Hernandez v. INS*, 528 F.2d 366, 368 (9th Cir.1975) (under facts of the case, impossible to prove deportability for illegal entry without statements made by alien following arrest).

however—in light of the alien's burden of proof, the requirement that the alien answer non-incriminating questions, the potential adverse consequences to the alien of remaining silent, and the fact that an alien's statement is admissible in the deportation hearing despite his lack of counsel at the preliminary interrogation— *Miranda* warnings would be not only inappropriate but could also serve to mislead the alien.

Chavez-Raya v. INS, 519 F.2d 397, 402 (7th Cir.1975).

In August 1992, the INS changed course in agreeing to a settlement in *Lopez v. INS,* No. CV 78–1912–WMB (C.D.Cal. Aug. 20, 1992), *digested at* 70 Interp.Rel. 151 (1993). The original *Lopez* plaintiffs were several aliens arrested in a 1978 INS raid on a Los Angeles shoe factory. They allegedly asked to consult with lawyers but were not allowed to; instead, they were forced to waive their rights and agree to immediate removal to Mexico. Saved by a last-minute temporary restraining order, they were ultimately found not deportable. The litigation continued as nationwide class action on behalf of all persons arrested by the INS without a warrant since 1978. It challenged the INS form used to advise class members of their rights, as well as the INS policy regarding their access to counsel. Under the settlement, the INS agreed to use new forms during a 30–month evaluation period. One new form advises aliens that they may speak with counsel, request a list of free and low-cost legal services, have a hearing before an immigration judge, obtain release on bond, be eligible for relief from deportation, and communicate with a consular or diplomatic officer of their home country. Another form asks all class members other than Canadians and Mexicans if they fear harm if they return home. The INS also agreed to suspend post-arrest interrogation temporarily (except to obtain basic biographical data) when the alien asks to consult counsel.

Does the *Lopez* settlement adequately balance the alien's interest in a fair proceeding and the government's interest in efficient and effective law enforcement? Does it address *Chavez-Raya* 's concern that the alien not be misled? Can you craft a better set of "warnings"?

Although *Miranda* 's bright-line test does not apply, the courts and the BIA will occasionally order the exclusion of prior statements on due process grounds where they conclude that the government's behavior violated fundamental fairness or that the circumstances surrounding the alien interrogation rendered the statements "involuntary." The following excerpt describes one such situation where evidence was ordered excluded.

[I]t appears that early in the evening of January 13, 1974, two of the appellant's [Ms. Navia–Duran's] housemates were detained by INS agents at a Boston restaurant, questioned about their alien status, and taken to their residence to get their identification papers. Ms. Navia–Duran's roommate, who was at home when the group arrived, was also questioned. The agents searched the apartment, including the appellant's bedroom, without warrant or consent, and allegedly seized some papers. Two of the three aliens were taken to INS offices, served with orders to show cause why they should not be deported, and held overnight in jail.

Later that same night, at approximately 10 p.m., Ms. Navia–Duran was approached from behind as she was about to enter her apartment. Without addressing her by name, a man identified himself as an INS agent and asked if she spoke English. Ms. Navia–Duran responded that she spoke Spanish. The agent requested identification, which she said was inside the apartment. Extremely frightened by this late-night approach and convinced that she had no choice but to cooperate, Ms. Navia–Duran opened her door and was followed in by this agent and by a second man who identified himself as Mr. Constance. Ms. Navia–Duran produced numerous documents, all of which were confiscated. The agents questioned her in Spanish for approximately one hour concerning her presence in the United States. During this period, Agent Constance told Ms. Navia–Duran that she must return to her native Chile immediately.

At approximately 11:30 p.m., the agents took Ms. Navia–Duran to the INS office and continued questioning her until 2 a.m. Constance showed her a calendar and told her that she must leave the country in two weeks. When the appellant protested that she needed more time, the agent reiterated that she must leave in two weeks; he characterized his offer as a fair deal for her. Throughout the early morning session, Constance insisted that she had no choice but to accept the two-week departure deadline. Fearing that she would not be permitted to go home until she cooperated, Ms. Navia–Duran signed a statement which admitted that she had entered this country on a three-month visitor's visa in 1974 and had never received an extension of time.

Navia-Duran v. INS, 568 F.2d 803, 805 (1st Cir.1977). *See, e.g., Matter of Garcia,* 17 I & N Dec. 319, 321 (BIA 1980).

Does the "due process" test, by being more flexible, provide a better accommodation between law enforcement needs and the rights of aliens than application of a strict *Miranda* rule?

Fourth Amendment

Under prevailing underlying substantive Fourth Amendment doctrine, an arrest may take place only if a police officer has probable cause to believe that an individual has committed a crime. Brief detentions, short of actual arrest, are permissible in some circumstances if a police officer has a reasonable suspicion of criminality. *Terry v. Ohio,* 392 U.S. 1, 88 S.Ct. 1868, 20 L.Ed.2d 889 (1968).

It is commonplace for INS officers to stop and question persons suspected of being aliens unlawfully in the country. The INA specifically grants INS officers the authority "to interrogate any alien or person believed to be an alien as to his right to be or remain in the United States." They are further authorized to arrest aliens unlawfully entering or unlawfully residing in the U.S. INA § 287(a). The Immigration Act of 1990 expanded INS enforcement authority by granting agency officers authority to arrest persons for any federal offense, provided that the officer is undertaking immigration enforcement activities at the time. INA § 287(a)(5).

Since aliens are protected by the Fourth Amendment, *Almeida-Sanchez v. United States,* 413 U.S. 266, 93 S.Ct. 2535, 37 L.Ed.2d 596 (1973), these enforcement powers are subject to constitutional constraint. The demands of the Fourth Amendment depend on both the kind of stop and the place where it occurs. In an interesting parallel to the border-interior distinction implicit in procedural due process analysis, the Supreme Court has been willing to recognize far greater power of law enforcement officials to search persons and property at the border than inside the country. Thus, a routine search at an official border inspection post may occur without probable cause or reasonable suspicion. *United States v. Ramsey,* 431 U.S. 606, 619, 97 S.Ct. 1972, 1980, 52 L.Ed.2d 617 (1977) ("This longstanding recognition that searches at our borders without probable cause and without a warrant are nonetheless 'reasonable' has a history as old as the Fourth Amendment itself"). Intrusive searches that go beyond a normal border search require some degree of reasonable belief that illegal activity is occurring. In *United States v. Montoya de Hernandez,* 473 U.S. 531, 105 S.Ct. 3304, 87 L.Ed.2d 381 (1985), the Supreme Court upheld the sixteen hour detention of an individual seeking to enter the U.S. based on customs officials' "reasonable suspicion" that the traveler was smuggling contraband in her alimentary canal. (For persons inside the United States, the Fourth Amendment would require that such detention be based upon a finding of "probable cause.")

Much INS enforcement activity takes places near, but not at, the border. Here the Court has applied the Fourth Amendment with more vigor. The Court has distinguished between stops made by "roving patrols" (that is, INS officers travelling in cars) and those made at "fixed checkpoints" near, but not at, the border. Roving patrols may conduct brief stops and questioning if an officer has a reasonable suspicion that a particular vehicle contains aliens unlawfully in the United States. *United States v. Brignoni–Ponce,* 422 U.S. 873, 95 S.Ct. 2574, 45 L.Ed.2d 607 (1975). Roving patrols may conduct arrests and full-scale searches only based on probable cause. *Almeida-Sanchez, supra.* At a fixed checkpoint, however, brief stops are permissible even without reasonable suspicion, *United States v. Martinez–Fuerte,* 428 U.S. 543, 96 S.Ct. 3074, 49 L.Ed.2d 1116 (1976). At a fixed check point, once a car and its riders have been held for secondary inspection, a search may occur only if the INS has probable cause to believe that criminal conduct is afoot. *United States v. Ortiz,* 422 U.S. 891, 95 S.Ct. 2585, 45 L.Ed.2d 623 (1975).

These are fine distinctions, and courts are usually willing to give considerable weight to the experience and expertise of INS officers in deciding whether or not reasonable suspicion or probable cause existed. Isn't it likely that the appearance of an individual (dress, national origin, language spoken) may figure prominently in an officer's assessment of the situation? Should the Court be crafting stricter standards in order to protect U.S. citizens and lawful resident aliens travelling near the border who may appear "foreign" to INS officers? Or do lengthy unprotected borders and huge numbers of unlawful entries each year demand that immigration officials have relatively unfettered authority to enforce the laws of the United States? Compare the IRCA anti-discrimination provisions, discussed in Section C of Chapter Three *supra.*

Brignoni-Ponce held that Hispanic appearance plus presence in an area where undocumented aliens frequently travel are not enough to justify a vehicle stop, 422 U.S. at 884–87, 95 S.Ct. at 2582–83. More recently, the INS settled a class action that alleged that the Border Patrol relied solely on Hispanic appearance in stopping, questioning, and detaining students, graduates, and staff of Bowie High School, located in El Paso right next to the U.S.–Mexico border. After a preliminary injunction, the INS agreed to provide information about and assistance with filing complaints against the Border Patrol. *See Murillo v. Musegades,* 809 F.Supp. 487 (W.D.Tex.1994), *digested at* 71 Interp.Rel. 987 (1994); *see also* 809 F.Supp. 487 (W.D.Tex. 1992) (preliminary injunction).[8]

Not all INS enforcement activity occurs at or near the border. Raids on places of employment well within the interior of the nation are common. The Supreme Court has held that the mere questioning of a person by a police officer does not trigger Fourth Amendment concerns provided that "in view of all the circumstances surrounding the incident, a reasonable person would have believed that he was * * * free to leave." *United States v. Mendenhall,* 446 U.S. 544, 554, 100 S.Ct. 1870, 1877, 64 L.Ed.2d 497 (1980). But is it likely that an alien stopped by an INS officer flashing a badge is going to feel free to leave? For a case that seems to blink reality by answering this question in the affirmative, see *INS v. Delgado,* 466 U.S. 210, 104 S.Ct. 1758, 80 L.Ed.2d 247 (1984), a decision that was probably based on concerns regarding the number of undocumented aliens entering and residing in the United States and the difficulties of effective enforcement of the INA. Actual detention of an alien for questioning during a factory or farm raid must be based on some reasonable, objective evidence that he or she is unlawfully in the United States. *See generally Illinois Migrant Council v. Pilliod,* 548 F.2d 715 (7th Cir.1977); *ILGWU v. Sureck,* 681 F.2d 624 (9th Cir.1982), *reversed on other grounds, INS v. Delgado,* *supra.* Moving away from the border in the other direction, *United States v. Verdugo–Urquidez,* 494 U.S. 259, 110 S.Ct. 1056, 108 L.Ed.2d 222 (1990), held that the Fourth Amendment does not apply to a search by American officials of a Mexican residence of a citizen and resident of Mexico.

We leave for criminal procedure courses the complicated question of the "warrant" requirement of the Fourth Amendment for interior enforcement operations. *See generally Blackie's House of Beef, Inc. v. Castillo,* 659 F.2d 1211 (D.C.Cir.1981), *cert. denied,* 455 U.S. 940, 102 S.Ct. 1432, 71 L.Ed.2d 651 (1982); *International Molders' and Allied Workers' Local No. 164 v. Nelson,* 674 F.Supp. 294 (N.D.Cal.1987). Importantly, IRCA amend-

---

8. For discussions of the constitutionality of the use of Hispanic appearance in INS decisions to stop and question persons, see Note, *Reexamining the Constitutionality of Workplace Raids After the Immigration Reform and Control Act of 1986,* 100 Harv. L.Rev.1979 (1987) ("*Harvard Note*"); Note, *The Immigration and Naturalization Service and Racially Motivated Questioning: Does Equal Protection Pick Up Where the Fourth Amendment Left Off?,* 86 Colum.L.Rev. 800 (1986).

ed the INA to require the INS to obtain a warrant before searching agricultural operations without the consent of the owner. INA § 287(e). More generally, the advent of employer sanctions may affect the warrant requirement for workplace raids. Previously, most such searches occurred with the consent of the employer; and, in any event, the employer was not potentially criminally liable for the hiring of undocumented workers. Does the existence of employer sanctions undercut relaxed standards for warrants based on the characterization of workplace raids as civil, regulatory searches? *See* Note, *Open-ended Warrants, Employers and the Simpson–Rodino Act,* 87 Colum.L.Rev. 817 (1987); *Harvard Note,* n. 8 *supra.*

Should evidence seized in violation of the Fourth Amendment be admissible in deportation hearings? In *INS v. Lopez–Mendoza,* 468 U.S. 1032, 104 S.Ct. 3479, 82 L.Ed.2d 778 (1984), the Supreme Court held that the Fourth Amendment's exclusionary rule does not apply in deportation proceedings. Justice O'Connor's majority opinion adopted a balancing approach, weighing "the likely social benefits of excluding unlawfully seized evidence against the likely costs." On the benefits side, she concluded that "several factors significantly reduce the likely deterrent value of the exclusionary rule in a civil deportation proceeding":

> * * * First, regardless of how the arrest is effected, deportation will still be possible when evidence not derived directly from the arrest is sufficient to support deportation. As the BIA has recognized, in many deportation proceedings "the sole matters necessary for the Government to establish are the respondent's identity and alienage—at which point the burden shifts to the respondent to prove the time, place and manner of entry." *Matter of Sandoval,* 17 I. & N. Dec., at 79. Since the person and identity of the respondent are not themselves suppressible, the INS must prove only alienage, and that will sometimes be possible using evidence gathered independently of, or sufficiently attenuated from, the original arrest. * * *

> The second factor is a practical one. In the course of a year the average INS agent arrests almost 500 illegal aliens. Over 97.5% apparently agree to voluntary deportation without a formal hearing. Among the remainder who do request a formal hearing (apparently a dozen or so in all, per officer, per year) very few challenge the circumstances of their arrests. * * * Every INS agent knows, therefore, that it is highly unlikely that any particular arrestee will end up challenging the lawfulness of his arrest in a formal deportation proceeding. When an occasional challenge is brought, the consequences from the point of view of the officer's overall arrest and deportation record will be trivial. In these circumstances, the arresting officer is most unlikely to shape his conduct in anticipation of the exclusion of evidence at a formal deportation hearing.

> Third, and perhaps most important, the INS has its own comprehensive scheme for deterring Fourth Amendment violations by its officers. Most arrests of illegal aliens away from the border

occur during farm, factory, or other workplace surveys. Large numbers of illegal aliens are often arrested at one time, and conditions are understandably chaotic. To safeguard the rights of those who are lawfully present at inspected workplaces the INS has developed rules restricting stop, interrogation, and arrest practices. These regulations require that no one be detained without reasonable suspicion of illegal alienage, and that no one be arrested unless there is an admission of illegal alienage or other strong evidence thereof. New immigration officers receive instruction and examination in Fourth Amendment law, and others receive periodic refresher courses in law. Evidence seized through intentionally unlawful conduct is excluded by Department of Justice policy from the proceeding for which it was obtained. See Memorandum from Benjamin R. Civiletti to Heads of Offices, Boards, Bureaus and Divisions, Violations of Search and Seizure Law (Jan. 16, 1981).[a] The INS also has in place a procedure for investigating and punishing immigration officers who commit Fourth Amendment violations. See Office of General Counsel, INS, U.S. Dept. of Justice, The Law of Arrest, Search, and Seizure for Immigration Officers 35 (Jan. 1983). The INS's attention to Fourth Amendment interests cannot guarantee that constitutional violations will not occur, but it does reduce the likely deterrent value of the exclusionary rule. Deterrence must be measured at the margin.

Finally, the deterrent value of the exclusionary rule in deportation proceedings is undermined by the availability of alternative remedies for institutional practices by the INS that might violate Fourth Amendment rights. The INS is a single agency, under central federal control, and engaged in operations of broad scope but highly repetitive character. The possibility of declaratory relief against the agency thus offers a means for challenging the validity of INS practices, when standing requirements for bringing such an action can be met.

Justice O'Connor then assessed the social costs of applying the exclusionary rule and concluded that they are "both unusual and significant":

* * * The first cost is one that is unique to continuing violations of the law. Applying the exclusionary rule in proceedings that are intended not to punish past transgressions but to prevent their continuance or renewal would require the courts to close their eyes to ongoing violations of the law. This Court has never before accepted costs of this character in applying the exclusionary rule.

---

a. Under the Attorney General's policy, reprinted in 58 Interp.Rel. 18 (1981), (1) evidence seized through an *intentional* violation of the Fourth Amendment will be excluded from the proceeding and the offending officer will be subject to "the highest administrative penalties available"; (2) evidence seized by a *reckless* violation of law will be excluded and the official will be subject to "administrative discipline" less stringent than that applied to intentional violators; and (3) officials who violate the Fourth Amendment through a negligent act or omission will ordinarily not be subject to administrative discipline.—eds.

* * * The constable's blunder may allow the criminal to go free, but we have never suggested that it allows the criminal to continue in the commission of an ongoing crime. When the crime in question involves unlawful presence in this country, the criminal may go free, but he should not go free within our borders.

Other factors also weigh against applying the exclusionary rule in deportation proceedings. The INS currently operates a deliberately simple deportation hearing system, streamlined to permit the quick resolution of very large numbers of deportation actions, and it is against this backdrop that the costs of the exclusionary rule must be assessed. The costs of applying the exclusionary rule, like the benefits, must be measured at the margin.

The average immigration judge handles about six deportation hearings per day. Neither the hearing officers nor the attorneys participating in those hearings are likely to be well versed in the intricacies of Fourth Amendment law. The prospect of even occasional invocation of the exclusionary rule might significantly change and complicate the character of these proceedings. * * *

* * * Immigration officers apprehend over one million deportable aliens in this country every year. A single agent may arrest many illegal aliens every day. Although the investigatory burden does not justify the commission of constitutional violations, the officers cannot be expected to compile elaborate, contemporaneous, written reports detailing the circumstances of every arrest. At present an officer simply completes a "Record of Deportable Alien" that is introduced to prove the INS's case at the deportation hearing; the officer rarely must attend the hearing. Fourth Amendment suppression hearings would undoubtedly require considerably more, and the likely burden on the administration of the immigration laws would be correspondingly severe.

Finally, the INS advances the credible argument that applying the exclusionary rule to deportation proceedings might well result in the suppression of large amounts of information that had been obtained entirely lawfully. INS arrests occur in crowded and confused circumstances. Though the INS agents are instructed to follow procedures that adequately protect Fourth Amendment interests, agents will usually be able to testify only to the fact that they followed INS rules. The demand for a precise account of exactly what happened in each particular arrest would plainly preclude mass arrests, even when the INS is confronted, as it often is, with massed numbers of ascertainably illegal aliens, and even when the arrests can be and are conducted in full compliance with all Fourth Amendment requirements.

468 U.S. at 1043–50.

Four Justices dissented from the Court's opinion. Justices Brennan and Marshall rejected the majority's balancing methodology, arguing that "the basis of the exclusionary rule does not derive from its effectiveness as a deterrent, but is instead found in the requirements of the Fourth

Amendment itself." *Id.* at 1051 (Brennan, J., dissenting). *See id.* at 1060–61 (Marshall, J., dissenting). Justice White, joined in substantial part by Justice Stevens, concluded that "the costs and benefits of applying the exclusionary rule in civil deportation proceedings do not differ in any significant way from the costs and benefits of applying the rule in ordinary criminal proceedings." *Id.* at 1060. (White, J., dissenting).

Notes

1. Are you satisfied with the empirical assumptions in the majority opinion regarding the costs and benefits of the exclusionary rule? Even if hard data on the issues were available, how does one assign values to the costs and benefits? *See generally* Kamisar, *Does (Did) (Should) the Exclusionary Rule Rest on a "Principled Basis" Rather than an "Empirical Proposition?,"* 16 Creighton L.Rev. 565, 645–67 (1983).

In discussing the "costs" that would be associated with application of an exclusionary rule in deportation proceedings, the Court mentions "the staggering dimension of the problem that the INS confronts" and concludes that "the likely burden on the administration of the immigration laws would be * * * severe." Is the majority saying that our immigration laws simply cannot be effectively enforced if INS officers are held to the dictates of the Fourth Amendment? Consider the remarks of BIA Member Ralph Farb, concurring in *Matter of Sandoval,* 17 I & N Dec. 70, 85 (BIA 1979):

> For Fiscal Year 1977, the Immigration and Naturalization Service reported that it had located 1,042,000 deportable aliens. Of these, 939,000, or 90%, were listed as having entered without inspection. That means that for the vast majority there was no reason to expect that the Immigration and Naturalization Service records contained prior evidence of their identity as aliens. I am not condoning or encouraging violation of Fourth Amendment rights in the immigration investigator's search for solid proof of identity. If it were done deliberately, discharge from Government service would be appropriate. I simply don't see how we can reasonably bar the use of illegally obtained convincing proof that a person is an alien with no right of presence, when that may be all that will ever be available to identify him. It would be inconsistent with the manifest intention of Congress that the Immigration and Naturalization Service know the location of every alien in the country.

2. The penultimate sentence of Justice O'Connor's opinion states: "[W]e do not deal here with egregious violations of Fourth Amendment or other liberties that might transgress notions of fundamental fairness and undermine the probative value of the evidence obtained." 468 U.S. at 1050–51, 104 S.Ct. at 3489. Chief Justice Burger did not join this portion of Justice O'Connor's opinion; but three other Justices in the majority did. When one considers the views of the four dissenting Justices, it seems safe to conclude that the sentence represents the view of a majority of the Court at that time.

When does this "egregious violation" exception allow aliens to invoke a Fourth Amendment exclusionary rule in deportation proceedings? In *Gonzalez-Rivera v. INS*, 22 F.3d 1441, 1449 (9th Cir.1994), the Ninth Circuit held that a vehicle stop based solely on the passengers' Hispanic appearance was a Fourth Amendment violation committed in "bad faith" because the law enforcement officer knew or reasonably should have known that his conduct would violate the Constitution. Therefore, the court ruled, the violation was "egregious" and required exclusion of the evidence obtained. *See also Orhorhaghe v. INS*, 38 F.3d 488, 501–04 (9th Cir.1994). Now consider that shortly before deciding *Lopez-Mendoza*, the United States Supreme Court limited the exclusionary rule in criminal cases generally. Under *United States v. Leon*, 468 U.S. 897, 922–23, 104 S.Ct. 3405, 3420–21, 82 L.Ed.2d 677 (1984), evidence may be admitted as long as the officer relied on a facially valid search warrant, even if the warrant is later found defective in violation of the Fourth Amendment. Combining *Leon* and *Gonzalez-Rivera*, compare the exclusionary rule's application in deportation and criminal proceedings.

c. *Special Deportation Procedures*

The INA provides special deportation procedures for several groups of aliens, for example: (1) alien crewmen who jump ship or overstay their shore leave, INA § 252(b); (2) certain aliens who unlawfully re-enter following deportation, INA § 242(f); (3) nonimmigrants who enter as visitors under the visa waiver pilot program discussed in Chapter Four *infra*, INA § 217(b)(4).

The recent trend has been a significant expansion in the use of these special procedures, largely to avoid what some find to be excessive or inefficient procedural protections for aliens in standard deportation proceedings. Predictably, the focus is on aliens deportable because of criminal convictions. In 1986, Congress enacted INA § 242(i), which simply instructs the Attorney General to begin deportation proceedings "as expeditiously as possible" after the date of a deportable conviction. Pub.L. 99–603, § 701, 100 Stat. 3359, 3445. In 1988, the Anti–Drug Abuse Act, Pub.L. 100–690, § 7347, 102 Stat. 4181, added INA § 242A, which you should now read. It establishes special expedited removal procedures for aliens with aggravated felony convictions. Aggravated felons are also limited to a shorter time period (30 days) for seeking judicial review of a deportation order.

The 1994 anti-crime legislation went one step further by adding new INA § 242A(b), which established an administrative deportation procedure for aliens who are aggravated felons without permanent resident status, and who are not eligible for any relief from deportation. Pub.L. 103–322, § 130004, 108 Stat. 1796, 2026–27. (In almost all cases, aliens without permanent resident status who have been convicted of an aggravated felony are therefore ineligible for any relief from deportation.) Section 242A(b) allows the Attorney General to issue an expedited deportation order without a hearing before an immigration judge. In order to allow the alien to seek the limited judicial review available to aliens deported under this procedure, the order cannot be executed for 30 days. Soon after new

§ 242A(b) became law, the 1994 Technical Corrections Act removed its requirement that the expedited order be supported by "clear, convincing, and unequivocal" evidence. Pub.L. 103–416, § 223, 108 Stat. 4305, 4322. Is this latest amendment to § 242A(b) constitutional under *Woodby*? Is the entire administrative deportation procedure constitutional under *Yamataya v. Fisher*?

Another significant development in 1994 was the advent of judicial deportation. You will recall that the 1990 Act ended judicial power to *prevent deportation* when it eliminated judicial recommendations against deportation ("JRAD's"). In the meantime, one appeals court ruled that a judge may *order deportation* in limited circumstances, *see United States v. Chukwara*, 5 F.3d 1420, 1423–24 (11th Cir.1993) (alien defendant deported as a condition of supervised release under 18 U.S.C.A. § 3583(d)). The 1994 Technical Corrections Act gave federal district courts the power to order deportation when sentencing an alien for a crime that makes him deportable. *See* INA § 241(a)(2)(A). Both the United States Attorney and the INS must seek the judicial deportation order. The alien defendant must receive notice and be given an opportunity to establish eligibility for relief from deportation.

Both judicial deportation and administrative deportation of aggravated felons without permanent resident status who are ineligible for relief from deportation are part of the linkage between criminal law and immigration law that inheres in deportation grounds for criminal activity. While we might therefore view judicial deportation as yet another procedure for deporting criminal aliens swiftly, judicial deportation differs from the new streamlined administrative deportation in one fundamental respect. It is taken for granted that the new administrative deportation, like any deportation procedure, does not include the procedural safeguards that are traditional in criminal cases. In fact, administrative deportation does not have the less extensive procedures that are traditional in standard deportation cases; arguably, this occurs only in cases with very limited (if any) grounds for contesting deportation. Judicial deportation goes further than streamlining deportation; it dispenses with a separate deportation procedure altogether. But with this step, judicial deportation brings deportation fully into the criminal process. Ironically, then, judicial deportation restores some of the protections that the trend toward special deportation procedures has been taking away. In theory, aliens subject to deportation for criminal activity may enjoy greater procedural safeguards—for example, the right to appointed counsel—than they would have in a standard deportation proceeding, at least when the government seeks a judicial deportation order.

These developments prompt some basic questions. How does judicial deportation affect the bedrock assumption that *Fong Yue Ting* is distinguishable from *Wong Wing*, and the time-honored rule that deportation is not "punishment"? And what *should* be the model for the deportation process? If we could accept the notion that deportation is a civil proceeding, perhaps we might prefer a less adversarial model to additional procedural protections within the familiar, lawyer-centered tradition. European countries often use such nonadversarial proceedings, with an active decisionmaking and minimal involvement by the parties' lawyers, even at times in criminal proceedings. The results are regarded, at least in those cultures, as fair. *See, e.g.,* Langbein, *The Criminal Trial Before the Lawyers,* 45 U.Chi.L.Rev. 263 (1975); Friendly, *Some Kind of Hearing,* 123 U.Pa.L.Rev. 1267, 1289–91. Should such a model be applied to immigration proceedings? Can adequate independence and professionalism of the adjudicators be assured? *See generally* Martin, *Due Process and Membership in the National Community: Political Asylum and Beyond,* 44 U.Pitt. L.Rev. 165, 219–21 (1983). But would such a model be appropriate with deportation focusing more and more on criminal aliens?

Finally, we call your attention to a bill pending in Congress as we go to press: S.390, 104th Cong., 1st Sess. This bill proposes The Omnibus Counterterrorism Act of 1995, the substantive provisions of which we mentioned on p. 531 *supra.* Section 201 of S.390 would establish a special deportation procedure for "terrorist activity" based on evidence presented *in camera* and *ex parte. Cf.* INA § 235(c), discussed at p. 402 *supra.* The government could invoke this special procedure by showing, *in camera* and *ex parte,* that the alien has been correctly identified and is deportable under INA § 241(a)(4)(B), and that use of the standard deportation procedures "would pose a risk to the national security of the United States." The cases would be heard by a new special court, made up of five federal district judges designated for five-year terms by the Chief Justice of the United States. While the evidence of "terrorist activity" would not be revealed to the alien or the public, a general summary of the evidence would normally (but not always) be made available.

SECTION C. DUE PROCESS, EXCLUSION AND DEPORTATION: TOWARDS A NEW APPROACH

As we explored in Chapter Four, the Supreme Court has been unwilling to subject statutory exclusion procedures to serious constitutional scrutiny. "Whatever the procedure authorized by Congress is," go the famous words of *Knauff* and *Mezei,* "it is due process as far as an alien denied entry is concerned." 338 U.S. 537, 544, 70 S.Ct. 309, 313, 94 L.Ed. 317 (1950); 345 U.S. 206, 212, 73 S.Ct. 625, 629, 97 L.Ed. 956 (1953). This abdication of judicial review at the border is in sharp contrast to the scrutiny that the Supreme Court is willing to apply in the deportation context. The decision in *Yamataya* in the early years of this century made clear that, as to aliens who have entered the country, "administrative officers, when executing the provisions of a statute involving the liberty of persons, may [not] disregard the fundamental principles that inhere in 'due process of law.'" 189 U.S. 86, 100, 23 S.Ct. 611, 614, 47 L.Ed. 721 (1903).

You should now be quite familiar with the curious results occasioned by a constitutional test that largely turns on the location of the alien. For example, an alien who arrives at the border with an immigrant visa and a job or family awaiting him in the United States is essentially unprotected by the Constitution's due process clause. However, an alien who is apprehended a few hours after making a surreptitious entry is afforded, as a matter of constitutional right, a hearing, an opportunity to present evidence and cross-examine witnesses, an unbiased decision-maker and, sometimes, counsel.

It is tempting to write off *Knauff* and *Mezei* as Cold War cases that are no longer entitled to our respect. They misread the cases they cited and cannot be squared with several earlier cases they did not cite. *See* Martin, *Due Process and Membership in the National Community: Political Asylum and Beyond,* 44 U.Pitt.L.Rev. 165, 173–75 (1983); Hart, *The Power of Congress to Limit the Jurisdiction of Federal Courts: An Exercise in Dialectic,* 66 Harv.L.Rev. 1362, 1386–96 (1953). Moreover, they are manifestly out of step with modern developments in constitutional law. But, at least as to first-time entrants, they continue to be viewed as the foundation of settled doctrine. *See, e.g., Landon v. Plasencia,* 459 U.S. 21, 103 S.Ct. 321, 74 L.Ed.2d 21 (1982).

Several rationales could conceivably justify the border/interior distinction. Indeed, two dissenting Justices in the first case to rule on the constitutionality of a deportation statute, *Fong Yue Ting v. United States,* 149 U.S. 698, 13 S.Ct. 1016, 37 L.Ed. 905 (1893), offered different theories as to why constitutional limits should apply to exercises of the deportation power but not the exclusion power. *See* pp. 27–35 *supra.*

Justice Brewer offered a *territorial* justification: the Constitution has no extraterritorial effect and thus aliens who are at the border but have not entered cannot claim its protection. Consider David Martin's critique of this theory:

> [The territorial] approach * * * requires an almost willful shutting of one's eyes to physical realities. In modern exclusion cases * * * the aliens involved will have been physically well inside the border for a significant period of time, either residing in detention facilities managed by the INS or else "paroled" into the United States * * *. More importantly, aliens in exclusion proceedings of whatever kind (as distinguished from those overseas in our consulates applying for permission to travel here) have always been at least within the territorial waters, even if they are detained on board ship while awaiting the admission decision.

Martin, *supra,* at 179.

Chief Justice Fuller, also dissenting in *Fong Yue Ting,* offered a second possible justification for the border/interior distinction. He argued that deportation, unlike exclusion, entailed the "deprivation of that which has been lawfully acquired." 149 U.S. at 762, 13 S.Ct. at 1041. In modern constitutional terms, one can interpret this statement in at least two ways. First, this rationale might be seen as an appeal to the "right-privilege" distinction. Second, we might read Fuller's statement as calling attention to the material and social *stake* that a resident alien has established in this country.

Neither interpretation, however, seems to sustain the current doctrine. First, it is unclear how we can distinguish an alien at the border from a resident alien in terms of rights or privileges. If we view a resident alien as having gained an entitlement to remain in the United States, at what point was such an entitlement acquired? One *could* choose the point of admission, but it is hardly obvious that this is a better point than, say, the time an immigrant visa is granted. Taking the earlier time, of course, would give us no cause for distinguishing some first-time entrants (that is, aliens who appear at the border with duly-issued visas) from permanent resident aliens (although it may give us good reason for distinguishing lawfully admitted aliens from surreptitious entrants—something that the current border/interior line does not.)

Alternatively, if we start by viewing the initial entrant as having only a privilege to enter this country, again it is not clear how we can distinguish the permanent resident alien. If entry is a privilege extended by a beneficent sovereign, what transmutes that act of grace into a right merely because an alien has accepted it? That is, is not the continued stay of an admitted alien also an act of grace that can be revoked at the sovereign's pleasure? *See Harisiades v. Shaughnessy,* 342 U.S. 580, 586–87, 72 S.Ct. 512, 517, 96 L.Ed. 586 (1952) (alien's stay in the United States "is not his right but is a matter of permission and tolerance").

If the "right-privilege distinction" is inadequate in explaining the current doctrine, perhaps the notion of "stake" can help us: in deciding what process is "due" an alien, it is permissible to take into account that alien's identification with, or ties to, the American community. This justification would recognize that permanent resident aliens have penetrated near to the core of American society; they have jobs, friends, and associations that often make them nearly indistinguishable from citizens. These substantial ties, so the argument might run, justify affording permanent resident aliens substantial process before we take that which has been "lawfully acquired" from them. Such reasoning also supports lesser protections for initial entrants—that is, those aliens who have not yet acquired a substantial stake in this society.

Although the "stake" theory may have a great deal of plausibility, it unfortunately cannot explain the way the Court has developed the border/interior distinction. Recall that under the current doctrine, an undocumented surreptitious entrant is granted greater protections than an alien who arrives at the border holding an immigrant visa. Furthermore it cannot explain *Mezei*: Mezei was a returning lawful resident who had a wife and family in this country.

These considerations lead us to suggest that the border/interior distinction be discarded. It is a nineteenth-century doctrine searching in vain for a twentieth century justification. A call for abandonment, however, should be coupled with an alternative proposal. We believe that a reasonable alternative could be based on the "stake" theory described above. The following is David Martin's development of such a theory:

> [T]he basic intuition * * * might be [stated] as follows: * * * we, as a national community, somehow *owe less* in the coin of procedural assurances to the first-time applicant for admission than we do to our fellow citizens or to permanent resident aliens,

or even to regular nonimmigrants who have been among us for awhile. This is not necessarily to say that we owe nothing; that would be to repeat the mistakes of *Knauff* and *Mezei*. Instead it is simply to assert that established community ties, which exist to varying degrees with respect to different categories of aliens, ought to count in deciding what process is due. Or perhaps the intuition is more accurately stated the other way around. We *owe more* procedural guarantees—a greater assurance of scrupulous factual accuracy—to citizens and permanent resident aliens than we do to aliens at the threshold of entry into the national community.

* * *

* * * [I]t is not novel to suggest that special, heightened obligations may grow up as a result of particular relationships. Families furnish the central examples, but other relationships, such as residence in the same neighborhood or town, or membership in the same organization, may also give rise to special obligations. We might, for example, justly criticize a neighbor for failing to join in a Saturday work session called to clean up litter along an adjoining highway. Even though he may never have agreed to be available for such efforts, we might consider that he has failed to meet an obligation that attaches simply because of our relation as neighbors. That obligation might, of course, be excused, and in this context, a far weaker reason than what is required to relieve some duty in the context of the family might suffice. Nevertheless, it is meaningful to consider that, absent valid excuse, he owes it to the neighbors to take part. Above all, we feel confident that he would not incur the same criticism if he failed to join a similar clean-up effort in the next county, even if he happened to learn of it well in advance. In those circumstances, no relevant relationship exists giving rise to an equivalent obligation.

* * *

To a significant degree, these relational obligations are linked to the concept of community. That concept is not a simple one, and there is a continuing dispute in the philosophical and sociological literature as to whether communities are mainly purposive or organic, whether they spring from common purposes and devotion to the same principles or instead derive from a shared history or a coincidence of sentiment fostered by organic historical development. We need not choose among these contending positions, but instead need only note the possible relevance of both principle and sentiment in the creation and maintenance of a community, including a national community. In either case, a large part of what we mean by "community" is that relational obligations exist and are to be honored. We may use the language of community instrumentally, for example as part of our appeal to a recalcitrant neighbor to join a clean-up crew: "This is a community effort" or "This is going to benefit the whole community." More to the point, if we describe a neighborhood as a community, rather than simply as a geographical location, we probably mean that this kind of interaction and sharing—this recognition and fulfillment of reciprocal obligations—takes place here.

We have long applied to the nation exactly this language of community. For example, in 1875, in *Minor v. Happersett*, [88 U.S. (21 Wall.) 162 (1875),] the Supreme Court was called upon to construe the meaning of the term "citizen" as used in the Constitution. In the course of concluding that the word conveys "the idea of membership of a nation, and nothing more," the Court wrote: "There cannot be a nation without a people. The very idea of a political community, such as a nation is, implies an association of persons for the promotion of their general welfare." The hallmark of this community, the Court recognized, is the concept of reciprocal obligations: "Each one of the persons associated becomes a member of the nation formed by the association. He *owes* it allegiance and is *entitled* to its protection."

* * *

* * * [O]ur notions of membership in the national community are more complex and multi-layered than can be captured in the concept of citizenship alone. The innermost members may be the only ones entitled to vote and hold office. But permanent resident aliens, members in the next wider circle of concentric communities that make up the nation—if one may indulge that image—are entitled by virtue of that membership alone to enter fully into virtually all other aspects of community life. * * *

Beyond the circle of permanent resident aliens, the mere fact of common residence, even illegal residence, establishes a certain measure of community membership. Undocumented aliens may of course be denied many benefits required to be extended to lawful permanent residents, but as to other advantages of life in this political community, denial is not allowed. * * *

In sum, it is common to recognize different levels of community membership, and to affirm that "the class of aliens is itself a heterogeneous multitude of persons with a wide-ranging variety of ties to this country." [*Mathews v. Diaz*, 426 U.S. 67, 78–79 (1976).] Or as the Court wrote in *Johnson v. Eisentrager* [, 339 U.S. 763, 770 (1950)]: "The alien, to whom the United States has been traditionally hospitable, has been accorded a generous and ascending scale of rights as he increases his identity with our society." * * * Levels of membership, then, may properly play a role in assessing what process is due, at least for purposes of decisions on the transcendent question of membership itself—which is what exclusion or deportation cases * * * constitute.

Martin, *supra,* at 191–95, 201–04.[9]

9. Consider Alex Aleinikoff's response to Martin:

[W]hat exactly is the "national community," and how is it that anyone—

Interestingly, the reasonableness of this line of analysis is supported, in part, by the case law itself. While the Supreme Court has continued to pay verbal homage to the border/interior distinction, in fact, the results of its cases approximate the doctrinal reorientation we propose.

Yamataya and its progeny make clear that permanent resident aliens are entitled to substantial protections under the due process clause. This accords with our approach, which recognizes the substantial ties to American society that permanent resident aliens are likely to develop. What about returning resident aliens? In our view, the fact that an alien has travelled abroad (so long as he or she has not abandoned residence here) does not generally affect the ties he or she has with this country. Accord-

citizen or alien—indicates his or her attachment to it? Professor Martin's notion of community begins with personal relationships and a neighborhood street-cleaning effort and quickly moves to a national community of persons united in a common commitment to the general welfare. I am not convinced that this shift can be made so easily. The idea of a political community sharing similar ideas of the meaning of membership and the scope of the common enterprise does not aptly describe a nation as diverse, as pluralistic as the United States. * * * Perhaps at some very abstract level, we can define a set of principles that most members of American society share, such as representative government or a rule of law. But is it not likely that aliens present in this country, or seeking entry, also share these values?

Furthermore, how do we measure commitment to the "national community? " Can one make reasonable assumptions about the level of commitment that various classes of aliens and citizens have to the American community? It is hardly clear that citizens, by the simple fact of birth in the United States, are any more committed, more loyal, to a "national community" than are aliens, most of whom have had to overcome substantial burdens to come to the United States. * * *

* * *

It seems that the problem is not so much in accepting Professor Martin's intuition that we "owe less in the coin of procedural assurances to the first-time applicant for admission than we do to our fellow citizens or to permanent resident aliens." Rather, it is trying to elaborate on that intuition in terms of membership in a national community. It is my belief that our intuition does not depend upon inchoate notions of mem-

bership. I think it is more easily explained as a generalization about the stake that certain groups of aliens have in entering or residing in the United States or in not being returned to their country of origin. In short, whereas Professor Martin would examine the notion of *community,* I would look at *community ties.* * * *

* * * The notion of "community ties," to me, indicates the actual relationships the individual has developed with a society: a family, friends, a job, association memberships, professional acquaintances, opportunities. "Community" is a more amorphous concept. It connotes a sense of identification with others as a group, a sense of common enterprise, a belief in the value of shared experiences and a shared future. Community ties are almost tangible; we can see interactions among people and membership in complex social and financial arrangements. But to see "community," we must catch a glimpse of the *Zeitgeist,* we must peer into people's hearts.

* * * [T]he "community ties" approach is consistent with our intuitional model of a description of aliens and citizens as falling within concentric circles. Although I have argued that viewing the circles as levels of "membership" is not sound, I believe that one can appropriately view the circles as proxies for the different kinds and degrees of community ties that persons in each circle are likely to have developed. Thus, citizens, in the innermost circle, are likely to have the greatest stake in remaining in the United States. Permanent resident aliens occupy the next circle, since they have had opportunities to find employment, make friends, and join community groups. An alien seeking entry for the first time is likely to be able to demonstrate far fewer existing ties to the community.

Aleinikoff, *supra,* at 240–45.

ingly, we believe that *Mezei* was wrongly reasoned and should be overruled. Although the Court has stopped short of overruling *Mezei,* not much of it appears to be left; *Plasencia* expressly states that returning residents "can invoke the Due Process Clause on returning to this country." 459 U.S. 21, 32, 103 S.Ct. 321, 329, 74 L.Ed.2d 21 (1982).[10]

Nor do we disagree with the Court's conclusion that lesser constitutional protections apply for initial entrants than resident aliens. Such a result is consistent with our analysis. We do take issue, however, with the statement for which *Knauff* is famous: that due process at the border is whatever Congress decides to give the alien. As a matter of common sense, one cannot take these words at face value. "[T]he Court really could not have meant *carte blanche* for Congress in the treatment of excludable aliens. Surely, had Congress revived trial by ordeal, or the ducking stool, or gladiatorial contests as the procedures for deciding who could enter, the Court—even the Court of the early 1950's—would have found a way to strike down such a practice." Martin, *supra,* at 173. Furthermore, we can see no reason why the United States government should be entirely free from core principles of fair play when acting on persons clearly within the borders of this country and subject to its jurisdiction. It is difficult to find an analogy to this hands-off approach in modern constitutional law, and we see nothing in the nature of the immigration process that demands a complete exception to general norms of due process.

Accordingly, while our theory may give the government substantial flexibility at the border when deciding whether aliens should be permitted to make an initial entry, we see no justification for the *Knauff* principle that Congress is free to do as it wishes. Again, *Plasencia* is significant. On the surface, it unfortunately reaffirms the holding of *Knauff* that "an alien seeking initial admission to the United States requests a privilege and has no constitutional rights regarding his application, for the power to admit or exclude aliens is a sovereign prerogative." 459 U.S. at 32, 103 S.Ct. at 329. At a more fundamental level, however, there is much in the opinion that not only undermines *Knauff*, but also signals adoption of a "stake" theory. Consider Hiroshi Motomura's analysis:

> * * * *Plasencia* was an important milestone because it opened the door for others, with less connection to the United States than returning permanent residents, to raise procedural due process claims. * * * [T]he basic concepts underlying *Plasencia* were simply too difficult to cabin. The statutory exclusion-deportation line was not constitutionally determinative, but rather aliens enjoyed degrees of "entitlement"—and in turn degrees of access to procedural due process rights—depending on the nature and extent of their attachment to the United States. *Plasencia* thus introduced a new analytical framework, allowing aliens to raise procedural due process claims that would have been futile before *Goldberg v. Kelly*. * * * Especially in the growing number of

10. The Court in *Plasencia* stated that it "need not now decide the scope of *Mezei;* it does not govern this case, for Plasencia was absent from the country only a few days, and the United States has conceded that she has a right to due process." 459 U.S. at 34, 103 S.Ct. at 330.

detention cases, aliens—including first-time entrants—could argue that statutes or other expressions of government policy gave them expectations of admission that qualified as "property" or "liberty" interests, which therefore entitled them to procedural due process protection under the three-factor *Eldridge* test. Judges were increasingly forced to reconcile the conflict between the new due process paradigm and the old way of thinking, typified by * * * *Knauff* * * *. With *Plasencia*, the procedural due process exception to the plenary power doctrine, for so long of more formal than practical import, began to take on real meaning.

Motomura, *The Curious Evolution of Immigration Law: Procedural Surrogates for Substantive Constitutional Rights*, 92 Colum.L.Rev. 1625, 1655–56 (1992).

Of course, to say that the due process clause applies at the border is not to say what process is due an initial entrant. That issue is usually considered within the three-part framework established by *Mathews v. Eldridge, see* p. 405 *supra*. In applying his analysis to initial entrants, David Martin has concluded:

> [E]xcludable aliens enjoy some measure of shared membership in a relevant community, simply by virtue of their common humanity and physical presence in our territorial jurisdiction. In short, they are not strangers to the Constitution. As human beings, they deserve fulfillment of the promise held out by *Yick Wo* [*v. Hopkins*; see p. 18 *supra*] and by the due process clause itself, which applies, in terms, to "persons." * * * [But while the] excludable alien is not a constitutional stranger, * * * he is not quite intimate family, either. The *Yick Wo* tradition is not offended by appropriately limited recognition of this distinction, so long as it affects only the gradation of due process protection and does not serve to cut off protection altogether. * * *

* * *

What is the minimum, then, that fairness should allow as to first-time applicants for admission? It is always hazardous to lay down a procedural code that purports to describe the content of due process in a particular context, because, as Judge Friendly has remarked, a legislative decision to improve one out of a list of safeguards might justify a reduction in other safeguards without transgressing basic fairness. Nevertheless, in most circumstances, aliens at the threshold of entry probably may insist upon the following: an unbiased decision-maker, notice of the proceedings and of the general grounds asserted by the government for denial of admission; a meaningful opportunity to dispute or overcome those grounds, orally or in writing; and a statement of reasons, even if oral and summary, for any adverse decision. Above all, courts should remain open to the legitimacy of highly informal adjudication of claims lodged by first-time applicants for admission. Assuming that the alien has had a real opportunity, however informal, to be heard on the crucial determinations—an opportunity missing in both *Knauff* and *Mezei*—courts should not generally import trial-type procedures or require heavily adversarial proceedings.

Martin, *supra*, at 216, 218–19.

Consider Alex Aleinikoff's response:

> The problem [with Martin's analysis] is that no distinction is made among immigrant, non-immigrant and undocumented aliens at the border. All are lumped together apparently because they have not yet lived in the national community; we "owe" them less because they have not been among us, we have not gotten to know or care about them. To me, however, these classes of aliens present distinct issues. To be granted an immigrant visa an alien must normally demonstrate that he or she has a close family relative in this country or is coming to perform a needed job. Generally, someone in the United States—a relative or employer—must have filed a petition on the alien's behalf. Aliens arriving with immigrant visas are entitled to stay as long as they wish (subject to deportation for misconduct). In short, they usually come to this country with a pre-existing stake awaiting them and with an intention to make the United States their permanent home. Most aliens entering the country with non-immigrant visas, on the other hand, come here as temporary visitors with a fixed time limit on their stays. Many must demonstrate that they have "no intention of abandoning" their residence in a foreign country. To be sure, non-immigrants may come with important business to conduct or studies to pursue; but generally the harm imposed upon a non-immigrant wrongfully denied entry is likely to be far less than an immigrant wrongfully excluded.

> Since undocumented aliens do not generally reveal their intentions when stopped at the border (unless they claim asylum), it is unclear what stake they may have in entry. They may have family here with whom they seek to live or may simply be seeking a short-term job. But another of the *Mathews* factors applies here: the likelihood that alternative procedures will produce fewer errors. Absence of a visa and a valid unexpired passport are grounds of exclusion. Thus it is unlikely that an undocumented alien—unless he or she claims asylum—will be able to establish eligibility to enter the United States no matter how many procedural rights are provided.

> Whether these differences in "personal stake" demand different procedures at the border as a constitutional matter requires careful analysis of the other elements of the *Mathews v. Eldridge* test: the increased accuracy of alternative procedures and the government's interest (including fiscal and administrative burdens). But these factors must be evaluated under Professor Martin's analysis as well. My only purpose here is to suggest that Martin's test of "membership in a national community" does not

seem to capture adequately relevant differences among classes of aliens seeking first-time entry.

Aleinikoff, *supra*, at 246–47.

In sum, while your three authors may disagree on particular applications of the general theory, we are in firm agreement that procedural due process analysis in immigration law should be fundamentally reoriented. The border/interior distinction, which has held sway since the 1950's, is based on no plausible rationale and is out of step with modern notions of due process. Happily, our approach, which focuses on the relationship of the alien to the community of which he is a part or which he seeks to join, requires more of a shift in judicial explanation than in result: the Court has moved away from the distinction without admitting it. It is time for the Court to go the final step and overrule *Knauff* and *Mezei*.

Are you convinced? What does our theory say about the due process rights of undocumented aliens residing in the United States? *See* Martin, *supra*, at 230–34 (treating them, for constitutional due process purposes, the same as first-time applicants at the border).

A Concluding Dialogue

Believer: You said we should talk again at the end of the deportation chapter and here we are.

Cynic: Yes. Have you read the essay just above?

Believer: Yes.

Cynic: Then you understand that my proposal for a unified immigration proceeding raises no serious constitutional issues.

Believer: It doesn't appear to. But are you suggesting that Congress ought to give all aliens the same hearing procedures?

Cynic: Not at all. I don't think that an alien who can make no colorable claim to be here should receive legal counsel at government expense or other extensive protections to help him contest deportability. There are real costs to guaranteeing a perfect process for all aliens. I would save limited resources for those who need them most—those who have acquired a substantial stake by their presence here.

Believer: What about resident undocumented aliens? Many have lived here for years and have substantial ties to our community. Would you take away from them what the law now guarantees?

Cynic: Due process applies, of course. But nothing in the due process clause prohibits putting the initial burden on the alien to show a prima facie right to be here. This would require the alien to proffer a valid visa, an I–94, a green card, some other form of documentation, or some reasonable explanation why such documents do not exist. It's not clear to me how a lawyer would help much here.

Believer: I'm not so sure. A lawyer could inform the alien of various avenues of relief available and could also warn the alien about the consequences of making certain statements.

Cynic: True. But, under current regulations, the immigration judge must often notify an alien of appropriate forms of relief from deportation.[11] And aliens are presently warned after the issuance of an order to show cause that anything they say may be used against them.[12] If after notification, an undocumented (and, hence, deportable) alien requests a form of relief and makes some showing of a reasonable probability of prevailing, then the alien should receive representation where the immigration judge determines counsel could be helpful in presenting the alien's claim. Certainly this would seem to satisfy *Mathews v. Eldridge*.

Believer: Sounds reasonable. You've made a believer out of me.

Questions

Did Believer give in too easily? Should he have been more cynical?

11. 8 C.F.R. § 242.17(a).   **12.** 8 C.F.R. § 287.3.

Chapter Seven

RELIEF FROM DEPORTATION

From 1981 to 1993 the INS averaged over one million apprehensions a year of aliens believed to be deportable. 1993 INS Statistical Yearbook, Table 58. Of these, only about 20,000 per year were actually deported (less than two percent of those apprehended). What happened to the other 98 percent? In some of the cases the INS decided not to initiate proceedings; in others the immigration judge determined that the government did not prove deportability; and in others the alien disappeared before or after the entry of an order of deportation. But these factors account for only a small part of the difference between apprehensions and deportations. The most significant factor is that the vast majority of deportable aliens are given the opportunity to leave the country *before* the issuance of a deportation order. For the years 1981 to 1993, an average of over 900,000 aliens per year chose this option, known as "voluntary departure." 1993 INS Statistical Yearbook, Table 59. Furthermore, each year thousands of aliens avoid deportation by taking advantage of one of a number of provisions in the INA that permit aliens, under specified conditions, to regularize their status.

This Chapter will examine the various provisions in the INA that provide relief from deportation. In the majority of deportation hearings, the eligibility for such relief is the only issue: the alien will concede deportability at the outset of the hearing and then request some form of relief from deportation. In examining these sometimes overlapping and highly discretionary forms of relief, ask yourself whether a more coherent process could be created to limit arbitrariness of implementation without sacrificing the flexibility needed to respond to humanitarian concerns.

SECTION A. VOLUNTARY DEPARTURE

1. WHY VOLUNTARY DEPARTURE?

If voluntary departure didn't exist we would have to invent it. The willingness of hundreds of thousands of aliens to waive a deportation hearing and leave the United States before a date certain saves the government untold enforcement resources. Indeed, it is a virtual certainty that the immigration system in this country would break down if all aliens who were apprehended as deportable were to request the deportation hearing the INA provides them.

This may explain why the government would desire a mechanism like voluntary departure. However, voluntary departure has a darker side as well: one court found and issued a permanent injunction against INS practices that coerced aliens into accepting voluntary departure to prevent them from applying for some other benefit—such as asylum—for which they might be eligible.[1] *Orantes-Hernandez v. Meese,* 685 F.Supp. 1488, 1511 (C.D.Cal.1988), *aff'd sub nom. Orantes–Hernandez v. Thornburgh,* 919 F.2d 549 (9th Cir.1990).

Why, though, would an alien voluntarily choose to leave instead of forcing the government to prove its case in a deportation hearing under the *Woodby* standard of clear, convincing and unequivocal evidence?

It is usual to answer this question by pointing to several provisions in the INA that create a legal incentive for the alien to choose voluntary departure. First and foremost is the fact that aliens who leave the country under an order of deportation and want to re-enter within five years after

---

1. The part of the injunction addressing voluntary departure reads as follows:

* * * IT IS HEREBY ORDERED that defendants, their agents and successors in office are permanently enjoined as follows:

1. Defendants shall not employ threats, misrepresentation, subterfuge or other forms of coercion, or in any other way attempt to persuade or dissuade class members when informing them of the availability of voluntary departure pursuant to INA § 242(b). The prohibited acts include, but are not limited to:

(a) Misrepresenting the meaning of political asylum and giving improper and incomplete legal advice to detained class members;

(b) Telling class members that if they apply for asylum they will remain in detention for a long period of time, without mentioning the possibility of release on bond or indicating that bond can be lowered by an immigration judge and that there are bond agencies which can provide assistance;

(c) Telling Salvadoran detainees the amount of bond given to other class members, without indicating that the bond amount ultimately depends upon the circumstances of the individual class member;

(d) Telling class members that their asylum applications will be denied, that Salvadorans do not get asylum, or that asylum is only available to guerillas or soldiers;

(e) Representing to class members that the information on the asylum application will be sent to El Salvador;

(f) Representing to class members that asylum applicants will never be able to return to El Salvador;

(g) Indicating that Salvadoran detainees will be transferred to remote locations if they do not elect voluntary departure;

(h) Advising Salvadorans of the negative aspects of choosing a deportation hearing without informing them of the positive options that are available;

(i) Refusing to allow class members to contact an attorney; and

(j) Making daily announcements at detention facilities of the availability of voluntary departure.

* * *

2. At the time any class member is processed, whether or not he or she is automatically processed for a hearing, Defendants shall inform the class member of the existence of his or her rights to be represented by an attorney, to request a deportation hearing, and to apply for political asylum. For those class members who are informed of the availability of voluntary departure pursuant to INA § 242(b), such notice shall be given before voluntary departure is discussed. * * *

deportation must obtain the Attorney General's permission to re-apply for admission. An alien who returns without such permission is excludable, *see* INA § 212(a)(6)(B), may in some circumstances be deported under summary procedures, *see* INA § 242(f), and is subject to a felony prosecution, *see* INA § 276. None of these provisions applies to an alien who voluntarily departs at his own expense before the entry of an order of deportation. Second, voluntary departure permits an alien to depart to a country of his choice (assuming that country will accept him). Furthermore, it saves him the potential expense, delay, and embarrassment of a deportation hearing.

While these statutorily based reasons no doubt account for many decisions to opt for voluntary departure, it is widely believed that a very different kind of factor plays the dominant role: the inability (or unwillingness) of the United States government to stop the surreptitious entry of aliens across the border. The vast majority of aliens granted voluntary departure are arrested for entering without inspection, and most have no colorable claim of lawful residence. Many of these aliens would rather accept the government's offer of a ride over the border than stay and fight deportation. As you will recall from the materials in Chapter Three, their chances of effecting another surreptitious entry are far greater than successfully contesting deportability in a hearing. The availability of voluntary departure, coupled with the realities of law enforcement and the rational decisions of aliens, creates a sequence at the border that is repeated over and over again: unlawful entry, apprehension, detention, return, and another unlawful entry.

2. THE STANDARDS FOR VOLUNTARY DEPARTURE

Two distinct sections of the statute, INA §§ 242(b) and 244(e), authorize the Attorney General to grant voluntary departure. At this point you should study these provisions. What is the difference between them? Why does the statute include both?

In answering these questions, it might help you to know that by regulation the Attorney General has delegated her authority under the two provisions to different classes of immigration officials. Under INA § 242(b), aliens not yet in deportation hearings may be granted relief by, *inter alia*, district directors, district officers who are in charge of investigations, officers in charge, and chief patrol agents. 8 C.F.R. § 242.5(a)(1). Relief under § 244(e), available after the beginning of a deportation hearing, is granted by an immigration judge. 8 C.F.R. §§ 242.17(b), 244.1.

An alien is ineligible for voluntary departure who within the previous five years has failed to leave on time pursuant to a grant of voluntary departure (barring "exceptional circumstances"), failed to appear at a properly noticed deportation or asylum hearing, or failed to report for deportation. *See* INA § 242B(e). Also, any alien who is deportable because of an aggravated felony conviction is ineligible for voluntary departure. *See* INA § 244(e)(2). (As discussed later in this Chapter, such aliens are also barred for five years from certain other forms of discretionary relief, including adjustment of status and suspension of deportation.)

Although the overwhelming number of grants of voluntary departure are made to effect the return of undocumented aliens who entered without inspection, voluntary departure is also used to permit some aliens to *stay* in the United States for a period of time without being subject to deportation proceedings. Thus, by regulation, an alien who is an immediate relative of a United States citizen or who has applied for an immigrant visa and has "a priority date for an immigrant visa not more than 60 days later than the date shown in the latest Visa Office Bulletin," may be granted voluntary departure (*i.e.*, permission to remain here) "until the American consul is ready to issue an immigrant visa." 8 C.F.R. § 242.5(a)(2)(vi)(C), (3). When the visa becomes available the alien may either leave the United States not subject to an order of deportation, pick up the visa overseas and return as a lawful immigrant, or in many cases adjust his status to permanent resident without having to leave the United States.

Perhaps the most startling, and controversial, form of voluntary departure was "extended voluntary departure" (EVD). This inelegant bit of Newspeak really meant extended voluntary non-departure, which the INS granted primarily to aliens who would otherwise be returned to countries undergoing civil war or other breakdowns in public order. The Immigration Act of 1990 Act replaced EVD with a similar device known as "temporary protected status" (TPS), which has been granted of late to aliens from Bosnia–Herzegovina, Liberia, Rwanda, and Somalia. Aliens from El Salvador formerly enjoyed TPS, which was replaced by a similar status known as "deferred enforced departure" (DED), which in turn expired December 31, 1994. *See* 59 Fed.Reg. 62751 (1994). Chapter Eight will treat TPS and DED in more detail.

In our examination of the various forms of relief from deportation, we will see that the granting of relief under both § 242(b) and § 244(e) usually involves two aspects: the meeting of statutory prerequisites for the relief and a favorable exercise of discretion by the Attorney General.

CAMPOS-GRANILLO v. INS

United States Court of Appeals, Ninth Circuit, 1993.
12 F.3d 849.

REINHARDT, CIRCUIT JUDGE:

* * *

Petitioner Carlos Adolfo Campos–Granillo is a 28–year-old citizen of Mexico who has resided in the United States almost continuously since June of 1983. He is married and has three children, all of whom live in the United States with him.[1] In April 1991, the INS issued Campos–Granillo an Order to Show Cause for entering the United States without inspection. He conceded deportability and filed an application for suspension of deportation under INA § 244(a)(1). In the alternative, he requested voluntary

---

1. His wife and the children (ages 10, 8, and 6 at the time of the hearing) are also Mexican citizens. They entered the U.S. in 1986 without inspection to live with petitioner. Petitioner paid an individual $300 to help them enter this country.

departure under INA § 244(e). Campos–Granillo received a hearing before an Immigration Judge.

At the hearing, Campos–Granillo testified that he had entered the United States in 1983 without inspection and that he had subsequently made several brief departures to Mexico.[4] Aside from those brief visits, however, Campos–Granillo had lived in this country uninterruptedly for eight years at the time of the hearing. His wife, children, and friends all reside within the United States, and Campos–Granillo testified that he had no close ties in Mexico. He has never been convicted of any felony.

During the suspension of deportation[a] phase of the hearing, the IJ found Campos–Granillo to be honest, law-abiding, and a person of good moral character. She stated:

> I have observed the respondent. I do believe he's been truthful during this hearing *and has no desire to necessarily disobey the laws if he can help it.*

She also concluded: "He would appear to qualify under the good moral character statutory requirement." Nonetheless, she found Campos–Granillo to be statutorily ineligible for suspension of deportation because he had not been physically present in the United States continuously for seven years. Campos–Granillos [*sic*] does not appeal this finding of statutory ineligibility.

During the voluntary departure phase of the hearing, Campos–Granillo testified that he would leave the United States voluntarily by the designated date if he were granted such relief. He also testified that he would try to return to the United States through legal means only and that he "will not think of" returning illegally. Finally, he testified that he had sufficient funds to finance his departure.

Despite Campos–Granillo's testimony and his good moral character, the IJ denied Campos–Granillo's request for voluntary departure as a matter of discretion. She based her decision primarily on a single phrase in his testimony—"I would have to return"—which she interpreted to mean that he would come back illegally.[7] She also gave consideration to

---

4. The dates and duration of his departures to Mexico were as follows: one month in April 1984, one and a half months in April 1985, one month in August 1985, and ten days in September 1985. Campos–Granillo testified that he was apprehended by the Border Patrol upon returning from his September 1985 departure and that he went back to Mexico. Nothing in the record indicates that a deportation proceeding was initiated, however, and he was not incarcerated. He returned to the United States three days after the incident.

a. Suspension of deportation is a form of relief from deportation provided by INA § 244, which we will discuss in detail later in this Chapter.—eds.

7. The following exchange took place between the government's attorney and peti-

tioner during the hearing: Q. Sir, if you leave this country, are you going to leave your wife and children behind or are you going to take them with you? A. It will be difficult. I have not thought about it yet because it will be difficult. If we ... if I return to Mexico, I don't have anything over there. Q. Well, if you go to Mexico, will you just come back through the hills again then as soon as you can? Like you've done before? A. I would try to obtain a document like I've been thinking about it because *I will not think of returning that way.* Q. Is it your understanding you can't get a green card if you don't get one here today? A. You mean that I know of? Q. Yes. A. *I don't know a lot about laws, but I would try to find a way through my work or through other people.* Q. Well, sir, if you're in Mexico and you find out you can't

his immigration history. Accordingly, the IJ ordered Campos–Granillo deported to Mexico.

Campos–Granillo filed an appeal with the BIA. The Board dismissed the appeal, affirming the IJ's judgment on both the suspension of deportation issue as well as the voluntary departure issue. Before this court, Campos–Granillo challenges only the voluntary departure order.

* * *

Where the BIA does not perform an independent review of the IJ's decision and instead defers to the IJ's exercise of his or her discretion, it is the IJ's decision that we review. In this case, the BIA merely listed factors that are generally considered in deportation hearings and ultimately deferred to the IJ's exercise of her discretion. * * *

* * *

Although administrative agencies have great latitude in exercising their discretion to grant or deny requests for voluntary departure, such discretion does not "strip the inquiry of all guideposts." *Mabugat v. INS*, 937 F.2d 426, 432 (9th Cir.1991). One such guidepost is the requirement that the agency "must weigh both favorable and unfavorable factors." *De la Luz v. INS*, 713 F.2d 545, 545 (9th Cir.1983).[8] The IJ is required to weigh favorable and unfavorable factors by "evaluat[ing] all of them, assigning weight or importance to each one separately and then to all of them cumulatively." *In re Edwards*, Interim Decision No. 3134 (available on Westlaw, 1990 WL 385757, FIM–BIA database), 1990 BIA LEXIS 8, at *22 (BIA 1990) (Morris, concurring). Mere conclusory statements by the IJ are insufficient—the reviewing court must see that the petitioner's claims have been "heard, considered, and decided." *Villanueva-Franco v. INS*, 802 F.2d 327, 330 (9th Cir.1986). This rule applies to the granting of discretionary relief in voluntary departure proceedings.

In this case, the record shows that the IJ based her determination solely on factors that were unfavorable to the petitioner—Campos–Granillo's somewhat ambiguous statement that he "would have to come back" in the future and his immigration history. The IJ determined:

> [I]n granting even the minimal relief of voluntary departure, I must consider [Campos–Granillo's] answers that were given during the relief phase of suspension as well as voluntary departure.

get a green card, and you can't come back ... legally, are you going to come through the hills again? A. My children will have to remain here because they will not be able to adapt in Mexico, and *I would have to return*. Based on this exchange, the IJ concluded that "the Court can only interpret that to mean that he would come back illegally."

8. Favorable factors include: family ties within the United States; residence of long duration in this country, particularly if residence began at a young age; hardship to the petitioner or petitioner's family if relief is not granted; service in the United States armed forces; a history of employment; the existence of business or property ties; evidence of value and service to the community; proof of rehabilitation if a criminal record exists; and other evidence attesting to good character.

Unfavorable factors include: the nature and underlying circumstances of the exclusion or deportation ground at issue; additional violations of the immigration laws; the existence, seriousness, and recency of any criminal record; and other evidence of bad character or the undesirability of the applicant as a permanent resident.

The respondent has a pattern of coming and going illegally. He also had his family smuggled into the United States and has now also stated that, if he cannot return legally, he will return through the hills because his family is here. I cannot condone that type of action since it is a violation of Immigration Laws.

Although the IJ had mentioned some favorable factors (e.g., Campos–Granillo's good moral character, his honesty, and his desire to obey the law) when determining that he was ineligible for suspension of deportation, there is no indication in her opinion that she considered *any* of those factors when deciding the voluntary departure issue. In the absence of a clear demonstration that the IJ considered both the positive and negative factors when making her discretionary decision not to grant voluntary departure, we are required to vacate and remand.

We note the critical nature of Campos–Granillo's somewhat ambiguous statement that he "will have to return." On remand, the IJ must evaluate that statement in light of Campos–Granillo's other statements about his desire to comply with the law. She must show that her interpretation is supported and not contradicted by the rest of the record. If, after making such an analysis, she once again determines that Campos–Granillo's statement means that he intends to return to this country *illegally*, then she must weigh that conclusion along with all of the other favorable and unfavorable factors in this case when exercising her discretion with respect to granting or denying voluntary departure.

* * *

We VACATE the BIA's order affirming the IJ's denial of Campos–Granillo's petition for voluntary departure, and we REMAND for proceedings not inconsistent with this opinion. * * *

* * *

Notes

1. On remand, can the immigration judge address the Ninth Circuit's concerns by simply providing a fuller account of her rationale for denying voluntary departure?

2. Lest you believe that federal courts readily overturn decisions by immigration judges and the BIA to deny voluntary departure, compare *Campos-Granillo* with *Carnejo-Molina v. INS*, 649 F.2d 1145 (5th Cir. 1981). Rosa Carnejo–Molina, a citizen of Chile, had entered the United States several times using a fraudulently obtained United States passport. In her deportation proceedings, she raised an evidentiary issue and requested a waiver of deportation and voluntary departure. The immigration judge found against her on all three issues, and she appealed. The Fifth Circuit rejected her claim that the immigration judge had not considered all favorable equities, among them that she had no criminal convictions or welfare history. The court concluded: "the judge exercised discretion in a manner that was neither arbitrary nor capricious, and * * * his decision

and that of the Board were supported by substantial evidence." *Id.* at 1151–52.

3. INA § 101(f) lists some persons who are *not* of "good moral character" (such as anyone convicted of an aggravated felony), but it doesn't give much of a clue as to what "good moral character" is. INA § 244(e) restricts voluntary departure to those who have been of "good moral character" for at least five years before applying. In *Hibbert v. INS,* 554 F.2d 17 (2d Cir.1977), the alien stressed that five years had passed since he had given the false testimony that made him not of "good moral character" under INA § 101(f). The Court responded: "The five-year period is not a statute of limitations; it is merely a threshold requirement for relief"; "It is necessary but not sufficient for a finding of good moral character." *Id.* at 20 & n.2. "Good moral character does not mean moral excellence and * * * is not destroyed by a 'single incident,'" but serious crimes are more than "'mere lapses.'" *Matter of Sanchez–Linn,* Int.Dec. 3156 (BIA 1991).

SECTION B.   PROSECUTORIAL DISCRETION

An alien who is deportable will not be deported if the government decides not to initiate proceedings against the alien. Decisions not to prosecute, which typically are said to fall under the heading of "prosecutorial discretion," may be based on a number of factors, such as lack of enforcement resources, compelling humanitarian concerns, or the imminent issuance of documentation that would regularize the alien's status. *See generally* Roberts, *The Exercise of Administrative Discretion Under the Immigration Laws,* 13 San Diego L. Rev. 144, 149–52 (1975).

This Section focuses on two formal acts of prosecutorial discretion: deferred action status and stays of deportation. You should be aware, however, that prosecutorial discretion is exercised in a more practically significant form in INS district offices every day, when decisions are made to target certain groups of aliens for deportation investigations (criminal aliens, for example), or to shift enforcement resources away from deportation altogether (to employer sanctions, for example).

The formal and informal exercise of prosecutorial discretion raises difficult issues, several of which are raised in the following materials. How does the agency establish uniformity of practice among several dozen district offices? Should an alien's ability to remain in the United States turn on the city in which he happens to reside? If the agency seeks to ameliorate potential arbitrariness by promulgating internal guidelines for the exercise of discretion, should those guidelines be enforceable by the courts?

1. DEFERRED ACTION STATUS

For a number of years, INS operated under an internal policy not to proceed against aliens presenting compelling humanitarian reasons to stay in the United States. INS placed such aliens in a "nonpriority" enforcement status—now generally known as "deferred action." Although the existence of the program was known, the actual guidelines used by INS to grant deferred action status did not come to light until the mid–1970's. The attorney for the alien responsible for the disclosure of the guidelines tells the story.

LEON WILDES, THE NONPRIORITY PROGRAM OF THE IMMIGRATION AND NATURALIZATION SERVICE GOES PUBLIC: THE LITIGATIVE USE OF THE FREEDOM OF INFORMATION ACT

14 San Diego L. Rev. 42, 42–49 (1976).

Had it not been for a certain rock musician and former *Beatle* named John Lennon, an article on the nonpriority program might never have been written. The research required a plaintiff willing to patiently await the outcome of numerous administrative requests for information and then to pursue a suit under the Freedom of Information Act (FOIA).[1] The entire program was so shrouded in secrecy that a former District Director of the Immigration and Naturalization Service (INS) actually denied the existence of the program. The *Operations Instruction* embodying the procedure was buried in the *Blue Sheets,* the INS internal regulations never made available to the public. The situation was a classic example of secret law.

* * *

Lennon came to the United States as a visitor in August 1971, and was permitted to remain until late February 1972. At that time the INS instituted deportation proceedings against him as an alleged overstay. Lennon claimed that the proceedings were instituted for political reasons. Among other things, he requested a grant of *nonpriority* status.

Nonpriority status is a euphemism for an administrative stay of deportation which effectively places an otherwise deportable alien in a position where he is not removed simply because his case has the lowest possible priority for INS action. Traditionally, the status was accorded to aliens whose departure from the United States would result in extreme hardship. Lennon and artist Yoko Ono, his wife, had come to this country to fight contested custody proceedings concerning Kyoko, Ono's daughter by a prior marriage. Lennon and Ono were completely successful on the law, with courts in several jurisdictions awarding them custody of Kyoko. However the father absconded with the child and could not be found. In the midst of the frantic search for the child, Lennon and Ono were subjected to expulsion proceedings. They felt, accordingly, that the equities involved in their continued search for the child justified the application for nonpriority status. Hardship notwithstanding, nonpriority status was never even given consideration, and the deportation proceedings relentlessly advanced.

Commencing on May 1, 1972, through extensive correspondence with the INS, Lennon made every conceivable effort to obtain the records relevant to nonpriority procedures before instituting suit in federal court.

1. 5 U.S.C.A. § 552 (1974).

However, after more than a year's correspondence, the records were not forthcoming. In fact, the Service stated that the data about nonpriority cases were "not compiled" although at no time did it deny the existence of either a nonpriority program or relevant records. Lennon's demands, made pursuant to the FOIA, continued until August 1973, with no response from the Service.

In his deportation proceedings, Lennon moved to depose a Government witness with knowledge of the program. His motion was rejected, however, because the immigration judge thought it irrelevant to any issue over which he could rule. Finally, when attempts to obtain the records through regular administrative channels failed, an action was instituted in district court, requesting injunctive relief pursuant to section (a)(3) of the FOIA. The suit was filed within a short time after filing a companion action against certain Government officials. The companion suit sought a hearing to determine whether such officials had conspired to prejudge an immigration case, to prejudge various applications for discretionary relief and the premature commencement of deportation proceedings against the plaintiff. Among the wrongs alleged was the Government's unexplained failure to consider Lennon's request for nonpriority classification.

* * *

When Lennon's FOIA action was instituted, the rules on nonpriority classification were contained in an INS *Operations Instruction* which was not available to the public. Subsequent to the action and as a direct result of it, this *Instruction* was transferred from the unpublished *Blue Sheets* to the published *White Sheets*.[17] The publication of this *Operations Instruction* was significant, for it was a formal, public acknowledgement by the INS that such a program existed. Even so, of much greater value to the litigant are the records of those cases in which nonpriority status was granted or denied. The records requested at the time of the action consisted of periodic reports by district directors. Each time a nonpriority decision was made the director had to record his reasons, forward his recommendation or decision to his regional commissioner, who then forwarded it to the Central Office in Washington, D.C., where an officer or a committee of officers acted on the decision and kept records.[18]

* * *

[In light of counsel's arguments for release of the records under the FOIA,] the Government decided that its most appropriate course would be to provide the plaintiff with the case histories of all extant approved nonpriority cases—1843 in number. Thus, for the first time, both the

---

17. The INS has available to the public in various district offices, including New York, and in the Central Office in Washington a volume containing the *Operations Instructions* of the INS for its employees. However, not all instructions are made available. Where a deletion has been made, Blue Sheets are inserted in the volume. * * * [The current version of the Operations Instructions as released to the public is available in Appendix volume 9 of GM & Y—eds.]

18. * * * [T]he *Operations Instruction* has recently been revised so that nonpriority applications are handled at the regional level rather than by a Central Office committee. This change was instituted on April 30, 1975, as a result of the litigation described herein.

procedures and the records of all known approved cases were made available to the public.[a]

The release of the INS Operations Instruction on deferred action status predictably led to claims by some aliens that the INS had violated its own regulations in denying their applications. Thus courts were forced to consider whether INS decisions taken pursuant to the Operations Instruction are reviewable; and, if so, what standard should be applied in reviewing agency refusals to confer the status.

The Operations Instruction, as originally drafted, provided that "[i]n every case where the District Director determines that adverse action would be unconscionable because of the existence of appealing humanitarian factors he *shall recommend* consideration for deferred action category." (Emphasis supplied.) The mandatory tenor of the language led the Ninth Circuit to conclude that the Instruction "far more closely resemble[d] a substantive provision for relief than an internal procedural guideline." *Nicholas v. INS,* 590 F.2d 802, 807 (9th Cir.1979). It therefore held that denials of deferred action status were subject to review—although the standard adopted by the court was highly deferential: "the decision of an INS District Director * * * will stand unless it so departs from an established pattern of treatment of others similarly situated without reason, as to be arbitrary and capricious, and an abuse of discretion." *Id.* at 808.

Other circuits rejected the *Nicholas* holding. Characterizing the O.I. as an internal guideline for the exercise of prosecutorial discretion, they concluded that it created no entitlement to deferred action status and that denials were not subject to judicial review. *Velasco-Gutierrez v. Crossland,* 732 F.2d 792 (10th Cir.1984); *Pasquini v. Morris,* 700 F.2d 658 (11th Cir.1983). *Cf. Heckler v. Chaney,* 470 U.S. 821, 105 S.Ct. 1649, 84 L.Ed.2d 714 (1985) (agency refusal to take enforcement action not reviewable under Administrative Procedure Act).

The INS responded to *Nicholas* by amending the Instruction in 1981. It now reads:

> The district director may, in his or her discretion, recommend consideration of *deferred action,* an act of administrative choice to give some cases lower priority and in no way an entitlement, in appropriate cases.
>
> The deferred action category recognizes that the Service has limited enforcement resources and that every attempt should be made administratively to utilize these resources in a manner

---

a. Lennon's immigration difficulties did not end with release of the information on deferred action cases. Both Lennon and Ono sought to adjust their status in the deportation hearing, and the INS concluded that each was eligible for an employment-based preference. However, Lennon was denied adjustment based on a prior conviction in England for possession of cannabis resin. The Second Circuit ultimately reversed, concluding that the prior offense made guilty knowledge irrelevant and thus did not come within the exclusion ground for drug convictions. *Lennon v. INS,* 527 F.2d 187 (2d Cir.1976).—eds.

which will achieve the greatest impact under the immigration laws. In making deferred action determinations, the following factors, among others, should be considered:

(A) the likelihood of ultimately removing the alien, including:

  (1) likelihood that the alien will depart without formal proceedings (e.g., minor child who will accompany deportable parents);

  (2) age or physical condition affecting ability to travel;

  (3) likelihood that another country will accept the alien;

  (4) the likelihood that the alien will be able to qualify for some form of relief which would prevent or indefinitely delay deportation;

(B) the presence of sympathetic factors which, while not legally precluding deportation, could lead to unduly protracted deportation proceedings, and which, because of a desire on the part of the administrative authorities or the courts to reach a favorable result, could result in a distortion of the law with unfavorable implications for future cases;

(C) the likelihood that because of the sympathetic factors in the case, a large amount of adverse publicity will be generated which will result in a disproportionate amount of Service time being spent in responding to such publicity or justifying actions;

(D) whether or not the individual is a member of a class of deportable aliens whose removal has been given a high enforcement priority (e.g., dangerous criminals, large-scale alien smugglers, narcotic drug traffickers, terrorists, war criminals, habitual immigration violators).

* * *

If the district director determines that a recommendation for deferred action should be made, it shall be made to the regional commissioner concerned on Form G–312, which shall be signed personally by the district director, and the basis for the recommendation shall be set forth therein specifically. Interim or biennial reviews should be conducted to determine whether approved cases should be continued or removed from deferred action category.

O.I. 242.1a(22).

How (and why) was the O.I. changed? Does the current wording of the O.I. undercut (or necessitate the overruling of) *Nicholas*? Should the issue of whether or not the Instruction creates a benefit affect the reviewability of the agency's decision? Should it affect the standard of review to be applied?

2. STAY OF DEPORTATION

By regulation, the district director has discretion to stay the deportation of an alien under an order of deportation "for such time and under such conditions as he may deem appropriate." 8 C.F.R. § 243.4. This authority is generally used to give the alien a reasonable amount of time to make arrangements prior to deportation; or to forestall deportation pending the outcome of a motion to reopen deportation proceedings. INS discretion in this regard is subject to limited judicial review. *See, e.g., Blancada v. Turnage,* 891 F.2d 688 (9th Cir.1989) (district director abused discretion in denying stay of deportation since the accompanying motion to reopen raised a nonfrivolous constitutional claim).

No deportation order may be executed while the time for filing an appeal to the BIA is running, or while an appeal to the BIA is pending. *See* 8 C.F.R. § 3.6(a). An automatic stay of deportation also comes with filing a petition for review in the Court of Appeals, except if the alien has been convicted of an aggravated felony, *see* INA § 106(a)(3).

In August 1994, the INS announced a less conventional use of stays of deportation, more akin to deferred action status. As discussed more fully in Chapter Eight *infra*, the INS, the BIA, and the courts have given divergent answers to the question whether to grant asylum based on opposition to coercive family planning practices in China. A recently adopted INS policy follows the more restrictive line of precedents, but it provides that for aliens who are ineligible for asylum "consideration will be given to granting * * * a stay of deportation," depending on the likelihood of involuntary abortion or sterilization or other harms. *See* 71 Interp.Rel. 1056, 1067 (1994). Should stays of deportation (or extended voluntary departure, deferred action status, and prosecutorial discretion, for that matter) be so used to provide something less than lawful admission to those who fail to qualify but who nonetheless seem to deserve some reprieve from deportation?

SECTION C. REGULARIZATION OF STATUS

Neither voluntary departure nor deferred action status is likely to be the alien's preferred form of relief from deportation. Most aliens who are deportable would like to remain in the United States in a lawful status, and many deportation cases pit the needs of law enforcement against the compelling human needs of an alien. Obviously, the longer an alien has lived in the United States—legally or illegally—the greater the ties he or she is likely to have established and the greater the hardship deportation will entail. The costs do not fall solely on the alien: employers may lose productive employees, neighborhoods may lose valued residents, and family and friends may be deprived of significant personal relationships. Because of the harshness that deportation may visit upon long-term residents, there have always existed avenues of relief for deportable aliens who have lived in the United States for a substantial period of time.

The INA provides a number of avenues of relief that authorize the Attorney General to confer lawful permanent resident status upon a deportable alien. For aliens who entered without inspection or as nonimmigrants, such relief makes them permanent resident aliens for the first time. For aliens who entered as immigrants, the Attorney General's action restores their prior lawful status. For all aliens, these forms of relief effectively wipe out the underlying basis for deportation.[2]

1. SUSPENSION OF DEPORTATION: INA § 244

*—dn't just put deport.
on hold—— it waives deport.
grd* & gives alien
lpr status*

We first consider INA § 244, commonly referred to as "suspension of deportation." The term derives from an early form of the provision under which the Attorney General was authorized to "suspend" deportation in particular cases upon a showing of "serious economic detriment" to an immediate relative of a deportable alien. Such action was then reported to Congress, which could mandate deportation by passing a concurrent resolution disapproving the suspension. If Congress did not do so during that session, the Attorney General "cancelled" deportation proceedings and accorded the alien lawful permanent residence. After 1952, the Attorney General's decision to suspend deportation was allowed to stand unless disapproved by a *single* House of Congress. Immigration and Nationality Act of 1952, Pub.L. No. 414, 66 Stat. 163, 214. In the landmark case of *INS v. Chadha,* 462 U.S. 919, 103 S.Ct. 2764, 77 L.Ed.2d 317 (1983), the Supreme Court ruled that the "legislative veto" in § 244 was unconstitutional; and in 1988 Congress amended the section to delete congressional participation in the suspension decision. Immigration Technical Corrections Act of 1988, Pub.L. No. 100–525, § 2(q), 102 Stat. 2609, 2613. Nonetheless, relief under § 244 is still called "suspension." As the language of the section makes clear, however, a grant of § 244 relief does not simply put an alien's deportation on hold. It waives the ground of deportation, terminates the deportation proceedings, and accords the benefited alien lawful resident status.

Let us draw your attention to several important aspects of § 244(a). First, notice the differences between both the classes of deportation grounds and the time periods specified in paragraphs (a)(1) and (a)(2). (Why would the statute so differentiate?) Second, aliens are ineligible for suspension of deportation who within the previous five years have failed to leave on time pursuant to a grant of voluntary departure (barring "exceptional circumstances"), failed to appear at a properly noticed deportation or asylum hearing, or failed to report for deportation. *See* INA § 242B(e). INA §§ 244(f) lists other aliens ineligible for suspension of deportation. *See also* the "good moral character" requirements in § 244(a). Third, the Attorney General has discretion to deny suspension even if an alien meets all the statutory prerequisites for relief. Finally, an alien who has entered the country without inspection may be eligible for suspension, though such entry or other immigration law violations may be a negative discretionary factor. *See, e.g., Ramirez–Gonzalez v. INS,* 695 F.2d 1208 (9th Cir.1983); *Pelupo de Toledo v. Kiley,* 436 F.Supp. 1090 (E.D.N.Y.1977).

In addition to the express grant of discretion, the explicit statutory guideposts in § 244 are themselves awash in a sea of discretion. Phrases

---

2. Adjustment of status can also serve as a form of relief from deportation, because it can be invoked by an alien in deportation proceedings before an immigration judge. We considered adjustment with the admission materials in Chapter Four, however, because adjustment is sought much more frequently outside proceedings, as a way of gaining permanent resident status without traveling abroad to obtain an immigrant visa.

like "good moral character," "extreme hardship," and "exceptional and extremely unusual hardship" are vague formulations. These phrases have gained some meaning, however, through administrative and judicial opinions. *See generally* Marks, *A Practitioner's Guide to Suspension of Deportation*, 93–6 Imm.Briefings (1993). In the following pages, we will consider the roles of Congress, the Department of Justice and the courts in giving content to these terms.

a. "Continuous" Physical Presence

Under paragraphs (a)(1) and (a)(2), an alien applying for suspension must have been "physically present in the United States for a continuous period" of seven and ten years, respectively.[3] The seven-year period in § 244(a)(1) is the period preceding the application for suspension. In contrast, the ten-year period in § 244(a)(2) starts to run only when the deportation ground arises and is therefore quite difficult to establish.

The "continuous" physical presence terminology appears to be substantially more restrictive than formulations found in other relief from deportation provisions in the INA. *See, e.g.,* § 212(c), discussed later in this Chapter ("lawful unrelinquished domicile"). For many years, the usual understanding was that only a "meaningfully interruptive" absence would keep an alien from meeting the "continuous physical presence" requirement. But in *INS v. Phinpathya,* 464 U.S. 183, 104 S.Ct. 584, 78 L.Ed.2d 401 (1984), the Supreme Court adopted a literal interpretation of the term "continuous physical presence." It held that an alien who had entered the United States in 1969 and taken a three month trip overseas in 1974 was not eligible for § 244 relief in 1977. Just two years later Congress acted to overturn the result in *Phinpathya* by adding a new paragraph (2) to INA § 244(b), which you should now read. You no doubt can identify the source of the language used by Congress to overcome *Phinpathya* as well as the humanitarian motivations behind the amendment.[4]

Note that § 244 does not require that an alien accrue seven years of continuous physical presence *before* deportation proceedings begin. Indeed, because of the number of levels of appeal and a sometimes slow-moving administrative and judicial system, the seven-year point is often reached while an alien's case is pending before an appellate tribunal. May the BIA or an immigration judge refuse to recognize seven years of physical presence brought about simply by the filing of appeals? Suppose the appeals were filed primarily for the purpose of forestalling deportation in order to satisfy the seven-year presence requirement? For the Supreme Court's answer, see *INS v. Rios–Pineda,* 471 U.S. 444, 105 S.Ct. 2098, 85 L.Ed.2d 452 (1985), excerpted p. 681 *infra. But cf. Gonzalez Batoon v. INS,* 791 F.2d 681, 684–86 (9th Cir.1986) (distinguishing *Rios-Pineda*).

3. INA § 244A(e) deals specifically with the application of the seven-year rule to aliens granted temporary protected status.

4. In *Rosenberg v. Fleuti,* 374 U.S. 449, 83 S.Ct. 1804, 10 L.Ed.2d 1000 (1963), the issue was whether a trip outside the U.S. was "meaningfully interruptive" of an alien's permanent *residence.* Does it make linguistic or scientific sense to talk of a "meaningful interruption" of *physical presence* in the U.S.?

What purposes are served by a statutory fixed minimum time? What about requiring that the seven years run before the issuance of the order to show cause? Would such a change serve the purposes of the statute more effectively? Would you favor such a change?

b. "Extreme Hardship" under § 244(a)(1)

Section 244(a)(1) requires an alien to demonstrate "extreme hardship to the alien or his *spouse, parent, or child,* who is a citizen of the United States or an alien lawfully admitted for permanent residence." (Emphasis supplied.) *Cf.* INA § 244(a)(2) (requiring "exceptional and extremely unusual hardship"). A literal reading of the italicized words would not allow consideration of harm to extended family members (such as a grandparent or nephew) or to other individuals for whom the alien has assumed a role comparable to that of an immediate family member. Is such a reading sensible? Does the specific list of individuals rule out an expansive reading of the language?

The Supreme Court has made clear that the "plain meaning" of the statute controls. In *INS v. Hector,* 479 U.S. 85, 107 S.Ct. 379, 93 L.Ed.2d 326 (1986) (*per curiam*), the Court reversed a decision of the Third Circuit that had ordered the BIA to consider whether an alien's relationship to her nieces was the "functional equivalent" of a parent-child relationship and, if so, to determine whether the nieces would experience extreme hardship if the alien were deported. The Court reasoned that "Congress has specifically identified the relatives whose hardship is to be considered, and then set forth unusually detailed and unyielding provisions defining each class of included relatives." Thus, "even if [the alien's] relationship with her nieces resembles a parent-child relationship, we are constrained to hold that Congress, through the plain language of the statute, precluded this functional approach to defining the term 'child.'"

What constitutes "extreme hardship"? Courts have repeatedly quoted Justice Brandeis' words that deportation may deprive a person "of all that makes life worth living." *Ng Fung Ho v. White,* 259 U.S. 276, 284, 42 S.Ct. 492, 495, 66 L.Ed. 938 (1922). Wouldn't deportation of most *de facto* resident aliens inflict "extreme hardship"—not only because of what an alien gives up here but also because of the different economic opportunities and standard of living he or she is likely to face in returning to most of the countries of the world? Yet, to grant this argument would effectively read the phrase out of statute, would it not?

How, then, can we arrive at an understanding of what circumstances constitute "extreme hardship"? The BIA and the courts have adopted some rules of thumb. For example, "a long line of authorities * * * state that while economic detriment is a factor for consideration, by itself it does not constitute extreme hardship." *Bueno-Carrillo v. Landon,* 682 F.2d 143, 146 (7th Cir.1982). Such "rules," however, are rarely determinative. Whether the alien has established "extreme hardship" is generally decided on a case-by-case basis, by looking at the particular circumstances of the applicant and the applicant's family—such as length of residence in the United States, family ties, age, medical needs of the alien or his dependents, and effects of deportation on economic and educational opportunities. *See* GM & Y §§ 74.07[5][f], 143.02[2]. How can an adjudicator value (or balance) these and other factors? Could we create a "point system" assigning particular values to various factors and requiring an alien to achieve a certain point total to establish "extreme hardship"? Would such a system be desirable?

Section 244 in Action

What follows are facts drawn from a suspension of deportation case. Regardless of any initial response you may have, the materials that follow will help you identify and answer the complex legal questions that these facts raise. Among these questions are: Have the statutory prerequisites for relief been met? If you were the immigration judge, how would you exercise your discretion to grant suspension of deportation? How would you view your mission? To "do justice"? Protect American borders? Help dependents of aliens who are United States citizens? How would your perspective on the purposes of § 244 affect your judgment as to which factors are pertinent to your decision?

Patricio Hernandez–Cordero and Maria Guadalupe Ortega de Hernandez are citizens of Mexico. They have resided continuously in the United States since they were married in 1985. The Hernandezes have four children: Victor (age 14), Patricio, Jr. (11), Lisa (9), and Veronica (8). Victor is a Mexican citizen; the youngest three children are United States citizens. Mr. Hernandez is deportable because he entered the United States without inspection. Mrs. Hernandez entered on a visitor's visa; she is deportable for having failed to depart at the end of her authorized stay.

The INS has stipulated that the Hernandezes are of good moral character. The Service concedes that the couple is "industrious, law-abiding, and the type [of people] that anyone would desire as a next-door neighbor." The family lives in Georgetown, Texas, where Mr. Hernandez built a home on a lot purchased in 1993. Mr. Hernandez is a self-employed carpenter, earning about $18,000 a year; and he has, through hard work and thrift, accumulated assets having a value of approximately $105,000. These assets include the family's home, a car, Mr. Hernandez's tools, and another piece of unimproved real estate for which they have paid in full.

The Hernandezes assert that they would suffer extreme hardship if deported to Mexico based on the following considerations:

(1) They would be forced to sell their home at a loss.

(2) The family would lose economic self-sufficiency because Mr. Hernandez would be unable to find in Mexico the kind of work at the same rate of remuneration that he has obtained in the United States. The evidence of economic hardship is supported by an affidavit from an economist who specializes in Latin America.

(3) Although the four children speak Spanish, they are currently enrolled in American schools, and none reads or writes Spanish. Three of the children have never visited or lived in Mexico. Six teachers have provided affidavits detailing the dimin-

ished educational opportunities available in Mexico and the serious emotional difficulty that the children would suffer if their parents were deported and they accompanied the family to Mexico.

(4) An affidavit from a licensed psychologist also concludes that the family would suffer severe emotional and psychological consequences if forced to return to Mexico.

(5) The family would leave behind many friends and relatives, a number of whom are prepared to vouch for the honesty and decency of the family. For example, Dan Johnson, the vice president of the bank that financed construction of the Hernandez home, would testify that "Patricio Hernandez and his family would be an asset to any country in which they chose to live. He takes pride in his work, and his word is his bond." And John Bryan, a ranch owner who employed both Mr. and Mrs. Hernandez in the past, would state: "I have had continuous contact with the Hernandez family since 1987. I consider them to be outstanding people who would be a great asset to American society. They are hard working, and persons of the highest moral caliber. They have assimilated themselves well into our society."

In response, the INS argues:

(1) The loss that would occur from sale of the house is a "self-inflicted wound" because it was built several months after deportation proceedings began.

(2) While economic opportunities in Mexico may not be as favorable in Mexico as in the United States, Mr. Hernandez is an able-bodied skilled craftsman; furthermore, mere economic hardship cannot constitute "extreme hardship" under the statute.

(3) The hardships of loss of friends and schooling opportunities are real, but they are hardly "extreme." Such hardship is likely to attend the deportation of any alien who has resided unlawfully in the United States for a number of years. Moreover, the Hernandezes have significant family ties in Mexico where their parents and most of their brothers and sisters reside. Finally, the children are bilingual, which should be of major assistance in integrating into Mexican life.

Motions to Reopen in Suspension of Deportation Cases

Many of the suspension of deportation cases in this Section arose after the alien sought suspension by moving to reopen deportation proceedings. Motions to reopen are common in suspension cases for at least two reasons. First, suspension under § 244(a)(1) requires seven years presence in the United States. An alien may not have lived here seven years prior to her deportation hearing, yet she may meet the time requirement while her case is on appeal or before the execution of the order of deportation. *See, e.g., INS v. Rios–Pineda,* 471 U.S. 444, 105 S.Ct. 2098, 85 L.Ed.2d 452 (1985); *Moore v. INS,* 715 F.2d 13 (1st Cir.1983) (*per curiam*). In such circumstances, the alien may file a motion to reopen the deportation proceeding in order to assert a § 244 claim. Second, a suspension claim often turns on the issue of whether or not the alien has established the requisite degree of hardship, and the degree of hardship is likely to increase the longer the alien remains in the United States. Thus it is often possible to allege new grounds of hardship that arise after the initial denial of the application but before appeals have been completed and deportation has occurred.

motion to reopen allows new evid. + material

If granted, a motion to reopen allows the moving party to submit new evidence (such as marriage to a U.S. citizen) on issues of deportability or relief from deportation. A motion to reopen may be filed before an immigration officer, an immigration judge, or the BIA, as appropriate. *See* 8 C.F.R. §§ 3.2, 103.5(a), 242.22. The motion must be supported by affidavits or other evidentiary material. It may not be granted unless the new evidence is material and "was not available and could not have been discovered or presented at the former hearing." 8 C.F.R. § 3.2, *see also* 8 C.F.R. § 242.22.

just a review for error

A motion to reconsider is different; it asks the decisionmaker (an immigration officer, an immigration judge, or the BIA) to review claimed errors in her earlier appraisal of the law or the facts. *See* 8 C.F.R. §§ 3.2, 103.5, 242.22. If a motion to reconsider is granted, the decisionmaker may affirm, modify or reverse the original decision made in the case.

The filing of a motion to reopen does not result in an automatic stay of the execution of an outstanding order of deportation. However, district directors, the BIA and immigration judges may stay deportation pending determination of the motion, if they are persuaded that a stay is justified. 8 C.F.R. §§ 3.8(a), 242.22, 243.4. *See generally* Gordon, *Appellate Immigration Practice: Appeals to the BIA and AAU,* 2 1992–93 Immigration & Nationality Handbook 522 (1992); Hurwitz, *Motion Practice Before the Board of Immigration Appeals,* 20 San Diego L.Rev. 79 (1982).

Motions to reopen have generated considerable controversy. For aliens, they are important devices for bringing new information before immigration authorities and for taking advantage of one of the numerous forms of relief from deportation. However, not only the INS but also Congress have grown concerned about the use of motion practice as a dilatory tactic to forestall deportation. The Immigration Act of 1990 required the Attorney General to submit a report to Congress "on abuses associated with the failure of aliens to consolidate requests for discretionary relief before immigration judges at the first hearing on the merits," and to issue regulations by May 1991 limiting (1) the time for filing motions to reopen or reconsider in deportation proceedings and (2) the number of such motions. 1990 Act, §§ 545(c), (d) (not codified in the INA). The accompanying Conference Report provided even more specific direction:

> The Attorney General, in developing these regulations, shall consider exceptions in the interest of justice. Unless the Attorney General finds reasonable evidence to the contrary, the regulations should state that such motions be made within 20 days of the date of the final determination in the proceeding and that such motions be limited to one motion to reopen and one motion to reconsider.

An exception for asylum claims which arise due to a change in circumstances in the country of the alien's nationality and after the initiation of the deportation proceedings, shall be considered.

H.R.Rep. No. 101–955, at 133 (1990).

The Attorney General's report, submitted in 1991, concluded that aliens were not engaging in such abuse and that there was no need to impose procedural restrictions. *See* 68 Interp.Rel. 907 (1991). These conclusions notwithstanding, in 1994 the Executive Office of Immigration Review proposed restrictive regulations as Congress had directed, *see* 59 Fed.Reg. 29386 (1994), *proposing to amend* 8 C.F.R. § 3.2. Under the proposed regulations, only one motion to reopen and one motion to reconsider may be filed, and they must be filed within 20 days of the decision in question. There are limited exceptions to the limit of one and the 20–day rule for motions to reopen (but not for motions to reconsider). Are these restrictions on the use of motions to reopen or reconsider a good idea?

Assume that an alien complies with these formal requirements, but the BIA denies a motion to reopen on the ground that the alien is not offering previously unavailable, material evidence. What standard should a court apply in reviewing that denial? In *INS v. Abudu*, 485 U.S. 94, 108 S.Ct. 904, 99 L.Ed.2d 90 (1988), the BIA denied Abudu's request that his deportation proceedings be reopened to allow him to apply for asylum. Abudu, a citizen of Ghana, had overstayed his student visa. After he pleaded guilty to drug charges in 1981, the INS initiated deportation proceedings, in which Abudu expressly declined to apply for asylum. In 1982 Abudu was ordered deported, and in 1984 the BIA dismissed his appeal. With judicial review pending, Abudu moved to reopen to apply for asylum in 1985. The Court summarized Abudu's argument as follows:

> [Abudu] claimed that he had a well-founded fear that if England did not accept him and he was returned to Ghana, his life and freedom would be threatened by the regime in power. His fear was based largely on the facts that after the current government seized power in 1981, it had carried out a systematic campaign of persecution against its political enemies and that respondent's brother and certain close friends were among the targets of that campaign. Moreover, in 1984, respondent had received an unsolicited and surprise visit from a former acquaintance who had become a high official in the Ghana government. The visitor invited respondent to return to Ghana, ostensibly because qualified physicians are in short supply, but respondent concluded that his visitor actually wanted to entice him to return in order to force him to disclose the whereabouts of his brother and other enemies of the government.

485 U.S. at 97, 108 S.Ct. at 908.

Writing for a unanimous Court (Justice Kennedy not participating), Justice Stevens upheld the Board's denial of Abudu's motion to reopen and discussed the appropriate judicial role:

Sct us:
3 grds where
BIA can
deny
mot. to reopen

There are at least three independent grounds on which the BIA may deny a motion to reopen. First, it may hold that the ①movant has not established a prima facie case for the underlying substantive relief sought. The standard of review of such a denial is not before us today * * *. Second, the BIA may hold that the movant has not introduced previously unavailable, material evidence② 8 CFR § 3.2 (1987), or, in an asylum application case, that the movant has not reasonably explained his failure to apply for asylum initially, 8 CFR § 208.11 (1987).ᵃ * * * We decide today that the appropriate standard of review of such denials is abuse of discretion. Third, in cases in which the ultimate grant of relief is discretionary, * * * the BIA may leap ahead, as it were, over the two threshold concerns (prima facie case and new evidence/reasonable explanation), and simply determine that even if they were met, the movant would not be entitled to the discretionary grant of relief. We have consistently held that denials on this third ground are subject to an abuse-of-discretion standard. *INS v. Rios–Pineda,* 471 U.S. 444, 105 S.Ct. 2098, 85 L.Ed.2d 452 (1985) (suspension of deportation); *INS v. Bagamasbad,* 429 U.S. 24, 97 S.Ct. 200, 50 L.Ed.2d 190 (1976) (adjustment of status).

We have discussed 8 CFR § 3.2 (1987), which is one of the two regulations before us today, in dicta:

> "[Section 3.2] is framed negatively; it directs the Board not to reopen unless certain showings are made. It does not affirmatively require the Board to reopen the proceedings under any particular condition. Thus, the regulations may be construed to provide the Board with discretion in determining under what circumstances proceedings should be reopened." *INS v. Jong Ha Wang,* 450 U.S. 139, 144, n. 5, 101 S.Ct. 1027, 1031, n. 5, 67 L.Ed.2d 123 (1981).

This footnote, and our subsequent citations of it, *INS v. Rios–Pineda, supra,* 471 U.S., at 449, 105 S.Ct., at 2101–2102; *INS v. Phinpathya,* 464 U.S. 183, 188, n. 6, 104 S.Ct. 584, 588–589, n. 6, 78 L.Ed.2d 401 (1984), stand for the proposition that the BIA has discretion to deny a motion to reopen even if the alien has made out a prima facie case for relief; that is, our prior glosses on § 3.2 have served as support for an abuse-of-discretion standard of review for the third type of denial, where the BIA simply refuses to grant relief that is itself discretionary in nature, even if the alien has surmounted the requisite thresholds of prima facie case and new evidence/reasonable explanation.

But even before reaching the ultimate decision on an alien's application for discretionary relief from deportation, or before reaching the point at which mandatory relief is called for in a withholding of deportation case, the BIA's discretion may be called

---

a. The asylum regulations were amended in 1990. The new sections on motions to reopen for purposes of filing for asylum, 8 C.F.R. §§ 208.4, 208.19, retain substantially the same requirement.—eds.

into play regarding the specific, evidentiary requirements of §§ 3.2 and 208.11. That is, in a given case the BIA may determine, either as a sufficient ground for denying relief or as a necessary step toward granting relief, whether the alien has produced previously unavailable, material evidence (§ 3.2), and, in asylum cases, whether the alien has reasonably explained his or her failure to request asylum initially (§ 208.11). We hold today that such decisions are subject to an abuse-of-discretion standard of review.

The reasons why motions to reopen are disfavored in deportation proceedings are comparable to those that apply to petitions for rehearing, and to motions for new trials on the basis of newly discovered evidence. There is a strong public interest in bringing litigation to a close as promptly as is consistent with the interest in giving the adversaries a fair opportunity to develop and present their respective cases. * * *

* * * [T]he Court of Appeals in this case purported to decide "whether [respondent] presented a *prima facie* case for reopening." In so doing, the Court of Appeals set out a standard for BIA motions to reopen deportation proceedings, see *supra,* at 6, that appears to have conflated the quite separate issues of whether the alien has presented a prima facie case for asylum with whether the alien has reasonably explained his failure to apply for asylum initially and has indeed offered previously unavailable, material evidence. To the extent that the reasoning of the Court of Appeals addresses the issue of reopening rather than the issue of prima facie case for asylum, it is not supported by our cases, and has been consistently rejected by other Circuits and by other panels in the Ninth Circuit. We have never suggested that all ambiguities in the factual averments must be resolved in the movant's favor, and we have never analogized such a motion to a motion for summary judgment. The appropriate analogy is a motion for a new trial in a criminal case on the basis of newly discovered evidence, as to which courts have uniformly held that the moving party bears a heavy burden. Moreover, this is the tenor of the Attorney General's regulations, which plainly disfavor motions to reopen. In sum, although all adjudications by administrative agencies are to some degree judicial and to some degree political—and therefore an abuse-of-discretion standard will often apply to agency adjudications not governed by specific statutory commands—INS officials must exercise especially sensitive political functions that implicate questions of foreign relations, and therefore the reasons for giving deference to agency decisions on petitions for reopening or reconsideration in other administrative contexts apply with even greater force in the INS context.

485 U.S. at 104–10, 108 S.Ct. at 912–15. The Court then rejected Abudu's claim that he explained his failure to apply for asylum initially and offered previously unavailable, material evidence:

We have no doubt that if respondent had made a timely application for asylum, supported by the factual allegations and exhibits set forth in his motion to reopen, the Immigration Judge would have been required to grant him an evidentiary hearing. We are equally convinced, however, that an alien who has already been found deportable has a much heavier burden when he first advances his request for asylum in a motion to reopen. In passing on the sufficiency of such a motion, the BIA is entitled to attach significance to its untimeliness, both for the purpose of evaluating the probability that the movant can prove his allegations and for the purpose of determining whether the movant has complied with the regulation requiring a reasonable explanation for the failure to request asylum during the deportation proceeding.

In this case we have no hesitation in concluding that the BIA did not abuse its discretion when it held that respondent had not reasonably explained his failure to apply for asylum prior to the completion of the initial deportation proceeding. The surprise visit in 1984 was admittedly an event with uncertain meaning, but it was neither arbitrary nor unreasonable for the BIA to regard it as not providing any significant additional support for a claim that respondent had not previously considered strong enough to prompt him to assert that he had a well-founded fear of persecution.

485 U.S. at 110–11, 108 S.Ct. at 915. In *INS v. Doherty*, 502 U.S. 314, 328–29, 112 S.Ct. 719, 727–28, 116 L.Ed.2d 823 (1992), the Supreme Court took a similarly narrow approach to what qualifies as previously unavailable, material evidence.

Obviously, if the BIA granted all motions to reopen, deportable aliens would have great incentives to file such motions irrespective of the underlying merits of their claims for relief. Accordingly, the BIA has established standards that require, *inter alia,* that aliens establish a *prima facie* case of extreme hardship before the motion to reopen will be granted and the § 244 claim will be considered. The 1994 proposed EOIR regulations include such an explicit requirement for all motions to reopen. *See* 59 Fed.Reg. 29387 (1994), *proposing to amend* 8 C.F.R. § 3.2.

In the following case the Supreme Court considered both the question of who has primary responsibility in defining "extreme hardship" and what standard the federal courts should apply in reviewing BIA denials of motions to reopen deportation proceedings. Here, the focus is an issue not addressed in *Abudu*: the "*prima facie* case" requirement.

INS v. JONG HA WANG

Supreme Court of the United States, 1981.
450 U.S. 139, 101 S.Ct. 1027, 67 L.Ed.2d 123.

PER CURIAM.

* * *

The § 244 issue usually arises in an alien's deportation hearing. It can arise, however, as it did in this case, on a motion to reopen after deportation has been duly ordered. The Act itself does not expressly provide for a motion to reopen, but regulations promulgated under the Act allow such a procedure. [The Court cites 8 C.F.R. § 3.2.] The regulations also provide that the motion to reopen shall "state the new fact to be proved at the reopened hearing and shall be supported by affidavits or other evidentiary material." 8 CFR § 3.8(a) (1979). Motions to reopen are thus permitted in those cases in which the events or circumstances occurring after the order of deportation would satisfy the extreme-hardship standard of § 244. Such motions will not be granted "when a *prima facie* case of eligibility for the relief sought has not been established." *Matter of Lam*, 14 I. & N. Dec. 98 (BIA 1972).

[handwritten: need prima facie case to get motion to reopen]

Respondents, husband and wife, are natives and citizens of Korea who first entered the United States in January 1970 as nonimmigrant treaty traders. They were authorized to remain until January 10, 1972, but they remained beyond that date without permission and were found deportable after a hearing in November 1974. They were granted the privilege of voluntarily departing by February 1, 1975. They did not do so. Instead, they applied for adjustment of status under § 245 of the Act, but were found ineligible for this relief after a hearing on July 15, 1975.[4] Their appeal from this ruling was dismissed by the Board of Immigration Appeals in October 1977. Respondents then filed a second motion to reopen their deportation proceedings in December 1977, this time claiming suspension under § 244 of the Act. Respondents by then had satisfied the 7-year-continuous-physical-presence requirement of that section. The motion alleged that deportation would result in extreme hardship to respondents' two American-born children because neither child spoke Korean and would thus lose "educational opportunities" if forced to leave this country. Respondents also claimed economic hardship to themselves and their children resulting from the forced liquidation of their assets at a possible loss. None of the allegations was sworn or otherwise supported by evidentiary materials, but it appeared that all of respondents' close relatives, aside from their children, resided in Korea and that respondents had purchased a dry-cleaning business in August 1977, some three years after they had been found deportable. The business was valued at $75,000 and provided an income of $650 per week. Respondents also owned a home purchased in 1974 and valued at $60,000. They had $24,000 in a savings account and some $20,000 in miscellaneous assets. Liabilities were approximately $81,000.

[handwritten: facts]
[handwritten: file for reopen]

The Board of Immigration Appeals denied respondents' motion to reopen without a hearing, concluding that they had failed to demonstrate a prima facie case that deportation would result in extreme hardship to either themselves or their children so as to entitle them to discretionary relief under the Act. The Board noted that a mere showing of economic detriment is not sufficient to establish extreme hardship under the Act.

---

4. Relief was denied because the immigration judge determined that visa numbers for nonpreference Korean immigrants were not available, thus rendering respondents ineligible for the requested relief. The immigration judge also stated that he would have denied the application given respondents' failure to move to Salt Lake City where Mr. Wang's sponsoring employer was located, thus causing doubt whether his services were in fact needed.

This was particularly true since respondents had "significant financial resources and there [was] nothing to suggest that the college-educated male respondent could not find suitable employment in Korea." With respect to the claims involving the children, the Board ruled that the alleged loss of educational opportunities to the young children of relatively affluent, educated Korean parents did not constitute extreme hardship within the meaning of § 244.

Ct App found prima facie case

The Court of Appeals for the Ninth Circuit, sitting en banc, reversed. 622 F.2d 1341 (1980). Contrary to the Board's holding, the Court of Appeals found that respondents had alleged a sufficient prima facie case of extreme hardship to entitle them to a hearing. The court reasoned that the statute should be liberally construed to effectuate its ameliorative purpose. The combined effect of the allegation of harm to the minor children, which the court thought was hard to discern without a hearing, and the impact on respondents' economic interests was sufficient to constitute a prima facie case requiring a hearing where the Board would "consider the total potential effect of deportation on the alien and his family." *Id.,* at 1349.

Sct + US reverses Ct App

The Court of Appeals erred in two respects. First, the court ignored the regulation which requires the alien seeking suspension to allege and support by affidavit or other evidentiary material the particular facts claimed to constitute extreme hardship. Here, the allegations of hardship were in the main conclusory and unsupported by affidavit. By requiring a hearing on such a motion, the Court of Appeals circumvented this aspect of the regulation, which was obviously designed to permit the Board to select for hearing only those motions reliably indicating the specific recent events that would render deportation a matter of extreme hardship for the alien or his children.[5]

Secondly, and more fundamentally, the Court of Appeals improvidently encroached on the authority which the Act confers on the Attorney General and his delegates. The crucial question in this case is what constitutes "extreme hardship." These words are not self-explanatory, and reasonable men could easily differ as to their construction. But the Act commits their

---

5. Other Courts of Appeals have enforced the evidentiary requirement stated in 8 CFR § 3.8 (1979). *See, e.g., Oum v. INS,* 613 F.2d 51, 54 (CA4 1980); *Acevedo v. INS,* 538 F.2d 918, 920 (CA2 1976). *See also Tupacyupanqui–Marin v. INS,* 447 F.2d 603, 607 (CA7 1971); *Luna-Benalcazar v. INS,* 414 F.2d 254, 256 (CA6 1969).

Prior to the present procedures, the grant or denial of a motion to reopen was solely within the discretion of the Board. *See Arakas v. Zimmerman,* 200 F.2d 322, 323–324, and n. 2 (CA3 1952). The present regulation is framed negatively; it directs the Board not to reopen unless certain showings are made. It does not affirmatively require the Board to reopen the proceedings under any particular condition. Thus, the regulations may be construed to provide the Board with discretion in determining under what circumstances proceedings should be reopened. *See Villena v. INS,* 622 F.2d 1352 (CA9 1980) (en banc) (Wallace, J., dissenting). In his dissent, Judge Wallace stated that INS had discretion beyond requiring proof of a prima facie case:

"If INS discretion is to mean anything, it must be that the INS has some latitude in deciding when to reopen a case. The INS should have the right to be restrictive. Granting such motions too freely will permit endless delay of deportation by aliens creative and fertile enough to continuously produce new and material facts sufficient to establish a prima facie case. It will also waste the time and efforts of immigration judges called upon to preside at hearings automatically required by the prima facie allegations." *Id.,* at 1362.

definition in the first instance to the Attorney General and his delegates, and their construction and application of this standard should not be overturned by a reviewing court simply because it may prefer another interpretation of the statute. Here, the Board considered the facts alleged and found that neither respondents nor their children would suffer extreme hardship. The Board considered it well settled that a mere showing of economic detriment was insufficient to satisfy the requirements of § 244 and in any event noted that respondents had significant financial resources while finding nothing to suggest that Mr. Wang could not find suitable employment in Korea. It also followed that respondents' two children would not suffer serious economic deprivation if they returned to Korea. Finally, the Board could not believe that the two "young children of affluent, educated parents" would be subject to such educational deprivations in Korea as to amount to extreme hardship. In making these determinations, the Board was acting within its authority. As we see it, nothing in the allegations indicated that this is a particularly unusual case requiring the Board to reopen the deportation proceedings.

The Court of Appeals nevertheless ruled that the hardship requirement of § 244 is satisfied if an alien produces sufficient evidence to suggest that the "hardship from deportation would be different and more severe than that suffered by the ordinary alien who is deported." 622 F.2d, at 1346. Also, as Judge Goodwin observed in dissent, the majority of the Court of Appeals also strongly indicated that respondents should prevail under such an understanding of the statute. *Id.,* at 1352. In taking this course, the Court of Appeals extended its "writ beyond its proper scope and deprived the Attorney General of a substantial portion of the discretion which § 244(a) vests in him." *Id.,* at 1351 (Sneed, J., dissenting from opinion).

The Attorney General and his delegates have the authority to construe "extreme hardship" narrowly should they deem it wise to do so. Such a narrow interpretation is consistent with the "extreme hardship" language, which itself indicates the exceptional nature of the suspension remedy. Moreover, the Government has a legitimate interest in creating official procedures for handling motions to reopen deportation proceedings so as readily to identify those cases raising new and meritorious considerations. Under the standard applied by the court below, many aliens could obtain a hearing based upon quite minimal showings. As stated in dissent below, "by using the majority opinion as a blueprint, any foreign visitor who has fertility, money, and the ability to stay out of trouble with the police for seven years can change his status from that of tourist or student to that of permanent resident without the inconvenience of immigration quotas. This strategy is not fair to those waiting for a quota." *Id.,* at 1352 (Goodwin, J., dissenting). Judge Goodwin further observed that the relaxed standard of the majority opinion "is likely to shift the administration of hardship deportation cases from the Immigration and Naturalization Service to this court." *Id.,* at 1351.

We are convinced that the Board did not exceed its authority and that the Court of Appeals erred in ordering that the case be reopened. Accordingly, the petition for certiorari is granted, and the judgment of the Court of Appeals is reversed.

So ordered.

JUSTICES BRENNAN, MARSHALL, and BLACKMUN would grant the petition for certiorari and give the case plenary consideration.

Notes

1. In *Wang*, there appear to be two interconnected issues: (a) whether the BIA should have reopened the deportation proceeding, and (b) whether the aliens had demonstrated extreme hardship. *Wang* has thus been interpreted to speak on both procedural and substantive aspects of judicial review in suspension cases. For example, *Wang* is routinely cited for the proposition that courts should exercise restraint in ordering the BIA to reopen deportation proceedings. *See, e.g., Mesa v. INS*, 726 F.2d 39, 41 (1st Cir.1984) (Board's decision not to reopen must be accepted by court unless arbitrary, capricious or an abuse of power). It is also regularly read to mean that the agency "has considerable discretion to decide what constitutes 'extreme hardship'." *See, e.g., Luna v. INS*, 709 F.2d 126, 127 (1st Cir.1983). Thus *Wang* broadly controls not only cases involving motions to reopen but also direct appeals from denials of suspension.

2. Several years after *Wang*, the Supreme Court's decision in *Chevron, U.S.A., Inc. v. Natural Resources Defense Council*, 467 U.S. 837, 104 S.Ct. 2778, 81 L.Ed.2d 694 (1984), p. 173 *supra*, established that a court should generally defer to an agency's construction of a statute where the statute is silent or ambiguous with respect to the precise question at issue. Judicial deference under *Chevron* may have a major substantive impact on implementation of a statute if the agency and the courts are likely to view the legislation from different perspectives. Such a difference in perspective seems to underlie the issues in *Wang*: the INS and BIA, acting primarily as law enforcement agencies, had adopted a strict standard of "extreme hardship" that the Ninth Circuit, looking at the provision through the eyes of the aliens, found too harsh. In effect, the Supreme Court held that Congress intended the agency's more hard-nosed approach to prevail.

Is it obvious that Congress thought that the law enforcement side of § 244 should outweigh its humanitarian aspects? If not, perhaps we would want to construct an adjudication structure that gives play to both concerns of § 244 by preserving a role for the courts to evaluate the evidence of a suspension claim. This is not to say that a reviewing court should substitute its judgment for that of the agency. That would be an overcorrection, tipping the balance too far in the direction of the alien just as the deference model may tip it too far toward enforcement objectives. Rather, the authority of a court to remand a case may ensure that a dialogue occurs between the agency and the court—a conversation that considers both law enforcement and humanitarian concerns. Is not such a dialogic process silenced by *Wang*?

Suspension of Deportation in the Post-*Wang* Era

Alexander Bickel has written that the "future will not be ruled; it can only possibly be persuaded." A. Bickel, The Least Dangerous Branch 98

(1962). Although Bickel was writing of important constitutional cases, his words are equally applicable to the reception of *Wang* in the lower federal courts. The Supreme Court's desire that the courts of appeals be far less intrusive in § 244 cases has not stopped the filing of appeals nor ended the remand of cases by appellate courts to the BIA. Faced with what they deem to be compelling humanitarian concerns, the courts have distinguished, explained, and perhaps misunderstood *Wang*. "Notwithstanding *Wang*," say the editors of the Harvard Law Review,

> the courts of appeals have developed standards of review that constrain the agency's discretion to deny suspension of deportation. The primary tools employed by the courts are the requirements that the Board of Immigration Appeals consider all evidence presented by the alien regarding the hardship she will face if deported, that the Board consider that evidence cumulatively, and that the Board "give reasons for its decisions showing that it has properly considered the circumstances." In addition, courts have held that the Board must reopen deportation proceedings to allow reconsideration of the hardship question whenever the alien comes forward with previously unavailable evidence that, considered cumulatively with the evidence already introduced, could conceivably support a finding of extreme hardship.

Note, *Developments in the Law—Immigration Policy and the Rights of Aliens,* 96 Harv.L.Rev. 1286, 1396 (1983).

Consider the following post-*Wang* Third Circuit panel decision.

RAVANCHO v. INS

United States Court of Appeals, Third Circuit, 1981.
658 F.2d 169.

SLOVITER, CIRCUIT JUDGE.

This case is before us on rehearing before the original panel following our exercise of our discretionary authority to recall the certified judgment issued in lieu of mandate, an action which we take only in "unusual circumstances." We followed that practice in this case so that we could consider the contention of respondent Immigration and Naturalization Service that our original decision is contrary to the subsequent decision of the Supreme Court in *INS v. Wang,* 450 U.S. 139, 101 S.Ct. 1027, 67 L.Ed.2d 123 (1981). On consideration of the parties' additional briefs and oral arguments, we believe that the primary basis for our original decision, that the Board abused its discretion in refusing to reopen the record to consider psychiatric data not available during previous hearings, is not foreclosed or undermined by the *Wang* decision, and we once again conclude a remand to the Board of Immigration Appeals is appropriate.

Zenaida Ravancho and her husband, Alejandro Ravancho, are both citizens of the Philippines who entered the United States on November 7, 1968 and December 19, 1968 respectively. On December 10, 1969, their daughter Patricia was born in the United States. Zenaida and Alejandro Ravancho were authorized to remain in the United States until February 7,

1974, but remained beyond their authorized stay * * *. At the hearings before the immigration judge on February 1, 1978 and on March 15, 1978, the Ravanchos conceded deportability and sought to establish that deportation should be suspended on the ground of "extreme hardship" as provided for in INA § 244(a)(2).

The Ravanchos proved, inter alia, that they are both presently employed; that they have had stable employment records, Mr. Ravancho having been employed as an engineering aide by the Wallace & Tiernan Company of Belleville, New Jersey, since December 1969, and Mrs. Ravancho having been employed by the New Jersey Bell Telephone Company as a keypunch operator since 1970; and that they have purchased a house in New Jersey. They sought to show economic hardship to them which would ensue if they were deported. They also sought to establish hardship to their child (then 8 years old) by their testimony at the hearing on March 15, 1978 that she knows no other life than that in the United States, is unable to speak the Philippine language, was a straight A student in school, and that her "life would be dramatically upset by being uprooted from her home, friends, and the only life she knows."

On October 24, 1978, the immigration judge denied the Ravanchos' applications for suspension of deportation. The judge concluded that the Ravanchos met the physical presence and good moral character requirements for relief under that statute, but had failed to satisfy their statutory burden of showing that extreme hardship would result. He stated:

> A careful review of all the facts as presented including the difficulties the respondents would have in attempting to obtain employment in their native Philippines, their family situation, the loss of the income that they have now in the United States and *the possible transfer of their United States citizen child to relocate in the Philippines* does not appear to satisfy the burden placed upon them to show that they would suffer extreme hardship under this Section of the law. *Such economic disadvantage* does not constitute the required statutory hardship. (emphasis added).

The Ravanchos' appeal to the Board of Immigration Appeals was dismissed on June 14, 1979. The Board held that the immigration judge properly found that the economic detriment the Ravanchos might suffer if deported to the Philippines would not amount to extreme hardship within the purview of the statute. The Board further stated in affirming the decision of the immigration judge: "We also find that their United States citizen child, born less than one year after her mother's arrival in this country as a nonimmigrant visitor, would not suffer extreme hardship."[2] The Ravanchos filed a Motion to Stay Deportation and to Reopen Proceedings on July 31, 1979. They attached to that motion a psychiatric evaluation of Patricia dated July 17, 1979, which had been made to evaluate the effect on Patricia's mental, physical and emotional stability of a return to the Philippines. They also filed an affidavit where they averred, as they

2. According to the record before us, the Ravanchos' daughter was born more than a year after her mother's arrival in the United States. Furthermore, the date of the child's birth more than ten years ago is patently unrelated to her current hardship.

had previously testified, that Mrs. Ravancho had a brother and sister who are both lawful permanent residents of the United States and that Mr. Ravancho has a sister who is also a lawful permanent resident of the United States.

[The BIA denied the motion.]

In our original decision, we held that a remand to the Board was appropriate because the Board

> appears to have considered the proffered psychiatrist's report in isolation, only in terms of whether, on its own, that report sufficed to demonstrate extreme hardship within the statutory terms. This is contrary to the requirement that the decision whether to suspend deportation must be made on a consideration of *all* relevant factors. The psychiatrist's report may well have been the increment which would have tipped the balance toward suspension. There is no indication in the Board's opinion that it evaluated the proffered evidence on this basis.

We also stated that the Board appeared to give too little weight to the psychological burden on Patricia, a factor that the immigration judge had erroneously subsumed in his discussion of "economic disadvantage". We concluded our observations with the statements:

> We recognize that the determination of whether petitioners have shown extreme hardship to warrant suspension of deportation is entrusted to the discretion of the immigration judge and Board, in the first instance. However, we hold that petitioners have produced evidence which, on its face, is relevant to that determination and which must be considered by the agency in the exercise of its discretion. (footnote omitted).

The thrust of the respondent's position on rehearing is that "[t]he decision in this case is incorrect because this court substituted its own judgment for that of the Board of Immigration Appeals in determining what will constitute extreme hardship warranting suspension of deportation," Respondent's Brief on Rehearing, p. 7, and thus is contrary to *I.N.S. v. Wang*, 450 U.S. 139, 101 S.Ct. 1027, 67 L.Ed.2d 123 (1981), decided after this court's original decision. Therefore our inquiry must focus upon the Supreme Court's *Wang* decision to determine whether it requires us to reverse our previous disposition remanding this matter to the Board.

* * *

We perceive substantial differences between the *Wang* case and that at issue here. In the first place, this case does not suffer from the first factor stressed by the Supreme Court, the failure of the Wangs to allege and support by affidavit or other evidentiary material "the particular facts claimed to constitute extreme hardship." On the contrary, in this case the Ravanchos filed the necessary affidavit and proffered as evidentiary material the psychiatric evaluation which related to "the particular facts claimed to constitute extreme hardship." Unlike the Wangs who apparently proffered merely a conclusory allegation about a general loss of educational opportunities for their children in Korea, the Ravanchos proffered specific evidence relating to a particular child.

We turn then to the more fundamental question of whether a decision by this court to remand constitutes an encroachment on the authority conferred by the Act on the Attorney General. The respondent views our original decision to remand as based on our observations with respect to the Board's construction of "extreme hardship". As shown by the previously quoted excerpts from our prior opinion, however, the primary basis for our original decision to remand was the failure of the Board to consider the newly proffered evidence in conjunction with that previously submitted in order to determine whether the circumstances justified exercise of the Board's discretion. It is not necessary to speculate whether our previous observations about the Board's narrow construction of "extreme hardship", which appeared to us to be inconsistent with Congressional intent,[6] would withstand scrutiny following the *Wang* decision, since our order granting rehearing withdrew the original opinion. In any event, as petitioners correctly note, those comments were not the ground on which we determined remand was appropriate. Instead, our decision then and now turns on the Board's action, when presented with material evidence previously unavailable, in considering such evidence in isolation in determining whether a prima facie case for reopening was established.

In this respect, this case differs markedly from *Wang* where there was no contention that the Board failed to consider the totality of all of the evidence presented before it. There, the only issue was the substantive evaluation to be given such evidence. The opinion of the Board in this case expressly indicates that reconsideration was denied only on the basis of an analysis of the newly proffered evidence. We express no view on the procedure to be followed by the Board where the petition merely seeks reconsideration based on rearguments with regard to evidence previously submitted. But where, as in this case, petitioners seek to reopen proceedings based on evidence which on its face showed it was not previously available,[7] then we believe the Board abused its discretion in failing to consider the cumulative effect of that evidence. In fact, at the oral argument before us, counsel for the respondent stated that it was the Board's position that in deciding whether there is a prima facie basis for reopening, the Board must consider all of the evidence, not merely the newly proffered evidence. Although counsel also suggested that we should conclude that the Board in fact followed that procedure, it is conceded that

---

6. A 1957 House Report refers to the Congressional intent "to provide for liberal treatment of children." *See* H.R.Rep.No. 1199, 85th Cong., 1st Sess. 7, *reprinted in* [1957] U.S.Code Cong. & Ad.News, 2016, 2020. In view of the grounds of our disposition of this case, we need not decide whether the effect of the *Wang* decision is to preclude all appellate consideration of the Board's determination whether a particular petitioner has demonstrated the requisite "extreme hardship." *See generally Brathwaite v. INS,* 633 F.2d 657, 659–60 (2d Cir.1980). We note that the statute does not explicitly so provide,

in contrast to other statutes where Congress has expressly committed certain determinations to unreviewable agency discretion. *See, e.g.,* 38 U.S.C. § 211(a) (1976) (decisions regarding veteran's benefits).

7. The psychiatric evaluation was made July 17, 1979 and referred to the drop in Patricia's grades during the school year which had just ended. This occurred substantially after the original hearing conducted by the immigration judge on March 15, 1978.

there is nothing in the Board's short statement that indicates that anything other than the newly proffered evidence was considered. The Board, after referring to the psychiatric report, stated *"This* is not the type of extreme hardship necessary for a grant of suspension of deportation and, accordingly, we will deny the respondents' request for reconsideration." (emphasis added). We must make our decision based on the Board's own articulation of its actions, rather than on the assumption of or reconstruction by its counsel.

Although respondent argues that the psychiatric evaluation does not demonstrate "severe hardship", we do not understand it to dispute the general proposition that psychological trauma may be a relevant factor in determining whether a United States citizen child will suffer "extreme hardship" within the statute. Thus, had this or any other relevant factor been disregarded by the immigration judge or the Board when the original determination was made, such action would constitute an abuse of discretion. Similarly, if petitioners present a petition to reopen with evidence which is material and was previously unavailable, and the substantive determination is one which must be made on the basis of a consideration of all of the relevant factors, a refusal to reopen would be justified only if the Board found that the cumulative effect of the new evidence could not have affected the decision. No such finding was made in this case.

Decisions as to what circumstances constitute "extreme hardship" require delicate balancing, and are rarely made by the Board on the basis of a single factor alone. * * * Indeed in this case, the Ravanchos may have been somewhat disadvantaged because the immigration judge inexplicably erroneously mischaracterized the state of the record by his statement that the Ravanchos have no close relatives in the United States.[8] As the respondent now concedes in its brief, "Mrs. Ravancho has a brother and sister who are lawful permanent residents of the United States, and Mr. Ravancho has a brother [sic] who is a lawful permanent resident." Mr. Ravancho's sister lives in New Jersey, as do the Ravanchos. In fact the record indicates they lived in adjoining towns at the time of the 1978 hearing. Respondent concedes that "close family ties and the interest in keeping families together are considerations in granting or denying applica-

---

8. The immigration judge stated:

The issue to be resolved is whether the deportation of the respondents *who have no close relatives in the United States* would constitute extreme hardship within the contemplation of the statute. (emphasis added)

The immigration judge's statement is particularly inexplicable in light of the fact that the relevant facts were presented not only in a document which might have been overlooked but by petitioners' testimony before that very judge that Mrs. Ravancho has a permanent resident brother in active service in the United States Navy, that she has a sister who is resident in the United States, and that Mr. Ravancho has a sister who is a lawful permanent resident of the United

States. In fact, the immigration judge's erroneous statement that the Ravanchos had no close relatives permanently resident in the United States was twice corrected by the petitioners at the hearing. Nonetheless, the report of the immigration judge again repeated the erroneous statement. The correct facts were again stated in the Ravanchos' affidavit on reopening, which set forth the following status of the family as of that date: Zenaida Ravancho's brother continues as a lawful permanent resident in military service, and has two children born in the United States. Her sister is a lawful permanent resident married to a United States citizen. Alejandro Ravancho's sister is a lawful permanent resident.

tions for suspension," but argues that the facts do not suggest that deportation in this case will adversely affect close family relationships. Whether that is so is not a determination to be made either by this court or the Board's counsel. It is one to which the immigration judge patently did not give any weight, in light of his mistaken statement that there were no such relatives in the United States, and it is one which the Board did not address because it limited its consideration to the psychiatric evaluation alone.

The Board has expressed the concern that a requirement that it review all prior evidence with each succeeding motion, no matter how insubstantial, would impose an unnecessary burden on the Board. We are not unaware of nor unsympathetic to the Board's problems in processing the substantial caseload before it. However, since the regulations themselves limit petitions to reopen to cases where there is material new evidence previously unavailable, 8 C.F.R. § 3.2, the Board itself has limited its reopening to preclude insubstantial motions.

We read the Supreme Court's *Wang* decision as reiterating the basic precept, which our prior opinion had also referred to, that Congress entrusted to the Attorney General, and not to the courts, discretion to determine whether a petitioner has shown extreme hardship to warrant suspension of deportation. We do not read that decision as foreclosing all judicial review regarding such matters, since such review is expressly provided in the statute. INA § 106.

While the scope of such review may be narrow, it extends at least to a determination as to whether the procedure followed by the Board in a particular case constitutes an improper exercise of that discretion. This court has previously held that where the record contains uncontradicted affidavits showing grounds for a suspension of deportation and yet lacks any reasoned evaluation by the INS of these grounds, an order to reopen is proper. *Martinez de Mendoza v. INS,* 567 F.2d 1222, 1224 (3d Cir.1977). We view this case in the same light.

Accordingly, we will grant review of the order of the Board and remand so that the Board can determine whether, taking into consideration all of the relevant factors on this record, the facts set forth in the psychiatric evaluation could not have affected the substantive decision on the petition for suspension of deportation, and whether reopening would be appropriate.

ALDISERT, CIRCUIT JUDGE, dissenting.

* * *

I.

Unlike the majority, I am unable to perform the court's reviewing function by selectively abstracting a few portions from the entire record before the Board. I am unable to do this because I recognize that the concept of discretion is founded on equitable considerations; a court that reviews for abuse of discretion, like the agency charged with its exercise, must view the totality of circumstances in reaching a decision. It cannot remove the question for decision from the larger context in which it is presented.

In their review of the record, the majority have glossed over a number of facts that I find quite revealing. For example, they ignore the deception of Mrs. Ravancho when she applied to the American consulate for a visa on September 26, 1968. At that time she claimed to be single and to be employed as a sales manager. In fact, she was married and had worked as an accounting clerk for the United States Navy. She repeated these falsehoods on January 21, 1969, when she applied for an extension of her visa.

The majority also ignore the record of the husband which parallels that of his wife. He first applied for a visa at the American consulate in the Philippines. After he was turned down he arranged for a "travel agency" to obtain a visa for him. He did not disclose the first rejection and, like his wife, he claimed before the authorities that he was single. Mr. Ravancho received a visa for business travel, but at the deportation hearing, he denied having any business in the United States. At the hearing, Mr. Ravancho at first denied seeking a visa from the embassy, but finally admitted that he had. Moreover, the evidence disclosed that the visa attached to his passport had been made out in the name of "Avan." The letters "r" and "cho" had been added in a different ink to change the name to "Ravancho."[1] When questioned about the alteration, Mr. Ravancho was evasive and denied knowing about it. After his arrival on December 19, 1968, he, too, applied for and received an extension of his stay, again representing that he was single. He claimed on the application for an extension of his visa that he wished to continue touring the country. The evidence disclosed that at the latest, he began working about six months later. Less than one year after this extension was granted, the Ravanchos' child, Patricia, was born. The immigration service thereafter granted another extension of their visas until February 7, 1974. Deportation proceedings for overstay were begun on December 5, 1977. These facts present a serious question about whether the petitioners are sincere in their application for reopening for the sake of their daughter, or whether they are stalling for an additional extension of an illegal stay *now amounting to over seven years.*

The majority have confused the question of statutory *eligibility* under INA § 244 and the question of whether the Board can consider the totality of the circumstances in exercising its *discretion.* * * *

II.

Turning now to the narrow focus of the majority's analysis and assuming the validity of that focus, I am unable to agree with their result. The Ravanchos have shifted emphasis in their petition to reopen, but their allegations remain substantially the same. They claim that they meet the statutory requirements, that they have relatives in this country, that they have behaved themselves while residents here, and that deportation would

---

1. Evidently this visa was one of many originating in the Philippines that had been altered in a similar manner.

psych.
eval
not mong

have a traumatic effect on their child. Their argument now, however, centers on the child and the excuse for their petition to reopen is a psychiatric evaluation of the effect of deportation on her.

In my view, the psychiatric evidence does not require the case to be reopened. Motions to reopen are governed by INS regulations, not by statute. They permit, but do not require, the service to re-examine a case previously decided when *significant* developments have occurred since the case was first heard.

This court has observed that the regulations bar consideration of evidence or contentions which could have been presented at the original proceeding. In the present case the record is barren of evidence suggesting that the adjustments Patricia would need to make in moving to the Philippines could not have been presented at that time. The utterly innocuous psychiatric report, set forth in pertinent part in the margin,[3] had significance only insofar as it confirmed the obvious: "the child will miss her friends in the United States and will have to adjust to life in the Philippines." I submit that the symptoms described in this report would parallel those of most ten year olds facing a move to a new neighborhood or to another part of the United States, let alone to a foreign country. In this regard, it should be kept in mind that the Ravanchos are natives of the Philippines with relatives and friends there who undoubtedly could ease the strain of adjustment for their daughter. To hold that this de minimis showing requires the Board to reopen a deportation hearing is to invite every deportable alien to challenge endlessly the Board's procedures. My views on this have not changed since the time the petition for review was originally presented. The Board implicitly found that the new evidence failed to meet the threshold requirement of materiality and, therefore, in my view, properly dismissed the motion.

---

3. The relevant portions of the report follow:

Psychiatric Evaluation of Patricia Ravancho
This 10 year old, fifth grade student was referred for psychiatric evaluation to determine [the] effect on her physical, mental and emotional stability if she is forced to return to the Philippines. Patricia was born in the United States and does not [speak] Tugallah.

. . . .

Interview with Patricia:

This clean, neat, well developed and well nourished, quiet, inhibited 10 year old sat anxiously awaiting her turn to be interviewed. She wrote her name very neatly in script, gave her age, grade, date of birth, address and school. Anxiety was revealed in her voice.

She was able to talk about her friends and her interests.

School has been all right for her except "arithmetic", "fractions", and "measurement".

This year her grades have gone down.

Fears are of "being frightened by other people", "heights", "bugs", "beetles", "wild animals", and "dying".

Ambition is to be a doctor.

When asked about her 3 wishes, she was able to state only one "Not have to go to the Philippines". When asked why she would not want to go there, she replied, "I would have to leave all of my friends whom I have known since kindergarten." She also mentioned the language problem, climate, and food.

Health: Health has been good. Sometimes she has trouble sleeping when weather is hot. Her insecurities were revealed in her HTP drawings. It took her a while to do the person, and she was so fearful of making a mistake that she traced the figure in the air first. When she called it "finished" there was no face or hands.

The house and tree showed isolation and inaccessibility.

Impression: Insecure child who relies on known friends and relatives for guidance and security.

The majority also consider significant the immigration judge's error in stating that the Ravanchos have no close relatives in the United States. The history of § 244 discloses that it was intended to deal with hardships to family relationships which would result from deportation. C. Gordon & H. Rosenfield, Immigration Law and Procedure § 7.9a (1980). The Ravanchos never attempted to demonstrate that they had any relationship with these family members, let alone that they would suffer from moving back to the country where their parents and other relatives live. Because there was no evidence of hardship either to the family members in the United States or to the Ravanchos, the error of the immigration judge was immaterial.[4]

III.

My principal disagreement with the majority, however, is their cavalier treatment of the Supreme Court's decision in *I.N.S. v. Wang*, 450 U.S. 139, 101 S.Ct. 1027, 67 L.Ed.2d 123 (1981) (per curiam). While not identical with the *facts* presented here, *Wang* addresses the specific *problem* before us in this case: the appropriate scope of judicial review of INS discretion. Unlike the majority, I read that decision broadly because I believe that the Court was deciding more than the issue presented by the precise facts before it. The Court was signalling to the courts of appeals the proper degree of deference to be accorded the Board's decisions on reopening. This reading is mandated because the Court did not stop with identifying the ninth circuit's error in ignoring the INS regulation requiring a petition to reopen to be supported by affidavits. That error alone would have justified the decision. Instead, the Court identified what it described as the circuit court's "fundamental" error of improvidently encroaching on the discretionary authority of the Attorney General and his designees. My reading of *Wang* convinces me that the majority here commit the same fundamental error as did the ninth circuit.[5]

4. The majority conclude that the Board did not consider the residence of these family members in its decision to reopen "because it limited its consideration to the psychiatric evaluation alone." I read the record differently. The residential status of the Ravanchos' relatives was set forth in the affidavit appended to their motion to reopen. The Board then considered both the affidavit and the psychiatric evaluation.

5. The majority attempt to distinguish *Wang* on the ground that there the Board undertook a cumulative review of the evidence presented, whereas here the Board reviewed only the new evidence. The majority indicates the Board's reference to the psychiatric report and its statement that "[t]his is not the type of extreme hardship necessary for a grant of suspension of deportation. . . ."

A reading of the entire paragraph reveals that this was not the case. The Board considered *both* the Ravanchos' affidavit which set forth the facts on which they based their initial petition for relief, *and* the psychiatric report:

> The only evidence submitted in support of the respondents' motion is *their own affidavit and a psychiatric evaluation of their ten-year-old United States citizen child.* This evidence does not establish the necessary hardship to the respondents or to their daughter for the purposes of relief from deportation under section 244 of the Immigration and Nationality Act, 8 U.S.C. 1254. Although the respondents have placed great reliance on the report of Dr. Prystowsky on their daughter, we find that it indicates no more than that the child will miss her friends in the United States and will have to adjust to life in the Philippines. This is not the type of extreme hardship necessary for a grant of suspension of deportation and, accordingly, we will deny the respondents' request for reconsideration.

Of particular relevance to the case before us is the language quoted by the Court in *Wang* from Judge Wallace's dissent in *Villena v. INS,* 622 F.2d 1352, 1362 (9th Cir.1980) (in banc), decided by the ninth circuit with *Wang:*

> If INS discretion is to mean anything, it must be that the INS has some latitude in deciding when to reopen a case. The INS should have the right to be restrictive. Granting such motions too freely will permit endless delays of deportation by aliens creative and fertile enough to continuously produce new and material facts sufficient to establish a prima facie case. It will also waste the time and efforts of immigration judges called upon to preside at hearings automatically required by the prima facie allegations.

Quoted 450 U.S. at 143 fn. 5, 101 S.Ct. at 1031 fn. 5. The Court quoted this language in connection with its recognition that the regulation providing for a procedure to reopen is framed negatively; it directs that the Board may not reopen absent a showing of specified conditions: "Thus the regulations may be construed to provide the Board with discretion in determining under what circumstances a proceeding should be reopened." *Id.* The Court then explained the legitimate government interest in limiting conditions on which reopening would be granted. The majority here, like the discredited ninth circuit *Wang* court, would require a reopening upon a minimal showing. *See* 450 U.S. at 144, 101 S.Ct. at 1031. This deprives the Board of its discretionary authority to determine under what circumstances reopening should be granted.

The majority pay only lip service to the legitimate interest of the government "in creating official procedures for handling motions to reopen deportation proceedings so as readily to identify those cases raising new and meritorious considerations." *Wang,* 450 U.S. at 145, 101 S.Ct. at 1031. The reason for according such procedures deference is clear: it is unfair to allow those aliens who have deliberately flouted the immigration laws to find shelter in those same laws, absent extraordinary circumstances, while requiring patient, law-abiding citizens of foreign states to follow the letter and spirit of the laws while awaiting a quota. The minimal showing that satisfies the majority will inevitably bring about further delays in this case, and worse, the decision invites any similarly situated alien to begin anew a groundless course of agency and judicial proceedings.

* * *

* * * What the majority have done is, in Karl Llewellyn's words, to treat the Supreme Court's decision in *Wang* as an "unwelcome precedent." Their grudging use of that decision seems to say that "[t]he rule holds only of redheaded Walpoles in pale magenta Buick cars." [6] I am confident that the majority's singular treatment of the Supreme Court's direction will have little precedential or institutional value in this or in other courts.

Notes

1. Numerous other § 244 cases have been remanded to the BIA, notwithstanding the holding (and implications) of *Wang. See, e.g., Jara-*

---

6. K. Llewellyn, *The Bramble Bush* 66–67 (1960).

Navarrete v. INS, 813 F.2d 1340, 1342 (9th Cir.1986) (BIA's "cursory and generalized analysis" of harm to U.S. citizen children constitutes abuse of discretion); *Cerrillo-Perez v. INS,* 809 F.2d 1419 (9th Cir.1987) (failure of BIA to consider hardship to alien's U.S. citizen children were they to remain in U.S. following alien's deportation); *Luna v. INS,* 709 F.2d 126 (1st Cir.1983) (alien established *prima facie* case of hardship warranting reopening and full consideration of § 244 claim); *Batoon v. INS,* 707 F.2d 399 (9th Cir.1983) (denial of motion to reopen reversed on ground that Board's opinion did not indicate consideration of important evidence); *Reyes v. INS,* 673 F.2d 1087 (9th Cir.1982) ("manifestly unfair" for BIA to disbelieve facts stated in affidavit submitted in support of motion to reopen). Are these cases consistent with the letter and spirit of *Wang?*

Of course, not all the cases have gone this way. *See, e.g., Hernandez–Patino v. INS,* 831 F.2d 750 (7th Cir.1987) (given BIA's authority to define "extreme hardship," Board need "merely follow established procedures, support conclusions with evidence and articulate reasons for its decisions"); *Hernandez-Cordero v. U.S.I.N.S.,* 819 F.2d 558 (5th Cir.1987) (en banc) (court may find abuse of discretion only where "the hardship is uniquely extreme, at or closely approaching the outer limits of the most severe hardship the alien could suffer and so severe that any reasonable person would necessarily conclude that the hardship is extreme"); *Leblanc v. INS,* 715 F.2d 685 (1st Cir.1983) (holding that BIA may deny motion to reopen as matter of discretion without determining whether alien has established prima facie case for relief); *Bueno-Carrillo v. Landon,* 682 F.2d 143 (7th Cir.1982) (upholding BIA finding of no extreme hardship).

Can the attempts by some lower courts to supervise suspension decisions succeed? Consider the following answer.

> In the long run * * * the techniques employed by the courts to control the Board's exercise of discretion may prove ineffective. The abuse-of-discretion standard devised by the courts of appeals does not significantly restrain the Board of Immigration Appeals: the Board may evade the teeth of the standard simply by taking care to include language in its opinions suggesting that the cumulative effect of all the evidence presented by the alien was insufficient to establish hardship. Unless one is confident that simply forcing the Board to articulate the factors it considered in reaching its decision will necessarily lead it to reach fairer and more humane results, the assertion that the post-*Wang* standard of review developed by the courts of appeals will serve as a real check on agency discretion seems unconvincing.

> Although the full consideration of all relevant facts is essential to proper exercise of administrative discretion, the manner in which that discretion is exercised is not determined solely by the deliberative process. The disagreement between the courts of appeals and the Board may ultimately be substantive rather than procedural: the cases strongly suggest that the courts have taken

a more generous view of the extent to which relief should be available to deportable aliens than has the Board. But because *Wang* seems to preclude the courts from enforcing their own substantive notions about the appropriateness of granting discretionary relief from deportation, the courts may be unable to affect anything more than the language in which the Board couches its conclusions. Thus, effective judicial control of agency discretion to deny relief from deportation may be a short-lived phenomenon.

Note, *Developments in the Law—Immigration Policy and the Rights of Aliens,* 96 Harv.L.Rev. 1286, 1397–98 (1983).

If this passage correctly identifies the judicial review in decisions like *Ravancho* as merely "procedural," and therefore inadequate to express underlying discomfort with the BIA's "substantive" views on the "extreme hardship," does it necessarily follow that judicial review will be ineffective? Should the courts' "own substantive notions" provide the test of effectiveness?

2. In *Matter of Kojoory,* 12 I & N Dec. 215, 219–20 (1967), the BIA stated that a claim by an alien that he will face persecution if returned home is irrelevant to extreme hardship under § 244 (although, of course, such a claim may provide the basis for withholding of deportation under § 243(h) or a grant of asylum under § 208). At least two circuit courts have accepted the BIA's position. *See Gebremichael v. INS,* 10 F.3d 28, 40 (1st Cir.1993); *Hee Yung Ahn v. INS,* 651 F.2d 1285, 1288 (9th Cir.1981). Is there a credible justification for this policy (other than a desire not to further complicate § 244 hearings)? *See* GM & Y § 74.07[5][f] ("the prospect of persecution seems to entail the highest degree of hardship").

Despite *Kojoory,* the BIA occasionally considers the risk of persecution in the course of deciding whether or not an alien has demonstrated extreme hardship under § 244. In such cases, courts have been willing to review the Board's evaluation of the persecution claim. *See, e.g., Kashefi–Zihagh v. INS,* 791 F.2d 708 (9th Cir.1986); *Zavala-Bonilla v. INS,* 730 F.2d 562 (9th Cir.1984).

c. *The Discretionary Aspect of § 244 Relief*

(i) *Administrative Discretion*

As the Supreme Court has noted, "[s]uspension of deportation is a matter of discretion and of administrative grace, not mere eligibility; discretion must be exercised even though statutory prerequisites have been met." *United States ex rel. Hintopoulos v. Shaughnessy,* 353 U.S. 72, 77, 77 S.Ct. 618, 621, 1 L.Ed.2d 652 (1957). Here we run into the same problems we faced in trying to pour content into the phrase "extreme hardship." What factors should the adjudicators consider in exercising the discretion the statute grants them? The cases indicate a number of factors that may be relevant. These include the alien's prior history of violations of the immigration laws, subversive activities, reliance on public assistance, and the absence of substantial ties in this country. *See, e.g., Vaughn v. INS,* 643 F.2d 35 (1st Cir.1981); GM & Y § 74.07[6]. What additional factors do you think could or should be considered?

Would it be advisable to promulgate regulations that would guide the exercise of discretion? In 1979, the INS issued proposed regulations that sought to identify factors to be considered in the exercise of discretion under INA § 245 (adjustment of status) and other provisions of the statute. 44 Fed.Reg. 36187–93 (1979). A year and a half later the project was abandoned; the INS explained:

> There is an inherent failure in any attempt to list those factors which should be considered in the exercise of discretion. It is impossible to list or foresee all of the adverse or favorable factors which may be present in a given set of circumstances. Listing some, even with the caveat that such list is not all inclusive, still poses a danger that the use of the guidelines may become so rigid as to amount to an abuse of discretion.

> In the exercise of discretion, all relevant factors are considered. The adverse factors are weighed against the favorable factors in the judgment and conscience of the responsible officials. Service officials are required to prepare a record justifying their actions when they deny a benefit in the exercise of administrative discretion. Summary and stereotyped denials are not acceptable.

> To avoid the possibility of hampering the free exercise of discretionary authority, the proposed rule is cancelled and a final rule will not be published.

46 Fed.Reg. 9119 (1981).

Maurice Roberts, former Chairman of the BIA, has argued that regulations to guide the exercise of discretion are both desirable and possible:

> [Discretion] is exercised by impressionable and fallible human beings at all levels of the administrative hierarchy. While the Act commits enforcement responsibility to the Attorney General and, upon his delegation, to the Commissioner of Immigration and Naturalization, in practice decision making has been delegated to and is exercised by a host of lesser officials. * * * In actual practice, most of the Service's decisions, which go out over the facsimile signatures of the various District Directors, are not made by the District Directors themselves, but are made in their name by adjudicators at various levels, who are not required to be lawyers or otherwise formally trained in the appraisal of evidence.

> In the absence of carefully considered and clearly articulated standards for the exercise of the various types of discretionary powers, the resulting decisions must necessarily vary with the personal attitudes and biases of the individual decision makers. Adjudicators with hard-nosed outlooks are likely to be more conservative in the evidentiary appraisals and in their dispensation of discretionary bounties than their counterparts with more permissive philosophies. It must be recognized as a fact of life that Service officers and Board members are no more immune than other persons to the influences that result in individual bias and predilection. To set up as a standard that a case must be

"meritorious" before discretion is favorably exercised in behalf of an eligible applicant is therefore illusory. Too many subjective elements go into the making of such a value judgment.

* * *

It should be possible to achieve greater uniformity of decision, while at the same time minimizing the opportunities for result-oriented adjudication based on an adjudicator's subjective feelings, by defining with greater precision not only the policies to be served but also the elements to be considered. It does not matter whether the guiding principles are laid down in published regulations or in the Board's published precedent decisions, which are binding on the Service. Certainly, greater care should be taken in thinking through and then defining those elements which should be considered "adverse" and those which can be properly juxtaposed in mitigation. Great [precision] need not completely strait-jacket the adjudicator or limit the range of elements which may properly be considered.

Of course, even with more precise definition of the relevant factors, the adjudicator must still determine how much weight to assign to each of the competing elements and in this appraisal his subjective notions can still come into play. It is at this point that clear policy statements become of overriding importance as a guide to action.

Uniformity of decision with mathematical precision is, of course, possible. Specific point values could be prescribed for each element deemed relevant, *e.g.,* so many minus points for a preconceived intent, so many for a wife abroad, so many for each minor child abroad, so many for being responsible for the break-up of the foreign marriage, so many for each intentional misstatement to the Service, etc. Plus points could be assigned for an American citizen or permanent resident wife, for each American child, for each year of the alien's residence here, and the like. An appropriate plus score could be fixed as a prerequisite to the favorable exercise of discretion. * * *

Any notion of such mechanical jurisprudence would, of course, be summarily rejected if seriously suggested. Yet, unless more realistic and specific guidelines are laid down, the opposite extreme becomes possible if it is left to each individual adjudicator to determine for himself, on the basis of his own subjective experiences and beliefs, just what factors in the alien's life should be determinative in exercising discretion and how much weight should be accorded each factor. An intolerant adjudicator could deny relief to aliens whose cultural patterns, political views, moral standards or life styles differed from his own. Worse still, a hostile or xenophobic adjudicator could vent his spleen on aliens he personally considered offensive without articulating the actual basis for his decision.

Unless standards are laid down which are not illusory and can be uniformly applied in the real world, we depart from even-handed justice and the rule of law. * * *

Roberts, *The Exercise of Administrative Discretion Under the Immigration Laws,* 13 San Diego L.Rev. 144, 147–48, 164–65 (1975).[5]

Do you agree with former Chairman Roberts? What are the costs and benefits of establishing guidelines for the exercise of discretion?

(ii) Judicial Review of Administrative Discretion in § 244 Cases

As the next case makes clear, the administrative agencies have broad authority to define circumstances under which discretionary relief will be granted or denied. Once again, the administrative action under review is a denial of a motion to reopen a deportation proceeding.

INS v. RIOS–PINEDA

Supreme Court of the United States, 1985.
471 U.S. 444, 105 S.Ct. 2098, 85 L.Ed.2d 452.

JUSTICE WHITE delivered the opinion of the Court.

* * *

Respondents, a married couple, are natives and citizens of Mexico. Respondent husband illegally entered the United States in 1972. Apprehended, he returned to Mexico in early 1974 under threat of deportation. Two months later, he and respondent wife paid a professional smuggler $450 to transport them into this country, entering the United States without inspection through the smuggler's efforts. Respondent husband was again apprehended by INS agents in 1978. At his request, he was granted permission to return voluntarily to Mexico in lieu of deportation. He was also granted two subsequent extensions of time to depart, but he ultimately declined to leave as promised. INS then instituted deportation proceedings against both respondents. By that time, respondent wife had given birth to a child, who, born in the United States, was a citizen of this country. A deportation hearing was held in December 1978. Respondents conceded illegal entry, conceded deportability, but requested suspension of deportation. The Immigration Judge, ruling that respondents were ineligible for suspension because they had not satisfied the requirement of seven years' continuous physical presence, ordered their deportation. Respondents appealed the order to the BIA, asserting a variety of arguments to establish that the deportation violated their rights or the rights of their child. The BIA rejected these arguments and dismissed the appeal.

5. *See also* Diver, *The Optimal Precision of Administrative Rules,* 93 Yale L.J. 65, 92–97 (1983) (concluding that "most of the reasons for discretionary grant or denial [by the INS] could be subjected to greater anterior specification without offending an applicant's humanity"). For other discussions of the tradeoffs involved in formulating legal principles as clear determinable rules or as policies and standards, *see* Kennedy, *Form and Substance in Private Law Adjudication,* 89 Harv. L.Rev. 1685, 1687–89, 1694–1701 (1976); Schuck, *When the Exception Becomes the Rule: Regulatory Equity and the Formulation of Energy Policy Through an Exceptions Policy,* 1984 Duke L.J. 163, 168–200, 289–300.

In July 1980, respondents filed a petition for review in the Court of Appeals, which automatically stayed their deportation pursuant to INA § 106(a)(3). Asking that the court order their deportation suspended, respondents asserted substantially the same claims rejected by the BIA: that the Immigration Judge should have given them *Miranda* warnings, that their deportation was an unlawful *de facto* deportation of their citizen child, and that respondent husband should have been considered present in the United States for seven years. In March 1982, 15 months after the briefs were filed, the Court of Appeals reversed the decision of the BIA and remanded the case for further proceedings. *Rios-Pineda v. United States Department of Justice,* 673 F.2d 225 (CA8). The Court of Appeals was of the view that during the pendency of the appeal, respondents had accrued the requisite seven years' continuous physical presence in the United States. *Id.,* at 227. Because of this development, the court directed the BIA to allow respondents 60 days to file a motion to reopen their deportation proceeding and cautioned the BIA "to give careful and thorough consideration to the . . . motion to reopen if, indeed, one is filed." *Id.,* at 228, n. 5. During the pendency of the appeals, respondent wife gave birth to a second citizen child.

Respondents then moved the BIA to reopen and requested suspension of deportation. They alleged that deportation would result in extreme hardship in that their two citizen children would be deprived of their right to an education in United States schools and to social assistance. Respondents also alleged general harm to themselves from their "low skills and educations" and the lower standard of living in Mexico.

The BIA denied the motion to reopen. First, the motion was not timely filed, as respondents had not served it on the proper official within the specified 60 days. Second, discretionary relief was unwarranted, since the additional facts—seven years' continuous physical presence and an additional child—were available only because respondents had delayed departure by frivolous appeals. Third, respondent husband's conduct in returning to the country only two months after his 1974 departure, respondents' payment to a professional smuggler to enter this country illegally, and respondent husband's refusal to depart voluntarily after promising to do so, all evinced a blatant disregard for the immigration laws, disentitling respondents to the favorable exercise of discretion.

The Court of Appeals reversed and directed the BIA to reopen the proceeding. *Rios-Pineda v. United States Department of Justice,* 720 F.2d 529 (CA8 1983). The motion to reopen, the panel concluded, was timely filed,[1] respondents had made out a prima facie case of hardship, and the factors relied on by the BIA did not justify its refusal to reopen. Although the court did not find merit in any of the legal arguments respondents had pressed during their prior appeals, their appeals were not frivolous. Neither could the BIA deny a motion to reopen because of respondents'

---

1. The issue of whether the motion to reopen was timely filed is not before this Court, and we assume, without deciding, that timely filing was established by service of the motion on the wrong official within the period required by the Court of Appeals' first decision. See 720 F.2d at 532.

disregard of the immigration laws, since such disregard is present in some measure in all deportation cases. *Id.,* at 534.

* * *

We have recently indicated that granting a motion to reopen is a discretionary matter with BIA. *INS v. Phinpathya,* 464 U.S. 183, 188, n. 6 (1984). Thus, even assuming that respondents' motion to reopen made out a prima facie case of eligibility for suspension of deportation, the Attorney General had discretion to deny the motion to reopen. *INS v. Jong Ha Wang,* 450 U.S. 139, 144, n. 5 (1981). We have also held that if the Attorney General decides that relief should be denied as a matter of discretion, he need not consider whether the threshold statutory eligibility requirements are met. *INS v. Bagamasbad,* 429 U.S. 24 (1976); see also *Jong Ha Wang,* 450 U.S., at 143–144, n. 5.

Given the Attorney General's broad discretion in this context, we cannot agree with the Court of Appeals' holding that denial of the motion to reopen was an impermissible exercise of that discretion. If, as was required by the regulations, respondents' motion to reopen was based on intervening circumstances demonstrating 7–year residence and extreme hardship, the Attorney General, acting through the BIA, nevertheless had the authority to deny the motion for two separate and quite adequate reasons.

First, although by the time the BIA denied the motion, respondents had been in this country for seven years, that was not the case when suspension of deportation was first denied; the seven years accrued during the pendency of respondents' appeals. The BIA noted that respondents' issues on appeals were without merit and held that the 7–year requirement satisfied in this manner should not be recognized. In our view, it did not exceed its discretion in doing so.

The Court of Appeals thought the appeal had not been frivolous because it had resulted in further proceedings. But this was true only because seven years of residence had accrued during the pendency of the appeal. No substance was found in any of the points raised on appeal, in and of themselves, and we agree with the BIA that they were without merit. The purpose of an appeal is to correct legal errors which occurred at the initial determination of deportability; it is not to permit an indefinite stalling of physical departure in the hope of eventually satisfying legal prerequisites. One illegally present in the United States who wishes to remain already has a substantial incentive to prolong litigation in order to delay physical deportation for as long as possible. The Attorney General can, in exercising his discretion, legitimately avoid creating a further incentive for stalling by refusing to reopen suspension proceedings for those who became eligible for such suspension only because of the passage of time while their meritless appeals dragged on.

The impact of any other rule is pointed out by this case. Respondents were apprehended in 1978, and they conceded deportability. Nonetheless, six years later they remain in the United States by virtue of their baseless appeals. In administering this country's immigration laws, the Attorney

General and the INS confront an onerous task even without the addition of judicially augmented incentives to take meritless appeals, engage in repeated violations, and undertake other conduct solely to drag out the deportation process. Administering the 7–year requirement in this manner is within the authority of the Attorney General. The Act commits the definition of the standards in the Act to the Attorney General and his delegate in the first instance, "and their construction and application of th[ese] standard[s] should not be overturned by a reviewing court simply because it may prefer another interpretation of the statute." *INS v. Jong Ha Wang, supra,* at 144.

Second, we are sure that the Attorney General did not abuse his discretion in denying reopening based on respondents' flagrant violation of the federal law in entering the United States, as well as respondent husband's willful failure to depart voluntarily after his request to do so was honored by the INS. The Court of Appeals' rejection of these considerations as "irrelevant" is unpersuasive. While all aliens illegally present in the United States have, in some way, violated the immigration laws, it is untenable to suggest that the Attorney General has no discretion to consider their individual conduct and distinguish among them on the basis of the flagrancy and nature of their violations. There is a difference in degree between one who enters the country legally, staying beyond the terms of a visa, and one who enters the country without inspection. Nor does everyone who illegally enters the country do so repeatedly and with the assistance of a professional smuggler. Furthermore, the Attorney General can certainly distinguish between those who, once apprehended, comply with the laws, and those who refuse to honor previous agreements to report for voluntary departure. Accordingly, we are convinced that the BIA did not abuse its discretion in denying reopening because of respondents' prior conduct.

This case, therefore, does not involve the unreasoned or arbitrary exercise of discretion. Here the BIA's explanation of its decision was grounded in legitimate concerns about the administration of the immigration laws and was determined on the basis of the particular conduct of respondents. In this government of separated powers, it is not for the judiciary to usurp Congress' grant of authority to the Attorney General by applying what approximates *de novo* appellate review. See *Jong Ha Wang,* 450 U.S., at 144–145; *Phinpathya,* 464 U.S., at 195–196. Because we conclude that here the refusal to reopen the suspension proceeding was within the discretion of the Attorney General, we reverse the decision of the Court of Appeals.

So ordered.

JUSTICE POWELL took no part in the consideration or decision of this case.

Notes

1. The Court states that "[a]dministering the 7–year requirement" as the BIA did in *Rios-Pineda* is "within the authority of the Attorney

General." What does the Court mean? Did the aliens lose because they failed to meet the seven-year requirement? (That is, if § 244 did not have a discretionary element, would the aliens still not have been entitled to relief?) Or did the aliens lose because the BIA is entitled to consider the filing of "frivolous" appeals as a negative factor when exercising its discretion? Or should we read *Rios-Pineda* as simply a case about motions to reopen—*i.e.*, that the BIA has discretion to deny such motions that are made possible only by abuse of the appeals process?

2. *Rios-Pineda* is yet another rather clear signal from the Supreme Court that the Court of Appeals should stop second-guessing the BIA's implementation of the discretionary aspects of the immigration laws. Here too, however, the lower courts have continued to find ways to express disapproval of the Board's actions. *See, e.g., Gonzalez Batoon v. INS*, 791 F.2d 681 (9th Cir.1986) (accrual of seven years of residence through filing of private bills is not equivalent to filing of frivolous appeals); *Sida v. INS*, 764 F.2d 1319 (9th Cir.1985), *superseded*, 783 F.2d 947 (9th Cir.1986) (period during pendency of appeals may count towards seven-year requirement).

3. Suppose a motion to reopen is not involved in a § 244 case. Is there then any room for judicial review of the exercise of administrative discretion? If the statute itself provides no standards, on what basis may a court determine that the adjudicators erred? Should we simply conclude, fortified by § 701 of the Administrative Procedure Act, *see* 5 U.S.C.A. § 701 (no judicial review where "agency action is committed to agency discretion by law"), that such decisions are not subject to judicial review? The (perhaps unsurprising) answer is no. Although APA § 701 excludes from judicial review actions committed by law to agency discretion, § 706 authorizes a court to set aside an agency action for "abuse of discretion." In the tussle that has ensued between these apparently conflicting provisions, reviewability has usually won out. *Citizens to Preserve Overton Park v. Volpe*, 401 U.S. 402, 410, 91 S.Ct. 814, 820, 28 L.Ed.2d 136 (1971) (§ 701 "is a very narrow exception * * * [and] is applicable in those rare instances where 'statutes are drawn in such broad terms that in a given case there is no law to apply.' "); *but cf. Heckler v. Chaney*, 470 U.S. 821, 105 S.Ct. 1649, 84 L.Ed.2d 714 (1985) (agency refusal to initiate enforcement action not subject to judicial review). *See generally* 3 K.C. Davis & R. Pierce, Administrative Law Treatise ch. 17 (3d ed. 1994).[6]

Judge Henry Friendly has written the definitive opinion on the reviewability of the discretionary aspect of the suspension of deportation decision.

6. For holdings in the immigration context that agency action is committed to agency discretion and thus not subject to judicial review, see *Dina v. Attorney General*, 793 F.2d 473 (2d Cir.1986) (USIA recommendation on waiver of two-year foreign residency requirement for J–1 visa holders); *Abdelhamid v. Ilchert*, 774 F.2d 1447 (9th Cir. 1985) (same); *Doherty v. Meese*, 808 F.2d 938 (2d Cir.1986) (Attorney General's decision under INA § 243(a) to deny deportation to country designated by alien, on finding that such deportation would be "prejudicial to the interests of the United States," is "essentially unreviewable"). A strikingly expansive reading of the "committed to agency discretion" doctrine appears in *Perales v. Casillas*, 903 F.2d 1043 (5th Cir.1990) (pre-deportation-hearing denial of voluntary departure and work authorization is unreviewable).

WONG WING HANG v. INS

United States Court of Appeals, Second Circuit, 1966.
360 F.2d 715.

handwritten margin note: "definitive opinion" of discretion for reviewing suspension of deport. decision

FRIENDLY, CIRCUIT JUDGE:

Wong Wing Hang asks us to set aside a final order of the Board of Immigration Appeals insofar as this denied, as a matter of discretion, his application under the Immigration and Nationality Act § 244, for suspension of a concededly valid order directing his deportation to Formosa.

handwritten margin note: fraudulent entry 1951

The petitioner, a 37–year old native and citizen of China, entered the United States in 1951 on a false claim that he was the son of a United States citizen. Two years later he fraudulently applied for a certificate of citizenship, and in December 1955, when questioned by a United States attorney, gave false information as to his identity and that of other Chinese immigrants. Shortly thereafter he furnished the correct information when called before a grand jury, and subsequently revealed his identity to the INS and surrendered his certificate. In 1956 he was indicted as a member of a conspiracy to perpetrate passport frauds for other Chinese, the last overt act being the giving of false testimony in court on December 12, 1955; he was convicted on a plea of guilty in 1961, and, receiving a suspended sentence, was placed on probation for a year.

handwritten margin note: 1963 applic. for susp. of deport.

In September 1963, the INS held proceedings to determine whether Wong should be deported for having entered the United States without inspection. Not disputing deportability, Wong applied for suspension. A hearing before a Special Inquiry Officer revealed that during the course of his probation Wong told his probation officer that his wife was in China and afterwards, in August 1962, when asked by an investigator of the INS where his wife and children were and whether they had ever entered the United States, stated under oath that they had never entered this country and were living in Kowloon; in fact, as Wong well knew, the wife and children had fraudulently entered Canada in 1958 as the spouse and children of a Canadian citizen and at the time of the statement to the investigator were visiting Wong in New York. The Special Inquiry Officer, after questioning Wong closely as to the extent of his wife's visits and whether she was spending most of the time here, reserved decision pending report of a character investigation being conducted by the Government. The following December, in the course of the investigation, the wife was found in Wong's apartment, having entered the United States two months before as a Canadian citizen saying she wanted to remain for three weeks or a month.

* * *

* * * Wong's application for suspension was denied not for ineligibility but because, in the language of the Special Inquiry Officer, "far from acting as a person who regretted his previous actions and was attempting to act in a law abiding fashion," Wong had "deliberately concealed the whereabouts and status of his wife and children" and had permitted his wife to enter the United States repeatedly with documents known to him to be fraudulent and to remain beyond the period of her admission. Wong complains that he is being penalized for protecting his wife and children as any husband and father would.

* * *

* * * [W]e turn for illumination to * * * the Administrative Procedure Act * * *. Here we encounter the familiar conflict between the preamble of [5 U.S.C.A. § 701] "Except so far as * * * agency action is by law committed to to agency discretion," and the command of [5 U.S.C.A. § 706] that the reviewing court shall "set aside agency action * * * found to be * * * arbitrary, capricious, an abuse of discretion, or otherwise not in accordance with law."

Some help in resolving the seeming contradiction may be afforded by the distinction drawn by Professors Hart and Sacks between a discretion that "is not subject to the restraint of the obligation of reasoned decision and hence of reasoned elaboration of a fabric of doctrine governing successive decisions" and discretion of the contrary and more usual sort, see The Legal Process 172, 175–177 (Tent. ed. 1958); only in the rare—some say non-existent—case where discretion of the former type has been vested, may review for "abuse" be precluded. An argument could be made that the change from the earlier versions of the suspension provision, "the Attorney General may suspend if he finds," 54 Stat. 672 (1940), 62 Stat. 1206 (1948), to its present form affords an indication that Congress meant to accord the Attorney General or his delegate *ad hoc* discretion of that sort. But the Attorney General himself has not thought so; applications for suspension of deportation, whether under § 244 or § 243(h) of the Immigration and Nationality Act, have long been subjected to various administrative hearing and appeal procedures, see the history recounted in Jay v. Boyd, 351 U.S. 345, 351–352, 76 S.Ct. 919, 100 L.Ed. 1242 (1956), with their concomitants of "the obligation of reasoned decision." Despite language in Jay v. Boyd, supra at 353–356, 76 S.Ct. 919, that could be read as supporting unreviewability of the ultimate exercise of discretion, the contrary view is implicit in United States ex rel. Hintopoulos v. Shaughnessy, 353 U.S. 72, 77, 77 S.Ct. 618, 1 L.Ed.2d 652 (1957), where the Court reviewed the discretionary denial of suspension and affirmed the agency decision because it did not represent an abuse of discretion and the reasons on which it was based were neither "capricious nor arbitrary." * * * This court has long held discretionary denials of suspension to be reviewable for "abuse."

What is not so clear is precisely what this means. In the absence of standards in the statute itself, proper administration would be advanced and reviewing courts would be assisted if the Attorney General or his delegate, without attempting to be exhaustive in an area inherently insusceptible of such treatment, were to outline certain bases deemed to warrant the affirmative exercise of discretion and other grounds generally militating against it. When we turn to the books, we find that "abuse of discretion" has been given two rather different meanings. In one version it appears as a sort of "clearly erroneous" concept, perhaps best expressed in Judge Magruder's formulation that "when judicial action is taken in a discretionary matter, such action cannot be set aside by a reviewing court unless it has a definite and firm conviction that the court below committed a clear error of judgment in the conclusion it reached upon a weighing of the relevant factors." In re Josephson, 218 F.2d 174, 182 (1 Cir.1954). *See* Pearson v. Dennison, 353 F.2d 24, 28 & n. 6 (9 Cir.1965). Under a more limited notion discretion is held to be abused only when the action "is arbitrary, fanciful or unreasonable, which is another way of saying that discretion is abused only where no reasonable man would take the view" under discussion. *See* Delno v. Market St. Ry. Co., 124 F.2d 965, 967 (9 Cir.1942). A narrower meaning seems more appropriate when a court is reviewing the exercise of discretion by an administrative agency or an executive officer as distinguished from hearing an appeal from a decision of a judge—particularly so when the relevant statute expressly confides "discretion" to the agency or officer; this assists in reconciling what conflict there is in * * * the APA. Without essaying comprehensive definition, we think the denial of suspension to an eligible alien would be an abuse of discretion if it were made without a rational explanation, inexplicably departed from established policies, or rested on an impermissible basis such as an invidious discrimination against a particular race or group, or, in Judge Learned Hand's words, on other "considerations that Congress could not have intended to make relevant." [United States ex rel. Kaloudis v. Shaughnessy, 180 F.2d 489, 491 (2d Cir.1950).]

Wong contends that the determination here comes under the first rubric since it is internally inconsistent—he was found to have possessed "good moral character" during the several years prior to his application for discretionary relief, yet was faulted for prevarication and concealment during that same period. But the answer lies in the very point so strongly pressed by him, that his falsehoods were prompted by the natural human motive to protect his wife and children and keep his family together. To say that such conduct does not demonstrate lack of good moral character but nevertheless may not demand a favorable exercise of discretion by the Immigration Service is by no means a self-contradiction. If the immigration authorities choose to say that a man who has gained entry by a false claim of United States citizenship and has cooperated with others in similar efforts, can win their favor only by a spotless record in later dealings with them, and apply this standard with an even hand, we cannot hold their decision to be so wanting in rationality as to be an abuse of the discretion which Congress vested in them.

The petition to review must therefore be denied.

Note

How can an alien prove that a discretion-based denial of § 244 relief—or any equivalent discretionary relief under the INA—departed from established policies or rested on a hidden impermissible basis? Would he be entitled to extensive discovery of INS internal documents (perhaps to be gathered nationwide, if the issue is departure from established policy), or to depositions of numerous INS officers? What threshold showing should be required before INS is subjected to these kinds of discovery burdens? A request for discovery in these circumstances can pose thorny problems for a court, because it is often hard to see how an alien could establish even a prima facie case of administrative flaws of this type without *first* obtaining highly burdensome discovery. Recall Leon Wildes' account of John Lennon's case, p. 648 *supra*. For one court's efforts to balance the relevant concerns, *see Munoz–Santana v. INS*, 742 F.2d 561 (9th Cir.1984).

2. WAIVER OF EXCLUSION GROUNDS IN DEPORTATION HEARINGS OF LONG–TERM PERMANENT RESIDENT ALIENS: INA § 212(c)

Take a close look at INA § 212(c) in the Statutory Supplement. You may wonder why we are discussing a waiver of exclusion grounds in a Chapter dealing with relief from deportation. The answer derives from *Francis v. INS*, 532 F.2d 268 (2d Cir.1976), a case which held that the equal protection component of the Fifth Amendment's due process clause requires extension of the exclusion waiver to similarly situated aliens in deportation hearings. To understand the case fully, we must examine a series of earlier administrative and judicial interpretations of § 212(c).

Section 212(c) is the descendant of the Seventh Proviso of § 3 of the 1917 Immigration Act, which authorized the waiver of grounds of exclusion for "aliens returning after a temporary absence to an unrelinquished United States domicile of seven consecutive years." This Proviso, which on its face only applies to re-entries, made its way into the deportation context in *Matter of L*, 1 I & N Dec. 1 (BIA & A.G. 1940). There the alien had been admitted in 1909 and was convicted of stealing a watch in 1924. At that time the deportation ground for crimes of moral turpitude was limited to crimes committed within five years of entry. Thus L was not deportable in 1924. In 1939 L left the United States to visit a seriously ill sister in Yugoslavia for two months. He was readmitted upon his return. Several months later he was arrested and placed in deportation proceedings. Why? Because § 19 of the 1917 Act included as a ground of deportation conviction of a crime involving moral turpitude "prior to entry." Thus, L, who would not have been deportable had he remained in the United States, was now deportable because he had been convicted of a crime prior to his re-entry in 1939. The re-entry doctrine had struck again.

L invoked the Seventh Proviso, asserting that the ground of exclusion was waivable at the time of entry. He therefore asked the Attorney General to apply the waiver provision in the deportation case. The Attorney General consented. Although the Attorney General recognized that the Act made no provision for such waivers outside of an exclusion proceeding, he concluded that "Congress [could not have] intended the immigration laws to operate in so capricious and whimsical a fashion":

> Granted that respondent's departure in 1939 exposed him on return to the peril of a fresh judgment as to whether he should be permitted to reside in the United States, such judgment ought not to depend upon the technical form of the proceedings. No policy of Congress could possibly be served by such irrational result.

> Had respondent obtained his readmission in 1939 by deceptive
> concealment of his prior conviction, the case would have been
> different.   But the record throws no doubt upon his good faith.
> This being so, he should be permitted to make the same appeal to
> discretion that he could have made if denied admission in 1939, or
> that he could make in some future application for admission if he
> now left the country.   To require him to go to Canada and reenter
> will make him no better resident of this country.   To require him
> to wait a year before reentry [following deportation], while his
> resources are exhausted and his shoe-shining business * * * is
> destroyed, will make him a worse one.

Accordingly, the Attorney General exercised the authority granted by the
Seventh Proviso *nunc pro tunc,* stating that such action under the circumstances of the case "amounts to little more than a correction of a record of
entry."   1 I & N Dec. at 5–6.

In the 1952 Act, the Seventh Proviso was amended slightly and
renumbered as § 212(c).   In an early interpretation of the new section, the
BIA concluded that the use of the Proviso in a deportation case survived
the revision of the statute.   *Matter of S.,* 6 I & N Dec. 392 (BIA 1954),
affirmed by the Attorney General, id. at 397 (1955).

The next expansion of the form of relief came in *Matter of G.A.,* 7 I &
N Dec. 274 (BIA 1956).   There the alien had been admitted in 1913 and
convicted of importation of 142 grains of marijuana in 1947.   He had last
re-entered the United States in 1952.   Several years later, G.A. was placed
in deportation proceedings on the basis of the 1947 drug conviction.   G.A.
requested a § 212(c) waiver in the deportation hearing, and the BIA found
him eligible for such relief.   It reasoned that the § 212(c) waiver would
have been exercised at the time of the alien's re-entry in 1952; and that
that waiver would have prevented initiation of a deportation proceeding
based on the same charge waived at time of entry.   The BIA therefore
analogized G.A.'s situation to that of the earlier cases: the waiver should
be available in the deportation proceeding when it could have been exercised at time of re-entry and would have wiped out the deportation ground.

While there is some surface plausibility to the BIA's reasoning in
Matter of G.A., the case is materially different from *Matter of L.* In *Matter
of L,* the alien was rendered deportable solely by operation of the re-entry
doctrine.   He was not deportable at the time he left the United States, nor
did he commit an act while outside the United States which would have
made him deportable upon return.   Section 212(c) seems clearly drafted to
ameliorate the capricious effects of the re-entry doctrine, and the situation
in *Matter of L* can reasonably be placed among them.

In *Matter of G.A.,* however, the alien's re-entry appears to work
capriciously *in his favor.* He was deportable irrespective of his re-entry.
Yet the BIA concluded that once he had left, the ground could have been
waived at readmission; thus it should also be waivable in a deportation
proceeding after re-entry.   Rather than triggering the ground of deportation, the re-entry triggered the waiver.

Now consider the alien who is a long-time resident and has never left the United States. Assume he commits a crime for which he is deportable—one that would also cause him to be excluded should he leave the country and try to re-enter. In his deportation hearing he invokes § 212(c), startling the immigration judge. When the judge states that § 212(c) only applies to returning residents, the alien claims that such an interpretation draws an arbitrary line between him and the alien in *Matter of G.A.* "Why should G.A. get the benefit of § 212(c)," asks the alien, "simply because he happened to leave the country? Both of us are deportable whether or not we leave and return. Can the immigration laws really mean that, although I am not eligible for relief from deportation now, I could become so by taking a month's vacation in Europe?" The immigration judge recognizes the seeming arbitrariness, but nonetheless denies the relief. "Section 212(c)," she states, "applies to returning residents in exclusion proceedings. I simply cannot read the section as authorizing relief in deportation proceedings to aliens who have never left the country." The alien responds, "I think your position violates standards of equal protection. You admit that, but for a fortuity, I am in the same position as G.A. No one made you read the section to apply to him. But once you do, you must now apply it on my behalf as well."

Who's correct? Read *Francis*.

FRANCIS v. INS

United States Court of Appeals, Second Circuit, 1976.
532 F.2d 268.

LUMBARD, CIRCUIT JUDGE:

* * *

Ernest Francis was admitted to this country as a permanent resident on September 8, 1961. Mr. Francis, a citizen and native of Jamaica, West Indies, is 55 years old, married and the father of a nine year old daughter. He is presently employed as a handyman and resides with his family in the Bronx. Petitioner's wife and daughter are citizens of the United States. His three brothers and one sister are also citizens. Petitioner's father, Joseph Francis, was, at the time of his death, a citizen of this country.

On October 20, 1971, following a plea of guilty, petitioner was convicted of criminal possession of dangerous drugs (marijuana). He was sentenced to a term of probation by the Supreme Court, Bronx County on December 14, 1971. Apart from this conviction and a twenty-five dollar fine for gambling in September, 1973, petitioner has no criminal record.

The Immigration and Naturalization Service ("INS") instituted a deportation proceeding against petitioner on December 6, 1972 by issuing an order to show cause and notice of hearing. The INS charged him with being deportable by reason of the marijuana conviction. * * *

Francis did not, and does not now, dispute his deportability * * *. Rather, he argues that he was eligible for discretionary relief under Section

212(c) of the INA, a provision which is primarily applicable to exclusion proceedings. * * *

On February 20, 1974, in an oral decision, the Immigration judge held that Section 212(c) consideration was not available and ordered petitioner deported. Petitioner appealed that decision to the Board on February 28, 1974. On August 15, 1974, the Board dismissed the appeal holding that petitioner was ineligible "for any form of discretionary relief from deportation."

Petitioner seeks a declaration from this court that he is eligible to apply to the Attorney General for discretionary relief under Section 212(c).

[The court then discusses administrative precedents including *Matter of L.* and *Matter of G.A.*]

The statutory interpretation which this petitioner complains of derives from the decision in *Matter of Arias–Uribe,* 13 I. & N.Dec. 696 (1971). There the Board declined to extend Section 212(c) to an otherwise eligible alien who had not departed the country since his narcotics conviction.

* * * In denying Section 212(c) treatment to the alien, the Board seized upon the change in language between the Seventh Proviso, which required that the alien be "returning [to the United States] after a temporary absence", and Section 212(c), which requires that the alien have "temporarily proceeded abroad voluntarily and not under an order of deportation." The Board viewed this as meaning that Congress intended by this clause to require an actual departure and return to this country.[4] In a brief per curiam opinion, the Ninth Circuit affirmed this construction of the statute. *Arias-Uribe v. INS,* 466 F.2d 1198 (1972). Although there is nothing in the legislative history of the 1952 Act which indicates that Congress intended to change prior case law in this respect, we agree with the Ninth Circuit that the Board's interpretation is consistent with the language of Section 212(c). See S.Rep.No. 1137, 82nd Cong., 2d Sess. (1952); H.R.No. 1365, 82nd Cong., 2d Sess. (1952); U.S.Code Cong. & Admin.News 1952, p. 1653.

It is the petitioner's contention that if this statutory construction is applied to his case, then he is deprived of the equal protection of the laws as guaranteed by the fifth amendment.[5] He argues that the statute as so applied creates two classes of aliens identical in every respect except for the fact that members of one class have departed and returned to this country at some point after they became deportable. Thus the distinction is not rationally related to any legitimate purpose of the statute.

---

4. The Board felt its position did not conflict with its interpretation in *Matter of Smith,* 11 I. & N. Dec. 325 (1965) which allowed Section 212(c) discretion to be applied in conjunction with a Section 245 adjustment of status without a physical departure. 13 I. & N. Dec. at 698–99. [Francis was not eligible for adjustment of status, and thus the benefits of *Matter of Smith,* because at the time § 245 relief was not available to natives of the Western Hemisphere.—eds.]

5. "[I]f a classification would be invalid under the Equal Protection Clause of the Fourteenth Amendment, it is also inconsistent with the due process requirement of the Fifth Amendment." *Johnson v. Robison,* 415 U.S. 361, 364 n. 4, 94 S.Ct. 1160, 1164, 39 L.Ed.2d 389, 396 (1974); *Bolling v. Sharpe,* 347 U.S. 497, 74 S.Ct. 693, 98 L.Ed. 884 (1954).

The authority of Congress and the executive branch to regulate the admission and retention of aliens is virtually unrestricted. Enforcement of the immigration laws is often related to considerations both of foreign policy and the domestic economy. Nevertheless "[i]n the enforcement of these policies, the Executive Branch of the Government must respect the procedural safeguards of due process...." *Galvan v. Press,* 347 U.S. 522, 74 S.Ct. 737, 98 L.Ed. 911 (1954).

It has long been held that the constitutional promise of equal protection of the laws applies to aliens as well as citizens, *Yick Wo v. Hopkins,* 118 U.S. 356, 6 S.Ct. 1064, 30 L.Ed. 220 (1886). * * * Although the right of a permanent resident alien to remain in this country has never been held to be the type of "fundamental right" which would subject classifications touching on it to strict judicial scrutiny, the Supreme Court has observed that "deportation can be the equivalent of banishment or exile.... " *Delgadillo v. Carmichael,* 332 U.S. 388, 391, 68 S.Ct. 10, 12, 92 L.Ed. 17, 19 (1947).

Under the minimal scrutiny test, which we consider applicable in this case, distinctions between different classes of persons "must be reasonable, not arbitrary, and must rest upon some ground of difference having a fair and substantial relation to the object of the legislation, so that all persons similarly circumstanced shall be treated alike." *Stanton v. Stanton,* 421 U.S. 7, 14, 95 S.Ct. 1373, 1377, 43 L.Ed.2d 688, 694 (1975).

In determining whether the Board's policy survives minimal scrutiny, the purpose of Section 212(c) must be examined. As the government notes in its brief, Congress was concerned that there be some degree of flexibility to permit worthy returning aliens to continue their relationships with family members in the United States despite a ground for exclusion. Realizing that these considerations apply with equal force to an alien who has already reentered, perhaps illegally, the Board chose to expand eligibility to that group. *Matter of G.A.,* 7 I. & N. Dec. 274 (1956). Thus an alien who had been convicted of two crimes involving moral turpitude and, therefore, was deportable under Section 241(a)(4), was eligible for Section 212(c) discretion because he was able to demonstrate that several months after his last conviction he left the country for a few hours to attend a funeral in Canada. *Matter of Edwards,* 10 I. & N. Dec. 506 (1963). The government has failed to suggest any reason why this petitioner's failure to travel abroad following his conviction should be a crucial factor in determining whether he may be permitted to remain in this country. Reason and fairness would suggest that an alien whose ties with this country are so strong that he has never departed after his initial entry should receive at least as much consideration as an individual who may leave and return from time to time.

It is the government's position that Congress has chosen to treat these two classes of aliens somewhat differently by providing a separate but analogous scheme of discretionary relief to the non-departing alien. Section 244(a)(2), allows the Attorney General to exercise discretion regarding certain deportable aliens who have been in the country for ten years following the act which was the ground for deportation.[7] This argument overlooks the fact that a deportable resident alien who briefly sojourns in Bermuda and then returns is eligible for discretionary consideration under Section 244(a)(2) as a non-departing alien. In addition, if otherwise qualified, he is eligible for Section 212(c) relief. *See Matter of G.A., supra.*

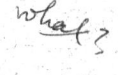

Fundamental fairness dictates that permanent resident aliens who are in like circumstances, but for irrelevant and fortuitous factors, be treated in a like manner. We do not dispute the power of the Congress to create different standards of admission and deportation for different groups of aliens. However, once those choices are made, individuals within a particular group may not be subjected to disparate treatment on criteria wholly unrelated to any legitimate governmental interest. We find that the Board's interpretation of Section 212(c) is unconstitutional as applied to this petitioner.

Accordingly, the petition is granted. The case is remanded to the Board so that the Attorney General's discretion under Section 212(c) may be exercised.

Notes

1. Although it seems clear that § 212(c) was intended to mitigate the harshness of the re-entry doctrine, *Francis* goes far beyond this purpose. It, in effect, provides a general power in the Attorney General to waive any ground of deportation analogous to an exclusion ground for long-time resident aliens. While this may seem like a sensible policy—a matter we will explore at the end of the Chapter—has not Congress already provided such a form of relief in § 244? Indeed, given the careful consideration in § 244 of the grounds that may be waived, the time period required for eligibility and the like, does not *Francis* create a new form of relief for deportable aliens quite at odds with the congressional scheme?

One answer to this is that *Francis* does not create a new avenue for relief; it simply demands equal treatment of similarly situated aliens. The Second Circuit essentially said to the agency: *if* you allow aliens like G.A. to apply for § 212(c) relief, then you must also allow aliens like Francis to do the same. The BIA, thus, could avoid *Francis* by simply overruling its decision in *Matter of G.A.* For example, it could conclude that § 212(c) relief should be available only to aliens who are rendered deportable *because* of a brief absence abroad and re-entry. The BIA, however, has not chosen to adopt this reformulation. Rather, in *Matter of Silva*, 16 I & N Dec. 26 (BIA 1976), it announced that it would abide by *Francis* and apply § 212(c) to aliens who had never left the United States. The BIA stated: "In light of the constitutional requirements of due process and equal protection of the law, it is our position that no distinction shall be made between permanent resident aliens who temporarily proceed abroad and non-departing permanent resident aliens." *Id.* at 30. *Francis* has become

---

7. Less than five years have elapsed since petitioner's conviction. Thus he is ineligible   for this discretionary provision.

the general rule. *See, e.g., Joseph v. INS*, 909 F.2d 605, 606 n.1 (1st Cir.1990); *Tapia-Acuna v. INS*, 640 F.2d 223, 225 (9th Cir.1981).

With the BIA's acquiescence in *Francis*, haven't an administrative agency and a federal court effectively amended the INA without Congress' participation?

2.   Would the *Francis* court have reached the same result if not just the BIA, but also Congress had expressly addressed this issue, codifying the results in *Matter of L.* and *Matter of G.A.*, but also making aliens who had never left the United States ineligible to use § 212(c)?

3.   Does § 212(c)'s requirement of *"lawful* unrelinquished domicile" mean that all seven years must have been preceded by a *lawful admission for permanent residence?* This issue can arise in two ways. First, an alien may reside here unlawfully for several years and then attain lawful permanent residence. It is established that all seven years of an alien's residence must be lawful for the alien to qualify for § 212(c) relief. *See Lok v. INS (Lok II)*, 681 F.2d 107, 109–10 (2d Cir.1982).

Second, some classes of aliens are able to maintain lawful domicile in the United States even though they are not permanent residents. These include some parolees and aliens admitted as refugees under INA §§ 207 and 208. Another large group consists of persons granted temporary resident status under the IRCA legalization programs. Most nonimmigrants cannot establish *lawful* domicile in this country because the definition in INA § 101(a)(15) of most classes of nonimmigrants requires them to have residences in foreign countries which they have no intention of abandoning. Also, certain foreign government officials may maintain lawful domicile in the United States. If aliens in any of these groups become lawful permanent residents, does their earlier time in the United States count toward the required seven years?

There is a split of authority on this question. At least two courts of appeals and the BIA have said no. *See Chiravacharadhikul v. INS*, 645 F.2d 248, 250–51 (4th Cir.1981), *cert. denied*, 454 U.S. 893, 102 S.Ct. 389, 70 L.Ed.2d 207 (1981); *Castillo-Felix v. INS*, 601 F.2d 459, 467 (9th Cir.1979); *Matter of Anwo*, 16 I & N Dec. 293, 296 (BIA 1977), *affirmed on other grounds per curiam*, 607 F.2d 435 (D.C.Cir.1979). The Second Circuit, however, has said that lawful domicile before attaining permanent resident status does count if the intent to remain is consistent with the immigration laws. *Lok v. INS*, 548 F.2d 37, 41 (2d Cir.1977) *(Lok I)*, as explained in *Lok II, supra*, 681 F.2d at 109 n.3. The BIA does not follow *Lok I* outside the Second Circuit, but other circuits have taken positions consistent with *Lok I. See, e.g., Castellon-Contreras v. INS*, 45 F.3d 149 (7th Cir.1995); *Melian v. INS*, 987 F.2d 1521, 1524 (11th Cir.1993). For an excellent discussion of the precedents and policies, see Wettstein, *Lawful Domicile for Purposes of INA § 212(c): Can It Begin With Temporary Residence?*, 71 Interp.Rel. 1273 (1994). Note that some of these non-permanent-resident statuses are arguably more like lawful permanent residence than others—for example, temporary residents under IRCA legalization—so answers may vary from category to category. What answer makes sense to you?

4. In counting the required seven years, the BIA and the federal appeals courts have struggled with the question when "lawful unrelinquished domicile" ends and the seven years stop accruing. Answers that have emerged include:

(a) when the order to show cause is issued, see, e.g., Matter of Diaz–Chambrot, 19 I & N Dec. 674, 675 (BIA 1988); Ballbe v. INS, 886 F.2d 306, 309 (11th Cir.1989), overruled in Jaramillo v. INS, 1 F.3d 1149, 1154–55 (11th Cir.1993); Marti-Xiques v. INS, 741 F.2d 350, 353 (11th Cir.1984), overruled in Jaramillo v. INS, 1 F.3d 1149, 1154–55 (11th Cir.1993);

(b) when the deportation order becomes "administratively final" in that the BIA decides the appeal, the appeal is waived, or the time for appeal expires, see, e.g., Matter of Lok, 18 I & N Dec. 101, 105–07 (BIA 1981), aff'd, Lok v. INS, 681 F.2d 107, 109–10 (2d Cir.1982); Jaramillo v. INS, 1 F.3d 1149, 1154–55 (11th Cir.1993).

(c) when judicial review of the BIA decision regarding deportation is final, see, e.g., Wall v. INS, 722 F.2d 1442, 1444–45 (9th Cir.1984), as modified by Avila–Murrieta v. INS, 762 F.2d 733, 735 (9th Cir.1985).

Alternative (b) has become the prevailing view. One additional possibility—when the deportable conduct occurred—was considered but rejected by the Eleventh Circuit in Marti-Xiques v. INS, 741 F.2d 350, 353 (11th Cir.1984), overruled in Jaramillo v. INS, 1 F.3d 1149, 1154–55 (11th Cir.1993). See generally GM & Y § 74.04[2][e]. A bill now pending in Congress, S. 269, 104th Cong., 1st Sess., would provide that the seven-year period stop accruing when the alien has received an order to show cause.

5. The seven-year accrual question is closely related to, yet distinct from, an eligibility issue. An alien may apply for relief under § 212(c) only if she is "lawfully admitted for permanent residence," a phrase that INA § 101(a)(20) defines as "the status of having been lawfully accorded the privilege of residing permanently in the United States as an immigrant in accordance with the immigration laws, such status not having changed." Assume that the alien had a "lawful unrelinquished domicile" for seven years but has been ordered deported, and that the BIA has affirmed the deportation order. Now she moves to reopen, either to apply for § 212(c) relief for the first time, or to present new evidence supporting a prior unsuccessful application for § 212(c) relief. Has the administratively final deportation order made her (1) no longer a permanent resident, thus (2) ineligible to apply, and thus (3) unable to reopen the proceedings?

The BIA and the several courts of appeal have answered "yes." See Matter of Cerna, Int.Dec. 3161 (BIA 1991), aff'd without opinion, Cerna v. INS, 979 F.2d 212 (11th Cir.1992). See, e.g., Nwolise v. United States INS, 4 F.3d 306, 310–12 (4th Cir.1993), cert. denied, 114 S.Ct. 888, 127 L.Ed.2d 82 (1994); Katsis v. INS, 997 F.2d 1067, 1072–74 (3d Cir.1993), cert. denied, 114 S.Ct. 902, 127 L.Ed.2d 93 (1994). Several other circuits have held that an alien can move to reopen in spite of an administratively final deportation order. See, e.g., Goncalves v. INS, 6 F.3d 830, 834–35 (1st

Cir.1993); *Henry v. INS*, 8 F.3d 426, 438–39 (7th Cir.1993); *Butros v. INS*, 990 F.2d 1142, 1145–46 (9th Cir.1993) (*en banc*).

Much of this uncertainty may be resolved by proposed regulations that would allow a motion to reopen to apply for § 212(c) relief if the alien was statutorily eligible before entry of the administratively final deportation order. *See* 59 Fed.Reg. 29386, 29388 (1994), *proposing to amend* 8 C.F.R. § 3.2.

6. Assume that alien G, a long-term permanent resident alien, has been convicted of selling a controlled substance (cocaine) and is deportable under § 241(a)(2)(B)(i). Does § 241 provide for waiver of the deportation ground? Under what terms is § 244 relief available? How about § 212(c)? Thoughtful answers to these questions should make clear to you the potency of § 212(c) relief. *See, e.g., Matter of Diaz–Chambrot*, 19 I & N Dec. 674 (BIA 1988).

7. Section 212(c) requires that an alien be returning "to a lawful unrelinquished domicile of seven consecutive years" in order to be eligible for relief. Contrast this phraseology with § 244(a)'s requirement that an alien be "physically present in the United States for a continuous period of not less than seven years immediately preceding the date of * * * application." "Domicile" connotes something more than mere physical presence, but it can be consistent with frequent, even lengthy absences: "[i]n general, the domicile of an individual is his true, fixed and permanent home and place of habitation. It is the place to which, whenever he is absent, he has the intention of returning." *Martinez v. Bynum,* 461 U.S. 321, 331, 103 S.Ct. 1838, 1844, 75 L.Ed.2d 879 (1983), *quoting Vlandis v. Kline,* 412 U.S. 441, 454, 93 S.Ct. 2230, 2237, 37 L.Ed.2d 63 (1973). *See Matter of Sanchez,* 17 I & N Dec. 218, 221 (BIA 1980) (domicile under § 212(c) requires intention of making United States one's home for the indefinite future).

How could an alien (1) satisfy § 212(c)'s requirement without satisfying § 244(a)'s, or (2) satisfy § 244(a)'s requirement without satisfying § 212(c)'s? Is there an underlying logic that explains why § 212(c) adopts "unrelinquished domicile" and § 244(a) "continuous physical presence"?

Beyond *Francis*?

After *Francis*, it was commonly understood that § 212(c) relief was available in deportation proceedings only where the INS invoked a deportation ground (*e.g.,* the drug offense in *Francis*) that had an exclusion counterpart. Thus, the alien who was deportable but not excludable (*e.g.,* for EWI) could not use § 212(c). The BIA surprised many observers by eliminating this restriction on § 212(c) relief in *Matter of Hernandez–Casillas*, Int.Dec. 3147 (BIA 1991). The BIA decision in *Hernandez–Casillas* announced that § 212(c) relief would be available in all deportation cases, except where the deportation ground was comparable to a nonwaivable exclusion ground.

Three months after the Board's decision in *Hernandez-Casillas*, the Commissioner of the INS requested that the BIA refer the case to the Attorney General for review pursuant to 8 C.F.R. § 3.1(h)(1)(ii). (The

Board withheld official publication of its decision pending review by the Attorney General.) Commissioner McNary spelled out his objections to the Board's decision in a lengthy memo to the Attorney General that requested not simply that the case be reversed, but also that the Attorney General overrule *Matter of Silva, Matter of M,* and *Matter of L,* and "limit availability of relief under section 212(c) to permanent residents who are applicants for admission to the United States seeking a waiver of excludability." 67 Interp.Rel. 354 (1990).

In March 1991, Attorney General Thornburgh issued his decision.

MATTER OF HERNANDEZ–CASILLAS

Attorney General, 1991.
Int.Dec. 3147.

The Immigration and Naturalization Service ("INS") has requested that I review the decision of the Board of Immigration Appeals * * * that a permanent resident alien who left the United States and then reentered illegally must be afforded the opportunity to seek discretionary relief from deportation under section 212(c) * * *.[1] For the reasons set forth below, I disapprove the Board's decision.

I.

1. The respondent, Joel Hernandez–Casillas, a citizen of Mexico, was admitted to the United States in 1967 as a permanent resident alien. On April 13, 1985, the respondent was arrested by border patrol agents after he reentered the United States by wading the Rio Grande River; the respondent was observed guiding a group of illegal aliens whom he planned to transport to the Austin, Texas area for a fee. The respondent was charged with violating INA § 275(a), which proscribes entry into the United States "at any time or place other than as designated by immigration officers." The respondent pled guilty to that charge and was convicted.

2. On April 13, 1985, the INS served the respondent with an order to show cause why he should not be deported pursuant to INA § 241(a)(2), which requires the deportation of any alien who has "entered the United States without inspection." The respondent contested the order to show cause in a deportation proceeding before an immigration judge. In that proceeding, the respondent sought discretionary relief under section 212(c) * * *.

* * *

By its terms, section 212(c) authorizes the Attorney General, in his discretion, to permit a permanent resident alien to reenter the United States after a brief trip abroad, even though the alien would otherwise come within certain of the statutory grounds for exclusion from this

1. While this appeal was pending, Congress enacted the Immigration Act of 1990. The 1990 Act will not affect the conclusions set forth herein, which will retain their general applicability to future cases. * * * Accordingly, all citations herein are to the INA as it existed prior to enactment of the 1990 Act.

country listed in section 212(a)—*i.e.*, grounds upon which the INS otherwise must bar an alien from entering the United States.[4] The only grounds for exclusion for which discretionary relief is unavailable under section 212(c) are those that concern the exclusion of undocumented nonimmigrants, *id.* INA § 212(a)(26), followers of totalitarian ideologies, *id.* INA § 212(a)(27)–(29), and graduates of unaccredited medical schools who "are coming to the United States principally to perform [medical] services," *id.* INA § 212(a)(32). In cases involving exclusion based upon these grounds, the Attorney General has no discretion and must exclude.

3. Although section 212(c) refers only to discretionary relief from grounds for exclusion, the Board, through a series of administrative decisions, has extended section 212(c) to authorize discretionary relief from grounds for deportation as well—*i.e.*, grounds upon which the INS must remove an alien from this country. In *Matter of Granados*, 16 I. & N. Dec. 726, 728 (BIA 1979), the Board held that discretionary relief under section 212(c) may be afforded in deportation cases "if [the] ground for deportation is also a ground of inadmissibility [*i.e.*, exclusion]" that may be waived by the Attorney General under section 212(c).

Applying *Granados* to this case, the immigration judge below denied the respondent's application for discretionary relief under section 212(c), because the ground for deportation asserted here—illegal entry—is not also a ground for exclusion made waivable by section 212(c).

4. On appeal to the Board, the respondent argued that the INS should be required to charge him with aiding another alien to enter the United States illegally—an offense that is a ground for both deportation and exclusion. The respondent further urged the Board to hold that where an alien is deportable under two grounds arising out of the same incident, section 212(c) permits the waiver of a ground not listed therein if the "more serious" ground would be waivable under that section.

5. The Board concluded that the respondent was entitled to seek discretionary relief under section 212(c), but rejected the respondent's reasoning:

> [The respondent's position is] a piecemeal approach to the problem ... which, if adopted, would likely raise new issues regarding which deportation grounds are "more serious" than others. Moreover, availability of section 212(c) relief under [the respondent's position] depends upon which charges happen to be made in a case and would result in situations like the one before us, where the alien desires to have a more serious charge of deportability lodged against him, so he can apply for a section 212(c) waiver.

---

4. * * * The grounds for exclusion overlap substantially with those for deportation. The grounds for deportation and exclusion are not identical, however. Some grounds for exclusion have no analogue in the grounds for deportation. *See, e.g., id.* INA § 212(a)(4), (6), (11) (exclusion based upon sexual deviance, contagious disease, or polygamy). Similarly, two grounds for deportation have no analogue in the grounds for exclusion. *See id.* INA § 212(a)(2) (illegal entry) & (14) (conviction of illegal possession of certain firearms).

Instead, the Board opted for what it described as a "cleaner, simpler" solution, holding that discretionary relief under section 212(c) is available in *all* deportation cases, except where the ground for deportation is also a ground for exclusion that the Attorney General may not waive under section 212(c).

The Board described its holding as an extension of the many administrative and judicial interpretations of section 212(c). The Board noted that discretionary relief under section 212(c) has long been available in deportation cases understood by the Attorney General and the Board to be the equivalents of exclusion proceedings. For example, when the INS has inadvertently permitted a permanent resident alien to reenter this country notwithstanding his excludability and, upon discovery of its error, has initiated deportation proceedings, the Attorney General and the Board have determined that the alien should not be placed in a worse position than if he had been excluded. In such cases, the Attorney General and the Board have permitted the alien to raise any claim for discretionary relief that the alien otherwise could have raised had he been excluded.

The Board further noted that, since a Second Circuit decision in 1976, relief under section 212(c) has been available in certain deportation proceedings in addition to those considered to be the equivalents of exclusion proceedings. * * * The Board subsequently adopted the Second Circuit's reasoning in *Francis*, without further elaboration upon the court's equal protection analysis. As a result of *Francis* and *Silva*, discretionary relief under section 212(c) became available for all grounds for deportation that also are grounds for exclusion made waivable by the terms of that section.

In *Matter of Granados*, the Board indicated that *Francis* and *Silva* represented the limit of its expansion of section 212(c) to deportation cases. The Board noted that "*Francis* expanded the class of aliens to whom section 212(c) relief is available [*viz.*, to deportable aliens who have not temporarily departed from the United States] but did not increase the statutory grounds to which section 212(c) relief may be applied." 16 I. & N. Dec. at 728. Because section 212(c), by its terms, permits the Attorney General to waive only particular grounds for exclusion, the Board reasoned that section 212(c) may not be used to obtain discretionary relief from "a ground of deportation which is not a ground of exclu[sion] listed under section 212(c)...." *Id.*

In the present case, however, the Board overruled its holding in *Granados* by reading section 212(c) as if it referred to the grounds for deportation set forth in section 241(a) as well as to the grounds for exclusion listed in section 212(a). The Board reasoned that:

> ... section 212(c) has long since been expanded to encompass many aliens not originally contemplated by the statute. We have concluded that the same fundamental fairness/equal protection arguments made in *Francis* ... can and should be invoked to make section 212(c) relief available to aliens deportable under any ground of deportability except those where there is a comparable ground of exclusion which has been specifically excepted from section 212(c) [*i.e.*, those grounds which the Attorney General may

not waive].... Having made the section 212(c) waiver, a form of relief ostensibly available only in exclusion proceedings, available in deportation proceedings, *we find no reason not to make it applicable to all grounds of deportability with the exception of those comparable to the exclusion grounds expressly excluded in section 212(c)*, rather than limiting it, as now, to grounds of deportability having equivalent exclusion provisions. *The two approaches are equally logical and bear equally little resemblance to the statute as written.*

The Board did not base its expansion of section 212(c) upon what it understood to be a constitutional requirement.

Applying its new approach to the present case, the Board concluded that the respondent should have been granted the opportunity to seek discretionary relief under section 212(c), because the ground for deportation asserted against the respondent is not a ground for exclusion placed beyond the Attorney General's discretionary powers by section 212(c). * * *

* * *

II.

The INS urges me to reverse the expansion of section 212(c) to deportation cases by giving effect to the plain language of that provision, which refers only to exclusion. Specifically, the INS requests that I disapprove, among other decisions, the Board's holding in *Silva*, which adopted the Second Circuit's decision in *Francis*.

For two reasons, I decline at this time to undertake a reexamination of these precedents and, accordingly, leave for another day the question of whether *Silva* should be disapproved. First, as the respondent and *amici* emphasize, and as the record confirms, the INS did not challenge the validity of *Silva* before the Board. As a result, the Board did not discuss this issue in its opinion. In the absence of compelling circumstances, I do not consider it prudent to resolve the validity of *Silva* without allowing the Board to explore that question in the first instance. Second, I need not reexamine *Silva* in order to decide the present case for, as I shall explain, even if I assume the validity of *Silva*, I nonetheless must disapprove the Board's decision here.

I conclude that the Board erred in holding that relief under section 212(c) may be afforded for grounds for deportation that are not grounds for exclusion made waivable by the terms of section 212(c). I reach this conclusion for two related reasons. First, the Board erred in concluding that its holding in *Silva* and its further expansion of section 212(c) in this case "bear equally little resemblance to the statute as written." *Silva* at least remains tied, albeit loosely, to the statutory text, because it permits waivers of only those grounds for deportation that Congress expressly made waivable in the related context of exclusion. Under *Silva*, therefore, the Attorney General may not waive a ground for deportation if it is not a ground for exclusion at all or if it is a ground for exclusion placed beyond the Attorney General's discretionary powers by the terms of section 212(c). In contrast, under the Board's holding in this case, only the latter limitation would remain. The Board's approach thus would take immigration practice even further from the statutory text, which refers only to grounds for exclusion.

The disruption to the statutory scheme that would be wrought by the Board's expansion of section 212(c) is apparent when one examines the provisions designed by Congress specifically to govern deportation cases. In section 244(a)(1) of the INA, Congress has expressly provided that the Attorney General may, in his discretion, suspend the deportation of an illegal entrant who "has been physically present in the United States for a continuous period of at least seven years," who "proves that during all of such period he was and is a person of good moral character," and who "is a person whose deportation would, in the opinion of the Attorney General, result in extreme hardship...." The showings of "good moral character" and "extreme hardship" required under section 244(a)(1) are, by contrast, not required under section 212(c). Extension of section 212(c) to deportation cases thus would further supplant the standard of proof specified by Congress for discretionary relief in such cases.

Second, the rationale articulated in *Francis* and *Silva* for expansion of discretionary relief under section 212(c) to deportation proceedings apart from those considered the equivalents of exclusion proceedings rests upon the conclusion that the constitutional guarantee of equal protection requires that expansion. Without evaluating the correctness of that conclusion, I am persuaded that the guarantee of equal protection does not requires the further departure from the terms of section 212(c) made by the Board in this case.

Under *Francis* and *Silva*, the guarantee of equal protection requires, at most, that an alien subject to deportation must have the same opportunity to seek discretionary relief as an alien who has temporarily left this country and, upon reentry, been subject to exclusion. The guarantee of equal protection, as understood by *Francis* and *Silva*, thus is satisfied if discretionary relief is available in deportation cases for all grounds that would be subject to waiver under section 212(c) were they asserted against the alien in exclusion proceedings. Under no plausible understanding of equal protection principles must discretionary relief be made available in deportation cases where the ground for deportation could not be waived if asserted in an exclusion case—or, as here, could not be asserted at all in an exclusion case. Accordingly, the Second Circuit in *Francis* and the Board in *Silva*, by concluding that equal protection principles require deviation from the literal terms of section 212(c), kept such deviations to what they understood as the constitutionally mandated minimum; that is, *Francis* and *Silva* require only that discretionary relief under section 212(c) be made available in deportation proceedings in which the asserted ground for deportation is also a ground for exclusion expressly subject to waiver under that section.

The constitutional guarantee of equal protection requires nothing more, as the Board itself concluded in *Granados*. Since that administrative decision, the constitutional soundness of *Granados* has been confirmed by the Ninth Circuit—the only court of appeals to address the question. *See Cabasug v. INS*, 847 F.2d 1321 (9th Cir.1988). In *Cabasug*, the INS ordered a permanent resident alien deported based upon his conviction for a firearm offense. On authority of *Granados*, the Board held that discretionary relief under section 212(c) was unavailable, because the particular ground for deportation has no counterpart among the grounds for exclusion. In the face of an equal protection challenge, the court upheld the Board's decision:

> [T]here exists no class of persons alike in carrying [the prohibited types of firearms], and deportable or not depending on the irrelevant circumstance of whether at some previous time they took a temporary trip out of the country. The gravamen of the equal protection violation identified in *Francis* was just such a distinction without a material difference. In the treatment of these weapons offenses, Congress has legislated no such distinction, nor has any administrative practice created one.

Id. at 1326. The same is true of illegal entrants, such as the respondent. Here, deportation turns not upon the "irrelevant circumstance" of whether the respondent has temporarily left the United States but, instead, upon the illegal nature of his reentry.[8]

Although the Ninth Circuit's decision in *Cabasug*—holding that the Constitution does not require discretionary relief under section 212(c) to be accorded from a ground for deportation that is not also a ground for exclusion made waivable under that section—is not controlling of its own force in the present case, I find Ninth Circuit's reading of section 212(c) more persuasive than that of the Board. * * * Absent some supervening affirmative justification based upon a requirement of the Constitution or other applicable law, neither the Board nor I may depart—or, in this instance, extend an earlier departure—from the terms of the statute we are bound to enforce.

* * *

Notes

1. The Attorney General's decision raises the question whether a deportation ground has an exclusion counterpart. *See, e.g., Matter of Wadud*, 18 I & N Dec. 182 (BIA 1984). The two most significant deporta-

---

8. The alien in *Cabasug* also argued that the determination to deny discretion under section 212(c) for a firearm offense but to permit such relief for other "more serious[ ]"grounds—for instance, "crimes of moral turpitude such as murder or rape"—was unconstitutional. 847 F.2d at 1326. The court rejected this further claim, stating:

> We ... do not agree with the implicit proposition that the Constitution requires Congress to lay out crimes on a spectrum, and grant at least as much

discretion for the less serious as for any more serious crimes.... Congress may fashion a sanction without discretionary mitigating features in order to deter a kind of conduct about which it is especially concerned. Congress may reasonably determine that a nondiscretionary moderate penalty will deter violators more effectively and more justly than a lesser risk of a harsher penalty.

Id. at 1327.

tion grounds without comparable exclusion grounds are entry without inspection and firearms violations.

As *Hernandez-Casillas* suggests, the BIA and the courts have rejected the argument that a permanent resident is eligible for § 212(c) relief if the INS might have charged (but in fact did not charge) a deportation ground with a comparable exclusion ground. For example, some permanent residents who are deportable for a firearms violation might also be deportable for a crime of moral turpitude, but they have been found ineligible for § 212(c) relief.

2. A permanent resident who cannot invoke § 212(c) to waive deportation for lack of a comparable exclusion ground may be eligible to apply for adjustment of status to permanent resident if she meets the requirements in INA § 245 (*e.g.*, that she be eligible for an immigrant visa that is immediately available and that she not be subject to an exclusion ground). *See Matter of Gabryelsky*, Int.Dec. 3213 (BIA 1993).

3. On remand, the Fifth Circuit upheld (without opinion) the Attorney General's decision and the subsequent BIA decision in *Hernandez-Casillas*. *See Hernandez–Casillas v. INS*, 983 F.2d 231 (5th Cir.1993). Most courts have agreed. *See, e.g., Rodriguez–Padron v. INS*, 13 F.3d 1455, 1459–60 (11th Cir.1994) (firearms violation); *Rodriguez v. INS*, 9 F.3d 408, 413–14 (5th Cir.1993) (firearms violation); *Leal-Rodriguez v. INS*, 990 F.2d 939, 949–52 (7th Cir.1993) (entry without inspection); *Campos v. INS*, 961 F.2d 309, 315–16 (1st Cir.1992) (firearms violation). But consider the following decision from the circuit that decided *Francis*.

BEDOYA-VALENCIA v. INS

United States Court of Appeals, Second Circuit, 1993.
6 F.3d 891.

MAHONEY, CIRCUIT JUDGE:

* * *

The facts in this case are uncontested. Bedoya–Valencia, a native and citizen of Colombia, first entered the United States as a lawful permanent resident in 1976. In 1983, he was convicted of possession of cocaine with intent to distribute in violation of 21 U.S.C. § 841(a)(1), and sentenced to four years imprisonment and six years special parole. In February 1984, the Immigration and Naturalization Service ("INS") issued an order to show cause charging Bedoya–Valencia as deportable under § 241 of the INA, for having been convicted of a narcotics offense.

At his deportation hearing in September 1986, Bedoya–Valencia conceded deportability and applied for discretionary relief from deportation under § 212(c). The parties consented to an adjournment of the proceedings until March 1987 to allow Bedoya–Valencia an opportunity to present evidence concerning his § 212(c) application. In conjunction with this initial proceeding, Bedoya–Valencia's alien registration card was retained by the INS.

In November 1986, while his deportation proceedings were pending, Bedoya–Valencia departed the United States and went to Colombia. Assertedly because the INS still retained Bedoya–Valencia's documentation as to his resident alien status, he evaded inspection upon his return to the United States in early 1988, and illegally reentered the country. Upon learning of Bedoya–Valencia's illegal reentry, the INS lodged an additional charge of deportability against him on October 11, 1991 for unlawful entry without inspection in violation of § 241(a)(1)(B). At his continued deportation hearing, Bedoya–Valencia conceded his deportability on the new charge and submitted a new application for § 212(c) relief.

The IJ found that Bedoya–Valencia was statutorily ineligible for § 212(c) relief. He based that determination upon the Attorney General's decision in *Hernandez-Casillas*, stating that "[t]he Attorney General unequivocally determined that entry without inspection, a conceded charge of deportability, is not waiveable by application for relief pursuant to [§ 212(c)]" because entry without inspection has no comparable ground of excludability under § 212(a).

Bedoya–Valencia appealed the IJ's decision to the BIA. He did not challenge the IJ's findings of deportability, but argued that the IJ erred in finding him ineligible for § 212(c) relief because: (1) the ground for deportation stated in § 241(a)(1)(B), entry without inspection, is analogous to the ground for exclusion stated in § 212(a)(7)(A), seeking admission without proper documentation; and (2) in any event, fundamental fairness requires that § 212(c) relief should be available to aliens charged with any ground for deportation or exclusion other than those specifically excepted by statute.

The BIA rejected Bedoya–Valencia's arguments. It viewed *Hernandez-Casillas* as having ruled that an alien deportable under § 241(a)(1)(B) is ineligible for § 212(c) relief because: (1) there is no ground of exclusion comparable to entry without inspection; (2) the limitation of § 212(c) waiver relief imposed by *Hernandez-Casillas* is consistent with constitutional guarantees of equal protection; and (3) a contrary ruling would unduly disrupt the statutory scheme. The BIA accordingly affirmed the decision of the IJ and dismissed Bedoya–Valencia's appeal.

* * *

Bedoya–Valencia argues on appeal that: (1) the deportation ground of entry without inspection is analogous to the exclusion ground of seeking admission without proper documentation, and he is accordingly eligible for § 212(c) relief; (2) if the statutory analogy is rejected, the case should be remanded for initial discretionary consideration of his claim for waiver of the narcotics ground of deportation, whose resolution might avoid any need to consider the constitutional issue otherwise presented by this appeal; and (3) in any event, due process and equal protection require that § 212(c) relief be available for an alien deportable on any ground other than those specifically precluded by § 212(c).

These issues are solely questions of law, and thus our review is plenary. In conducting that review, however, deference must be accorded to the views of the Attorney General, who is charged with the administration of the INA and whose rulings with respect to questions of immigration law are controlling within the executive branch.

* * *

Bedoya–Valencia first contends that he is entitled to a § 212(c) hearing because entry without inspection is analogous to a ground for exclusion, failure to present proper documents for admission. We disagree.

[The court quotes INA §§ 212(a)(7)(A)(i) and 241(a)(1)(B).]

The issue is to be determined by a standard of "substantial[ ] equivalen[ce]." *Campos*, 961 F.2d at 313 n.6. This standard is not satisfied by a comparison of these provisions. Entry without inspection involves a calculated avoidance of the admission procedure; it is hardly equivalent to an invocation of that procedure that is undermined by faulty documents.

Bedoya–Valencia argues that he did not present himself for inspection when he returned to the United States because he lacked proper admission documents. That may be true, but it does not render the resulting illegal entry substantially equivalent, as a matter of statutory definition, to the motivating lack of documentation.

* * *

In *Francis*, we invoked the implicit equal protection guarantee of the Fifth Amendment due process clause * * *. We therefore concluded that the discretionary waiver that § 212(c) allowed in favor of a returning alien in exclusion proceedings must also be accorded his more sedentary counterpart in deportation proceedings. We did so even though Congress had "provid[ed] a separate but analogous scheme of discretionary relief to the non-departing alien." *Id.* at 273.

The BIA subsequently applied the *Francis* rule nationally in *In re Silva*, 16 I. & N. Dec. 26, 30 (BIA 1976). That rule has now been adopted in the First, Fourth, Fifth, Sixth, Seventh, Ninth, and Tenth Circuits.

In *Francis*, however, the ground of deportation was a narcotics conviction, for which there was a substantially equivalent ground of exclusion. Thus, *Francis* did not address the situation presented by this appeal—a ground of deportation, entry without inspection, for which there is no analogous ground of exclusion.

The Attorney General determined in *Hernandez-Casillas* that the *Francis* rule should not be extended to allow § 212(c) relief in such situations. His ruling was affirmed by the Fifth Circuit, without opinion. Three other circuits concur.

* * *

We view the matter differently. *Francis* was decided over seventeen years ago, and addressed a situation that had been the subject of similarly ameliorative administrative decisions since 1940. The Department of Justice declined to seek review of the *Francis* decision by the Supreme Court, and the BIA promptly adopted the *Francis* rule nationally. As noted *supra*, seven circuits have since explicitly adopted the *Francis* rule, and no circuit has embraced a different rule. Further, since *Francis* was decided, Congress has not addressed either the issue to which *Francis* was addressed or the variant of the issue that is presented by this appeal.

* * *

The only clearly discernible Congressional intention regarding the denial of § 212(c) waivers is that they are not available in exclusion proceedings to aliens who are excludible because of security and related grounds or because of international child abduction, or have served a term of imprisonment of at least five years upon conviction of one or more aggravated felonies. * * *

In reversing the BIA [in *Hernandez-Casillas*] and ruling that § 212(c) waivers are available only for grounds of deportation for which there are substantially equivalent grounds of exclusion, the Attorney General stated that only two grounds of deportation fail to satisfy this requirement, entry without inspection, and certain firearm offenses. There is, however, at least one other nonequivalent ground of deportation—willful failure to notify the Attorney General of a change of address.

In thus limiting the § 212 relief available in deportation proceedings, the Attorney General did not address the Congressional purposes underlying the enactment of the immigration laws. Rather, * * * he articulated a determination not to depart further from the statutory text, and the absence of any constitutional (equal protection) mandate to do so.

As a result of *Francis* and *Silva*, building upon a history of administrative decisions, there has already been a considerable departure from the text of § 212(c), which now applies to deportation as well as exclusion proceedings despite the absence of any textual justification for this extension. Further, since Congress considered only grounds for exclusion when it enacted § 212(c), it could not conceivably have had any intent regarding the availability of § 212(c) discretion to a resident alien charged with illegal entry. Indeed, any such intention would be logically impossible. As the Seventh Circuit pointed out in *Leal-Rodriguez*, "entry without inspection [is] a ground for deportation which, as a matter of logic, cannot be a ground for exclusion, since the moment the violation occurs the offender is already inside the United States." 990 F.2d at 949. This analysis also applies to the deportation ground of wilful failure to notify the Attorney General of a change of address.

Absent any Congressional indication to the contrary, we believe that coherence and consistency are promoted by allowing the exercise of § 212(c) discretion with respect to the deportation ground of entry without inspection. *Francis* effected a significant alteration of the legal framework in this area, and in the absence of any Congressional revisitation of that framework in the aftermath of *Francis*, courts must cope with the interstitial issue posed by grounds of deportation that have no counterparts among the statutory grounds for exclusion. At least with respect to entry without inspection, a ground of deportation that could not conceivably have such an analogue, there is no basis in statutory text or legislative purpose to preclude the modest extension of the *Francis* rule that Bedoya–Valencia seeks on this appeal.

We recognize, of course, as we did in *Francis*, the paramount authority of the executive and legislative branches of our national government with respect to immigration matters, and the correspondingly limited role of the judiciary. *See Fiallo v. Bell*, 430 U.S. 787, 792, 97 S.Ct. 1473, 1478, 52 L.Ed.2d 50 (1977). We also recognize, however, that federal courts can play an important role in interstitial implementation of a legislative design, especially when that design has already been altered by a constitutionally based court decision.

The ruling that we make today poses no challenge to the legislative and executive branches, or to the Attorney General's special role within the executive branch with respect to legal interpretation of the immigration statutes. We note that this opinion addresses the ramifications of a prior constitutional decision of this court, rather than the original statute concerning whose interpretation the Attorney General has conceded expertise. We note also that the Attorney General regards the legitimacy of this court's opinion in *Francis* as an open question, despite its adoption by seven circuit courts in addition to the one that initially announced it. In sum, * * * we undertake only to achieve coherence regarding the impact of our prior ruling in *Francis* upon a ground of deportation that, by logical necessity, can have no counterpart ground of exclusion.

The INS points out that the prevention of illegal entry is an important policy of our immigration laws. All of the statutory grounds for deportation, however, are rooted in considerations of public policy. We are confident that the Attorney General and her delegates will accord those considerations appropriate weight in their exercise of § 212(c) discretion. We hold only that Bedoya–Valencia is entitled to that exercise.

* * *

Notes

1. Which ruling in *Hernandez-Casillas*—that of the BIA or that of the Attorney General—do you find more persuasive, either as a matter of policy or as a reading (or reconstruction) of congressional intent?

2. How persuasive is the argument (rejected by the Attorney General in *Hernandez-Casillas* and by the federal appellate decisions in the other cases cited in note 3 on p. 704 *supra*, but not reached by the Second Circuit in *Bedoya-Valencia*) that the Constitution requires that § 212(c) relief be available for any deportation ground other than those specifically precluded by § 212(c) itself? Is it irrational and therefore unconstitutional to deny permanent residents convicted of firearms violations the opportunity to seek § 212(c) relief when permanent residents convicted of more serious crimes may apply?

3. In retrospect, does the course of events after *Francis* cast doubt on the wisdom of judicial intervention in that case?

Section 212(c) in Action

The discretionary nature of the waiver presents difficult issues—of administrative discretion and judicial review of the exercise of that discretion—that are similar to the issues discussed earlier in this Chapter in the suspension of deportation context. Consider the following facts.

[Luis Guillen–Garcia, a 41–year-old native of Mexico and lawful permanent resident of the United States,] has resided in the United States since the age of fourteen. He is married to a United States citizen and has five children, all of whom are United States citizens. Additionally, his parents are lawful permanent residents, and he has four siblings who are citizens and three siblings who are lawful permanent residents.

On May 10, 1974, Mr. Guillen was convicted of two counts of aggravated battery for causing great bodily harm to another individual, and of one count of aggravated battery through the use of a deadly weapon. He was sentenced to five years of probation. On April 18, 1984, Mr. Guillen was convicted of attempted murder and was sentenced to ten years imprisonment, but served only four and a half years of the sentence and was then placed on probation for the remainder of his term.

* * * Mr. Guillen conceded that he was deportable, but requested a waiver of inadmissibility under section 212(c) of the Act.

At the waiver hearing, Mr. Guillen testified that he was innocent of the crimes for which he had been convicted. He stated that he had pleaded guilty to the aggravated battery charges on the advice of his public defender, who informed him that he would receive probation by doing so. According to Mr. Guillen, the incident leading to his conviction occurred when he and some friends had attended a dance, at which a fight ensued when other men tried to take away Mr. Guillen's and his friends' dates. He testified that a distant cousin had a gun, which his cousin fired and then placed in Mr. Guillen's hands. At that time, a police officer saw Mr. Guillen with the gun, told him to discard it, and then arrested him. Mr. Guillen further testified that he did not then own and has never owned a gun.

As to the attempted murder conviction, Mr. Guillen testified that he had gone out to buy a soft drink and encountered a group of men fighting on the street. He stated that he asked them to let him pass, but he was shot in the back and leg, lost consciousness, and woke up in the hospital. On cross-examination, Mr. Guillen claimed that he believed he had been shot by an unidentified police officer. Although he was convicted of attempted murder following a jury trial, Mr. Guillen denied possessing a weapon at any time during the night in question. Mr. Guillen testified that, after his conviction, he was under the impression that his public defender was going to pursue an appeal on his behalf but none was filed.

Mr. Guillen testified that, while in prison, he worked as a cook and was paid approximately $100.00 per month, about half of which he retained for his own use, and the remainder of which he sent to his wife. During cross-examination of Mrs. Guillen, however, she stated that her husband had sent her money only for one year during his prison term. Mr. Guillen stated that he earned diplomas in welding and mechanics while incarcerated, that he was visited about twice a month by relatives, and that he studied the Bible during his free time. After his release from prison, Mr. Guillen was employed by C.E. Smith in lawn maintenance. Subsequently, he was employed by Parent Petroleum, where he has a long employment history. Since his release from prison, Mr. Guillen testified that his wife and children have not received any public assistance and that he and his family are active in a Bible class sponsored by the church they attend.

Mr. Guillen further testified that he has left the United States only once since he began to reside here, and that his wife and children had lived in Puerto Rico for approximately one year when her mother and father were in ill health. According to Mr. Guillen, his children attended school in Puerto Rico but did not adjust well because they did not speak Spanish fluently and had difficulty making friends. Mr. Guillen stated that his wife and children would not accompany him if he were deported to Mexico, that his wife has no relatives there, and that he has only one relative there, an uncle whom he has never met. He further testified that he doubted his wife alone would be able to support herself and their children if he were deported.

During the hearing, Mrs. Guillen and two of the Guillens' children also testified concerning the hardship that would befall them if Mr. Guillen were deported. Mrs. Guillen further testified that their oldest daughter had developed ulcers and psychiatric problems during Mr. Guillen's incarceration. In addition, she testified that she has a steady factory job earning approximately $4.50 per hour, and that she lives very close to her brother and sister-in-law. Finally, in response to a question by the IJ, Mrs. Guillen indicated that, to her knowledge, her husband has never owned a gun.

Numerous relatives also testified or submitted affidavits to the effect that the Guillens have a close-knit family and that Mr. Guillen tends either to stay at home or to attend family functions. Mr. Guillen's parents testified that they were ill, that their son and other children live close to them and help them out, and that Mr. Guillen contributes about $20.00 per week toward their support. Letters from Mr. Guillen's church and employer attested to his good character and work record. Finally, a letter from his parole officer stated that Mr. Guillen was under minimum supervision at the time of the hearing, although during cross-examination Mr. Guillen stated that he had personally spoken to his parole officer only on two occasions.

Would you grant relief under § 212(c)? How, if at all, does your approach to this question differ from your approach to the suspension of deportation fact situation on p. 656 *supra*?

Matter of Marin, 16 I & N Dec. 581 (BIA 1978), is often cited for its list of factors relevant to § 212(c) determinations. *Marin* listed as adverse factors:

> the nature and underlying circumstances of the exclusion [or deportation] ground at issue, the presence of additional significant violations of this country's immigration laws, the existence of a criminal record and, if so, its nature, recency, and seriousness, and the presence of other evidence indicative of a respondent's bad character or undesirability as a permanent resident of this country.

Id. at 584. *Marin* then listed as favorable factors:

> family ties within the United States, residence of long duration in this country (particularly when the inception of residence occurred while the respondent was of young age), evidence of hardship to the respondent and family if deportation occurs, service in this country's Armed Forces, a history of employment, the existence of property or business ties, evidence of value and service to the community, proof of a genuine rehabilitation if a criminal record exists, and other evidence attesting to a respondent's good character (e.g., affidavits from family, friends, and responsible community representatives).

Id. at 584–85.

We alert you to the fact that the BIA has been particularly reluctant to grant § 212(c) relief to aliens who have drug convictions. Consider the following passage from a court decision in a § 212(c) case:

> The INS at oral argument was asked to provide the panel with decisions of the BIA exercising 212(c) discretion in favor of an alien convicted of a drug offense so the Court could have some understanding of the manner in which the Board exercises its discretion. Although more than three thousand of BIA's decisions have been published, the INS has provided the panel with only a single decision [which involved] one attempted sale of cocaine valued at $20.

Gonzalez v. INS, 996 F.2d 804, 810 (6th Cir.1993). Of course, this statement does not necessarily capture decisionmaking by immigration judges. The BIA responded to the Sixth Circuit by pointedly refuting the suggestion that it "engages in a 'de facto' policy of denying section 212(c) relief to aliens convicted of a single and serious drug offense." *See Matter of Burbano*, Int.Dec. 3229 (BIA 1994).

For more on § 212(c), see Yale-Loehr, *An Overview of INA § 212(c)*, 95–2 Imm.Briefings (1995); Rosenberg & Sabagh, *A Practitioner's Guide to INA § 212(c)*, 93–4 Imm.Briefings (1993).

3. REGISTRY: INA § 249

Section 249 of the INA, which you should now study, establishes a form of relief for deportable aliens, generally referred to as "registry." Gordon, Mailman and Yale-Loehr describe the purpose and history of the registry provision as follows:

> Registry originated with the Act of March 2, 1929. Originally it related to aliens who had arrived before the temporary quota law of May 19, 1921, and permitted creation of a record of lawful entry for permanent residence on behalf of those who could meet certain prescribed conditions. The purpose was to legalize the residence of aliens who had entered improperly before that date, or whose entry record could not be located, but whose deportation was precluded by the statute of limitations then in effect. The registry statute was codified in the Nationality Act of 1940. The only significant change was to advance the controlling date to July 1, 1924, the effective date of the basic quota law.

> In its studies that preceded the 1952 Act, the Senate Judiciary Committee expressed approval of the registry procedure and recommended that it be retained. This recommendation was followed, and the registry requirements and procedure were continued without any significant change. A major revision in 1958 advanced the cutoff date to June 28, 1940 and eliminated the complete disqualification of those subject to deportation. Instead the 1958 amendment disqualified only those inadmissible for certain aggravated grounds. Elimination of the disqualification of deportables has made this procedure for administrative adjustment of status available to many who previously were deportable as overstayed nonimmigrants or as illegal entrants. In 1965 the cutoff date was again advanced to June 30, 1948. In 1986 the cutoff date for registry was again advanced to January 1, 1972. The Immigration Act of 1990 limited registry by providing that for 5 years it is not available to aliens found deportable in absentia, remaining in the U.S. after a scheduled departure, failing to appear for deportation after proper notice of the consequences, or failing to appear for an asylum hearing despite proper notice.

> Although the principal purpose of registry originally was to aid persons who wished to be naturalized, the record of lawful entry established in such proceedings is recognized as valid for all purposes under the immigration and naturalization laws. In effect it has become a form of statute of limitations for illegal entrants, based on affirmative grant of discretion to applicants who satisfy specified eligibility requirements.

GM & Y § 54.01.*

The impact of the advancement of the cut-off date was immediate. In FY 1986, fewer than 100 aliens were granted § 249 relief. In FY 1987, 8,060 aliens qualified for registry, and in FY 1988, the number almost quadrupled, to 39,999. Since then, the number has steadily declined, to 938 in FY 1993. 1993 INS Statistical Yearbook, Table 4. In a general sense, registry was the precursor of the legalization programs that were enacted in 1986 as part of IRCA which, as discussed in Chapter Three *supra*, led to permanent residency for far greater numbers.

4. PRIVATE BILLS

In the early years of our immigration laws, private bills were the primary form of relief from deportation. Such bills have often been used to create humanitarian flexibility in a law that, if applied as written, would produce harsh results. Furthermore, "private bills have frequently been the forerunners of significant amendments to existing general immigration laws":

> Before the Immigration and Nationality Act accorded "nonquota" status to spouses of American citizens irrespective of their ancestry, Asian spouses of American citizens were subject to quota restrictions. The stationing of American servicemen in the Far East and the resulting marriages between American citizens and alien spouses of Asian ancestry led to the introduction and passage of a considerable number of private bills according the individual Asian spouse "nonquota" status. The increasing volume of this type of private bills led eventually to public legislation giving "nonquota" status to the spouses of American servicemen irrespective of their ancestry and later led to the provision in the Immigration and Nationality Act which placed alien spouses of all American citizens on equal footing irrespective of race. Similarly, the provision of the Act of September 3, 1954 exempting petty offenders from the excluding provisions of the general law was preceded by a series of private bills seeking relief in cases of individual aliens, mostly alien wives of American servicemen who, during the post-war period, had been convicted for minor offenses.

E. Harper, Jr. & R. Chase, Immigration Laws of the United States 657–59 (1975).[7]

The prospects for passage of a private bill are poor. In the 102d Congress, 71 bills were introduced and 11 passed; in the 101st Congress,

---

7. A former General Counsel of the Senate Judiciary Committee provides another example:

A private bill can be transformed into a public law. The metamorphosis begins when it is amended on the floor of either House to take on the substance of a public bill. A perfect example is P.L. 95–579 of November 2, 1978. In embryonic form as S. 2247, it was a private bill to exempt an elderly female alien from the English literacy requirements in Section 312. After passing the Senate, it was amended by the House to provide a general statutory waiver of the literacy requirements for all naturalization applicants over 50 years of age with 20 or more years of lawful residence on the date of filing the petition. The Senate concurred in the House amendment, the President signed, and it became a law. [See INA § 312(1).]

Rawitz, *In the Hands of Congress: Suspension of Deportation and Private Bills,* 57 Interp.Rel. 76, 80 (1980).

127 were introduced and 7 passed. 1993 Statistical Yearbook, Table 79. Also, mere introduction of a private bill does not automatically guarantee a stay of deportation, as it once did. Now, after introduction of a private bill, the House or Senate Judiciary Committee may issue a request for a report from the INS on the alien beneficiary. Under Operations Instruction 107.1c, "a stay of deportation will generally be authorized" by INS after of a committee's request for a report. If this happens, the alien may be able to forestall deportation for a considerable period of time, irrespective of the private bill's ultimate chance for passage. However, rules of the relevant House and Senate Subcommittees limit the circumstances under which requests for INS reports will be made.

5. ESTOPPEL

Suppose the conduct of the government is a contributing cause of the alien's deportability—for example, because the alien has relied upon bad advice from the government or because the government has taken so long to adjudicate a matter that the alien's condition has changed. Or suppose the government has misled an excludable alien into believing that his entry and residence in the United States are lawful. Should the government be estopped from deporting the alien? The traditional answer, consistent with basic principles of administrative law, is usually not: "When the Government is unable to enforce the law because the conduct of its agents has given rise to an estoppel, the interest of the citizenry as a whole in obedience to the rule of law is undermined. It is for this reason that it is well-settled that the Government may not be estopped on the same terms as any other litigant." *Heckler v. Community Health Services of Crawford County, Inc.*, 467 U.S. 51, 60, 104 S.Ct. 2218, 2224, 81 L.Ed.2d 42, 52 (1984). The Court added, however: [W]e are hesitant * * * to say that there are *no cases* in which the public interest in ensuring that the Government can enforce the law free from estoppel might be outweighed by the countervailing interest of citizens in some minimum standard of decency, honor, and reliability in their dealings with their Government. 467 U.S. at 60, 104 S.Ct. at 2224, 81 L.Ed.2d at 52. *See generally* 2 K.C. Davis & R. Pierce, Administrative Law Treatise Ch. § 13.1 (3d ed. 1994); W. Gellhorn, C. Byse, P. Strauss, T. Rakoff & R. Schotland, Administrative Law: Cases and Comments 522–30 (8th ed. 1987). This notion is clearly evident in § 241(a)(1) of the INA, which renders deportable aliens who were excludable at the time of entry; notions of estoppel are not deemed to prevent the government from correcting a prior incorrect admission of the alien. *See, e.g., Santiago v. INS*, 526 F.2d 488 (9th Cir.1975) (*en banc*), *cert. denied*, 425 U.S. 971, 96 S.Ct. 2167, 48 L.Ed.2d 794 (1976).

While the general principle that there is no estoppel against the government is still intact, at least one Supreme Court decision has left open the question whether INS could be estopped if an alien demonstrates the traditional elements required for estoppel as well as "affirmative misconduct" on the part of the agency. Here was the situation in *INS v. Miranda*, 459 U.S. 14, 103 S.Ct. 281, 74 L.Ed.2d 12 (1982):

> Respondent Horacio Miranda, a citizen of the Philippines, entered the United States in 1971 on a temporary visitor's visa.

After his visa expired, he stayed in this country, eventually marrying Linda Milligan, a citizen of the United States, on May 26, 1976. Shortly thereafter, Milligan filed a visa petition with the Immigration and Naturalization Service (INS) on respondent's behalf. She requested that he be granted an immigrant visa as her spouse. Respondent simultaneously filed an application requesting the INS to adjust his status to that of a permanent resident alien. Section 245(a) of the Immigration and Nationality Act of 1952 conditions the granting of permanent resident status to an alien on the immediate availability of an immigrant visa. Milligan's petition, if approved, would have satisfied this condition.

The INS did not act on either Milligan's petition or respondent's application for 18 months. Following the breakup of her marriage with respondent, Milligan withdrew her petition in December 1977. At that point, the INS denied respondent's application for permanent residence because he had not shown that an immigrant visa was immediately available to him. The INS also issued an order to show cause why he should not be deported.

At a deportation hearing, respondent conceded his deportability but renewed his application for permanent resident status because of his marriage to Milligan. Although the marriage had ended, he claimed that a previous marriage was sufficient to support his application. The Immigration Judge rejected this claim, concluding that the immediate availability of an immigrant visa was a necessary condition to respondent's application. Since Milligan had withdrawn her petition for an immigrant visa before the INS had acted on it, respondent was ineligible for permanent resident status.

Respondent appealed the decision to the Board of Immigration Appeals. For the first time, he raised the claim that the INS was estopped from denying his application because of its "unreasonable delay." He argued that the "failure to act was not only unreasonable, unfair and unjust but also an abuse of governmental process if the delay was deliberate." The Board rejected respondent's claim. It found "no evidence of any 'affirmative misconduct'" and no basis for an equitable estoppel.

The Court of Appeals for the Ninth Circuit reversed, holding that "[t]he unexplained failure of the INS to act on the visa petition for an eighteen-month period prior to the petitioner's withdrawal * * * was affirmative misconduct by the INS." *Miranda v. INS*, 638 F.2d 83, 84 (9th Cir.1980). The Supreme Court summarily reversed the Ninth Circuit:

> * * * [T]he evidence that the Government failed to fulfill its duty in this case is at best questionable. The only indication of negligence is the length of time that the INS took to process respondent's application. Although the time was indeed long, we cannot say in the absence of evidence to the contrary that the delay was unwarranted. Both the number of the applications received by the INS and the need to investigate their validity may

make it difficult for the agency to process an application as promptly as may be desirable. * * *

* * * An increasingly important interest, implicating matters of broad public concern, is involved in cases of this kind. Enforcing the immigration laws, and the conditions for residency in this country, is becoming more difficult. Moreover, the INS is the agency primarily charged by Congress to implement the public policy underlying these laws. Appropriate deference must be accorded its decisions.

This case does not require us to reach the question * * * whether affirmative misconduct in a particular case would estop the Government from enforcing the immigration laws. Proof only that the Government failed to process promptly an application falls far short of establishing such conduct.

459 U.S. at 18–19, 103 S.Ct. at 283–84.

6. ADDITIONAL FORMS OF RELIEF

INA § 208 (asylum) and § 243(h) (withholding of deportation) allow otherwise deportable aliens to remain in the United States if they can demonstrate that they are likely to be persecuted upon return to their home countries. And in 1987, Congress enacted legislation permitting certain aliens in extended voluntary departure during the five-year period ending November 1, 1987, to adjust to permanent resident status. We will consider these provisions in detail when we explore all of the INA's refugee provisions together in Chapter Eight.

7. RELIEF IN THE CONTEXT OF JUDICIAL DEPORTATION

As discussed in Chapter Six *supra*, § 224 of the 1994 Immigration and Nationality Technical Corrections Act, Pub.L. 103–416, 108 Stat. 4305, 4322–23, added new INA § 242A(d), which gives United States district courts jurisdiction to order deportation when an alien is sentenced for a criminal conviction. You should now study § 242A(d)(2), which gives the court jurisdiction to grant or deny relief from deportation. Would you expect this new procedure for relief in the context of judicial deportation to expand or restrict the availability of relief?

SECTION D. A CONCLUDING QUESTION

Does it make sense for the INA to have so many different and overlapping forms of relief from deportation? Viewed together, they display no obvious underlying theory of which aliens merit relief from what kinds of deportation grounds: the list of waivable grounds varies from section to section (*compare* § 244(e) *with* § 212(c) and § 244(a)); the period of residence required for each is not the same (*compare* § 212(c) *with* § 244(a)(2) and § 249); and even the description of that residence is not uniform. *See, e.g.,* § 212(c) (unrelinquished domicile); § 244(a) (continuous physical presence); § 249 (continuous residence). Moreover, some individual deportation grounds have their own waiver provisions. See, e.g.,

§ 241(a)(1)(E) (alien smuggling), § 241(a)(1)(H) (misrepresentation). Do these differences represent legislative fine-tuning or historical happenstance?

Consider the following hypothetical legislative proposal.

Section 1. Except as provided in Section 2, all provisions for relief from deportation are hereby repealed.

Section 2. The Attorney General may waive any ground of deportation and adjust the status of an alien on whose behalf the ground is waived to that of lawful permanent resident if the Attorney General determines that such waiver and adjustment are justified by humanitarian concerns or are otherwise in the national interest.

Section 3. A determination by the Attorney General under Section 2 shall not be set aside by a court unless it is arbitrary or capricious.

If you were a member of Congress, would you support the proposal? If not, what additional legislative guidelines would you add? Would you distinguish between (1) immigrants and nonimmigrants; (2) aliens who were admitted and aliens who entered without inspection; and (3) aliens who have resided here for a short while and those who are long-time residents?

An alternate (or additional) route would be to eliminate discretionary relief altogether and enact a statute of limitations on deportation instead. Do you find this proposal satisfactory?

How would you resolve the tension that we have traced throughout this Chapter: the conflict between the twin goals of establishing clear rules to limit executive branch discretion and creating avenues of relief flexible enough to respond to the particular facts of each alien's case?

Chapter Eight

REFUGEES AND
POLITICAL ASYLUM

SECTION A. INTRODUCTION

1. THE CONTROVERSY

A refugee, in the usual conception, is among the world's most unfortunate people. Besides being a victim—of persecution, war, or natural disaster—a refugee has also been uprooted, forced to leave familiar territory because of that same oppression or destruction. But paradoxically, under modern international law, to be a refugee—a recognized refugee—is also to assume a position of privilege. Refugees, unlike millions of other deprived people throughout the globe, benefit from distinctive programs for relief and assistance, and often from arrangements for distant resettlement. A specialized office of the United Nations, the UN High Commissioner for Refugees (UNHCR), with an annual budget running over a billion dollars and a large staff that includes dozens of lawyers known as protection officers, watches over their treatment and seeks to find durable solutions.

Nearly a hundred nations, moreover, have become parties to treaties[1] that set forth specific, and sometimes quite extensive, legal protections for refugees. Domestic legal provisions in many nations augment these requirements, spelling out the circumstances under which refugees who have reached their territory may claim political asylum—which usually entails indefinite rights to resettle and establish a new life in the receiving nation, even if the refugee violated the regular provisions of the immigration laws in the course of arriving there. In spite of these paradoxical advantages, however—or more likely, because of them—the legal conception of refugee is narrower than the usual popular conception. The most common legal

---

1. The two most important treaties are the Convention relating to the Status of Refugees, *done* July 28, 1951, 189 U.N.T.S. 137 [hereinafter cited as UN Convention]; and the Protocol relating to the Status of Refugees, *done* Jan. 31, 1967, 19 U.S.T. 6223, T.I.A.S. No. 6577, 606 U.N.T.S. 267 [hereinafter cited as UN Protocol], reproduced in the Statutory Supplement. For useful general treatments of the international law relating to refugees, *see* J. Hathaway, The Law of Refugee Status (1991); G. Goodwin–Gill, The Refugee in International Law (1983), and A. Grahl–Madsen, The Status of Refugees in International Law (2 vols. 1966, 1972).

definitions of "refugee" focus only on persecution. They do not recognize economic deprivation or natural disasters, or even the outbreak of military hostilities in the homeland, as the source of refugee status.

Thus there is an inherent tension that runs through all political and legal decisionmaking on refugee and asylum questions in the United States. The notion of refugee evokes sympathy. The possibility of resulting privileges, especially a potential right to resettle indefinitely, evokes suspicion that the unworthy are trying to claim that status.[2]

Compounding the difficulty is the inherent vagueness of the governing legal standard for deciding just who is a "refugee." Under the usual legal definitions, a "refugee" is someone who demonstrates "a well-founded fear of persecution" in his or her homeland. But when is a fear well-founded? What is persecution? What kind of evidence is necessary to prove the needed facts? When the standard is this vague, there remains plenty of room for manipulation, by those who favor a less generous policy as well as by those who favor a more generous one.

As more and more asylum-seekers have reached the United States, this built-in tension in American immigration law has become more glaringly apparent. This Chapter therefore treats subjects that are among the most controversial in the whole immigration field.[3] Some of the harshness of the debate, as well as some flavor of the genuinely difficult dilemmas involved, comes through in the following selection of charges and countercharges:

> As far as many of the detained Haitians are concerned, the main difference is * * * between black refugees and white ones. "I think they're holding me because I'm black," says Francesca Dorgille, who left an infant son behind in her search for prosperity, only to wind up at Fort Allen [a detention center in Puerto Rico]. "If I were white, they would let me free." Many of the Haitians' American supporters agree that race is a prime factor; this, they suggest, was the "shock" that led to last summer's new policies [mandating detention for nearly all excludable aliens, even those who have applied for asylum]. * * *

> [T]he suspicion lingers that if 15,000 white Poles fleeing the crackdown showed up in New York Harbor, they would not be

---

2. One judge referred to asylum applications as "this most sensitive of human claims in the international community." *Reyes-Arias v. INS*, 866 F.2d 500, 504 (D.C.Cir.1989) (Starr, J.).

3. Serious controversies also persist in Western Europe over the treatment of asylum-seekers and decisions to grant or deny asylum to particular groups or individuals. *See generally, e.g.*, Int'l Centre for Migration Policy Development, The Key to Europe—a Comparative Analysis of Entry and Asylum Policies in Western Countries (1994); The New Asylum Seekers: Refugee Law in the 1980s (D. Martin ed. 1988); W. Smyser, Ref-

ugees: Extended Exile 92–121 (1987) (especially the chapter on "The Jet People"); Fullerton, *Restricting the Flow of Asylum-Seekers in Belgium, Denmark, the Federal Republic of Germany, and the Netherlands: New Challenges to the Geneva Convention relating to the Status of Refugees and the European Convention on Human Rights*, 29 Va.J. Int'l L. 35 (1988); Aleinikoff, *Political Asylum in the Federal Republic of Germany and the Republic of France: Lessons for the United States*, 17 U.Mich.J.L.Ref. 183 (1984); Avery, *Refugee Status Decision–Making: The Systems of Ten Countries*, 19 Stan. J. Int'l L. 235 (1983).

shipped off to * * * Fort Allen—a comparison the Haitians themselves make over and over again.

Refugees or Prisoners?, Newsweek, February 1, 1982, at 28–29.*

[Writing of "asylum as a growth industry":] The "asylum strategy" has become well-known in countries of out-migration, and increasing numbers of persons ineligible for refugee or immigrant admission are choosing to enter the country illegally (or on temporary visitors' visas) in order to claim asylum.

Teitelbaum, *Political Asylum in Theory and Practice,* 76 The Public Interest 74, 77–78 (1984).

The Haitians' advocates, however, argue that a great many of the refugees are victims of repression. Even those who had no trouble before they left Haiti could be viewed as traitors for seeking asylum here, claims Kurzban [one of the lawyers for the Haitians]. Thus, he asserts, they have as much right to stay as Cubans who fled Castro or Nicaraguans who fled the Sandinists. The government's efforts to expel the Haitians, he says, come from a blend of racism and loyalty to Duvalier's regime.

* * *

Inman [General Counsel of INS] dismisses these statements with an angry wave. "This is *war*," he declares. "The war is to in effect eliminate the definition of refugee and to open our borders to anybody that wants to come in and have a worldwide equalization of wealth and property." Kurzban and the [other lawyers for the Haitians], he says, "are orchestrating some massive program to open our doors for all immigration."

Bruck, *Springing the Haitians,* The American Lawyer, September 1982, at 36, 39.

Dessine asked a question he had asked before, one that comes in a perpetual refrain from incarcerated Haitians: "Why are we in jail? We are not criminals. Can you explain it?"

"I said that this administration doesn't want you here but that I don't agree, and I'm doing everything I can," says Levine [Dessine's pro bono lawyer].

He shakes his head. "You can't really answer that. As far as I'm concerned they're in a concentration camp. You can call them detainees, but you can call black white. It makes me ashamed to be an American."

Id. at 36.

[I]n other respects, the [West's asylum] system is nearing breakdown. The cost is huge: Sweden alone spends more on the care and maintenance of asylum-seekers than the entire annual budget of the UNHCR, whose responsibility is to the whole world's refugees. The real issue, however, is numbers. Even though the western countries took on an extra 1,000 administrative staff in 1988, they cannot cope with the flood of applicants. As a result, asylum-seekers are in effect becoming immigrants. The question that follows is whether immigrants should be accepted on this foot-in-the-door principle, or whether it should be a more orderly affair that gives consideration to the historical obligations of the host country, family reunification and the nature of the state being abandoned.

The Year of the Refugee, *The Economist,* Dec. 23, 1989, at 17, 26.

2. OVERVIEW

We consider together in this Chapter the important legal provisions relating to refugees. You should keep in mind, however, that an alien's successful claim that she is a refugee may lead to permanent residence in the United States through two quite different paths. Although courts and commentators often fail to make the distinction when speaking of U.S. refugee programs, this failure only compounds a confusion that is already too widespread. Each path has its own distinctive set of procedures, constraints, and legal and policy dilemmas. We will often refer to them generically, and with some imprecision, as "overseas refugee programs" and "political asylum," respectively.

Overseas refugee programs are analytically akin to the material we covered in Chapter Three relating to admissions. We focused in that Chapter on two broad characteristics that serve as the basis for permission to migrate permanently to the United States (in addition to good fortune in the diversity lottery): family ties and labor needs. Refugee status constitutes a third and completely independent characteristic that may be the basis for an alien's securing, while she remains in a foreign country, permission to immigrate to the United States. Unlike a preference immigrant or an immediate relative, she will not receive an immigrant visa, *see* INA §§ 207(c), 211(c), but this is merely a minor paperwork detail. Typically those who gain admission through the overseas refugee programs are located in a refugee camp in a foreign country at the time of their selection, but with increasing frequency they are now selected and processed while still within their countries of origin.[4]

The statutory provisions governing such admissions changed rather frequently for 35 years after World War II, as Congress and the executive branch struggled to find a framework that would provide a reasonable degree of control and predictability, while at the same time retaining

4. See INA § 101(a)(42)(B). In this respect, U.S. law applies a broader definition of refugee than does the leading international treaty, the UN Convention, *supra* note 1, which considers no one a refugee unless he or she is outside the home country. The difference is of minor importance, however, because the refugees will obviously be outside the home country before they are actually admitted to the United States. Moreover, in practice, a program to bring refugees directly from their country of origin can be established only in special circumstances, for that country must agree to allow the emigration in a category that implicitly insults or condemns its policies, through the required U.S. finding that the government persecutes or at least tolerates persecution. *See* Martin, *The Refugee Act of 1980: Its Past and Future,* in Transnational Legal Problems of Refugees, 1982 Mich.Y.B. Int'l L.Stud. 91, 101–04.

adequate flexibility to respond to new crises. With the Refugee Act of 1980,[5] the United States seems to have achieved a relatively stable statutory framework for accommodating these contradictory ends, at least to the extent of establishing, year by year, the number of refugee admissions and the allocation of those admission spaces among refugee groups. INA § 207. Debate persists, however, over funding of resettlement and transitional support, exact selection procedures, the role of domestic interest groups in establishing admissions priorities, and the application of the refugee definition or other standards after the end of the Cold War.

The second path to permanent residence based on refugee status comes through filing a claim for political asylum at our borders or inside the United States, and as indicated, this remains a highly controversial subject. We are still far from having a statutory framework and administrative apparatus widely regarded as adequate and reliable for coping with political asylum applications—although major administrative changes adopted in 1990 and 1994 (*see* 55 Fed.Reg. 30674 (1990), 59 *id.* 62284 (1994)) hold promise to ease some of the lingering problems. The controversy derives from the very nature of the process. Unlike beneficiaries of the overseas refugee programs, who do not reach U.S. soil until they have been processed, screened, selected, and plied with documents in some other country, applicants for asylum reach the territorial United States on their own and only then claim protection against involuntary return. Some applicants enter on nonimmigrant visas and overstay. Others enter without inspection before filing their claims somewhere in the interior. Still others ask for asylum at a border post or on the beach where they first encounter the border patrol. And a handful are nonimmigrants still in status who file, for example, because a sudden political change at home makes it risky for them to return.

Because of this characteristic, there is no reasonable way to screen asylum applications in advance nor to impose strict limits on the overall number of applicants. Of course, not all applicants will manage to prove their entitlement to asylum. In fact, the percentage of successful applications historically has run roughly between 15 and 30 percent. But in nearly all circumstances the applicants will remain in the United States while their claims are adjudicated.

Adjudication has proved to be a lengthy and tangled process, owing both to inadequacies in administration and to a complex interaction between the courts and the political branches. The result has been a series of significant problems in deciding what arrangements should be made for the care and maintenance of the applicants, over the months or years that may pass while the adjudication proceeds. Should they be detained? If not, should they be allowed to work? What kinds of public assistance should be provided? Moreover, as noted before, because the governing standards are vague and difficult to apply, there is ample room for controversy about whether political considerations have intruded on the decisions.

5. Pub.L. No. 96–212, 94 Stat. 102 (1980)   U.S.C.A.).
(codified at various sections of 8, 22

Political asylum (*see* INA §§ 208, 243(h)) is analytically akin to the provisions for relief from deportation that we examined in Chapter Seven, but it is potentially more potent than any of the provisions reviewed there. For one thing, a political asylum claim can provide relief from exclusion as well as deportation; its protection extends to parolees and to persons apprehended before they ever make a recognized entry. Beyond this, there is no waiting period before one qualifies, and a grant of asylum may lead rather directly to permanent residence rights. Moreover, if the alien establishes entitlement to protection by demonstrating that his life or freedom would be threatened in his home country, both statutory law and treaty requirements forbid the application of many of the usual exclusion criteria and other eligibility qualifications.

All these features—the difficulty of imposing control over numbers, the delays in the adjudication process, the potency of a successful asylum claim, and charges of political manipulation of the system—give rise to the divisive legal and policy issues concerning political asylum.[6]

3. THE REFUGEE DEFINITION: AN INTRODUCTION

Crucial to the operation of both overseas refugee programs and the political asylum adjudication system is the statutory definition of refugee. Section 101(a)(42)(A) of the INA defines "refugee" as:

> any person who is outside any country of such person's nationality or, in the case of a person having no nationality, is outside any country in which such person last habitually resided, and who is unable or unwilling to return to, and is unable or unwilling to avail himself or herself of the protection of, that country because of persecution or a well-founded fear of persecution on account of race, religion, nationality, membership in a particular social group, or political opinion * * *.

This language, based on Article I of the UN Convention relating to the Status of Refugees, as modified by Article 1 of the 1967 Protocol, gives rise to immensely rich controversies over meaning and implementation. The same is true of the closely related language in INA § 243(h), which is based on Article 33 of the Convention.

Before plunging into those controversies, it may be worthwhile to place them in context. One well-regarded estimate placed the world's refugee total at over 16.2 million in 1993. U.S. Comm. for Refugees, World Refugee Survey: 1994 at 40–41 (1994). A great many of these people, however,

6. Besides the sections we will consider in detail here, there are at least two other legal provisions whose implementation may require an assessment of the threat of persecution faced by the applicant in her home country. INA § 212(e) bars many exchange visitors—beneficiaries of "J" visas—from returning to the United States as permanent residents until they have spent two years back in the home country, but a proviso permits the waiver of this requirement for aliens who show "exceptional hardship" or demonstrate that they would be "subject to persecution on account of race, religion, or political opinion." Secondly § 13 of the Act of September 11, 1957, 8 U.S.C.A. § 1255b, allows the adjustment of status of certain diplomats (beneficiaries of "A" and "G" visas) to lawful permanent resident status if "the alien has shown compelling reasons demonstrating * * * that the alien is unable to return to the [home] country," and meets certain other criteria.

would not come close to satisfying the U.S. definition above, or the UN Convention definition from which it derives, for they have not fled targeted persecution as such. Some of the largest concentrations of "refugee" populations (as they are popularly understood)—for example, Afghan refugees in Pakistan and Iran, Liberians in Cote d'Ivoire, or Somalis in Kenya and Ethiopia—consist primarily of people who fled civil war and ethnic strife, or perhaps some combination of natural disasters (such as drought) and human-caused suffering.

Why does the prevailing legal definition not include such victims? What political choices underlie the narrower approach? Should the legal definitions be more expansively interpreted so as to afford coverage to a larger proportion of them—given that they are often popularly thought of as refugees? Alternatively, should the present U.S. and UN definitions be explicitly amended in pursuit of this aim? On the other hand, does the existing UN definition perform a worthwhile function when used for limited purposes? Does it make sense to count certain populations as refugees for some purposes but not for others? For which purposes?

The following readings explore some of these issues and provide background for considering the legal and policy questions that will preoccupy us throughout the Chapter. The first reading, by Professor Astri Suhrke, explores a variety of conceptions of refugee. In the second, Professor Suhrke and her co-authors advocate a conception of refugee broader than the UN definition—a conception which, they assert, is "consistent with ethical considerations" but also realistic in light of late twentieth century global politics. The third reading provides background on the UN definition, reflects on the ways in which refugee conceptions can be misunderstood or misapplied, and suggests how the prevailing definition should be implemented.

ASTRI SUHRKE, GLOBAL REFUGEE MOVEMENTS AND STRATEGIES OF RESPONSE

U.S. Immigration and Refugee Policy: Global and Domestic Issues 157–162.
(M. Kritz ed. 1983).

The definitional question is crucial because persons identified as refugees typically have special protection and benefits that are not accorded those identified as migrants. This preferential status is recognized in international law on the grounds that the refugee is a person in need who cannot turn to his government for protection. The international community consequently is obliged to render assistance, even if this means limiting the customary rights of states to decide the terms of entry and sojourn of individuals. The principal international definitions at present are the U.N. concepts that were formulated in the immediate post-World War II period, largely in response to European refugee flows. Contemporary movements, by contrast, originate primarily in the Third World. This has raised questions about the relevance of conventional concepts to current realities.

Concern over definitions is closely related to the notion that refugee flows have increased at a rapid pace in recent years, and will probably continue to do so in the future. Increased demand for assistance generates pressures to adjust the definition of beneficiaries, particularly in view of the resource restraints evident in many industrialized countries today. Fears that huge international flows of destitute persons will be a permanent feature of the future partly stem from the appearance of large flows at present—including the Indochinese, the Somalis, the Cubans, the Haitians, and the Afghans. However, it may be rash to conclude that these flows constitute a pattern and a trend, rather than a coincidence causing a temporary peak.

* * *

A refugee can be defined in three ways: legally (as stipulated in national or international law); politically (as interpreted to meet political exigencies); and sociologically (as reflecting an empirical reality). A legal definition must limit the numbers demanding assistance, otherwise the very existence of a refugee program may be jeopardized. On the other hand, it should also be sufficiently broad to accommodate people requiring international protection. Historically, this has been the concept of a refugee in international law; the current concern is to what extent new situations have arisen that are not adequately recognized by legal norms. A brief review of the types of legal norms now in existence indicates the trade-offs associated with each.

The principal international definition is that of the United Nations, which has been adopted by many nations. The U.N. definition limits the numbers in many ways. Only persons who are outside their country of origin qualify. The key criterion determining refugee status is persecution, which usually means an act of government against individuals, thereby excluding those fleeing from generalized conditions of insecurity and oppression, as well as victims of nature-made disasters. Persecution, moreover, is generally interpreted to mean loss of certain rights, as opposed to exploitation, which implies failure to enjoy those rights in the first place. Masses of poverty-stricken and powerless people in the Third World therefore are excluded. * * *

Nor does the U.N. definition specifically cite economic factors as a reason for persecution. This omission has reinforced conventional notions to the effect that persons who leave their country for political reasons are refugees, while those who move for economic reasons are migrants. International lawyers maintain, however, that, if membership in a particular economic class is the main reason for persecution, the person in question would qualify as a refugee. This interpretation opens the way for a potentially very large number of applicants, including the poverty-stricken masses. The main corrective lies in arguing, as is customarily done, that systematic economic deprivation does not constitute persecution.

The limitations in the U.N. definition also reflect the political climate at the time it was adopted (1951). The concept of rights parallels that put forth in the 1948 Universal Declaration of Human Rights; political, civic, and legal rights are stressed, while economic rights are much less prominent. Refugees from European colonialism—that is, majority victims of minority rule—are not accounted for explicitly. The emphasis on loss of existing rights implied in the term persecution tends to favor disposed elites, while persons who normally possess few, if any, rights would not as readily qualify.

The U.N. definition is vulnerable to attack from two directions. First, as a product of Western liberal thinking and Western political supremacy in the early 1950s, it reflects particularist notions of needs and rights. Can this be the basis for a definition that aspires to universality? Second, contemporary population outflows from many Third World countries consist of persons who flee generalized conditions of insecurity and oppression, as well as the economic refugees who seek to escape severe economic deprivation. These people typically cannot count on the protection of their government to provide basic physical, economic, or political security. Their need may be equal to those who are persecuted in the sense of the U.N. definition.

Slightly broader definitions have been adopted to accommodate some of these categories of need. The most important is the 1969 Convention of the Organization of African Unity (OAU) which stipulates that persons fleeing generalized conditions of insecurity and oppression due to colonial rule, or for other reasons, should be viewed as refugees.[a] A similar provision has not been adopted by any country outside Africa, even though these types of outflows are a common result of instability in many Third World nations. However, the UNHCR has for some time included such flows under its mandate, as a matter of administrative practice.

The reasons behind the OAU innovation may help to explain why other states have been reluctant to follow suit. African states were prepared to accept the additional obligations resulting from a broadened definition partly because wars of independence were a major cause of mass outflows. African solidarity and mutual assistance in the name of independence was a moral imperative. Ethnic groups frequently cut across state boundaries and made it easy to accept new arrivals. Repatriation, moreover was—and is—a frequent solution. Many conflicts were solved in a way that enabled the displaced persons to return home (that is, the end of colonial rule), and refugee movements did not typically flow from very poor to very rich states. The refugees, consequently, had no strong incentives to remain in the country of first asylum once the conflict at home had subsided.

A few European countries have experimented with a definition that is broader than that of the United Nations. The criteria for refugees [are] relaxed to include persons who require assistance on humanitarian grounds generally, but those who qualify are usually given benefits equivalent to a second-class status, or B–status. The concept remains controversial, but it does reflect the needs of many Third World groups that flee generalized

a. The OAU definition restates the UN definition and then adds a second paragraph:

The term "refugee" shall also apply to every person who, owing to external aggression, occupation, foreign domination or events seriously disturbing public order in either part or the whole of his country of origin or nationality, is com-

pelled to leave his place of habitual residence in order to seek refuge in another place outside his country of origin or nationality.

Organization of African Unity Convention Governing the Specific Aspects of Refugee Problems in Africa, art. 1, *entered into force*, June 20, 1974, 1001 U.N.T.S. 45.—eds.

conditions of insecurity and oppression. Giving limited benefits to such groups could help to protect the integrity of a more generous policy designed for those who are most victimized. On the other hand, is it feasible and desirable to have first- and second-class refugees, any more than it is to have first- and second-class citizens? It is further objected that even B–status programs will attract hordes of destitute Third World nationals that the rich countries cannot reasonably accommodate. While humanitarian reasons could be interpreted narrowly to keep the numbers down, considerations of equity will likely generate pressures in the other direction.

There are two kinds of more narrow definitions: a highly politicized one that requires that the applicant must only meet certain political criteria, and one that limits asylum or refugee status to the political activist.

The first category is exemplified by U.S. law prior to 1980 and current legislation in most communist countries. The principal criterion in the U.S. definition was that a person leaving a communist country *ipso facto* was a refugee. Need was inferred to apply categorically to all such persons. In communist countries, asylum provisions typically stipulate that the beneficiary must have struggled on behalf of the working class or a similar cause. One presumed advantage of a politicized definition is that the numbers and kinds of beneficiaries can be regulated with relative ease, because there is no pretense in the first place that refugee policy should be equitable and relative to need. However, if one category of established beneficiaries suddenly swells, this can create problems and force a reevaluation of terms: should these be treated as refugees or as migrants? Another problem is that politicized definitions usually reflect hostile relations between the sending and the receiving countries; hence there is little alternative but to accept all outflows as refugees, since a return process cannot easily be arranged. U.S. problems with Indochinese and Cuban arrivals are cases in point.

Another way of limiting the definition is to include only political activists. This concept is contained in most Latin American treaties, which limit asylum to persons who have committed a political crime. Past refugee movements in the region mainly consisted of political activists, and generous asylum provisions involved few obligations. The typical exile was educated and had independent means, his asylum frequently was temporary, and the total number was low. At present, however, a new pattern is emerging in Latin America, similar to that in Africa. Mass flows of common people spill across national boundaries due to internal strife. This is a challenge to the traditional Latin American concept of asylum, and to the kinds of legal, socioeconomic and political rights that have been associated with refugee status in the region. So far, Latin American scholars and policymakers are only beginning to explore ways of meeting that challenge.

* * *

Existing legal norms define need primarily with respect to the causes that led the person to flee. The numbers are then limited partly by stipulating types of causes, for instance, political activism, political dissidence, and ethnic minority status. Some critics argue that it is more meaningful to build a definition around the concept of need, regardless of causes. This means discarding the distinction between those who are actively persecuted and those who flee generalized conditions of insecurity, between persecuted minorities and majorities, between "refugees-in-place," who have been unable to leave and those who have left, between economic and political reasons for leaving, and so on. People in all these categories would be potentially eligible for refugee status, and the final determination would be based on an assessment of relative need. Such a concept would be relevant to contemporary realities, indeed, to any reality. The numbers could be limited according to the degree of need, it is argued. A refugee program may not be the most appropriate response for all these situations, but the important point is that some groups of very vulnerable persons would not *a priori* be excluded from consideration.

ARISTIDE R. ZOLBERG, ASTRI SUHRKE, & SERGIO AGUAYO, ESCAPE FROM VIOLENCE: CONFLICT AND THE REFUGEE CRISIS IN THE DEVELOPING WORLD

Pp. 269–72 (1989).

Our analysis of contemporary refugee movements [has] delineated three sociological types of refugees: (1) the activist, (2) the target, and (3) the victim. * * * [T]he classic activists are dissenters and rebels whose actions contribute to the conflict that eventually forces them to flee. The targeted refugees are individuals who, through membership in a particular group, are singled out for violent action. And the victims are randomly caught in the cross fire or are exposed to generalized social violence. What all three have in common is fear of immediate violence—violence resulting from conflict between state and civil society, between opposing armies, or conflict among ethnic groups or class formations that the state is unable or unwilling to control. Whether the individuals are activists or passive bystanders simply caught in the conflict is immaterial from the point of view of their immediate security. Their need clearly could be the same regardless of the cause, and has demonstrably been so in many of the cases analyzed. It follows that in a historical and normative sense, the three types of refugees are equally deserving. The activist, the target, and the victim have an equally valid claim to protection from the international community.

The international refugee regime has to some extent recognized the moral equivalence of the three types. The U.N. Convention's definition accommodates the first two but has no provision for the victim. On the other hand, victims were in practice recognized as refugees in the European experience, both in earlier centuries and after World War II. The victims were also acknowledged in the institutional response to Third World refugees through the expanded mandate of the UNHCR in the 1960s and the general practices of first asylum countries in Asia, Africa, and Latin America. Legal codes in Africa and Latin America were also adjusted to allow for mere "victims" (in the 1969 OAU convention and the 1984

Cartagena Declaration). The UNHCR introduced the notion of "victims of violence" in the mid–1980s to plead for asylum seekers in other regions.

From this perspective, the restrictive tendencies evident in North American and West European asylum practices in the 1980s, toward a narrow interpretation of the convention's criterion of persecution as the basis for refugee status, are highly questionable and have been deplored by UNHCR officials. To deny "mere victims" the opportunity to escape from violence is not only morally untenable but runs counter to broader historical trends. It is also open to charges of discrimination on racial and political grounds, as the restrictive tendencies have been most clearly evident with respect to spontaneous asylum seekers of non-European origin who come from noncommunist states.

* * *

An optimal policy would start from the explicit premise of moral equivalence among all three refugee types; the administration of protection and services should also be formal and explicit rather than leaving the beneficiary to an uncertain or semilegal status. Equally important, however, is the need to limit the number of prospective beneficiaries. It will be recalled that with the development toward a universal definition of refugees in the 1930s, it was stressed that some "exact definitions" were necessary to prevent the number of refugees from multiplying *ad infinitum*. Half a century later the point has, if anything, become more self-evident. Because it represents a privileged form of migration, refugee status can be given to only a limited number of people. The question then arises whether the concept of violence lends itself to discriminating interpretations that permit setting priorities.

We submit that it can and that the central ranking principle must be the immediacy and degree of life-threatening violence. Those most exposed must be given preferential access to protection, which becomes the most basic of rights. Farther along in the queue, relief could be given as far as resources and political will permit. More specifically, this would mean that priority be given to individuals or groups who find themselves in extremely threatening situations: civilians in battle areas, likely targets of death squads and pogroms, political prisoners under threat of torture, members of rebel or dissident groups on "wanted" lists, and the like. Proscription on cultural expressions such as lack of freedom of religion would come much farther down on the list, except when it is associated with life-threatening forms of violence.

Situations in which the economic prerequisites for sustaining life have suddenly been removed equally constitute life-threatening violence, and such victims need protection. This definition would include the poverty-stricken masses of the developing world, the victims of structural violence who are systematically pressed toward starvation levels, and the victims of drought and famine, with or without the compounded effect of warfare. It may be objected that such a definitional basis of refugee is totally unrealistic; in particular, the resource-rich countries of the North would not want to relieve famine or massive poverty in the South by means of a large-scale relocation of people.

The objection seems unfounded. Most victims of famine and starvation who today cross international borders remain in neighboring countries, where their claims to life-sustaining support generally are recognized by the international relief or refugee regime. Groups accused of being economic refugees who have claimed asylum in the industrialized countries are not the ones who are most economically destitute and would hardly be admitted as victims of violence even if economically based violence were included in the definition[.] * * *

The rule must be that victims of economic, that is, structural, violence must be helped first in their own country. Observance of the *in situ* clause,[a] * * * is necessary to prevent neighboring and often poor developing countries from becoming overloaded by an influx of desperately poor people seeking relief and not to encourage an international restructuring of populations that in an age of nation-states is politically unacceptable.

DAVID A. MARTIN, REFORMING ASYLUM ADJUDICATION: ON NAVIGATING THE COAST OF BOHEMIA

138 U.Pa.L.Rev. 1247, 1253–57, 1270–79 (1990).

* * *

Classically, the right of asylum under international law belonged to states and not to individuals. Sovereigns were considered to have the right or prerogative to grant protection against return of those they chose to shelter. This framework shamed itself in the world's woefully inadequate response in the 1930s and 1940s to those who were fleeing Nazi persecution. From the ashes of World War II arose an international structure that signalled a determination, measured but genuine, to do more for refugees.

* * *

[T]he 1951 Convention Relating to the Status of Refugees * * * established a definition that has become the centerpiece of most Western asylum adjudication systems, including that of the United States. * * *

The 1951 Convention, a cautious and more limited treaty than is often appreciated, provides relatively few actual guarantees to refugees illegally present in the country of haven (as most asylum seekers now are).[15] In

a. In an earlier chapter, the authors discuss the "*in situ* clause," based on a distinction borrowed from Michael Walzer, in these terms:

> [T]he key issue from the perspective of concerned humanitarians is not only whether the movement is involuntary and essentially political but also whether the immediate, intense suffering of the victims can be relieved by helping them in their own country—through policies of their own government or combined with favorable external initiatives—or if relief is possible only by enabling them to move abroad—that is, by providing them

with a refuge. * * * [This approach makes it possible, for example,] to distinguish refugees from persons who move as a consequence of natural disaster. Most victims of malnutrition and slow starvation in the developing world should not be considered as refugees because most of them can be assisted *in situ* in their own countries.

Id. at 33.—eds.

15. The 1951 Convention does provide a host of impressively detailed guarantees for refugees lawfully present, but a decision that the person is a Convention refugee does not

particular, it does not guarantee asylum, in the sense of a durable lawful residence status, even for those duly adjudged to be refugees under its provisions. Thus even today there is no individual right of asylum under international law.[16] What the Convention does require, however, even for refugees illegally present, is *nonrefoulement*—a technical term for protection, deriving from Article 33 of the Convention, against return to a country "where [the refugee's] life or freedom would be threatened on account of his race, religion, nationality, membership of a particular social group or political opinion." Article 33 affords a limited and country-specific protection, and the receiving nation technically remains free to send a refugee on to other countries, rather than granting asylum on its soil.

Nevertheless, since 1951 most Western countries, to their credit, have set up asylum claims systems that essentially combine the determination of refugee status under the 1951 Convention definition with the discretionary act of providing durable status, or asylum. An affirmative refugee status determination thus routinely leads not only to the limited protection against return contemplated by Article 33, but also to the full range of protections embraced within the notion of asylum.[19] In this sense, we have come close to a system that guarantees an individual right of asylum to those who somehow establish physical presence on the soil of such Western countries and also prove that they satisfy the Convention definition.

That these admirable features of the system go beyond the strict requirements of international law, however, should remind us of their fragility. They cannot be taken as inevitable constants. Instead, it must be an ever-present concern of wise policy to shape asylum measures, including adjudication systems, so as to maximize continued domestic

ipso facto result in lawful presence. *See Report of the Ad Hoc Comm. on Statelessness and Related Problems,* U.N.Doc. E/1618/Corr. 1; E/AC.32/5/Corr. 1 (1950), at 47. [The drafters of the treaty there stated:

The expression "lawfully within their territory" throughout this draft Convention would exclude a refugee who while lawfully admitted has overstayed the period for which he was admitted or was authorized to stay or who has violated any other condition attached to his admission or stay.]

The major purpose of the Convention, as the name suggests, was to clarify questions of status for the World War II refugees already in place. As Professor Goodwin–Gill has explained:

The 1951 Convention was originally intended to establish, confirm or clarify the legal status of a known population of the displaced. This met the needs of the time, and most provisions focus on assimilation, or are premised on lawful residence or tolerated presence. There is nothing on asylum, on admission, or on resettlement.

Goodwin–Gill, *The Future of International Refugee Law,* Refugees, Oct. 1988, at 28.

16. An abortive effort was made in the 1970s to draft a convention that would go further toward international legal guarantees of political asylum for refugees. But this effort was abandoned when a 1977 conference of government representatives appeared likely to weaken even those minimal guarantees derived from the 1951 Convention and the 1967 Protocol. See Weis, *The Draft United Nations Convention on Territorial Asylum,* 50 Brit.Y.B.Int'l L. 151–71 (1979).

19. See Hofmann, *Asylum and Refugee Law,* in The Legal Position of Aliens in National and International Law 2045, 2058–59 (J. Frowein & T. Stein eds. 1987). In fact Western nations (with a few exceptions, like Austria, traditionally viewed as transit countries) rarely find third countries willing to take refugees off their hands. Given that the refugees are present and, under article 33, cannot be sent to the only country normally obligated to take them in (the country of nationality), it is clearly better if they early attain a secure new status that allows them to rebuild a normal life.

support. The systems' inability to cope effectively with growing numbers of asylum seekers over the last decade now threatens that foundation.

* * *

Although Americans (along with most of the Western world) are virtually united in a commitment to protect refugees, they are far from united in a common conception of "refugee." Everyday parlance tends to treat anyone fleeing life-threatening conditions as a refugee, whether the source of the threat be natural disaster, foreign invasion, civil unrest, or deliberate persecution. The legal framework of course employs a narrower concept than this journalistic usage, and the 1951 Convention definition might be expected to provide the basis for a unified common understanding, built around the phrase "well-founded fear of persecution." But this phrase too can also take on a variety of shapes, from highly expansive to narrowly crabbed, often depending, it seems, on whether the speaker wishes to include or exclude a particular group of claimants.

* * *

Compounding [the problem of agreed interpretation] are the images we (both citizens and government officials) bring to judgments about asylum policy. [Under the case law, the] legal standard looks, in most cases, toward a finely calibrated individualized judgment of the risk of persecution the applicant would face in the homeland. The judgment must be based, to some extent, on general information about human rights conditions in the home country. But the primary reliance will fall, most of the time, on information specific to that individual.

Public debate on asylum policy, however, proceeds in cruder terms. Partisans are often ready to make sweeping judgments, by nationality, about the merit of large groups of asylum seekers. Two leading schools of thought have been prominent in the debate. The first, which has long dominated actual outcomes, assumes that virtually anyone from a Communist country would face persecution upon return. Holders of this view find it nearly unthinkable that the government could contemplate deportation. A second school makes similar assumptions about Central American countries, particularly El Salvador and Guatemala.

a. The essential problem. This kind of stereotyping or oversimplification is unfortunately commonplace—and to a significant extent inevitable—in public debate and policy decisions. In a classic work, Walter Lippmann explored comprehensively the influence on policy of these "pictures in our heads." [81] In explaining how easily policymakers can err by relying on their own misconceptions about foreign lands, he wrote:

> [T]he real environment is altogether too big, too complex, and too fleeting for direct acquaintance. We are not equipped to deal with so much subtlety, so much variety, so many permutations and combinations. And although we have to act in that environment, we have to reconstruct it on a simpler model before we can manage with it. To traverse the world men must have maps of

81. W. Lippmann, Public Opinion 3 (1960).

the world. Their persistent difficulty is to secure maps on which their own need, or someone else's need, has not sketched the coast of Bohemia.[82]

The "coast of Bohemia" problem bedevils both public debate and adjudication in the asylum field. But perhaps the image for our purposes should be shifted from the littoral to the physiographical. Few nations enjoy a political geography characterized by a reliably fertile plain of steady human rights observance. Outcroppings of abuses appear, sometimes intermittent hills, sometimes whole mountain ranges of severe persecution. The partisans in refugee debates—as well as adjudicators and judges under the current system—are too often inclined, in looking at nations to which they are favorably disposed, to mistake mountains for hills—or plains. The same people, in looking at nations to which they are hostile or for whose exiles they have (understandably) developed sympathy, often picture mountains where they should see hills, and then rush to the conclusion that that nation's exiles are refugees. Whatever the actual geography, it is also easy to forget that many people in those distant nations continue to inhabit the valleys even when the mountains loom large and forbidding.

b. Boxes vs. spectrums. A related and persistent misunderstanding compounds the difficulties in achieving a sensible and widely supported asylum policy, and it also occasionally complicates adjudication. Much of the debate proceeds as though there are two sharply different categories of persons who find their way into the asylum adjudication system in this country: refugees, on the one hand, and economic migrants (or simply "illegal aliens") on the other. A recent book on U.S. refugee policy (in other respects quite thorough and insightful) reflects this attitude:

> Refugees are neither immigrants nor illegal migrants, although, like immigrants, they have forsaken their homelands for new countries and, like illegal migrants, they may enter those new countries without permission. But a refugee is, in the end, *unlike either.* Both the immigrant and the illegal migrant are drawn to a country. *The refugee is not drawn but driven;* he seeks not to better his life but to rebuild it, to regain some part of what he has lost.[84]

Even if this sharply dichotomous view might, at one time, have captured the realities of refugee flows, it does not offer a helpful way to approach today's asylum caseload. Today's dilemma is both tragic and surpassingly difficult precisely because, among current asylum applicants, refugees are so much like illegal migrants. Only an indistinct and difficult line separates those who should succeed on their asylum applications from those who should not. That is, most of those applying in the United States today were both drawn and driven, and they chose to come in response to a complex mix of political and economic considerations. Asylum seekers are not so different from the rest of us. We have a hard time deciding,

---

82. Id. at 16. For those who are rusty on their Eastern European geography, Bohemia is located in western Czechoslovakia. It has no coast.

84. [N.L. Zucker & N.F. Zucker, The Guarded Gate: The Reality of American Refugee Policy] xiv (emphasis added).

particularly when we make difficult, life-altering decisions, and when we finally do choose a course of action, we act from a mix of motives.

* * *

* * * [In judging an asylum claim under definitions derived from the UN Convention, we do not need to find that the applicant] was only driven, nor assess what his primary motivation was, nor the immediately precipitating event. The best way to understand asylum adjudication is to focus on the degree of risk he would face when he returns. If the risk of persecution is sufficiently substantial, his fear is well-founded, even if it was his need for funds to feed his children that sent him on the particular boat trip at the particular time. That he stayed home until economic considerations tipped the balance in his decision may be relevant—but only for the light it casts on the separate question concerning the degree of risk he truly faces. His refugee claim is not forever tainted because he thought about jobs in Miami or the need for money to feed his family.

* * *

If all asylum applicants did fit neatly into one of two boxes—refugee or economic migrant—the adjudicative task would certainly be simplified. The job would simply be to unmask the impostors, those economic migrants who are base enough to pose as something they are not. Unfortunately some people with authority over asylum decisions in Western countries sometimes speak of adjudications as though they did present such a morality play. They hasten to label as abusive, frivolous, or lawless those claims that simply fall short of the necessary showing.

But the world is not that simple. Asylum adjudication, it must be recognized, is at best a crude and incomplete way to respond to the complex realities that the world presents. Our legal structure, for ultimately sound reasons, demands a simple yes or no answer to the asylum claim. But the dichotomous character of the results should not obscure the complexity onto which that yes-or-no grid is forced. Asylum seekers present a spectrum of situations, with only subtle shadings distinguishing the risk levels they face. Adjudication must draw a line at some point on that spectrum. And it must do so with care, so that it protects those whose risks exceed the threshold, even if they happen to have joined a migration stream made up principally of those less severely threatened, who therefore lack, in this technical sense, a well-founded fear of persecution.

Notes

1. The readings take differing approaches toward economic deprivation as a basis for refugee-type protections. Under what circumstances should severe economic conditions result in mandated protection in a foreign country, under Martin's approach? Under Zolberg, Suhrke, and Aguayo's formulation? When does the *"in situ* clause" the latter authors discuss take effect and justify a proposed haven state's rejection of the asylum seekers' claims?

2. Most of the time the safe haven provided to "victims" outside the borders of their countries of origin has resulted from ad hoc political efforts

undertaken by the receiving states and international organizations. (We will discuss this in greater detail in connection with our examination of the U.S. practice of safe haven in Section D *infra*.) Particularly in recent years receiving states have resisted efforts to characterize such practices as legally required rather than simply desirable measures undertaken whenever conditions permit—including conditions having to do with the overall numbers and relative burdens imposed by the asylum seekers. Consider the advantages and disadvantages of incorporating such practices more thoroughly in a binding legal regime—which would, in effect, extend the currently operative UN definition to include victims of war and civil strife. How would you formulate the relevant standards in a way that lends itself to legal rather than political implementation?

3.   Similarly, the world has for many years marshaled assistance to persons displaced within their own countries by armed conflict or natural disaster, but such efforts have usually been ad hoc, without a clear legal framework structuring international action or firmly legitimating it, for example, even over the objection of the national government. As the number of internally displaced has mounted dramatically over the last decade, to an estimated 25 million in 1994, several efforts have been underway, particularly through the United Nations, to establish a firmer legal foundation for this work. *See* Plender, *The Legal Basis of International Jurisdiction to Act with Regard to the Internally Displaced*, 6 Int'l J.Ref.L. 345 (1994); *Comprehensive study on the human rights issues related to internally displaced persons,* UN Doc. E/CN.4/1993/35 (1993).

4.   There exists a rich and growing literature on the philosophical and legal conceptions of "refugee." For a very selective sampling see, *e.g.,* J. Hathaway, The Law of Refugee Status (1991); H. Adelman, Canada and the Indochinese Refugees 4–16 (1982); Hathaway, *A Reconsideration of the Underlying Premise of Refugee Law*, 31 Harv.Int'l L.J. 129 (1990); Martin, *The Refugee Concept: On Definitions, Politics, and the Careful Use of a Scarce Resource*, in Refugee Policy: Canada and the United States 30 (H. Adelman ed.1991); Singer & Singer, *The Ethics of Refugee Policy,* in Open Borders?   Closed Societies?: The Ethical and Political Issues 111 (M. Gibney ed. 1988); Schacknove, *Who is a Refugee?,* 95 Ethics 274 (1985); Note, *Political Legitimacy in the Law of Political Asylum,* 99 Harv.L.Rev. 450, 459–64 (1985).

SECTION B.   OVERSEAS REFUGEE PROGRAMS

1.   THE LEGAL FRAMEWORK

Only with the end of World War II was there much systematic attention in the United States to admission programs for refugees.[7] By directive in 1945, President Truman ordered priority use of regular immi-

---

7. Much of the impetus for new American and international efforts after the war derived from a recognition that pre-war efforts, especially on behalf of Jewish refugees, were shamefully inadequate. *See generally* J. Simpson, The Refugee Problem (1939); D. Wyman, Paper Walls: America and the Refugee Crisis, 1938–1941 (1968); H. Feingold, The Politics of Rescue: The Roosevelt Administration and The Holocaust, 1938–1945 (1970).

gration quota numbers for the admission of some of the millions of displaced persons left stranded by World War II. In 1948, Congress passed the first significant refugee legislation in American history in order to meet the same problem. The Displaced Persons Act [8] of that year provided a temporary program for the admission of over 200,000 people from the categories specified in the legislation (the ceiling was raised to 400,000 in later legislation). Throughout the next decade, Congress enacted other statutes providing specific numbers of admission spaces for designated groups of refugees. Each measure was conceived as a one-time response to known problems and did not set up an ongoing statutory mechanism to treat future episodes.[9]

When the Soviet Union put down the Hungarian revolution in 1956, its action sent hundreds of thousands across the borders, mainly to Austria, and generated pressure for a quick United States response. But adequate admission provisions were unavailable to offer resettlement and thereby assist the overburdened first-asylum countries. The Eisenhower Administration finally decided to act anyway, and it chose to bring over 30,000 Hungarian refugees here using the Attorney General's parole power. The same approach was employed after Fidel Castro came to power in Cuba. Beginning in the early 1960's, parole was used increasingly for the thousands of Cubans who sought refuge in the United States.

From the executive branch's standpoint, the parole power was outstandingly convenient. It allowed for flexible response to developing crises without the need for new legislation. But its use carried certain disadvantages. Parole, as you recall from our discussion in Chapter Three, is technically not an admission of the alien. A parolee remains constructively at the border and is subject to exclusion rather than deportation proceedings if the government later chooses to remove the individual—even years later. Moreover, when the Hungarian and Cuban programs began, there was no direct way to adjust the status of a parolee to permanent resident status, even though both programs clearly were intended to bring the refugees here for a permanent stay and the beginning of a new life in a new country. Congress eventually cured the latter problem by special statutes authorizing adjustment of status for Hungarians and Cubans.[10] But more and more members of Congress asserted that the parole power was being misused to bring in large groups of refugees without direct legislative approval.

8. Displaced Persons Act of 1948, Ch. 647, 62 Stat. 1009.

9. *See, e.g.,* Refugee Relief Act of 1953, Ch. 336, 67 Stat. 400; Act of Sept. 11, 1957, Pub.L. No. 85–316, § 15, 71 Stat. 639, 643–44; Refugee Fair Share Law, Pub.L. No. 86–648, 74 Stat. 504 (1960). *See generally* N.L. Zucker & N.F. Zucker, The Guarded Gate: The Reality of American Refugee Policy (1987); G. Loescher & J. Scanlan, Calculated Kindness: Refugees and America's Half-Open Door, 1945–Present (1986); Congres-

sional Research Service, 96th Cong., 2d Sess., Review of U.S. Refugee Resettlement Programs and Policies (Comm.Print, Senate Comm. on the Judiciary, 1980).

10. Act of July 25, 1958, Pub.L. No. 85–559, 72 Stat. 419 (providing for adjustment of status of Hungarians who had been in the United States at least two years); Act of Nov. 2, 1966, Pub.L. No. 89–732, 80 Stat. 1161 (providing similar adjustment opportunity for Cubans).

The Hungarian and Cuban programs also taught an additional lesson. These two episodes disabused Americans of any notion that refugee problems would disappear once World War II's displaced persons had all found new homes. Some permanent provision for refugee programs, available to meet new crises, would have to be made.

The landmark 1965 immigration amendments provided the occasion for major changes. In addition to the six regular preference categories which that Act established for deciding admission priorities in place of the old national origins quotas, Congress adopted a new seventh preference designed to be a permanent provision for overseas refugee resettlement programs. It made available for refugees up to six percent of the annual numerically limited immigration numbers, but the provision applied only to refugees as precisely defined therein. A person could qualify for this program only by establishing that he had "fled" persecution in a "Communist or Communist-dominated country" or a "country within the general area of the Middle East." [11] This seventh preference provision was often called "conditional entry," because its beneficiaries did not come in on immigrant visas. They entered in a somewhat more tenuous status known as "conditional entrant," which in most respects, save the name, was identical to parole. But importantly, the 1965 law provided for fairly routine adjustment out of conditional entrant status to permanent resident status two years after initial arrival.

Congressional committee reports accompanying the 1965 amendments stated that parole was not to be used in the future for large groups of refugees, now that permanent provision for such admissions had been made through the seventh preference. This legislative history, however, had stunningly little effect. President Johnson announced a major new parole program for Cubans during the very ceremony, held at the base of the Statue of Liberty, in which he signed the 1965 Act into law. That program came to be known as the Freedom Flights, because the Administration negotiated arrangements with the Cuban government allowing direct air travel from Havana to Florida. By the time Cuba halted the program in 1973, over 700,000 Cubans had immigrated to the United States since Fidel Castro's rise to power. When the Freedom Flights ended, the controversy over the use of parole for refugees diminished for awhile. But in 1975 the Administration used its parole power to bring in over 100,000 Vietnamese who fled when Saigon fell. After a lull in 1976 and 1977, the exodus from Indochina picked up again and reached enormous proportions in the late 1970's. The United States responded with large new refugee paroles.

The permanent seventh preference provision (which by 1978 allowed the admission of 17,400 people a year) was plainly not adequate to meet the high numerical demand experienced in times of refugee emergencies. Moreover, by this time the United States had established other, but much

---

11. Immigration and Nationality Act Amendments of 1965, Pub.L. No. 89–236, § 3, 79 Stat. 911, 913, amending § 203(a)(7) of the INA. This section also authorized admission of "persons uprooted by catastrophic natural calamity", but that provision was never used. *See generally* Parker, *Victims of Natural Disasters in United States Refugee Law and Policy,* in Transnational Legal Problems of Refugees, *supra* note 4, at 137.

smaller, refugee resettlement programs for persons not from Communist countries or from the Middle East—such as modest programs for former political prisoners from Argentina and Chile. The evident inadequacy of the seventh preference, coupled with lingering doubts about the legitimacy of using the parole power for refugees, convinced Congress and the executive branch of the need for new legislation. Their combined efforts led to the Refugee Act of 1980, which establishes the current framework for admissions.

The Refugee Act repealed the old, numerically limited, seventh preference in its entirety. It had become apparent that a single fixed ceiling, applicable every year, simply would not fit the variable needs created by the rise and fall of refugee flows. At the same time, congressional drafters of the Refugee Act were unwilling to leave refugee admissions totally ungoverned by numerical limits fixed in some systematic fashion. That is, although they wanted to avoid a single numerical ceiling applicable year in and year out, they did not want to treat refugee admissions in the same fashion as immediate relatives, an admission category governed only by qualitative and not numerical criteria. The Refugee Act therefore established a third broad admission structure governed by a decisionmaking system quite different from quota immigration and the numerically unlimited system for immediate relatives. Before we explore its operation, you may wish to review the current provisions that govern overseas refugee programs, INA §§ 101(a)(42), 207 and 209.

Annually, before the beginning of the fiscal year, the President is required to consult with the Judiciary Committees of the Congress on the executive branch's plans for refugee admissions. The Act lays out in some detail the procedures to be observed in this consultation process, and it specifies a variety of reports and data to be presented to Congress. Following consultation, the President issues a determination that sets a total numerical ceiling applicable for the next fiscal year. That Presidential Determination also allocates this total among various refugee groups, formally based on a decision as to which refugees are of "special humanitarian concern." As a result of the allocations, not all who might meet the statutory definition of "refugee" in INA § 101(a)(42) are to be considered equally eligible to migrate to the United States. Some groups, though clearly meeting the definition, might be refused an allocation of numbers altogether—based on a judgment, for example, that conditions may soon settle down in the home country allowing voluntary repatriation, or that local settlement in the first asylum country is preferable to distant resettlement, or that this group has sufficient opportunities to resettle in distant lands other than the United States. The formal Presidential Determinations, however, have tended to use very broad regional allocation categories. More precise criteria for selection and priorities are included in the annual consultation documents submitted to Congress, and in guidelines issued to field officers.

Under guidelines used through 1994, the first priority was reserved for those in immediate danger of loss of life and certain others such as political prisoners. Only a tiny fraction of annual admissions fell within this category. The next four priority groups all required some kind of earlier tie to the United States, by family, education, or employment. The final priority, known as P–6, potentially covered all others found to meet the refugee definition. In most regions of the world, P–6 processing was unavailable; only the first five priorities (sometimes only the first four) were deemed eligible for the U.S. refugee program. *See* Refugee Reports, Dec. 31, 1993, at 6–7, for a more complete description. Is this an appropriate way to target limited refugee admission spaces? How would you change the priority system? What *should* be the basis for refugee selections?

A new system was announced in September 1994, which will expand Priority One to include cases referred by a U.S. embassy or by UNHCR, including persons in immediate danger of loss of life, former political prisoners, UNHCR-referred vulnerable cases, such as women at risk or torture survivors, and those from UNHCR's list of persons for whom other durable solutions are unavailable and whose first asylum situation is not feasible for the long term. For an account of UNHCR's priorities for resettlement, see Troeller, *UNHCR Resettlement as an Instrument of International Protection,* 3 Int'l J. Refugee L. 564 (1991). The U.S.'s first priority will also include "groups of special concern to the U.S. to be established as needed by nationality." For FY 1995 those groups were specified categories from Bosnia, Burma, Cuba, Haiti (later suspended), Iran, Laos, Vietnam, and the former Soviet Union. Refugee Reports, Oct. 27, 1994, at 8; *id.,* Dec. 31, 1994, at 6–7. Nongovernmental organizations (NGOs) active in refugee resettlement generally responded favorably to the changes, which may orient admissions more toward need (especially as viewed by UNHCR) and away from prior U.S. ties. But concern lingers about how the new system will work in practice. Moreover, it now appears that as many as 80 percent of current admissions will fall within the first priority—perhaps diminishing the usefulness of the idea of priorities. *Id.* at 9–12.

PRESIDENTIAL DETERMINATION NO. 95–1
OF OCTOBER 1, 1994

59 Fed.Reg. 52393.

Memorandum for the Secretary of State

In accordance with Section 207 of the Immigration and Nationality Act, as amended and after appropriate consultation with the Congress, I hereby make the following determinations and authorize the following actions:

> The admission of up to 112,000 refugees to the United States during FY 1995 is justified by humanitarian concerns or is otherwise in the national interest; provided, however, that this number shall be understood as including persons admitted to the United States during FY 1995 with Federal refugee resettlement assistance under the Amerasian immigrant admissions program,[a] as provided below.

---

a. This is an admissions program for certain out-of-wedlock children fathered by Americans, primarily U.S. soldiers who were in Southeast Asia during the Vietnam War.

The 110,000 funded admissions shall be allocated among refugees of special humanitarian concern to the United States as described in the documentation presented to the Congress during the consultations that preceded this determination and in accordance with the following regional allocations; provided, however, that the number located to the East Asia region shall include persons admitted [under the Amerasian immigrant program;] provided further that the number allocated to the former Soviet Union shall include persons admitted who were nationals of the former Soviet Union, or in case of persons having no nationality, who were habitual residents of the former Soviet Union, prior to September 2, 1991:

Africa 7,000
East Asia 40,000
Former Soviet Union/Eastern Europe 48,000
Latin America/Caribbean 8,000
Near East/South Asia 5,000
Unallocated (funded) 2,000

The 2,000 unallocated federally funded numbers shall be allocated as needed. Unused admissions numbers allocated to a particular region within the 110,000 federally funded ceiling may be transferred to one or more other regions if there is an overriding need for greater numbers for the region or regions to which the numbers are being transferred. You are hereby authorized and directed to consult with the judiciary committees of the Congress prior to any such use of the unallocated numbers or reallocation of numbers from one region to another.

The 2,000 privately funded admissions are not designated for any country or region and may be used for refugees of special humanitarian concern to the United States from any region provided that private resources are available to fund the reasonable cost of their admission and resettlement.

* * *

An additional 10,000 refugee admissions numbers shall be made available during FY 1995 for the adjustment to permanent resident status under Section 209(b) of the Act of aliens who have been granted asylum in the United States under Section 208 of the Act, as this is justified by humanitarian concerns or is otherwise in the national interest. An estimated 8,500 aliens were granted asylum during FY 1994 under Section 208 of the Act.

Such Amerasian children are often the victims of discrimination and abuse in their home countries. Under special statutory authority, INA § 204(f) and Pub.L. No. 100-202, § 101(e), 101 Stat. 1329 (1987), as amended, 8 U.S.C.A. § 1101 note, such offspring (now in their teens or older) and certain immediate family members may immigrate to the United States even without the sponsorship or knowledge of the U.S. father.—eds.

In accordance with Section 101(a)(42) of the Act and after appropriate consultation with the Congress, I also specify that, for FY 1995, the following persons may, if otherwise qualified, be considered refugees for the purpose of admission to the United States within their countries of nationality or habitual residence:

    a. Persons in Vietnam

    b. Persons in Cuba

    c. Persons in Haiti

    d. Persons in the former Soviet Union

You are authorized and directed to report this Determination to the Congress immediately and to publish it in the Federal Register.

William J. Clinton

Notes

1. Work through this Presidential Determination and satisfy yourself as to the significance of each provision. Consider especially the paragraph relating to persons still "within their countries of nationality or habitual residence." Review INA § 101(a)(42)(A) and the definitional provision of the UN Convention Relating to the Status of Refugees, from which this part of the statutory definition was derived. Why do you suppose the UN provision is limited to persons outside their country of nationality or habitual residence? Would it be a good idea to change the international definition so as to include all people who have a well-founded fear of persecution, even if they have not managed to cross their own national boundaries? Why does INA § 101(a)(42)(B) broaden the definition only "in such circumstances as the President after appropriate consultation * * * may specify"? On these and other questions concerning the operation of the provisions governing overseas refugee programs, *see* Martin, *supra* note 4, at 101–104.

2. Note that the Presidential Determination includes numbers for "privately funded admissions." This approach was first used in the Determination for 1987, as a partial response to the federal budget squeeze. It enables private groups to secure admission for certain individuals by pledging to provide the services usually underwritten by the federal government. (The first use of these provisions came in 1988 when 684 Cubans entered under the sponsorship of the Cuban American National Foundation. Refugee Reports, Oct. 14, 1988, at 8. In succeeding years, however, only a few hundred of the numbers were actually claimed; few sponsors were willing to take on the commitment, particularly for the refugees' health care.) Is this a wise use of admission spaces? Does this approach allow wealthy groups to distort what should be public decisions on refugee admission priorities, as detractors charge, thus further slanting admissions in favor of groups with important domestic constituencies and away from those having the greatest need? How should need be assessed in this context? Or does this approach expand opportunities for resettlement by

allowing higher admissions ceilings than limited budgets would otherwise permit, as supporters contend?

———

Refugee emergencies, of course, might also spring up anew in the middle of a fiscal year. The Refugee Act makes provision for "unforeseen emergency refugee situations" by authorizing a new round of consultations followed by a new Presidential Determination in such circumstances. INA § 207(b). That new Determination may add further admission numbers, but in the succeeding fiscal year (which begins the following October), admission spaces to meet that particular crisis are supposed to be worked into the regular consultation process and the standard Presidential Determination issued at the beginning of the new admissions period.

For example, the original Presidential Determination for fiscal year 1988 authorized overseas admissions up to 72,500. A new Determination in May 1988 added 15,000 admissions, all for refugees from Eastern Europe and the Soviet Union (bringing the total for that allocation category to 30,000 for the fiscal year). Presidential Determination No. 88–16, 53 Fed.Reg. 21,405 (1988). In October, regular overseas admissions for FY 1989 were set at 94,000, including 24,500 for Eastern Europe and the Soviet Union. Presidential Determination No. 89–2, 53 Fed.Reg. 45,249 (1988). But rising emigration from the U.S.S.R. forced early reallocations, at the expense of admissions from Southeast Asia, and eventually President Bush issued a new emergency determination in June 1989, bringing the total admissions to 116,500, of which 50,000 were available for East European and Soviet refugees. Presidential Determination No. 89–15, 54 Fed.Reg. 31,493 (1989). Did these emergency admissions, particularly in 1989, comply with the INA § 207(b) requirements of a finding that "an unforeseen emergency refugee situation exists" and that admission "is justified by grave humanitarian concerns or is otherwise in the national interest"?

Refugee admissions since the enactment of the Refugee Act are summarized in Table 8.1; most of the data are taken from Refugee Reports, Dec. 31, 1994, at 9. Note that in some years actual admissions fell far below the ceiling established at the beginning of the fiscal year.

Once the numbers and allocations are established, the Attorney General has authority under INA § 207(c) to admit persons who meet the relevant allocation criteria. Unlike most other forms of permanent immigration, there is no requirement that the process be initiated by a petition in the United States (from a family member or potential employer). Usually the alien can initiate the process herself, but only at U.S. overseas facilities designated as refugee processing posts. Some of the exclusion provisions from § 212(a) are waived for all refugees, and the Attorney General has the authority, in individual cases, to waive most of the others. INA § 207(c)(3).

Table 8.1
Refugee Admissions, 1980–1995

Fiscal Year	Actual Admissions	Original Ceiling	Revised Ceiling
1980	207,116	231,700	
1981	159,252	217,000	
1982	97,355	140,000	
1983	61,681	90,000	
1984	71,113	72,000	
1985	68,045	70,000	
1986	62,440	67,000	
1987	64,828	70,000	
1988	76,487	72,500	87,500
1989	107,238	94,000	116,500
1990	122,326	125,000	
1991	112,811	131,000	
1992	132,173	142,000	
1993	119,482	132,000	
1994	112,573	121,000	
1995		112,000	

A beneficiary of the overseas refugee program, once selected and given the necessary documents for travel to the United States, enters in a new immigration status, created by the Refugee Act of 1980 and known, sensibly enough, as "refugee." In some respects this status resembles parole for the first year after entry, because such a "refugee" can be removed through exclusion rather than deportation proceedings if a ground for expulsion is discovered.[12] But virtually all who are in this "refugee"

12. Congress accomplished this through some easily missed subtleties in § 209(a). That section provides that aliens "admitted to the United States under Section 207"— that is, in refugee status—return after a year of physical presence in the United States "to the custody of the Service for inspection and examination for admission to the United States as an immigrant *in accordance with the provisions of sections 235, 236, and 237*" (emphasis added). Any who do not pass this second round of screening are thus held for exclusion proceedings, because the referenced sections govern exclusion, not deportation. (Incidentally, the custody prescribed is constructive only; refugees have never been physically seized at this stage, to our knowledge.)

The BIA clarified the operation of some of these provisions in *Matter of Garcia–Alzuga-ray,* 19 I & N Dec. 407 (BIA 1986). It held that an alien admitted as a refugee under INA § 207 is not paroled but is instead "admitted conditionally." Therefore exclusion proceedings before an immigration judge may not be held unless the District Director has

first terminated the refugee status, after an examination, or else the alien has been denied permanent resident status following the district director's examination prescribed by INA § 209(a)(1). Moreover, termination is permitted only on the ground that the alien was not a refugee, as defined in INA § 101(a)(42), at the time of initial entry.

The phrasing of these sections raises some interesting questions under the usual doctrines for applying due process to aliens. As we indicated in Chapters Four and Five, due process entitlements may turn on whether or not one has accomplished an entry—which is usually the same as asking whether one is in exclusion or deportation proceedings. Here the statute says that refugees have been "admitted," and yet it puts them in exclusion proceedings. Which level of due process entitlement do they enjoy? The issue has never arisen in any reported case. Perhaps if it did, it would present an occasion for realizing, and thus eliminating, the arbitrariness of the basic due process doctrines under which we currently operate.

status may adjust routinely to lawful permanent resident status after one year. INA § 209(a). This adjustment of status is also retroactive in effect, so that the clock starts running toward qualification for citizenship from the initial date of arrival in the United States. § 209(a)(2). Persons who enter as part of our overseas refugee programs also are eligible for a broad range of federal assistance and retraining programs provided under INA §§ 411–414 (added by the Refugee Act). *See generally Chu Drua Cha v. Noot,* 696 F.2d 594 (8th Cir.1982); *Nguyen v. U.S. Catholic Conference,* 548 F.Supp. 1333 (W.D.Pa.1982), *affirmed,* 719 F.2d 52 (3d Cir.1983).

There are two other threshold requirements for admission as a "refugee," however, that must claim our attention here. These are *individual* qualifications, and an applicant for inclusion in the refugee program must satisfy an immigration officer that they are met, even if she clearly falls within one of the geographical allocation groups and admission numbers are available.

First, she is ineligible if she is "firmly resettled" in a third country. This requirement reserves U.S. refugee program spaces for those who have not already received and pursued resettlement offers elsewhere. In 1971 the Supreme Court approved INS's application of such a requirement even though the statutes at the time did not explicitly disqualify firmly resettled refugees. The "central theme of U.S. refugee legislation," the Court held, has been "the creation of a haven for the world's *homeless* people," not simply the maintenance of a preference for people who at one time had to flee persecution. *Rosenberg v. Yee Chien Woo,* 402 U.S. 49, 55, 91 S.Ct. 1312, 1315, 28 L.Ed.2d 592 (1971) (emphasis added). Congress restored the "firmly resettled" language to the text of the INA when it passed the Refugee Act, *see* INA § 207(c)(1), and regulations have clarified the application of the concept. 8 C.F.R. §§ 207.1(b) (overseas refugee programs); 208.15 (asylum). *See generally Matter of Lam,* 18 I & N Dec. 15 (BIA 1981); *Matter of Portales,* 18 I & N Dec. 239 (BIA 1982); *Matter of Soleimani,* Int.Dec. 3118 (BIA 1989) (modifying *Lam* and *Portales*).

Second, and more important, the officer must find that the applicant is a "refugee" within the statutory definition, INA § 101(a)(42). The key element of the definition is the requirement of a "well-founded fear of persecution on account of race, religion, nationality, membership in a particular social group, or political opinion." There was wide support in Congress for this more universal definition at the time when the Refugee Act was under consideration—especially in comparison to the old limitations that applied to the seventh preference. The former provisions limiting overseas refugee programs to persons who fled Communist countries or countries in the Middle East were widely denounced as "geographic and ideological discrimination."

Nevertheless, several questions can be raised regarding the wisdom of limiting overseas refugee programs by requiring that all beneficiaries meet this UN definition. For one thing, although the United States became a party to the Protocol in 1968 (and hence became derivatively bound by all the important provisions of the Convention), nothing in the Convention or Protocol obligates a country to use this definition in its *admission* decisions. The Convention, as its name suggests, is largely devoted to resolving questions about the status of persons *already physically present* in the territory of a contracting state who are determined to be "refugees," and most of its articles address matters like rights to education, public assistance, or employment.

Therefore, properly understood, the UN treaties create important obligations for the United States, but virtually all of those obligations relate to the *asylum* program rather than to the overseas refugee program. The Convention and Protocol, by their terms, do not require states parties to admit anyone. On the other hand, they clearly were not meant to narrow the discretion of states to choose to admit persons based on other humanitarian considerations. A few other industrialized nations that are parties to the Convention and Protocol have statutory provisions expressly allowing the admission, as part of overseas refugee programs, of needy people who may not technically meet the UN definition of refugee. *See, e.g.,* Canadian Immigration Act, 1976, 25–26 Eliz. II, Ch. 52, § 6(2) (providing for admission, without regard to other regulations under the Act, of Convention refugees and also of groups "designated by the Governor in Council as a class, the admission of members of which would be in accordance with Canada's humanitarian tradition with respect to the displaced and the persecuted").[13]

Against this background, is it sound for the United States to employ the same definition to govern overseas programs as the one used in the political asylum context? Further, should the definition used in the overseas program (and possibly the definition used for political asylum purposes as well) be expanded in light of significant changes the world has experienced since the UN definition was drafted in 1951? Reconsider the views of Zolberg, Suhrke and Aguayo, *supra* p. ___, as well as the policy considerations set forth in the following readings.

DAVID A. MARTIN, THE REFUGEE ACT OF 1980: ITS PAST AND FUTURE

1982 Mich.Y.B.Int'l L.Stud. 91, 101, 111–114.

[The Refugee] Act limits resettlement [as part of U.S. overseas refugee programs] to those who meet the United Nations definition of "refugee," derived from the 1951 Convention relating to the Status of Refugees * * *. This definition forms the basis for a growing body of international law which, in the view of the bill's proponents, deserved to be strengthened and built upon. There was little controversy over the definition's adoption. Indeed, because its use eliminated the geographic restrictions that marred the conditional entry provisions, it was widely welcomed.

In some respects, however, this definition serves to narrow eligibility for U.S. programs, because it excludes certain people who had been eligible

---

13. For a useful discussion of this provision in actual practice, see Hathaway, *Selective Concern: An Overview of Refugee Law in Canada,* 33 McGill L.J. 676 (1988). *See also* Meissner, *Class II Refugees: An Answer to a Growing Need,* World Refugee Survey: 1986 in Review, at 22 (1987) (proposing a similar system for U.S. overseas refugee admissions).

under earlier refugee legislation and, indeed, who are popularly thought of as "refugees." The UN definition does not embrace those who flee natural disasters, nor, in most cases, those displaced by military operations or civil strife. (People who stream away from a battlefront generally are not fleeing persecution targeted at them, but rather are seeking personal safety.) The theory behind this technical limitation on the refugee category is apparently that the bombs will cease falling, the floods will recede, but persecution is implacable. Obviously such a generalization has sharp limits, but, as an exceedingly general rule of thumb, the theory is useful. It distinguishes those uprooted persons who are more likely to be able to pick up the pieces of their lives again in the place where they originated, and who therefore have less need of resettlement in a distant land. The drafters of the Refugee Act sought ways to contain the claims on inevitably limited U.S. resettlement opportunities, and this restriction provided one such method.

Little thought was given during consideration of the Refugee Act, however, to the difficulty inherent in making the individualized and fine-grained determination of likely persecution which the UN definition seems to require.

* * *

[T]he Refugee Act expressly links the grant of asylum to the applicant's satisfying Part A of the statute's refugee definition. There is nothing surprising in this linkage, since Part A essentially restates the Convention definition, which by treaty already governed asylum determinations. A problem arises, however, because this is exactly the definition that sets the threshold qualifications for the U.S. overseas refugee programs. Critics have charged vociferously that the *de facto* standard applied overseas is far more relaxed than that applied to asylum applicants. Vietnamese boat people, they claim, benefit from a presumption that all who risked their lives at sea faced persecution at home and therefore meet the refugee definition. Yet Haitians, who also crossed the seas in flimsy boats but happened to land directly in the United States, enjoy no similar presumption. To claim asylum, they must show more than the simple fact of flight or the existence of human rights abuses in Haiti. They must provide evidence that they themselves are likely to be singled out for persecution on return, and their stories will be minutely scrutinized.

These critics are right. There is, *de facto*, a difference in the application of the "well-founded fear of persecution" standard. Administration pronouncements often try to dodge the issue by pointing to the formal (but routine) INS finding that the UN refugee definition is met by each beneficiary of overseas programs. As the provisions are actually administered, however, the UN definition poses a significantly higher hurdle for asylum applicants. Overseas refugee staffs devote very little attention to the question of likely persecution; INS and State Department officials involved in passing on asylum claims examine that issue in great detail.

The interesting question, however, is what conclusions to draw from this revelation of a dual standard. In quest of consistency, one might relax the scrutiny of asylum claims, thereby reducing the showing of likely persecution required of an applicant. A demonstration that the home government often abuses human rights, for example, might be sufficient without any demonstration that the individual is a likely target. But the practical consequences of such a change in asylum scrutiny could easily be enormous.

Asylum constitutes a wild card in the immigration deck. No other provision of the INA opens such a broad potential prospect of U.S. residency to aliens without the inconvenience of prescreening or selection. An alien may enter in flagrant disregard of U.S. immigration laws, but if he meets the asylum test, he is entitled to stay in the United States indefinitely and to advance toward permanent residence here. By the very nature of the UN Protocol commitment, the United States is not entitled to apply other criteria in deciding whether to extend this protection—criteria such as family ties, other U.S. connections, or employment skills, routinely applied to other intending immigrants. If the alien proves a well-founded fear of persecution, then, by law, he or she cannot be returned to the home country.

This system need not be alarming, if wisely administered. Asylum became an immigration law loophole for good reasons. Returning people to situations where they are almost sure to face persecution, no matter how they reached U.S. shores, would flatly contradict American tradition. * * *

[But because] the "well-founded fear of persecution" standard is the only criterion the Protocol permits parties to apply (assuming that the applicant is neither a spy nor a criminal), there are strong incentives to administer that standard with scrupulous care and to insist on more than a showing of general abuses by the home government. The UNHCR handbook on determination of refugee status generally indicates such a circumscribed and individualized standard, and American judicial decisions support that approach. A relaxation of asylum scrutiny is thus unlikely.

The second option for bringing consistency to U.S. application of the UN refugee definition is to tighten scrutiny overseas. In fact, large populations in temporary asylum areas probably do contain many who could not prove entitlement if subjected to asylum-type scrutiny. Particularly as it becomes known that the United States and other attractive countries are resettling large numbers from the first-asylum camps, migrants are surely drawn there for reasons other than fear of persecution.

Any tightening in overseas scrutiny, however, would require a much greater commitment of staff and resources. As asylum processing demonstrates, establishing with reasonable confidence that an applicant fears persecution and that the fear is well-founded requires careful interviewing, steps to verify the events claimed as the basis of the fear, and ultimately a difficult assessment of the applicant's credibility. American field staff is already stretched thin in applying the other, more accessible, screening criteria currently employed. Devoting additional resources to a more finely-tuned application of the refugee definition is not worthwhile, for a simple reason. Finding a Vietnamese national in Malaysia or an Eastern European in Frankfurt to be a refugee within the UN definition furnishes only the first step in a process that may or may not lead to resettlement in the United States. Physical distance virtually assures that that person will not come to the United States unless selected for the resettlement program, and the Refugee Act's allocation provisions clearly authorize the use of other screening criteria. The practical imperative for stringent application of the refugee definition is therefore minor. Screening can be done, and in its most important respects will continue to be done, on the basis of other criteria.

The availability of other screening criteria overseas, coupled with the inevitable difficulty and expense entailed in scrupulous application of the refugee definition in any context, amply justifies the *de facto* difference in application of the "refugee" definition. And justified or not, the divergence is quite likely to continue.

As long as the statute, however, formally applies the same definitional test to asylum and refugee determinations, this inconsistency will remain a powerful fulcrum for complaints about denials of asylum. The only adequate remedy for the problem would be an amendment to the Act to separate the two standards, recognizing forthrightly the different imperatives that govern review of the respective applicants' compliance with the refugee definition.

Notes

1. Martin suggests that the differential application of the definition—stringently in asylum processing but generously in overseas programs—is justified because of the contrasting arrangements that can be made to control the overall numbers of people admitted in either fashion. But is this disparity really justifiable? Should it make so much difference whether a putative refugee happens to land in Thailand, rather than the United States, as a first-asylum country? Is the claimed justification just a pleasant way of disguising ideological discrimination in the application of a standard Congress meant to apply impartially to all people seeking haven?

Before the Refugee Act was passed, the parole power was used predominantly to bring in refugees from Marxist countries (even though parole, unlike conditional entry, was not formally limited to refugees from Communist countries and the Middle East). From 1968 (the date of U.S. accession to the UN Protocol) through 1980, parole was used to admit 7,150 people from non-Communist countries and 608,365 from Communist countries. Helton, *Political Asylum under the 1980 Refugee Act: An Unfulfilled Promise,* 17 U.Mich.J.L.Ref. 243, 248 (1984). A glance at the Presidential Determination reprinted above reveals that refugees from present or former Communist states still claim the overwhelming majority of refugee admission spaces. Is this allocation justified? Helton argues that standards Congress meant to be "uniform and neutral" have been rendered "subservient to foreign and domestic policy considerations." *Id.* at 243.[14]

14. Consider, however, Congress's reaction to recent changes in the Soviet Union, described below. Is Congress still interested, as of 1989, in uniform and neutral applica- tion of refugee standards? Should this matter in assessing the administrative implementation of a statute passed in 1980?

2.   On the other hand, is there really anything wrong with an ideological refugee policy? Perhaps the statute ought to be more candid about the de facto requirements, but if it were, would such an approach, historically favoring the enemies of our clearest international adversaries, be undesirable? Morally wrong? Might these questions depend on the overall numbers seeking refuge? On the severity of the treatment that the various groups of refugees can expect in their home countries if returned, or on their treatment in the country of first asylum, if they are forced to remain there?

The political theorist Michael Walzer—who is clearly not a Cold Warrior himself—has treated these questions at length in his book *Spheres of Justice: A Defense of Pluralism and Equality* (1983). His conclusions are surprisingly favorable to an "ideological" refugee admission policy. Many of the dilemmas have no satisfactory answers, he acknowledges, but he offers in part the reflections that follow:

> Toward some refugees, we may well have obligations of the same sort that we have toward fellow nationals. This is obviously the case with regard to any group of people whom we have helped turn into refugees. The injury we have done them makes for an affinity between us: thus Vietnamese refugees had, in a moral sense, been effectively Americanized even before they arrived on these shores. But we can also be bound to help men and women persecuted or oppressed by someone else—if they are persecuted or oppressed because they are like us. Ideological as well as ethnic affinity can generate bonds across political lines, especially, for example, when we claim to embody certain principles in our communal life and encourage men and women elsewhere to defend those principles. * * * [C]onsider the thousands of men and women who fled Hungary after the failed revolution of 1956. It is hard to deny them a similar recognition [as a kind of kin], given the structure of the Cold War, the character of Western propaganda, the sympathy already expressed with East European "freedom fighters." These refugees probably had to be taken in by countries like Britain and the United States. The repression of political comrades, like the persecution of co-religionists, seems to generate an obligation to help, at least to provide a refuge for the most exposed and endangered people. Perhaps every victim of authoritarianism and bigotry is the moral comrade of a liberal citizen: that is an argument I would like to make. But that would press affinity too hard, and it is in any case unnecessary. * * * [W]hen the number increases, and we are forced to choose among the victims, we will look, rightfully, for some more direct connection with our own way of life. * * * Once again, communities must have boundaries; and however these are determined with regard to territory and resources, they depend with regard to population on a sense of relatedness and mutuality. Refugees must appeal to that sense. One wishes them success; but in

particular cases, with reference to a particular state, they may well have no right to be successful.

Id. at 49–50.

2. THE OVERSEAS REFUGEE PROGRAM IN OPERATION

Martin, writing in 1981, assumed that the differential application of the definition as between asylum processing and overseas refugee processing would persist quietly. This proved to be poor prophecy. In late 1981 and more systematically in 1988, INS began moving toward applying the definition with the same rigor in both settings. Each time the change resulted in considerable public controversy.

a. Indochina, 1981

In 1981 the change was initiated at a fairly low level in the INS bureaucracy. A new District Director, Joseph Sureck, took over as head of the Hong Kong district office, then the office with authority over processing for Indochinese refugees. He ordered that immigration officers tighten up their application of the definition, in order to render it consistent with the application of the definition in asylum cases. Apparently neither the State Department nor any higher level of the Justice Department had been consulted; it was simply a matter of applying the statute, and the statute uses the same definition of "refugee" in both settings.

Suddenly thousands of Indochinese boat people and land escapees found their applications for refugee status provisionally denied, on the ground that they could not individually document reasons to fear persecution. This result slowed resettlements out of the camps and complicated diplomatic relations with countries of first asylum, whose governments were counting on a steady outflow to resettlement countries, as well as with other resettlement countries. It also outraged the voluntary organizations who had been closely involved in the resettlement and sponsorship process. In consequence, the shift promptly attracted the personal attention of both the Attorney General and the Secretary of State, and the involvement of the congressional committees with jurisdiction over immigration matters.

After months of review and deliberation, new guidelines were implemented that generally restored, in practice, the status quo ante. Most of the Indochinese in the camps would again be adjudged to satisfy the refugee definition (although they might well still be denied a space in the U.S. resettlement program because of a failure to meet other selection criteria). Although the guidelines placed some emphasis on "case by case" determinations, they also established certain categories of applicants determined "to share common characteristics that identify them as targets of persecution in their particular countries." Indochinese who fit into such a category did not need to offer further proof of individualized persecution. No similar presumptions were available to asylum applicants. *See generally* House Comm. on the Judiciary, 97th Cong., 2d Sess., Refugee Issues in Southeast Asia and Europe (Comm.Print 1982); *INS Guidelines for Over-*

seas Processing of Refugees Evaluated, Problems Identified, Refugee Reports, September 7, 1984, at 1–3.

b. Soviet Refugees

The later moves toward rigor in applying the refugee definition in overseas processing, taken in 1988 and 1989, resulted from decisions at the highest levels of government, and not from the loose-cannon initiative of a single district director. The focus of the changes fell on Soviet refugees, and, to a lesser extent, on other Eastern Europeans.

For many decades, Soviet emigration controls were a particular target of U.S. human rights policy, with special emphasis on their application to Soviet Jews. For example, the Jackson–Vanik amendment of 1974, 19 U.S.C.A. § 2432, conditioned extension of certain trading benefits to Communist countries on a formal presidential determination that the country honors rights of emigration. (This congressional initiative thereby torpedoed much of Henry Kissinger's policy of détente with the U.S.S.R.). The Soviets resented that pressure, and pointedly kept exits at a very low level for several years thereafter.

In the late 1970s, however, the Soviet government began to permit Soviet Jews, and a handful of others, to emigrate in much higher numbers. Jews were allowed to leave only on Israeli travel documents, officially for reasons of reunifying with family in Israel. Early contingents in the 1970s in fact went to Israel in overwhelming proportions, but by 1979 as many as two-thirds of those exiting "broke off" from the path to Israel as soon as they reached Vienna. Most then went on to Rome where they spent a period of months, supported by the U.S. refugee program, while the necessary further processing occurred before actual movement to this country. In 1979, over 50,000 Soviet émigrés came to the United States through this process (adding to the pressures on refugee admissions that year, and further spurring the drive for new refugee legislation).

The Soviet government responded to its more adversarial relationship with the Reagan administration, beginning in 1981, with sharp cuts in emigration. Nevertheless, throughout this period, refugee applicants from the Soviet Union still benefited from virtually automatic approval of their refugee claims. With the advent of *glasnost* and *perestroika* under Mikhail Gorbachev in the latter part of the decade, however, the numbers able to exit began rising again, and a few other groups, particularly Armenians and certain non-Jewish religious minorities, also gained such permission. It also became possible, in a growing number of cases, to process applicants in Moscow.

Against this background, the U.S. government decided to take a closer look at the legal validity of the near-automatic approval of Soviet refugee applications.[15] In August 1988, Attorney General Edwin Meese wrote to

---

15. The break-off rate in Vienna had also risen to 90 percent, and this created increasing friction in our relations with Israel. Israel definitely wanted the additional population, and forcefully pointed out that the people involved had secured exit permission from the USSR by representing that they were in fact going to Israel. (Other critics also pointed out that the United States usually disqualifies from overseas refugee programs those

National Security Council advisor Colin Powell: "Changes must be made in our Soviet refugee admissions program.   * * * Current practices * * * appear not to conform with the requirements" of the Refugee Act of 1980. He directed a transition to "the proper statutory processing of Soviets," meaning careful case-by-case evaluation of the persecution claims of each individual applicant. Refugee Reports, April 28, 1989, at 1. This memorandum marked the beginning of a systematic INS effort to apply the "worldwide refugee definition" consistently in all settings, involving asylum or overseas processing; the change therefore also resulted in higher denial rates for Indochinese.

The transition did not go smoothly. Hundreds of Soviet Jews in Rome, fully expecting steady processing for resettlement, suddenly found their applications denied. Likewise, many applicants in Moscow were turned down, even though, having previously secured exit documents from Soviet authorities, they had already given up their jobs and apartments in the expectation of resettlement. The voluntary organizations assisting these groups protested vigorously, emphasizing the hardships visited on people who had relied on an implicit American promise of resettlement. Some members of Congress joined the protest, particularly because of the Administration's failure to consult before changing the processing.

The executive branch's response to these hardships and complaints was an offer to parole into the United States, at the rate of 2000 per month, any Soviet applicant whose refugee claim was denied. This initiative reduced but did not still the objections. Parolees were ineligible for the federal funding the Refugee Act authorizes for persons admitted as refugees. Moreover, no regular procedure existed for eventually adjusting status to lawful permanent resident. See 65 Interp.Rel. 1286 (1988); Refugee Reports, April 28, 1989, at 1. (These problems are quite similar to those generated by the extensive use of parole in the 1970s—which had led to the Refugee Act's limitation on the parole power in such circumstances. Is the use of parole for rejected Soviet refugee applicants consistent with the statute? Consider INA § 212(d)(5)(B).)

The administration recognized that parole was a short-term response. In mid–1989 it introduced legislation that would have created a new "special immigrant" category for up to 30,000 people a year, for five years. The President would be authorized, following consultation with Congress, to designate the class of aliens to be admitted, based on a determination that their admission "is deemed * * *, for foreign policy reasons to be in the national interest." H.R. 2646, 101st Cong., 1st Sess. (1989). See Refugee Reports, April 28, 1989, at 3. This approach held many similarities to the Canadian "designated class" approach, mentioned above, but with one important difference. The U.S. special immigrants would not have benefited from the federally-funded assistance programs available to refugees.

The administration also moved to phase out all processing of Soviets in Rome (which was costing $34 million a year), transferring all decisionmak-

refugees who have an opportunity to resettle   Post, Sept. 14, 1988, at A2; id., Oct. 23,
in another democratic state.) See Wash.   1988, at A33.

ing on such refugee applications to Moscow. And it began alerting all potential applicants in Moscow not to give up employment or take other actions in reliance on resettlement until their processing was concluded. Denial rates rose in Moscow, until they averaged 73.6 percent from October 1988 through August 1989. Refugee Reports, Sept. 22, 1989, at 4. Denied applicants still came within the parole promise, but the backlog for that benefit grew rapidly.

Many members of Congress reacted negatively to the Administration's bill proposing a new special immigrant category, in part for fear that it gave the President 30,000 admissions that he could dole out freely to placate domestic constituencies. This worry was fueled by recognition that the proposed process would not be subject to the usual budget discipline, because such admissions, like paroles, had to be supported by the private sector. The Administration bill therefore made little headway. A variety of other bills were introduced, taking different approaches toward reinstating a more generous admissions policy for Soviets. Rep. Bruce Morrison (D–Conn.), then chair of the House Subcommittee on Immigration, Refugees, and International Law, offered a bill, H.R. 2022, 101st Cong., 1st Sess., whose initial versions would have created a presumption that all Soviet Jews and Pentecostals continued to suffer persecution and therefore qualified as refugees. *See* 66 Interp.Rel. 397–400 (1989). (Morrison had earlier objected to the Administration bill on the ground that it would "explicitly politicize who could come into the U.S. who aren't immigrants or refugees." *Id.* at 399. Was his proposal subject to the same objection?)

When the House took up Morrison's bill, other members warned of "an avalanche of legislation to grant special, preferential refugee and immigration status to select groups," contrary to the spirit and intent of the Refugee Act. Others retorted that such legislation was necessary only because of the administration's dereliction in ending an earlier system that had worked reasonably well. In any event, amendments that would grant preferential consideration to other groups began to appear. A few such proposals were rejected, but active members of the Ukrainian Catholic and Ukrainian Orthodox Churches, and a specified list of Indochinese were also given their own presumptions. Then Rep. Gerald Klecska (D–Wisc.) offered an amendment for similar treatment of Polish nationals. It passed the House by an overwhelming margin—ironically, in the same month that the Solidarity opposition movement took over a majority of the seats in the lower house of the Polish parliament after free elections, and not long before Solidarity ally Tadeusz Mazowiecki became prime minister of Poland. Refugee Reports, July 28, 1989, at 1–4.

The Senate rejected the Klecska amendment, but went along with most of what the House had passed, incorporating the new provisions in the foreign operations appropriations bill for fiscal year 1990, Pub.L. No. 101–167, § 599D, 103 Stat. 1195, 1261 (1989).[16] Commonly known as the Lautenberg amendment, this measure applies only to the overseas refugee

---

16. Section 599E of the same act also authorized adjustment of status to lawful permanent resident, after physical presence of at least one year, for Soviet and Indochinese nationals paroled into the United States.

program (INA § 207), not to asylum determinations. It was initially made effective only through September 1990, but was later extended in successive stages and is now valid through September 1996. Pub.L.No. 103–236, § 512, 108 Stat. 382, 466 (1994).

Notes

1. Look closely at the language of the Lautenberg amendment, reprinted in the Statutory Supplement. What is your evaluation of this approach? How does it differ from the kind of legislation that Martin, in 1981, suggested might be desirable? Should more discretion be given to the executive branch? Should less? How should a member of one of the designated groups establish "a credible basis for concern about the possibility of such persecution"? How far into the future (or the past) does this formulation reach?

2. Why did Congress apparently find it so important to bring persons admitted in these circumstances under the specific umbrella of the "refugee" label, rather than accepting them as special immigrants under the framework suggested by the Bush Administration, or even as parolees? Should a higher value be placed on preserving the integrity of the refugee category, by insisting on consistent application of a "worldwide refugee definition" without presumptions? Which approach, Congress's or the Bush Administration's, is more subject to political manipulation? Which better promotes candor about the true grounds for admission decisions?

3. The Soviet Union disappeared from the map in 1991, the governments of the successor nations generally owe their positions to elections, and the Communist Party of the USSR itself has been disbanded. Nonetheless, Congress has regularly extended the Lautenberg amendment since these changes—and the former Soviet Union continues to claim the largest allocation of refugee admissions. *See* Presidential Determination No. 95–1, *supra* p. 739. (Unlike earlier years, however, very few refugees are admitted from the former Warsaw Pact states of eastern Europe.) Why? What does this pattern say about U.S. domestic politics? Can the current priority for ex-Soviet refugees be justified? Virtually all who come under this part of the allocation enter as a result of in-country processing in Moscow. Does this fact raise further questions about the nature of these admissions? Has this part of the refugee program been turned into a de facto immigration category, rather than a refugee program helping people escape persecution? Those who support continuing refugee admissions from the former Soviet Union usually point to the rise of nationalist extremists in Russia and the risk of a resurgence in anti-Semitism. These risks are real, but do they adequately distinguish the case from current victims such as Liberians who have fled to Guinea or Côte d'Ivoire, or Rwandans in Zaire or Tanzania? Are there other reasons to emphasize resettlement as a solution for ex-Soviets but not for the latter groups? Is the Soviet Union a special case, owing to longstanding adversarial relations with the United States? Or, on a more limited basis, should a special commitment to ex-Soviet Jews be sustained?

4. Although Congress in 1989 accepted the view that the United States should respond generously to the new opportunities for emigration from the Soviet Union, a few voices raised questions about such a response. First, improved human rights observance, which includes permitting people to leave, perhaps should lead to *reduced* admissions, rather than increases, or at least to closer scrutiny of persecution claims. *See* Refugee Reports, Sept. 22, 1989, at 6 (reporting on comments made at hearings).

Second, some have raised doubts about whether increased emigration might not actually retard human rights improvements in the home country. A leader of the Armenian–American community in California, for example, questioned increases in refugee admissions of Armenians in the late 1980s: "when Armenians on any part of our historical homeland leave Armenia, they go against the struggle, against our goals." Refugee Reports, June 24, 1988, at 12. (By 1994, however, after the Soviet Union's collapse and with a bitter war underway between the now independent countries of Armenia and Azerbaijan, leading Armenian groups in the United States petitioned to add Armenians to the categories benefiting from the Lautenberg amendment. Refugee Reports, Oct. 17, 1994, at 12–13.)

Doris Meissner, then Senior Associate at the Carnegie Endowment and since 1993 Commissioner of the INS, has made the point more sharply, in reflecting on the hundreds of thousands of Cubans and Vietnamese admitted to the United States:

> The fact that Cuba and Vietnam have been among the slowest nations in the communist world to change is not unrelated to this exodus. Unwittingly, and with the best intentions, our refugee policy has provided a means for these nations to export the critical mass of people most likely to challenge the system from within and spark political and economic reform.

Meissner, *Let the Contras Find a Haven Rebuilding Peace in Nicaragua, Not Living in the U.S.,* Los Angeles Times, Sept. 11, 1989, § 2, at 5, col. 2.

Should admission levels be reduced on this basis? Would limiting Soviet admissions now make a mockery of earlier U.S. efforts (dating back to Jackson–Vanik and beyond) to encourage an end to tight exit controls in the Soviet Union? Or would it simply bring the policy into line with the U.S. approach toward a host of other countries, especially in Latin America, whose governments have always honored the "right to leave" but whose nationals have not been readily admitted to the United States?

The right to leave, as formulated in international human rights instruments, has never been accompanied by a clear right to enter some other country. Ad hoc political efforts, until now, have generally minimized the need to confront that disharmony, because places were found for many who managed to exit. But increasing restrictiveness around the globe in the mid–1990s makes the tension ever more evident. How should it be resolved?

c. *Indochinese Refugees*

As is evident from the history recounted early in this section, American experience with Indochinese refugees, and particularly Vietnamese, has played a major role in shaping the law and practice of our overseas refugee programs. Since 1975, America has accepted over one million Indochinese refugees, and several hundred thousand have found permanent refuge in other Western countries. But profound new difficulties and challenges arose in the late 1980s.

In 1979, the UN High Commissioner for Refugees called a major refugee conference in Geneva to deal with the situation in Southeast Asia. This call was stimulated by a stunningly rapid rise in outflows from Indochina beginning in 1978 (sometimes exceeding 50,000 a month), and also by the harsh response sometimes taken by the first asylum countries of the region who were beginning to feel overwhelmed. Reports had proliferated of boats pushed off from shore or forced repatriation across land borders, with frequent loss of life. At the 1979 conference, a rough accommodation was reached, whereby countries in the region agreed to continue providing temporary first asylum, resettlement countries essentially pledged to resettle all thus accommodated, and Vietnam undertook to rein in smuggling rings that promoted the exodus. Vietnam also agreed to establish an Orderly Departure Program (ODP), allowing those who wished to leave a safer and more humane alternative. ODP provided for processing of cases while the applicants remained in Vietnam, followed by more direct air transportation of approved applicants to their countries of refuge. These arrangements worked reasonably well from 1980 to 1987, as departures from asylum countries to resettlement countries outpaced arrivals. Meantime over 150,000 people resettled through ODP, about half in the United States. See Robinson, *Sins of Omission: The New Vietnamese Refugee Crisis,* World Refugee Survey—1988 in Review, at 5 (1989); *Country Reports,* id., at 55.

But in about 1987, further problems arose. Resettlement offers from distant countries, including the United States, were dropping, a trend often blamed on "compassion fatigue." Disputes between Vietnam and the United States over the operation of ODP also slowed departures through that route, and a backlog of over 700,000 applicants developed. Concurrently, direct arrivals in the first asylum countries of the region began increasing, overtaking resettlements. Moreover, a growing proportion of the arrivals were coming from the north of Vietnam, thus lacking the ties with the United States that would have enabled them to be included within U.S. resettlement priorities. A new bit of jargon, "long-stayers," developed to categorize those in the refugee camps who had little prospect of resettlement. By 1988, Malaysia, Thailand and Indonesia reportedly were pushing boats off to sea again and complaining about the failure of resettlement countries to do their part under the 1979 arrangements.

Perhaps because of these episodes, boat arrivals in Hong Kong took a dramatic jump in 1988, ultimately exceeding 9200 people arriving in May 1989 alone. Officials voiced increasing skepticism about the refugee bona fides of the arrivals, and conflict with the local population grew to near explosive levels (exacerbated by the Hong Kong policy of rejecting summarily all Chinese who managed to cross the border from the People's Republic). By September 1989, that small British dependency harbored over 55,000 asylum seekers. In order to deter future arrivals, most were housed in austere (and sometimes terrible) accommodations known as "closed camps." *See* Refugee Reports, Sept. 22, 1989, at 9–12. Hong Kong became the focus of the new debates over Indochinese refugees.

In June 1988, Hong Kong began a policy of screening all new arrivals, reviewing their claims individually to see whether they met the 1951 Convention definition. Only those who passed this test would be eligible for resettlement in distant countries; others would be encouraged to repatriate voluntarily. Critics charged that the screening was inadequate and that deteriorating conditions in the closed camps were inhumanely used as a device to coerce acceptance of repatriation. Nevertheless, Hong Kong persisted in its policy, gradually introducing improvements in the screening. UNHCR became involved in training adjudicators and monitoring the process, and an appeals procedure was made available to denied applicants.

Despite the criticism, screening of this sort became a model for the entire Southeast Asian region, under the "Comprehensive Plan of Action" (CPA) adopted at a second Geneva conference held in June 1989. *See* Refugee Reports, July 18, 1989, at 6; *id.*, Sept. 22, 1989, at 12; Bari, *Refugee Status Determination under the Comprehensive Plan of Action (CPA): A Personal Assessment*, 4 Int'l J. Refugee L. 487 (1992). (The full text of the CPA is reprinted at 1 Int'l J. Refugee L. 574 (1989).) Western countries promised to continue resettlement offers in order to clear the camps of "long-stayers," but new arrivals would all be judged according to the Convention standard, and only those who passed the screening would remain eligible for resettlement. The rest were supposed to repatriate to Vietnam.

At that 1989 Geneva conference, the British government, noting that only a few dozen of the more recent arrivals ruled ineligible for resettlement had voluntarily returned to Vietnam, expressed its determination to begin involuntary repatriations—but only of those found not to be refugees. The first such returns took place in December 1989. The White House denounced the action: "The U.S. position is that involuntary repatriation is unacceptable until conditions improve in Vietnam." British Prime Minister Thatcher offered this retort: "Those countries who are protesting their return would do far better if they offered to take some of them." Strauss, *Hong Kong Expulsions to Continue*, Wash.Post, Dec. 13, 1989, at A27, A30. Nevertheless, Britain temporarily suspended further involuntary repatriations, but it vowed to resume them if other solutions were not found. Thereafter, Hong Kong continued to repatriate those who volunteered to return rather than continue life in the bleak "closed camps," and they also found it possible to do the same with those deemed "acquiescent non-volunteers," another inventive term to add to the jargon. *See generally Human Rights and Forced Repatriation*, Int'l J. Refugee L. 137–171 (Special Issue, Sept. 1990).

Notes

1. Can the U.S. government's position in 1989, objecting to Hong Kong's forced repatriations, be reconciled with U.S. treatment of asylum

seekers deported to, say, Haiti or El Salvador, after being found not to qualify as Convention refugees? Was there a basis for distinguishing the two situations? Or was it simply a matter of who bears the residual responsibility if return is not accomplished?

2. If you were an official of the British government, what would you have done during this period about Vietnamese asylum seekers in Hong Kong? In deciding on your approach, consider the dynamics of the Indochinese refugee migration, as reflected in the following passage from an article by James Fallows, written on the basis of several months of travels through Asia.

> What kind of deplorable country must they be running if everyone wants to leave? In the case of Cambodia under Pol Pot, using refugees to draw dire conclusions about the regime was clearly justified. But after seeing Burma and Vietnam back to back, my idea about the meaning of the Vietnamese boat people has changed.

> * * *

> [B]ad treatment does not automatically make people into refugees. To say this the other way around, the people who do leave by boat are not necessarily the ones who have suffered most. They may simply be the ones for whom this gamble makes the most practical sense * * *. Life in Vietnam, though terrible, may not be that much worse than life in many other countries. The rewards for leaving may simply be better.

> From what I could see, life in Burma is, for most people, fully as hopeless as life in Vietnam. Burma does not have enormous re-education camps, but then most Vietnamese are not in the camps either. For many Filipinos, life is worse than it is for nearly all Vietnamese. China is both poor and repressive. Bangladesh has every problem a country can have. But Vietnam, Cambodia, and Laos are the only Asian countries from which hundreds of thousands flee. Why? The basic reason, I think, is that if Burmese or Filipinos leave, they're sent back home. They're not presumed to be political refugees, they're not processed for resettlement in the West. For them, becoming a refugee is pointless; for a Vietnamese, it is a risky but sensible step to take.

Fallows, *No Hard Feelings?*, The Atlantic Monthly, Dec. 1988, at 71, 77–78.

Other studies also support a finding that high expectations about resettlement played a major role in stimulating the outflow from Vietnam in the 1970s and 1980s (without necessarily negating that a proportion of the flow qualified as genuine refugees). See Robinson, *supra,* at 8; Suhrke, *Indochinese Refugees: The Law and Politics of First Asylum,* 467 The Annals 102 (1983). Is it desirable—and is it possible, humanely—to break through this cycle of expectation? How would you go about doing so?

However one views the debate over the CPA, the Plan had its intended effect. Outflow from Vietnam, which reached 71,000 in 1989, the year the CPA was adopted, fell to 55 in 1992 and 777 in 1993. During this period, over 60,000 returned to Vietnam from the camps after being screened out under the terms of the Plan. Roughly the same number remained behind, as of February 1994, but the pace of returns had reached a new record of 2,844 that January. At a CPA steering committee meeting in February 1994, the U.S. government announced that it would no longer object to mandatory return of screened-out refugees "in accordance with international law and practice, as a supplement to the preferred solution of voluntary returns." Refugee Reports, Feb. 18, 1994, at 6–10. *See* Symposium, *Focus on the Comprehensive Plan of Action*, 5 Int'l J. Refugee L. 507 (1993). Key documents relevant to the CPA appear at *id.* 617–46.

These developments have prompted abundant talk about an "end game" for the Indochinese refugee program. The camps in Hong Kong, the Philippines, Indonesia, Thailand, and Malaysia may be largely emptied by the end of 1995, and even the ODP will probably be greatly reduced. By then nearly all former inmates of the Vietnamese re-education camps—long a priority group for inclusion in the ODP—will have been resettled, and the same will be true of Amerasian children and their families. *See* Deffenbaugh, *Resettlement as Protection: New Directions in the U.S. Refugee Program*, Refugee Reports, Apr. 29, 1994, at 10–15. Other relatives of those previously resettled in the United States as refugees could of course still make use of ODP resettlement, but should a special program continue for these cases, or should they be expected to wait in line for normal immigration under the preference categories or as immediate relatives? Should the overall refugee admission numbers be reduced once the Indochinese program winds down? Or should those numbers be transferred elsewhere? Where?

In 1995, while the United States made 112,000 admission spaces available for overseas refugee resettlement, UNHCR identified only 37,000 persons worldwide whom it deemed in need of resettlement, a considerable decline from earlier years. UNHCR Resettlement Section, Assessment of Global Resettlement Needs for Refugees in 1995 (Dec. 1994). In the late 1990s, how should the State Department decide which refugees are of "special humanitarian concern"?

SECTION C. POLITICAL ASYLUM

1. INTRODUCTION

From the very beginning of federal immigration laws, Congress has recognized that special exemptions may be necessary for otherwise deportable or excludable aliens who have become political enemies of the government in the nation to which they would be sent. In 1875, when Congress provided that convicts would be excludable, it exempted persons who had been convicted of political offenses. Similar exemptions appeared with regularity in later laws.[17]

---

17. *See, e.g.,* Act of March 3, 1875, Ch. 141, § 5, 18 Stat. 477; Act of August 3, 1882, Ch. 376, § 4, 22 Stat. 214; Act of March 3, 1891, Ch. 551, § 1, 26 Stat. 1084; Act of Feb.

In 1950, Congress adopted the first clearcut political asylum provision exempting aliens from deportation "to any country in which the Attorney General shall find that such alien would be subjected to physical persecution." Internal Security Act of 1950, Ch. 1024, § 23, 64 Stat. 987, 1010. Early court decisions ostensibly imposed onerous factfinding responsibilities on the Attorney General under this provision. *See, e.g., Sang Ryup Park v. Barber,* 107 F.Supp. 605 (N.D.Cal.1952); *Harisiades v. Shaughnessy,* 187 F.2d 137, 142 (2d Cir.1951), *affirmed on other grounds,* 342 U.S. 580, 72 S.Ct. 512, 96 L.Ed. 586 (1951). As a result, Congress rewrote the provision when it drafted the Immigration and Nationality Act in 1952. Section 243(h) of that Act authorized the Attorney General, *in his discretion,* to withhold deportation of an alien within the United States who was subject to physical persecution in his country of nationality. In 1958, the Supreme Court construed this provision rather rigidly, holding that it covered only aliens in deportation proceedings and afforded no protection for a parolee even if she were equivalently jeopardized. *Leng May Ma v. Barber,* 357 U.S. 185, 78 S.Ct. 1072, 2 L.Ed.2d 1246 (1958). But eventually INS found ways to afford parallel protection to people in exclusion proceedings, through special use of the parole power when it deemed that the persecution claim was valid.

You will recall that the old seventh preference provision, added by the 1965 immigration act amendments, as well as some of its predecessor provisions for overseas programs, treated as refugees only people who fled Communist countries or countries in the general area of the Middle East. Arrangements for the withholding of deportation or for equivalent protections through the parole power were never formally subject to the same limitations. It remains clear, nevertheless, that these asylum-type provisions were administered for many years under the strong influence of Cold War assumptions. Successful asylum claimants were, in overwhelming proportions, refugees from Communist countries.

In 1968, the United States became a party to the United Nations Protocol relating to the Status of Refugees, and so became derivatively bound by all of the important substantive provisions of the UN Convention relating to the Status of Refugees.[18] Congress enacted no changes in the statutory provisions relating to asylum at that time, because the Departments of State and Justice had assured the Senate, while it was considering ratification, that the Protocol could be implemented without requiring any changes in the immigration laws. It is questionable, however, whether the Senators fully appreciated the consequences of our accepting the treaty. What had previously been purely discretionary provisions permitting, but not requiring, the Attorney General to withhold deportation were transformed into firm legal obligations. The treaty recognizes no discretion to return an alien if he proves he is a refugee and comes within Article 33's protection against *refoulement* (the French term commonly used to refer to

20, 1907, Ch. 1134, § 2, 34 Stat. 898, 899; Immigration Act of 1917, Ch. 29, § 3, 39 Stat. 874, 877.

18. *See* UN Convention and Protocol, *supra* note 1.

the return of refugees in such circumstances). *See* Note, *The Right of Asylum under United States Law,* 80 Colum.L.Rev. 1125 (1980).

Moreover, the executive branch's testimony had merely stated that the treaty could be implemented under existing *statutes.* It did not promise that the earlier administrative criteria for the exercise of discretion could remain unchanged once the treaty became law. (Nor did it promise the opposite; it was simply silent on this crucial question.) The BIA had ruled many years before ratification that an alien would be accorded discretionary relief under § 243(h) only if he demonstrated "a clear probability of persecution." Soon after ratification of the Protocol, litigants began to argue that this standard was too severe, and that the touchstone should be "a well-founded fear of persecution," as set forth in Article 1 of the UN Convention—presumably a standard somewhat easier to satisfy. The Board ultimately decided that no change was warranted, despite the new treaty obligation. *Matter of Dunar,* 14 I. & N. Dec. 310 (1973).

More significant changes in the actual implementation of political asylum protections came in the wake of the Kudirka incident in 1970. A Lithuanian seaman named Simas Kudirka managed to escape in U.S. territorial waters from a Russian vessel to a Coast Guard cutter, the *Vigilant,* tied alongside for a discussion of fishing rights. After a series of miscalculations and missed communications, and with stunning blindness to the likely political fallout, the Coast Guard permitted Soviet crewmen to come aboard, forcibly seize Kudirka, and return him to the Russian ship.[19] As a result of the ensuing outcry, the Nixon Administration launched a major review of all U.S. arrangements for political asylum. This process eventually resulted in formal regulations and guidelines issued by several agencies, including the State Department and INS.[20] The INS regulations,

---

19. *See* Mann, *Asylum Denied: The Vigilant Incident,* 62 U.S. Naval War College Int'l L.Stud. 598 (1980); Goldie, *Legal Aspects of the Refusal of Asylum by U.S. Coast Guard on 23 November 1970, id.,* at 626.

Remarkably, an incident quite similar to the Kudirka incident occurred in October 1985, but this time on U.S. soil. A Soviet seaman, Miroslav Medvid, jumped ship in Louisiana and attempted to ask for political asylum. Because of apparent problems in translation (accompanied by INS agents' failure to follow established procedures), he was forcibly returned to his vessel. Controversy erupted the next day when the return came to light. The U.S. government then refused to let the ship leave port until Medvid was again interviewed and told of his right to remain here if he wished. Eventually he was taken to shore, accompanied by other ship's officers, and allowed to remain overnight. Meantime he was interviewed several times and given a psychiatric evaluation. In view of his continued insistence by this time that he wished to go home, he was ultimately allowed to depart with his ship. A variety of judicial and congressional investigations took place. (Interestingly, the first witness at one

of the hearings was Simas Kudirka, who had been allowed to emigrate from the U.S.S.R. after several years in prison.) *See, e.g., Medvid by Jeziersky v. New Orleans Police Dept.* 621 F.Supp. 503 (E.D.La.1985) (denying temporary restraining order sought by seaman's alleged "next friends" that would have blocked ship's departure); *The Case of Miroslav Medvid: Hearings on H.Res. 314 Before the House Comm. on Foreign Affairs,* 99th Cong., 2d Sess. (1985); Sen. Subcomm. on Immigration and Refugee Policy, 99th Cong., 2d Sess., The Miroslav Medvid Incident, October 24–29, 1985 (Comm.Print No. 99–179, 1986).

20. The policy of the State Department is still in force in essentially the same form adopted in 1972. *See* Public Notice 351, 37 Fed.Reg. 3447 (1972); modified, Public Notice 728, 45 Fed.Reg. 70,621 (1980). One feature deserves special mention: the specific disavowal of the custom of diplomatic asylum. Diplomatic asylum is a practice, rejected by most countries around the world but accepted by many Latin American states, whereby certain threatened persons (usually members of a political elite endangered by a

issued in 1974, were the first to spell out in detail the procedures to be followed when applying for political asylum. In ensuing years, INS made several changes in these regulations, many of them in response to the pressure of litigation.[21]

Although by 1980 the controversy over the provisions for political asylum and their implementation was mounting, Congress did not use the occasion of the Refugee Act to undertake a thorough review of these arrangements. Congressional attention was preoccupied with the overseas refugee programs. Nevertheless, the Act made a few important improvements respecting political asylum. For example, the word "asylum" had never before appeared in the immigration laws of the United States. To be sure, successful applicants who proved the required degree of threatened persecution in the homeland were protected against involuntary return, but there had been no immigration status clearly available to reflect that decision and clarify the beneficiary's right to stay indefinitely.

The Refugee Act added a new § 208 to the INA, specifically curing the earlier omission and establishing what amounts to a new immigration status—"asylum" status. This status can be provided, in the discretion of the Attorney General, to applicants in the United States who show that they meet the UN definition of refugee—that is, who have a "well-founded fear of persecution" if returned to their home countries. The status of "asylee," as it is called in the regulations, 8 C.F.R. Part 208, differs in important respects from the status of "refugee"—meaning here those who have entered as part of the overseas programs. For example, the asylum provisions of the INA (§§ 208 and 209(b)) place greater emphasis on continuing review of conditions in the asylee's home country. "Asylum" status may be terminated if circumstances change abroad so that the threat of persecution is ended. "Refugee" status carries no equivalent vulnerability. *See* INA §§ 207(c)(4), 208(b), 209(a), 209(b)(3). Moreover, although asylees are provided a mechanism for adjusting to lawful permanent resident status after one year in the United States, the Refugee Act expressly limited the number of adjustments to a maximum of 5,000 per

sudden change of government) are offered initial shelter in a diplomatic mission, and, ordinarily, are then provided a safe-conduct pass that will permit their removal to the territory of the asylum country. *See generally* The Asylum Case, 1950 I.C.J. 266. Official U.S. policy, however, does allow for short-term harborage in diplomatic facilities under some circumstances—for example, to protect persons pursued by an angry mob. *See* 2 A. Grahl–Madsen, The Status of Refugees in International Law 6 (1972) (commenting on this practice of "temporary refuge" in diplomatic facilities).

The stated policy often presents difficult practical problems in implementation, once asylum-seekers (seeking haven against the host government rather than mob violence) have managed to enter U.S. diplomatic facilities. Though there is no legal requirement

for sheltering them, at times the likely domestic political consequences of ejection have prompted the Department to allow a lengthy stay in an embassy. For example, in the late 1970s a family of Pentecostals remained in the American embassy in Moscow for several years before arrangements were finally concluded to move them to the United States. *See generally* Nash, *Contemporary Practice of the United States Relating to International Law: Diplomatic Asylum*, 75 Am.J.Int'l L. 142 (1981); Note, *Diplomatic Asylum in the United States and Latin America: A Comparative Analysis*, 13 Brooklyn J.Int'l L. 111 (1987).

21. The history of regulatory and statutory provisions is recounted in Martin, *Reforming Asylum Adjudication: On Navigating the Coast of Bohemia*, 138 U.Pa.L.Rev. 1247, 1294–98 (1990).

year—raised to 10,000 in 1990—and the executive branch need not make the full number available in any given year. In contrast, there is no ceiling on the adjustments of persons who are in "refugee" status. (*Compare* INA § 209(a)(2) *with* § 209(b).)

It is important to recognize that this is a ceiling on asylee *adjustments* only; there is no annual limit on the number of initial grants of asylum. Moreover, since 1980 Presidents have invariably made available the full quota of adjustment spaces every year. (Take another look at Presidential Determination No. 95–1, p. 739 *supra*, to review the provisions for asylees.) The ceiling of 5000, which did not receive much attention during Congress's consideration of the Refugee Act of 1980, appeared adequate at the time to provide for asylum caseloads, which were running below 3000 annual filings with INS through late 1978. But the asylum application rate reached considerably higher levels through the 1980s, and 5000 proved inadequate to keep pace with the number of recognized asylees who wanted to adjust to permanent resident status. Backlogs as long as 31 months developed. In the Immigration Act of 1990, Congress took note of these problems. It therefore raised the ceiling on asylee adjustments to 10,000 per year, and also wiped out the backlog by exempting all asylees who had applied for adjustment on or before June 1, 1990 from any such ceiling.[22] 1990 Act, § 104(c).

The Refugee Act also modified § 243(h) of the INA, the provision that had since 1952 given the Attorney General discretion to withhold the deportation of aliens subject to persecution. First, this provision was expressly expanded so as to include aliens in exclusion proceedings (although it is still often referred to as "withholding of deportation"). Second, it was changed from a discretionary to a mandatory provision. Return now must be withheld if the alien shows that his "life or freedom would be threatened * * * on account of race, religion, nationality, membership in a particular social group, or political opinion." This language is taken directly from Article 33 of the UN Convention. Certain exceptions to this mandatory obligation appear in § 243(h)(2), serving generally to disqualify spies, dangerous criminals, and persons who themselves participated in the persecution of others. Do these exceptions place us in violation of the treaty? Congress intended to avoid any such result, and the legislative history states explicitly that the exceptions are to be construed consistently with exceptions to the Protocol's protections. *See* Articles 1(F) and 33(2) of the UN Convention. But the wording of § 243(h)(2)(A), disqualifying those who have "ordered, incited, assisted or otherwise participated in" persecution of others, is extraordinarily broad.[23] To what provisions in the Convention does it correspond?

---

22. Congress also included another rather curious grandfather provision in § 104(d) of the 1990 Act. It allows adjustment to permanent resident status for any person who was granted asylum before the date of enactment (Nov. 29, 1990), "who is no longer a refugee because of a change in circumstances in a foreign state," and who would qualify for adjustment but for INA § 209(b)(2) or (3).

Why do you suppose Congress added this provision? Think about the "changes in circumstances" in foreign states that occurred within the year or so preceding this enactment. Is such special treatment justified?

23. The apparent breadth of this exception reflects its provenance, for the language mirrors the language of former § 241(a)(19), a particularly strict provision directed at Nazi

Asylum Procedures

Under the regulations, an alien applies for asylum-type protections under either § 208 or § 243(h) by filing Form I–589 (in triplicate). 8 C.F.R. §§ 208.3, 208.4. In addition to asking why the applicant is seeking asylum and what he or she thinks would happen upon return to the home country, the form requires the applicant to provide other information that may throw further light on the claim. It asks, for example, about past activities and organizational affiliations, current whereabouts and condition of family members, and the circumstances of departure and travel to the United States. *See* 71 Interp.Rel. 1617–31 (1994) for a copy of the form as modified in late 1994 (also reprinted in the Supplement). Many applicants also provide additional material, sometimes quite voluminous, including affidavits, news accounts, or human rights reports from nongovernmental organizations like Amnesty International.

Asylum applications can follow two different paths, usually called "affirmative applications" and "defensive applications," depending on the pendency of exclusion or deportation proceedings against the alien. Applicants not currently in proceedings may file the I–589 affirmatively by mail with an INS regional service center. (In recent years roughly 90 percent of asylum applications have been affirmative claims.) The RSC staff checks that the application is complete and, if so, schedules the alien for an interview with an INS officer, which is to be carried out in a "nonadversarial manner." 8 C.F.R. § 208.9. For many years the INS officers adjudicating affirmative claims were part of the examinations staff in the district office, and the decision was issued in the name of the District Director. In 1990, however, INS issued new asylum regulations, 55 Fed. Reg. 30,674 (July 27, 1990), which took this function from the district office.

persecutors. (This ground for deportation is now incorporated, using similar wording, in § 241(a)(4)(D) [insofar as it refers to § 212(a)(3)(E)(i)].) During the 1970's, several former Nazi collaborators were discovered in the United States, many of them having entered in the late 1940's under the Displaced Persons program, usually by concealing their true identities. Because of the passage of time, there had been difficulties in securing their deportation under the regular provisions of the immigration laws. Congresswoman Elizabeth Holtzman took the lead in pushing for their removal, and § 241(a)(19) was adopted in 1978 under legislation known as the Holtzman Amendment. Persons deportable under this provision are explicitly declared ineligible for most forms of relief from deportation, including withholding under § 243(h) and suspension under § 244.

As § 241(a)(19) and the successor provision have been interpreted by the BIA, they provide for the removal of those who assisted the Nazis in persecution, even if they did so involuntarily and under duress. *See Matter*

of Fedorenko, 19 I & N Dec. 57 (BIA 1984); *Matter of Laipenieks,* 18 I & N Dec. 433 (BIA 1983), *reversed, Laipenieks v. INS,* 750 F.2d 1427 (9th Cir.1985) (holding that "active personal involvement in persecutorial acts needs to be demonstrated" for a finding of deportability under this provision). It is not yet clear whether the BIA would interpret the parallel language in § 243(h)(2) in such a draconian fashion. *See Matter of McMullen,* 19 I & N Dec. 90, 95–97 (BIA 1984), *affirmed,* 788 F.2d 591 (9th Cir.1986). But it is doubtful whether such a harsh construction, however appropriate it might be for Nazi collaborators, would be consistent with Article 1(F) of the UN Convention. Language identical to that of INA § 243(h)(2)(A) in the second sentence of § 101(a)(42) likewise excepts persecutors from the statute's definition of "refugee." Application of that exception, particularly to Cambodian applicants for the overseas programs, provoked considerable controversy. *See* Note, *From Treblinka to the Killing Fields: Excluding Persecutors from the Definition of "Refugee,"* 27 Va.J.Int'l L. 823 (1987).

In recognition of the complexity and uniqueness of asylum decision-making, INS assigned the task instead to a specialized "corps of professional asylum officers who are to receive special training in international human rights law, conditions in countries of origin, other relevant national and international refugee laws." 8 C.F.R. § 208.1(b). Asylum officers are accountable to the INS Central Office and have no direct connection with the district offices. They are based in eight asylum offices located in cities throughout the country that have high concentrations of asylum applicants, and they occasionally ride circuit to hear claims at other places. Asylum officers make their decisions on the basis of the application form, the information presented during the interview, and possibly other information from the State Department or "other credible sources, such as international organizations, private voluntary agencies, or academic institutions." 8 C.F.R. § 208.12(a). They are supported by their own central documentation center, *see id.* § 208.1(c), which makes wide-ranging information about country conditions and legal developments available to the officers on-line. *See* Beyer, *Affirmative Asylum Adjudication in the United States*, 6 Geo. Imm. L.J. 253 (1992); Beyer, *Establishing the United States Asylum Officer Corps: A First Report*, 4 Int'l J. Refugee L. 455 (1992) (two interesting and revealing articles by the first director of the central Asylum Office).

If exclusion or deportation proceedings are already underway, the applicant presents a "defensive" claim that is heard exclusively by the immigration judge. 8 C.F.R. § 208.2(b). Typically the alien makes known at master calendar (the first appearance in immigration court) her wish to assert asylum (or withholding) as a defense to removal, and the judge then grants a specified period of time for completion of the I–589, to be filed with the clerk of the immigration court. The matter is then heard in the more formal setting of the immigration court, with examination and cross-examination by the alien's counsel (if she has one) and the INS trial attorney. And if the applicant applies for asylum only after the issuance of an exclusion or deportation order, the claim must be raised by means of a motion to reopen filed with the IJ or BIA, as appropriate. The motion "must reasonably explain the failure to request asylum prior to the completion of the exclusion or deportation proceeding." *Id.* § 208.4(c)(4). *See INS v. Abudu*, 485 U.S. 94, 108 S.Ct. 904, 99 L.Ed.2d 90 (1988).

Until 1995, asylum officers issued fairly lengthy decision letters to denied applicants, explaining the reasons for the denial. These applicants then had no direct appeal rights, but they could renew the claim before the immigration judge once they were haled into immigration court for exclusion or deportation proceedings. The judge would consider the matter *de novo*. Typically this meant that the process started over again, involving a new I–589, and considerable additional delay. In order to streamline asylum procedures, and also to respond to criticism about "two bites at the apple" for affirmative claimants, the Justice Department adopted major regulatory reforms in December 1994 (taking effect January 4, 1995). 59 Fed.Reg. 62284 (1994). The regulations do not eliminate the two separate forums for the hearing of asylum claims, but they introduce much closer linkage between them, and they endeavor to eliminate unproductive procedures so that the system can once again become current with incoming receipts. (*See* Table 8.2, *infra,* for information on receipts and backlogs. While waiting for their interviews under the prior system—which could mean years—the applicants enjoyed work authorization and were shielded against removal; this situation was believed to foster abuse.)

Under the new procedures, asylum officers no longer deny claims, in most instances. Instead, their function is to grant meritorious cases (assumed for planning and budgeting purposes to run at 20–30 percent of affirmative filings) and to *refer* the rest to immigration court, with minimal paperwork that does not have to explain in detail the reasons for the referral.[24] 8 C.F.R. § 208.14(b). At the same time, the new system places emphasis on promptly serving "referred" applicants with charging documents that specify the date for appearance in immigration court, *see id.* § 208.18(b). Moreover, the asylum officer transmits the pre-existing I–589, with its attachments, to the immigration court along with copies of the charging documents. Although applicants can of course supplement their claims in immigration court and put on additional witnesses, using the original application form in both settings is meant to enhance efficiency and save time. Immigration judges will then decide referred cases in the normal way, granting some asylum claims and giving rejected applicants a full statement of reasons.

The intent of the new procedures is to provide a genuine opportunity to bona fide asylum claimants, but to discourage others by making it clear that weak claims will only lead to early commencement of immigration court proceedings and probably to the prompt entry of an exclusion or deportation order. The reforms have been accompanied by a doubling of the asylum officer corps (to over 300 officers) and a nearly-comparable growth in the ranks of immigration judges. *See* Beyer, *Reforming Affirmative Asylum Processing in the United States: Challenges and Opportunities,* 9 Am.U.J. Int'l L. & Pol'y 43 (Special Issue 1994); 71 Interp.Rel. 1577 (1994). As a further deterrent to weak claims, the 1994 regulations changed the system for granting work authorization to asylum applicants. Now claimants may not even apply for work authorization (unless asylum is granted) until 150 days after filing the initial asylum claim, and they may not receive it if the immigration judge denies asylum before the 180th day. 8 C.F.R. § 208.7. (We will consider the employment authorization issue more closely at pp. 882–84, *infra.*)

The immigration judge's decision (on either a defensive asylum claim or a referred claim) is appealable to the Board of Immigration Appeals. Most of the time, any judicial review of the decision comes at this stage, after the Board has ruled, *see Kashani v. Nelson,* 793 F.2d 818 (7th Cir.1986); *Yim Tong Chung v. Smith,* 640 F.Supp. 1065 (S.D.N.Y.1986), but there have been exceptions when judicial review was deemed proper at

---

24. Asylum officers will still issue full decisions, granting or denying asylum, in the case of crewmen, stowaways, or aliens ruled excludable based on confidential information under INA § 235(c). 8 C.F.R. §§ 208.14(b)(3), 253.1(f). And if the alien is still in status (*e.g.,* as a nonimmigrant student) at the time of filing, the officer will also either grant or deny asylum. *Id.* § 208.14(b)(4). In the latter circumstances a referral to immigration court would not be appropriate, because the alien is not prima facie excludable or deportable; but applications from in-status aliens make up a very small percentage of asylum office caseload.

an earlier stage because of the nature of the issues raised—particularly when it was alleged that there had been major procedural defaults in the early stages of the asylum proceedings. *See, e.g., Haitian Refugee Center v. Smith,* 676 F.2d 1023, 1033–36 (5th Cir.1982), discussed in Chapter Nine; *Orantes-Hernandez v. Thornburgh,* 919 F.2d 549 (9th Cir.1990). Judicial review takes place initially either in the district court or the court of appeals, depending on whether the applicant is in exclusion or deportation proceedings, respectively.

Information about asylum applications is supposed to remain confidential, both to protect family members and friends still in the home country, and to help assure that the mere fact of filing for asylum will not add in any measure to the risks that might be faced by the applicant. Both INS and the State Department have taken steps to safeguard such information, *see, e.g.,* 60 Interp.Rel. 917–18 (1983), but this policy of confidentiality has been implemented unevenly. Some courts have expressed concern about the use of names and identifying information in public administrative and judicial proceedings. *See, e.g., Perez–Alvarez v. INS,* 857 F.2d 23, 24 (1st Cir.1988). The 1990 regulations contained new provisions meant to provide better assurance of confidentiality, 8 C.F.R. § 208.6, and the BIA now usually excises the names from published decisions in asylum cases, referring to the alien only by initials.

Trends and Statistics

INS received asylum applications in the 1970s at a rate of between 1900 and 5800 per year. *See* 1986 INS Statistical Yearbook, Table 27 (1987). Shortly after the adoption of the Refugee Act, however, the fledgling asylum provisions in the statute were sorely tested by an unexpected combination of geopolitical developments. The Mariel boatlift brought approximately 125,000 asylum seekers from Cuba in the spring and summer of 1980, at a time when several thousand Haitian applications were being received. The Shah's fall in Iran also resulted in thousands of applications from Iranians in the United States during 1980 and 1981, and the fall of Somoza led to a similar receipt of Nicaraguan applications. *See* Meissner, *Reflections on the Refugee Act of 1980,* in The New Asylum Seekers: Refugee Law in the 1980s, at 57, 60–63 (D. Martin ed. 1988). As a result, INS developed a backlog of cases that exceeded 170,000, and only by a major priority effort in 1983 and 1984 was that backlog cleared. Substantial questions have been raised about the fairness of that clearance process, however, particularly as it applied to Central American asylum seekers. See *id.* at 63–64.[25]

25. Controversy raged for many years over the low approval rates for asylum seekers from some countries, particularly El Salvador (2 to 3 percent in INS district offices in the 1980s) and Guatemala (less than 2 percent). In 1990, the Department of Justice agreed to a massive settlement of civil litigation that alleged bias in the adjudication of Salvadoran and Guatemalan asylum claims.

American Baptist Churches v. Thornburgh, 760 F.Supp. 796 (N.D.Cal.1991). The settlement provided for readjudication of virtually all such claims filed in the 1980s (perhaps 150,000 cases). In addition, all class members (Salvadorans in the United States as of September 19, 1990 and Guatemalans here as of October 1, 1990, but excluding aggravated felons), whether or not they had previously

For a few years after the backlog clearance, the application rate appeared to stabilize, at around 20,000–25,000. This was considerably higher than the experience of the 1970s, but after the 1980 peak, it appeared a politically manageable level. Beginning in 1988, however, a strong upward trend began, mostly involving nationals of Nicaragua, El Salvador, Guatemala and Honduras. *See* 1993 INS Statistical Yearbook 77. The reasons are not clear, but some of the increase may be a delayed effect of the Immigration Reform and Control Act of 1986. By most counts, several hundred thousand people from those Central American nations were living in the United States in undocumented status before 1986, and most probably encountered little difficulty in securing work, thereby enjoying a kind of *de facto* asylum. After 1986, IRCA's employer sanctions provisions made it more difficult for them to continue such an existence without papers. Asylum came to be recognized as one way to obtain such papers, at least temporarily, because the IRCA regulations mandated issuance of employment authorization to aliens who filed a "nonfrivolous" asylum application. *See* Martin, *The End of De Facto Asylum: Toward a Humane and Realistic Response to Refugee Challenges,* 18 Calif.W.Int'l L.J. 161 (1987–88); 69 Interp.Rel. 756 (1992) (INS guidelines for deciding whether a claim is frivolous). (As noted, the 1994 regulations introduced new restrictions on employment authorization.)

Table 8.2 shows the trends in asylum applications and the growing backlogs that have fortified recent efforts to streamline and reform the system. Table 8.3 indicates leading source countries in 1994. Do any of the countries listed there surprise you? Do any omissions surprise you?

Other events also added to a sense of urgency, even panic, over asylum reform that descended on Washington in 1993. Large ships bearing hundreds of smuggled Chinese asylum seekers arrived on both coasts, the most notable being the *Golden Venture*, which ran aground off Long Island in June 1993. *See Matter of G—,* Int.Dec. 3215 (BIA 1993), discussed at pp. 476–81 *supra.* Other such ships were detected far offshore and diverted to Mexico or Guatemala. *See* Suro, *Guatemala Agrees to Facilitate Repatriation of Illegal Chinese Immigrants,* Wash. Post, Apr. 29, 1994, at A3. Also, news accounts attributed acts of terrorism, including the World Trade Center bombing and the shootings outside CIA complex in northern Virginia, to persons who had won lengthy stays in the United States by filing asylum applications. A host of bills proposing changes in asylum procedures, some of them quite radical, were introduced in Congress. *See* 70 Interp.Rel. 581, 612, 738, 898, 1397 (1993). Then in 1994, new crises over asylum seekers from Haiti and Cuba, discussed *infra,* also added to the concern. None of the bills were adopted in the 103d Congress, but asylum

filed for asylum, were protected against deportation, received work authorization, and were entitled to have their cases considered by the then-new corps of specialist asylum officers created under the 1990 regulations. The settlement contained special provisions for notice to class members and for outside monitoring, and the government expressly reaffirmed that border enforcement and for-eign policy concerns have no bearing on deciding asylum cases. *See* 67 Interp.Rel. 1480 (1990). The Bush administration, however, never adequately budgeted for the greatly augmented caseload caused by the *ABC* settlement, and readjudication appears unlikely to begin in any serious way until late 1995. *See* 71 Interp.Rel. 1586 (1994); Section D *infra.*

Table 8.2
Asylum Cases Filed with INS, FY 1984–95

Fiscal Year	Cases Pending Beginning FY	Cases Filed with INS	Cases Completed
1984	165,998	24,295	54,320
1985	138,601	16,622	28,528
1986	126,311	18,889	45,792
1987	99,408	26,107	44,785
1988	80,730	60,736	68,357
1989	73,109	101,679	102,795
1990	71,993	73,637	48,342
1991	97,288	56,310	16,552
1992	137,046	103,964	21,996
1993	223,709	144,166	34,228
1994*	327,385	147,605	54,196
1995*	420,794		

* Data are preliminary.

Source: INS Asylum Division, Preliminary FY 1994 Statistical Package, Oct. 28, 1994. [26]

Table 8.3
Asylum Applications Filed with INS, FY 1994
Leading Source Countries*

1.	Guatemala	34,630
2.	El Salvador	18,543
3.	China	10,930
4.	Mexico	9,791
5.	Haiti	9,354
6.	Nicaragua	4,673
7.	India	4,571
8.	Honduras	4,436
9.	Bangladesh	3,584
10.	Pakistan	3,339

* The top 10 nationalities accounted for 70 percent of applications filed.

Source: INS Asylum Division, Preliminary FY 1994 Statistical Package, Oct. 28, 1994.

26. Table 8.2 reflects the number of cases, but a single case may include several family members applying together. Thus the number of asylum seekers is higher than the number of cases.

Although the pattern varies greatly by nationality, the overall grant rate by the Asylum Office was 37.6% in FY 1992, 21.8% for FY 1993 and 22.1% for FY 1994. Moreover, the statistics in Table 8.2 count only cases received in INS district offices, not those filed with immigration judges. In FY 1993, immigration judges received 13,594 cases, granted 1,626, and denied 5,393, for an approval rate of 23.2%. In FY 1994, they received 18,246, granted 1,699, and denied 7,600, yielding an approval rate of 18.3%. (The data do not show how many of these are renewals of claims initially denied by INS.) Refugee Reports, Dec. 31, 1993, at 13; *id.*, Dec. 31, 1994, at 13. The December issue of each year's Refugee Reports contains comprehensive data, including a detailed breakdown, by nationality, of asylum cases received, granted, and denied, for INS asylum officers and for immigration judges.

reform, of both procedures and substantive standards, may remain a key point of controversy in coming years. Keep these elements of the policy context in mind as you read the materials in this Section.

2. THE RELATIONSHIP BETWEEN § 208 AND § 243(H): STANDARDS FOR ANALYZING THE THREAT AN APPLICANT FACES IN THE HOMELAND

Both INA § 208 and § 243(h) point toward similar kinds of protection for what might initially seem to be the same class of persons threatened with persecution in their homelands. Just how the two provisions interrelate, however, has been the subject of major debate. This question has also provided the occasion for the first Supreme Court decisions to consider the Refugee Act of 1980, *INS v. Stevic,* 467 U.S. 407, 104 S.Ct. 2489, 81 L.Ed.2d 321 (1984), and *INS v. Cardoza–Fonseca,* 480 U.S. 421, 107 S.Ct. 1207, 94 L.Ed.2d 434 (1987), considered below. Those cases focused on this question: What *degree of threat or risk* in the homeland must an applicant prove before being found to meet the threshold qualification for protection under these sections? But lingering in the background is a second question that we will treat in detail in Part 3 of this Section. Note that the 1980 Refugee Act transformed § 243(h), governing withholding of deportation (or *nonrefoulement*), into a mandatory provision, whereas § 208, providing for asylum status, is discretionary. The second question is this: What standards should the immigration authorities use in exercising the *discretion* § 208 gives them in deciding whether to grant asylum? How freely may they deny such a benefit to those who have satisfied the statutory eligibility requirements by meeting the refugee definition in INA § 101(a)(42)? Be alert as you read the following cases, and particularly *Cardoza–Fonseca,* to what the courts have to say, if only in passing, about the discretion issue.

a. *Salim*

The Board's first significant effort to delineate the differences between the two sections came in a case focusing on standards for the exercise of discretion. *Matter of Salim,* 18 I & N Dec. 311 (BIA 1982). The applicant was from Afghanistan, and he was found to satisfy the refugee definition, because he had been a member of rebel groups opposed to the Soviet-supported Afghan regime and, further, because he might be dragooned to fight under Soviet command. But he had spent some time in Pakistan before coming to the United States, and he got here by fraudulent use of someone else's passport.

The Board explained its understanding of the relationship between §§ 208 and 243(h):

> Section 243(h) relief is "country specific" and accordingly, the applicant here would be presently protected from deportation to Afghanistan pursuant to section 243(h). But that section would

> not prevent his exclusion and deportation to Pakistan or any other hospitable country under section 237(a) if that country will accept him. In contrast, asylum is a greater form of relief. When granted asylum, the alien may be eligible to apply for adjustment of status to that of a lawful permanent resident pursuant to section 209 of the Act, after residing here one year, subject to numerical limitations and the applicable regulations. See 8 C.F.R. § 209.

Id. at 315. The Board went on to grant withholding with respect to Afghanistan, but to affirm the denial of asylum in the exercise of discretion, primarily because of the fraud. *See* pp. 793–95 *infra.*[27]

b. *Stevic and Cardoza–Fonseca*

The Supreme Court elaborated on the relationship between the two sections in two cases that arose against the following background. Since the 1950s the BIA had required applicants for relief under § 243(h) (then the principal, and for a time the only, avenue for asylum-type relief available under the INA) to demonstrate a "clear probability of persecution" before their application would be granted. This standard was initial- ly established as a criterion governing the exercise of the discretion given to the Attorney General by the original wording of § 243(h). When such protection became, in effect, mandatory after U.S. accession to the UN Protocol in 1968—for persons meeting the standards of Article 33 of the Convention—litigants claimed that the Board was required to relax that criterion. The Board disagreed. In *Matter of Dunar,* 14 I. & N.Dec. 310 (BIA 1973), it determined that the treaty worked no change in the governing standards, and it continued to employ the "clear probability" test.

Not long after the Refugee Act was passed in 1980, litigants renewed the argument. The Court of Appeals for the Second Circuit ruled that Congress, by amending the asylum provisions and conforming their language more closely to the wording of the treaty, intended to ease the requirements for proving entitlement to asylum in this country. *Stevic v. Sava,* 678 F.2d 401 (2d Cir.1982). Although it declined to specify in detail the new criteria, it indicated that "asylum may be granted, and under Section 243(h), deportation must be withheld, upon a showing far short of a 'clear probability' that an individual will be singled out for persecution." The court reached this conclusion after a lengthy review of the history of the legal provisions, both domestic and international, governing political asylum. Although its reasoning would seem to suggest that the Board's practice had been in error ever since 1968, when the United States became a party to the Protocol, the court's actual holding was more limited. It ruled only that, in passing the Refugee Act in 1980, Congress intended to require that the BIA end its former administrative practice and adopt a more generous standard for asylum and withholding of deportation. The Third Circuit, however, sustained the Board's "clear probability" approach,

---

27. The Board later modified *Salim's* holding so as to greatly reduce discretionary denials, even in cases involving some manipulation of the procedures, if the applicant meets the refugee definition. *Matter of Pula,* 19 I & N Dec. 467 (BIA 1987), considered *infra* p. 797.

Rejaie v. INS, 691 F.2d 139 (3d Cir.1982), and the Supreme Court granted certiorari in *Stevic* to resolve the conflict.

One feature of these appellate cases—indeed virtually all such litigation since *Dunar*—deserves special mention. Litigants, lower courts, and the BIA had almost uniformly assumed that the threshold standard was the same for both asylum under § 208 and withholding under § 243(h). *See, e.g., Zavala–Bonilla v. INS*, 730 F.2d 562, 563 n. 1 (9th Cir.1984); *Matter of Lam*, 18 I & N Dec. 15, 17 n. 3 (BIA 1981); *Matter of Martinez–Romero*, 18 I & N Dec. 73, 77 n. 5 (BIA 1981). The *Stevic* case was therefore argued in the Supreme Court on this assumption. It was thought that the Court would simply have to choose a governing formulation, to apply in both of these related settings.

The Supreme Court's approach in *INS v. Stevic*, 467 U.S. 407, 104 S.Ct. 2489, 81 L.Ed.2d 321 (1984) therefore came as a surprise. *See generally* Helton, *Stevic: The Decision and its Implications*, 3 Imm.L.Rep. 49 (1984). Justice Stevens, writing for a unanimous Court, laid considerable stress on a fact the parties had given little notice: in the procedural posture of the *Stevic* case, the alien was seeking only withholding under § 243(h). Therefore the only issue considered to be properly before the Court was the standard that should govern under § 243(h), and the opinion proceeded to pay close attention to the precise wording of that section. The Court stated that it was leaving for another day consideration of the § 208 test, although lengthy dictum strongly hinted that an easier standard might govern there. Further suggesting a sharp distinction between the two sections, the Court declared "mistaken" the court of appeals' "premise that every alien who qualifies as a 'refugee' under the statutory definition [referred to in § 208] is also entitled to a withholding of deportation under § 243(h)." 467 U.S., at 428, 104 S.Ct. at 2500.

In evaluating the requirements for § 243(h), the Court relied largely on a plain-language approach to statutory interpretation:

> The section literally provides for withholding of deportation only if the alien's life or freedom "would" be threatened in the country to which he would be deported; it does not require withholding if the alien "might" or "could" be subject to persecution.

Id. at 422, 104 S.Ct. at 2497. As a result, the Second Circuit's lower threshold was rejected and the Board's "clear probability" approach approved, but only for applying § 243(h). Moreover, the *Stevic* Court applied a gloss to "clear probability" that makes it a somewhat less daunting standard than the words might initially convey. *Stevic* held that "clear" is surplusage and that the standard requires only a showing that "it is more likely than not that the alien would be subject to persecution." *Id.* at 424 and n. 19, 104 S.Ct. at 2498 and n. 19.

(Note the exact language used by the Court in these quotations from *Stevic*. Is "would be subject to persecution" equivalent to "would be persecuted"? Moreover, the statutory language in § 243(h) is "life or freedom would be *threatened*," but the court pays little attention to the final word in this phrase when it juxtaposes "would" against "might" or "could.")

Predictably, litigation resumed immediately after *Stevic,* now carefully targeting the § 208 issue that the Supreme Court had avoided. Again the courts of appeals reached disparate results. The BIA surveyed these decisions in *Matter of Acosta,* 19 I & N Dec. 211 (BIA 1985), and then announced that it would continue to apply a unitary standard:

> One might conclude that "a well-founded fear of persecution," which requires a showing that persecution is likely to occur, refers to a standard that is different from "a clear probability of persecution," which requires a showing that persecution is "more likely than not" to occur. As a practical matter, however, the facts in asylum and withholding cases do not produce clear-cut instances in which such fine distinctions can be meaningfully made. Our inquiry in these cases, after all, is not quantitative, *i.e.,* we do not examine a variety of statistics to discern to some theoretical degree the likelihood of persecution. Rather, our inquiry is qualitative: we examine the alien's experiences and other external events to determine if they are of a kind that enable us to conclude the alien is likely to become the victim of persecution. In this context, we find no meaningful distinction between a standard requiring a showing that persecution is likely to occur and a standard requiring a showing that persecution is more likely than not to occur. * * * Accordingly, we conclude that the standards for asylum and withholding of deportation are not meaningfully different and, in practical application, converge.

Id. at 229.

In 1987, the § 208 issue returned to the Supreme Court.

INS v. CARDOZA–FONSECA

Supreme Court of the United States, 1987.
480 U.S. 421, 107 S.Ct. 1207, 94 L.Ed.2d 434.

JUSTICE STEVENS delivered the opinion of the Court.

Since 1980, the Immigration and Nationality Act has provided two methods through which an otherwise deportable alien who claims that he will be persecuted if deported can seek relief. Section 243(h) of the Act requires the Attorney General to withhold deportation of an alien who demonstrates that his "life or freedom would be threatened" on account of one of the listed factors if he is deported. In *INS v. Stevic,* 467 U.S. 407 (1984), we held that to qualify for this entitlement to withholding of deportation, an alien must demonstrate that "it is more likely than not that the alien would be subject to persecution" in the country to which he would be returned. The Refugee Act of 1980, 94 Stat. 102, also established a second type of broader relief. Section 208(a) of the Act authorizes the Attorney General, in his discretion, to grant asylum to an alien who is unable or unwilling to return to his home country "because of persecution or a well-founded fear of persecution on account of race, religion, nationality, membership in a particular social group, or political opinion." § 101(a)(42).

In *Stevic*, we rejected an alien's contention that the § 208(a) "well-founded fear" standard governs applications for withholding of deportation under § 243(h).[1] Similarly, today we reject the Government's contention that the § 243(h) standard, which requires an alien to show that he is more likely than not to be subject to persecution, governs applications for asylum under § 208(a). Congress used different, broader language to define the term "refugee" as used in § 208(a) than it used to describe the class of aliens who have a right to withholding of deportation under § 243(h). The Act's establishment of a broad class of refugees who are eligible for a discretionary grant of asylum, and a narrower class of aliens who are given a statutory right not to be deported to the country where they are in danger, mirrors the provisions of the United Nations Protocol Relating to the Status of Refugees, which provided the motivation for the enactment of the Refugee Act of 1980. In addition, the legislative history of the 1980 Act makes it perfectly clear that Congress did not intend the class of aliens who qualify as refugees to be coextensive with the class who qualify for § 243(h) relief.

I

Respondent is a 38–year–old Nicaraguan citizen who entered the United States in 1979 as a visitor. After she remained in the United States longer than permitted, and failed to take advantage of the Immigration and Naturalization Service's (INS) offer of voluntary departure, the INS commenced deportation proceedings against her. Respondent conceded that she was in the country illegally, but requested withholding of deportation pursuant to § 243(h), and asylum as a refugee pursuant to § 208(a).

To support her request under § 243(h), respondent attempted to show that if she were returned to Nicaragua her "life or freedom would be threatened" on account of her political views; to support her request under § 208(a), she attempted to show that she had a "well-founded fear of persecution" upon her return. The evidence supporting both claims related primarily to the activities of respondent's brother who had been tortured and imprisoned because of his political activities in Nicaragua. Both respondent and her brother testified that they believed the Sandinistas knew that the two of them had fled Nicaragua together and that even though she had not been active politically herself, she would be interrogated about her brother's whereabouts and activities. Respondent also testified that because of her brother's status, her own political opposition to the Sandinistas would be brought to that government's attention. Based on these facts, respondent claimed that she would be tortured if forced to return.

The Immigration Judge applied the same standard in evaluating respondent's claim for withholding of deportation under § 243(h) as he did in evaluating her application for asylum under § 208(a). He found that she had not established "a clear probability of persecution" and therefore was

---

1. We explained that the Court of Appeals' decision had rested "on the mistaken premise that every alien who qualifies as a 'refugee' under the statutory definition is also entitled to a withholding of deportation under § 243(h). We find no support for this conclusion in either the language of § 243(h), the structure of the amended Act, or the legislative history." *INS v. Stevic*, 467 U.S., at 428.

not entitled to either form of relief. On appeal, the Board of Immigration Appeals (BIA) agreed that respondent had "failed to establish that she would suffer persecution within the meaning of section 208(a) or 243(h) of the Immigration and Nationality Act."

In the Court of Appeals for the Ninth Circuit, respondent did not challenge the BIA's decision that she was not entitled to withholding of deportation under § 243(h), but argued that she was eligible for consideration for asylum under § 208(a), and contended that the Immigration Judge and BIA erred in applying the "more likely than not" standard of proof from § 243(h) to her § 208(a) asylum claim. Instead, she asserted, they should have applied the "well-founded fear" standard which she considered to be more generous. The court agreed. Relying on both the text and the structure of the Act, the court held that the "well-founded fear" standard which governs asylum proceedings is different, and in fact more generous, than the "clear probability" standard which governs withholding of deportation proceedings. 767 F.2d 1448, 1452–1453 (1985). Agreeing with the Court of Appeals for the Seventh Circuit, the court interpreted the standard to require asylum applicants to present " 'specific facts' through objective evidence to prove either past persecution or 'good reason' to fear future persecution." *Id.*, at 1453 (citing *Carvajal–Munoz v. INS*, 743 F.2d 562, 574 (CA7 1984)). The court remanded respondent's asylum claim to the BIA to evaluate under the proper legal standard. We granted certiorari to resolve a circuit conflict on this important question.

II

The Refugee Act of 1980 established a new statutory procedure for granting asylum to refugees. The 1980 Act added a new § 208(a) to the Immigration and Naturalization Act of 1952. * * *

Under this section, eligibility for asylum depends entirely on the Attorney General's determination that an alien is a "refugee," as that term is defined in § 101(a)(42), which was also added to the Act in 1980. [The Court then sets forth the text of INA § 101(a)(42)(A).] Thus, the "persecution or well-founded fear of persecution" standard governs the Attorney General's determination whether an alien is eligible for asylum.[5]

In addition to establishing a statutory asylum process, the 1980 Act amended the withholding of deportation provision,[6] § 243(h). Prior to 1968, the Attorney General had discretion whether to grant withholding of deportation to aliens under § 243(h). In 1968, however, the United States agreed to comply with the substantive provisions of Articles 2 through 34 of the 1951 United Nations Convention Relating to the Status of Refugees. Article 33.1 of the Convention, which is the counterpart of § 243(h) of our

5. It is important to note that the Attorney General is *not required* to grant asylum to everyone who meets the definition of refugee. Instead, a finding that an alien is a refugee does no more than establish that "the alien *may* be granted asylum *in the discretion of the Attorney General.*" § 208(a) (emphasis added).

6. Asylum and withholding of deportation are two distinct forms of relief. First, as we

have mentioned, there is no entitlement to asylum; it is only granted to eligible refugees pursuant to the Attorney General's discretion. Once granted, however, asylum affords broader benefits. * * * [The Court then quotes the passage from *Matter of Salim* appearing on pp. 770–71 *supra*.]

statute, imposed a mandatory duty on contracting States not to return an alien to a country where his "life or freedom would be threatened" on account of one of the enumerated reasons. Thus, although § 243(h) itself did not constrain the Attorney General's discretion after 1968, presumably he honored the dictates of the United Nations Convention.[8] In any event, the 1980 Act removed the Attorney General's discretion in § 243(h) proceedings.

In *Stevic* we considered it significant that in enacting the 1980 Act Congress did not amend the standard of eligibility for relief under § 243(h). While the terms "refugee" and hence "well-founded fear" were made an integral part of the § 208(a) procedure, they continued to play no part in § 243(h). Thus we held that the prior consistent construction of § 243(h) that required an applicant for withholding of deportation to demonstrate a "clear probability of persecution" upon deportation remained in force. Of course, this reasoning, based in large part on the plain language of § 243(h), is of no avail here since § 208(a) expressly provides that the "well founded fear" standard governs eligibility for asylum.

The Government argues, however, that even though the "well-founded fear" standard is applicable, there is no difference between it and the "would be threatened" test of § 243(h). It asks us to hold that the only way an applicant can demonstrate a "well-founded fear of persecution" is to prove a "clear probability of persecution." The statutory language does not lend itself to this reading.

To begin with, the language Congress used to describe the two standards conveys very different meanings. The "would be threatened" language of § 243(h) has no subjective component, but instead requires the alien to establish by objective evidence that it is more likely than not that he or she will be subject to persecution upon deportation.[10] *See Stevic, supra.* In contrast, the reference to "fear" in the § 208(a) standard obviously makes the eligibility determination turn to some extent on the subjective mental state of the alien.[11] "The linguistic difference between the words 'well-founded fear' and 'clear probability' may be as striking as that between a subjective and an objective frame of reference.... We simply cannot conclude that the standards are identical." *Guevara Flores v. INS,* 786 F.2d 1242, 1250 (CA5 1986), [*cert. denied,* 480 U.S. 930, 107 S.Ct. 1565, 94 L.Ed.2d 757 (1987)]; see also *Carcamo–Flores v. INS,* 805 F.2d 60, 64 (CA2 1986); [*Cardoza–Fonseca,*] 767 F.2d, at 1452.

That the fear must be "well-founded" does not alter the obvious focus on the individual's subjective beliefs, nor does it transform the standard

---

8. While the Protocol constrained the Attorney General with respect to § 243(h) between 1968 and 1980, the Protocol does not *require* the granting of asylum to anyone, and hence does not subject the Attorney General to a similar constraint with respect to his discretion under § 208(a).

10. "The section literally provides for withholding of deportation only if the alien's life or freedom 'would' be threatened in the country to which he would be deported; it does not require withholding if the alien

'might' or 'could' be subject to persecution." *Stevic,* 467 U.S., at 422.

11. The BIA agrees that the term "fear," as used in this statute, refers to "a subjective condition, an emotion characterized by the anticipation or awareness of danger." *Matter of Acosta,* Interim Decision No. 2986, p. 14 (Mar. 1, 1985) (citing Webster's Third New International Dictionary 831 (16th ed. 1971)).

into a "more likely than not" one. One can certainly have a well-founded fear of an event happening when there is less than a 50% chance of the occurrence taking place. As one leading authority has pointed out:

> "Let us ... presume that it is known that in the applicant's country of origin every tenth adult male person is either put to death or sent to some remote labor camp ... In such a case it would be only too apparent that anyone who has managed to escape from the country in question will have 'well-founded fear of being persecuted' upon his eventual return." 1 A. Grahl–Madsen. The Status of Refugees in International Law 180 (1966).

This ordinary and obvious meaning of the phrase is not to be lightly discounted. * * *

III

[The Court then found this reading confirmed by an examination of the history of the Refugee Act and of the UN Convention and Protocol.]

* * *

The origin of the Protocol's definition of "refugee" is found in the 1946 Constitution of the International Refugee Organization (IRO). See 62 Stat. 3037. The IRO defined a "refugee" as a person who had a "valid objection" to returning to his country of nationality, and specified that "fear, based on reasonable grounds of persecution because of race, religion, nationality, or political opinions ..." constituted a valid objection. See IRO Constitution Annex 1, Pt. 1, § C1(a)(i). The term was then incorporated in the United Nations Convention Relating to the Status of Refugees, 189 U.N.T.S. 150 (July 28, 1951). The Committee that drafted the provision explained that "[t]he expression 'well founded fear of being the victim of persecution ...' means that a person has either been actually a victim of persecution or can show good reason why he fears persecution." The 1967 Protocol incorporated the "well-founded fear" test, without modification. The standard, as it has been consistently understood by those who drafted it, as well as those drafting the documents that adopted it, certainly does not require an alien to show that it is more likely than not that he will be persecuted in order to be classified as a "refugee."

In interpreting the Protocol's definition of "refugee" we are further guided by the analysis set forth in the Office of the United Nations High Commissioner for Refugees, Handbook on Procedures and Criteria for Determining Refugee Status (Geneva, 1979). The Handbook explains that "[i]n general, the applicant's fear should be considered well-founded if he can establish, to a reasonable degree, that his continued stay in his country of origin has become intolerable to him for the reasons stated in the definition, or would for the same reasons be intolerable if he returned there."

The High Commissioner's analysis of the United Nations' standard is consistent with our own examination of the origins of the Protocol's definition, as well as the conclusions of many scholars who have studied the matter.[24] There is simply no room in the United Nations' definition for concluding that because an applicant only has a 10% chance of being shot, tortured, or otherwise persecuted, that he or she has no "well-founded fear" of the event happening. As we pointed out in *Stevic,* a moderate interpretation of the "well-founded fear" standard would indicate "that so long as an objective situation is established by the evidence, it need not be shown that the situation will probably result in persecution, but it is enough that persecution is a reasonable possibility." 467 U.S., at 424–425.

In *Stevic,* we dealt with the issue of withholding of deportation, or *nonrefoulement,* under § 243(h). This provision corresponds to Article 33.1 of the Convention. Significantly though, Article 33.1 does not extend this right to everyone who meets the definition of "refugee." Rather, it provides that "[n]o Contracting State shall expel or return ('refouler') a *refugee* in any manner whatsoever to the frontiers of territories *where his life or freedom would be threatened* on account of his race, religion, nationality, membership or a particular social group or political opinion." Thus, Article 33.1 requires that an applicant satisfy two burdens: first, that he or she be a "refugee," *i.e.,* prove at least a "well-founded fear of persecution"; second, that the "refugee" show that his or her life or freedom "would be threatened" if deported. Section 243(h)'s imposition of a "would be threatened" requirement is entirely consistent with the United States' obligations under the Protocol.

Section 208(a), by contrast, is a discretionary mechanism which gives the Attorney General the *authority* to grant the broader relief of asylum to refugees. As such, it does not correspond to Article 33 of the Convention, but instead corresponds to Article 34. That Article provides that the contracting States "shall as far as possible facilitate the assimilation and naturalization of refugees...." Like § 208(a), the provision is precatory; it does not require the implementing authority actually to grant asylum to all those who are eligible. Also like § 208(a), an alien must only show that he or she is a "refugee" to establish eligibility for relief. No further showing that he or she "would be" persecuted is required.

Thus, as made binding on the United States through the Protocol, Article 34 provides for a precatory, or discretionary, benefit for the entire class of persons who qualify as "refugees," whereas Article 33.1 provides an entitlement for the subcategory that "would be threatened" with persecution upon their return. This precise distinction between the broad class of refugees and the subcategory entitled to § 243(h) relief is plainly revealed in the 1980 Act. See *Stevic,* 467 U.S., at 428, n. 22.

* * *

24. See 1 A. Grahl–Madsen, The Status of Refugees in International Law 181 (1966) ("If there is a real chance that he will suffer persecution, that is reason good enough, and his 'fear' is 'well-founded.'"); G. Goodwin–Gill. The Refugee in International Law 22–24 (1983) (balance of probability test is inappropriate; more appropriate test is "reasonable chance," "substantial grounds for thinking," or "serious possibility"); see generally Cox, "Well–Founded Fear of Being Persecuted": The Sources and Application of a Criterion of Refugee Status, 10 Brooklyn J. Int'l Law 333 (1984).

IV

The INS makes two major arguments to support its contention that we should reverse the Court of Appeals and hold that an applicant can only show a "well-founded fear of persecution" by proving that it is more likely than not that he or she will be persecuted. We reject both of these arguments: the first ignores the structure of the Act; the second misconstrues the federal courts' role in reviewing an agency's statutory construction.

First, the INS repeatedly argues that the structure of the Act dictates a decision in its favor, since it is anomalous for § 208(a), which affords greater benefits than § 243(h), to have a less stringent standard of eligibility. This argument sorely fails because it does not take into account the fact that an alien who satisfies the applicable standard under § 208(a) does not have a *right* to remain in the United States; he or she is simply *eligible* for asylum, if the Attorney General, in his discretion, chooses to grant it. An alien satisfying § 243(h)'s stricter standard, in contrast, is automatically entitled to withholding of deportation. In *Matter of Salim,* 18 I. & N. Dec. 311 (1982), for example, the Board held that the alien was eligible for both asylum and withholding of deportation, but granted him the more limited remedy only, exercising its discretion to deny him asylum. See also *Walai v. INS,* 552 F.Supp. 998 (S.D.N.Y.1982); *Matter of Shirdel,* Interim Decision No. 2958 (BIA Feb. 21, 1984). We do not consider it at all anomalous that out of the entire class of "refugees," those who can show a clear probability of persecution are *entitled* to mandatory suspension of deportation and *eligible* for discretionary asylum, while those who can only show a well-founded fear of persecution are not *entitled* to anything, but are *eligible* for the discretionary relief of asylum.

There is no basis for the INS's assertion that the discretionary/mandatory distinction has no practical significance. Decisions such as *Matter of Salim, supra,* and *Matter of Shirdel, supra,* clearly demonstrate the practical import of the distinction. Moreover, the 1980 Act amended § 243(h) for the very purpose of changing it from a discretionary to a mandatory provision. Congress surely considered the discretionary/mandatory distinction important then, as it did with respect to the very definition of "refugee" involved here. The House Report provides:

> "The Committee carefully considered arguments that the new definition might expand the numbers of refugees eligible to come to the United States and force substantially greater refugee admissions than the country could absorb. However, merely because an individual or group comes within the definition will not guarantee resettlement in the United States."

This vesting of discretion in the Attorney General is quite typical in the immigration area, see, *e.g., INS v. Jong Ha Wang,* 450 U.S. 139 (1981). If anything is anomalous, it is that the INS now asks us to restrict its discretion to a narrow class of aliens. Congress has assigned to the Attorney General and his delegates the task of making these hard individualized decisions; although Congress could have crafted a narrower definition, it chose to authorize the Attorney General to determine which, if any, eligible refugees should be denied asylum.

The INS's second principal argument in support of the proposition that the "well founded fear" and "clear probability" standard are equivalent is that the BIA so construes the two standards. The INS argues that the BIA's construction of the Refugee Act of 1980 is entitled to substantial deference, even if we conclude that the Court of Appeals' reading of the statutes is more in keeping with Congress' intent.[29] This argument is unpersuasive.

The question whether Congress intended the two standards to be identical is a pure question of statutory construction for the courts to decide. Employing traditional tools of statutory construction, we have concluded that Congress did not intend the two standards to be identical. In *Chevron U.S.A. Inc. v. Natural Resources Defense Council, Inc.,* 467 U.S. 837 (1984), we explained:

> "The judiciary is the final authority on issues of statutory construction and must reject administrative constructions which are contrary to clear congressional intent. [Citing cases.] If a court, employing traditional tools of statutory construction, ascertains that Congress had an intention on the precise question at issue, that intention is the law and must be given effect." *Id.,* at 843, n. 9 (citations omitted).

The narrow legal question whether the two standards are the same is, of course, quite different from the question of interpretation that arises in each case in which the agency is required to apply either or both standards to a particular set of facts. There is obviously some ambiguity in a term like "well-founded fear" which can only be given concrete meaning through a process of case-by-case adjudication. In that process of filling " 'any gap left, implicitly or explicitly, by Congress,' "the courts must respect the interpretation of the agency to which Congress has delegated the responsibility for administering the statutory program. But our task today is much narrower, and is well within the province of the judiciary. We do not attempt to set forth a detailed description of how the "well-founded fear" test should be applied.[31] Instead, we merely hold that the Immigration Judge and the BIA were incorrect in holding that the two standards are identical.

* * *

Deportation is always a harsh measure; it is all the more replete with danger when the alien makes a claim that he or she will be subject to death or persecution if forced to return to his or her home country. In enacting

---

29. In view of the INS's heavy reliance on the principle of deference as described in *Chevron U.S.A. Inc. v. Natural Resources Defense Council, Inc.,* 467 U.S. 837 (1984), we set forth the relevant text [the Court then quotes the passage set forth in Chapter Three, p. 173 *supra*].

31. How "meaningful" the differences between the two standards may be is a question that cannot be fully decided in the abstract, but the fact that Congress has prescribed two different standards in the same Act certainly implies that it intended them to have significantly different meanings.

* * *

the Refugee Act of 1980 Congress sought to "give the United States sufficient flexibility to respond to situations involving political or religious dissidents and detainees throughout the world." Our holding today increases that flexibility by rejecting the Government's contention that the Attorney General may not even consider granting asylum to one who fails to satisfy the strict § 243(h) standard. Whether or not a "refugee" is eventually granted asylum is a matter which Congress has left for the Attorney General to decide. But it is clear that Congress did not intend to restrict eligibility for that relief to those who could prove that it is more likely than not that they will be persecuted if deported.

The judgment of the Court of Appeals is

Affirmed.

JUSTICE BLACKMUN, concurring.

I join the Court's opinion and judgment. Thus, I accept its "narrow" conclusion that "the Immigration Judge and the BIA were incorrect in holding that the [standards for withholding of deportation and granting asylum] are identical." In accordance with this holding, the Court eschews any attempt to give substance to the term "well-founded fear" and leaves that task to the "process of case-by-case adjudication" by the INS, the agency in charge of administering the immigration laws. I write separately and briefly to emphasize my understanding that, in its opinion, the Court has directed the INS to the appropriate sources from which the agency should derive the meaning of the "well-founded fear" standard, a meaning that will be refined in later adjudication. This emphasis, I believe, is particularly needed where, as here, an agency's previous interpretation of the statutory term is so strikingly contrary to plain language and legislative history.

* * *

JUSTICE SCALIA, concurring in the judgment.

I agree with the Court that the plain meaning of "well founded fear" and the structure of the Immigration and Nationality Act (Act) clearly demonstrate that the "well-founded fear" standard and the "clear probability" standard are not equivalent. I concur in the judgment rather than join the Court's opinion, however, for two reasons. First, despite having reached the above conclusion, the Court undertakes an exhaustive investigation of the legislative history of the Act.

* * *

[T]here is simply no need for the lengthy effort to ascertain the import of the entire legislative history. And that effort is objectionable not only because it is gratuitous. I am concerned that it will be interpreted to suggest that similarly exhaustive analyses are generally appropriate (or, worse yet, required) in cases where the language of the enactment at issue is clear. I also fear that in this case the Court's conduct of that inquiry will be interpreted as a betrayal of its assurance that it does "not attempt to set forth a detailed description of how the well-founded fear test should be applied."

I am far more troubled, however, by the Court's discussion of the question whether the INS's interpretation of "well-founded fear" is entitled to deference. Since the Court quite rightly concludes that the INS's interpretation is clearly inconsistent with the plain meaning of that phrase and the structure of the Act, there is simply no need and thus no justification for a discussion of whether the interpretation is entitled to deference. See *Chevron U.S.A. Inc. v. Natural Resources Defense Council, Inc.,* 467 U.S. 837, 842–843 (1984) ("If the intent of Congress is clear, that is the end of the matter; for the court, as well as the agency, must give effect to the unambiguously expressed intent of Congress" (footnote omitted)). Even more unjustifiable, however, is the Court's use of this superfluous discussion as the occasion to express controversial, and I believe erroneous, views on the meaning of this Court's decision in *Chevron.* *Chevron* stated that where there is no "unambiguously expressed intent of Congress," *id.,* at 843, "a court may not substitute its own construction of a statutory provision for a reasonable interpretation made by the administrator of an agency," *id.,* at 844. This Court has consistently interpreted *Chevron*—which has been an extremely important and frequently cited opinion, not only in this Court but in the Courts of Appeals—as holding that courts must give effect to a reasonable agency interpretation of a statute unless that interpretation is inconsistent with a clearly expressed congressional intent. The Court's discussion is flatly inconsistent with this well-established interpretation. The Court first implies that courts may substitute their interpretation of a statute for that of an agency whenever, "[e]mploying traditional tools of statutory construction," they are able to reach a conclusion as to the proper interpretation of the statute. But this approach would make deference a doctrine of desperation, authorizing courts to defer only if they would otherwise be unable to construe the enactment at issue. This is not an interpretation but an evisceration of *Chevron.*

* * *

JUSTICE POWELL, with whom THE CHIEF JUSTICE and JUSTICE WHITE join, dissenting.

Many people come to our country because they fear persecution in their homeland. Congress has provided two forms of relief for such people: asylum, see Immigration and Nationality Act of 1952, § 208(a), and withholding of deportation, see § 243(h). The Board of Immigration Appeals (BIA) has concluded that there is no practical distinction between the objective proofs an alien must submit to be eligible for these two forms of relief. The Court rejects this conclusion. Because I believe the BIA's interpretation of the statute is reasonable, I dissent.

I

The Court's opinion seems to assume that the BIA has adopted a rigorous mathematical approach to asylum cases, requiring aliens to demonstrate an objectively quantifiable risk of persecution in their homeland that is more than 50%. The Court then argues that such a position is inconsistent with the language and history of the Act. But this has never been the BIA's position. Thus, it is useful to examine the BIA's approach in some detail before evaluating the Court's rejection of the BIA's approach. After all, the BIA is the tribunal with the primary responsibility for applying the Act, and the greatest experience in doing so.

The BIA's interpretation of the statutory term "well-founded fear" appears in *Matter of Acosta,* Interim Decision No. 2986 (BIA Mar. 1, 1985). Under the BIA's analysis, an immigration judge evaluating an asylum application should begin by determining the underlying historical facts. The burden of persuasion rests on the applicant, who must establish the truth of these facts by a preponderance of the evidence. See *id.,* at 7 (citing, *inter alia,* 1A C. Gordon & H. Rosenfield, Immigration Law & Procedure § 5.10b, p. 5–121 (rev. ed. 1986)).

Once the immigration judge has decided what historical facts the applicant has demonstrated, he then decides whether those facts meet the definition of "refugee" set forth in § 101(a)(42)(A) of the Act. The major point of contention in this case concerns that section's requirement that the fear be "well-founded." In *Acosta,* the BIA adhered to the interpretation of that language it had developed in *Matter of Dunar,* 14 I. & N. Dec. 310 (1973):

> " '[T]he requirement that the fear be "well-founded" rules out an apprehension which is purely subjective.... Some sort of showing must be made and this can ordinarily be done only by objective evidence. The claimant's own testimony as to the facts will sometimes be all that is available; *but the crucial question is whether the testimony, if accepted as true, makes out a realistic likelihood that he will be persecuted.' '' Acosta, supra,* at 18–19 (quoting *Dunar, supra,* at 319) (emphasis added by *Acosta* Board).

The *Acosta* Board went on to caution:

> "By use of such words [as 'realistic likelihood'] we do not mean that 'a well-founded fear of persecution' requires an alien to establish to a particular degree of certainty, such as a 'probability' as opposed to a 'possibility,' that he will become a victim of persecution. Rather as a practical matter, what we mean can best be described as follows: the evidence must demonstrate that (1) the alien possesses a belief or characteristic a persecutor seeks to overcome in others by means of punishment of some sort; (2) the persecutor is already aware, or could easily become aware, that the alien possesses this belief or characteristic; (3) the persecutor has the capability of punishing the alien; and (4) the persecutor has the inclination to punish the alien." *Acosta, supra,* at 22.

Finally, the *Acosta* opinion compared this "realistic likelihood" standard to the "clear probability" standard applied to applications for withholding of deportation. The BIA's comments are insightful:

[JUSTICE POWELL then quotes from the passage from *Acosta* reprinted *supra,* p. 773.]

In sum, contrary to the Court's apparent conclusion, the BIA does not contend that both the "well-founded fear" standard and the "clear probability" standard require proof of a 51% chance that the alien will suffer persecution if he is returned to his homeland. The BIA plainly eschews analysis resting on mathematical probabilities. Rather, the BIA has adopted a four-part test requiring proof of facts that demonstrate a realistic likelihood of persecution actually occurring. The heart of the *Acosta* decision is the BIA's empirical conclusion, based on its experience in adjudicating asylum applications, that if the facts establish such a basis for an alien's fear, it rarely will make a difference whether the judge asks if persecution is "likely" to occur or "more likely than not" to occur. If the alien can establish such a basis, he normally will be eligible for relief under either standard.

II

* * *

With respect to the issue presented by this case, I find the language far more ambiguous than the Court does. Respondent contends that the BIA has fallen into error by equating the objective showings required under §§ 208(a) and 243(h). The Court notes that the language of § 208(a) differs from the language of § 243(h) in that it contemplates a partially subjective inquiry. From this premise, the Court moves with little explanation to the conclusion that the objective inquiries under the two sections necessarily are different.

In reaching this conclusion, the Court gives short shrift to the words "well-founded," that clearly require some objective basis for the alien's fear. The critical question presented by this case is whether the objective basis required for a fear of persecution to be "well-founded" differs *in practice* from the objective basis required for there to be a "clear probability" of persecution. Because both standards necessarily contemplate some objective basis, I cannot agree with the Court's implicit conclusion that the statute resolves this question on its face. In my view, the character of evidence sufficient to meet these two standards is a question best answered by an entity familiar with the types of evidence and issues that arise in such cases. Congress limited eligibility for asylum to those persons whom "the Attorney General determines" to be refugees. See § 208(a). The Attorney General has delegated the responsibility for making these determinations to the BIA. That Board has examined more of these cases than any court ever has or ever can. It has made a considered judgment that the difference between the "well-founded" and the "clear probability" standards is of no practical import: that is, the evidence presented in asylum and withholding of deportation cases rarely, if ever, will meet one of these standards without meeting both. This is just the type of expert judgment—formed by the entity to whom Congress has committed the question—to which we should defer.

The Court ignores the practical realities recognized by the expert agency and instead concentrates on semantic niceties. It posits a hypothetical situation in which a government sought to execute every 10th adult male. In its view, fear of such executions would be "well-founded" even if persecution of a particular individual would not be "more likely than not" to occur. But this hypothetical is irrelevant; it addresses a mathematically demanding interpretation of "well-founded" that has no relation to the

BIA's actual treatment of asylum applications. Nor does it address the validity of the BIA's judgment that evidence presenting this distinction will be encountered infrequently, if ever.

Common sense and human experience support the BIA's conclusion. Governments rarely persecute people by the numbers. It is highly unlikely that the evidence presented at an asylum or withholding of deportation hearing will demonstrate the mathematically specific risk of persecution posited by the Court's hypothetical. Taking account of the types of evidence normally available in asylum cases, the BIA has chosen to make a *qualitative* evaluation of "realistic likelihoods." As I read the *Acosta* opinion, an individual who fled his country to avoid mass executions might be eligible for both withholding of deportation *and* asylum, whether or not he presented evidence of the numerical reach of the persecution. Nowhere does the Court consider whether the BIA's four-element interpretation of "well-founded" is unreasonable. Nor does the Court consider the BIA's view of the types of evidentiary presentations aliens generally make in asylum cases.

In sum, the words Congress has chosen—"well-founded" fear—are ambiguous. They contemplate some objective basis without specifying a particular evidentiary threshold. There is no reason to suppose this formulation is inconsistent with the analysis set forth in *Acosta*. The BIA has concluded that a fear is not "well-founded" unless the fear has an objective basis indicating that there is a "realistic likelihood" that persecution would occur. Based on the text of the Act alone, I can not conclude that this conclusion is unreasonable.

* * *

Notes

1. The majority and particularly the concurrences are convinced that the "plain language" or "plain meaning" of the two sections mandates a differential standard of proof for §§ 208 and 243(h). The majority emphasizes that the language of § 243(h) is "would," not " 'might' or 'could' be subject to persecution" (footnote 10, quoting *Stevic*). But, as noted earlier, this juxtaposition of the language is not fully responsive to the actual wording.

Section 243(h) extends its protection to aliens whose "life or freedom would be *threatened* " on the specified grounds. Consider the Court's own example of an alien returning to a country where the government is killing or jailing every tenth adult male. Assuming that the alien is a male, obviously he has a well-founded fear of persecution on return. But how does the plain language of § 243(h) apply here? Wouldn't we say with equal conviction that this man's life or freedom would be *threatened* on return?

2. In part IV of its opinion, the Court cites *Matter of Salim, supra,* in support of its holding that asylum under § 208 should be held open to a wider class of applicants than is § 243(h). After all, the Court emphasizes, not all who meet the threshold of the refugee definition will achieve

asylum. Asylum remains discretionary, and *Salim,* in the Court's view, illustrates the importance of the distinction between mandatory and discretionary provisions.

But the Court seems to have overlooked an important difference between the setting of *Salim* and *Cardoza–Fonseca*—a difference that demonstrates a troubling gap in the law following *Stevic* and *Cardoza–Fonseca*. *Cardoza–Fonseca*, unlike *Salim*, was ruled ineligible for § 243(h) relief under the more demanding standard approved in *Stevic*. She is no longer challenging that decision. If, upon remand, she is found to be a refugee but denied asylum in the exercise of discretion, she faces serious consequences. Unlike *Salim*, she can call on no mandatory provision of law to shield her against return to the country where she fears persecution, and where, upon this hypothesis, the adjudicators consider her fear well-founded. Denying asylum to Salim means only that he may be sent to a third country, or failing that, may remain here in an uncertain legal limbo without a secure immigration status. It is not a happy state of affairs, but at least the law keeps him away from his potential persecutors. Apparently the Supreme Court now countenances returning a recognized "refugee," provided that she falls short of the standard for § 243(h). Is this sound policy? Is it what Congress had in mind? Would the drafters of the UN treaties have intended to permit such a result? Isn't Article 33's protection against *refoulement* the *raison d'être* for an international scheme of refugee protection? Or are there other policy objectives that might account for the distinction the Court draws?

3. The Court in *Cardoza–Fonseca* writes: "That the fear must be 'well-founded' does not alter the obvious focus on the individual's subjective beliefs." (Other parts of the opinion, however, lay greater stress on objective risks.) The UNHCR's *Handbook on Procedures and Criteria for Determining Refugee Status* goes somewhat further, placing a relatively strong emphasis on the subjective component of the definition in its advice on how to determine refugee status. The Handbook states:

> The term "well-founded fear" * * * contains a subjective and an objective element, and in determining whether well-founded fear exists, both elements must be taken into consideration. * * * The subjective character of fear of persecution requires an evaluation of the opinions and feelings of the person concerned. It is also in the light of such opinions and feelings that any actual or anticipated measures against him must necessarily be viewed. Due to variations in the psychological make-up of individuals and in the circumstances of each case, interpretations of what amounts to persecution are bound to vary.[29]

29. Office of the United Nations High Commissioner for Refugees, *Handbook on Procedures and Criteria for Determining Refugee Status* 12, 14 (2d ed. 1988; UN Sales No. HCR/IP/4/Eng.Rev. 1). This Handbook has played an important role in U.S. asylum practice, having been cited on various occasions by the Board and the courts as an authoritative guide to relevant standards under the UN treaties and hence under U.S. law. Nevertheless the preface to the Handbook states that the work "has been conceived as a practical guide and not as a treatise on refugee law," *id.* at 1, and some of the guidelines as they emerged from the UN committee process are so painstakingly balanced

Is this a sound way to administer the asylum provisions of the immigration laws? Did Congress intend immigration judges to expend adjudication resources on close inquiry into the psychological makeup of individual applicants? Shouldn't equivalent showings of objective risk lead to equal results, whatever the varying states of mind of the claimants? In his treatise on the refugee definition, Professor Hathaway argues that attention to subjective fears "is neither historically defensible nor practically meaningful." Examining the drafting history, he concludes:

> While the word "fear" may imply a form of emotional response, it may also be used to signal an anticipatory appraisal of risk. That is, a person may fear a particular event in the sense that she apprehends that it may occur, yet she may or may not * * * stand in trepidation of it actually taking place. * * * [T]he term "fear" was employed to mandate a forward-looking assessment of risk, not to require an examination of the emotional reaction of the claimant.

J. Hathaway, The Law of Refugee Status 65–66 (1991).

c. The BIA's Response to Cardoza–Fonseca

The Board moved quickly to conform its practice to *Cardoza–Fonseca*. In *Matter of Mogharrabi*, 19 I & N Dec. 439 (BIA 1987), it took note of the Supreme Court's direction that the standards for §§ 208 and 243(h) are "significantly different." 480 U.S., at 448 n. 31, 107 S.Ct. at 1222 n. 31. It then surveyed the efforts of earlier lower court decisions to describe that difference. A small portion of that survey is reprinted here, along with the approach the Board ultimately selected (*id.* at 444–47):

> In *Diaz–Escobar v. INS*, 782 F.2d 1488 (9th Cir.1986), the Ninth Circuit attempted to refine its requirement that there be both subjective and objective showings, * * * [concluding] "[w]hat is critical is that the alien prove his fear is subjectively genuine and objectively reasonable." The inquiry into the reasonableness of an applicant's fear was also alluded to by the Ninth Circuit in *Garcia–Ramos v. INS*, 775 F.2d 1370 (9th Cir.1985), where the court stated that the well-founded fear standard "implicates a requirement of objective reasonableness. In other words, there must be some basis in reality or reasonable possibility that a petitioner would be persecuted."

* * *

> [T]he Fifth Circuit offered a somewhat more concrete definition. The court held, "[a]n alien possesses a well-founded fear of persecution if a reasonable person in her circumstances would fear persecution if she were to be returned to her native country." [*Guevara Flores v. INS*, 786 F.2d 1242, 1249 (5th Cir.1986).] This reasonable person standard was subsequently adopted by the Second Circuit, in *Carcamo–Flores v. INS*, 805 F.2d 60 (2d Cir.1986).

as to be of little utility. *See* Martin, *supra* note 21, at 1283 n. 100.

We agree with and adopt the general approach set forth by the Fifth Circuit; that is, that an applicant for asylum has established a well-founded fear if he shows that a reasonable person in his circumstances would fear persecution. As noted by the Second Circuit, this "reasonable person standard appropriately captures the various formulations that have been advanced to explain the well-founded fear test." *Carcamo–Flores v. INS*, [805 F.2d 60, 68 (2d Cir.1986)]. It is a standard that provides a "common sense" framework for analyzing whether claims of persecution are well-founded. Moreover, a reasonable person may well fear persecution even where its likelihood is significantly less than clearly probable.

* * *

Where the country at issue in an asylum case has a history of persecuting people in circumstances similar to the asylum applicant's, careful consideration should be given to that fact in assessing the applicant's claims. A well-founded fear, in other words, can be based on what has happened to others who are similarly situated. The situation of each person, however, must be assessed on its own merits.

We note that although our decision in *Matter of Acosta*[, 19 I & N Dec. 211 (BIA 1985),] has been effectively overruled by *INS v. Cardoza–Fonseca*, insofar as *Acosta* held that the well-founded fear standard and the clear probability standard may be equated, much of our decision remains intact, and good law. Indeed, we still find in *Acosta* some guidance regarding the meaning of a well-founded fear. In *Acosta*, we set forth four elements which an applicant for asylum must show in order to establish a well-founded fear of persecution. What we required was that the evidence establish that

> (1) the alien possesses a belief or characteristic a persecutor seeks to overcome in others by means of punishment of some sort; (2) the persecutor is already aware, or could easily become aware, that the alien possesses this belief or characteristic; (3) the persecutor has the capability of punishing the alien; and (4) the persecutor has the inclination to punish the alien.

Matter of Acosta, supra, at 226.

In our view, these requirements, for the most part, survive the Supreme Court's decision in *Cardoza–Fonseca*, and are still useful guidelines in assessing an asylum application. However, we have determined that one small but significant change in these requirements should be made in view of the Court's ruling. The second requirement should be changed by omitting the word "easily." Thus, it is enough for the applicant to show that the persecutor could become aware that the applicant possesses the belief or characteristic in question. The omission of the word easily lightens the applicant's burden of proof and moves the requirements as a whole into line with *Cardoza–Fonseca*. Of course, all these requirements must now be considered in light of the lower burden of proof which will be imposed on asylum applicants generally.

It must also be remembered that an alien who succeeds in establishing a well-founded fear of persecution will not necessarily be granted asylum. He must also show that the feared persecution would be on account of his race, religion, nationality, membership in a particular social group, or political opinion. Thus, for example, aliens fearing retribution over purely personal matters, or aliens fleeing general conditions of violence and upheaval in their countries, would not qualify for asylum. Such persons may have well-founded fears, but such fears would not be on account of their race, religion, nationality, membership in a particular social group, or political opinion. Finally, an applicant for asylum must also show that he merits the relief as a matter of discretion.

While under *Matter of Acosta, supra,* we were able to consider an application for asylum and withholding of deportation as, for most purposes, one, this approach requires some modification after *INS v. Cardoza–Fonseca, supra.* Given that the core of evidence and testimony presented in support of the asylum and withholding applications will in almost every case be virtually the same, such evidence and testimony may still be presented in a single hearing. However, in actually adjudicating the applications, a clear delineation of the findings should be made as to each application. We anticipate that as a general rule the asylum application, with its lower burden of proof, will be adjudicated first. If the applicant is found eligible for asylum, and worthy of the relief as a matter of discretion, there may be no need to determine as well whether a clear probability of persecution exists.

Exercise

The readings above have covered a variety of formulations of the standard for claiming asylum-type protections under § 208 or § 243(h). They can probably be grouped as follows, from the most demanding to the least, although some of the rankings are arguable:

1. A. clear probability of persecution

    B. persecution is more likely than not

2. well-founded fear of persecution, understood as:

    A. reasonable possibility of persecution

    B. good reason to fear persecution

    C. a reasonable person in such circumstances would fear persecution upon return to the homeland. *Mogharrabi*

Test your understanding of the various versions and their implications for concrete cases by applying them to the following hypotheticals.

Hypothetical A. (1) Alien A was a local leader in a teacher's organization that began a campaign of criticism against the authoritarian government in Ruritania and called for democratic reforms. The government has denounced the protests, but so far has done nothing further.

(2) Same facts, but now the Ruritanian government has shown some signs that it will crack down on opponents. So far, however, it has arrested only labor union leaders.

(3) Same facts, but Ruritania now branches out beyond labor leaders and seizes three top officials at the national level in the teacher's organization, holding them without charge for 10 days, then releasing them. Local leaders have not been bothered.

Hypothetical B. (1) Alien B was a simple farmer in Montana province in Fredonia. That province has just come under the control of a local militia chief who has a reputation for ruling with an iron hand.

(2) Same facts, but now B adds that the bodies of two activists were found, decapitated, on the main street of the province's capital city shortly before he left for the United States.

(3) Same facts, but B adds that he attended an antigovernment demonstration three years ago at which the two activists gave a speech.

(4) Same facts, but B adds that he helped organize that demonstration, although he has been inactive since then.

(5) Same facts, but B adds that he was a lower-echelon leader in the organization to which the two activists belonged.

Questions

Do you find some discontinuities between the "reasonable person" standard of *Mogharrabi* and the "persecution is a reasonable possibility" formulation that appears in *Cardoza–Fonseca?* Isn't it possible that a reasonable person would harbor a fear of persecution on return to the homeland, even if the risk of persecution was not such that outside observers would label it a "reasonable possibility?" Wouldn't any reasonable person have some fear of persecution if returning to Guatemala, Peru, or Iran? To what extent do the policy considerations canvassed in Section A, *supra,* properly play a role in deciding when a possibility of persecution should be labeled "reasonable"—that is, in setting the threshold degree-of-threat requirement higher or lower before holding that a claimed fear of persecution is well-founded? Is it appropriate to lower the threshold in times when applicant numbers are low and raise it to limit asylum grants or deter asylum seekers in times of high influx?

d. Current Standards

Before *Stevic* and *Cardoza–Fonseca,* the Board routinely announced a requirement that the applicant for asylum "must demonstrate a likelihood that he individually will be singled out and subjected to persecution." *Matter of Sibrun,* 18 I & N Dec. 354, 358 (BIA 1983). Numerous court decisions, both before and after those Supreme Court decisions, have likewise employed the "singling out" formulation, or similar ones like "a specific threat to the petitioner." See, e.g., *Carvajal–Munoz v. INS,* 743 F.2d 562, 573–74 (7th Cir.1984); *Artiga Turcios v. INS,* 829 F.2d 720, 723 (9th Cir.1987); *Cruz–Lopez v. INS,* 802 F.2d 1518, 1521 (4th Cir.1986) (all three using the "singled out" language); *Ananeh–Firempong v. INS,* 766 F.2d 621, 627 (1st Cir.1985) ("specific threat"). In *Ananeh–Firempong,* Judge Breyer explained the policy reasons underlying such requirements:

> [W]e recognize the need to require an alien * * * to offer reasonably specific information showing a real threat of individual persecution. Otherwise, given the unfortunately large number of repressive governments throughout the world, Congress's offer of haven to refugees present in the United States could severely weaken its more general legislative effort to impose overall limitations upon immigration.

Id. at 627 (applied specifically to § 243(h) relief, but the policy considerations are relevant also to § 208). The Seventh Circuit has also pursued this theme: "the requirement that an asylum applicant demonstrate that he or she has a reasonable fear of being *singled out* for persecution 'is no doubt driven by Congress' concern that a more lenient and compassionate policy would qualify the entire population of many war torn nations for asylum.' " *Milosevic v. INS,* 18 F.3d 366, 373–74 (7th Cir.1994), quoting *Sivaainkaran v. INS,* 972 F.2d 161, 165 (7th Cir.1992).

Is the singling out test still appropriate after *Cardoza–Fonseca,* or is it too stringent? If not, what level of individualized threat would you require? For a thorough consideration, see Blum, *The Ninth Circuit, and the Protection of Asylum Seekers Since the Passage of the Refugee Act of 1980,* 23 San Diego L.Rev. 327, 343 (1986).

The 1990 Regulations

The 1990 asylum regulations incorporated new substantive standards for establishing refugee status and thus meeting the threshold requirement for asylum under § 208. They largely avoid use of the BIA's formulation asking whether a "reasonable person in [the asylum applicant's] circumstances would fear persecution." Instead the central element in the asylum standard set by the regulations asks whether "there is a reasonable possibility of actually suffering such persecution if he were to return to [the home] country." 8 C.F.R. § 208.13(b)(2). The provision also rejects the "singling out" requirement, if the applicant shows a pattern or practice of "persecution of groups of persons similarly situated to the applicant" and "establishes his own inclusion in and identification with such group of persons such that his fear of persecution upon return is reasonable." *Id.* A similar rejection of "singling out" applies to withholding of deportation under § 243(h), although in the context of an overarching requirement that the applicant for withholding show that "it is more likely than not that he would be persecuted on account of race, religion, nationality, membership in a particular social group, or political opinion." *Id.* § 208.16.

[margin annotation: SHIFTS FOCUS FROM INDIV. TO GROUP]

Check the language relating to the "singling out" standard in 8 C.F.R. §§ 208.13 and 208.16 carefully, in order to consider the following decision. In *Kotasz v. INS,* 31 F.3d 847, 850 (9th Cir.1994), the applicant was a Hungarian who had been frequently arrested in the 1980s for anti-communist activities and beaten during detention. The BIA rejected his claim with these words: "there is no evidence in the record that [he] was singled out for persecution—rather he was arrested with numerous other demonstrators and incarcerated for a short period of time." Under the regulations, is the BIA decision legally correct? For a highly useful discussion of the singling out standard and the relevance of group membership in many types of asylum claims, see the court's decision in *Kotasz*.

Past Persecution

The central question in asylum adjudication is essentially forward-looking, trying to determine what is likely to happen to the individual in the future if he returns to the home country. *See* J. Hathaway, The Law of Refugee Status 65–80 (1991). But past persecution may of course hold great relevance in making this difficult prediction; applicants frequently spend considerable time describing threats or mistreatment they or others like them received before their departure. The Board considered certain issues involving past persecution in *Matter of Chen*, Int.Dec. 3104 (BIA 1989):

> If an alien establishes that he has been persecuted in the past for one of the five reasons listed in the statute, he is eligible for a grant of asylum. The likelihood of present or future persecution then becomes relevant as to the exercise of discretion, and asylum may be denied as a matter of discretion if there is little likelihood of present persecution.

Id. at 4. The Board went on to state that proof of past persecution establishes a rebuttable presumption that the individual has reason to fear persecution in the future.

The 1990 regulations codified the Board's evidentiary approach:

> If it is determined that the applicant has established past persecution, he shall be presumed also to have a well-founded fear of persecution unless a preponderance of the evidence establishes that since the time the persecution occurred conditions in the applicant's country of nationality or last habitual residence have changed to such an extent that the applicant no longer has a well-founded fear of being persecuted if he were to return.

8 C.F.R. § 208.13(b)(1)(i).

Moreover, in U.S. law past persecution is of more than evidentiary value in making predictions about future danger. To begin with, the statute appears to be more favorable toward claims based solely on past persecution than is the UN Convention. The INA definition recognizes refugee status when one is outside the country of origin "because of *persecution or* a well-founded fear of persecution." INA § 101(a)(42)(A) (emphasis added). Compare the phrasing of the definition in Article 1(A)(2) of the Convention. Does U.S. law then contravene the treaty? Consider in this connection subsections (5) and (6) of Article 1(C). Are they relevant? *See generally Skalak v. INS*, 944 F.2d 364 (7th Cir.1991) (Posner, J.).

The regulations further clarify the possibility of asylum for those who have suffered past persecution even if it is clear that they are not endangered in the future. As a matter of initial authorization, they provide: "An applicant *shall* be found to be a refugee * * * if he can establish that he has suffered persecution in the past in [his home country] * * * and that he is unable or unwilling to return * * * owing to such persecution." 8 C.F.R. § 208.13(b)(1) (emphasis added). Discretionary denial of asylum to such a "refugee" is nonetheless possible (*id.* § 208.13(b)(1)(ii)):

> An application for asylum shall be denied if the applicant establishes past persecution under this paragraph but is determined not also to have a well-founded fear of future persecution * * *, unless it is determined that the applicant has demonstrated compelling reasons for being unwilling to return to his [home country] arising out of the severity of the past persecution.

This provision is consistent with *Chen*, where the BIA ruled that in some circumstances, even if there is little likelihood of future persecution, asylum may be warranted for humanitarian reasons, particularly if the past persecution was "atrocious." Int.Dec. 3104, at 5. In the *Chen* case itself, the Board concluded that asylum was merited, owing largely to the harsh treatment that the applicant and his family had received in the 1960s and 1970s at the hands of the Red Guards during the Cultural Revolution in the People's Republic of China.

In the years since 1990, past persecution has become an even more prominent focus in asylum cases under the terms of these regulations. Moreover, perhaps because of the many striking changes of government that have recently taken place throughout the world, a substantial number of applicants invoke the "compelling reasons" provision. What might be "compelling reasons" for a grant of asylum when there is little risk of future persecution? If asylum is denied in the exercise of discretion, does past persecution, without any future threat, guarantee *nonrefoulement* protection under INA § 243(h)?

3. DISCRETIONARY DENIALS OF ASYLUM UNDER § 208

The Supreme Court in *Cardoza–Fonseca* considered it anomalous that the Attorney General wished to confine to a narrow class of aliens his ability to exercise the discretion granted him by INA § 208. After our discussion of discretion in Chapter Seven, this stance may not seem so curious to you. (Sometimes discretion is a burden, and administrators might well prefer bright-line rules that make a difficult decision process more straightforward.) But in any event, the Court relied heavily on the discretionary nature of that section in explaining why Congress would provide a more generous standard as the test for § 208's "greater form of relief."

a. *Early Administrative Use of Discretion Under § 208*

The BIA has taken various approaches toward the exercise of such discretion, and its doctrines have, as usual, met with a mixed reception in the courts of appeals. The first significant case was *Matter of Salim,* 18

I & N Dec. 311 (BIA 1982), discussed briefly at p. 770 *supra*. The alien was from Afghanistan, but he had spent some time in Pakistan and came to the United States on fraudulently acquired papers. The Board found that he qualified for § 243(h) withholding, because of the persecution threatened in Afghanistan, and met the eligibility requirement for asylum under § 208. But emphasizing that asylum relief is a matter of discretion, it held:

> Attempting entry into the United States by way of fraudulently obtained documentation has consistently been considered a strong negative discretionary factor. * * * [T]he public interest requires that we do not condone this applicant's attempt to circumvent the orderly procedures that our government has provided for refugees to immigrate lawfully. The fraudulent passport was obtained after the applicant had escaped from Afghanistan, with the sole purpose of reaching this country ahead of all the other refugees awaiting their turn abroad. This is not the case where an alien was forced to resort to fraudulently obtained documentation in order to escape or prevent being returned to the country in which he fears persecution. *See Matter of Ng,* 17 I & N Dec. 536 (BIA 1980). This Board finds that the fraudulent avoidance of the orderly refugee procedures that this country has established is an extremely adverse factor which can only be overcome with the most unusual showing of countervailing equities. This case before us does not present such equities. Consequently, the application for asylum relief will be denied as a matter of discretion.

18 I & N Dec. at 315–16.

The chief reason for the Board's unfavorable exercise of discretion with respect to asylum under § 208 was Salim's "fraudulent avoidance of the orderly refugee procedures this country has established." This statement implies that Salim's default consisted of jumping the queue—that if he had simply waited his turn he could have immigrated as part of our overseas refugee programs for Afghans. But there were over two million Afghan refugees in Pakistan at the time of Salim's departure. Only a few thousand U.S. resettlement spaces were being provided each year for this population, governed by specific screening criteria and selection priorities. It is likely that Salim would never have qualified, no matter how patient he might have been.

A high percentage of aliens who apply for asylum, moreover, will be out of compliance with the regular provisions of our laws—thus will have "misused our immigration laws to gain an advantage over all other similarly situated" persons. *Salim, supra,* at 314. Can this factor then serve as a justifiable basis for an unfavorable exercise of discretion under § 208?

Most asylum applicants, however, will not have even a remote prospect of going to a third country if their applications for asylum are denied. In the overwhelming majority of cases, the only options consist of indefinite stay in the United States or else return to the country of nationality. Is the possible availability of a return to Pakistan here a justifiable ground for denying Salim asylum under § 208, even though relief under § 243(h) is granted? What should happen to Salim if Pakistan refuses to accept his return and no other country, other than Afghanistan, will take him in? May he be held in detention in the United States indefinitely? Check Article 31 of the UN Convention. Does it provide much assistance in answering this question?

In some cases, INS sent Afghan nationals back to India or Pakistan, accompanied by U.S. agents, but without the ordinarily requisite documents, in an effort to secure their return. INS took this somewhat unusual step because those two countries would rarely agree in advance to take such persons off the hands of a wealthy North American or European country, and so would not provide travel documents, but often would accept the Afghans once they actually arrived. If the country refused the landing, however, individuals might fly back and forth several times before the sending country abandoned its efforts. *See generally Walai v. United States INS,* 552 F.Supp. 998 (S.D.N.Y.1982); *Amanullah v. Cobb,* 862 F.2d 362 (1st Cir.1988). Similar episodes in Europe (antedating the Afghan crisis), usually involving disputes over which country was the "country of first asylum," gave birth to a label for such standoffs: "refugees in orbit." *See* Melander, *Refugees in Orbit,* 16 A.W.R. Bull. 59 (1978); Vierdag, *The Country of "First Asylum": Some European Aspects,* in The New Asylum Seekers, *supra* note 3, at 73.

Those Afghans not accepted for return by India or Pakistan faced a prospect of indefinite detention in the United States, in view of their excludable status and the denial of asylum under § 208. Following litigation, INS eventually developed policy guidelines authorizing—but not mandating—release after 30 days of individuals protected by § 243(h) for whom return to a country other than the country of nationality cannot be arranged. *See Singh v. Nelson,* 623 F.Supp. 545, 552 (S.D.N.Y.1985); 60 Interp.Rel. 536 (1983); Helton, *The Proper Role of Discretion in Political Asylum Determinations,* 22 San Diego L.Rev. 999, 1009 (1985). The 1990 asylum regulations also mandate reconsideration, in certain circumstances, of a discretionary asylum denial to those who qualify for withholding under § 243(h), when there are limited opportunities for the alien to go to a third country. 8 C.F.R. § 208.16(c)(4).

b. Discretion, According to the Ninth Circuit

In *Hernandez–Ortiz v. INS,* 777 F.2d 509, 519 (9th Cir.1985), the court took a much more limited view than did the BIA in *Salim* of legitimate grounds for denying asylum in the exercise of discretion.

We have not previously delineated the factors, or "legitimate concerns" that the Board may consider when denying asylum to an alien who has established refugee status. We note, however, that 8 C.F.R. § 208.8(f)(1) (1985) lists a small number of factors that require the denial of relief, *e.g.,* "the alien, having been convicted by a final judgment of a particularly serious crime, constitutes a danger to the community of the United States." [a]

---

a. This paragraph of the regulations at the time, 8 C.F.R. § 208.8(f)(1) (1985), restated, virtually word for word, the exceptions to nonrefoulement protection set forth in § 243(h)(2) (which you may wish to consult at this point). It also added two other

The regulation also specifies one factor that would justify the discretionary denial of asylum: "there is an outstanding offer of resettlement by a third nation where the applicant will not be subject to persecution and the applicant's resettlement in a third nation is in the public interest." 8 C.F.R. § 208.8(f)(2) (1985). The factors mentioned in section 208.8 of the regulations are substantial factors involving the national interest or the welfare of the community, or they are factors relating to the existence of other means of ensuring the safety and security of the alien. Although we need not, at this time, define precisely the kinds of legitimate concerns that may serve as a basis for the Board's determinations, it would appear that, where the Board has not identified an alternative source of refuge, it can deny asylum only on the basis of genuine compelling factors—factors important enough to warrant returning a bona fide refugee to a country where he may face a threat of imminent danger to his life or liberty.

Hernandez–Ortiz obviously contemplates a very limited role for discretionary denials of asylum, unless it is clear that the alien can be sent to a safe third country. But *Hernandez–Ortiz* was decided two years before the Supreme Court's decision in *Cardoza–Fonseca*. The Supreme Court's vision of the Attorney General's discretion under § 208 appears considerably more capacious. In its closing paragraph, *supra*, the Court emphasizes that its holding "increases" the government's "flexibility" to respond to situations involving persecution throughout the world. Does this language effectively overrule the limits on discretionary denials of asylum that the Ninth Circuit imposed in *Hernandez–Ortiz?*

In this connection, imagine that the Department of Justice issued the following hypothetical press release:

The Attorney General announced today that the INS will promulgate regulations denying asylum, in the exercise of discretion, to all nationals of Afghanistan, Guatemala, and El Salvador. Afghani nationals, although they claim our sympathy, have access to secure asylum in the immediate region, and should not be allowed to circumvent our orderly procedures for immigration and overseas refugee processing. With respect to Guatemala and El Salvador, democratically elected governments there are making every effort to curb human rights abuses and build a solid future for all their citizens. These efforts should not be undercut by siphoning off productive members of the population to this country, causing a "brain drain." Moreover, recent large increases in the number of asylum applicants in the United States require us to reserve our limited capacity to provide asylum for those most gravely endangered, such as those who meet the more demanding

factors mandating denial of asylum: (1) if the alien does not meet the refugee definition (an unnecessary provision, as he then would not qualify for asylum in any event), and (2) if the alien has been firmly resettled in a for-

eign country. The 1990 and 1994 asylum regulations recast the provisions for mandatory and discretionary denial, which now appear in 8 C.F.R. § 208.14.—eds.

test of INA § 243(h) by showing a "clear probability of persecution."

In every possible case, but with due regard to the requirements of § 243(h), persons in the categories mentioned above will be promptly deported.

Would such a policy be lawful under *Cardoza–Fonseca?* Would it be lawful under *Hernandez–Ortiz?* What judicially imposed limits on discretionary denials of asylum, if any, would be consistent with *Cardoza–Fonseca?*

c. The BIA's Approach to Discretion After Cardoza-Fonseca

Some observers worried that the Board would respond to *Cardoza–Fonseca* by tightening the standards for discretionary grants of asylum. *See* Anker & Blum, *New Trends in Asylum Jurisprudence: The Aftermath of the U.S. Supreme Court Decision in INS v. Cardoza–Fonseca,* 1 Int'l J. Refugee L. 67 (1989). Such an approach might result in large-scale deportation of persons found to meet the definition of "refugee" but who failed to qualify for nonrefoulement under § 243(h). Or, if the claimants did satisfy the latter standards, following a discretionary denial they would fall into the legal limbo that awaits such people, given that the United States has little chance of sending them to third countries. *See generally* Anker, *Discretionary Asylum: A Protection Remedy for Refugees under the Refugee Act of 1980,* 28 Va.J.Int'l L. 1 (1987).

The Board's approach, however, has trended in the opposite direction. Shortly after *Mogharrabi,* the Board issued the following decision, importantly modifying some of the doctrine of *Salim.*

MATTER OF PULA

Board of Immigration Appeals, 1987.
19 I & N Dec. 467.

In a decision dated December 1, 1986, the immigration judge found the applicant excludable [for misrepresentation and lack of required documents]. He granted the applicant's applications for withholding of deportation to Albania and Yugoslavia under section 243(h) of the Act, but he denied the applicant's application for asylum under section 208 of the Act and ordered that the applicant be excluded and deported from the United States. The applicant has appealed from the denial of his application for asylum. The Immigration and Naturalization Service has appealed from the grant of the application for withholding of deportation to Yugoslavia. The applicant's appeal will be sustained, and the Service's appeal will be dismissed.

The applicant is a 26–year–old married male native of Albania and citizen of Yugoslavia. He arrived in the United States on June 5, 1986, and was placed in exclusion proceedings. The applicant does not contest on appeal his excludability under * * * the Act. We are satisfied from a review of the record that the applicant received a fair hearing and that his excludability has been clearly established. The only issues to be decided by

ISSUE

the present appeal are whether the immigration judge's denial of asylum and grant of withholding of deportation to Yugoslavia were proper.

The applicant testified that he was born in Albania and fled to Yugoslavia with his family as a refugee when he was 5 years old. He said that he left Yugoslavia in 1986 to avoid further encounters with police officials who, on numerous occasions since 1979, had detained, interrogated, and physically abused him for hours or days at a time. He stated that the police insisted that he was involved in the political activities of the Albanian minority in Yugoslavia, although he denied the accusation. He said that the police sought information from him about such matters as his contacts with his Albanian family and friends, Albanian anti-government demonstrations, and discussions among local Albanian university students. He also testified that one of the periods of detention occurred in 1982 after he approached Yugoslav authorities to request travel documents to visit his sister in the United States. The applicant explained that the police accused him of planning to go to the United States to participate in anti-Yugoslav demonstrations with Albanians here.

The applicant further advised that in 1985 Yugoslav authorities did issue him a titre de voyage[2] so he could travel out of the country, but the American Embassy denied his application for a visa. According to the applicant, he was told at the embassy that the titre de voyage did not guarantee his return to Yugoslavia. The applicant testified that he subsequently relinquished his refugee status and reluctantly accepted Yugoslav citizenship in order to qualify for a Yugoslav passport. He said that he left Yugoslavia on April 20, 1986, as soon as he managed to obtain the passport. He stated that he took a train to Brussels, Belgium, although he had made application to Yugoslav authorities only for permission to visit Turkey. He testified that he believed that the authorities would have denied him the passport if they had known that he intended to go to the United States. He also said that he was afraid to apply again for a visa at the American Embassy because most of the employees there were Yugoslav nationals who might be agents for the Government of Yugoslavia.

In addition, the applicant testified that he stayed in Brussels for 6 weeks with a man who had been a friend of his family in Albania and Yugoslavia. He said that his friend made a telephone call on his behalf to a refugee organization in Italy to inquire about whether he could obtain residency in an Italian refugee camp. According to the applicant, his friend was informed by the organization that citizens of Yugoslavia were not accepted as refugees in European states. The applicant also said that while he was in Brussels he applied for a tourist visa at the American Embassy, but his application was denied and he was told to go to Yugoslavia to apply for a visa. He testified that he did not ask for asylum[a] at the American Embassy because he did not know that he could do so.

2. A titre de voyage is a travel document issued in lieu of a passport under provisions of the United Nations Convention Relating to the Status of Refugees, July 28, 1951, 189 U.N.T.S. 150.

a. Technically, he could ask there only to be included in the U.S. overseas refugee program, not for asylum.—eds.

The applicant also stated that one day while he was discussing his situation in an Albanian coffee house in Belgium, a stranger there offered to sell him a titre de voyage for $1,000. He said that he gave the man his photograph and paid him the money 2 days later, when he returned with a titre de voyage issued by the Government of Belgium which had a tourist visa to the United States already entered. The applicant advised that the titre de voyage had been issued in the name of someone whom he did not know.

The applicant further testified that on June 5, 1986, he flew with his titre de voyage from Belgium to New York. He said that during a 2–to 3–hour stopover at the airport in Amsterdam, he mailed his Yugoslav passport to a cousin in the United States to avoid having it in his possession when he landed in New York. He explained that his inability to speak English made him concerned that immigration officials might discover the passport and put him on a plane to Yugoslavia before he could tell them about his desire for asylum. The applicant also stated that he did not dispose of the Yugoslav passport altogether because he planned to use it later to corroborate his account of events for his asylum request. In addition, the applicant advised that when he arrived in New York, language differences did in fact prevent him and the immigration officer from communicating and, as a result, he did not tell the officer anything or sign any statements.

The applicant also testified that he chose to flee to the United States because he had relatives here. He stated that he had a sister and two uncles who were lawful permanent residents of the United States, and cousins who were United States citizens. He further advised that his wife, who was still living in Yugoslavia with their daughter, also had an uncle and cousins in the United States. The record reflects that many of the applicant's relatives traveled from such places as upstate New York, Texas, and California on multiple occasions to attend the applicant's hearings in New York City.

In his decision, the immigration judge stated that if the facts as described by the applicant were true, they established without a doubt that the applicant had been persecuted in the past and faced a clear probability of persecution in the future. The immigration judge then made a specific finding that the applicant's testimony was credible, noting that he had observed the applicant testify for approximately 8 hours over a period of 2 days. He accordingly found that the applicant had established his eligibility for withholding of deportation to Yugoslavia and Albania. The immigration judge further found, however, that the applicant was not eligible for asylum as a matter of discretion because the equity of his many relatives legally in the United States did not overcome the adverse factor of his having sought admission to the United States by use of a purchased travel document.

* * *

We find no merit in the assertion by the Service that the immigration judge erred in assessing the applicant's credibility. The immigration judge found the applicant to be credible after observing his demeanor and listening to his testimony for 8 hours over a period of 2 days. The finding of an immigration judge with respect to the credibility of witnesses appearing before him will ordinarily be given great weight. *Wing Ding Chan v. INS,* 631 F.2d 978 (D.C.Cir.1980), *cert. denied,* 450 U.S. 921 (1981); *Vasquez–Mondragon v. INS,* 560 F.2d 1225 (5th Cir.1977); *Matter of Magana,* 17 I & N Dec. 111 (BIA 1979); *Matter of Teng,* 15 I & N Dec. 516 (BIA 1975); *Matter of T–,* 7 I & N Dec. 417 (BIA 1957). We have carefully examined the record in this case and conclude that the immigration judge's determination is correct. In view of the detail, consistency, and candor of the applicant's lengthy testimony, we do not find that his credibility is impeached by the minor discrepancies in his written asylum application, which was prepared with the assistance of interpreters.

We further agree with the immigration judge's conclusion that if the applicant's testimony is true, it establishes that the applicant has been persecuted. We have considered the Service's argument that some of the actions of Yugoslav authorities towards the applicant, *i.e.,* granting him citizenship and issuing him a passport, appear inconsistent with an intent to persecute. Yet because the record reflects that those authorities nevertheless have persecuted the applicant, these apparent inconsistencies in treatment provide an insufficient basis, under the facts of this case, for rejecting the applicant's persecution claim. We conclude, therefore, that a reasonable person in the applicant's circumstances would fear persecution if returned to Yugoslavia, and that the applicant has established his statutory eligibility for asylum.

We turn now to the issue of whether the applicant merits asylum in the exercise of discretion. In *Matter of Salim,* [18 I & N Dec. 311 (BIA 1982),] we denied asylum as a matter of discretion to an alien who was excludable * * * and who attempted to circumvent the orderly procedures provided for refugees to immigrate lawfully. We found the fraudulent avoidance of orderly refugee procedures to be an extremely adverse factor which could only be overcome with the most unusual showing of countervailing equities.

* * *

[W]hile we find that an alien's manner of entry or attempted entry is a proper and relevant discretionary factor to consider in adjudicating asylum applications, we agree with the applicant that *Matter of Salim, supra,* places too much emphasis on the circumvention of orderly refugee procedures. This circumvention can be a serious adverse factor, but it should not be considered in such a way that the practical effect is to deny relief in virtually all cases. This factor is only one of a number of factors which should be balanced in exercising discretion, and the weight accorded to this factor may vary depending on the facts of a particular case. We therefore withdraw from *Matter of Salim* insofar as it suggests that the circumvention of orderly refugee procedures alone is sufficient to require the most unusual showing of countervailing equities.

Instead of focusing only on the circumvention of orderly refugee procedures, the totality of the circumstances and actions of an alien in his flight from the country where he fears persecution should be examined in determining whether a favorable exercise of discretion is warranted. Among those factors which should be considered are whether the alien passed through any other countries or arrived in the United States directly from his country, whether orderly refugee procedures were in fact available to help him in any country he passed through, and whether he made any attempts to seek asylum before coming to the United States. In addition, the length of time the alien remained in a third country, and his living conditions, safety, and potential for long-term residency there are also relevant. For example, an alien who is forced to remain in hiding to elude persecutors, or who faces imminent deportation back to the country where he fears persecution, may not have found a safe haven even though he has escaped to another country. Further, whether the alien has relatives legally in the United States or other personal ties to this country which motivated him to seek asylum here rather than elsewhere is another factor to consider. In this regard, the extent of the alien's ties to any other countries where he does not fear persecution should also be examined. Moreover, if the alien engaged in fraud to circumvent orderly refugee procedures, the seriousness of the fraud should be considered. The use of fraudulent documents to escape the country of persecution itself is not a significant adverse factor while, at the other extreme, entry under the assumed identity of a United States citizen with a United States passport, which was fraudulently obtained by the alien from the United States Government, is very serious fraud.

In addition to the circumstances and actions of the alien in his flight from the country where he fears persecution, general humanitarian considerations, such as an alien's tender age or poor health, may also be relevant in a discretionary determination. A situation of particular concern involves an alien who has established his statutory eligibility for asylum but cannot meet the higher burden required for withholding of deportation. Deportation to a country where the alien may be persecuted thus becomes a strong possibility. In such a case, the discretionary factors should be carefully evaluated in light of the unusually harsh consequences which may befall an alien who has established a well-founded fear of persecution; the danger of persecution should generally outweigh all but the most egregious of adverse factors.

Each of the factors mentioned above will not, of course, be found in every case. An applicant for asylum has the burden of establishing that the favorable exercise of discretion is warranted. *Matter of Shirdel,* Interim Decision 2958 (BIA 1984). Therefore, the alien should present evidence on any relevant factors which he believes support the favorable exercise of discretion in his case. In the absence of any adverse factors, however, asylum should be granted in the exercise of discretion.

In the case before us, the applicant attempted to enter the United States with a fraudulent document. Yet we note that the applicant had inquired about obtaining refugee status in Europe, only to be informed that the Yugoslav citizenship which he had recently accepted presented an obstacle to his being recognized by European countries as a refugee. Further, the record reflects that the applicant resorted to the purchase of the fraudulent document only after he was unsuccessful in several attempts at acquiring a visa to enter the United States legally to ask for asylum. We find no basis for doubting the applicant's testimony that he failed to request asylum at the American Embassy because he did not know that he could do so. In addition, the applicant remained in Belgium for only 6 weeks and was in the Netherlands for only a few hours; it does not appear that he was entitled to remain permanently in either country. Moreover, he decided to seek asylum in the United States because he had many relatives legally in the United States to whom he could turn for assistance. Although only the applicant's sister would typically be characterized as a "close" relative, the record reflects that many of his other relatives are also particularly supportive and concerned about him. We note that the applicant seems to have no significant ties to any other countries except for Albania and Yugoslavia, where he fears persecution. Based on the foregoing factors, therefore, we find that asylum should be granted in the exercise of discretion. We further find it unnecessary to decide whether the applicant has also established a clear probability of persecution in Yugoslavia for the purpose of section 243(h) of the Act. *See Matter of Mogharrabi.*

Accordingly, the applicant's appeal will be sustained and the Service's appeal will be dismissed. * * * The applicant is granted asylum pursuant to section 208 of the Immigration and Nationality Act, as amended, and the exclusion proceedings are terminated.

[A separate opinion by Board Member Heilman, concurring in part and dissenting in part, is omitted.]

Notes

1. Under *Salim* the Board considered the use of false documents such a strongly negative factor that it nearly always outweighed other positive factors bearing on the exercise of discretion. *Pula* properly corrects that tendency. But does *Pula* too readily dismiss other factors that should be considered in the exercise of discretion, even ûnder *Hernandez–Ortiz?* Above all, could Pula return to Belgium?

The Board gives this possibility scant attention, apparently accepting Pula's assertion that citizens of Yugoslavia "were not accepted as refugees in European states." But this is an exceedingly odd conclusion. Unlike India and Pakistan, discussed in subpart a. of this Section, all West European states are parties to the UN Convention, and domestic asylum systems there frequently go beyond the minimum strictly required in the treaties. Belgium has a fully functioning asylum adjudication system of this description. *See* Johnson, *Refugee Law Reform in Europe: The Belgian Example,* 27 Colum.J. Transnat'l L. 589 (1989). Yugoslavs could not be excluded per se. The relatively inhospitable stance toward Yugoslav asylum claims (if that was in fact the case) probably reflected a judgment that few such claims were valid on the facts, based on conditions then prevailing in Yugoslavia. Should this situation count in Pula's *favor* for purposes of BIA decisions?

Moreover, the United States had at the time a relatively generous overseas refugee program operative in Europe, open primarily to people from East European countries. Naturally there could be no guarantee that Pula's application would be successful, but should he be completely excused from inquiring into such possibilities from Belgium? The Board imposes remarkably little in the way of a duty of inquiry.

2. *Matter of Soleimani,* Int.Dec. 3118 (BIA 1989), further continued a trend toward permitting favorable exercises of discretion in increasingly diverse circumstances. The Board ruled that a finding that an alien was firmly resettled in a third country—in this case, Israel—does not necessarily render her ineligible for a discretionary grant of asylum. Ties to a third country, whether or not they amount to "firm resettlement," are a factor to be evaluated in exercise of discretion, but may be outweighed by other factors. Soleimani, an Iranian national, had family in the United States. Although she had spent approximately 10 months in Israel, where she could have claimed full citizenship under Israel's Law of Return, asylum was granted. Is this outcome consistent with the general approach taken in *Hernandez–Ortiz?* Why shouldn't Soleimani be required to pursue immigration to the United States through ordinary channels, perhaps based on her family ties? After receiving asylum under § 208, could she eventually adjust status to lawful permanent resident? *See* INA § 209(b)(4). The 1990 regulations apparently overruled *Soleimani,* however, by expressly providing for mandatory denial of asylum when an applicant has been firmly resettled. The provision now appears in 8 C.F.R. § 208.14(d)(2). Review this provision now, and consider *id.* § 208.15, defining "firm resettlement."

d. The Issue of Transit Through Third Countries

Should a person be denied asylum in the exercise of discretion if he traveled through third countries on his way to the United States—third countries to which he might have appealed for asylum, or from which he might have applied for resettlement in the United States as a refugee under INA § 207? Such an idea has appeared in various forms in recent years, as the numbers of asylum seekers from El Salvador, Guatemala, Nicaragua, and other relatively nearby states reached high levels. *See, e.g.,* S. 474, 101st Cong., 1st Sess. (1988) (bill offered by Senator Gramm (R–Tex.) that would provide, in essence, for summary rejection of asylum and § 243(h) applications filed by Western Hemisphere applicants, without having to reach the merits of the persecution claims, if they had transited other countries with which the U.S. has consular relations); 66 Interp.Rel. 478 (1989) (reporting on a draft "Asylum Anti–Abuse Act" prepared at the working level in INS, but never formally proposed to Congress).

This issue is often confused with the question of "firm resettlement" under the regulations, *see* 8 C.F.R. § 208.15, but it is analytically distinct.[30] This country would have the power and the legal right under the UN Convention and Protocol to deny asylum in such circumstances, even if the alien's connection with the third country was rather fleeting and did not

---

30. Note that the statute applies "firm resettlement" as a bar only to inclusion in the overseas program, INA § 207(c)(1), but regulations since 1980 have incorporated this concept, in some form, into the standards for asylum cases.

amount to resettlement. The question is whether such a step would be wise policy.

Should the fact of transit cast doubt on the bona fides of the persecution claim? Should asylum be denied on this basis to deter what *Salim* called the "circumven[tion of] the orderly procedures that our government has provided for refugees to immigrate lawfully"? What provision has been made under § 207 for Central American refugees? More importantly, what would happen to persons denied asylum under some such transit doctrine? The United States may lawfully deny asylum under the treaties, but under what circumstances could it avoid passing on the issues raised by Article 33 of the Convention? Shouldn't the focus be less on where the alien has been in the past, and instead more on what countries, other than the country of nationality, might take the person in for the future? (If this is the case, Mexico is not likely to be any more receptive than were India and Pakistan toward the idea of taking people off the hands of a wealthy country. Mexico's own policy toward Central American asylum seekers is often rather severe. *See, e.g.,* S. Aguayo & P. Weiss Fagen, Central Americans in Mexico and the United States (1988); J. Friedland & J. Rodriguez y Rodriguez, Seeking Safe Ground: The Legal Situation of Central American Refugees in Mexico (1987).)

Significantly, the 1994 regulations have apparently restricted the use of discretionary denials in these circumstances, confining them to cases where the alien will be assured in the third country of "a full and fair procedure for determining his or her asylum claim in accordance with a bilateral or multilateral arrangement with the United States governing such matter." 8 C.F.R. § 208.14(e). This goes considerably beyond the protections ordinarily accorded in other countries, including under the Dublin and Schengen agreements entered into by many European nations. For contrasting assessments of the European arrangements, see Hathaway, *Harmonizing for Whom? The Devaluation of Refugee Protection in the Era of European Economic Integration*, 26 Cornell Int'l L.J. 719 (1993); Neuman, *Buffer Zones Against Refugees: Dublin, Schengen, and The German Asylum Amendment*, 33 Va.J.Int'l L. 503 (1993); Hailbronner, *Perspectives of a Harmonization of the Law of Asylum after the Maastricht Summit*, 29 Common Mkt.L.Rev. 917 (1992).

4. BOOTSTRAP REFUGEES

The beneficiaries of the old seventh preference for refugees (repealed by the Refugee Act of 1980) had to show that they "fled" because of a fear of persecution. The current statutory definition of "refugee" (in INA § 101(a)(42)(A)), like the UN definition from which it is derived, contains no equivalent requirement. The claimant need only show that he is now outside the country where the threat exists and is unwilling to return or otherwise claim the protection of that country, based on a well-founded fear of persecution.

Clearly the new language makes better provision for one type of potential asylum claim. Sometimes prominent political figures, travelling outside the country after a routine departure at a time when they faced no threats, find themselves jeopardized by a coup d'etat or other drastic political change that occurred at home during their absence. If the threat is genuine, it would be hypertechnical to deny asylum because of the timing of their journey abroad. The UNHCR Handbook, *supra* note 29, at 22, refers to such persons as refugees *"sur place."*

But suppose that the asylum applicant does not assert that there have been any dramatic changes in the political scene at home. Suppose he admits he was in no danger before he left, but does claim that he would now be persecuted because (a) he left without permission or deviated from the prescribed terms of his exit visa, and that the home government imposes severe sanctions for such violations of its travel laws, (b) he is now at risk because of political activities that began only after arrival in the United States, or (c) he is at risk simply because the home government will regard the fact that he has applied for political asylum as punishable political opposition.

Does such an applicant merit asylum, if he can prove his allegations? If so, he will in a sense have picked himself up by his own bootstraps, since he created the conditions that validate the claim at a time when he was otherwise in no danger. The prospect of rewarding manipulative behavior by applicants has prompted concern about bootstrapping, and in any event such claims pose real dilemmas for those who must decide on individual applications.

Consider first the situation based on application of the home country's travel laws (category (a) above). The general consensus seems to be that mere application of such sanctions would not support a claim to asylum. Other nations are entitled to have exit laws more severe than we would find acceptable, and the populace must comply, just as it must with other police regulations. But various aggravating factors might change this outcome. For example, if the law is applied with excessive severity, and particularly if it seems to be applied discriminatorily, this fact may validate the asylum claim. *See Sovich v. Esperdy,* 319 F.2d 21, 29 (2d Cir.1963); UNHCR Handbook, *supra* note 29, at 16. *Cf. Coriolan v. INS,* 559 F.2d 993, 1000 (5th Cir.1977). *See also* 70 Interp.Rel. 498, 507–08 (1993) (memorandum from INS General Counsel discussing such circumstances). Whether a particular country's laws fit this description can be a very tough call. Some decisions also suggest that prosecution under the illegal departure laws may constitute persecution if the applicant's motive in leaving was political, although this theory has been somewhat submerged in recent years. *See Matter of Janus and Janek,* 12 I & N Dec. 866, 876 (BIA 1968); *Kovac v. INS,* 407 F.2d 102, 104–05 (9th Cir.1969); *Berdo v. INS,* 432 F.2d 824, 845–47 (6th Cir.1970).

Assertions under category (b) and (c) above are probably more vexing. The connection to political persecution is more direct, but the bootstrapping seems more blatant in such a case—or at least the potential for manipulation is more troublesome. Why didn't the person simply keep quiet here or abstain from claiming asylum, since he was otherwise in no difficulty at home?

Professor Grahl–Madsen, in his treatise on international refugee law, suggests that a distinction can be drawn between actions which are taken out of genuine political motives or which inadvertently result in some political danger, on the one hand, and similar acts committed "for the sole purpose of creating a pretext for invoking a fear of persecution," on the other. In his view, a consensus exists that applicants in the latter case may be denied refugee status, under the general legal principle requiring good faith. 1 A. Grahl–Madsen, *supra* note 1, at 247–52 (1966).

To our knowledge, this principle has not been used, as such, in American practice. Should it be? How would such bona fides be determined? Is it any comfort, if the person is persecuted on return, to know that he brought it on himself by committing a political act that he need not have committed? Isn't the threat equally avoidable for virtually anyone persecuted because of political opinion—even those who escape only after their political activities have put them in danger and hence would unquestionably merit refugee status? After all, in most circumstances, they *could* simply have kept their political opinions to themselves.[31]

The UNHCR Handbook makes clear that persons may become refugees *sur place* based on their own actions abroad, even if there are no changes in the political scene at home. It goes on to say, however, that in such cases there should be "careful examination of the circumstances. Regard should be had in particular to whether such actions may have come to the notice of the authorities of the person's country of origin and how they are likely to be viewed by those authorities." Handbook, *supra* note 29, at 22. For similar approaches, *see Sanchez–Trujillo v. INS,* 801 F.2d 1571, 1580 (9th Cir.1986); *Matter of Vigil,* 19 I & N Dec. 572, 579 (BIA 1988).

The Board has sometimes seemed more doctrinaire: "For the most part [we have] not considered that joining protest groups or making public statements after entering the United States supports a withholding of deportation under section 243(h)." *Matter of Nghiem,* 11 I & N Dec. 541, 544 (1966). In any event, much of the time, the courts and the Board have looked closely at the available evidence to determine whether the applicant was politically active, or was in some way viewed as a known opponent of the government, *before* departing from the home country. *See, e.g., Matter of Williams,* 16 I & N Dec. 697, 701 (BIA 1979); *Gena v. INS,* 424 F.2d 227, 233 (5th Cir.1970). *See also Cisternas–Estay v. INS,* 531 F.2d 155 (3d Cir.1976), *cert. denied,* 429 U.S. 853, 97 S.Ct. 145, 50 L.Ed.2d 127 (1977) (asylum denied to Chilean who had held a press conference in the United States to denounce the Pinochet regime shortly after initial denial of his asylum claim; application had previously rested on a fear of persecution at the hands of the Allende government, which Pinochet overthrew). Is this approach too severe? Other authorities suggest greater receptivity to such claims. *See Ghadessi v. INS,* 797 F.2d 804, 807–08 (9th Cir.1986); *Sakhavat v. INS,* 796 F.2d 1201, 1203–04 (9th Cir.1986); *Haitian Refugee Center v. Civiletti,* 503 F.Supp. 442, 477, 480–81 (S.D.Fla.1980), *modified sub nom.*

31. The situation is different with asylum applications based on "involuntary" grounds of persecution like race or nationality—and possibly religion as well. Consider again the distinction drawn by Zolberg, Suhrke, and Aguayo, p. 728 *supra,* between activists and targets.

Haitian Refugee Center v. Smith, 676 F.2d 1023 (5th Cir.1982); J. Hathaway, *supra* note 1, at 33–39; Note, *Basing Asylum Claims on a Fear of Persecution Arising from a Prior Asylum Claim*, 56 Notre Dame Law. 719 (1981).

In 1981, several senators introduced a bill proposing changes in the law in order to reduce the possibilities for abuse or manipulation by bootstrap asylum claimants. The sponsors evidently were concerned because a large proportion of Haitian asylum claims then pending asserted no danger before departure but only a fear based on the fact of the time spent in the United States. The bill would have amended § 208 to authorize a grant of asylum only if the Attorney General determined that the applicant "is a refugee within the meaning of section 101(a)(42)(A) and if such alien establishes the acquisition of such refugee status which is based on facts existing before his departure from his [home] country." S. 776, 97th Cong., 1st Sess. (1981).

This bill never reached the Senate floor, but in your opinion, should such a measure be adopted? Would it be consistent with the UN Convention and Protocol? Should similar restrictions be imposed on § 243(h)? How would the bill have affected each of the various scenarios described here involving applicants who were not in danger at the time of departure from the home country?

5. WHAT IS PERSECUTION?

a. Overview

Neither the Convention refugee definition nor its analogue in U.S. law offers clarification of what is meant by "persecution." Should persecution be understood as encompassing only threats to life or freedom, building on the specification in Article 33 of the Convention and INA § 243(h)? Courts have sometimes suggested such an equivalency. *See, e.g., McMullen v. INS*, 658 F.2d 1312, 1315 (9th Cir.1981) ("likelihood of persecution, i.e., a threat to life or freedom"). But others have suggested that persecution goes beyond these limitations to include, as the UN Handbook phrases it, "other serious violations of human rights." *See, e.g., Cardoza–Fonseca v. INS*, 767 F.2d 1448, 1452 (9th Cir.1985), *affirmed*, 480 U.S. 421, 107 S.Ct. 1207, 94 L.Ed.2d 434 (1987). If such expansion is appropriate, which human rights are covered, and how serious must any infringement be? The Universal Declaration of Human Rights, UNGA Res. 217A(III) (1948), speaks importantly of rights that protect life and liberty, but it also includes mention of a right to own property, a right to take part in government, a right to social security, a right to an adequate standard of living, even a right to rest and leisure. For an elegant and comprehensive theory of "persecution" based on the international human rights instruments and offering criteria for determining when particular rights count for purposes of refugee determinations, see J. Hathaway, *supra* note 1, at 99–134. For a critique of the Hathaway theory, see Martin, *Book Review*, 87 Am.J. Int'l L. 348 (1993).

The Ninth Circuit has offered this definition:

"Persecution" occurs only when there is a difference between the persecutor's views or status and that of the victim; it is oppression which is inflicted on groups or individuals because of a difference that the persecutor will not tolerate.

Hernandez–Ortiz v. INS, 777 F.2d 509, 516 (9th Cir.1985). Does this help? The House Judiciary Committee, in a different but related context (the Committee report accompanying the bill that eventually added the deportation ground aimed at Nazi persecutors, now INA § 241(a)(4)(D)), stated that the general standard of persecution is "the infliction of suffering or harm, under government sanction, upon persons who differ in a way regarded as offensive (*e.g.,* race, religion, political opinion, etc.) in a manner condemned by civilized governments." Quoted in *Schellong v. INS,* 805 F.2d 655 (7th Cir.1986). How far does this take us? Which governments are civilized?

Perhaps a more helpful definition was offered by Judge Posner in *Osaghae v. INS,* 942 F.2d 1160, 1163 (7th Cir.1991): " 'Persecution' means, in immigration law, punishment for political, religious, or other reasons that our country does not recognize as legitimate." The task in this section of the materials, then, is to identify a workable notion of when this country is prepared to declare another nation's punishments illegitimate. Some cases are easy, but a great many fall at the margin and present surprisingly difficult issues.

Often the definitional question arises in a setting where the government of the country of origin applies criminal or other procedurally regular sanctions in pursuit of a policy aim it deems legitimate, or indeed vital, but that is not shared by other nations. The asylum state may then have to pass judgment on the validity of the underlying policy. How should it do so? What values should it apply? Should it impose its values, in this limited sense, on the policy choices of the other state? Is it possible to devise an approach that does not require value choices about the substantive rightness of the underlying policy—e.g., an approach that focuses only on procedural defects or invidious discrimination in implementation?

The following case and later notes explore these issues. (The case was decided by the BIA in 1989 before the Chinese government ordered the Tiananmen Square massacre in June 1989.)

MATTER OF CHANG

Board of Immigration Appeals, 1989.
Interim Decision No. 3107.

[The immigration judge found the respondent deportable and denied his applications for asylum and withholding of deportation.]

* * * [T]he respondent, a 33–year–old native and citizen of the People's Republic of China, made the following assertions. In his application for asylum, the respondent indicated that he was an anti-Communist who fled his homeland "because of Communist domination of China"; that he did not base his asylum claim on conditions in China that affected his freedom more than the rest of the country's population; and that neither he nor any member of his immediate family had "ever been mistreated by the authorities of his home country." His asylum application did not reference any claim to asylum based on his country's population control measures and he did not allege any mistreatment arising from such policies.

At his deportation hearing, the respondent testified that he was afraid of persecution in China; that people there were "mobilized" and "forced to do the bidding of the government"; that he and his wife were not given any work to do; that he and his wife were forced to flee from their commune because they had two children and did not agree to stop having more children; and, that they disagreed with China's family planning policies because "in the countryside, especially in the farming areas, we need more children." He indicated that the "government" wanted him to go to a clinic to be sterilized, that he thought the operation would "harm" his body, that he did not want to be sterilized, and that if he returned to China he would be forced to submit to the operation. He testified that his wife was supposed to go to the clinic but did not do so because she was ill. He testified that he did not know what would have happened if his wife had gone to the clinic. He further testified that he did not mention his opposition to China's birth control policies on his asylum application because "nobody had asked [him]" and because he was not very "conversant" in expressing himself and did not understand English.

On appeal, the respondent, through counsel, states that the facts of the case are that he and his wife were ordered by their commune to submit to sterilization operations after the birth of their second child, that his wife was able to "postpone" the operation due to illness, but that he fled China because he had no choice other than to submit to the surgery.

In conjunction with the appeal, the respondent also submitted a letter from the Library of Congress dated November 23, 1987, transmitting to the Immigration and Naturalization Service a report entitled "Population Control in the People's Republic of China." The report was apparently requested by the Service in connection with another matter.[1] According to the report, the People's Republic of China ("PRC") has no national law on population control per se. The constitution provides that the state shall carry out family planning to control the size of the population and that spouses have the duty to carry out family planning. The Marriage Law of 1980 sets minimum marriage ages and places responsibility for birth control on both partners. The provinces and the cities governed directly by the state have enacted their own regulations on population control, but the population control program is guided by a joint directive of the Chinese Communist Party and the state entitled "On the Further Implementation of Family Planning Work" of February 1982. The policy provides that state cadres and urban residents are allowed one child per couple, with

1. Counsel for the respondent states that the Service is aware of this report. The sources cited in the report were not furnished to the Board in connection with this appeal and it is not known whether they were furnished to the Service by the Library of Congress. The Service, however, has not object-ed to consideration of this report. On appeal, respondent has also referenced newspaper articles and various other non-legal sources which were not offered into evidence at the hearing and whose texts have not been made available to this Board. These latter sources will not be considered.

exceptions when special permission is granted. In rural areas generally the one-child rule is applied, except that where there are special difficulties, such as the birth of a handicapped child who cannot work, application to have a second child can be made. In no case is a third birth to be permitted. The rules are more leniently applied to families of non-Han ethnic minority groups. Late in 1985, it was announced that the one-child rule would be relaxed, and that in some areas a second child would be permitted if the first was a girl and in other special circumstances. The mechanics of the implementation of the program are by and large locally determined. Economic sanctions, peer pressure, and propaganda are used to insure compliance. Single child families receive health and educational benefits for the child. Couples who continue pregnancies which are not allowed may suffer the suspension of wages, fines, loss of seniority for promotion, and so forth. Couples are urged to undergo birth control operations (sterilization). Wages are sometimes paid during a rest period after sterilization, and cash rewards have been used to encourage sterilization. The Chinese Government has consistently denied supporting any use of force to obtain compliance with birth quotas. The transmittal letter forwarding the report states that punishment in the form of a sterilization operation is not provided for in Chinese law, though local officials may have used the one-child campaign to carry out a private vendetta.

Counsel also relies on the 1985 and 1987 [U.S. State Department] Country Reports on Human Rights Practices, Joint Committee of the Senate and the House of Representatives, 99th Congress, 2d Session (1986), and 100th Congress, 2d Session (1988) ("Country Reports"), respectively. The 1985 Country Report on the PRC indicates that "[r]eported instances of family planning malpractice occur mostly in rural areas, where local officials have sometimes translated the policy into rigid quotas. Chinese authorities say they take measures against local officials who violate the Government's policy in this regard, but there have been few reports of punishment of such offenders." 1985 Country Reports at 741. According to the 1987 report, provinces are allowed to make their own regulations regarding implementation of the one-child policy as long as overall birth-rates match the state-imposed goals. In the past, local officials coerced significant numbers of women into having abortions. In 1987 the Chinese Government stressed repeatedly that it does not condone forced abortions or sterilizations. Chinese authorities have said that they take measures against local officials who violate the Government's policy. Despite central government efforts to prevent the imposition of rigid quotas, local government officials and peers reportedly continue to exert pressure on some persons seeking to have second children. Economic pressure on families with more than two children can be severe and can include loss of party membership, loss of job, difficulty in purchasing state-supplied seed, fertilizer, and fuel and other sanctions. 1987 Country Reports at 666.

* * *

The respondent's position on appeal is that he has a well-founded fear of persecution based on the likelihood he would face mandatory sterilization, that he has a reasonable fear of persecution as a member of a "particular social group" (namely, persons who actually oppose the government policy of "one child per family"), and that he is eligible for withholding of deportation under section 243(h) of the Act because he has demonstrated a clear probability of being sterilized if returned to China.

We do not find that the "one couple, one child" policy of the Chinese Government is on its face persecutive. China has adopted a policy whose stated objective is to discourage births through economic incentives, economic sanctions, peer pressure, education, availability of sterilization and other birth control measures, and use of propaganda. Chinese policymakers are faced with the difficulty of providing for China's vast population in good years and in bad. The Government is concerned not only with the ability of its citizens to survive, but also with their housing, education, medical services, and the other benefits of life that persons in many other societies take for granted. For China to fail to take steps to prevent births might well mean that many millions of people would be condemned to, at best, the most marginal existence. The record reflects that China was in fact encouraged by world opinion to take measures to control its population.

There is no evidence that the goal of China's policy is other than as stated, or that it is a subterfuge for persecuting any portion of the Chinese citizenry on account of one of the reasons enumerated in section 101(a)(42)(A) of the Act. The policy does not prevent couples from having children but strives to limit the size of the family. It appears that exceptions are made so that couples facing certain hardships may have another child. The policy applies to everyone but expressly protects, and indeed is more leniently applied to, minority (non-Han) peoples within China. It appears to impose stricter requirements on Party members (state cadres) than on some non-Party members. The Chinese Government has stated that it does not condone forced sterilizations and that its policy is to take action against local officials who violate this policy.

The population problem arising in China poses a profound dilemma. We cannot find that implementation of the "one couple, one child" policy in and of itself, even to the extent that involuntary sterilizations may occur, is persecution or creates a well-founded fear of persecution "on account of race, religion, nationality, membership in a particular social group, or political opinion." This is not to say that such a policy could not be implemented in such a way as to individuals or categories of persons so as to be persecution on account of a ground protected by the Act. To the extent, however, that such a policy is solely tied to controlling population, rather than as a guise for acting against people for reasons protected by the Act, we cannot find that persons who do not wish to have the policy applied to them are victims of persecution or have a well-founded fear of persecution within the present scope of the Act.

Thus, an asylum claim based solely on the fact that the applicant is subject to this policy must fail. An individual claiming asylum for reasons related to this policy must establish, based on additional facts present in his case, that the application of the policy to him was in fact persecutive or that he had a well-founded fear that it would be persecutive on account of one of the five reasons enumerated in section 101(a)(42)(A). For example, this might include evidence that the policy was being selectively applied against members of particular religious groups or was in fact being used to punish individuals for their political opinions. This does not mean that all who show that they opposed the policy, but were subjected to it anyway, have demonstrated that they are being "punished" for their opinions. Rather, there must be evidence that the governmental action arises for a reason other than general population control (*e.g.*, evidence of disparate, more severe treatment for those who publicly oppose the policy). Finally, if the applicant claims that the punishment occurred at the hands of local officials, he must normally show that redress from higher officials was unavailable or that he has a well-founded fear that it would be unavailable.

We note that the respondent has not shown that mandatory sterilization is or was authorized under regulations or programs in effect in Fukien province, whence he came, or that forced sterilization has in fact occurred in his locality. The Country Report for 1987 reflects that 48.8% of the births in China in 1986 were second, third, or later births, which indicates that millions of persons in China were allowed or chose to have more than one child in that year. It also is support for the Chinese claim that the one-child policy is not routinely enforced by mandatory sterilization and abortion. The sole evidence at the hearing regarding this respondent's claim was his asylum application itself and his testimony. His testimony was simply not sufficiently detailed to provide a plausible and coherent account of the basis of his asylum claim and was contradicted by other information in the record. His asylum application undermines his testimony as it disclaims any mistreatment by the Government and does not refer to any fear stemming from China's population control measures. However, even if we accept the characterization of the evidence as set forth by the respondent on appeal (*i.e.,* that he and his wife wished to have more than two children and he would be forced to undergo mandatory sterilization if returned to China), we would not find that evidence sufficient in itself to support a well-founded fear of persecution on account of a reason enumerated in section 101(a)(42)(a) of the Act. The respondent has not asserted or established that he was treated differently from other Chinese with respect to application of the "one couple, one child" policy, or that its application in his case was in reality a guise to achieve a governmental goal other than general population control.

Such a showing cannot be made by arguing that there is a "particular social group" made up of those persons who "actually" oppose the policy of "one couple, one child," and that the evidence that this "group" is persecuted is simply the fact that the policy is applied to them despite their opposition to it. If a law or policy is not inherently persecutive (as would be, for example, a law enacted to punish individuals because of their religious beliefs), one cannot demonstrate that it is a persecutive measure simply with evidence that it is applied to all persons, including those who do not agree with it. This is true even where questions of conscience or religion may be involved. In the United States, there are numerous cases upholding the imposition of religiously neutral laws against persons whose religious beliefs conflicted with them. *See, e.g., United States v. Lee,* 455

U.S. 252 (1982) (imposition of Social Security taxes against Amish persons whose religious beliefs forbade payment of the taxes or receipt of the benefits did not interfere with the free exercise of their religion); *United States v. Merkt,* 794 F.2d 950, 954–57 (5th Cir.1986), *cert. denied,* 480 U.S. 946 (1987) (conviction for illegally transporting aliens not barred by first amendment although defendants contended they were religiously motivated in conducting "sanctuary" activities), and cases cited therein.

The respondent submits that the freedom to have children is an absolute right under the 14th amendment to the United States Constitution and, for that reason, countries that abridge this right must be found to be engaging in acts of persecution. The resolution of the constitutional issues that could arise if the population problems underlying the implementation of the "one couple, one child" policy in China were to occur in the United States is a matter of speculation that it is hoped this country need never address. However, the fact that a citizen of another country may not enjoy the same constitutional protections as a citizen of the United States does not mean that he is therefore persecuted on account of one of the five grounds enumerated in section 101(a)(42)(A) of the Act.

The respondent points out that Congress has chosen to provide financial aid only to countries that employ voluntary family planning techniques. It has prohibited the use of such aid to coerce or provide any financial incentive to any person to undergo sterilization, or for the performance of involuntary sterilizations as a method of family planning, or for biomedical research relating to methods of performing abortions or involuntary sterilization as a means of family planning. However, the fact that Congress may strongly disapprove of a foreign country's policy does not mean that Congress has found that the policy involves "persecution on account of race, religion, nationality, membership in a particular social group or political opinion."

The respondent submits that involuntary sterilization is both a violation of fundamental human rights and a denial of the "right to life, liberty, and ... security" within the meaning of 22 U.S.C. § 2151n(a) (1982), which restricts the use of international development funds in countries which engage in a consistent pattern of gross violations of internationally recognized human rights. However, even if involuntary sterilization was demonstrated to be a violation of internationally recognized human rights, that fact in itself would not establish that an individual subjected to such an act was a victim of persecution "on account of race, religion, nationality, membership in a particular social group, or political opinion." We are satisfied that if an individual demonstrated a well-founded fear that such an act would occur "on account of" a reason protected by the Act, the "refugee" definition in section 101(a)(42) of the Act would be met.

The issue before us is not whether China's population control policies, in whole or in part, should be encouraged or discouraged to the fullest extent possible by the United States and the world community. The issue is whether the respondent demonstrates persecution or a well-founded fear of persecution on account of race, religion, nationality, membership in a particular social group, or political opinion simply with evidence that he and his wife desire to have more than two children and that, because of China's population control measures, he may be subjected to mandatory sterilization. Where there is no evidence that the application of the policy is a subterfuge for some other persecutive purpose, we do not find that he demonstrates eligibility for asylum by this evidence alone. Whether these policies are such that the immigration laws should be amended to provide temporary or permanent relief from deportation to all individuals who face the possibility of forced sterilization as part of a country's population control program is a matter for Congress to resolve legislatively.

On the record before us we find that the respondent's claims are insufficient to establish that he has a well-founded fear of persecution on account of one of the five grounds enumerated in section 101(a)(42)(A) of the Act.

* * *

Notes

1. *Chang* can be evaluated in two separate lights. First, there is some evidence that the Chinese population control policy is enforced only through "[e]conomic sanctions, peer pressure, and propaganda." [32] *Chang* indicates that these kinds of economic sanctions and pressure alone do not amount to persecution. Do you agree? At what point would economic sanctions rise to the level of persecution? In *Kovac v. INS*, 407 F.2d 102, 107 (9th Cir.1969), the court ruled that "deliberate imposition of substantial economic disadvantage for reasons of race, religion or political opinion" would suffice to justify political asylum. Does this go too far? How would you give the *Kovac* standard operational content? *See generally* Blum, *The Ninth Circuit and the Protection of Asylum Seekers Since the Passage of the Refugee Act of 1980,* 23 San Diego L.Rev. 327, 344 (1986). Denial of the right to practice a chosen profession and assignment to a lesser occupation for political reasons occurred rather frequently in Eastern Europe (at least until recent years). Such restrictions appear to be human rights violations, but are they persecution of a sort that should justify a right of relocation under refugee law? How about denial of entry into certain universities because of ethnic or religious affiliations (as often happened to Soviet Jews)? Denial of entry into any university?

---

32. The fact that more coercive measures would violate stated national policy of the Chinese government suggests that individuals threatened with stronger action may have remedies short of relocating outside the country (such as appealing to national authorities, or perhaps moving elsewhere within China).

Consider also the following views, expressed in a letter to the editor responding to a press account that asylum had been granted to a Chinese couple who feared forced abortion or sterilization:

What Americans fail to realize is that Chinese couples can choose to have more than one child. * * * [In localities where] one child is still the guideline, parents who choose to have a second child know they will pay the government 10 percent of their wages for seven years [rising to 20 percent for a third child]. * * * This is a choice available to every couple and known to all Chinese citizens. The Chinese couple in the Associated Press article was fleeing a known tax for having a second child.

Letter from Sarah G. Epstein, Wash.Post., May 25, 1990, at A20.

Second, the BIA in *Chang* apparently also considers the case on an assumption that more serious consequences await the applicant, possibly including sterilization or his wife's forced abortion. Even so, it appears unwilling to find that these consequences amount to persecution on account of one of the five reasons stated in the definition. Such sanctions could constitute persecution in some settings, but apparently not if they are applied to virtually all in the population who fail to go along with the national policy. Persecution, in this conception, apparently requires some sort of invidious discrimination. Do you agree? If you consider this a good rule of thumb in general, what limits would you place upon it? Think of how the definition would apply to people who escaped Cambodia under Pol Pot, whose Khmer Rouge, in power from 1975 to 1979, attempted to purge their country of all Western influence, and who killed over a million of their countrymen in the process (often in quite indiscriminate fashion).

2. Consider the Board's treatment of the claim that those who oppose the one-child policy amount to a "particular social group." Is the BIA's position persuasive? Is the claimant's position tautological—because all who violate *any* national law could be characterized as a particular group manifesting opposition to the law, and the sanctions would of course then fall only on such a group? What about the BIA's exception for actions that are "inherently persecutive?" On what values does one draw in making that assessment? Should U.S. constitutional values (such as the Fifth and Fourteenth Amendments' protection of personal childbearing decisions) carry substantial weight in that process? *See generally* Note, *Coercive Population Control Policies: The Need for a Conscientious Objector Provision for Asylum Seekers*, 30 Va. J. Int'l L. 1007 (1990).

3. Finally, consider the following comments, taken from an article that analyzes *Chang* and many of the other cases in this section (Aleinikoff, *The Meaning of "Persecution" in United States Asylum Law*, 3 Int'l J. Refugee L. 5, 12–13, 27 (1991)):

> Courts and commentators tend to see the "persecution" issue primarily in terms of the level of harm imposed on an individual. The UNHCR *Handbook on Procedures and Criteria for Determining Refugee Status* is typical. In its brief discussion, it notes that
>
>> [t]here is no universally accepted definition of "persecution," and various attempts to formulate such a definition have met with little success. From Article 33 of the 1951 Convention, it may be inferred that a threat to life or freedom on account of race, religion, nationality, political opinion or membership in a particular social group is always persecution. Other serious violations of human rights—for the same reasons—would also constitute persecution. [UNHCR Handbook, *supra* note 29, para. 51.]
>
> Two considerations are at work in this paragraph: (1) the harm imposed must be of a serious nature; and (2) the harm must be imposed for one of the designated reasons for it to qualify as persecution within the terms of the Convention. The first point is sensible enough; surely neither international law nor the dramatic

relief provided by U.S. asylum law need concern itself with minor inconveniences inflicted upon individuals, irrespective of the motive of the inflicter.

The second point, however, requires some further reflection. Why is the definition of persecution necessarily linked to the five specified grounds? My sense is that this gets at something other than just the level of harm—call it a "qualitative" or "normative" aspect of the definition of persecution. That is, persecution connotes unacceptable, unjustified, abhorrent infliction of harm, not simply a particular degree of harm. To see this, compare the case of an individual sentenced to life imprisonment for having committed murder with the case of a person sentenced to ten years in prison for having circulated a pamphlet opposing the government. The first case is unlikely to be seen as persecution; the second might well.

The *Handbook*'s use of the five grounds in its explication of "persecution," then, signals the unjustifiable, intolerable aspect of the infliction of harm. One's race or religion cannot provide an acceptable reason for the imposition of serious injury. But while one can understand how the existence of one of the five grounds might signal the qualitative aspect of the definition of persecution, it is not at all clear that persecution ought to be so limited—or, more importantly, that an applicant must be able to establish conclusively that one of the five grounds is at work in order to establish persecution. Persecution might well be given a "free-standing" meaning that requires judgments about both the degree of and justifications for the harm, but not one that necessarily invokes the five grounds as the test of the qualitative aspect.

* * *

[T]he issue of persecution necessarily includes a normative, qualitative judgment about the degree of, and justification for, the harm imposed on an individual or group * * *.

Later Developments Involving Chinese Family Planning Policy

In November 1989 Congress overwhelmingly passed a bill in response to the Tiananmen Square killings and the general crackdown on the democracy movement in the People's Republic the previous June. Most of the provisions focused on the situation of Chinese students in this country, for example waiving the usual requirement that J–1 exchange visitors (a category that included most such students and other visiting Chinese scholars) return and live at least two years in the home country before becoming U.S. permanent residents or adjusting to certain other nonimmigrant statuses. *See* INA § 212(e). But at the urging of Senator Armstrong (R–Colo.), an amendment was included to provide asylum to people like Chang. *See* 66 Interp.Rel. 1290 (1989). Congress agonized over the exact wording, apparently concerned about a potential bootstrapping problem if the legislation mandated asylum for anyone who simply declared, even after coming to the United States, his or her opposition to the Chinese policy. As adopted, the legislation would have required INS to give "careful consideration" to asylum applicants from the PRC who express "a fear of persecution upon return to China related to China's 'one couple, one child' family planning policy." It also provided:

> If the applicant establishes that such applicant has refused to abort or be sterilized, such applicant shall be considered to have established a well-founded fear of persecution, if returned to China, on the basis of political opinion consistent with [INA § 101(a)(42)(A)].

Emergency Chinese Relief Act of 1989, H.R. 2712, § 3(a), 101st Cong., 1st Sess. (1989).

President Bush vetoed the bill, not because of disagreement with its substance, but because he thought that statutory codification of such measures would interfere with ongoing diplomatic initiatives. To mollify opposition, however, he ordered implementation of all the bill's provisions by executive action. With respect to the Armstrong measure he went even further. His formal Memorandum of Disapproval, issued at the time of the veto, stated: "I have directed that enhanced consideration be provided under the immigration laws for individuals from *any country* who express a fear of persecution upon return to their country related to that country's policy of forced abortion or coerced sterilization." 66 Interp.Rel. 1331 (1989) (emphasis added). Is this step lawful under the existing immigration laws, or was statutory amendment required? If you were the INS officer asked to draft guidance or regulations to implement the President's directives, how would you proceed? In particular, is the stated policy inherently open to bootstrapping? Should that be a matter of concern?

In late January 1990, the Attorney General issued interim regulations on these matters. 55 Fed.Reg. 2803 (1990). *Interpreter Releases* speculated that the Department of Justice resorted to formal regulations, signed by Attorney General Thornburgh, in order to overcome and effectively overrule *Matter of Chang,* 67 Interp.Rel. 117 (1990). *See also* 66 *id.* 1316, 1388 (1989). President Bush then referred to these regulations in the Executive Order he issued in April 1990 to compile and formalize all the Administration's policy initiatives affecting PRC nationals in the United States. Executive Order 12711, § 4, 55 Fed.Reg. 13897 (1990). *See* 69 Interp.Rel. 311 (1991) (implementing guidance from the INS General Counsel).

The Executive Order included a grant of "deferred enforced departure" through January 1, 1994, to Chinese citizens in this country before April 11, 1990—essentially permission to stay, with work authorization. Before that status expired, Congress passed special legislation to grant full permanent resident status to most of the PRC nationals covered by the order. Chinese Student Protection Act, Pub.L.No. 102–404, 106 Stat. 1969 (1992). *See Lin v. Meissner,* 855 F.Supp. 4 (D.D.C.1994) (describing CSPA and holding that PRC nationals who entered without inspection may not benefit from the Act, even though they were covered by E.O. 12711).

Meantime, however, great confusion was being sown regarding the status of the *Chang* decision. The Justice Department finally promulgated its long-awaited comprehensive revision of asylum regulations in July 1990. The focus of those regulations, which had been debated for years, was the creation of the specialist corps of asylum officers within INS, but the new rules comprehensively replaced all of 8 C.F.R. Part 208, thus inadvertently superseding the January 1990 regulations governing these PRC cases. When the problem came to light, INS sent guidance to its officers directing them to continue following the January 1990 approach. But such guidance could not bind the BIA. Ultimately Attorney General Barr signed regulations in January 1993 essentially reinstating the January 1990 regulations. They were scheduled for publication in the Federal Register on January 25, three days after President Clinton's inauguration. But the new Administration issued orders forbidding the publication of new regulations until they had been approved by a Clinton-appointed agency head. As a result, the Barr regulations have never been published.

Hoping to clarify the situation, the BIA certified two PRC cases to Attorney General Reno so that she could rule whether *Chang* remained the governing rule. In a mystifying move, however, she decided that the merits did not have to be reached and rescinded her order granting review. 70 Interp.Rel. 1631 (1993). The Board thereupon returned to its practice of applying *Chang*, and it had a great many occasions to do so, because of a significant increase in Chinese applications in this country. *See Matter of G—*, Int.Dec. 3215 (BIA 1993), *supra* pp. 476–81. Many Chinese asylum applicants apparently arrive here by means of smuggling rings, which charge as much as $30,000 per passenger and often hold the individuals in near-bondage until the debt is paid. *See* Suro, *Chinese Smuggling Grows, Forcing U.S. Reassessment*, Wash. Post, June 2, 1994, at A1. And as noted earlier, a few highly publicized boat arrivals in 1993, including the grounding of the *Golden Venture* near Long Island, had made these questions highly visible and controversial. Meantime, courts were reaching disparate results in PRC family planning cases, including many *Golden Venture* cases themselves. *Compare, e.g., Di v. Carroll*, 842 F.Supp. 858 (E.D.Va.1994); and *Xin-Chang v. Slattery*, 859 F.Supp. 708 (S.D.N.Y.1994) (ruling in favor of the applicant; *Xin-Chang*, unlike other courts to reach the issue, finds that Barr's Jan. 1993 regulations applied even though they were never formally published); *with Zheng v. INS*, 44 F.3d 379 (5th Cir.1995); *Chen v. Carroll*, 858 F.Supp. 569 (E.D.Va.1994); and *Chen v. Slattery*, 862 F.Supp. 814 (E.D.N.Y.1994) (essentially approving *Chang*).

Finally, after a long interagency review process, in which the concern about adopting a policy that might promote smuggling contended with concern over human rights abuses committed under China's family planning policies, the Clinton administration staked out its position on these cases in August 1994. Asylum officers were instructed to follow *Chang* and *Matter of G—*, but a form of "extraordinary humanitarian relief" would be available "outside the asylum context." Wash. Post, Aug. 7, 1994, at A10 (quoting Deputy Associate Attorney General Phyllis Coven). District directors were instructed to consider granting a stay of deportation, with work authorization, in the following circumstances:

when the alien has expressed a credible fear of returning to the PRC and his claim falls into any of the following three categories: (1) the person, upon return to the PRC, is faced with imminent danger of forced abortion or involuntary sterilization; (2) the person has suffered or would suffer severe harm for refusing to submit to an abortion or sterilization; or (3) the person has suffered or would suffer severe harm because he violated other unreasonable family planning restrictions. This latter category * * * would not, however, include a person who has one child, expresses an intention to have a second child, and speculates that this will result in severe harm.

The memorandum goes on to emphasize that the implementing officers must carefully evaluate the alien's credibility. 71 Interp.Rel. 1066–70 (1994). And Ms. Coven stated: "The smugglers may test us but they will fail and the message will go out loud and clear that this is not an open gate but that relief will be provided only in very extraordinary and credible cases." Wash. Post, *supra*. Is the message loud and clear? Does this policy improve matters? How should one decide if an applicant is credible? What exactly are the district directors supposed to determine under this memo?

U.S. policy on Chinese asylum seekers is thus somewhat schizophrenic. At the same time that it opens up an avenue for extraordinary relief over and above asylum, the government is engaging in maritime and intelligence measures to locate Chinese smugglers' ships far offshore and divert them to other countries which apparently have an easier time arranging prompt repatriation. *See* Suro, *On Immigration, A Question of Fairness*, Wash. Post, Dec. 20, 1994, at A3; Suro, *Guatemala Agrees to Facilitate Repatriation of Illegal Chinese Immigrants*, Wash. Post, Apr. 29, 1994, at A3; 70 Interp.Rel. 344 (1993). Why is it so difficult to create a unified and harmonious policy on these issues? Does the problem stem from the difficulty in assessing claims based on China's population control policies under any of the standards considered in this part? Does it come instead from the scope of potential immigration from the most populous country in the world? Is this attention to practical consequences and political limitations a legitimate factor to consider in shaping asylum doctrine?

b. *Coup Plotters*

In the decision reviewed in *Dwomoh v. Sava*, 696 F.Supp. 970 (S.D.N.Y.1988), the BIA, over a dissent, denied political asylum to an applicant who had been caught in the early stages of a coup plot against the government in Ghana (which itself came to power through a successful coup led by Flight Lieutenant Jerry Rawlings in December 1981). The applicant had been detained and mistreated, without trial, but eventually escaped, made his way to the United States, and sought asylum. The court described the BIA's ruling as follows:

> The BIA takes the position that a person can qualify for refugee status if he faces prosecution for openly *espousing* anti-government views, but that he cannot so qualify if he faces

not allowed

prosecution for *acting* on those views, where his action takes the
form of a politically motivated attempt to overthrow the government by violent means.   Without considering the fact that in
totalitarian governments a person may have only one chance to
express or act upon anti-government views, and that the only
means of effecting political change may be to overthrow the
government, the BIA compared Ghana to the United States and
stated that both countries have the right to enforce their laws
against treason and insurrection, even by imposition of the death
penalty.   On the question of whether the beatings and one year's
detention of Mr. Dwomoh without permitting him contact with the
outside world constitute "persecution on account of ... political
opinion" within the Congressional definition, the BIA stated, " ...
he was subjected to mistreatment due to his refusal to provide
information about the attempted *coup d'état*, not because of any
political view he may hold."   In determining whether the punishment petitioner faced and faces is persecution on account of
political opinion, the BIA relied both on its view that governments
have the right to enforce laws against treason, and a statement in
a publication of the United Nations High Commissioner for Refugees that persons fleeing from punishment for common law offenses are not normally refugees.

The court reversed:

In evaluating the nature of the crime with which Mr. Dwomoh
is charged and the punishment he may face, the BIA noted
American laws against treason and insurrection.   The *UNHCR
Handbook* notes that in evaluating the laws and punishments of
other countries, it is often useful to compare those laws to national
legislation; in this case, however, the comparison was inapt.   The
United States has procedures whereby citizens can change their
form of government peaceably.   In Ghana, where no such procedures exist,[11] a coup may be the only means by which political
change can be effected.   In addition, while it is true that the
United States has laws against treason, and punishes violators of
those laws severely, United States law also provides due process
protections.   No United States citizen is punished for treason
without a formal charge, and the opportunity for a full trial and
appeal.   Mr. Dwomoh has no such protections; he might be
executed without ever having been charged, no less tried.

* * *

An accurate assessment of the political conditions existing in
the particular country at the time the political crime is committed

---

11. According to the United States State
Department:

The PNDC under Chairman Rawlings
exercises total executive, legislative, judicial, and administrative power in Ghana
(PNDC Law 42).   There are no elections
to governing organs and no current procedure by which citizens can freely and
peacefully change their laws, officials, or
form of government.

* * *

is central to the determination of whether prosecution for a political crime constitutes persecution under the guidelines set forth by the UNHCR. It may be that as a general rule prosecution for an attempt to overthrow a lawfully constituted government does not constitute persecution. However, the UNHCR does not view that general rule as applicable in countries where a coup is the only means through which a change in the political regime can be effected.

[handwritten margin note: But don't apply where coup only means]

Notes

1. In *Matter of Izatula,* Int.Dec. 3127 (BIA 1990), the Board cited the court decision in *Dwomoh* with approval. The immigration judge had ruled that the applicant, a national of Afghanistan, would merely be subject to "prosecution," not persecution, for his assistance to the mujahedin rebels in that country and his resistance to conscription into the Afghan army. The Board disagreed. Quoting a State Department human rights country report on Afghanistan, it found that "Afghanistan is a totalitarian state," and "[c]itizens have neither the right nor the ability peacefully to change their government." It went on to rule: "there is no basis in the record to conclude that any punishment imposed by the Afghan Government would be a legitimate exercise of sovereign authority." *Id.,* at 8. Therefore Izatula was awarded asylum.

Two members concurred specially, on the ground that the threatened punishment was disproportionate to Izatula's offenses, in view of the routine torture meted out in Afghan prisons. Board member Vacca then criticized the grounds relied on by the majority:

> In effect, the majority finds that the Afghan government is illegitimate and therefore incapable of imposing a lawful punishment. * * * [T]he majority wades in dangerous waters when it presumes to make judgments as to the legitimacy of sovereign nations by scrutinizing their political systems. Clearly the President of the United States has constitutional authority to formulate and conduct foreign policy[.] * * * To hold that some governments may create laws affecting crimes, adjudicate criminal cases and impose punishments upon offending citizens and other governments may not[,] depending upon the nature of their political systems[,] is patently absurd. The right of all nations to recruit soldiers and maintain armies to protect themselves from enemies within or without their borders is recognized as fundamental in international law. This sovereign right is not limited to countries whose internal political structures are democratic.

Id. at 10–11. For useful discussions of *Izatula,* see Blum, *License to Kill: Asylum Law and the Principle of Legitimate Governmental Authority to "Investigate Its Enemies,"* 28 Willamette L.Rev. 719, 746–48 (1992); Note, *Refugee Determinations: A Consolidation of Approaches to Actions by Nongovernmental Forces,* 33 Va.J.Int'l L. 927 (1993). Blum reports that *Izatula's* doctrine has not been applied in other cases.

2.   The court in *Dwomoh* mentions both the absence of procedures for peaceful change of government and the lack of due process protections in any trial of coup plotters. But presumably coup plotters would still be punished in authoritarian states with better judicial procedures. Is the second element therefore essential to the ruling? Or should coup plotters be entitled to protection based only on a showing that the home state lacks effective and meaningfully contested elections?

3.   How much of a real option must the voters enjoy before *Dwomoh* ceases to apply? After all, even Ceausescu's Romania held elections, albeit utterly meaningless ones. Consider the following description of the situation of state X, taken from the 1983 State Department country reports (an earlier number in the series on which the *Dwomoh* court relies for its information about the situation in Ghana). Should coup plotters in state X qualify for asylum? (See footnote 33, p. 828 *infra*, to learn which country this is.)

> The [ABC political party, which has controlled the government for over fifty years] dominates politics at the federal, state, and local levels but opposition parties are both allowed and encouraged by the government as outlets for criticism and dissatisfaction. They have not, however, been able successfully to challenge the [ABC] politically in presidential and gubernatorial elections and some observers note that [X] remains virtually a one party state. Opposition party opportunities have been thwarted by nationwide [ABC] voting strength and organizational power, by the party's maneuvers to co-opt and/or divide the opposition, and, the opposition claims, by electoral fraud.

U.S. Dept. of State, Country Reports on Human Rights Practices for 1983, at 624 (Jt.Comm.Print, 98th Cong., 2d Sess., February 1984).

4.   Should a participant in the failed 1991 coup attempt staged by old-line Communists against Soviet President Mikhail Gorbachev be considered eligible for asylum, assuming he managed to escape to the United States?

c.   *Conscientious Objectors*

Many nations have compulsory military service laws. Some recognize exemptions for those conscientiously opposed to military service, but exemptions take many forms. Some nations allow no such exemptions. In what circumstances should punishment for noncompliance with these laws be considered persecution, thus supporting a grant of asylum to those who resist military service?

The BIA denied a motion to reopen to a national of El Salvador who wished to claim asylum based on his fear of punishment for failure to serve in the Salvadoran military. *Matter of A–G–*, 19 I & N Dec. 502 (BIA 1987). It explained:

> The respondent argues that he will refuse to serve in the "terrorist" military and that his refusal is based on his political beliefs. He then contends that he would likely suffer severe penalties including death at the hands of the death squads for his

refusal, because he would be suspected of anti-government sympathies. He also argues that it would be against his moral values to serve in an army which has engaged in violations of human rights. He alleges that the immigration judge failed to consider his argument that he was not obliged at all to serve in an army which violates human rights. He argues that his position is similar to that of the alien granted asylum in *Matter of Salim,* 18 I & N Dec. 311 (BIA 1982), in that his claim is more than a mere refusal to serve in his country's military.

* * *

We hold to the long-accepted position that it is not persecution for a country to require military service of its citizens. Exceptions to this rule may be recognized in those rare cases where a disproportionately severe punishment would result on account of one of the five grounds enumerated in section 101(a)(42)(A) of the Act, or where the alien would necessarily be required to engage in inhuman conduct as a result of military service required by the government. *See* Office of the United Nations High Commissioner for Refugees, *The Handbook on Procedures and Criteria for Determining Refugee Status Under the 1951 Convention and the 1967 Protocol Relating to the Status of Refugees* 39–41 (Geneva, 1979). We conclude that the respondent has not brought forward evidence that his refusal to serve would result in disproportionately severe punishment for an impermissible reason or that the activity in which he might be involved has been condemned by the international community as contrary to the basic rules of human conduct.

The respondent contends that his refusal to serve is a valid political opinion and a moral conviction which is supported by international law. He asserts that the actions of the Salvadoran Army violate international law and have been condemned by the international community. Although incidents involving the Salvadoran Army have been reported, which undoubtedly involve the violation of the rights of noncombatants and international law, there is no evidence that these incidents represent the policy of the Salvadoran Government or that the respondent would be required to engage in such actions as a member of the armed forces. The statements of opinion of Americas Watch to the contrary in the record may indeed be the belief of those who represent that organization. Such statements of opinion of private unofficial bodies do not constitute evidence of condemnation by recognized international governmental bodies, which would be necessary at a minimum for us to accept this argument. For an example of a statement of opinion of a recognized international governmental body, see the resolution concerning the status of persons refusing service in military or police forces used to enforce apartheid. G.A.Res. 33/165, 33 U.N. GAOR Supp. (No. 45) at 154, U.N.Doc. A/33/45 (1979). Thus, the Government of El Salvador has the same right as other governments to require military service and to

enforce that requirement with reasonable penalties.   The case of
the claimant in *Matter of Salim, supra,* [a national of Afghanistan]
is distinguishable from that of the respondent because the former
was refusing to serve, not in an army controlled by his own
government, but in one which was "under Soviet command."
A panel of the Court of Appeals for the Fourth Circuit initially
reversed. *M.A. v. INS,* 858 F.2d 210, 215 (4th Cir.1988).

Failure to serve in the military may also be the expression of a
political opinion, subjecting the evader to the same punishment as
any other draft evader.   When this occurs, the applicant should
ordinarily be denied refugee status because the draft is generally
recognized as lawful.   There is, however, an exception to this
general rule:

> There are, however, also cases where the necessity to
> perform military service may be the sole ground for a claim to
> refugee status, i.e. when a person can show that the perfor-
> mance of military service would have required his partic-
> ipation in military action contrary to his genuine political,
> religious or moral convictions, or to valid reasons of con-
> science.

> Not every conviction, genuine though it may be, will
> constitute a sufficient reason for claiming refugee status after
> desertion or draft-evasion.   It is not enough for a person to be
> in disagreement with his government regarding the political
> justification for a particular military action.   Where, however,
> the type of military action, with which an individual does not
> wish to be associated, is condemned by the international
> community as contrary to basic rules of human conduct,
> punishment for desertion or draft-evasion could, in the light of
> all other requirements of the definition, in itself be regarded
> as persecution.

[UNHCR] *Handbook* ¶¶ 170–71.   It is the possibility that an
unwilling conscriptee may be associated with the commission of
atrocities which places him in a different predicament from that of
a conscriptee who merely disagrees with the political justification
of a conflict.

* * *

We think that the Board has made the petitioner's burden
unduly harsh.   An applicant for political asylum should not be
required to prove that he would be compelled to commit atrocities.
It is unlikely that such a standard could ever be met.   Paragraph
171 of the *Handbook* focuses instead on the *association* with
certain types of military action as the relevant inquiry.   Whether
an individual will be associated with condemned conduct will
depend largely on how widespread it has become, and it follows
that the likelihood that an individual would be forced to participate in atrocities increases as the atrocities become more wide-

spread. We therefore think that the appropriate inquiry is to consider the pervasiveness of atrocities. We think also that petitioner has presented sufficient evidence from a wide variety of sources to show that atrocities committed against the civilian population by the military are frequent and widespread.

We also decline to adopt the Board's requirement that there be proof that the acts of atrocity with which M.A. does not want to be associated are the policies of the Salvadoran government. It is sufficient that M.A. show that the Salvadoran government is unwilling or unable to control the offending group, here, the armed forces.

* * *

Similarly, we do not think that M.A. must wait for international bodies such as the United Nations to condemn officially the atrocities committed by a nation's military in order to be eligible for political asylum. Paragraph 171 of the *Handbook* shelters those individuals who do not wish to be associated with military action "condemned by the international community as contrary to basic rules of human conduct...." These basic rules are well documented and readily available to guide the Board in discerning what types of actions are considered unacceptable by the world community [citing the Geneva Conventions of 1949].

The court of appeals then granted the government's petition for rehearing en banc and eventually ruled 6–5 to sustain the BIA's ruling. *M.A. v. INS,* 899 F.2d 304 (4th Cir.1990) (en banc). The majority stated (*id.,* at 312–313):

The Board did not abuse its discretion in denying M.A.'s motion to reopen for failure to establish prima facie eligibility for political asylum. It properly focused upon the fact that, at bottom, M.A. was a draft resister who claimed that his justified refusal to serve in the Salvadoran military would result in his persecution. International law and Board precedent are very clear that a sovereign nation enjoys the right to enforce its laws of conscription, and that penalties for evasion are not considered persecution.

* * *

M.A. claims that the military in which he might be forced to serve has committed acts that are contrary to the basic rules of human conduct. The Board was within its discretion in rejecting this claim based on M.A.'s failure to present cognizable evidence that the alleged atrocities he wanted to avoid were perpetrated as a result of the policies of the Salvadoran military or government. Misconduct by renegade military units is almost inevitable during times of war, especially revolutionary war, and a country as torn as El Salvador will predictably spawn more than its share of poignant incidents. Without a requirement that the violence be connected with official governmental policy, however, *any* male alien of draft age from just about any country experiencing civil strife could establish a well-founded fear of persecution. The Refugee Act does not reach this broadly.

M.A. did, of course, bring forth evidence from prominent private organizations such as Amnesty International and Americas Watch. These organizations have condemned the Salvadoran military and security forces for committing violent acts against all sectors of Salvadoran society. They report that the Salvadoran military engages in "extrajudicial execution on noncombatant civilians, individual death squad-style killings, 'disappearances,' arbitrary detention and torture." Moreover, they contend that the military violence is carried out pursuant to a deliberate policy of the Salvadoran government designed to further that government's political interests.

* * *

[But a] standard of asylum eligibility based solely on pronouncements of private organizations or the news media is problematic almost to the point of being non-justiciable. * * * Although we do not wish to disparage the work of private investigative bodies in exposing inhumane practices, these organizations may have their own agendas and concerns, and their condemnations are virtually omnipresent. Taken alone, they do not suffice to overturn the Board's judgment in M.A.'s case.[6]

It is, of course, the role of private organizations and news reports to energize the political branches. But that is quite a different thing from requiring the courts in each instance to evaluate independently the accusations of private organizations to determine whether they set forth conditions adequate to overturn the Board's discretionary judgment. This responsibility would require us to make immigration decisions based on our own implicit approval or disapproval of U.S. foreign policy and the acts of other nations. Courts could be put in the position of ruling, as a matter of law, that a government whose actions have not been condemned by international governmental bodies engages in persecution against its citizens. * * * Such a role for the courts would transform the political asylum process from a method of individual sanctuary left largely to the political branches into a vehicle for foreign policy debates in the courts.

6. The dissent's charge that the majority considers the reports of private organizations to be "biased, standardless, and of little probative value" is wholly misplaced. We respect the role of these organizations in documenting human rights abuses, but we are not about to use these reports as the basis for overturning the judgment of the Board or for issuing judicial condemnations of the conduct of foreign governments, especially where the Board itself found no evidence of international governmental condemnation in this case. As to "standardlessness," we have never said that the reports themselves are standardless, but rather that the use of these reports to overturn the Board here would leave judges in a world that is barren of guidance for the legal judgments they purport to reach. As to the probativeness of this evidence, we do not say that the Board should not consider it, only that its method of evidentiary assessment did not constitute the abuse of discretion that would justify our overturning its judgment. * * *

A vigorous dissent restated many of the points in the panel opinion, questioning in particular the deferential review standard employed. "It is precisely the politicization of the asylum process that troubles me, and suggests that heightened deference to the Board is unwarranted." *Id.,* at 319 (Winter, J., dissenting). The dissent also defended reliance on reports of private human rights organizations, against the majority's concern that such action would invade foreign policy reserved to the political branches. "Even if such reliance constituted in some way an indirect condemnation of the government in question, the Congress has explicitly empowered the federal judiciary to review and, if necessary, to correct INS determinations of the asylum standard." *Id.,* at 323.

Notes

1. Consider carefully the doctrine prescribed in paras. 170–171 of the UNHCR Handbook, quoted early in the excerpt from the initial panel's decision in *M.A. v. INS*. Did the panel accurately apply that doctrine? Did the en banc majority? For a case where the "association" with military atrocities was far closer, see *Barraza Rivera v. INS*, 913 F.2d 1443 (9th Cir.1990).

2. Has the Board in *A–G–* adequately distinguished its decision in *Matter of Salim, supra* p. 770?

3. Canada has granted asylum in circumstances somewhat similar to *M.A.*, to an applicant who deserted the Mexican army to avoid further involvement in his army unit's duties, namely, as found by the Board, the extrajudicial execution of prisoners. *Cruz v. Canada (Minister of Employment & Immigration)*, 10 Imm.L.R.(2d) 47 (Imm.Appeal Board 1988).

4. The en banc majority in *M.A.* suggests that adjudicators, or at least the courts, should not rely on the reports of nongovernmental human rights organizations. But regulations issued by the Department of Justice a few months after that decision specifically provide that INS asylum adjudicators "may rely on * * * other credible sources, such as international organizations, private voluntary agencies, or academic institutions." 8 C.F.R. § 208.12(a).

5. The alien in *M.A.* is a "selective conscientious objector," to use the terminology often applied in the United States during the Vietnam War. That is, he did not claim to be opposed to war in any form, but only to the particular uses of military force employed by the Salvadoran military at the time. U.S. law has usually allowed Americans who conscientiously oppose all war to avoid military service, subject to an obligation to perform alternative noncombatant service, while denying that option to selective objectors.

Should nonselective religious objectors be recognized as refugees, if they leave a country that makes no allowance for any such exemptions? The Board has denied asylum in these circumstances, to Salvadoran applicants who asserted that, as Jehovah's Witnesses, they were opposed to all war:

[T]here is nothing in this record which indicates that the Salvadoran conscription law does not offer exceptions from mandatory service to conscientious objectors because the intent of the law is to persecute Jehovah's Witnesses, or members of any other religious group which is opposed to military service and war. Nor is there evidence that the conscription laws were enacted or are applied in a persecutory manner, *e.g.*, with only those with religious objections being punished for their refusal to join the military.

Matter of Canas, 19 I & N Dec. 697, 708 (BIA 1988). The Ninth Circuit reversed. *Canas-Segovia v. INS,* 902 F.2d 717, 723 (9th Cir.1990), *vacated and remanded for reconsideration in light of* Elias–Zacarias, *infra,* 112 S.Ct. 1152 (1992), *reaffirmed in part on imputed political opinion grounds,* 970 F.2d 599 (9th Cir.1992). *See generally* Note, *Asylum for Unrecognized Conscientious Objectors to Military Service: Is There a Right not to Fight?,* 31 Va. J. Int'l L. 447 (1991).[33]

6. "PERSECUTION ON ACCOUNT OF . . ." (INCLUDING VARIOUS PROBLEMS IN APPLYING REFUGEE STANDARDS IN CIVIL WAR SITUATIONS)

The preceding materials already suggest the close links the Board sometimes requires between the allegedly persecuting act of the government and the precise basis or motive for the oppression, before the government's threat can be accepted as a valid foundation for asylum under § 208. Some of this linkage may be implicit in the very notion of "persecution" itself, as the attempted definitions that open the preceding subsection of this Chapter indicate. That is, harsh sanctions do not usually amount to persecution unless they are inflicted on the basis of some characteristic that is thought not to justify such a response. Someone imprisoned at hard labor after a valid conviction for armed robbery is not being persecuted.

Beyond this, the statute itself explicitly calls for attention to these linkages. Section 101(a)(42)(A), which provides the definition governing § 208, speaks explicitly of "persecution or a well-founded fear of persecution on account of race, religion, nationality, membership in a particular social group, or political opinion." Similarly, § 243(h) extends *nonrefoulement* protection only where the "alien's life or freedom would be threatened in such country on account of race, religion, nationality, membership in a particular social group, or political opinion." What kind of connection to one of the five grounds must be shown to meet these standards?

Several observers expected some narrowing effort on the part of the BIA in response to *Cardoza–Fonseca,* to reduce the possible exposure of the

---

33. In the materials on Coup Plotters, *supra,* p. 822, State X is Mexico; the ABC party is the Institutional Revolutionary Party (PRI). Since 1983, when the quoted material was written, the role of opposition parties in Mexico has strengthened considerably, and the PRI won the 1988 presidential election by a very narrow margin. Controversy continues, however, over charges of vote fraud and other manipulation by the PRI. U.S. Dept. of State, Country Reports on Human Rights Practices for 1988, at 637 (Jt.Comm.Print (S.Prt. 101–3), 101st Cong., 1st Sess., February 1989).

United States to large numbers of aliens who might successfully claim asylum once the qualifying threshold was made easier to surmount. Many expected that narrowing to come in the way seemingly invited by the Supreme Court, through wider use of discretionary denials. Instead, as we saw in *Matter of Pula, supra,* the Board moved in the opposite direction, making discretionary denials far less common. But the narrowing impulse found expression in other ways, most prominently in a growing insistence by the BIA that the alien demonstrate convincingly that the harm he fears is "on account of" one of the five grounds. *See* Anker & Blum, *supra,* 1 Int'l J.Refugee L. 67. Several courts have resisted this administrative approach. Consider, as you read through the following materials, which approach best reflects congressional intent in passing the Refugee Act. Which best reflects the purposes of the refugee treaties?

a. *Neutrality and Imputed Political Opinion*

In *Matter of Acosta,* 19 I & N Dec. 211 (BIA 1985), the alien, a former taxi driver in San Salvador, had received death threats from the guerrillas in that country because he refused to take part in work stoppages they were sponsoring. The Board wrote (*id.* at 234–35):

> * * * The fact that the respondent was threatened by the guerrillas as part of a campaign to destabilize the government demonstrates that the guerrillas' actions were undertaken to further their political goals in the civil controversy in El Salvador. However, conduct undertaken to further the goals of one faction in a political controversy does not necessarily constitute persecution "on account of political opinion" so as to qualify an alien as a "refugee" within the meaning of the Act.
>
> As we have previously discussed, the term "persecution" means the infliction of suffering or harm in order to punish an individual for possessing a particular belief or characteristic the persecutor seeks to overcome. It follows, therefore, that the requirement of "persecution on account of political opinion" means that the particular belief or characteristic a persecutor seeks to overcome in an individual must be his political opinion. Thus, the requirement of "persecution on account of political opinion" refers not to the ultimate political end that may be served by persecution, but to the belief held by an individual that causes him to be the object of the persecution. * * *
>
> In the respondent's case there are no facts showing that the guerrillas were aware of or sought to punish the respondent for his political opinion; nor was there any showing that the respondent's refusal to participate in the work-stoppages was motivated by his political opinion. Absent such a showing the respondent failed to demonstrate that the particular belief the guerrillas sought to overcome in him was his political opinion. Therefore he does not come within this ground of persecution.

The Ninth Circuit has taken a far different approach. It reversed the Board's decision in a somewhat similar case involving another Salvadoran asylum applicant and ordered the Board both to grant withholding of deportation and to consider the applicant eligible for asylum. *Bolanos-Hernandez v. INS*, 767 F.2d 1277 (9th Cir.1984). On the question whether the threatened harm was based on "political opinion," the court wrote (*id.* at 1286–87):

> The government concedes that Bolanos has consciously chosen not to join either of the contending forces in El Salvador because he wishes to remain neutral, yet it argues that any persecution Bolanos might suffer would not be because of his political opinion. We find it somewhat difficult to follow the government's argument. The government contends that Bolanos' decision to remain politically neutral is not a political choice. There is nothing in the record to support this contention. Presumably the government is suggesting either that neutrality is always apolitical or that an individual who chooses neutrality must establish that the choice was made for political reasons. We disagree with both of these contentions.

> Choosing to remain neutral is no less a political decision than is choosing to affiliate with a particular political faction. * * * When a person is aware of contending political forces and affirmatively chooses not to join any faction, that choice is a political one. A rule that one must identify with one of two dominant warring political factions in order to possess a political opinion, when many persons may, in fact, be opposed to the views and policies of both, would frustrate one of the basic objectives of the Refugee Act of 1980—to provide protection to all victims of persecution regardless of ideology. Moreover, construing "political opinion" in so short-sighted and grudging a manner could result in limiting the benefits under the ameliorative provisions of our immigration laws to those who join one political extreme or another; moderates who choose to sit out a battle would not qualify.

> The government's second suggestion is equally unconvincing. The motive underlying any political choice may, if examined closely, prove to be, in whole or in part, non-political. Certainly a political affiliation may be undertaken for non-political, as well as political, reasons. A decision to join a particular political party may, for example, be made to curry favor, gain social acceptability, advance one's career, or obtain access to money or positions of power. Similarly, a decision to remain neutral may be made, in whole or in part, for non-political reasons. However, the reasons underlying an individual's political choice are of no significance for purposes of sections 243(h) and 208(a) and the government may not inquire into them. Whatever the motivation, an individual's choice, once made, constitutes, for better or for worse, a manifestation of political opinion.

> * * * It does not matter to the persecutors what the individual's motivation is. The guerrillas in El Salvador do not inquire into the reasoning process of those who insist on remaining

neutral and refuse to join their cause. They are concerned only with an act that constitutes an overt manifestation of a political opinion. Persecution because of that overt manifestation is persecution because of a political opinion.

In *Bolanos–Hernandez* the Ninth Circuit helped launch a line of analysis often referred to as "imputed political opinion." In *Hernandez–Ortiz v. INS,* 777 F.2d 509 (9th Cir.1985), the court expanded on this analysis, and suggested a presumption that should operate in such circumstances. Hernandez–Ortiz had moved to reopen her case based on additional information that became available after her initial deportation hearing in 1980. (Some of the information related to her own treatment in 1982 when she was erroneously deported while her case was awaiting judicial review; a few weeks later she was able to return to the United States at U.S. government expense.) The BIA denied the motion to reopen, but the court of appeals reversed. Because of the procedural posture of the case, the court assumed that the facts she alleged were true. Under that account, in November 1980,

> Hernandez–Ortiz's brother—a teacher—and his wife were murdered in El Salvador by Salvadoran security forces. * * * [In] November 1982, Salvadoran soldiers entered her grandparents' grocery store, threatened them with submachine guns, and robbed them of both goods and the store's gross receipts for the day. In June 1983, * * * her brother-in-law's wife was kidnapped late at night by members of the Salvadoran National Guard who beat her and threw salt and sand in her eyes. The Guardsmen returned to Hernandez–Ortiz's brother-in-law's house and threatened to kill both her brother-in-law and his wife.

777 F.2d, at 512.

The court dealt with the "political opinion" issue as follows:

> The Board * * * concluded that neither Hernandez–Ortiz nor any of her relatives has ever been harmed "on account of race, religion, nationality, membership in a particular social group, or political opinion." A clear probability that an alien's life or freedom is threatened, without any indication of the basis for the threat, is generally insufficient to constitute "persecution" and thus to preclude the Attorney General from deporting the alien. There must also be some evidence that the threat is related to one of the factors enumerated in section 243(h). Although Hernandez–Ortiz opposes the current regime in El Salvador, the Board concluded that she failed to demonstrate that any threat to her life or freedom was related to her political opinion. The Board based this conclusion on the fact that Hernandez–Ortiz did not allege that she or any of her relatives was a member of any political groups or "had ever participated in the current conflict in El Salvador."

> Section 243(h) could be read as providing that only the alien's race, religion, nationality, membership in a particular social group, or political opinion, not the persecutor's, can be considered in

determining whether oppressive conduct constitutes persecution. However, we do not believe the section may properly be given so restrictive or mechanical a construction. "Persecution" occurs only when there is a difference between the persecutor's views or status and that of the victim; it is oppression which is inflicted on groups or individuals because of a difference that the persecutor will not tolerate. For this reason, in determining whether threats or violence constitute political persecution, it is permissible to examine the motivation of the persecutor; we may look to the political views and actions of the entity or individual responsible for the threats or violence, as well as to the victim's, and we may examine the relationship between the two.

In this case it is the forces of the government that are inflicting the threats and violence. When a government exerts its military strength against an individual or a group within its population and there is no reason to believe that the individual or group has engaged in any criminal activity or other conduct that would provide a legitimate basis for governmental action, the most reasonable presumption is that the government's actions are politically motivated. Here, numerous incidents were all directed at members of the same family. Because the killings, kidnapping, beating, threats, robbery, and harassment were all inflicted by government forces, the inference that they were connected and politically motivated is an appropriate one.

A government does not under ordinary circumstances engage in political persecution of those who share its ideology, only of those whose views or philosophies differ, at least in the government's perception. It is irrelevant whether a victim's political view is neutrality, as in *Bolanos–Hernandez,* or disapproval of the acts or opinions of the government. Moreover, it is irrelevant whether a victim actually possesses any of these opinions as long as the government believes that he does. *See Argueta* [*v. INS,* 759 F.2d 1395, 1397 (9th Cir.1985)](death threat based on persecutors' *erroneous* belief that alien was a member of a guerrilla organization is sufficient to establish clear probability of persecution based on political opinion); *see also* [*UNHCR*] *Handbook,* p. 7, at ¶¶ 80–83 (government's persecution of persons to whom it attributes certain political opinions is persecution on account of political opinion). In most societies, a failure to take sides or to articulate a political opinion does not ordinarily trigger retribution. However, when through legally cognizable inferences or otherwise, an alien establishes a *prima facie* case that he is likely to be persecuted because of the government's belief about his views or loyalties, his actual political conduct, be it silence or affirmative advocacy, and his actual political views, be they neutrality or partisanship, are irrelevant; whatever the circumstances, the persecution is properly categorized as being "on account of ... political opinion."

777 F.2d, at 516–17.

Notes

1. *Hernandez–Ortiz* established a strong presumption that certain kinds of threats are to be treated as being "on account of" political opinion. Is this presumption appropriate or does it go too far? Under it, does *any* form of threatened harsh treatment necessarily come within § 208 or § 243(h)?

2. As a policy matter, should a citizen's choice to remain neutral in the midst of a vicious civil war be protected through the mechanism of political asylum? In such a setting, a great contest is underway for the future of the country. Should citizens simply be expected to take a stand in the midst of such tragic circumstances, and abide any consequences? Think about how you might have reacted to a stance of purported neutrality during the American Civil War. (For an intriguing quasi-fictional treatment of these questions, see William Safire's novel, *Freedom* (1988), exploring the position of former U.S. Vice President and then Senator John Breckenridge, who attempted after the firing on Fort Sumter to adhere to a kind of neutrality in favor of "the Union as it was" but ultimately became a Confederate general.)

3. *M.A. v. INS*, 899 F.2d 304, 315 (4th Cir.1990) (en banc), discussed *supra* p. 825, involved a Salvadoran who wished to avoid conscription into the national army because of its human rights violations in the course of fighting the civil war there. The majority opinion stated: "It is unclear whether neutrality can be considered a 'political opinion' within the meaning of the Refugee Act." The court in *Perlera–Escobar v. EOIR*, 894 F.2d 1292, 1298 (11th Cir.1990), another Salvadoran case, raised a similar question in describing approvingly what it read as the applicable BIA doctrine: "In the context of a civil war, * * * the BIA has declined to apply the principle that a desire to remain neutral is an expression of a political opinion for purposes of asylum and withholding of deportation. The BIA's position is no doubt based upon the fact that adoption of such an interpretation would create a sinkhole that would swallow the rule."

A separate opinion by Judge Sneed in *Mendoza Perez v. INS*, 902 F.2d 760, 767–68 (9th Cir.1990), puts a sharper edge on these points, in the course of criticizing earlier Circuit doctrine and comparing it to that of several other Circuits:

> The Ninth Circuit has held that political neutrality is a political opinion for purposes of [INA § 243(h)]. This holding eviscerates the political opinion requirement of the statute. It means that a politically inactive alien, and perhaps most illegal aliens are, may now gain the protection of asylum. * * * The core idea of political activism underlies the concept of "refugee" status. * * * We distort the meaning of an important requirement for refugee status when we permit political aloofness to serve as an active "political opinion," that endangers its holder. It also demeans the true martyr for whom asylum was intended.

Professor Hathaway takes a strikingly different view. He criticizes Canadian cases that have ruled against the claimant because of "the objective unimportance of the claimant's political acts, her own inability to characterize her actions as flowing from a particular political ideology, or even an explicit disavowal of the views ascribed to her by the state." J. Hathaway, *supra* note 1, at 155–56. This focus is misguided, he argues, provided the proof of likely persecution is sufficient. The point of refugee law is to "establish a surrogate protection system for those whose membership in the national community has been fundamentally denied," and not simply "to protect persons on the basis of personal merit," such as the actual possession of some well-considered political opinion. *Id.* at 157.

Which view do you find more persuasive? Which better accords with the statute and treaty? What vision of the underlying purposes of, and policy constraints affecting, political asylum undergirds Sneed's position? Hathaway's?

4. *In Matter of Juan* (BIA 1989), a nonprecedent decision reported in Refugee Reports, Nov. 17, 1989, at 13, the applicant was a fifteen-year-old Kanjobal Indian from Guatemala. In 1982 government soldiers appeared in his village with a list of names of people who allegedly had given corn to the guerrillas. Juan's father, whose name was on the list, was taken and found decapitated the next day. Shortly thereafter the guerrillas entered the village and abducted Juan's mother. She was found dead the next day. The immigration judge denied asylum, but the BIA, somewhat reluctantly, reversed, stating that it was bound in this case by Ninth Circuit precedents regarding "imputed political opinion."

Two members dissented, in an opinion by Board member Heilman, arguing vigorously that asylum should not be granted. He wrote: "The only reason to speak in terms of imputed political opinion is to 'pigeon-hole' the case within one of the five categories set forth in the law for asylum. * * * It seems a bit absurd in these circumstances to try to divine some 'imputation' of opinion, as if the individual's political views would save or condemn him." He concluded that the government was more interested "in making examples and intimidating the population" than in inflicting persecution because of political opinion. *Id.* at 14.

This passage distills the essence of the debate over this issue and the Board's doctrine applying the "on account of" language in the definition. Did Congress intend to protect only those who are targeted because of explicit political opinion they chose to adopt or express? If so, the Ninth Circuit's case law is wrong. Or should the Refugee Act be understood to protect all those who have been or are likely to be targeted by politically motivated persecution, even if unfairly or even if only to make an example that might intimidate others? What vision of the underlying purposes of, and policy constraints affecting, political asylum undergirds Heilman's position? What vision underlies the Ninth Circuit's position?

INS v. ELIAS–ZACARIAS

Supreme Court of the United States, 1992.
502 U.S. 478, 112 S.Ct. 812, 117 L.Ed.2d 38.

Justice Scalia delivered the opinion of the Court.

The principal question presented by this case is whether a guerrilla organization's attempt to coerce a person into performing military service necessarily constitutes "persecution on account of ... political opinion" under § 101(a)(42) of the Immigration and Nationality Act.

ISSUE

I

Respondent Elias–Zacarias, a native of Guatemala, was apprehended in July 1987 for entering the United States without inspection. In deportation proceedings brought by petitioner Immigration and Naturalization Service (INS), Elias–Zacarias conceded his deportability but requested asylum and withholding of deportation.

The Immigration Judge summarized Elias–Zacarias' testimony as follows:

"[A]round the end of January in 1987 [when Elias–Zacarias was 18], two armed, uniformed guerrillas with handkerchiefs covering part of their faces came to his home. Only he and his parents were there.... [T]he guerrillas asked his parents and himself to join with them, but they all refused. The guerrillas asked them why and told them that they would be back, and that they should think it over about joining them.

"[Elias–Zacarias] did not want to join the guerrillas because the guerrillas are against the government and he was afraid that the government would retaliate against him and his family if he did join the guerrillas. [H]e left Guatemala at the end of March [1987] ... because he was afraid that the guerrillas would return."

The Immigration Judge understood from this testimony that Elias–Zacarias' request for asylum and for withholding of deportation was "based on this one attempted recruitment by the guerrillas." She concluded that Elias–Zacarias had failed to demonstrate persecution or a well-founded fear of persecution on account of race, religion, nationality, membership in a particular social group, or political opinion, and was not eligible for asylum. She further concluded that he did not qualify for withholding of deportation.

The Board of Immigration Appeals (BIA) summarily dismissed Elias–Zacarias' appeal on procedural grounds. Elias–Zacarias then moved the BIA to reopen his deportation hearing so that he could submit new evidence that, following his departure from Guatemala, the guerrillas had twice returned to his family's home in continued efforts to recruit him. The BIA denied reopening on the ground that even with this new evidence Elias–Zacarias had failed to make a prima facie showing of eligibility for asylum and had failed to show that the results of his deportation hearing would be changed.

The Court of Appeals for the Ninth Circuit, treating the BIA's denial of the motion to reopen as an affirmance on the merits of the Immigration Judge's ruling, reversed. The court ruled that acts of conscription by a nongovernmental group constitute persecution on account of political opinion, and determined that Elias–Zacarias had a "well-founded fear" of such conscription. We granted certiorari.

II

* * * The BIA's determination that Elias–Zacarias was not eligible for asylum must be upheld if "supported by reasonable, substantial, and probative evidence on the record considered as a whole." INA § 106(a)(4). It can be reversed only if the evidence presented by Elias–Zacarias was such that a reasonable factfinder would have to conclude that the requisite fear of persecution existed.[1]

The Court of Appeals found reversal warranted. In its view, a guerrilla organization's attempt to conscript a person into its military forces necessarily constitutes "persecution on account of ... political opinion," because "the person resisting forced recruitment is expressing a political opinion hostile to the persecutor and because the persecutors' motive in carrying out the kidnapping is political." The first half of this seems to us untrue, and the second half irrelevant.

 Even a person who supports a guerrilla movement might resist recruitment for a variety of reasons—fear of combat, a desire to remain with one's family and friends, a desire to earn a better living in civilian life, to mention only a few. The record in the present case not only failed to show a political motive on Elias–Zacarias' part; it showed the opposite. He testified that he refused to join the guerrillas because he was afraid that the government would retaliate against him and his family if he did so. Nor is there any indication (assuming, *arguendo,* it would suffice) that the guerrillas erroneously *believed* that Elias–Zacarias' refusal was politically based.

As for the Court of Appeals' conclusion that the guerrillas' "motive in carrying out the kidnapping is political": It apparently meant by this that the guerrillas seek to fill their ranks in order to carry on their war against the government and pursue their political goals. But that does not render the forced recruitment "persecution on account of ... political opinion." * * * The ordinary meaning of the phrase "persecution on account of ... political opinion" in § 101(a)(42) is persecution on account of the victim's political opinion, not the persecutor's. If a Nazi regime persecutes Jews, it is not, within the ordinary meaning of language, engaging in persecution on account of political opinion; and if a fundamentalist Moslem regime persecutes democrats, it is not engaging in persecution on account of religion. Thus, the mere existence of a generalized "political" motive

---

1. Quite beside the point, therefore, is the dissent's assertion that "the record in this case is more than adequate to *support the conclusion* that this respondent's refusal [to join the guerrillas] was a form of expressive conduct that constituted the statement of a 'political opinion,' " (emphasis added). To reverse the BIA finding we must find that the evidence not only supports that conclusion, but *compels* it—and also compels the further conclusion that Elias–Zacarias had a well-founded fear that the guerrillas would persecute him *because of* that political opinion.

underlying the guerrillas' forced recruitment is inadequate to establish (and, indeed, goes far to refute) the proposition that Elias–Zacarias fears persecution on account of political opinion, as § 101(a)(42) requires.

Elias–Zacarias appears to argue that not taking sides with any political faction is itself the affirmative expression of a political opinion. That seems to us not ordinarily so, since we do not agree with the dissent that only a "narrow, grudging construction of the concept of 'political opinion'" would distinguish it from such quite different concepts as indifference, indecisiveness and risk-averseness. But we need not decide whether the evidence compels the conclusion that Elias–Zacarias held a political opinion. Even if it does, Elias–Zacarias still has to establish that the record also compels the conclusion that he has a "well-founded fear" that the guerrillas will persecute him because of that political opinion, rather than because of his refusal to fight with them. He has not done so with the degree of clarity necessary to permit reversal of a BIA finding to the contrary; indeed, he has not done so at all.[2]

Elias–Zacarias objects that he cannot be expected to provide direct proof of his persecutors' motives. We do not require that. But since the statute makes motive critical, he must provide some evidence of it, direct or circumstantial. And if he seeks to obtain judicial reversal of the BIA's determination, he must show that the evidence he presented was so compelling that no reasonable factfinder could fail to find the requisite fear of persecution. That he has not done.

The BIA's determination should therefore have been upheld in all respects, and we reverse the Court of Appeals' judgment to the contrary.

It is so ordered.

JUSTICE STEVENS, with whom JUSTICE BLACKMUN and JUSTICE O'CONNOR join, dissenting.

Respondent refused to join a guerrilla organization that engaged in forced recruitment in Guatemala. He fled the country because he was afraid the guerrillas would return and "take me and kill me." After his departure, armed guerrillas visited his family on two occasions searching for him. In testimony that the hearing officer credited, he stated that he is still afraid to return to Guatemala because "these people" can come back to "take me or kill me."

---

2. The dissent misdescribes the record on this point in several respects. For example, it exaggerates the "well-foundedness" of whatever fear Elias–Zacarias possesses, by progressively transforming his testimony that he was afraid the guerrillas would " 'take me or kill me,' " into, first, "the guerrillas' *implied threat* to 'take' him or to 'kill' him," (emphasis added), and, then, into the flat assertion that the guerrillas "*responded by threatening* to 'take' or to 'kill' him" (emphasis added). The dissent also erroneously describes it as "undisputed" that the cause of the harm Elias–Zacarias fears, if that harm should occur, will be "the guerrilla organization's displeasure with his refusal to join them in their armed insurrection against the government." The record shows no such concession by the INS, and all Elias–Zacarias said on the point was that he feared being taken or killed by the guerrillas. It is quite plausible, indeed likely, that the taking would be engaged in by the guerrillas in order to augment their troops rather than show their displeasure; and the killing he feared might well be a killing in the course of resisting being taken.

It is undisputed that respondent has a well-founded fear that he will be harmed, if not killed, if he returns to Guatemala. It is also undisputed that the cause of that harm, if it should occur, is the guerrilla organization's displeasure with his refusal to join them in their armed insurrection against the government. The question of law that the case presents is whether respondent's well-founded fear is a "fear of persecution on account of ... political opinion" within the meaning of § 101(a)(42) of the Immigration and Naturalization Act.

* * *

Today the Court holds that respondent's fear of persecution is not "on account of ... political opinion" for two reasons. First, he failed to prove that his refusal to join the guerrillas was politically motivated; indeed, he testified that he was at least in part motivated by a fear that government forces would retaliate against him or his family if he joined the guerrillas. Second, he failed to prove that his persecutors' motives were political. In particular, the Court holds that the persecutors' implicit threat to retaliate against respondent "because of his refusal to fight with them," is not persecution on account of political opinion. I disagree with both parts of the Court's reasoning.

I

A political opinion can be expressed negatively as well as affirmatively. A refusal to support a cause—by staying home on election day, by refusing to take an oath of allegiance, or by refusing to step forward at an induction center—can express a political opinion as effectively as an affirmative statement or affirmative conduct. Even if the refusal is motivated by nothing more than a simple desire to continue living an ordinary life with one's family, it is the kind of political expression that the asylum provisions of the statute were intended to protect [quoting from the *Bolanos-Hernandez* excerpt on p. 830, *supra*].

* * *

The narrow, grudging construction of the concept of "political opinion" that the Court adopts today is inconsistent with the basic approach to this statute that the Court endorsed in *INS v. Cardoza–Fonseca.*

* * *

Similar reasoning should resolve any doubts concerning the political character of an alien's refusal to take arms against a legitimate government in favor of the alien. In my opinion, the record in this case is more than adequate to support the conclusion that this respondent's refusal was a form of expressive conduct that constituted the statement of a "political opinion" within the meaning of § 208(a).[5]

---

5. Here, respondent not only engaged in expressive conduct by refusing to join the guerrilla organization but also explained that he did so "[b]ecause they see very well, that if you join the guerrillas ... then you are against the government. You are against the government and if you join them then it is to die there. And, then the government is against you and against your family." Respondent thus expressed the political view that he was for the government and against the guerrillas. The statute speaks simply in

II

It follows as night follows day that the guerrillas' implied threat to "take" him or to "kill" him if he did not change his position constituted threatened persecution "on account of" that political opinion. As the Court of Appeals explained in *Bolanos-Hernandez, supra:*

> "It does not matter to the persecutors what the individual's motivation is. The guerrillas in El Salvador do not inquire into the reasoning process of those who insist on remaining neutral and refuse to join their cause. They are concerned only with an act that constitutes an overt manifestation of a political opinion. Persecution because of that overt manifestation is persecution because of a political opinion."[6]

It is important to emphasize that the statute does not require that an applicant for asylum prove exactly why his persecutors would act against him; it only requires him to show that he has a "well-founded fear of persecution on account of ... political opinion." As we recognized in *INS v. Cardoza Fonseca*, the applicant meets this burden if he shows that there is a " 'reasonable possibility' " that he will be persecuted on account of his political opinion (quoting *INS v. Stevic*). Because respondent expressed a political opinion by refusing to join the guerrillas, and they responded by threatening to "take" or to "kill" him if he did not change his mind, his fear that the guerrillas will persecute him on account of his political opinion is well founded.[7]

Accordingly, I would affirm the judgment of the Court of Appeals.

Notes

1. Does the decision in *Elias-Zacarias* overrule the doctrine of imputed political opinion? INS General Counsel Grover Joseph Rees issued a lengthy opinion in 1993 maintaining that it did not. 70 Interp.Rel. 498 (1993). The question was left open, he opined, because the Court "explicitly recognized" that the alien there had not put that question in issue, citing

terms of a political opinion and does not require that the view be well developed or elegantly expressed.

6. The Government has argued that respondent's statement is analogous to that of a person who leaves a country to avoid being drafted into military service. The INS has long recognized, however, that the normal enforcement of selective service laws is not "persecution" within the meaning of the statute even if the draftee's motive is political. Thus, while holding that an Afghan soldier who refused to fight under Soviet command qualified as a political refugee, *Matter of Salim*, 18 I. & N.Dec. 311 (BIA 1982), the INS has adhered "to the long-accepted position that it is not persecution for a country to require military service of its citizens." *Matter of A–G-*, 19 I. & N.Dec. 502, 506 (BIA 1987); cf. United Nations High Commissioner for Refugees, Handbook on Procedures and Criteria for Determining Refugee Status ¶ 167 (1979) ("Fear of prosecution and punishment for desertion or draft-evasion does not in itself constitute well-founded fear of persecution under the [1967 United Nations Protocol Relating to the Status of Refugees]").

7. In response to this dissent, the Court suggests that respondent and I have exaggerated the "well-foundedness" of his fear. The Court's legal analysis, however, would produce precisely the same result no matter how unambiguous the guerrillas' threatened retaliation might have been. Moreover, any doubts concerning the sinister character of a suggestion to "think it over" delivered by two uniformed masked men carrying machine guns should be resolved in respondent's favor.

this passage: "Nor is there any indication (assuming, *arguendo*, it would suffice) that the guerrillas erroneously *believed* that Elias–Zacarias' refusal was politically based." Rees then concluded that the imputed political opinion doctrine should be sustained because it serves the objectives of the statute. He illustrated his point by an example based on the analogous notion of imputed religious belief (*id.* at 501–02):

> Thus [without some doctrine of "imputed opinion"], a Mr. Rosenberg whom the Nazi government of Germany had sentenced to the gas chamber because it erroneously believed him to be a Jew, but who had somehow made it to the United States to apply for asylum, would not qualify for asylum. No matter how clear it might be that the government was going to kill him upon his return, and that the killing would be specifically motivated by a desire to do unpleasant things to Jews, such persecution would not be "on account of ... religion" unless the government happened to be correct about Rosenberg's religion. This result is hardly compelled by the language of the statute; the most straightforward meaning of the words "persecution ... on account of ... religion" would appear to encompass a program specifically intended to stamp out Judaism even though implementation of the program should lead to some persecution of non-Jews. Nor does it seem appropriate to ascribe to Congress an unarticulated intention to generate such harsh results.

> Nevertheless, as the Court underscored in *Elias-Zacarias*, prosecution and punishment under a law of general applicability will not ordinarily constitute persecution "on account of" one of the five statutory grounds. The "imputed political opinion" exception to this rule arises only when there is evidence that the law and/or its enforcement are motivated in whole or in part by a desire to punish or deter one of the five characteristics protected by the asylum and refugee laws.

> Such evidence may be either direct or circumstantial. Direct evidence would consist of statements by the persecutor to the effect that violators of the law are to be regarded and punished not just as ordinary lawbreakers but as political enemies. * * * Circumstantial evidence has most commonly consisted of punishment so severe as to seem obviously directed at real or perceived enemies rather than at ordinary lawbreakers.

Id. at 501–02. For similar conclusions, arguing that *Elias-Zacarias* is highly fact-specific, see Anker, Blum & Johnson, *The Supreme Court's Decision in* INS v. Elias–Zacarias: *Is There Any "There" There?*, 69 Interp.Rel. 285 (1992).

2. On the other hand, the BIA has read the decision broadly, as a mandate for restrictively analyzing the motivation of the alleged persecutor. *See, e.g., Matter of R—*, Int.Dec. 3195 (BIA 1992) (rejecting claim by Sikh asylum seeker from the Punjab, despite evidence of mistreatment by Indian police: "the record reflects that the purpose of the mistreatment was to extract information about Sikh militants, rather than to persecute

the applicant 'because' of his political opinions or the mere fact that he was a Sikh''); *Matter of T—*, Int.Dec. 3187 (BIA 1992) (similarly rejecting claim by Sri Lankan Tamil). Many courts, however, have remanded BIA decisions that labored too hard to find that mistreatment simply amounts to legitimate law enforcement or otherwise strained to read the persecutor's motives narrowly. *See, e.g., Shirazi–Parsa v. INS*, 14 F.3d 1424 (9th Cir.1994); *Perkovic v. INS*, 33 F.3d 615 (6th Cir.1994). Several have also supported the notion that "imputed political opinion" remains a viable basis for asylum. *See, e.g., Nasseri v. Moschorak*, 34 F.3d 723 (9th Cir.1994); *Rajaratnam v. Moyer*, 832 F.Supp. 1219 (N.D.Ill.1993). For a useful discussion of the BIA cases, see Blum, *License to Kill: Asylum Law and the Principle of Legitimate Governmental Authority to "Investigate its Enemies,"* 28 Willamette L.Rev. 719 (1992).

3. Is the presumption set forth in *Hernandez-Ortiz* still valid after *Elias-Zacarias*?

Elias-Zacarias and Judicial Review

Elias-Zacarias may have had its most noticeable impact in shaping the standards—or at least the language—used by courts in reviewing factual determinations in asylum and withholding cases.

Because the benefits of § 243(h) are mandatory for those who qualify, it has long been held that courts review denials of withholding under a "substantial evidence" test. Courts also generally review the factual decisions on threshold eligibility for asylum under § 208 under the same test, but review discretionary denials of asylum under the somewhat more deferential "abuse of discretion" standard. *See, e.g., Bolanos–Hernandez v. INS*, 767 F.2d 1277, 1282 n. 9 (9th Cir.1984); *Carvajal–Munoz v. INS*, 743 F.2d 562, 567 (7th Cir.1984); *Cruz–Lopez v. INS*, 802 F.2d 1518, 1519 n. 1 (4th Cir.1986). *But see Marroquin–Manriquez v. INS*, 699 F.2d 129, 133 (3d Cir.1983), *cert. denied*, 467 U.S. 1259, 104 S.Ct. 3553, 82 L.Ed.2d 855 (1984) (suggesting that the more deferential "abuse of discretion" standard should be used in judicial review of all such issues, because of the "necessary application of expertise in the determination that a fear of persecution is well-founded"). *See also Ananeh–Firempong v. INS*, 766 F.2d 621, 624 (1st Cir.1985) (acknowledging that courts should give the Attorney General "considerable leeway" in asylum cases, but rejecting the "special judicial mood of extraordinary caution" advocated by the dissent). *See generally* Legomsky, *Political Asylum and the Theory of Judicial Review*, 73 Minn. L.Rev. 1205 (1989).[34]

After *Elias-Zacarias*, courts now regularly state the standard for reviewing factual determinations with words like these: "To reverse the

---

34. Some asylum cases suggest an even more deferential stance toward administrative decisions in the asylum process. *Perlera–Escobar v. EOIR*, 894 F.2d 1292, 1299 (11th Cir.1990) ("What constitutes a political opinion under the [Refugee Act's definition of 'refugee'] is a political question which the courts are not especially qualified to decide."); *M.A. v. United States I.N.S.*, 899 F.2d 304, 309 (4th Cir.1990) (en banc) ("[W]e must be sensitive to the inherently political nature of the decision whether or not to deport. * * * The arguments for a deferential abuse of discretion standard are thus multitudinous and compelling.").

BIA's determination, the evidence must *compel* the conclusion that [the applicant] had a well-founded fear of persecution on account of his political opinions." *Sotelo-Aquije v. Slattery*, 17 F.3d 33, 35 (2d Cir.1994) (emphasis added). Is this a gloss on the "substantial evidence" test or a new and more deferential standard? Consider the following view:

> [*Elias-Zacarias*] stated that the Board may be reversed only if the evidence the petitioner presented "was so compelling that no reasonable fact-finder could fail to find the requisite fear of persecution." It is a matter of observation that in current briefing of asylum cases the INS relies on this language and appears to believe that it has a force which somehow casts the balance in the Board's favor.
>
> Acknowledging the vividness of style with which the standard was presented in *Elias-Zacarias*, we do not find that without saying so the Supreme Court intended to change the normal principles of administrative review and put the INS's [*sic*] factual determinations in the same category as those made by a prison official administering a prison.

Ghebllawi v. INS, 28 F.3d 83, 85–86 (9th Cir.1994). Is this wishful thinking by a notably activist court? For a critique of the deferential stance in *Elias-Zacarias* and other Supreme Court cases, see Johnson, *Responding to the "Litigation Explosion": The Plain Meaning of Executive Branch Primacy Over Immigration*, 71 N.C.L.Rev. 413 (1993).

b. Civil War Situations: The Effect on Political Asylum Determinations

A variety of related issues can arise in cases involving claimants from countries embroiled in civil war or widespread insurrection. The following materials present the Board's approach and the reactions of several courts.

Fuentes and Risks From Nongovernmental Actors
MATTER OF FUENTES

Board of Immigration Appeals, 1988.
19 I & N Dec. 658.

In a decision dated August 14, 1984, the immigration judge found the respondent deportable as charged, denied his applications for asylum and withholding of deportation, but granted him voluntary departure. The respondent has appealed from that decision. The appeal will be dismissed.

The respondent is a 33–year–old native and citizen of El Salvador who entered the United States in 1982 without inspection. He conceded deportability at his hearing. The sole issue on appeal concerns his eligibility for asylum and for withholding of deportation.

The respondent maintains that he will be persecuted and harmed by leftist insurgents in El Salvador on account of his association with the Government of El Salvador. He testified that he was a member of the national police in El Salvador from 1967 to 1980 and a guard at the United

States Embassy from 1980 until 1982. In both capacities, the respondent and his fellow officers were attacked by guerrillas on several occasions. In one incident, for example, while checking the highways, guerrillas assaulted his police group and killed one of his fellow officers. On another occasion, four guerrillas in an automobile machine-gunned the Embassy while he was standing guard. When the guerrillas returned for a second attack, they were captured.

The respondent further testified that many inhabitants of his hometown had joined the guerrillas and they were very active in that area. The guerrillas there knew him by name, knew he was a member of the police, and had threatened him personally while he was a member of the national police. He stated that the government was unable to protect him in El Salvador and he had fled to avoid being killed. The respondent additionally testified that two of his relatives, who had been "local commanders," had committed suicide because of their fear of the guerrillas.

In addition to his own testimony, the respondent presented two witnesses who had known him in El Salvador. They testified that, the situation in his hometown was very dangerous; that it was an area of ongoing fighting between the military and the guerrillas; that the guerrillas there killed people for "having been" in the military; that the guerrillas knew of the respondent's past service; that he would be punished or "disappear" if he returned to his hometown even if he was no longer in service; and that the government could not protect him. One of the two witnesses also stated that the guerrillas had the names of the people who had been in the service and would immediately find out if the respondent returned to his hometown.

* * *

Based upon our review of the record, we find that the respondent has failed to demonstrate his eligibility for asylum and, consequently, also has not satisfied the higher burden of proof necessary to establish eligibility for withholding of deportation.

There are two related, but distinct, bases underlying this respondent's asylum claim. The first is his fear arising from the events that occurred while he was a policeman and guard in El Salvador prior to his departure in 1982. The second aspect of his claim is the fear that he will face persecution as a *former* national policeman if he returns to El Salvador.

We do not find that the respondent can demonstrate a well-founded fear of persecution "on account of" one of the grounds specified in the Act based on the events that occurred while he was a policeman and guard in El Salvador from 1967 to 1982. In so holding, we find that dangers faced by policemen as a result of that status alone are not ones faced on account of race, religion, nationality, membership in a particular social group, or political opinion.

There is presently a political struggle ongoing in El Salvador, the ultimate objective of which is supremacy of one side over the other. The guerrillas, whom the respondent fears, appear intent on overthrowing the government. The government's obvious intent is to thwart the guerrillas' objectives. Unfortunately, violence appears inherent to such revolutionary struggles. Guerrillas often engage in violence, not only against military targets, but also against civilian institutions that, whether intentionally or not, support domestic stability and the strength of the existing government. Policemen are by their very nature public servants who embody the authority of the state. As policemen around the world have found, they are often attacked either because they are (or are viewed as) extensions of the government's military forces or simply because they are highly visible embodiments of the power of the state. In such circumstances, the dangers the police face are no more related to their personal characteristics or political beliefs than are the dangers faced by military combatants. Such dangers are perils arising from the nature of their employment and domestic unrest rather than "on account of" immutable characteristics or beliefs within the scope of sections 101(a)(42)(A) or 243(h) of the Act. Accordingly, we do not find that the respondent has demonstrated a well-founded fear of persecution "on account of" one of the grounds protected by the Act by virtue of the attacks and dangers he faced as a policeman and guard in El Salvador prior to his departure in 1982.

We note that if one were to find that a policeman or guerrilla was a victim of "persecution" within the scope of the Act based solely on the fact of an attack by one against the other, then it would follow that the attacker had participated in an act of "persecution" that would forever bar him or her from relief under sections 208(a) or 243(h). Such a "broad" interpretation of the concept of persecution "on account of race, religion, nationality, membership in a particular social group, or political opinion" would have the actual effect of greatly narrowing the group of persons eligible for asylum and withholding. Virtually all participants on either side of an armed struggle could be characterized as "persecutors" and would thereby be ineligible for asylum or withholding of deportation. The concept of "persecution" has not been so broadly defined.

The second aspect of the respondent's claim is his fear arising from his status as a former member of the national police. This is in fact an immutable characteristic, as it is one beyond the capacity of the respondent to change. It is possible that mistreatment occurring because of such a status in appropriate circumstances could be found to be persecution on account of political opinion or membership in a particular social group. For example, where hostilities have ceased, an asylum applicant who is subject to mistreatment because of a past association may be able to demonstrate a well-founded fear of persecution on account of a ground protected by the Act. We note that an applicant does not bear the unreasonable burden of establishing the exact motivation of a "persecutor" where different reasons for actions are possible. However, an applicant does bear the burden of establishing facts on which a reasonable person would fear that the danger arises on account of his race, religion, nationality, membership in a particular social group, or political opinion. The Government may also introduce supporting or contradictory evidence regarding both the potential for mistreatment and the reasons therefor.

In this case, the facts surrounding the possible danger faced by the respondent if he returns to his hometown and, more specifically, the reasons for that danger are not clearly developed. Although the respondent testified that he fears harm if he returns to El Salvador, his testimony relates to events that occurred while he was an active member of the government forces prior to his departure from El Salvador. One of his witnesses stated that the respondent would face danger if he returned to his hometown but was unable to testify to any instances of individuals endangered for having been in the military service. The final witness, however, did testify that the guerrillas in the respondent's hometown knew of those "who served in the military" and the respondent would "disappear" if he returned. But this witness also testified that the town was in a situation of strife between the army and the guerrillas with "terrible" fighting ongoing.

On this record, we do not find that the respondent has adequately demonstrated a well-founded fear of "persecution" on account of his status as a former policeman; rather, the record would indicate a danger that one with ties to a participant in a violent struggle might expect if he ventures into an area of open conflict. We note that participants in an ongoing armed struggle may well have reasons for refusing to tolerate the presence of "past" opponents in territories under their control or under dispute, unrelated to persecution on account of a protected status (*e.g.*, the most fundamental question of whether or not such individuals are in fact no longer taking part in the hostilities either overtly or covertly).

Even if one assumes the respondent's claim in this respect has been otherwise demonstrated, however, we do not find an asylum claim based on nongovernmental action adequately established where the evidence the respondent presents is directed to so local an area of his country of nationality. Although the respondent expressed a general fear of returning to El Salvador, his specific evidence focuses on the danger he would face if he returned to his hometown, where he is known by guerrillas and the conflict is still ongoing. The record in fact indicates that the respondent resided in San Salvador for 2 years prior to his departure from El Salvador and only visited his mother on weekends at his hometown when he had permission.

Because we do not find that the respondent has demonstrated his eligibility for the requested relief from deportation, the appeal will be dismissed.

ORDER: The appeal is dismissed.

Notes

1. The Board in *Fuentes* suggests that the alien could avoid the risk of harm by moving to another part of El Salvador, rather than returning to his hometown. *See also Etugh v. INS*, 921 F.2d 36 (3d Cir.1990) (ineligible for asylum because the scope of alleged persecution is "not national"). Is this "domestic flight alternative" doctrine, as it is sometimes known, appropriate in applying §§ 208 and 243(h)? What kinds of assurances should an adjudicator look for before accepting that the domestic alternative is sufficiently safe? *See Sotelo–Aquije v. Slattery*, 17 F.3d 33, 37 (2d

Cir.1994) (questioning the doctrine but in any event distinguishing *Fuentes*); J. Hathaway, *supra* note 1, at 133–34 (accepting the doctrine but insisting that it be limited to those "for whom the reality of protection [elsewhere in the country] is *meaningful* "). The doctrine implies that if both San Salvador and San Diego are reasonably safe refuges, preference should be given to the former, because it is in the person's own country. Is this too much to ask of one who already had to flee familiar territory? On the other hand, given that the individual has already chosen to leave his hometown, should this doctrine be seen as a sensible way to preserve the politically limited asylum resource for those who truly need it? He would have to uproot in either case.

2. Ordinarily asylum cases involve claims of likely persecution at the hands of the government. Although the Board rules against the applicant in *Fuentes,* it seems quite prepared to assume that, in a proper case, harm caused by guerrillas can amount to persecution. Should this be so? The Board's assumption, in any event, is in keeping with established case law. As the Ninth Circuit explained in *McMullen v. INS,* 658 F.2d 1312, 1315 n. 2 (9th Cir.1981), "persecution within the meaning of § 243(h) includes persecution by non-governmental groups * * * where it is shown that the government of the proposed country of deportation is unwilling or unable to control that group."

When is a government unable to control a persecuting group? This is a more complicated question than it might initially seem. In all countries, violent crime occurs to a greater or lesser degree, despite control efforts by the government. No one can be completely guaranteed protection against some such criminal activity. If a threatened violent crime has a political cast to it, must the potential harm be considered persecution of a kind that might give rise to a valid asylum claim? *Compare Zayas–Marini v. INS,* 785 F.2d 801 (9th Cir.1986) (death threats that resulted from private dispute and "personal animosity" do not meet requirements for asylum despite some doubts about Paraguayan government's willingness or ability to prevent their realization) *with Lazo–Majano v. INS,* 813 F.2d 1432 (9th Cir.1987) (rape and long-term mistreatment of his housekeeper by army sergeant held persecution based on political opinion). What if the persecutor's motives are mixed, partly based on personal reasons, partly on political reasons? For a helpful discussion of mixed motivations, see generally *Maikovskis v. INS,* 773 F.2d 435, 448 (2d Cir.1985); *id.* at 450 (Newman, J., concurring in part and dissenting in part).

Maldonado–Cruz and "Military Discipline"

In *Matter of Maldonado–Cruz,* 19 I & N Dec. 509 (BIA 1988), the applicant claimed he had been kidnapped and forced to join a guerrilla unit in El Salvador. He took an early opportunity to escape, but feared the guerrillas would kill him for having deserted if he returned to El Salvador. The Board found that any such harm would simply be a form of military discipline, and not persecution on account of any of the grounds specified in the Act. It explained (*id.* at 513, 516–17):

In analyzing a claim of persecution made in the context of a civil war, it is necessary to look to the motivation of the group threatening harm. Even though guerrillas may have the political strategy of overthrowing the government by military means, this does not mean that they cannot have objectives within that political strategy which are attained by acts of violence, but whose motivation is not related to any desire to persecute.

Historically, civil wars or revolutions have always contained strong currents of violence, threats, destruction, intimidation, and indeed ruthlessness. Individuals harmed by such violence or threats of harm in a civil war situation are not necessarily persecuted "on account of" the five categories enumerated in section 101(a)(42)(A) of the Act.

* * *

The record is devoid of any evidence that the guerrillas, who initially recruited the respondent to their cause, have any motivation to harm him because he holds views contrary to their political objectives. The threat against the respondent is consequently part of a military policy of the guerrilla organization, inherent in the nature of the organization, and a tool of discipline necessary to the continued functioning of the organization. The threat is therefore neither an act of persecution nor evidence of persecution by the guerrilla organization against the respondent on account of political opinion, or on any other ground set forth in the Refugee Act of 1980. *See Matter of Acosta, supra,* at 211.

* * *

The respondent's problem is not that the guerrillas are motivated to hate him because of political views they "impute" to him, but rather is that he has breached their discipline in a way that cannot remain unpunished. They might deal with an informer or a rapist in the same manner, if it suited their military or political needs. A guerrilla organization may therefore have a rational basis to punish deserters, devoid of any intent to inflict harm on account of political opinion. There is no reason in logic or fact to find otherwise.

The analysis applied here is, in addition, virtually identical to that applied in the case of a deserter from a conventional military force, for example, a deserter from the Salvadoran Army.

In sharp contrast to the BIA's position, the Ninth Circuit was inclined to view such situations as follows:

Because nongovernmental groups lack legitimate authority to conscript persons into their armies, their acts of conscription are tantamount to kidnapping and constitute persecution. The persecution is properly categorized as "on account of political opinion," because the person resisting forced recruitment is expressing a political opinion hostile to the persecutor and because the persecutor's motive in carrying out the kidnapping is political.

Zacarias v. INS, 921 F.2d 844, 850 (9th Cir.1990), *reversed sub nom. INS v. Elias–Zacarias*, 502 U.S. 478, 112 S.Ct. 812, 117 L.Ed.2d 38 (1992).[35]

In reversing the Ninth Circuit in *Zacarias*, the Supreme Court did not expressly deal with the first sentence from the Ninth Circuit opinion quoted above. Should it have? Isn't it odd for the highest judicial body to be, in essence, recognizing the legitimacy of an insurgent movement trying to topple a government that the U.S. executive branch supported?[36]

On the other hand, would it be right for asylum adjudication to accord legitimacy only to the established government in a situation of civil conflict? Perhaps the asylum provisions should be implemented in a manner that emphasizes nonideological application, a theme that figured prominently in the debates on the Refugee Act. Classic international law doctrines of neutrality required that both sides in a civil war be given equal treatment as "belligerents" once the conflict had reached the stage of a genuine contest for governance of the state. *See* L. Henkin, R. Pugh, O. Schachter, & H. Smit, *International Law: Cases and Materials* 874–76, 940–49 (3d ed.1993). Does a nonideological asylum policy then require the Board's approach to "military discipline"? Or would it require instead asylum for all persons facing possible forced recruitment by either side? Is the BIA's position in *Maldonado–Cruz* consistent with its approval of asylum for an Afghan draft evader, on the grounds that the Afghan government lacked legitimacy, in *Matter of Izatula*, Int.Dec. 3127 (BIA 1990), discussed *supra* p. 821?

A Middle Ground?

Judge (now Justice) Stephen Breyer's opinion for the Court in *Novoa–Umania v. INS*, 896 F.2d 1 (1st Cir.1990), which involved a Salvadoran applicant claiming a risk of persecution from both the guerrillas and the government, carved out a middle doctrinal position that may hold promise for developing sound standards to implement political asylum protections in the difficult circumstances presented by civil wars:

> We assume, as the Board apparently did, that in appropriate circumstances "neutrality" may fall within the scope of the statute's words "on account of ... political opinion." Nonetheless, we do not see how a petitioner such as Novoa, claiming asylum on the

35. The Board had applied its understanding of Fifth Circuit case law in *Maldonado–Cruz*, because that was where the alien was then detained. The BIA acknowledged that it was not applying the Ninth Circuit's standards, derived from cases like *Bolanos–Hernandez, supra.* Before he sought judicial review, Maldonado–Cruz was released, and he returned to California, where he had lived before his apprehension. His petition for review therefore was lodged with the Ninth Circuit, which applied its own case law and reversed the BIA. *Maldonado–Cruz v. INS*, 883 F.2d 788 (9th Cir.1989).

36. For a stunning example of a nearly inexplicable hard-line decision, using highly restrictive "on account of" doctrine in affirming the denial of asylum in a case where credibility was not questioned and the risks faced by the Salvadoran asylum applicant seem quite extreme, see *Campos–Guardado v. INS*, 809 F.2d 285 (5th Cir.1987). *See also* Martin, *Comparative Policies on Political Asylum: Of Facts and Law*, 9 In Defense of the Alien 105, 108 (1987) ("restrictive legal doctrine is a compensating mechanism—compensating for inadequate means within the system to assess the facts of the case competently").

basis of "neutrality," could bring himself within the statute's terms unless he can demonstrate that a reasonable person would fear one of the following: 1) that a group with the power to persecute him intends to do so specifically because the group dislikes neutrals, or 2) that such a group intends to persecute him because he will not accept its political point of view, or 3) that one or more such groups intend to persecute him because each (incorrectly) thinks he holds the political views of the other side.

* * *

The most difficult evidentiary question is whether or not the facts demonstrate a "well-founded" fear that the guerrillas would persecute Novoa, either because he refuses to accept their point of view or because they believe he supports the government. On the one hand, the record shows that the guerrillas threatened to kill Novoa (unless he told them who had guns) in August 1979 and again (if he voted) in March 1982; in April 1983 they pressured him by threatening to take everything he had; in October 1983 they questioned and beat his cousin; and, on several occasions during this time, they spoke and acted as if they thought he supported the government. On the other hand, the 1979 who-has-guns death threat seems tied to a particular place and circumstance. The 1982 do-not-vote threat is eight years old, seems similarly tied, and lacks accompanying evidence showing the guerrillas held a grudge; there is no indication, for example, that they subsequently injured others who voted (though they apparently were near or controlled the relevant village for a time). The 1983 threats are described only in vague terms, permitting an inference that they amounted to no more than recruitment efforts similarly related to a particular time and place. One would also find support for a "time-bound local circumstance," rather than a "grudge, threatening special persecution years later," interpretation of these events in the fact that Novoa, after these events, while living in San Salvador, returned to his native village without incident to look after his property.

Id., at 3–4. Acknowledging that the issue was a close one, the court wound up sustaining the BIA's ruling against the alien:

[I]n light of our examination of the record, we think the Board in this case could have found the threats at issue here less "viewpoint based," more context specific, more likely to reflect battlefield exigencies, and consequently less likely to reflect a well-founded fear of a continued threat of persecution based upon a political viewpoint, than the threats in the relevant Ninth Circuit cases.

Id., at 5. *See also Subramaniam v. District Director,* 724 F.Supp. 799, 802 (D.Colo.1989) (denying asylum to Tamil asylum seeker who fled civil war in Sri Lanka).

c. Membership in a Particular Social Group

"Membership in a particular social group" may be the most vague or elusive of the five factors listed in the statute. How should it be understood? (You may wish to reconsider, in this connection, the Board's treatment of one kind of "social group" claim, in *Matter of Chang,* Int.Dec. 3107 (BIA 1989), *supra* p. 808.)

In general, the Board has imposed the following standards in judging asylum claims based on alleged membership in a particular social group: "the common characteristic that defines the group * * * must be one that the members of the group cannot change, or should not be required to change because it is fundamental to their individual identities or consciences." *Matter of Acosta,* 19 I & N Dec. 211, 233 (BIA 1985) (rejecting asylum claim based on membership in an organization of taxi drivers that refused to participate in a guerrilla-called work stoppage). On what basis does one decide that a mutable characteristic is so fundamental that a person should not be required to change it?

The court in *Sanchez–Trujillo v. INS,* 801 F.2d 1571 (9th Cir.1986) confronted another form of "particular social group" claim. There the petitioners argued that they feared persecution in El Salvador as members of the following group: "young, urban, working class males of military age who had never served in the military or otherwise expressed support for the government." *Id.* at 1573. (This was a common theme in many Salvadoran cases in the 1980s.) In rejecting this claim, the court reasoned:

> We may agree that the "social group" category is a flexible one which extends broadly to encompass many groups who do not otherwise fall within the other categories of race, nationality, religion, or political opinion. Still, the scope of the term cannot be without some outer limit.
>
> The statutory words "particular" and "social" which modify "group," indicate that the term does not encompass every broadly defined segment of a population, even if a certain demographic division does have some statistical relevance. Instead, the phrase *"particular social* group" implies a collection of people closely affiliated with each other, who are actuated by some common impulse or interest. Of central concern is the existence of a voluntary associational relationship among the purported members, which imparts some common characteristic that is fundamental to their identity as a member of that discrete social group.[7]

7. We do not mean to suggest that a persecutor's perception of a segment of a society as a "social group" will invariably be irrelevant to this analysis. But neither would such an outside characterization be conclusive. The Refugee Act did not comprehend "refugee" status for everyone who fears adverse treatment by a foreign government, but only when the fear of persecution is on account of "race, religion, nationality, membership in a particular social group, or political opinion." For example, an individual who fears persecution because of a personal dispute with a foreign government official is not entitled to "refugee" status, as the anticipated mistreatment would not be on account of "political opinion" as required by the statute. *Zayas–Marini v. INS,* 785 F.2d 801, 805–07 (9th Cir.1986). Likewise, what constitutes a "particular social group," as opposed to a mere demographic division of the population, must be independently determined through the application of the statutory term in a particular context.

Perhaps a prototypical example of a "particular social group" would consist of the immediate members of a certain family, the family being a focus of fundamental affiliational concerns and common interests for most people. In *Hernandez–Ortiz,* 777 F.2d at 516, we regarded evidence of persecution directed against a family unit as relevant in determining refugee status, noting that a family was "a small, readily identifiable group." As a contrasting example, a statistical group of males taller than six feet would not constitute a "particular social group" under any reasonable construction of the statutory term, even if individuals with such characteristics could be shown to be at greater risk of persecution than the general population.

Likewise, the class of young, working class, urban males of military age does not exemplify the type of "social group" for which the immigration laws provide protection from persecution. Individuals falling within the parameters of this sweeping demographic division naturally manifest a plethora of different lifestyles, varying interests, diverse cultures, and contrary political leanings. As the IJ said in his written decision, "This [class of young, working class, urban males] may be so broad and encompass so many variables that to recognize any person who might conceivably establish that he was a member of this class is entitled to asylum or withholding of deportation would render the definition of 'refugee' meaningless."

In sum, such an all-encompassing grouping as the petitioners identify simply is not that type of cohesive, homogeneous group to which we believe the term "particular social group" was intended to apply. Major segments of the population of an embattled nation, even though undoubtedly at some risk from general political violence, will rarely, if ever, constitute a distinct "social group" for the purposes of establishing refugee status. To hold otherwise would be tantamount to extending refugee status to every alien displaced by general conditions of unrest or violence in his or her home country. Refugee status simply does not extend as far as the petitioners would contend.

Id. at 1576–77. Compare the court's analysis to the Board's "unchangeable characteristic" approach. Are there other modes of analysis that should be adopted instead? *See* Helton, *Persecution on Account of Membership in a Social Group as a Basis for Refugee Status,* 15 Colum.Hum.Rts.L.Rev. 39 (1983); Graves, *From Definition to Exploration: Social Groups and Political Asylum Eligibility,* 26 San Diego L.Rev. 739 (1989); Fullerton, *Persecution Due to Membership in a Particular Social Group: Jurisprudence in the Federal Republic of Germany,* 4 Geo.Imm.L.J. 381 (1990). We will return to some of these issues in connection with the *Fatin* case *infra.*

d. *Applying the Standards: Gender-based Asylum Claims*

So far in this section we have taken the "refugee" definition apart in an effort to explore its component parts. But as is apparent from earlier readings, many cases present interconnected issues of policy and law that touch upon considerations raised in multiple subparts of this chapter. The case that follows pursues many such inquiries, in considering a kind of claim that is increasingly encountered in asylum adjudication, both here and abroad: claims based in some fashion on gender. For a comprehensive discussion, with citations to much of the literature, see Goldberg, *Asylum Law and Gender–Based Persecution Claims*, 94–9 Imm.Briefings (1994); Love, *Equality in Political Asylum Law: For a Legislative Recognition of Gender–Based Persecution*, 17 Harv. Women's L.J. 133 (1994).

FATIN v. INS

United States Court of Appeals, Third Circuit, 1993.
12 F.3d 1233.

ALITO, CIRCUIT JUDGE:

Parastoo Fatin has petitioned for review of an order of the Board of Immigration Appeals (the "Board" or "BIA") requiring her to depart or be deported from the United States. * * *

I.

The petitioner is a native and citizen of Iran. On December 31, 1978, approximately two weeks before the Shah left Iran, the petitioner entered the United States as a nonimmigrant student. She was then 18 years old. She attended high school in Philadelphia through May 1979, and the following September she enrolled in Spring Garden College, also in Philadelphia.

In May 1984, apparently while still attending college, she applied to the Immigration and Naturalization Service District Director for political asylum pursuant to Section 208(a) of the Immigration and Nationality Act ("INA"), by submitting a completed INS Form I 589. In response to question 31 on this form, which asked what she thought would happen to her if she returned to Iran, she wrote: "I would be interrogated, and I would be forced to attend religious sessions against my will, and I would be publicly admonished and even jailed." In answer to question 34, which asked about any organization in Iran to which she or any immediate family member had ever belonged, she wrote:

> I personally belonged to a student group that favored the Shah. We refused to demonstrate with the students who favored Khomeni. I refused to wear a veil which was a sign or badge that I favor Khomeni. My cousin ... is now a refugee living in Paris France. He was formerly one of the guards for the Shah.

* * *

[In 1987, in proceedings before the immigration judge, she] reiterated and expanded upon the statements in her initial asylum application concerning the treatment of her relatives in Iran, adding that one of her cousins had subsequently been killed in a demonstration and that her brother was in hiding in order to avoid the draft. She also elaborated upon her political activities prior to coming to the United States, stating that she had been involved with a student political group and with a women's rights group associated with the Shah's sister.

When her attorney asked her why she feared going back to Iran, she responded: "Because of the government that is ruling the country. It is a strange government to me. It has different rules and regulation[s] th[a]n I have been used to." She stated that "anybody who [had] been a Moslem" was required "to practice that religion" or "be punished in public or be jailed," and she added that she had been "raised in a way that you don't have to practice if you don't want to." She subsequently stated that she would be required "to do things that [she] never had to do," such as wear a veil. When asked by her attorney whether she would wear a veil, she replied:

A. I would have to, sir.

Q. And if you didn't?

A. I would be jailed or punished in public. Public mean by whipped or thrown stones and I would be going back to barbaric years.

Later, when the immigration judge asked her whether she would wear a veil or submit to arrest and punishment, she stated:

If I go back, I would try personally to avoid it as much as I could do.... I will start trying to avoid it as much as I could.

The petitioner also testified that she considered herself a "feminist" and explained:

As a feminist I mean that I believe in equal rights for women. I believe a woman as a human being can do and should be able to do what they want to do. And over there in ... Iran at the time being a woman is a second class citizen, doesn't have any right to herself....

After the hearing, the immigration judge denied the petitioner's applications for withholding of deportation, asylum, and suspension of deportation. Addressing her request for withholding of deportation, the immigration judge stated that, although she would be subject to the same discriminatory treatment as all other women in Iran, there was "no indication that there is a likelihood that the Iranian government would be particularly interested in this individual and that they would persecute her." Similarly, with respect to her renewed request for asylum, the judge stated:

Respondent has offered no objective indic[i]a which would lead the Court to believe that there is a possibility that she would be persecuted upon return to Iran. Respondent has not been politi-cal[ly] active in the United States nor openly opposed to the Khomeni Government. It would appear that her fear of return to Iran while indeed understandable is based upon uncertainty and the unknown. In addition, it would appear that the respondent's fear upon return to Iran is her apparent dislike for the system and her belief that she as a woman would be subject to the severe restrictions presently imparted on Iranian[s] in that country.

Respondent therefore contends that her beliefs as a "feminist" would be compromised. While the Court is very much sympathetic to the respondent's desire not to return to Iran, nonetheless, in applying the law to include case law, the Court is compelled to find that the respondent has failed to sustain her burden of proof necessary to be accorded asylum in the United States.

* * *

Lost in front of Imm. Judge

Petitioner then appealed to the Board of Immigration Appeals. In her brief, she argued that she feared persecution "on account of her membership of a particular social group, and on the basis of her political opinion." Her brief identified her "particular social group" as "the social group of the upper class of Iranian women who supported the Shah of Iran, a group of educated Westernized free-thinking individuals." Her brief also stated that she had a "deep[ly] rooted belief in feminism" and in "equal rights for women, and the right to free choice of any expression and development of abilities, in the fields of education, work, home and family, and all other arenas of development." In addition, her brief observed that she would be forced upon return to Iran "to practice the Moslem religion." Her brief stated that "she would try to avoid practicing a religion as much as she could." Her brief added that she had "the personal desire to avoid as much practice as she could," but that she feared that "through religious ignorance and inexperience she would be unable to play the role of a religious Shi'ite woman." Her brief contained one passage concerning the requirement that women in Iran wear a veil in public:

> In April 1983, the government adopted a law imposing one year's imprisonment on any women caught in public without the traditional Islamic veil, the Chador. However, from reports, it is clear that in many instances the revolutionary guards ... take the law into their own hands and abuse the transgressing women....

Her brief did not discuss the question whether she would comply with the law regarding the wearing of a chador. Nor did her brief explain what effect submitting to that requirement would have upon her.

In the section of her brief devoted to political opinion, she mentioned her political activities while in Iran, as well as her current "deep-rooted beliefs in freedom of choice, freedom of expression [and] equality of opportunity for both sexes."

The Board of Immigration Appeals dismissed the petitioner's appeal. The Board noted that she had argued that she was entitled to relief "as a member of the social group composed of upper-class Iranian women" and as a person who "was educated in the western tradition." Rejecting this argument, the Board stated that there was no evidence that she would be "singled out" for persecution. Instead, the Board observed that she would be "subject to the same restrictions and requirements" as the rest of the population. The Board also noted that there had been "a considerable passage of time since [she] was in high school and participated in political activities." In addition, the Board stated that her claims were based on circumstances that had arisen since her entry into this country and that "[s]uch claims are dimly viewed."

After the Board issued its order requiring her voluntary departure or deportation, the petitioner filed the current petition for review.

II.

* * *

Both courts and commentators have struggled to define "particular social group." Read in its broadest literal sense, the phrase is almost completely open-ended. Virtually any set including more than one person could be described as a "particular social group." Thus, the statutory language standing alone is not very instructive.

Nor is there any clear evidence of legislative intent. * * *

* * * When the Conference of Plenipotentiaries was considering the [UN Convention relating to the Status of Refugees] in 1951, the phrase "membership of a particular social group" was added to this definition as an "afterthought." The Swedish representative proposed this language, explaining only that it was needed because "experience had shown that certain refugees had been persecuted because they belonged to particular social groups," and the proposal was adopted. Conference of Plenipotentiaries on the Status of Refugees and Stateless Persons, Summary Rec. of the 3d Mtg., U.N. Doc. A/CONF.2/SR.3 at 14 (Nov. 19, 1951). Thus, neither the legislative history of the relevant United States statutes nor the negotiating history of the pertinent international agreements sheds much light on the meaning of the phrase "particular social group."

Our role in the process of interpreting this phrase, however, is quite limited. As the Supreme Court has explained, the Board of Immigration Appeals' interpretation of a provision of the Refugee Act is entitled to deference pursuant to the standards set out in *Chevron U.S.A., Inc. v. Natural Resources Defense Council, Inc.*, 467 U.S. 837, 104 S.Ct. 2778, 81 L.Ed.2d 694 (1984). * * *

Here, the Board has interpreted the phrase "particular social group." In *Matter of Acosta*, 19 I. & N. Dec. 211, 233 (BIA 1985), the Board noted that the United Nations Protocol refers to race, religion, nationality, and political opinion, as well as membership in a particular social group. Employing the doctrine of ejusdem generis, the Board then reasoned that a particular social group refers to "a group of persons all of whom share a common, immutable characteristic." The Board explained:

> The shared characteristic might be an innate one such as sex, color, or kinship ties, or in some circumstances it might be a shared past experience such as former military leadership or land ownership. The particular kind of group characteristic that will qualify under this construction remains to be determined on a case-by-case basis. However, whatever the common characteristic that defines the group, it must be one that the members of the group either cannot change, or should not be required to change

because it is fundamental to their individual identities or consciences.

We have no doubt that this is a permissible construction of the relevant statutes, and we are consequently bound to accept it.

With this understanding of the phrase "particular social group" in mind, we turn to the elements that an alien must establish in order to qualify for withholding of deportation or asylum based on membership in such a group. We believe that there are three such elements. The alien must (1) identify a group that constitutes a "particular social group" within the interpretation just discussed, (2) establish that he or she is a member of that group, and (3) show that he or she would be persecuted or has a well-founded fear of persecution based on that membership.

she only meets 1st 2 elements

In the excerpt from *Acosta* quoted above, the Board specifically mentioned "sex" as an innate characteristic that could link the members of a "particular social group." Thus, to the extent that the petitioner in this case suggests that she would be persecuted or has a well-founded fear that she would be persecuted in Iran simply because she is a woman, she has satisfied the first of the three elements that we have noted. She has not, however, satisfied the third element; that is, she has not shown that she would suffer or that she has a well-founded fear of suffering "persecution" based solely on her gender.

In *Acosta*, the BIA discussed the meaning of the term "persecution," concluding that "the pre-Refugee Act construction" of that term should still be followed. Heeding this construction, the BIA interpreted "persecution" to include threats to life, confinement, torture, and economic restrictions so severe that they constitute a threat to life or freedom. By contrast, the BIA suggested that "[g]enerally harsh conditions shared by many other persons" do not amount to persecution. Among the pre-Refugee Act cases on which the BIA relied was *Blazina v. Bouchard*, 286 F.2d 507, 511 (3d Cir.), *cert. denied*, 366 U.S. 950, 81 S.Ct. 1904, 6 L.Ed.2d 1242 (1961), where our court noted that the mere "repugnance of . . . a governmental policy to our own concepts of . . . freedom" was not sufficient to justify labelling that policy as persecution. Thus, we interpret *Acosta* as recognizing that the concept of persecution does not encompass all treatment that our society regards as unfair, unjust, or even unlawful or unconstitutional. If persecution were defined that expansively, a significant percentage of the world's population would qualify for asylum in this country—and it seems most unlikely that Congress intended such a result.[10]

In this case, the evidence in the administrative record regarding the way in which women in Iran are generally treated is quite sparse. We

10. We are convinced that the BIA's interpretation of "persecution," like its interpretation of "particular social group," is permissible and thus must be followed. In ordinary usage, the term "persecution" denotes extreme conduct. For example, *The Random House Dictionary of the English Language* 1444 (2d ed. 1987) defines the term to mean "a program or campaign to exterminate, drive away, or subjugate a people because of their religion, race, or beliefs." We are aware of nothing indicating that Congress intended to depart from the ordinary meaning of the term "persecution." Moreover, authoritative interpretations of the United Nations Convention and Protocol also recognize that the concept of persecution refers to extreme conduct. *See, e.g.,* United Nations High Commissioner for Refugees, *Handbook of Procedures*, §§ 51, 54, 55.

certainly cannot say that "a reasonable factfinder would have to conclude," based on that record, that the petitioner, if returned to Iran, would face treatment amounting to "persecution" simply because she is a woman. *See INS v. Elias–Zacarias*, ___ U.S. ___, ___, 112 S.Ct. 812, 815, 117 L.Ed.2d 38 (1992). While the amici supporting the petitioner have called to our attention articles describing the harsh restrictions placed on all women in Iran, the facts asserted in these articles are not part of the administrative record. "Only the record of the administrative proceeding itself is pertinent and relevant in this type of action."

The petitioner's primary argument, in any event, is not that she faces persecution simply because she is a woman. Rather, she maintains that she faces persecution because she is a member of "a very visible and specific subgroup: Iranian women who refuse to conform to the government's gender-specific laws and social norms." This definition merits close consideration. It does not include all Iranian women who hold feminist views. Nor does it include all Iranian women who find the Iranian government's "gender-specific laws and repressive social norms" objectionable or offensive. Instead, it is limited to those Iranian women who find those laws so abhorrent that they "refuse to conform"—even though, according to the petitioner's brief, "the routine penalty" for noncompliance is "74 lashes, a year's imprisonment, and in many cases brutal rapes and death."

Limited in this way, the "particular social group" identified by the petitioner may well satisfy the BIA's definition of that concept, for if a woman's opposition to the Iranian laws in question is so profound that she would choose to suffer the severe consequences of noncompliance, her beliefs may well be characterized as "so fundamental to [her] identity or conscience that [they] ought not be required to be changed." *Acosta*. The petitioner's difficulty, however, is that the administrative record does not establish that she is a member of this tightly defined group, for there is no evidence in that record showing that her opposition to the Iranian laws at issue is of the depth and importance required.

The Iranian restriction discussed most prominently in the petitioner's testimony was the requirement that women wear the chador or traditional veil, but the most that the petitioner's testimony showed was that she would find that requirement objectionable and would seek to avoid compliance if possible. When asked whether she would prefer to comply with that law or suffer the consequences of noncompliance, she stated only that she "would try to avoid" wearing a chador as much as she could. Similarly, her brief to the BIA stated only that she would seek to avoid Islamic practices "as much as she could." She never testified that she would refuse to comply with the law regarding the chador or any of the other gender-specific laws or social norms. Nor did she testify that wearing the chador or complying with any of the other restrictions was so deeply abhorrent to her that it would be tantamount to persecution. Instead, the most that emerges from her testimony is that she would find these requirements objectionable and would not observe them if she could avoid doing so. This testimony does not bring her within the particular social group that she has defined—Iranian women who refuse to conform with those requirements even if the consequences may be severe.

The "particular social group" that her testimony places her within is, instead, the presumably larger group consisting of Iranian women who find their country's gender-specific laws offensive and do not wish to comply with them. But if the petitioner's "particular social group" is defined in this way, she cannot prevail because the administrative record does not satisfy the third element described above, i.e., it does not show that the consequences that would befall her as a member of that group would constitute "persecution." According to the petitioner, she would have two options if she returned to Iran: comply with the Iranian laws or suffer severe consequences. Thus, while we agree with the petitioner that the indicated consequences of noncompliance would constitute persecution, we must still inquire whether her other option—compliance—would also constitute persecution.

In considering whether the petitioner established that this option would constitute persecution, we will assume for the sake of argument that the concept of persecution is broad enough to include governmental measures that compel an individual to engage in conduct that is not physically painful or harmful but is abhorrent to that individual's deepest beliefs. An example of such conduct might be requiring a person to renounce his or her religious beliefs or to desecrate an object of religious importance. Such conduct might be regarded as a form of "torture" and thus as falling within the Board's description of persecution in *Acosta*. Such a requirement could constitute "torture" or persecution, however, only if directed against a person who actually possessed the religious beliefs or attached religious importance to the object in question. Requiring an adherent of an entirely different religion or a non-believer to engage in the same conduct would not constitute persecution.[11]

Here, while we assume for the sake of argument that requiring some women to wear chadors may be so abhorrent to them that it would be tantamount to persecution, this requirement clearly does not constitute persecution for all women. Presumably, there are devout Shi'ite women in Iran who find this requirement entirely appropriate. Presumably, there are other women in Iran who find it either inconvenient, irritating, mildly objectionable, or highly offensive, but for whom it falls short of constituting persecution. As we have previously noted, the petitioner's testimony in this case simply does not show that for her the requirement of wearing the chador or complying with Iran's other gender-specific laws would be so profoundly abhorrent that it could aptly be called persecution. Accordingly, we cannot hold that she is entitled to withholding of deportation or asylum based on her membership in a "particular social group."

The petitioner also argues that she is entitled to withholding of deportation or asylum based on her "political opinion," but her brief treats

---

11. We do not suggest that an alien could establish that he or she would be persecuted or has a well-founded fear of persecution based solely on his or her subjective reactions. Presumably, conduct could not constitute persecution or "torture" within *Acosta* unless an objective requirement is also satisfied.

this argument as essentially the same as her argument regarding membership in a particular social group.   *   *   *

*   *   *

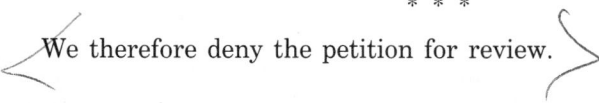

We therefore deny the petition for review.

Notes

1. The court rejects the asylum claim here, largely because of the state of the record and the way in which petitioner chose to frame the "social group." Is the court too inflexible in defining the relevant group? If you were Fatin's counsel, how should you have framed the issues?

2. The *Fatin* court also betrays some concern about the numerical consequences of expansive doctrine governing claims like this one: "If persecution were defined that expansively, a significant percentage of the world's population would qualify for asylum in this country—and it seems most unlikely that Congress intended such a result." But does the court's doctrine truly guard against such an outcome? That is, won't it be rather easy for future applicants to allege more carefully that certain traditional practices are "abhorrent" or that their objections are "profound"? How can an asylum officer or immigration judge test such a claim?

3. For other cases raising highly similar issues, see, *e.g.*, *Fisher v. INS*, 37 F.3d 1371 (9th Cir.1994) (ruling for applicant); *Safaie v. INS*, 25 F.3d 636 (8th Cir.1994) (ruling against applicant). *See also Gomez v. INS*, 947 F.2d 660 (2d Cir.1991) (rejecting "social group" claim characterized as "women who have been previously battered and raped by Salvadoran guerillas"); *Lazo-Majano v. INS*, 813 F.2d 1432 (9th Cir.1987) (holding that woman raped and battered by employer, a sergeant in the Salvadoran army, had established persecution on account of political opinion); *Campos-Guardado v. INS*, 809 F.2d 285 (5th Cir.1987) (rejecting asylum claim by Salvadoran woman who had been raped and threatened by masked gunmen after they murdered her relatives in her presence). For reference to Guidelines adopted by UNHCR and by the Canadian Immigration and Refugee Board for asylum claims based on gender, see Goldberg, *supra*, at 16. Similar guidelines have been submitted to INS in the hope that they will stimulate INS to develop its own. Kelly, Anker & Beasley, *Guidelines for Women's Asylum Claims*, 71 Interp.Rel. 813 (1994).

4. Similar claims of persecution on account of membership in a particular social group can arise on the basis of sexual orientation. The BIA accepted such a claim by a Cuban national in *Matter of Toboso-Alfonso*, Int.Dec. 3222 (BIA 1990), and the Attorney General ordered in 1994 that the decision be published as a precedent decision. The INS Asylum Office has also issued guidance on such cases, based on a claim filed by a Mexican national. The INS memo states that sexual orientation appears to meet the *Acosta* standards for a "particular social group," but it goes on to caution: "Our finding that 'particular social group' under the refugee definition can, under certain circumstances, be defined by homosexual orientation, does not imply a 'group,' blanket, or other generic determination regarding the asylum eligibility of Mexicans, homosexuals, or any

other nationality or group. The [office's] decision does not obviate the need for individualized assessments under the entire refugee definition for all cases." 71 Interp.Rel. 652–53 (1994). *See also id.* at 490, 1515; 70 *id.* 1100 (1993).

7. THE EXCEPTION CLAUSES

The Board in *Fuentes* suggested that it should apply a narrow notion of persecution and a narrow understanding of when persecution is "on account of" one of the five factors, lest large numbers of people from strife-torn countries be disqualified because of their own involvement as "persecutors" under the exception clauses of the statute and the treaties. *See* INA §§ 101(a)(42) (second sentence), 243(h)(2)(A); 8 C.F.R. §§ 208.13(c), 208.16(c)(2)(i). Does this conclusion necessarily follow? If so, is this a valid consideration supporting the Board's approach in *Fuentes*?

See code

The exception clauses of INA § 243(h)(2), and the parallel provisions governing discretion under 8 C.F.R. § 208.14, can present challenging interpretive issues. (Are they consistent with U.S. treaty obligations? *See* p. 763 & n.23 *supra.*) At least two of the clauses were employed in the lengthy *McMullen* litigation, involving a former Provisional Irish Republican Army member who had been involved in blowing up a British barracks and in supplying arms used in other PIRA violence. The Board found McMullen disqualified from asylum and withholding on numerous grounds. *Matter of McMullen*, 19 I & N Dec. 90 (BIA 1984). The court of appeals affirmed, but the majority did so solely on the basis of McMullen's commission of a "serious nonpolitical crime" outside the United States, citing INA § 243(h)(2)(C). *McMullen v. INS*, 788 F.2d 591 (9th Cir.1986). The concurring judge found application of that provision troubling because, in his view, McMullen's "personal culpability" for the PIRA crimes at issue had not been adequately shown. He would have affirmed instead on the basis of § 243(h)(2)(A), because McMullen's role in supplying arms to the PIRA clearly amounted to "assistance" in the persecution of others based on political opinion.

The PIRA's crimes obviously had an important political element, being directed at forcing the British government to end its sovereignty over Northern Ireland. How could they then be characterized as nonpolitical? This provision regarding serious nonpolitical crimes is similar to provisions in most extradition treaties banning the return of those who are sought by the requesting state in order to be tried for "political offenses." But both the judicial and executive branches have found it difficult to apply this concept consistently in the extradition setting, especially to so-called "relative political offenses," acts that would be common crimes (murder, theft, property destruction), but which are allegedly committed for political ends. The issue has spawned an enormously complex and often contradictory body of case law. *See* Note, *Extradition Reform and the Statutory Definition of Political Offenses*, 24 Va.J.Int'l L. 419, 429–32 (1984); *Eain v. Wilkes*, 641 F.2d 504, 519 (7th Cir.), *cert. denied*, 454 U.S. 894, 102 S.Ct. 390, 70 L.Ed.2d 208 (1981); *Quinn v. Robinson*, 783 F.2d 776 (9th Cir.) *cert. denied*, 479 U.S. 882, 107 S.Ct. 271, 93 L.Ed.2d 247 (1986); *Matter of Requested Extradition of Smyth*, 863 F.Supp. 1137 (N.D.Cal.1994). The

BIA drew selectively on some of this case law in *Matter of McMullen, supra,* to hold that a crime is political only if the "political aspect" outweighs its "common-law character"; atrocious acts or violence grossly out of proportion to the objective would not meet this test.

It is also worth noting that the political offense exception to extradition is not coextensive with the shelter provided by the political asylum provisions of the immigration laws. Occasionally, an alien fugitive has escaped extradition because the magistrate ruled that the requesting state sought him for an offense of a political character, only to be adjudged deportable nonetheless, sometimes after the denial of a political asylum application. *See, e.g.,* O'Higgins, *Disguised Extradition: The Soblen Case,* 27 Mod. L.Rev. 521 (1964); *INS v. Doherty,* 502 U.S. 314, 112 S.Ct. 719, 116 L.Ed.2d 823 (1992) (clearing the way for ultimate deportation (not extradition) of Doherty, another PIRA member, to Northern Ireland); 69 Interp.Rel. 223 (1992) (reporting on Doherty's deportation, following over eight years of litigation, during which time Doherty was incarcerated in the United States); *Matter of McMullen,* 17 I. & N. Dec. 542 (BIA 1980) (finding magistrate's ruling against extradition not binding in asylum case), *reversed on other grounds,* 658 F.2d 1312 (9th Cir.1981), *asylum denial approved after remand,* 788 F.2d 591 (9th Cir.1986). In fact, McMullen was eventually ruled extraditable as well, when new extradition proceedings were brought after the U.S.-U.K. extradition treaty was amended to narrow the category of crimes that could be considered political offenses. *See In re Extradition of McMullen,* 989 F.2d 603 (9th Cir.), *cert. denied,* ___ U.S. ___, 114 S.Ct. 301, 126 L.Ed.2d 249 (1993). For critical commentary on the *Doherty* decision, *see* Fitzpatrick & Pauw, *Foreign Policy, Asylum and Discretion,* 28 Willamette L.Rev. 751 (1992).

Is there any reason to have the same basic commodity—protection against return to a state where the individual fears severe consequences—thus governed by discontinuous standards in asylum and extradition proceedings? *See generally* G. Goodwin–Gill, *supra* note 1, at 78–81. How should these issues be approached?

For other cases exploring the exception clauses, precluding asylum or withholding of deportation when the alien has committed "a serious nonpolitical crime" or a "particularly serious crime" (what is the difference between the two?; look closely at INA § 243(h)(2)), *see, e.g., Ramirez–Ramos v. INS,* 814 F.2d 1394 (9th Cir.1987) (rejecting a balancing test that would weigh the seriousness of the crime against the gravity of the threatened persecution); *Crespo–Gomez v. Richard,* 780 F.2d 932 (11th Cir.1986) (ineligible because of possession of cocaine for sale); *Mahini v. INS,* 779 F.2d 1419 (9th Cir.1986) (similar holding for possession of heroin with intent to distribute). For further consideration of the "persecutor" exception, see *Matter of Rodriguez–Majano,* 19 I & N Dec. 811 (BIA 1988).

The 1990 Act added language to INA § 243(h)(2) providing that an aggravated felony, as defined in § 101(a)(43), is to be considered a "particularly serious crime." It also specified that those convicted of aggravated felonies "may not *apply for* or be granted asylum." INA § 208(d) (emphasis added). This clear statutory specification has quieted many controversies over the exception clauses, including an earlier dispute over whether INA § 243(h)(2)(B), requires two separate findings: conviction of a particularly serious crime and dangerousness to the community. *See Beltran–Zavala v. INS*, 912 F.2d 1027 (9th Cir.1990) (holding that two findings are required). After the amendment, courts are apparently unanimous that conviction of an aggravated felony, per se, precludes withholding. *See, e.g., Feroz v. INS*, 22 F.3d 225 (9th Cir.1994); *Martins v. INS*, 972 F.2d 657 (5th Cir.1992). *See also* 8 C.F.R. § 208.16(c)(2)(ii), as amended by the Dec. 1994 regulations (adopting the per se rule for aggravated felons). *But see* 69 Interp.Rel. 570 (1992) (letter from Sen. Kennedy, chair of the Senate subcommittee, asserting that the 1990 amendment was not meant to preclude a separate inquiry into dangerousness).

Exercise: The Asylum Standards Applied

To cement your understanding of the preceding materials on political asylum, and to appreciate the task facing those who must adjudicate asylum claims, assume that you are an immigration judge required to rule on the case of the following hypothetical applicant, named Rodriguez, a citizen of Guatemala. Consider how the standards governing asylum under INA § 208 and *nonrefoulement* under § 243(h) apply in light of the evidence available at each step, and then see whether your result would change given the new information provided in the following step (the evidence should be treated as cumulative). What other information do you need or want in order to make these determinations? Consider as well how the standards *should* apply; should they be changed to provide, or to eliminate, protection for any of the following situations? What policy considerations lead you to reach each such conclusion?

1. Rodriguez states that he lives in a village that has been fought over in the civil war, changing hands from government to guerrillas many times, and many poor farmers like himself have been killed in the fighting.

2. He adds that his own house has been destroyed in the war.

3. His brother was killed in the fighting.

4. Another brother was killed by government forces because he was a known labor union organizer.

5. Rodriguez himself spoke out once in the village square against the misdeeds of both the government and the guerrillas.

6. Rodriguez spoke out numerous times against the contending parties.

7. Rodriguez also served as a union organizer for several years.

8. He had been specifically warned by friends that government-related death squads were out to get him.

9. He received such a warning from a sympathetic government official.

10. He relates all the above, and states that he had lived under threats for several years. He finally decided to come to the United States,

however, only when a severe drought ruined the crops for the growing season, and he felt he had to try something else to feed his family.

11. Although his immediate departure was occasioned by the drought, Rodriguez still fears greatly for his family's safety back home.

12. Rodriguez travelled through Mexico and stayed there several months before coming on to the United States.

13. Rodriguez was brought into the United States by a *coyote* or alien smuggler.

14. He assisted the smuggler in pulling together a large group of Salvadorans then living in Mexico to make the clandestine crossing.

15. Rodriguez was paid $1000 by the smuggler for his role in organizing the group.

16. When first apprehended by INS in the United States, he falsely claimed he was an American citizen.

17. After applying for asylum, Rodriguez posted bond and received work authorization pending the hearing (including a ruling on his asylum application). Rodriguez then moved without informing INS of his new address and failed to show up for his hearing. Bond was forfeited. INS located him again seven months later and a new hearing was then scheduled. (Under new provisions added in 1990, aliens who fail to appear for a scheduled asylum hearing may be held ineligible for certain other forms of relief. INA § 242B(e)(4). Is this provision too severe? Not severe enough?)

18. Rodriguez has been charged with possession of two kilos of marijuana, and the state prosecutor is considering further counts in connection with the discovery of the marijuana in his apartment (during the seven months when his whereabouts were unknown to INS).

8. THE FACTS AND THE PROCEDURES

a. The Factfinding Challenge

So far we have been looking primarily at legal questions—assuming that we had an adequate account of the facts, and endeavoring to make sense of how the legal standards fit. But such an assumption glosses over one of the major difficulties in asylum cases.

> [T]he asylum determination rests on uniquely elusive grounds. It will usually turn on facts which are strikingly inaccessible by U.S. courts and agencies. Applicants typically base their claims on events in a distant land, about which the U.S. Government may otherwise have no information—matters such as their own past political activities, or abuses visited on them or their families and friends. Bona fide applicants are unlikely to have left their homelands with corroborating documentation in hand or with supporting witnesses. On the other hand, fraudulent applicants can probably count on the government's inability to produce evidence disproving their stories. Asylum determinations therefore revolve critically around a determination of the applicant's

credibility. Moreover, even if past events can be established with some certainty, the crucial determination does not stem directly from these factual findings of the classical sort. Instead, one must venture into the realm of prediction to decide whether a given showing of the prevalence of persecution in the home country makes a particular applicant's fear well-founded. Applications present a continuum, running from clearly legitimate claims, through borderline cases from countries where all residents are exposed to some risk of persecution, to fanciful fears and bogus applications. The process, however, demands a flat yes or no answer in each case. Because of the large gray area, political considerations—the U.S. Government's hostility or friendship for the allegedly persecuting regime—might easily affect the results. And even where the government is committed to avoiding that practice, it will be hard-pressed to prove that political considerations did not intrude.

Martin, *The Refugee Act, supra* note 4, at 115. *See also* Smith & Hake, *Evidence Issues in Asylum Cases,* 90–10 Imm. Briefings (1990).

In response to these factual challenges, the Board and several courts at one time appeared to impose a stringent requirement that the alien's statements be corroborated by "objective evidence," which were contrasted with "the alien's own speculations and conclusional statements." *Matter of Sibrun,* 18 I & N Dec. 354, 358 (BIA 1983). *See also, e.g., Dally v. INS,* 744 F.2d 1191, 1195–96 (6th Cir.1984).

Beginning at least with *Matter of Acosta* and *Matter of Mogharrabi, supra,* however, the Board has shown much more understanding of the dilemma faced by bona fide asylum seekers, many of whom will have little direct evidence beyond their own statements to support the specific facts that underlie their claims. Under these later cases, the alien's own uncorroborated testimony is no longer so readily dismissed as self-serving. It can be sufficient to justify a favorable ruling, without specific corroboration, provided that the "testimony is believable, consistent, and sufficiently detailed to provide a plausible and coherent account of the basis for his fear." *Mogharrabi,* 19 I & N Dec. 439, 445.[37] The courts now generally support this approach. *See, e.g., Dawood–Haio v. INS,* 800 F.2d 90, 96–97 (6th Cir.1986); *Canjura–Flores v. INS,* 784 F.2d 885, 888–89 (9th Cir. 1985); *Cardoza–Fonseca v. INS,* 767 F.2d 1448, 1453 (9th Cir.1985), *affirmed,* 480 U.S. 421, 107 S.Ct. 1207, 94 L.Ed.2d 434 (1987) ("That the objective facts are established through the credible and persuasive testimony of the applicant does not make those facts less objective"). And the 1990 asylum regulations officially adopted this doctrine as well. 8 C.F.R. §§ 208.13(a), 208.16(b).

Court decisions vary considerably, however, in the degree to which they will probe the credibility findings of the immigration judge or the BIA.

---

37. See also *Matter of Fefe,* Int.Dec. 3121 (BIA 1989) (because of the importance of such testimony and possible questions that the immigration judge may wish to ask, a claim should not be adjudicated solely on the written submissions; the alien must testify under oath at the hearing).

Compare, e.g., Diaz–Escobar v. INS, 782 F.2d 1488, 1492 (9th Cir.1986) (courts must defer to immigration judge's "express and implied determination concerning credibility" even if INS offered no testimony that rebutted applicant's statements), *and Sarvia–Quintanilla v. United States INS,* 767 F.2d 1387, 1395 (9th Cir.1985) (immigration judge, who alone is in position to observe tone and demeanor, is "uniquely qualified to decide whether an alien's testimony has about it the ring of truth") *with Damaize–Job v. INS,* 787 F.2d 1332, 1338 (9th Cir.1986) (negative credibility finding rejected for lack of "legitimate, articulable basis to question [the applicant's] credibility"); *Aguilera–Cota v. United States INS,* 914 F.2d 1375, 1381–82 & n. 7 (9th Cir.1990) (immigration judge "must not only articulate the basis for a negative credibility finding, but those reasons must be substantial and must bear a legitimate nexus to the finding"; "a petitioner's admission that he lied to the INS about his citizenship does not support a negative credibility finding" (these rulings provoked a sharp dissent)); *and Hartooni v. INS*, 21 F.3d 336 (9th Cir.1994) (discounting immigration judge's expression of doubt about alien's credibility for failure to make "findings of fact regarding which, if any, of her specific claims were questionable").

Do *Damaize–Job, Aguilera–Cota,* and *Hartooni* go too far? Under them, can any alien from a troubled country simply walk in to immigration court, tell a clever story (taking care to avoid overt internal contradictions), and then force INS to come up with specific disproof of the factual claims, on pain of reversal by the Ninth Circuit? *Cf. Mendoza Perez v. INS*, 902 F.2d 760, 766 (9th Cir.1990) (Sneed, J., concurring) (lamenting "the erosion of external corroboration requirements" and the Ninth Circuit's "departure from the general rule of deference to administrative decisions"). In a case reviewing findings of the National Labor Relations Board, the court described the scope of review as follows: "The Board's findings are not lightly overturned. Its acceptance of an ALJ's findings regarding witness credibility will not be reversed unless those findings are 'hopelessly incredible.'" *Pergament United Sales, Inc. v. NLRB*, 920 F.2d 130, 138 (2d Cir.1990). What reasons favor giving immigration judges similar deference in asylum cases? What reasons disfavor such an approach? (Outside studies have often been critical of the fairness and effectiveness of the procedures used, by both immigration judges and INS examiners, in hearing and deciding asylum claims. *See, e.g.,* Anker, *Report of the Findings and Recommendations of An Empirical Study of Adjudication Before the Immigration Court,* 2 Int'l J.Refugee L. 252 (1990); Nat'l Asylum Study Project, An Assessment of the Asylum Process of the Immigration and Naturalization Service (1993).)

It may be helpful to break the factual determination down into three parts, each of which presents its own challenges: (1) classic retrospective factfinding about past events specific to the claimant—adjudicative facts, in the terminology developed by Professor Kenneth Culp Davis;[38] (2) broader determinations about the practices of the government or other alleged persecutors in the home country—properly deemed legislative facts; and

---

38. See 3 K. Davis, Administrative Law Treatise, ch. 15 (2d ed. 1980). The terminology is more completely explained in the *Zamora* case, *infra.*

(3) finally, an informed prediction, not truly a finding, about the degree and type of danger the applicant is likely to face upon return.

The cases usually have not carefully separated these elements. The first element is in reality the focus of the cases cited above, for the alien's detailed and specific testimony is most likely to be useful in establishing the adjudicative facts specific to his case. For example, was he in fact, as he claims, beaten by the police shortly before he left the home country? Was he really held for the 10 days he asserts? Close questioning of the applicant, probing the detail, consistency, and coherence of the account, is probably the best way to gain insight into these matters.[39] The third element, the prediction about future harm, as we have seen, usually derives from an assessment of past threats or abuse, the nature of the risk asserted, and the extent to which any threat is focused or targeted on the applicant or others similarly situated.

The remaining element, legislative facts or "country conditions," deserves further attention.

> The second critical element of factfinding requires determinations about broader patterns of governmental behavior in the home country. For example, the asylum applicant may prove to the factfinder's satisfaction, through his own detailed testimony, that he was active as a union organizer for two years before leaving for the United States and that he heard stories of arrests of organizers in nearby towns before he left. But in order to assess the risk that the individual would face on return, the adjudicator must also learn from some source about relevant legislative facts. Does the government regard union organizers as opponents, subject to suppression? If so, what forms does the suppression take? Loss of a job or limitation of schooling options for organizers' children might not amount to persecution (even though it would constitute a human rights violation), but beatings, jailings, or killings in reprisal for peaceful union activity certainly would. If there have been some reports of such violence, how widespread are the abuses? Were they based on the victim's union affiliation or on some other characteristic? In other words, is the current applicant relevantly similar to other persecution victims? And has there been a material change in the country since those events, such as a complete revamping of the police forces responsible for the earlier abuses, including reliable disciplining of the violators?

> Each of these questions will be difficult to answer, both because such patterns change over time, sometimes quite quickly, and because persecutors do not spell out the range of characteristics they seek in their victims. If the available information shows any substantial level of persecution of union activists, then uncer-

---

39. Allowance must be made, however— and this is no easy task—for cross-cultural differences that may impede this examination process. *See* Kälin, *Troubled Communications: Cross–Cultural Misunderstandings in* *the Asylum Hearing,* 20 Int'l Migration Rev. 230 (1986); Pfeiffer, *Credibility Findings in INS Asylum Adjudications: A Realistic Assessment,* 23 Tex. Int'l L.J. 139 (1988).

tainties should be resolved in the individual's favor. Thus, the claimant should receive the "benefit of the doubt" commonly prescribed in works on refugee law. But the benefit of the doubt is hardly a magic formula, somehow dispensing with a need to reach a judgment about country conditions.

The individual applicant will not necessarily be in a position to provide insight on these wider matters, although the process should certainly allow for whatever assistance he or his counsel can provide. * * *

Legislative facts should not be regarded, however, as simply something the adjudicator looks up or examines *after* he has completed the proceedings addressed to finding the adjudicative facts, even though much of his knowledge about country conditions will doubtless come from documentary sources rather than live testimony. Knowledge of political developments and patterns of persecution contributes toward making the final predictive judgment about risks faced if the individual returns home, but perhaps more importantly, such knowledge can also play a useful role in developing and assessing the adjudicative facts themselves.

This second use of knowledge about country conditions is often overlooked, but it remains crucial. An adjudicator thus equipped can better pick out those parts of the applicant's story that are most relevant, and can ask specific questions that will flesh out the testimony in the most helpful fashion. Such expert questioning can also help expose inconsistencies and falsehoods more effectively. Since there are so few other checks on the asylum seeker's story (given that he is likely to be the only available witness to the key events), the system badly needs to make use of whatever other tools might be available for such assessment. But equipping adjudicators with such expertise is not just a device for spotting weaknesses or magnifying contradictions. Properly applied, it can also assist confused or inarticulate applicants present fully the particularized information that will cast positive light on their claims. All this argues for making sure, to the maximum extent possible, that the adjudicators are themselves highly knowledgeable about country conditions.

Martin, *Reforming Asylum Adjudication, supra* note 21, 138 U.Pa.L.Rev., at 1282–85.

With this background, consider the following holding of the BIA, in the case of an applicant from India who based his claim on his membership in the Dal Khalsa, a Punjabi independence movement. *Matter of Dass*, Int.Dec. 3122, at 6–8 (BIA 1989). The immigration judge rejected his claim, and he appealed, asserting that the judge "erroneously ignored my testimony that the lives of Dal Khalsa's are in danger only because I could not provide government publications." The Board held him accountable for the lack of such information:

First, the general rule regarding the consideration of asylum applications by immigration judges and the Board, as with other matters in deportation and exclusion proceedings, is that they must be evaluated based on matters of record (*i.e.,* based on the evidence introduced by the parties to the case under consideration). As the asylum applicant bears the evidentiary burden of proof and persuasion, where there are significant, meaningful evidentiary gaps, applications will ordinarily have to be denied for failure of proof.

Secondly, in determining whether an asylum applicant has met his burden of proof, we have recognized the difficulties that may be faced by aliens in obtaining documentary or other corroborative evidence to support their claims of persecution. Consequently, in *Matter of Mogharrabi, supra,* we held that the lack of such evidence will not necessarily be fatal to an application. We noted, as have various courts of appeals, that an alien's own testimony may in some cases be the only evidence available, and it can suffice where the testimony is believable, consistent, and sufficiently detailed to provide a plausible and coherent account of the basis for his alleged fear. *See, e.g., Carvajal–Munoz v. INS,* 743 F.2d 562, 574 (7th Cir.1984); *Matter of Mogharrabi, supra.* These cases, however, do not stand for the proposition that the introduction of supporting evidence is purely an option with an asylum applicant in the ordinary case. Rather, the general rule is that such evidence should be presented where available. *See Bolanos–Hernandez v. INS,* 767 F.2d 1277, 1285–86 (9th Cir.1984) (comparing "lack of direct corroboration of specific threats" to general corroboration of "whether there is reason to take the threat seriously"); *Sarvia–Quintanilla v. INS,* 767 F.2d 1387, 1392 (9th Cir.1985); *Carvajal–Munoz v. INS, supra; Sanchez v. INS,* 707 F.2d 1523, 1529 (D.C.Cir.1983); *Matter of Mogharrabi, supra.* If an intelligent assessment is to be made of an asylum application, there must be sufficient information in the record to judge the plausibility and accuracy of the applicant's claim. Without background information against which to judge the alien's testimony, it may well be difficult to evaluate the credibility of the testimony.

* * *

Particularly when the basis of an asylum claim becomes less focused on specific events involving the respondent personally and instead is more directed to broad allegations regarding general conditions in the respondent's country of origin, corroborative background evidence that establishes a plausible context for the persecution claim (or an explanation for the absence of such evidence) may well be essential. The more sweeping and general a claim, the clearer the need for an asylum applicant to introduce supporting evidence or to explain its absence. Furthermore, there is a greater likelihood that corroborative evidence will be available if the claim is of longstanding, widespread persecution.

Is this an appropriate requirement to place on an individual applicant, in view of the relative capacities of the applicant and the government to provide information on country conditions as opposed to adjudicative facts specific to the individual?

b. The Role of the State Department

For many years, it has been recognized that neither immigration judges, BIA members, nor district office examiners were likely to possess special expertise regarding conditions in a particular applicant's home country. Accordingly, the U.S. asylum system has addressed the need for country condition information primarily by drawing on the expert knowledge available in the U.S. Department of State. (The BIA in *Dass, supra,* relied significantly on a State Department advice letter in rejecting the asylum claim presented there.) But litigants, for understandable reasons, have often challenged the practice of awaiting a Department letter in every case, as the regulations once required. *See* 8 C.F.R. §§ 208.7, 208.10 (1987). The critics raised complaints about both political bias and due process, the latter because the author of the letter is never made available for cross-examination at the hearing or by way of deposition (and in view of the volume of cases, could not be). *See generally Matter of Exilus,* 18 I & N Dec. 2 (1982) (noting these problems, but approving use of letters in view of applicant's opportunity to rebut by presenting his own evidence in response); *Edmond v. Nelson,* 575 F.Supp. 532, 536–37 (E.D.La.1983) (generally approving *Exilus* approach).

In *Zamora v. INS,* 534 F.2d 1055 (2d Cir.1976), Judge Henry Friendly considered such challenges to the use of State Department letters and helped clarify the use of "country condition" information in asylum cases:

> We think solution of the problem lies in Professor Kenneth Culp Davis' famous distinction between adjudicative and legislative facts. The attitude of the country of prospective deportation toward various types of former residents is a question of legislative fact, on which the safeguards of confrontation and cross-examination are not required and on which the IJ needs all the help he can get. He cannot expect much from the applicants who, as Judge Waterman wrote in *Sovich v. Esperdy,* 319 F.2d 21, 29 (2 Cir. 1963), are often "unlettered persons who have been away from their native countries for many years" and "typically have available to them no better methods for ascertaining current political conditions abroad than does the average citizen." The worse complexion the alien puts on his previous conduct or the character of the present regime, the greater will be the likelihood that he may indeed be persecuted if his § 243(h) application fails; hence he might logically be under some compulsion to understate his case—although perusal of these and other petitions scarcely indicates such a tendency. Also, the greater the likelihood of persecution in the foreign country, the less will be the possibility of obtaining information from relatives or friends who are still there. Only rarely will an applicant be able to locate and enlist the services of an expert on conditions in the foreign country * * * .

Counsel for the INS may not be much better off. The obvious
source of information on general conditions in the foreign country
is the Department of State which has diplomatic and consular
representatives throughout the world. While there is undoubted
truth in the observation in *Kasravi [v. INS]*, 400 F.2d at 677 n. 1,
as to there being some likelihood of the Department's tempering
the wind in comments concerning internal affairs of a foreign
nation, it is usually the best available source of information and
the difficulty could be mitigated by not spreading its views on the
record, as [the regulations permit in limited circumstances.] We
therefore see no bar to the admissibility of statements of the
Department of State or its officials abroad which inform the IJ and
the Board of Immigration Appeals of the extent to which the
nation of prospective deportation engages in "persecution on account of race, religion, or political opinion" of the class of persons
to whom an applicant under § 243(h) claims to belong, and reveal,
so far as feasible, the basis for the views expressed, but do not
attempt to apply this knowledge to the particular case, as the
[Department] does in making recommendations with respect to
requests for political asylum.

The difficulty with introducing [the State Department] letters
into hearings under § 243(h) is that they do both too little and too
much. The ones in these cases and in others that we have seen
give little or nothing in the way of useful information about
conditions in the foreign country. What they do is to recommend
how the district director should decide the particular petitioner's
request for asylum. When these letters are introduced into the
§ 243(h) inquiry, they present [the Department's] conclusion as to
an adjudicative fact, based, in the present examples, solely on the
alien's own statements and phrased in the very language of the
§ 243(h) standard. Adjudication in the withholding process is,
however, the task of the IJ and the Board of Immigration Appeals.
Particularly in light of the difficulties confronting the alien in
proving his case, there is a risk that such communications will
carry a weight they do not deserve. It should not be difficult for
the INS and the Department of State to conform their practices in
the future to the views here expressed.

Id. at 1062–63.

McLeod v. INS, 802 F.2d 89 (3d Cir.1986), provided further analysis of
the use of State Department materials. The court there permitted "official
notice" of certain information derived from Department materials, ruling
that "official notice" is a broader concept than "judicial notice," because
the former allows consideration of a wider range of accepted facts that are
within the agency's area of expertise. *Id.* at 93 n. 4.

Despite Judge Friendly's optimism about the ready conformance of
INS and State Department practices to the guidelines *Zamora* lays down,
the opinion had little impact in this regard. State Department letters
continued to take a position on the merits of the individual application

under review (although they were often form letters that provided little detailed information explaining why the Department reached its conclusions). *See Asylum Adjudications: An Evolving Concept and Responsibility for the Immigration and Naturalization Service* 58 (INS Staff Study, mimeo, June 1982). *See also Hotel and Restaurant Employees Union, Local 25 v. Smith*, 594 F.Supp. 502, 510–14 (D.D.C.1984) (partially distinguishing *Zamora*, the court approves use of individual advisory opinions in Salvadoran cases; the court's opinion provides considerable information on how the advisory opinions were prepared), *aff'd by an equally divided court*, 846 F.2d 1499 (D.C.Cir.1988). In another respect, however, *Zamora* did affect the practices of immigration judges; they have usually been careful to recite in opinions denying asylum that they were not influenced by a negative advisory opinion from State, instead reaching their own conclusions. *See, e.g., Barraza Rivera v. INS*, 913 F.2d 1443, 1447–48 (9th Cir.1990). And occasionally there have been cases where a decision runs counter to the State Department recommendation. *See, e.g.,* 60 Interp.Rel. 26, 106 (1983) (reporting on IJ decisions granting asylum to a Nicaraguan and an Afghan applicant, respectively, despite negative letters from the State Department); *Zavala-Bonilla v. INS*, 730 F.2d 562 (9th Cir.1984) (reversing IJ denial of asylum in case of a Salvadoran as to whom State had issued an advisory opinion favoring asylum).[40] Nevertheless, evidence suggests that the impact of a negative letter was still considerable. *See, e.g.,* the *Asylum Adjudications* study, *supra*, at 62; Avery, *supra* note 3, at 333; *Martin, Reforming Asylum Adjudication, supra* note 21, at 1310–13, 1330–34.

The State Department has taken other steps, however, that come closer to meeting Judge Friendly's prescriptions. Under a statutory mandate (adopted to promote human rights diplomacy and not with a view to providing information in immigration proceedings), the Department now prepares annual reports on the human rights practices of governments around the world. These are submitted to Congress and published each February as Committee Prints. Copies are disseminated to INS district offices, immigration courts, and libraries; they are widely available. These reports contain the Department's judgments about the observance of human rights, country by country. The discussion is broken down by topic to consider, for example, torture and other cruel or inhuman treatment, arbitrary arrests and detentions, civil and political rights, economic conditions, etc.[41]

40. *Zavala-Bonilla* states several times that the State Department letter should have been regarded "with deference." 730 F.2d, at 566–67. The court also considered that letter especially significant "in light of the fact, acknowledged by the Government at oral argument, that Salvadorans rarely receive a State Department opinion supportive of a political asylum application." *Id.* at 567. *Zamora* is never discussed. Are the two cases inconsistent?

41. A further move in the direction of Judge Friendly's suggestions resulted from

what was originally a budgetary measure. The State Department decided in 1988 that it would no longer routinely provide an individual letter in asylum cases. Instead, its response may take one of three forms: (1) a sticker affixed to the papers returned to the Justice Department, saying that State has nothing to add to the information already in the annual country reports—now used in a majority of cases; (2) a generic fact sheet meant as a supplement to the country report, giving greater detail, for example, on treatment of a particular ethnic group or developments since the most recent country report;

Presumably these annual country reports set forth "legislative facts," as *Zamora* prescribes, but some of the reports, particularly on Central American countries, remained controversial. Moreover, even when the facts and evaluations set forth in the State Department report were not seriously contested, in most cases they plainly do not obviate further close inquiry by the adjudicator into the individualized facts bearing on the particular asylum seeker's case. And mere possession of such a report does not transform the examiner or immigration judge into an expert well-equipped to use the legislative facts in assessing credibility and thus reaching a judgment about adjudicative facts, nor in making the ultimate prediction about the threats facing the individual upon return.

The 1990 reforms of asylum procedures were based in part on INS's recognition of these problems in appropriately drawing on country condition information. Those regulations removed the adjudication function from the district offices, and created a separate corps of specialist asylum officers supported by its own documentation center charged with compiling information from both governmental and nongovernmental sources. 8 C.F.R. § 208.12. And the December 1994 regulations finally removed the requirement that asylum officers and immigration judges must wait a prescribed period to give the State Department an opportunity to provide its views on a case. 8 C.F.R. § 208.11, as amended. The State Department does continue to receive one copy of the I–589 application form, however, and retains the option to submit its comments, which are made a part of the administrative record unless they are classified for national security reasons. But State is expected to play a much reduced role under the new system.

c. *Later Controversies over Administrative Notice*

In 1988–91, major changes of government occurred in countries that had been the source of a large number of asylum claimants in the United States, including most of Eastern Europe, the Soviet Union, Ethiopia, Nicaragua, and others. The BIA held that it could take administrative notice of these changes, and it frequently relied on such information to reject asylum claims that had been long pending. The resulting petitions for judicial review raised a host of challenges, both substantive and procedural, to the validity of the Board's practice, but the central controversy came to focus on procedural issues. Specifically, does due process require the BIA to give the alien an opportunity to challenge the noticed facts or their significance with regard to the specific asylum claim *before* the decision becomes final?

The Seventh Circuit held that such an opportunity was not required, because an alien disadvantaged by the taking of administrative notice could challenge the result by means of a motion to reopen that would specifically set forth the matter in dispute. *Kaczmarczyk v. INS*, 933 F.2d 588 (7th Cir.1991), *cert. denied*, 502 U.S. 981, 112 S.Ct. 583, 116 L.Ed.2d 608 (1991). Seven other circuits appear to have adopted this holding. *See Gomez–Vigil v. INS*, 990 F.2d 1111, 1114–15 (9th Cir.1993) (Aldisert, J., concurring).

---

(3) an individual letter. *See* 53 Fed.Reg. 2893 (1988).

Cf. 5 U.S.C.A. § 556(e), part of the Administrative Procedure Act, which appears to allow decisions based on administrative notice, as long as the decision is subject to a later challenge by the affected party, on his or her own initiative: "When an agency decision rests on official notice of a material fact not appearing in evidence in the record, a party is entitled, on timely request, to an opportunity to show the contrary." But the Ninth Circuit reached a different conclusion in *Castillo-Villagra v. INS,* 972 F.2d 1017 (9th Cir.1992), and its rule has been accepted in *de la Llana–Castellon v. INS,* 16 F.3d 1093 (10th Cir.1994).

The *Castillo-Villagra* court affirmed a fairly broad use of administrative notice by the BIA, because in this way, the "tribunal learns from its cases." 972 F.2d, at 1026–27. But taking notice must be "fair in the circumstances." Particularly where the significance of the noticed facts is arguable, the agency must warn the parties of its plans. Its failure to do so in this case (involving a Nicaraguan who feared persecution from the Sandinistas, who in the meantime had fallen from power through an election) violated the Fifth Amendment's due process clause. "The availability of a motion to reopen was not adequate, because the agency might have denied it, and deportation would not have been automatically stayed by the motion." *Id.* at 1029. *Kaczmarczyk* had noted this potential problem, but it announced that the court would presume that "the Board will exercise its discretion to stay the execution of its decision until it has had an opportunity to rule on the applicant's motion." 933 F.2d at 597 n.9. The Ninth Circuit disagreed. "We are not satisfied that we can make this presumption, in view of the 'broad discretion' the agency has to deny motions for rehearing, which are 'disfavored.'" 972 F.2d at 1030, quoting *INS v. Doherty,* 112 S.Ct. 719, 724 (1992).

In his separate opinion in *Gomez-Vigil, supra,* Judge Aldisert criticized *Castillo-Villagra* with asperity. He viewed the decision as one of "exceptional importance" because of its implications for all fields of administrative law, and he labeled it a "draconian extension of orthodox Due Process teachings stemm[ing] from the view that the Board's discretionary power to grant or deny a stay of deportation affords the petitioners no protection * * * pending a motion to reopen." 990 F.2d at 1114. "The petitioners have a federal court remedy [via habeas corpus proceedings] to afford immediate, around-the-clock protection against any INS action that might implement deportation proceedings before a Due Process right has been vindicated." *Id.* at 1117. Which view do you find more persuasive? *See generally* Tome, *Administrative Notice of Changed Country Conditions in Asylum Adjudication,* 27 Colum. J.L. & Soc. Probs. 411 (1994).

9. DETERRENCE OF ASYLUM SEEKERS

The boatlift from the Cuban port of Mariel in 1980, which brought 125,000 Cuban asylum seekers to the United States within the span of a few months, started many people thinking about how to avoid such "mass asylum" situations in the future. The Select Commission on Immigration and Refugee Policy was deeply affected by this event, which occurred in the midst of its two-year investigations. Ultimately, it offered several suggestions on the subject:

Considering the possible recurrence of mass first asylum situations and the exponential growth in new asylum applicants other than Cubans and Haitians, the Select Commission has made a series of recommendations as to how the United States should attempt to manage such emergencies. These recommendations stem from the view of most Commissioners that:

- The United States, in keeping with the Refugee Act of 1980, will remain a country of asylum for those fleeing oppression.

- The United States should adopt policies and procedures which will deter the illegal migration of those who are not likely to meet the criteria for acceptance as asylees. Therefore, asylee policy and programs must be formulated to prevent the use of asylum petitions for "backdoor immigration."

- The United States must process asylum claims on an individual basis as expeditiously as possible and not hesitate to deport those persons who come to U.S. shores—even when they come in large numbers—who do not meet the established criteria for asylees.

* * *

The Select Commission [recommends that an interagency planning body] develop contingency plans for opening and managing federal asylum processing centers, where asylum applicants would stay while their applications were processed quickly and uniformly. Although some Commissioners who voted against this proposal believe that the existence of such centers could act as an incentive to those using asylum claims as a means of gaining entry to the United States, the Commission majority holds that these centers could provide a number of important benefits:

- Large numbers of asylum applications could be processed quickly. No delays would result because addresses were unknown or because of the time required to travel to an examination site;

- Staff whose training and experience make them uniquely qualified to deal with mass asylum situations could be provided;

- Applicants could be centrally housed, fed and given medical aid;

- Law enforcement problems, which might arise as a result of a sudden influx of potential asylees, could be minimized;

- Resettlement of those applicants who, for a variety of reasons, were not accepted by the United States would be facilitated by providing a setting for the involvement of the U.N. High Commissioner for Refugees and the regional mechanism the Commission has proposed to deal with migration issues.

- Ineligible asylum applicants would not be released into communities where they might later evade U.S. efforts to deport them or create costs for local governments; and

- A deterrent would be provided for those who might see an asylum claim as a means of circumventing U.S. immigration law. Applicants would not be able to join their families or obtain work while at the processing center.

SCIRP, Final Report 165–68 (1981).

Detention of Asylum Seekers

The Select Commission called for developing new facilities called "asylum processing centers," in part for the purpose of deterring marginal or abusive claims. Despite the polite label, wouldn't such facilities in reality be detention centers (or even concentration camps, as attorney Levine called them at the beginning of this Chapter)? Is such detention consistent with international law, especially as reflected in the UN Convention and Protocol? Check the Convention, with special attention to Articles 9, 26, and 31.

The Commission assumes that an applicant's stay in the centers will be relatively short, and that confinement can end as soon as a decision is reached on the application. But experience has shown that final, enforceable decisions on asylum applications often require months or years. How long could or should applicants be held in such centers if the Commission's hopes about quick processing do not become reality? How long if asylum is denied and return or distant resettlement arrangements cannot be made because other governments fail to cooperate?

We explored some of these questions in Chapter Four, pp. 445–73 *supra*, with particular attention to the constitutional issues. The judicial response has been mixed. But that is only the beginning of the inquiry. Is detention a good idea as a matter of policy?

Early in its tenure, the Reagan administration made detention a key element in its overall approach to the problem of illegal migration. The new policy was announced in Attorney General Smith's initial congressional testimony presenting the administration's proposed immigration reform legislation. Stating that we, as a nation, "have lost control of our borders," Smith emphasized: "We must more effectively deter illegal immigration to the United States—whether across our expansive borders or by sea." *Administration's Proposals on Immigration and Refugee Policy, Joint Hearing before the House Subcomm. on Immigration, Refugees, and Int'l Law and the Sen. Subcomm. on Immigration and Refugee Policy*, 97th Cong., 1st Sess. 6 (1981). He outlined the components of the legislative package, and laid special stress on two of them, "the reform of exclusion proceedings, and the necessity of detaining illegal aliens pending exclusion." *Id.* at 11.

Many of the components of the administration's reform package required congressional action before they could be effectuated—especially sanctions for employers of unauthorized aliens, which did not pass until

1986. But the administration began implementing its detention plans right away, simply by ending the custom of paroling most aliens in exclusion proceedings—a custom which had prevailed since Ellis Island closed in 1954. Eventually a court ruled that the new practice was invalid because the administration had not conformed to the notice-and-comment rulemaking requirements of the Administrative Procedure Act. *Louis v. Nelson,* 544 F.Supp. 973 (S.D.Fla.1982). *See also Bertrand v. Sava,* 684 F.2d 204 (2d Cir.1982) (sustaining the new detention practices as applied to a class of Haitian asylum applicants held in New York). But INS thereupon immediately promulgated new detention regulations in conformance with the APA procedures. *See* 47 Fed.Reg. 30,044 (1982) (interim rule); 47 Fed.Reg. 46,493 (1982) (final rule), codified at 8 C.F.R. §§ 212.5, 235.3. This general approach (if not all of its potential applications) survived numerous court challenges, discussed in Chapter Four, *supra.*

The 1982 regulations still apply, and they establish a presumption that undocumented aliens in exclusion proceedings will be incarcerated throughout the course of those proceedings (usually including judicial review). Overwhelmingly, the impact of this detention policy has fallen on asylum applicants. Moreover, many asylum applicants in deportation proceedings have also had to remain in detention while the adjudication process was underway, because they could not post the bond set under INA § 242(a). In succeeding years, however, limited INS detention space has required the release of many people covered by the regulations. In response, and in cooperation with several private organizations that assist asylum seekers, INS developed a pilot project to allow for release of selected asylum seekers who appeared to have plausible asylum claims and to pose a minimal risk of absconding, after screening by Asylum Pre–Screening Officers (APSOs). The agency considered the results from the pilot project to be mixed, but it nonetheless adopted similar standards for application nationwide in 1992. *See* 69 Interp.Rel. 252, 503, 527 (1992); Ortiz Miranda, *An Agenda for the Commission on Immigration Reform,* 29 San Diego L.Rev. 701, 731–32 (1992); *Noorani v. Smith,* 810 F.Supp. 280 (W.D.Wash.1993).

Other arguably deterrent INS practices affecting detained aliens have been challenged in litigation, with some success. In *Orantes–Hernandez v. Meese,* 685 F.Supp. 1488 (C.D.Cal.1988), *affirmed sub nom. Orantes–Hernandez v. Thornburgh,* 919 F.2d 549 (9th Cir.1990), the district court certified a nationwide class of all Salvadorans "eligible to apply for political asylum" who have been or will be taken into custody by INS. After lengthy trial proceedings, the court found that various INS actions had had the coercive effect of inducing aliens to withdraw their asylum applications. These practices ranged from "subtle persuasion to outright threats and misrepresentations. Many class members were intimidated or coerced to accept voluntary departure even when they had unequivocally expressed a fear of returning to El Salvador." Further, "INS processing officers engaged in a pattern and practice of misrepresenting the meaning of political asylum and of giving improper and incomplete legal advice which denied class members meaningful understanding of the options presented and discouraged them from exercising valuable rights." 685 F.Supp. at 1494. The court also found, *id.* at 1497–98, that INS was not following a policy the government had earlier announced: namely, promptly beginning full asylum processing whenever an individual expressed fear of return, whatever the exact words used. *See Ramirez–Osorio v. INS,* 745 F.2d 937, 944 (5th Cir.1984).

The coercive practices were adjudged a matter of INS policy, "approved, authorized and/or ratified by INS personnel at all levels." And the court concluded that the practices violated constitutional and statutory rights of the class members. 685 F.Supp., at 1504–05. Based on these findings and conclusions, the court ordered extensive relief, including formal advisal, at the time of initial processing of any detained Salvadoran, of rights to have a hearing, to secure counsel and to apply for asylum; limitations on transfers between detention centers; improved access to telephones; accurate lists of free legal services; improved access to clients and to the detention centers by counsel and paralegals; and much else. (For accounts of the trial and of other episodes in this legal battle, including contempt proceedings wherein INS was found to have violated a 1982 preliminary injunction, see 66 Interp.Rel. 1172 (1989); 65 *id.* 462 (1988); Refugee Reports, May 20, 1988, at 8–11.) But the *Orantes–Hernandez* court did not require an end to detention of asylum applicants.

Detention of excludable aliens who are applying for asylum has been challenged in several other cases, but the detention has usually been upheld. *See, e.g., Amanullah v. Nelson,* 811 F.2d 1 (1st Cir.1987); *Singh v. Nelson,* 623 F.Supp. 545 (S.D.N.Y.1985). The latter case held that the detention regulations and guidelines did not amount to an abuse of discretion. They were instead rationally related to INS's goal of deterring the arrival of people who lack documents or would "circumvent the procedures governing lawful immigration to this country." *Id.* at 556. Moreover, "[a]lthough the lengthy process of pursuing an asylum application may present petitioners with the discouraging prospect of prolonged incarceration, such detention is not inconsistent with the right to apply for asylum created by the Refugee Act." *Id.* at 558. The court also gave consideration to Article 31 of the UN Convention in these circumstances, holding that detention pending a decision on refugee *bona fides* was not forbidden. It held further that Article 31 protects only refugees coming directly from the country of persecution, not those like petitioners (Afghans who transited through Pakistan or India) who passed through other countries. *Id.* at 559–61. For discussion of detention issues, *see* Schmidt, *Detention of Aliens,* 24 San Diego L.Rev. 305 (1987); Helton, *The Legality of Detaining Refugees in the United States,* 14 N.Y.U.Rev.L. & Soc.Change 353 (1986).

Detaining nearly all excludable aliens and many deportable aliens while adjudication proceeds certainly may deter marginal asylum applicants. Is this a valid goal of public policy? If so, when should detention be employed to serve such an end? Does detention overdeter—that is, close down the prospect of asylum for people the United States should be trying to protect, or induce people already here to withdraw meritorious applications? Could a more precise and discriminating deterrent be devised? Should it? What other changes in the overall system for treatment and processing of asylum claimants might better serve the same basic ends?

Interdiction

In addition to its new detention policies, in October 1981 the Reagan administration also adopted a program of Coast Guard interdiction of boats in the waters between Haiti and the United States, clearly meant to cut down on the number of asylum seekers. The documents establishing the program carefully stated that no genuine refugees were to be returned to Haiti, *see* Proclamation 4865, 46 Fed.Reg. 48107 (1981); Executive Order 12324, 46 Fed.Reg. 48109 (1981), and INS agents were stationed aboard the Coast Guard cutter in order to interview the passengers of any interdicted boats. Up until the Haitian coup of September 1991, 22,716 Haitians had been stopped and interviewed in this fashion. Only 28 were allowed to proceed to the United States for further pursuit of an asylum claim. Refugee Reports, Feb. 28, 1994, at 13.

Critics voiced strong objections to the interdiction program:

Interdiction represents a radical departure from normal inspection and inquiry procedures which afford an alien the opportunity to present his or her case, through counsel, to an immigration judge. As to refugees, interdiction runs afoul of the obligations under the domestic withholding provision and its international law correlative—Article 33 of the Protocol relating to the Status of Refugees—to refrain from refoulement. * * *

A refugee who would otherwise undergo persecution might be returned upon interdiction without any recourse simply because of an inability to articulate the reasons feared, or to persuade an on-ship inspector that the fear is well-founded, or simply because he or she is afraid to speak to authorities. This is particularly so since there would be no access to counsel under these circumstances.

A refugee fleeing persecution after a stressful and surreptitious journey often lacks the documentary resources, the psychological reserve, and even perhaps the willingness to persuade someone of the integrity of his or her asylum claim. Indeed, the *Handbook on Procedures and Criteria for Determining Refugee Status* of the United Nations High Commissioner for Refugees, used by the United States in the analysis of asylum claims, emphasizes the difficulties experienced by aliens in pursuing asylum at a national border: "[The applicant for refugee status] finds himself in an alien environment and may experience serious difficulties, technical and psychological, in submitting his case to the authorities of a foreign country, often in language not his own." The *Handbook* recommends taking special care in processing such applications.

Helton, *Political Asylum Under the 1980 Refugee Act: An Unfulfilled Promise,* 17 U.Mich.J.L.Ref. 243, 255–56 (1984). *See also* Lawyers Comm. for Human Rights, Refugee Refoulement: The Forced Return of Haitians Under the U.S.-Haitian Interdiction Agreement (1990); Legomsky, *The*

Haitian Interdiction Programme, Human Rights, and the Role of Judicial Protection, Int'l. J. Refugee L. 181 (Special Issue, Sept. 1990).

The Helton article raises two issues regarding interdiction as it was practiced during the 1980s. First, to what extent are true asylum candidates returned to Haiti because of inhibitions that prevent them from voicing their claims? This raises subsidiary questions. Is the role of counsel at this stage as significant as Helton suggests? Should we be as solicitous of potential claimants as the UNHCR Handbook seems to call for, or may we assume that those with legitimate fears will resist return in some way that will signal their fears and thus prompt further processing? In a somewhat similar setting, you recall, Simas Kudirka, the Lithuanian sailor who bolted from a Soviet ship in 1970 (mentioned earlier in this Chapter), fought vigorously before he was finally overcome and physically bound and gagged by the Soviet seamen sent to retrieve him. There was no mistaking that he feared return. *See* Mann, *supra* note 19.

But Kudirka's experience raises the second set of questions. Even if we can envision an interdiction system fairly run with appropriate inquiries made before anyone is returned, how sure can we be that any particular program operates fairly? Interdiction, after all, is carried out on the high seas, away from the scrutiny of the press and the public—and perhaps out of the reach of the federal courts. *See Haitian Refugee Center, Inc. v. Gracey,* 600 F.Supp. 1396 (D.D.C.1985) (holding that plaintiffs had standing to challenge the interdiction program, but finding no cognizable violations of statutes, treaties, or the constitution), *affirmed on other grounds,* 809 F.2d 794 (D.C.Cir.1987) (lack of standing). *Cf.* Motomura, *Haitian Asylum Seekers: Interdiction and Immigrants' Rights,* 26 Cornell Int'l L.J. 695, 709–14 (1993) (suggesting that interdicted aliens should be treated as having reached the "functional equivalent of the border"). Are there other administrative checks that might provide assurances of fair implementation? Or is this objection so basic that interdiction should be abandoned— at least short of true emergencies?

Major changes in the interdiction program took place in 1991. Initially, INS announced new procedures to assure more careful and thorough questioning of interdicted aliens. *See* 68 Interp. Rel. 804 (1991); Alvarez, *Haitians Get Longer Hearings at Sea,* Miami Herald, March 16, 1991, at Bl. But these innovations were overtaken by major political changes inside Haiti.

Jean–Bertrand Aristide, who had become President early that year after Haiti's first internationally certified fair elections, was ousted in a military coup in September. The Organization of American States imposed an embargo on Haiti in response, and eventually the United Nations provided for a stronger set of global sanctions against the regime. Aristide had been wildly popular among Haiti's poor, and boat departures nearly disappeared during his tenure. But after the coup, and in the wake of the deprivations imposed by sanctions, thousands more Haitians took to the seas in search of haven elsewhere. The interdiction controversy became a major public issue. As the numbers outran the capacity of shipboard processing, the U.S. government initially began taking the Haitians to the

U.S. naval base at Guantanamo, Cuba, for INS screening (about 100 miles across the Windward Passage from Haiti). Members of INS's new Asylum Officer corps performed the initial reviews. Roughly one-third of those interviewed were found to have a "credible fear" of persecution and so were approved for onward travel to the mainland U.S. where full adjudication of the application could occur.[42]

Several aspects of the screening and interdiction process were challenged in litigation. In the initial stages, the government largely succeeded in reversing adverse district court decisions. *See, e.g., Haitian Refugee Center, Inc. v. Baker*, 949 F.2d 1109 (11th Cir.1991); 953 F.2d 1498 (11th Cir.1992), *cert. denied*, 112 S.Ct. 1245 (1992). When returns to Haiti of screened-out applicants resumed in March 1992, after temporary court stays were lifted, the outflow declined temporarily. But then large-scale boat traffic reappeared in May, and the Bush Administration decided that the Guantanamo screening was no longer feasible. President Bush issued Executive Order 12807, 57 Fed. Reg. 23133 (1992), authorizing direct return of interdicted individuals to Haiti, without any screening. Haitians who believed they were threatened in their home country were invited to apply at the U.S. embassy in Port-au-Prince for in-country screening and possible inclusion in a U.S. refugee program for direct departures.

The new Executive Order was ruled unlawful in *Haitian Centers Council, Inc. v. McNary*, 969 F.2d 1350 (2d Cir.1992), but the Supreme Court stayed the injunction and set an expedited schedule for its review. In the meantime, President Clinton, who had harshly criticized the Bush policy during the presidential campaign, surprisingly announced just before his inauguration that he would continue the interdiction—apparently to avoid a sudden outflow of Haitian boats built in anticipation of his taking office. In a much-awaited ruling, in June 1993, the Supreme Court sustained the interdiction policy (on an 8–1 vote) and held that neither the Refugee Convention nor INA § 243(h) applies to actions on the high seas. *Sale v. Haitian Centers Council, Inc.*, ___ U.S. ___, 113 S.Ct. 2549, 125 L.Ed.2d 128 (1993). Justice Stevens wrote for the majority: "While we must, of course, be guided by the high purpose of both the treaty and the statute, we are not persuaded that either one places any limit on the President's authority to repatriate aliens interdicted beyond the territorial seas of the United States. * * * 'This case presents a painfully common situation in which desperate people, convinced that they can no longer remain in their homeland, take desperate measures to escape. Although the human crisis is compelling, there is no solution to be found in a judicial remedy.'" *Id.* at 2567, quoting Judge Edwards' concurrence in *Gracey, supra.* For summaries of these developments, including legislation that was proposed (unsuccessfully) to alter the U.S. interdiction policy, see 69 Interp. Rel. 149, 213, 249, 672 (1992); Refugee Reports, June 19, 1992, at 11; *id.*, Jan. 29, 1993, at 1; *id.*, June 30, 1993, at 1. *See also* Frelick,

---

42. Approximately 250 of the "screened in" Haitians were not permitted to enter the United States because they tested positive for HIV, the AIDS virus. They remained in detention in Guantanamo, but litigation ultimately won their release, and they were brought to this country. *Haitian Centers Council, Inc. v. Sale*, 823 F.Supp. 1028 (E.D.N.Y.1993).

Haitian Boat Interdiction and Return: First Asylum and First Principles of Refugee Protection, 26 Cornell Int'l L.J. 675 (1993); *Koh, Reflections on* Refoulement *and* Haitian Centers Council, 35 Harv. Int'l L.J. 1 (1994); Koh, *The Human Face of the Interdiction Program,* 33 Va. J. Int'l L. 483 (1993); Note, *Litigating as Law Students: An Inside Look at* Haitian Centers Council, 103 Yale L.J. 2337 (1994).

President Clinton had justified his continuation of the interdiction program in part by emphasizing the new diplomatic steps his Administration was taking to force the junta to leave power and restore Aristide. For awhile this new activity seemed to bear fruit, as the generals agreed in July 1993 to a gradual process for the transfer of power. But they reneged on the deal in October (when the United States was preoccupied, and somewhat cowed, by disastrous developments in the UN intervention in Somalia). The embargo was tightened, and general threats of more forceful military action, under UN authority, were uttered. But little real progress took place. In April 1994, Randall Robinson, an activist who had been instrumental in the effort to end apartheid in South Africa, announced a hunger strike until Haitian interdiction ended. President Clinton yielded and in May announced a change. He did not want to return to the "credible fear" screening employed in 1991–92; the cases of the screened-in Haitians were still making their slow way through the asylum adjudication system in the United States. Instead, interdicted Haitians were to be taken to a ship anchored in Jamaica (and perhaps later to other sites on islands in the region) for full refugee screening. Those found to have a well-founded fear of persecution were to be brought to the United States in full "refugee" status, under INA § 207, the provision that governs overseas refugee programs. The rest would be repatriated.

These arrangements proceeded for a few weeks after their commencement in June, but the numbers began to overwhelm the processing capacity. Once again Guantanamo was opened as an interviewing and temporary lodging site. When the outflow reached as high as 3000 per day, however, the Administration announced a significant change of course. On July 5, 1994, the President stated that Haitians would no longer be allowed to resettle in the United States, but instead would be taken to "safe havens" in the region. Guantanamo would be the first of such sites—and as it turned out, the only one needed for Haitians. Refugee screening was ended; any who wished to stay would be allowed to (save for some residual efforts to remove persons with criminal records).

The effect on the outflow from Haiti was dramatic. Within two weeks the rate fell below 200 a week. Meantime, many Haitians chose to repatriate rather than remain in the bleak tent cities of Guantanamo. Then on September 19, U.S. military forces entered Haiti under UN authority, and by October 15, Aristide was back in the Presidential Palace in Port-au-Prince. By December 1, as a result of voluntary repatriations, the Haitian safe haven held fewer than 5,000 persons. In late December, the U.S. government announced that conditions in Haiti were generally safe for return, and it offered cash and job-training incentives to those who repatriated voluntarily by January 5, 1995. Nearly 700 accepted. The remaining 3,900 were screened and then were involuntarily returned unless they showed substantial reasons for believing that they would face serious harm not arising out of a personal dispute if returned to Haiti. UNHCR objected to the "cursory" screening process and the use of a standard not known to international law—and so refused involvement in the repatriation. (Is this a valid objection? Would the standard applied here include all Convention refugees?) By March, fewer than 100 Haitians remained behind, pending further investigation. *See* Refugee Reports, Jan. 31, 1995, at 5–7; Suro, *U.S. Policy Changed with Guantanamo Safe Havens,* Wash. Post, Feb. 5, 1995, at A24.

The use of offshore safe havens will be considered in greater detail in Section E *infra.* For more on humanitarian intervention, which can serve as one possible response to refugee emergencies, see, *e.g.,* Enforcing Restraint: Collective Intervention in Internal Conflicts (L. Damrosch ed. 1993); Law and Force in the New International Order (L. Damrosch & D. Scheffer eds. 1991); To Loose the Bands of Wickedness: International Intervention in Defense of Human Rights (N. Rodley ed. 1992); Martin, *Strategies for a Resistant World: Human Rights Initiatives and the Need for Alternatives to Refugee Interdiction,* 26 Cornell Int'l L.J. 753 (1993).

Denial of Work Authorization

Many INS officers have argued for years that the nearly automatic availability of work authorization during the pendency of any "nonfrivolous" asylum application, under regulations in effect through 1994, provided a magnet that encouraged large numbers of meritless asylum claims. This concern increased in 1991–93, as the number of INS applications grew by 200 percent, and as INS began seeing large numbers of virtually identical "boilerplate" applications—which seem plausible on their face but wind up having nothing to do with the realities of the named applicant. These were apparently being generated and filed, for a fee, by immigration "advisers" who counted on INS's inability ever to schedule an interview. (Boilerplate applications accounted for a great many of the applications by Mexican nationals filed in 1994, when Mexico climbed to fourth place on the top ten countries list.)

Some INS officers have thus proposed that work authorization should not be provided routinely during the adjudication period. *See* Martin, *Reforming Asylum Adjudication, supra* note 21, 138 U.Pa.L.Rev., at 1373 (reporting comments during INS interviews); 66 Interp.Rel. 3, 4 (1989). Such a change would indeed limit an artificial attraction of the process. But it had always been stymied by concern about the impact of such a change on genuine refugees awaiting judgments on their asylum claims. It was not immediately clear how such persons should survive in the meantime. Most federally funded assistance programs are not open to aliens whose status is otherwise unlawful, even if they have filed a nonfrivolous asylum claim. *See Sudomir v. McMahon,* 767 F.2d 1456 (9th Cir.1985); Wheeler, *Alien Eligibility for Public Benefits: Part I,* 88–11 Immigration Briefings (1988). Would denial of work authorization thus necessitate detention, simply to assure subsistence for a destitute applicant? *See* Martin, *supra,* at 1374–76 (sketching possible alternatives, less harsh than detention, based roughly on the West German model, but acknowledging many disadvantages, including greater cost to the taxpayer, in the short run, than release with work authorization).

Noting the lack of tolerable alternatives for an asylum seeker's subsistence under the present statutory system, courts have stepped in to halt INS practices that appeared likely to leave many applicants without work authorization during substantial periods while applications were pending. These cases generally held such impositions to be an unlawful burden on the statutory right to apply for asylum. *See, e.g., Diaz v. INS*, 648 F.Supp. 638 (E.D.Cal.1986) (under former regulations that made work authorization discretionary, court substantially limited district director's discretion to refuse such authorization); *Doe v. Meese*, 690 F.Supp. 1572 (S.D.Tex. 1988); *Alfaro–Orellana v. Ilchert*, 720 F.Supp. 792 (N.D.Cal.1989). If you were the Attorney General, how would you deal with these issues?

The 1994 asylum reforms, described at greater length at p. 765 *supra*, addressed these problems in two ways. Principally, by making the system more efficient and by doubling the staff, the Justice Department expects to be able to reach a point in 1995 where it can schedule all incoming cases for a prompt interview. Those whose cases cannot be granted by the asylum officer will be placed into deportation proceedings (with a few minor exceptions). Boilerplate applications will thus be detected early, and presumably persons with weak claims will be deterred from filing.

Second, the December 1994 reforms changed the arrangements for work authorization. Previous regulations theoretically allowed for up to 90 days processing time before INS had to issue the EAD (employment authorization document). But in most cases, particularly those that could not be scheduled for an interview, the EAD was issued much earlier. Nearly all affirmative asylum applicants therefore accompanied the I–589 with an application for work authorization, and a high percentage were rewarded with a wholly bona fide work authorization, because the caseload precluded anything but a hasty paper screening for "frivolousness."

In order to "decouple" the mere act of applying for asylum from work authorization, the new regulations do not permit the alien to *file* for an EAD until 150 days have elapsed after the filing of a complete asylum application, and alien-caused delays do not count toward the running of the clock. The INS then has 30 days from the date of the EAD request to issue the document, unless the claim has been adjudicated in the meantime. Of course, an EAD will issue promptly at any point when the claim is granted; and if the claim has been finally rejected by the immigration judge during that period, no EAD will issue. 8 C.F.R. § 208.7, as amended.

How is the asylum applicant supposed to survive in the meantime? INS data derived from applications filed in 1992–93 showed that over three-quarters of applicants had been in the United States for more than six months before applying; presumably they could continue whatever arrangements sustained them before applying. (Doubtless many have been working unlawfully or with false employment documents.) Is this an adequate response? How would you have dealt with the expanding asylum caseload and the apparent abuse, at least by a segment of the applicant population and their advisors, of the earlier work authorization provisions? Congress also used the 1994 crime bill to add a new subsection (e) to INA § 208: "An applicant for asylum is not entitled to employment authorization except as may be provided by regulation in the discretion of the Attorney General." Does this statutory change immunize the 1994 EAD regulations to court challenges like those in *Diaz, Doe v. Meese,* or *Alfaro-Orellana, supra?*

Summary Exclusion

Developments in mid–1993 (a growing backlog of unadjudicated applications, reported abuses by asylum seekers appearing at Kennedy airport in New York without documents that they must have had to board the plane, the discovery of several large ships smuggling Chinese asylum seekers to the United States, and the alleged involvement of asylum applicants in terrorist acts at the World Trade Center in New York and the CIA headquarters in northern Virginia) spawned legislative proposals for far more extensive changes to asylum procedures. Many of them included proposals to provide for a summary procedure at the border for excludable aliens who apply for asylum. The Clinton Administration announced on July 27, 1993, its own bill for "expedited exclusion" of certain categories of excludable aliens, especially those arriving with false documents, without the documents they presented to board the airplane in the foreign airport, or aboard an interdicted ship brought into a U.S. port. S. 1333, 103d Cong., 1st Sess. (1993). Such aliens claiming asylum would be interviewed promptly by an experienced asylum officer to determine whether a "credible fear," as defined in the bill, exists. If so, the case would be assigned for full adjudication of the claim in the normal course. If not, sharply limited administrative and judicial review would be available, and the entire procedure should be concluded within a matter of days or weeks. *See* 70 Interp. Rel. 582, 899, 965, 1001, 1551 (1993).

Would you support such changes? What would you propose instead to deal with possible "asylum emergencies," as they were sometimes called during the debate over these issues? As it happened, the Clinton administration later retreated somewhat from its earlier proposal, asking instead that Congress provide it with standby authority to invoke summary exclusions when the Attorney General declared an immigration emergency under specified criteria. *See* 71 *id.* 897 (1994). The Senate Judiciary Committee approved a bill in this form, but no further action was taken. *Id.* at 1053. New summary exclusion bills can be expected, however, in 1995.

SECTION D.   SAFE HAVEN

To establish an asylum claim, an applicant ordinarily must show some likelihood that he or she would be targeted for persecution on account of one of the five statutory grounds. Consequently, as we saw in Section C 6, *supra,* those who flee war zones or civil strife often cannot establish the necessary proof, even though they are usually referred to, in common parlance, as "refugees." They have not been targeted; they simply got in the way of the fighting.

This may be an understandable approach for implementing the fixed and open-ended legal obligation the United States undertook when it became a party to the UN Protocol. But shouldn't there be a way to provide at least a minimal level of protection—some type of safe haven—in a broader range of circumstances? Persons who flee anarchy, war, or civil strife present strong humanitarian claims, at least to receive temporary permission to remain within the confines of U.S. borders for as long as the fighting continues. And their claims are of course stronger whenever some risk of persecution also underlies their resistance to return, even if the proof is insufficient to win protection under § 208, § 243(h), or the UN Convention and Protocol.[43]

For years, some groups received a form of ad hoc protection under the label of "extended voluntary departure" (EVD), essentially an exercise of prosecutorial discretion.[44] When the Attorney General decided, usually on the advice of the State Department, to grant blanket EVD to nationals of a certain country, this action meant that INS would take no action to force departure for as long as the policy remained in effect. But EVD also often meant that INS took note of the probable illegality of the alien's presence. (If the alien could qualify for other, less tenuous, categories—for example through marriage to an American citizen—he would have every incentive to claim the conventional immigration status.)

Under the work authorization regulations adopted to implement IRCA, beneficiaries of EVD received automatic and unrestricted work authorization. 8 C.F.R. § 274a.12(a)(11). Some disputes continue over exactly which federally funded public assistance programs otherwise closed to

---

43. Several scholars have argued that international humanitarian law or other aspects of customary international law forbid nations to return persons to countries beset by war or civil strife. *See, e.g.,* Perluss & Hartman, *Temporary Refuge: Emergence of a Customary Norm,* 26 Va.J.Int'l L. 551 (1986); Goodwin–Gill *and the New Asylum Seekers,* 26 Va.J.Int'l L. 897 (1986); Note, *The Agony and the Exodus: Deporting Salvadorans in Violation of the Fourth Geneva Convention,* 18 N.Y.U.J. Int'l L. & Pol. 703 (1986). *See also* Heyman, *Redefining Refugee: A Proposal for Relief for the Victims of Civil Strife,* 24 San Diego L.Rev. 449 (1987). Some of these views were challenged in Hailbronner, *Non–Refoulement and "Humanitarian" Refugees: Customary International Law or Wishful Legal Thinking?,* 26 Va.J.Int'l L. 857 (1986); Martin, *Effects of International Law on Migration Policy and Practice: The Uses of Hyprocrisy,* 23 Int'l Migration Rev. 547, 564–68 (1989).

The Board rejected the claim that international law prohibited return to countries in-

volved in civil war in *Matter of Medina,* 19 I & N Dec. 734 (BIA 1988). Courts reached conclusions similar to the Board's in *Echeverria–Hernandez v. INS,* 923 F.2d 688 (9th Cir.1991), and *American Baptist Churches v. Meese,* 712 F.Supp. 756, 769–71 (N.D.Cal. 1989). In a case involving somewhat different international law claims, however, an immigration judge ruled that Salvadorans, though ineligible for asylum, could not be sent back to their home country. *Matter of Santos,* reported in 67 Interp.Rel. 982 (1990).

44. EVD "status," despite the confusing label, is largely equivalent to parole—a discretionary arrangement meant to cut through other technical requirements and meant to be granted and terminated with relative ease. Because of the intricacies associated with the entry doctrine, however, parole cannot be given to people who have already entered the country. And most of the people for whom safe haven has been a significant issue have already made an entry, either as nonimmigrants or as surreptitious entrants.

"illegal aliens" are open to aliens benefiting from EVD.[45]   But clearly Congress has provided no special program for federal assistance like that available to refugees under INA §§ 411–414.   *Cf. Holley v. Lavine,* 553 F.2d 845 (2d Cir.1977), *cert. denied,* 435 U.S. 947, 98 S.Ct. 1532, 55 L.Ed.2d 545 (1978).   No routine mechanism existed for eventual adjustment from EVD to lawful permanent resident status.

EVD: The Historical Pattern

Further review of the history of the use of EVD will enable a better understanding of the safe haven arrangements that are currently available. A 1982 INS staff study located 15 occasions since 1960 in which extended voluntary departure had been granted to aliens because of disturbed conditions in the home country.   *Asylum Adjudications: An Evolving Concept and Responsibility for the Immigration and Naturalization Service* 66–68 (mimeo, June 1982).   The terms varied widely, as did the decision-making background.   A description of several selected uses of EVD, and related measures, derived primarily from *id.* and from a 1981 letter from the Acting Commissioner to Senator Edward Kennedy, reprinted in 128 Cong.Rec. S831–32 (daily ed. Feb. 11, 1982), may usefully introduce the subject.

• In July 1977, the State Department recommended blanket EVD for Ethiopian nationals then in the United States.   Many of the beneficiaries had been in the country since before the 1974 overthrow of the Emperor, Haile Selassie, and in any event the country was then in the midst of a bloody series of purges known as the Red Terror.   EVD was granted in one-year increments, and was continually extended until 1981.   In 1981 the Deputy Secretary of State sent a letter to INS indicating that conditions had stabilized in Ethiopia and that the blanket policy should be ended. INS sent out a policy wire conforming to the recommendation.   *See* 58 Interp.Rel. 482–83 (1981).   This change touched off widespread criticism, led by several members of Congress, arguing that conditions were still extremely dangerous because of both the continued civil war and the regime's unabated human rights abuses.   In an embarrassing reversal, INS and State reinstated EVD for Ethiopians six months after the initial cancellation, but only for Ethiopians who had arrived before June 1980. The reinstatement letter indicated that the tight exit controls in effect in Ethiopia as of that date justified such a policy; people who left thereafter would almost surely have the blessing of the government and so would not merit special protection.   *See* 59 Interp.Rel. 456 (1982).   After the mid–1980s, extensions of EVD for Ethiopians were handled case-by-case; INS reported that it knew of none still in that status as of February 1989.   69 *id.* 898 n.8 (1992).

• In April 1978, the Department of State recommended EVD for Ugandans in the United States, because of the savagery of the Idi Amin regime then ruling the country, and because of the spreading violence in opposition.   Amin was overthrown in 1979, but conditions remained unset-

45.   *See* Wheeler, *Alien Eligibility for Public Benefits, Part 1,* 88–11 Imm.Briefings 3 (1988);   Part 2, 88–12 *id.* 16–17.

tled thereafter, and State declined for several years to change its recommendation. *See, e.g.,* 61 Interp.Rel. 899 (1984). Conditions finally improved sufficiently following the establishment of the Museveni government in 1986 for the United States to rescind blanket EVD for Ugandans. 63 Interp.Rel. 649 (1986). *See generally* U.S. Committee for Refugees, *World Refugee Survey: 1986 in Review* 3, 48–49 (1987). Most Ugandans who previously benefited from EVD became eligible for permanent resident status under 1987 legislation described below.

• In March 1979, the State Department recommended blanket EVD for nationals of Iran, then experiencing the turmoil associated with the ouster of the Shah and the eventual return of the Ayatollah Khomeini. When the U.S. embassy in Teheran was seized and American diplomats were taken hostage in November 1979, however, EVD status was abruptly cancelled as part of the overall U.S. response to the crisis. *See Yassini v. Crosland,* 618 F.2d 1356 (9th Cir.1980). (Asylum claims of course could still be lodged, and the State Department ultimately decided not to process advisory letters on Iranians for so long as the hostage situation continued. This practice achieved functionally the same result as EVD for those Iranians who filed a Form I–589; they would not be removed until those claims were adjudicated, and no claims were processed until after the hostages were released in January 1981.)

• In June 1979 the State Department recommended EVD for nationals of Nicaragua. A civil war had been underway in that country for several months by the time this recommendation was issued, and the dictator, Anastasio Somoza, was overthrown about a month after the policy went into effect. With extensions, EVD status lasted until September 1980, at which time State advised that conditions had stabilized to the point that further extensions were unnecessary.

• In December 1981, the Polish government declared martial law and seized many of the labor union activists whose Solidarity union movement had previously won important concessions from the Polish government. Many Poles departed for other European countries, and the State Department moved promptly to recommend to INS a grant of blanket EVD to Polish nationals within the United States who resisted return (with exceptions for those with a third-country residence or a criminal conviction in the United States). The INS agreed, and this policy was continued even after martial law ended in Poland. At first the policy applied only to persons who arrived before December 24, 1981, but in 1984 its reach was expanded to include those who arrived no later than July 21, 1984. *See* 61 Interp.Rel. 899–900, 1070 (1984). A series of short-term extensions (all maintaining the 1984 cut-off date for arrivals) ensued. The State Department recommended termination in 1987 because of improved political conditions in Poland, but Attorney General Meese kept extending the EVD policy, in the expectation of legislation allowing permanent residence for the covered Poles. Such a bill passed in late 1987, and EVD for Poles finally ended on March 1, 1989. 66 Interp.Rel. 38, 512 (1989).

• Beginning in December 1980, EVD was provided to all nationals of Afghanistan, owing to the war between the Afghan government—then supported by Soviet troops—and various Afghan resistance movements. See 62 Interp.Rel. 106 (1985). EVD apparently remained in force for some time after the Soviets pulled out, for Afghans who arrived before December 2, 1980. *See* 65 Interp.Rel. 964 (1988). But after the mid–1980s, extensions of EVD for Afghans were handled case-by-case; INS reported that it knew of none still in that status as of February 1989. 69 *id.* 898 n.8 (1992).

• By the mid–1980s, the Reagan Administration was coming under increasing pressure to grant EVD (again) to Nicaraguans. Advocates of this step pointed forcefully to the Administration's strong opposition to the Sandinista regime ruling Nicaragua, and argued that anything short of EVD would be inconsistent with the U.S. government's support for the Nicaraguan *contras*. The Administration resisted, largely because it worried that EVD for Nicaraguans would create irresistible pressure for EVD for Salvadorans (an issue to be considered below). But the Supreme Court's decision in *Cardoza–Fonseca* in early 1987 afforded the basis for a new policy announcement on Nicaraguans by Attorney General Meese. Under that policy, all denied Nicaraguan applicants were essentially invited to reapply under the *Cardoza–Fonseca* standards, and all were guaranteed work authorization pending a new decision on the claim. The result was functionally quite similar to what EVD would have provided, particularly given adjudication delays, but without the kind of precedent that was feared, because the Meese policy statement technically only restated existing asylum law and certainly did not directly provide EVD. District directors also apparently took the Attorney General's hint, and the grant rate for Nicaraguan asylum applications climbed sharply. *See* 64 Interp.Rel. 821, 920 (1987).

• In June 1989, the Chinese government cracked down brutally on a budding democracy movement; the events in Tiananmen Square in Beijing were viewed on televisions around the world. The Bush Administration responded by immediately suspending forced departures of Chinese nationals, for a period of at least one year. Apparently still worried about creating an EVD precedent, however, the administration issued policy statements that went out of their way to avoid EVD terminology. The plan was referred to instead as "deferral of enforced departure." *See* 66 Interp.Rel. 676 (1989). When pressed to explain how such DED differed from EVD, the acting General Counsel of INS conceded, "There is no difference in practical effect with EVD." Refugee Reports, July 28, 1989, at 10. In succeeding months, Congress and the President competed to offer other sorts of benefits as well to Chinese, including measures that would make it easier to adjust to permanent resident status. Eventually President Bush formalized his DED policy, applicable to all Chinese in the United States at some point between June 5, 1989 and April 11, 1990. E.O. 12711, 55 Fed.Reg. 13897 (April 11, 1990). It deferred departure until January 1, 1994 for all Chinese nationals in the country on the date of the order. The Chinese Student Protection Act, Pub.L.No. 102–404, 106 Stat. 1969 (1992), however, eventually allowed most DED beneficiaries to become lawful permanent residents. *See* pp. 816–17 *supra*.

Special EVD Legislation

There was no regular provision for beneficiaries of EVD eventually to become lawful permanent residents. The basic idea underlying EVD policy has always been that the stay is temporary, and that the individuals will go home once circumstances justify termination of the status. But in 1987 Congress enacted a special provision allowing certain EVD beneficiaries a 21–month period in which to apply for temporary resident status (the same status initially given the beneficiaries of legalization under IRCA, see INA § 245A), and eventually for permanent resident status. Pub.L. No. 100–204, § 902, 101 Stat. 1331 (1987). The program was opened only to members of nationality groups granted EVD during the five-year period preceding enactment. This meant that only nationals of Poland, Afghanistan, Ethiopia, and Uganda could benefit. Moreover, an applicant had to show entry before July 21, 1984 and continuous residence since then. If you think you've seen that cut-off date before, it is because you have. That is the date that limited EVD for Poles, and its appearance here reflects the fact that the legislation, as introduced by Senator Jesse Helms (R–N.C.), at first was meant to benefit only Poles; it was expanded, however, during the course of congressional consideration. See 64 Interp.Rel. 1391, 1392 (1987); 65 id. 269 (1988); 8 C.F.R. § 245a.4 (implementing regulations). Over 5500 people applied for these benefits—fewer than expected. About 70 percent of them were from Poland. 67 Interp.Rel. 72 (1990).[46]

The Salvadoran Controversy and "Temporary Protected Status"

Much of the debate over safe haven has focused on nationals of El Salvador, during its long-running civil war. For many years, the U.S. government staunchly resisted calls for extending EVD status to Salvadorans, for a variety of reasons that appear from the following materials. The controversy took place on two levels—first, a debate over the facts concerning the real dangers in El Salvador, and second, a debate over the standards that should be employed in deciding which groups merit safe haven. Advocates for granting such status argued that the general level of fighting and human rights abuses in the home country paralleled that experienced in Nicaragua, for example, when EVD was granted in 1979. They also argued that the real risks faced by most of the Salvadorans

---

46. Mention should also be made of a somewhat similar legalization program for Cuban–Haitian Entrants. As indicated *supra*, pp. 382–83, the Carter administration responded to the 1980 Mariel boatlift from Cuba (and the simultaneous arrival of thousands of Haitians by sea) by adopting a policy of not forcibly returning any such persons who arrived before a certain cut-off date (originally in 1980, later extended to 1982). Because of their manner of arrival, virtually all such aliens were excludable rather than deportable. Thus the nonreturn policy took the form of parole, rather than EVD. Unlike most other such policies, however, it was clear from the beginning that this population was being allowed to stay permanently. From 1980 onward, therefore, the executive branch sought legislation to regularize their status, but nothing passed until such a measure was included in IRCA in 1986. It allowed persons in this category a two-year application period, and they would move directly to permanent resident status (in fact, recorded retroactively to January 1, 1982), rather than first spending time as a temporary resident alien. IRCA § 202, Pub.L. No. 99–603, 100 Stat. 3359.

exceeded those faced by others who had been protected by EVD, especially Polish nationals.

Because of pressure in the 1980s for a changed EVD policy, congressional committees held hearings, and a labor union filed, on behalf of its Salvadoran members, an equal protection lawsuit against the administration's denial of EVD. To the surprise of many, this lawsuit survived the government's first motion for summary judgment. *Hotel and Restaurant Employees Union, Local 25 v. Smith,* 563 F.Supp. 157 (D.D.C.1983). (For incisive commentary on the opinion, *see* Schuck, *The Transformation of Immigration Law,* 84 Colum.L.Rev. 1, 58–62 (1984).) Seventeen months later, after discovery had taken place, the district court changed its approach significantly and granted the government's renewed motion for summary judgment. The court apparently concluded that judicial review of EVD decisions is precluded because of the exclusive authority granted to the executive branch to judge foreign policy interests and to exercise prosecutorial discretion. 594 F.Supp. 502 (D.D.C.1984), *affirmed by an equally divided* court, 846 F.2d 1499 (D.C.Cir.1988). The opinion commented further:

> For a Court to order EVD in this case would set a far-reaching precedent, wholly within the prerogatives of Congress, and might then apply to all situations of widespread fighting, destruction and the breakdown of public services and order throughout the world. Also, such situations as famine, drought, or other natural disasters might at any time also raise "humanitarian" concerns, wherever they might occur. To require the Attorney General to grant blanket EVD status to all such nationals would be to open up irresponsibly the floodgates to illegal aliens, without regard to foreign policy and internal immigration concerns, or, of equal importance, to the concerns of American working men and women in the United States and our taxpayers generally.

Id. at 508.[47]

When a group of 89 members of Congress wrote to the Attorney General and the Secretary of State in April 1983 asking that EVD be provided for Salvadorans, the Administration responded with the following letter. It was carefully drafted with an eye toward both the current political controversy and the pending *Employees Union* litigation (mindful, at the time, of the court's *first* ruling, 563 F.Supp. 157, which had held that the standards for EVD decisions were readily ascertainable and presented no "political questions" of a kind that rendered the dispute nonjusticiable).

July 19, 1983

Dear Congressman:

This is in response to your letter of April 28, 1983, concerning El Salvador and requesting that Salvadoran nationals be provided

---

47. For a contrary view, apparently countenancing limited judicial review of EVD decisions, see *Gurbisz v. INS,* 675 F.Supp. 436 (N.D.Ill.1987). *See also* Note, *Extended Voluntary Departure: Limiting the Attorney General's Discretion in Immigration Matters,* 85 Mich.L.Rev. 152 (1986).

temporary sanctuary in the United States. The delay in this response has been due to our taking a close look at the situation. I share your concern about the disturbances in areas of El Salvador, and the unfortunate plight of the Salvadoran nationals who have been displaced from their homeland. However, after careful consideration and review, I have concluded that the present circumstances do not warrant a granting of "extended voluntary departure" to El Salvadorans presently in the United States illegally.

As your letter points out, there have been occasions when the Attorney General, in consultation with the Secretary of State, has determined to delay temporarily expulsion of aliens of particular nationalities. Although somewhat of a misnomer, this form of discretionary relief from enforcement of our immigration laws most often has been referred to as "extended voluntary departure." Because of the serious foreign and domestic policy ramifications of withholding the expulsion of illegal aliens on nationality-based classifications, grants of such relief have been rare and limited to those cases where, in the judgment of the senior Executive Branch officials responsible for such policy, the best interests of the United States are served by such extraordinary measures.

It is true, as you further point out, that "extended voluntary departure" has been granted to nationals of Ethiopia, Nicaragua, Poland, and Uganda, at times when such countries were experiencing significant civil disturbances. It is inaccurate, however, to assume that there exists any specific criterion or criteria, such as the occurrence of violence or political instability, by which grants of "extended voluntary departure" are determined. As reflected in our immigration laws, it is an unfortunate reality that our country cannot provide sanctuary to all foreign nationals whose homelands are experiencing political or economic misfortune. The decisions made as to "extended voluntary departure" are reached on a situation by situation basis and are not readily susceptible to comparison or generalization. Each determination is based on examination of a variety of factors unique to each country's situation.

Because of our shared concern regarding the citizens of El Salvador, I requested new and additional advice of the Secretary of State on this matter. By recent letter, Secretary Shultz has responded that in his judgment our present U.S. efforts to assist the Salvadoran people constitute the most constructive course of action in light of our foreign policy interests, and that the Department of State does not recommend that "extended voluntary departure" be granted to Salvadoran nationals in the United States.

In addition to the counsel provided by Secretary Shultz, I have carefully considered a number of other factors. As you know, it is estimated that there are hundreds of thousands of illegal Salvadoran aliens already in the United States. This is but one facet of the current crisis in which our country is experiencing a floodtide of illegal immigrants. A grant of "extended voluntary departure" to the Salvadorans undoubtedly would encourage the migration of many more such aliens. Because of the present and potential political and economic instability in other countries in close geographic proximity to the United States, any grants of conditional immigration benefits must be considered in light of its potential inducement to further influxes of illegal immigrants. Our recent experiences with the mass migrations of Cuban and Haitian nationals to the United States have underscored the need for proper concern in such matters for the finite capacity of our country's law enforcement and social support systems. It is also clear that, notwithstanding our improving economy, the continuing problems of unemployment and budget deficits can only be exacerbated by any action which would increase substantially the number of people competing for employment and social services.

I have also considered the fact that there are adequate alternatives by which the Salvadoran nationals may seek relief. For example, as you know, our immigration laws provide various specific procedures whereby aliens may lawfully secure the right to enter and remain in the United States, including application for asylum where there is a properly demonstrated claim of fear of individual persecution in the alien's homeland. This is not to suggest that grants of "extended voluntary departure" and asylum are based upon the same considerations and criteria; however, I do view it as significant that the provisions of the Immigration and Nationality Act contain numerous forms of relief for which aliens may apply to remain in the United States. Both the number of Salvadoran aliens and past experience suggest the possibility that many such aliens may seek to remain in the United States for economic improvement as well as the fact that many such aliens passed through third countries which would afford sanctuary were that the sole objective of the migrants. Thus, I believe it appropriate to address the Salvadorans' request for relief on an individual by individual basis, as is the normal course under our immigration laws.

Finally, as you know, the Department of State has made periodic reports on the conditions in El Salvador and has concluded that, while serious problems remain, the risk to the general citizenry from civil disturbance is not prevalent throughout the country and, in some areas, the risk has diminished.

Although it is my judgment under the present circumstances not to institute a discretionary grant of relief from enforcement of our immigration laws to all Salvadoran nationals now in the United States, I have attempted to convey the serious attention that has been given to the matters raised in your letter. Please be assured that we shall continue to monitor the situation carefully, and will make every effort to ensure the fair and humane administration of our immigration laws and policies with respect to the many Salvadoran and other aliens now in our country.

> Sincerely,
> William French Smith
> Attorney General

Though the letter tries to downplay the notion that there are any specific criteria for EVD decisions, what rough standards are implicit from the letter? Are they valid? What would you add to the list? What would you subtract? Compare the following proposal, from the testimony of Congressman Mike Lowry presented in House hearings held in April 1984.

Although the context of violence is indisputable, it is difficult to obtain full documentation of the degree of risk that our current policy presents to deported Salvadoran refugees. However, the Center for Immigration Rights has studied a list of 2500 deportees. The preliminary results indicate that 50 appeared on death lists compiled by independent Salvadoran human rights organizations. That is to say, about 2% of the deportees studied were killed. Because the records are not always reliable, the total number of victims in this group could be higher.

It seems to me that there is only one responsible and humane way of reacting to this finding. That is to recognize that 2% is far too high a figure to be acceptable to us, as Americans whose government deported these individuals as a matter of policy. I do not mean to suggest that those 50 individuals were killed because they had been refugees. I do mean to suggest that their chances of dying violent deaths were far greater because we sent them back to El Salvador than if they had been allowed to stay in the United States, temporarily, until conditions in their country improve.

It was reported in one of the Seattle newspapers that a spokesman for the Immigration and Naturalization Service responded to this study with this statement: "Just because those people were returned and may have become innocent victims of some level of random violence in El Salvador does not mean the judgment on their asylum claims was inaccurate."

That is exactly the point. Asylum is appropriate for people who face threats of individual persecution. It may well have not been appropriate for those 50 Salvadorans. Yet they lost their lives in acts of violence. That is why we should grant extended voluntary departure status to those Salvadorans who remain in the United States, rather than processing them on a case-by-case basis for an asylum status designed to help a category of people with different problems.

Simply put, if we have reason to believe that a policy of deporting refugees from the United States may lead to death for 2% of them, it seems to me that a study of this policy is not too much to ask, and that while the study is going on, the policy should be suspended. That is what H.R. 4447 [the bill that was the subject of the House hearings] would do: It would suspend the deportation of Salvadorans from the U.S. pending a study of the conditions they face.

Temporary Suspension of Deportation of Certain Aliens, Hearing before the Subcomm. on Immigration, Refugees, and International Law, House Comm. on the Judiciary, 98th Cong., 2d Sess., at 44 (April 12, 1984). What are Congressman Lowry's standards for granting EVD? What other groups could be expected to meet them? Don't his standards ethically require an affirmative *admissions* policy for large numbers of Salvadorans, rather than simply a policy of non-return? What was the proposed study supposed to discover?

Later Legislative and Administrative Developments

On several occasions in the late 1980s, the House of Representatives considered and passed legislation that would have suspended the deportation of Salvadorans in the United States. Known as the DeConcini–Moakley bill, the legislation at various times included other nationalities (such as Nicaraguans and Chinese) thought to be deserving of some form of safe haven. During this period the measure failed of passage in the Senate. In 1987 Congressman Mazzoli, then chair of the House subcommittee on immigration matters, proposed an alternative to the country-specific relief of DeConcini–Moakley, instead establishing a general statutory framework for what would remain discretionary executive-branch decisions to grant temporary safe haven. *See generally* Note, *Temporary Safe Haven for De Facto Refugees from War, Violence, and Disasters,* 28 Va.J.Int'l.L. 509 (1988).

Both these legislative initiatives reached fruition in the Immigration Act of 1990. Adopting Congressman Mazzoli's proposal, Congress added § 244A to the INA, which authorizes the Attorney General to grant "temporary protected status" (TPS) to nationals of foreign states in which armed conflict, natural disaster, or other circumstances pose a serious threat to personal safety or the ability of the state to handle the return of aliens. TPS may be granted for no more than 18 months, but may be extended if the Attorney General finds that the reasons for the initial granting of the status continue. Work authorization accompanies TPS status. Take a close look at subsection (h) of § 244A. What problem does this (rather extraordinary) piece of legislation address? Why do you think it was added? Would you have supported it? For a thorough treatment of the application process and other TPS issues, see Lawyers Comm. for Human Rights, Handbook on Obtaining Temporary Protected Status (1991).

The DeConcini–Moakley approach was also adopted by Congress in the 1990 Act. Section 303(a) of the Act (not codified in the INA) provides: "El Salvador is hereby designated under section 244A(b) of the [INA]." To be eligible for TPS, a Salvadoran must have been continuously physically present in the United States since September 19, 1990. This statutory provision of TPS for Salvadorans was valid for 18 months, through June 1992, but the statute allowed for the renewal of TPS for Salvadorans under the general authority of § 244A.

As it turned out, the war in El Salvador ended in January 1992 as a result of a UN-brokered settlement. President Cristiani of El Salvador nevertheless asked President Bush to extend TPS beyond the statutory expiration date of June 30, 1992, so that returnees would not overwhelm the process of national reconstruction. Instead, the government decided to provide "deferred enforced departure" (DED) for Salvadorans through June 30, 1993. As noted earlier, this status appears to be functionally equivalent to TPS for most purposes (it clearly includes work authorization), but it is not statutorily based and hence is not subject to the reporting requirements of INA § 244A. See 69 Interp. Rel. 600 (1992). In June 1993, President Clinton then extended Salvadoran DED through the end of 1994. 58 Fed. Reg. 32157 (1993). In December 1994 the administration announced that there would be no further extensions of DED, because "the political and human rights situation inside El Salvador has improved significantly." But it did provide a transition period, by automatically extending their work authorizations for nine months. 59 Fed. Reg. 62751 (1994); 71 Interp.Rel. 1586 (1994). *See also id.* at 1322 (State Department cable discussing the effect of a likely termination of DED and noting that remittances from Salvadorans in the United States are estimated at $840 million annually).

No mass returns are expected, because most DED Salvadorans can have asylum applications heard de novo under the settlement reached in *American Baptist Churches v. Thornburgh*, 760 F.Supp. 796 (N.D.Cal. 1991), described in note 25 *supra*. As "backlog" cases, these applications will occupy a low priority for asylum officers as they strive principally to achieve quick turn-around on newly filed asylum claims. And many Salvadorans are nearing the seven years' presence required to file for suspension under INA § 244. Some observers believe that the Salvadoran experience renders future provision of TPS less likely, because for so many Salvadorans the stay will not prove to be truly temporary, despite a surprisingly successful negotiated peace in El Salvador. Should this be viewed as a problem? Are there other ways to improve the odds that TPS can truly be temporary? Or is it unrealistic to expect temporariness if the safe haven period lasts beyond—what?—one year? three years?

In February 1991, the Department of Justice announced the granting of temporary protected status, under the ordinary provisions of the new § 244A to aliens in the United States from Kuwait, Lebanon and Liberia. 56 Fed.Reg. 12745 (1991); 68 Interp.Rel. 214 (1991). TPS for Kuwait was allowed to lapse in 1992, over a year after Kuwait was liberated from the Iraqi invaders, and that for Lebanon was ended in April 1993, 70 Interp. Rel. 175 (1993), but Lebanese were granted a highly liberal voluntary departure policy through December of that year. *Id.* at 215, 1063. TPS for Liberians has been extended through March 28, 1995, 59 Fed. Reg. 9997 (1994); INS estimates that about 4000 Liberians benefit from the status. 71 Interp.Rel. 319 (1994). Somalis who arrived before September 16, 1991 were provided with TPS in 1991, 68 Interp. Rel. 1191 (1991). The status has been extended through September 1995, but INS estimates only about 350 beneficiaries. 71 *id.* 1150. Bosnians present as of August 10, 1992, have also been added to the list, 69 Interp. Rel. 969 (1992), and the Bosnian designation has been extended into July 1995, but without moving up the initial cut-off date for qualifying (only about 300 Bosnians in the U.S. have done so). 71 Interp.Rel. 930–31 (1994). Rwandans were granted TPS in June 1994. 59 Fed.Reg. 29440 (1994). Evidently the Salvadoran experience has not completely ended the use of TPS—but note how distant are the recently designated countries, and how few of their citizens appear to be in the United States. *See generally* B. Frelick & B. Kohnen, Filling the Gap: Temporary Protected Status (U.S. Comm. for Refugees Issue Paper 1994) (also reporting that 187,000 Salvadorans initially registered for TPS).

Cuba and the Use of Offshore Safe Havens

One of the most troubling points of the Haitian interdiction program, described in the previous Section, has always been the sharp contrast between the treatment of Haitians and the boat people from the next island over, Cuba. During much of the time that the U.S. Coast Guard was interdicting Haitians and returning some or all of them, other Coast Guard cutters were patrolling nearby waters to pick up Cubans who had slipped past government guards and managed to get their rafts past the twelve-mile limit. Until summer 1994, Cuban rafters picked up this way were taken to Florida, where they were warmly greeted and put on a fast-track toward permanent residency, without having to demonstrate a well-founded fear of persecution.

This grand-daddy of all safe haven programs dates back to the early years of Castro's revolution, when the U.S. government essentially decided to allow all Cubans to enter and to stay as long as was necessary. Many were paroled in; those who had already made an entry became some of the first beneficiaries of EVD. When it became apparent that the Castro government would not quickly fade away, Congress enacted the Cuban Adjustment Act of 1966, Pub.L.No. 89–732, 80 Stat. 1161. It provides that the status of Cubans who have been "inspected and admitted or paroled into the United States subsequent to January 1, 1959, * * * may be adjusted by the Attorney General, in his discretion and under such regulations as he may prescribe, to that of an alien lawfully admitted for permanent residence" after one years' physical presence in the United States (originally two years). This was taken by generations of Cuban–Americans and many politicians to be an open-ended entitlement for all Cubans who could make it to U.S. soil. Is that a fair reading? What is the significance of the discretion explicitly vested in the Attorney General?

The Mariel boatlift in 1980, which brought some 125,000 Cubans, sorely tested the limits of U.S. (and Florida) hospitality, but the 1966 Act remained unchanged and the flow remained low as Cuba thereafter maintained close enforcement of its exit controls. Then in August 1994 Fidel Castro responded to internal unrest—as he had often done before—by trying to create a new migration crisis for the United States. Guards stopped patrolling the beaches of northern Cuba, and eager rafters by the thousands set off for the high seas in flimsy home-made craft. Governor

Chiles of Florida, in the middle of a hard-fought election campaign, declared a state of emergency and pushed the federal government to act.

The Clinton administration responded fairly quickly, setting in motion a chain of events that has basically ended the open-door policy for Cubans. Instead of bringing the Cubans to the United States, the administration opted to use the model of offshore safe haven that had recently proven so effective, see p. 881 *supra,* in discouraging further departures from Haiti (the Cuban crisis began about five weeks after Clinton announced that departing Haitians would receive temporary safe haven in Guantanamo— nothing more). Rescued Cuban rafters were taken to a separate camp in Guantanamo, and later some were moved to a safe-haven camp in Panama paid for and operated by the U.S. government. Initially this change in policy seemed to have little effect on departures from Cuba, but after about 10 days the numbers began to decline. Before the dissuasive effect was fully tested, however, Cuba and the United States reached a migration-only agreement on September 9. Cuba agreed to end departures "using mainly persuasive means," and the United States agreed to take a minimum of 20,000 Cubans for permanent, orderly migration each year, after advance screening and selection in Havana. *See* 71 Interp.Rel. 1091, 1213, 1236–37 (reprinting the agreement), 1409, 1474 (1994). (These unprecedented arrangements for annual orderly migration have drawn court challenges, but administration officials assert that this was the price that had to be paid to bring an end to 35 years of inequitable policy and the expectations that had been generated.)

By the end of the summer, then, far greater parity had been brought to the treatment of Cubans and Haitians (and a democratically elected President had been returned to Haiti as a result of armed U.S. intervention). Two agonizing immigration crises had been mastered fairly speedily, as these things go, through the use of offshore safe haven. Some officials waxed enthusiastic about this practice. Is this enthusiasm warranted? Consider the following views:

> The newest innovation in the West's refugee tool-kit is really just a form of temporary protection: offshore safe haven funded by the United States but located in places like Guantanamo or Panama, with little prospect for the beneficiaries ever to resettle in the U.S. From an official's perspective, this variant carries many advantages. The individuals are confined to a known area, making it easy to locate them when the protection period ends. Because the safe havens are not on U.S. soil, the individuals' ultimate return, even involuntarily, will be hard to tie up in federal court. And because life there is not nearly as comfortable as residence in the United States, the asylum seekers are much more likely to self-select. That is, once the no-resettlement policy is believably understood, it is probable that only people who are truly threatened will seek such safe haven. To those for whom economic motives predominate, boredom in a tent city in Guantanamo will seem far less attractive than sticking it out in Cap Haitien or Havana, whereas residence in Miami would have the opposite effect. Moreover, no officer has to apply the difficult

Convention refugee standard in costly individual adjudications. And from a humanitarian perspective, the practice is clearly superior to the kind of blanket interdiction imposed on Haitians from 1992 to May 1994: *nonrefoulement* is honored without scaring Florida officials.

And yet, and yet. These advantages still come at a high price. The very monotony of existence in the safe havens stunts human development and creates persistent risks of riot and disorder—familiar problems in third-world refugee camps, but relatively novel in American experience. And the ongoing costs of housing, feeding, and providing medical care to thousands of idle people mount up quickly. The United States has never been good at simply warehousing innocent people, and we should not be anxious to acquire the habit.

Offshore safe havens, in short, may be highly useful and legitimate measures for responding to emergencies—that was certainly their genesis. But here more than ever it is important that their use be truly temporary. In the Haitian instance this condition seemed to obtain as of July when Guantanamo opened for these purposes, because the junta's departure, resulting from either the embargo or an intervention, was clearly on the horizon. And after the U.S. intervention, most Guantanamo Haitians have returned home. But Cuba was always a much more difficult case. Perhaps Castro's government will succumb to internal discontent; the legal migration stream out of Havana, though now expanded under the New York agreement that resolved this summer's crisis, will not provide much of a safety valve. But overthrow seems most unlikely in the short term. A difficult judgment now looms about the increasingly restive Cubans in U.S.-funded safe havens.

Martin, *Political Asylum in the West: Dying or Recuperating?*, _____ (1995).

Chapter Nine

JUDICIAL REVIEW

Decisions under the immigration laws can carry the most telling personal consequences known to the federal administrative process. To be sure, a ratemaking order or a broadcast licensing proceeding might mean millions of dollars in profit or loss to the contending parties—sums far beyond what one encounters in the immigration field. But those on the losing side, even in such titanic administrative battles, can go home and relieve their disappointment among family and friends. Immigration decisions, in contrast, often bear directly on just where home will be, and on which family members and friends will share daily in life's triumphs and losses.

In light of the potential stakes, both the alien and ultimately the government have the strongest reasons for wanting to be sure that such decisions are done correctly. To serve this end, complex mechanisms for administrative review have evolved, varying considerably depending on the precise application or decision at issue. The basic structure of administrative review is sketched in Chapter Two.[1]

---

1. You may wish to review that Chapter at this point, as the materials to follow presuppose a basic familiarity with the scheme of administrative review. In essence, practice within the Justice Department involves two main avenues for such review. The Board of Immigration Appeals hears appeals from the most potent administrative decisions—orders of exclusion and deportation, which are handed down initially by immigration judges—and also reviews a handful of other categories of decisions. Many of the latter never go before an immigration judge. For example, INS district directors and regional service centers (RSCs) decide on visa petitions. If they deny a petition founded on alleged family relationships, the petitioner may ask the BIA to review the denial. Many other decisions reached by district directors are appealable, not to the Board, but to the Administrative Appeals Unit (AAU) in the Central Office (for example, visa petitions based on occupational preferences). Some decisions of the district directors or RSCs (*e.g.*, denial of an extension of stay sought by a nonimmigrant) are not appealable. Others are not strictly appealable but may be filed *de novo* with the immigration judge once deportation proceedings begin (*e.g.*, applications for adjustment of status). For a highly useful summary, *see* Ruthizer, *Administrative Appeals of Immigration Decisions: A Practitioner's Guide*, 88–1 Imm. Briefings 1 (1988). For a thoughtful analysis and critique of the distribution of administrative and judicial review authorities, *see* Legomsky, *Forum Choices for the Review of Agency Adjudication: A Study of the Immigration Process*, 71 Iowa L. Rev. 1297 (1986) (based on a study done for the Administrative Conference of the United States, which then adopted recommendations for change in the administrative structure, 1 C.F.R. § 305.85–4 (1989), but found the proposed changes in judicial

But Americans have probably always harbored a measure of distrust for bureaucrats, even those who serve in purely corrective or appellate roles. Perhaps as a result, the federal courts, staffed with life-tenured judges, have come to be seen as the ultimate guarantors of administrative reliability. Whether or not this great faith in the bench's capacity is always well-placed, *see* Schuck, *The Transformation of Immigration Law,* 84 Colum.L.Rev. 1, 62 and *passim* (1984), nonetheless this judicial role is a well-entrenched feature of modern life. Under doctrines worked out over the last forty years or so, federal agency actions are now presumptively subject to review in the courts, *Abbott Laboratories v. Gardner,* 387 U.S. 136, 140–41, 87 S.Ct. 1507, 1510, 1511, 18 L.Ed.2d 681 (1967). (Several recent Supreme Court decisions have emphasized, however, that this principle is "just a presumption" and should be considered overcome in several categories of cases where Congress has implicitly intended to foreclose review. *See Lincoln v. Vigil,* ___ U.S. ___, 113 S.Ct. 2024, 2030, 124 L.Ed.2d 101 (1993).)

The Administrative Procedure Act (APA), enacted in 1946 (Pub.L. No. 404, 60 Stat. 237), provides the foundation for most such judicial review. (Selected sections of the Act appear in the Statutory Supplement.) The review framework is highly flexible, at least so long as the statutes establishing the administrative project do not expressly eliminate or channel the judicial role. The APA states a general rule that persons "adversely affected or aggrieved by agency action" are entitled to judicial review. 5 U.S.C.A. § 702. In the absence *or inadequacy* of specialized provisions for judicial review set forth in the statutes governing a particular agency, a person adversely affected by agency action may seek review using "any applicable form of legal action, including actions for declaratory judgments or writs of prohibitory or mandatory injunction or habeas corpus, in a court of competent jurisdiction." 5 U.S.C.A. § 703. Litigants in immigration cases at various times have attempted to make use of all these possibilities for review of various decisions under the immigration laws.

But the interest in accuracy of administration—an interest shared, in the end, by the alien and the government (whether or not this is always remembered and observed by particular officials cloaked with governmental authority)—is not the only force that impels the people involved to go into court. Even aliens with no colorable claim to the benefit at issue may have a strong interest in stringing out the procedures as long as possible. For in nearly every case, the alien remains in the United States as long as the

---

review more controversial, *see* 63 Interp. Rel. 1192 (1986)).

Outside of the Justice Department, other agencies have their own review systems. For example, the Department of Labor subjects initial decisions on labor certification to review by a panel of administrative law judges (ALJs) known as the Board of Alien Labor Certification Appeals (BALCA). The ALJs are employees of the Department, but maintain a measure of independence, under statutes establishing the ALJ system for the federal government. *See* 5 U.S.C.A. §§ 3105, 5372, 7521. (Immigration judges, although

they perform functions similar to those performed by ALJs in many agencies and enjoy equivalent independence, are not ALJs governed by this statutory scheme.)

The cases in this Chapter will generally set forth clearly enough the administrative review mechanism applicable to the particular determination at issue. But it will be worthwhile each time to reflect on how those mechanisms fit into the overall scheme, to consider whether other administrative mechanisms would work better, and to ponder how any such administrative changes would or should affect judicial review.

process of review—both administrative and judicial—continues. And even when a particular chain of review seems to have come to an end, it remains possible to ask some decisionmaker along the way to reopen or reconsider the earlier decision, based on a claim of new information or new legal arguments. Reconsideration might be erroneously denied; it is impossible to design an adjudication system so perfect as to exclude that contingency. And so the theoretical foundation is laid for a new chain of review, testing whether or not such an error has occurred.

Here, then, as in other areas of immigration law, we encounter a familiar tension. We do not want to stint on measures meant to assure accurate and humane application of the system. At the same time we do not want to foster manipulation by well-counseled aliens seeking only to prolong a stay to which they are not entitled. How can the appropriate balance be achieved? At different stages in our history, Congress, the courts, and the agencies have provided different answers to this underlying riddle. It suggests several subsidiary questions. At what stage in the administrative proceedings should review take place? What form of action is appropriate? Which judicial forum should hear the case? What if the same or similar issues have been heard before? What should be the standard for judicial review? The materials in this Chapter touch on these questions.[2]

SECTION A. BACKGROUND

From the beginning, federal immigration statutes have regularly provided that orders of executive branch officers in deportation and exclusion cases are to be "final."[3] Some early Supreme Court decisions seemed to

---

2. This Chapter is selective; it gives detailed consideration to only a few issues of major significance that appear from the cases considering judicial review of immigration decisions. Most of the opinions excerpted at length, however, evince some attention to the whole list of questions set forth in the text.

Also, you may find a few of those questions familiar ones, especially those dealing with the standard or scope of review of administrative action. Should the courts reverse an administrative decision when they determine that the findings are not supported by "substantial evidence" on the record? (And just what does "substantial evidence" mean anyway?) Or should courts reverse only when there has been an "abuse of discretion" or administrative action deemed "arbitrary and capricious" (formulations usually considered more deferential to the administrators)? *See generally Citizens to Preserve Overton Park v. Volpe,* 401 U.S. 402, 413–16, 91 S.Ct. 814, 822, 823, 28 L.Ed.2d 136 (1971).

The answer may vary depending on the precise statutory provision at issue. Moreover, each of these formulations may carry its own specific connotations and implications,

again depending on the precise nature of the substantive scheme. Consequently, we have found it more logical to consider some issues of this sort in other Chapters, because the questions can be so closely linked to an understanding of the substantive provisions of the INA. *See, e.g., Wong Wing Hang v. INS,* 360 F.2d 715 (2d Cir.1966), at p. 686 *supra* (a leading decision both on the meaning of suspension of deportation under § 244 and also on standards for review of administrative decisions under statutes explicitly vesting an administrator with discretion). More detailed consideration of the intricate disputes over scope of review is standard fare in general administrative law courses; we will not try to cover the same ground.

3. For a summary, *see Heikkila v. Barber,* 345 U.S. 229, 233–35, 73 S.Ct. 603, 605, 606, 97 L.Ed. 972 (1953). The INA still contains such language. *See* §§ 236(c), 242(b). Interestingly, the only significant provisions establishing a different structure appeared in the Chinese exclusion laws, which envisioned a judicial determination of deportability. Once general deportation provisions were applied to Chinese aliens, however, the judicial proce-

read that specification in its harshest literal sense, as though it precluded any possible judicial role.[4] But that phase did not last long. Soon the courts began to entertain cases challenging the decisions of the administrators in exclusion and deportation cases. Often the substantive standard for review was extraordinarily deferential to the administrators, when viewed from a modern perspective, but the immigration authorities did not always prevail. In any event, the mere fact of judicial consideration was significant, in the face of the statute's command of finality.[5]

These cases allowing judicial review present an apparent puzzle. Federal courts are courts of limited jurisdiction, and they must ordinarily trace their power to hear a case to a specific congressional authorization. The early immigration statutes merely set forth the administrative arrangements and purported to make the resulting orders final. Clearly *they* bestowed no review authority on the courts. Indeed, it was not until 1961 that any general provisions for judicial review appeared in our immigration laws. Just how did the courts manage to assume jurisdiction?

The answer derives from the brute requirements of the process of deportation and exclusion. An unwilling alien could not (and obviously still cannot) be removed without being physically restrained at some point. Classically, such physical restraint—custody—is the foundation for issuance of the Great Writ, the writ of habeas corpus, a remedy guaranteed in the text of the Constitution.[6] The early review cases were all habeas corpus cases, and for decades, the writ of habeas corpus provided the only avenue for court review of exclusion and deportation orders.

The exclusiveness of habeas review answered many of the questions we posed earlier, often by drawing on the common law doctrines relating to habeas corpus. The scope of review in such cases was relatively narrow,

---

dure fell into disuse. *See* GM & Y § 81.01[2] n.7; *Ng Fung Ho v. White,* 259 U.S. 276, 279–81, 42 S.Ct. 492, 493–94, 66 L.Ed. 938 (1922).

4. *See, e.g., Nishimura Ekiu v. United States,* 142 U.S. 651, 660, 664, 12 S.Ct. 336, 340, 35 L.Ed. 1146 (1892); *Lem Moon Sing v. United States,* 158 U.S. 538, 549, 15 S.Ct. 967, 971, 39 L.Ed. 1082 (1895); *Fok Yung Yo v. United States,* 185 U.S. 296, 305, 22 S.Ct. 686, 689, 46 L.Ed. 917 (1902).

5. *See, e.g., Yamataya v. Fisher (The Japanese Immigrant Case),* 189 U.S. 86, 100–02, 23 S.Ct. 611, 614, 615, 47 L.Ed. 721 (1903); *Chin Yow v. United States,* 208 U.S. 8, 12, 28 S.Ct. 201, 202, 52 L.Ed. 369 (1908); *Gegiow v. Uhl,* 239 U.S. 3, 9, 36 S.Ct. 2, 60 L.Ed. 114 (1915). For a general summary of these developments, *see* Hart, *The Power of Congress to Limit the Jurisdiction of the Federal Courts: An Exercise in Dialectic,* 66 Harv. L.Rev. 1362, 1389–96 (1953).

6. Article I, section 9, clause 2 states: "The privilege of the Writ of Habeas Corpus shall not be suspended, unless when in Cases of Rebellion or Invasion the public Safety may require it." It can be quite difficult to decide just what restrictions on the writ will constitute an invalid "suspension," especially when restrictions are accompanied by the opening of other procedural avenues for a prisoner to test the confinement. *See generally Swain v. Pressley,* 430 U.S. 372, 97 S.Ct. 1224, 51 L.Ed.2d 411 (1977).

The habeas corpus remedy was also the subject of federal statutes well before the first immigration acts were passed, and sometimes it is not clear whether particular features of habeas practice as we have come to know them derive from constitutional command or from statutory refinement. *See* Saltzburg, *Habeas Corpus: The Supreme Court and the Congress,* 44 Ohio St.L.J. 367 (1983). Most of the time it has not been important to make such distinctions; habeas practice in immigration cases has conformed in general to the outlines established in the general federal habeas provisions. 28 U.S.C.A. § 2241 et seq. But some proposals for immigration reform, including bills that passed the Senate in 1982 and 1983, would have limited the writ in deportation and exclusion cases to its minimum content "under the Constitution." Specifying that content would not be easy.

frequently expressed as follows: the courts would inquire whether the hearing conformed to minimum due process requirements, whether there was any evidence to support the conclusion, and whether the statutory requirements had been properly construed.[7] Furthermore, the exclusivity of the habeas corpus remedy minimized the chances of interrupting the administrative process with premature review or burdening it with repetitious litigation. Custody often began only at the end of the process; and a familiar prerequisite to issuance of the writ was the petitioner's exhaustion of other available remedies.

But litigants still sought other avenues into the courts, for a simple reason. The very foundation of the high regard Anglo–American jurisprudence has maintained for the habeas corpus remedy—its availability at the moment when a person was restrained of his or her liberty—also resulted in its major disadvantage. As habeas was ordinarily understood until recent years, the alien could not petition for the writ until he was actually in physical custody. By then he may have had to sell his belongings, bid farewell to family and friends, and wait from his jail cell for the court's decision.

In 1934, Congress passed the Declaratory Judgment Act, 28 U.S.C.A. § 2201, allowing litigants in certain circumstances to seize the initiative for securing a judicial hearing in a federal court earlier than was otherwise possible, provided the plaintiff presented "a case of actual controversy within [the court's] jurisdiction." At one point it appeared that aliens might use that procedure to contest immigration rulings without having to undergo physical custody. *See McGrath v. Kristensen,* 340 U.S. 162, 168–71, 71 S.Ct. 224, 228–30, 95 L.Ed. 173 (1950). But a few years later, when the issue was squarely presented, the Supreme Court disavowed such a conclusion. In *Heikkila v. Barber,* 345 U.S. 229, 73 S.Ct. 603, 97 L.Ed. 972 (1953), the Court staunchly reaffirmed the exclusiveness of the habeas remedy (except in extremely narrow circumstances):

> Congress may well have thought that habeas corpus, despite its apparent inconvenience to the alien, should be the exclusive remedy in these cases in order to minimize opportunities for repetitious litigation and consequent delays as well as to avoid possible venue difficulties connected with any other type of action.

Id. at 237, 73 S.Ct. at 607. *See also Shung v. Brownell,* 346 U.S. 906, 74 S.Ct. 237, 98 L.Ed. 405 (1953).

But it turned out that the *Heikkila* doctrine was quite short-lived. The case arose in 1950, before passage of the INA but after the APA had been enacted, and Heikkila tried to claim declaratory review not only under the Declaratory Judgment Act, but also under the APA. *See* 5 U.S.C.A. §§ 701–706. The Court ruled against him on both grounds. But crucially, its holding applied only to the immigration laws extant in 1950 (the most important being the Immigration Act of 1917). The Court did not decide the effect of the 1952 INA, even though that law was already on the books by the time the decision issued.

---

7. *See, e.g., Kwock Jan Fat v. White,* 253 U.S. 454, 457–58, 40 S.Ct. 566, 567, 64 L.Ed. 1010 (1920); *United States ex rel. Rongetti v. Neelly,* 207 F.2d 281, 284 (7th Cir.1953).

In 1955 the Court decided that the new INA made a profound difference. *Shaughnessy v. Pedreiro,* 349 U.S. 48, 75 S.Ct. 591, 99 L.Ed. 868 (1955). The 1952 Congress had not specifically exempted future immigration decisions from the judicial review provisions of the 1946 APA. Because the APA itself established a presumption that later-enacted administrative statutes would be subject to APA requirements, the congressional silence was considered determinative.[8] From that moment on, declaratory and injunctive relief were to be available under the APA to test deportation orders under the INA. In 1956 the Court reached the same conclusion with respect to exclusion cases. *Brownell v. Shung,* 352 U.S. 180, 77 S.Ct. 252, 1 L.Ed.2d 225 (1956).

For immigration litigants, these were wonderful developments. Aliens could at last clearly contest exclusion and deportation orders without having to go to jail. Congress, however, was less pleased with the results. Although many members were prepared to afford some mechanism for court review of deportation orders in advance of custody, the key committees feared that the procedures made available under *Pedreiro* would be abused to string out court review beyond all reasonable bounds. *See, e.g.,* H.R.Rep. 1086, 87th Cong., 1st Sess., 28–32 (1961). Several tales of delay and manipulation were presented in the congressional testimony. But one case stands out—that of Carlos Marcello, a reputed racketeer who had been brought to the United States from Italy at the age of one but had never become a citizen. INS had been trying to deport him since virtually the moment in 1952 when the INA became effective. A deportation order became administratively final in 1953, but court orders had prevented its execution. One committee report reprinted the text of a letter detailing Marcello's use of the courts to impede deportation:

March 25, 1959

Hon. Sam J. Ervin, Jr.,

U.S. Senate.

Dear Senator Ervin: It has been called to my attention that yesterday at the hearing of the Senate Select Committee on Improper Activities in the Labor and Management Field you made

---

8. *Pedreiro* did not decide that all provisions of the APA applied to all aspects of implementation under the 1952 INA. In fact, the same year the Court reached the opposite conclusion regarding the application of the rather stringent separation-of-function requirements the APA establishes for agency adjudicators. These were held inapplicable to special inquiry officers, because INA § 242(b) contains its own (watered-down) set of requirements on this subject. *See Marcello v. Bonds,* 349 U.S. 302, 75 S.Ct. 757, 99 L.Ed. 1107 (1955).

As a result, although the INA postdates the APA, the APA applies only in patchwork fashion to decisions under the INA. Indeed, this patchwork quality was augmented in 1961 when Congress enacted special judicial review provisions as § 106 of the INA. That section, which will claim most of our attention throughout this Chapter, exempts exclusion and deportation orders from the procedural specifications of the APA governing judicial review. Specifically, it forbids review of such orders in declaratory actions brought in accordance with the APA. But observe that § 106 provides special and exclusive judicial review channels only for exclusion and deportation orders; it leaves APA procedures applicable to judicial review of other decisions under the immigration laws. (The APA's requirements for public notice and opportunity for comment in advance of rulemaking, 5 U.S.C.A. § 553, also apply to the promulgation of regulations under the INA.)

inquiries concerning the deportation proceedings against Carlos Marcello. I thought you would be interested in knowing the steps the Department of Justice has taken to rid the country of this undesirable alien. Attached herewith is a summary of the chronology of the litigation involved in these proceedings.

You will notice that on six separate occasions Marcello has instituted various suits in the district courts of the United States raising issues incident to the deportation order. Each case has been contested vigorously. On several occasions, he has sought review in the court of appeals, and on three occasions has been to the Supreme Court of the United States. Although the deportation order has been successfully defended on all occasions, and the Government has been successful on most of the other issues raised, it has been under court-imposed restraint from deporting Marcello during much of this time.

During periods when there was no court imposed restraint, deportation has not been possible because of the lack of an Italian passport, without which deportation was not possible. In August 1955 when travel documentation was available and Marcello had been directed to surrender for deportation, the Italian consul at New Orleans revoked the passport on the day he was to be deported. Thereafter, further litigation was instituted and was decided favorably to the Government. After continuous negotiations, the Italian authorities on October 31, 1956, issued another passport which was limited in time. However, on the day before its issuance, Marcello filed a new suit and obtained a temporary restraining order preventing deportation.

Another suit was instituted by Marcello to delay deportation and, in addition, he started proceedings in the Italian courts for a judgment declaring him not to be a citizen of Italy, as a result of which the Italian Foreign Office was enjoined from issuing any travel documents until that suit is terminated. Nevertheless, the Government has continued to exert every effort for the issuance of an Italian passport and I have personally participated in this effort.

At the present time the deportation order against Marcello is still outstanding. In his last effort to delay deportation, he applied for an administrative stay on the ground that he would suffer physical persecution if deported to Italy. When this was denied and the Government's position upheld in the U.S. District Court for the District of Columbia, he sought review in the court of appeals. The latter court held that the Immigration Service had not given him adequate time to collect and present evidence in support of his claim that he would be subject to persecution. He was given such an opportunity and on February 20, 1959, the Service denied the requested relief.

Although presently there is no pending litigation, deportation cannot be effected because no passport is available. If this obstacle is overcome there is no guarantee that deportation can be expeditiously effected. On the basis of past experience it is expected that Marcello will attempt other delaying tactics in the courts.

In connection with the delays often encountered in effecting deportation, I would like to call your attention to the fact that the administration for the past 5 years has sought legislation which would strengthen our immigration laws by limiting judicial review of deportation orders within reasonable bounds so as to avoid its repeated use solely as a delaying tactic.

* * *

I urge the Congress to enact this much needed legislation at the earliest possible moment.

> Sincerely,
> William P. Rogers,
> Attorney General

H.R.Rep. No. 565, 87th Cong., 1st Sess. 6–7 (1961). The committee reprinted the Attorney General's chronology, updating it with references to later events, including the three new federal actions Marcello had filed between 1959 and mid–1961. The committee also noted "that Marcello's repetitious court proceedings are principally begun (with their accompanying requests for interim stays) just when the Government manages to obtain a travel document and is about to enforce departure—many years after the order of deportation was entered." *Id.* at 11.[9]

After considering all these developments, Congress ultimately added section 106 to the INA in order to restructure the judicial review arrangements. Act of Sept. 26, 1961, Pub.L. No. 87–301, § 5, 75 Stat. 651. This enactment constituted the first specific statutory provision governing the judicial review of exclusion and deportation orders. At this point you should consult the text of § 106.

Consider first the changes Congress wrought for exclusion cases. Section 106(b) restores habeas corpus as the exclusive means for review of exclusion orders. Early declaratory review, as authorized by the 1956 *Shung* decision, *supra,* under the authority of the APA, was thus foreclos-

---

9. The chronology also reveals some questionable government behavior in INS's ceaseless efforts to remove Marcello. *See United States ex rel. Marcello v. District Director,* 634 F.2d 964, 966 (5th Cir.1981), *cert. denied* 452 U.S. 917, 101 S.Ct. 3052, 69 L.Ed.2d 421 (1981) ("arguably Marcello was shanghaied to Guatemala" by INS in 1961, although he soon reentered without inspection). That 1981 Fifth Circuit decision, which is excerpted later in this Chapter, reprints the committee's chronology as an appendix to the opinion and also reveals some of the later developments in the Marcello saga. *See also Marcello v. INS,* 449 F.2d 349 (5th Cir.1971).

One further irony arose in 1983. Marcello was convicted and sentenced to seven years' imprisonment for racketeering, but remained at large pending appeal. The Justice Department's organized crime strike force then sought and received an emergency mandate for his immediate imprisonment, based on a sealed affidavit indicating that he "planned to flee the country rather than serve" his sentence. N.Y. Times, April 16, 1983, at A6. INS had sought the former outcome for over 30 years, only to be thwarted by its own Department! Released from prison in 1989, Marcello died at his New Orleans home March 2, 1993. L.A. Times, March 5, 1993, at A3.

ed. Congress evidently accepted that aliens in the excludable category would have to submit to custody before gaining access to the courts. Interestingly, however, Congress viewed the changes implemented by this subsection primarily in procedural terms. It apparently did not intend that the return to exclusive habeas review should drastically limit the range of issues or narrow the standard of review to be applied when the courts finally did take jurisdiction of the case. (And in practice, the fact that exclusion orders are reviewed by means of habeas corpus does little to differentiate the reviewing court's role in exclusion cases from its role in deportation cases; the standard for review and the range of issues the court can consider are quite similar.) Petitions for the writ of habeas corpus in exclusion cases are almost invariably filed in the federal district courts, and the action proceeds according to the usual rules applicable to habeas actions. *See generally* 28 U.S.C.A. § 2241 et seq. The losing party at the district court level may appeal that determination to the court of appeals and, if unsuccessful at that stage, may petition for certiorari in the Supreme Court.

As for review of deportation orders, § 106(a) took a wholly new approach and did not relegate deportable aliens to the old habeas procedure. Section 106(a) provides that the procedure prescribed by the Hobbs Act (now codified at 28 U.S.C.A. Chapter 158) "shall apply to, and shall be the sole and exclusive procedure for, the judicial review of all final orders of deportation * * * pursuant to administrative proceedings under Section 242(b) of this Act or comparable provisions of any prior Act * * *."[10] The Hobbs Act, which also governs review for several other administrative agencies, including the Federal Communications Commission, the Federal Maritime Commission, the Interstate Commerce Commission, and others, takes the reviewing role out of the district courts and places it in the courts of appeals. Review is initiated by a petition for review filed in the appropriate circuit; such petitions must ordinarily be filed no later than 90 days after the issuance of a final deportation order. § 106(a)(1). Service of the petition on the INS automatically stays deportation of the alien, although the court has authority to vacate the stay if INS moves for such

---

10. INA § 106(a)(10) does, however, preserve the availability of habeas for "any alien held in custody." Just how this provision is to fit with the "sole and exclusive procedure" established in the earlier parts of the subsection has posed some knotty issues, which we will consider in connection with the *Marcello* and *Daneshvar* cases in Section E below.

The Supreme Court's decision in *United States v. Mendoza–Lopez,* 481 U.S. 828, 107 S.Ct. 2148, 95 L.Ed.2d 772 (1987) also undercuts to some extent the exclusiveness of the review procedure established by § 106. In that case an alien was charged with a criminal violation of INA § 276 for reentering after a previous deportation without the necessary advance permission. The Court held that § 276 does not authorize a challenge to the earlier deportation order in the criminal proceeding, but the due process clause of the Constitution does require permitting such collateral attack "where the deportation proceeding effectively eliminates the right of the alien to obtain judicial review." The courts of appeals have wrestled with how to implement *Mendoza–Lopez,* and they have tended to require a strong showing of both fundamental errors and prejudice before granting relief. *See, e.g., United States v. Proa–Tovar,* 975 F.2d 592 (9th Cir.1992); *United States v. Holland,* 876 F.2d 1533, 1536 (11th Cir.1989) (citing cases from several circuits). Few defendant aliens, perhaps none, have surmounted the prejudice hurdle. *See United States v. Viera–Candelario,* 797 F.Supp. 117, 119 (D.R.I.1992).

relief. INA § 106(a)(3).[11]

Although this enactment, like the APA-based declaratory review it replaced, allows aliens to secure judicial review without submitting to the rigors of physical custody, Congress believed that three other central features of INA § 106 would limit the opportunities for delay and manipulation. First, there is a strict requirement that all administrative remedies be exhausted before review is available (a prescription that applies with equal force to exclusion cases). INA § 106(c). Second, the law specifically requires that every petition for review or for habeas corpus must state whether the validity of the challenged order has been previously determined in any judicial action. If so, further review is forbidden, unless certain narrow conditions are met. *See* § 106(c) (second and third sentences); *Toma v. Turnage,* 825 F.2d 1400 (9th Cir.1987). And finally, § 106(a) eliminates one layer of court review—the district courts, which had been the initial forum for judicial involvement both before and after *Pedreiro.* The courts of appeals are directed to carry out their reviewing functions strictly on the basis of the administrative record, *see* § 106(a)(4), and there can be no new factfinding at this stage.[12] As a result, there is only one further layer of direct review for an alien who is unsuccessful in the court of appeals: a petition for certiorari to the U.S. Supreme Court.

The rest of this Chapter considers the modern review provisions in greater detail.

SECTION B. PETITIONS FOR REVIEW OF ORDERS OF DEPORTATION

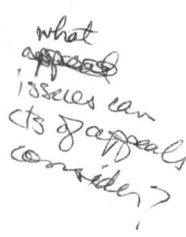

what ~~appeals~~ *issues can Cts of appeals consider?*

Despite its length and detail, INA § 106(a) leaves many questions unanswered. Most of the questions arise because a potentially deportable alien, in addition to contesting deportability, may also seek a variety of other benefits, stays, or other forms of relief from deportation, and he may do so before, during, or after the actual deportation hearing. Once the

---

11. Before the 1990 Act, aliens had six months to petition for review. That Act also restricted the time period even further for certain subclasses. If an alien wishes to challenge an order entered *in absentia* under INA § 242B(c), he must file a petition for review within 60 days. § 242B(c)(4). Persons convicted of an aggravated felony must petition for review within 30 days, § 106(a)(1), and, quite significantly, Congress deleted the automatic stay for this class, requiring them instead to persuade a court that a stay should be entered. *See, e.g., Ignacio v. INS,* 955 F.2d 295 (5th Cir.1992); *Jenkins v. INS,* 32 F.3d 11 (2d Cir.1994). Timely filing is usually considered a mandatory jurisdictional prerequisite to the hearing of the appeal. *See Karimian–Kaklaki v. INS,* 997 F.2d 108 (5th Cir.1993). *But cf. Gonzalez–Julio v. INS,* 34 F.3d 820 (9th Cir.1994) (finding regulations allowing only 10 days to appeal to BIA violat-

ed due process when notice of appeal had to be mailed from Hawaii); *Hernandez-Rivera v. INS,* 630 F.2d 1352 (9th Cir.1980) (extra time for appeal to BIA allowed, despite regulations, where immigration judge purported to grant extension on which the alien relied).

12. The statute provides a special exception to these requirements when the petitioner makes a nonfrivolous claim to U.S. nationality. If the issue cannot be resolved strictly as a matter of law, the case is transferred to a district court for de novo judicial factfinding on this question. INA § 106(a)(5). *See Agosto v. INS,* 436 U.S. 748, 98 S.Ct. 2081, 56 L.Ed.2d 677 (1978). In *Ng Fung Ho v. White,* 259 U.S. 276, 42 S.Ct. 492, 66 L.Ed.2d 938 (1922), the Court held that de novo judicial decision is required in these circumstances under the due process clause, at least as to persons within the United States. See Chapter Ten at p. 1080.

court of appeals then receives a petition for review, exactly what issues are within its reviewing reach? The determination of deportability alone? Decisions to deny discretionary relief? All decisions on potential relief, or only those passed on by an immigration judge? Should the court instead take jurisdiction and try to resolve all complaints the deportable alien might have about decisions under the immigration laws that at any time have gone against him? Or should it perhaps limit this function simply to those matters that arose before or during the hearing in immigration court, leaving to another forum resolution of issues that arose later?

The Supreme Court struggled with these questions in an important triad of cases that reached it within a few years after the enactment of the 1961 INA amendments. We reprint here the third decision of the group, *Cheng Fan Kwok,* for it adequately recounts the outcome of the other two cases, *Foti* and *Giova.* But pay close attention to precisely what the Supreme Court held in its first two encounters with § 106(a).

CHENG FAN KWOK v. INS

Supreme Court of the United States, 1968.
392 U.S. 206, 88 S.Ct. 1970, 20 L.Ed.2d 1037.

Mr. Justice Harlan delivered the opinion of the Court.

The narrow question presented by this case is whether jurisdiction to review the denial of a stay of deportation, if the pertinent order has not been entered in the course of a proceeding conducted under § 242(b) of the Immigration and Nationality Act, is, under § 106(a) of the Act, vested exclusively in the courts of appeals. The question arises from the following circumstances.

Petitioner, a native and citizen of China, evidently entered the United States in 1965 as a seaman. The terms of his entry permitted him to remain in this country for the period during which his vessel was in port, provided that this did not exceed 29 days. See INA § 252(a). He deserted his vessel, and remained unlawfully in the United States. After petitioner's eventual apprehension, deportation proceedings were conducted by a special inquiry officer under the authority of § 242(b). Petitioner conceded his deportability, but sought and obtained permission to depart the United States voluntarily.[4] Despite his protestations of good faith, petitioner did not voluntarily depart, and was ultimately ordered to surrender for deportation. He then requested a stay of deportation from a district director of immigration, pending the submission and disposition of an application for adjustment of status under 8 U.S.C. § 1153(a)(7) (1964 ed., Supp. II).[a] The

4. We note, as we did in Foti v. Immigration and Naturalization Service, 375 U.S. 217, 84 S.Ct. 306, 11 L.Ed.2d 281, that the "granting of voluntary departure relief does not result in the alien's not being subject to an outstanding final order of deportation." [This is so because the immigration judge entered an "alternate order of deportation." See pp. 593–94 n. a *supra.*—eds.]

a. Formerly INA § 203(a)(7)—the old seventh preference—which then permitted the adjustment of status of certain persons, *inter alia,* those who demonstrated that they feared persecution in "any Communist or Communist-dominated country." The seventh preference was repealed by the Refugee Act of 1980, which fashioned a completely different structure for political asylum and

district director concluded that petitioner is ineligible for such an adjustment of status, and denied a stay of deportation.

Petitioner thereupon commenced these proceedings in the Court of Appeals for the Third Circuit, petitioning for review of the denial of a stay. The Court of Appeals held that the provisions of § 106(a), under which it would otherwise have exclusive jurisdiction to review the district director's order, are inapplicable to orders denying ancillary relief unless those orders either are entered in the course of a proceeding conducted under § 242(b), or are denials of motions to reopen such proceedings. The court dismissed the petition for want of jurisdiction. We granted certiorari because the courts of appeals have disagreed as to the proper construction of the pertinent statutory provisions. For reasons that follow, we affirm.

[handwritten margin notes: 3d Cir → here, aff'd; holdi: review denied b/c lack jdn]

I.

It is useful first to summarize the relevant provisions of the Immigration and Nationality Act and of the regulations promulgated under the Act's authority. Section 242(b) provides a detailed administrative procedure for determining whether an alien may be deported. It permits the entry of an order of deportation only upon the basis of a record made in a proceeding before a special inquiry officer, at which the alien is assured rights to counsel, to a reasonable opportunity to examine the evidence against him, to cross-examine witnesses, and to present evidence in his own behalf. By regulation, various forms of discretionary relief may also be sought from the special inquiry officer in the course of the deportation proceeding; an alien may, for example, request that his deportation be temporarily withheld, on the ground that he might, in the country to which he is to be deported, "be subject to persecution * * *." See 8 U.S.C. § 1253(h) (1964 ed., Supp. II).[b]

Other forms of discretionary relief may be requested after termination of the deportation proceeding. The regulations thus provide that an alien "under a final administrative order of deportation" may apply to the district director "having jurisdiction over the place where the alien is at the time of filing" for a stay of deportation. 8 CFR § 243.4. The stay may be granted by the district director "in his discretion." Ibid. If the stay is denied, the denial "is not appealable" to the Board of Immigration Appeals. Ibid.

Section 106(a) provides that the procedures for judicial review prescribed by the Hobbs Act, 64 Stat. 1129, 68 Stat. 961, "shall apply to, and shall be the sole and exclusive procedure for, the judicial review of all final orders of deportation heretofore or hereafter made against aliens ... pursuant to administrative proceedings under section 242(b) of this Act...." These procedures vest in the courts of appeals exclusive jurisdiction to review final orders issued by specified federal agencies. In situations to which the provisions of § 106(a) are inapplicable, the alien's

the admission of refugees. See Chapter Eight.—eds.

b. INA § 243(h) still permits withholding of deportation in these circumstances, but

the wording has been altered somewhat. See Chapter Eight.—eds.

remedies would, of course, ordinarily lie first in an action brought in an appropriate district court.

The positions of the various parties may be summarized as follows. We are urged by both petitioner and the Immigration Service to hold that the provisions of § 106(a) are applicable to the circumstances presented by this case, and that judicial review thus is available only in the courts of appeals. The Immigration Service contends that § 106(a) should be understood to embrace all determinations "directly affecting the execution of the basic deportation order," whether those determinations have been reached prior to, during, or subsequent to the deportation proceeding. In contrast, amicus[9] urges, as the Court of Appeals held, that § 106(a) encompasses only those orders made in the course of a proceeding conducted under § 242(b) or issued upon motions to reopen such proceedings.

II.

This is the third case in which we have had occasion to examine the effect of § 106(a). In the first, Foti v. Immigration and Naturalization Service, 375 U.S. 217, 84 S.Ct. 306, 11 L.Ed.2d 281 [1963], the petitioner, in the course of a proceeding conducted under § 242(b), conceded his deportability but requested a suspension of deportation under § 244(a)(5). The special inquiry officer denied such a suspension, and petitioner's appeal from the denial was dismissed by the Board of Immigration Appeals. Petitioner commenced an action in the district court, but the action was dismissed on the ground that, under § 106(a), his exclusive remedy lay in the courts of appeals. He then petitioned for review to the Court of Appeals for the Second Circuit, but it dismissed for want of jurisdiction. A divided court held en banc that the procedures of § 106(a) were inapplicable to denials of discretionary relief under § 244(a)(5). * * * On certiorari, we reversed, holding that "all determinations made during and incident to the administrative proceeding conducted by a special inquiry officer, and reviewable together by the Board of Immigration Appeals ... are ... included within the ambit of the exclusive jurisdiction of the Court of Appeals under § 106(a)."

In the second case, Giova v. Rosenberg, 379 U.S. 18, 85 S.Ct. 156, 13 L.Ed.2d 90, petitioner moved before the Board of Immigration Appeals to reopen proceedings, previously conducted under § 242(b), that had terminated in an order for his deportation. The Board denied relief. The Court of Appeals for the Ninth Circuit concluded that the Board's denial was not embraced by § 106(a), and dismissed the petition for want of jurisdiction. On certiorari, this Court held, in a brief per curiam opinion, that such orders were within the exclusive jurisdiction of the courts of appeals.

Although Foti strongly suggests the result that we reach today, neither it nor Giova can properly be regarded as controlling in this situation. Unlike the order in Foti, the order in this case was not entered in the course of a proceeding conducted by a special inquiry officer under § 242(b); unlike the order in Giova the order here did not deny a motion to

---

9. Since the Immigration Service had aligned itself with petitioner on this question, the Court invited William H. Dempsey, Jr., Esquire, a member of the Bar of this Court, to appear and present oral argument as amicus curiae in support of the judgment below.

reopen such a proceeding. We regard the issue of statutory construction involved here as markedly closer than the questions presented in those cases; at the least, it is plainly an issue upon which differing views may readily be entertained. In these circumstances, it is imperative, if we are accurately to implement Congress' purposes, to "seiz[e] everything from which aid can be derived." Fisher v. Blight, 2 Cranch 358, 386, 2 L.Ed. 304.

*106
intent*

It is important, first, to emphasize the character of the statute with which we are concerned. Section 106(a) is intended exclusively to prescribe and regulate a portion of the jurisdiction of the federal courts. As a jurisdictional statute, it must be construed both with precision and with fidelity to the terms by which Congress has expressed its wishes. Utah Junk Co. v. Porter, 328 U.S. 39, 44, 66 S.Ct. 889, 892, 90 L.Ed. 1071. Further, as a statute addressed entirely to "specialists," it must, as Mr. Justice Frankfurter observed, "be read by judges with the minds of . . . specialists."

We cannot, upon close reading, easily reconcile the position urged by the Immigration Service with the terms of § 106(a). A denial by a district director of a stay of deportation is not literally a "final order of deportation," nor is it, as was the order in *Foti,* entered in the course of administrative proceedings conducted under § 242(b).[11] Thus, the order in this case was issued more than three months after the entry of the final order of deportation, in proceedings entirely distinct from those conducted under § 242(b), by an officer other than the special inquiry officer who, as required by § 242(b), presided over the deportation proceeding. The order here did not involve the denial of a motion to reopen proceedings conducted under § 242(b), or to reconsider any final order of deportation. Concededly, the application for a stay assumed the prior existence of an order of deportation, but petitioner did not "attack the deportation order itself but instead [sought] relief not inconsistent with it." Mui v. Esperdy, 371 F.2d 772, 777 (C.A.2nd Cir.). If, as the Immigration Service urges, § 106(a) embraces all determinations "directly affecting the execution of" a final deportation order, Congress has selected language remarkably inapposite for its purpose. As Judge Friendly observed in a similar case, if "Congress

---

11. We find the emphasis placed in dissent upon the word "pursuant" in § 106(a) unpersuasive. First, § 106(a) was evidently limited to those final orders of deportation made "pursuant to administrative proceedings under section 242(b)" simply because Congress preferred to exclude from it those deportation orders entered without a § 242(b) proceeding. This would, for example, place orders issued under INA § 252(b) by which the Immigration Service may revoke a seaman's conditional permit to land and deport him, outside the judicial review procedures of § 106(a). Perhaps this suggests, as *amicus* urges, that § 106(a) was intended to be limited to situations in which quasi-judicial proceedings, such as those under § 242(b), have been conducted. It certainly indicates that the reference in § 106(a) to § 242(b) proceedings was intended to limit, and not to broaden, the classes of orders to which § 106(a) may be applied. Second, it must be reiterated that § 106(a) does not, as the dissenting opinion suggests, encompass "all orders" entered pursuant to § 242(b) proceedings: it is limited to "final orders of deportation." The textual difficulty, with which the dissenting opinion does not deal, is that the order in question here neither is a final order of deportation, nor is it, as was the order in *Foti,* "made during the same proceedings" in which a final order of deportation has been issued. This cannot be overcome merely by examination of the meaning of the word "pursuant."

had wanted to go that far, presumably it would have known how to say so." Ibid.

The legislative history of § 106(a) does not strengthen the position of the Immigration Service. The "basic purpose" of the procedural portions of the 1961 legislation was, as we stated in *Foti,* evidently "to expedite the deportation of undesirable aliens by preventing successive dilatory appeals to various federal courts...." Congress prescribed for this purpose several procedural innovations, among them the device of direct petitions for review to the courts of appeals. Although, as the Immigration Service has emphasized, the broad purposes of the legislation might have been expected to encompass orders denying discretionary relief entered outside § 242(b) proceedings, there is evidence that Congress deliberately restricted the application of § 106(a) to orders made in the course of proceedings conducted under § 242(b).

Thus, during a colloquy on the floor of the House of Representatives, to which we referred in *Foti,* Representative Moore, co-sponsor of the bill then under discussion, suggested that any difficulties resulting from the separate consideration of deportability and of discretionary relief could be overcome by "a change in the present administrative practice of considering the issues ... piecemeal. There is no reason why the Immigration Service could not change its regulations to permit contemporaneous court consideration of deportability and administrative application for relief." In the same colloquy, Representative Walter, the chairman of the subcommittee that conducted the pertinent hearings, recognized that certain forms of discretionary relief may be requested in the course of a deportation proceeding, and stated that § 106(a) would apply to the disposition of such requests, "just as it would apply to any other issue *brought up in deportation proceedings.*" Similarly, Representative Walter, in a subsequent debate, responded to a charge that judicial review under § 106(a) would prove inadequate because of the absence of a suitable record, by inviting "the gentleman's attention to the law in section 242, in which the procedure for the examiner is set forth in detail."

We believe that, in combination with the terms of § 106(a) itself, these statements lead to the inference that Congress quite deliberately restricted the application of § 106(a) to orders entered during proceedings conducted under § 242(b), or directly challenging deportation orders themselves. This is concededly "a choice between uncertainties," but we are "content to choose the lesser." Burnet v. Guggenheim, 288 U.S. 280, 288, 53 S.Ct. 369, 371, 77 L.Ed. 748.

We need not speculate as to Congress' purposes. Quite possibly, as Judge Browning has persuasively suggested, "Congress visualized a single administrative proceeding in which all questions relating to an alien's deportation would be raised and resolved, followed by a single petition in a court of appeals for judicial review...." Yamada v. Immigration & Naturalization Service, 384 F.2d 214, 218. It may therefore be that Congress expected the Immigration Service to include within the § 242(b) proceeding "all issues which might affect deportation." Ibid. Possibly, as *amicus* cogently urges, Congress wished to limit petitions to the courts of appeals to situations in which quasi-judicial hearings had been conducted. It is enough to emphasize that neither of these purposes would be in any fashion impeded by the result we reach today. We hold that the judicial review provisions of § 106(a) embrace only those determinations made during a proceeding conducted under § 242(b), including those determinations made incident to a motion to reopen such proceedings.[16]

This result is entirely consistent with our opinion in *Foti*. There, it was repeatedly stated in the opinion of THE CHIEF JUSTICE that the order held reviewable under § 106(a) had, as the regulations required, been entered in the course of a proceeding conducted under § 242(b). * * * It was emphasized that "the administrative discretion to grant a suspension of deportation," the determination involved in *Foti*, "has historically been consistently exercised as an integral part of the proceedings which have led to the issuance of a final deportation order." * * * A suspension of deportation "must be requested prior to or during the deportation hearing." Moreover, it was explicitly recognized that, although modification of the pertinent regulations might "effectively broaden or narrow the scope of review available in the Courts of Appeals," this was "nothing anomalous."[17] An essential premise of *Foti* was thus that the application of § 106(a) had been limited to orders "made during the same proceedings in which deportability is determined...."

The *per curiam* opinion in *Giova* did not take a wider view of § 106(a). The denial of an application to reopen a deportation proceeding is readily distinguishable from a denial of a stay of deportation, in which there is no attack upon the deportation order or upon the proceeding in which it was entered. Petitions to reopen, like motions for rehearing or reconsideration, are, as the Immigration Service urged in *Foti*, "intimately and immediately associated" with the final orders they seek to challenge. Thus, petitions to reopen deportation proceedings are governed by the regulations applicable to the deportation proceeding itself, and, indeed, are ordinarily presented for disposition to the special inquiry officer who entered the deportation order.[19] The result in *Giova* was thus a logical concomitant of the construction of § 106(a) reached in *Foti;* it did not, explicitly or by implication, broaden that construction in any fashion that encompasses this situation.

The result we reach today will doubtless mean that, on occasion, the review of denials of discretionary relief will be conducted separately from the review of an order of deportation involving the same alien. Nonetheless, this does not seem an onerous burden, nor is it one that cannot be avoided, at least in large part, by appropriate action of the Immigration Service itself. More important, although "there is no table of logarithms

---

16. We intimate no views on the possibility that a court of appeals might have "pendent jurisdiction" over denials of discretionary relief, where it already has before it a petition for review from a proceeding conducted under § 242(b).

17. The opinion of the Court emphasized, in addition, that "[c]learly, changes in administrative procedures may affect the scope and content of various types of agency orders and

thus the subject matter embraced in a judicial proceeding to review such orders."

19. See 8 CFR § 242.22. If, however, the order of the special inquiry officer is appealed to the Board of Immigration Appeals, a subsequent motion to reopen or reconsider is presented to the Board for disposition. The motion in *Giova* was presented to the Board and decided by it.

for statutory construction," it is the result that we believe most consistent both with Congress' intentions and with the terms by which it has chosen to express those intentions.

Affirmed.

MR. JUSTICE WHITE, dissenting.

If the special inquiry officer had possessed jurisdiction to issue a stay order pending petitioner's efforts to obtain discretionary relief from the District Director, I take it that his denial of the stay, like a refusal to re-open, would have been appealable to the Court of Appeals. But, as I understand it, no stay could have been granted by the hearing officer and it was sought from the District Director as an immediate consequence of there being outstanding a final order of deportation, which, if executed, might moot the underlying request for relief from the District Director. Section 106 does not limit judicial review in the Court of Appeals to orders entered "in the course of" § 242(b) proceedings, but extends it to all orders against aliens entered "pursuant" to such proceedings, that is, at least as Webster would have it,* "acting or done in consequence" of the § 242(b) proceedings. Except for the order of deportation, there would have been no occasion or need to seek a stay. It hardly strains congressional intention to give the word "pursuant" its ordinary meaning in the English language. If there are reasons based on policy for the court's contrary conclusion, they are not stated. I would reverse the judgment.

Notes

1. The majority acknowledges a substantial congressional policy that is somewhat undercut, at the very least, by the Court's interpretation of § 106(a): the broad legislative purpose "to expedite the deportation of undesirable aliens by preventing successive dilatory appeals to various federal courts." Justice White, in dissent, suggests that the majority could locate no countervailing policy reasons that would justify its conclusion. But the majority does not rest solely on linguistic analysis. It at least hints at certain policies that are served by its holding. What are those policies? Are they weighty enough to justify the outcome, especially when the Court agrees that it was faced with "a choice between uncertainties." If you were redrafting the statute, how would you choose to provide for review in these situations?

2. The Court extends a none too subtle invitation to the Justice Department to change its regulations if it is really so intensely interested in assuring that deportable aliens have only one avenue of appeal to the courts. Nevertheless, over twenty years later, the regulations still essentially reserve to the district directors much of the authority to issue post-order stays of deportation. 8 C.F.R. § 243.4. Why do you suppose the Department has maintained this structure for decisionmaking? (Consider

---

* Merriam–Webster, Webster's New International Dictionary, Second Edition, unabridged (1957), defines "pursuant" as:

"1. Acting or done in consequence or in prosecution (of anything); hence, agreeable; conformable; following; according ...

"2. That is in pursuit or pursuing...."

the usual scenarios in which such a stay may be needed and the probable logistics involved in securing such an order. *See generally Matter of Santos*, 19 I & N Dec. 105 (BIA 1984).) Should it now change?

————

Cheng Fan Kwok clearly prevents a court of appeals from reviewing a *post*-deportation-order decision by the immigration authorities when it is considering a petition under § 106(a) (unless that decision happens to arise on a motion to reopen or to reconsider). But what about *pre*-order determinations under the immigration laws, if they were made outside the § 242(b) hearing? Sometimes such decisions are intimately linked with the issues in the deportation proceedings, and to that extent, the case may be stronger for allowing judicial review as part of the review of the order itself. Under § 106(a), can the court of appeals review the propriety of the earlier determination? The next case considers this question.

KAVASJI v. INS

United States Court of Appeals, Seventh Circuit, 1982.
675 F.2d 236.

Per Curiam.

Petitioner Ardesheer P. Kavasji seeks review of a final order of deportation issued against him by the Board of Immigration Appeals on September 3, 1980. The Board of Immigration Appeals affirmed the decision of an Immigration Law Judge [*sic*] which held that the petitioner was deportable * * * since Kavasji had remained in the United States beyond the period authorized by the terms of his admission as a nonimmigrant student.

Ardesheer P. Kavasji is a twenty-five year old citizen and national of Pakistan who entered the United States on September 4, 1970 to study engineering at the Indiana Institute of Technology at Fort Wayne, Indiana. Kavasji was authorized as a nonimmigrant student to remain in the United States until July 30, 1979. In the early part of 1979, Kavasji sought to transfer from the Indiana Institute of Technology to Huntington College in Huntington, Indiana. To that end Kavasji requested permission from the Immigration and Naturalization Service ("INS") to transfer schools and to extend his stay in this country. In February 1979, Kavasji and his attorney prepared and mailed to the INS office in Huntington, Indiana a Form I–538 petition to transfer and a Form I–20 from Huntington College as required by INS regulation. According to Kavasji's counsel, the application for a transfer and extension were either lost in the mail or lost by the INS. Consequently, Kavasji never received authorization from the INS to transfer schools or to remain beyond July 30, 1979.[a]

Kavasji nonetheless attended Huntington College without an application being filed. About August 10, 1979, Kavasji submitted another appli-

---

a. INS regulations were later amended to assign more of the authority over school transfer and extension of a student's stay to "designated school officials," thereby reducing INS's paperwork and the risk of lost applications. *See* 8 C.F.R. § 214.2(f).—eds.

cation for an extension of stay and a transfer of schools with the assistance of the Dean of Students of Huntington College. That application was denied on November 1, 1979 by the INS for the express reason that Kavasji violated his nonimmigration status by remaining in the United States beyond his authorized stay. Accordingly, the INS district director ordered Kavasji to depart by December 1, 1979.[b]

When Kavasji failed to leave the country by December 1, 1979, the INS commenced deportation proceedings against him. To that end the INS issued an Order to Show Cause dated January 7, 1980 charging that Kavasji was subject to deportation * * * for having remained in the United States for a longer time than permitted.

At the deportation hearing before an Immigration Law Judge on March 5, 1980, Kavasji admitted all of the allegations in the Order to Show Cause, including the fact that he had received a Form I–541 notification that his application for an extension was denied on November 1, 1979 because he was deemed an overstay. Kavasji's counsel argued that the district director's decision to deny an extension of a temporary stay was arbitrary and capricious in light of the fact that Kavasji had attempted in February of 1979 to obtain permission to transfer and to extend his stay. The hearing was adjourned in order to give Kavasji an opportunity to present his case to the district director for reconsideration of the earlier denial of his request for a temporary stay.

Upon the resumption of the deportation hearing proceedings Kavasji's attorney stated that the district director refused to reconsider Kavasji's case. His attorney again contended that the district director acted arbitrarily and capriciously and moved to terminate the proceedings. The Immigration Law Judge held that he had no jurisdiction to review the district director's denial of a temporary stay because the matter was strictly within the discretion of the district director. Accordingly, the Immigration Law Judge refused to admit evidence and argument concerning an alleged abuse of discretion by the district director.

In the Decision of the Immigration Law Judge dated May 15, 1980, the motion to terminate the proceedings submitted by Kavasji's counsel was denied on the ground that under relevant regulations of the Immigration and Naturalization Service there is no jurisdiction for the Immigration Law Judge to review the denial by the district director of an application for transfer of schools or extension of stay, citing 8 C.F.R. 103.1(n); 8 C.F.R. 214.1(c). It was further noted that under relevant regulation no appeal lies from the decision of the district director. 8 C.F.R. 214.2(f)(7). The Immigration Law Judge held that a nonimmigrant alien becomes deportable as an "overstay" when the period of his admission expires, unless he receives a grant of an extension of stay from the district director. Accordingly, Kavasji was found deportable by clear, convincing, and unequivocal evidence.

On appeal the Board of Immigration Appeals upheld the Immigration Law Judge's findings and conclusions and granted Kavasji until October 30,

---

b. District directors can't issue deportation orders. What do you suppose the court—rather inartfully—is describing here? —eds.

1980 to depart voluntarily. On October 6, 1980 Kavasji filed this petition for review.

In this petition for review Kavasji claims that the action taken by the district director was a manifest abuse of discretion. Also Kavasji claims that it was error for the Immigration Law Judge to refuse to permit evidence pertinent to certain lost documents or concerning the alleged arbitrary and capricious action of the district director. Thus petitioner contends that the denial of the request to terminate the proceedings was improper and that deportability was not proven by clear, convincing, and unequivocal evidence.

The respondent INS on the other hand contends that this court does not have jurisdiction to review the district director's denial of the request for a transfer and extension of stay. The respondent is correct in this contention. Under § 106(a) of the Immigration and Nationality Act, this court's jurisdiction extends to "final orders of deportation ... made against aliens within the United States pursuant to administrative proceedings under § 242(b)." The Supreme Court in *Cheng Fan Kwok v. INS* held that the discretionary denial by a district director of a stay of deportation is not reviewable as a final order of deportation because Congress restricted the application of § 106(a) to orders entered during deportation proceedings conducted under § 242(b), or directly challenging deportation orders themselves.

Since the applications to the district director for an extension of a temporary stay and to transfer were not submitted pursuant to a proceeding under § 242(b), nor were they incident to a motion to reopen such a proceeding, this court is without jurisdiction to review the district director's denial of the applications in question.

Although petitioner attempts to distinguish *Cheng* on the basis that the present case does not involve a denial of a stay of deportation as in *Cheng* but rather a denial of an extension of a temporary stay, petitioner does not show how that distinction is significant for the purpose of demonstrating that the discretionary determination by the district director in this case was made during the course of deportation proceedings. In short, Kavasji's challenge to the actions of the district director properly belongs in the district court. *See, e.g., Richards v. INS*, 554 F.2d 1173 (D.C.Cir.1977).

Finally, the regulations make clear that the Immigration Law Judge had no jurisdiction to review the district director's discretionary actions taken in this case. Therefore it was not error for the Immigration Law Judge to refuse to consider the evidence pertinent to Kavasji's claim that the district director abused its discretion.

The petitioner does not otherwise challenge the basis of the decision of the Immigration Law Judge. In any event, it is clear that the deportability of Kavasji was established by clear, convincing, and unequivocal evidence. Therefore the order of the Immigration and Naturalization Service requiring petitioner to depart voluntarily [*sic*] is affirmed.

Notes

1. Would it be possible for INS to avoid the prospect of piecemeal review in these circumstances by changing its regulations? What kinds of changes would bring the issues Kavasji wants to raise within the reach of the court of appeals? What might be the disadvantages of such changes? Should the regulations be modified in such a fashion?

2. *Kavasji* reflects the predominant view among the courts on the question of jurisdiction to review immigration determinations made outside the forum of a § 242(b) proceeding—even if those determinations were handed down earlier and form a crucial link in the chain of events that ultimately led to the finding of deportability. But there are a few exceptions. For example, in *Bachelier v. INS,* 625 F.2d 902 (9th Cir.1980), the court considered, as part of a review proceeding under § 106, the propriety of an earlier decision, under INA § 246, to rescind an adjustment of status previously granted under § 245. Under the regulations, rescission is adjudicated by an immigration judge, but the rescission proceedings are wholly separate from the deportation proceedings (which may or may not be instituted once permanent resident status is rescinded). To be sure, in *Bachelier,* if the earlier rescission order was valid, there was no real dispute over the alien's deportability—but the same was true of Kavasji, if the district director's denial of his application for transfer and extension of stay was likewise legally valid. The *Bachelier* court provides only a rather cryptic statement of reasons for extending its jurisdiction in this fashion (and in any event it found against the alien on the merits). Are *Bachelier* and *Kavasji* inconsistent? Are there any pertinent reasons for distinguishing the two situations? *See generally* Note, *Jurisdiction to Review Prior Orders and Underlying Statutes in Deportation Appeals,* 65 Va.L.Rev. 403 (1979). *See also Gottesman v. INS,* 33 F.3d 383 (4th Cir.1994) (disagreeing with *Bachelier,* court of appeals finds it has no jurisdiction to consider underlying rescission order on petition for review under § 106(a)).

Jurisdiction Under *Chadha*

The majority rule, as applied in *Kavasji,* marks out a bright line that is usually quite easy to apply. Jurisdiction extends to "orders entered during deportation proceedings conducted under § 242(b)." If the matter was not decided during such proceedings, review must be had elsewhere; the issue cannot come up as part of proceedings in the courts of appeals under § 106(a).

But that bright-line rule poses a problem when the alien levels a constitutional challenge at her deportation proceedings, and particularly when she claims that the underlying statute is itself unconstitutional. Under longstanding practice (similar to the practice of other administrative agencies, *see Califano v. Sanders,* 430 U.S. 99, 109, 97 S.Ct. 980, 986, 51 L.Ed.2d 192 (1977)), immigration judges and the BIA consider themselves to be without authority to hear constitutional challenges to the statutes they administer. Thus no matter how forcefully the alien protests that the provision is unconstitutional, and no matter how persuasive her position, there will be no determination on the matter as part of the proceedings under § 242(b). Is she then foreclosed from raising her constitutional claim in the court of appeals?

This jurisdictional issue reached the Supreme Court in *INS v. Chadha,* 462 U.S. 919, 103 S.Ct. 2764, 77 L.Ed.2d 317 (1983). There the alien petitioner, Chadha, initially had been granted suspension of deportation by an immigration judge under INA § 244, but the House of Representatives voted a resolution disapproving suspension, exercising its purported one-house veto authority under § 244(c)(2) (as it then read). Chadha contended that this legislative veto was unconstitutional. The Justice Department clearly agreed with Chadha on the merits of the constitutional issue; it had been arguing the point for years on behalf of Presidents of both political parties, both in the courts and before Congress. Nevertheless the Department decided that it had to go ahead and proceed with routine deportation of Chadha until directed otherwise by a court. Thus when the deportation order was entered following the purported House veto, Chadha petitioned for review under § 106(a). The Supreme Court ultimately used this case for its landmark ruling that legislative vetoes are unconstitutional, but first it had to deal with the tricky jurisdictional question posed by *Cheng Fan Kwok.*

Consider as you read the following passage from *Chadha* (the entirety of the Court's discussion of this jurisdictional issue) whether Kavasji could now insist, under *Chadha's* holding, that the court of appeals reach the merits of his challenge to the district director's denial of his transfer petition. We will then take up one court's post-*Chadha* attempt to determine what the Supreme Court meant in a case whose facts are much like *Kavasji.*

It is contended that the Court of Appeals lacked jurisdiction under § 106(a) of the Act. That section provides that a petition for review in the Court of Appeals "shall be the sole and exclusive procedure for the judicial review of all final orders of deportation ... made against aliens within the United States pursuant to administrative proceedings under section 242(b) of this Act." Congress argues that the one-House veto authorized by § 244(c)(2) takes place outside the administrative proceedings conducted under § 242(b), and that the jurisdictional grant contained in § 106(a) does not encompass Chadha's constitutional challenge.

In *Cheng Fan Kwok v. INS,* this Court held that "§ 106(a) embrace[s] only those determinations made during a proceeding conducted under § 242(b), including those determinations made incident to a motion to reopen such proceedings." It is true that one court has read *Cheng Fan Kwok* to preclude appeals similar to Chadha's. See *Dastmalchi v. INS,* 660 F.2d 880 (CA3 1981).[11]

---

11. Under the Third Circuit's reasoning, judicial review under § 106(a) would not extend to the constitutionality of § 244(c)(2) because that issue could not have been tested during the administrative deportation pro-ceedings conducted under § 242(b). *Dastmalchi v. INS,* 660 F.2d 880 (CA3 1981). The facts in *Dastmalchi* are distinguishable, however. In *Dastmalchi,* Iranian aliens who had entered the United States on nonimmi-

However, we agree with the Court of Appeals in this case that the term "final orders" in § 106(a) "includes all matters on which the validity of the final order is contingent, rather than only those determinations actually made at the hearing." 634 F.2d, at 412. Here, Chadha's deportation stands or falls on the validity of the challenged veto; the final order of deportation was entered against Chadha only to implement the action of the House of Representatives. Although the Attorney General was satisfied that the House action was invalid and that it should not have any effect on his decision to suspend deportation, he appropriately let the controversy take its course through the courts.

This Court's decision in *Cheng Fan Kwok, supra,* does not bar Chadha's appeal. There, after an order of deportation had been entered, the affected alien requested the INS to stay the execution of that order. When that request was denied, the alien sought review in the Court of Appeals under § 106(a). This Court's holding that the Court of Appeals lacked jurisdiction was based on the fact that the alien "did not 'attack the deportation order itself but instead [sought] relief not inconsistent with it.'" Here, in contrast, Chadha directly attacks the deportation order itself and the relief he seeks—cancellation of deportation—is plainly inconsistent with the deportation order. Accordingly, the Court of Appeals had jurisdiction under § 106(a) to decide this case.

462 U.S., at 937–39.

MOHAMMADI–MOTLAGH v. INS

United States Court of Appeals, Ninth Circuit, 1984.
727 F.2d 1450.

HUG, CIRCUIT JUDGE:

Majid Mohammadi–Motlagh petitions for review of an order of deportation. He was found deportable because he violated the conditions of his nonimmigrant visa by transferring schools without obtaining prior permission. Mohammadi–Motlagh claims the District Director erred in refusing his transfer request. Because we are without jurisdiction to review that claim, we affirm the decision of the Board of Immigration Appeals.

Mohammadi–Motlagh, a native and citizen of Iran, entered the United States in January 1979 as a nonimmigrant student. He was authorized to study at the American Language and Cultural Institute in New York and later given permission to transfer to Wagner College, also in New York. In January 1980 Mohammadi–Motlagh transferred to the College of Great Falls in Montana. He neither sought nor received INS permission to make

grant student visas challenged a regulation that required them to report to the District Director of the INS during the Iranian hostage crisis. The aliens reported and were ordered deported after a § 242(b) proceeding.

The aliens in *Dastmalchi* could have been deported irrespective of the challenged regulation. Here, in contrast, Chadha's deportation would have been *cancelled* but for § 244(c)(2).

the transfer prior to enrolling at the college.[a] In August 1980, after attending the college for several months, Mohammadi–Motlagh filed an application for permission to transfer. The District Director denied the request, noting that Mohammadi–Motlagh had been "in unauthorized attendance at the College of Great Falls for some seven months prior to submitting the instant request."

The INS then issued an order to show cause, charging that Mohammadi–Motlagh was subject to deportation for failure to comply with the conditions of his nonimmigrant status. In a hearing before an immigration judge, Mohammadi–Motlagh attempted to argue the merits of his transfer request. He claimed that transferring without prior permission was justified and that the delay in filing the transfer request occurred despite his best efforts to comply with the application requirement. The immigration judge did not consider these contentions because he concluded he had no jurisdiction to review the District Director's denial of Mohammadi–Motlagh's request. He found Mohammadi–Motlagh deportable and granted him voluntary departure. The BIA also refused to review the District Director's decision, citing 8 C.F.R. § 214.2(f)(7) (1982). It dismissed Mohammadi–Motlagh's appeal and ordered his voluntary departure within fifteen days.

Mohammadi–Motlagh's petition for review first challenges the refusals of the immigration judge and the BIA to review the decision of the District Director. The refusals were based on an interpretation of 8 C.F.R. § 214.2(f)(7), which provides that "[n]o appeal shall lie from the decision" of the District Director denying permission to transfer to another school. This interpretation is entitled to deference. *Tooloee v. INS,* 722 F.2d 1434, 1436 (9th Cir.1983); *Ghorbani v. INS,* 686 F.2d 784, 791 (9th Cir.1982). We have held the conclusion that the denial of an appeal right deprives the immigration judge and BIA of jurisdiction is not unreasonable. *Id.* We therefore reject Mohammadi–Motlagh's claim.

Mohammadi–Motlagh next contends we have jurisdiction to review the District Director's decision. In *Ghorbani,* we were presented with an almost identical factual situation. We held the District Director's decision was not a final order reviewable under INA § 106(a). *Id.* Following our decision in *Ghorbani,* the Supreme Court decided *INS v. Chadha,* 462 U.S. 919, 103 S.Ct. 2764, 77 L.Ed.2d 317 (1983), *aff'g* 634 F.2d 408 (9th Cir.1980). We must consider how *Chadha* affected our jurisdictional analysis in *Ghorbani.*

In *Ghorbani* our analysis began with section 106(a), which confers on the courts of appeals exclusive jurisdiction to review final orders of deportation made pursuant to administrative proceedings under § 242(b). We noted the Supreme Court had narrowly construed the instances in which courts of appeals could assume pendent jurisdiction over discretionary decisions made incident to the final deportation order. Two circumstances in which the use of pendent jurisdiction was justified were identified in

---

a. Today such INS permission for a transfer would not usually be required. The regulations now call instead for actions and decisions by specifically designated school officials, under far more general supervision of INS. 8 C.F.R. § 214.2(f)(8).—eds.

Ghorbani: (1) when there has been a factual hearing on the issue of discretionary relief or (2) when such a hearing is unnecessary.

In *Chadha,* we held pendent jurisdiction permitted review of the House of Representatives' veto of the suspension of Chadha's deportation. 634 F.2d at 413. We defined pendent jurisdiction as encompassing certain determinations "on which the final order of deportation is contingent." *Id.* We then reviewed a purely legal question: the constitutionality of the one-house veto. Our review was made without the benefit of a prior administrative record. The immigration judge and the BIA had not considered this question since they lack authority to determine constitutional issues. However, review was possible without an administrative record since only a question of law was presented. *Ghorbani,* 686 F.2d at 790.

The Supreme Court's decision in *Chadha* approved our assumption of pendent jurisdiction. The Court emphasized that Chadha would not have been deported but for the veto. It thus sanctioned our definition of the class of cases encompassed by the grant of pendent jurisdiction. The Court did not consider, as we were required to in *Ghorbani,* the instances in which utilization of pendent jurisdiction is justified. Because it was presented with a purely legal question, the application of pendent jurisdiction to factual questions was not before the Court. *Chadha* therefore does not signify that the Court has retreated from the narrow construction of section 106(a) adopted in *Cheng Fan Kwok v. INS,* 392 U.S. 206, 216, 88 S.Ct. 1970, 1976, 20 L.Ed.2d 1037 (1968). Our jurisdictional analysis in *Ghorbani* is consistent with each of these Supreme Court cases and thus remains viable.

As in *Ghorbani,* Mohammadi–Motlagh asserts challenges to the District Director's decision that raise factual questions as to whether discretion was properly exercised. The BIA lacked authority to hear and determine these factual issues and did not do so. We are therefore without jurisdiction to consider these claims. They must be raised in the first instance in the district court. * * *

The decision of the BIA is Affirmed.

Notes

1. The doctrine of pendent jurisdiction is usually associated with questions of federal court jurisdiction to consider state law claims for which there is otherwise no jurisdictional basis. The Supreme Court has held that federal courts may exercise pendent jurisdiction to hear such claims, despite the absence of an independent jurisdictional foundation, when the state claim shares "a common nucleus of operative fact" with a federal law claim over which the court clearly has cognizance. *See United Mine Workers v. Gibbs,* 383 U.S. 715, 725, 86 S.Ct. 1130, 1138, 16 L.Ed.2d 218 (1966). But exercise of such jurisdiction is discretionary, and the pendent cause of action is considered "a separate but parallel ground for relief." *Id.* at 722, 726, 86 S.Ct. at 1136, 1139. *Cf. Hagans v. Lavine,* 415 U.S. 528, 548, 94 S.Ct. 1372, 1385, 39 L.Ed.2d 577 (1974) (jurisdiction under 28 U.S.C.A. § 1343 to hear constitutional claim also authorizes exercise of

pendent jurisdiction to hear related federal statutory claim; the opinion suggests that courts should more readily exercise pendent jurisdiction to hear other federal claims than they would to consider state law claims, owing to considerations of comity in a federal system).

Is the pendent jurisdiction rubric a helpful framework for making sense of the Supreme Court's unelaborated notion of "contingency"? Isn't a pendent claim the antithesis of what actually happened in the *Chadha* case? (Chadha's constitutional argument wasn't parallel and separate; it was fundamental to the deportation order itself.) The Ninth Circuit's decision in *Chadha,* moreover, which is quoted in the key passage of the Supreme Court's jurisdictional holding, never makes use of the "pendent jurisdiction" notion, nor does the Supreme Court itself. *Cf. Ghorbani v. INS, supra,* 686 F.2d at 792 (Poole, J., concurring specially) (agreeing with the decision that the court lacked jurisdiction under § 106(a) to consider the district director's earlier ruling, but protesting application of the "pendent jurisdiction" terminology). *See also Martinez De Mendoza v. INS,* 567 F.2d 1222, 1224–25 & n. 5 (3d Cir.1977), where the court of appeals took jurisdiction under § 106(a) to consider a post-order denial of a stay of deportation by the district director. That case seems to fit more comfortably into customary notions of pendent jurisdiction, as the opinion notes, although the court ultimately does not rely on the pendent jurisdiction theory as the basis for its power to decide the particular substantive issue.

Whether one uses this terminology or not, are the tests employed in *Mohammadi-Motlagh* sound means for deciding the reach of jurisdiction in the courts of appeals under the "contingency" rule?

2.   Other courts have been as reluctant as *Mohammadi-Motlagh* to go further and apply *Chadha* so as to reach pre-deportation-order rulings, although their precise formulations for making sense of the "contingency" rule have differed. *See, e.g., Ghaelian v. INS,* 717 F.2d 950 (6th Cir.1983); *Gurbisz v. INS,* 675 F.Supp. 436 (N.D.Ill.1987). As noted in *Gurbisz,* "a broad interpretation of [the *Chadha*] decision would involve a dramatic change in the scope of § 106(a)," *id.* at 439 n. 3; consequently the courts have simply not felt confident enough to usher in such changes. It therefore appears that under *Chadha* as currently applied, jurisdiction under § 106(a) reaches outside the issues determined in the § 242(b) hearing only when the alien challenges the constitutionality of the underlying statute. Because constitutional attacks face such serious doctrinal hurdles in the immigration field, *Chadha* appears unlikely to have wide application. Nevertheless, arguments for a broader understanding of the "contingency" rule remain available to litigants in the several circuits that have not yet passed on the issue, albeit without much encouragement from cases decided to date. *But see Ruginski v. INS,* 942 F.2d 13, 15 (1st Cir.1991) (in a somewhat murky opinion, the court apparently makes use of the "contingency" doctrine to review a legalization denial by the Legalization Appeals Unit in the course of § 106(a) review).

Ongoing Problems with the Doctrine
of *Cheng Fan Kwok*

Surveying the cases on jurisdiction under § 106(a), one court commented drily, "The jurisdictional provisions of the Immigration and Nationality Act are not models of clarity." *Williams v. INS,* 795 F.2d 738, 742 (9th Cir.1986). Given all the intricacies of practice under § 106(a), the judicial resources expended in resolving issues that arise, and the possible consequences for aliens if they guess badly and choose the wrong court in seeking judicial review, should the petition-for-review procedure be retained? Recall the reasons underlying Congress's choice of this device. Are they still being served? If not, what should be done to overcome the problems?

If the principal concern focuses on the litigation resources consumed in highly technical (and minimally productive) battles over whether a particular issue should be decided in the district court or the court of appeals, two possible solutions suggest themselves. Judge Henry Friendly long championed one of them. After reviewing the jurisdictional confusion and the attendant delays caused by § 106(a), he wrote: "The clear answer to this problem is to place appeals from all final deportation orders back in the district courts, and expect the courts of appeals to give expeditious treatment to those orders of the district courts that are appealed." H. Friendly, *Federal Jurisdiction: A General View,* 175–76 (1973).

Testifying before Congress ten years later, Maurice Roberts, editor of *Interpreter Releases* and former chairman of the BIA, argued for the second solution:

> INA § 106(a) [should be amended] to make it clear that in reviewing a final order of deportation the court shall review every challenged INS determination relevant to the alien's status, regardless of whether the determination was made as part of the deportation proceedings or preceded or followed it. Under the present provision, as construed in *Cheng Fan Kwok,* only those issues raised and determined in the deportation hearing before the immigration judge and considered on appeal by the BIA are reviewable in the Court of Appeals. This makes for bifurcation of review, which § 106(a) was designed to eliminate. A one-package review of all related issues in the Court of Appeals under § 106(a) would make more sense.

The Immigration Reform and Control Act of 1983, Hearings Before the Subcomm. on Immigration, Refugees, and International Law of the House Comm. on the Judiciary, 98th Cong., 1st Sess. 955 (1983).[13]

---

13. Roberts has also been a leading advocate for the creation of a separate Article I court system (with both "trial" and "appellate" levels) as the exclusive forum for review of decisions under the immigration laws—save for ultimate review authority in the Supreme Court on petition for certiorari. *See* Roberts, *Proposed: A Specialized Statutory Immigration Court,* 18 San Diego L.Rev. 1 (1980). The Select Commission on Immigration and Refugee Policy endorsed this basic idea in 1981, *see* SCIRP, Final Report, 248–

Judge Friendly's suggestion could not be implemented without statutory changes, and the Roberts proposal, if it is to take effect, is perhaps best implemented by Congress as well. But there remain judicial opportunities, without statutory amendment, to accomplish much of what Roberts advocates, through bolder use by the courts of appeals of two doctrines available to minimize the bifurcation of deportation-related review. First, courts could make more ambitious use of *Chadha's* "contingency" rule. It would not do violence to the Supreme Court's formulation of that rule to read it broadly enough that the court of appeals might reach and review virtually any pre-deportation-order decision that went against the alien's interests. Second, courts could pick up more completely on the possibilities for use of "pendent jurisdiction," hinted at in footnote 16 of *Cheng Fan Kwok*. Despite *Mohammadi–Motlagh,* the doctrine of pendent jurisdiction need not be linked in any way to the "contingency rule." The courts of appeals, once properly seised of a case under § 106(a), could use this framework to consider any issue sharing "a common nucleus of operative fact." Most discretionary relief, whether sought before or after the deportation hearing would appear likely to satisfy this test. Professor Legomsky has argued persuasively for such an approach. Legomsky, *supra* note 1, at 1328, 1367–68.

The principal obstacle to either of these judicial remedies appears to be the reluctance of the courts of appeals to consider matters which might have received inadequate factual development at the administrative stage. *See Olaniyan v. District Director,* 796 F.2d 373, 376 (10th Cir.1986); Currie & Goodman, *Judicial Review of Federal Administrative Action: Quest for the Optimum Forum,* 75 Colum.L.Rev. 1, 35–36 (1975). This reluctance in turn assumes that adequate administrative records will be available only when factual issues were first aired in the quasi-judicial forum of the immigration court or the BIA.

But that assumption (a theme that also appears in *Cheng Fan Kwok* itself) deserves closer scrutiny. Factual issues are routinely resolved in a variety of administrative settings that do not conform to classic trial-type procedures, and the APA certainly contemplates judicial review, on the available administrative record, of much of such "informal" decisionmaking. *See Camp v. Pitts,* 411 U.S. 138, 142–43, 93 S.Ct. 1241, 1244, 36 L.Ed.2d 106 (1973); Gardner, *The Informal Actions of the Federal Government,* 26 Am.U.L.Rev. 799 (1977); Martin, *Mandel, Cheng Fan Kwok and Other Unappealing Cases: The Next Frontier of Immigration Reform,* 27 Va.J.Int'l L. 803, 809 (1987). The Supreme Court has emphasized exactly this possibility for review in the courts of appeals on just such a record, in a case that involved the Hobbs Act, but in a non-immigration setting.

In *Florida Power & Light Co. v. Lorion,* 470 U.S. 729, 105 S.Ct. 1598, 84 L.Ed.2d 643 (1985), the underlying agency decision (a decision by the

50 but Congress has not chosen to pursue it. For a critique, see Legomsky, *supra* note 1, at 1386–96. Interest in proposals of this type may run high in coming years, as all three branches of government seek ways to cope with an expected quantum leap in administrative decisions, resulting both from increased enforcement activities and from reform of asylum procedures that will enable decisions on a backlog of over 400,000 applications accumulated by 1995.

Nuclear Regulatory Commission *not* to initiate enforcement action requested by a petitioner), had been taken without a hearing. Partly for this reason, the court of appeals had ruled that the petitioner must seek judicial review in the district court, and that the Hobbs Act review provisions ordinarily applicable to the Commission's decisions did not govern. The Supreme Court reversed, expressing concern that the lower court's approach would result in a counterproductive bifurcation of judicial review. *Id.* at 743. The Court explained:

> Perhaps the only plausible justification for linking initial review in the court of appeals to the occurrence of a hearing before the agency would be that, absent a hearing, the reviewing court would lack an adequate agency-compiled factual basis to evaluate the agency action and a district court with factfinding powers could make up that deficiency. Such a justification cannot, however, be squared with fundamental principles of judicial review of agency action. "[T]he focal point for judicial review should be the administrative record already in existence, not some new record made initially in a reviewing court." * * *

> If the record before the agency does not support the agency action, if the agency has not considered all relevant factors, or if the reviewing court simply cannot evaluate the challenged agency action on the basis of the record before it, the proper course, except in rare circumstances, is to remand to the agency for additional investigation or explanation. * * * Moreover, a formal hearing before the agency is in no way necessary to the compilation of an agency record. * * * The APA specifically contemplates judicial review on the basis of the agency record compiled in the course of informal agency action in which a hearing has not occurred.

Id. at 743–44, 105 S.Ct. at 1606–07.

After considering these proposals, what changes you would make, if any, in the current judicial review scheme?

SECTION C.   REVIEW IN THE DISTRICT COURT

Both *Cheng Fan Kwok* and *Kavasji* state that the aliens involved should have gone into the district court to secure judicial review of their particular complaints. But exactly how does one get there? Federal courts remain courts of limited jurisdiction, and plaintiffs must plead and prove their jurisdictional basis.

The Administrative Procedure Act, as we have noted, establishes a broad presumption that administrative actions are reviewable.[14] But the

---

14. A few decisions under the immigration laws, however, have been held unreviewable under the provision of the APA denying judicial review in those relatively rare circumstances where "agency action is committed to agency discretion by law." 5 U.S.C.A. § 701(a)(2). *See, e.g., Doherty v. Meese,* 808 F.2d 938, 943 (2d Cir.1986) (judicial review is precluded for Attorney General's refusal to deport individual (alleged PIRA terrorist) to country he designated (Ireland), based on determination under § 243(a) that such depor-

Supreme Court held, after years of controversy in the lower courts, that the APA did not itself constitute an independent grant of jurisdiction. *Califano v. Sanders*, 430 U.S. 99, 103, 97 S.Ct. 980, 983, 51 L.Ed.2d 192 (1977). A litigant seeking district court review must anchor his claim elsewhere, although, once he does so, he can usually take advantage of the other general provisions of the APA governing judicial review.

One important potential jurisdictional foundation is 28 U.S.C.A. § 1331, which vests in the district courts general federal question jurisdiction. Until 1976, § 1331 imposed a jurisdictional amount requirement: district court jurisdiction attached only if the amount in controversy exceeded $10,000. Since immigration disputes usually involve personal stakes not easily translated into dollar figures, this could have been a difficult barrier. But in 1976, Congress amended the section to eliminate the monetary requirement where suit was brought against the United States, a federal agency, or an official or employee sued in official capacity. Pub.L. No. 94–574, § 2, 90 Stat. 2721 (1976). (Section 1 of the same statute amended the APA to make clear that sovereign immunity should not bar otherwise proper suits brought to secure judicial review of agency action. *See* 5 U.S.C.A. § 702, as amended.) Then in 1980 Congress determined that "arising under" jurisdiction should no longer depend on the monetary stakes, no matter who the defendant might be. Pub.L. No. 96–486, § 2(a), 94 Stat. 2369 (1980). That amendment changed § 1331 to a simple and direct grant of power. It now reads in full: "The district courts shall have original jurisdiction of all civil actions arising under the Constitution, laws, or treaties of the United States."

One might expect that this change would greatly simplify litigation of immigration disputes in the district courts, and for the most part it has. But there are some remaining complications. Most importantly, § 1331 does not override other specialized arrangements for review of agency determinations; § 1331 jurisdiction is still subject to preclusion-of-review statutes enacted by Congress. *See Califano v. Sanders*, 430 U.S. at 105, 97 S.Ct. at 984. This means, for example, that an alien who wants to lodge a direct challenge to an order directing his deportation must still adhere to the requirements of § 106(a) (the "sole and exclusive procedure" for such review); he must file a petition for review in the court of appeals.[15]

tation would be prejudicial to U.S. interests). Most such cases, however, have refused review of decisions by the USIA rejecting requested waivers of the two-year residence in the home country required of exchange visitors—beneficiaries of J visas—by § 212(e) before they are able to take up permanent residence or certain other nonimmigrant statuses in the United States. *See, e.g., Slyper v. Attorney General,* 827 F.2d 821 (D.C.Cir. 1987), *cert. denied,* 485 U.S. 941, 108 S.Ct. 1121, 99 L.Ed.2d 281 (1988); *Dina v. Attorney General,* 793 F.2d 473 (2d Cir.1986); *Abdelhamid v. Ilchert,* 774 F.2d 1447 (9th Cir. 1985). *Contra: Chong v. Director, USIA,* 821 F.2d 171 (3d Cir.1987) (review not precluded by § 701(a)(2), but scope of review is "severe-

ly limited"). Until recently, the USIA appeared quite satisfied with this situation and refused requests to give specific reasons for waiver denials, persisting in boilerplate invocation of "program, policy and foreign policy aspects" in its decision letters. *See* 65 Interp.Rel. 379–80 (1988). For a rather aggressive application of the nonreviewability doctrine, see *Perales v. Casillas* 903 F.2d 1043 (5th Cir.1990) (decision to grant voluntary departure and work authorization has been committed to agency discretion by law).

15. This subordination to preclusion-of-review provisions apparently also accounts for the continued refusal of most courts to review the denial of a visa by a United States consul. *See generally Pena v. Kissinger,* 409

But that may not be the only obstacle to the use of § 1331, for the INA contains another jurisdictional provision, INA § 279, deriving from the original enactment in 1952. Read that section closely. The last three sentences suggest that Congress was preoccupied with granting jurisdiction in cases where the government would be the plaintiff (such as in proceedings to collect on a bond forfeiture). Indeed, it might even have been possible at one time to read the statute as a grant of judicial authority *only* when the United States was a plaintiff. But the courts have not moved in this direction at all; § 279 has been read as a grant of district court jurisdiction in a wide variety of settings.

Perhaps the most perplexing questions derive from the limitation in § 279 to causes "arising under any of the provisions *of this subchapter.*" The reference is to Subchapter II ("Immigration") of the INA, which includes §§ 201 through 293. Thus excluded from the jurisdictional grant are sections 101 through 106 (which are part of Subchapter I, General), all of Subchapter III, Nationality and Naturalization, and Subchapter IV, Refugee Assistance.

This restriction proved fatal to the plaintiffs' attempt in *Chen Chaun–Fa v. Kiley,* 459 F.Supp. 762 (S.D.N.Y.1978), to secure early judicial review in the district court. The plaintiffs had unsuccessfully petitioned the district director for political asylum. At the time, prior to passage of the Refugee Act of 1980, there was no specific statutory provision for political asylum,[16] and the petition had been filed under what was then 8 C.F.R. Part 108. The district court determined that it had no jurisdiction. After quoting the language of the first sentence of § 279, the court stated:

> Because this section appears in subchapter II of the Act, the jurisdiction of the district courts is limited to causes arising under subchapter II.
>
> Plaintiffs' request that this Court review the decision of the INS District Director denying political asylum does not present a claim arising under subchapter II. Plaintiff's asylum claims were submitted pursuant to the regulations set out in 8 C.F.R. Part 108. The statutory basis for these regulations is section 103 of the Act [the general grant of authority to the Attorney General to administer and enforce the immigration laws], a provision contained in the *first* subchapter of the Act. Thus, section 279 fails on its face to confer jurisdiction on this Court.

459 F.Supp. at 764. This holding on the application of § 279 also worked to foreclose relief under 28 U.S.C.A. § 1331:

> The only jurisdictional basis alleged by plaintiffs in their complaint is 28 U.S.C. section 1331. This section confers jurisdic-

---

F.Supp. 1182 (S.D.N.Y.1976), considered in detail in Chapter Three, p. 363.

16. There was a closely related provision in § 243(h), however, which authorized the withholding of deportation of aliens who would be subject to persecution in their homelands. But the court evidently treated this as a wholly separate form of relief, or at least as a provision unavailable as a subchapter II hook for jurisdiction under § 279. On the complex interrelationships between political asylum and withholding of deportation under § 243(h), *see* Chapter Eight.

tion on federal courts to review agency action, subject, however, to preclusion of review statutes created by Congress. *See Califano v. Sanders.* This exception to judicial review of agency decisions clearly applies here.

> We find that Congress intended to limit judicial review to those claims arising under subchapter II of the Immigration and Nationality Act. This conclusion is based on the legislative history of section 279 which evidences a deliberate attempt to narrow the jurisdiction of the district court.

Id. at 765. A footnote contained the court's entire discussion of that legislative history (*id.* at 764 n. 6):

> Congress' intent to limit jurisdiction to causes arising under the second subchapter appears to have been deliberate. In 1917, the Act vested the district courts with jurisdiction of all causes arising under any of the provisions of the *Act*. In 1940, this was amended to causes arising under any of the provisions of the *Chapter*. Jurisdiction was further restricted in 1952 when the jurisdictional section was amended to include only causes arising under the second subchapter of the Act.

Do you find this holding persuasive? [17] Does § 279 read like a preclusion-of-review statute? (It is, at the very least, worded quite differently from § 106(a) and (b), which are unambiguously intended to preclude review of deportation and exclusion orders in any other manner than the course specified therein.) If the court's ruling is correct, then any immigration decisions based solely on title I of the INA—including any decisions based on regulations adopted solely under the Attorney General's general authority bestowed by § 103—will escape judicial review. Does the legislative history the court recites demonstrate a deliberate congressional decision to foreclose district court review altogether in these circumstances? What would be Congress's reason for limiting review in this fashion?

Cf. Martinez v. Bell, 468 F.Supp. 719, 726 & n. 6 (S.D.N.Y.1979) (similarly suggesting that the limitations on review under § 279 would restrict review under § 1331); *Karmali v. INS,* 707 F.2d 408 (9th Cir.1983) (approving jurisdiction in the district court to review denial of intracompany transferee visa application under INA § 101(a)(15)(L), because denial also implicated § 214(c), which is within title II); *Yim Tong Chung v. Smith,* 640 F.Supp. 1065, 1069 n. 11 (S.D.N.Y.1986) (work authorization—before enactment of IRCA—could only be provided pursuant to § 103; court therefore lacked jurisdiction under § 279 or 28 U.S.C. § 1331 to consider denial); *Gurbisz v. INS,* 675 F.Supp. 436, 439–40 n. 5 (N.D.Ill. 1987) (extended voluntary departure is a power exercised by the Attorney General under INA § 103, but denial of EVD implicates deportation provisions of § 242 and is therefore reviewable under § 279).

---

17. The court also based its dismissal on a more solidly grounded ruling that the plaintiffs had not adequately exhausted administrative remedies, since they could essentially renew their asylum claims before the immigration judge in deportation proceedings and then, if unsuccessful, secure judicial review in the court of appeals. 459 F.Supp. at 765.

Whatever complications holdings like *Chen Chaun–Fa* may introduce upon occasion, most immigration disputes do arise under title II of the INA. Thus, most of the time a plaintiff seeking relief in the district court will have little difficulty invoking jurisdiction under either § 279 or 28 U.S.C.A. § 1331—or both—provided only that she is not directly challenging an exclusion or deportation order, for which § 106 unambiguously provides exclusive review channels. (She will also have to be sure she has standing to bring the suit—that is, that she is a proper party with a sufficient personal stake to initiate the action. *See* GM & Y § 81.01[3]. In 1990 the Gordon & Mailman treatise listed the following matters which have been held reviewable in the district courts:

> denials of visa petitions, registry, benefits under the agricultural workers program, waivers for exchange visitors, denial of parole to entry applicant, of approval for a school qualified to accept nonimmigrant students, or withdrawal of such approval, change from one nonimmigrant status to another, denial of a labor certification, improper seizure or retention of the alien's passport, denial of extension of temporary stay, of asylum claim, claim of arbitrary, discriminatory, and unconstitutional action in bringing deportation proceeding when prosecutive discretion usually exercised to withhold deportation proceedings in similar cases, exclusion from a list of companies authorized to conduct immigration medical examinations, breach of immigration bond, denial of advance parole, and adjustment of status.

Gordon & Mailman, Immigration Law and Procedure § 8.23 (1990 ed.). The list probably does not exhaust the possibilities.

But if all these matters are subject to review in the district courts, when should or must review be sought? Congress thought it important to confine the period for bringing a petition for review under § 106(a) to 90 days after entry of the deportation order. Does any comparable statute of limitations restrict actions under § 279? Could Kavasji go back even today and demand district court review of the denial of his transfer application? As a matter of policy, should he be allowed to?

A Pictorial Summary

Figure 9.1, adapted from D. Martin, Major Issues in Immigration Law 104–105 (Fed.Jud.Center 1987), summarizes the major avenues for administrative and judicial review of issues that arise under the immigration laws, as we have explored them in this Chapter. For more complete descriptions of the review process, including less common patterns not depicted in the Figure, and for citations to the relevant statutes and regulations, see Legomsky, *supra* note 1, at 1303–12; Patrick, *Tell it to the Judge—Judicial Review of Immigration Decisions,* 88–10 Imm. Briefings (1988).

Figure 9.1

Major Patterns of Administrative and Judicial
Review Under the Immigration Laws

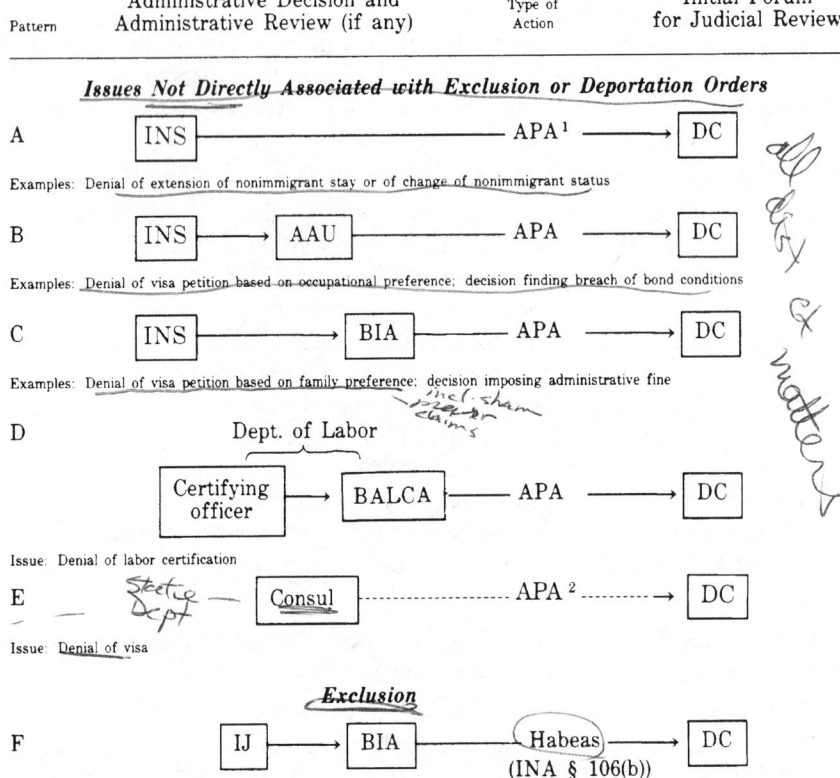

Pattern	Administrative Decision and Administrative Review (if any)	Type of Action	Initial Forum for Judicial Review

Issues Not Directly Associated with Exclusion or Deportation Orders

A   INS ——————————————— APA[1] ——→ DC

Examples: Denial of extension of nonimmigrant stay or of change of nonimmigrant status

B   INS ——→ AAU ——————— APA ——→ DC

Examples: Denial of visa petition based on occupational preference; decision finding breach of bond conditions

C   INS ——————→ BIA ——— APA ——→ DC

Examples: Denial of visa petition based on family preference; decision imposing administrative fine

D   Dept. of Labor

   Certifying officer ——→ BALCA ——— APA ——————→ DC

Issue: Denial of labor certification

E   Consul ---------------- APA[2] ------→ DC

Issue: Denial of visa

Exclusion

F   IJ ——→ BIA ———— Habeas ——→ DC
                            (INA § 106(b))

Issues: Excludability and certain waivers or other forms of relief open to excludable aliens

ABBREVIATIONS: INS = officers of the Immigration and Naturalization Service (includes examiners in district offices or regional service centers, and INS asylum officers); IJ = immigration judge; AAU = Administrative Appeals Unit (exercising authority officially vested in INS Associate Commissioner for Examinations); BIA = Board of Immigration Appeals; BALCA = Board of Alien Labor Certification Appeals; DC = U.S. district court; CA = U.S. court of appeals.

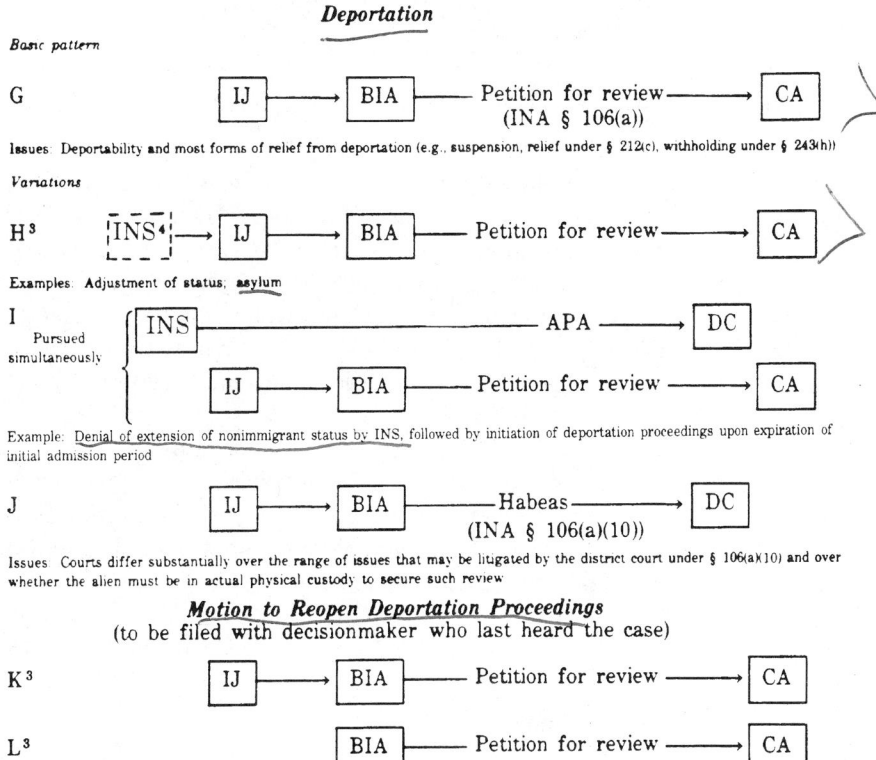

Deportation

Basic pattern

G   IJ ⟶ BIA ⟶ Petition for review ⟶ CA
                                   (INA § 106(a))

Issues: Deportability and most forms of relief from deportation (e.g., suspension, relief under § 212(c), withholding under § 243(h))

Variations

H[3]   INS ⟶ IJ ⟶ BIA ⟶ Petition for review ⟶ CA

Examples: Adjustment of status; asylum

I   INS ⟶ APA ⟶ DC
   Pursued
simultaneously   IJ ⟶ BIA ⟶ Petition for review ⟶ CA

Example: Denial of extension of nonimmigrant status by INS, followed by initiation of deportation proceedings upon expiration of initial admission period

J   IJ ⟶ BIA ⟶ Habeas ⟶ DC
                                (INA § 106(a)(10))

Issues: Courts differ substantially over the range of issues that may be litigated by the district court under § 106(a)(10) and over whether the alien must be in actual physical custody to secure such review

Motion to Reopen Deportation Proceedings
(to be filed with decisionmaker who last heard the case)

K[3]   IJ ⟶ BIA ⟶ Petition for review ⟶ CA

L[3]   BIA ⟶ Petition for review ⟶ CA

Stay of Deportation [5]

M[3]   INS ⟶ Usually habeas ⟶ DC
                              (INA § 106(a)(10))
                                 or APA

---

[1] Action for declaratory or injunctive relief in accordance with the Administrative Procedure Act (APA); jurisdiction is usually based on Immigration and Nationality Act (INA) § 279 or 28 U.S.C. § 1331.

[2] Authority is divided as to permissibility of judicial review.

[3] A similar pattern is possible, but less common, in exclusion cases, in which case the initial forum for judicial review is clearly the district court.

[4] If the benefit has been sought before INS, the application is renewable before the IJ, who will consider it de novo. But there is ordinarily no requirement that the alien apply to INS first; in fact, application to INS may be barred if exclusion or deportation proceedings have already begun. If application is made only to the IJ, consideration of the issue conforms to pattern G.

[5] When a stay is sought in connection with a motion to reopen, application may also be made, under certain circumstances, to the IJ or the BIA. Jurisdiction to review the BIA's denial of a stay (or reversal of an IJ's grant of such a stay) is ordinarily held to lie in the district court, as in pattern M.

SECTION D.   OTHER RESTRICTIONS ON JUDICIAL REVIEW

1. EXHAUSTION OF REMEDIES AND RIPENESS DOCTRINE

A fundamental principle of administrative law ordinarily requires a party to exhaust available administrative remedies before invoking a court's authority to review the decision. The exhaustion rule "is based on the need to allow agencies to develop the facts, to apply the law in which they are particularly expert, and to correct their own errors. The rule ensures that whatever judicial review is available will be informed and narrowed by the agencies' own decisions. It also avoids duplicative proceedings, and often the agency's ultimate decision will obviate the need for judicial intervention." *Schlesinger v. Councilman*, 420 U.S. 738, 756–57, 95 S.Ct. 1300, 1312–13, 43 L.Ed.2d 591 (1975). Occasionally this principle blocks premature district court review of immigration decisions when an alien seeks the court's aid under general grants of jurisdiction set forth in INA § 279 and 28 U.S.C.A. § 1331, even though neither of those sections specifically mentions the exhaustion requirement.[18] *See, e.g., Sweet Life, Inc. v. Dole*, 876 F.2d 402, 407–09 (5th Cir.1989) (denial of H–2 labor certification); *Rafeedie v. INS*, 880 F.2d 506, 513 (D.C.Cir.1989) (discussing "the prudential exhaustion requirement that the courts routinely apply to putative challengers of agency action").[19]

18. The Supreme Court has noted, however, that there are circumstances where "the interests of the individual weigh heavily against requiring administrative exhaustion," and may overcome the administrative interests. *McCarthy v. Madigan*, 112 S.Ct. 1081, 1087 (1992). The Court also ruled in 1993 that in actions brought under the APA, federal courts may not, under § 10(c) of that Act, 5 U.S.C.A. § 704, impose an exhaustion requirement when exhaustion is not expressly required by statute or agency rule. *Darby v. Cisneros*, 113 S.Ct. 2539, 2548 (1993).

19. Particularly complicated exhaustion questions may arise when the alien complains about an INS officer's denial of a form of relief for which application may be renewed before the immigration judge once deportation proceedings begin. The principal (perhaps the only) examples are adjustment of status under INA § 245 and asylum under § 208 (and the opportunity for renewal, strictly speaking, in asylum cases is greatly reduced under regulations that took effect in January 1995; see Chapter Eight). The immigration judges do not review the INS officer's decision; they consider the issue *de novo* based on a new record compiled in the immigration court. Hence, under a strict application of *Cheng Fan Kwok*, the court of appeals will not be able to pass upon the legality of the INS decision upon review of an order of deportation under § 106(a).

Most courts nevertheless invoke the exhaustion principle and require that judicial review be deferred until after the immigration judge and the BIA have considered the matter. Although neither forum will, strictly speaking, consider any claims of error made by the INS officer, owing to the *de novo* character of the immigration judge's consideration, a grant of the relief sought would obviously moot any further dispute. Moreover, any arguably invalid exercise of INS discretion to deny the benefit would be "overtaken" by the immigration judge's subsequent exercise of discretion, which would itself be fully reviewable in the court of appeals. *See, e.g., Randall v. Meese*, 854 F.2d 472, 478–82 (D.C.Cir.1988); *Augoustinakis v. INS*, 693 F.Supp. 1554 (S.D.N.Y.1988) (both collecting cases). *Contra* (apparently): *Jaa v. INS*, 779 F.2d 569 (9th Cir.1986).

But note that the renewal option is not a remedy that the alien is fully at liberty to exhaust, for aliens cannot initiate deportation proceedings. Some courts have therefore sensibly allowed review in the district court of the denial of a renewable application, without requiring exhaustion, where an order to show cause has not yet been served. *See, e.g., Nasan v. INS*, 449 F.Supp. 244 (N.D.Ill. 1978).

When a petitioner seeks judicial review of an exclusion or deportation order under INA § 106, however, he must contend not just with the general principle, but also with a specific statutory requirement set forth in § 106(c): "An order of deportation or exclusion shall not be reviewed by any court if the alien has not exhausted the administrative remedies available to him as of right under the immigration laws and regulations * * *." The following case depicts the usual implementation of this provision.

BAK v. INS

United States Court of Appeals, Third Circuit, 1982.
682 F.2d 441.

PER CURIAM:

Petitioners arrived in this country as visitors for pleasure from Poland, Josef Bak in November 1979 and Teresa Dworniczak in March 1980. Both overstayed the times appointed for their departure, and the Immigration and Naturalization Service (INS) instituted deportation proceedings. On September 8, 1980, both were found deportable for overstays * * * and were granted the right to depart voluntarily prior to January 8, 1981. Petitioners did not appeal these decisions by the immigration judge to the Board of Immigration Appeals; in fact, they both specifically waived this right.

Petitioners subsequently requested that the immigration judge reopen their deportation proceedings so that they could apply for political asylum in the United States. On March 20, 1981, the immigration judge denied these motions to reopen, on the ground that "no new facts are available, which were not available at the original deportation hearing." Petitioners did not appeal this decision to the Board of Immigration Appeals either; instead, they filed petitions for review with this Court pursuant to INA § 106.

The INS has moved to dismiss these consolidated appeals, claiming that the Court is without jurisdiction to entertain the petitions. We agree.

At the outset, we note that we have no jurisdiction to review the immigration judge's original deportation orders. Section 106(a)(1) clearly provides that "a petition for review may be filed not later than six months from the date of the final deportation order." [a] Petitioners here are out of time: they received their orders to deport on September 8, 1980, but delayed filing this appeal until July 14, 1981, more than six months later.

The fact that we have no jurisdiction to review the underlying deportation orders does not end our inquiry, however, for petitioners moved before the immigration judge to reopen their deportation proceedings. These motions were denied on March 20, 1981, and the present petitions were filed within six months of this latter date. The general rule is that a motion to reopen deportation proceedings is a new, independently reviewa-

---

a. The statute was amended in 1990 to reduce this time period, in most cases, to 90 days.—eds.

ble order within the jurisdiction of the court of appeals pursuant to section 106. *Giova v. Rosenberg,* 379 U.S. 18, 85 S.Ct. 156, 13 L.Ed.2d 90 (1964), *reversing* 308 F.2d 347 (9th Cir.1962); *see Bufalino v. Immigration and Naturalization Service,* 473 F.2d 728, 737 (3d Cir.1973) (Adams, J., concurring) (while ordinarily "the right to appeal from an order of deportation is extinguished when the six-month period expires," a court of appeals "may review judgments on motions to reopen"; therefore, limited jurisdiction was present to consider whether the INS abused its discretion in denying petitioner's motion to reopen); *see also Jacobe v. Immigration and Naturalization Service,* 578 F.2d 42 (3d Cir.1978) (Service's refusal to reopen proceedings was subject to review for abuse of discretion).

Despite this general rule, we have no jurisdiction to review petitioners' motions to reopen in the matter *sub judice,* because petitioners failed to exhaust their administrative remedies—that is, they did not appeal the immigration judge's refusal to reopen their proceedings to the Board of Immigration Appeals. Section 106(c) of the Act explicitly proscribes judicial review of an order of deportation if the alien "has not exhausted the administrative remedies available to him as of right under the immigration laws and regulations." Because petitioners never sought review by the Board of the immigration judge's denial of their motions to reopen, we have no jurisdiction to entertain these appeals. *See Jacobe, supra,* 578 F.2d at 44 ("Failure to exhaust administrative remedies results in a lack of jurisdiction in the Court of Appeals").

Anticipating this outcome, petitioners argue that they should not be obligated to exhaust, because to do so would be "futile." Petitioners contend that exhaustion is not necessary if an order is challenged solely on an issue of law. They claim that the immigration judge, in refusing to reopen their proceedings, did so because he was absolutely bound by Service regulations (specifically, 8 C.F.R. §§ 103.5 & 242.22), and that the Board, had it confronted their appeals, would have arrived at precisely the same result because of these regulations. Thus petitioners seek protection under the rule of *Beltre v. Kiley,* 470 F.Supp. 87, 89 (S.D.N.Y.1979). In that case, the court deemed exhaustion unnecessary because the INS district director reached a decision mandated by an INS definitional regulation; the court found, therefore, that if the matter had been presented to the Board, it could not help but have rendered the same decision. *Beltre* is inapplicable here, however. The regulations about which petitioners complain merely provide for the possibility of reopening a deportation proceeding, and direct the immigration judge to reopen only if evidence that is "material and was not available and could not have been discovered or presented" at the original hearing is proffered. These regulations did not in any sense "dictate" the outcome of petitioners' motions. The Board, had an appeal been brought to it, quite conceivably could have determined that the immigration judge erred in not opening the proceedings anew, in view of the showing made to him by petitioners. This case, then, is unlike *Beltre,* in which the decision of the Board was foreordained because of explicit regulatory mandates. Here, the Board could have reversed the immigration judge, and thus exhaustion is necessary under section 106(c) and *Jacobe.*[1]

We conclude that we have no jurisdiction to review any of petitioners' claims having to do with the validity of their underlying deportation orders. With respect to the motions to reopen, we dismiss these petitions because petitioners failed to exhaust their administrative remedies.

Notes

1. The *Bak* case refers to two judge-made exceptions to the exhaustion requirement: when pursuit of the additional remedies would be "futile," and when there is a convincing showing of "fundamental errors." Are these exceptions consistent with the statute? Aren't errors that are convincingly fundamental the kind most likely to be corrected in the administrative review process without having to draw on judicial resources? *See also Sweet Life v. Dole,* 876 F.2d 402, 409 (5th Cir.1989) (warning against equating pessimism with futility).

2. In *Townsend v. United States Dept. of Justice,* 799 F.2d 179 (5th Cir.1986), the alien had filed a formal appeal to the BIA, but he had neither submitted a brief there nor otherwise detailed the precise reasons for his appeal, despite extensions granted for this purpose. In accordance with a recent tightening of its practice in such cases, *see Matter of Valencia,* 19 I & N Dec. 354 (BIA 1986), the BIA summarily dismissed his administrative appeal because "the reasons for the appeal have not been meaningfully identified on the Notice of Appeal." On judicial review, the court then treated the alien's inadequate filing as a failure to exhaust administrative remedies, and so dismissed the petition for review. Other circuits have not considered such a default by the alien a failure to exhaust remedies under § 106(c). They have therefore gone ahead to consider the merits of the appeal, but nearly all have found the BIA dismissal fully justified in these circumstances. *See, e.g., Athehortua–Vanegas v. INS,* 876 F.2d 238 (1st Cir.1989) (collecting cases); *Toquero v. INS,* 956 F.2d 193 (9th Cir.1992) (holding that BIA's practice did not violate due process). For an exception reversing the BIA dismissal, *see Medrano–Villatoro v. INS,* 866 F.2d 132 (5th Cir.1989).

The Board continues to implement *Valencia* with considerable strictness. The message to practitioners is clear: specify the claimed IJ errors in some detail in the notice of appeal, or else be sure to file a timely brief containing the necessary information.

The *HRC* Exception

In *Haitian Refugee Center v. Smith,* 676 F.2d 1023 (5th Cir.1982), the court established a significant potential exception to the exhaustion requirement. The plaintiffs there, a class of over 4000 deportable Haitians

---

1. We note that this is not a situation in which the exhaustion requirement might be waived as the result of a convincing showing that "fundamental errors" were committed in the administrative proceedings, *see McLeod v. Peterson,* 283 F.2d 180 (3d Cir. 1960).

who had sought political asylum in the United States, claimed that they were denied due process and equal protection in the course of accelerated processing carried out by INS. As the district court had summarized the issues, "the gravamen of the plaintiffs' complaint is that INS [including immigration judges] instituted a program 'to achieve expedited mass deportation of Haitian nationals irrespective of the merits of an individual Haitian's asylum application and without regard to the constitutional, treaty, statutory, and administrative rights of the plaintiff class."

Because regular deportation processing, including review by the BIA, had not been concluded in most of the cases by the time the district court ruled, the complaint obviously presented significant questions under the dictate of § 106(a) that petitions for review in the court of appeals should be the "sole and exclusive procedure" for review of deportation orders, and under the exhaustion-of-remedies requirement codified in § 106(c). The Fifth Circuit nonetheless ruled that the district court had jurisdiction:

> Notwithstanding any surface appeal to the government's argument [that *Foti* and *Cheng Fan Kwok* require review only in the court of appeals,] we are convinced that insofar as the first three counts set forth matters alleged to be part of a pattern and practice by immigration officials to violate the constitutional rights of a class of aliens they constitute wrongs which are independently cognizable in the district court under its federal question jurisdiction.[22] Although a court of appeals may have sole jurisdiction to review alleged procedural irregularities in an individual deportation hearing *to the extent these irregularities may provide a basis for reversing an individual deportation order,* that is not to say that a program, pattern or scheme by immigration officials to violate the constitutional rights of aliens is not a separate matter subject to examination by a district court and to the entry of at least declaratory and injunctive relief. The distinction we draw is one between the authority of a court of appeals to pass upon the merits of an individual deportation order and any action in the deportation proceeding to the extent it may affect the merits determination, on the one hand, and, on the other, the authority of a district court to wield its equitable powers when a wholesale, carefully orchestrated, program of constitutional violations is alleged.

> In concluding that the district court had jurisdiction over the first three counts, we wish to emphasize the factual uniqueness of this case. Our holding is not to be construed as permitting a constitutional challenge in the district court based on a procedural ruling in a deportation proceeding with which an alien is dissatisfied. We refuse to condone any such end-run around the administrative process. Casting as a constitutional violation an interlocutory procedural ruling by an immigration judge will not confer jurisdiction on the district court. Such a result would indeed

---

22. 28 U.S.C. § 1331(a). The district court is also given jurisdiction over claims arising under the immigration statutes. INA § 279.

defeat the congressional purpose behind the enactment of section 106(a)—the elimination of dilatory tactics by aliens challenging deportation orders in piecemeal fashion. Congress resolved this problem by consolidating jurisdiction over challenges to final orders of deportation in one court, the court of appeals. We do not intend by our holding today to emasculate that solution, and given the narrowness of our holding, we do not expect such a result.

* * *

The government also contends that the procedural errors challenged in counts one through three and in counts four through sixteen are subject to internal agency review and, therefore, are not subject to judicial review prior to exhaustion of available administrative remedies.[24] As a general rule parties are required to pursue administrative remedies before resorting to the courts to challenge agency action. We agree with the district court, however, that the exhaustion requirement is not a jurisdictional prerequisite but a matter committed to the sound discretion of the trial court. *NLRB v. Industrial Union of Marine and Shipbuilding Workers,* 391 U.S. 418, 419, 426 n. 8, 88 S.Ct. 1717, 1719, 1723 n. 8, 20 L.Ed.2d 706 (1968); *see Ecology Center of Louisiana, Inc. v. Coleman,* 515 F.2d 860, 865–66 (5th Cir.1975). For a number of reasons, we conclude that the district court did not abuse its discretion in exercising jurisdiction notwithstanding any failure of the plaintiffs to exhaust administrative remedies.

The policies advanced by allowing the administrative process to run its full course are not thwarted by judicial intervention in this case. Among those policies are (1) allowing the agency to develop a more complete factual record; (2) permitting the exercise of agency discretion and expertise on issues requiring this; (3) preventing deliberate disregard and circumvention of established agency procedures; and (4) enhancing judicial efficiency and eliminating the need for judicial vindication of legal rights by giving the agency the first opportunity to correct any error. *McKart v. United States,* 395 U.S. 185, 193–95, 89 S.Ct. 1657, 1662–63, 23 L.Ed.2d 194 (1969); *see Ecology Center of Louisiana, Inc.,* 515 F.2d at 866.

With respect to the plaintiffs' attack on actions taken by immigration judges (counts 1–3), further development of the factual record via completion of deportation hearings and subsequent appeal to the BIA would not significantly aid judicial review; to the extent these procedural irregularities are alleged to constitute part of a scheme denying the due process and equal protection rights of the Haitians, they raise legal and not factual issues. Moreover, they present the kind of issues on which the INS possesses no particular expertise. In addition, there is no danger

---

24. The members of the plaintiff class are at varying stages in the administrative process.

that the exercise of jurisdiction will promote disregard of agency procedures since we have indicated above that it is the rare case in which jurisdiction to review procedural rulings made in a deportation hearing properly lies in the district court.

676 F.2d. at 1032–35.

Notes

1.   The court concludes that the exhaustion of remedies requirement "is not a jurisdictional prerequisite but a matter committed to the sound discretion of the trial court," citing a labor law case and an environmental law case.   But the court here was not simply adapting a common-law doctrine to make it work in a particular setting.   It had before it a specific statutory requirement.   Other courts have ruled expressly that the exhaustion requirement in INA § 106(c) is jurisdictional and cannot be waived. *See, e.g., Dhangu v. INS,* 812 F.2d 455, 460 (9th Cir.1987), *Gallanosa by Gallanosa v. United States,* 785 F.2d 116, 119 (4th Cir.1986); *Bothyo v. INS,* 783 F.2d 74, 76–77 (7th Cir.1986); *Garcia–Mir v. Smith,* 766 F.2d 1478, 1486–89 (11th Cir.1985), *cert. denied sub nom. Marquez–Medina v. Meese,* 475 U.S. 1022, 106 S.Ct. 1213, 89 L.Ed.2d 325 (1986).

The Fifth and Eleventh Circuits, original homes of the *Haitian Refugee Center* doctrine (the Eleventh Circuit was carved from the old Fifth after that case began) continue to display confusion on this matter.   Decisions going each way have appeared, without attempting to distinguish or explain contrary circuit precedent. *See, e.g., Haitian Refugee Center v. Meese,* 791 F.2d 1489, 1498–99 (11th Cir.1986) (reaffirming original *Haitian Refugee Center* doctrine in the course of awarding attorneys' fees; no discussion of *Garcia–Mir*); *Townsend v. United States Dept. of Justice,* 799 F.2d 179, 181 (5th Cir.1986) (exhaustion is jurisdictional; no mention of original *Haitian Refugee Center* case).

2.   Take a close look at the court's detailed reasons for excusing the plaintiffs' failure to exhaust administrative remedies, in the last paragraph of the excerpt above.   Why is it that counts 1–3 are seen to raise legal rather than factual issues?   Is this a fair characterization?   The BIA was not specifically named as a party to the claimed conspiracy to deny constitutional, statutory, and administrative rights.   Why does the court assume that no relief would be forthcoming if plaintiffs had to pursue appeals to the Board before coming into court?

––––––––––

The *Haitian Refugee Center (HRC)* court emphasizes the "factual uniqueness" of this case and bravely asserts that its exception to the exhaustion requirement should be taken as a narrow one, which will not become an avenue for avoiding the strictures of § 106.   Nevertheless, in succeeding years numerous district courts deployed this doctrine to hear early challenges to alleged patterns of INS behavior said to violate constitution or statute. In 1989, the District of Columbia Circuit gathered the citations to numerous such decisions and characterized them as follows:

> Although the Fifth Circuit emphasized the narrowness of its holding and promised not to condone any "end-run around the administrative process," the application of *HRC v. Smith* has proliferated to the point where it now more nearly resembles a gaping hole in the middle of the INS's defensive line.

Ayuda, Inc. v. Thornburgh, 880 F.2d 1325, 1336 (D.C.Cir.1989), *vacated for reconsideration in light of* McNary, *infra,* 111 S.Ct. 1068 (1990).[20] The *Ayuda* court amplified its critique:

> If appellees are correct [regarding the availability of the *HRC* exception, when the case presents "broad challenges to an INS policy or legal position that could apply to many cases,"] such a challenge could be brought not only by an organization alleging an independent injury, but by an individual alien, * * * a group of aliens, or an organization representing their interests. These potential plaintiffs would thereby gain significant litigating advantages. For one thing—as happened in this very case—the district court could avoid the difficult analytical problem of discerning the relationship between the "abuse of discretion" scope of review that applies in the courts of appeals and the normal scrutiny given agency interpretations of their organic statutes. More importantly, such an action, particularly if it includes a request for an injunction, could offer the opportunity decisively to influence the INS's behavior all over the country—and do so quickly. * * *
>
> Whether or not the judicial review provisions * * * preclude direct recourse to the district court to challenge the INS's construction of the statute embodied in a regulation depends, of course, on congressional intent. Paradoxically, appellees' construction of those * * * provisions suggests that Congress wished to channel to the courts of appeals only the application of the statute in presumably less important individual cases while reserving to initial district court review (albeit subject to subsequent appeal) the much more important cases involving broad questions of statutory construction that would apply to a whole class of

---

20. In a 1990 case the Ninth Circuit almost completely eviscerated INA § 106(a), by tolerating a truly audacious "end run." A single immigration judge in California had begun to impose onerous filing requirements on asylum applicants. Rather than pursue their complaints about this procedure by means of appeals to the BIA after the entry of a deportation order, a group of aggrieved plaintiffs instead sued in district court for injunctive relief, alleging a pattern or practice. In the meantime, another unsuccessful asylum applicant who had been victimized by the filing requirements had his case heard by the BIA, which ruled the procedures invalid.

The BIA then granted motions to reopen *filed by INS* in all other pending cases affected by the immigration judge's unjustified practice.

Even though the BIA could—and did—correct the challenged practice via administrative appeal, the Ninth Circuit held that "individual administrative appeals did not provide a practical remedy"! Hence the *HRC* exception applied, the district court had jurisdiction, and the plaintiffs' lawyers were entitled to attorneys' fees paid by the government under the Equal Access to Justice Act. *Montes v. Thornburgh,* 919 F.2d 531 (9th Cir.1990).

aliens. * * * [W]e do not believe Congress intended that result
* * *.[5]

* * *

The flaw in the district court's analysis, in our view, is its assumption that every aggrieved party must have a remedy under the statute. It did not consider that Congress sometimes intends to preclude suits by certain classes of plaintiffs, *see* 5 U.S.C. § 701(a)(1) (1982) (judicial review under the APA not available when precluded by statute), and we think a "balanced approach to statutory construction," *Block v. Community Nutrition Inst.,* 467 U.S. 340, 350, 104 S.Ct. 2450, 2456, 81 L.Ed.2d 270 (1984), reveals that a congressional purpose * * * to preclude judicial review by anyone, except in the deportation context, is " 'fairly discernible in the statutory scheme.' "

Id. at 1330–31, 1340. Rejecting the *HRC* doctrine, the court of appeals in *Ayuda* held that the district court lacked jurisdiction.

Which approach, *HRC* or *Ayuda,* better serves the purposes of judicial economy and efficiency? Which better comports with congressional intent? The Supreme Court granted certiorari in the following case in view of the incipient conflict in the circuits. The Court's decision here involves a different statutory provision from the one involved in the original *HRC* case in 1981, but one that is intimately linked with INA § 106.

McNARY v. HAITIAN REFUGEE CENTER, INC.

Supreme Court of the United States, 1991.
498 U.S. 479, 111 S.Ct. 888, 112 L.Ed.2d 1005.

JUSTICE STEVENS delivered the opinion of the Court.

[The plaintiffs in this class action alleged a pattern or practice of procedural due process violations by the INS in its administration of the special agricultural worker (SAW) legalization program enacted as part of the Immigration Reform and Control Act of 1986 (IRCA), INA § 210. They sought injunctive relief in the district court. The governing jurisdictional provision, INA § 210(e), provides in relevant part: "There shall be no administrative or judicial review of a determination respecting an application for adjustment of status [legalization] under this section except in accordance with this subsection," and "There shall be judicial review of such a denial only in the judicial review of an order of exclusion or deportation under section 106."]

* * *

The plaintiffs sought relief on behalf of a class of alien farmworkers who either had been or would be injured by unlawful practices and policies

---

5. In enacting section 106 itself, Congress seems to have been more broadly concerned with "unjustified" litigation, even "unjustified attacks upon the constitutionality of the Immigration and Nationality Act" by "astute attorneys who know how to skillfully exploit the judicial process." Of course, jurisdiction could not turn on the justification (merits) of a claim, but Congress' concern about attorneys' skill in using the judicial process to frustrate deportation proceedings by such devices as forum shopping seems relevant to the *HRC v. Smith* exception—and perhaps even more pertinent to the instant case.

adopted by the INS in its administration of the SAW program. The complaint alleged that the interview process was conducted in an arbitrary fashion that deprived applicants of the due process guaranteed by the Fifth Amendment to the Constitution. Among other charges, the plaintiffs alleged that INS procedures did not allow SAW applicants to be apprised of or to be given opportunity to challenge adverse evidence on which denials were predicated, that applicants were denied the opportunity to present witnesses on their own behalf, that non-English speaking Haitian applicants were unable to communicate effectively with LOs [Legalization Offices] because competent interpreters were not provided, and that no verbatim recording of the interview was made, thus inhibiting even any meaningful administrative review of application denials by LOs or regional processing facilities.

After an evidentiary hearing, the District Court ruled that it had jurisdiction, that the case should proceed as a class action, and that a preliminary injunction should issue.

* * *

The Court of Appeals affirmed. * * *

In their certiorari petition, petitioners did not seek review of the District Court's rulings on the merits or the form of its injunctive relief. Our grant of certiorari is therefore limited to the jurisdictional question.

* * *

Petitioners' entire jurisdictional argument rests on their view that respondents' constitutional challenge is an action seeking "judicial review of a determination respecting an application for adjustment of status" and that district court jurisdiction over the action is therefore barred by the plain language of § 210(e)(1) of the amended INA. The critical words in § 210(e)(1), however, describe the provision as referring only to review "of *a determination* respecting *an application* "for SAW status (emphasis added). Significantly, the reference to "a determination" describes a single act rather than a group of decisions or a practice or procedure employed in making decisions. Moreover, when § 210(e)(3) further clarifies that the only judicial review permitted is in the context of a deportation proceeding, it refers to "judicial review of *such a denial* "—again referring to a single act, and again making clear that the earlier reference to "a determination respecting an application" describes the denial of an individual application. We therefore agree with the District Court's and the Court of Appeals' reading of this language as describing the process of direct review of individual denials of SAW status, rather than as referring to general collateral challenges to unconstitutional practices and policies used by the agency in processing applications.

This reading of the Reform Act's review provision is supported by the language in § 210(e)(3)(B) of the INA, which provides that judicial review "shall be based solely upon the administrative record established at the time of the review by the appellate authority and the findings of fact and determinations contained in such record shall be conclusive unless the applicant can establish abuse of discretion or that the findings are directly contrary to clear and convincing facts contained in the record considered as a whole." This provision incorporates an assumption that the limited review provisions of § 210(e) apply only to claims that have been subjected to administrative consideration and that have resulted in the creation of an adequate administrative record. However, the record created during the SAW administrative review process consists solely of a completed application form, a report of medical examination, any documents or affidavits that evidence an applicant's agricultural employment and residence, and notes, if any, from an LO interview—all relating to a single SAW applicant. Because the administrative appeals process does not address the kind of procedural and constitutional claims respondents bring in this action, limiting judicial review of these claims to the procedures set forth in § 210(e) is not contemplated by the language of that provision.

Moreover, the "abuse of discretion" standard of judicial review under § 210(e)(3)(B) would make no sense if we were to read the Reform Act as requiring constitutional and statutory challenges to INS procedures to be subject to its specialized review provision. Although the abuse-of-discretion standard is appropriate for judicial review of an administrative adjudication of the facts of an individual application for SAW status, such a standard does not apply to constitutional or statutory claims, which are reviewed *de novo* by the courts. The language of § 210(e)(3)(B) thus lends substantial credence to the conclusion that the Reform Act's review provision does not apply to challenges to INS's practices and procedures in administering the SAW program.

Finally, we note that had Congress intended the limited review provisions of § 210(e) of the INA to encompass challenges to INS procedures and practices, it could easily have used broader statutory language. Congress could, for example, have modeled § 210(e) on the more expansive language in the general grant of district court jurisdiction under Title II of the INA by channeling into the Reform Act's special review procedures "all causes ... arising under any of the provisions" of the legalization program. 66 Stat. 230, INA § 279. It moreover could have modeled § 210(e) on 38 U.S.C. § 211(a), which governs review of veterans' benefits claims, by referring to review "on all questions of law and fact" under the SAW legalization program.

Given Congress' choice of statutory language, we conclude that challenges to the procedures used by INS do not fall within the scope of § 210(e). Rather, we hold that § 210(e) applies only to review of denials of individual SAW applications. Because respondents' action does not seek review on the merits of a denial of a particular application, the District Court's general federal question jurisdiction under 28 U.S.C. § 1331 to hear this action remains unimpaired by § 210(e).

* * *

Petitioners place their principal reliance on our decision in *Heckler v. Ringer,* 466 U.S. 602, 104 S.Ct. 2013, 80 L.Ed.2d 622 (1984). The four respondents in *Ringer* wanted to establish a right to reimbursement under the Medicare Act for a particular form of surgery that three of them had undergone and the fourth allegedly needed. They sought review of the

Secretary's policy of refusing reimbursement for that surgery in an original action filed in the District Court, without exhausting the procedures specified in the statute for processing reimbursement claims. The District Court dismissed the case for lack of jurisdiction because the essence of the complaint was a claim of entitlement to payment for the surgical procedure. With respect to the three respondents who had had the surgery, we concluded that "it makes no sense" to construe their claims "as anything more than, at bottom, a claim that they should be paid for their BCBR [bilateral carotid body resection] surgery," *id.,* at 614, 104 S.Ct., at 2021, since success in their challenge of the Secretary's policy denying reimbursement would have the practical effect of also deciding their claims for benefits on the merits. "Indeed," we noted, "the relief that respondents seek to redress their supposed 'procedural' objections is the invalidation of the Secretary's current policy and a 'substantive' declaration from her that the expenses of BCBR surgery are reimbursable under the Medicare Act." *Ibid.* Concluding that respondents' judicial action was not "collateral" to their claims for benefits, we thus required respondents first to pursue their administrative remedies. In so doing, we found it significant that respondents, even if unsuccessful before the agency, "clearly have an adequate remedy in § 405(g) for challenging [in the courts] all aspects of the Secretary's denial of their claims for payment for the BCBR surgery." *Id.,* at 617, 104 S.Ct., at 2022–23.

Unlike the situation in *Heckler,* the individual respondents in this action do not seek a substantive declaration that they are entitled to SAW status. Nor would the fact that they prevail on the merits of their purportedly procedural objections have the effect of establishing their entitlement to SAW status. Rather, if allowed to prevail in this action, respondents would only be entitled to have their case files reopened and their applications reconsidered in light of the newly prescribed INS procedures.

Moreover, unlike in *Heckler,* if not allowed to pursue their claims in the District Court, respondents would not as a practical matter be able to obtain meaningful judicial review of their application denials or of their objections to INS procedures notwithstanding the review provisions of § 210(e) of the amended INA. It is presumable that Congress legislates with knowledge of our basic rules of statutory construction, and given our well-settled presumption favoring interpretations of statutes that allow judicial review of administrative action, see *Bowen v. Michigan Academy of Family Physicians,* 476 U.S. 667, 670, 106 S.Ct. 2133, 2135, 90 L.Ed.2d 623 (1986), coupled with the limited review provisions of § 210(e), it is most unlikely that Congress intended to foreclose all forms of meaningful judicial review.

Several aspects of this statutory scheme would preclude review of respondents' application denials if we were to hold that the District Court lacked jurisdiction to hear this challenge. Initially, administrative or judicial review of an agency decision is almost always confined to the record made in the proceeding at the initial decisionmaking level, and one of the central attacks on INS procedures in this litigation is based on the claim that such procedures do not allow applicants to assemble adequate records.

As the District Court found, because of the lack of recordings or transcripts of LO interviews and the inadequate opportunity for SAW applicants to call witnesses or present other evidence on their behalf, the administrative appeals unit of the INS, in reviewing the decisions of LOs and regional processing facilities, and the courts of appeals, in reviewing SAW denials in the context of deportation proceedings, have no complete or meaningful basis upon which to review application determinations.

Additionally, because there is no provision for direct judicial review of the denial of SAW status unless the alien is later apprehended and deportation proceedings are initiated, most aliens denied SAW status can ensure themselves review in courts of appeals only if they voluntarily surrender themselves for deportation. Quite obviously, that price is tantamount to a complete denial of judicial review for most undocumented aliens.

Finally, even in the context of a deportation proceeding, it is unlikely that a court of appeals would be in a position to provide meaningful review of the type of claims raised in this litigation. To establish the unfairness of the INS practices, respondents in this case adduced a substantial amount of evidence, most of which would have been irrelevant in the processing of a particular individual application. Not only would a court of appeals reviewing an individual SAW determination therefore most likely not have an adequate record as to the pattern of INS' allegedly unconstitutional practices, but it also would lack the factfinding and record-developing capabilities of a federal district court.

* * *

It therefore seems plain to us, as it did to the District Court and the Court of Appeals, that restricting judicial review to the courts of appeals as a component of the review of an individual deportation order is the practical equivalent of a total denial of judicial review of generic constitutional and statutory claims.

* * *

The strong presumption in favor of judicial review of administrative action is not overcome either by the language or the purpose of the relevant provisions of the Reform Act.

The judgment of the Court of Appeals is affirmed.

It is so ordered.

CHIEF JUSTICE REHNQUIST, with whom JUSTICE SCALIA joins, dissenting.

Congress has carefully limited the judicial review available under the Immigration Control and Reform Act of 1986 (Reform Act) in language which "he who runs may read." The Court, with considerable and obvious effort, finds a way to avoid this limitation, because to apply the statute as written could bar judicial review of respondents' constitutional claims. The statute as written is, in my view, constitutional, and there is therefore no need to rewrite it.

* * *

[Section 210(e) states,] as clearly as any language can, that judicial review of a "determination respecting an application for adjustment of status under this section" may not be had except in accordance with the provisions of the subsection. The plain language of subsection (3)(A) provides that judicial review of a denial may be had only in connection with review of an order of exclusion or deportation. The Court chooses to read this language as dealing only with "direct review of individual denials of SAW status, rather than as referring to general collateral challenges to unconstitutional practices and policies used by the agency in processing applications." But the accepted view of judicial review of administrative action generally—even when there is no express preclusion provision as there is in the present statute—is that only "final actions" are reviewable in court. The Administrative Procedure Act provides:

> "[F]inal agency action for which there is no other adequate remedy in a court [is] subject to judicial review. A preliminary, procedural, or intermediate agency action or ruling not directly reviewable is subject to review on the review of the final agency action." 5 U.S.C. § 704.

The Court's reasoning is thus a classic non sequitur. It reasons that because Congress limited judicial review only of what were in effect final administrative decisions, it must not have intended to preclude separate challenges to procedures used by the agency before it issued any final decision. But the type of judicial review of agency action which the Court finds that Congress failed to preclude is a type not generally available even without preclusion. In the light of this settled rule, the natural reading of "determination respecting an application" in § 210(e) encompasses both final decisions and procedures used to reach those decisions. Each of respondents' claims attacks the process used by Immigration and Naturalization Service (INS) to make a determination respecting an application.

We have on several occasions rejected the argument advanced by respondents that individual plaintiffs can bypass restrictions on judicial review by purporting to attack general policies rather than individual results. For instance, in *United States v. Erika, Inc.*, 456 U.S. 201, 102 S.Ct. 1650, 72 L.Ed.2d 12 (1982), we found that in the context of the "precisely drawn provisions" of the Medicare statute, the provision of judicial review for awards made under Part A of the statute, coupled with the omission of judicial review for awards under Part B, "provides persuasive evidence that Congress deliberately intended to foreclose further review of such claims." *Id.*, at 208, 102 S.Ct., at 1654 (citations omitted). Similarly, in *Heckler v. Ringer*, 466 U.S. 602, 104 S.Ct. 2013, 80 L.Ed.2d 622 (1984), we addressed a challenge to a ruling issued by the Secretary of Health and Human Services that precluded payment under Medicare for a particular medical procedure. * * * We expressly rejected the contention—also urged by the respondents here—that "simply because a claim somehow can be construed as 'procedural,' it is cognizable in federal district court by way of federal-question jurisdiction." *Id.*, at 614, 104 S.Ct., at 2021.

It is well settled that when Congress has established a particular review mechanism, courts are not free to fashion alternatives to the specified scheme. In creating the Reform Act and the SAW program, Congress balanced the goals of the unprecedented amnesty programs with the need "to insure reasonably prompt determinations" in light of the incentives and opportunity for ineligible applicants to delay the disposition of their cases and derail the program. The Court's ponderously reasoned gloss on the statute's plain language sanctions an unwarranted intrusion into a carefully drafted congressional program, a program which placed great emphasis on a minimal amount of paperwork and procedure in an effort to speed the process of adjusting the status of those aliens who demonstrated their entitlement to adjustment. "If the balance is to be struck anew, the decision must come from Congress and not from this Court." *Ringer, supra,* 466 U.S., at 627, 104 S.Ct., at 2028.

* * *

The Court bases its conclusion that district courts have jurisdiction to entertain respondents' pattern and practice allegations in part out of "respect [for] the 'strong presumption that Congress intends judicial review of administrative action.'" This presumption, however, comes into play only where there is a genuine ambiguity as to whether Congress intended to preclude judicial review of administrative action. In this case two things are evident: First, in drafting the Reform Act, Congress did not preclude all judicial review of administrative action; as detailed earlier, Congress provided for judicial review of INS action in the courts of appeals in deportation proceedings, and in the district courts in orders of exclusion. Second, by enacting such a scheme, Congress intended to foreclose all other avenues of relief. Therefore, since the statute is not ambiguous, the presumption has no force here.

The Court states that this presumption of judicial review is particularly applicable in cases raising constitutional challenges to agency action since respect for the presumption avoids "'the "serious constitutional question" that would arise if a federal statute were construed to deny any judicial forum for a colorable constitutional claim.'" I believe that Congress intended to preclude judicial review of such claims in this instance, and that in this context it is permissible for it to do so.

In the Reform Act, Congress enacted a one-time amnesty program to process claims of illegal aliens allowing them to obtain status as lawful residents. Congress intended aliens to come forward during the limited, 12–month eligibility period because "[t]his is the first call and the last call, a one-shot deal." 132 Cong.Rec. 33217 (1986) (remarks of Sen. Simpson). If an alien failed to file a legalization application within the 12–month period, the opportunity was lost forever. To further expedite this unique and unprecedented amnesty program and to minimize the burden on the federal courts, Congress provided for limited judicial review.

Given the structure of the Act, and the status of these alien respondents, it is extremely doubtful that the operation of the administrative process in their cases would give rise to any colorable constitutional claims. "'An alien who seeks political rights as a member of this Nation can rightfully obtain them only upon terms and conditions specified by Congress. Courts are without authority to sanction changes or modifications; their duty is rigidly to enforce the legislative will in respect of a matter so vital to the public welfare.' " *INS v. Pangilinan,* 486 U.S. 875, 884, 108 S.Ct. 2210, 2216, 100 L.Ed.2d 882 (1988) (quoting *United States v. Ginsberg,* 243 U.S. 472, 474, 37 S.Ct. 422, 425, 61 L.Ed. 853 (1917)).

Respondents are undoubtedly entitled to the benefit of those procedures which Congress has accorded them in the Reform Act. But there is no reason to believe that administrative appeals as provided in the Act— which simply have not been resorted to by these respondents before suing in the District Court—would not have assured them compliance with statutory procedures. The Court never mentions what colorable constitutional claims these aliens, illegally present in the United States, could have had that demand judicial review. The most that can be said for respondents' case in this regard is that it is conceivable, though not likely, that the administrative processing of their claims could be handled in such a way as to deny them some constitutional right, and that the remedy of requesting deportation in order to obtain judicial review is a burdensome one. We have never held, however, that Congress may not, by explicit language, preclude judicial review of constitutional claims, and here, where that body was obviously interested in expeditiously processing an avalanche of claims from noncitizens upon whom it was conferring a substantial benefit, I think it may do so.

Notes

1. Suppose you had represented a SAW applicant during the legalization process. Because the Supreme Court's decision did not come down until after the application period closed, at the time of application you of course could not be certain whether class actions in the district court would ultimately be allowed. If you believed that your client was being denied the statutory and constitutional rights at issue in this case (see the first quoted paragraph in the majority opinion), what would you have done in the individual SAW proceedings to preserve such claims for administrative appeal and possibly judicial review? Presumably some issues would be easier to capture and record than others, but couldn't you have created some basis for later pursuit of those claims? Even as to the generic claims, wouldn't it have been possible for the Legalization Appeals Unit to provide some sort of relief? If the reviewing body (either agency or appellate court) considered the record inadequate to pass on some of the claims, what should it do? (In this connection, reconsider *Florida Power & Light Co. v. Lorion, supra* p. 926.)

2. The majority notes that, as the government construes the statute, aliens would have to surrender for deportation in order to secure judicial review. It then comments: "Quite obviously, that price is tantamount to a complete denial of judicial review for most undocumented aliens." Is this so obvious? Judicial review is not denied. It is just costly. (It imposes a cost, however, that is consistent with Congress's general message in IRCA: Legalize or leave. *See* Martin, *Judicial Review of Legalization Denials,* 65

Interp.Rel. 757, 760 (1988).) If the alien petitions for such review and prevails, obviously he avoids—as he should—having to pay that cost. If he loses, he faces deportation, but his loss signifies that the courts agree that he did not have a meritorious defense to deportation anyway. Why should such people receive extra protection against measures designed to assure compliance with the underlying immigration laws?

3. The SAW program provides a kind of amnesty: despite illegality, a qualified alien will be given special forgiveness that permits him to stay. One has no claim of right to an amnesty; it is a legislative gratuity. In this context, could Congress have made amnesty or legalization a purely administrative process with no possibility for judicial review? Could it preclude judicial review of constitutional claims?

Reno v. Catholic Social Services, Inc.

HRC v. McNary did not spell the end of the controversy over the *HRC* exception, nor indeed over the role of the courts in considering class action challenges to certain INS practices and procedures in the legalization programs adopted in 1986. The later history of the *Ayuda* case is illustrative. On remand for reconsideration in light of *McNary*, the *Ayuda* court read the *McNary* decision narrowly, as dealing only with collateral challenges, usually of a procedural nature. Therefore it ruled again that the district court was without jurisdiction to consider the plaintiffs' challenge, because it went to INS's substantive interpretation of a provision governing the main legalization program under INA § 245A. The court also ruled that plaintiffs had not satisfied a jurisdictional requirement of exhaustion of remedies, and that the issue was not ripe for review. *Ayuda, Inc. v. Thornburgh*, 948 F.2d 742 (D.C.Cir.1991), *rehearing en banc denied*, 958 F.2d 1089 (D.C.Cir.1992), *vacated and remanded for reconsideration in light of* CSS *decision, infra*, 113 S.Ct. 3026 (1993). But at the same time other circuits were taking a more expansive view of *McNary* to authorize extensive class-wide relief to those apparently disadvantaged by certain legalization regulations interpreting and applying IRCA. *See, e.g., Catholic Social Services, Inc. v. Thornburgh*, 956 F.2d 914 (9th Cir.1992).

The Supreme Court granted certiorari in the latter case, and its ruling appeared to restrict the practical impact of *McNary* quite substantially. Initially, the Court reaffirmed its position, based on *McNary*, that jurisdiction existed to entertain a class-action challenge to INS's regulations despite INA § 245A(f)(1), because the plaintiffs' challenge did not refer to or rely on the denial of any individual application. (Section 245A(f)(1) is the judicial review provision for the main legalization program, worded quite similarly to the jurisdictional provision at issue in *McNary*, reprinted in the bracketed paragraph at the beginning of that case *supra*.) The *CSS* opinion goes on to say, however, that that INA section "is not the only jurisdictional hurdle in the way of" the plaintiffs, "whose claims still must satisfy the jurisdictional and justiciability requirements that apply in the absence of a specific Congressional directive." In particular, the controversy must be " 'ripe' for judicial resolution," which means that the administrative action must have been "felt in a concrete way by the challenging parties." This might be a major barrier for many in the plaintiff class:

> The regulations * * * limit access to a benefit created by the Reform Act but not automatically bestowed on eligible aliens. Rather, the Act requires each alien desiring the benefit to take further administrative steps, and to satisfy criteria beyond those addressed by the disputed regulations. It delegates to the INS the task of determining on a case-by-case basis whether each applicant has met all of the Act's conditions, not merely those interpreted by the regulations in question. * * * [A] class member's claim would ripen only once he took the affirmative steps that he could take before the INS blocked his path by applying the regulation to him.
>
> Ordinarily, of course, that barrier would appear when the INS formally denied the alien's application on the ground that the regulation rendered him ineligible for legalization. A plaintiff who sought to rely on the denial of his application to satisfy the ripeness requirement, however, would then still find himself at least temporarily barred by the Reform Act's exclusive review provisions, since he would be seeking "judicial review of a determination respecting an application." [INA § 245A(f)(1).] The ripeness doctrine and the Reform Act's jurisdictional provisions would thus dovetail neatly, and not necessarily by mere coincidence. Congress may well have assumed that, in the ordinary case, the courts would not hear a challenge to regulations specifying limits to eligibility before those regulations were actually applied to an individual. * * * [The plaintiffs here] do not argue that this limited scheme would afford them inadequate review of a determination based on the regulations they challenge * * * ; their situation is thus different from that of the "17 unsuccessful SAW applicants" in *McNary*, whose procedural objections, we concluded, could receive no practical judicial review within the [comparable] scheme established by [INA § 210(e)].

Reno v. Catholic Social Services, Inc., ___ U.S. ___, ___, 113 S.Ct. 2485, 2495–97, 125 L.Ed.2d 38 (1993).

The Supreme Court remanded the *CSS* case, however, to allow a determination of whether some plaintiffs were actually prevented from receiving such an individual determination as a result of INS's "front-desking" policy—a stated policy whereby the legalization assistant at the front desk of the legalization office might refuse to accept a proffered application even for initial filing, in reliance on the challenged regulation. (The front-desking policy was adopted largely as a way of saving money for the potential applicants, by turning away meritless applications before the individual had to tender the legalization fee of $185. The subclass that might be able to show it was front-desked is likely to be considerably smaller than the class originally certified in these cases.) The mere existence of the front-desking policy was not sufficient to leap the ripeness hurdle, however. "[O]nly those class members (if any) who were front-desked have ripe claims over which the District Courts should exercise jurisdiction * * *." Id. at 2500.[21]

The Supreme Court's decision in *CSS* has certainly made it more difficult for plaintiffs to get class action lawsuits past the initial hurdles of jurisdiction and justiciability, and will ordinarily require that challenges to regulations and practices be channeled through individual deportation appeals. For an excellent map of the rather confusing jurisdictional terrain after *McNary* and *CSS*, see *Yang v. Reno*, 852 F.Supp. 316 (M.D.Pa.1994) (denying class certification and finding no jurisdiction under 28 U.S.C. § 1331 for challenge to specific asylum case-law doctrine), *affirmed sub nom. Yi v. Maugans*, 24 F.3d 500 (3d Cir.1994).

Is this channeling a good or a bad thing? Consider the new doctrine's impact on the work of pro bono lawyers who wish to challenge INS policies. *See Naranjo–Aguilera v. INS*, 30 F.3d 1106, 1114 (9th Cir.1994) (class action challenge to certain regulations implementing the SAW program ordered dismissed for lack of jurisdiction; court comments on impact on counsel). Recall that appointed counsel is unavailable in individual deportation proceedings, and that even if the alien prevails in that forum, she cannot, unlike most other litigants against the government, obtain government reimbursement of attorney's fees under the Equal Access to Justice Act, 28 U.S.C. § 2412. *Ardestani v. INS*, 502 U.S. 129, 112 S.Ct. 515, 116 L.Ed.2d 496 (1991) (holding EAJA inapplicable to deportation cases). (EAJA permits fee shifting in successful actions against the government, when the government's position was not "substantially justified.") Ironically, EAJA has been available in *HRC*-style class action challenges, sometimes leading to awards of several hundred thousand dollars. *See, e.g., Haitian Refugee Center v. Meese*, 791 F.2d 1489 (11th Cir.1986), *opinion amended*, 804 F.2d 1573 (11th Cir.1986) (awarding $441,000 plus interest to plaintiffs in original *HRC* litigation). Why bar EAJA awards in the less expensive setting while leaving open large awards in class actions? Could a better balance between the concerns of the *Ayuda* court and the needs of the pro bono bar be struck? Consider a hypothetical bill to amend the statutes to curtail such class actions but to permit (1) EAJA awards to aliens who prevail in deportation cases, or (2) appointed counsel in deportation cases, perhaps after some threshold showing.

The Supreme Court remanded *Ayuda* yet again, for reconsideration in light of *CSS*. 113 S.Ct. 3026 (1993). The court of appeals again found that jurisdiction was absent and that the organizational plaintiffs lacked standing. In its view, the *CSS* decision extended general ripeness doctrine "so as to severely limit *McNary*, and thus neatly came, by a somewhat modified route, to our [original] resolution of the boundary issue." *Ayuda, Inc. v. Reno*, 7 F.3d 246, 249 (D.C.Cir.1993), *rehearing en banc denied*, 14 F.3d 61 (1994). This time, on the third round, the Supreme Court simply

---

21. The Court also left the door open to the possibility of other exceptions: "Although we think it unlikely, we cannot rule out the possibility that further facts would allow class members who were not front-desked to demonstrate that the front-desking policy was nevertheless a substantial cause of their failure not to apply [*sic*], so that they can be said to have had the [challenged regulations] applied to them in a sufficiently concrete manner to satisfy ripeness concerns." 113 S.Ct. at 2500 n.28.

denied certiorari. ___ U.S. ___, 115 S.Ct. 70, 130 L.Ed.2d 26 (1994). *See also INS v. Legalization Assistance Project,* ___ U.S. ___, 114 S.Ct. 422, 126 L.Ed.2d 410 (1993) (O'Connor, J., in chambers) (staying order of district court in a case similar to *CSS,* on grounds of its likely reversal; district court had distinguished *CSS* because plaintiffs there were individuals whereas its plaintiffs were organizations). The *CSS* litigation continues at a very slow pace, with bitter skirmishing between the parties. *See* 72 Interp.Rel. 207, 237 (1995).

2. DEPARTURE FROM THE COUNTRY WHILE REVIEW IS PENDING

Section 106(c) not only denies review rights when an alien fails to exhaust remedies. It also states: "An order of deportation or exclusion shall not be reviewed by any court if the alien * * * has departed from the United States after issuance of the order." [22] What does this requirement mean, and why did Congress include it? What if the alien's departure is forced upon him by pressing business, by illness in the family, by a need for indispensable personal medical treatment, or by alleged government misbehavior?

In *Mendez v. INS,* 563 F.2d 956 (9th Cir.1977), INS executed a deportation order about one month after it had become final. This was permissible, for § 106 grants no automatic stay during the time period allowed for filing the petition for review to the courts of appeals. *See* INA § 106(a)(8). A stay takes effect automatically (subject to being vacated by the court of appeals) only when the petition is served on INS. *Id.* § 106(a)(3). But here INS provided no notice of the impending removal to the alien's counsel of record, as it was required to do under the regulations. Violation of the regulation was uncontested. INS nevertheless contended that the court lacked jurisdiction to consider the case because of the departure preclusion in § 106(c). The court responded (563 F.2d, at 958–59):

> We are of the opinion that "departure" in the context of § 106 cannot mean "departure in contravention of procedural due process." We hold that "departure" means "legally executed" departure when effected by the government. We base our holding on the Supreme Court's decision in *Delgadillo v. Carmichael,* 332 U.S. 388, 68 S.Ct. 10, 92 L.Ed. 17 (1947). In that case the Court held that an alien does not make an "entry" into the United States when he had no intent to "depart," or left involuntarily.
> * * *

22. In parallel fashion, the regulations bar BIA consideration of an appeal or a motion to reopen or reconsider if the alien has departed from the country. 8 C.F.R. §§ 3.2, 3.3(a), 3.4. Curiously, however, an immigration judge *is* permitted to proceed to issuance of a deportation order, even if it is known that the alien has already left the country. *See Joo v. INS,* 813 F.2d 211, 212 (9th Cir. 1987) (per curiam); 63 Interp. Rel. 36 (1986); 64 *id.* 231 (1987). *Matter of Keyte,* Int.Dec. 3128 (BIA 1990), holds that the departure rule of 8 C.F.R. § 3.4 does not apply to exclusion cases, but in *Matter of Okoh,* Int.Dec. 3227 (BIA 1994), the Board ruled that the rule does bar a motion to reconsider after an exclusion order has been executed.

Appellee's contention that its decisions are immune from judicial review when the alien is physically out of the country— without regard to the manner in which this "departure" was accomplished—is just such a "captious interpretation" [of the kind condemned in *Delgadillo*]. Appellee's argument would serve to thwart the jurisdiction of this court in a case where the alien has been "kidnapped" and removed as easily as it would apply to this case involving deportation in derogation of procedural due process.

* * *

Nor is it necessary to invoke constitutional grounds in order to dispose of this appeal. Courts have looked with disfavor upon actions taken by federal agencies which have violated their own regulations. * * *

Here, failure to notify appellant's counsel amounted not only to a violation of 8 C.F.R. 292.5(a), but also to appellant's right to counsel as provided in INA § 242(b). We order the Immigration and Naturalization Service to admit appellant into the United States, granting appellant the same status he held prior to the May 15, 1975 deportation. This will permit appellant to pursue any administrative and judicial remedies to which he is lawfully entitled.

Notes

1. In *Umanzor v. Lambert,* 782 F.2d 1299, 1303 (5th Cir.1986), the court suggested that "*Mendez* has become a sinkhole that has swallowed the rule" of INA § 106(c). In dictum, it wrote:

> We entertain serious reservations regarding the "*Mendez* exception" for, if the exception is taken to its logical conclusion, *any* error or procedural defect at any point in the alien's deportation saga (from his arrest, hearing, BIA hearing, habeas proceeding in district court or appeal to the appropriate circuit court, to his final departure from the United States) would render the departure illegal. This being so, any later *allegation* of procedural error by a deported alien would force the district court and the circuit courts to review the entire matter, despite the express determination of Congress that no such reviews should take place.

Are these concerns valid? Can they be alleviated by measures short of eliminating the *Mendez* exception?

The Fifth Circuit eventually acted on the reservations expressed above, when it squarely rejected the *Mendez* doctrine in *Quezada v. INS*, 898 F.2d 474 (5th Cir.1990), as did the Tenth Circuit in *Saadi v. INS*, 912 F.2d 428 (10th Cir.1990), and the Second Circuit in *Roldan v. Racette*, 984 F.2d 85 (2d Cir.1993) (summarizing cases on both sides of the issue). Under this view, the court lacks jurisdiction in any case if the alien has departed, no matter what the alien claims about possible violations of rights in the course of his deportation. The Third and Eighth Circuits, however, have tried to stake out a middle ground, allowing review "if the record reveals a colorable due process claim." *Camacho-Bordes v. INS*, 33 F.3d 26, 28 (8th Cir.1994), accepting doctrine of *Marrero v. INS*, 990 F.2d 772 (3d Cir.1993).

2. The departure rule of § 106(c) creates strong incentives for courts to grant their own stays of deportation (or find administrative denial of such a stay to be an abuse of discretion), particularly in connection with an alien's attempt to obtain reopening or reconsideration. Such pressures exist even if the motion is filed at the last possible moment and appears to be of dubious merit, for denial of a stay may preclude any ruling on the merits whatsoever, much less possible later judicial review. *See, e.g., Anderson v. McElroy*, 953 F.2d 803, 805–06 (2d Cir.1992); *Blancada v. Turnage*, 891 F.2d 688, 690 (9th Cir.1989); *Dill v. INS*, 773 F.2d 25, 31 (3d Cir.1985).

In light of these dynamics, consider the following proposal for changing the departure rule and in fact requiring some people to depart before litigation is concluded.

> The rule barring appeals and motions from abroad generated little discussion when section 106 was enacted, and has drawn little attention since then. It is high time we questioned it. Many European countries somehow manage admirably with rules that allow appeals even after departure. In consequence, they have developed elaborate rules for deciding whether an appeal or other filing will suspend the execution of the deportation order. Such "suspensive effect," as it is ordinarily called, is usually not automatic. In fact, in Great Britain, aliens in certain circumstances are *refused* the right to appeal *until* they depart—strikingly, the complete opposite of the American system.

> Moreover, in terms of real effect on the litigation, waiting in San Jose, Costa Rica, for example, for the BIA to rule on an appeal or a motion to reopen is not so different from waiting in San Diego, California. The distance from the BIA is roughly the same, and nearly all decisions are based solely on an administrative record already compiled, along with papers that the parties file by mail. The only real advantage of the current system, from the government's point of view, would seem to be that the approach of section 106(c) yields a fixed endpoint beyond which further appeals and reopenings cannot take place. But surely we could find other ways to achieve that worthy end: for example, firmer rules limiting the time in which such filings could be offered.

> Above all, permitting appeals and motions from abroad would win for our system greater flexibility in another important respect. Because the issues may still be heard whether or not the alien remains in the country, it becomes thinkable to insist that at least some people *must* leave while later proceedings are underway. If we allowed appeals and motions from abroad, stays would turn on other questions—more particularized questions that go to the precise situation of the individual alien and perhaps the strength of his case.

Here then is the tentative proposal. We should amend section 106(c) to permit appeals from abroad (and similarly to allow at least some motions to reopen). But in return, we should require most aliens to leave after losing before the BIA—or maybe even after losing before the immigration judge. This latter rule, however, would be subject to a strictly limited discretionary authority in courts and certain agency officials to stay deportation in compelling cases. I would also hasten to add that certain categories of cases should be placed outside the rule altogether. Obviously, an alien who has filed a nonfrivolous asylum application should be permitted to remain, without exception, pending full completion of review. Also, in my view, such a system should allow persons who were once admitted for lawful permanent residence to remain throughout.

But in other sorts of cases, involving people who entered without inspection or as nonimmigrants, mandatory early departure makes a fair amount of sense. After all, it simply means a wait back in the home country for the ultimate decision, not complete denial of a ruling on the merits. And removal, as noted earlier, should not significantly impair the individuals' ability to conduct further litigation, because in most instances the administrative record will already have been compiled, and arrangements for filing the necessary additional papers could be made before leaving. * * *

Perhaps the greatest benefit would be a long-run reduction in the workload of our adjudication and review system. Although this proposal permits some filings from abroad not now accepted, those additions should be more than offset by the virtual disappearance of appeals and motions filed only for the purpose of delaying the date of removal. Whereas such filings can now buy months or years in this country, under the new system they would buy nothing but added expense and possible added attorney's fees. Thus the individual would have to apply a more appropriate calculus in deciding just how strong his case appears and therefore whether further litigation is worthwhile. Decisions would turn, as they should, on the strength of the case, not on the chance that such a filing will artificially extend a clearly undeserved residence here.

Those who have legitimate claims of course should be able to pursue them and see them through all the stages of adjudication and review. An important part of this tentative proposal is therefore that successful appellants would return to this country at government expense. (This could apply, with some modification, to reopening as well.) This guarantee not only reflects simple fairness. It would also provide an added incentive for the Justice Department to look carefully at every appealed case or motion to reopen, before actual deportation, to see whether the Department would consent to a stay of deportation. If the decision from which appeal is taken appears substantially questionable, it will make financial (as well as humanitarian) sense to allow the alien to remain. But again, these are exactly the persons who should be allowed to stay, while those with almost no chance of success should be discouraged from clogging the system with baseless appeals and motions.

Martin, *Mandel, Cheng Fan Kwok, and Other Unappealing Cases: The Next Frontier of Immigration Reform,* 27 Va.J.Int'l L. 803, 816–19 (1987). *See also* Spiro, *Leave for Appeal: Departure as a Requirement for Review of Deportation Orders,* 25 San Diego L.Rev. 281 (1988).

3. The 1990 Act amended INA § 106(a)(3) to eliminate, in cases involving persons convicted of aggravated felonies, the automatic stay of deportation that usually accompanies petitions for review. Instead the courts of appeals have authority to decide whether a discretionary stay should be permitted. The stakes are high, because absent a stay, the alien is very likely to fall victim to the departure rule before the merits of his petition can be heard. Nevertheless, discretionary stays remain rare in such cases. Congress has foreclosed most forms of relief for deportation to this uniquely disfavored class of deportation respondents; hence it is difficult for aggravated felons to demonstrate a substantial possibility of success on appeal. *See, e.g., Jenkins v. INS,* 32 F.3d 11 (2d Cir.1994); *Ignacio v. INS,* 955 F.2d 295 (5th Cir.1992).

3. THE EFFECT OF MOTIONS TO REOPEN ON ADMINISTRATIVE AND JUDICIAL REVIEW

The case of *Bak v. INS,* p. 935 *supra,* reflects many of the salient rules that apply when an alien seeks reopening or reconsideration of exclusion or deportation proceedings. First, at present there is no time limit on filing such a motion. Protection against abuse of this device ostensibly derives from the relatively stringent substantive standards observed before the motion will be granted. *See generally INS v. Wang,* 450 U.S. 139, 101 S.Ct. 1027, 67 L.Ed.2d 123 (1981), considered in Chapter Seven, *supra.* Second, the motion is filed with whichever authority, BIA or immigration judge (or in other sorts of cases, INS officer), last considered the matter. *See* 8 C.F.R. §§ 3.2, 3.23(b), 103.5, 242.22. Bak, for example, properly filed his motion to reopen with the immigration judge, because he had waived his rights to take the initial deportation order up to the BIA. Third, in deportation cases, the alien has a new 90–day period after the denial of a motion to reopen or reconsider during which to seek review in the court of appeals under § 106(a). Under the doctrine observed by most courts, however, that denial does not then give the court of appeals authority to reach the merits of the original deportation order. The court considers only whether the BIA abused its discretion in denying the motion (or approving the immigration judge's denial of the motion). Finally, the pendency of a motion to reopen or reconsider with the administrative authorities does not operate to stay deportation. The alien must instead seek a discretionary stay from the IJ or BIA, as the case may be, or from an INS district director. 8 C.F.R. §§ 3.2, 3.3(a), 3.4, 3.23(b)(2), 242.22, 243.4.

Ongoing Controversies

Time limits. Should there be a time limit on filing motions to reopen? The availability of last-minute motions of this sort has drawn criticism as an easily exploited avenue of abuse, and Congress manifested concern about this issue in the 1990 Act. Section 545(d) of that Act directs the Attorney General to issue regulations establishing, *inter alia*, "a maximum time period for the filing of such motions." Proposed rules were finally promulgated, after considerable delay, in June 1994. 59 Fed.Reg. 29368 (1994). They would limit aliens to one motion to reopen and one motion to reconsider, and any such motion must be filed within 20 days of the decision at issue, except for asylum claims based on a showing of changed circumstances. The rules have not yet been made final. Would this change be good policy? In what circumstances might an alien wish to file a later motion? Or to put the issue another way, what scenarios for substantive relief from deportation would be effectively foreclosed by this procedural change?

Timing of judicial review. If the alien files a motion to reopen or reconsider within the 90–day period after the BIA acts on his appeal, must he also file a petition for review by that deadline in order to preserve his right to have the court consider the merits of the initial BIA ruling? The Ninth and Eleventh Circuits will dismiss such a petition, on the ground that the pending motion makes the underlying decision nonfinal and thus nonappealable. *See Ogio v. INS*, 2 F.3d 959 (9th Cir.1993); *Fleary v. INS*, 950 F.2d 711 (11th Cir.1992). The alien must instead delay petitioning until the BIA has ruled on the motion to reopen. Of course, at that point the court of appeals has jurisdiction, under this view, to review both the motion denial and the merits of the original deportation order. *Chudshevid v. INS*, 641 F.2d 780, 784 (9th Cir.1981).

Most other circuits that have considered the issue take precisely the opposite position, requiring a petition for review within the 90–day period if the original order is to be reviewed, even if a motion to reopen or reconsider is pending, and a second petition if the motion is denied and the alien then wants judicial review of that denial. *See, e.g., Stone v. INS*, 13 F.3d 934 (6th Cir.1994) (collecting cases on both sides of the issue), *cert. granted*, ___ U.S. ___, 114 S.Ct. 2098, 128 L.Ed.2d 661 (1994); *Nocon v. INS*, 789 F.2d 1028 (3d Cir.1986). And the Fifth and D.C. Circuits have tried to carve out a middle position, finding that only "good faith petitions" toll the time for seeking judicial review. *Pierre v. INS*, 932 F.2d 418 (1991); *Attoh v. INS*, 606 F.2d 1273 (D.C.Cir.1979).

Which of these positions makes the most sense? INA § 106(a)(6), added in 1990, provides for the consolidation of any review of a motion to reopen or reconsider with review of the deportation order. Which circuit court position is most consistent with this subsection? Should the third sentence of § 704 of the APA influence your choice among the circuits? One of the positions leaves the alien vulnerable to removal by INS before his claims can be fully heard. Which one? Why?

This division of views, which has persisted for many years, has been confusing for alien petitioners and their counsel, because choosing the wrong path can mean losing any right to meaningful court review. Presumably the Supreme Court's decision in *Stone, supra,* will end the uncertainty.

Stays. Giova v. Rosenberg, 379 U.S. 18, 85 S.Ct. 156, 13 L.Ed.2d 90 (1964), a brief per curiam decision discussed in *Cheng Fan Kwok,* p. 911 *supra,* has wound up tempting manipulation (by either aliens or immigration authorities) connected with motions to reopen. Under that decision, denials of such motions by the BIA in connection with deportation proceedings are not reviewable in the district courts but instead must be heard in the courts of appeals under INA § 106(a). This may mean a second (or even third) round of automatic stays under § 106(a)(3). Or it could mean that an alien who let the statutory period for appealing the original BIA order lapse can now forestall removal anyway by means of a last-minute motion to reopen.

Note, however, that the pendency of a motion to reopen before the BIA itself does not stay deportation. Therefore movants typically couple their motions with a request to the BIA for a stay of deportation. Apparently in order to avoid falling too easily into the Giova situation (although without directly acknowledging this dynamic), the Board now commonly follows this pattern: it denies the stay, usually on the basis that the movant has not shown a substantial likelihood of success on the merits, but it issues no ruling on the motion itself at that time, nor indeed until months later. The movant is therefore left vulnerable to the operation of the departure rule of § 106(c), unless he earlier petitioned for review of the initial BIA decision on the deportation order itself.

What is he to do? The only remedy left then may be to seek judicial review of the denial of the stay request. But in what forum? The decisions have almost uniformly held that the courts of appeals have no jurisdiction under INA § 106(a) in these circumstances, although those courts might have ancillary jurisdiction over the stay denial once the motion to reopen or reconsider is actually decided—provided that the alien remains in the country that long. *See, e.g., Dhangu v. INS,* 812 F.2d 455, 457–59 (9th Cir.1987) (collecting cases on the issue); 65 Interp.Rel. 725 (1988). Some courts base this conclusion explicitly on the policy ground that they wish to avoid application of the automatic stay provisions of § 106(a)(3), because then the "potential for abusive delay is obvious." *Gando–Coello v. INS,* 857 F.2d 25, 26 (1st Cir.1988), quoting *Bonilla v. INS,* 711 F.2d 43, 44 (5th Cir.1983).

But this jurisdictional holding leaves the district courts with a potentially difficult discretionary determination, and the court decisions reviewing stay denials in these circumstances are strikingly diverse. Because denial of a stay, coupled with the departure rule, may foreclose any consideration whatever of the merits of the motion to reopen, some courts have been quite ready to find that the immigration authorities abused their discretion in refusing a stay. *See, e.g., Blancada v. Turnage,* 891 F.2d 688 (9th Cir.1989); *Lopez–Alegria v. Ilchert,* 632 F.Supp. 932 (N.D.Cal.1986).

But others, focusing instead on the risk of abusive delay won by aliens through manipulating these rules, have imposed higher barriers to judicial relief. *See, e.g., Garay v. Slattery*, 23 F.3d 744 (2d Cir.1994) (alien may not receive judicial review of IJ's denial of stay unless he has exhausted remedies by seeking the same from INS district director, who also has authority to stay deportation pending a motion to reopen). Some courts have readily reversed because of the BIA's failure to provide an adequate explanation of its reasons for denying a stay, *see, e.g., Anderson v. McElroy*, 953 F.2d 803, 806 (2d Cir.1992); *Butros v. INS*, 804 F.Supp. 1336, 1339 (D.Ore.1991), whereas another court found no requirement that the Board explain its stay denials, *Narayan v. Ilchert*, 799 F.Supp. 1047, 1051 (N.D.Cal.1992).

SECTION E. HABEAS CORPUS IN DEPORTATION CASES

Most of this Chapter has considered the complexities that arose because of Congress' attempt to force all judicial review of deportation orders (and at least some related matters) into the courts of appeals under § 106(a). But a rather obscure provision buried at the end of that subsection seems to leave open a significant path for review in the district court. Section 106(a)(10) states simply that "any alien held in custody pursuant to an order of deportation may obtain judicial review thereof by habeas corpus proceedings." Just how wide a path into the district courts does this import? The next two cases consider that question and reach sharply different conclusions. The first case, incidentally, features Carlos Marcello—the same Carlos Marcello so much on the mind of Congress in 1961 when it passed § 106. In 1981 he was still making creative use of the possibilities for judicial review.

UNITED STATES EX REL. MARCELLO v. DISTRICT DIRECTOR

United States Court of Appeals, Fifth Circuit, 1981.
634 F.2d 964, cert. denied, 452 U.S. 917, 101 S.Ct. 3052, 69 L.Ed.2d 421 (1981).

GEE, CIRCUIT JUDGE:

Carlos Marcello, a foreign national permanently resident in the United States, was first ordered deported in 1953, almost thirty years ago, on the basis of a 1938 marijuana conviction. The order was not executed until 1961, however, when it was apparently executed illegally: arguably Marcello was shanghaied to Guatemala without prior notice to him or his attorney by means of a Guatemalan birth certificate that the Immigration and Naturalization Service (INS) may have known was a forgery. About a month later, Marcello reentered the United States without permission and, later in 1961, was the subject of another deportation order, this one based both on the 1938 conviction and the illegal entry after the apparently irregular 1961 deportation. The validity of neither the 1953 order nor of the 1961 order, insofar as it rests on the 1938 conviction, is contested here.

In 1972, Marcello filed an application for suspension of deportation, and in 1976 the Board of Immigration Appeals (Board) denied the application on two independent grounds: that Marcello had not shown the good moral character required for suspension by INA § 244(a) and that the Board did not choose to exercise its discretion to suspend deportation. The Board relied primarily on a 1968 conviction for assault and expressly stated that it did not consider Marcello's reentry after the 1961 deportation.

Marcello then filed this habeas action in federal district court. The court, after concluding that it had habeas jurisdiction, found that the Board both erred in finding that Marcello lacked good moral character and abused its discretion in denying suspension of deportation. The court vacated the Board's decision and remanded the cause for a determination of the validity of the 1961 deportation and a reassessment of Marcello's character. 472 F.Supp. 1199. We reverse.

Although the facts of Marcello's case are relatively straightforward, we find the legal issues posed by astute counsel on both sides both doubtful and difficult. We treat them in what seems to us their logical order.

Is Habeas Available as a Remedy?

Commendably, as a matter of advocacy, the government's first contention goes for the jugular. It urges us to hold that the district court lacked jurisdiction to pass on this matter at all. The contention is not without force, and the reasons why we must reject it require some explication.

In 1961, concerned by the lengthy delays in deportations occasioned by developing judicial precedent, the Congress attempted to streamline these arrangements. It did so by enacting § 106, which provides that the courts of appeals are to be the "sole" organs of review for final deportation orders and thus restricts resort to the district courts in such cases. The legislative purpose and background of this statute are extensively reviewed in *Foti v. Immigration Service,* 375 U.S. 217, 84 S.Ct. 306, 11 L.Ed.2d 281 (1963), and need not be further discussed here except in the one respect that is material.

The sweep of section 106 could not be a clean one because of Article I, section 9 of the Constitution, providing, among other things, that the Great Writ should not be suspended unless rebellion or invasion was in progress. This Congress recognized in section [106(a)(10)]of the statute, which provides that an "alien held in custody pursuant to an order of deportation" can seek judicial relief via habeas corpus. The government urges upon us that since Marcello is not presently "held in custody," but merely subjected to reporting requirements and travel restrictions, habeas relief is not available to him.

It is true that in 1961, when the amending act was passed, "custody" for habeas purposes meant primarily physical detention by the government. Since most aliens subject to deportation orders are not physically detained, the habeas exception to exclusive review in the courts of appeals was then a minor one. Since 1961, however, the Supreme Court has expanded the concept of custody for habeas proceedings after conviction to encompass any significant restraint on liberty, including parole, *Jones v. Cunningham,*

371 U.S. 236, 83 S.Ct. 373, 9 L.Ed.2d 285 (1963), and release on one's own recognizance, *Hensley v. Municipal Court,* 411 U.S. 345, 93 S.Ct. 1571, 36 L.Ed.2d 294 (1973). If this broader notion of custody applies generally to habeas under section [106(a)(10)], then the court below had jurisdiction, habeas commencing in the district court remains an alternative vehicle of review in most deportation proceedings, and the judicial reform that Congress attempted to bring about by enacting section 106—elimination of the district court step in review of deportation orders—is in great part stultified.

* * *

The legislative history of section 106 leaves little doubt that by enacting it Congress meant to establish two mutually exclusive modes for reviewing deportation orders: a general scheme of statutory review for cases where the alien was not "held in custody" and a provision for habeas review where he was. The Report of the House Committee provides on its first page that:

> The bill provides that with certain specified exceptions (made necessary by the unique subject matter of the bill), all the provisions of the act of December 29, 1950 (64 Stat. 1129, 68 Stat. 961; 5 U.S.C. 1031 et seq.), shall apply to and be the sole and exclusive procedure for judicial review of orders of deportation. In substance, an alien aggrieved by such an order may seek judicial review by filing a petition in the U.S. circuit court of appeals. The writ of habeas corpus is specifically reserved to an alien held in custody pursuant to an order of deportation.

Also included in the report is the text of a letter from then Deputy Attorney General, now Justice, Byron R. White to the chairman of the committee explaining, in response to his request, the Justice Department's view of the legislation and providing in pertinent part:

> Aliens seeking review of administrative orders should be given full and fair opportunity to do so, but the present possibilities of review pose undesirable obstacles to deportation of aliens who have been ordered deported and have had their day in court. An alien subject to a deportation order, having lost his case in a declaratory judgment or injunction proceeding may thereafter sue out of a writ of habeas corpus when taken into custody. Moreover, as the law now stands, it is possible to seek relief by habeas corpus repeatedly.

> The bill proposes to meet this problem by providing an exclusive method of review of deportation orders for aliens not in custody. This would be by petition for review in the appropriate court of appeals. The procedure is generally as prescribed by the act of December 29, 1950 (64 Stat. 1129; 68 Stat. 961; 5 U.S.C. 1031), relating to judicial review of orders of Federal agencies. The bill also provides "any alien held in custody pursuant to an order of deportation may obtain judicial review thereof by habeas corpus proceedings." In order to meet the problem of repeated

proceedings, no petition for review by the court of appeals or for habeas corpus may be entertained if the validity of the deportation order has been previously determined in any civil or criminal proceeding unless (1) the petition presents grounds which the court finds could not have been presented in the prior proceeding, or (2) the court finds that the remedy provided by the prior proceeding was inadequate or ineffective to test the validity of the order. Administrative findings of fact in deportation cases are made conclusive if supported by reasonable, substantial, and probative evidence.

Also in order to speed up the judicial review, the special statutory review proceeding provided in the bill must be instituted not later than 6 months from the date of the final order of deportation. At the present time there is no time limitation applicable to judicial review.

Finally, in the portion of the report entitled "Analysis of the Bill" it is asserted that "[t]he bill carefully preserves the writ of habeas corpus to an alien detained in custody pursuant to a deportation order."

It is apparent, therefore, that Congress meant by enacting section 106 to provide for two modes of review, one for those "held in custody" and one for those not so held. It remains for us to inquire what was intended by the phrase "held in custody." We think the statutory pattern and structure make plain that what was meant is actual, physical custody in a place of detention. Until that had occurred, we do not think the remedy of review by habeas corpus proceedings was meant to apply but rather that of review by direct appeal.

Examining the pattern of the statute, as well as legislative material such as the Justice Department letter quoted in part above, leaves little room for doubt that Congress attempted to severely limit the availability of habeas review. The basic pattern of review is meant to be by petition to the appellate court, not by resort to habeas in the district court.

Section [(a)(8)]of § 106, separated from section [(a)(10)], which preserves the habeas remedy to those "held in custody" only by a housekeeping provision, provides:

> nothing in this section shall be construed to require the Attorney General to defer deportation of an alien after the issuance of a deportation order because of the right of judicial review of the order granted by this section, or to relieve any alien from compliance with subsections (d) and (e) of section 242. Nothing contained in this section shall be construed to preclude the Attorney General from detaining or continuing to detain an alien or from taking him into custody pursuant to subsection (c) of section 242 at any time after the issuance of a deportation order[.]

Subsections (c), (d), and (e) of section 242, referred to above, provide respectively for a six-month period following the order of deportation or of the reviewing court for deportation of the alien, with authorization to the Attorney General to provide places of detention for those taken into custody; for mandatory supervision of aliens against whom final orders of deportation have been outstanding for so much as six months; and for criminal penalties for those seeking to evade deportation.

* * *

Thus, we view a congressional pattern for deportation proceedings that contemplates:

First, a final administrative deportation order;

Second, a six-month period [a] thereafter during which review in the court of appeals may be sought and during which the Attorney General may seek to deport the alien, with or without taking him into physical custody;

Third, mandatory and restrictive supervision of those aliens remaining here after the six-month period; and

Fourth, judicial review by means of habeas corpus proceedings for aliens held in custody.

Viewing this plan, it is at once plain that the Congress, when enacting section 106, did not see the mere existence of an outstanding deportation order against an alien as placing him in the status of "held in custody." Had it done so, a main procedural innovation of the enactment—eliminating resort to the district courts in the majority of cases—would have been an entire futility from its outset, since habeas in the district court would have been immediately available to all persons ordered deported, without any further assertion of "custody" over them, and resort to the district court routinely had, doubtless, by the delay-minded.

THE GOVERNMENT CONTENTION HERE

Reasoning from the above premises, the government contends that habeas is not available to Marcello here, since at the time his petition was filed he was not in physical custody. As we noted at the outset, the argument has force, a force derived from its congruence with apparent congressional intent in crafting and enacting the statutory plan.

At the time this petition was filed, when Marcello was subject only to the deportation order, we do not doubt that resort to the court of appeals was available to him as a remedy. Nor do we doubt that, having once so appealed, his right to obtain review in that mode would not have been disturbed by his being taken into "custody." If it were in the Attorney General's power to destroy the appellate remedy by moving under section [106(a)(8),] quoted above, to seize an appellant, it would be of little value indeed. Nor, once such an appeal has been lodged, would the alien be well advised to dismiss it upon coming into custody and institute habeas proceedings in its stead. Such a course—indeed a mere failure to appeal at all within the six-month period provided—would raise immediate questions of deliberate bypass of statutory remedies, and should the occurrence of

a. The Immigration Act of 1990 reduced this period, in most circumstances, to 90 days.—eds.

such a bypass be determined, habeas relief would likely be held unavailable as well—except perhaps for matters excepted by section 106(c).[10]

Here, however, the converse has occurred; Marcello filed his habeas petition at a time when, arguably, he was merely subject to a deportation order and not "held in custody." Perhaps a timely motion to dismiss, timely acted upon, might have forestalled this present cause before "custody" attached. This did not take place, however; and if the Supreme Court's expanded concepts of custody apply here, then Marcello presently is and for a long time has been in that condition.[11] We can discern little, if any, practical difference between the condition of Marcello and that of Hensley, who was held by the Court to have been in custody for habeas purposes. *Hensley v. Municipal Court,* 411 U.S. 345, 93 S.Ct. 1571, 36 L.Ed.2d 294 (1973). We conclude that since Marcello is presently in custody, though perhaps he was not for section 106 purposes when this habeas petition was filed, we have jurisdiction of his appeal.

Next, the government urges us to discern and apply to Marcello's attempt to obtain relief in this case, pursuant to 28 U.S.C. § 2241, the exhaustion requirements that are applied in actions brought pursuant to sections 2254 (state criminal convictions) and 2255 (federal ones). Only when the alien has availed himself of the normal mode of appeal provided him by section 106, it is said, should the courts entertain a plea for the extraordinary relief of habeas corpus. There is force and reason in this contention as well; however, to apply it now would be to bar Marcello from any review whatever, the six-month period for an appeal having long passed. Absent a finding of deliberate bypass of the direct appeal,[12] we do not believe such an outcome just or appropriate.

Finally, the government argues persuasively that Congress intended by section 106 to restrict habeas review to the constitutional minima, both as to availability and as to scope of review. There can be no doubt that there

---

10. Those "which the court finds could not have been presented in such prior proceeding, or the court finds that the remedy provided by such prior proceeding was inadequate or ineffective to test the validity of the order."

In the analogous context of 28 U.S.C. § 2255, we have often observed that a deliberate bypass of the provided remedy of a federal appeal generally forecloses raising by the extraordinary means of habeas issues that could have been asserted in the foregone appeal. We have specifically held under § 2255, moreover, that "habeas will not be permitted to substitute for an appeal when the choice to seek habeas relief is made to seize some legal or tactical advantage." The quest for such a tactical advantage—an added stage of review with its resulting delays—will doubtless usually be apparent in such cases as this.

11. We recognize that in *Cunningham* and *Hensley,* the parole and release cases discussed above in text, the release from (or absence of) physical custody occurred during

the habeas proceeding, so that a holding that these events terminated custody would have aborted the ongoing habeas proceedings. The Court lays no special stress on this circumstance, however, and in *Hensley* the petitioner had in fact never been in physical custody at any time after the conviction as to which he sought the writ. The conditions of his custody, moreover, appear less stringent than those applied here to Marcello. *See* 411 U.S. at 348, 93 S.Ct. at 1573. Marcello is under supervised parole, which requires him to report quarterly to the INS and notify it whenever he intends to leave Louisiana for more than 48 hours. Hensley seems to have been subject to no reporting requirements except to appear when ordered to do so. *Id.*

12. The court below did not make such a finding. In the circumstances of this case, and in view of Marcello's long experience with the laws governing deportation and his demonstrated ability in evading them, we might almost do so as a matter of law.

exists a constitutional core of habeas corpus authority, derived from the Common Law, guarded by Article I, section 9, and proof against congressional or executive tampering save in the event of invasion or rebellion. The statutory enactments overlaying the Great Writ—28 U.S.C. §§ 2241, 2254, and 2255—are, the argument runs, congressional additions to its scope that may be limited or withdrawn at the pleasure of the Congress so long as the constitutional core is not disturbed. This, according to the government, is what was done by section 106: a more than adequate statutory appellate remedy was provided, together with a highly restricted version of habeas—one embodying only the constitutional core, added solely to render the enactment constitutionally viable.

We agree with the government that such a plan and purpose would be a rational and probably desirable one. The difficulty here is that there is little or no indication, either in the statute or the legislative history, that it was the *congressional* plan and purpose in enacting section 106. To the contrary, as we have noted above, these materials seem to indicate that the Congress contemplated alternative methods of obtaining review, one available to aliens not "held in custody" and the other to those who were. We see little logic and less fairness in laying it down that the scope of review available to an alien may be narrowed by the occurrence of an event quite beyond his control, the action of the Attorney General in taking him into custody. Rather than such an effect, what Congress intended, we think, was to abolish in as many cases as possible the district court step in direct appeals and the employment by the alien of *both* modes of review successively. Our conclusion in this line is reinforced by the simple language of section [106(a)(10)], providing that "judicial *review*" of the deportation order may be had in habeas corpus proceedings by an alien in custody.

Thus, it appears that the government's attacks on jurisdiction and propriety of review here must, perhaps unfortunately, fail.

The Merits

Our standard of review of the order of the Board denying suspension of deportation, then, is the same as that on direct appeal of a final order of deportation. It is whether "reasonable, substantial, and probative evidence on the record considered as a whole" supports the order. § 106(a)(4). That question is one of law as to which we review the district court's decision free of the trammels of the clearly erroneous standard. The district court concluded that substantial evidence did not support the order. We disagree.

In a majority opinion, the Board dismissed Marcello's application for suspension of deportation, both for failure to establish statutory eligibility and in the exercise of its discretion. It did so on the basis of numerous facts detailed therein, all of which are supported by substantial evidence in the record and most of which are not seriously disputed. Among these are a 1938 drug conviction, a 1930 state conviction for assault and robbery, and a 1968 felony conviction for assault on a federal officer. In view of these matters, we cannot say that the Board's decision that Marcello failed to establish good moral character for the requisite ten-year period is unsupported by substantial evidence. Nor can we conclude that the Board's

BIA correct in finding no evid. for good moral; and BIA but wt abuse discret'n

discretion to deny suspension was abused, a ground independent of the statutory prerequisites. *United States ex rel. Hintopoulous v. Shaughnessy,* 353 U.S. 72, 77 S.Ct. 618, 1 L.Ed.2d 652 (1957).

* * *

The judgment of the district court is Reversed and that of the Board is Affirmed.

DANESHVAR v. CHAUVIN

United States Court of Appeals, Eighth Circuit, 1981.
644 F.2d 1248.

ARNOLD, CIRCUIT JUDGE.

Bizhan Daneshvar appeals the dismissal by the district court of that portion of his petition for writ of habeas corpus in which he sought judicial review of an order of the United States Immigration and Naturalization Service (INS) which required his deportation from the United States. The district court concluded that it lacked jurisdiction to review final deportation orders of the INS in a habeas corpus proceeding. We affirm.

Appellant Daneshvar is an Iranian citizen who entered this country as a nonimmigrant student, eventually enrolling at the University of Arkansas at Little Rock in June of 1978. His student status gave him a right to remain in the United States until June 29, 1979. On November 29, 1979, the INS issued a show cause order, pursuant to 8 C.F.R. § 242.1, alleging that Daneshvar had failed to maintain his nonimmigrant student status and was therefore subject to deportation. At a hearing held on January 9, 1980, Daneshvar appeared with an attorney and admitted that he was deportable. The immigration judge subsequently ordered his deportation but permitted Daneshvar to leave the United States voluntarily. Daneshvar did not appeal the judge's order.

Daneshvar, however, did not leave the United States within the time allowed. He instead filed a motion to reopen or reconsider the deportation order. On September 12, 1980, while the motion to reopen was still pending, Daneshvar was arrested by the United States Border Patrol, acting pursuant to the deportation order,[2] and placed in jail. On September 14, 1980, Daneshvar petitioned the district court for a writ of habeas corpus. He claimed that the order of deportation in his case threatened to deprive him of liberty without due process of law because, among other reasons, he did not understand English well enough to appreciate the nature of the proceedings against him. The district court moved with appropriate solicitude for the right of personal liberty. The court admitted Daneshvar to bail, perhaps feeling that his motion to reopen, which had been pending for some four months, was not being treated with reasonable expedition. In addition, the district court ordered the INS not to deport Daneshvar until further order of the district court or of a court of appeals

---

2. The filing of a motion to reopen or for reconsideration does not stay the execution of   a deportation order. 8 C.F.R. § 242.22.

having jurisdiction. In all other respects, however, the petition was dismissed for want of jurisdiction. The district court held that its habeas jurisdiction was limited to review of ancillary or preliminary actions of the INS (for example, its taking Daneshvar into custody while delaying a ruling on his motion to reopen), and that the courts of appeals had exclusive jurisdiction to review the final order of deportation itself. A partial final judgment was entered under Fed.R.Civ.P. 54(b), and Daneshvar then appealed.[4]

Daneshvar argues that the district court had jurisdiction to consider the validity of the deportation order itself. He relies on two provisions of law. First, Section 279 of the Immigration and Nationality Act of 1952, provides:

> The district courts of the United States shall have jurisdiction of all causes, civil and criminal, arising under any of the provisions of this subchapter.

The reference to "this subchapter" denotes Subchapter II of Chapter 12 of Title 8 of the United States Code, and includes 8 U.S.C. §§ 1151–1362 [INA §§ 201–293]. In addition, we are cited to Section [106(a)(10)]:

> any alien held in custody pursuant to an order of deportation may obtain judicial review thereof by habeas corpus proceedings.

The government, on the other hand, relies on another portion of Section 106(a), * * * under which petitions for review in a court of appeals are

> the sole and exclusive procedure for, the judicial review of all final orders of deportation. . . .

The question presented here is whether the district courts have jurisdiction to review final orders of deportation when the plaintiff's form of action is habeas corpus. The answer is not immediately clear from the language of the three statutes involved, pertinent parts of which we have quoted. These provisions present, to say the least, a question of interpretation. We have no great difficulty with the suggestion that § 279, a general grant of jurisdiction to the district courts of cases arising under the immigration title of the 1952 Act, is applicable here. *Foti v. Immigration & Naturalization Serv.*, 375 U.S. 217, 84 S.Ct. 306, 11 L.Ed.2d 281 (1963), suffices to dispose of this contention. There, the Supreme Court explained that Section 106(a) of the Act, as added by the 1961 amendment, was intended to make a definite change in pre-existing law, including § 279. "The key feature of the congressional plan . . . was the elimination of the previous initial step in obtaining judicial review—a suit in a District Court—and the resulting restriction of review to Courts of Appeals, subject only to the certiorari jurisdiction of this Court." * * * "[T]he declared purpose of § 106(a) [is] to eliminate the District Court stage of the judicial review process in an effort to prevent dilatory tactics." * * * *Foti* holds

---

4. In addition to appealing to this Court, the appellant has filed with the United States Court of Appeals for the Sixth Circuit an appeal from the denial by the INS of his motion to reopen or reconsider the deportation order, which was denied on September 16, 1980. This case was pending in the Sixth Circuit at the time of the oral argument in the instant appeal before this Court.

that discretionary determinations of the Attorney General, relating to the suspension of deportation under § 244(a)(5) of the Act, are, like final orders of deportation themselves, reviewable exclusively in the courts of appeals.

Later cases elaborate the line between final orders of deportation reviewable only in courts of appeals, and certain other kinds of orders reviewable in district courts. See *Immigration & Naturalization Serv. v. Stanisic*, 395 U.S. 62, 68 n. 6, 89 S.Ct. 1519, 1523 n. 6, 23 L.Ed.2d 101 (1969) (denial by the Attorney General of an application to withhold deportation, under Section 243(h) of the Act, to a country where the alien would be subject to persecution, is reviewable in the district courts, "[b]ecause the ... determination [to deny the application] was not pursuant to § 242(b)," the provision specifically referred to in the 1961 amendment);[a] *Cheng Fan Kwok v. Immigration & Naturalization Serv.*, 392 U.S. 206, 215, 88 S.Ct. 1970, 1975, 20 L.Ed.2d 1037 (1968) (" ... Congress quite deliberately restricted the application of § 106(a) to orders entered during proceedings conducted under § 242(b), or directly challenging deportation orders themselves" (footnote omitted)); *Giova v. Rosenberg*, 379 U.S. 18, 85 S.Ct. 156, 13 L.Ed.2d 90 (1964) (per curiam) (courts of appeals have exclusive jurisdiction to review denials of motions to reopen § 242(b) deportation proceedings); *Mendez v. Major*, 340 F.2d 128 (8th Cir.1965); *Chadha v. Immigration & Naturalization Serv.*, 634 F.2d 408 (9th Cir. 1980) (review of final deportation orders includes review of matters upon which the final order is contingent); *Reyes v. Immigration & Naturalization Serv.*, 571 F.2d 505 (9th Cir.1978).

Some of the distinctions drawn by these cases among different types of orders relating to deportation are hard to follow, at least for us. But the common thread running through all the cases is that judicial review of final orders of deportation, when the question of deportability is in question, is exclusively in the courts of appeals. This is so even when deportability under the statute is conceded, but the alien plaintiff claims that the statute itself is unconstitutional. *Shodeke v. Attorney General*, 391 F.Supp. 219 (D.D.C.1975). In the instant case deportation proceedings were commenced under Section 242(b) of the Act, and the final order of deportation was entered in those proceedings. Attempts by Daneshvar to contest the validity of this order fall squarely within Section 106(a), and that specific, later-enacted provision must prevail, as the Supreme Court held in *Foti*, over the earlier-enacted general grant of jurisdiction to the district courts.

It remains to consider the habeas corpus provision, Section [106(a)(10)], which is on its face an exception to the general rule of exclusivity set out in Section 106(a). Daneshvar argues that the habeas corpus paragraph must be given the effect of creating district-court jurisdiction, even to review final orders of deportation, when the affected person is in custody. Although that construction of the statute is unquestionably one that the words will bear, we decline to accept it. The proper solution to this problem, we think, is explained by Judge Becker in *United States ex*

---

a. Under regulations adopted after *Stanisic* was decided, applications for relief under § 243(h) are now adjudicated, in many circumstances, as part of the deportation hearing before the immigration judge. *See* Chapter Eight.—eds.

not merits

rel. Parco v. Morris, 426 F.Supp. 976, 978 n. 4 (E.D.Pa.1977). There, habeas corpus jurisdiction in the district courts was upheld where plaintiff was not seeking review of the merits of the deportation order itself, but only to contest the denial of a stay of deportation. "Habeas corpus is an appropriate proceeding to review the denial of discretionary relief from deportation where deportability itself is not in issue." "Custody," in the present context, refers not only to confinement in jail, as in Daneshvar's case, but also that restriction of movement resulting from any final order of deportation. *United States ex rel. Parco v. Morris, supra,* 426 F.Supp. at 978 n. 4. The suggestion that Section [106(a)(10)]be construed to create district-court habeas jurisdiction whenever the petitioner is in custody, while the general language of Section 106(a) would confer jurisdiction on courts of appeals to review final orders of deportation at the suit of petitioners who are not in custody, does not, therefore, make a great deal of sense. Under this interpretation, the exception would swallow the rule. Since the issuance of a final order of deportation itself subjects the affected person to "custody" for habeas purposes, it is hard to see what, if anything, would be left of the courts of appeals' exclusive jurisdiction. It makes more sense, and furthers the congressional purpose to avoid delay, explained in *Foti,* to construe Section 106(a) to confer exclusive jurisdiction on courts of appeals in all cases where the validity of a final order of deportation is drawn in question, and to limit Section [106(a)(10)]to review of the denial of discretionary relief where deportability itself is not an issue.

The district court's memorandum and order, accompanying the judgment from which this appeal is taken, dismissed for want of jurisdiction "the petitioner's request for review of the administrative determinations regarding his deportation." This decision was based on what we hold to be a correct construction of the jurisdictional statutes, and the judgment is

Affirmed.[6]

Notes

1. Both courts note that concepts of "custody" have expanded in habeas corpus cases handed down since Congress enacted § 106 in 1961. The key decisions were *Jones v. Cunningham,* 371 U.S. 236, 83 S.Ct. 373, 9 L.Ed.2d 285 (1963), which held that a former prisoner on parole was sufficiently in custody to claim federal jurisdiction in habeas, and *Hensley v. Municipal Court,* 411 U.S. 345, 93 S.Ct. 1571, 36 L.Ed.2d 294 (1973), which reached the same conclusion as to a person at large on his own recognizance in advance of the commencement of his sentence. But those cases are not immigration cases. The first paragraph of each opinion states that the Supreme Court was called upon there to construe the meaning of "custody" in a specific federal statute, 28 U.S.C.A. § 2241.

6. Appellant, we assume, remains at large on the bond fixed by the district court, and is protected by that court's order of October 6, 1980, enjoining appellees from deporting him. In view of the fact that Daneshvar has a petition for review of the order denying his motion to reopen pending in the Sixth Circuit, pursuant to which his deportation has been stayed by that court, he may no longer need the protection of the injunction entered by the district court in this case. * * *

Although that statute is obviously closely related to the habeas provisions in INA § 106, must we assume that Congress intended to base the reach of the immigration provision on the changing boundaries of the other remedy?

At the very least the fundamental setting is quite different. Section 2241 governs when state prisoners may have access to the federal courts by means of habeas corpus. Had the parolee in *Jones* been found not to be in custody, for example, he might never have had an opportunity to raise his constitutional claims in a federal forum. The aliens in the two cases here clearly have, or had, opportunities for federal court review, by means of the regular petition for review envisioned by § 106(a). Would this difference support a distinction in the way that "custody" is understood in the two settings?

Daneshvar does not seem aware of this possible difference. In this respect, it is in the company of several other courts, which have rather hastily assumed that the Supreme Court's expanded custody notions automatically applied with equal vigor to § 106(a)(10). *See, e.g., Flores v. INS,* 524 F.2d 627 (9th Cir.1975); *Sotelo-Mondragon v. Ilchert,* 653 F.2d 1254 (9th Cir.1980); *United States ex rel. Parco v. Morris,* 426 F.Supp. 976, 978 n. 4 (E.D.Pa.1977).

The *Marcello* court, in contrast, is apparently aware of the potential distinctions. Moreover, it devotes several paragraphs to showing why the 1961 Congress unmistakably intended that habeas be available to deportation respondents only when they are actually taken into physical custody. Just why then does the court end up finding Marcello sufficiently in custody to invoke the habeas remedy, given the limited restrictions on his liberty described in footnote 11? The third paragraph of the section of the court's opinion headed "The Government Contention Here" contains the crucial passages, but there the court's musings sound a bit like T.S. Eliot's *The Love Song of J. Alfred Prufrock.* The shift from "if" to "since" (referring to application of the *Hensley* standards) is so subtle as to elude recognition.[23] But the question remains: should the *Hensley* standards govern here? Would a strict physical custody requirement narrow the otherwise formidable loophole that § 106(a)(10) potentially represents in a more useful and constructive manner than the *Daneshvar* approach, which focuses instead on narrowing the scope of issues to be raised?

Whatever the murkiness of the ruling in *Marcello* itself, the Fifth Circuit now appears to treat it as imposing a strong physical custody requirement. In *Umanzor v. Lambert,* 782 F.2d 1299, 1302 (5th Cir.1986), the court described the former decision as holding that Congress requires "actual, physical custody in a place of detention" before jurisdiction arises under INA § 106(a)(10). *See also El–Youssef v. Meese,* 678 F.Supp. 1508 (D.Kan.1988) (adopting *Marcello* approach over *Daneshvar,* on the understanding that habeas is then available only to individuals actually "de-

---

23. The same poetic talents are displayed when the court discusses the exhaustion of remedies and "deliberate bypass" doctrines. Just why is it, again, that Marcello is not precluded from habeas corpus review on these grounds? Other decisions have been more willing to reject habeas petitions under § 106(a)(10) on the ground of deliberate bypass. *See, e.g., Okechukwu v. United States,* 825 F.Supp. 139 (S.D.Tex.1993); *Singh v. INS,* 825 F.Supp. 143 (S.D.Tex.1993).

tained"). *But cf. Williams v. INS,* 795 F.2d 738 (9th Cir.1986) (apparently accepting *Marcello* approach as to the wide range of issues reachable on habeas, but accepting as well the expanded *Jones/Hensley* concept of "custody").

2. The *Daneshvar* court strives for an interpretation of INA § 106(a)(10) that will avoid having the exception (district court review on habeas) swallow the rule (court of appeals review). But it is far from apparent that the court has succeeded. Its guideline appears to be as follows: Direct challenges to deportability can be considered only in the courts of appeals; denial of discretionary relief that does not implicate deportability can be considered in the district courts.

The problem arises because the latter category is potentially vast. Indeed, only a small minority of deportation respondents challenge deportability itself. Such a challenge would require a genuine factual dispute such as, for example, whether a permanent resident alien who became a public charge did so from causes that "have arisen since entry." INA § 241(a)(5). Most deportations, however, involve those who entered without inspection or overstayed a nonimmigrant admission—matters that usually admit of easy proof and rarely provoke factual contests. Even when lawful permanent residents are served with an order to show cause, deportation is usually based on criminal convictions that are not subject to collateral attack in the deportation proceeding.

The overwhelming majority of deportation respondents, then, admit deportability but seek to remain in the United States based on some form of relief, such as suspension under § 244, or asylum under § 208, or a § 212(c) waiver. All these relief issues would appear to be reviewable in a district court on habeas under *Daneshvar,* even though they are exactly the same kinds of issues that could be raised in the courts of appeals upon a petition to review, under the holdings in *Foti* and *Giova.* Some courts have applied *Daneshvar* in just such a sweeping manner, and without any requirement that the applicant be in actual physical custody. *See, e.g., Salehi v. District Director,* 796 F.2d 1286 (10th Cir.1986).

The *Daneshvar* framework might be more workable if it further subdivided the categories of "discretionary relief where deportability itself is not an issue." The first subcategory would consist of those forms of discretionary relief passed on by the immigration judge in the § 242(b) hearing and reviewable under *Foti* or *Giova* in the courts of appeals under § 106(a). The second would comprise those forms of discretionary relief that are not incorporated into the § 242(b) proceedings, and which therefore must be heard by the district courts under *Cheng Fan Kwok.* The first set of issues, under this reformulated *Daneshvar* framework, could only be heard by the courts of appeals and could not be reached on habeas under § 106(a)(10). The second, unreachable on petition for review, would be exactly the kinds of matters district courts should consider under § 106(a)(10). Of course, these issues could probably also be heard in district court in actions for declaratory or injunctive relief under the APA, with jurisdiction founded on 28 U.S.C.A. § 1331 or possibly INA § 279. Would such a reworking of *Daneshvar* more appropriately honor congressional intent? Is it a better approach for these purposes than *Marcello,* as construed in *Umanzor* and *El–Youssef?*

The court in *Galaviz-Medina v. Wooten,* 27 F.3d 487, 492 (10th Cir.1994), *cert. denied,* ___ U.S. ___, 115 S.Ct. 741, 130 L.Ed.2d 643 (1995), appears to have taken a view quite similar to the reworked *Daneshvar* framework suggested in this Note. It disallowed habeas review when the alien wishes to challenge deportability or "the denial of discretionary relief made as part of the underlying deportation hearings." Such challenges must go to the court of appeals under INA § 106(a)(1), within the time limits specified. The full import of *Galaviz* is somewhat unclear, however, because another part of the decision states that review under § 106(a)(10) allows only for "claims which are cognizable under traditional habeas proceedings such as allegations of constitutional due process or equal protection violations."

3. Whatever the proper scope of habeas review in dealing with deportation orders and forms of relief, it is clear that § 106(a)(10) is finding increasing acceptance as the principal, and perhaps sole, source of jurisdiction to review discretionary decisions by district directors, immigration judges, or the BIA to deny a stay of deportation, particularly when such stays are sought in connection with a motion to reopen or reconsider which has not yet been finally adjudicated (discussed in Section D.3 of this Chapter). *See, e.g., Dhangu v. INS,* 812 F.2d 455, 457–59 (9th Cir.1987); *Lemos-Garcia v. Weiss,* 797 F.Supp. 126 (D.Conn.1991) (both summarizing cases on this point).

Chapter Ten

CITIZENSHIP

Congress enacted the first federal nationality and citizenship law in 1790, 85 years before it initiated federal regulation of immigration. This timing reflects the different treatment accorded the two realms of governmental competence in the Constitution itself. Although federal authority to control immigration, as we have seen, must be derived by implication from other portions of the constitutional text or from certain structural features of the nation it created, the Constitution explicitly vests in Congress the power to "establish an uniform Rule of Naturalization." Art. I, Sec. 8, cl. 4.[1]

This venerable field of law presents a host of interesting historical, philosophical, constitutional, administrative and technical issues worthy of a more extended treatment than we can provide here. This chapter, therefore, will be even more selective than the earlier chapters on immigration. We shall examine briefly the rules governing acquisition of U.S. citizenship by birth and by naturalization, and we shall look at the modern rules governing loss of nationality.[2] In each setting we consider a few of

---

1. The requirement of uniformity should not be read as a broad equal protection guarantee—that is, as an authorization to courts to strike down naturalization requirements whenever different conditions are prescribed for various categories of aspiring citizens. In fact, such varying requirements are an established feature of our naturalization laws. The Framers mandated "an uniform Rule" in order to change the confusing practice that had prevailed under the Articles of Confederation, when each state separately enacted its own naturalization rules. *See* The Federalist No. 42 (J. Madison); J. Kettner, *The Development of American Citizenship,* 1608–1870, at 213–32 (1978). Judicial decisions generally have refused to find that the Constitution requires more of Congress than geographic uniformity in this sense. *See, e.g., Samras v. United States,* 125 F.2d 879 (9th Cir.1942), *cert. denied,* 317 U.S. 634, 63 S.Ct. 34, 87 L.Ed. 511 (1942). Under the prevailing in-

terpretation, moreover, even certain kinds of geographic disparities are allowed. *See Petition of Lee Wee,* 143 F.Supp. 736 (S.D.Cal. 1956) (gambling offenses preclude a finding of good moral character necessary for naturalization, even though the same behavior would not have been criminal in a nearby locality).

2. We will generally use "citizenship" and "nationality" as equivalent terms here. There is, however, a potential distinction, worth noting in passing, between a "citizen" of the United States, who ordinarily enjoys full rights of participation in the national polity, and a noncitizen "national" of the United States, who owes allegiance to this country but does not enjoy the full measure of such political rights. *See* INA § 101(a)(21), (22) (defining the terms "national" and "national of the United States"). In addition, at times in our history some noncitizen nationals did not have the right of

---

the important cases establishing or explaining the governing standards, or illustrating their implementation. But we begin with a rather impressionistic review of the concept of citizenship itself. What does it mean? What should it mean? Why the intense interest in its acquisition or loss?

SECTION A. IS CITIZENSHIP IMPORTANT?

American citizenship is the major objective of many aliens who come to the United States—the ultimate culmination of the American immigration process. Naturalization ceremonies tend to be occasions for great joy, the outpouring of emotion, heartfelt expressions of attachment to the new citizens' new land.

On the other hand, large numbers of resident aliens seem quite indifferent to the blandishments of U.S. citizenship. Many never make the change, remaining here indefinitely, as they are entitled to do, in permanent resident status. Others eventually become U.S. citizens, but plainly find little reason to hurry to change their nationality. Although patterns vary considerably by country of origin, the median number of years of residence before naturalization has held quite steady at eight, and over a quarter of the 240,252 people who naturalized in 1992 had come to the United States before 1980. 1992 INS Statistical Yearbook 127–28, 146. An intensive study of the 1977 immigration cohort found that only 38.7 percent of that group had naturalized by 1992 (but the study was not able

free movement from the outlying territory to the "metropolitan" United States. *See* Philippine Independence Act of 1934, Ch. 84, § 8, 48 Stat. 462 (providing that Filipinos, who were at the time U.S. nationals, were to be treated as aliens for purposes of the immigration laws).

The distinction between citizen and mere national was far more important around the turn of the century, when the United States acquired numerous outlying territorial possessions, principally as a result of the Spanish–American War. The local populations were held to American allegiance, but were not considered citizens. The Supreme Court struggled, in a series of decisions that came to be known as the Insular Cases, with questions of personal status and constitutional protections in such circumstances, finally accepting a somewhat reduced level of protection in those territories held not to be "incorporated" into the United States. *See, e.g., Balzac v. Porto Rico*, 258 U.S. 298, 42 S.Ct. 343, 66 L.Ed. 627 (1922); *Gonzales v. Williams*, 192 U.S. 1, 24 S.Ct. 177, 48 L.Ed. 317 (1904); G & R §§ 11.3b, 12.7; Coudert, *The Evolution of the Doctrine of Territorial Incorporation*, 26 Colum.L.Rev. 823 (1926). The continued vitality of the incorporation doctrine is unclear. *See Reid v. Covert*, 354 U.S. 1, 14, 77 S.Ct. 1222, 1229, 1 L.Ed.2d 1148 (1957) (plurality opinion); *Torres v.*

Puerto Rico, 442 U.S. 465, 468–70, 99 S.Ct. 2425, 2428–29, 61 L.Ed.2d 1 (1979); and *id.* at 475–76 (Brennan, J., concurring in the judgment). *See also United States v. Verdugo–Urquidez*, 494 U.S. 259, 110 S.Ct. 1056, 108 L.Ed.2d 222 (1990) (plurality opinion) (Fourth Amendment does not apply to search by American officials of Mexican residence of a Mexican citizen and resident). For an excellent overview of these issues, see Neuman, *Whose Constitution?*, 100 Yale L. J. 909 (1991).

In recent decades, the nationality questions associated with U.S. territories have become relatively insignificant (even though other associated political issues have remained complex, *see, e.g.,* Time for Decision: The United States and Puerto Rico (J. Heine ed. 1984)). Congress has gradually either granted full citizenship to the local population, as happened, for example, with Puerto Rico, or passed legislation leading to the independence of the territory, as happened with the Philippines. Today only American Samoa and Swains Island constitute outlying possessions of the United States for purposes of the nationality laws, and essentially only the local inhabitants there constitute noncitizen nationals. *See* INA § 101(a)(29). *See generally* A. Leibowitz, Defining Status: A Comprehensive Analysis of United States Territorial Relations (1989).

to adjust for those who failed to naturalize owing to death or emigration). *Id.* at 128.

Moreover, the Supreme Court sometimes seems to be of two minds on the issue. An important line of equal protection cases, beginning with *Graham v. Richardson,* 403 U.S. 365, 91 S.Ct. 1848, 29 L.Ed.2d 534 (1971), purposely made the difference between citizen and alien count for a good deal less than it traditionally had. In many settings, the very distinction amounts, the Court has said, to a "suspect classification," and States may employ the distinction between aliens and citizens only if they demonstrate compelling reasons for doing so. *See* p. 162 *supra.*

Not too many years before that, however, the same Court, after a decade of sharp division, concluded that a person could not be involuntarily deprived of U.S. citizenship. *Afroyim v. Rusk,* 387 U.S. 253, 87 S.Ct. 1660, 18 L.Ed.2d 757 (1967). In that case, and in preceding cases that laid the groundwork for such a holding (to be reviewed later in this Chapter), several Justices wrote at length about the preciousness of citizenship status. *See, e.g., Trop v. Dulles,* 356 U.S. 86, 101, 78 S.Ct. 590, 598, 2 L.Ed.2d 630 (1958) (plurality opinion) (deprivation of citizenship "is a form of punishment more primitive than torture, for it destroys for the individual the political existence that was centuries in the development"); *Kennedy v. Mendoza–Martinez,* 372 U.S. 144, 160, 83 S.Ct. 554, 563, 9 L.Ed.2d 644 (1963) ("American citizenship * * * is 'one of the most valuable rights in the world today' ").

Which view is correct? Is citizenship important? Should it be? For what purposes? The debate is an ancient one. The readings that follow reflect some of its main contours.

ALEXANDER M. BICKEL, CITIZEN OR PERSON?: WHAT IS NOT GRANTED CANNOT BE TAKEN AWAY

The Morality of Consent, Ch. 2 (1975).

In the view both of the ancients and of modern liberal political theorists, the relationship between the individual and the state is largely defined by the concept of citizenship. It is by virtue of his citizenship that the individual is a member of the political community, and by virtue of it that he has rights. Remarkably enough—and as I will suggest, happily—the concept of citizenship plays only the most minimal role in the American constitutional scheme.

* * *

There is a great deal to the Hobbesian notion that we are all really subjects held to obedience, if no longer by divine command then by a simple fear of our fellows. To the extent that this explanation does not fit our situation or ought not, to the extent that it is not the true or the good explanation, liberal as well as classic thought has considered us citizens who owe obedience, as we owe allegiance, chiefly because we are self-governing, and as self-governing because we are citizens. When they freed themselves from subjection, the makers of the French Revolution called each other citizen, denoting their participation in the state; so the communists later called each other comrade, denoting their common allegiance to an ideology, a movement.

Both classic and later liberal statements of the duty to obey law thus subsume the concept of citizenship, even though not as a wholly necessary or sufficient condition. Also subsumed are the clarity and economy of the law to be obeyed, and of the process by which that law is formed. The classic among classics is, of course, the statement of Socrates as reported in the *Crito:* "In war as in the court of justice, and everywhere, you must do whatever your state and your country tell you to do, or you must persuade them that their commands are unjust." It is the citizen who has the standing to persuade his fellow citizens that what they are doing is unjust. Our own system does not resemble the one subsumed in the statement of Socrates in clarity or in economy of application, and not in the immediacy with which the citizen can affect the process of law-formation. That makes a difference; so, also, although less directly and certainly, does the striking ambivalence, the great ambiguity that has surrounded the concept of citizenship in our law and in our tradition.

The original Constitution, prior to Reconstruction, contained no definition of citizenship and precious few references to the concept altogether. The subject was not entirely ignored by the Framers. They empowered Congress to make a uniform rule of naturalization. But, wishing to attract immigrants, they rejected nativist suggestions for strict naturalization requirements, such as long residence. They plainly assumed that birth as well as naturalization would confer citizenship but they made nothing depend on it explicitly, aside from a few offices: president, congressman, senator, but notably not judge. State citizenship provided one, but only one of several, means of access to federal courts (under the diversity jurisdiction) and conferred the not unqualified right, under the privileges and immunities clause of article IV, section 2, to be treated generally by each state in the same fashion as its own citizens were treated. Discrimination on the sole ground of not holding citizenship in a given state is forbidden; discrimination on other and reasonable grounds is, however, allowed. Discriminations on the basis of residence, which is different in concept from citizenship, are permitted; and where state citizenship is a reasonable requirement, as for officeholding, discrimination is not prohibited. But if no special reason restricts a privilege sensibly to the state's own citizens, the state must extend it to the citizens of other states as well.

There is no further mention of citizenship in the Constitution before the Civil War amendments, even though there were plenty of occasions for making rights depend on it. The Preamble speaks of "We the people of the United States," not, as it might have, of we the citizens of the United States at the time of the formation of this union. And the Bill of Rights throughout defines rights of people, not of citizens. * * * To be sure, implicitly, the citizen had a right freely to enter the country, whereas the alien did not; and implicitly also the citizen, while abroad, could be held to an obligation of allegiance and might under very specific conditions be found guilty of the crime of treason for violating it, while the alien generally could not. But these were hardly critical points, as the Framers

demonstrated by saying nothing explicit about them. It remains true that
the original Constitution presented the edifying picture of a government
that bestowed rights on people and persons, and held itself out as bound by
certain standards of conduct in its relations with people and persons, not
with some legal construct called citizen. This idyllic state of affairs was
rudely disturbed by the crisis of the 1850s. Like so much else, it foundered
on the contradiction of slavery. A majority of the Supreme Court seized on
the concept of citizenship in the *Dred Scott* case,[1] in a futile and misguided
effort, by way of a legalism and an unfounded legalism at that, to resolve
the controversy over the spread of slavery.

Dred Scott, the slave of one John Sandford in Missouri, brought suit in
the Circuit Court of the United States for his freedom. * * * However,
Scott could come into federal court only by claiming to be a citizen of
Missouri; Sandford, who held Scott in Missouri, was himself a citizen of
New York. Scott could not be a citizen of Missouri, Sandford said, because
he was "a negro of African descent, whose ancestors were of pure African
blood, and who were brought into this country and sold as slaves." If Scott
was not a citizen of Missouri, there could be no federal jurisdiction, and
that was an end of the matter. The significance of citizenship was in
question. * * *

In the Supreme Court the majority opinion was written by Chief
Justice Roger Taney, Marshall's successor, * * * [who was] a political
progressive—if that is a correct designation for a Jacksonian populist—an
economic liberal, and a racist who persuaded himself by mid-life that
slavery was not only a necessary evil, if that, but right as well. Taney
combined personal kindness with public ferocity, he freed his own slaves
and cared for them afterward, but he was opposed politically to any large-
scale manumission. He was an able man, broken on the rack of slavery.
Dred Scott, Taney held, could not be a citizen, not because he was a slave
but because, even if he were a free man, he was "a negro of African
descent, whose ancestors were of pure African blood, and who were brought
into this country and sold as slaves." The words "people of the United
States" and "citizens" are synonymous terms, he held, used interchangeably in the Constitution: "They both describe the political body who,
according to our republican institutions, form the sovereignty, and who
hold the power and conduct the government through their representatives.
They are what we familiarly call the [single] 'sovereign people' and every
citizen is one of this people, and a constituent member of this sovereignty."

At the time of the framing of the Constitution Taney continued, even
free Negroes were not viewed as being a portion of "this people," the
constituent membership of the sovereignty. They were not viewed as
citizens or as entitled to any of the rights and privileges the Constitution
held out to citizens. In this Taney was probably wrong, as the dissenters, I
think, demonstrated. Taney's Constitution held out rights and privileges
to citizens, even though the document itself holds out few to citizens as
such, does not bother to define the status of citizenship, and altogether
appears to set very little store by it. Taney, by an *ipse dixit,* argued that

4. Scott v. Sandford, 60 U.S. (19 Howard)
393 (1857).

when the Constitution says "people" it means the same thing as citizens. Yet the Constitution says citizens rarely, and people most of the time, and never the two interchangeably.

When the Constitution was formed, Taney said, Negroes were "considered as a subordinate and inferior class of beings, who had been subjugated by the dominant race, and, whether emancipated or not, yet remained subject to their authority, and had no rights or privileges but such as those who held the power and the Government might choose to grant them." Now, this is a perversion of the complex, guilt-ridden, and highly ambivalent attitude of the Framers toward slavery, and of their vague, and possibly evasive and culpably less than candid expectation of some future evolution away from it. It is possible to have some compassion for the Framers in their travail over the contradiction of slavery. It is not possible to have compassion for Taney's hardening of the Framers' position, his stripping it of its original aspirations to decency as well as of its illusions, and his reattribution to the Framers of the position thus altered. * * *

The original Constitution's innocence of the concept of citizenship was thus violated in the *Dred Scott* case, in an encounter with the contradiction of slavery. A rape having occurred, innocence could never be restored. But remarkably enough, after a period of reaction to the trauma, we resumed behaving as if our virginity were intact and with a fair measure of credibility at that. Fewer than four months after the Thirteenth Amendment became law, in December 1865, Congress enacted the Civil Rights Act of 1866. With the express intention of overruling *Dred Scott,* the act declared that "all persons born in the United States and not subject to any foreign power, excluding Indians not taxed, are hereby declared to be citizens of the United States." This was the first authoritative definition of citizenship in American law. It had become necessary to make clear that race and descent from slaves was no ground of exclusion. * * * The *Dred Scott* decision used the concept of citizenship negatively, as exclusionary. It indicated who was not under the umbrella of rights and privileges and status and thus entrenched the subjection of the Negro in the Constitution. The Civil Rights Act of 1866 was equally negative; *Dred Scott* had to be exorcised. In the process, as a matter of syntactic compulsion, of stylistic necessity, as a matter of the flow of the pen, the concept of citizenship was revived.

When the same Congress that passed the 1866 Civil Rights Act wrote the Fourteenth Amendment, it forbade any state to "abridge the privileges or immunities of citizens of the United States." The author of this phrase was John A. Bingham, a Representative from Ohio, a Republican of abolitionist antecedents. He was a type that frequently occurred in our political life, a man of enthusiastic rhetorical bent, on the whole of generous impulse, and of zero analytical inclination or capacity. A Republican colleague in the House recalling quite specifically the privileges and immunities clause, and that it came from Bingham, said: "Its euphony and indefiniteness of meaning were a charm to him." The only explanation of this clause that was attempted in the long course of the congressional debate on the amendment came from Bingham, and it confirms his contemporaries' estimate of him—it was highly confused. As an afterthought, by amendment in the Senate of the text passed in the House, a definition of citizenship modeled on the Civil Rights Act of 1866 was added: "All persons born or naturalized in the United States and subject to the jurisdiction thereof [which may exclude the children of foreign ambassadors, and means little, if anything, more than that], are citizens of the United States and of the state wherein they reside."

The *Dred Scott* decision had to be effectively, which is to say constitutionally, overruled by a definition of citizenship in which race played no part. So, in a fashion no one quite understood but everyone apparently found necessary, *Dred Scott* was exorcised. That having been done, the rest of section 1 of the Fourteenth Amendment made no further reference to citizens. * * *

At this stage of our history we stood at a point where the status of citizenship might have become all-important, not because of a deliberate, reasoned decision, but owing to the particular dialectic of the *Dred Scott* case, which one may view as an accident, and of the natural reaction to it. Actually, the concept of citizenship, once inserted in the Fourteenth Amendment, survived as a drafting technique in three later constitutional amendments which safeguard the right to vote against particular infringements. But on the whole the development was away from this concept— owing to yet another accident.

This other accident was the decision in the *Slaughter-House Cases*[12] of 1873, in which the Supreme Court for the first time construed the newly enacted Fourteenth Amendment. The first reading of the great Reconstruction amendment had nothing to do with Negroes, slavery, civil rights, or in any other way with the aftermath of the Civil War. The case arose instead out of a more than ordinarily corrupt enactment of the Louisiana legislature in 1869, which created a slaughtering monopoly in New Orleans. * * *

The main purpose of the Fourteenth Amendment's definition of citizenship, Justice Samuel F. Miller began for the Court, was to overrule the *Dred Scott* case and "to establish the citizenship of the negro." In addition, the definition clarified what Miller thought was a previously open but hardly world-shaking question: whether a person born not in a state, but in a territory or in the District of Columbia, who was therefore not a citizen of any state, could be a citizen of the United States. He could be. The Fourteenth Amendment made sure there would be no limbo.

But what could be meant by privileges and immunities of citizens of the United States? The sole purpose of the privileges and immunities clause of the original Constitution, article IV, section 2, said Justice Miller, was "to declare to the several States, that whatever those rights, as you grant or establish them to your own citizens, or as you limit or qualify or impose restrictions on their exercise, the same, neither more nor less, shall be the measure of rights of citizens of other States within your jurisdiction." But the rights themselves did not depend on the federal govern-

12. Slaughter–House Cases, 83 U.S. (16 Wallace) 36 (1872).

ment for their existence or protection. Their definition and their limitation lay within the power of the states.

Was the Fourteenth Amendment, by creating national citizenship, meant to work the radical change * * * of making basic relationships between the individual and the state turn on federal law? * * * Miller answered for the majority with a vigorous negative. The purpose of the privileges and immunities clause was to define, secure, and protect the citizenship of the newly freed slaves, that and no more. It was a close decision; the Court divided 5 to 4.

Was the privileges and immunities clause, then, entirely meaningless? Why did the draftsman put it in? We know why—because John A. Bingham liked the sound of it. But that is not good enough. Statutory and particularly constitutional enactments must be invested with some meaning, which Miller proceeded to do. National citizenship, he said, confers the right to come to the seat of government, a right protected for inanimate things, and for aliens as well, by the commerce clause; the right to seek (though probably not to claim) the protection of the government when outside the United States; the right to use the navigable waters of the United States, which under international law may be forbidden to aliens. That was about it.

* * *

The decision in the *Slaughter-House Cases,* however narrowly reached, has stuck so far as the argument proceeding from the privileges and immunities clause is concerned. And what it did was to bring us back to where we started. It concluded the flurry of the *Dred Scott* case, came around just about full circle, and left matters almost as they were before that episode. While we now have a definition of citizenship in the Constitution we still set very little store by it.

* * *

The consequences of the decision in the *Slaughter-House Cases* with respect to the role played in our polity by the concept of citizenship have followed with inexorable logic. Although the Fifteenth, Nineteenth, and Twenty-sixth Amendments guarantee the right to vote in terms of citizenship, and the right to vote is now generally a function of United States citizenship, it was not always, and in some states not recently, so; and in any case it is not the Constitution that ties even that most symbolically charged act of participation in governance to the status of citizenship. There have been other, aberrant departures from the logic of the *Slaughter-House Cases.* But when challenged they are most often found to be insupportable contradictions, and are eliminated.

[Bickel then reviews several cases in the line that spawned the potent equal protection doctrine of *Graham v. Richardson,* 403 U.S. 365 (1971), which shields aliens from most State law discrimination, unless the State can demonstrate a compelling governmental interest.]

That is not quite an end of the matter. Resident aliens are under the protection of our Constitution substantially no less than citizens, but conditions may be attached to entry permits, and in time of war even resident enemy aliens may be subject to fairly harsh restrictions. But that is a consequence, I suggest, of our perception of the meaning of foreign citizenship and of the obligations it may impose more than it is a consequence of the significance of the status of citizen in our own domestic law. * * * The citizen has a right as against the whole world to be here. The alien does not, although once the alien is permanently resident his right to remain, if qualified, is substantial and covered by constitutional protections. The decision of who may enter and remain as of right must be made by every nation-state in a world of nation-states, else it places its existence at risk. Citizenship can be and is made, though rarely, the basis for the extraterritorial application of domestic law (such as the draft, the tax law, rules requiring appearance in court) and, most significantly, for the extraterritorial reach of the quintessential crime of allegiance, the crime of treason, which is defined by the Constitution closely and narrowly in terms of persons, not citizens.

* * *

* * * Special qualifications for naturalization do exist and are enforced. Good moral character is one. However, qualifications that seek to pour ideological and political meaning into the concept of citizenship meet with judicial resistance. Nor has Congress been permitted to define the allegiance of those already citizens by providing for their involuntary expatriation—the involuntary loss of citizenship—upon commission of acts inconsistent with allegiance. Such acts by citizens and even by noncitizens may be punished, but loss of citizenship cannot be predicated on them. And the irony is that in the decisions that denied a power to impose involuntary expatriation and thus seemed to follow the tradition of denuding the concept of citizenship in our law of any special role and content, the Supreme Court returned to a rhetoric of exalting citizenship which echoes the Taney opinion in *Dred Scott.*

In the early years of the Republic, Hamilton and his followers believed that, like British subjects, Americans should be tied indissolubly to the state; a right of voluntary expatriation would encourage subversion. But voluntary expatriation has long been permitted by our law. Jefferson supported such a right, and in the end his view prevailed. In 1868 Congress, having for the first time defined citizenship, passed a statute still on the books providing, in warm language, that "the right of expatriation is a natural and inherent right of all people, indispensable to the enjoyment of the rights of life, liberty and the pursuit of happiness," and was not to be denied. We had, after all, fought in 1812 against British claims that immigrants from Great Britain who were sailors in our navy could be treated by the British as deserters because they had never lost their British nationality, and in the 1860s we were indignant at British treatment of naturalized Irish–Americans arrested in Ireland for participation in anti-British activities.

Congress listed as expatriating behavior such acts as voting in a foreign political election or deserting from the armed forces in time of war, or, for a naturalized citizen, taking up permanent residence in the country of his or her birth.   In the end the Court held them all unconstitutional,[35] although there is some slight evidence that the Court as now constituted might be willing to some extent to rethink the whole question.[36]   The Court said, in effect, in these cases holding the involuntary expatriation statutes unconstitutional, that Congress may not put that much content into the concept of citizenship.   It seemed to reaffirm the traditional minimal content of the concept of citizenship, the minimal definition of allegiance. But its language was at war with its action.   "This government was born of its citizens," wrote Chief Justice Earl Warren,

> it maintains itself in a continuing relationship with them, and, in my judgment, it is without power to sever the relationship that gives rise to its existence.   I cannot believe that a government conceived in the spirit of ours was established with power to take from the people their most basic right.
>
> Citizenship *is* man's basic right for it is nothing less than the right to have rights.   Remove this priceless possession and there remains a stateless person, disgraced and degraded in the eyes of his countrymen.   He has no lawful claim to protection from any nation, and no nation may assert rights on his behalf.   His very existence is at the sufferance of the state within whose borders he happens to be.   [As if our government were in the habit of beheading people for not being citizens!]   In this country the expatriate would presumably enjoy, at most, only the limited rights and privileges of aliens....
>
> The people who created this government endowed it with broad powers....   But the citizens themselves are sovereign, and their citizenship is not subject to the general powers of their government.[37]

Citizenship, Warren concluded, is "that status, which alone assures the full enjoyment of the precious rights conferred by our Constitution."   Ten years later, when these views came to command a majority,[38] Justice Black wrote: "In our country the people are sovereign and the Government cannot sever its relationship to the people by taking away their citizenship."   And: "Its citizenry is the country and the country is its citizenry."

All this, as we have seen, is simply not so.   It is not so on the face of the Constitution, and it certainly has not been so since the *Slaughter-House Cases* of 1873.   The Warren language was a regression to the confusions of Bingham and, what is worse, to the majority opinion in *Dred*

---

35.   *Afroyim v. Rusk*, 387 U.S. 253, 87 S.Ct. 1660, 18 L.Ed.2d 757 (1967); *Schneider v. Rusk*, 377 U.S. 163, 84 S.Ct. 1187, 12 L.Ed.2d 218 (1964).

36.   *See Rogers v. Bellei*, 401 U.S. 815, 91 S.Ct. 1060, 28 L.Ed.2d 499 (1971). [*But see Vance v. Terrazas*, 444 U.S. 252, 100 S.Ct. 540, 62 L.Ed.2d 461 (1980) (to be considered later in this Chapter), decided several years after Bickel's essay was written.—eds.]

37.   *Perez v. Brownell*, 356 U.S. 44, 64–65, 78 S.Ct. 568, 579–80, 2 L.Ed.2d 603 (1957)

(footnotes omitted) (Warren, Black, and Douglas dissenting).   This dissent within the decade became the prevailing view.   The Chief Justice took his clue from an unguarded comment by Brandeis, made in a quite different context, to the effect that deportation of one who claims to be a citizen may result in the loss of "all that makes life worth living."   *Ng Fung Ho v. White*, 259 U.S. 276, 284 (1922).

38.   *Afroyim v. Rusk*, 387 U.S. 253, 87 S.Ct. 1660, 18 L.Ed.2d 757 (1967).

Scott v. Sandford, which held that the terms "people of the United States" and "citizens" are synonymous and that they "both describe the political body who according to our republican institutions form the sovereignty." Who said, "They are what we familiarly call the single 'sovereign people,' and every citizen is one of this people and a constituent member of the sovereignty"? Roger B. Taney did, and Earl Warren and Hugo L. Black echoed it a century later, unwittingly to be sure. Who said that noncitizens "had no rights or privileges but such as those who held the power and the government might choose to grant them"? Roger B. Taney, to the same curious later echo.

No matter to what purpose it is put and by whom, this is regressive. Its thrust is parochial and exclusive. A relationship between government and the governed that turns on citizenship can always be dissolved or denied. Citizenship is a legal construct, an abstraction, a theory. No matter what the safeguards, it is at best something given, and given to some and not to others, and it can be taken away. It has always been easier, it always will be easier, to think of someone as a noncitizen than to decide that he is a nonperson, which is the point of the *Dred Scott* case. Emphasis on citizenship as the tie that binds the individual to government and as the source of his rights leads to metaphysical thinking about politics and law, and more particularly to symmetrical thinking, to a search for reciprocity and symmetry and clarity of uncompromised rights and obligations, rationally ranged one next and against the other. Such thinking bodes ill for the endurance of free, flexible, responsive, and stable institutions and of a balance between order and liberty. It is by such thinking, as in Rousseau's *The Social Contract,* that the claims of liberty may be readily translated into the postulates of oppression. I find it gratifying, therefore, that we live under a Constitution to which the concept of citizenship matters very little, that prescribes decencies and wise modalities of government quite without regard to the concept of citizenship. It subsumes important obligations and functions of the individual which have other sources—moral, political, and traditional—sources more complex than the simple contractarian notion of citizenship. "The simple governments," wrote Burke, "are fundamentally defective, to say no worse of them." Citizenship is at best a simple idea for a simple government.

SUGARMAN v. DOUGALL

Supreme Court of the United States, 1973.
413 U.S. 634, 93 S.Ct. 2842, 37 L.Ed.2d 853.

MR. JUSTICE REHNQUIST, dissenting.

[Justice Rehnquist's dissent applies both to *Sugarman v. Dougall,* 413 U.S. 634, 93 S.Ct. 2842, 37 L.Ed.2d 853 (1973) (wherein the Court invalidated New York's law barring aliens from state civil service jobs) and *In re Griffiths,* 413 U.S. 717, 93 S.Ct. 2851, 37 L.Ed.2d 910 (1973) (holding that Connecticut could not make citizenship a requirement for admission to the bar).]

* * *

The Court, by holding in these cases and in *Graham v. Richardson*, 403 U.S. 365, 91 S.Ct. 1848, 29 L.Ed.2d 534 (1971), that a citizen-alien classification is "suspect" in the eyes of our Constitution, fails to mention, let alone rationalize, the fact that the Constitution itself recognizes a basic difference between citizens and aliens. That distinction is constitutionally important in no less than 11 instances in a political document noted for its brevity. Representatives, U.S. Const. Art. I, § 2, cl. 2, and Senators, Art. I, § 3, cl. 3, must be citizens. Congress has the authority "[t]o establish an uniform Rule of Naturalization" by which aliens can become citizen members of our society, Art. I, § 8, cl. 4; the judicial authority of the federal courts extends to suits involving citizens of the United States "and foreign States, Citizens or Subjects," Art. III, § 2, cl. 1, because somehow the parties are "different," a distinction further made by the Eleventh Amendment; the Fifteenth, Nineteenth, Twenty–Fourth, and Twenty–Sixth Amendments are relevant only to "citizens." The President must not only be a citizen but "a natural born Citizen," Art. II, § 1, cl. 5. One might speculate what meaning Art. IV, § 2, cl. 1, has today.

Not only do the numerous classifications on the basis of citizenship that are set forth in the Constitution cut against both the analysis used and the results reached by the Court in these cases; the very Amendment which the Court reads to prohibit classifications based on citizenship establishes the very distinction which the Court now condemns as "suspect." The first sentence of the Fourteenth Amendment provides:

> "All persons born or naturalized in the United States and subject to the jurisdiction thereof, are citizens of the United States and of the State wherein they reside."

In constitutionally defining who is a citizen of the United States, Congress obviously thought it was doing something, and something important. Citizenship meant something, a status in and relationship with a society which is continuing and more basic than mere presence or residence. The language of that Amendment carefully distinguishes between "persons" who, whether by birth or naturalization, had achieved a certain status, and "persons" in general. That a "citizen" was considered by Congress to be a rationally distinct subclass of all "persons" is obvious from the language of the Amendment.

* * *

PETER H. SCHUCK, MEMBERSHIP IN THE LIBERAL POLITY: THE DEVALUATION OF AMERICAN CITIZENSHIP

Immigration and the Politics of Citizenship in Europe and
North America 51, 60–65 (W.R. Brubaker ed.1989).

* * * There is merit in Bickel's observation; indeed, it is probably truer today than in 1973 when he made it. For United States citizenship—relative to most other countries and to earlier periods in American history—is notably easy to obtain, difficult to lose, and confers few legal or economic advantages over the status of permanent resident alien.

* * *

But the devaluation of citizenship only serves to raise a further question: so what? Should we be concerned that American citizenship has manifestly little appeal for many aliens, or should we instead view this development with indifference or even satisfaction?

There are at least four dangers lurking in a devalued citizenship. The first is *political*: a concern for the quality of both the governmental process and the policy outcomes that it generates. Sound governance demands that those who are affected by the business of government participate in its decisions. The consent that invigorates liberal democracy must be as broad as the society that is coerced and governed in it name. But if millions of adult individuals subject to the exercise of governmental power are noncitizens who are legally disabled from voting, politicians have little incentive to learn about and respond to their claims. Under those conditions, the gap between power and accountability widens and the potential for exploiting noncitizens grows. When vitally affected interests remain voteless and (to that extent) voiceless, policy decisions are seriously deformed.

A second danger of a devalued citizenship is *cultural* in nature. An effective society—one that can accomplish its common goals, facilitate the private ends of its members, and nourish its systems of values—requires that newcomers achieve at least a modest degree of assimilation into its culture. At a minimum, this must involve attaining competence in the common language in which that culture expresses and changes itself, but it also demands some comprehension of the nation's institutions and traditions. If newcomers do not value citizenship, if they fail to acquire the mastery of language and social knowledge that citizenship requires, they jeopardize their own well-being and (if they are sufficiently numerous) that of their adopted society. They create practical obstacles to the success of their own projects, while encouraging others to view them as strangers rather than as collaborators, as outsiders rather than as integrated members of the community.

The third danger created by the devaluation of citizenship is *spiritual* in nature. Democracy is more than a mechanism for governmental decisions, more than a technology for getting the public's work done well. It is also a normative order, an ethos that legitimates certain process values and nourishes particular ways of thinking about the means and ends of politics. Its success depends upon the discipline of self-restraint; a willingness to sacrifice advantages and share burdens; a concern for the public interest; the capacity to inspire and accept leadership, a reverence for law; and pride in one's political community.

A polity that devalues citizenship may discourage the development and diffusion of these civic virtues. Although citizenship cannot guarantee any of these virtues, it seems to be a necessary or at least instrumental condition for most of them. If noncitizens can claim the same benefits that citizens enjoy without having to bear the obligations of full membership, they may acquire an "entitlement mentality" that can erode those virtues. Most noncitizens are manifestly law-abiding and socially productive; they are presumably no less altruistic than other people. But by withholding their participation in and commitment to our civic life, they decline to be public-spirited in the fullest sense. To that extent, they may impoverish the democratic spirit of their communities.

A final danger concerns the *emotional* consequences of devalued citizenship. Fred Schauer has noted that citizenship serves as an especially important bond among individuals in a polyglot society like ours in which there are relatively few other affective linkages or commonalities. The ethnic, wealth, gender, religious, and lingual differences that divide us, Schauer points out, are inherently difficult for individuals to control or change. Citizenship, in contrast, is a status that can enable us to transcend these more enduring differences and achieve some common ground. If citizenship is to perform this special office, it must be accessible to all. But if it becomes too readily accessible, it may lose much of its capacity to bind us together in a meaningful, emotionally satisfying community.

Schauer's observation is really a point about how national communities are constituted and kept cohesive. Michael Walzer has hinted at a underlying emotional dynamic of such communities in his assertion that "Neighborhoods can be open only if countries are at least potentially closed." This suggestion, if true, has an important implication for citizenship. If we need the warmth and immediacy of parochial attachments to feel truly human, if there are spatial limits to our capacity for communal spirit, then citizenship may be a way to crystallize those attachments and define their outer boundaries. A liberal society committed to the equality and due process principles seeks to rationalize and bureaucratize relationships among individuals and with the state by appealing to universal, abstract standards. At the same time, its members commonly feel a heightened need for some refuge from that universalizing impulse, some enclave in which they can define themselves and their allegiances more locally and emotionally.

National citizenship is certainly not the only haven from universality, and it has never been the most satisfying one; for most people, that succor is more fully provided by family, friendships, neighborhoods, ethnicity, religion, and other less cosmopolitan attachments. But if, as Bickel showed, citizenship has not been particularly important in American law, it has surely affected how Americans feel about and define themselves and others. As citizenship's value and significance decline, therefore, we should expect that people's more parochial loyalties may loom correspondingly larger and may be asserted with greater intensity. Such a shift may yield neighborly pride, ethnic solidarity, and other emotional satisfactions. But it may also encourage a retreat from civic commitment toward some darker feelings that are never wholly absent from American life: xenophobia, petty localism, intolerances, and privatistic self-absorption.

The existence of these dangers reinforces a point that is often obscured by the liberal, minimalist conception of citizenship celebrated by Bickel and dominant in American law: society's interest in the value of citizenship transcends the valuation that the individuals in that society place upon it. Even if aliens' decisions to forego naturalization were truly voluntary and fully informed—indeed, even if those choices did not expose them to political exploitation or injustice at the hands of citizens—society might be justified in concluding that in the aggregate those choices debase, perhaps even imperil, the quality of its political life. Put another way, the level of political, and hence social, assimilation that aliens find perfectly congenial may seem inadequate from society's point of view.

* * *

We live in an increasingly integrated world. * * * It would be premature, nonetheless, to conclude that national citizenship today is anachronistic. I have suggested that it provides a focus of political allegiance and emotional energy on a scale capable of satisfying deep human longings for solidarity, symbolic identification, and community. Such a focus may be especially important in a liberal ethos whose centrifugal, cosmopolitan aspirations for global principles and universal human rights must somehow be balanced against the more parochial imperatives of organizing societies dominated by more limited commitments to family, locality, region, and nation.

Notes

1. Both Bickel and Rehnquist describe the same set of constitutional references to the citizenship concept, yet they reach radically different conclusions about the Framers' understanding of, and reliance on, that status. Which characterization strikes you as more persuasive? Is the glass half empty or half full?

2. Chief Justice Warren, whose opinion in *Perez* is excerpted and sharply criticized by Bickel, cited the philosopher and political thinker Hannah Arendt in support of his general understanding of the importance of citizenship. In the relevant passage of her noted work *The Origins of Totalitarianism* 293–95 (1951), she begins with a thorough review of the situation of stateless people in Europe between the two world wars and of "displaced persons" immediately after World War II. She writes: "The Rights of Man, supposedly inalienable, proved to be unenforceable—even in countries whose constitutions were based upon them—whenever people appeared who were no longer citizens of any sovereign state." These people lost their homes and suffered the loss of government protection, but the real problem was deeper. "The calamity of the rightless is not that they are deprived of life, liberty, and the pursuit of happiness, or of equality before the law and freedom of opinion—formulas which were designed to solve problems *within* given communities—but that they no longer belong to any community whatsoever." In the displaced person camps "their freedom of opinion is a fool's freedom, for nothing they think matters anyhow." They suffer "the loss of the relevance of speech (and man, since Aristotle, has been defined as a being commanding the power of speech and thought), and the loss of all human relationship (and man, again since Aristotle, has been thought of as the 'political animal,' that is one who by definition lives in a community), the loss, in other words, of some of the most essential characteristics of human life." Do these arguments provide a more effective counter to Bickel's assertions? *See also* Rosen, *The War*

on Immigrants, The New Republic, Jan. 30, 1995, at 22, 25 (calling Bickel's account of the constitutional history "airbrushed and unpersuasive").

3. Which of the four dangers identified by Schuck as flowing from the devaluation of citizenship is the most important? Has devaluation gone too far?

4. Other useful discussions of these and related issues may be found in M. Walzer, Spheres of Justice: A Defense of Pluralism and Equality 31–63 (1983); the other essays in Immigration and the Politics of Citizenship in Europe and North America (W. Brubaker ed. 1989); Hammar, *Citizenship: Membership of a Nation and of a State,* 24 Int'l Migration 735 (1986); *Symposium: Law and Community*, 84 Mich.L.Rev. 1373 (1986) (particularly the articles by Professors Levinson, Aleinikoff, and Schauer); Neuman, *Justifying U.S. Naturalization Policies,* 35 Va.J.Int'l L. 237 (1994), and the commentaries on Neuman's article by Professors *Legomsky*, Martin, and Schuck, *id.* at 279–332.

5. A significant round of debate over the meaning of citizenship was prompted by the publication of P. Schuck & R. Smith, *Citizenship Without Consent: Illegal Aliens in the American Polity* (1985). Professors Schuck and Smith argue that our understanding of citizenship should be brought more into line with America's basic devotion to the principle of consent. Rather than relying so heavily on what they call "ascriptive" rules that assign citizenship based on accidental features of birth, they propose a greater role for consent to citizenship—consent both by the individual and by the polity. *See id.* at 9–41.

To this end, they urge serious reconsideration of several current practices. To reinforce the reality of express consent by the individual to his or her citizenship status, they suggest a procedure whereby every citizen, upon reaching age eighteen, would receive a notice explicitly informing him or her of the right to expatriate, and also discussing the consequences. Those who did nothing would remain citizens. Professors Schuck and Smith would also make the voluntary surrender of citizenship an easier process. Expatriation now usually requires renunciation before a U.S. consul in a foreign country, and expatriates are likely to lose their rights of residence in the United States. The authors instead would allow such individuals a continuing right of residence. *Id.* at 116–24.

To reinforce the notion of *governmental* consent to citizenship, they urge reconsideration of our present *jus soli* rules (citizenship based on birth within the territory). They argue first that the Fourteenth Amendment should not be read as imposing quite so broad a rule of birthright citizenship as is currently understood. *Id.* at 72–89. It should be read instead as consenting to citizenship by birth in the territory only for children born to citizens or lawful permanent residents. Congress could of course choose to extend birthright citizenship to a wider class, but it would not do so by constitutional compulsion. Any legislation applying a rule of *jus soli* broader than the constitutional minimum, as they understand it, would then come only after deliberation by the current citizenry; it would thus amount to an important exercise of societal consent. "[T]he boundaries of the political community, for better or for worse, [would be] matters of self-conscious public choice." *Id.* at 129. Finally, as a means of responding to the critical issue of illegal migration, they propose serious consideration of new statutes barring birthright citizenship to children born on U.S. soil to aliens illegally present (and perhaps to nonimmigrants as well). *Id.* at 90–115.

The book sparked lively debate, concerning both its conclusions regarding the meaning of the Fourteenth Amendment, and the policy consequences of the statutory changes set forth. *See, e.g.,* Martin, *Membership and Consent: Abstract or Organic?,* 11 Yale J. Int'l L. 278 (1985) (questioning the sharp dichotomy drawn between ascriptive and consensual principles, and expressing particular concern about the political consequences if the children of illegal aliens were placed outside our *jus soli* rules); Schuck & Smith, *Membership and Consent: Actual or Mythic?—A Reply to David A. Martin,* 11 Yale J. Int'l L. 545 (1986); Neuman, *Back to* Dred Scott?, 24 San Diego L.Rev. 485 (1987) (challenging Schuck and Smith's reading of the history and meaning of the Fourteenth Amendment's citizenship provisions); Schwartz, *The Amorality of Consent,* 74 Calif.L.Rev. 2143 (1986) (asserting that "the book is wrong as a matter of political and moral theory").

Governor Pete Wilson of California has called for a constitutional amendment to prevent the children of illegal migrants from obtaining birthright U.S. citizenship, as have several legislators, and the 104th Congress appears quite likely to consider bills to this effect. *See* Note, *The Birthright Citizenship Amendment: A Threat to Equality,* 107 Harv.L.Rev. 1026 (1994).

SECTION B. ACQUISITION OF NATIONALITY BY BIRTH

Two basic principles for the acquisition of nationality at birth are known to international practice: the *jus soli,* literally right of land or ground—conferment of nationality based on birth within the national territory; and the *jus sanguinis,* or right of blood—the conferment of nationality based on descent, irrespective of the place of birth. *See generally* Harvard Research in International Law, *Nationality,* 23 Am. J.Int'l L. 27–29 (Special Supp.1929). Anglo–American nationality law is fundamentally based on the *jus soli,* although both principles have played a role in the transmission of United States citizenship ever since the first nationality statute was passed. Act of March 26, 1790, Ch. 3, 1 Stat. 103.

Jus Soli

We consider here first the *jus soli.* As is evident from Professor Bickel's essay earlier in this chapter, citizenship based on birth in the national territory is rooted in the language of the first sentence of the Fourteenth Amendment. Adopted in 1868, that provision states: "All persons born or naturalized in the United States, and subject to the jurisdiction thereof, are citizens of the United States and of the State wherein they reside." But what does it mean to be born "subject to the jurisdiction thereof"?

The Supreme Court's first holding on the subject suggested that the court would give a restrictive reading to the phrase, potentially disqualifying significant numbers of persons born within the physical boundaries of the nation. In *Elk v. Wilkins,* 112 U.S. 94, 5 S.Ct. 41, 28 L.Ed. 643 (1884), the court ruled that native Indians were not U.S. citizens, even if they later severed their ties with their tribes. The words "subject to the jurisdiction thereof," the Court held, mean "not merely subject in some respect or degree to the jurisdiction of the United States, but completely subject to their political jurisdiction, and owing them direct and immediate allegiance." Most Indians could not meet the test. "Indians born within the territorial limits of the United States, members of, and owing immediate allegiance to, one of the Indian tribes, (an alien though dependent power,) although in a geographical sense born in the United States, are no more 'born in the United States and subject to the jurisdiction thereof,' * * * than the children of subjects of any foreign government born within the domain of that government * * *." *Id.* at 102.

Congress eventually passed legislation overcoming the direct effects of this holding. The Allotment Act of 1887 conferred citizenship on many Indians who resided in the United States, and later statutes expanded the scope of the grant. Since at least 1940 (and possibly since 1924—the application of the statute enacted that year to Indians born thereafter was unclear), all Indians born in the United States are U.S. citizens at birth. *See* GM & Y § 92.03[3][e], INA § 301(b).

But in the meantime, in the years following *Elk,* the Chinese exclusion laws were being tightened. The question arose whether children born in the United States to Chinese parents would be citizens under *Elk* 's reading of the Fourteenth Amendment. After all, opponents of such citizenship pointed out, Chinese had always been excluded from naturalization,[3] and the Chinese exclusion laws themselves restated that bar. Did the impossibility of their parents' obtaining U.S. citizenship also somehow render such persons not subject to the jurisdiction of the United States, within the meaning of the Fourteenth Amendment, at the time of their birth?

The Supreme Court's answer came in a case involving one Wong Kim Ark, born in San Francisco to Chinese parents who had taken up residence in this country under treaties that initially had encouraged such migration. Excluded from entry in 1895 on returning from a brief visit to China, Wong Kim Ark claimed a right to admission as a citizen, based on the locus of his birth. In a landmark decision, a divided Supreme Court held that the words "born in the United States and subject to the jurisdiction thereof" should be given an expansive reading; hence Wong Kim Ark was indeed a citizen by virtue of the Fourteenth Amendment. Both the majority and dissenters wrote lengthy scholarly opinions examining common law and

3. The original naturalization laws opened citizenship only to "free white persons." In 1870, in the wake of the Civil War, Congress extended naturalization eligibility to "persons of African descent." Western Hemisphere natives were included in 1940. Not until 1943 were Chinese made eligible for naturalization—a somewhat belated token of support extended to a World War II ally. Only in 1952 were all racial and national origin bars eliminated from the naturalization laws. INA § 311. *See generally* GM & Y §§ 94.01[2], 94.03[5].

civil law rules for the acquisition of citizenship at birth. After quoting the key constitutional language, the majority held:

> As appears upon the face of the amendment, as well as from the history of the times, this was not intended to impose any new restrictions upon citizenship, or to prevent any persons from becoming citizens by the fact of birth within the United States, who would thereby have become citizens according to the law existing before its adoption. It is declaratory in form, and enabling and extending in effect. Its main purpose doubtless was, as has been often recognized by this court, to establish the citizenship of free negroes, which had been denied in the opinion delivered by Chief Justice Taney in *Dred Scott v. Sandford*, (1857) 19 How. 393; and to put it beyond doubt that all blacks, as well as whites, born or naturalized within the jurisdiction of the United States, are citizens of the United States. But the opening words, "All persons born," are general, not to say universal, restricted only by place and jurisdiction, and not by color or race * * *.

* * *

The decision in *Elk v. Wilkins* concerned only members of the Indian tribes within the United States, and had no tendency to deny citizenship to children born in the United States of foreign parents of Caucasian, African or Mongolian descent, not in the diplomatic service of a foreign country.

The real object of the Fourteenth Amendment of the Constitution, in qualifying the words, "All persons born in the United States," by the addition, "and subject to the jurisdiction thereof," would appear to have been to exclude, by the fewest and fittest words, (besides children of members of the Indian tribes, standing in a peculiar relation to the National Government, unknown to the common law,) the two classes of cases—children born of alien enemies in hostile occupation, and children of diplomatic representatives of a foreign State—both of which, as has already been shown, by the law of England, and by our own law, from the time of the first settlement of the English colonies in America, had been recognized exceptions to the fundamental rule of citizenship by birth within the country.

* * *

This sentence of the Fourteenth Amendment is declaratory of existing rights, and affirmative of existing law, as to each of the qualifications therein expressed—"born in the United States," "naturalized in the United States," and "subject to the jurisdiction thereof"—in short, as to everything relating to the acquisition of citizenship by facts occurring within the limits of the United States. But it has not touched the acquisition of citizenship by being born abroad of American parents; and has left that subject to be regulated, as it had always been, by Congress, in the exercise of the power conferred by the Constitution to establish an uniform rule of naturalization.

United States v. Wong Kim Ark, 169 U.S. 649, 676, 682, 688, 18 S.Ct. 456, 467, 469, 472, 42 L.Ed. 890 (1898).

Some of the language of the majority opinion seemed to leave open the status of children born within the United States to alien parents only temporarily present within the national borders. But in fact the *Wong Kim Ark* decision has served to establish for the United States a "general rule of universal citizenship" by birth, as it is called by a leading immigration treatise, GM & Y § 92.03[2][a]. Birth in the territorial United States, even to parents fresh across the border after an illegal entry, results in U.S. citizenship. The only exceptions to this *jus soli* rule are exceedingly narrow: birth to foreign sovereigns and accredited diplomatic officials[4]; birth on foreign public vessels—meaning essentially warships, not commercial vessels—even while they are located in U.S. territorial waters (we wonder: does this ever happen?); birth to alien enemies in hostile occupation of a portion of U.S. territory. *See* GM & Y § 92.03[3][d].

Special considerations may apply, however, in determining the effect of birth in an outlying territory of the United States. The issue is whether birth there resulted in full citizenship or only in status as a noncitizen national. *See* note 2, *supra.* Care must be taken to consult the relevant rules in effect for the particular territory at the time of the birth, and, if full citizenship was not granted, to track later developments affecting the status of the territory and its inhabitants.[5] Sometimes the governing rules, in light of intervening changes in the political status of the territory, can be exceedingly complex. *See* GM & Y § 92.04. As of today, however, the regular *jus soli* rules are in effect in all territories except American Samoa and Swains Island—meaning that children now born in any U.S. territorial possessions except those two become full citizens at birth.

Jus Sanguinis

Since 1790 Congress has made special provision for the transmission of U.S. nationality *jure sanguinis* to children born abroad to American parents. The current *jus sanguinis* rules are set forth in INA §§ 301(c), (d), (e), (g), (h); 308(2), (4); and 309. The most important relate to children born outside U.S. territory to parents either one or both of whom are U.S. citizens. If both are citizens, the child acquires citizenship at birth,

4. Birth on U.S. soil to a diplomat does entitle the child to permanent resident status in the United States, subject to certain administrative requirements. *See Nikoi v. Attorney General,* 939 F.2d 1065 (D.C.Cir.1991) (holding that absences of 11 and 16 years, though begun while the petitioners were minors, resulted in abandonment of resident status).

5. Filipinos, for example, were noncitizen nationals of the United States from 1899 to 1946, but became aliens when independence was granted to the Philippines in the latter year and their allegiance was declared trans-

ferred to the new nation. *See Rabang v. Boyd,* 353 U.S. 427, 77 S.Ct. 985, 1 L.Ed.2d 956 (1957). In the early 1990s several deportation respondents from the Philippines defended on the basis that they were U.S. citizens, because their parents, born in the Philippines while it was a U.S. territory, were born "in the United States, and subject to the jurisdiction thereof" within the meaning of the Fourteenth Amendment. The Ninth Circuit rejected the claim, over a vigorous dissent by Judge Pregerson. *Rabang v. INS,* 35 F.3d 1449 (9th Cir.1994).

provided only that one of the parents had a residence in the United States at some time prior thereto. INA § 301(c).[6] *See Weedin v. Chin Bow,* 274 U.S. 657, 47 S.Ct. 772, 71 L.Ed. 1284 (1927) (parental residence must precede birth of the child). If one parent is an alien, however, then the citizen parent must have been physically present in the United States for a total of five years before the birth, including at least two years after the age of fourteen. Certain kinds of government and military service abroad count as physical presence in the United States for these purposes. § 301(g).

These current rules are fairly straightforward, but until 1978 the statute included several other provisos, rendered even more complicated for ready application by the fact that the rules had been modified frequently over the years. *See* GM & Y § 93.01[3]–[5]. The complexities result from evolving congressional views about how a fairly consistent aim should be achieved. From the beginning, Congress has sought to avoid the creation of a class of expatriates who may transmit U.S. citizenship to their children indefinitely, even though the family has had no close contact with actual life in the United States for generations. The issue has been what type of contact, on the part of the parents and/or the child, should be required.

Congress has employed two principal means toward this end. First, American citizen parents lacking a specified period of historical residence in the United States have been unable to transmit citizenship to their children. Second, from 1934 until 1978, the child had to establish his or her own residence in the United States for a specified number of years within stated periods, or else lose the citizenship acquired at birth. The length of residence and the ages during which residence had to be established have been altered several times.

The first type of limitation, concerning parental residence before the child's birth, has raised few constitutional issues. The second came under attack after *Afroyim v. Rusk,* 387 U.S. 253, 87 S.Ct. 1660, 18 L.Ed.2d 757 (1967), imposed strict constitutional limits on the power of Congress to deprive persons of U.S. citizenship involuntarily. But the Supreme Court, by a vote of five to four, eventually held that Congress retained the power to impose such a residence requirement as a "condition subsequent" on persons who are U.S. citizens by virtue of their birth to U.S. nationals abroad. *Rogers v. Bellei,* 401 U.S. 815, 91 S.Ct. 1060, 28 L.Ed.2d 499 (1971).

Despite the judicial endorsement of this type of post-acquisition residence requirement, Congress chose in 1978 to remove all such provisions from the immigration laws. Current law therefore relies solely on *parental* residence requirements to avoid the indefinite perpetuation of U.S. citizenship *jure sanguinis* within families that realistically have lost touch with

---

6. The statute provides that the term "residence" means "the place of general abode; the place of general abode of a person means his principal, actual dwelling place in fact, without regard to intent." INA § 101(a)(33). This objective test of residence was adopted in reaction to administrative rulings which had found that even temporary sojourn in the United States, lasting no more than a few days, might fulfill the parental residence requirements of earlier statutes. *See, e.g., Matter of E.,* 1 I & N Dec. 40 (AG 1941); *Matter of V.,* 6 I & N 1 (AG 1954).

their American roots. Act of Oct. 10, 1978, Pub.L. No. 95–432, 92 Stat. 1046. This change has considerably simplified the operation of current *jus sanguinis* rules, but Congress, as has been its usual practice when amending the citizenship rules, did not make its amendment retroactive. Persons who had already lost their citizenship under the earlier residency requirements thus remain denationalized, and those who did not qualify for citizenship under the rules extant on the date of birth usually cannot benefit from later statutory liberalization.[7] To determine whether a person born outside the territorial jurisdiction is a United States citizen, therefore, it is not enough to consult the present INA, unless of course the birth occurred after enactment of the latest amendments. One must check carefully the precise requirements in effect at the time of the birth of the individual in question, and also see whether any requirements for later residence in the United States have been fulfilled. *See, e.g., Runnett v. Schultz*, 901 F.2d 782 (9th Cir.1990). For summaries of the relevant rules, broken down by date of birth, *see* GM & Y § 93.02[5][c]; 66 Interp.Rel. 444 (1989) (reprinting charts used by the State Department, showing the different rules that apply for legitimate and illegitimate children born during the various time periods).

Problems

1. Your clients, a married couple, are Presbyterian missionaries in Botswana in southern Africa. They are both children of missionaries; the husband was born in Ghana and the wife in the Philippines, but both

---

7. A 1993 decision applying modern gender discrimination doctrine to *jus sanguinis* restrictions has led to a 1994 INA amendment that is an important exception to the nonretroactivity rule. In *Wauchope v. U.S. Dept. of State*, 985 F.2d 1407 (9th Cir.1993), the plaintiff had been born in Canada in 1931 to a Canadian father and a U.S. citizen mother. At the time, U.S. statutory law allowed the transmission of citizenship *jure sanguinis* by U.S. citizen fathers but not mothers. The plaintiff challenged this restriction on equal protection grounds, and the court ruled in her favor. The case, however, does not discuss *Mackenzie v. Hare*, 239 U.S. 299, 36 S.Ct. 106, 60 L.Ed. 297 (1915), summarized in Section D *infra*, a 1915 ruling by the Supreme Court that explicitly approved other related gender-based distinctions in U.S. nationality laws despite their highly unfavorable effect on women. Gender discrimination in a host of settings had been easily upheld in the Supreme Court against equal protection challenge until 1970, *see, e.g., Goesaert v. Cleary*, 335 U.S. 464, 69 S.Ct. 198, 93 L.Ed. 163 (1948) (upholding Michigan law forbidding most women from becoming licensed bartenders), and the offending statute had been repealed in 1934. The *Wauchope* court gave no consideration to whether modern rulings should be applied with full retroactivity

in a way that would essentially overrule *Mackenzie.*

Despite these potential doctrinal problems, Congress accepted the result in *Wauchope* and used the 1994 Technical Corrections Act to codify certain rules for implementing it. The Act adds INA § 301(h), and then carefully specifies the circumstances under which the change in law is to be applied retroactively. Pub.L.No. 103–416, § 101(b)-(d), 108 Stat. 4305 (1994). It allows the children of the disadvantaged U.S. citizen mothers to take advantage of the retroactive change in the rules, but not to allow transmission to further generations (unless the first generation also met the usual U.S. residence requirements for transmission, normally five years). Is this restriction on transmission constitutional, or should the first generation's failure to meet the U.S. residence requirements be seen as a "fruit of the poisonous tree"?

The same 1994 Act also added a new INA § 324(d), which allows former *jus sanguinis* citizens who lost that status as a result of the pre-1978 statutes upheld in *Bellei, supra*, to regain U.S. citizenship upon taking the oath prescribed in INA § 337 (thereby renouncing other national allegiances).

acquired U.S. citizenship at birth. They are expecting a baby next month, and it will be born in Botswana. Will the child have U.S. citizenship?

2. Your client was born in the United States, but his parents moved to Switzerland when he was two, and he has spent most of his life in Europe. He has been living with a French woman in Paris for the past three years, and she recently discovered that she is pregnant. The child is due in five months. This event has prompted the couple to talk more earnestly about a subject they have discussed for a long time but never acted upon: whether they should get married. They haven't yet decided. In any event he wants to make sure that the child has U.S. citizenship.

a. He asks whether he has to move to the United States with his "fiancée" to accomplish this aim. He is not sure he could even arrange this in time because she has no passport and no U.S. visa. What do you advise?

b. The couple may decide anyway to stay in France, "to be absolutely certain," he says, "that the baby has French citizenship too." Is there any way that the he can arrange for the child also to have U.S. nationality if it is born in Paris? Does he have to marry the mother to accomplish this? (What other factual information might you have to obtain to answer his questions?)

SECTION C.   NATURALIZATION AND DENATURALIZATION

1. ACQUIRING U.S. CITIZENSHIP THROUGH NATURALIZATION

As a country of immigration, the United States from its earliest days has made provision for the relatively easy acquisition of citizenship by persons born with another nationality. A brief review of the history of U.S. naturalization legislation will throw considerable light on the current scheme.

CHARLES GORDON, STANLEY MAILMAN, AND STEPHEN YALE-LOEHR, IMMIGRATION LAW AND PROCEDURE
Vol. 4, § 94.01[2] (rev. ed. 1994).*

* * *

In the original statute of March 26, 1790, Congress prescribed that a free white alien who had resided in the United States for 2 years, including residence of one year in any State, might be naturalized by any common law court of record, provided he was of good moral character and took an oath to support the Constitution. Five years later the 1790 statute was repealed by the Act of January 29, 1795, which re-enacted most of its provisions, with the following additions: The period of required residence in the United States was increased to 5 years; federal courts were also empowered to grant naturalization; a formal declaration of intention 3 years before admission to citizenship was made a prerequisite; applicants were required to renounce their former allegiance and to swear allegiance to the United States; and it was prescribed that the applicant establish to the satisfaction of the court that he was attached to the Constitution of the United States and well disposed to the good order and happiness of the United States.

The statutory requirements for naturalization formulated at this juncture resembled very closely the substantive requirements now generally prescribed. However, the 1795 law was short lived. The country had entered a period of reaction characterized by outbursts against aliens. One product of this interlude of hysteria was the enactment of the Alien and Sedition acts; another was the Act of June 18, 1798 which repealed the lenient provisions of the 1795 statute, and announced more restrictive naturalization requirements. The period of required residence was increased to 14 years in the United States and 5 years in a State; a declaration of intention at least 5 years old was prescribed; all aliens were required to register; and residence for the purposes of naturalization could be proved only upon production of a certificate of registry. Naturalization of alien enemies was prohibited. Clerks of court were required to transmit to the Secretary of State abstracts of declarations of intention filed in their courts.

Fortunately this interval of reaction soon ended. The Act of April 14, 1802 repealed the 1798 statute and restored the reasonable requirements of the 1795 law, which have remained in effect through almost two centuries. The 1802 law also introduced the requirement of witnesses to support the application for naturalization.

* * *

Although the early laws established acceptable substantive requirements, they were silent concerning the procedure to be followed. There were thousands of naturalization courts throughout the country, most of which were local courts in the various states, and each tribunal determined the procedure it would pursue in applications for naturalization. There was no centralized federal agency charged with the responsibility of enforcing the naturalization statutes.

This situation may have been adequate when there were few courts and a moderate quota of applicants for naturalization. With the expansion of immigration and the consequent augmentation in the number of aliens who sought naturalization, serious shortcomings in the naturalization process became evident. The absence of procedural standards and safeguards bred wide divergences in the practices of different naturalization courts, in the records they maintained, and in the type of evidence of citizenship they issued. The courts had no facilities to investigate the applications presented to them and many of the court officials were not scrupulous in insisting upon compliance with the requirements fixed by law.

As a result of these conditions, widespread frauds developed, which frequently made a mockery of the naturalization process. It was a notorious practice in many courts, for example, regularly to naturalize large groups of aliens on the eve of a political election. In many instances mill owners would load large numbers of alien employees into trucks a day or two before an election and transport them to the local court so that they might be naturalized in time to vote—presumably for the right candidate. Frequently the courts would approve the applications of persons who had no familiarity with American language or traditions, who could not meet the qualifications fixed by law, and who had no conception of the meaning of the naturalization process.

On March 1, 1905 President Theodore Roosevelt appointed a Commission to investigate the abuses in the naturalization process and to recommend appropriate revisions. As the result of the report of this Commission, Congress enacted the basic Naturalization Act of June 29, 1906. Under this statute the courts retained the ultimate authority to grant or deny citizenship, but administrative supervision over naturalization was vested in a federal agency (originally the Bureau of Immigration and Naturalization in the Department of Commerce and Labor). Among the statute's innovations were the following:

- Power to naturalize was removed from State courts of inferior jurisdiction.

- Every petitioner for naturalization who arrived in the United States after June 29, 1906 had to obtain an official certificate of his lawful admission, and it was required that such certificate be attached to and made part of the petition for naturalization.

- Uniform naturalization forms were prescribed.

- Uniform naturalization fees were fixed and clerks of court were required to account for such fees.

- It was directed that duplicates of all naturalization documents filed in and issued by the courts be transmitted to the Bureau of Immigration and Naturalization.

- Every applicant was required to sign the petition in his own handwriting and to speak the English language if physically able to speak.

- Each petition was to be supported by two citizen witnesses who would testify to the applicant's general qualifications for citizenship.

- Courts were prohibited from hearing or granting any petition until the expiration of 90 days after its filing, and then only on a stated day fixed by rule of court for the hearing of naturalization cases; and hearings on petitions for naturalization were prohibited within 30 days before a general election.

- Provision was made for court proceedings to cancel certificates of naturalization that were fraudulently or illegally procured.

* * *

The Nationality Act of 1940 was enacted as a codification and revision of all existing nationality laws, following a comprehensive study and report of a committee appointed by President Franklin D. Roosevelt and consisting of the Secretary of State, the Attorney General, and the Secretary of Labor. The nationality code adopted by Congress on October 14, 1940 followed closely the recommendations of this committee and included the following principal revisions:

- Provision was made for appointment of designated naturalization examiners by the Commissioner and for extension of the designated examiner system to the State courts.

- The required waiting period after filing the petition for naturalization was reduced from 90 days to 30 days and the period immediately prior to general elections during which naturalization was prohibited was increased from 30 days to 60 days.

- Authorization was granted for naturalization of natural children and adopted children on petition of their citizen parent or parents.

- The racial restrictions on naturalization were eased by adding descendants of races indigenous to the Western Hemisphere as a new class of eligibles in addition to white persons and persons of African nativity or descent. On December 17, 1943 Chinese persons or persons of Chinese descent were added as a fourth class of persons eligible for naturalization.

* * *

The last major milestone in the historical pattern was the Immigration and Nationality Act of 1952, which is now the basic statute for immigration and nationality. * * * Among the major changes effected by the 1952 Act were the following:

- The racial qualifications for naturalization were completely eliminated, and the statute specifically prohibited denial of naturalization because of race or sex.

- The statute, incorporating an enactment of 1950, specifically prohibited the naturalization of certain members of subversive groups.

- A specific disqualification was prescribed for aliens who had sought relief and had been relieved from military service on the ground of alienage.

- Naturalization was precluded for aliens against whom a deportation proceeding or order was outstanding.

- Special provision was made for the naturalization of aliens who had performed military service during certain periods of hostilities.

- The declaration of intention and the certificate of arrival were eliminated as requirements for naturalization.

- The grounds for expatriation and denaturalization were enlarged.

———

Naturalization Procedures

As Gordon and Mailman's account indicates, the United States historically has assigned the naturalization function to the courts, including state courts. Gradually, in response to abuses or other systemic difficulties, Congress grafted on to this system an administrative screening and support mechanism, principally through the use of designated naturalization examiners—employees of INS who made recommendations to the courts regarding the disposition of naturalization petitions. As a result, the court's decisionmaking role became perfunctory in the vast majority of cases.

In the Immigration Act of 1990, Congress significantly amended title III of the INA and thereby brought an end to the blanket role of courts in the naturalization process, making naturalization (after October 1, 1991) almost entirely an administrative procedure under the authority of the Attorney General. Courts are still generally involved in administering the citizenship oath, however, and an especially powerful form of judicial review is available when the administrators deny a naturalization petition. These changes are accomplished primarily in INA § 310 (setting forth the basic administrative procedure and the judicial review provisions), § 335 (examination of application for naturalization), and § 336 (hearing before an immigration officer if application is denied at the examination stage). Of lesser importance are the procedural provisions of §§ 318, 331–334, and 337–348. Consider those provisions carefully before reading further.

A House committee report explained the reasons for the change:

> By vesting authority for naturalization with the Attorney General, the applicant will be relieved of onerous paperwork burdens, confusing divisions of responsibilities between the Courts and the Department of Justice, and unduly lengthy processing times to achieve their goal of acquiring U.S. citizenship.

> Removal of the 200–year–old naturalization process from the Judiciary is not a step taken lightly by the Committee. The Committee notes the important role the Courts have performed in the past of welcoming citizens to the U.S. However, the increasing volume of citizenship applicants and heavy dockets of the Courts in other areas leads the Committee to consider a more streamlined process for those aspiring to citizenship. The quagmire only serves to discourage potential citizens from making application and deprives this country of a traditional source of productive and informed citizenry.

* * *

Lengthy delays in the Judiciary can also be attributed to the increased volume of applications as well as the number of other cases referred to the courts. In fact, a majority of cases pending in the naturalization area were in the courts and not in the Immigration Service. The impact on the Courts has a dual effect: it presents logistical as well as paperwork burdens. Logistical difficulties involve accommodating large numbers of applicants in limited space as well as conducting more frequent ceremonies.

* * *

With respect to the Court function in the naturalization process, the Committee notes that its major role is ceremonial and there are few instances where the recommendation of INS is not granted. In fact, in FY 1988, 242,000 persons were naturalized and only 767 statutorily denied.

H.R.Rep. No. 101–187, at 8–10 (1989).

Under the system established by the 1990 Act, an application for naturalization goes to an INS officer who examines the applicant and makes a formal determination to grant or deny. INA § 335. That examiner has authority to conduct a wide-ranging investigation and to subpoena witnesses and documents, but in most cases the examination will probably consist primarily of an interview of the applicant. If the application is approved, the oath of allegiance can be administered by a court or by the Attorney General's delegate, in accordance with INA § 310(b).

If the examiner denies the application, he or she must state the reasons.[8] The applicant may then request a further hearing before an "immigration officer," who must be of equal or higher grade level to the examiner who initially denied the application. INA § 336(a), 8 C.F.R. § 336.2(b). This second officer has the discretion to schedule a full de novo hearing, or to "utilize a less formal review procedure, as he or she deems reasonable and in the interest of justice." *Id.* The latter course is likely if it appears that the problem can be resolved routinely—for example, by administering another test of English language capability or knowledge of U.S. government. *See* 68 Interp.Rel. 166 (1991). If the administrative appeal still results in a denial, the applicant can seek judicial review, in accordance with the general provisions of the Administrative Procedure Act, in the federal district court having jurisdiction over the place of his residence. INA § 310(c). (State courts will no longer have any role in naturalization decisionmaking.) The court's review "shall be *de novo,* and the court shall make its own findings of fact and conclusions of law." *Id.* The House committee explained that "citizenship is the most valued governmental benefit of this land and applicants should receive full recourse to the Judiciary when the request for that benefit is denied." H.R.Rep. No. 101–187, *supra,* at 14. Upon judicial review, full authority

---

8. Also, if no decision issues within 120 days from the time of the interview, the applicant may go to court for a judicial determination of the application or for remand with instructions—presumably directing prompt processing by INS. INA § 336(b). This was one of several congressional changes designed to make the naturalization process less intimidating or discouraging for potential citizens. *See, e.g.,* § 332(h) (prescribing an outreach program, including work with community organizations); 68 Interp.Rel. 166, 170–71 (1991).

for both decisionmaking and administering of the oath will lie with the court. *Id.*

The Basic Substantive Provisions

In connection with the following readings, you should review the sections setting forth those substantive requirements, INA §§ 311–331, and 337, with special attention to §§ 312, 313, 316, and 337.

DAVID WEISSBRODT, IMMIGRATION LAW AND PROCEDURE IN A NUTSHELL
299–316 (3d ed. 1992).

B. REQUIREMENTS OF NATURALIZATION
(1) Residence and Physical Presence

Section 316(a) of the Immigration and Nationality Act requires that, except as otherwise provided, no person shall become a U.S. citizen by being naturalized unless (1) he or she[a] has resided continuously in the United States for five years as a lawfully admitted permanent resident, (2) during the five years immediately prior to filing the petition for naturalization he or she has been physically present in the United States for at least half of the time, and (3) he or she has resided within the district in which he or she filed the petition for at least three months. [The petitioner must also reside continuously within the United States from the date of the petition up to the time of admission to citizenship.] INA § 316. The purpose of the residency requirements is to create a reasonable period of "probation" that will enable candidates to discard their foreign attachments, to learn the principles of the U.S. system of government, and to develop an identification with the national community.

To comply with the statute a legal residence is necessary; a valid statutory residence prior to naturalization cannot be founded on an illegal entry into the country. Congress has defined "residence" under the 1952 Act to mean "the place of general abode ... [a person's] principal actual dwelling place in fact, without regard to intent." INA § 101(a)(33). The question of residence thus turns on a determination of where an applicant has held the status of lawful permanent resident alien, not on declarations of where he or she intends to live.

An applicant for citizenship need not show that he or she stayed at the claimed residence each day of the five year statutory period. Temporary absences from the place of abode—even from the United States—do not alone break the continuity of an applicant's residence. Absence from the United States for less than six months during the statutory period [does] not affect continuous residence, while an absence of more than six months but less than one year presumptively breaks the continuity. INA § 316(b). The applicant can overcome the presumption by "establish[ing] to the satisfaction of the Attorney General that he did not in fact abandon his

---

a. For aesthetic reasons, we have changed the neologism "s/he" in the original to "he or   she" and "her/his" to "his or her" wherever they appear in this excerpt.—eds.

residence during such period." An absence from the United States for one year or more will as a matter of law break the continuity of residence; the applicant will be required to complete a new period of residence after he or she returns to the United States.

As an exception to the physical residency requirement, persons who expect to be away from the United States for a year or more in service of the United States government, a recognized U.S. institution of research, a U.S. corporation engaged in foreign trade and commerce, a public international organization of which the United States is a member by treaty or statute, or a religious organization, may apply for permission to be absent without breaking their residence for purposes of naturalization. Before seeking such exception * * *, an applicant must continuously reside in the United States—following lawful admission—for one year or more. INA §§ 316(b), 317.

* * *

The exemption to the one year absence limitation concerning continuity of residence, which is provided for certain applicants (INA § 316(b)(1)), does not relieve such persons from the requirement of physical presence within the United States for one-half of the statutory five year period. INA § 316(c). Persons employed by the United States government, however, are exempted completely from the physical presence requirements of section 316(a). INA § 316(c).

* * *

(2) Age

To apply for naturalization an applicant must generally have attained the age of eighteen years. INA § 334(b)(1). * * * [C]hildren [younger than this generally] acquire citizenship at the time their parents are naturalized; they are not subject to the five-year waiting period. Their naturalization is by operation of law; hence, no application or proceeding is necessary. The child's status is called derivative citizenship. [The 1994 Technical Corrections Act also rewrote INA § 322 to simplify the process whereby parents may obtain a certificate of citizenship for children who somehow did not otherwise obtain U.S. nationality. At least one parent must be a U.S. citizen who has been physically present in the United States for five years, and the child must be under 18, in the legal custody of the citizen parent, and physically present in the United States pursuant to a lawful admission. The procedure is also available to foreign-born children adopted before the age of 16.]

(3) Literacy and Educational Requirements

Unless he or she is physically unable to do so through blindness or deafness, an applicant for naturalization must be able to speak and understand simple English, as well as read and write it. INA § 312[(a)(1)]. * * * [The Act now exempts from this requirement] any person who was over the age of fifty years *at the time of filing their petition,* and who had been lawfully admitted for permanent residence for periods totalling twenty years [or over fifty-five and had lived in the United States for at least fifteen years]. * * *

The statute further requires "a knowledge and understanding of the fundamentals of the history, and of the principles and form of government, of the United States." INA § 312[(a)(2)]. Each person applying for naturalization, including the older persons mentioned above, must pass an examination demonstrating the requisite knowledge of the United States. An interpreter or sign language may be used to test the applicant's knowledge of United States history, principles, and form of government, if he or she is exempt from the literacy requirement. 8 C.F.R. § 332.11(b). The Immigration Service generally applies the educational requirements in a lenient manner with due consideration given to such factors as the extent of petitioner's education, background, age, and length of residence in the United States. 8 C.F.R. § 312.2. Moreover, the regulations provide for second and third opportunities to pass the examinations. 8 C.F.R. § 312.3. [The 1994 amendments exempt from the language and citizenship requirements persons "unable because of physical or developmental disability or mental impairment to comply therewith." They also direct the Attorney General to give "special consideration" regarding compliance with the civics requirement to persons over 65 who have lawfully resided for at least 20 years. INA § 312(b).]

The power of Congress to establish these literacy requirements has withstood constitutional challenge. In *Trujillo-Hernandez v. Farrell* [503 F.2d 954] (5th Cir.1974), petitioner brought a class action, attacking the statute on equal protection grounds. The Court of Appeals for the Fifth Circuit held that a direct attack on Congress' exercise of its naturalization power was foreclosed and nonjusticiable, as such power was part of the foreign relations responsibilities committed to the Congress.

(4) Good Moral Character

An applicant for naturalization must show that, during the five year statutory period before filing and up until the final hearing of the naturalization petition, he or she "has been and still is a person of good moral character...." INA § 316(a). The burden of establishing good moral character falls upon the petitioner, as an applicant must prove his or her eligibility for citizenship in every respect. *Berenyi v.* [*District Director,* 385 U.S. 630, 87 S.Ct. 666, 17 L.Ed.2d 656 (1967).]

Courts have struggled with the issue of what constitutes good moral character. Judge Learned Hand stated that it is a "test, incapable of exact definition; the best we can do is to improvise the response that the 'ordinary' man or woman would make, if the question were put whether the conduct was consistent with a 'good moral character'." *Posusta v. United States* [285 F.2d 533] (2d Cir.1961). Prior to 1952, no attempt had been made to define good moral character by statute. Then in the 1952 Act, Congress chose to define by enumerated exclusions what would *preclude* a finding of good moral character. [INA § 101(f).]

* * *

The fact that a person is not within the classes enumerated does not preclude a finding for other reasons that he or she lacks the requisite good moral character.

* * *

(5) Attachment to Constitutional Principles

An applicant must show that he or she is "attached to the principles of the Constitution of the United States, and well disposed to the good order and happiness of the United States." INA § 316(a). The purpose behind this requirement is the admission to citizenship of only those persons who are in general accord with the basic principles of the community. *Petition of Sittler* [197 F.Supp. 278] (S.D.N.Y.1961). Courts have defined attachment to the Constitution as a belief in representative democracy, a commitment to the ideals embodied in the Bill of Rights, and a willingness to accept the basic social premise that change only be effected in an orderly manner. Similarly, a favorable disposition to the good order and happiness of the United States has been characterized as a belief in the political processes of the United States, a general satisfaction with life in the United States, and a hope for future progress and prosperity. Neither requirement is thought to preclude a belief that change in our form of government within constitutional limits is desirable.

* * *

Although the general requirements of attachment to the Constitution allow judicial discretion in evaluating a case on its own facts, several statutes enacted in 1952 specifically and automatically preclude naturalization of certain persons. Individuals belonging to the Communist Party or other totalitarian groups, * * * and persons who—irrespective of membership in any organization—advocate the overthrow of the United States government by force or violence or other unconstitutional means may not obtain naturalization. INA § 313(a)(4). An applicant is not disqualified, however, if he or she can show that the membership in the prescribed organization is or was involuntary. INA § 313(d). Moreover, if the applicant can establish that such membership or affiliation occurred and terminated prior to the alien's attaining sixteen years of age, or such membership or affiliation was by operation of law or for purposes of obtaining employment, food, or other essentials, he or she may yet qualify for naturalization. In *Grzymala-Siedlecki v. United States* [285 F.2d 836] (5th Cir.1961), therefore, petitioner's enrollment in the Polish Naval Academy, which automatically conferred Communist Party membership, did not disqualify him from naturalization where the college education was necessary to the applicant's earning a livelihood in Poland.

A few courts have added another exception to the disqualification for Communist membership. Such membership or affiliation does not disqualify an applicant unless it is or was a "meaningful association." The Supreme Court had held, in the context of deportation proceedings, that a "meaningful association" signifies at minimum "[an] awareness of the

Party's political aspect." *Rowoldt v. Perfetto* [355 U.S. 115, 78 S.Ct. 180, 2 L.Ed.2d 140] (1957). * * *

An applicant may escape the preclusion statute if more than ten years have passed, between his or her membership in the subversive organization or the act of advocating overthrow of the government, and the filing of the petition for naturalization. INA § 313(c).

Section 314 of the INA permanently precludes the naturalization of anyone who, during the time that the U.S. "has been or shall be at war," deserts the U.S. armed forces or leaves the country with the intent of avoiding the military draft, and is convicted of that offense by a court-martial or a court of competent jurisdiction. * * *

INA § 315(a) provides that an alien who seeks or obtains exemption from service in the armed forces on the ground that he or she is an alien becomes permanently ineligible for citizenship, unless the alien had served in the military of a country having a treaty with the United States. INA § 315(a)[, 315(c)]. Selective Service records are conclusive on the issue of whether an alien secured the exemption because of alienage. INA § 315(b).

(6) Oath of Allegiance to the United States

Related to the requirement that an applicant be attached to the Constitution of the United States, he or she also must take an oath of renunciation and allegiance in ["a public ceremony before the Attorney General or a court with jurisdiction under section 310(b)."] Section 337(a) of the INA requires that the applicant pledge (1) to support and bear true faith and allegiance to the Constitution of the United States; (2) to renounce all allegiance to any foreign state or sovereign; (3) to support and defend the Constitution and laws of the United States against all enemies, foreign and domestic; (4) to bear arms on behalf of the United States when required by law, or to perform noncombatant service in the armed forces, or to perform civilian work of national importance when required by law. INA § 337.

If an applicant can show by clear and convincing evidence, that he or she is opposed to the bearing of arms, the applicant may revise the pledge to perform only noncombatant services in the armed forces. Similarly, if the applicant can show by the same standard of proof that he or she opposes any type of service in the armed forces by reason of "religious training and belief," he or she may pledge merely to perform important civilian work. INA § 337(a).

The present statute was designed to codify judicial decisions relieving conscientious objectors of naturalization requirements to bear arms. The moral stand taken by conscientious objectors frequently resulted in the denial of their naturalization petitions between the world wars—a result the Supreme Court affirmed in *United States v. Schwimmer* [279 U.S. 644, 49 S.Ct. 448, 73 L.Ed. 889 (1929)] and *United States v. Macintosh* [283 U.S. 605, 51 S.Ct. 570, 75 L.Ed. 1302 (1931)]. In the 1946 case of *Girouard v. United States* [328 U.S. 61, 66 S.Ct. 826, 90 L.Ed. 1084], however, the Court overruled these prior cases and held that religious objection to bearing arms was not of itself incompatible with allegiance to the United States. Congress adopted the Supreme Court's holding by enacting the statute currently in effect.

* * *

[The Act also relaxes certain of the usual naturalization requirements for special classes of applicants. The most important are spouses "living in marital union with the citizen spouse," for whom the residency requirement is reduced to three years (§ 319); children of U.S. citizens (several of the usual requirements are relaxed, §§ 322, 337(a), for those infrequent cases where the child did not automatically acquire U.S. citizenship under the *jus soli* or *jus sanguinis* rules nor by derivation at the time when his or her parents were naturalized); and current or former members of the armed forces (§§ 328, 329).]

Problems

Advise your client in the following situations:

1. (a) Your client, A, was lawfully admitted to the United States 40 months ago under the second preference, as the spouse of a lawful permanent resident alien, B. B naturalized one year later. A wants to become a citizen as soon as possible. When is the earliest that she can *apply*? What are the procedural steps she needs to follow? Must she file any papers now?

(b) What if for two years B has held a job in Chicago while A works in Los Angeles? (They try to get together every weekend, but sometimes have to spend two or three weeks apart.)

2. Your client, C, entered as a lawful permanent resident on January 1 six years ago. He now wishes to naturalize. He has travelled extensively since taking up residence here, although he has owned the same condominium overlooking Central Park in Manhattan throughout the period; he always stays there when he is in New York. Here are his travel records:

Year 1: 2 months in Japan on business, October–November

Year 2: 6 weeks in San Francisco, February to March, interrupted by two or three weekends back in New York; 7 months in the Netherlands Antilles on business, April through November

Year 3: one month hiking in The Wind River Wilderness Area in Wyoming during the summer

Year 4: departure for Japan on business in March, remaining there into year 5

Year 5: continuation of Japan trip through mid-February, then on to Bali in Indonesia for pleasure, returning to New York from Bali in May; trip to Canada for two weeks in October

Year 6: a two-week business trip to Europe in January, two more weeks in April, and numerous week-long business trips to Arizona and California throughout the year.

When may he naturalize? Could you have speeded up the process if he had consulted you before taking any of the trips? He may have returned to New York for a couple of weekends in year 4, in the midst of his Japan trip, but he can't remember for sure. Would that make any difference?

3. Your client, D, was a member of the Communist party in Bulgaria, as were all persons in her profession (attorney) in her home town. During her youth she was a devoted Marxist–Leninist, but had become quietly disaffected with the party in her twenties. She was finally able to leave seven years ago, at age 40. After a year in a refugee facility in Austria, she was then admitted to the United States as a refugee. Is she now eligible for naturalization?

4. Your client, E, was born in Mexico but came here lawfully with his parents, both Mexican citizens, as an infant nearly 40 years ago. He believes they came as "nonpreference" aliens. His father deserted the family when E was 3, and E has few memories of him. E's mother naturalized when he was 10. He did not attend her ceremony, because it was held during the school day. Must he naturalize if he wants to be a U.S. citizen? How can he obtain evidence of his citizenship status?

PETITION FOR NATURALIZATION OF KASSAS

United States District Court, Middle District of Tennessee, 1992.
788 F.Supp. 993.

HIGGINS, District Judge.

* * *

The petitioner is a native citizen of Syria, who was lawfully admitted for permanent residence in the United States as of March 27, 1987. The petitioner is an adherent of the Islamic religious faith. The Service objects to the petitioner's naturalization on the grounds that: (1) the petitioner has failed to establish that he is eligible to take the oath of allegiance required by section 337(a) of the Immigration and Nationality Act; and (2) the petitioner has failed to establish that he is attached to the principles of the Constitution of the United States and is well disposed to the good order and happiness of the United States as required by Section 316(a). The specific issue is whether the petitioner can and will swear, without any mental reservation, by taking the Oath of Renunciation and Allegiance, to "bear arms on behalf of the United States when required by the law." INA § 337(a)(5)(A).

According to the record, at his preliminary investigation by the Service, the petitioner testified that he would be willing to take the full oath of allegiance to the United States; however he expressed reservations about bearing arms on behalf of the United States against persons of the Islamic faith or a predominately Islamic country.

The petitioner was questioned in more detail on this matter at his preliminary examination which was held immediately thereafter. It was the petitioner's belief that if he killed a member of the Islamic faith or if he in turn were killed by a member of the Islamic faith, he would be condemned to hell. The only exception to this would be if an Islamic country attacked or invaded the United States. Petitioner was unclear as to what exactly constituted an "Islamic Country." The petitioner was clear that he would be willing to bear arms against India or China, but not Iran. Additionally, at the hearing before the Court, petitioner testified that there were no conditions under which he would bear arms, except as allowed by Islamic law.[1]

Section 316(a) of the Act provides that no person shall be naturalized unless he is "attached to the principles of the Constitution of the United States, and well disposed to the good order and happiness of the United States." Congress has recognized that some people have deeply held religious beliefs which prohibit them from bearing arms under any circumstances, and thus has provided that where a person is opposed to bearing arms as a result of his religious training and beliefs, he may nevertheless be naturalized upon the taking of a modified oath. INA § 337(a).

The legislative history of the Immigration and Nationality Act of 1952 reveals that when Congress recognized the exemption from the military service for conscientious objectors, it intended to place the naturalized citizen on equal footing with the native born citizen. The House and Senate conferees also determined that the eligibility for a modified oath would be determined in accordance with the standards used under the Selective Service Act of 1948.

The record indicates that petitioner's reasons opposing the bearing of arms is [sic] a result of his religious training and beliefs. The Service argues that petitioner is not eligible for an exemption from swearing to section (5)(A) of the Oath, because he is opposed only to some, but not all wars. In *Gillette v. United States*, 401 U.S. 437, 443, 91 S.Ct. 828, 832, 28 L.Ed.2d 168, 176 (1971), the Supreme Court held that a similarly based exemption from military service is only available where the individual is opposed to "participation in war in any form."

Considering this legislative background and in view of the identical wording in both the selective service and naturalization exemptions, the Service asserts that the petitioner does not qualify for a modified oath. The petitioner, by reserving his right to make future decisions regarding his participation in the armed forces of the United States, has demonstrated that he cannot take this obligation, the oath of allegiance, without mental reservations. Furthermore, the Service argues the petitioner has failed to establish that he is attached to the principles of the Constitution as required by section 316(a). The petitioner, by reserving unto himself when he will or will not serve in the armed forces, is, in effect, stating when he will or will not obey the law.

The Court has fully considered the record and the testimony of the petitioner. The petitioner's testimony at the preliminary investigation,

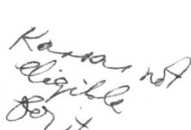

---

1. It appears to the Court that the petitioner has switched his position from that advanced before the examiner to the effect that he could bear arms on behalf of the United States except as to Islamic nations, and that advanced before the Court to the effect that he is precluded by his religion from killing anyone except as provided by Islamic law and is willing to perform noncombatant service.

and at the preliminary examination, along with his testimony before the Court, indicates the petitioner is only opposed to some, but not all war.

The Court finds that the petition of Mahmoud Kassas for naturalization should be denied.

PRICE v. INS

United States Court of Appeals, Ninth Circuit, 1992.
962 F.2d 836, cert. denied, ___ U.S. ___, 114 S.Ct. 683, 126 L.Ed.2d 650 (1994).

BEEZER, CIRCUIT JUDGE:

John Eric Price appeals the district court's denial of his petition for naturalization. The district court's order was based on Price's refusal to list all organizations with which he has ever been affiliated. Price argues that the Attorney General does not have statutory authority to require him to supply such a list and that such authority would be unconstitutional. We affirm.

John Price is a native of England and a citizen of the United Kingdom. He was granted lawful resident alien status in the United States in 1960, and has worked and resided in the United States since then.

On April 21, 1984, Price applied to petition for naturalization. Price answered all questions on the application except Question 18, which reads: "List your present and past membership in or affiliation with every organization, association, fund, foundation, party, club, society or similar group in the United States or in any other country or place, and your foreign military service. (If none, write 'None.')." In the space provided for an answer to this question, Price wrote "Please see attached statement." The attached statement is a legal brief contending that Question 18 violates Price's First Amendment right of association.

Price answered negatively all parts of Question 19, which asked whether he was or had ever been a member of or associated with the Communist Party, had ever knowingly aided or supported it, or had ever "advocated, taught, believed in, or knowingly supported or furthered the interests of Communism."

* * *

The Immigration and Naturalization Act [sic] gives the Attorney General the authority to "prescribe the scope and nature of the examination of petitioners for naturalization as to their admissibility to citizenship." INA § 332(a). The examination of petitioners must be limited to

> inquiry concerning the applicant's residence, physical presence in the United States, good moral character, understanding of and attachment to the fundamental principles of the Constitution of the United States, ability to read, write and speak English, and other qualifications to become a naturalized citizen as required by law.

Within these limits, the Attorney General has the authority to require an applicant for naturalization to aver to "all facts which in the opinion of the

Attorney General may be material to the applicant's naturalization," INA § 335(a) (emphasis added), and to designate INS employees to take "testimony concerning any matter touching or in any way affecting the admissibility of any petitioner for naturalization." INA § 335(b) (emphasis added). Thus the Attorney General is given very broad authority to make inquiries as long as they are related in some way to the naturalization requirements.

* * *

The INS argues that limiting examination to asking petitioners whether they are members of organizations of the type described in section 313(a) requires the INS to rely on petitioners' own determinations whether particular organizations are of the prohibited type, rather than allowing the Service to make that determination, and does not address the possibility that a petitioner may wrongly believe that an organization with which he is affiliated does not fall within section 313(a).

* * *

The INS also argues that membership in types of organizations not described in section 313(a) may be relevant to other requirements of naturalization such as duration of residence, good moral character or being "well disposed to the good order and happiness of the United States." "The government is entitled to know of any facts that may bear on an applicant's statutory eligibility for citizenship, so it may pursue leads and make further investigation if doubts are raised." *Berenyi v. District Director, INS*, 385 U.S. 630, 638, 87 S.Ct. 666, 671, 17 L.Ed.2d 656 (1967). It is completely reasonable to assume that knowing the organizations with which a petitioner is associated will be relevant to one or more of the requirements for citizenship. * * *

"[A]n alien seeking initial admission to the United States requests a privilege and has no constitutional rights regarding his application, for the power to admit or exclude aliens is a sovereign prerogative." *Landon v. Plasencia*, 459 U.S. 21, 32, 103 S.Ct. 321, 329, 74 L.Ed.2d 21 (1982). However, "once an alien gains admission to our country and begins to develop ties that go with permanent residence, his constitutional status changes accordingly." *Id.* It has long been recognized that resident aliens enjoy the protections of the First Amendment. * * *

However, the protection afforded resident aliens may be limited. The Supreme Court recently stated that the cases establishing constitutional protection for aliens within the territory of the United States "are constitutional decisions of this Court expressly according differing protection to aliens than to citizens, based on our conclusion that the particular provisions in question were not intended to extend to aliens in the same degree as to citizens." *United States v. Verdugo–Urquidez*, 494 U.S. 259, 110 S.Ct. 1056, 1064, 1065, 108 L.Ed.2d 222 (1990) (citations omitted). Additionally, the Court has historically afforded Congress great deference in the area of immigration and naturalization. * * * *Fiallo v. Bell*, 430 U.S. 787, 792, 796, 97 S.Ct. 1473, 1477, 1480, 52 L.Ed.2d 50 (1977) (quotations omitted). "[I]n the exercise of its broad power over immigration and naturalization,

'Congress regularly makes rules that would be unacceptable if applied to citizens.'" *Id.* at 792, 97 S.Ct. at 1478 (quoting *Mathews v. Diaz*, 426 U.S. 67, 80, 96 S.Ct. 1883, 1891, 48 L.Ed.2d 478 (1976)).

The INS relies on *Kleindienst v. Mandel*, 408 U.S. 753, 92 S.Ct. 2576, 33 L.Ed.2d 683 (1972) [*supra,* p. 345] for the proposition that Price's first amendment rights invoke at most only limited judicial review. * * *

Price argues that because *Kleindienst* involved exclusion rather than naturalization, it does not control his case. However, the determination of who will become a citizen of the United States is at least as "peculiarly concerned with the political conduct of government," as the decision of who will be allowed to enter, if not more so. While a resident alien may not participate in the process of governing the country, naturalized citizens may. Naturalization decisions, therefore, deserve at least as much judicial deference as do decisions about initial admission.[5] Furthermore, although Price is justified in expecting the greatest degree of constitutional protection afforded a non-citizen, the protection afforded him under the First Amendment certainly is not greater than that of the citizen plaintiffs in *Kleindienst*. For these reasons, the *Kleindienst* standard is appropriate in this case.

Price argues that he is not challenging the political decision underlying the determination of the substantive requirements for naturalization, but that he challenges instead the method of inquiry, which, in the case of Question 18, chills his freedom of association. Because of this posture, he contends, greater judicial scrutiny is appropriate.

A similar claim was rejected in *Kleindienst*. * * * The Court applied only limited judicial scrutiny and held that the requirements of the First Amendment were met because the reasons for refusing to grant the waiver were "facially legitimate and bona fide."

Applying this limited standard of review to the Attorney General's decision to ask Question 18 is also appropriate because "[n]o alien has the slightest right to naturalization unless all statutory requirements are complied with." *See Fedorenko v. United States*, 449 U.S. 490, 506, 101 S.Ct. 737, 747, 66 L.Ed.2d 686 (1981). Additionally, "the burden is on the applicant to show his eligibility in every respect." *See Berenyi*, 385 U.S. at 637, 87 S.Ct. at 671.[7]

* * *

5. The importance of the naturalization process was the basis for the district court's alternative holding that even under a more demanding First Amendment analysis, the government has a compelling interest in asking questions such as Question 18 that outweighs any First Amendment right a petitioner for naturalization may have.

7. In deportation hearings, the government must prove its case by "clear, unequivocal and convincing evidence." *Berenyi*, 385 U.S. at 636, 87 S.Ct. at 670 (quotation omitted). The fact that the alien carries the burden in naturalization proceedings helps to explain why, despite the sliding-scale theory of alien rights, [derived from *Johnson v. Eisentrager*, 339 U.S. 763, 771, 70 S.Ct. 936, 940, 94 L.Ed. 1255 (1950), which stated that an alien is "accorded a generous and ascending scale of rights as he increases his identity with our society,"] aliens at naturalization are not necessarily entitled to the full protection of the First Amendment arguably afforded in deportation hearings. *See Harisiades v. Shaughnessy*, 342 U.S. 580, 592, 72 S.Ct. 512, 520, 96 L.Ed. 586 (1952) (upholding the deportation of a member of the Communist

Because a petitioner might be mistaken about whether an organization is of the type prohibited by section 313(a) and because Question 18 could reasonably reveal information relevant to other requirements for naturalization, the Attorney General's decision that Question 18 is relevant to determining qualification for naturalization is facially legitimate and bona fide.

The district court's denial of Price's petition for naturalization is affirmed.

NOONAN, CIRCUIT JUDGE, dissenting:

The Immigration Service propounds a question to persons seeking naturalization that would be intolerable if asked by a government agency of an American citizen. It is an intimidating question. It chills the right of free association guaranteed by the First Amendment.

The Immigration Service's answer is that aliens are different. They are second class people. No doubt for some purposes this characterization is the harsh truth. Since the abolition of slavery aliens are the only adults subject to treatment as second class people in the United States.

* * * [Deference to Congress over the admission of aliens] is defensible when the alien is outside the United States and seeking to enter this country. *Kleindienst.* It is also appropriate to give deference to Congress and the Executive Branch in matters which "may implicate our relations with foreign powers." *Fiallo.*

The case, however, is substantially different when the alien is a resident and a resident of long standing—in the present case 30 years. Realistically such a person has been conducting himself like an American for a very long time. His reactions to an intolerable inquiry are similar to those of a citizen. Rightly so. He has imbibed the air of freedom which permeates our culture. He insists upon a right not to be treated as a second class person where freedom of association is concerned.

* * *

The power of Congress to set standards for naturalization is very large, but like every other power of government it is circumscribed; it is not absolute. In *Girouard v. United States*, 328 U.S. 61, 66 S.Ct. 826, 90 L.Ed. 1084 (1946), the Court refused to construe as mandatory a requirement made by Congress that a petitioner for naturalization swear to support the Constitution by taking up arms in defense of this country. The Court did so because otherwise the statute would have been held as unconstitutional.

In the present case the Immigration Service and this court have construed the statute in such a way that it is unconstitutional. As construed, the statute permits the Immigration Service to undertake an inquiry far broader than any governmental necessity warrants. * * *

Party under the then-applicable First Amendment test); *Parcham v. INS,* 769 F.2d 1001, 1005–06 (4th Cir.1985) (First Amendment protection applies in a deportation hearing); *American–Arab Anti-Discrimination Committee v. Meese,* 714 F.Supp. 1060 (C.D.Cal.1989) (same). Further support for this result is found in the fact that admission of an alien to citizenship is at least as fundamental to the identity of the nation as is the initial decision of whom to admit.

A narrowly tailored question could be asked of any petitioner without infringing on First Amendment rights. A petitioner could be asked if he had belonged to any organizations dedicated to the overthrow of the government or advocating or using terrorism or if he belonged to any foreign military, paramilitary or intelligence organization. Such a question would have an obvious relevance to the government's legitimate concerns. A question without bounds as to association has no relation to governmental concerns.

The Immigration Service says that the government is concerned with the petitioner's "character." Beyond excluding persons committed to subversion or terror or under the orders of a foreign government, there is no conceivable way that the government can measure a person's character. Persons of all kinds of character make up the United States. The Immigration Service cannot design some fine test by which only persons of outstanding character will be admitted as citizens. In reality we must take our applicants for citizens, as we take our citizens themselves, as a mix of people. That is the way immigrants have come to the United States and peopled it and that is the way it will always be.

The statute is without rational purpose and, infringing severely on the right of free association, it is unconstitutional. I respectfully dissent.

Notes

1. Is the *Price* majority correct to analogize applications for naturalization to applications for admission (*i.e.*, to exclusion cases) for the purpose of deciding what level of First Amendment scrutiny to apply? Should the requirement of a complete answer to question 18 be held to meet a higher standard anyway? Judge Noonan seems to suggest that the government has no business deciding on the character of prospective citizens. Does this mean that the "attachment" and "good moral character" requirements are unconstitutional? Can the result in *Kassas* be squared with the First Amendment's protection of freedom of religion?

2. During the 1980s, petitions for naturalization ranged from a low of 171,073 in FY 1981 to a high of 305,981 in 1985. 1993 INS Statistical Yearbook, Table 45, p. 134. FY 1992 and 1993 saw a significant increase, as the cohort of immigrants legalized under IRCA became eligible for citizenship (and had significant incentives to naturalize in order to bring in family members delayed by the backlogs in the second preference). In 1992, 342,269 petitions were filed, *id.*, whereas the 1993 total climbed to 522,298. In 1992, 240,252 persons were naturalized, in 1993, 314,681. *Id.*

In recent decades, the reported denial rate in naturalization cases has run between one and three percent, *see* 1992 INS Statistical Yearbook, Table 45; 1981 INS Statistical Yearbook, Table 19, p. 50. Fiscal years 1992 and 1993 stand out, however, because the data reported in the Yearbooks show a denial rate exceeding 7%—figures that may reflect backlog clearances but anyway are still subject to adjustment, because certain INS offices had not fully reported naturalization data at the time the Yearbooks were compiled. 1992 INS Statistical Yearbook 124; 1993 *id.*

127. The overwhelming majority of reported denials have been based on two reasons: lack of prosecution or withdrawal of the petition by the petitioner, leaving only a tiny fraction denied on other specified grounds under the INA. *See* 1981 INS Statistical Yearbook, Table 30, p. 82. Recent INS yearbooks, however, have ceased reporting the reasons for denial, and studies have raised questions about the completeness of the statistics and possible practices by INS that may discourage some people, particularly those with more difficult cases, from pursuing their naturalization applications to a final decision on the merits. *See* H.R.Rep. No. 101–187, at 11–13 (1989); New Citizens in Limbo?: One in Three Applicants for U.S. Citizenship Neither Pass Nor Fail (NALEO Background Paper # 8, mimeo 1988).

3. A 1985 study of naturalization procedures provides useful insights into the process. D. North, The Long Gray Welcome: A Study of the American Naturalization Program (1985). It also casts doubt on some widely held beliefs. For example, naturalization is apparently a more forbidding and difficult process than is often assumed, and U.S. procedures compare unfavorably in many respects with the more welcoming stance taken by other countries like Canada. *See id.* at 46–57. The current Commissioner of Immigration, Doris Meissner, announced that encouragement of naturalization would be a major priority during her tenure in office. 70 Interp.Rel. 1471–72 (1993).

2. DENATURALIZATION

A key feature of the Naturalization Act of 1906 was the creation of a procedure to take away citizenship if a later judicial proceeding determined that the naturalization was illegally or fraudulently acquired. This procedure has changed little since that time. Denaturalization proceedings may be brought only by United States Attorneys, not by private parties, and only when based on an affidavit of good cause, which is ordinarily prepared by officials of the Immigration Service. *See United States v. Zucca,* 351 U.S. 91, 76 S.Ct. 671, 100 L.Ed. 964 (1956). The current statutory provision for denaturalization appears in § 340 of the INA.[9]

---

9. Generally, an order granting naturalization by a court of competent jurisdiction (state or federal), like any other judgment, cannot be collaterally attacked if the order is valid on its face, even when the contesting party claims fraud in the procurement of the judgment. But a naturalization order, again like other judgments, is subject to *direct* attack, and the established means for direct attack is through the independent denaturalization proceedings prescribed in INA § 340(a). The Justice Department always brings such proceedings in federal district court, however, even if the original order issued from a state court (as was possible before the 1990 amendments). How can such an action be considered a direct attack?

This conceptual conundrum has caused the Supreme Court considerable difficulty in de-

ciding on the exact nature of judicial naturalization and denaturalization proceedings, and in determining how each should be deemed to fit with other statutory and constitutional requirements governing the roles of state and federal courts. Highlights of the Court's theoretical and practical meanderings may be traced from *Johannessen v. United States,* 225 U.S. 227, 32 S.Ct. 613, 56 L.Ed. 1066 (1912) (which initially approved the new denaturalization remedy, using a theory that later proved troublesome), through *United States v. Ness,* 245 U.S. 319, 38 S.Ct. 118, 62 L.Ed. 321 (1917); *Tutun v. United States,* 270 U.S. 568, 46 S.Ct. 425, 70 L.Ed. 738 (1926); and *Bindczyck v. Finucane,* 342 U.S. 76, 72 S.Ct. 130, 96 L.Ed. 100 (1951).

For many years, it was also possible for naturalized citizens to lose their citizenship, not for defects in the original grant, but because of certain actions following naturalization—actions which had been declared by Congress to result in such forfeiture. Most of these grounds of expatriation applied equally to naturalized and native-born citizens, but a few imposed more stringent requirements on those who had gained citizenship by naturalization. Occasionally the loss of citizenship in this manner has also been called denaturalization, but we will avoid that terminology here. We will use the term "denaturalization" to mean only the revocation of the citizenship of a naturalized alien based on <u>fraud or illegality in the</u> original naturalization. Any other deprivation of citizenship, whether applied to native-born or naturalized citizens, will be called "expatriation." [10]

The standards and procedures applied in denaturalization proceedings differ from those in the naturalization setting. *See generally* GM & Y §§ 100.01, 100.02. Most importantly, the burden of proof shifts to the government. In a major decision handed down in 1943, *Schneiderman v. United States*, 320 U.S. 118, 63 S.Ct. 1333, 87 L.Ed. 1796, a divided Court established important standards that the government must meet in a denaturalization proceeding. Schneiderman had been naturalized in 1927, and the naturalization court found, as the statutes then and now require, that he was "attached to the principles of the Constitution of the United States and well disposed to the good order and happiness of the United States." Later, Schneiderman became prominent in the leadership of the Communist Party, of which he had been a member since at least 1924. Though he had never been arrested for lawless acts, the government brought a denaturalization proceeding in 1939, claiming that his membership and his advocacy of Marxist doctrine demonstrated that he lacked the necessary attachment at the time of naturalization. The lower courts agreed and ordered denaturalization, but the Supreme Court reversed:

> This is not a naturalization proceeding in which the Government is being asked to confer the privilege of citizenship upon an applicant. Instead the Government seeks to turn the clock back twelve years after full citizenship was conferred upon petitioner by a judicial decree, and to deprive him of the priceless benefits that derive from that status. In its consequences it is more serious than a taking of one's property, or the imposition of a fine or other penalty. For it is safe to assert that nowhere in the world today is the right of citizenship of greater worth to an individual than it is in this country. It would be difficult to exaggerate its value and importance. By many it is regarded as the highest hope of civilized men. This does not mean that once granted to an alien, citizenship cannot be revoked or cancelled on legal grounds under appropriate proof. But such a right once conferred should not be taken away without the clearest sort of justification and proof.

---

10. As will become clear in Section D, over the last thirty years the Supreme Court has progressively imposed tighter constitutional limitations on Congress's power to expatriate unwilling citizens, whether native-born or naturalized. But none of the decisions in this series has seriously questioned Congress's authority to protect the integrity of the original naturalization process by permitting later deprivation of citizenship that was acquired illegally or through fraud.

So, whatever may be the rule in a naturalization proceeding (see *United States v. Manzi,* 276 U.S. 463, 467, 48 S.Ct. 328, 329, 72 L.Ed. 654), in an action instituted under § 15 for the purpose of depriving one of the precious right of citizenship previously conferred we believe the facts and the law should be construed as far as is reasonably possible in favor of the citizen. Especially is this so when the attack is made long after the time when the certificate of citizenship was granted and the citizen has meanwhile met his obligations and has committed no act of lawlessness. * * *

* * *

* * * If a finding of attachment can be so reconsidered in a denaturalization suit, our decisions make it plain that the Government needs more than a bare preponderance of the evidence to prevail. The remedy afforded the Government by the denaturalization statute has been said to be a narrower one than that of direct appeal from the granting of a petition. *Tutun v. United States,* 70 U.S. 568, 579, 46 S.Ct. 425, 427, 70 L.Ed. 738; *cf. United States v. Ness,* 245 U.S. 319, 325, 38 S.Ct. 118, 121, 62 L.Ed. 321. *Johannessen v. United States* states that a certificate of citizenship is "an instrument granting political privileges, and open like other public grants to be revoked if and when it shall be found to have been unlawfully or fraudulently procured. It is in this respect closely analogous to a public grant of land * * *." 225 U.S. 227, 238, 32 S.Ct. 613, 615, 56 L.Ed. 1066. To set aside such a grant the evidence must be "clear, unequivocal, and convincing"—"it cannot be done upon a bare preponderance of evidence which leaves the issue in doubt". *Maxwell Land–Grant Case (United States v. Maxwell Land–Grant Co.),* 121 U.S. 325, 381, 7 S.Ct. 1015, 1029, 30 L.Ed. 949. This is so because rights once conferred should not be lightly revoked. And more especially is this true when the rights are precious and when they are conferred by solemn adjudication, as is the situation when citizenship is granted. The Government's evidence in this case does not measure up to this exacting standard.

320 U.S. at 122–23, 125, 63 S.Ct. at 1335, 1337.

CHAUNT v. UNITED STATES

Supreme Court of the United States, 1960.
364 U.S. 350, 81 S.Ct. 147, 5 L.Ed.2d 120.

Opinion of the Court by MR. JUSTICE DOUGLAS, announced by MR. JUSTICE HARLAN.

Petitioner, a native of Hungary, was admitted to citizenship by a decree of the District Court in 1940. Respondent filed a complaint to revoke and set aside that order as authorized by § 340(a) of the Immigration and Nationality Act of 1952, on the ground that it had been procured "by concealment of a material fact or by willful misrepresentation." The complaint stated that petitioner had falsely denied membership in the

Communist Party and that by virtue of that membership he lacked the requisite attachment to the Constitution, etc., and the intent to renounce foreign allegiance. It also alleged that petitioner had procured his naturalization by concealing and misrepresenting a record of arrests. The District Court cancelled petitioner's naturalization, finding that he had concealed and misrepresented three matters—his arrests, his membership in the Communist Party, and his allegiance. The Court of Appeals affirmed, reaching only the question of the concealment of the arrests. The case is here on a writ of certiorari.

One question, on a form petitioner filled out in connection with his petition for naturalization, asked if he had ever been "arrested or charged with violation of any law of the United States or State or any city ordinance or traffic regulation" and if so to give full particulars. To this question petitioner answered "no." There was evidence that when he was questioned under oath by an examiner he gave the same answer. There was also evidence that if his answer had been "yes," the investigative unit of the Immigration Service would check with the authorities at the places where the arrests occurred "to ascertain ... whether the full facts were stated."

The District Court found that from 10 to 11 years before petitioner was naturalized he had been arrested three times as follows:

(1) On July 30, 1929, he was arrested for distributing handbills in New Haven, Connecticut, in violation of an ordinance. He pleaded not guilty and was discharged.

(2) On December 21, 1929, he was arrested for violating the park regulations in New Haven, Connecticut, by making "an oration, harangue, or other public demonstration in New Haven Green, outside of the churches." Petitioner pleaded not guilty. Disposition of the charge is not clear, the notation on the court record reading "Found J.S." which respondent suggests may mean "Judgment Suspended" after a finding of guilt.

(3) On March 11, 1930, he was again arrested in New Haven and this time charged with "General Breach of the Peace." He was found guilty by the City Court and fined $25. He took an appeal and the records show "nolled April 7, 1930."

Acquisition of American citizenship is a solemn affair. Full and truthful response to all relevant questions required by the naturalization procedure is, of course, to be exacted, and temporizing with the truth must be vigorously discouraged. Failure to give frank, honest, and unequivocal answers to the court when one seeks naturalization is a serious matter. Complete replies are essential so that the qualifications of the applicant or his lack of them may be ascertained. Suppressed or concealed facts, if known, might in and of themselves justify denial of citizenship. Or disclosure of the true facts might have led to the discovery of other facts which would justify denial of citizenship.

On the other hand, in view of the grave consequences to the citizen, naturalization decrees are not lightly to be set aside—the evidence must indeed be "clear, unequivocal, and convincing" and not leave "the issue ...

in doubt." *Schneiderman v. United States,* 320 U.S. 118, 125, 158, 63 S.Ct. 1333, 1336, 1352, 87 L.Ed. 1796; *Baumgartner v. United States,* 322 U.S. 665, 670, 64 S.Ct. 1240, 1243, 88 L.Ed. 1525. The issue in these cases is so important to the liberty of the citizen that the weight normally given concurrent findings of two lower courts does not preclude reconsideration here, for we deal with "judgments lying close to opinion regarding the whole nature of our Government and the duties and immunities of citizenship." *Baumgartner v. United States, supra,* 671, 64 S.Ct. 1243, 1244. And see *Klapprott v. United States,* 335 U.S. 601, 612 and (concurring opinion) 617, 69 S.Ct. 384, 389, 391, 93 L.Ed. 266.

While disclosure of them was properly exacted, the arrests in these cases were not reflections on the character of the man seeking citizenship. The statute in force at the time of his naturalization required that "he has behaved as a person of good moral character, attached to the principles of the Constitution of the United States, and well disposed to the good order and happiness of the United States" during the previous five years. These arrests were made some years prior to the critical five-year period. They did not, moreover, involve moral turpitude within the meaning of the law. No fraudulent conduct was charged. They involved distributing handbills, making a speech, and a breach of the peace. In one instance he was discharged, in one instance the prosecution was "nolled," and in the other (for making a speech in a park in violation of city regulations) he apparently received a suspended sentence. The totality of the circumstances surrounding the offenses charged makes them of extremely slight consequence. Had they involved moral turpitude or acts directed at the Government, had they involved conduct which even peripherally touched types of activity which might disqualify one from citizenship, a different case would be presented. On this record the nature of these arrests, the crimes charged, and the disposition of the cases do not bring them, inherently, even close to the requirement of "clear, unequivocal, and convincing" evidence that naturalization was illegally procured within the meaning of § 340(a) of the Immigration and Nationality Act.

It is argued, however, that disclosure of the arrests made in New Haven, Connecticut, in the years 1929 and 1930 would have led to a New Haven investigation at which leads to other evidence—more relevant and material than the arrests—might have been obtained. His residence in New Haven was from February 1929 to November 1930. Since that period was more than five years before his petition for naturalization, the name of his employer at that time was not required by the form prepared by the Service. It is now said, however, that if the arrests had been disclosed and investigated, the Service might well have discovered that petitioner in 1929 was "a district organizer" of the Communist Party in Connecticut. One witness in this denaturalization proceeding testified that such was the fact. An arrest, though by no means probative of any guilt or wrongdoing, is sufficiently significant as an episode in a man's life that it may often be material at least to further enquiry. We do not minimize the importance of that disclosure. In this case, however, we are asked to base materiality on the tenuous line of investigation that might have led from the arrests to the alleged communistic affiliations, when as a matter of fact petitioner in this same application disclosed that he was an employee and member of the International Workers' Order, which is said to be controlled by the Communist Party. In connection with petitioner's denial of such affiliations, respondent argues that since it was testified that the IWO was an organization controlled and dominated by the Communist Party, it is reasonable to infer that petitioner had those affiliations at the time of the application. But by the same token it would seem that a much less tenuous and speculative nexus with the Communist Party, if it be such, was thereby disclosed and was available for further investigation if it had been deemed appropriate at the time. It is said that IWO did not become tainted with Communist control until 1941. We read the record differently. If the Government's case is made out, that taint extended back at least as far as 1939. Had that disclosure not been made in the application, failure to report the arrests would have had greater significance. It could then be forcefully argued that failure to disclose the arrests was part and parcel of a project to conceal a Communist Party affiliation. But on this record, the failure to report the three arrests occurring from 10 to 11 years previously is neutral. We do not speculate as to why they were not disclosed. We only conclude that, in the circumstances of this case, the Government has failed to show by "clear, unequivocal, and convincing" evidence either (1) that facts were suppressed which, if known, would have warranted denial of citizenship or (2) that their disclosure might have been useful in an investigation possibly leading to the discovery of other facts warranting denial of citizenship.

There are issues in the case which we do not reach and which were not passed upon by the Court of Appeals. Accordingly the judgment will be reversed and the cause remanded to it so that the other questions raised in the appeal may be considered.

It is so ordered.

M R. J USTICE C LARK, with whom M R. J USTICE W HITAKER and M R. J USTICE S TEWART join, dissenting.

Petitioner swore in his application for naturalization that he had never been under arrest when in fact he had been arrested in New Haven, Connecticut, on three separate occasions within an eight-month period. * * * Both the District Court and the Court of Appeals have found that petitioner's falsification "was an intentional concealment of a material fact and a willful misrepresentation which foreclosed the Immigration and Naturalization Service and the district court from making a further investigation as to whether he had all the qualifications for citizenship . . . ." These findings, as such, are not disputed. It is nowhere suggested, for example, that the petitioner's falsehoods were the result of inadvertence or forgetfulness—that they were anything but deliberate lies. This Court, however, brushes these findings aside on the ground [1] that the arrests

1. The Court says that "[t]he totality of the circumstances surrounding the offenses charged makes them of extremely slight consequence." However, it overlooks the fact that neither the content of the handbills or of the harangue in the park nor the nature of the conduct leading to the conviction in the city court for a general breach of the peace appears in the record. Time has served petitioner well, for even the disposition of the

"were not reflections on the character of the man seeking citizenship." The Swiss philosopher Amiel tells us that "character is an historical fruit and is the result of a man's biography." Petitioner's past, if truthfully told in his application, would have been an odorous one. So bad that he dared not reveal it. For the Court to reward his dishonesty is nothing short of an open invitation to false swearing to all who seek the high privilege of American citizenship.

[handwritten margin note: dishonesty shld = denial of citizenship]

The Court first says that arrests of this nature, "the crimes charged, and the disposition of the cases do not bring them, inherently, even close to the requirement of 'clear, unequivocal, and convincing' evidence that naturalization was illegally procured." The Court, of course, knows that this is not the applicable test where one has deliberately falsified his papers and thus foreclosed further investigation. This basis for the reversal, therefore, misses the point involved and should have been of no consequence here.

The test is not whether the truthful answer in itself, or the facts discovered through an investigation prompted by that answer, would have justified a denial of citizenship. It is whether the falsification, by misleading the examining officer, forestalled an investigation which *might have resulted* in the defeat of petitioner's application for naturalization. The Courts of Appeals are without disagreement on this point and it is, of course, a necessary rule in order to prevent the making of misrepresentations for the very purpose of forestalling inquiry as to eligibility. The question as to arrests is highly pertinent to the issue of satisfactory moral character, the *sine qua non* of good citizenship. Petitioner's false answer to the question shut off that line of inquiry and was a fraud on the Government and the naturalization court. The majority makes much of the fact that the arrests occurred prior to the five-year statutory period of good behavior, but that is of no consequence. Concealment at the very time of naturalization is the issue here and that act of deliberate falsification before an officer of the Government clearly relates to the petitioner's general moral character. Indeed, the Congress has long made it a felony punishable by imprisonment for a maximum of five years. Certainly this does not fall within a class of peccadilloes which may be overlooked as being without "reflections on the character of the man seeking citizenship." In fact it strips an offender of all civil rights and leaves a shattered character that only a presidential pardon can mend.

The Court concludes that the false denial of prior arrests was "neutral" because the petitioner revealed in his preliminary application that he was an employee of the International Workers Order, which the Court adds, "is said to be controlled by the Communist Party." What the Court fails to point out is that the sole evidence, in this record, as to the International Workers Order was presented in 1955, 15 years after petitioner's deception of the examiner. * * * The truth of the matter is that in his final naturalization application petitioner said he was employed by

cases is not too clear. But to extrapolate the character of petitioner's conduct solely from these meager circumstances smacks of the psychic. Moreover, to say that the offenses "did not ... involve moral turpitude" is gratuitous. This Court has never so held.

the "Fraternal Benefit Society of Internation [*sic*]Workers Order," a name which would lead one to believe that it was an insurance society. * * *

As I read the record, it clearly supports the findings of the two courts below. Even if petitioner had told the truth, and the conduct causing the arrests was found not to relate to his present fitness for naturalization, it does not follow that citizenship would have been awarded. It might well have been that in checking on the handbills, the harangue in the public park, and the general breach of the peace the investigator would have been led to discover that petitioner was, in 1940, a leader in the Communist Party. I think it more logical than not that the Government would have discovered petitioner's Communist affiliations through such an investigation, and that the deliberate falsification in 1940 forestalled this revelation for 15 years. But whether or not that be the case, the Government was entitled to an honest answer from one who sought admission to its citizenship. We should exact the highest standards of probity and fitness from all applicants. American citizenship is a valuable right. It is prized highly by us who have it and it is sought eagerly by millions who do not. It is asking little enough of those who would be vested with its privileges to demand that they tell the truth.

I would affirm.

Notes

1. The *Chaunt* majority relies on the doctrine of *Schneiderman*, which requires the government to prove its case in a denaturalization proceeding by "clear, unequivocal, and convincing" evidence. But is that requirement relevant here? From all that appears in the opinions, the government's proof was solid, and apparently Chaunt does not here dispute the fact of his arrests or the willfulness of his misrepresentations when the form asked about them.

2. If this is not a case about inadequate factual showings, then, what exactly is the theory of the majority opinion? Is it based on a decision that the lies were not material? The statute provides for denaturalization when citizenship was procured "by concealment of a material fact or by willful misrepresentation." Has the majority misread the statute when it applies the notion of materiality to a case of misrepresentation, rather than concealment? If the naturalization form had merely asked "Are there any other matters bearing on good moral character that we ought to know about?" instead of asking specifically about arrests, the issue would be concealment and materiality would be relevant. But that is not this case.

3. How would the majority have responded if Chaunt's arrests (and hence his misrepresentations) had come to light 15 days after the naturalization proceedings, rather than approximately 15 years later? Perhaps *Chaunt* amounts to a crude judicial attempt to fashion a de facto statute of limitations, in light of the harsh consequences of denaturalization when a relatively minor flaw in the naturalization proceedings is unearthed after many years of unblemished citizenship. If so, does this approach work? Does such an effort represent a legitimate judicial role?

4. Is the Court serious when it says that "[f]ull and truthful response to all relevant questions required by the naturalization procedure is, of course, to be exacted, and temporizing with the truth must be vigorously discouraged"? Doesn't *Chaunt* encourage applicants to conceal or even lie about troublesome parts of their past, whenever there is doubt whether the hidden information would disqualify them? If their deception is successful, then the relevance of the information will be tested only under the stringent standards that apply in *denaturalization* proceedings, if indeed it is ever unearthed and tested at all. Is this what the Court meant? Is it a sound way to construe the statute?

In succeeding years, the lower courts struggled with the meaning and application of *Chaunt,* as the next two cases reveal.

IN RE PETITION OF HANIATAKIS

United States Court of Appeals, Third Circuit, 1967.
376 F.2d 728.

FREEDMAN, CIRCUIT JUDGE.

This is an appeal by the United States from an order granting a petition for naturalization. The appellee, whose petition was granted by the court below, has presented no argument to us, although we had sought to have her present her views.

Petitioner is a twenty-two year old native of Greece who has been a lawful permanent resident of the United States since June 4, 1956. In 1964, she applied for naturalization in her maiden name in the District Court for the Western District of Pennsylvania. The standard procedure, which she followed, required her first to present a written application to file a petition for naturalization and later to be examined under oath in regard to it, after which she swore to the application as corrected by the hearing examiner, and finally to file the verified petition itself.[a] In her written application of June 9, 1964, again during her oral examination under oath by the hearing examiner on June 17, and also in the petition for naturalization, filed on the same date, petitioner stated that she was unmarried. In fact, however, she had been married on May 18, 1964 to a Greek seaman who had been arrested for illegal entry into the United States on June 10, and had voluntarily returned to Greece on August 3. Petitioner had also falsely stated her prior places of residence, declaring both in her written application and her oral statements under oath that she had been a resident of Pennsylvania continuously since her entry into the United States, although for part of that time she had been a resident both of Indiana, where she had been married, and of Ohio.

After an investigation by the Immigration and Naturalization Service had revealed the fact of her marriage, a further preliminary examination

---

a. The 1990 Act implemented a somewhat different application process as part of a change to a largely administrative naturalization procedure. See p. 1000 *supra.*—eds.

was held at which petitioner acknowledged the falsity of her statement that she was unmarried. She explained that she had concealed her marriage out of fear that her naturalization would be held up for five more years if the fact of her marriage to another alien had been revealed. Her explanation makes her conduct all the more tragic, for the Immigration and Naturalization Service declares that her marriage to another alien would not have affected her application.

As a result of her testimony the hearing examiner concluded that petitioner had testified falsely to obtain benefits under the Immigration and Nationality Act, and that she was consequently ineligible for naturalization, because she lacked the "good moral character" required by the Act for admission to citizenship. The District Court, however, granted the petition for naturalization in petitioner's married name, feeling bound to follow the decision of another judge of the same court in Petition for Naturalization of Sotos, 221 F.Supp. 145 (W.D.Pa.1963). It concluded that petitioner's false testimony did not affirmatively demonstrate the absence of "good moral character," since her misrepresentations were not material and the facts concealed would not themselves have been a barrier to her naturalization. 246 F.Supp. 545 (W.D.Pa.1965). The United States appeals from this ruling.

Section 316(a)(3) of the Immigration and Nationality Act provides that no person shall be naturalized unless, *inter alia,* he "has been and still is a person of good moral character" during the five-year period immediately preceding the date of filing of his petition for naturalization and the period thereafter until admission to citizenship. Section 101(f) of the Act specifies a number of instances in which an applicant shall not be regarded to be of good moral character. Among those is the case of "one who has given false testimony for the purpose of obtaining any benefits under this chapter." This section is mandatory in its terms.

Petitioner's false answers were given both in the written application and in the petition for naturalization. Were this all, we would be required to determine whether false statements in applications or other written documents sworn to before an officer duly authorized to administer oaths would constitute "false testimony," which the statute makes conclusive proof of lack of good moral character. The same false statements, however, were given orally as testimony at the preliminary investigation, and this brings the case clearly within the proscription of the statute. The remaining question, therefore, is whether we should narrow the plain words of the statute and read into it an exception which would distinguish between material and immaterial matters in the giving of false testimony.

The federal courts have consistently refused to draw a distinction between materiality and immateriality of false testimony in cases where such a distinction would have had clear application. See Berenyi v. District Director, 385 U.S. 630, 87 S.Ct. 666, 17 L.Ed.2d 656 (1967); Stevens v. United States, 190 F.2d 880 (7 Cir.1951); Del Guercio v. Pupko, 160 F.2d 799 (9 Cir.1947). The statute is not concerned with the significance or materiality of a particular question, but rather, as the Supreme Court has recently indicated in Berenyi v. District Director, intends that naturalization should be denied to one who gives false testimony to facilitate naturalization.

The reason for denying naturalization whenever false testimony is given in an attempt to gain it goes beyond a judgment that one who gives false testimony to deceive the government is by that fact unworthy of the privileges of citizenship; it is also based on the practical ground that a false answer to a query which on its face appears innocuous may effectively cut off a line of inquiry which might have revealed further facts bearing on the petitioner's eligibility for citizenship. Having asked a question which it deems significant to determine the qualifications of one seeking citizenship, the government is entitled to full disclosure. Berenyi v. District Director, supra at 638, 87 S.Ct. 666. See also United States v. Montalbano, 236 F.2d 757, 759–760 (3 Cir.1956), cert. denied, sub nom. Genovese v. United States, 352 U.S. 952, 77 S.Ct. 327, 1 L.Ed.2d 244 (1956), involving revocation of citizenship. Indeed, the contention that the misrepresentations made here were immaterial is quite misleading, for the failure to give truthful answers regarding marital status has been deemed a "material fact" under § 340(a) of the Act, which permits the more drastic action of cancellation of naturalization where it has been "procured by concealment of a material fact or by willful misrepresentation." See, e.g., United States v. D'Agostino, 338 F.2d 490, 491 (2 Cir.1964).

Both the court below and the court in Petition for Naturalization of Sotos, 221 F.Supp. 145 (W.D.Pa.1963), relied upon Chaunt v. United States, 364 U.S. 350, 81 S.Ct. 147, 5 L.Ed.2d 120 (1960), in concluding that false testimony given to facilitate naturalization does not bar naturalization unless the concealed matter itself would bar it. There the Supreme Court refused to revoke and set aside the naturalization twenty years before of an American citizen even though he had failed to reveal, as then required by the naturalization form, that he had previously been arrested. Although the Court's decision in *Chaunt* rested upon the immateriality of the false testimony, this does not help the petitioner here. To begin with, the provision of the Act involved in *Chaunt*, § 340(a), specifically required that the fact concealed be "material." Moreover, in *Chaunt* the government attempted to withdraw the privileges of citizenship from one who had already been admitted to their benefits. What is involved here, on the other hand, is the decision whether the petitioner should be admitted to the benefits of that citizenship. Much turns on this distinction, since the immigration law historically has chosen to afford greater protections to those who have been admitted to citizenship. Thus, the Supreme Court recently declared in the *Berenyi* case, *supra*, 385 U.S. at 636–637, 87 S.Ct. at 610:

> "When the Government seeks to strip a person of citizenship already acquired, or deport a resident alien and send him from our shores, it carries the heavy burden of proving its case by 'clear, unequivocal, and convincing evidence.' But when an alien seeks to obtain the privileges and benefits of citizenship, the shoe is on the other foot. He is the moving party, affirmatively asking the Government to endow him with all the advantages of citizenship. Because that status, once granted, cannot lightly be taken away,

the Government has a strong and legitimate interest in ensuring that only qualified persons are granted citizenship. For these reasons, it has been universally accepted that the burden is on the alien applicant to show his eligibility for citizenship in every respect. This Court has often stated that doubts 'should be resolved in favor of the United States and against the claimant.' E.g., United States v. Macintosh, 283 U.S. 605, 626 [51 S.Ct. 570, 75 L.Ed. 1302]."

Falling as she does within the class of those seeking citizenship, petitioner was obliged to prove her suitability for it. This, unfortunately, she has not done.

The judgment of the district court will be reversed.

UNITED STATES v. SHESHTAWY

United States Court of Appeals, Tenth Circuit, 1983.
714 F.2d 1038.

McKay, Circuit Judge.

Adel Sheshtawy, a naturalized citizen of the United States, appeals a district court decision to revoke his citizenship and cancel his certificate of naturalization.

The appellant initially sought naturalization in 1978; however, his naturalization was delayed because his character witnesses had not known him for the requisite period of time. Approximately three weeks before the appellant's rescheduled naturalization hearing, he was arrested and charged with concealing stolen property. Shortly after the arrest, he received a standard form questionnaire from the Immigration and Naturalization Service, which he was required to fill out in order to update the information on his application for a petition for naturalization. The third question asked whether he had ever been arrested, which he falsely answered "no." As instructed, the appellant took the form with him to his naturalization hearing, where he turned it in to a naturalization examiner and was ultimately naturalized. About six weeks later, the state trial judge, at the end of the preliminary hearing, dismissed the criminal charges against the appellant, finding that no crime had been committed. At some later date, the INS discovered that the appellant had been arrested, and these proceedings were commenced.

In revoking the appellant's citizenship, the trial court held that disclosure of the arrest would have caused a substantial delay in the appellant's naturalization pending investigation, that the appellant willfully answered the arrest question falsely in order to avoid the consequences that a true answer might have had on his naturalization thereby facilitating his acquisition of citizenship, and that the defendant willfully misrepresented and concealed a material fact.

This case is squarely governed by principles established in *Chaunt v. United States,* 364 U.S. 350, 81 S.Ct. 147, 5 L.Ed.2d 120 (1960). There, the Supreme Court held that the government carries a heavy burden when it seeks to revoke citizenship under INA § 340(a) for the willful misrepresentation or concealment of a material fact.[1] For a fact to be "material," the government must "show by 'clear, unequivocal, and convincing' evidence either (1) that facts were suppressed which, if known, would have warranted denial of citizenship or (2) that their disclosure might have been useful in an investigation possibly leading to the discovery of other facts warranting denial of citizenship." *Id.* at 355, 81 S.Ct. at 150.

In this case, the government made no claim that the arrest itself would have resulted in a denial of citizenship. Nor did the government attempt to show that an investigation would have turned up other facts warranting a denial of citizenship. Rather, it argues that *Chaunt* requires only that disclosure might have led to the discovery of disqualifying facts—that is, that an investigation would have been undertaken.[2] Thus, the substance of the government's position, which the trial court accepted, is that the test for materiality

> is not whether the truthful answer in itself, or the facts discovered through an investigation prompted by that answer, would have justified a denial of citizenship. It is whether the falsification, by misleading the examining officer, forestalled an investigation which *might have resulted* in the defeat of petitioner's application for naturalization.

Id. at 357, 81 S.Ct. at 151 (Clark, J., dissenting) (emphasis supplied). This test, however, was the one espoused by the *Chaunt* dissent and rejected by the majority.

In *Fedorenko v. United States,* 449 U.S. 490, 101 S.Ct. 737, 66 L.Ed.2d 686 (1981), the Court avoided reviewing a similar construction of the *Chaunt* test by the Fifth Circuit, by choosing to resolve the case on a different theory. In his concurring opinion, however, Justice Blackmun carefully reviewed the *Chaunt* test and concluded that it requires that the government demonstrate the existence of actual disqualifying facts—facts that themselves would have warranted denial of petitioner's citizenship. *Id.* at 523–26, 101 S.Ct. at 755–57 (Blackmun, J., concurring).[3] While there has been substantial disagreement over the meaning of *Chaunt,*[4] its characterizations by Justice Blackmun appear to us to be correct, and until

1. * * * The Court has read both the willfulness and materiality requirements as applying to both concealments and misrepresentations. *See, e.g., Fedorenko v. United States,* 449 U.S. 490, 493, 101 S.Ct. 737, 740, 66 L.Ed.2d 686 (1981).

2. There is evidence in the record that had the INS known of the appellant's arrest, it would have delayed the naturalization decision and conducted an investigation that would have consisted of a tape-recorded interview with the appellant, an examination of the police reports, and probably a recommendation that the investigative department make a complete check of the appellant's moral character.

3. Justice Stevens' view of the *Chaunt* test substantially coincides with that of Justice Blackmun. He reads *Chaunt* as requir-

ing that disclosure would have led to an investigation, that a disqualifying circumstance actually exist, and that it would have been discovered in the investigation. *Fedorenko,* 449 U.S. at 537, 101 S.Ct. at 762 (Stevens, J., dissenting). Thus, although the Court declined to follow what is essentially the version of *Chaunt* for which the government argues on this appeal, only two of the justices specifically rejected it; and Justice White was the only one who embraced it, *id.* at 528, 101 S.Ct. at 758 (White, J., dissenting).

4. *Compare La Madrid–Peraza v. INS,* 492 F.2d 1297, 1298 (9th Cir.1974) *with United States v. Oddo,* 314 F.2d 115, 118 (2d Cir.), *cert. denied,* 375 U.S. 833, 84 S.Ct. 50, 11 L.Ed.2d 63 (1963).

Chaunt as thus interpreted has been rejected or overturned by the Supreme Court, we must follow it.

At issue in these cases is a balance of the importance of securing the stability and security of naturalized citizenship against the risk, arguably posed by *Chaunt,* of encouraging lying in connection with applications for citizenship. Our reading of *Chaunt* is unlikely to provide persons who have in their background a clearly disqualifying experience with additional incentive to lie, since their citizenship would be revoked even under our interpretation of *Chaunt.* Nor does *Chaunt* encourage persons with no doubtful experiences in their lives to lie. The only group possibly affected are those who are uncertain whether a particular event would disqualify them from naturalization. We believe the *Chaunt* Court considered this tension and, in effect, concluded that even though there may be some who are encouraged to lie, the importance of putting naturalized citizenship well beyond the danger of unwarranted revocation justifies the adoption of so severe a test.

Since the government does not claim to have established facts that would have warranted denial of the appellant's citizenship, it has not met *Chaunt* 's rigorous test, and revocation under section 340(a) is not justified.

The government alternatively argues that revocation is justified because the appellant did not meet all of the statutory prerequisites to naturalization. Only "a person of good moral character" is eligible for naturalization, INA § 316(a)(3), and "one who has given false testimony for the purpose of obtaining any benefits under this chapter" cannot be found to be a person of good moral character, § 101(f)(6). Since the appellant lied to gain naturalization benefits, the government argues that he was not of good moral character and therefore ineligible for naturalization.

We believe, however, that in denaturalization proceedings, section 101(f)(6) applies only to false testimony concerning material facts. In *Fedorenko,* the Supreme Court construed a section of the Displaced Persons Act, providing that any person who made a willful misrepresentation in order to gain benefits under that Act—i.e., admission to the United States—should thereafter not be admissible, to apply only to material misrepresentations. The Court simply noted that materiality is required to revoke citizenship for concealments or misrepresentations under section § 340(a) and asserted that "[l]ogically, the same principle should govern the interpretation of this provision of the DPA." The wording of section 101(f)(6) closely tracks that of the statute in *Fedorenko,* and the context within which we are construing the statute—that is, denaturalization of a citizen—and the interests at stake are the same. We therefore conclude that *Fedorenko* compels reading a materiality requirement into section 101(f)(6) when it is invoked for denaturalization purposes.[6]

---

6. Both the Second and Third Circuits have refused to read a materiality requirement into § 101(f)(6); however, both of those cases involved naturalization, not denaturalization, proceedings so that the important interest of the naturalized citizen in retaining his or her citizenship was not implicated. *See Kovacs v. United States,* 476 F.2d 843, 845 (2d Cir.1973); *In re Haniatakis,* 376 F.2d 728, 730 (3d Cir.1967). They are therefore inapposite in the denaturalization context.

The remaining question is the legal standard for materiality under section 101(f)(6). Although the Court in *Fedorenko* refrained from deciding whether the *Chaunt* test for materiality applied to misrepresentations on visa applications, it reaffirmed the test's applicability to determine the materiality of misrepresentations on citizenship applications. Thus, *Chaunt* is the controlling authority for materiality decisions under section 101(f)(6), and the government's case under this section must fail for the reasons set out *ante*.

McWilliams, Judge, dissents.

It is incongruous that Sheshtawy should be rewarded for his dishonesty. If Sheshtawy had answered the question truthfully and informed the authorities that he had been recently arrested on a charge of concealing stolen goods, such disclosure *might* have been useful in an investigation *possibly leading* to the discovery of other facts warranting denial of citizenship. Such meets the second test in *Chaunt v. United States,* 364 U.S. 350, 81 S.Ct. 147, 5 L.Ed.2d 120 (1960), as I read that case. I would affirm the trial court.

Questions

Is it possible to construct a theory under which *Haniatakis* and *Sheshtawy* are consistent? If Sheshtawy can get away with a deliberate lie because the matter involved turns out not to have been a disqualifying factor in an application for naturalization, why shouldn't Haniatakis enjoy the same forgiveness? Can the timing of the discovery legitimately make so much difference? If you were a member of Congress, what changes, if any, would you make in the naturalization and denaturalization provisions in light of *Chaunt, Berenyi, Haniatakis, Fedorenko,* and *Sheshtawy?*

KUNGYS v. UNITED STATES

Supreme Court of the United States, 1988.
485 U.S. 759, 108 S.Ct. 1537, 99 L.Ed.2d 839.

Justice Scalia delivered the judgment of the Court, the opinion of the Court as to Parts I, II–A, and III–A, and an opinion joined by Chief Justice Rehnquist and Justice Brennan as to Parts II–B and III–B, and by Justice O'Connor as to Part III–B.

Juozas Kungys seeks our review of a judgment and opinion of the Third Circuit remanding his case for the completion of deportation proceedings. The issues presented are: first, whether certain misrepresentations or concealments made by Kungys in connection with his naturalization proceeding were material within the meaning of INA § 340 and *Chaunt v. United States,* 364 U.S. 350, 81 S.Ct. 147, 5 L.Ed.2d 120 (1960); and second, whether those misrepresentations, made under oath and in the form of forged documents, rendered Kungys' citizenship "illegally procured" under INA §§ 101(f)(6), 316(a)(3) and 340(a), because they established that he lacked the requisite good moral character when he was naturalized 34 years ago.

I

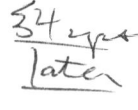

Petitioner applied for an immigration visa in Stuttgart, Germany, in 1947. In 1948, the visa was issued, and he came to the United States; he was naturalized as a citizen in 1954. In 1982, the United States, acting through the Office of Special Investigations of the Department of Justice, filed a complaint pursuant to INA § 340(a) to denaturalize him. The United States advanced three grounds. First, it attempted to show that Kungys had participated in executing over 2,000 Lithuanian civilians, most of them Jewish, in Kedainiai, Lithuania, between July and August of 1941. As proof of this claim, the United States offered in evidence three video-taped depositions taken for use in this case in the Soviet Union. After determining that for numerous reasons the Soviet-source depositions were inherently unreliable, the District Court admitted them only for the limited purpose of showing that the atrocities actually occurred. The District Court then held that the admissible evidence was insufficient to sustain the charges that Kungys had participated in the Kedainiai atrocities.

Second, the United States attempted to show that, in applying for his visa and in his naturalization petition, Kungys had made false statements with respect to his date and place of birth, wartime occupations, and wartime residence. The District Court found that these misrepresentations had been made but held them not to be material within the meaning of § 340(a), as illuminated by language in *Chaunt v. United States, supra.*

Third, the United States argued that Kungys' citizenship had been "illegally procured" under § 340(a) because when he was naturalized he lacked the good moral character required of applicants for citizenship by § 316(a). In support of this theory, the United States asserted that Kungys' false representations, whether or not material, were sufficient to show that he had given false testimony to obtain immigration or naturalization benefits, which INA § 101(f)(6) makes determinative of lack of good moral character. The District Court ruled that the false statements at issue were not covered by § 101(f)(6) because they were not material.

Having rejected each of the three asserted grounds for denaturalization, the District Court entered judgment for Kungys. The United States appealed. The Third Circuit declined to pass on the United States' submission that the first asserted ground (participation in the Kedainiai atrocities) was wrongfully rejected because of error in failing to admit unqualifiedly the Soviet-source depositions. It reversed, however, the District Court's rejection of the second ground, concluding that Kungys' willful misrepresentation of the date and place of his birth in connection with his applications for visa and naturalization (which was no longer disputed), was material for purposes of the "concealment or misrepresentation" provision of § 340(a). Finally, the Third Circuit upheld the District Court's rejection of the third asserted ground for deportation, agreeing that in order to establish "illegal procurement" under § 340(a) on account of lack of good moral character under § 101(f)(6), false testimony must be shown to have been material.

* * *

II

A

* * * This Court has previously suggested, and the parties do not dispute, that [§ 340(a)] requires misrepresentations or concealments that are both willful and material. See *Fedorenko v. United States,* 449 U.S. 490, 507–508, n. 28, 101 S.Ct. 737, 747–748, n. 28, 66 L.Ed.2d 686 (1981). So understood, the provision plainly contains four independent requirements: the naturalized citizen must have misrepresented or concealed some fact, the misrepresentation or concealment must have been willful, the fact must have been material, and the naturalized citizen must have procured citizenship as a result of the misrepresentation or concealment. It is no longer in dispute that the first two of these requirements were met here, since petitioner now concedes that he willfully misrepresented the date and place of his birth in his naturalization proceeding in 1954 as well as in applying for his visa in 1947.[5]

* * * In *Chaunt v. United States,* we held that a naturalized citizen who had willfully and falsely stated during the naturalization process that he had never been arrested could nevertheless not be denaturalized pursuant to § 340. * * * [The Court in *Chaunt,*] in summarizing its holding, states that "the Government has failed to show by 'clear, unequivocal, and convincing' evidence either (1) that facts were suppressed which, if known, would have warranted denial of citizenship or (2) that their disclosure might have been useful in an investigation possibly leading to the discovery of other facts warranting denial of citizenship." The efforts to make this formulation the test for materiality have not met with notable success. Not only have the Courts of Appeals failed to arrive at a single interpretation, but our one attempt to dispel their confusion, *Fedorenko,* seemingly produced at least three variants on this Court [citing the concurring and dissenting opinions.]

With the wisdom of experience, we now conclude that the attempts to construct a standard from the *Chaunt* dicta have been both unnecessary and unfortunate. The term "material" in § 340(a) is not a hapax legome-

---

5. The Government asserted that the purpose of the misrepresentations was to distance Kungys from Kedainiai, where atrocities had occurred, and to make it more difficult to identify him as one of the perpetrators. Kungys contended that even greater atrocities had occurred in the city he falsely listed as his birthplace; and that the age difference (two years) was of little consequence for identification purposes. Kungys asserted that he had lied concerning his date and place of birth in obtaining identity documents from the Nazis to go from Lithuania to Germany—the purpose of the dissembling at that time being to place him above the age of conscription and to avoid the risk of persecution for his participation in the Lithuanian resistance movement. (Vydaudas Vidiekunas, a leader of the resistance movement validated Kungys' account of his participation.) Kungys asserted that in applying for his visa he simply repeated the information contained on his identity documents, believing the falsities inconsequential for United States immigration purposes; and that with similar belief he conformed his naturalization petition to his visa application.

non. Its use in the context of false statements to public officials goes back as far as Lord Coke[.] * * * Given these common-law antecedents, it is unsurprising that a number of federal statutes criminalizing false statements to public officials use the term "material." * * * The federal courts have long displayed a quite uniform understanding of the "materiality" concept as embodied in such statutes. The most common formulation of that understanding is that a concealment or misrepresentation is material if it "has a natural tendency to influence, or was capable of influencing, the decision of" the decisionmaking body to which it was addressed. While we have before us here a statute revoking citizenship rather than imposing criminal fine or imprisonment, neither the evident objective sought to be achieved by the materiality requirement, nor the gravity of the consequences that follow from its being met, are so different as to justify adoption of a different standard. "Where Congress uses terms that have accumulated settled meaning under either equity or the common law, a court must infer, unless the statute otherwise dictates, that Congress means to incorporate the established meaning of these terms."

One might perhaps view the *Chaunt* test as not a repudiation of the established meaning of "material," but as an attempt to craft a more precise test for what constitutes "a natural tendency to influence" a naturalization decision. Surely, however, there is no less need for precision in the criminal context than in the denaturalization context. The more general formulation is preferable there, as we think it is here, because the judgment in question does not lend itself to mechanical resolution. The disagreement between the District Court and the Court of Appeals in *Fedorenko* turned on whether the *Chaunt* test required that, had the truth been told, an investigation *would* have resulted which *would* have disclosed disqualifying facts, or rather that an investigation *would* have resulted which *might* have disclosed disqualifying facts. *Fedorenko,* 449 U.S., at 528, 101 S.Ct., at 758 (WHITE, J., dissenting). But if the ultimate question is "natural tendency to influence," it would seem to make little difference whether the probabilities of investigation and resulting disclosure, respectively, are 100%–20%, 20%–100%, 51%–51%, or even 30%–30%. It has never been the test of materiality that the misrepresentation or concealment would *more likely than not* have produced an erroneous decision, or even that it would *more likely than not* have triggered an investigation. Thus, while the *Chaunt* formulation may be an adequate explanation of why the misrepresentation in that case was judged not to have had a natural tendency to influence the decision, it does not necessarily facilitate judgment in the infinite variety of other factual patterns that may emerge * * *. We think it safer in the naturalization context, as elsewhere, to fix as our guide the central object of the inquiry: whether the misrepresentation or concealment was predictably capable of affecting, *i.e.,* had a natural tendency to affect, the official decision. The official decision in question, of course, is whether the applicant meets the requirements for citizenship, so that the test more specifically is whether the misrepresentation or concealment had a natural tendency to produce the conclusion that the applicant was qualified. This test must be met, of course, by evidence that is clear, unequivocal, and convincing. See, *e.g., Schneiderman v. United States,* 320

U.S. 118, 158, 63 S.Ct. 1333, 1352–1353, 87 L.Ed. 1796 (1943). Though this formulation may seem less verbally precise than *Chaunt*, in application it may well produce greater uniformity, since judges are accustomed to using it, and can consult a large body of case precedent.

[The opinion then rules that the issue of materiality is an issue of law, not one of fact.]

* * *

B

We turn, then, to whether the one misrepresentation on which the trial court's finding was considered and upheld by the Third Circuit—misrepresentation of the date and place of Kungys' birth—was material under the foregoing test. As discussed earlier, Kungys made that misrepresentation in both the 1947 visa proceeding and the 1954 naturalization proceeding. But insofar as application of the "concealment or misrepresentation" clause of § 340(a) is concerned, we find it improper to address the 1947 episode. Unlike § 101(f)(6), which covers false testimony "for the purpose of obtaining *any* benefits" under the immigration and naturalization laws, the "concealment or misrepresentation" clause of § 340(a) applies only where the *order and certificate of naturalization* . . . were procured by concealment of a material fact or by willful misrepresentation." Procurement of other benefits, including visas, is not covered. Especially in light of this contrast with § 101(f)(6), we are unpersuaded by the Government's argument that a misrepresentation in the visa proceeding "procures" the naturalization because it obtains United States residence, which in turn is a prerequisite to naturalization. The same argument could be made with respect to a misrepresentation that effects free enrollment in a reading course, which produces the prerequisite of English literacy. Such analysis stretches the "concealment or misrepresentation" clause of § 340(a) beyond its intent, which we think limited to falsehoods or deceptions in the naturalization proceeding.

Looking, therefore, solely to the question whether Kungys' misrepresentation of the date and place of his birth in his naturalization petition was material within the meaning of § 340(a), we conclude that it was not. There has been no suggestion that those facts were themselves relevant to his qualifications for citizenship. Even though they were not, the misrepresentation of them would have a natural tendency to influence the citizenship determination, and thus be a misrepresentation of material facts, if the true date and place of birth would predictably have disclosed other facts relevant to his qualifications.[9] But not even that has been found here.   * * *

9. Justice Stevens minimizes the substance of what we require by describing it as no more than a showing "by clear and convincing evidence that the true facts would have led to further investigation." But further investigation would not occur—and its predictability could assuredly not be clear and convincing—if the facts at issue were not such as gave cause to believe that the applicant was not qualified. We are not talking about investigations by detective hobbyists, but by public officials seeking only evidence concerning citizenship qualifications.

It seems to us not so clear that, had Kungys explained his earlier misstatement of date and place of birth as he has here, see n. 5, *supra,* the discrepancy would likely have produced either "outright denial" or an investigation, or that an investigation would have produced the described outcome. But even a high probability that one or another of those consequences would have resulted from the discrepancy does not establish that Kungys' misrepresentation was material. Section 340(a) imposes denaturalization for "concealment *of a material fact*"; and the materiality requirement implicit in the misrepresentation provision likewise relates to misrepresentation *of a material fact.* Thus, for purposes of determining the natural tendency of a misrepresentation to affect a decision under § 340(a), what is relevant is what would have ensued from official knowledge of the misrepresented fact (in this case, Kungys' true date and place of birth), not what would have ensued from official knowledge of inconsistency between a posited assertion of the truth and an earlier assertion of falsehood. * * * What must have a natural tendency to influence the official decision is the misrepresentation itself, not the failure to create an inconsistency with an earlier misrepresentation; the failure to state the truth, not the failure to state what had been stated earlier. The Government has failed to establish clearly, unequivocally, and convincingly that Kungys' misrepresentation of the date and place of his birth had this natural tendency.

We leave it to the Third Circuit on remand to determine whether the other misrepresentations or concealments that the District Court found to have been made in 1954 were supported by the evidence and material to the naturalization decision under the standard we have described—bearing in mind the unusually high burden of proof in denaturalization cases. If so, it will have to reach the fourth § 340(a) issue described in our earlier analysis: whether Kungys "procured" his citizenship by means of those misrepresentations or concealments. That requirement demands, first of all, that citizenship be obtained as a result of the application process in which the misrepresentations or concealments were made. The difficult question, and that on which we part company with JUSTICE STEVENS' opinion concurring in the judgment (concurrence), is what it demands beyond that. We do not agree with petitioner's contention that it requires the Government to establish that naturalization would not have been granted if the misrepresentations or concealments had not occurred. If such a "but for" causation requirement existed in § 340(a), it is most unlikely that a materiality requirement would have been added as well—requiring, in addition to distortion of the decision, a natural tendency to distort the decision. Moreover, the difficulty of establishing "but for" causality, by clear, unequivocal, and convincing evidence many years after the fact, is so great that we cannot conceive that Congress intended such a burden to be met before a material misrepresentation could be sanctioned. We do think, however, that the "procured by" language can and should be given some effect beyond the mere requirement that the misrepresentation have been made in the application proceeding. Proof of materiality can sometimes be regarded as establishing a rebuttable presumption. Though the "procured by" language of the present statute cannot be read to *require* proof of disqualification, we think it can be read to express the notion that one who obtained his citizenship in a proceeding where he made material misrepresentations was *presumably* disqualified. The importance of the rights at issue leads us to conclude that the naturalized citizen should be able to refute that presumption, and avoid the consequence of denaturalization, by showing, through a preponderance of the evidence, that the statutory requirement as to which the misrepresentation *had a natural tendency* to produce a favorable decision was in fact met. Such a construction gives ample meaning to both the "materiality" and "procured by" requirements.

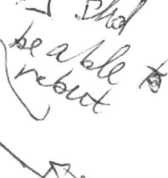

JUSTICE STEVENS' concurrence would adopt a requirement of "but for" causality, emphasizing the necessity that the Government establish, at least, that the misrepresenting applicant was in fact not qualified to be naturalized. * * * It makes nonsense of the statute to say that its misrepresentation provision can only be the basis of denaturalization if the Government establishes *in addition* a factor that is itself, without misrepresentation, a basis for denaturalization anyway [under the "illegally procured" provision of § 340(a).] On JUSTICE STEVENS' concurrence's reading, the law says, in effect: Citizenship you obtain by lying may be revoked, but only for a reason other than lying. This is likely to have the congressionally desired deterrent effect upon only the most dim-witted of prevaricators. But worse than making an enigma of the statute, JUSTICE STEVENS' concurrence's position makes a scandal of the results the statute achieves: Proof that an applicant lied when he said he was not an SS officer at Dachau would not suffice for denaturalization without clear, unequivocal, and convincing proof—after 40 years of disappearing evidence—that he was guilty of war crimes.

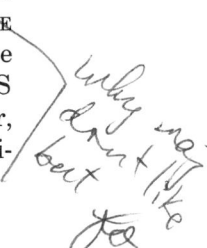

III

A

The United States argues, as an alternative basis for affirming the Third Circuit's upholding of denaturalization, that Kungys' misrepresentations, made under oath and in the form of forged documents, rendered his citizenship "illegally procured" under INA §§ 101(f)(6), 316(a)(3), and 340(a). As discussed earlier, the alleged ground of "illegal procurement" is that Kungys lacked the requisite good moral character in 1954, at the time of his naturalization, because he had given false testimony for the purpose of obtaining benefits in both the visa and naturalization proceedings, in violation of § 101(f)(6). In connection with this aspect of the judgment, we address only the issue considered (and resolved in the affirmative) by the Third Circuit: whether § 101(f)(6) contains a materiality requirement for false testimony. We hold that it does not.

Under § 101(f)(6), a person shall be deemed not to be of good moral character if he "has given false testimony for the purpose of obtaining" immigration or naturalization benefits. On its face, § 101(f)(6) does not distinguish between material and immaterial misrepresentations. Literally read, it denominates a person to be of bad moral character on account of having given false testimony if he has told even the most immaterial of lies with the subjective intent of obtaining immigration or naturalization benefits. We think it means precisely what it says.

* * * A literal reading of the statute does not produce draconian results, for several reasons. First, "testimony" is limited to oral statements made under oath. The United States concedes that it does not include "other types of misrepresentations or concealments, such as falsified documents or statements not made under oath." Second, § 101(f)(6) applies to only those misrepresentations made with the subjective intent of obtaining immigration benefits. As the Government acknowledges:

> "It is only dishonesty accompanied by this precise intent that Congress found morally unacceptable. Willful misrepresentations made for other reasons, such as embarrassment, fear, or a desire for privacy, were not deemed sufficiently culpable to brand the applicant as someone who lacks good moral character." Supplemental Brief for United States 12.

Obviously, it will be relatively rare that the Government will be able to prove that a misrepresentation that does not have the natural tendency to influence the decision regarding immigration or naturalization benefits was nonetheless made with the subjective intent of obtaining those benefits. This is especially so since the invalidating intent, like all other factual matters necessary to support denaturalization, must be proved by " 'clear, unequivocal, and convincing' evidence which does not leave 'the issue in doubt.' " Third, unlike the misrepresentation clause of § 340(a), the false testimony provisions of § 101(f)(6) do not apply to "concealments." With all these built-in limitations, and given the evident purpose of the provision, we see no reason for straining to avoid its natural meaning.

* * *

B

Accordingly, it is clear that the Third Circuit erred in importing a materiality requirement into § 101(f)(6). Nevertheless, we cannot affirm denaturalization under that section because the question whether any misrepresentation made by Kungys constituted "false testimony for the purpose of obtaining" immigration or naturalization benefits cannot be answered without resolving an additional question of law and an additional question of fact. The former, which we choose not to resolve ourselves, since the case must be remanded in any event, is whether Kungys' misrepresentations constituted "testimony." The latter, which must be resolved by the trier of fact, is whether in making the misrepresentations Kungys possessed the subjective intent of thereby obtaining immigration or naturalization benefits. We are unpersuaded by the United States' argument that Kungys' so-called pattern of lies establishes the illegal subjective intent of his alleged false testimony as a matter of law.

For the reasons stated, the judgment of the Third Circuit is reversed and the case remanded for further proceedings consistent with this opinion.

It is so ordered.

JUSTICE KENNEDY took no part in the consideration or decision of this case.

JUSTICE BRENNAN, concurring.

I join the Court's opinion. I write separately, however, to spell out in more detail the showing I believe the Government must make to raise a presumption of ineligibility. The Court holds that a misrepresentation is material if it has "a natural tendency to produce the conclusion that the applicant was qualified" for citizenship. A misrepresentation or concealment can be said to have such a tendency, the Court explains, if honest representations "would predictably have disclosed other facts relevant to [the applicant's] qualifications." Proof by clear, unequivocal, and convincing evidence that the misrepresentation had this tendency raises a presumption of ineligibility, which the naturalized citizen is then called upon to rebut.

I agree with this construction of the statute. I wish to emphasize, however, that in my view a presumption of ineligibility does not arise unless the Government produces evidence sufficient to raise a fair inference that a statutory disqualifying fact actually existed. It is this fair inference of ineligibility, coupled with the fact that the citizen's misrepresentation necessarily frustrated the Government's investigative efforts, that in my mind justifies the burden-shifting presumption the Court employs. Evidence that simply raises the possibility that a disqualifying fact might have existed should not entitle the Government to the benefit of a presumption that the citizen was ineligible, for as we have repeatedly emphasized, citizenship is a most precious right, and as such should never be forfeited on the basis of mere speculation or suspicion. I therefore would not permit invocation of the presumption of disqualification in circumstances where it would not otherwise be fair to infer that the citizen was actually ineligible.

Because nothing in the Court's opinion is inconsistent with this standard, I join it.

JUSTICE STEVENS, with whom JUSTICE MARSHALL and JUSTICE BLACKMUN join, concurring in the judgment.

* * *

I

Over a quarter of a century ago, in *Chaunt v. United States,* the Court considered a case in which the District Court found that petitioner had concealed his membership in the Communist Party as well as three arrests that, had they been disclosed, would have led to further investigation by the Immigration Service. Although the dissenting justices thought that Chaunt's failure to tell the truth about his arrest record was sufficient reason to revoke his citizenship, the majority came to the contrary conclusion. It held that the Government had failed to prove "either (1) that facts were suppressed which, if known, would have warranted denial of citizenship or (2) that their disclosure might have been useful in an investigation possibly leading to the discovery of other facts warranting denial of citizenship." Thus we announced a test for whether citizenship was procured by a material misrepresentation that required the Government to prove the existence of a disqualifying fact. This result was compelled both by the statute's requirement that the misrepresentation be material and by the requirement that it procure citizenship. * * *

"Material" means "having real importance" or "great consequences." Webster's Ninth New Collegiate Dictionary 733 (1983). The adjective "material" is widely used to distinguish false statements that are actionable at law from those that are not. In the context of criminal false statements, the term "material" has been said to require that the false statement be one that had "a natural tendency to influence, or was capable of influencing, the decision of" the decisionmaking body to which it was addressed. In tort law, a misrepresentation is material if "a reasonable man would attach importance to its existence or nonexistence in determining his choice of action in the transaction in question." In contract law, a misrepresentation is material if "it would be likely to induce a reasonable person to manifest his assent."

In all of these contexts, the use of the word "material" serves to distinguish the trivial from the substantive, drawing the line between statements that appear to be capable of influencing an outcome and those that do not. It is reasonable to assume that the term serves the same role in the denaturalization statute. It guarantees that trivial misstatements do not result in the loss of citizenship by making actionable only those that are capable of influencing the decision whether to confer citizenship. This principle may be stated more specifically. Unlike the decision to enter a contract or to do some act in detrimental reliance on the assertion of another, the decision whether to grant citizenship is an objective one. The applicant either does or does not possess the requisite qualifications. The process relies on facts, not hunches or intuitions. Thus, in the denaturalization context, the only statements that are capable of influencing the outcome are those that conceal disqualifying facts or that prevent or hinder the discovery of disqualifying facts. Our statement in *Chaunt* was not a rejection of the traditional definition of materiality, it was merely an acknowledgment of the realistic consequences of that term's use in the context of an objective decisionmaking process.

* * *

Thus the Government cannot prevail in a denaturalization action based on a false statement in an application for a naturalization certificate unless it can prove by clear, unequivocal, and convincing evidence the existence of a disqualifying fact. To prove that a misrepresentation was material, the Government must prove that the statement concealed a disqualifying fact or hindered the discovery of a disqualifying fact. Further, the existence of a disqualifying fact is a necessary element of the Government's proof of reliance. Unless a disqualifying fact existed, it cannot be said that a misrepresentation "procured" citizenship. Section 340(a) does not allow an individual who was in all ways qualified to be an American citizen to be deprived of that citizenship because of a false statement that did not prevent the discovery of a fact that would have affected his or her eligibility to become a United States citizen. Together and separately, the materiality and procurement requirements reflect congressional intent that citizenship status not be taken away unless the Government proves that the person was not qualified to hold that status at the time it was obtained.

In his separate opinion in *Fedorenko v. United States,* JUSTICE BLACK-
MUN correctly pointed out that as construed by our decision in *Chaunt* the
misrepresentation ground of § 340(a) requires that the Government "prove
the existence of disqualifying facts." Until today, JUSTICE WHITE was the
only Member of the Court to have disagreed with this reading of the
Chaunt opinion. Even today, it is not clear whether the Court disagrees
with this interpretation of *Chaunt,* or simply rejects it based on its current
notion of "the wisdom of experience."

In my opinion, the wisdom of experience has provided firm support for
Chaunt 's holding. Our construction of the denaturalization statute must
be animated by our longstanding recognition of the severity of the sanction
being sought. I firmly believe that denaturalization is far too heavy a
sanction to impose on an otherwise innocent citizen for making false
statements in 1948 and 1953. Without evidence of any wrongdoing before
he came to the United States in 1948 or after he acquired his citizenship in
1954, the revocation of petitioner's citizenship—a punishment that is
tantamount to exile or banishment—is patently excessive.

* * *

[T]oday the Court announces a new burden-shifting presumption that
lowers the standard of proof required for the Government to prevail in a
denaturalization proceeding. Under the Court's test, a misrepresentation
or concealment is material if it concerned a fact that was relevant to the
naturalization decision or if the true facts "would predictably have disclosed other facts relevant to [the citizen's] qualifications." A fact may be
relevant if it would have led to an investigation. Thus the Government
becomes entitled to the presumption that the citizen was not qualified to
become a citizen, that is, to the presumption that citizenship was "procured by" the misrepresentation, if it shows by clear and convincing
evidence that the true facts would have led to further investigation. The
citizen then bears the burden of "showing, through a preponderance of the
evidence, that the statutory requirement as to which the misrepresentation
had a natural tendency to produce a favorable decision was in fact met."
Since under the Court's test the Government is never required to identify a
specific disqualifying fact, apparently the citizen must refute the existence
of every disqualifying fact that might have been revealed by an investigation. The Government need not introduce any proof whatsoever suggesting the existence of a disqualifying fact.

Though joining the Court's opinion, JUSTICE BRENNAN would require
more. He would not allow the Government the benefit of the presumption
unless it first produced "evidence sufficient to raise a fair inference that a
statutory disqualifying fact actually existed." Although JUSTICE BRENNAN
imposes a burden of production on the Government, he agrees with the
majority that the burden of ultimate persuasion rests with the defendant.
Under JUSTICE BRENNAN's approach, however, the defendant at least has the
benefit of knowing specifically what disqualifying fact must be rebutted.
Both approaches require the defendant to rebut the existence of the
presumed disqualifying fact—even demonstrating that there is a completely

innocent explanation for the misrepresentation would not be sufficient to rebut the presumption.

Neither the majority's nor JUSTICE BRENNAN'S formulation of shifting burdens is faithful to our previous recognition of the special burden the Government must bear when it seeks to denaturalize an American citizen or to our previous rejection of default judgments in denaturalization proceedings.

* * *

II

The reasons why the Court has required the Government to carry a heavy burden of proof in denaturalization cases apply equally to the argument that petitioner is subject to denaturalization because his false statements demonstrate that he lacked good moral character in 1953.

* * * The Government contends that it is not necessary for it to establish that petitioner's false statements were material to denaturalize him under this provision. Under the Government's theory, the mere fact that the statements were false is sufficient to compel petitioner's denaturalization if they were made under oath and with the subjective intention of obtaining a benefit—any benefit, no matter how trivial—under the naturalization laws. Because I am convinced that a materiality requirement is implicit in § 101(f)(6), I reject this contention.

* * *

In addition to requiring materiality, [§ 101(f)(6) requires] that the false statement have been made for the purpose of obtaining a benefit under the immigration and naturalization laws. The Government would have us adopt a subjective test of the individual's motive in any particular case, thus forcing the factfinder to inquire of the defendant in each case why the particular falsehood was asserted and insuring that many citizenship determinations would boil down to credibility battles. An objective test is far more reasonable. Under an objective approach, a false testimonial statement would be considered made "for the purpose of obtaining any benefits under [the immigration laws]" if it in fact had the effect of giving the defendant a benefit under the immigration laws. An objective test would eliminate the necessity of inquiring in each case whether a person lied about his or her date of birth for personal reasons, such as mere vanity, or to conceal information that would lead to the denial of a visa or certificate of naturalization. If the false statement as to age actually had the effect of obtaining for the individual a benefit he or she would not otherwise have enjoyed, then, and only then, would American citizenship have been "illegally procured." An objective test is more consistent with the heavy burden of proof borne by the Government in denaturalization cases and with the severity of the sanction. Because states of mind are notoriously difficult to prove, an objective test also has the critical virtue of diminishing the risk of erroneous determinations.

It is obvious that there is some overlap between the scope of the misrepresentation and illegally procured clauses of § 340(a). That the

Government may in some cases be able to choose one of two available paths for denaturalizing a citizen for essentially the same conduct, however, does not suggest that either of the paths should be made more lenient than Congress intended.

III

The Government attempted to prove the existence of a disqualifying fact before the District Court by introducing videotaped deposition testimony, which it asserted proved petitioner's participation in the Kedainiai atrocities. The District Court found the deposition testimony unreliable and admitted the depositions only for the limited purpose of establishing that the atrocities occurred.[12] Because the Court of Appeals did not address the propriety of this ruling, I would vacate its judgment and remand the case for further proceedings not inconsistent with this opinion.

Justice O'Connor, concurring in part and dissenting in part.

I join Parts I, II–A, and III of Justice Scalia's opinion in this case. For the reasons given in Part II of Justice White's opinion, however, I dissent from Part II–B of Justice Scalia's opinion. In my view, when the correct standard of materiality is applied to the facts of this case, the misrepresentations made by petitioner are properly viewed as material.

Justice White, dissenting.

* * *

Although I agree with Parts I, IIA, and IIIA of the Court's opinion, I disagree with other parts and with the result it reaches. I therefore dissent.

I

I would affirm the judgment below and grant the Government's petition for denaturalization. The Court holds, and I agree, that there was error in the holding below that petitioner's misrepresentations must be material in order to constitute sufficient grounds for finding that petitioner lacks "good moral character" under § 101(f)(6). As the Court states, the statute "does not distinguish between material and immaterial misrepresentations," but instead "denominates a person to be of bad moral character on account of having given false testimony if he has told even the most immaterial of lies with the subjective intent of obtaining immigration or naturalization benefits." In addition to the language of § 101(f)(6), which in itself compels this conclusion, the legislative history of the 1961 amendments to the statute, shows that Congress sought to *broaden,* not restrict, the grounds upon which naturalization could be revoked.[1]

---

12. The difference between this case and the Court's hypothetical concerning an SS officer at Dachau, is critical. Proof by clear and convincing evidence that a naturalized citizen concealed his official status at Dachau would establish his lack of good moral character. In this case, however, there is no such proof of any official or unofficial connection between petitioner and the atrocities at Kedainiai.

1. Prior to 1952, "illegal procurement" constituted grounds for revoking a citizen's naturalization. When Congress enacted § 340 of the Immigration and Nationality Act of 1952, it dropped, without explanation, the "illegal procurement" provision, adding in its stead the "concealment of a material fact" or

In this connection, we must bear in mind the necessity of striking an appropriate balance between the serious consequences that attend loss of citizenship and the need for "strict compliance with all the congressionally imposed prerequisites to the acquisition of citizenship." *Fedorenko v. United States,* 449 U.S. 490, 506, 101 S.Ct. 737, 747, 66 L.Ed.2d 686 (1981). We need not decide in this case whether § 101(f)(6) would bar naturalization of an individual who offered a single piece of false testimony in only one instance or who later offered a reasonable explanation for why misstatements were made; we also need not decide whether such a construction of the statute would be inconsistent with a proper balancing of the two important but opposing considerations set out above. There may well be cases in which a single willful but immaterial misrepresentation would be insufficient to establish lack of good character, but would constitute grounds for denaturalization if it were material. Similarly, there are cases like this one in which repeated and numerous willful misrepresentations justify a finding of lack of good moral character notwithstanding that the misrepresentations may not involve material facts.

Here, the petitioner's false testimony was not confined to one occasion, nor did it concern only a single piece of evidence. And at no time before or during the naturalization process did petitioner voluntarily step forward and attempt to explain the reasons for his various misrepresentations. To the contrary, the facts as found by the District Court demonstrate clearly, unequivocally, and convincingly that the petitioner engaged in a pattern of repeated misrepresentations and nondisclosures at both the visa application stage and during his naturalization proceedings. * * * The congressional mandate expressed in § 101(f)(6) speaks clearly to such a pattern of falsehoods, and that statute would have precluded a determination in 1954 that petitioner possessed "good moral character." Accordingly, the petitioner lacked an essential prerequisite to becoming a naturalized citizen, and he is now subject to denaturalization for having "illegally procured" his citizenship. § 340(a).

Despite its recognition that materiality is not required by § 101(f)(6), the Court declines to uphold the judgment below, and remands the case for further consideration of one point of law and one point of fact. Neither point is at all substantial. The point of law is whether petitioner's misrepresentations constituted "testimony" within the meaning of the statute. As the Court notes, the term "testimony" in § 101(f)(6) has been

"willful misrepresentation" language. The deleted provision was reinserted in § 340(a) by the 1961 amendments, Pub.L. 87–301, § 18, 75 Stat. 656. The House Report accompanying the amendments noted that "[e]limination of the illegality ground bars denaturalization under section 340 unless it is proved that the naturalized person has been guilty of wrongdoing amounting to concealment of a material fact or willful misrepresentation. . . ." H.R.Rep. No. 1086, 87th Cong., 1st Sess., p. 38 (1961), U.S.Code Cong. & Admin.News 1961, p. 2982. The Report explained that "[p]roof of concealment of material facts or willful misrepresentation . . . is fraught with difficulty," *id.,* at 39, U.S.Code Cong. & Admin.News 1961, p. 2983, and that the amendment to § 340(a) was necessary because "[t]he congressional mandate that no person shall be naturalized unless possessed of certain qualifications is ineffectual unless there is also statutory provision for revoking citizenship where the prerequisites did not in fact exist." *Ibid.* These statements evince clear congressional intent that "illegal procurement" be maintained as a *separate* basis for denaturalization, and do not sanction collapsing § 101(f)(6) into the willful and material misrepresentation or concealment provision of § 340(a).

construed as referring only to oral evidence, and thus as excluding the written documents submitted by petitioner in his naturalization petition. Yet petitioner in this case did make oral misrepresentations: he testified falsely when he swore under oath before a naturalization examiner that the contents of his naturalization forms were true. Furthermore, he had testified falsely in order to obtain his visa into this country.

The point of fact is whether petitioner made these misrepresentations "for the purpose of obtaining any benefits" under the immigration and naturalization laws. There is no difficulty about this point either. The willful misrepresentations at issue here were made in the context of petitioner's naturalization petition and were made earlier at the visa stage. The fact that the misrepresentations were willful, coupled with the fact that they were made during proceedings and on documents required for immigration and naturalization purposes—indeed, the very proceedings and documents that petitioner was required to complete in order to "obtai[n]" the "benefits" he sought of gaining naturalization—satisfies the elements of § 101(f)(6). * * *

II

Because the Court declines to affirm the decision below on the basis of § 101(f)(6), it finds it necessary to revisit the definition of the term "material" as it is used in § 340(a). The Court today holds that the proper test of materiality is whether the misrepresentations "had a natural tendency to influence the decisions of the INS." I do not disagree with this definition, but the Court's application of the definition in this case is flawed.

To begin with, the Court finds it proper under § 340(a) to consider only the misrepresentations petitioner made in his naturalization proceedings but not those made in his earlier visa proceedings. The view of the United States is much more persuasive: the misrepresentations made by petitioner at the visa stage were instrumental to his procuring naturalization, for by obtaining the visa petitioner obtained lawful admission to residence in this country, which is one requirement for naturalization under § 318. See also *Fedorenko,* 449 U.S., at 518–520, 101 S.Ct., at 753–754 (BLACKMUN, J., concurring in judgment). The Court responds that by that logic, *any* misrepresentation that helps an individual to obtain *any* prerequisite to naturalization, such as English literacy, would be considered material. These two things, however, are not the same, and the Court's supposed extension of its logic is merely foolish. * * * [It] is not mere residence in this country that is a prerequisite to naturalization, but residence after being "lawfully admitted." § 318. It makes no sense, on the other hand, to speak of proceedings to attain "lawful" literacy skills or a "lawful" understanding of American history and government, as required under § 312, and the statute does not speak in these terms but instead manifests complete and understandable indifference as to how the individual came by those proficiencies. * * *

Even if I were to accept the proposition that we should consider only the materiality of the misrepresentations that petitioner made in the naturalization proceedings, those misrepresentations surely had a natural tendency to influence the decisions of the INS. * * * I would ask not only whether these misrepresentations of fact would have a natural tendency to influence the decisions of the INS, but also whether the fact of these misrepresentations *itself* would have had such a tendency. In other words, the proper inquiry is not only whether the true date and place of birth, in isolation, would have aroused suspicion, but whether an investigation would have ensued had petitioner revealed the true facts and thereby disclosed the discrepancy between them and the false statements in his supporting documents. * * *

The Court of Appeals arrived at the same conclusion, and the United States supports this construction of the statute, which is a sound one. The materiality of misrepresentations may be, but need not be, established by considering the true facts alone. It also may be shown by a comparison between those true facts and the false assertions made about those same matters. * * * For whether a misrepresentation has actually been made is itself a matter of fact, and in certain circumstances this fact alone may possess great significance. Unless a court is to pretend that petitioner's lies themselves are not facts, it defies reality to conclude that "official knowledge of the misrepresented fact," means only that the INS now knows how to correct the lies but must not take into account the fact that those lies have been told.

For these reasons, I would affirm the decision below on this ground also. At the very least I note that it is open to the trier of fact on remand to consider whether knowledge of petitioner's repeated and numerous misrepresentations would have had a natural tendency to influence the decisions of the INS.

* * *

I respectfully dissent.

Notes

1. *Kungys* was eagerly awaited in the hope that it might settle the long-running battles over the meaning of *Chaunt*. The fractured result hardly achieved this end. A majority appears to agree on a new verbal formula for materiality: *i.e.,* a natural tendency to influence or affect the official decision. But Justice Scalia (joined by Justice Rehnquist and perhaps Justice Brennan) seems worlds apart from Justices O'Connor and White in the way he applies it.

Justice Stevens' test is certainly clearer and easier to apply in the future; it would end all confusion surrounding *Chaunt*. Consider the kinds of incentives it creates, however, for permanent resident aliens who are about to apply for naturalization and who believe that some fact in their past, about which the naturalization forms ask, probably disqualifies them from citizenship (or even know for certain that it does disqualify them). Are these incentives overcome by others that will encourage truth-telling? Does his objective test "also [have] the critical virtue of diminishing the risk of erroneous determinations," as he claims?

Justice White's tests are also probably more easily administered, and certainly help induce truthfulness in visa and naturalization proceedings. The major potential objection to his approach arises in looking at a case long after the naturalization, when false information comes to light only after the person has experienced many years of productive and honest citizenship (and may have a sympathetic explanation for the earlier misrepresentations). Does his test have an escape hatch for such situations?

2. Why is it apparently so difficult for the Supreme Court to achieve a clear majority opinion on the standards for materiality under INA § 340(a) and for good moral character under § 101(f)(6)? What are the specific (and often conflicting) policy objectives that the different members of the Court seek to accomplish through the development of such standards? Are there better ways to accomplish them? If you were a member of Congress and felt it was high time for a legislative response to end the years of judicial confusion on these issues, how would you draft a new § 340(a)? For useful reflections on these issues and on *Kungys,* see Wolf, *Fraud and Materiality: Has the Supreme Court Redefined Immigration and Naturalization Fraud?,* 62 Temple L.Rev. 481 (1989).

3. The remand in *Kungys* produced no further trial. Instead Kungys agreed to a consent judgment of denaturalization in return for a government pledge not to seek deportation. 66 Interp.Rel. 1287 (1988).

SECTION D.   EXPATRIATION

As indicated in Section C, denaturalization proceedings constitute one important way in which U.S. citizenship today may be taken away. In such proceedings, the government must establish, under a fairly stringent standard of proof, that the original naturalization was acquired illegally or through fraud. But through the years, Congress also added to the nationality statutes various provisions to deprive individuals of citizenship status based on specified behavior not related to defects in the acquisition process. Whether the citizen subjectively intended to surrender citizenship when the allegedly expatriating behavior occurred was usually irrelevant.

The Supreme Court wrestled for several decades with the constitutionality of these grounds for involuntary expatriation.[11] The divisions among the Justices were bitter, and for a while, as we shall see, the results in the cases, sometimes sustaining the expatriation provisions, sometimes striking them down, traced an odd pattern. But today the Court has apparently reached unanimity on the basic substantive doctrine, although skirmishing may still be possible regarding some of the procedural details. The materials to follow reveal the historical development of the statute and the constitutional rulings.

11. We use the term "involuntary expatriation" here to mean a loss of citizenship imposed on persons based on certain behavior, such as lengthy residence abroad or marriage to a foreign national, whether or not they subjectively wished to surrender their citizenship thereby. But supporters of the practice have often noted that such expatriation is not involuntary in the strongest sense. That is, American statutes have never tried to deprive persons of citizenship except on the basis of actions (moving overseas, marrying, etc.) that the citizen voluntarily performed—with statutory notice, even if not willing acceptance, of the consequences.

DONALD K. DUVALL, EXPATRIATION UNDER UNITED
STATES LAW, *PEREZ* TO *AFROYIM*: THE SEARCH
FOR A PHILOSOPHY OF AMERICAN CITIZENSHIP

56 Va.L.Rev. 408, 411–17 (1970).

HISTORICAL DEVELOPMENT OF EXPATRIATION LAW

When ratified in 1789, the Constitution contained no definition of
citizenship or provision for its loss, but merely authorized Congress "[t]o
establish an uniform Rule of Naturalization." Subsequently, the Supreme
Court held that while this constitutional provision gave the naturalized
citizen the same rights as a native, it did not authorize Congress to enlarge
or abridge those rights.

The rule of *jus soli*—citizenship by birth within the country—was first
given statutory expression in section 1 of the Civil Rights Act of 1866, the
substance of which was adopted as the fourteenth amendment during the
same year. Previously, the *jus soli* rule had been generally applied on the
basis of the English common law, which had been adopted by the United
States as its main body of law after independence. Likewise, the rule of *jus
sanguinis*—citizenship by blood relation to citizen parent—was statutorily
recognized * * *. Although the United States followed a liberal immigration and naturalization policy based on both the *jus soli* and *jus sanguinis*
rules during its formative years, before 1907 there was no general statute
governing expatriation. As might be expected in an expanding new nation,
the United States until the Civil War was primarily concerned with
assimilating its millions of immigrants and establishing the legal primacy of
national citizenship over state citizenship.

The scope of US citizenship was further beclouded in the early days
because the judiciary felt bound to apply the adopted English common law
of indefeasible perpetual allegiance, which precluded renunciation of citizenship without the consent of the sovereign. Great Britain's adherence to
this rule in its impressments on the high seas of naturalized American
seamen, formerly of British nationality, contributed to the War of 1812.
And events of 1868 further aggravated Anglo–American friction, when the
British failed to respect the rights of naturalized US citizens involved in
criminal activities with the Fenian movement in Ireland. These incidents
led to the passage of the Expatriation Act of 1868,[31] which, *inter alia,*
declared "the right of expatriation" to be an "inherent right of all people,"
thus enabling naturalized Americans to cast off, at least under United
States law, the claims to allegiance advanced by their states of origin. The
Act further extended to naturalized citizens traveling abroad "the same
protection of persons and property that is accorded to native-born citizens
in like situations," and declared that whenever a US citizen was unjustly
deprived of his liberty by or under the authority of any foreign government,
the President had the duty to extend protection in appropriate ways short
of war.

---

31. Ch. 249, 15 Stat. 223.

While the Act of 1868 clarified the right of expatriation and was construed to include the citizen's right to shed his citizenship, it provided no specific method for exercising that right. Furthermore, even though naturalization under the domestic law of the United States required the citizen to "renounce and adjure" all allegiance to his former sovereign, effective protection of US naturalized citizens abroad still depended upon reciprocal recognition by foreign states of the exclusive nature of voluntarily acquired American citizenship. Accordingly, in 1868 the United States began negotiating bilateral treaties [known as the Bancroft Treaties] with various foreign states to protect the status of its naturalized citizens on a reciprocal basis in an effort to reduce or eliminate the conflicting claims of different sovereignties arising out of dual nationality. Some of these treaties, including the current multilateral Rio Treaty of 1906, provided not only for mutual acceptance of the right to abandon one nationality and acquire another but also that two years continuous residence by a naturalized citizen in his former country gave rise to a rebuttable presumption of intention to remain permanently. Prolonged return to the state of origin was therefore grounds for treating the citizen as having renounced his naturalized citizenship.

Pursuant to the report of a Citizenship Board appointed by the Secretary of State in 1906, Congress enacted the Expatriation Act of 1907,[38] the first general statute providing for loss of US nationality. Section 2 of the Act of 1907 provided for the expatriation of any national who obtained naturalization in a foreign state or took an oath of allegiance to a foreign state. Section 3 of the Act provided for the expatriation of an American woman who married a foreigner. These provisions attempted to prevent dual nationality, which had previously led to conflicting national claims upon the allegiance of the US citizen whenever he returned, even temporarily, to his former country, or voluntarily entered the military or civil service of a third state.

The constitutionality of the 1907 Act was first tested in the landmark decision of *Mackenzie v. Hare*,[40] in which the Supreme Court upheld the power of Congress to expatriate, during the period of coverture, a female US citizen who obtained foreign nationality by marriage to a foreign national, because such action was a "necessary and proper" implementation of the "inherent power of sovereignty" in foreign relations, especially under "conditions of national moment." [a] Conceding that expatriation

---

38. Ch. 2534, 34 Stat. 1228.

40. 239 U.S. 299, 36 S.Ct. 106, 60 L.Ed. 297 (1915). Act of Sept. 22, 1922, ch. 411, § 3, 42 Stat. 1022, and Act of March 3, 1931, ch. 442, §§ 4(a), (b), 46 Stat. 1511, eliminated marriage to a foreigner as an expatriating act.

a. Eliminating the gender discrimination in U.S. citizenship law (manifested perhaps most objectionably in that portion of the 1907 Act upheld in *Mackenzie*) was a prominent objective of the women's suffrage movement. An important change was provided just two years after the 19th Amendment became part

of the Constitution. The Cable Act of Sept. 22, 1922, 422 Stat. 1021, ended automatic deprivation of citizenship upon marriage to a foreign husband and allowed women expatriated under prior law to regain U.S. citizenship through naturalization. Later statutes through 1930 further eased the requirements for this special procedure. *See Di Iorio v. Nicolls*, 182 F.2d 836, 839–40 (1st Cir.1950). Finally the Act of May 24, 1934, 48 Stat. 797, provided that any child born abroad to one American citizen parent—rather than simply to American fathers—could obtain U.S. citizenship, provided a few other gender-neutral

could not be imposed "without the concurrence of the citizen," the Court inferred assent from the fact that the expatriating act had been "voluntarily entered into, with notice of the consequences." In sum, the concept of voluntary renunciation of citizenship proclaimed in the 1868 Expatriation Act was interpreted in *Mackenzie* to include voluntary performance of an expatriating act without regard to whether the citizen actually intended or desired to lose his US nationality.[43] By extending the meaning of "voluntary," the Court apparently sought to reconcile the intent of Congress to minimize international frictions arising out of dual nationality with the statutory guarantee and tradition of voluntary expatriation.

The 1938 Report of the President's Commission on Revision and Codification of the Nationality Laws led to the Nationality Act of 1940.[45] This Act, the first comprehensive codification of the nationality laws, substantially increased the number of actions which, when performed voluntarily, would automatically result in the loss of US nationality.[46] The increased number of statutory provisions relating to loss of nationality may be explained in several ways. First, most of the provisions were codifications of existing statutory or common law which had evolved from established diplomatic and administrative practice. Second, the 1940 Act was drafted and approved at a time of economic stress and increasing security-consciousness caused by the onset of World War II. Third, World War I and its aftermath had produced a complete reversal of America's traditional "open door" immigration policy, thus leading to stricter requirements for acquisition and retention of US nationality.

Following World War II, the stage was again set for retrenchment and consolidation of the nationality laws. The post-war climate and Cold War

conditions of U.S. residency were met by the parent and (later) by the child. These changes did not have retroactive effect, however.—eds.

43. For an explicit exposition of this objective standard of voluntary expatriation, see *Savorgnan v. United States*, 338 U.S. 419, 70 S.Ct. 292, 94 L.Ed. 287 (1950).

45. Ch. 876, 54 Stat. 1137.

46. Specifically, the Act provided for loss of United States nationality in the following ways:

For any national, native or naturalized, by

1. Obtaining naturalization in a foreign state.

2. Taking an oath of allegiance to a foreign state.

3. Entering or serving in the armed forces of a foreign state while a national thereof without legal authorization.

4. Holding any office, post or employment in the government of a foreign state or any subdivision thereof.

5. Voting in a political election in a foreign state.

6. Formal renunciation before a US diplomatic or consular officer in a foreign state.

7. Formal renunciation in the United States approved by the Attorney General during wartime.

8. Court martial conviction and discharge from armed forces for desertion during wartime.

9. Court martial or civil court conviction for treason, attempting by force to overthrow, or bearing arms against the United States.

10. Departing from or remaining outside of the United States during wartime for purpose of evading training and service in armed forces.

For nationals born abroad (retention provision), by

11. Failing to take up permanent residence in the United States before attaining 16 years of age, subject to certain exceptions.

For naturalized US nationals, by

12. Fraudulent naturalization.

13. Residing continuously for 3 years in foreign state of birth or for 5 years in any other foreign state, with certain exceptions.

hyper-security-consciousness produced the Immigration and Nationality Act of 1952, which Congress approved over President Truman's veto. Essentially a reenactment of the pertinent provisions of the 1940 Act, the 1952 law made few significant changes in loss of nationality. The Act added a section permitting expatriation of persons who acquired dual nationality at birth and "voluntarily sought or claimed benefits" of their foreign nationality and resided in the foreign state for three continuous years after age 22. It also created a non-rebuttable presumption of voluntariness for each of the statute's expatriating acts when performed by a national of a foreign state, who had been physically present in such state for at least ten years.

In 1961 Congress added a statutory standard of proof—preponderance of the evidence—necessary to prove performance of an expatriating act or to rebut the usual presumption of voluntariness. This standard was a relaxation of that previously required by the Supreme Court in *Gonzales v. Landon*[53] and *Nishikawa v. Dulles*,[54] where the Court had imposed upon the Government the burden of proving the act and its voluntariness by clear, unequivocal and convincing evidence.

Another substantial change in the construction of the expatriation provisions of the 1952 Act occurred in 1962, when the Attorney General ruled[55] that in the absence of clear and compelling statutory language, he was "unwilling to attribute to Congress an intention that the United States citizenship of an individual should be forfeited by reason of actions taken at a time when he was unaware of his citizenship." Finally, the Expatriation Act of 1954[57] amended the Immigration and Nationality Act of 1952 by adding, as additional grounds for expatriation, conviction of certain existing crimes, including rebellion and insurrection, seditious conspiracy and advocating the overthrow of the Government in any manner proscribed by law.

———

For many years, the *Mackenzie v. Hare* decision seemed to have settled the question of Congress's broad powers over expatriation. But as a leading commentator has remarked, "[t]his apparent consensus was resoundingly shattered in 1958, * * * when the court decided three cases in which reargument had been directed after argument during the previous term had failed to produce decisions." Gordon, *The Citizen and the State: Power of Congress to Expatriate American Citizens*, 53 Geo.L.J. 315, 326–27 (1965). A sharply divided Court sustained one ground of expatriation, held another unconstitutional, and vacated a third expatriation order on procedural grounds. *Perez v. Brownell* was the first of the trilogy.

---

53. 350 U.S. 920, 76 S.Ct. 210, 100 L.Ed. 806 (1955) (per curiam) (proof of the act).

54. 356 U.S. 129, 78 S.Ct. 612, 2 L.Ed.2d 659 (1958) (proof of voluntariness).

55. Freddie Norman Chatty–Suarez, 9 I. & N. Dec. 670 (1962).

57. Ch. 1256, § 2, 68 Stat. 1146.   * * *

PEREZ v. BROWNELL

Supreme Court of the United States, 1958.
356 U.S. 44, 78 S.Ct. 568, 2 L.Ed.2d 603.

MR. JUSTICE FRANKFURTER delivered the opinion of the Court.

[Perez, the petitioner, was born in Texas in 1909, and thus became a citizen of the United States at birth. He had lived most of his life, however, in Mexico, where he voted in a political election in 1946. The lower courts held that he had lost his U.S. citizenship under, inter alia, § 401(e) of the Nationality Act of 1940, as amended, which provided:

> A person who is a national of the United States, whether by birth or naturalization, shall lose his nationality by:

* * *

> (e) Voting in a political election in a foreign state or participating in an election or plebiscite to determine the sovereignty over foreign territory * * *.

[Justice Frankfurter begins his opinion with a lengthy review of American expatriation laws and practices, pointing out the usual connection between expatriation grounds and the conduct of foreign affairs. The specific provision at issue here was one of the newer additions to the list, enacted only in 1940. It came in large measure as a response to the participation of numerous American citizens in a 1935 plebiscite on the annexation of the Saar region to Hitler's Germany. The chairman of the House Committee on Immigration and Naturalization remarked at one point during hearings on the proposed law: "I know we had a lot of Nazis, so-called American citizens, go to Europe who have voted in the Saar for the annexation of territory to Germany, and Germany says that they have the right to participate and to vote, and yet they are American citizens." (Quoted in the dissenting opinion of Chief Justice Warren, 356 U.S. at 76.) Later, on the House floor, the chairman explained the intention behind the expatriation provisions included in the bill (there were many others in addition to the voting provision): "this bill would put an end to dual citizenship and relieve this country of the responsibility of those who reside in foreign lands and only claim citizenship when it serves their purposes." (Quoted in Justice Frankfurter's opinion, *id.* at 55.)]

* * *

The first step in our inquiry must be to answer the question: what is the source of power on which Congress must be assumed to have drawn? Although there is in the Constitution no specific grant to Congress of power to enact legislation for the effective regulation of foreign affairs, there can be no doubt of the existence of this power in the law-making organ of the Nation. *See* United States v. Curtiss–Wright Export Corp., 299 U.S. 304, 318, 57 S.Ct. 216, 220, 81 L.Ed. 255; Mackenzie v. Hare, 239 U.S. 299, 311–312, 36 S.Ct. 106, 108, 60 L.Ed. 297. The States that joined together to form a single Nation and to create, through the Constitution, a Federal Government to conduct the affairs of that Nation must be held to have granted that Government the powers indispensable to its functioning effectively in the company of sovereign nations. The Government must be able not only to deal affirmatively with foreign nations, as it does through the maintenance of diplomatic relations with them and the protection of

American citizens sojourning within their territories. It must also be able to reduce to a minimum the frictions that are unavoidable in a world of sovereigns sensitive in matters touching their dignity and interests.

The inference is fairly to be drawn from the congressional history of the Nationality Act of 1940, read in light of the historical background of expatriation in this country, that, in making voting in foreign elections (among other behavior) an act of expatriation, Congress was seeking to effectuate its power to regulate foreign affairs. The legislators, counseled by those on whom they rightly relied for advice, were concerned about actions by citizens in foreign countries that create problems of protection and are inconsistent with American allegiance. Moreover, we cannot ignore the fact that embarrassments in the conduct of foreign relations were of primary concern in the consideration of the Act of 1907, of which the loss of nationality provisions of the 1940 Act are a codification and expansion.

Broad as the power in the National Government to regulate foreign affairs must necessarily be, it is not without limitation. The restrictions confining Congress in the exercise of any of the powers expressly delegated to it in the Constitution apply with equal vigor when that body seeks to regulate our relations with other nations. Since Congress may not act arbitrarily, a rational nexus must exist between the content of a specific power in Congress and the action of Congress in carrying that power into execution. More simply stated, the means—in this case, withdrawal of citizenship—must be reasonably related to the end—here, regulation of foreign affairs. The inquiry—and, in the case before us, the sole inquiry— into which this Court must enter is whether or not Congress may have concluded not unreasonably that there is a relevant connection between this fundamental source of power and the ultimate legislative action.

Our starting point is to ascertain whether the power of Congress to deal with foreign relations may reasonably be deemed to include a power to deal generally with the active participation, by way of voting, of American citizens in foreign political elections. Experience amply attests that in this day of extensive international travel, rapid communication and widespread use of propaganda, the activities of the citizens of one nation when in another country can easily cause serious embarrassments to the government of their own country as well as to their fellow citizens. We cannot deny to Congress the reasonable belief that these difficulties might well become acute, to the point of jeopardizing the successful conduct of international relations, when a citizen of one country chooses to participate in the political or governmental affairs of another country. The citizen may by his action unwittingly promote or encourage a course of conduct contrary to the interests of his own government; moreover, the people or government of the foreign country may regard his action to be the action of his government, or at least as a reflection if not an expression of its policy.

It follows that such activity is regulable by Congress under its power to deal with foreign affairs. And it must be regulable on more than an *ad hoc* basis. * * *

The question must finally be faced whether, given the power to attach some sort of consequence to voting in a foreign political election, Congress, acting under the Necessary and Proper Clause, Art. I, § 8, cl. 18, could attach loss of nationality to it. Is the means, withdrawal of citizenship, reasonably calculated to effect the end that is within the power of Congress to achieve, the avoidance of embarrassment in the conduct of our foreign relations attributable to voting by American citizens in foreign political elections? The importance and extreme delicacy of the matters here sought to be regulated demand that Congress be permitted ample scope in selecting appropriate modes for accomplishing its purpose. The critical connection between this conduct and loss of citizenship is the fact that it is the possession of American citizenship by a person committing the act that makes the act potentially embarrassing to the American Government and pregnant with the possibility of embroiling this country in disputes with other nations. The termination of citizenship terminates the problem. Moreover, the fact is not without significance that Congress has interpreted this conduct, not irrationally, as importing not only something less than complete and unswerving allegiance to the United States but also elements of an allegiance to another country in some measure, at least, inconsistent with American citizenship.

Of course, Congress can attach loss of citizenship only as a consequence of conduct engaged in voluntarily. See Mackenzie v. Hare, 239 U.S. 299, 311–312, 36 S.Ct. 106, 108, 60 L.Ed. 297. But it would be a mockery of this Court's decisions to suggest that a person, in order to lose his citizenship, must intend or desire to do so. The Court only a few years ago said of the person held to have lost her citizenship in Mackenzie v. Hare, supra: "The woman had not intended to give up her American citizenship." Savorgnan v. United States, 338 U.S. 491, 501, 70 S.Ct. 292, 298, 94 L.Ed. 287. And the latter case sustained the denationalization of Mrs. Savorgnan although it was not disputed that she "had no intention of endangering her American citizenship or of renouncing her allegiance to the United States." What both women did do voluntarily was to engage in conduct to which Acts of Congress attached the consequence of denationalization irrespective of—and, in those cases, absolutely contrary to—the intentions and desires of the individuals. Those two cases mean nothing—indeed, they are deceptive—if their essential significance is not rejection of the notion that the power of Congress to terminate citizenship depends upon the citizen's assent.

* * *

Judgment affirmed.

MR. CHIEF JUSTICE WARREN, with whom MR. JUSTICE BLACK and MR. JUSTICE DOUGLAS join, dissenting.

* * *

Generally, when congressional action is challenged, constitutional authority is found in the express and implied powers with which the National Government has been invested or in those inherent powers that are necessary attributes of a sovereign state. The sweep of those powers is surely broad. In appropriate circumstances, they are adequate to take away life itself. The initial question here is whether citizenship is subject to the exercise of these general powers of government.

What is this government, whose power is here being asserted? And what is the source of that power? The answers are the foundation of our Republic. To secure the inalienable rights of the individual, "Governments are instituted among Men, deriving their just powers from the consent of the governed." I do not believe the passage of time has lessened the truth of this proposition. It is basic to our form of government. This Government was born of its citizens, it maintains itself in a continuing relationship with them, and, in my judgment, it is without power to sever the relationship that gives rise to its existence. I cannot believe that a government conceived in the spirit of ours was established with power to take from the people their most basic right.

Citizenship *is* man's basic right for it is nothing less than the right to have rights. Remove this priceless possession and there remains a stateless person, disgraced and degraded in the eyes of his countrymen. He has no lawful claim to protection from any nation, and no nation may assert rights on his behalf. His very existence is at the sufferance of the state within whose borders he happens to be. In this country the expatriate would presumably enjoy, at most, only the limited rights and privileges of aliens, and like the alien he might even be subject to deportation and thereby deprived of the right to assert any rights. This government was not established with power to decree this fate.

The people who created this government endowed it with broad powers. They created a sovereign state with power to function as a sovereignty. But the citizens themselves are sovereign, and their citizenship is not subject to the general powers of their government. Whatever may be the scope of its powers to regulate the conduct and affairs of all persons within its jurisdiction, a government *of* the people cannot take away their citizenship simply because one branch of that government can be said to have a conceivably rational basis for wanting to do so.

The basic constitutional provision crystallizing the right of citizenship is the first sentence of section one of the Fourteenth Amendment. It is there provided that "All persons born or naturalized in the United States, and subject to the jurisdiction thereof, are citizens of the United States and of the State wherein they reside." United States citizenship is thus the constitutional birth-right of every person born in this country. * * * Under our form of government, as established by the Constitution, the citizenship of the lawfully naturalized and the native-born cannot be taken from them.

* * *

It has long been recognized that citizenship may not only be voluntarily renounced through exercise of the right of expatriation but also by other actions in derogation of undivided allegiance to this country. While the essential qualities of the citizen-state relationship under our Constitution preclude the exercise of governmental power to divest United States citizenship, the establishment of that relationship did not impair the principle that conduct of a citizen showing a voluntary transfer of allegiance is an abandonment of citizenship. Nearly all sovereignties recognize that acquisition of foreign nationality ordinarily shows a renunciation of citizenship. Nor is this the only act by which the citizen may show a voluntary abandonment of his citizenship. Any action by which he manifests allegiance to a foreign state may be so inconsistent with the retention of citizenship as to result in loss of that status. In recognizing the consequence of such action, the Government is not taking away United States citizenship to implement its general regulatory powers, for, as previously indicated, in my judgment citizenship is immune from divestment under these powers. Rather, the Government is simply giving formal recognition to the inevitable consequence of the citizen's own voluntary surrender of his citizenship.

* * *

* * * Mackenzie v. Hare should not be understood to sanction a power to divest citizenship. Rather this case, like Savorgnan, simply acknowledges that United States citizenship can be abandoned, temporarily or permanently, by conduct showing a voluntary transfer of allegiance to another country.

* * *

The fatal defect in the statute before us is that its application is not limited to those situations that may rationally be said to constitute an abandonment of citizenship. In specifying that any act of voting in a foreign political election results in loss of citizenship, Congress has employed a classification so broad that it encompasses conduct that fails to show a voluntary abandonment of American citizenship. * * * Voting in a foreign election may be a most equivocal act, giving rise to no implication that allegiance has been compromised. Nothing could demonstrate this better than the political history of this country. It was not until 1928 that a presidential election was held in this country in which no alien was eligible to vote. Earlier in our history at least 22 States had extended the franchise to aliens. It cannot be seriously contended that this Nation understood the vote of each alien who previously took advantage of this privilege to be an act of allegiance to this country, jeopardizing the alien's native citizenship. How then can we attach such significance to any vote of a United States citizen in a foreign election? It is also significant that of 84 nations whose nationality laws have been compiled by the United Nations, only this country specifically designates foreign voting as an expatriating act.

* * *

[Separate dissenting opinions by Justices Douglas and Whittaker are omitted.]

Questions

What is Justice Frankfurter's test for deciding the constitutionality of expatriation provisions? Should this particular provision, apparently not adopted by any other nation in the world, be held to meet that test? How would expatriation of voters in foreign elections avoid national embarrassment or entanglement in disputes? What kinds of disputes are anticipated? With whom? If this statute passes muster, what kinds of statutes would fail?

A Note on Dual Nationality

The *Perez* majority defers to Congress at least in part because of what it regards as legitimate concerns about problems arising from dual nationality. Some further background may help in evaluating the seriousness of such problems and the appropriateness of the remedies adopted in far-reaching expatriation statutes of the kind that the United States has had through most of this century.

It is clear that dual nationality may in some circumstances place the individual involved in the most serious kind of high-stakes dilemma. *Kawakita v. United States,* 343 U.S. 717, 72 S.Ct. 950, 96 L.Ed. 1249 (1952), affirmed the treason conviction—and death sentence—imposed on a dual national of Japan and the United States. Finding himself in Japan when war broke out between his two countries in 1941, Kawakita served as an interpreter for a company for which American prisoners of war were forced to work. There was extensive evidence that he engaged in serious mistreatment of the prisoners. He was tried and convicted, however, not for war crimes under general international standards, but for treason against the United States, an offense which by definition can be committed only by someone who owes allegiance to this nation.

In considering his appeal, the Supreme Court, per Mr. Justice Douglas, first rejected his claim that certain of his actions in Japan amounted to an effective renunciation of his U.S. citizenship, relying in large part on the findings of the jury. Then it proceeded to consider the requirements imposed on a dual national, "a status long recognized in law," in time of war (*id.* at 733–36):

> One who has a dual nationality will be subject to claims from both nations, claims which at times may be competing or conflicting. The nature of those claims has recently been stated as follows:
>
> > "A person with dual nationality may be subjected to taxes by both states of which he is a national. He is not entitled to protection by one of the two states of which he is a national while in the territorial jurisdiction of the other. Either state not at war with the other may insist on military service when the person is present within its territory. In time of war if he supports neither belligerent, both may be aggrieved. If he supports one belligerent, the other may be aggrieved. One state may be suspicious of his loyalty to it and subject him to the disabilities of an enemy alien, including sequestration of his property, while the other holds his conduct treasonable."

Orfield, *The Legal Effects of Dual Nationality,* 17 Geo.Wash. L.Rev. 427, 429.

Dual nationality, however, is the unavoidable consequence of the conflicting laws of different countries. One who becomes a citizen of this country by reason of birth retains it, even though by the law of another country he is also a citizen of it. He can under certain circumstances be deprived of his American citizenship through the operation of a treaty or an act of Congress; he can also lose it by voluntary action. But American citizenship, until lost, carries obligations of allegiance as well as privileges and benefits. For one who has a dual status the obligations of American citizenship may at times be difficult to discharge. An American who has a dual nationality may find himself in a foreign country when it wages war on us. The very fact that he must make a livelihood there may indirectly help the enemy nation. In these days of total war manpower becomes critical and everyone who can be placed in a productive position increases the strength of the enemy to wage war. Of course, a person caught in that predicament can resolve the conflict of duty by openly electing one nationality or the other and becoming either an alien enemy of the country where he resides or a national of it alone. Yet, so far as the existing law of this country is concerned, he need not make that choice but can continue his dual citizenship. It has been stated in an administrative ruling of the State Department that a person with a dual citizenship who lives abroad in the other country claiming him as a national owes an allegiance to it which is paramount to the allegiance he owes the United States. That is a far cry from a ruling that a citizen in that position owes no allegiance to the United States. Of course, an American citizen who is also a Japanese national living in Japan has obligations to Japan necessitated by his residence there. There might conceivably be cases where the mere nonperformance of the acts complained of would be a breach of Japanese law. He may have employment which requires him to perform certain acts. The compulsion may come from the fact that he is drafted for the job or that his conduct is demanded by the laws of Japan. He may be coerced by his employer or supervisor or by the force of circumstances to do things which he has no desire or heart to do. That was one of petitioner's defenses in this case. Such acts—if done voluntarily and willfully—might be treasonable. But if done under the compulsion of the job or the law or some other influence, those acts would not rise to the gravity of that offense. The trial judge recognized the distinction in his charge when he instructed the jury to acquit petitioner if he did not do the acts willingly or voluntarily "but so acted only because performance of the duties of his employment required him to do so or because of other coercion or compulsion." In short, petitioner was held accountable by the jury only for performing acts of hostility toward this country which he was not required by Japan to perform.

If he can retain that freedom and still remain an American citizen, there is not even a minimum of allegiance which he owes to the United States while he resides in the enemy country. That conclusion is hostile to the concept of citizenship as we know it, and it must be rejected. One who wants that freedom can get it by renouncing his American citizenship. He cannot turn it into a fair-weather citizenship, retaining it for possible contingent benefits but meanwhile playing the part of the traitor. An American citizen owes allegiance to the United States wherever he may reside.

Manifestly, dual nationality can impose difficult choices on the persons who hold that status. In time of war, they may have to judge with exquisite care what kind of support to provide to the country in which they are then resident, at risk of death for treason in one nation or the other, should they go too far or not far enough.[12] *See generally* N. Bar–Yaacov, Dual Nationality 54–62 (1961). But does the existence of those problems justify provisions in U.S. law decreeing *involuntary* expatriation of U.S. citizens, based on certain objective behavior, since even under *Kawakita* they retain the option of voluntary renunciation of citizenship at all times? What difference does it make to the government? Even if Kawakita had never been a U.S. citizen, presumably he could still have committed the same cruelties against American POW's.

Most of the arguments in favor of the expatriating provisions of the original 1952 Act have not rested on scenarios like that involved in *Kawakita*. Instead, they have looked to entanglements that may result from this government's attempts to provide diplomatic protection under circumstances of real or perceived dual nationality—that is, involving U.S. nationals who also have extensive connections with the other nation involved. In order to assess the risks and consequences of such conflicts, one must understand just what is meant by "diplomatic protection." A classic work in the field, E. Borchard, The Diplomatic Protection of Citizens Abroad (1919), summarizes (*id.* at v–vi):

> The individual abroad finds himself in legal relation to two countries, the country of which he is a citizen, and the country in which he resides or establishes his business. From the point of view of the one, he is a citizen abroad; from the point of view of the other, he is an alien. The common consent of nations has established a certain standard of conduct by which a state must be guided in its treatment of aliens. In the absence of any central authority capable of enforcing this standard, international law has authorized the state of which the individual is a citizen to vindicate his rights by diplomatic and other methods sanctioned by international law. This right of diplomatic protection constitutes,

---

12. As it happened, Kawakita's death sentence was later commuted to life imprisonment by President Eisenhower. He was pardoned in 1963, on condition that he be deported immediately to Japan and never re- turn. Kelly, *Dual Nationality, the Myth of Election, and a Kinder, Gentler State Department*, 23 U.Miami Inter–Am.L.Rev. 421, 431 (1991–92).

therefore, a limitation upon the territorial jurisdiction of the country in which the alien is settled or is conducting business.

The standard of treatment which an alien is entitled to receive is incapable of exact definition. The common practice of the civilized nations and the adjudication of conflicts between nations, particularly by arbitration, arising out of alleged violations of the rights of citizens abroad, have nevertheless developed certain fundamental principles from which no nation can depart without incurring international responsibility to the national state of the person injured. The right which every state possesses to protect its citizens abroad is correlative to its obligation to accord foreigners a measure of treatment satisfying the requirements of international law and applicable treaties, and to its responsibility for failure to accomplish this duty. Practice has demonstrated that the mere fact that aliens have been granted the rights authorized by local law, and equality of treatment with natives, is not necessarily regarded as a final compliance with international obligations, if the local measure of justice and administration in a given case falls below the requirements of the international standard of civilized justice, although it is always a delicate proceeding, in the absence of extraterritoriality, to charge that a rule of municipal law or administration fails to meet the international standard.

Citizens abroad, therefore, have in the vindication of their rights an extraordinary legal remedy not open to natives. However just it may be to confine the alien to the rights granted by local law, predicating state liability merely upon the state's failure to make its grant effective, practice has shown that nations of the Western European type are unwilling unreservedly to concede the application of this principle to some of the weaker countries of the world. While tacitly undertaking to abide by the local law, a rule supported by principle, international practice has given aliens a reserved power, after the vain exhaustion of local remedies, to call upon the diplomatic protection of their own government, if their rights, as measured not necessarily by the local, but by the international, standard have been violated. The citizen abroad has no legal right to require the diplomatic protection of his national government. Resort to this remedy of diplomatic protection is solely a right of the government, the justification and expediency of its employment being a matter for the government's unrestricted discretion. This protection is subject in its grant to such rules of municipal administrative law as the state may adopt, and in its exercise internationally to certain rules which custom has recognized.

What exactly does a government do when it is engaged in diplomatic protection? The term embraces a wide variety of actions. At its simplest level, protection consists simply of informal diplomatic or consular contacts with local officials to help straighten out a misunderstanding involving a national. If the matter is not resolved, however, protection can escalate to a higher level of diplomatic negotiation, perhaps accompanied or followed by the formal presentation of a claim for redress, which under some circumstances may be submitted to arbitration or trial before an international tribunal.

At the extreme, diplomatic protection may entail the use of armed force or a full-scale declaration of war. The War of 1812 resulted at least in part from dual nationality problems. Great Britain at the time followed the theory of perpetual allegiance, and refused to recognize the claimed American nationality of its subjects who had been naturalized in the United States. The resulting forcible impressment of American sailors into British service inflamed local passions and helped to bring on hostilities. Naturally, diplomatic protection, even when pushed to that extreme, does not invariably secure *actual* protection of the individual's interests. Moreover, at any stage the government involved is considered to have discretion to abstain from pressing the claim any further. *See id.* at 435–56, 590–91.[13]

In view of these difficulties, numerous states have entered into treaties to reduce or eliminate dual nationality. The Council of Europe also adopted a Convention on the Reduction of Cases of Multiple Nationality in 1963, which has 13 parties. 634 U.N.T.S. 221 (1963). Most of the bilateral treaties provide for a right of option to be exercised at a stated age or date; in default, the person will be deemed a citizen only of the state where he or she resides. R. Donner, The Regulation of Nationality in International Law 201–04 (2d ed.1994). (For a discussion of several such U.S. treaties negotiated in the 1860s and 1870s, see *Perkins v. Elg*, 307 U.S. 325, 59 S.Ct. 884, 83 L.Ed. 1320 (1939); James, *Expatriation in the United States: Precept and Practice Today and Yesterday*, 27 San Diego L.Rev. 853, 865–71 (1990).) The U.S. State Department ruled for many years that dual national children who took up residence with their parents in the other country of nationality had to make an "election" at age 21, by returning to reside here, on pain of losing U.S. citizenship. *Elg, supra*, describes this State Department practice in some detail and seems to approve it, but later the Supreme Court ruled that election could not be required, because Congress had never seen fit to incorporate such a limitation in statute. *Mandoli v. Acheson*, 344 U.S. 133, 73 S.Ct. 135, 97 L.Ed. 146 (1952).

---

13. It should also be noted that the concept of diplomatic protection has been in considerable flux since the days when Borchard wrote, producing changes associated in part with the end of colonialism and the increased assertiveness of Third World nations. Controversy is particularly intense over the content of the "international standard" to be applied to the behavior of host governments, especially in connection with matters like the expropriation of foreign-owned property. *See generally* International Law of State Responsibility for Injuries to Aliens (R. Lillich ed. 1983); Restatement Third, Restatement of the Foreign Relations Law of the United States §§ 711–713 (1987). Also, the former doctrine that a country may not extend diplomatic protection to a dual national against the other country of nationality, *see* E. Borchard, *supra,* at 575–91, has eroded, in favor of a rule recognizing that the country of "effective" or "dominant" nationality is entitled to pursue a claim. *See* McDougal, Lasswell, and Chen, *Nationality and Human Rights: The Protection of the Individual in External Areas*, 83 Yale L.J. 900, 987–91 (1974); Restatement, *supra,* § 713, Comment c. *See generally* P. Weis, Nationality and Statelessness in International Law (2d ed. 1979). Nevertheless, whatever the standard to be applied or the precise circumstances in which it can be invoked, the practice of diplomatic protection undeniably remains an important feature of modern international relations.

anti-dual
nat. pol.
may be
changing.

Opinion on these issues may be undergoing a significant change, however, in many countries formerly in the forefront of the efforts to curb dual nationality. Increasing global mobility has led to many more cross-national marriages, a major cause of dual nationality (for both spouses and children, depending on the law of the spouses' home countries). Also, children born in *jus soli* states to resident foreigners are also likely to have multiple nationalities. One important sign of the altered atmosphere is a 1993 Protocol adopted by the Council of Europe to the aforementioned Convention, which "represents a complete change of policy in regard to certain cases of dual nationality." Donner, *supra*, at 213. Although not yet widely ratified, the Protocol essentially encourages states to permit the retention of the original nationality by spouses who marry a national of a state party, and by young people born and/or long-resident on the territory who will acquire the nationality of that state. *Id.* at 212–16. The latter measure is in part a response to the significant "second generation problem" in European states that do not recognize the *jus soli* but have large permanent resident alien populations as a result of earlier guest-worker programs. *See generally* Hammar, *Dual Citizenship and Political Integration*; 19 Int'l Migration Rev. 438 (1985); Immigration and the Politics of Citizenship in Europe and North America (W.R. Brubaker ed.1989); *Symposium*, 35 Va.J.Int'l L. 237–332 (1994).

In light of this brief discussion, how great a problem—for the nation in its conduct of foreign affairs, not the individual—is dual nationality today? How persuasive are the arguments based on dual nationality in support of expatriation provisions in any country's nationality laws? What other solutions to the difficulties are available, short of involuntary expatriation? Should dual nationality instead be tolerated or even encouraged? Should Congress enact a requirement for dual nationals to elect one nationality or the other upon attaining majority?

———

2.

deserters
still
citizens

On the same day that *Perez* was decided, the court struck down, also by a vote of five to four, a section of the nationality laws that was meant to strip citizenship from those convicted of desertion from the military during time of war. *Trop v. Dulles*, 356 U.S. 86, 78 S.Ct. 590, 2 L.Ed.2d 630 (1958). Chief Justice Warren wrote the plurality opinion, joined by the other three *Perez* dissenters. He repeated his view that Congress lacked the power to expatriate, but also found the statute invalid on a separate ground. This provision was intended by its framers, he determined, to be a punishment; as such, it was subject to the Eighth Amendment. And because denationalization in these circumstances involves "the total destruction of the individual's status in organized society," it amounted to cruel and unusual punishment that could not stand. Justice Brennan, the crucial swing vote, concurred separately. As his agreement with the majority in *Perez* indicated, he believed that Congress had the power to expatriate. But he found this particular provision wanting because "the requisite rational relation between the statute and the war power does not appear." The other four members of the *Perez* majority dissented.

In the third expatriation case decided that day, *Nishikawa v. Dulles*, 356 U.S. 129, 78 S.Ct. 612, 2 L.Ed.2d 659 (1958), the Court reversed an expatriation ruling without having to reach the constitutional issues. The lower court had ruled that a dual national's service in the Japanese army during World War II resulted in his expatriation, over his claim that his service was involuntary because he was conscripted by his other country of nationality. A majority of the Supreme Court determined that once the issue of duress was raised, the statute required the government to shoulder the burden of proving that the allegedly expatriating behavior had been performed voluntarily. Moreover, the government would have to make its case by clear, unequivocal, and convincing evidence, "[b]ecause the consequences of denationalization are so drastic * * *." Justice Black attached a concurring opinion reiterating the view he and Justice Douglas had favored in both *Perez* and *Trop*: that Congress lacks power to expatriate and that *Mackenzie v. Hare* should be overruled to the extent that it was inconsistent with this position.

The 1958 trilogy thus revealed a badly divided court, and it established no clearly prevailing framework for deciding when involuntary expatriation was permissible. Indeed, the results of the three cases seem intuitively backwards. The rather innocent act of voting in a Mexican election (about which Mexico had made no complaint) resulted in forfeiture of citizenship. Yet a wartime deserter and a citizen who served with an enemy army escaped the same fate.

In 1963, the Court returned to the same arena, but the decision cast little new light on the contours of the doctrine. At issue in *Kennedy v. Mendoza–Martinez*, 372 U.S. 144, 83 S.Ct. 554, 9 L.Ed.2d 644 (1963) was the section of the statute decreeing expatriation for those who left or remained outside the United States during time of war to evade military service. By a vote of five to four, the Court held this provision unconstitutional, following an approach similar to that of the *Trop* plurality. The majority first examined the legislative history and concluded that the statute employed expatriation as a punishment. As such, the sanction could not be employed without prior observance of the procedural safeguards guaranteed by the Fifth and Sixth Amendments, meaning "a prior criminal trial and all its incidents."

The following year, the Court considered a provision that decreed loss of U.S. citizenship for a naturalized citizen who returned to reside in his native country for three years (implementing a practice quite common in treaties meant to minimize dual nationality). *Schneider v. Rusk*, 377 U.S. 163, 84 S.Ct. 1187, 12 L.Ed.2d 218 (1964). The majority struck down the section, by a vote of five to three, with Justice Brennan not participating. Justice Douglas's brief majority opinion restated his belief that Congress lacked power to expatriate. Acknowledging that this position "has not yet commanded a majority of the entire Court," however, he ultimately rested the invalidation on a different ground. The statute, he wrote, "proceeds on the impermissible assumption that naturalized citizens as a class are less reliable and bear less allegiance to this country than the native born." (Is this a fair characterization? Are assumptions made about "naturalized citizens as a class"? Or is the assumption instead merely that the small subclass of naturalized citizens who live for a long period in their native countries are more likely to experience conflicting allegiances than others who have no such prior tie—and so should be put to a choice of ending the residence in that country or forfeiting citizenship? Is such an assumption irrational? Is it even unreasonable?)

The majority then applied its understanding of the *Perez* standards under the Fifth Amendment due process clause. It concluded that the statute contravened equal protection principles embraced in that clause: "The discrimination aimed at naturalized citizens drastically limits their rights to live and work abroad in a way that other citizens may. It creates indeed a second-class citizenship." Congress henceforth would not be permitted to distinguish between naturalized and native-born citizens for purposes of expatriation, although it could still provide for denaturalization if the original naturalization was tainted with fraud or other illegality, properly proven.

In 1967, the Court returned to the precise ground of expatriation that had been upheld in *Perez:*

AFROYIM v. RUSK

Supreme Court of the United States, 1967.
387 U.S. 253, 87 S.Ct. 1660, 18 L.Ed.2d 757.

Mr. Justice Black delivered the opinion of the Court.

Petitioner, born in Poland in 1893, immigrated to this country in 1912 and became a naturalized American citizen in 1926. He went to Israel in 1950, and in 1951 he voluntarily voted in an election for the Israeli Knesset, the legislative body of Israel. In 1960, when he applied for renewal of his United States passport, the Department of State refused to grant it on the sole ground that he had lost his American citizenship by virtue of § 401(e) of the Nationality Act of 1940 which provides that a United States citizen shall "lose" his citizenship if he votes "in a political election in a foreign state." Petitioner then brought this declaratory judgment action in federal district court alleging that § 401(e) violates both the Due Process Clause of the Fifth Amendment and § 1, cl. 1, of the Fourteenth Amendment which grants American citizenship to persons like petitioner. Because neither the Fourteenth Amendment nor any other provision of the Constitution expressly grants Congress the power to take away that citizenship once it has been acquired, petitioner contended that the only way he could lose his citizenship was by his own voluntary renunciation of it. Since the Government took the position that § 401(e) empowers it to terminate citizenship without the citizen's voluntary renunciation, petitioner argued that this section is prohibited by the Constitution. [The lower courts held for the government.] * * *

Petitioner, relying on the same contentions about voluntary renunciation of citizenship which this Court rejected in upholding § 401(e) in *Perez,* urges us to reconsider that case, adopt the view of the minority there, and overrule it. That case, decided by a 5–4 vote almost 10 years ago, has been a source of controversy and confusion ever since, as was emphatically recognized in the opinions of all the judges who participated in this case below. Moreover, in the other cases decided with and since *Perez,* this Court has consistently invalidated on a case-by-case basis various other statutory sections providing for involuntary expatriation. It has done so on various grounds and has refused to hold that citizens can be expatriated without their voluntary renunciation of citizenship. These cases, as well as many commentators, have cast great doubt upon the soundness of *Perez.* Under these circumstances, we granted certiorari to reconsider it, 385 U.S. 917, 87 S.Ct. 232, 17 L.Ed.2d 142. In view of the many recent opinions and dissents comprehensively discussing all the issues involved, we deem it unnecessary to treat this subject at great length.

* * *

First we reject the idea expressed in *Perez* that, aside from the Fourteenth Amendment, Congress has any general power, express or implied, to take away an American citizen's citizenship without his assent. This power cannot, as *Perez* indicated, be sustained as an implied attribute of sovereignty possessed by all nations. Other nations are governed by their own constitutions, if any, and we can draw no support from theirs. In our country the people are sovereign and the Government cannot sever its relationship to the people by taking away their citizenship. Our Constitution governs us and we must never forget that our Constitution limits the Government to those powers specifically granted or those that are necessary and proper to carry out the specifically granted ones. The Constitution, of course, grants Congress no express power to strip people of their citizenship, whether in the exercise of the implied power to regulate foreign affairs or in the exercise of any specifically granted power. And even before the adoption of the Fourteenth Amendment, views were expressed in Congress and by this Court that under the Constitution the Government was granted no power, even under its express power to pass a uniform rule of naturalization, to determine what conduct should and should not result in the loss of citizenship. On three occasions, in 1794, 1797, and 1818, Congress considered and rejected proposals to enact laws which would describe certain conduct as resulting in expatriation. * * *

[Justice Black then spends several pages describing these proposals and reprinting excerpts from the congressional debates.]

* * *

Although these * * * statements may be regarded as inconclusive and must be considered in the historical context in which they were made, any doubt as to whether prior to the passage of the Fourteenth Amendment Congress had the power to deprive a person against his will of citizenship once obtained should have been removed by the unequivocal terms of the Amendment itself. It provides its own constitutional rule in language calculated completely to control the status of citizenship: "All persons born or naturalized in the United States ... are citizens of the United States...." There is no indication in these words of a fleeting citizenship, good at the moment it is acquired but subject to destruction by the Government at any time. Rather the Amendment can most reasonably be read as defining a citizenship which a citizen keeps unless he voluntarily relinquishes it. Once acquired, this Fourteenth Amendment citizenship was not to be shifted, canceled, or diluted at the will of the Federal Government, the States, or any other governmental unit.

It is true that the chief interest of the people in giving permanence and security to citizenship in the Fourteenth Amendment was the desire to protect Negroes. The *Dred Scott* decision, 19 How. 393, 15 L.Ed. 691, had shortly before greatly disturbed many people about the status of Negro citizenship. But the Civil Rights Act of 1866 had already attempted to confer citizenship on all persons born or naturalized in the United States. Nevertheless, when the Fourteenth Amendment passed the House without containing any definition of citizenship, the sponsors of the Amendment in the Senate insisted on inserting a constitutional definition and grant of citizenship. * * *

* * * Though the framers of the Amendment were not particularly concerned with the problem of expatriation, it seems undeniable from the language they used that they wanted to put citizenship beyond the power of any governmental unit to destroy. In 1868, two years after the Fourteenth Amendment had been proposed, Congress specifically considered the subject of expatriation. Several bills were introduced to impose involuntary expatriation on citizens who committed certain acts. With little discussion, these proposals were defeated. * * *

* * *

Because the legislative history of the Fourteenth Amendment and of the expatriation proposals which preceded and followed it, like most other legislative history, contains many statements from which conflicting inferences can be drawn, our holding might be unwarranted if it rested entirely or principally upon that legislative history. But it does not. Our holding we think is the only one that can stand in view of the language and the purpose of the Fourteenth Amendment, and our construction of that Amendment, we believe, comports more nearly than *Perez* with the principles of liberty and equal justice to all that the entire Fourteenth Amendment was adopted to guarantee. Citizenship is no light trifle to be jeopardized any moment Congress decides to do so under the name of one of its general or implied grants of power. In some instances, loss of citizenship can mean that a man is left without the protection of citizenship in any country in the world—as a man without a country. Citizenship in this Nation is a part of a cooperative affair. Its citizenry is the country and the country is its citizenry. The very nature of our free government makes it completely incongruous to have a rule of law under which a group of citizens temporarily in office can deprive another group of citizens of their citizenship. We hold that the Fourteenth Amendment was designed to, and does, protect every citizen of this Nation against a congressional forcible destruction of his citizenship, whatever his creed, color, or race. Our holding does no more than to give to this citizen that which is his own, a constitutional right to remain a citizen in a free country unless he voluntarily relinquishes that citizenship.

Perez v. Brownell is overruled. The judgment is

Reversed.

MR. JUSTICE HARLAN, whom MR. JUSTICE CLARK, MR. JUSTICE STEWART, and MR. JUSTICE WHITE join, dissenting.

* * *

The Court today overrules *Perez,* and declares § 401(e) unconstitutional, by a remarkable process of circumlocution. First, the Court fails almost entirely to dispute the reasoning in *Perez;* it is essentially content with the conclusory and quite unsubstantiated assertion that Congress is without "any general power, express or implied," to expatriate a citizen "without his assent." [1] Next, the Court embarks upon a lengthy, albeit incomplete, survey of the historical background of the congressional power at stake here, and yet, at the end, concedes that the history is susceptible to "conflicting inferences." * * *

I can find nothing in this extraordinary series of circumventions which permits, still less compels, the imposition of this constitutional constraint upon the authority of Congress. I must respectfully dissent.

There is no need here to rehearse Mr. Justice Frankfurter's opinion for the Court in *Perez;* it then proved and still proves to my satisfaction that § 401(e) is within the power of Congress. It suffices simply to supplement *Perez* with an examination of the historical evidence which the Court in part recites, and which provides the only apparent basis for many of the Court's conclusions. As will be seen, the available historical evidence is not only inadequate to support the Court's abandonment of *Perez,* but, with due regard for the restraints that should surround the judicial invalidation of an Act of Congress, even seems to confirm *Perez'* soundness.

* * *

The most pertinent evidence from this period upon these questions has been virtually overlooked by the Court. Twice in the two years immediately prior to its passage of the Fourteenth Amendment, Congress exercised the very authority which the Court now suggests that it should have recognized was entirely lacking. In each case, a bill was debated and adopted by both Houses which included provisions to expatriate unwilling citizens.

1. It is appropriate to note at the outset what appears to be a fundamental ambiguity in the opinion for the Court. The Court at one point intimates, but does not expressly declare, that it adopts the reasoning of the dissent of THE CHIEF JUSTICE in *Perez.* THE CHIEF JUSTICE there acknowledged that "actions in derogation of undivided allegiance to this country" had "long been recognized" to result in expatriation, *id.,* at 68; he argued, however, that the connection between voting in a foreign political election and abandonment of citizenship was logically insufficient to support a presumption that a citizen had renounced his nationality. *Id.,* at 76, 78 S.Ct. at 586. It is difficult to find any semblance of this reasoning, beyond the momen-

tary reference to the opinion of THE CHIEF JUSTICE, in the approach taken by the Court today; it seems instead to adopt a substantially wider view of the restrictions upon Congress' authority in this area. Whatever the Court's position, it has assumed that voluntariness is here a term of fixed meaning; in fact, of course, it has been employed to describe both a specific intent to renounce citizenship, and the uncoerced commission of an act conclusively deemed by law to be a relinquishment of citizenship. Until the Court indicates with greater precision what it means by "assent," today's opinion will surely cause still greater confusion in this area of the law.

In the spring and summer of 1864, both Houses debated intensively the Wade–Davis bill to provide reconstruction governments for the States which had seceded to form the Confederacy. Among the bill's provisions was § 14, by which "every person who shall hereafter hold or exercise any office . . . in the rebel service . . . is hereby declared not to be a citizen of the United States." Much of the debate upon the bill did not, of course, center on the expatriation provision, although it certainly did not escape critical attention. Nonetheless, I have not found any indication in the debates in either House that it was supposed that Congress was without authority to deprive an unwilling citizen of his citizenship. The bill was not signed by President Lincoln before the adjournment of Congress, and thus failed to become law, but a subsequent statement issued by Lincoln makes quite plain that he was not troubled by any doubts of the constitutionality of § 14. Passage of the Wade–Davis bill of itself "suffices to destroy the notion that the men who drafted the Fourteenth Amendment felt that citizenship was an 'absolute.'"

Twelve months later, and less than a year before its passage of the Fourteenth Amendment, Congress adopted a second measure which included provisions that permitted the expatriation of unwilling citizens. Section 21 of the Enrollment Act of 1865 provided that deserters from the military service of the United States "shall be deemed and taken to have voluntarily relinquished and forfeited their rights of citizenship and their rights to become citizens. . . ." * * * [I]t was never suggested in either debate that expatriation without a citizen's consent lay beyond Congress' authority.

* * *

* * * [Nothing in the debates on the Citizenship Clause of the Fourteenth Amendment] supports the Court's assertion that the clause was intended to deny Congress its authority to expatriate unwilling citizens. The evidence indicates that its draftsmen instead expected the clause only to declare unreservedly to whom citizenship initially adhered, thus overturning the restrictions both of *Dred Scott* and of the doctrine of primary state citizenship, while preserving Congress' authority to prescribe the methods and terms of expatriation.

* * *

Once obtained, citizenship is of course protected from arbitrary withdrawal by the constraints placed around Congress' powers by the Constitution; it is not proper to create from the Citizenship Clause an additional, and entirely unwarranted, restriction upon legislative authority. The construction now placed on the Citizenship Clause rests, in the last analysis, simply on the Court's *ipse dixit,* evincing little more, it is quite apparent, than the present majority's own distaste for the expatriation power.

I believe that *Perez* was rightly decided, and on its authority would affirm the judgment of the Court of Appeals.

Notes

Justice Black seems almost to concede that the historical materials on which he relies have been rendered suspect by the patient historical research of Justice Harlan (of which only a portion is reprinted here). The last textual paragraph in the majority opinion retreats to an invocation of "the language and the purpose of the Fourteenth Amendment" as the real ground of decision. But does the language by itself support the majority's conclusions? If not, how can we know the purpose apart from inquiry into the historical views of the drafters?

Even those who share, in Justice Harlan's words, "the present majority's distaste for the expatriation power" might wish to have some more solid basis for the conclusion reached by the majority in *Afroyim*. Can you construct such a basis? Reconsider Chief Justice Warren's dissent in *Perez*. How does it differ in reasoning, or at least in emphasis, from Justice Black's majority opinion in *Afroyim?* Does it furnish a more reliable foundation for the conclusions reached? *See generally* C. Black, Structure and Relationship in Constitutional Law (1969).

————

The durability of *Afroyim* was called into question by a holding, again reached by a five-four margin, handed down four years later, after two Justices had retired and been replaced by new appointees. *Rogers v. Bellei*, 401 U.S. 815, 91 S.Ct. 1060, 28 L.Ed.2d 499 (1971). Bellei was born in Italy in 1939 to an Italian father and an American mother. Because the mother had resided in the United States for more than 10 years before his birth, she could transmit U.S. citizenship to him *jure sanguinis*. But the statute then operative also imposed a "condition subsequent" on children obtaining citizenship this way; they had to come to the United States and reside here for a minimum of five years between the ages of 14 and 28. Bellei had not met this condition, but he argued that, under *Afroyim*, Congress lacked the power to deprive him of citizenship.

The majority, per Justice Blackmun, ruled for the government:

The central fact, in our weighing of the plaintiff's claim to continuing and therefore current United States citizenship, is that he was born abroad. He was not born in the United States. He was not naturalized in the United States. And he has not been subject to the jurisdiction of the United States. All this being so, it seems indisputable that the first sentence of the Fourteenth Amendment has no application to plaintiff Bellei. He simply is not a Fourteenth–Amendment-first-sentence citizen. His posture contrasts with that of Mr. Afroyim, who was naturalized in the United States and with that of Mrs. Schneider, whose citizenship was derivative by her presence here and by her mother's naturalization here.

The plaintiff's claim thus must center in the statutory power of Congress and in the appropriate exercise of that power within the restrictions of any pertinent constitutional provisions other than the Fourteenth Amendment's first sentence.

* * *

[I]t is conceded here both that Congress may withhold citizenship from persons like plaintiff Bellei and may prescribe a period of residence in the United States as a condition *precedent* without constitutional question.

* * *

We feel that it does not make good constitutional sense, or comport with logic, to say, on the one hand, that Congress may impose a condition precedent, with no constitutional complication, and yet be powerless to impose precisely the same condition subsequent. Any such distinction, of course, must rest, if it has any basis at all, on the asserted "premise that the rights of citizenship of the native born and of the naturalized person are of the same dignity and are coextensive," *Schneider v. Rusk,* and on the announcement that Congress has no "power, express or implied, to take away an American citizen's citizenship without his assent," *Afroyim v. Rusk.* But, as pointed out above, these were utterances bottomed upon Fourteenth Amendment citizenship and that Amendment's direct reference to "persons born or naturalized in the United States." We do not accept the notion that those utterances are now to be judicially extended to citizenship not based upon the Fourteenth Amendment and to make citizenship an absolute. That it is not an absolute is demonstrated by the fact that even Fourteenth Amendment citizenship by naturalization, when unlawfully procured, may be set aside. *Afroyim v. Rusk,* 387 U.S., at 267 n. 23, 87 S.Ct., at 1667.

Justice Black, joined by Douglas and Marshall, wrote a furious dissent claiming that the majority had overruled *Afroyim.* He rejected the majority's view of the Fourteenth Amendment's language as a "technical reading." In his view, "the word 'in' as it appears in the phrase 'in the United States' was surely meant to be understood in two somewhat different senses: one can become a citizen of this country by being born *within* it or by being naturalized *into* it." Justice Brennan based his dissent on "the complete lack of a rational basis for distinguishing among citizens whose naturalization was carried out within the physical bounds of the United States, and those who, like Bellei, may be naturalized overseas."

As noted in Section B, however, Congress chose not long after the *Bellei* decision to repeal (but without retroactive effect) all conditions subsequent applicable to persons gaining U.S. citizenship *jure sanguinis.* Under current law, someone born abroad in a situation like Bellei's need never establish residence in the United States in order to preserve his citizenship. He will probably have to do so, however, if he wishes to transmit citizenship to his own children.

Doubt about the vitality of *Afroyim* lingered after *Bellei*, but Justice Black was proved resoundingly wrong in 1980. The following case seems to have brought relative stability to the constitutional doctrine governing expatriation.

VANCE v. TERRAZAS

Supreme Court of the United States, 1980.
444 U.S. 252, 100 S.Ct. 540, 62 L.Ed.2d 461.

Mr. Justice White delivered the opinion of the Court.

Section 349(a)(2) of the Immigration and Nationality Act (Act) provides that "a person who is a national of the United States whether by birth or naturalization, shall lose his nationality by ... taking an oath or making an affirmation or other formal declaration of allegiance to a foreign state or a political subdivision thereof." The Act also provides that the party claiming that such loss of citizenship occurred must "establish such claim by a preponderance of the evidence" and that the voluntariness of the expatriating conduct is rebuttably presumed. § 349(c), as added, 75 Stat. 656.[a] The issues in this case are whether, in establishing loss of citizenship under § 349(a)(2) a party must prove an intent to surrender United States citizenship and whether the United States Constitution permits Congress to legislate with respect to expatriation proceedings by providing the standard of proof and the statutory presumption contained in § 349(c).

I

Appellee, Laurence J. Terrazas, was born in this country, the son of a Mexican citizen. He thus acquired at birth both United States and Mexican citizenship. In the fall of 1970, while a student in Monterrey, Mexico, and at the age of 22, appellee executed an application for a certificate of Mexican nationality, swearing "adherence, obedience, and submission to the laws and authorities of the Mexican Republic" and "expressly renounc[ing] United States citizenship, as well as any submission, obedience, and loyalty to any foreign government, especially to that of the United States of America, ..." The certificate, which issued upon this application on April 3, 1971, recited that Terrazas had sworn adherence to the United Mexican States and that he "has expressly renounced all rights inherent to any other nationality, as well as all submission, obedience, and loyalty to any foreign government, especially to those which have recognized him as that national." Terrazas read and understood the certificate upon receipt.

A few months later, following a discussion with an officer of the United States Consulate in Monterrey, proceedings were instituted to determine whether appellee had lost his United States citizenship by obtaining the certificate of Mexican nationality. Appellee denied that he had, but in December 1971 the Department of State issued a certificate of loss of nationality. The Board of Appellate Review of the Department of State, after a full hearing, affirmed that appellee had voluntarily renounced his

---

a. This presumption now appears in § 349(b).—eds.

United States citizenship. As permitted by § 360(a) of the Act, appellee then brought this suit against the Secretary of State for a declaration of his United States nationality. Trial was *de novo.*

rule

The District Court recognized that the first sentence of the Fourteenth Amendment, as construed in *Afroyim v. Rusk,* " 'protect[s] every citizen of this Nation against a congressional forcible destruction of his citizenship' " and that every citizen has " 'a constitutional right to remain a citizen … unless he voluntarily relinquishes that citizenship.' " A person of dual nationality, the District Court said, "will be held to have expatriated himself from the United States when it is shown that he voluntarily committed an act whereby he unequivocally renounced his allegiance to the United States." Specifically, the District Court found that appellee had taken an oath of allegiance to Mexico, that he had "knowingly and understandingly renounced allegiance to the United States in connection with his Application for a Certificate of Mexican Nationality," and that "[t]he taking of an oath of allegiance to Mexico and renunciation of a foreign country [*sic*]citizenship is a condition precedent under Mexican law to the issuance of a Certificate of Mexican Nationality." The District Court concluded that the United States had "proved by a preponderance of the evidence that Laurence J. Terrazas knowingly, understandingly and voluntarily took an oath of allegiance to Mexico, and concurrently renounced allegiance to the United States," and that he had therefore "voluntarily relinquished United States citizenship pursuant to § 349(a)(2) of the … Act."

dist ct
– renounced

In its opinion accompanying its findings and conclusions, the District Court observed that appellee had acted "voluntarily in swearing allegiance to Mexico and renouncing allegiance to the United States," and that appellee "knew he was repudiating allegiance to the United States through his actions." The court also said that "the declaration of allegiance to a foreign state in conjunction with the renunciatory language of United States citizenship 'would leave no room for ambiguity as to the intent of the applicant.' "

Ct App
– rv'd

block
Cong. pwr

The Court of Appeals reversed. As the Court of Appeals understood the law—and there appears to have been no dispute on these basic requirements in the Courts of Appeals—the United States had not only to prove the taking of an oath to a foreign state, but also to demonstrate an intent on appellee's part to renounce his United States citizenship. The District Court had found these basic elements to have been proved by a preponderance of the evidence; and the Court of Appeals observed that, "[a]ssuming that the proper [evidentiary] standards were applied, we are convinced that the record fully supports the court's findings." The Court of Appeals ruled, however, that under *Afroyim v. Rusk,* Congress had no power to legislate the evidentiary standard contained in § 349(c) and that the Constitution required that proof be not merely by a preponderance of the evidence, but by "clear, convincing and unequivocal evidence." The case was remanded to the District Court for further proceedings.

The Secretary took this appeal under 28 U.S.C. § 1252. Because the invalidation of § 349(c) posed a substantial constitutional issue, we noted probable jurisdiction.

II

The Secretary first urges that the Court of Appeals erred in holding that a "specific intent to renounce U.S. citizenship" must be proved "before the mere taking of an oath of allegiance could result in an individual's expatriation." His position is that he need prove only the voluntary commission of an act, such as swearing allegiance to a foreign nation, that "is so inherently inconsistent with the continued retention of American citizenship that Congress may accord to it its natural consequences, *i.e.,* loss of nationality." We disagree.

* * *

The Secretary argues that *Afroyim* does not stand for the proposition that a specific intent to renounce must be shown before citizenship is relinquished. It is enough, he urges, to establish one of the expatriating acts specified in § 349(a) because Congress has declared each of those acts to be inherently inconsistent with the retention of citizenship. But *Afroyim* emphasized that loss of citizenship requires the individual's "assent," in addition to his voluntary commission of the expatriating act. It is difficult to understand that "assent" to loss of citizenship would mean anything less than an intent to relinquish citizenship, whether the intent is expressed in words or is found as a fair inference from proved conduct. *Perez* had sustained congressional power to expatriate without regard to the intent of the citizen to surrender his citizenship. *Afroyim* overturned this proposition. It may be, as the Secretary maintains, that a requirement of intent to relinquish citizenship poses substantial difficulties for the Government in performance of its essential task of determining who is a citizen. Nevertheless, the intent of the Fourteenth Amendment, among other things, was to define citizenship; and as interpreted in *Afroyim,* that definition cannot coexist with a congressional power to specify acts that work a renunciation of citizenship even absent an intent to renounce. In the last analysis, expatriation depends on the will of the citizen rather than on the will of Congress and its assessment of his conduct.

* * *

[W]e are confident that it would be inconsistent with *Afroyim* to treat the expatriating acts specified in § 349(a) as the equivalent of or as conclusive evidence of the indispensable voluntary assent of the citizen. "Of course," any of the specified acts "may be highly persuasive evidence in the particular case of a purpose to abandon citizenship." *Nishikawa v. Dulles,* 356 U.S. 129, 139, 78 S.Ct. 612, 618, 2 L.Ed.2d 659 (1958) (Black, J., concurring). But the trier of fact must in the end conclude that the citizen not only voluntarily committed the expatriating act prescribed in the statute, but also intended to relinquish his citizenship.

* * *

III

With respect to the principal issues before it, the Court of Appeals held that Congress was without constitutional authority to prescribe the standard of proof in expatriation proceedings and that the proof in such cases must be by clear and convincing evidence rather than by the preponderance standard prescribed in § 349(c). We are in fundamental disagreement with these conclusions.

In *Nishikawa v. Dulles,* 356 U.S. 129, 78 S.Ct. 612, 2 L.Ed.2d 659 (1958), an American-born citizen, temporarily in Japan, was drafted into the Japanese Army. The Government later claimed that, under § 401(c) of the Nationality Act of 1940, 54 Stat. 1169, he had expatriated himself by serving in the armed forces of a foreign nation. The Government agreed that expatriation had not occurred if Nishikawa's army service had been involuntary. Nishikawa contended that the Government had to prove that his service was voluntary, while the Government urged that duress was an affirmative defense that Nishikawa had the burden to prove by overcoming the usual presumption of voluntariness. This Court held the presumption unavailable to the Government and required proof of a voluntary expatriating act by clear and convincing evidence.

Section 349(c) soon followed; its evident aim was to supplant the evidentiary standards prescribed by *Nishikawa.* The provision "sets up rules of evidence under which the burden of proof to establish loss of citizenship by preponderance of the evidence would rest upon the Government. The presumption of voluntariness under the proposed rules of evidence, would be rebuttable—similarly—by preponderance of the evidence, ..." H.R.Rep. No. 1086, 87th Cong., 1st Sess., 41, U.S.Code Cong. & Admin.News, p. 2985 (1961).

We see no basis for invalidating the evidentiary prescriptions contained in § 349(c). *Nishikawa* was not rooted in the Constitution. The Court noted, moreover, that it was acting in the absence of legislative guidance. Nor do we agree with the Court of Appeals that, because under *Afroyim* Congress is constitutionally devoid of power to impose expatriation on a citizen, it is also without power to prescribe the evidentiary standards to govern expatriation proceedings. Although § 349(c) had been law since 1961, *Afroyim* did not address or advert to that section; surely the Court would have said so had it intended to construe the Constitution to exclude expatriation proceedings from the traditional powers of Congress to prescribe rules of evidence and standards of proof in the federal courts. This power, rooted in the authority of Congress conferred by Art. 1, § 8, cl. 9, of the Constitution to create inferior federal courts, is undoubted and has been frequently noted and sustained.

* * * [S]ince Congress has the express power to enforce the Fourteenth Amendment, it is untenable to hold that it has no power whatsoever to address itself to the manner or means by which Fourteenth Amendment citizenship may be relinquished.

We are unable to conclude that the specific evidentiary standard provided by Congress in § 349(c) is invalid under either the Citizenship Clause or the Due Process Clause of the Fifth Amendment. It is true that in criminal and involuntary commitment contexts we have held that the Due Process Clause imposes requirements of proof beyond a preponderance of the evidence. *Mullaney v. Wilbur,* 421 U.S. 684, 95 S.Ct. 1881, 44

L.Ed.2d 508 (1975); *Addington v. Texas*, 441 U.S. 418, 99 S.Ct. 1804, 60 L.Ed.2d 323 (1979). This Court has also stressed the importance of citizenship and evinced a decided preference for requiring clear and convincing evidence to prove expatriation. *Nishikawa v. United States, supra.* But expatriation proceedings are civil in nature and do not threaten a loss of liberty. Moreover, as we have noted, *Nishikawa* did not purport to be constitutional ruling, and the same is true of similar rulings in related areas. *Woodby v. INS*, 385 U.S. 276, 285, 87 S.Ct. 483, 487, 17 L.Ed.2d 362 (1966) (deportation); *Schneiderman v. United States*, 320 U.S. 118, 125, 63 S.Ct. 1333, 1336, 87 L.Ed. 1779 (1943) (denaturalization). None of these cases involved a congressional judgment, such as that present here, that the preponderance standard of proof provides sufficient protection for the interest of the individual in retaining his citizenship. Contrary to the Secretary's position, we have held that expatriation requires the ultimate finding that the citizen has committed the expatriating act with the intent to renounce his citizenship. This in itself is a heavy burden, and we cannot hold that Congress has exceeded its powers by requiring proof of an intentional expatriating act by a preponderance of evidence.

IV

* * *

It is important at this juncture to note the scope of the statutory presumption. Section 349(c) provides that any of the statutory expatriating acts, if proved, are presumed to have been committed voluntarily. It does not also direct a presumption that the act has been performed with the intent to relinquish United States citizenship. That matter remains the burden of the party claiming expatriation to prove by a preponderance of the evidence. As so understood, we cannot invalidate the provision.[9]

* * * [T]he Court in *Nishikawa*, because it decided that "the consequences of denationalization are so drastic" and because it found nothing indicating a contrary result in the legislative history of the Nationality Act of 1940, held that the Government must carry the burden of proving that the expatriating act was performed voluntarily.

Section 349(c), which was enacted subsequently, and its legislative history make clear that Congress preferred the ordinary rule that voluntariness is presumed and that duress is an affirmative defense to be proved by the party asserting it. * * * The rationality of the procedural rule with respect to claims of involuntariness in ordinary civil cases cannot be doubted. To invalidate the rule here would be to disagree flatly with Congress on the balance to be struck between the interest in citizenship and the burden the Government must assume in demonstrating expatriating conduct. It would also constitutionalize that disagreement and give the

---

9. The Secretary asserts that the § 349(c) presumption cannot survive constitutional scrutiny if we hold that intent to relinquish citizenship is a necessary element in proving expatriation. The predicate for this assertion seems to be that § 349(c) presumes intent to relinquish as well as voluntariness.

We do not so read it. Even if we did, and even if we agreed that presuming the necessary intent is inconsistent with *Afroyim*, it would be unnecessary to invalidate the section insofar as it presumes that the expatriating act itself was performed voluntarily.

Citizenship Clause of the Fourteenth Amendment far more scope in this context than the relevant circumstances that brought the Amendment into being would suggest appropriate. Thus we conclude that the presumption of voluntariness included in § 349(c) has continuing vitality.

V

In sum, we hold that in proving expatriation, an expatriating act and an intent to relinquish citizenship must be proved by a preponderance of the evidence. We also hold that when one of the statutory expatriating acts is proved, it is constitutional to presume it to have been a voluntary act until and unless proved otherwise by the actor. If he succeeds, there can be no expatriation. If he fails, the question remains whether on all the evidence the Government has satisfied its burden of proof that the expatriating act was performed with the necessary intent to relinquish citizenship.

The judgment of the Court of Appeals is reversed, and the case is remanded for further proceedings consistent with this opinion.

So ordered.

* * *

Mr. Justice Marshall, concurring in part and dissenting in part.

I agree with the Court's holding that a citizen of the United States may not lose his citizenship in the absence of a finding that he specifically intended to renounce it. I also concur in the adoption of a saving construction of INA § 349(a)(2) to require that the statutorily designated expatriating acts be done with a specific intent to relinquish citizenship.

I cannot, however, accept the majority's conclusion that a person may be found to have relinquished his American citizenship upon a preponderance of the evidence that he intended to do so. The Court's discussion of congressional power to "prescribe rules of evidence and standards of proof in the federal courts," is the beginning, not the end, of the inquiry. It remains the task of this Court to determine when those rules and standards impinge on constitutional rights. As my Brother Stevens indicates, the Court's casual dismissal of the importance of American citizenship cannot withstand scrutiny. * * *

For these reasons I cannot understand, much less accept, the Court's suggestion that "expatriation proceedings ... do not threaten a loss of liberty." Recognizing that a standard of proof ultimately " 'reflects the value society places' "on the interest at stake, *Addington v. Texas,* 441 U.S. 418, 425, 99 S.Ct. 1804, 1809, 60 L.Ed.2d 372 (1979), I would hold that a citizen may not lose his citizenship in the absence of clear and convincing evidence that he intended to do so.

Mr. Justice Stevens, concurring in part and dissenting in part.

The Court today unanimously reiterates the principle set forth in *Afroyim v. Rusk,* that Congress may not deprive an American of his citizenship against his will, but may only effectuate the citizen's own intention to renounce his citizenship. I agree with the Court that Congress may establish certain standards for determining whether such a renunciation has occurred. It may, for example, provide that expatriation can be proved by evidence that a person has performed an act that is normally inconsistent with continued citizenship and that the person thereby specifically intended to relinquish his American citizenship.

I do not agree, however, with the conclusion that Congress has established a permissible standard in § 349(a)(2). Since we accept dual citizenship, taking an oath of allegiance to a foreign government is not necessarily inconsistent with an intent to remain an American citizen. Moreover, as now written, the statute cannot fairly be read to require a finding of specific intent to relinquish citizenship. The statute unambiguously states that

"a national of the United States ... shall lose his nationality by—

. . .

"(2) taking an oath or making an affirmation or other formal declaration of allegiance to a foreign state or a political subdivision thereof."

There is no room in this provision to imply a requirement of a specific intent to relinquish citizenship. The Court does not attempt to do so, nor does it explain how any other part of the statute supports its conclusion that Congress required proof of specific intent.[1]

I also disagree with the holding that a person may be deprived of his citizenship upon a showing by a mere preponderance of the evidence that he intended to relinquish it. The Court reasons that because the proceedings in question are civil in nature and do not result in any loss of physical liberty, no greater burden of proof is required than in the ordinary civil case. Such reasoning construes the constitutional concept of "liberty" too narrowly.

The House Report accompanying the 1961 amendment to the Immigration and Naturalization Act of 1952 refers to "the dignity and the priceless value of U.S. citizenship." That characterization is consistent with this Court's repeated appraisal of the quality of the interest at stake in this proceeding. In my judgment a person's interest in retaining his American

---

1. It could perhaps be argued that a specific intent requirement can be derived from INA § 349(c). That subsection creates a rebuttable presumption that any expatriating act set forth in subsection (a) was performed "voluntarily." The term "voluntary" could conceivably be stretched to include the concept of a specific intent to renounce one's citizenship. While the person seeking to retain his citizenship would thus have the burden of showing a lack of specific intent, such a construction would at least provide a statutory basis for bringing the issue of intent into the proceeding. The majority apparently would not be willing to accept such a construction in order to salvage the statute, however, inasmuch as it rejects the Secretary's argument that, if there is a requirement of specific intent, it is also subject to the presumption applicable to voluntariness.

The majority's assumption that the statute can be read to require specific intent to relinquish citizenship as an element of proof is also contradicted by the Court's treatment in *Afroyim* of a different subsection of the same statute. Like the subsection at issue here, subsection (a)(5) provided that an American automatically lost his nationality by performing a specific act: in that case, voting in a foreign election. If the majority's analysis in this case was correct, the Court in *Afroyim* should not have invalidated that provision of the statute; rather, it should merely have remanded for a finding as to whether Afroyim had voted in a foreign election with specific intent to relinquish his American citizenship. That the Court did not do so is strong evidence of its belief that the statute could not be reformed as it is today.

citizenship is surely an aspect of "liberty" of which he cannot be deprived without due process of law. Because the interest at stake is comparable to that involved in *Addington v. Texas,* 441 U.S. 418, 99 S.Ct. 1804, 60 L.Ed.2d 372 [which dealt with involuntary civil commitment], essentially for the reasons stated in The Chief Justice's opinion for a unanimous Court in that case, I believe that due process requires that a clear and convincing standard of proof be met in this case as well before the deprivation may occur.

Mr. Justice Brennan, with whom Mr. Justice Stewart joins as to Part II, dissenting.

The Court holds that one may lose United States citizenship if the Government can prove by a preponderance of the evidence that certain acts, specified by statute, were done with the specific intent of giving up citizenship. Accordingly, the Court, in reversing the judgment of the Court of Appeals, holds that the District Court applied the correct evidentiary standards in determining that appellee was properly stripped of his citizenship. Because I would hold that one who acquires United States citizenship by virtue of being born in the United States, U.S.Const., Amdt. 14, § 1, can lose that citizenship only by formally renouncing it, and because I would hold that the act of which appellee is accused in this case cannot be an expatriating act, I dissent.

I

This case is governed by *Afroyim v. Rusk. Afroyim,* emphasizing the crucial importance of the right of citizenship, held unequivocally that a citizen has "a constitutional right to remain a citizen ... unless he voluntarily relinquishes that citizenship." "[T]he only way the citizenship ... could be lost was by the voluntary renunciation or abandonment by the citizen himself." The Court held that because Congress could not "abridge," "affect," "restrict the effect of," or "take ... away" citizenship, Congress was "without power to rob a citizen of his citizenship" because he voted in a foreign election.

The same clearly must be true of the Government's attempt to strip appellee of citizenship because he swore an oath of allegiance to Mexico. Congress has provided for a procedure by which one may formally renounce citizenship.[2] In this case the appellant concedes that appellee has not renounced his citizenship under that procedure. Because one can lose citizenship only by voluntarily renouncing it and because appellee has not formally renounced his, I would hold that he remains a citizen. Accordingly, I would remand the case with orders that appellee be given a declaration of United States nationality.

---

2. INA § 349(a)(5) provides that "a national of the United States whether by birth or naturalization, shall lose his nationality by ... making a formal renunciation of nationality before a diplomatic or consular officer of the United States in a foreign state, in such form as may be prescribed by the Secretary of State." The Secretary of State has pre- scribed such procedures in 22 CFR § 50.50 (1979). See Department of State, 8 Foreign Affairs Manual § 225.6 (1972). Congress also provided for renunciation by citizens while in the United States [during time of war. § 349(a)(6).] This last provision is not relevant to our case.

II

I reach the same result by another, independent line of reasoning. Appellee was born a dual national. He is a citizen of the United States because he was born here and a citizen of Mexico because his father was Mexican. The only expatriating act of which appellee stands accused is having sworn an oath of allegiance to Mexico. If dual citizenship, *per se,* can be consistent with United States citizenship, *Perkins v. Elg,* 307 U.S. 325, 329, 59 S.Ct. 884, 887, 83 L.Ed. 1320 (1939),[5] then I cannot see why an oath of allegiance to the other country of which one is already a citizen should create inconsistency. One owes allegiance to any country of which one is a citizen, especially when one is living in that country. *Kawakita v. United States,* 343 U.S. 717, 733–735, 72 S.Ct. 950, 960–961, 96 L.Ed. 1249 (1952). The formal oath adds nothing to the existing foreign citizenship and, therefore, cannot affect his United States citizenship.

Notes

1. Are the dissenters in *Terrazas* right concerning the procedural issue? Does the Court's approval of the preponderance standard and the presumption of voluntariness represent a significant retreat from its earlier judgments about the preciousness of U.S. citizenship? Why or why not?

2. How do the views of Justice Marshall and Justice Stevens differ? Which is more persuasive on the question of statutory construction? Consider INA § 356 in connection with your answer. Justice Brennan says that citizens may lose that status "only by formally renouncing it." Review the contents of Terrazas' oath of allegiance to Mexico. Why is Brennan in dissent?

3. Suppose Terrazas had been able to show that he executed the renunciation oath—after reading it—only because a Mexican citizenship certificate was required in order to secure a specific job in Mexico. He asserts that, subjectively, his strongest wish throughout the whole process was to retain his dual nationality. Suppose further that he spoke of this wish to many witnesses at the time; hence there is adequate factual support for his assertion. He was not motivated by a desire to surrender his U.S. affiliation, but instead by his desire to get a job. Could he then, consistently with the Constitution, be considered expatriated? What does it mean to find that an individual had a "specific intent to renounce U.S. citizenship"? *See Richards v. Secretary of State,* 752 F.2d 1413, 1421–22 (9th Cir.1985); *Parness v. Shultz,* 669 F.Supp. 7 (D.D.C.1987).

4. In a case involving Rabbi Meir Kahane, the State Department attempted to expand the bases on which an intent to relinquish citizenship could be found. Kahane was a U.S. citizen by birth and a former activist with the militant Jewish Defense League. His actions in the United States led to a federal firearms conviction in 1971. He moved to Israel later that

5. *Rogers v. Bellei,* 401 U.S. 815, 91 S.Ct. 1060, 28 L.Ed.2d 499 (1971), is not to the contrary. Bellei's citizenship was not based on the Fourteenth Amendment, and the issue before the Court was whether Bellei could lose his statutory citizenship for failure to satisfy a condition subsequent contained in the same statute that accorded him citizenship.

year, and became an Israeli citizen under the Law of Return—a process that does not require express renunciation of other allegiances. Kahane became active in politics, and in 1984 was elected to the Israeli Parliament, the Knesset, as head of the right-wing Kach party.

Accepting an office under a foreign government was an expatriating act listed in INA § 349(a)(4). Aware of this, and apparently concerned that his 1971 conviction would then prevent even brief visits to the United States, Kahane communicated on several occasions with the State Department around the time when he took his oath of office, insisting that he did not intend by that act to give up his U.S. citizenship. The State Department's Board of Appellate Review nonetheless found that he had committed the expatriating act with intent to relinquish U.S. citizenship. It examined other evidence of his actions, writings, and speeches, and concluded that he had shifted his allegiance to Israel; actions, the Board suggested, speak louder than words.

Kahane challenged this decision in court, which ruled rather readily against the State Department:

> If the [expatriating] act stands alone, with no proof of intent adduced by either side, a court may conclude that the preponderance of the evidence shows an intent to relinquish citizenship. When the act is accompanied by evidence of intent, either direct or circumstantial, the situation seems to this court somewhat different. Since citizenship is "beyond the power of any governmental unit to destroy," [quoting *Afroyim*] it may well be that a declaration of intent to retain citizenship, made simultaneously with commission of the expatriating act, will suffice to preserve the actor's citizenship.

Kahane v. Shultz, 653 F.Supp. 1486, 1493 (E.D.N.Y.1987). In a footnote, the Court rejected the government's attempted analogy to intent to commit a crime. The Court conceded that a person may be convicted of a crime even though he states at the time that he had no intent to commit the act.

> But an actor who states that he wishes to remain a citizen is making a statement about *his own status.* * * * This court is inclined to believe that the statement "I wish to remain a citizen" cannot be a "lie" and that an actor who made the declaration contemporaneously with the expatriating act would automatically preserve his citizenship.

Id. at 1493 n. 7 (emphasis in original).

Is this a sound reading of *Terrazas?* If so, is it good public policy? Should there be room under our Constitution for rules that forbid assumption of an office under a foreign government, on pain of giving up U.S. citizenship? Could Congress constitutionally enforce such rules by criminal or (other) civil sanctions?

In early 1988, the Knesset passed a law providing that its members could be citizens only of Israel. To hold on to his seat, Kahane executed an express "Oath of Renunciation" of U.S. citizenship before a U.S. consul in Jerusalem. A few weeks later the Israeli Supreme Court barred the Kach party, on other grounds, from running in the November 1988 election. Kahane thereupon sought to revoke his renunciation. Getting nowhere with the State Department, he returned to federal district court, claiming that the Israeli law amounted to compulsion that vitiated the voluntariness of the expatriating act, namely, the oath of renunciation. The court ruled against him on the law and denied a preliminary injunction. *Kahane v. Secretary of State,* 700 F.Supp. 1162 (D.D.C.1988). Kahane remained expatriated. Expatriation did not have the expected effect on Kahane's ability to travel to the United States, however—tragically, as it turned out. He was admitted in 1990 for a speaking tour, but he was assassinated while in New York City. *N.Y. Times,* Nov. 6, 1990, at A1.

For a discussion of the first Kahane case, and further reflections on various theories that might underlie loss-of-citizenship doctrine, see Aleinikoff, *Theories of Loss of Citizenship,* 84 Mich.L.Rev. 1471 (1986).

5. In the 1986 INA Amendments, Pub.L. No. 99–653, 100 Stat. 3655, Congress finally brought the language of § 349 into line with the Supreme Court's expatriation rulings. It changed the operative language of § 349(a), which contains the list of expatriating acts, to provide that U.S. citizens shall lose their nationality only by "voluntarily performing any of the following acts *with the intention of relinquishing United States nationality.*" (Emphasis added.)

6. In 1978, several inmates of a state prison in Lucasville, Ohio, wrote to the State Department renouncing their U.S. citizenship and claiming status as citizens of the Soviet Union. Apparently they believed that they might in this way secure the diplomatic interposition of their alleged new country of nationality to protect the human rights they claimed were violated by their incarceration. These letters were clearly meant to be direct expressions of specific intent to terminate U.S. nationality. Yet the State Department refused to consider the inmates as validly expatriated. *See* INA §§ 349(a)(5), (6), 351(a); 22 C.F.R. § 50.50.

What policies are reflected in the provisions of the statute just cited? *See generally Gillars v. United States,* 182 F.2d 962, 981–83 (D.C.Cir.1950); *Davis v. District Director,* 481 F.Supp. 1178 (D.D.C.1979). Do these policies make sense in the conditions of the modern world? However prudent they may be, are they constitutionally valid? That is, in light of the priority *Terrazas* places on the individual's voluntary decisions about his or her own citizenship status, is it permissible to require the commission of specified objective acts (which some persons may have difficulty performing) in addition to an unambiguous expression of intent to renounce?

Procedures in Expatriation Cases

Terrazas reflects the usual way in which a controversy over expatriation arises and is resolved. A U.S. consulate, upon learning that a potentially expatriating act has occurred, investigates the facts and files a report with the Department of State. If the Department agrees that expatriation has occurred, a copy of the consulate's Certificate of Loss of

Nationality (CLN) is then sent to the Attorney General and to the individual. *See* INA § 358; 22 C.F.R. § 50.41. The person may appeal the decision to the Board of Appellate Review (BAR) of the State Department within one year. *Id.* Part 7; § 50.52. It may also happen that the loss-of-nationality issue is adjudicated when a person applies for a U.S. passport. Passport denial may also be appealed to the BAR. *Id.* §§ 7.3, 7.6, 50.42. The State Department procedures employed in loss-of-citizenship cases are usefully summarized in James, *The Board of Appellate Review of the Department of State: The Right to Appellate Review of Administrative Determinations of Loss of Nationality,* 23 San Diego L.Rev. 261 (1986), with particular attention to the case law and practice of the BAR. *See also* Endelman, *How to Prevent Loss of Citizenship,* 89–11 & 89–12 Imm.Briefings (1989).

If the finding of expatriation is sustained by the BAR, the person may contest the issue in federal court. Under INA § 360(a), claimants within the United States may obtain a full judicial determination of a citizenship claim by means of a declaratory judgment action in accordance with 28 U.S.C.A. § 2201. The action must be initiated within five years after the final administrative denial of a right or privilege of citizenship by any department or agency. Claimants outside the United States are granted by the INA only a procedure permitting them to travel to this country to have the citizenship issue tried in the relatively disadvantageous setting of an exclusion proceeding. Judicial review then is available only on habeas corpus, without provision for de novo judicial determination of a rejected citizenship claim. *Id.* § 360(b), (c).

These statutory distinctions follow the contours of Supreme Court doctrine in the matter. In *Ng Fung Ho v. White,* 259 U.S. 276, 42 S.Ct. 492, 66 L.Ed. 938 (1922), the Court held that persons *within* the United States who make supported claims to U.S. citizenship may not be deported strictly on the basis of an administrative finding against their claims. There must be a de novo judicial decision on the citizenship allegation. The ruling rested on the Fifth Amendment's due process clause, and the Court adverted to the "difference in security of judicial over administrative action." *Id.* at 285. But if such claimants are not within the country— and specifically if they are in exclusion proceedings—final administrative determination of the citizenship claim is permissible, under *United States v. Ju Toy,* 198 U.S. 253, 25 S.Ct. 644, 49 L.Ed. 1040 (1905), and judicial review in this setting remains quite deferential to the administrators. *DeBrown v. Dept. of Justice,* 18 F.3d 774 (9th Cir.1994).[13]

Despite the INA's limitations applicable to claimants outside the country, however, later court decisions have made it possible for such persons to obtain a full judicial determination of a citizenship claim, by means of

---

13. A claim of U.S. citizenship may also arise by way of a defense in a deportation proceeding, in which case the issue is resolved by the immigration judge and, upon appeal, the BIA, without the direct involvement of the State Department. If the BIA rejects the claim and the alien files a petition for review in the court of appeals, INA § 106(a)(5) makes special provision for transfer, if the claim to citizenship status is nonfrivolous, to the district court for a hearing de novo.

ordinary declaratory judgment proceedings. *See Rusk v. Cort,* 369 U.S. 367, 82 S.Ct. 787, 7 L.Ed.2d 809 (1962).

The State Department's New Leaf

In 1990, the State Department adopted a new statement of evidentiary standards to be applied in expatriation cases. They reflect a wholly new attitude far more hospitable to dual citizenship than in earlier years, when the Department often tried to read as narrowly as possible any Supreme Court decisions that restricted expatriation. The standards provide in part:

[The actions listed in INA § 349(a)] can cause loss of U.S. citizenship only if performed voluntarily and with the intention of relinquishing U.S. citizenship. *The Department has a uniform administrative standard of evidence based on the premise that U.S. citizens intend to retain United States citizenship when they obtain naturalization in a foreign state, subscribe to routine declarations of allegiance to a foreign state, or accept non-policy level employment with a foreign government.*

* * *

In light of the administrative premise discussed above, a person who:

(1) is naturalized in a foreign country;

(2) takes a routine oath of allegiance; or

(3) accepts non-policy level employment with a foreign government

and in so doing wishes to retain U.S. citizenship need not submit prior to the commission of a potentially expatriating act a statement or evidence of his or her intent to retain U.S. citizenship since such an intent will be presumed.

When such cases come to the attention of a U.S. consular officer, the person concerned will be asked to complete a questionnaire to ascertain his or her intent toward U.S. citizenship. Unless the person affirmatively asserts in the questionnaire that it was his or her intention to relinquish U.S. citizenship, the consular officer will certify that it was *not* the person's intent to relinquish U.S. citizenship and, consequently, find that the person has retained U.S. citizenship.

* * *

The premise that a person intends to retain U.S. citizenship is *not* applicable when the individual:

(1) formally renounces U.S. citizenship before a consular officer;

(2) takes a policy level position in a foreign state;

(3) is convicted of treason; or

(4) performs an act made potentially expatriating by statute accompanied by conduct which is so inconsistent with retention of U.S. citizenship that it compels a conclusion that the individual intended to relinquish U.S. citizenship. (Such cases are very rare.)

Cases in categories 2, 3, and 4 will be developed carefully by U.S. consular officers to ascertain the individual's intent toward U.S. citizenship.

* * *

An individual who has performed *any* of the acts made potentially expatriating by statute who wishes to lose U.S. citizenship may do so by affirming in writing to a U.S. consular officer that the act was performed with an intent to relinquish U.S. citizenship. Of course, a person always has the option of seeking to formally renounce U.S. citizenship in accordance with Section 349(a)(5) INA.

67 Interp.Rel. 1092, 1093 (1990) (emphasis in original); *see also id.* at 799–800.

Are the provisions numbered (2) and (3) in the fourth quoted paragraph consistent with the Constitution as interpreted in *Afroyim* and *Terrazas?* How would the Department's new evidentiary standards apply in cases like those described in note 3 *supra* p. 1077, *i.e.,* to someone who takes an oath of allegiance to another nation, including an express renunciation of U.S. citizenship, as part of a naturalization ceremony before an administrative officer of that other nation, but who subjectively wishes to retain U.S. nationality as well?

One recent article reports that "formulas of renunciation contained in naturalization oaths are now considered [by U.S. consular officials] merely pro forma declarations, without any indication of intention to give up U.S. citizenship." Kelly, *Dual Nationality, the Myth of Election, and a Kinder, Gentler State Department*, 23 U.Miami Inter–Am.L.Rev. 421, 446 (1991–92). Suppose you are consulted by a client who wants to take a particular job overseas that requires the nationality of the host country. She finds that she can naturalize there, but must take a renunciatory oath in order to do so. She wants the job but also wishes to retain her U.S. citizenship and seems happy to know that the State Department apparently won't slap her with a CLN after the ceremony. How would you advise her? Is perjury a problem? *See id.* at 448–51. Is the State Department's treatment of such oaths permissible under congressional enactments? Review the language of INA § 349(a)(1) and consider it in connection the wording of our naturalization oath, set forth in INA § 337.

For a further indication of the Department's change of course, now permitting a far easier finding of duress that would nullify a renunciation of citizenship, see James, *Cult-Induced Renunciation of United States Citizenship: The Involuntary Expatriation of Black Hebrews*, 28 San Diego L.Rev. 645 (1991).

Expatriation and Denaturalization: Some Statistics

For fiscal year 1981, INS records showed a total of 1,537 persons expatriated, 1,446 of these on the grounds of naturalization in a foreign state. U.S. Dept. of Justice, 1981 Statistical Yearbook of the Immigration and Naturalization Service, Table 35, p. 90. By 1985, those totals had declined to 585 and 426, respectively (another ground, renunciation of nationality, had climbed from 7 cases to 72 over that period). 1985 *id.*, Table NAT 6, p. 173. These figures may be of limited utility, however, (except for giving a rough idea of relative importance of the various grounds of expatriation), because the State Department, not the INS, plays the key role in most expatriation cases, principally through its issuance of Certificates of Loss of Nationality. Perhaps for this reason, INS statistical yearbooks ceased providing expatriation data after 1985. The State Department reported in 1990 that it processes about 4,500 potential loss-of-citizenship cases annually. About 800, on the average, are found to have lost their citizenship, approximately 200 of these on the basis of express renunciation. 67 Interp.Rel. 1094 (1990).

The INS Statistical Yearbook provides no comparable figures for denaturalizations (which, as you recall, are imposed only on the ground of fraud or illegality in the original grant). But if one may judge from the volume of reported cases, denaturalizations almost surely increased in the 1980s and 1990s. The increase resulted from a systematic effort, carried out by the Office of Special Investigations (OSI) of the Department of Justice, to locate former Nazis and Nazi collaborators who entered the United States illegally, or by fraud or misrepresentation, in the period following World War II. The *Kungys* case, *supra,* is the fruit of one such effort. *See also, e.g., Fedorenko v. United States,* 449 U.S. 490, 101 S.Ct. 737, 66 L.Ed.2d 686 (1981); *United States v. Schellong,* 717 F.2d 329 (7th Cir.1983), *cert. denied,* 465 U.S. 1007, 104 S.Ct. 1002, 79 L.Ed.2d 234 (1984); *United States v. Koreh*, 856 F.Supp. 891 (D.N.J.1994). For an interesting account of the Nazi denaturalization and deportation cases, written by a former head of the Office of Special Investigations, see A. Ryan, Quiet Neighbors: Prosecuting Nazi War Criminals in America (1984). For the story of Canada's efforts along these lines, *see* D. Matas, Justice Delayed: Nazi War Criminals in Canada (1987).

Two celebrated removals, following denaturalization, of persons allegedly involved in Nazi persecution occurred in the 1980s. In one, Karl Linnas was deported to the Soviet Union, where he had earlier been sentenced to death in absentia. He died in a hospital in Leningrad while further proceedings were pending. See p. 578 *supra.* In the other, John Demjanjuk, believed to be the notorious "Ivan the Terrible" from the Treblinka death camp in Poland, was extradited to Israel to stand trial for his acts. The U.S. courts found that the Israeli courts had criminal jurisdiction under the international law principle of universal jurisdiction, which permits all nations to try perpetrators of war crimes and crimes against humanity. *See In re Extradition of Demjanjuk,* 612 F.Supp. 544 (N.D.Ohio 1985), *habeas corpus denied sub nom. Demjanjuk v. Petrovsky,*

612 F.Supp. 571 (N.D.Ohio 1985), *affirmed,* 776 F.2d 571 (6th Cir.1985), *cert. denied,* 475 U.S. 1016 (1986). Demjanjuk's earlier denaturalization proceedings were reported in *United States v. Demjanjuk,* 518 F.Supp. 1362 (N.D.Ohio 1981), *affirmed* 680 F.2d 32 (6th Cir.1982), *cert. denied,* 459 U.S. 1036, 103 S.Ct. 447, 47 L.Ed.2d 602 (1982). In Israel, Demjanjuk was convicted and sentenced to death, but new evidence became available after the collapse of the Soviet Union suggesting that the torturer was one Ivan Marchenko, not Demjanjuk. The Israeli Supreme Court eventually sustained his appeal and disallowed further prosecution based on other alleged involvement with Nazi persecution. *See* Kozinski, *Sanhedrin II: the Case of Ivan Demjanjuk,* The New Republic, Sept. 13, 1993, at 16.

Meantime the Sixth Circuit Court of Appeals in the United States sua sponte reopened the extradition proceedings and eventually vacated its 1985 judgment because of prosecutorial misconduct (failure to disclose exculpatory evidence) that amounted, in its view, to fraud on the court. 10 F.3d 338 (6th Cir.1993), *cert. denied sub nom. Rison v. Demjanjuk,* ___ U.S. ___, 115 S.Ct. 295, 130 L.Ed.2d 205 (1994). A few months earlier, in an extraordinary procedure, the court had issued a writ of habeas corpus essentially requiring that Demjanjuk be readmitted to the United States "while this court proceeds to unravel the legal ramifications of this unprecedented case." 1993 WL 394773 (6th Cir.1993).

SECTION E.   A CONCLUDING PROBLEM: CITIZENS, ALIENS, AND THE RIGHT TO VOTE

Should permanent resident aliens be entitled to vote in state and federal elections? This question forces us to consider what we mean by the concept of "citizenship." The preceding Chapters have suggested a number of possible answers: citizens are those people who have the power and authority to write the membership (immigration and naturalization) rules of a society—and its other rules; citizens are those people whom a nation cannot send home (deport); citizens are those people who owe a nation allegiance and are entitled to that nation's protection.

Running through each of these descriptions is the idea of membership in a *political community*—a group of human beings united by, and for, self-governance. The Supreme Court has expressed this view of citizenship as follows:

> The exclusion of aliens from basic governmental processes is not a deficiency in the democratic system but a necessary consequence of the community's process of political self-definition. Self-government, whether direct or through representatives, begins by defining the scope of the community of the governed and thus of the governors as well: aliens are by definition outside of this community.

Cabell v. Chavez–Salido, 454 U.S. 432, 439–40, 102 S.Ct. 735, 740, 70 L.Ed.2d 677 (1982).

If this view accurately captures the essence of citizenship, then it is understandable why we, as a society, have little trouble denying aliens the right or privilege of voting in state and federal elections. To guarantee aliens a right to vote, so the argument might run, would destroy one of the few remaining distinctions between aliens and citizens and would fatally undermine our understanding of a nation as a self-governing political community.

Counterarguments, however, are possible. The Supreme Court, at least in the nineteenth century, recognized that the terms "voter" and "citizen" were not coterminous. *Minor v. Happersett,* 88 U.S. (21 Wall.) 162, 22 L.Ed. 627 (1875) (upholding state law denying women the right to vote). Furthermore, throughout the nineteenth century a number of states extended voting rights to aliens. Rosberg, *Aliens and Equal Protection: Why Not the Right to Vote?,* 75 Mich.L.Rev. 1092, 1093–1100 (1977). And in recent years some communities have sought to extend the franchise in local elections to resident aliens. *See* Raskin, *Legal Aliens, Local Citizens: The Historical, Constitutional and Theoretical Meanings of Alien Suffrage,* 141 U.Pa.L.Rev. 1391 (1993).

Consider the following attempt to uncouple the concepts of voting and citizenship.

GERALD M. ROSBERG, ALIENS AND EQUAL PROTECTION: WHY NOT THE RIGHT TO VOTE?

75 Mich.L.Rev. 1092, 1127–1135 (1977).

Immigrants who have arrived recently in the United States may know little about this country's institutions of government or about the issues on which election campaigns are fought. They can certainly learn about these matters, and it would not take very long for many of them to gain this knowledge. But in all likelihood many immigrants are also largely ignorant of this country's values and traditions and therefore cannot have developed an appreciation of or commitment to them. The naturalization requirement for voting could be seen as responsive to this concern in two different ways. First, the durational residence feature gives the immigrant an opportunity to develop a feel for American values and traditions. Second, the act of naturalization itself represents a formal and solemn commitment to the country, its values, and its institutions. The testing of a prospective citizen's loyalty, knowledge, and character is critical, under this view, not so much because it screens out the undeserving candidate but rather because it makes the attainment of naturalization difficult and meaningful. The judicial setting and the oath of renunciation and allegiance (with its grand language about foreign princes and potentates and bearing true faith and allegiance to the United States) drive home to the new citizen the significance of the occasion. It all adds up to a very deliberate and ritualized act of opting into the community and accepting its values and traditions as one's own.

In my view, this argument is the most substantial one that can be made in defense of the citizenship qualification for voting. And yet it is by no means free of difficulty. If everything is going to turn on a sense of commitment to the country's values and traditions, it would seem important to know exactly what values and traditions * * * we have in mind. * * *

The very fact that neither candidate in an election wins all the votes is in itself a good indication that the electorate is already divided on fundamental value questions. Political analysts typically assume that different segments of American society—Catholics, Chicanos, blue-collar workers, Polish–Americans—have their own values and traditions that influence their voting behavior. To which set of values and traditions are the aliens expected to commit themselves? Do we exclude them from the polls until they have narrowed the choice to two—the Democratic tradition and the Republican tradition—and then turn them loose to make a free choice between Alexander Hamilton and Thomas Jefferson? Or is it rather that the central value and tradition of this country is that there is no central value and tradition? Perhaps aliens are entitled to hold whatever views they want, but they cannot be allowed to vote until they have come to understand and cherish the fact that they may hold whatever views they want. One has an intuitive sense that an alien who has not been socialized in the United States will lack certain characteristics or attitudes that are fundamentally American. But given the diversity of socialization experiences available in the United States, this intuition would seem a rather treacherous foundation on which to build an argument of compelling state interest.

Instead of trying to determine the substantive content of the country's values and traditions, one might do better to focus on the act of commitment to the United States that naturalization apparently involves. In terms of values, culture, and language, resident aliens may be indistinguishable from at least some group of American citizens. And their loyalty may be beyond question, at least in the sense that they think well of the country and wish it no harm. But what may be lacking is a willingness on the part of resident aliens to identify themselves with the country and its people and to give up once and for all their attachment to the countries in which they were born. The unnaturalized alien is perhaps holding something back, refusing to join in. * * *

[But] it is simply not correct to say that unnaturalized aliens have made no commitment to the United States. In contrast to native-born citizens, whose commitment, if any, is tacit, resident aliens have committed themselves knowingly and voluntarily. They have all had to make considerable effort to qualify for an immigrant visa, which is ordinarily a good deal harder to obtain than a certificate of naturalization. Even after proving themselves qualified, they have had to wait months and even more often years for a visa to become available. And they have given up their homes in the countries of their birth and resettled in the United States. Moreover, most resident aliens had ties to the United States even before they arrived, for they have tended to follow their countrymen and kinsmen in chains of migration. * * *

* * *

* * * We have come to accept and even cherish the fact that many citizens will retain what Justice Frankfurter called "old cultural loyalty" [125] to another country, and the line between cultural matters and political matters is known to be indistinct. The internment during the Second World War of persons of Japanese ancestry—citizen and alien alike—is a powerful reminder of how far we have been willing to go on the supposition that national origin may be much more accurately predictive of loyalty than is citizenship. In short, it is hard to see what it is about resident aliens that makes us insist on excluding them from the polls for want of the necessary commitment to the United States.

Yet it may be objected that the net effect of this kind of argument is to deny the existence of any distinction at all between the citizen and the alien. If the alien is indistinguishable from the citizen in terms of knowledge of affairs in the United States, loyalty, and commitment to the people and institutions of the United States, and if for that reason the alien has a constitutional right to vote, then it may appear that the concept of citizenship has been robbed of all its meaning. Plainly, nothing that I have said would jeopardize the distinction between the citizen and the nonresident alien. But one might insist that under the view presented here resident aliens would in effect be naturalized as of the moment they take up residence in the United States. Much of the difficulty arises, however, from the assumed equation of citizenship and voting. My argument is not that resident aliens look like citizens, so therefore they must be citizens. It is rather that in pertinent respects resident aliens are enough like citizens that it may be unconstitutional to distinguish between them in allocating the right to vote.

Citizens have historically enjoyed certain rights and undertaken certain obligations that resident aliens did not share. Every time one of those rights or obligations is passed on to aliens the gap between citizens and aliens narrows. If we are determined to maintain a gap, to preserve a sense of "we" and "they," we could disqualify aliens from owning land or deny them welfare benefits or make them all wear green hats. The imposition of these disabilities on aliens may seem intolerable. But why should it be any more tolerable to make the burden of preserving the distinction between citizens and aliens fall exclusively on the right to vote, the most precious right of all?

Moreover, extending the franchise to aliens would not, in fact, completely close the gap between citizens and aliens, since voting is not the only distinction between the two that survives the Supreme Court's recent decisions on the rights of aliens. By the terms of the Constitution itself aliens are ineligible to hold certain offices in the government of the United States. Aliens do not have the same right as citizens to gain admission to the United States. Citizens born abroad can take up residence in this country whenever they desire. Citizens can abandon their residence in the United States without fear of losing their right to return. Aliens, on the other hand, gain the right to reside in the United States only upon compliance with the stringent terms of the immigration laws. And resi-

---

125. * * * *Baumgartner v. United States,*
322 U.S. 665, 674 (1944).

dent aliens who abandon their domicile in this country will not necessarily be readmitted. When citizens travel outside the United States they carry American passports, and they expect and ordinarily receive the diplomatic protection of the United States when the need for it arises. Aliens, even resident aliens, have no right to call upon the United States for that protection and would not receive it in any case. Citizens are entitled to have the government represent their interests in international tribunals. Aliens have no such right, and under international law the government would be barred from representing them even if it had any interest in doing so. Citizens are generally free from any obligation to register with the government or to inform the government regularly of their whereabouts. Aliens are subject to rather elaborate reporting requirements. Citizens can be held to account in American courts for conduct overseas in some circumstances where aliens apparently cannot. Citizens can confer an immigration preference on their relatives overseas in a considerable number of situations where aliens cannot.

* * * Considering the primacy of the right to vote one could reasonably argue that it is distinctions like these that should bear the burden of differentiating citizens from aliens, and not the distinction between voting and not voting. We could, in other words, grant the right to vote to resident aliens and still leave them readily distinguishable from citizens. Yet that result would remain unacceptable to those who believe that allowing aliens to vote would eviscerate the concept of citizenship. Their assumption must be that political rights are inherently and properly rights of citizenship, whereas civil rights have no necessary connection with citizenship and properly belong to "persons." In the earliest part of the country's history, however, the assumption was precisely the reverse: citizenship "carried with it civil rights but no political privileges." [128] Citizenship, and in particular naturalization, was thought important because it determined whether or not a new settler would be able to own and convey land. Even today, * * * the Supreme Court insists that citizenship as such confers no right to vote. Indeed, it would seem anomalous to equate citizenship with voting so long as we separate the power to make persons citizens from the power to make persons voters. The former power inheres in the national government, the latter in the states.

Yet I cannot deny the existence of a widespread assumption that the right to vote is not only a right of citizenship, but the quintessential right of citizenship. And the conferral of the right to vote on aliens would undermine that assumption. But where does the assumption come from, and why should we insist on preserving it? Intuitively, it seems that there must be some explanation for the assumption. After all, the very fact that it is so widespread may be an indication that it responds to some important inner need of citizens to distinguish themselves from what are perceived to be outsiders, even where the outsiders are their neighbors. But I do not believe that it is possible to articulate an explanation for this assumption without moving the discussion to a level of extremely high abstraction and without putting a great deal of weight on symbolic values. To sustain the

---

128. Start, *Naturalization in the English Colonies in North America,* in American Historical Assn., Annual Report for the Year 1893, at 319 (1894).

disenfranchisement of aliens on the strength of that kind of reasoning would be fundamentally inconsistent, it seems to me, with our ordinary approach in determining which state interests are compelling. I am reluctant to conclude that, because I have so much difficulty articulating the state's interest, it must be less than compelling. But I am confident at least that the validity of laws denying aliens the vote is by no means self-evident. It is surely not enough to tip one's hat at the state interest in having knowledgeable and loyal voters and let it go at that.

Questions

Suppose the Supreme Court were to decide that state laws denying permanent resident aliens the right to vote in state elections violate the Equal Protection Clause. Would such a ruling rob citizenship of all its meaning? Is the right to participate in political affairs the only remaining significant difference between U.S. citizens and permanent resident aliens? What *does* it mean to be a *citizen* of the United States?

*

Index

References are to Pages

ADMINISTRATIVE REVIEW
Generally, 107–114, 899–901, 931–933.
Confidential information, 400.
Motion to reconsider, 372–374, 658–659.
Motion to reopen, 373–74, 657–78, 681–685.

ADMISSION PROCEDURES
Adjustment of status, 175–186, 372, 433–445, 743–744.
Adjustment of status, rescission of, 444–445.
Appeal, 430.
Border processing, 400–401, 413–418, 427–433.
Confidential information, 386–396, 401–404.
Constitutional questions, 385–412, 445–473.
Constitutional standard for evaluation of, 150–166.
Criticisms, 385–386.
Hearings, 386–396, 401–410.
History, 122–123, 137–138.
Immigrants, 424–426, 427–433.
Labor certification, 118, 128–29, 136, 192–220.
Nonimmigrants, 421–423, 427–433.
Prevailing wage requirement, 206–208.
Re–entry rights of an alien, 389–396, 405–411.
Referral, 429.
Visas, 100, 103–105, 115–117, 421–427, 431–432.

AGENCIES AND OFFICERS
Administrative Appeals Unit (AAU), 114.
Attorney General, 101, 112.
Board of Alien Labor Certification Appeals (BALCA), 118.
Board of Immigration Appeals (BIA), 111–114.
Border Patrol, 103, 272–273, 315–318.
Commissioner of Immigration and Naturalization, 101.
Consular officers, 115–117.
Department of Justice, 100–115.
Department of Labor, 118.
Department of State, 115–117, 135.
District Offices of INS, 102–103.
Executive Office of Immigration Review (EOIR), 110–113, 115, 596.
Immigration and Naturalization Service (INS), 100–114, 115.
Immigration inspectors, 103.

AGENCIES AND OFFICERS—Cont'd
Immigration lawyers, 105–107, 119–121.
Immigration officers, 427–428.
Office of Chief Administrative Hearing Officer (OCAHO), 115.
Public Health Service (PHS), 118.
Regional Adjudication Centers, 104.
Regional Service Centers, 104–105.
Special Counsel for Immigration–Related Unfair Employment Practices, 115.
Special Inquiry Officers (Immigration Judges), 107–112, 429–430.
United States Information Agency (USIA), 118–119.
Visa Office, 116–117.

ASYLUM
See Refugees and Political Asylum.

BONDS
See Deportation; Law Enforcement, Detention.

BRACERO PROGRAM
See Nonimmigrants; Undocumented Aliens and Illegal Migration.

CITIZENSHIP
See also Evidence and Evidentiary Standards; Expatriation; Naturalization and Denaturalization.
Generally, 974–1089.
Allotment Act of 1887, p. 991.
Acquisition at birth, 977, 990–996.
Chinese exclusion laws, 991–993.
Civil Rights Act of 1866, p. 979–980.
Congress' power, 974.
Consent, 989–990.
Constitutional law, generally, 974–990, 994–995.
Definition, 974, 985, 989–990.
Deprivation, 994.
Derivative, 1003.
Discrimination, on basis of, 977, 984–985.
Dred Scott decision, 978–980.
Dual nationality, 1055–1060, 1081–1082.
Equal protection, 976, 981, 995.
Expatriation, 982–983, 989, 994–995, 1045–1084.
First amendment, 1010–1015.
Fourteenth amendment, 979, 985, 988–993.
Good moral character, 982, 1004–1005.

CITIZENSHIP—Cont'd
History, 974, 977–984.
Indians, 991–992.
Insular cases, 974–975.
Jus sanguinis principle, 990, 993–995, 1046.
Jus soli principle, 125, 990–993, 1046.
Nationality, 974–975.
Naturalization, 982, 991, 996–1015, 935, 945, 1084–1089.
Right to vote, 1084–1089.
Significance, 975–990,1002.
State, 977.
Uniformity, 974.

CONSTITUTIONAL LAW
Bill of attainder, 574–576.
Chadha jurisdiction, 919–924.
Citizenship, 974, 976–985, 988–995.
Deportation power of Congress, 512.
Due process, 108–109, 155, 156, 385–412, 438–439, 445–473, 518–521, 553–555, 559, 576–578, 582–586, 590, 595–604, 612, 616–620, 629–639, 692–694, 937–940.
Eighth amendment, 1060.
Equal protection, 17–19, 155–161, 161–166, 512, 577–578, 692–694, 890, 937–940, 976, 981, 984–985.
Ex post facto clause, 513, 522–524, 531–534.
Expatriation, 1045–1084.
Fifteenth amendment, 981.
Fifth amendment (Due process), 445–473, 525, 616–620, 1061–1062.
First amendment, 343–356, 361, 522.
Fourteenth amendment, 978–985, 988–993, 1053, 1062–1068, 1071.
Fourth amendment, 620–627.
Habeas corpus, 525.
Nineteenth amendment, 981.
Privileges and immunities clause, 977.
Slaughter House cases, 981.
Sources of power to control immigration, 1, 7–40.
Thirteenth amendment, 979.
Twenty–sixth amendment, 981.
Void for vagueness doctrine, 552–559.

DEFINITIONS
Beneficiary, 124.
Chain migration, 191.
Child under INA, 125, 161.
Deportation, 20, 475.
Entry, 474, 481–482, 489–491, 496.
Exclusion, 20.
Expatriation, 956.
Family reunification categories, 125–128.
Immediate relatives, 125–126.
Interim Decisions, 114.
Involuntary expatriation, 1045.
Jus sanguinis principle, 993–995.
Labor schedules, 194–195.
Lawful permanent residents (LPRs), 122.
Moral turpitude, 542–559, 564.
Naturalization and denaturalization, 1016.
Nonimmigrant, 229.
Operations Instructions (OIs), 114–115.

DEFINITIONS—Cont'd
Parent under INA, 125.
Parolee, 737.
Per–country ceilings, 134–135.
Permanent resident aliens (PRAs), 122.
Petitioner, 124.
Primary inspection, 427–428.
Priority dates, 135–136.
Push–pull factors, 70.
Refugee, 718–719, 723–735.
Returning resident, 21.
Special immigrants, 126.
Spill–down, 127.
Suspension of deportation, 653.
Visa multiplier effect, 191.
Visa petition, 124.
Visas, 115–116.

DEPORTATION
Aggravated felony, 559–561.
Arrest, 587, 618.
As punishment, 512, 575.
Bill of attainder, 574–576.
Bond, 588–591.
Constitutional limitations, 511–535, 572–580, 582–586, 595–596, 598–604, 617–639.
Conviction for certain crimes, 564–569.
Conviction for possession of firearms, 560.
Crimes in general, 540–542.
Crimes involving moral turpitude, 487–490, 542–559, 568–69.
Defined, 511.
Detention of criminals, 585, 590, 591.
Document fraud, 539–540.
Drug addicts, users and dealers, 559–564.
Due process, 518–521, 553–555, 558, 576–578, 582–586, 590, 595–604, 612, 616–620, 629–639.
Due process and the border–interior distinction, 624–639.
Entry without inspection, 537–539, 698–704.
Equal protection, 578.
Evidentiary rules, 606–627.
Ex post facto clause, 513, 522–524, 531–534.
Excludable at time of entry, 536–537.
Expedited administrative, 627–628.
Expungement of conviction for crimes, 565.
Extradition, 576–577.
Failure to maintain nonimmigrant status, 539.
Fifth amendment, 525, 617–620.
First amendment, 522.
Fourth amendment, 620–627.
Grounds, 527, 535–582.
Habeas corpus, 525, 907–920.
Hearings, 582–616.
Hearings, difference from exclusion, 475–476.
Interpreters for hearings, 592–593.
Judicial, 627–628.
Judicial review, 575–578.
    Summary chart, 931–933.
Nazis, 534, 572–580.
Order to show cause, 587–588, 617.
Procedures, 582–629.
Prostitution, 607.

DEPORTATION—Cont'd
Right to legal counsel, 587–594, 597–606.
Sixth amendment, 525.
Special deportation procedures, 627–629.
Standards of proof, 606–617.
Statistics, 536, 597.
Statute of limitations, 410, 411, 580–582.
Statutory history of moral turpitude, 542–544.
Subversives, 513–526, 582.
Undocumented aliens, 537–538.
Void for vagueness doctrine, 556–557.
Waiver of grounds, 537.

DETENTION
See Law Enforcement; Refugees and Political Asylum, Deterrent measures.

DOMICILE
See Residence, Domicile, Physical Presence.

DUE PROCESS
See Constitutional law.

ENTRY
Burden of proof, 482–484.
Generally, 476–486.
Constitutional significance, 399–400, 402–404, 452–473.
Criteria, 441.
Definition, 474, 478–479, 489–491, 496, 536.
Re-entry, 537.
Re-entry doctrine, 486–505.
Re-entry doctrine, reform of, 492–495, 497–505.

EVIDENCE AND EVIDENTIARY STANDARDS
Citizenship, 1000–1002, 1015–1029, 1069–1077.
Deportation, 606–627.
Motion to reopen, 678–681.
Political asylum, 759–766.

EXCLUSION
See also Admission Procedures.
Based on national security, 343–362.
Chinese exclusion laws, 2–5, 17–20.
Congress' power of, 20.
Congressional action, 357–359.
Departure, effect on review, 953–957.
First amendment applied to waivers, 345–353.
Fraud (willful misrepresentation), 375–379.
Grounds, 193–194, 339–343, 398–400.
Hearings, 386–396, 405–412, 429–433.
History, 343–344.
Homosexuals, 340.
Judicial review, 906–908, 931–933, 953–957.
Parole, 379–384, 709, 710, 720, 721.
Public charge, 370–375.
Standing, 368–370.
Summary, 431–433, 884.
Visa denials, 362–368.
Waiver of grounds, 341, 689–711.

EXPATRIATION
See also Deportation, Crimes involving moral turpitude.
Generally, 982–983, 989, 994, 1045–1084.
Bancroft Treaties, 1047.
Constitutional law, 1045–1047, 1049–1055.
Defined, 1016.
Dual nationality, 1055–1062.
Duress, 1061.
Eighth amendment, 1060.
Expatriation acts, 1046–1049.
Fifth amendment (due process), 1060–1061.
Fourteenth amendment, 1053, 1062–1068, 1071.
History, 1046–1049.
Immigration and Nationality Act of 1952, pp. 1048–1049.
Intent requirement, 1073–1076.
Involuntary, defined, 1045.
Nationality Act of 1940, 1048, 1050.
Physical presence requirements, 1067–1068.
Procedures, 1079–1081.
Sixth amendment, 1061.
Standard of proof, 1049, 1061, 1072–1082.
Statistics, 1083–1084.
Voluntariness requirement, 1047–1048, 1052–1055, 1056–1057, 1060–1082.
Voting in foreign election, 1049–1055, 1062–1067.

FRAUD
See Law enforcement; Marriage fraud.

"GOOD MORAL CHARACTER", 550, 644–646, 647, 654, 688, 982, 1004–1005.
See also Deportation, Crimes involving moral turpitude.

GREEN CARD
See Registration of Aliens.

HISTORY
Adjustment of status, 433–434.
Americanization, 51, 52.
Board of Immigration Appeals (BIA), 112–113.
Border processing, 414–418.
Burlingame Treaty, 3, 4.
Ceilings, 59–60.
Chinese immigration, 2–5, 6, 7, 17–20.
Citizenship, 974, 976–984.
Deportation, 511–512, 526–527, 591–592.
Diversity, 129–130, 137–141.
Ellis Island, 412–421.
Exclusion, 47–48, 340.
Expatriation, 993–996.
Fifth amendment, 525.
From Mexico and Central America, 58, 276–278.
Great Depression, 54, 55.
Immigration Act of 1921, pp. 53, 54.
Immigration Act of 1924, p. 54.
Immigration Act of 1965, p. 58.
Immigration Act of 1990, p. 62.
Immigration and Naturalization Service (INS), 101.

HISTORY—Cont'd
Immigration Reform and Control Act, 61.
Literacy testing, 49, 50, 52.
Marriage fraud amendments, 62.
McCarran–Walter Act, 57.
National origins quotas, 51, 53–58, 122–123, 129–130, 137–140, 159, 419–420.
Naturalization, 996–1000.
Origin of U.S. Immigration, 1821–1987, 137–138.
Political asylum, 759–770.
Refugee Act of 1980, 60.
Refugees, 55, 56, 60, 63, 735–739.
Safe haven, 886–889, 894–898.
Special Inquiry Officers (Immigration Judges), 107–111.
Subversives, 513–518.
Undocumented aliens, 276–278.
U.S. immigration, generally, 40–66.
Visa requirements, 419–421.
World War II, 55, 56.

IMMIGRANTS
See also Preference system.
Admission procedures, 424–433.
Assimilation, 226–229.
Backlogs, 189–192.
Diversity programs, 124, 129–131, 148–149, 225–229.
Immediate relatives, 123, 124, 125, 131–134, 166.
Immigrants since 1960, 138–150.
Investors, 129, 223–225.
Migrant workers, 1960–1980, 141–142.
Special immigrants, 126, 129, 427.
Statistics, 62, 64–65, 126, 131, 133–134, 138, 146–149.
Subject to numerical limitations, 123, 125–136, 189–192.
Unskilled workers, 128–129.

INTERNATIONAL LAW, 3, 4, 718, 723–735, 777–778, 805–806, 821, 848.

JUDICIAL REVIEW
Generally, 899–973.
Administrative discretion, review of, 345–352, 362–368, 430–431, 457–460, 490, 575–578, 644–646, 664–688, 691–694.
Administrative Procedure Act (APA), 362, 685, 687, 900, 903–904, 927–928, 932–933.
Chadha jurisdiction, 919–924.
"Contingency" rule, 924, 926.
Declaratory judgment, 903.
Departure during pending review, 953–957.
Deportation orders, generally, 907–927, 935–953.
Detention, 445–473, 875–877.
District courts, 925, 927–931.
Exclusion and deportation orders, 397–400, 906–927, 934–937, 953–957.
Exhaustion of remedies, 934–953.
Exceptions, 937–953.
Federal question jurisdiction, 928–931.

JUDICIAL REVIEW—Cont'd
Habeas corpus, 386, 389–400, 902–903, 906–907, 960–973.
Hobbs Act, 907.
HRC exception, 937–953.
Interdiction of boats, 878–881.
Motion to reopen, 935–937.
Motion to reopen deportation proceedings, 935–937.
Naturalization decisions, 1016–1045.
Naturalization procedures, 1000–1002, 1015–1017.
Pendent jurisdiction, 923–924, 926.
Petition to review deportation order, 572–578, 599–604, 607, 611.
Political asylum applications, 766–767.
Post–deportation order review, 908–916.
Pre–deportation order review, 871–874.
Preclusion–of–review statutes, 916–919.
Res judicata, 432.
Scope of review, 150–166.
Standing, 368–370.
Summary chart, 932–933.
Visa denials, 362–370.

LAW ENFORCEMENT
See also Marriage Fraud.
Arrest, 587–588.
Bond, 588–590.
Border, 271–274, 315–318, 642.
Detention, 389–396, 429, 445–473, 588–591.
Fraud (including sham marriages), 175–189, 208–212, 296, 375–379, 437–438, 443–444, 546–549, 554–555.
Immigration Reform and Control Act (IRCA), 293–315.

LEGAL IMMIGRATION REFORM
Ceilings and floors, 131–135, 192.
Diversity programs, 129–131.
Undocumented aliens, 431.

MARRIAGE FRAUD
See also Law Enforcement, Fraud.
Generally, 175–179, 181–189, 616–618.
Ethical responsibilities of an attorney, 179–181.
Immigration Marriage Fraud Amendments (IMFA), 62, 184–189, 443–444.
Sham divorces, 183–184.

MIGRATION
Push–pull factors, 70.
Theories of, 66–74, 139–146, 278–283.

MORAL FOUNDATIONS AND CONSTRAINTS
Developing immigration policy, 74–99.

NATIONAL ORIGINS QUOTAS
See History.

NATURALIZATION AND DENATURALIZATION
Age requirements, 1003.
Attachment to constitutional principles, 1005–1006.

NATURALIZATION AND DENATURALIZA-TION—Cont'd

Defined, 1016.

Expatriation, as distinguished from, 1016.

False statements, materiality of, 1017–1045.

Good moral character, 1004–1005, 1017–26, 1035–1036, 1040–1044.

History, 996–1000.

Immigration and Nationality Act of 1952, 1002–1007, 1019, 1024, 1029–1045.

Judicial procedures, 1000–1001.

Judicial review, 1017–1045.

Literacy and education requirements, 1003–1004.

Nationality Act of 1940, p. 999.

Naturalization Act of 1906, p. 998.

Oath of allegiance requirement, 1006–1007.

Requirements, generally, 1002–1007.

Residence and physical presence requirements, 1002–1003.

Standard of proof, generally, 1016, 1017–1022, 1026–1027, 1037–1041.

Standards and procedures for, 1016–1017.

Statistics, 1014–1015, 1083–1084.

NONIMMIGRANTS

Generally, 229–270.

Academic students (F), 233–236.

Adjustment to immigrant status, 433–445.

Admission procedures, 423, 427–433.

Admissions procedures, 421–423.

Agricultural workers (H–2A), 243–244.

Athletes (P), 248.

Attestation, 247.

Bracero program, 277.

Business and entrepreneurial, 240–270.

Categories, 229–231.

Defined, 229.

Distinguished merit and ability (H–1B), 245–248.

Entertainers (P), 248.

Exchange visitors (J), 236–239.

Extraordinary ability (O), 248.

Intracompany transferees (L), 248–250.

North American Free Trade Agreement, 270.

Nurses (H–1A), 245.

Statistics, 230–231.

Students and scholars, 233–240.

Temporary visitors for business (B), 260–270.

Temporary workers (H–2B), 244–245.

Treaty traders (E), 250–260.

PREFERENCE SYSTEM

Generally, 122–129.

"After-acquired" spouses and children, 128.

Adopted children, 154, 174.

Application of foreign law, 166–170, 174–175.

Application of state laws, 175.

Ceilings and floors, 131–135, 189–192.

Child, 125–128, 150–161, 166–175.

Families of permanent residents, 127.

Family preferences, 126–128.

Family reunification categories, 125–128, 131–136, 166–175, 189–192.

Illegitimate child, 150–161, 166–175.

Immediate relatives, 132–135, 721.

PREFERENCE SYSTEM—Cont'd

Immigrants subject to numerical limitations, 125–136.

Legitimated child, 166–175.

Marriage, 175–189.

Occupational preferences, 128–129, 220–223.

Parent, 125, 150–161, 166–175.

Priorities, 135–136.

Spouse, 125–128.

Stepchild, 160–161.

PROFESSIONAL RESPONSIBILITY, 179–181, 209–212.

REFUGEES AND POLITICAL ASYLUM

See also Evidence and Evidentiary standards.

Generally, 126, 718–898.

Administrative notice, 872–873.

Applications, confidentiality, 767.

"Asylum" status, 762.

Bootstrap, 804–807.

Burmese, 758.

Chinese, 476–484, 808–819.

Civil war situations, 842–849.

Conscientious objectors, 822–828.

Coup plotters, 819–822.

Cubans, 446–452, 465–473, 736–737, 873–875, 896–898.

De facto, 746–748.

Definition, 718–719, 723–735, 742–745, 746, 807–816, 819–863.

Deterrent measures, 873–884.

Discretion to withhold deportation, 763, 770–787.

Discretionary denials of asylum, 793–804.

Economic migrants, 719, 729–730, 733–734.

Exceptions, 860–862.

Extended voluntary departure (EVD), 643, 716, 885–896.

Extradition, 576–577.

Firmly resettled, 744, 803–804.

Gender-based claims, 851–860.

Haitians, 446–449, 452–465, 719–720, 746, 807, 878–882, 896–898.

History, 735–739, 759–770, 884–889, 894–896.

Indochinese, 750–751, 755–759.

Judicial review, 766–767, 825–827, 835–842.

Lautenberg Amendment, 753–755.

Neutrality and imputed political opinion, 829–842.

Orderly Departure Program (ODP), 755–759.

Organization of African Unity (OAU), 726, 728.

Overseas refugee programs, 721–722, 735–759.

Past persecution, relevance of, 792–793.

Persecution, 770–793, 807–828.

Political asylum, generally, 721–723, 759–884.

Procedures for asylum applications, 764–767, 863–873.

Profile, 144–145.

Refoulement and nonrefoulement, 731, 770, 828.

REFUGEES AND POLITICAL ASYLUM
  —Cont'd
Refugee Act of 1980, 738–748, 752, 762–764.
Safe haven, 884–898.
Salvadorans, 822–834, 842–851, 876–877, 889–896.
Seventh preference (conditional entry), 737–738, 744, 748, 804.
Sexual orientation, 859–860.
Social group, 850.
Soviets–Eastern Europeans, 751–755.
Special humanitarian concern, 738.
Standards for adjudication, 770–793, 863–873.
State Department role, 869–872, 886–887.
Statistics, 742–743, 767–770.
Temporary protected status (TPS), 63, 889–896.
Tiananmen Square, 816, 888.
UN Convention Relating to the Status of Refugees, 730–734, 745–746, 760–761, 762.
Unforeseen emergency refugee situations, 742.
UNHCR, 718, 728–729, 747, 756–757, 759, 805–806, 827.
"Well founded fear of persecution", 746–747, 770–789.
Withholding of deportation, 716, 829–830, 835–839, 842–845, 860–862.

REGISTRATION OF ALIENS (including "green cards"), 182–183, 426.

RELIEF FROM DEPORTATION
  See also Refugees and Political Asylum.
Adjustment of status, 433–445.
Administrative discretion, 664–665, 678–681, 683–689.
Administrative procedures for, 865.
Asylum, 716.
Constitutional challenges (*Chadha* jurisdiction), 919–921.
"Contingency" rule, 924, 926.
Continuous physical presence, 654–655, 694–697, 716.
Deferred action status (nonpriority status), 587–588, 647–651.
Departure, effect of on review, 953–957.
Discretionary relief, 910.
Eligibility for government financial assistance, 339.
Estoppel, 714–716.
Extended voluntary departure (EVD), 643, 716, 707, 885–896.
Extreme hardship, 655–667.
Family Unity policy, 296.
General legalization program, 294–296.

RELIEF FROM DEPORTATION—Cont'd
Habeas corpus review, 960–973.
Immigration Reform and Control Act (IRCA), 293–315.
Judicial review, 664–678, 681–689, 691–694.
Summary chart, 932–933.
Judicial review of legalization denials, 296.
Judicial review of orders, 906–927, 935–953.
Lawful unrelinquished domicile, 654, 689–697.
Legislative history, 913–914.
Motion to reopen, 657–685.
Pendent jurisdiction, 923–924, 926.
Private bills, 713–714.
Registry, 712–713.
Replenishment Agricultural Workers (RAW), 126, 296.
Review of constitutional claims, 937–953.
Special Agricultural Workers (SAW), 126, 295–296.
State legalization impact–assistance grants (SLIAG), 339.
Stay of deportation, 651–652, 658, 668, 714.
Suspension of deportation, 653–689, 914.
Use of waiver of exclusion, 689–711, 716–717.
Voluntary departure, 560, 587, 592, 640–647.
Withholding of deportation, 716, 829–830, 835–839, 842–845, 860–862.

RESIDENCE, DOMICILE, PHYSICAL PRESENCE, 341, 492–495, 500–505, 654–655, 694–697, 712.

STATUTORY CONSTRUCTION, 166–174, 349–350, 482, 490–497, 535, 544–545, 666, 689–711.

STOWAWAYS, 433, 485.

UNDOCUMENTED ALIENS AND ILLEGAL MIGRATION
  Generally, 270–339.
Antidiscrimination provisions, 298–307, 318–321.
Bracero program, 277.
Deportation, 537–538.
Discrimination from sanctions, 115.
Effects of, 283–293.
Employer sanctions, 297–315, 318–322.
Estimates, 274–275.
History, 276–278.
Kinship networks, 278–283.
Mexican, 271–273, 275–283.
Monitoring and sunset provisions, 304–307.
Public benefits, 323–339.
Reasons for, 275–283.
Reforms to control, 293–339.

†

0-314-06104-5

90000

9 780314 061041